SOCIAL PSYCHOLOGY

SECOND EDITION

John Sabini

UNIVERSITY OF PENNSYLVANIA

W · W · NORTON & COMPANY

New York · London

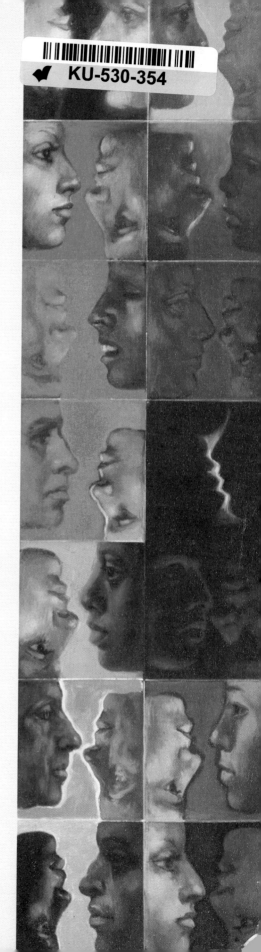

The text of this book is composed in Photina with the display set
in Futura Condensed
Composition by University Graphics, Inc.
Manufacturing by Québecor, Hawkins
Book design by Jack Meserole
Cover art: Colleen Browning, *Encounters* (1975), ACA Galleries, New York
City. Courtesy of the artist.

Acknowledgments and copyrights appear on pp. A61–A63, which
constitute a continuation of the copyright page.

Library of Congress Cataloging-in-Publication Data
Sabini, John, 1974–
    Social psychology / John Sabini.—2nd ed.
      p.   cm.
    Includes bibliographical references and index.
    1. Social psychology. I. Title.
HM251.S19 1994
302—dc20   94-36074
                                                    CIP

ISBN 0-393-96609-7

W. W. Norton & Company, Inc., 500 Fifth Avenue, New York, N.Y. 10110
W. W. Norton & Company Ltd., 10 Coptic Street, London WC1A 1PU

  2 3 4 5 6 7 8 9 0

To Debbie, thanks.

CONTENTS IN BRIEF

CONTENTS

PART **ONE**
GROUP DYNAMICS

PART **Two**

THE SELF

PART **FOUR**
ENDURING
RELATIONSHIPS

PART **FIVE**
ATTITUDES

PREFACE

The newspaper reporter and the mystery writer are both storytellers. But they tell their stories in quite different ways. The reporter's discipline is, to mix clichés, to put the bottom line right up front. The story starts with a strong lead paragraph, one that tells the who, what, where, when, and why of what happened. The remaining paragraphs provide detail and background—things the reader can decide to pursue or ignore, depending on her interest in the topic. Whether the reader reads on or not, she has gotten the most important facts from the first paragraph. The reporter's aim is to give the reader as much information as he can, as economically as possible. But putting the most important facts in the lead paragraph is the *last* thing a mystery writer would do. The mystery writer expects—demands—her reader to read the whole piece; her aim is to lead, and even mislead, her reader's thinking along the path to the resolution. *How* the reader gets to the criminal is the crucial issue for the mystery writer. Textbooks can be written either way. This one is modeled on the mystery novel.

Behind this decision to borrow from Agatha Christie lies a conception of science and of liberal education. It is a cliché that the satisfaction scientists derive from pursuing truth is much the same as Sherlock Holmes's; the reason it has become a cliché is that it is true. The satisfaction of science *is* the satisfaction of a detective. I hope that you as a reader can share that satisfaction. Given this idea of what science is, I was drawn to the style of a mystery novel.

A second reason to prefer the detective story model is a conception of what a liberal education is about. One thing it is about is conveying to the student some small fraction of the knowledge our culture, and for that matter our species, has accumulated. This aim could easily, perhaps more easily, be accomplished in a newspaper format. But there is another aim of a liberal education: to train the student to think about whatever the subject matter of the course happens to be. One way to do that is by tracing the thinking of the people who created the field. And this means following the detective's reasoning, rather than merely remembering the who, what, when, where, and why of what he discovered.

The discussions in this text, then, move from question to answer, but the path traveled from one to the other is not always the most direct one. Where it digresses from the direct path, it is to follow actual inquiry. These digressions embody the logic used by practicing scientists; they do so better than do direct paths—which are known primarily to crows.

When I wrote the first edition of this text, there was one Soviet Union and two Germanies. Things change. It is the responsibility of textbooks to chronicle the changes in the part of the world the textbook calls its own. I have attempted in this second edition to chronicle the changes that have occurred in social psychology over the last three years. But at the same time, I have tried not to lose the historical approach that guided the first edition.

In addition to bringing each of the chapters of the first edition up-to-date, I made two important changes in the second edition. The first has to do with gender. In the first edition, there was a chapter on gender that discussed psychological differences between men and women, gender roles, and gender stereotypes. It made sense to collect these phenomena in one place. Unfortunately, however, that organization meant that gender stereotypes were treated in a different chapter from other stereotypes—for example, racial stereotypes. But many social psychologists believe that the same mechanisms are involved in all stereotypes, and that therefore the material on gender stereotyping should be in the same chapter as the material on racial stereotyping.

Putting everything to do with gender in one place has another unfortunate consequence—it also divorced gender roles from sex, and it makes sense to think about gender roles in relation to sexual behavior.

To solve these problems, in this second edition the chapter on gender has been removed. The material on gender stereotypes is now to be found in the prejudice chapter (Chapter 4), and the material on gender roles is in a chapter called ''Sex and Gender'' (Chapter 12). I, like many authors before me, wish I could have arranged the material both ways! Perhaps one day books will be published in such a way that this will be possible.

The second major change has to do with culture. Since the first edition, there has been an increasingly forceful movement within social psychology to examine our discipline in cross-cultural perspective. In the first edition, I responded to this impulse by including an epilogue on just that topic. But in the interim, it became increasingly clear to me that culture deserved a more complete treatment. So this second edition contains a chapter about culture, specifically focused on the question: Is the Western conception of a self broadly shared, or is it a uniquely Western idea?

COVERAGE

This book is intended to be a fairly complete account of what appears in the literature of social psychology. As such, it contains too much material to be covered in a one-semester course—or, at least, I have not been able to cover everything in my one-semester course. There is room, then, for individual taste in which topics to cover and which to leave to the curiosity of the student.

In deciding what to include, I have tried to avoid believing that only the latest findings of social psychology are worth thinking about. The classic studies are, to my mind, just as interesting. Thus I have tried to include both.

This book is organized into five parts. Each part addresses some broad subarea of social psychology. How these five parts are arranged follows from the emphasis of the text. The emphasis is distinctly on the *social* in social psychology. For that reason, the text begins with the material traditionally known as *group dynamics* (Part One: Social Influence, Groups and Task Performance, Intergroup Conflict). It ends with a discussion of what is, perhaps, the most individual topic in social psychology—*attitudes* (Part Five: Attitudes and Attitude Change, and Attitudes and Behavior). So the movement is from the social to the individual.

The second part of the book is about *the self;* consistent with the book's emphasis, it first treats the self from a social perspective. The opening chapter of that part explores how people think about other people. Chapter 6 focuses on the self in social interaction—that is, on self-presentation—and Chapter 7 focuses on emotion. The final chapter in this part treats the self in cultural perspective.

Part Three is about four prominent *social motives:* altruism, justice, sex, and aggression. Also included in this third part is a chapter on strategic interaction (interpersonal competition). The reason for its inclusion along with the social motives also has to do with the social emphasis of the book. In treating the social motives, it was natural to turn to a discussion of their evolutionary roots, but a satisfactory understanding of the evolution of sexuality (or altruism) must itself be focused on natural selection as a *social* entity, as competition among members of the same species for reproductive success. As it happens, evolution from this perspective is itself a kind of strategic interaction—not among individuals, but among genes. The neat dovetailing of reasoning, and indeed findings, at these very different levels of analysis suggested that the chapter on strategic interaction (although it was not about a specific social motive) ought to be included with discussions of social motives.

Part Four focuses on *interpersonal relationships.* The first chapter discusses interpersonal attraction; the next discusses the development (and dissolution) of relationships, especially marriage.

This organization is, however, not the only one it makes sense to follow. Indeed, the chapters are meant to make sense no matter the order in which they are read. Certainly the order of the parts can be switched. Part Five, for example, can be covered as the second section (or even the first!) for those who would prefer to cover attitudes earlier in the course. Other chapters can also be moved about.

As in the previous edition, Susan Rakowitz has prepared an Instructor's Manual and Test Item File, which has all sorts of useful information about how to put this book to good use. Maury Silver has prepared a Study Guide to help students master the material of the book; it covers the same ground but with a different pattern.

ACKNOWLEDGMENTS

Now comes the time for me to pay back the many kindnesses I have received—not to mention criticisms—over the many years it took to write this book. The following reviewers helped on the previous edition: Teresa M. Amabile, *Brandeis University*; Craig A. Anderson, *University of Missouri-Columbia*; C. Daniel Batson, *University of Kansas*; Steven J. Breckler, *John Hopkins University*; Linda Carli, *College of the Holy Cross*; Martin Daly, *McMaster University*; Alan Fridlund, *University of California-Santa Barbara*; Theodore L. Gessner, *George Mason University*; James L. Hilton, *University of Michigan*; Lynn Kahle, *University of North Carolina*; Diane Mackie, *University of California-Santa Barbara*; Clark McCauley, *Bryn Mawr College*; David A. Schroeder, *Fullbright College at University of Arkansas*; R. Lance Shotland, *Pennsylvania State University*; Janet T. Spence, *University of Texas at Austin*; Mark P. Zanna, *University of Waterloo*; Dolf Zillmann, *Indiana University*.

For the Second Edition, a new group of professional reviewers was kind enough to offer their advice. I am, of course, terribly grateful to them, though I remain responsible for the errors they couldn't talk me out of. They are: David M. Buss, *University of Michigan*; Shelly Chaiken, *New York University*; Margaret S. Clark, *Carnegie Mellon University*; Joan F. DiGiovanni, *Western New England College*; Alan Fridlund, *University of California-Santa Barbara*; William K. Gabrenya, *Florida Institute of Technology*; William P. Gaeddert, *SUNY Plattsburgh*; James L. Hilton, *University of Michigan*; Larry A. Hjelle, *SUNY Brockport*; Marianne E. Jaeger, *Temple University*; Clark McCauley, *Bryn Mawr College*; Joan Miller, *Yale University*; Valerie J. Steffen, *University of Idaho*.

Next comes Mark Boggs, a friend of mine and of this book. He was always willing to give me his uncommonly wise advice—would I had taken it better.

Then comes Susan Rakowitz, who in preparing the Instructor's Manual read the book seriously enough to save me from so many embarrassments; thanks, Susan, thanks for taking it seriously.

And there is Paul Rozin, another friend of this book and its author, and a dear colleague, someone who repeatedly came to their aid just when they needed it most.

Loud thanks too go to Jay Schulkin for his support, encouragement, and enthusiasm over so many years. His loyalty is a great gift.

How can I repay Henry and Lila Gleitman? First there is their friendship—textbook authors need friendship badly, but there is so much more than that. There is their confidence in me, but there is more yet. Mostly there is their being examples of textbook writers, teachers, and intellectuals. What I am most grateful for is their being such wonderful exemplars.

Norton has been wonderfully generous in providing editorial help over the years; this project has profited mightily from the contributions of Ed Barber, Don Fusting, Sandy Lifland, and Hank Smith. Cathy Wick has added her talents to this second edition. It is a pleasure to thank her for her countless good ideas—especially the ones I first resisted and then took. As with the first edition, Deborah Malmud deserves most of the credit for the images that illustrate these pages; once again my book has profited much from her taste and creativity.

Now I get to thank the three people closest to the book. The first was Stanley Milgram. The book started out being his, then ours, and finally, with his untimely death, mine. He read early drafts, criticized prose, and kept critics at bay. But what he really did was mentor me in the broadest sense of the term. I thank him.

Now we come to two people who at times no doubt felt all too close to the book, Debbie Kossman and Maury Silver. They were called upon to do two things: keep me honest and keep me going. The first required critical eyes, minds, and ears; the second, the ability to offer encouragement. I thank them, and appreciate them, for being wonderful at one and adequate at the other.

John Sabini

Philadelphia, Pennsylvania
August, 1994

OCIAL PSYCHOLOGY

SECOND EDITION

CHAPTER 1

Introduction

Social psychologists, like other scientists, try to figure out how things work—what makes them go the way they go. Social psychologists in particular try to figure out how our social lives work; they want to know how we think about, feel for, and act toward other people. But social psychologists are not alone in trying to figure this out. Cultural anthropologists, sociologists, historians, political scientists, even economists, biologists, and philosophers have the same general aim. So how is social psychology different from these other fields?

There are no clear and important dividing lines. Some of the work you will read about in this book has been done by anthropologists, sociologists, historians, political scientists, and even economists, biologists, and philosophers. So much for clear lines. But still, there are differences in emphasis among these fields. The most important difference is this: social psychology is more concerned with the individual than are many of these other fields.

ROMANTIC LOVE

Take romantic love—surely that is a part of our social lives. How does it work; what makes it go? An anthropologist might point out that not all cultures have such a notion, and a historian might mention that even Western culture hasn't always had such a notion. And this suggests a very important point about romantic love: that if we had not grown up hearing about it from every radio we have ever passed, we wouldn't find it as big a part of our social lives. But, now, what question does the anthropologist or historian or sociologist raise about romantic love?

1

For workers in these fields, the key questions are about romantic love as an element of culture. They want to know how romantic love fits into any culture that has it. They want to know how it came to be when it came to be—again as a cultural entity. But the social psychologist has a different emphasis. She is concerned with what makes romantic love work from the point of view of the individual. This is not to say that the social psychologist is concerned with every Sally and Harry, and the particularities of their unique experiences when they fall in love. That is the province of novelists, playwrights, poets, screenwriters—quite a lot of novelists, playwrights, poets, and screenwriters, as a matter of fact. No, the social psychologist is interested in the principles, not the particularities. She wants to know what it is about human nature that determines with whom, where, when, how, and why people fall in love.

Romantic love is a bit like mortar. Mortar holds bricks together—no mortar, no buildings. City planners are very interested in buildings, because buildings are a crucial part of cities. But the city planner isn't very interested in how mortar actually works; just so long as it does, in fact, hold the bricks together. Similarly, romantic love helps create families; anthropologists and sociologists are vitally concerned with families because families are crucial parts of cultures. But sociologists and anthropologists aren't all that concerned with how romantic love works, just so long as it does. Still, somebody had better worry about how it works—that's the social psychologist.

This book isn't about, or just about, romantic love. But many of its chapters are about the psychological principles that romantic love draws upon. We can think about the substance of social psychology by decomposing romantic love into its elements. First of all, being in love with someone involves having certain thoughts about the person you are in love with. It also involves trying to get the person you are in love with to have certain thoughts about you. Thus, principles that govern our thinking about other people are relevant to romantic love; these principles are the topic of Chapter 5. How we get other people to think certain things about us is taken up in Chapter 6. One subtopic of social psychology, then, is the question of how we come to know other people and how we help to shape their knowledge of us.

But romantic love isn't just a matter of having thoughts. Passion is in-

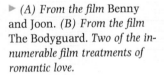 (A) From the film Benny and Joon. (B) From the film The Bodyguard. Two of the innumerable film treatments of romantic love.

volved too; in particular, sexual passion. That is the topic of Chapter 12. In that chapter, we will examine sexual desire from a cultural and biological perspective. Love also involves altruism, altruism toward the beloved (see Chapter 9). And to be fair to the facts, love's course sometimes involves aggression, the topic of Chapter 13. All of these basic social motives have a role to play in love, as well as in the rest of our social lives. The passions of romantic love are also emotional in a richer sense, and Chapter 7 discusses emotions in a broader perspective. There we will see how cognition and physiology come together to produce emotion, and how the emotions produced give rise to a key element of romantic love—emotional expression. So while thinking about people is one subtopic of social psychology, another branch of the field is concerned with social motives and emotions.

For romantic love to flourish, Sally and Harry must be attracted to each other. What principles govern who is attracted to whom, not just romantically but more generally? That is the topic of Chapter 14. Being attracted to people, having desires toward them, profoundly affects our evaluations of them, leads us to have certain attitudes toward them. How attitudes are formed and changed is the topic of Chapter 16. And how these attitudes relate to behavior is the concern of Chapter 17. Finally, romance may lead to real relationships and often enough to marriage. How relationships develop (and, sadly, deteriorate) is the topic of Chapter 15.

While we're on the topic of Romeo and Juliet, remember that they had a bit of a problem. Their families didn't get along. The Montagues and the Capulets were not each other's favorite people. They suffered from a certain prejudice toward each other. And social psychologists have long been concerned with prejudice—its sources and cures. What we have learned about it is in Chapter 4.

Although being in love with someone is a deeply personal experience, you may have noticed that people are rarely content simply to notice their love's virtues. They want other people too to notice them—actually people often grow quite testy when others don't see those virtues in quite the same way. This strong desire to see the world as others see it and the sometimes none-too-charming implications of that desire are the concern of Chapter 2.

Finally there is flirtation. Flirtation is many things; for one, it is great fun. But another thing it is is a strategic interaction, that is, an interaction in which Harry tries by his behavior toward Sally to get her to act in certain ways toward him. Love isn't a game, but it often has game-like qualities. How people act in situations of this sort is covered in Chapter 11.

There is one topic that, at least in our culture, has nothing whatever to do with romantic love but is a part of social psychology, and while I am cataloguing, I should mention it: group problem solving. One of the concerns of social psychologists is how individuals get together in small groups to solve problems; this is covered in Chapter 3. Juries are examples of such groups, and included in that chapter is a discussion of how juries work.

METHODS OF SOCIAL PSYCHOLOGY

What are the methods social psychologists use to find out how things work? As you will see, there is no one method; social psychologists use all kinds.

And well they should, since the means of answering a question must be suited to the specifics of the question. But there is one method that is highly distinctive of social psychology, a method occasionally used by researchers in other disciplines but used centrally in social psychology: the controlled experiment. To appreciate social psychology, it is crucial to understand the logic, power, and limitations of experimentation.

The Experimental Method

It is not at all mysterious why social psychologists have turned to experiment. Experiments are the best tools we have to determine *causal* relations, and in the end, figuring out how things work is a matter of answering causal questions. To see this, we need to be concrete and focus on an example.

DOES BRAINSTORMING ENHANCE CREATIVITY? AN EXPERIMENTAL APPROACH

An advertising executive, Alexander Osborn, popularized a technique he called "brainstorming." Brainstorming, Osborn argued, is a way for organizations to use social groups to maximize creativity. To brainstorm is to bring groups of people together and give them a specific kind of instruction, which stresses that everyone is to contribute any idea, good or bad, that occurs to him. The notion behind this is that it is useful to separate the solution of a problem into two distinct phases, phases that are often run together. In the first phase, you generate possible solutions; in the second phase, you evaluate those solutions to see which is best. The brainstorming idea is that it is best to instruct people *not* to evaluate their ideas until they have generated lots and lots of them. To do that you have to get people to contribute ideas, even possibly off-the-wall ideas, so that you later have a large pool to pick from (Osborn, 1957). In a brainstorming group, each person can hear everybody else's fresh ideas, develop them, and perhaps take them in new, more creative directions.

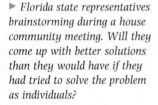

▶ *Florida state representatives brainstorming during a house community meeting. Will they come up with better solutions than they would have if they had tried to solve the problem as individuals?*

So Osborn had a theory, or at least a claim. It was that by using brainstorming groups, organizations would be able to increase their creativity substantially—in places Osborn suggests they will be able to *double* their creativity. And Osborn has been persuasive. Apparently, brainstorming groups are quite widely used in industry, and especially in advertising agencies. But social psychologists are by temperament a somewhat skeptical group, and they have been, from Osborn's first pronouncements, quite interested in whether brainstorming actually works. Does brainstorming lead to enhanced creativity?

As I mentioned above, the preferred technique for answering this is controlled experimentation. Let us see, now, how we might conduct a controlled experiment to determine whether brainstorming enhances the creativity of an organization.

One thing we surely need to do is to conduct some brainstorming sessions in just the way that Osborn describes his technique. But to find out whether brainstorming increases creativity, we want to compare the creative output of these brainstorming groups with—well, with what? What we want to know precisely is: Do the brainstorming groups produce more creative ideas than they would have produced had they not been given the brainstorming instructions? We want to know this because the causal claim that brainstorming increases creativity comes down to the claim that groups given brainstorming instructions are more creative than they would have been had they not been given those instructions. But how can we tell how creative they would have been had they not been given brainstorming instructions? The best we can do is to use *other groups* as stand-ins, as stand-ins for what the brainstorming groups would have done had they not been given brainstorming instructions.

So what we will do is construct two kinds of groups. One kind will be given brainstorming instructions, and the other will be given whatever instructions groups would have been given had Osborn never written his book. We will then compare the output of the two kinds of groups. If the brainstorming groups out-create the others, then we will have some reason to take Osborn's claim seriously. If they don't, then we will have reason to be skeptical. And if several experiments return positive results, then our confidence in Osborn's technique should be very great indeed; whereas if they all flop, then we should feel quite safe in dismissing Osborn's claim. This is the essential logic of controlled experimentation.

Let me pause here to note some terminology and to highlight some key points of the experimental method. Terminology comes first.

First, the people who take part in experiments are referred to as **subjects.** Next, the difference between the ways the two groups of subjects are treated, that is, whether they get the brainstorming instructions or the standard instructions, is called the **independent variable.** The independent variable is what the experimenter manipulates (varies); it is the suspected cause of something else. Third, in order to tell if the brainstorming groups are more creative than the others, we need to assess (measure) the amount of creative output from the two groups. This measured effect (or possible effect) is called the **dependent variable.** So the independent variable is the (putative) cause the experimenter manipulates directly; the dependent variable is the (putative) effect that the experimenter observes.

Independent variable: what the experimenter manipulates directly

Dependent variable: a variable that *might* be affected by manipulating the independent variable

An experiment is often an attempt to find out whether changes in the independent variable cause changes in the dependent variable!

Fourth, I have referred to the idea that Osborn was advancing as a claim or theory, but in the context of an experiment this proposition—that brainstorming increases productivity—is called a **hypothesis.** A hypothesis is a proposition that is being tested in an experiment; the results of the experiment either support or fail to support the hypothesis. Finally, the brainstorming groups in this sort of study are called the **experimental groups,** while the groups treated in the standard way are called the **control groups.** Enough of terminology, on to highlights.*

Crucial to this experiment is determining the creativity of the two groups. If someone claimed that a certain vitamin made people taller, it would be easy to decide how to measure the dependent variable—a yardstick would do nicely. And sometimes in social psychology it is possible to find dependent variables that are that easy to measure; in fact, how hard someone pulls on a rope is a dependent variable discussed later in this book. But usually one cannot spell out the dependent variable in physical terms, so often—as is the case in brainstorming groups—one is left with using human raters to measure the dependent variable. The raters must make a judgment, in this case a judgment about how creative the proposed solutions are.

Next, it is absolutely vital that the experimental and control groups be treated identically *except for the independent variable.* Indeed, the logic of experimentation is that there be two groups the same in *every* way except for the difference in the independent variable; then and only then can we attribute the differences observed in the dependent variable (if there are any) to the causal influence of the independent variable. So everything we do to the two groups must be the same, except that the brainstorming group gets the brainstorming instructions, while the control group gets the standard instructions.

Suppose that this were not so. Suppose that, for example, the experimenter were also nicer and warmer to the experimental group than to the control group. If the results were that the brainstorming group performed better than the experimental group, we would not know whether this was because of the brainstorming instructions or because of the added warmth.

MATCHING AND RANDOMIZING

Now, a specific problem with all of this may have occurred to you. Let us suppose that the experimental group did produce more creative solutions. Maybe this wasn't because of the brainstorming instructions but instead because all the creative people happened to be in the experimental group. If the people in the experimental group were more creative than those in the control group, then of course they would produce more creative solutions *regardless of instructions.* How can we guard against this problem?

The first solution is to try to match the subjects in the experimental and control groups for creativity; that is, we might try to assign equal numbers of creative people to the experimental and control groups. If we had a way of knowing with passing accuracy who is creative and who isn't, we might well try this. But unfortunately, we are far from perfect in our ability to pick out the creative people in advance. So what other tool can we use?

---

*I will treat the discussion in this and the following two sections as if there were two groups in the experiment. Most experiments have many groups, but the general principles are the same, and it is easier to write (and read) about two groups.

In this circumstance, the best tool we have is **random assignment of the subjects to conditions.** That is, we assign subjects to the experimental and control groups with the aid of some randomizing device; flipping a coin is just fine. Can randomization guarantee that all the creative people don't wind up in one group while all the duller people wind up in the other? No, it can't guarantee it, but it does make it unlikely. And the larger the number of subjects in each group the *more* unlikely it becomes that all of one kind (any kind) of subject are in one group while all of another kind (any kind) are in the other. (Suppose you had ten playing cards, and you used a coin flip to decide which of two piles each card would go into. It is not very likely that all of the reds would wind up in one pile while all of the blacks wind up in the other. But it is much less likely that they would divide that way if you had a hundred cards, and much less likely still if you had a thousand.)* So random assignment is the crucial element of an experiment; it is the best technique we have for being sure that the difference in the dependent variable (or variables) that we observe was caused by the difference in the independent variable rather than by something extraneous. One last highlight, then we shall look at some actual experiments on brainstorming.

Random assignment of subjects to conditions is crucial in establishing that it is differences in the independent variable that produce differences in the dependent variable.

GENERALIZING FROM PARTICULAR SUBJECTS TO PEOPLE IN GENERAL

Suppose we find that the group with the brainstorming instructions was more creative. Does this mean that brainstorming will work on everybody? In the technical language of experimentation, this is a problem of **generalization.** Typically an experimenter wishes that her subjects were a random sample of the world's population; if this were the case, then the experimenter would be entitled to generalize the results found in the experiment to everybody. But it is impossible, obviously, to do experiments on random samples of the world's population. In fact, many experiments reported in this book were carried out on nonrandom samples of largely white, largely middle-class American college sophomores enrolled in social psychology courses. To whom can we generalize from these subjects? This is a sticky and hotly debated matter within the discipline of social psychology. Some would argue, and indeed have argued most stridently, that it is always unreasonable to generalize the results of any of these studies to broader populations (see, for example, Jahoda, 1988). But others would argue that though as a logical matter one cannot generalize very broadly, as a matter of practical wisdom, whether one generalizes from college sophomores to broader populations isn't so clear. So what should one make of the results to be reported in the chapters of this book?

Well, first, though much of the research reported here used undergraduates, many studies have used more broadly selected (and more broadly representative) subjects. You should pay special attention to results derived from

*As you may have noticed from this example, the probability of dividing the cards randomly into black and red piles grows smaller as the number of cards increases, *but* it never reaches zero. The analogy is that we can never be dead certain we didn't wind up with the creative people in one group and the dullards in the other. But the point is, there are ways to estimate how likely it is that the observed difference in creative ideas was due to this sort of chance effect rather than to the brainstorming. So, though we can't be certain the brainstorming worked, we can give the odds that it worked. In psychology, results are usually not reported in the professional literature unless the odds are at least 19 to 1 that the observed effect on the dependent variable was due to the independent variable rather than to chance.

a broader selection of subjects. Then too, though most of the experiments were performed on undergraduates, most of the **phenomena** reported in these pages used broader selections of subjects. This is because the typical strategy investigators use is to begin an investigation with undergraduates—as a practical matter, they are easier to find—but then to extend the inquiry to other subjects. Few phenomena discovered in the laboratory with undergraduates survive without being tested on other samples in other contexts. Social psychologists find it especially encouraging when results from various samples *converge*. When this happens, we can be quite confident we have found something real. Still, very few of the phenomena reported in these pages have been studied in anything like a random sample of the world's cultures. And this makes generalization to human nature hazardous.

There is another point well worth remembering. Much about an experiment will be bound to its particular time and place. For example, some real studies have asked subjects to come up with names that appeal to American undergraduates; other experiments conducted in Germany have asked subjects to think about what Germany should do to reduce unemployment among guest workers. These are highly culture-bound issues. So too, no doubt, is the absolute number of ideas that the subjects came up with. But these details were *not* the focus of the investigations. The focus was on the *relation between* the experimental condition and the number of ideas produced. Thus, the relevant question is: Is the relationship discovered in an experiment—the relationship between what the experimenter varied from condition to condition and the subjects' responses—likely to vary from sample to sample of subjects?

Well, *that* surely depends on what exactly is under investigation. Some social psychologists, for example, are concerned with describing the fundamental processes that characterize human memory as those memorial processes are involved in thinking about other people. It is at least plausible that fundamental memorial processes are the same for American undergraduates as they are for people from all cultures of the world. Perhaps, by the way, they aren't, but it is *plausible* to believe that they are. Other social psychologists are interested in questions like: How does a person's physical attractiveness matter to his romantic (and other) relationships? Surely it would *not* be wise to imagine that the answer to this question will not vary from culture to culture. Since most of the research reported in these pages has not been replicated (repeated) in anything like all cultures of the world, the reader—and indeed the author—has no choice but to use her common sense in deciding how broadly to generalize results.

TWO ACTUAL EXPERIMENTS ON BRAINSTORMING

So, do brainstorming instructions work? In one experiment, student groups of four males and three females met to dream up new brand names that would appeal to male students at their university. The brand names were to be for cigars, automobiles, and deodorants. Some of the groups were given brainstorming instructions; they were told (over and over again) that they should say out loud any idea that occurred to them. They should not worry about how good or bad the idea was, and they should not criticize each other's ideas, either explicitly or by sneering, laughing, or snickering. The other groups were told to be critical. They were told to produce *good* ideas; not just any ideas, and especially not silly ideas.

It is easy enough to tell whether the brainstorming groups produced *more* names than the other groups—they did. But were the names more creative? How can we tell that? Remember that the subjects were told to produce names that would appeal to undergraduates. So it was fairly easy to determine whether the brainstorming groups did better work: a panel of undergraduates were asked to say how much each name appealed to them. Thus, each member of the panel rated each name for its appeal. Now suppose the members of the panel knew which ideas came from the brainstorming group and which came from the control group, and suppose the panelists wanted the brainstorming group to do better. It would be very easy for them to bias the results by overrating the brainstorming ideas and underrating the control ideas. Of course, you might, as experimenter, try to fix this by telling the panelists to be very careful to be unbiased, but this would not rule out the possibility that they would be biased in favor of their favorite group *despite* their efforts to be unbiased—sometimes bias is a quite unconscious matter. And harping at the panelists might have another, equally undesirable, result: they might bend over backward in favor of the group they are rooting against. That, after all, is just as bad as being biased in favor of the other group.

The solution to this problem isn't harping at people, but rather a structural solution: suppose you have the panelists rate the ideas without knowing which ideas came from which group. Now bias *cannot* come into play. Panelists who rate things without knowing which condition of the experiment was responsible for them are said to be *blind* to the experimental condition. Keeping the subjects in an experiment blind, as the researchers did in this study, is an excellent idea, one that experiments try, so far as possible, to implement.

How did the experiment turn out? Did brainstorming unleash creativity? Well, the brainstorming groups did produce more ideas. Did they come up with more creative ideas? No. They produced just about as many really good ideas as did the other groups. But they produced many more *low-quality* ideas than did the control groups (see Figure 1.1; Weisskopf-Joelson & Elisio, 1961). Brainstorming increased the chaff without increasing the wheat, thus reducing the ratio of wheat to chaff. These results suggest, then, that brainstorming groups are useful only if one wants to generate lots of ideas and isn't terribly concerned about their quality.

This experiment compared brainstorming groups with other kinds of groups. But is this the comparison we should make if we want to know whether brainstorming increases creativity? Or, at least, is it the only comparison we should make? Osborn argued that brainstorming increased creativity, but compared with what? We might also be interested in comparing brainstorming groups with brainstorming individuals. Imagine that you are an advertising executive trying to maximize the number of creative solutions from your six-person staff. Should you assemble all of them in a room, give them brainstorming instructions, and let them go at it, or should you put each person in his own room with a pad and let him work? After an hour, will you have more ideas from the group or will you get more ideas by pooling the contributions of the six people working alone?

FIGURE 1.1 ▬▬▬▬
BRAINSTORMING

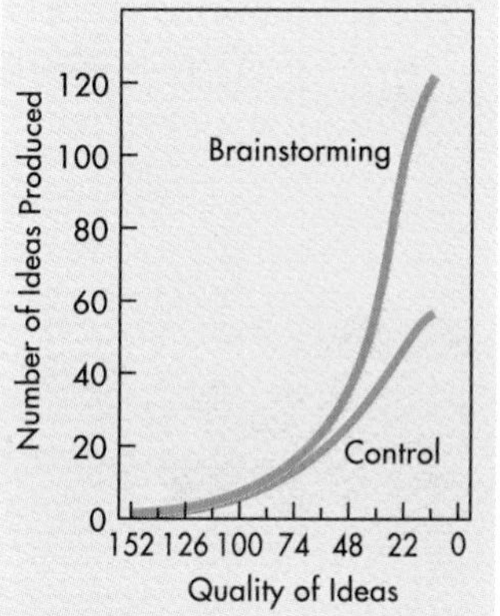

▲ *The number of ideas of various levels of quality produced in a brainstorming group and a control group. The brainstorming group produced a greater number of ideas, but most of them were of poor quality. (From Weisskopf-Joelson & Elisio, 1961)*

In an experiment meant to answer this question, groups of five, seven, or nine subjects discussed the following problem: What would happen if people had an extra thumb? They were to write down as many consequences of such an interesting anatomical alteration as they could think of. The number of answers they produced was compared with the number found by pooling the answers from five, seven, or nine individuals working alone. The results were quite clear: more solutions were produced by the individuals than by the groups. And as the number of people in the groups increased, this difference increased. The wholes were much less than the sums of their parts, and as the size of the group grew, the whole got smaller and smaller relative to its parts (Bouchard & Hare, 1970). Indeed, this finding is the general result from studies of brainstorming: groups are less productive than the same number of individuals working alone (Lamm & Trommsdorff, 1973).* I point this out in part because it is a reasonably interesting fact about brainstorming groups, but also because it illustrates a central fact about experiments: they address relatively narrow issues. An experiment cannot tell us whether brainstorming groups are good or bad in some absolute sense; it can tell us, however, whether brainstorming groups produce more or less creative solutions than X. What X is must be determined by the experimenter's purposes.

So far we have seen that, and to some degree how, experiments help us answer *whether* something causes something else. More typically, however, experiments are put to a different purpose. They are used *analytically*, to determine not whether something works but *how* something works—or fails to work. They help us to determine *what about something* leads to its having the causal effects it has. Suppose we wanted to know what it was about brainstorming groups that interfered with individual performance. Could we do that?

■■■■■■■■■■■■
Brainstorming groups typically produce *fewer*, and fewer *good*, ideas than do people working alone under brainstorming instructions.
■■■■■■■■■■■■

HOW GROUPS INTERFERE WITH PRODUCTIVITY

The first step is to think through the possibilities. Ivan Steiner has proposed that in general there are two types of reasons for groups to fail to measure up to the individuals who comprise them. One is motivational: people may simply work less hard in a group. The second kind of problem is failure of coordination. Sometimes coordination is an easy matter: if two people are to lift a table, then they just have to be sure to lift at the same time. But if they are going to build a house, they need to coordinate a lot more. The various steps in building a house have to be done in the right order; it is very expensive to finish the walls off *before* you put the pipes in. Might coordination be the problem in brainstorming groups?

In one quite clever experiment, some subjects worked individually on the problem of how to reduce unemployment; other subjects worked on the same problem in a brainstorming group. In a third condition, subjects were alone in cubicles, but they were treated in one way as if they were a group: they were to speak their ideas into microphones, but only one microphone was "live" at any moment. Thus, although the subjects couldn't hear each other's ideas, they also couldn't speak while another subject was talking. This, of

*In experiments of this sort, brainstorming groups produce fewer total ideas and, in particular, fewer good ideas than individuals working alone.

course, is what happens (for the most part) in real brainstorming groups; only one person speaks at a time.

The actual brainstorming group, as usual, contributed fewer ideas than did the individuals working alone; the interesting finding was that the subjects who were alone but who could speak only when others were silent were just about as bad (see Figure 1.2; Diehl & Stroebe, 1987; Diehl & Stroebe, 1991). This suggests that the problem with brainstorming has something to do with being interrupted in one's speech (and presumably one's thinking) while other people are talking. Whatever benefits brainstormers may derive from hearing others' ideas are apparently not as great as the burden imposed by having to interrupt one's train of thought to listen to them.

This experiment, then, compared three groups of subjects: individuals, brainstormers, and other subjects treated in one way, but not all ways, like a brainstormer. It found that these "pseudo" brainstormers showed the same deficits as the real brainstormers. This finding provides evidence that the pseudo-brainstorming groups contain an "active" ingredient of the brainstorming condition: in particular, they contain a key element, interference, crucial for the performance deficits.

Showing that you can produce the brainstorming deficit in performance by introducing the interference brainstorming imposes even without the group is one way of showing that you have located an active ingredient in the brainstorming problem. But another way would be by demonstrating that if you leave the brainstorming group intact but remove the active ingredient, then the problem goes away. One group of researchers has done something just like this. They have developed computer software that allows people to interact with one another and see others' solutions on their computer screens, but it also allows them to offer their own solutions anytime they like. Groups interacting in this way are not interfered with, and they do *not* perform worse than individuals using the same software (they don't do better either). So this software seems to solve the brainstorming problem, or, as we shall see, one of the brainstorming problems, by removing interference (Gallupe, Bastianutti, & Cooper, 1991). And solving the problem gives us confidence that interference is an active ingredient in the brainstorming problem.

There is evidence, however, that interference isn't the only reason that brainstorming groups underperform individuals given brainstorming instructions. Some investigators believe that in brainstorming groups, each individual works no harder than the least hardworking member of the group; that is, each member in the group compares himself with the least effective other member and tries no harder than that. These investigators have shown that giving brainstorming groups explicit high standards to live up to also overcomes the brainstorming deficit, and this suggests that there is a motivational as well as a technical basis to the problem with brainstorming groups (Paulus & Dzindolet, 1993). So there may be more than one active ingredient in the brainstorming group's tendency to impede performance.

Experiments have two principal roles: (1) they can provide evidence of causal efficacy, and (2) they can be used to analyze social circumstances to determine the active ingredient of some manipulation. It is because experiments are so well suited to these aims that such a great premium is placed on experiments in social psychology.

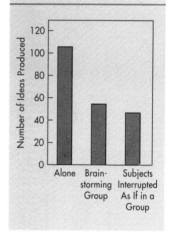

FIGURE 1.2

BRAINSTORMING AND "PSEUDO" BRAINSTORMING

▲ The total number of ideas produced when subjects worked alone, were combined into a brainstorming group, or were alone but allowed to speak only when no other member was speaking. Such "pseudo" brainstorming groups are about as insufficient as real brainstorming groups. (Data from Diehl & Stroebe, 1987)

Regardless of why brainstorming groups interfere with productivity, it is very clear now *that* they interfere with productivity when compared with individuals working alone. So it is quite clear that the wise businessperson should not use brainstorming *groups;* she would be better off with individuals, each in his room with a notepad (or hand-held computer) brainstorming alone. Yet as I mentioned above, brainstorming groups are still widely used in the advertising and industrial world (Stroebe, Diehl, & Abakoumkin, 1992). Their usefulness is part of the popular wisdom. This is a case where the popular wisdom is just flat wrong. The experiments we have reviewed show, beyond a reasonable person's doubts, that, Osborn's arguments notwithstanding, brainstorming isn't a very effective way for executives to spend their money and—what comes down to the same thing—their employees' time. The social psychologist using the experimental method is often in the position of refuting popular wisdom. In Chapter 2, which discusses Stanley Milgram's experiments on obedience to authority, we will encounter a series of experiments that fly in the face of popular wisdom and that have far more upsetting implications for all of us than do the experiments we have reviewed so far on brainstorming.

One reason that executives are wrong about brainstorming groups might be that they put *other people* in them; they don't necessarily participate themselves. Perhaps people who are part of brainstorming groups have a better grasp of how they work. Indeed, we often hear that only people who have had some sort of experience are in a position to judge it. Is this so? No. At least not for brainstorming. The fact is that several studies have shown that people who have been through brainstorming experiments get everything wrong too. Specifically, people who work alone under brainstorming instructions believe that they would have had more ideas had they been part of a brainstorming group, while people who have been in a brainstorming group do *not* believe that they would have had more ideas working alone (Stroebe, Diehl, & Abakoumkin, 1992; Paulus, Dzindolet, Poletes, & Camacho, 1993). As we have seen, just the reverse is true. So the truth about brainstorming groups isn't revealed just by being part of them. There is in this a general lesson.

Our experiences are always of some concrete set of circumstances. People in brainstorming groups experience the groups. Those who work alone experience that. But causal questions are inherently comparative; for example, the question of whether brainstorming groups increase creativity is inherently about what happens in brainstorming groups *in comparison with what happens when individuals work alone.* So the subjects in these experiments have only half the experience they need to answer the causal question. The subjects in the brainstorming group lack the experience of working alone; the subjects who work alone lack the experience of being in the group (see Sabini & Silver, 1981, for more on this).

Another reason to be skeptical of the claim that only people who have been through an experience can evaluate it is that people immersed in some strong experience may well pay attention to the wrong aspect of it, so even if they have had the relevant comparative experience, they might still answer the causal question wrong. Subjects in brainstorming groups, for example, typically report that they enjoyed the experience, while subjects who work alone typically report that they don't enjoy that. No doubt subjects with both experiences would prefer the groups to working alone, and they might well confuse their relative enjoyment of the two experiences with their relative productivity in the two circumstances. So for these two reasons, and others too, it isn't wise to accept even firsthand testimonials in the face of well-done, conflicting research. Experiments are just too powerful to be ignored, regardless of the popular wisdom.

The Correlational Method

The experiment isn't the only tool social psychologists use. There are times when we simply can't experiment.

Suppose we were interested, as some social psychologists are, in the impact of physical attractiveness on various kinds of relationships, including romantic relationships. How could we approach such a question experimentally? Well, one narrower question we might ask is: How much does physical attractiveness matter to first dates, when people barely know one another? To find out, we might randomly assign people to go out on dates with people who are either very attractive or less so, and see how much it matters in terms of their eagerness to date that person again. It is not easy to do such an experiment, but it is possible. And indeed, such experiments have been carried out (see Chapter 14). But there is a limitation to such research.

Suppose we wanted to know whether (and how much) the physical attractiveness of one's spouse matters to one's satisfaction with marriage *over the long run.* How could we find this out experimentally?

We would have to assign some people to be married to attractive people and others to be married to unattractive people, randomly, and then see what happened over the long run. But in our culture, at least, people will just not put up with having their marital partners assigned to them—by anyone, let alone randomly. Thus, there is simply no way of approaching this question experimentally. But we can gather evidence by using a different method, the **correlational method.**

Suppose for the moment we were interested in whether women married to attractive men were happier in their marriages than women married to unattractive men. To answer this question, we would have to (1) measure how attractive each husband was and (2) determine how happy each wife was with her marriage. We would then like to know whether, and to what degree, these two factors were related. The statistic designed for this purpose is called a **correlation coefficient.** A correlation coefficient is a number that can take on any value from (and including) $+1$ through 0 to -1. It tells us the *degree of relation* between two variables. A correlation of $+1$ means that the two variables are perfectly related in the positive direction. If we obtained a correlation of $+1$ in the study just described, it would mean that the more attractive a husband was, the happier his wife was with their marriage. That is, a correlation of $+1$ would mean that the *only thing that mattered* to a wife's satisfaction in marriage was her husband's attractiveness.* A correlation of

*This does not imply that attractiveness caused satisfaction; it could be the reverse. Or it could be that something else besides attractiveness caused both satisfaction and dissatisfaction, but it would mean that personality, say, could not matter to satisfaction *unless* it also made the husband more (or less) attractive in his wife's eyes.

−1 would mean just the reverse, that the two variables were still perfectly related but in the opposite direction. It would mean that the *more* attractive a husband was, the *less* happy his wife was, and it would also mean that the only thing that mattered to her was his attractiveness.

A correlation of 0, on the other hand, would mean that the two variables were utterly unrelated; it would mean that overall—for the group as a whole—attractive husbands had neither happier nor less happy wives than did unattractive husbands. A correlation coefficient, then, gives us two kinds of information. The *sign* of the coefficient tells us the direction of the relation between two variables—whether one goes up or down as the other increases. The magnitude, or **absolute value,** of the coefficient tells us the degree to which the two variables are related.

In the empirical world, variables are rarely related to each other perfectly. If they are, it is probably for an uninteresting reason. For example, if you take 100 people and write down their ages and the years they were born, the correlation between these two variables will be −1; that is, as the date of birth increases, the age goes down. But this isn't a fact about the world at all, rather it is a fact about arithmetic. In the social world, correlations rarely exceed 0.5. This should not depress anyone; it is simply a way of saying that the social world is complex, and the degree to which anything we would care to measure relates to *any one other thing* we care about is not likely to be very strong. Even in studies of first dates, the correlation between judges' ratings of how attractive a person is and how much his date would like to go out with him again is, as we shall see, just about 0.5. This just means that even here other things matter too.

Correlation coefficients, then, tell us the degree and direction of relations between two variables. But they do not tell us directly about causality. To see why, consider two variables; call them *A* and *B*. Suppose *A* and *B* are correlated 0.5; what does this tell us about causality? It might mean that *A* has a causal influence on *B*, or that *B* has a causal influence on *A*. Or it might mean neither of those; it might merely mean that some third variable, *C*, has a causal influence on both.

Suppose we did a study in which we had people judge the pleasantness of personalities of their friends. And suppose we also measured how attractive those friends were, and we found them correlated 0.3—positively and modestly. What would this tell us?

Well, it might mean that how attractive someone is affects our judgment of her personality: a person's attractiveness has a causal effect on our judgment of her personality. But the causal direction might be just the reverse. It might be that when we like a person's personality, we tend to judge her to be more attractive. Thus, while the correlation tells us that the variables are related, the correlation does not tell us what causes what. Or consider this. There is a hefty correlation between a child's shoe size and her general knowledge of the world. But this is neither because having big feet makes her smart, nor because being smart makes her have big feet. Rather it is because a third factor, age, causes both her feet and her knowledge about the world to grow. (The correlation is much less than 1, since more than age affects both one's foot size and one's knowledge of the world.)

In general, then, correlational studies tell us if two things are related, but they cannot by themselves tell us which causes which. Of course, there are times when one direction or the other is implausible as a causal sequence. Developing lung cancer and smoking cigarettes are correlated. This might mean that smoking causes cancer or that cancer causes smoking. The former is vastly more plausible than the latter.

Suppose we were interested, as Stanley Schachter was, in whether being anxious leads people to want to socialize. We might approach this problem correlationally. We might gather a group of subjects—say, students right before an exam—and measure how anxious they are, and we could also measure (somehow) how much they want to socialize. If this correlation were positive, then we would know that anxiety and socializing were related. But we wouldn't know why. It might be because the more anxious people are, the more they want to socialize; it might be because wanting to socialize makes people anxious; or it might be because some third factor (say, being an only child) makes people want to socialize *and also* makes them likely to be anxious. An experimental approach (the one Schachter selected—see Chapter 14), on the other hand, would take a group of subjects and *randomly* make some of them anxious while not making the others anxious. Then we would measure how eager each group was to socialize. If, as we shall see is true, the anxious group wants to socialize more than does the less anxious group, we can be confident that anxiety—the (independent) variable the experimenter randomly assigned—has a causal impact on the (dependent) variable the experimenter did not assign, in this case socializing.

These, then, are the two principle methods of social psychology: experimental and correlational approaches. The details of how these are used—often together in the same study—and their subtleties and complexities are beyond the scope of this chapter, and indeed this book.

Two variables, A and B, may be correlated because

- *A* causes *B*;

- *B* causes *A*; or

- some other variable causes *both* A and B.

Thus, showing that A and B are correlated does *not* show that A causes B.

PART ONE

GROUP DYNAMICS

The three chapters of this part are about how individuals relate to groups. In Chapter 2, we consider how being exposed to a group affects the way people think, feel, and act toward aspects of their immediate situation. As we shall see, groups sometimes have a powerful, dramatic effect. This influence extends from the perception of simple physical stimuli to the understanding of moral conflicts, and even to decisions about what is or is not an emergency.

Chapter 3 focuses on a different aspect of group life: how groups perform the tasks they have been given. In this chapter, we explore how groups make use of—or fail to make use of—the resources of their members, and leaders, in performing group tasks.

Chapter 4 focuses on relations between groups. It is hardly news that people tend to be prejudiced *in favor of* members of their own racial and ethnic groups and *against* outsiders. In this chapter, we explore some cultural, motivational, and cognitive bases of such prejudice. ■

CHAPTER 2

Social Influence

As Hans Christian Andersen tells it, there once was a very vain emperor; so vain was he that he spent all his money on clothes. This particular emperor had the misfortune of meeting up with some clever swindlers. They made him an offer he couldn't refuse; they proposed to weave him the finest clothes ever to be seen. To produce their remarkable goods, they would need lots of money and vast quantities of the most precious of materials: gold and silk. As part of their ruse, the swindlers told the emperor that their clothes had a wonderful feature in addition to splendor: the clothes would be perfectly invisible to fools.

As you might imagine, it took quite some time to weave such wonderful material, and the emperor grew anxious about the state of the project. So from time to time, he sent trusted emissaries to look into how the project was going. The emissaries were shown yards and yards of splendid fabric—which, of course, they could not see. But, not wanting to be thought fools, they reported back that the weaving was coming along nicely. Given these favorable reports, the emperor had quite a shock when the clothes arrived: he couldn't see a thing—not a stitch. But he acted, of course, as if they really were the finest clothes he had ever seen. And, as you might imagine, so too did his trusted aides. Thus did the emperor set out on a royal procession in a state unusual for an emperor, at least in a procession.

The townspeople were startled to see their emperor thus attired, but which of them was foolish enough to express surprise? So they too pretended to see these finest ever garments. Unfortunately for the emperor, however, there was one among the crowd unconcerned with being seen as a fool—a child, a child who rudely enough announced the emperor's nakedness. To the chagrin of the emperor, the child's innocent remark freed the rest of the towns-

▲ *Illustration from "The Emperor's New Clothes." The emperor parades through the streets without clothes until one small child remarks, "But he has nothing on."*

people from their burden of pretending to see what was so clearly not there, and they joined the general chorus of comment on the emperor's foolishness.

Why was the emperor taken in by such an obvious swindle? Was it just because the swindlers told him that his failure to see the garments made him a fool? No, the story suggests that there was another element: the emperor's belief that other people *did* see the fabric. The emperor was trapped because he was led to believe that his failure to see the fabric was a consequence of his personal inadequacy—after all, his aides saw the gold and silk!

Andersen's famous story illustrates the central theme of this chapter, and a fundamental form of social influence: we are influenced by other people's perceptions because we expect to see the same world everyone else does.* When we find ourselves in apparent disagreement with everyone else, we are in a very difficult position. To let on to that disagreement is to risk revealing our own foolishness. The story captures the fact that our behavior is influenced not only by our own perceptions, but also by what we think other people perceive.

We will start our discussion of social influence with a phenomenon very close to Andersen's story, a series of brilliant and classic experiments by Solomon Asch designed to find out what people will do when they are asked to express their perceptions, and those perceptions are clearly at odds with what everybody else seems to see. We will ask with Asch whether people in that situation will conform—go along with other people's opinions—or stick with their own perceptions. We will also discuss the role Andersen assigned to the child; what effect a lone dissenter from the popular opinion really has. Does a dissenter, as Andersen suggests, free people to express their real views?

Fortunately for us, not to mention emperors, we are rarely in a situation in which our senses are in flagrant conflict with what everyone else says. But we are more commonly in situations of some ambiguity, situations that aren't so clear. We shall look at how this fundamental form of social influence works there, at how we are influenced by others' views about more ambiguous matters. We will also look at the role of groups of minorities who seem to have a different view from the majority. We will ask whether they too have influence.

The first section of this chapter, then, has to do with how other people's perceptions of the physical world affect our responses to that world. But our assumption that there is one world we all perceive has an impact on a much broader set of judgments. Thus, the remaining sections of the chapter examine social influence on much more complex issues.

The first case we will look at has to do with people's judgments of the amount of risk it is appropriate to accept when making an important decision; here other people's judgments certainly affect our decisions. Next we examine situations in which someone needs our help. These are circumstances in which we might expect people to act regardless of how other people perceive things. But social influence derived from the assumption of a shared reality works here too. People are reluctant to act in an emergency unless they are sure it really is an emergency, unless they are sure other people see it as an emergency too.

---

*This is not the *only* form of social influence. Indeed, the whole of this book is about social influence. But this is one, and perhaps the most fundamental, form of social influence.

Finally we will look at social influence over moral choices. We will take up an important series of studies in which people are given a choice of doing what they see as the right thing to do or going along with the immoral orders of an authority. We shall see that here too, to a degree that no one imagined possible, social influence has a powerful effect. Along these lines, we will also see how social influence can contribute to brutality in a study of how ordinary people act when assigned the roles of prisoner or guard.

Western culture places great value on independence. This stress on the individual takes many forms. For one thing, we expect people to make moral choices based on what they themselves think is right or wrong. For another, we believe in democracy, the idea that governments (and other organizations) act most wisely when they allow each person to express his views. Democratic organization *allows* people a say in what happens to them, but it also imposes a demand: it demands that each person express her independent views. So our culture expects each of us to be his "own person," expects us to reach moral and political decisions on our own.

But the idea that people make moral and political decisions on their own is a bit naive. We all know that sometimes, at least, people's judgments and behavior are influenced by what they believe other people think. An adolescent deciding whether to take drugs or have sex, for example, doesn't decide in a social vacuum; rather, she decides in the context of her impression of what her friends and other peers are doing. And there is every reason to believe that senators on the floor of the Capitol are also influenced by what their peers, other senators, think. Even though we may conceive of ourselves as rugged individuals, we know that we often act as we do in part, at least, because of our knowledge of how other people have acted.

An adolescent who would rather not take drugs but who believes that all his friends do, or a senator personally opposed to a bill but who knows that it is overwhelmingly popular with her peers, faces a choice, a choice between being independent or going along with a group, conforming. By ***conforming,*** social psychologists mean acting at odds with one's beliefs or perceptions because other people are acting in that way. Because these moments of drama are so important to our personal and political lives, social psychologists have devoted a good bit of attention to understanding the forces that determine whether and when a person will remain independent or go along with a group. And as part of that research, they have introduced an important distinction between two very different kinds of conformity.

Consider our senator for a moment. Imagine that she opposes a certain bill, but as the roll call progresses, she finds that she is the only one who opposes it. And when her turn comes, she votes for it too. Now this could happen in two different ways. Perhaps she voted for the bill even though she still didn't think the bill was a good idea. In this case, she has *complied* with the group's position. On the other hand, perhaps she really had her mind changed by listening to her colleagues. In this case, she can be said to have *internalized* the group's position. ***Compliance*** is a matter of going along with a group behaviorally, without being persuaded that the group is correct. ***In-***

Compliance involves going along with influence publicly while remaining privately unconvinced.

Internalization involves being privately persuaded whether one goes along publicly or not.

ternalization implies that the person privately accepts the position her behavior endorses (Kelman, 1958). So compliance implies conformity at the behavioral level only, while internalization refers to a deeper social influence in which the person's private opinions as well as her behavior are changed.

We begin our study of conformity research with the brilliant series of experiments carried out by Solomon Asch (1952). Asch was not the first investigator to study conformity, but his approach was the most direct and dramatic. We will later return to some earlier examples of research on conformity. The contrast between this earlier work and the Asch studies will help us appreciate both.

CLASSIC FINDINGS IN SOCIAL PSYCHOLOGY: THE ASCH EXPERIMENT

▲ *Solomon Asch.*

To understand the Asch experiment, it is best to approach it from the point of view of a subject. Imagine, if you will, that you have been asked by a distinguished professor of psychology to take part in an experiment on visual perception. You arrive at the appointed hour to find six other students there. Some of them are acquaintances of yours, others are strangers. The seven of you are invited to take seats around a table. The experimenter explains that your task will be simple. He places a card on an easel and points to a vertical line on the left side of the card labeled "S" and to three on the right labeled "A," "B," and "C" (see Figure 2.1). Your task is simply to call out the letter corresponding to the line on the right that is the same length as the line labeled "S." As you look at the card, the task does seem simple; it is perfectly obvious that "B" is the right answer—the other answers aren't even close.

The experimenter now asks the first person to give his opinion, and not surprisingly that person says "B." Indeed, the next five people say "B." Now it is your turn, and of course you say "B." Certainly nothing wrenching has happened so far. At the end of this trial, the experimenter removes the card from the easel and replaces it with another. Again the answer is obvious; again everyone who goes before you gives the right answer, and so do you. The experiment seems so easy that you prepare yourself to be politely bored for the next half hour or so.

The experimenter now puts the third card up. This one looks just as easy as the first two; again "B" is the obviously right answer. But the first person says "A," which is clearly, laughably, wrong. You are surprised when you hear "A." You hadn't expected that. You think to yourself, "There must be something wrong with him; maybe he can't see very well." But the next person says "A" too. Now you're not surprised anymore. You're more than that; you're confused. Then, all too quickly, the other four people answer, and they all say "A." Now it's your turn. What can you do? Your eyes give you a clear answer to the experimenter's simple question: "B" is obviously right. But all of those people said "A." There is something wrong here; either you can't see, or you misunderstood the instructions, or something else is going on. Maybe *they* got the instructions wrong; maybe *they* can't see. But how likely is that? After all, they all gave the *same* wrong answer. And what a fool you'll be if you answer "B" and "A" *is* the right answer. They'll probably laugh at you. You know how funny the first person looked to you when you first heard him say "A." Yet the answer still seems clear: it's "B." You are torn, on the spot. The experimenter is looking at you. He wants your answer now. Will you go along, or let on that you are a fool?

RESULTS OF THE EXPERIMENT

If you are like the typical subject, you will give the right answer on this trial. But as the experiment continues, you will find yourself at odds with the group over many of the cards. On some of the trials, the pressure will just be too much for you, so you will give in and go along with the group. In fact, about a third of the subjects (all college students) went along with the group (conform) on a majority of the trials in which they saw the answer one way but the group answered another. On the other hand, about one-quarter of the subjects remained independent of the group on all trials, and the rest conformed on a few of the trials but not on the others (Asch, 1956). Overall, one-third of the judgments were in error, while two-thirds were correct. These error rates take on significance when we realize that other subjects tested alone on the same stimuli got the answers right on all but about 2 percent of the cases (see Figure 2.2).

Were subjects in general independent, or did they conform? There is no simple answer to this question; this is no fairy tale. On the one hand, most of the subjects' *responses* were independent (two-thirds of them; on the other hand, most *subjects* (three-quarters) conformed at least once out of the twelve critical trials. If you expect people to conform, then you should be surprised at the rates of independence. But if you expect people to be independent (which Asch did), then you should be surprised at the degree of conformity (Friend, Rafferty, & Bramel, 1990).

DIFFERENCES IN WHO CONFORMS

Rates of conformity are not always the same; they vary depending on personality differences, gender, and nationality. For example, authoritarian subjects (people especially conventional in their outlook) conform more than less authoritarian, less conventional subjects (Crutchfield, 1955). (See Chapter 4 for a discussion of authoritarianism.) And female subjects typically conform slightly more than male subjects, a fact that may be connected with women's typically lower status in institutions (Eagly & Carli, 1981; Eagly, Wood, & Fishbaugh, 1981; Eagly, 1983; Eagly & Chrvala, 1986). Further, there is some evidence that rates of conformity among American and British students have declined of late (Nicholson, Cole, & Rocklin, 1985). Still, in the Asch situation, in which the facts were very clear and the group had no material power over the individual, there was a substantial measure of conformity across all groups tested.

Why Do People Conform?

The number of subjects who conform isn't the only important fact of the Asch experiment. At least as important is the fact that *all* of the subjects found the experience upsetting; to some degree, all of them were made ill at ease, confused, a bit afraid. As Marie Jahoda (1959) pointed out, although only some of the subjects conformed, all of them felt pressure to go along with the group,

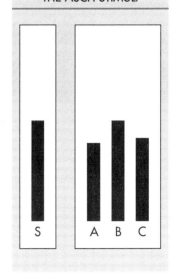

FIGURE 2.1
THE ASCH STIMULI

▲ *Pictured here are stimulus cards drawn to scale similar to those used in Solomon Asch's experiment. (Asch, 1956)*

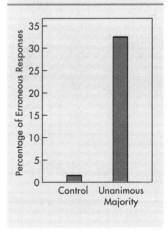

FIGURE 2.2
CONFORMITY TO A UNANIMOUS MAJORITY

▲ *Number of erroneous responses to a unanimous majority compared with responses in subjects who were tested alone with the same stimuli. (Data from Asch, 1952)*

A B C

▲ *Subjects in the Asch experiment. (A) The real subject (center) listens with the confederates to the instructions. (B) After the confederates unanimously agree to an answer that doesn't make sense to the subject, he leans forward to look more closely at the stimuli. (C) After twelve trials, the subject explains that he has to trust his own senses even if it means that his answer will differ from everyone else's.*

▲ *From the Alfred Hitchcock film* Rear Window. *James Stewart witnesses something he thinks was a murder; or was it? Only he saw it. How far does one trust one's own impressions?*

to praise the emperor's fine outfit. So let us turn our attention back to this pressure, this kind of social influence. Where does this power of the group come from? Why do people conform?

CONFORMITY AND OBJECTIVITY

Asch's subjects (like the emperor's) were so upset because they were forced to doubt two things they could not afford to doubt: (1) their own senses and (2) that they see the same world everyone else sees. Ordinarily we trust our senses. Certainly we can learn about cases where we shouldn't trust them—optical illusions, mirages in the desert, trick photography, and so on. But to live our lives in an ordinary, untroubled way, we must trust our senses in all but the most unusual circumstances. And we must also trust that we perceive the same world everybody else does. The possibility of our having any relations at all with other people depends on this. Imagine what it would be like if you couldn't trust the other students in the lecture hall to see it as a lecture hall; suppose they acted as if it were the cafeteria. And suppose they treated the cafeteria like a lecture hall. Suppose your whole life were like that; you could never trust other people to see anything as you did. The world would quite literally be an asylum for you. This is the predicament Asch's subjects were in.

You may be wondering how Asch's subjects found themselves in this predicament in the first place. How did the first six people come to give the wrong answer if the judgment was so easy? In fact, the first six people were accomplices of the experimenter, ***confederates,*** to use the usual term, who deliberately gave the wrong answer. Asch's actual subjects didn't realize this for two reasons: (1) the experiment is much more stressful for participants than for those of us who merely read about it, and (2) the Asch experiment was conducted in the early 1950s before the use of confederates and rigged situations became commonplace in psychology, before subjects became suspicious of experimenters. We can be reasonably sure, then, that Asch's subjects saw the situation as real, and we can be reasonably sure that the influence the experiment displays is real. Had the subjects figured the experiment out, they would have experienced less pressure and made fewer errors.

Our treatment of the Asch experiment has focused on the subjects' confusion, and it has attributed their conformity to that confusion. But there is more to the subjects' experience than being confused. After all, confused or not, the subjects were supposed to report the answer *as they saw it.* They believed that there was a right answer and even if they were confused about what the right answer really *was,* they should have had little doubt about what they *saw.* So, confused or not, they should have given the right answer, though perhaps with little conviction. Is there something more in the subjects' experience that explains why they couldn't cut through their confusion to give this answer?

Perhaps they were just afraid to say what they thought in front of the other subjects. Maybe they were afraid that they would be laughed at, or that they would be thought fools or blind. These fears were not far-fetched. In one version of the experiment, a confederate was instructed to give the wrong answer in the presence of sixteen subjects who gave the right answer. In this condition, the subjects found the confederate's behavior ludicrous; in fact, they openly laughed at him. Indeed, the situation was so ludicrous that the experimenter, who had set the situation up in the first place, found himself laughing too (Asch, 1952; see also Schachter, 1951).

To the degree that subjects are influenced because they accept the other subjects as sources of information about the world, they are responding to what has been called **informational pressure.** To the degree that they change their answer because of their fear that other people will laugh at them or harm them in some other way, they are responding to what has been called **normative pressure** (Deutsch & Gerard, 1955).*

To determine whether the subjects conformed simply because they used the group as a source of information, Asch arranged another condition in which the real subjects were led to believe that they were late; the confederates were already at work. They were told that because they were late, they couldn't really be part of the group; therefore they wouldn't give their judgments aloud. But they could take part in the experiment anyway. They were to write down everybody else's answers and also record the answer they would have given had they had an opportunity to speak. They were to pass on their own answers (and the record they made of the other subjects' answers) directly to the experimenter. These subjects, then, needn't have feared being laughed at by the other subjects, since the other subjects wouldn't know their answers. If these subjects gave the wrong answers, it was because they were genuinely confused rather than afraid of looking like fools to the others. On the other hand, if they gave the right answers, the conformity we saw in the original experiment probably was the result of a fear of looking foolish.

Subjects in this condition gave more wrong answers than subjects tested *alone,* but fewer wrong answers than those who had to answer *aloud.* This suggests that to some degree subjects gave wrong answers for both reasons: because they were confused, and because they were afraid of looking foolish before the other subjects. Both informational and normative pressure work to produce conformity; both are mechanisms of social influence.

AMBIGUITY: THE SHERIF EXPERIMENT

Another experiment—actually performed much earlier than Asch's—also illustrates social influence, but it is in other ways quite different from Asch's. Subjects in Muzafer Sherif's experiment (undergraduate and graduate stu-

Informational influence involves persuasion and internalization.

Normative influence involves coercion and compliance.

---

*Although the Asch experiment didn't provide for it, responding in a certain way to gain some reward would also be an example of normative influence.

dents) were brought into a small laboratory one at a time, and were offered a seat (Sherif, 1935). The experimenter explained that the research they would be taking part in had to do with people's perception of motion. The subjects were told that they would be asked to judge how far a small light moved. The room was darkened, and the subjects were shown the light at the front of the room. They were told that at a certain point the experimenter would move the light, and they were to report on a slip of paper just how far they thought it had moved. Although this task sounds easy, it isn't, because in a darkened room it is very difficult to judge distance. Another reason the task was harder than it seems is that the experimenter didn't actually move the light. Rather, he relied on a well-known optical illusion called the **auto-kinetic effect:** when someone stares at a stationary point of light long enough, it appears to move. So the subjects, unbeknownst to themselves, were trying to estimate the extent of an optical illusion.

Each subject did the best she could with this problem—she guessed. Once she had written her guess down, the experimenter repeated the procedure. The subject had to guess again how far the light moved, and she typically guessed a substantially different distance from her first guess. But as the hundred or so trials progressed, the subject became consistent in her "judgments"; she began making estimates within a reasonably narrow range. Over time, each subject came to home in on some estimate, as if she were actually getting the hang of it. But given that this is an optical illusion, there is no reason for us to expect much consistency among the subjects in the distances they homed in on. And there wasn't. One subject might settle on around four inches, another on about two inches. Each subject made her separate peace with the phenomenon.

In the second, social phase of the experiment, Sherif took subjects who had been in the first phase separately and now put them in the room together. He asked them this time to call out their estimates after each trial. So here we have Tom and Harry. Tom when judging by himself estimated that the light had moved two inches. Harry guessed around four inches. What happened when they were together?

Very quickly their judgments converged; very quickly they influenced each other; very quickly they adopted a common standard. Thus, subjects who at the beginning of their joint session had quite differing views came, by the end, to share an at least rough consensus as to the "facts of the matter." Sherif intended this demonstration to illustrate the way in which social interaction leads people to merge their individual views into a common, shared standard or **norm.** He saw the formation of a common norm as an essential element of all group life, and another example of social influence.

We saw that the influence in the Asch experiment grew out of the subjects' believing that there was a right answer. Did the influence in the Sherif experiment also grow out of the subjects' assuming (erroneously, as it happens) that there was a right answer?

Sherif addressed this question directly. He told some subjects in the group session that the movement was an optical illusion, that there was no right answer. In this case, by and large, the subjects' judgments did *not* converge; rather the subjects stuck with the judgments they had made when alone. So the influence in the Sherif experiment, as in the Asch experiment, required the assumption of a single reality (Sherif, 1935; Alexander, Zucker, & Brody,

1970). Still, there are differences between the Asch and Sherif experiments, and it is as important to see the differences as it is to see the similarities.

THE ASCH AND SHERIF EXPERIMENTS COMPARED

The Sherif experiment gave subjects as ambiguous a task as we can imagine; Asch's task was perfectly clear. This difference in the nature of the judgment the subjects were asked to make had important consequences.

In the Sherif experiment, each subject knew several things. First, he knew that he didn't know the right answer—he knew that he was guessing. He also knew that the other subjects were in no worse (or better) position to judge the right answer than he was; so he knew that they were also guessing. Therefore, it was reasonable for subjects to believe that the truth might lie somewhere in the middle; it was reasonable for them to take account of each other's views. This is not to say that the subjects thought all of this out explicitly. No doubt, many of them didn't. But still, it was reasonable for them to act this way. In the Asch experiment, however, the subjects did not believe they were guessing. It seemed to them that there *was* a right answer, and that they could see it quite clearly. The Sherif stimuli, in other words, were objectively ambiguous; the Asch stimuli were objectively clear. Second, because Sherif's subjects could give any distance as an answer, they could strike a compromise between their guess and their partners'. But Asch gave his subjects only three possible answers; they could not compromise.

There are other important differences between the Sherif and Asch experiments. Asch's subjects, once they learned that the "other subjects" were confederates, realized that they had caved in to social pressure. Indeed, finding the view of themselves as "conformists" unattractive, Asch's subjects typically underestimated the degree to which they had been influenced. Often they denied that they had been influenced at all, when they had in fact given several wrong answers (Tuddenham & McBride, 1959). But Sherif's subjects had no reason to criticize themselves once they learned that the movement was an optical illusion—they had acted quite reasonably in the face of a maximally ambiguous stimulus.

The difference in ambiguity had further effects on the subjects as the experiment unfolded. Asch's subjects were, as mentioned, quite tense, disturbed, even scared by the disagreement. They were forced by the disagreement they faced to see how important assumptions about a shared world are. Sherif's

> **Sherif experiment:**
>
> • Maximally ambiguous stimuli
>
> • Subjects are quite calm
>
> • Conformity leads to internalization
>
> **Asch experiment:**
>
> • Perfectly clear stimuli
>
> • Subjects are very tense
>
> • Conformity does not lead to internalization

A

B

◀ *(A) David Koresh and his wife. (B) The Davidian compound in flames: conformity pressure at its worst.*

subjects were in a different state. The assumption of a single world affected them too, but in a calmer, more ordinary way. It is upsetting to face disagreement only when the matter seems to be so clear as to preclude the possibility of disagreement. Disagreement over the clearly ambiguous causes no such powerful emotions.

As we saw, when Asch's subjects were tested again on the same stimuli out of the presence of the group, they mostly gave the right answers. Their experience of judging in the presence of the group didn't affect their understanding of lines, their length, or the meaning of the notion "same size." But Sherif's subjects were more permanently affected. Subjects brought back to the lab up to one year later and tested alone still relied on the norms they had formed as part of the group; they tended to give the same answers they had given as part of the group a year before (Rohrer, Baron, Hoffman, & Swander, 1954). Sherif's subjects, in contrast to Asch's, *internalized* the frame of reference they had absorbed from the group. Social influence about ambiguous matters, then, is more subtle, quieter, less dramatic, but more enduring.

Last, the social influence in the Asch experiment was heightened by unanimous majorities. A minority in the Asch experiment, on the other hand, had influence only if it was in agreement with the obvious facts of the matter. But in the Sherif experiment, influence was more symmetric. Thus, we should expect that at least with some matters, minorities as well as majorities are able to exert influence.

What Reduces Conformity?

There are various ways in which conformity can be reduced. For example, where people don't doubt their perception of reality, conformity is less likely. Lee Ross conducted an experiment to illustrate just this point. In his experiment, subjects were faced with confederates making different responses to stimuli as in Asch's experiment. But in contrast to Asch's subjects, Ross's subjects *could* reconcile those different responses with a single reality. Ross's subjects were offered a reward for giving the correct answer, but they were told that the "other subjects" were taking part in the experiment under different rules. They were told that the *other subjects* would receive bonuses if they guessed certain lines and if those guesses turned out to be right. So in this version of the experiment, when the subject sees the confederates give the obviously wrong answer, the subject can say to herself, "Well, their answer certainly doesn't look right to me, but maybe they are giving it because they will win a bonus if it *does* turn out to be right. Maybe they're just playing a long shot." Here conformity was reduced substantially below the level in the standard condition (see Figure 2.3; Ross, Bierbrauer, & Hoffman, 1976). It isn't disagreement per se, then, that is so important to conformity; it is the belief that the disagreement indicates real differences in perception.

PREFERENCES

I have argued that Asch's subjects felt all the pressure they felt, and conformed to the degree they conformed, because they assumed that they lived in the same, real world as the other subjects did. I have argued that this is a fundamental form of social influence. But it isn't a very interesting kind of influence if it works only for judgments of line length.

FIGURE 2.3

CONFORMITY WHEN DIFFERENCES MAKE SENSE

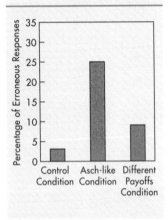

▲ *Conformity will vary depending on whether subjects can account for why other people are responding to the world differently. The figure shows conformity when different responses did not make sense (the Asch-like condition) and conformity when different responses did make sense (the different payoffs condition), all compared with erroneous responses when tested alone using the same stimuli (the control condition). (Data from Ross, Bierbrauer, & Hoffman, 1976)*

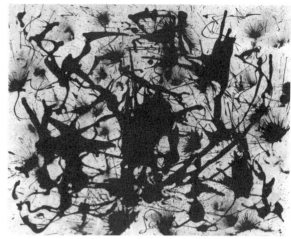

A

B

▲ *(A) A child's drawing and (B) a Jackson Pollock painting. Is one art and the other not? However one answers, to engage the question at all is to take "What is art?" to be an objective matter.*

Richard Crutchfield (1955) repeated Asch's experiment using a slightly different method with a variety of stimuli. He used the kinds of stimuli Asch used, but he also used a number of other tasks: determining the areas of geometric figures, completing series of numbers, giving the meanings of vocabulary items, and so on. Crutchfield, like Asch, found a considerable degree of conformity (see also Santee & Maslach, 1982; Maslach, Santee, & Wade, 1987). But Crutchfield also included questions that didn't produce conformity; knowing what does *not* produce influence is as informative as is knowing what does.

Crutchfield showed subjects two simple drawings and asked them which they preferred. He knew from pretests with other subjects that one of the drawings was much more popular than the other. But he arranged it so that each subject thought that a majority actually preferred the less favored one. The subjects remained independent; the popular drawing in the pretests remained popular among these subjects. These results support our interpretation that the pressure to conform arises not from some general desire to be like everyone else, but from a fear of being wrong about a clear, objective matter. People are willing to be different; they just don't want to be crazy. The subjects apparently believed that when they were asked which drawing they liked, they were not being asked about an objective matter, and hence they were liberated from pressure to conform. This basic form of social influence works on matters of fact, not matters of taste. Indeed, to call something a matter of taste is to call it something subjective.*

THE LONE DISSENTER

The Catholic Church has long understood the power of a unanimous group. When the church considers canonizing someone, elevating him to sainthood,

---

*You may be wondering about modern art. Am I really claiming that the art world is immune from conformity pressure? No. But art dealers, art purchasers, art critics, artists themselves, and many of us who simply enjoy modern art do not see modern art as a matter of taste; rather, they (we) see it (however appropriately or inappropriately) as a domain of objective value. They (we) believe that some modern art really is better than others, and because they see judgments of artistic worth as matters of fact, conformity pressure has an opening (Wolfe, 1975).

FIGURE 2.4

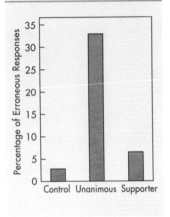

CONFORMITY WITH A
SINGLE SUPPORTER

▲ *Conformity when faced with a unanimous majority and a single supporter and in a control condition in which the subjects were tested alone using the same stimuli. (Data from Asch, 1956)*

a group is convened to consider the moral life of the candidate. In recognition, however, of the way that pressures might develop to suppress evidence of wrongdoing on the part of the candidate saint, there is always one member of the group, the devil's advocate, who is charged with reporting whatever facts weigh against canonization. The devil's advocate not only brings discrediting facts to the attention of the group, but more important, makes it possible for others to express their own reservations. Of course, this lone dissenter will have little influence if the other members don't have any reservations of their own. But if they do, the devil's advocate can liberate others to express their own perceptions.

Asch too found evidence of the power of a lone dissenter. In a variant of his procedure, he had a number of confederates give the wrong answer, but included one confederate who, like the child in the story of the emperor's new clothes, gave the right answer. Thus, the subject had an ally. Having a partner reduced the rate of conformity by about three-quarters (see Figure 2.4). Indeed, in another version of the experiment, Asch included a confederate who, like the other confederates, gave the wrong answer, but the answer he gave was *further* from the right answer than the majority's answer. In this condition, the rate of conformity was also reduced below the level produced by the unanimous majority (Asch, 1956). Vernon Allen has documented this ability of a lone dissenter (even a visually impaired confederate who answered randomly) to reduce the pressure of the group in an extensive series of experiments using a variety of stimuli (Allen, 1965a, 1965b, 1975; Allen & Levine, 1969, 1971). The powerful social influence evident in conformity studies, then, isn't a matter of majority rule.

Further research has shown that seeing someone remain independent in the face of a unanimous majority can induce the courage such action requires even on a different task. In one study, subjects were exposed to a confederate who relentlessly answered "green" to a series of blue slides when others present (correctly) judged them to be blue. Other subjects simply saw four confederates answer "blue." Then subjects from both conditions were exposed to a majority who consistently judged red slides to be orange. Those who had previously seen a confederate hold out in giving his (erroneous) "green" opinion were now more willing to answer with a truthful "red" when all about them answered "orange" than were subjects who had not witnessed the lone dissenter (Nemeth & Chiles, 1988).

MINORITY INFLUENCE

Many important social movements of our times have begun with small numbers of people who challenged the existing assumptions of the majority. The civil rights, women's rights, and gay rights movements had their start with small numbers of people convinced that their positions were better in accord with the moral facts of the matter than were the views of the majority. And all of these movements have, at least to some degree, succeeded; they have caused the majority to reexamine its position and see that it was not in accord with moral right and wrong (see Nemeth & Wachtler, 1973, 1983; Maass & Clark, 1984; Nemeth, 1986).

In addition to the results from the lone dissenter, Asch also developed other evidence about the impact of minorities. In one version of his experiment, Asch had nine confederates give the wrong answer in the presence of eleven naive subjects. There was no conformity; the eleven subjects stuck to their guns, *but* the tone of their reaction to the deviants was very different from the reaction to the single deviate—no one laughed. The majority was puzzled at the disagreement, but respectful (Asch, 1952). So the fact that a substantial number of people gave a patently wrong answer wasn't enough to change anyone's mind, but it was enough to confer respectability on the minority view. This much power a consistent minority has, even a minority endorsing a position that is patently wrong. Serge Moscovici set out to show that in the right circumstances minorities exert even greater influence.

The Moscovici Experiment   Moscovici's research procedure, like those we have already looked at, involved having subjects make judgments in the presence of a group. He used judgments of color rather than of line length. In particular, the subjects were exposed to a light that control subjects (tested alone) almost always called "blue." He showed this stimulus to experimental subjects in the presence of a minority of confederates who called it "green." His question was: What is the impact of these minorities on the majority?

Since blue shades into green, even though a subject would call the stimulus "blue" when asked alone, it is unlikely that she would be *bewildered* to find someone else calling it "green." The situation is very different from Asch's, where subjects *were* bewildered at the confederates' responses. But Moscovici's subjects probably didn't find the question as ambiguous as Sherif's subjects did either. So the majority was faced with a minority that gave what seemed to them a wrong, but plausible, answer. Now let us turn to the exact procedure and the results.

Moscovici made up six slides, all of the same blue color. But three of the slides were bright and three were dim. He then created groups of four subjects and two confederates. The subjects and confederates were first given a test of color vision. This was done for two reasons: (1) to exclude from the study

Conformity is *reduced* when

- subjects can understand the difference between their own responses and the majority's;

- subjects are asked to express their taste rather than their perception of facts;

- at least one other person gives the correct answer;

- at least one other person gives an answer that is incorrect, but different from the incorrect one given by the majority.

FIGURE 2.5
CONFORMITY TO A
CONSISTENT AND
INCONSISTENT MINORITY

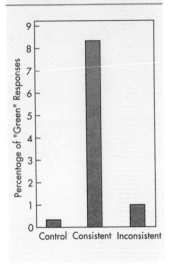

▲ *The responses of subjects calling a blue stimulus "green" varied depending on whether they were tested alone (control condition), with a minority saying "green" consistently (consistent condition), or a minority saying "green" inconsistently (inconsistent condition). (Data from Moscovici, Lage, & Naffrechoux, 1969)*

Minorities sometimes have a direct effect on majorities, influencing their immediate, public behavior.

Minorities can also have a latent effect on majorities, influencing their later, private opinions.

any subject who was color blind and (2) to convince the subjects that the confederates weren't color blind. He then instructed the groups on their task: they were to judge aloud both the color and brightness of the slides.

In one condition, the confederates consistently claimed that the slides were green; in another condition, they randomly varied between calling them "blue" and "green." One measure of social influence was the number of subjects who went along with the minority and called the slides "green" (see Figure 2.5). When the confederates were consistent, 8.4 percent of the subjects' answers were "green," in contrast to 0.25 percent when the subjects were tested alone. Thus, the consistent confederates did have influence. The confederates who responded randomly produced a very small and unreliable increase in "green" responding (1.25 percent).

After this phase of the experiment was over, the experimenter introduced the subjects to a second experimenter, who, he said, had nothing to do with the experiment they had just taken part in, but who was also interested in color vision. This second experiment tested the subjects on a series of colors in the blue-green range and noted just where the subjects drew the line between blue and green. The investigators found that subjects exposed to the *consistent* minority shifted the point at which they cut up the spectrum; they called more stimuli "green" (and fewer "blue") than did the control group not exposed to the confederates. This effect was seen even among subjects who in the first phase of the experiment had not been influenced, who had labeled all of the stimuli "blue."

Thus, the consistent minority affected the subjects in two quite different ways. First, it caused some of the subjects to change their overt responses. Second, it affected a larger number of subjects by causing them to alter the way they looked at the blue-green distinction; it caused them to broaden their conception of green. The first effect has been referred to as the ***direct effect*** of minorities; the second has been called a ***latent effect*** of minorities (Moscovici, Lage, & Naffrechoux, 1969). For Moscovici, these results illustrate the way that minorities can cause the majority to reconsider its views and look at the world in a different way. In his study, the minority had influence only when it consistently gave "green" as a response to the blue stimulus. Other investigators have found that the minority need not be rigidly consistent; what is important is that the minority seem consistent and certain (Nemeth, Swedlund, & Kanki, 1974).

Moscovici has also argued that the *kind* of influence minorities exert is quite different from the kind majorities are capable of. The pressures Asch's subjects were under made them turn away from the stimulus. Perhaps minorities do not have this effect; in fact, it is plausible that they have just the reverse effect. They may get people to consider the matter more thoroughly. Perhaps, as Moscovici has proposed, finding a minority of people challenging the accepted view calls attention to the issue under discussion, and it may do so in a reasonably pressure-free way. And this may indeed lead to the majority's noticing things it hadn't noticed before. There is evidence, for example, that subjects recall atypical responses by a minority better than they recall atypical answers from a majority (Nemeth, Mayseless, Sherman, & Brown, 1990). And studies that have looked at attitude change, rather than judgments of color, suggest that majorities and minorities do differ in the kinds of influence they exert.

A

B

C

Other research has found, as we might expect, that minorities that are able to refute the arguments of a majority are more likely to persuade than those that can't, and that the more members of the majority who defect, the more likely the remaining members are to defect too (Clark, 1990). Insofar as minority influence rests on the ability to refute arguments, then it too rests on an assumption of objectivity, the assumption that arguments that persuade me ought to persuade you too. The social influence that comes from the assumption of objectivity is available for all to use—majority and minority alike.

The social influence we have seen so far has involved subjects who are faced with a simple judgment, a judgment of a simple physical quantity. But social influence works on a much broader set of issues than how long a line is, or how far a point source of light has moved. In the subsequent sections of this chapter, we shall consider social influence in domains richer than physical judgment. We begin by looking at a body of research concerned with how being part of a group engaging in discussion affects individuals' views.

▲ *(A) Albert Einstein challenged the dogma of his day in science, as did (B) Gertrude Stein, and (C) Josephine Baker, in the world of art. All were minorities of one.*

RISKY SHIFT

The literature on group discussion and decision began rather modestly in the early 1960s with research conducted as part of a master's degree program by a graduate student studying management at MIT. James Stoner was interested in documenting something that observers of groups strongly believed, that groups are more conservative than individuals. They are, everyone believed, more conservative in the sense that they are less willing than individuals to take risks. It was widely believed that if you asked individuals to choose a course of action and then brought them together as a group, the decisions made by the group would be *less risky* than the average of the decisions made by the people when judging alone. This is, obviously, a topic of concern to management, since so much of the decision making in corporations is carried out by committees. The thought was that their proclivity to have decisions made by committees doomed large corporations to a stodgy conservatism,

TABLE 2.1

SAMPLE ITEM FROM THE RISKY SHIFT QUESTIONNAIRE

Mr. A, an electrical engineer, who is married and has one child, has been working for a large electronic corporation since graduating from college 5 years ago. He is assured of a lifetime job with a modest, though adequate, salary, and liberal pension benefits upon retirement. On the other hand, it is very unlikely that his salary will increase much before he retires. While attending a convention, Mr. A is offered a job with a small, newly founded company which has a highly uncertain future. The new job would pay more to start and would offer the possibility of a share in the ownership if the company survived the competition of the larger firms.

Imagine that you are advising Mr. A. Listed below are several probabilities or odds of the new company's proving financially sound.

PLEASE CHECK THE *LOWEST* PROBABILITY THAT YOU WOULD CONSIDER ACCEPTABLE TO MAKE IT WORTHWHILE FOR MR. A. TO TAKE THE NEW JOB.

- The chances are 1 in 10 that the company will prove financially sound.
- The chances are 3 in 10 that the company will prove financially sound.
- The chances are 5 in 10 that the company will prove financially sound.
- The chances are 7 in 10 that the company will prove financially sound.
- The chances are 9 in 10 that the company will prove financially sound.
- Place a check here if you think Mr. A should not take the new job no matter what the probabilities.

that it led to a sapping of the innovative, risky, entrepreneurial spirit that Americans are so fond of acclaiming.

To demonstrate this conservatism, Stoner made use of a questionnaire (see Table 2.1). The questionnaire asked subjects to imagine that they had been asked for advice by someone who was considering a risky course of action. For example, one item had to do with an engineer who was earning a decent salary but had an offer to go with a new firm where he might make much more money. The problem was that, like all new firms, it might just fail. So he faced a dilemma—stay where he was at his current salary but with substantial security, or change jobs accepting greater risk but with hopes of greater gain. Now what a person should do in such a case obviously depends on the odds that the new company will fail: If it is a sure thing that the new company will do well, then he should go; if it is a sure thing that the company will fail, then he should stay. But life rarely involves sure things. So the question is: At just what odds of success would you advise him to move? And this was the question Stoner asked his subjects—what are the *minimum acceptable odds* at which you would advise him to take the new job?

Stoner asked his subjects, other students in the management school, to answer this question for twelve dilemmas. He then brought groups of them together and told the groups that they should discuss each of the problems until they reached a unanimous consensus as to what odds they as a group would accept. He compared the average odds the groups decided on with the average odds the same subjects had endorsed as individuals. He expected to find that the groups' averages would be higher than the individuals'—that is, the groups would accept less risk. He found just the reverse. He found that the groups on average were riskier than the individuals on ten of the twelve items (Stoner, 1961). This finding became immortalized as the ***risky shift.***

Most master's theses do not reach a very wide audience, or have much impact on the research of other investigators. But Stoner's finding captured the imagination of a wide group of investigators; literally hundreds of experiments were carried out exploring the phenomenon. Part of the enthusiasm had to do with the counterintuitiveness of the finding. Stoner had discovered that a cultural truism was wrong, and finding that people are wrong about something stimulates the imagination. But another part of the enthusiasm had to do with the robustness of the phenomenon. Research using the same questionnaire across a variety of subject groups, countries, and cultures repeatedly found the same result—groups were riskier than individuals (for reviews, see Cartwright, 1971; Pruitt, 1971).

Explanations of Risky Shift

Because of the replicability of the result, social psychologists were convinced that risky shift was a real phenomenon, something worth investigating. One of the most interesting and important explanations was put forward by Roger Brown (Brown, 1965, 1974).

SOCIAL COMPARISON

Brown suggested that the risky shift might best be explained by ***social comparison theory.*** Social comparison theory, as proposed by Leon Festinger (1954), concerns two central ideas: shared reality and self-evaluation. The first idea lies at the heart of this chapter: when people are confused about the nature of the shared world they live in, they look to other people's opinions to help them understand that world. But there is a second aspect of social comparison theory, which involves self-evaluation.

People worry about whether they are good or bad people in the vast variety of ways that a person can be good or bad. So, for example, a person may be concerned to know whether she is smart or dumb, beautiful or ugly, gen-

◄ *Would these streakers streak alone, or is their risk taking connected to their being part of a group?*

erous or cheap. For these kinds of issues, other people are doubly relevant. First, we may use other people's judgments *about* us to help us determine what is true of us; so one way to find out whether we are smart is to consult other people's opinions of our intelligence. In this way, judgments about ourselves are no different from judgments about any other facet of the world. Second, since beauty, intelligence, and even generosity are at least in part relative matters, we judge ourselves against others. To be beautiful is to some degree to be more attractive than other people. To be smart is to be smarter than other people. To be generous is to give more than other people give. Thus, in assessing our worth, other people are important to us, not just as independent sources of judgment, but also as relevant others to compare ourselves with. Now what, you may be wondering, does all of this have to do with the risky shift?

Brown argued that in our culture, being a risk taker is a valued trait, especially, perhaps, for young males (Dahlbäck, 1990). He argued that we like to see ourselves as people who are willing to take risks to achieve things we want. He proposed that when individuals make their solitary judgments of the minimal acceptable odds, they see themselves as risk takers, more willing than the next guy to take risks. But when the group discusses the dilemmas, most subjects find out that they were really no more risk taking than the next guy. As a consequence, they shift the risk they endorse in the risky direction. Thus, social comparison leads to shifts in the culturally valued direction, toward risk.

A variety of evidence has been established in support of Brown's account of the risky shift. For example, in one study, subjects were asked to rate their own desired level of risk as well as what level of risk they think other people would find acceptable (see Figure 2.6). The subjects for the most part erroneously believed that they were greater risk takers than their peers (Wallach & Wing, 1968). So people do tend to see themselves as riskier than the next guy. In another study, subjects were asked to specify their own level of risk, the average other person's, and the amount of risk the person they admired most would take. The results were that subjects saw themselves as more willing to take risks than the average other student, but less willing to take risks than the person they admired most (Levinger & Schneider, 1969). So people see themselves as having room for improvement.

The first fly in the ointment is this: if social comparison is the mechanism of the risky shift, then there ought to be a shift toward the culturally valued end of the continuum when groups discuss *any* issue. Imagine that some subjects were asked to contribute money to a charity, and then they were asked to discuss how much a person *should* contribute. Since generosity is a culturally valued trait, we would expect that in the group discussion subjects would outdo themselves trying to be generous, so a group discussion should produce a "generous shift." Well, it doesn't. An experiment conducted in just this manner found a "stingy shift" after group discussion (Baron, Roper, & Baron, 1974).

The second and bigger problem is that the explanation of risky shift gives no real role to the group *discussion* in producing the risky shift. As Brown explains it, the shift occurs simply because the subjects are informed of the others' initial judgments. If all there is to the risky shift is social comparison,

FIGURE 2.6

RISK AS VALUE

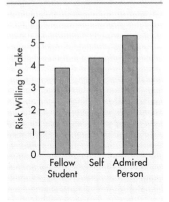

▲ *The amount of risk subjects believed a fellow student would take, they themselves would take, and the person they admired most would take. Subjects believed that taking risks is an admirable thing to do. (Data from Levinger & Schneider, 1969)*

then so long as the subjects found out the other subjects' judgments, the risky shift would happen; actual discussion of the dilemma would add nothing. But in a study conducted by Allan Teger and Dean Pruitt (1967), there was a condition in which subjects did not discuss the problems; they simply learned of the other people's judgments. There was also a condition in which they heard each other's judgments first, and then discussed the problems. Teger and Pruitt found that there was a risky shift in the condition without the discussion, but it was *smaller* than in the condition with a discussion. This suggests that while social comparison may be sufficient to produce the risky shift, it isn't the only mechanism involved.

PERSUASIVE ARGUMENT

Another explanation of the risky shift, advanced by Eugene Burnstein and Amir Vinokur, focuses on the effect of the discussion itself. In their view, it is the arguments brought out in the discussion that matter, not just the exchange of initial views. In one study addressed to this claim, after subjects had individually filled out the risk questionnaire, they were given some information to read. Half the subjects read about the initial judgments of one other person; the other half read about the initial judgments of five other people. In all cases, the judgments they read were quite risky. But the subjects read more than initial judgments. They also read arguments (supposedly generated by other subjects) in favor of a riskier course. Half the subjects read five arguments in favor of greater risk; half read twenty-five arguments. Social comparison theory would predict that the more other subjects' initial judgments subjects read, the more they would shift. Burnstein and Vinokur, on the other hand, proposed that what would matter was the number of arguments, not the number of other people's initial judgments. Their results in fact indicated a relatively small effect of the number of other subjects' judgments and a much larger effect of the number of persuasive arguments (see Figure 2.7; Burnstein, Vinokur, & Trope, 1973). This evidence makes a case for, as Burnstein and Vinokur call it, **persuasive argument theory.**

SOCIAL COMPARISON VERSUS PERSUASIVE ARGUMENT

One way to think about these accounts of the risky shift is that they are *competing explanations* of the same phenomenon, that if one of them is true, then the other isn't. But as some have argued, this may not be so; they may both be components of the risky shift (Blascovich, Ginsburg, & Veach, 1975). It is also true that the two accounts have much in common; let us step back to see what they share.

Roger Brown's account relies on the assumption that taking risks is a cultural value, and the evidence seems to be that it is. But the Burnstein and Vinokur approach assumes that there are more and better arguments in favor of taking risks than there are in being conservative. One would hardly expect this to be true unless taking risks were a cultural value. So both approaches share an emphasis on risk as value. Indeed, each approach seems to emphasize a different aspect of social comparison.

Recall that social comparison theory has two aspects. First, people compare what they think about the world with what other people think about the world. Second, they compare themselves with other people in order to

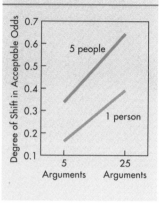

FIGURE 2.7

RISK INDUCED BY ARGUMENTS AND PEOPLE

▲ *Increasing both the number of people endorsing a risky course and the number of arguments they offered increased subjects' willingness to take risk. (Data from Burnstein, Vinokur, & Trope, 1973)*

- Social comparison theory explains risky shift by claiming that people compare themselves with other people and want to be thought riskier.

- Persuasive argument theory explains risky shift by claiming that people compare the arguments they hear with the arguments they already know.

decide how virtuous they are. Brown's account focuses on the second aspect of social comparison theory. The Burnstein and Vinokur account focuses on the first, on the fact that since we do think there is a right thing to do, we listen to the arguments other people make and are influenced by them. Both accounts see the risky shift as an outgrowth of our seeing other people and their arguments as relevant to our own thinking and behavior. Both accounts rely, in the end, on the kind of social influence we have been discussing.

The Demise of Risky Shift

Something curious has happened to the risky shift. First, recall that in Stoner's original work, the group discussion led to greater risk taking on ten of the twelve items. But it didn't lead to a risky shift on the other two. Indeed, there was evidence of a cautious shift, a shift toward a more conservative group judgment on these two items. At the time, no one made very much of this; it was just supposed that it was a matter of chance that the risky shift didn't emerge on two of the items. But as experience mounted, it became clear that these two items quite reliably resulted in a shift toward conservatism. These results weren't a matter of chance, but had to do with something about the items. Moreover, it proved possible to write new items that also produced a conservative shift. Indeed, Clark McCauley conducted a field experiment demonstrating a cautious shift in a natural setting.

McCauley went to a local race track and intercepted bettors at the $2 window after they had placed their bets. He then created groups of three bettors, and told them he would place another $2 bet on whatever horse they agreed on. The risky shift would predict that groups of gamblers would shift from sure things to long shots, but the data revealed the reverse shift. The bettors were more *conservative* as a group than they had just been as individuals (McCauley, Stitt, Woods, & Lipton, 1973). Thus, a shift toward risk simply cannot be counted on as the outcome of a group discussion.

GROUP POLARIZATION

The evidence is that there is a reliable effect of group discussions. Group discussions produce one of two things: either a risky or a conservative shift. Groups do become more extreme, more **polarized.** And, it seems, this effect is not confined just to discussions about what degree of risk to accept. For example, in one study, French students became more extreme in their attitudes about Charles de Gaulle and American foreign policy as a result of group discussion (Figure 2.8; Moscovici & Zavalloni, 1969; see also Doise, 1969; Myers & Bishop, 1971; Myers & Bach, 1974). The risky shift is gone, but group polarization has replaced it as a well-documented phenomenon of group discussion (see Isenberg, 1986, for a review). Now the question is, what account can we offer of group polarization?

As it turns out, the same explanations we offered for risky shift can be applied to group polarization. Both Brown's social comparison ideas and Burnstein and Vinokur's persuasive argument theory can be, and have been, applied to the group polarization effect (Madsen, 1978; Laughlin & Earley, 1982). Brown would argue that people try to outdo each other endorsing the right side of the issue. Thus, as a consequence, the group ends up with a more extreme view than it began with. Burnstein and Vinokur would argue that people offer lots of arguments in the discussion, and therefore the group winds up in a more extreme and convinced posture than the one in which it began. Both views would hold that the groups end up with less divergence of opinion than they started with. Thus, although the risky shift may have disappeared, the social influence mechanisms discovered through it are still with us.

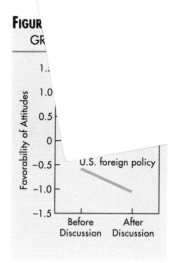

▲ *Group discussion induced attitude polarization. Positive attitudes (toward de Gaulle) became more positive, and negative attitudes (toward U.S. foreign policy) became more negative after a group discussion. (Data from Moscovici & Zavalloni, 1969)*

CLASSIC FINDINGS IN SOCIAL PSYCHOLOGY: BYSTANDER INTERVENTION

On the evening of March 13, 1964, a woman named Kitty Genovese was murdered outside her apartment building in Kew Gardens, Queens. Her assailant attacked her, left, returned, and then killed her. This brutal attack took about a half hour, all told. In all of that time, no one answered her screams either by coming to her aid or even by calling the police. Worse yet, a subsequent investigation by the press revealed that more than thirty people had *watched* the crime from their apartment windows facing the courtyard in which she was killed. Why did no one render even the most passive assistance?

Ambiguity of Emergencies

The press had a simple answer to why no one helped Kitty Genovese. They attributed the failure to the notorious apathy from which, they were sure, New Yorkers suffer. This answer, at least at first glance, seems satisfying. If thirty or so people watched someone else being stabbed and didn't raise a hand to help, then they must not have cared much about her being murdered.

But there was some reason to believe that the story wasn't quite that simple. For one thing, these thirty people didn't just ignore what went on; they stood at their windows and watched. That isn't a sign of apathy. But if they weren't apathetic, then what were they?

Bibb Latané and John Darley suggested that the people watching the attack on Kitty Genovese were confused, and that this confusion led to their inhibition from acting (Latané & Darley, 1970). But what were they confused about, and why did this confusion prevent them from helping Kitty Genovese? Understanding why they were confused and inhibited brings us back to social influence.

Let's start by seeing why they might have been confused. They were, one imagines, sitting in their living rooms watching television, reading the paper, balancing their checkbooks, or whatever, when they heard noises from the street. Perhaps at first they tried to ignore the noises, hoping they were nothing, hoping they would go away. But the noises didn't stop. So eventually they walked to their windows to see what was going on. But what did they see? They saw a man and a woman arguing, screaming. What *should* you do if you hear noises, go to your window to see what is happening, and then see a man and a woman arguing? Should you call the police? Should you go downstairs yourself to see what's going on? It's not clear; at least in a big city it's not so clear. Knowing how it turned out, we know that they should have intervened, but should they have known that then? After all, maybe it was just a quarrel between friends. And if it was just an innocent quarrel, then it was none of the onlookers' business. This, of course, is true of many emergencies.

By definition, emergencies are situations of crisis that arise out of tranquillity; deciding just when something is an emergency, therefore, is often difficult. So let us suppose the witnesses were confused about whether it really was an emergency. What could they do to find out? What test could they use?

'UNCONSCIOUS' PERSON ON STREET (PART OF PSYCHOLOGY EXPERIMENT)

'UNCONCERNED' PASSERBY (ALSO PART OF EXPERIMENT)

'UPSET VIEWER (SHE TOO IS PART OF EXPERIMENT)

S.harris

Emergencies aren't things one can measure with a ruler; we have no chemical tests for emergencies. The most obvious thing for the onlookers to do was to find out what other people were thinking. But how could they do that? Well, they could look at what other people, who also must have heard the screams, were doing. They could look at, and through, other windows that faced the courtyard. In those windows, what they saw were other people. And what were those people doing? They were looking back at them. This suggested to the witnesses that all was well. After all, those other people in the windows weren't running downstairs to see what was happening. Apparently those other people didn't think there was an emergency going on beneath them. Thus, the witnesses misread each other's passivity as a sign that they were convinced that nothing was very wrong, when, in fact, it was just a sign that no one was *sure* something *was* wrong.

PLURALISTIC IGNORANCE

Latané and Darley suggested that while Kitty Genovese was being killed, she was watched by thirty or so people who were far from apathetic. They were people who were intently watching both what was happening to her and each other for a clue as to how to interpret what was happening. Kitty Genovese was a victim, then, of what has been called ***pluralistic ignorance,*** a state in which people mistake each other's beliefs by misinterpreting their behavior, and then use that misinterpretation as evidence for what must be true. The witnesses, through their passivity, influenced each other to believe the passivity was appropriate.

Notice that this analysis rests on an assumption. It rests on the assumption that these witnesses believed that situations either are or are not emergencies; that whether something is an emergency is a matter of fact. The witnesses acted as if they were subjects in a Sherif experiment using other people's responses in their ambiguous situation to help them figure out what the real facts were. In the Sherif experiment, the subjects influenced each other by explicitly stating their impressions; in the Kitty Genovese case, the witnesses influenced each other not through their explicit statements but through their behavior.

Recently Deborah Prentice and Dale Miller have called attention to some interesting examples of pluralistic ignorance that crop up on college campuses. One example is regrettably common to college classrooms. It goes like this. Sometimes lecturers get the impression—from the reaction of their audience—that their lecture might not be as perfectly clear as they hoped it would be. Most lecturers want to know whether this impression is correct; they really do. So the natural impulse at such moments is to stop and ask students directly, "Is this clear? Do you have any questions?" All too often, at least in my experience, however, this leads to a very disappointing response—blank stares. Why?

The reason may be pluralistic ignorance: I know from my own experience as a student that at such moments *nothing* was going to get me to admit that I didn't understand—or, at least, nothing was going to get me to be the *first* person to admit I didn't understand. So in response to such direct questions, I would sit there quietly no matter how confused I was (hoping, of course, that someone else would ask what I wanted to know). But in hindsight, I am now sure I was not unique in being confused at least in some of those moments. In hindsight, I recognize that everyone else was acting just as I did. The upshot was that no one, no one at all, would ask a question even if everyone, yes everyone, was confused. And *worst of all,* since each of us would see that no one else asked a question, each of us would become convinced that we were the only person in the class not understanding. And that, of course, would make us even less likely to ask a question now or in the future. (It is exactly to prevent this that instructors sometimes inhibit their impulse to ask the class if it is confused!) So pluralistic ignorance may account for the absence of student questions just when they are most needed. The other example Prentice and Miller pointed to also takes place on campus, but not in classrooms.

The liberal consumption of alcohol is perceived to be the social norm on some college campuses; that is, it seems to students on these campuses that it is simply assumed that alcohol will be consumed at social events. But Prentice and Miller argued that on these campuses there might be many students who are themselves quite uncomfortable with casual alcohol use, but who believe that they are different from the norm, that *everybody else* is comfortable with it. If this is so, then there is pluralistic ignorance about the local social norm; people are responding to what they think everyone thinks is appropriate rather than to an actual consensus of individual opinions.

To show that this was the case on one campus, Prentice and Miller asked 132 undergraduates to indicate on an eleven-point scale ranging from "not at all comfortable" on one end to "very comfortable" on the other how comfortable *they* personally were with alcohol use and also how comfortable they thought *the average student on their campus* was. The results were that the students thought that the average other student would rate herself at a seven on degree of comfort, which is closer to "very comfortable" than to "not at all comfortable." But how comfortable *was* the average student really; that is, what was the average of the students' reports about how comfortable they were personally? The answer was 5.33—significantly less comfortable than they thought the average student was. Thus, for the most part, the typical student thought herself to be less comfortable with the degree of alcohol use than the average other student. The students, one must assume, had private qualms about all the alcohol that is used, but failed to voice those qualms, and thus allowed for a (false) perception that people were happy with things the way they were.

Prentice and Miller went on to ask what happens over time when the perceived norm and private personal opinions are at variance. They followed some of their subjects over the course of the sophomore year to find out what happened to their perceived norms and their personal attitudes. The answer was different for men and women. At the end of the fall semester, the men in the sample had shifted their private attitudes toward what they perceived to be the social norm. That is, they became more comfortable with the level of drinking on campus. What they thought (erroneously) at the beginning of the year was the consensus about alcohol use became the consensus over the course of the year. But the same change in personal opinions toward the perceived norm didn't occur for the women in the sample, who remained in pluralistic ignorance. That is, they continued to have unexpressed private reservations, and they continued to imagine that other people didn't have those reservations (Prentice & Miller, 1993).

In the Kitty Genovese case, we see an example of pluralistic ignorance in the heat of action—in circumstances where an immediate response to an unexpected event was called for. But the evidence Prentice and Miller present about attitudes toward alcohol suggests that pluralistic ignorance can endure even over extended periods of time so long as—for whatever reason—people do not publicly express their private attitudes.

Pluralistic ignorance involves

- mistakenly inferring a person's beliefs from behavior;

- a resulting false consensus.

DIFFUSION OF RESPONSIBILITY

Latané and Darley offered an additional reason for the witnesses' inaction in the Genovese case. The second reason they called **diffusion of responsibility.**

If someone had decided that there really was an emergency, then that person surely would have known that *someone* should do something—come to the victim's aid or at least call the police. But that still wouldn't settle the question of just *who* should do something. There is an important difference between knowing that *someone* should act and knowing that *you* should act. The problem is that everyone watching may have believed that someone was responsible to act, but everyone may also have believed that *someone else* was the someone who was responsible. This logic is diffusion of responsibility.

Latané and Darley argued that had only one person been watching the assault, that person would have known it was his place to do something. But since many people watched, and knew other people were watching, none of them felt uniquely responsible to help.

Experimental Findings

All that we have observed so far has been speculation, a story that makes sense of what happened one night in Kew Gardens. Latané and Darley weren't interested in finding out whether the story they told about this particular event in Kew Gardens was the right one, however; rather, they were concerned to see whether the principles of pluralistic ignorance and diffusion of responsibility are sound. Thus, they conducted a series of experiments to determine whether bystanders in general are inhibited by these factors.

WHERE THERE'S SMOKE THERE'S FIRE

Latané and Darley invited Columbia University undergraduates to what was advertised as a study of the experience of going to college in an urban environment. Subjects were invited to an office one at a time and given a questionnaire to fill out. As they were filling it out, what appeared to be smoke poured out of the ventilator (actually it wasn't smoke, but the same vapor used in billboards in Times Square to produce the illusion of cigarette smoke). Sensibly enough, the subjects quickly left the room to report the smoke.

But in another condition, the results were quite different. Now the subject was asked to fill out the questionnaire not alone, but with two other people who were confederates of the experimenter. These confederates behaved in a most amazing manner—they simply continued to fill out the questionnaire in the face of smoke that eventually became so dense that it made reading quite difficult! What would the subjects do in the face of this competing evidence—the evidence of their senses that there was a fire somewhere and the evidence that the "other subjects" didn't seem upset by it? Well, eventually most of the subjects did leave the room and report the smoke (see Figure 2.9). But they took considerably longer to leave than did the subjects tested alone. And some subjects didn't leave at all; they were still there shrouded in smoke when the experimenter called the experiment off. The subjects were inhibited from acting in the face of an emergency by the passivity of the others. And note that in this case it wasn't someone else's life that was on the line; it was their own lives—there is no question of apathy here.

There was one more condition in this experiment. In this condition, more like the Kitty Genovese murder, the subject filled out the questionnaire not in the presence of two confederates, but in the presence of two other real subjects. If Latané and Darley's analysis of the Genovese case was right, then here too the subjects should be slower to react to the smoke than they were when tested alone. And indeed they were. They weren't as slow as when tested with two stubbornly passive confederates, but they were slower than when tested alone. These strangers, then, did inhibit each other from reacting to what certainly looked like a fire. Pluralistic ignorance can lead to inhibition. But what about diffusion of responsibility; is that a real phenomenon?

FIGURE 2.9
PLURALISTIC IGNORANCE

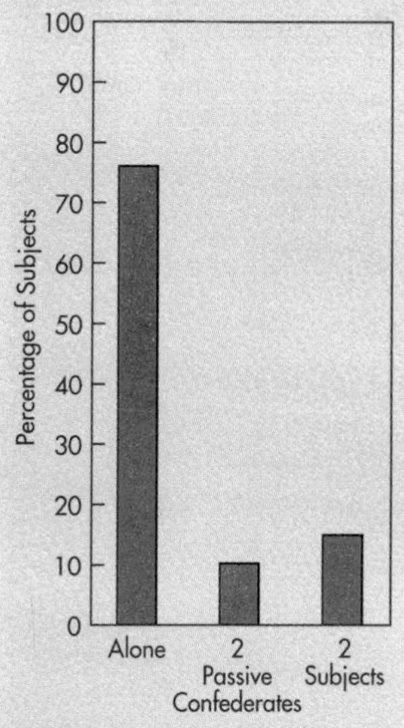

▲ Percentage of subjects responding to smoke within two minutes when alone, with two passive confederates, and with two other subjects present. (Data from Latané & Darley, 1968)

Another study with Columbia undergraduates looked for diffusion of responsibility. In one condition, when the subject arrived at the office, she was told that she would be having a discussion of urban college life with one other subject. She was led to a one-person cubicle, given headphones, and shown a microphone. The experimenter explained that she and the "other subject" were simply to take turns talking to each other about urban college life. The discussion would be tape-recorded, and the experimenter would listen to it later. Thus, the subject was led to believe that she and the other subject would *not* be overheard at the time of the discussion.

After a time, the subject thought she heard the other subject being shown to his cubicle. Actually, the subject heard a tape recording; there was no other subject there. The tape spoke first, and on it the confederate explained that his problem in living in the city was that he was an epileptic. He sometimes had serious seizures, especially when under stress from his studies. Then it was the subject's turn. She had a chance to talk about her experiences for a few minutes. Then it was the confederate's turn again, and he returned to the theme of his seizures.

He began to describe them rather calmly, but as he spoke, it became obvious that he was having a seizure at that very moment. In his increasingly incoherent talk, he explicitly asked for help, and at the end of the talk he raised, in a scream, his fear of dying. After 125 seconds, the tape stopped, and the subject could hear nothing through the earphones. As you might imagine, the subject was very likely to come to the victim's aid. Indeed, 85 percent did so within 125 seconds, and the average time it took for a response was just under a minute.

Other conditions were run in an identical fashion except the subject was led to believe that in addition to herself and the epileptic, one or four other subjects were participating in the discussion. Thus, the experiment allowed a test of the diffusion of responsibility notion. According to that idea, if the subject believes that there is another subject there with her and the epileptic, then she will be less likely, or slower, to help than if she knows she is the only one who can help. And if she knows there are four others who could just as well help, she will be slower still. And this is just what happened.

For example, 62 percent of the subjects who knew there was another subject in a position to help came to the victim's aid, and only 31 percent of those who thought there were four other people came to rescue the epileptic (Darley & Latané, 1968). Also the more people present, the slower witnesses were to respond, if they responded at all (see Figure 2.10). The results, then, are strong support for the notion of diffusion of responsibility.

The results of this experiment (and others like it) suggest that there is merit in Latané and Darley's account of what happened to Kitty Genovese. But more important for our purposes, they highlight two facts about the kind of social influence we have been considering: (1) it happens in situations where what is at issue is more complicated than a simple physical measurement, and (2) it has the power to affect us even when what is at issue is as important to us as whether there is a fire in the building. Just as Asch's subjects would have given the right answer had they been left to their own devices, Latané and Darley's subjects when left to their own devices did the right thing. But if they were in the presence of other people, subjects in both

FIGURE 2.10

DIFFUSION OF RESPONSIBILITY

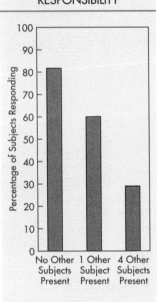

▲ *Number of subjects responding to an epileptic having a seizure when alone, with one other subject, or with four other subjects. (Data from Darley & Latané, 1968)*

experiments took account of the other people's perceptions and were inhibited from doing the right thing. These experiments also illustrate the fact that social influence increases with the number of people present.

Stanley Milgram's research on obedience to malevolent authority is surely the most dramatic in social psychology; some would consider it the most significant. For these reasons, we shall examine it in detail. Milgram's research was influenced by questions within the discipline of social psychology and questions arising from broader concerns. It is important to see both influences, and how they came together.

THE ASCH EXPERIMENT AND HUMAN SIGNIFICANCE

The Asch experiments were quite powerful demonstrations of social influence, but they had a weakness. Some critics said, "Well, yes, people were influenced. But the matter was so trivial; so what if one line was the same size as the other? Who cares?" A demonstration like Asch's would be much more powerful if something of importance hung on what the subjects said. So Milgram set out to design an experiment that would be like the Asch experiment but that would attach importance to the subjects' responses.

This idea occurred to him. Suppose he changed the Asch experiment in the following way. Instead of having the subjects judge the length of the lines, he had a confederate give answers to Asch's question. The subjects' task would be to shock the confederate if he got the answer wrong. Now to make the situation like Asch's, other confederates (assigned the same task as the subject) would administer a shock on some trials in which the answer the confederate gave was clearly and obviously right. The subject therefore would find himself in the same position as subjects in the Asch experiment: he could either give an honest response or go along with the confederates giving the wrong answer. The difference is that this time if the subject caved in to a majority, he would also be unfairly shocking someone.

This was a clever idea, but it was never carried out. The reason it was never carried out is that Milgram realized that he needed to run a control group. He needed to know how willing subjects would be to shock someone *without* the confederates. And answering that question became an important research program in its own right. The shape of that research program, however, was also determined by something quite far from the laboratories of social psychologists.

EICHMANN IN JERUSALEM

In a courtroom in Jerusalem, Adolf Eichmann was placed on trial for his part in the Holocaust. Eichmann was the Nazi official most directly responsible for the logistics of the Holocaust, the slaughter of 8 million Jews, Gypsies, gays, Communists, and Christian Scientists. He had been captured by Israeli officials who tracked him down in Argentina. Hannah Arendt, a philosopher, was sent to Jerusalem by the *New Yorker* magazine to report on the trial, which she did in a series of quite controversial articles. Arendt's account of Eich-

▲ *Stanley Milgram.*

A

B

▲ *(A) Close-up of Adolf Eichmann, on trial in a Jerusalem courtroom in 1961 for his role in the perpetration of the atrocities of the Holocaust in Hitler's Germany. (B) An overview of the courtroom where Eichmann was tried.*

mann depicted him as an extraordinary man in only one way: his ordinariness. This was not something the world wanted to hear.

The Holocaust is surely unsurpassed in the dreary chronicle of human evil. One expects, even wants, its organizers to be different from the rest of us; one wants them to wear their evil. Hitler was such an obviously Satanic character. People wanted Eichmann to be one too. They wanted him, like Hitler, to bubble over with his hatred of the Jews. They wanted him to be a man ruled by his passions, horrifying passions.

But Eichmann was none of these things. He was, instead, a very mild-mannered man. He explained to his Jewish captors, apparently without guile, that he himself had nothing in particular against the Jews, and that he certainly had gotten along with the few Jews he had worked with early in his job. So, he was asked, if he didn't hate the Jews, how could he have done what he did? He explained that the reason was really very simple—he was ordered to. Again and again he was pressed with the question of why he had done it, and again and again he replied that he did it because he was ordered to.

Eichmann's answer was incomprehensible to those who asked the question. The interrogators simply couldn't understand how someone could have organized the death of 8 million people just because he was told to. So they kept asking the question. But their repeating the question was equally incomprehensible to Eichmann; he couldn't understand why they thought there must be more to it than that. It had never occurred to him to think about whether being ordered to was a good enough reason to do what he did.

Arendt's readers were quite upset with this portrait of Eichmann, and there are many reasons to find it upsetting. The most important reason is that it eroded the difference between Eichmann and the rest of us. If Eichmann could become so deeply involved in the Holocaust without any strong hatred, just because he was ordered to, them maybe the rest of us could too. This disturbing possibility contributed to the acrimony over the publication of Arendt's report, first as articles in the *New Yorker,* and then as a book, *Eichmann in Jerusalem,* tellingly subtitled *A Report on the Banality of Evil* (Arendt, 1965). But was Arendt right? Could any of us be induced to torture, even kill, just by being ordered to do so? The control group that Milgram as we shall see, addressed this question.

Milgram brought subjects, attracted to the experiment by an ad in a New Haven paper, to a laboratory and told them they were there to take part in an experiment on human learning. Their particular role, determined by drawing lots, was to consist of delivering electric shock to a learner—an avuncular-looking, middle-aged gentleman—each time he made an error in learning associations between paired words. The subjects saw their "fellow subject" strapped into a chair; they saw electrode paste and electrodes attached to his arm. They heard the experimenter say that the paste was to avoid blisters and burns. In some cases, they heard their pupil-to-be tell the experimenter that he had a slight heart condition. And they both heard the experimenter reassure them that although the shocks might be painful, they would cause no permanent tissue damage.

With the learner now prepared to receive the shocks, the experimenter turned his attention to the teacher. The experimenter conducted the teacher to another room and showed him the machine with which he was to deliver the "punishment," an impressive-looking device with thirty switches marked from 15 to 450 volts in 15-volt increments. Below the numerical labels were others characterizing the shocks. These ranged from "SLIGHT SHOCK" at the low end to "INTENSE SHOCK" in the middle, through "DANGER: SEVERE SHOCK," and finally to a simple, stark "XXX" beneath the last two switches. So that the teacher would have a better appreciation for the learner's experience, the experimenter gave him a sample shock of 45 volts, which was within the slight shock range and was only one-tenth of the shock that would be delivered by the finally lever.

The experimenter then explained the way the experiment would work. The instructions were a bit complicated. The teacher was to read the learner lists of word pairs. Then he was to read the first word of each pair back to the learner with four other words, one of which was the correct completion of the pair. The learner was to answer this multiple-choice test by pressing one of four buttons to indicate his impression of the right answer. Thus, the teacher first read to the learner, "Blue-box, nice-day, wild-duck," and so on, and then read him, "Blue-sky, ink, box, lamp." The learner was to press the

▲ *The learner in the Milgram experiment.*

◀ *The legend below the switches on the Milgram shock machine.*

▲ (A) The Milgram shock machine. (B) The learner being strapped into his chair. (C) The subject being instructed about the experiment.

A button if he thought "sky" was the word originally paired with "blue," and so on. A light in front of the shock box informed the teacher of the learner's choice.

The final instruction was that the teacher was to give the learner a 15-volt shock for his first wrong answer, and was to shock him again every time he made a mistake. The teacher was to increase his punishment one shock level (15 volts) for every wrong answer. The learner was a confederate of the experimenter; the only real shock delivered was the sample shock given to the teacher. But the teacher, the real subject, didn't know this.

The experimental sessions began innocuously enough; the learner got some of the pairs right, but he soon made an error and was given a 15-volt shock. Such a shock, had it been real, would have been so slight as to cause neither the learner nor the teacher distress. And indeed, until 75 volts, the teacher had no indication that he was causing the learner much pain. But at 75 volts, the learner grunted in pain. The teacher could hear the grunt through the wall separating them. At 120 volts, the learner shouted to the experimenter that the shocks were becoming painful. The innocuousness of the beginning had passed.

At 150 volts, the teacher and learner crossed an important border when the learner, and now we would do better to call him "the victim," screamed, "Experimenter get me out of here! I won't be in the experiment anymore! I refuse to go on!" This response made it clear both that the shocks had become very painful and, perhaps more important, that the learner was no longer a willing participant. He was now a captive of the experimenter and his agent—the teacher/subject.

The learner continued to cry out in pain, with his cries increasing in intensity, becoming agonized screams once the shocks reached 270 volts. At this point, it would not be an exaggeration to say that the experimenter and teacher were engaged in torture.

At 300 volts, the learner shouted in desperation that he would no longer respond to the word pairs. The experimenter matter-of-factly informed the subject to treat no response as if it were an error, and to go on administering shock. From this point on, the subject heard no more from the learner; he did not know whether the learner was even still conscious. And he knew that since the experimenter was in the room with him, not with the victim, the experimenter couldn't tell either whether the victim was conscious—or even alive. The subject could certainly see that the torture had become pointless torture; whatever else was true, since the learner was no longer answering, he was surely no longer taking part in a learning experiment. When the subject reached the end of the shock board, he was told to continue using the last lever for all subsequent "mistakes." The pointless torture now became of indeterminate sentence. The subjects were, of course, physically free to leave the experiment, to relieve the victim's suffering; the victim was strapped in, but nothing barred the subjects' escape.

PREDICTIONS ABOUT THE EXPERIMENT

The point of the experiment was to investigate factors that control our willingness to obey an authority's commands when those commands are contrary to widely shared moral sentiments, sentiments about hurting people against their will. Milgram expected that very few, if any, subjects would continue in the experiment to shocks of 450 volts. He expected that to get subjects to obey, he would have to reduce the intensity of the cries of agony from the victim. Other experts agreed. Samples of psychiatrists, graduate students, and faculty members in the behavioral sciences all predicted that no more than 2 or 3 percent of subjects would continue to the end. When similar samples were asked to predict *their own* behavior, *none* predicted that she would continue to the end. Thus, expectations about what would happen in the experiment were clear; all samples expected subjects to become defiant at some point. But what actually happened?

RESULTS OF THE EXPERIMENT

Twenty-six of the forty male subjects who took part in the experiment continued to the end; exactly the same number of women, twenty-six out of forty, continued to the end (see Figure 2.11). The fully obedient subjects stopped administering the 450-volt shocks to the victim only when *the experimenter* told them to stop.

There have been several replications of the experiment in other countries. The rates of obedience vary from place to place, but the general fact is that in all countries, subjects obey at rates we would never expect (Kilham & Mann, 1974; Mantell & Panzarella, 1976; Shanab & Yahya, 1977). The phenomenon is robust enough and general enough to merit our careful attention.

Explanations of Obedience

There are two questions that must concern us: (1) Why did so many people obey the experimenter's unconscionable commands? and (2) Why did no one expect them to? It is clear from the results of the experiment that the Milgram situation lets loose some powerful social influences, but it is also clear from the predictions people made that we are, in the main, unaware of these forces. Let us look, then, for details of the experimental setting that might have contributed to obedience.

SLIPPERY SLOPES

One important feature of the situation is that although subjects end up giving extraordinary levels of shock, they begin with perfectly innocuous amounts. The first switch, after all, is only 15 volts, a barely perceptible shock. And the shock increases by a mere 15 volts with each error. Although it is clear that giving someone 450 volts is a very different matter from giving him 15 volts, it is not so clear just where the innocuous becomes the unconscionable; it is not so clear just where the subject ought to stop. The very gradual increase in the level of shock is a slippery slope from the innocent to the evil; it is slippery enough for most subjects to slide down. But it apparently doesn't seem so slippery from outside the experiment.

THE OBJECTIVITY OF THE EXPERIMENTER

The CBS television network once produced a "docudrama" on the Milgram experiment. Although it was for the most part faithful to the actual experiment, it departed in some ways. One way was in the demeanor of the experimenter. In the CBS version, when a subject protested, the experimenter appealed to him to continue. The experimenter cajoled, wheedled, and so on.

Obedience in the Milgram experiment vastly exceeded the predictions of

- a sample of residents of New Haven;

- a sample of Yale psychology graduate students;

- a sample of Yale psychiatrists.

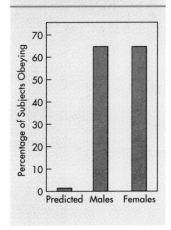

FIGURE 2.11
RESULTS OF THE MILGRAM EXPERIMENT

▲ *Predicted versus actual obedience for males and females. (Data from Milgram, 1974)*

But in fact the experimenter acted in a quite different way. The experimenter was supremely matter-of-fact. If the real subject protested against the order to shock (and many subjects did), the real experimenter said, ''Please continue.'' If the subject protested again, the experimenter said, ''The experiment requires that you continue.'' Further protest was met by ''It is absolutely essential that you continue,'' and if necessary the experimenter finally said, ''You have no choice, you must go on.'' Notice how impersonal, how bureaucratic these replies are; there is no hint of a personal involvement on the experimenter's part. This is important to an understanding of why the subject continued.

Obedience in the Milgram experiment is *not* a matter of the subject's giving over his will to the experimenter; rather, it is a matter of the experimenter's persuading the subject that he has a *moral* obligation to continue. And the moral aspect of the experimenter-subject relationship is sustained in part by the impersonal nature of the experimenter's demeanor. The experimenter is objective; he presents himself to the subject as an unbiased, disinterested observer concerned only to interpret the experiment's requirements for the subject. The experimenter acts as if he is simply presenting the social-moral world to the subject as he sees it. The power of this posture is apparently lost on those not currently facing it.

Stressing the objectivity of the experimenter as a crucial element in the subjects' obedience highlights the parallels between the kind of social influence we saw in the Asch experiment and the obedience seen in the Milgram experiment. It is important to appreciate just what those parallels are. In the Asch experiment, the subject enters the laboratory with a fairly good sense of how long a line is; in the Milgram experiment, he enters with, one imagines, a good sense of how far it is reasonable to shock someone. In the Asch experiment, the subject runs into six people *just like himself* who disagree; in the Milgram experiment, the subject runs into a single authority with a very different sense of what is morally proper. In both cases, subjects find themselves under great stress and pressure because of these different views, and in both cases, significant numbers of subjects give in.

FIGURE 2.12

REDUCING OBEDIENCE

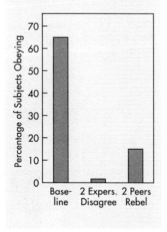

▲ *Obedience when in the presence of two experimenters who disagreed or two peers who rebelled, compared with obedience when in the presence of one experimenter and no peers. (Data from Milgram, 1974)*

Reducing Obedience

Milgram carried out a variety of variations on his basic experiment in which subjects were substantially less willing to obey the experimenter. We can learn about the forces producing obedience by a close examination of circumstances that reduce it.

DISAGREEING EXPERIMENTERS AND REBELLING PEERS

Recall that in the Asch experiment if a single other person gave the right answer, then conformity was dramatically reduced. In one condition of the Milgram experiment, when the subject arrived for the experiment, he met not one but two experimenters. At the crucial 110-volt point, where the victim cried out in pain, one of the experimenters told the subject to stop, while the other ordered him to continue. In this condition, *every* subject stopped (see Figure 2.12). Thus, just as the pressure to conform in the Asch experiment relied on unanimity among the confederates, so too does the pressure to obey depend on unanimity among the authorities. Disagreement calls into question whether the authorities are able to provide a definitive interpretation of the objective requirements of the situation, and thus allows the subject to act in accord with his own interpretation.

The subjects' belief in the authoritativeness of the experimenter's interpretation can be upset in other ways too. In another condition of the Milgram experiment, three "subjects" were involved in giving the shock; two were confederates. One of these "other subjects" disobeyed the experimenter at 150 volts, and refused to continue; the other disobeyed at 210 volts. In this condition, 10 percent of the subjects themselves continued to the end. Thus, if the subject is caused to doubt the experimenter's interpretation, he is much more likely to refuse to continue.

OBEDIENCE AND EMBARRASSMENT

In one additional condition, the experimenter wasn't in the room with the subject as the experiment unfolded; his instructions were conveyed by a tape-recorded message (see Figure 2.13). The subject could also talk to the experimenter by phone. Now from the point of view of informational influence, whether the experimenter was present or talking over the phone is irrelevant. But when the experimenter was absent, the rate of obedience declined: nine (as opposed to twenty-six) subjects continued to the end. Why?

Perhaps the experimenter's presence is important for this reason. If the experimenter is in the same room, in order for the subject to quit, he has to confront the experimenter directly. He can't just quit; he has to explain why he is quitting. But what reason can he offer? Some subjects tried to withdraw by saying that they couldn't continue, or didn't want to continue, or were too uncomfortable to continue. These explanations didn't work very well because the experimenter countered them by claiming that the subject had an *obligation* to continue; ironically, the subject was trapped into offering a "selfish" reason for quitting, while the experimenter offered a "moral" reason for continuing.

What kind of justification *should* the subject have offered for leaving? A moral one: "I am quitting because continuing is wrong, morally wrong." But this implies a criticism of the experimenter for ordering the subject to continue. And this is apparently very hard to do. It is embarrassing. When the experimenter is in another room, the subjects are spared this embarrassment. One contributing cause of this terrible obedience, then, may be that it is just very embarrassing to tell someone off (Milgram, 1974; Sabini & Silver, 1982). When the experimenter wasn't present, subjects were spared this embarrassment, and they obeyed less. Thus, the experimenter exerted normative as well as informational pressure.

DISTANCE FROM THE VICTIM

In the version of the Milgram experiment with which we began, the subject could hear the screams of the victim through the walls of the laboratory, but he could not see the victim. In other versions, Milgram moved the victim closer and closer to the subject. In the most intimate version, the subject had to hold the victim's hand on the shock plate (through a sheet of Mylar insulation so that the subject wouldn't feel the shock). Reducing the distance between subject and victim had a dramatic effect: when the subject had to

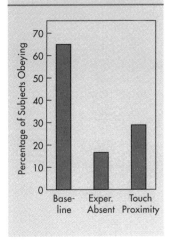

FIGURE 2.13

OBEDIENCE AND EMBARRASSMENT

▲ *Obedience when the experimenter was in another room, when the subject was actually touching the victim, and in the baseline condition. (Data from Milgram, 1974)*

▲ *The learner screams in pain during the touch proximity condition of the Milgram experiment.*

■■■■■■■■■■■

Obedience in the Milgram experiment was *substantially reduced* when

• two experimenters disagreed as to whether the subject should continue to deliver shocks;

• the "fellow subjects" refused to continue in the experiment;

• the experimenter was in a different room from the subject and communicated with the subject only by phone;

• the subject was told to hold the victim's hand on the shock plate.

■■■■■■■■■■■

hold the hand of the victim on the shock plate, obedience was reduced to twelve out of forty subjects. But why does closeness reduce obedience?

It is important to realize that the closeness of the victim in no way alters the *moral* issue embodied in the situation; it is no more moral to shock a distant victim than a close one. So closeness contributes to disobedience in another way. One reasonable interpretation is that closeness to the victim makes it more difficult for the subjects to administer the shock. Perhaps it makes it harder just because it is difficult for subjects to listen to someone screaming in pain. It seems that we humans are so constructed that certain cues, like the sound of someone screaming, are aversive to us (see Chapter 11). Distance from the victim typifies both modern weaponry and modern bureaucracies. Warfare is increasingly a matter of killing someone with long-range means. The modern warrior overcomes with distance this natural inhibition against harming another.

Subjects' Justifications for Their Obedience

We have examined the Milgram experiment for sources of the subjects' obedience. And we have focused on four aspects: (1) the gradual escalation of the voltage, (2) the experimenter's posture as the interpreter of the objective requirements of the situation, (3) the embarrassment it would cause the subjects to tell the experimenter off, and (4) the distance the subject is removed from the victim. But how did the *subjects* see the experiment? What features were salient to them? What did they offer as reasons for obeying? And how do their explanations fit with those we have just considered? We shall examine three issues the subjects raised: legitimacy, fairness, and responsibility. These features of the situation were important in the subjects' own accounts of their obedience. But, as we shall see, the subjects' explanations for why they obeyed cannot be taken at face value.

LEGITIMACY

One factor that was surely salient to the subjects, and one they commonly mentioned after the experiment was over, was the setting: Yale University. Subjects, not unreasonably, suggested that such an august university as Yale couldn't possibly be involved with something evil. But is this really why they

▼ *The setting for the Bridgeport version of the Milgram experiment. (A) The experiment took place just above and to the left of Austin's. (B) Inside the Bridgeport office.*

A

B

obeyed? To find out, Milgram moved the experiment to the offices of "Research Associates of Bridgeport," a company described as doing consumer research for industry. Research Associates of Bridgeport had marginally respectable offices (plastic drapes on the windows) in a run-down office building in the downtown shopping area of Bridgeport, Connecticut. This change in the setting of the experiment did have an effect on the rates of obedience (see Figure 2.14). The number of fully obedient subjects declined from twenty-six to nineteen out of a total of forty. But although this is a reduction, it isn't a significant one in either the statistical or more general sense. Now what are we to conclude from this?

It is unlikely that the original subjects were lying. They probably honestly believed that if the experiment had not been at Yale, they wouldn't have participated. They may have believed this, but they were wrong. Yale's respectability had little to do with the obedience. This is not to say that if the lab had posted "Organized Crime of Bridgeport" on the door the subjects would have entered, but the results do show that no special signs or symbols of legitimacy were needed to produce obedience.

FAIRNESS

When asked why they had obeyed the experimenter, many subjects replied that they had obeyed because the experiment was "fair." It's a bit difficult to see what the subjects might mean here. It's hard to see in what sense the experiment was fair—what's fair about torturing someone! But there is a limited sense in which the experiment *was* fair.

When the subjects first entered the lab, the experimenter explained to them that one of them would be the teacher and the other the learner. Then he asked if either had a preference. The subject and the victim always said no. So the experimenter explained that they would decide who was teacher and who was learner by lot. The drawings were rigged, so that the subject was always the teacher, but the subject didn't know they were rigged. The experiment was fair, then, in the very limited sense that the learner freely agreed to be in the experiment and, so far as the subject knew, became the learner rather than the teacher by the luck of the draw.

But does this fairness matter, or do the subjects just think it matters? To address this question, Milgram set out to make the experiment less fair (see Figure 2.14). He did this by having the learner tell the experimenter that although he was willing to be in the experiment, he had a heart condition and insisted that the experimenter terminate the experiment when he (the learner) wanted him to. In earshot of the real subject, the experimenter grunted his acceptance of this prior condition. As usual, at 150 volts the learner demanded to be released. In this way, he called upon the experimenter to live up to the contract he had agreed to. If the fairness of the experiment is crucial in winning subjects' cooperation, then there should be substantially less obedience in this condition, since ordering the subject to continue in the face of the broken prior contract is hardly fair.

In this condition, sixteen out of forty subjects obeyed to the end. This is fewer than the twenty-six who obeyed in the standard condition, but it is still a surprising degree of obedience. The evidence indicates, then, that fairness, just as a connection with Yale, played some role in determining obedience, but it doesn't tell the whole story of why subjects obeyed.

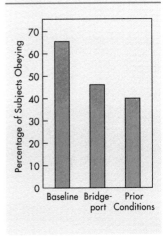

FIGURE 2.14

OBEDIENCE WITH REDUCED LEGITIMACY

▲ *Obedience in the baseline condition, in the Bridgeport setting, and where there were prior conditions—when the learner entered the experiment with the explicit understanding that the experimenter would stop the experiment when the learner asked him to because of his (the learner's) heart condition. (Data from Milgram, 1974)*

Some of the subjects in the course of the experiment asked the experimenter: "Who is responsible here? Who is responsible for shocking the victim?" And the experimenter always replied, "I am responsible." So on the face of it, subjects obeyed because they saw the experimenter, not themselves, as responsible for the torture. But this leads us to another question: How could they have come to see themselves as not responsible? After all, responsibility is not like a car, something that someone owns, something that the owner has control over, something that can be given to other people or taken from them. In the moral sense, we *just are* responsible for our actions; other people can't make us more or less so. When Jesse James was about to hold up the Northfield Bank, he couldn't just go up to a stranger and say, "Why don't you help me blow up the vault? Don't worry, if we get caught, I'll assume full responsibility." We can all see this is absurd. Yet Milgram's subjects didn't see the absurdity of the experimenter's absolving them of responsibility. Why?

Lee Hamilton has investigated people's beliefs about responsibility within a hierarchy. Her findings indicate that people do tend to pass responsibility up the ranks of a hierarchy, thus exonerating subordinates (Hamilton, 1978). It should be pointed out, however, that 82 percent of subjects who heard a description of the Milgram experiment assigned some responsibility to the subject for shocking the victim (Hamilton, 1986). Thus, people *not* in the Milgram experiment see the subjects as responsible for their action, even if in the heat of the action the subjects saw themselves as not responsible.

Why are the subjects not sensitive to the facts of responsibility? Milgram's subjects' sense of legitimacy and fairness played some role in determining obedience; the subjects' beliefs that they weren't responsible for what went on there probably mattered too. But how did the subjects come to believe all of these things? We have to ask this because shocking the learner *wasn't* legitimate; it *wasn't* fair; the subjects *were* responsible. The subjects see the experiment as fair and legitimate and themselves as not responsible because *this is the interpretation the experimenter offers.* The subjects see the experimenter as the authoritative interpreter of the objective moral order. This is where the social influence lies.

Social Influence and Arendt's Questions

Is the pressure we saw in the Asch experiment intense enough to operate in a case where the subject's behavior matters? Certainly. Was Arendt right? Could any one of us have been Eichmann? Certainly the Milgram experiment doesn't prove we could. There are many differences between what Eichmann did and what Milgram's subjects did. Still, before Milgram gathered his results, no one, no one at all, thought that most people would obey. Everyone he asked simply assumed that people would do the obviously morally right thing and quit. But most people didn't quit. Most people obeyed to an immoral and even senseless extreme. At the very least, the Milgram experiment makes it much harder for us to *assume* that we couldn't be Eichmann. The Milgram experiments are, at the very least, an antidote to moral self-complacency (Milgram 1963, 1964, 1965a, 1965b, 1974).

The Ethics of the Social Influence Experiments

The Milgram experiment sparked a rather heated debate about the ethics of experimentation (Baumrind, 1964). It is important to see just what the ethical issues involved in experimentation are, and the Milgram experiment brings them to the fore.

In the CBS docudrama, one of the experimental subjects has a nervous breakdown because of the experiment. Obviously it would be ethically unacceptable for a researcher to expose subjects to a risk of such magnitude, at least once the researcher had reason to believe there was such risk. But after the real experiment, none of the subjects suffered such a breakdown. Indeed, Milgram had a psychiatrist follow up forty of his subjects, and there was no evidence of psychopathology produced by being a subject in the experiment. Long-term harm, however, is not the only ethical issue.

The subjects in the Milgram experiment were unquestionably exposed to significant short-term stress; they were placed in a very difficult position. Is it ethical to expose subjects to intense, short-term stress? There seem to be three issues involved here. The first is: Is the research important? If it isn't, then such stress is unjustifiable. The second question is: Is the subject free to terminate the experiment at any time? Certainly the subject (as opposed to the victim) was free to leave the experiment. The third issue is: Does the subject freely consent to being in the experiment?

If the subject is to be exposed to even transient stress, she must consent to exposing herself to that stress. But if that consent is to be informed, then she must know what the experiment is about. And the subjects in the experiments described so far did not know what the experiments were about. Nor could they know. Obviously, were they to be informed of the details, the experiments would be of no interest. Is there any solution to this problem? Perhaps there is. If the experimenter can inform the subject of the purpose of the experiment concretely enough so that she can decide whether or not to participate, and if the experimenter can explain the degree of stress involved, then it seems to me that the experimenter has discharged his ethical obligations without invalidating the research.

BRUTALITY

Philip Zimbardo was interested in why prisons are such violent and degraded places. This doesn't sound like a very difficult question to answer; there are obvious reasons they would be violent and degraded. For one thing, prisoners aren't on average very nice people; that's why they're in prison. Then too, if you were a sadist, someone who took pleasure in another's pain, where would you look for employment? Prisons seem like a good bet. This is not to say that all, most, or even many prison guards are sadists, but it is likely that a higher percentage of prison guards are than are members of the population at large. These factors seem, even one at a time, adequate to account for prison violence, so there seems to be little mystery about why prisons are violent. But Zimbardo thought, and wanted to show, that there are other reasons adequate to produce prison violence even if those just mentioned weren't true.

The Zimbardo Experiment

Zimbardo took over the basement of the Psychology Department of Stanford University. There he constructed a mock prison that was to be the site of a two-week study of the effects of prison on the behavior of subjects pretending to be prisoners and other subjects pretending to be guards. To populate his prison, Zimbardo placed an ad in the local newspaper asking for male college students willing to participate in a two-week study of prison life. They were to be paid $15 per day. Seventy applicants answered the ad. They were carefully screened for evidence of psychological disorder. Twenty-four college students from all over the United States and Canada who passed these tests remained.

Twelve of these young men were assigned at random to be prisoners; twelve were assigned to be guards. In this prison, then, all of the guards and prisoners were college students. None had been convicted of a crime. All knew they were being paid to take part in an experiment. None showed signs of sadism. All knew that chance alone separated guards from prisoners. In other words, the features so obviously likely to produce brutality in real prisons were missing here. But Zimbardo did make his prison experience as like prisons as he could in other ways.

The "prisoners" were picked up from their homes in real police cars. They really were lined up spread-eagle against the police cars and frisked. They were carried off in a car with a siren that really did wail. They were really fingerprinted. Then they were stripped and de-loused. Imagine what it is like to be stripped in front of strangers and then subjected to a procedure designed to remove the lice you are, obviously, suspected of carrying! Next they were given stocking caps to wear, to conceal their then fashionably long hair. The prisoners were also given gowns that looked like dresses; they had no underwear. Zimbardo's prison, then, did all it could to degrade its prisoners.

Now real prisons don't give prisoners stocking caps or make male prisoners wear dresses, but they do degrade their inmates. And what Zimbardo wanted to show was the effect of this degradation on the behavior of prisoners and guards. So in his role-playing variant, he used whatever techniques he could to achieve the same end.

The guards too were treated as far as possible as real guards. They were given uniforms, nightsticks, reflecting sunglasses, and most important, au-

▼ (A) A "prisoner" being "arrested," (B) being frisked, and (C) in his cell.

A

B

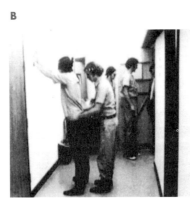

C

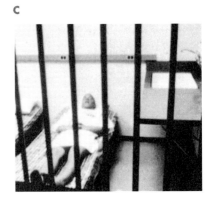

thority over the prisoners. Then the guards were set loose over the prisoners. What happened?

Quite a lot happened. The prisoners staged a rebellion. The guards retaliated. The guards withheld food from those who wanted it; they forced food on those who went on a hunger strike. They subjected their prisoners to physical punishment—push-ups and sleep deprivation. They made the prisoners do stupid and degrading tasks, such as cleaning toilets with their bare hands. They put people in solitary confinement. They forced their prisoners to ask permission to go to the bathroom, and they sometimes denied permission, forcing the prisoners to use buckets in their cells. Thus, they forced the prisoners to live in the smell of their own excrement. In short, as Zimbardo expected and hoped to show, the guards recreated much of the squalor and degradation of real prisons. The guards became more and more brutal. They did this even though none of the obvious reasons for brutality in real prisons were present. Most important, both the guards and the prisoners knew that but for the flip of a coin their places would have been reversed.

The prisoners became so demoralized by all of this that Zimbardo was forced to stop the experiment after only six days, a week earlier than he had expected to end it. Zimbardo's demonstration worked too well, in a sense, at demonstrating the way that the degradation intrinsic to prisons breeds further degradation and further brutality (Zimbardo, 1971). What features of the situation can we identify that promoted this brutality and degradation?

Explanations of the Brutality

There are two subtly different ways of asking about what went on in the Zimbardo study. One question is: Why were the guards so brutal? The other is: Why weren't the guards inhibited from being brutal? The first question is easy to answer. The guards were provoked to brutality by a variety of things. Most important, perhaps, the prisoners did rebel. So it is not surprising that the guards wanted to punish the prisoners. What is somewhat surprising is that their punishing the prisoners got so out of hand. After all, each of us in our everyday lives encounters plenty of provocations. We all encounter drivers who cut us off, pushy salespeople who call us to sell this, that, and the other thing, rudeness of every type, and so on. If we attacked everyone we had a momentary impulse to attack, life would indeed be like a jungle. But it isn't—even in New York. Most of our impulses to attack pass without action, or any other residue. Why?

Most of us most of the time refrain even from harsh words, let alone harsh actions, because we know it is wrong to hurt others or to use force to get our way. But in prisons, as in mental hospitals, things aren't that simple. In a prison, guards are entitled, and know they are entitled, to use (at least minimal amounts of) force to restrain unruly prisoners. The rule they must follow is to use "minimal force," not "no force." But it is difficult to know how much force is just enough. Thus, each guard must answer the question: How far should I go in "disciplining" these truculent prisoners? Guards in the Zimbardo experiment slid from reasonable force to brutality. They slid down a slippery slope of the sort we saw in relation to the Milgram experiment. And

► *How much force is just enough? Will this policeman go from reasonable force to brutality?*

as in the analysis offered of the Milgram experiment, it pays to look at the factors that facilitated the slide. They seem to be of two general sorts.

DEGRADATION

The first is the degradation that Zimbardo inflicted on the prisoners. As humans, we have the right to be treated in a decent, reasonable way. But there is a difference between having a right and being able to get others to treat us as someone with that right. There is evidence in the Zimbardo experiment, and far more evidence, far more tragic evidence, in accounts of both Nazi and Stalin's concentration camp survivors, that once a person has been degraded, it is far easier to do whatever one wants to him, to ignore his humanity and even his basic human rights. We are ordinarily unaware of the degree to which our being treated as civilized, decent, autonomous, moral agents depends on our ability to look and act like such agents. To the degree that we make it impossible for other people to look and act that way, we make it easy to treat them as less than human.

Franz Stangl, the commandant of Treblika, one of the Nazi extermination camps, was asked, "Why . . . if they were going to kill [the prisoners] anyway, what was the point of all the humiliation, why the cruelty?" "To condition those who actually had to carry out the policies," he answered. "To make it possible for them to do what they did." Degradation breeds brutality (Sereny, cited in Des Pres, 1976. See Des Pres, 1976, and Sabini & Silver, 1982, for more on degradation and brutality).

MORAL DRIFT

There was also another kind of influence working to produce brutality, a kind of influence much closer to the central theme of this chapter. Let us look for the ways the guards influenced each other in the Zimbardo experiment.

After the experiment was halted by Zimbardo, he arranged for sessions where the "guards" and "prisoners" exchanged views with one another. The prisoners pointed out that there seemed to be three kinds of guards. There were "good guards," who were, in various ways, kind and helpful to the prisoners; "average guards," who weren't very helpful, but who also didn't engage in much in the way of brutality themselves; and "bad guards," who instigated much of the brutality. When the hostages returned from Iran in 1980, they too reported that their captors were of these three types. And there are even accounts from Auschwitz written by some of the very small number of survivors that speak of "good guards." The escalating brutality, then, seems to have corresponded to the inclinations of the bad guards. This leads us to wonder why the bad guards seemed to have disproportionate influence. From what we have seen so far, we have no reason to expect this disproportionate influence.

Sherif saw his experiment on the autokinetic effect as a model of how social norms emerge in a group. Recall that in his experiment, a group of people faced with a difficult, ambiguous matter, about which they had different initial views, reached a consensus that was a compromise of their original views. They influenced each other so that in the end each accepted a compromise frame of reference. He thought of his experiment as a model for how individuals who were part of a larger group reached an understanding about any sort of ambiguous matter. If his experiment had been a model for what went on in the Zimbardo experiment, then what would have happened?

We know that Zimbardo's subjects too were faced with an ambiguous issue—exactly how much force is a guard allowed to use to maintain order in a prison? We would expect, then, that a shared, stable consensus would have been reached here too. In other words, we would expect that the good and bad guards would have reached some stable compromise about what was permissible. This didn't happen. Had it happened, there would have emerged some idea about what the limits of acceptable behavior were for the bad guards. They would have found themselves inhibited at some point in what they themselves found morally acceptable. But, instead, the brutality escalated. In particular, the bad guards became more and more brutal as the experiment progressed. Why didn't a consensus emerge?

The emergence of consensus in the Sherif experiment was dependent on each subject's expressing his opinion. If all of those subjects who thought the light moved only a little didn't express that view, then we could hardly expect their opinions to enter into the formation of the consensus. But, of course, all of the subjects' views did enter into the consensus because the experimenter asked each subject her view. When we turn to the Zimbardo experiment (or Auschwitz), we see that there was no experimenter present to solicit opinions; thus, it was easy for some people's views not to find expression. Worse, there was a systematic bias in whose views were expressed.

Systematic bias occurred because as one of the bad guards turned a fire extinguisher on the prisoners, for example, he did two things at once. At the same time he assaulted the prisoner, he also expressed his moral view of such behavior. He announced that to his mind such behavior was acceptable. He didn't do this in words, of course; rather, his behavior made it clear. For a Sherif-like consensus to emerge, this view would have to be countered by its opposite, by an expression of the view that such behavior was unacceptable. Perhaps many of the good guards felt this way, but they didn't say it. The good guards, then, contributed to a sort of pluralistic ignorance of the kind

Brutality by guards in the Zimbardo experiment was disinhibited by

- derogation of the prisoner;

- moral drift.

we saw in the Latané and Darley experiment. Anyone looking at the overt behavior of the good guards would assume they *condoned* what they saw.

Why didn't the good guards cut through the pluralistic ignorance by telling the bad guards in so many words that what they were doing was wrong? Perhaps the good guards felt they had no right to tell other people what to do. At least in this culture, we seem to be quite inhibited about saying to someone, "What you are doing is wrong, morally wrong." Remember that none of Milgram's subjects made this clear moral statement either. Yet remaining silent in the face of immoral action contributes to that immorality. And a failure to express disapproval of an immoral action means that our disapproval doesn't enter into the formation of a shared, objective social consensus.

WRAP-UP

Social influence expresses itself in many ways. But a common theme emerges. When people interact, the usual consequence is a convergence of opinion. This convergence may be toward error as in the Asch experiments on conformity, toward the mean as in the Sherif experiment on the autokinetic effect, or toward greater risk, and typically toward views more extreme than the group members had prior to the discussion. Social influence may result in the inhibition of action as in Latané and Darley's studies of bystander intervention. Obedience and brutality are the outcome of social influence in the Milgram and Zimbardo studies. But through all these differences, we find people believing that there is one world, one moral order, one virtuous way of living. This assumption means that, excepting matters of taste, if we interact with other people, we must in some way deal with their views, be open to influence from them.

SUMMARY

1. In a series of experiments by Solomon Asch, subjects were asked to make simple, clear judgments about the relative length of several lines. But six confederates gave the same, obviously wrong, answer. This situation produced confusion and discomfort for the subjects and conformity to the incorrect answer for most subjects on at least some trials.

2. Experiments conducted by Muzafer Sherif have documented conformity to the opinions of others in the context of an extremely ambiguous judgment about the motion of a light. Subjects (erroneously) believed that the judgment they were asked to make was about a matter of fact. But because in this experiment the stimuli were more ambiguous, subjects experienced less stress than in the Asch experiment, and *internalized* their new answers.

3. Conformity to an incorrect majority has been found with a variety of judgments of fact, but not with judgments that are clearly known to be matters of taste. We expect differences in matters of taste.

4. The tendency to conform and the social influence that causes it are substantially reduced if at least one other person gives the right answer, or if subjects can understand why they are in disagreement with the group.

5. Serge Moscovici has demonstrated that minorities can have substantial impact on majorities regarding the judgment of whether some blue-green stimuli are really green or really blue. The impact of a minority is heightened if the minority seems to be consistent in its judgments.

6. In many cases, groups of people will endorse a riskier course of action than the average of the preferences of individuals. This seems to be in part a matter of subjects' wanting to see themselves as willing to take risks and in part a matter of being more persuaded by arguments in risky action than by arguments for more conservative approaches. Recent research suggests that this tendency is part of a more general tendency of groups to polarize their members' judgment.

7. Bibb Latané and John Darley have shown in a series of experiments that social influence may inhibit people from aiding someone in need of help: (1) people are slow to respond in an emergency until they are convinced that other people present also see the situation as an emergency, and (2) when several people witness an emergency—and know that others are also witnessing it—they may suffer from *diffusion of responsibility.* All may agree that someone should help, but each may believe that it isn't his responsibility.

8. Stanley Milgram has shown that a majority of subjects brought to a laboratory (under a suitable pretext) will administer extremely dangerous shocks to a protesting victim because they have been ordered to do so by an experimenter.

9. Subjects' willingness to obey seems to arise from two fundamental sources: (1) they accept the authority's interpretation of moral right and wrong in this situation, even though it contradicts their own sense, and (2) they are unwilling to confront the experimenter's immorality directly.

10. Philip Zimbardo showed in the context of a mock prison that college students randomly assigned to be "guards" would engage in substantial brutality toward other college students randomly assigned to be "prisoners." The silence of the guards who had private reservations about the brutality may have influenced the guards without such reservations by creating the illusion that they too found the behavior morally tolerable.

CHAPTER 3

Groups and Task Performance

This chapter has a rather practical focus. Much of the work of our culture is performed by individuals working as part of a group. Committees, rather than emperors, really run the world. Because groups perform so much of our culture's work, it is natural to want to understand how they do that work. In this chapter, we will examine a variety of influences on how groups (and the individuals who comprise them) perform tasks.

To start, we need to be clear about just what a group is. There are all kinds of groups. For example, in a sense, left-handed people make up a group; they certainly are a group to a company that designs gadgets specifically for left-handers. But in this chapter, we will ignore groups like this and focus instead on face-to-face groups—collections of people that, at least on occasion, assemble in one place. Such groups are sometimes called ***primary groups.*** But even within this narrower definition, there is an enormous range of collections of people we refer to as groups.

Consider a number of people playing video games in the same room. This collection of people is more or less face-to-face, but it is just barely a social group; the players interact only in that they are able to observe each other. Such people doing something in one another's presence, but without substantial communication, are called ***co-actors.*** You might imagine that being a member of a group in this minimal sense would have no effect on your performance, but this isn't so. We begin, then, with a discussion of how performing in the presence of co-actors affects individuals' performance.

Co-actors lack one crucial element that groups in a stronger, fuller sense have: a common goal. A committee appointed to plan next year's production of gadgets is more thoroughly a group because the people in it work together toward a single goal. The later sections of this chapter examine collections of people that are groups in this stronger sense of sharing a common goal.

Some groups—say, a group of students working on a joint project—are created for a single, temporary purpose. Such single-occasion groups are called *ad hoc groups.* Being a part of an ad hoc group can affect performance in a variety of ways; one important effect is on workers' motivation. As we shall see in the section on social loafing, members of ad hoc groups in some, but not all, circumstances fail to pull their weight—literally!

GROUP PORTRAIT OF 15 TOTAL STRANGERS WHO JUST HAPPENED TO BE ON THE SAME BUS

Other groups, like the Supreme Court, persist over time; true, its membership changes slowly as members retire and new members are appointed, but still the Court remains as an enduring group. Almost every group has a leader. And we will address several questions about leaders. We will ask: Are there personality characteristics that distinguish good from bad leaders? We will also ask: What kinds of *behavior* do good and bad leaders exhibit? After all, leaders can only lead by exhibiting behavior of some kind. And we surely will want to know what makes for effective (and ineffective) leader behavior. We will examine the kinds of power that some leaders have, and look at how they exercise it.

Enduring groups differ from one another in various ways. One way is in how *cohesive* they are. Cohesiveness has to do with how tightly connected to a group its members are. In this chapter we will ask: What makes groups cohesive? And what are the consequences of being cohesive (or not) on a group's performance? Cohesiveness, as we shall see, is a mixed blessing.

One advantage that groups are often thought to have is that they are sometimes less biased as a whole than their members—groups sometimes cancel out their members' biases. But they don't always work this way, and we shall look a bit at when they do and when they don't.

There is one remaining, crucial determinant of a group's performance—the task the group is given to do. We shall also, therefore, be concerned with how a group's task affects its performance.

In the final section of this chapter, we will look in some detail at one extremely important kind of ad hoc group: juries. We will review what social psychologists have discovered about how these groups function.

CLASSIC FINDINGS IN SOCIAL PSYCHOLOGY: SOCIAL FACILITATION

Suppose your instructor gave you the following choice: either you can take your final exam as students usually do, in a room full of other students also taking the exam, or you can take it all by yourself alone in a room. Which should you choose?

Your first impulse might be to say that it really doesn't matter. After all, no matter which way you choose, you will be performing as an individual; in neither case will you be allowed to consult with other people. But Robert Zajonc has proposed that it *does* matter how you take the exam. He has argued

According to Robert Zajonc, the mere presence of others

- innately produces arousal, which

- facilitates the performance of well-practiced or simple tasks;

- interferes with the performance of novel or complex tasks.

that we are so thoroughly social creatures that merely being in the presence of other people, even if we are prevented from interacting with them, has an effect on us.

Zajonc has argued that we humans (and other organisms as well) are so constructed that being in the presence of others of our species is arousing. He argues that being around other people works like a cup of coffee: it is stimulating. Very well, but how does being stimulated affect performance? Drawing on research from the animal laboratory, Zajonc has argued that being aroused affects performance in a complex way. In particular, arousal *enhances* the performance of well-learned responses, or simple tasks, but *inhibits* the performance of novel, poorly mastered, or complex tasks. Thus, Zajonc suggests, which choice you should make depends on how well you have mastered the course material. If you have really studied hard and have the material under control, then elect to take the exam around other students; their presence will facilitate your performance. But if you really haven't studied and don't know the material, take the test alone; the presence of all of those people will only disrupt your performance (Zajonc, 1965).

Zajonc tested his theory in a variety of experiments in which subjects were exposed to novel tasks. In practice trials, the subjects were given lots of practice alone with some of the tasks, but very little practice with others. In the second phase of the experiment, they performed the tasks again. Some of the subjects did this again alone; others did it in the presence of other people who, Zajonc told the subjects, were observers who had asked to see the experiment. The observers did just that; they sat there and watched without comment. Zajonc found, as he expected, that the presence of other subjects enhanced performance on the well-practiced tasks but inhibited performance on the less well-practiced tasks (Zajonc & Sales, 1966). And Zajonc later showed the same effects on other species. The (unfortunately) domestic cockroach will emit more dominant, or practiced, responses in the presence of other cockroaches and suppress less well-learned responses (see Figure 3.1; Zajonc, Heingartner, & Herman, 1969). Zajonc's research nicely captured a basic fact of social psychology: **social facilitation,** the facilitation of practiced re-

▶ *Practicing ballet without an audience.*

64 GROUPS AND TASK PERFORMANCE (3)

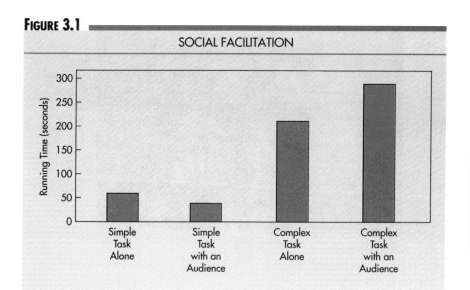

FIGURE 3.1

SOCIAL FACILITATION

◀ Audience effects on simple (runway) and complex (maze) tasks for the domestic cockroach. (Data from Zajonc, Heingartner, & Herman, 1969)

sponses by an audience. He also spawned an immense amount of subsequent research. Has that research supported his claim?

Well, not every study that has looked for social facilitation has found it (see Manstead & Semin, 1980). Does that mean the phenomenon isn't real? Not necessarily. There can be lots of reasons why any particular study, using only a small number of subjects, fails to show even a real phenomenon. To determine whether a phenomenon is real in the face of conflicting results, one should combine the results from all of the studies into a single analysis. Such a technique is called **meta-analysis.** And a meta-analysis has been carried out on the social facilitation literature.

The analysis looked at 241 experiments. All told, these experiments used the staggering total of 23,970 subjects. The analysis made it reasonably clear that social facilitation does exist (Bond & Titus, 1983). There is indeed a tendency for simple, well-learned tasks to be facilitated by the presence of others, but for more complex, less well-mastered tasks to be inhibited. But the effect is fairly small; having an audience will, even in the best of circumstances, help your grade only a few points.

Explanations of Social Facilitation

The research we have reviewed so far documents the existence of social facilitation, but it hasn't said much about *why* it happens.

THE MERE PRESENCE EXPLANATION

Zajonc offered a very simple explanation for social facilitation. We are born with the tendency to become aroused in the presence of others; it is part of our genetic inheritance. He argued that because **conspecifics** (other members of our species) provide many of the rewards and punishments we receive, evolution has endowed us with an innate response to the presence of conspecifics—we become aroused. And arousal produces social facilitation. This

▶ A novice violinist will probably do worse when in front of an audience, while more practiced violinists when probably do better.

position has been dubbed the ***mere presence account,*** because it holds that merely being in the presence of others *no matter what they are doing* produces the effect. Zajonc's explanation has a certain appeal. It is first of all simple, and all other things being equal, one should prefer a simple explanation to a complex one. The argument also has a degree of plausibility. It does seem that it would be generally useful for creatures big and small to be especially sensitive to what others of their same kind are up to. But many researchers have thought the explanation too simple, and have proposed other, *more cognitive* explanations for why the presence of others leads to social facilitation.

THE EVALUATION APPREHENSION EXPLANATION

Nickolas Cottrell carried out an experiment similar to the one Zajonc had used to demonstrate social facilitation. He too had subjects performing alone or with two spectators watching. But in one condition of his experiment, the two other people in the room were wearing blindfolds; they were really "merely present." (They were supposedly waiting to be in a color perception experiment and had to wear the blindfolds as they waited.) So this experiment had three conditions. The subjects (1) performed alone, (2) performed in the presence of spectators, or (3) performed in the presence of two other people who could *not* observe their performance. The experiment found, as Zajonc's had, that the tendency to emit well-practiced responses (and suppress rarely practiced ones) was increased by the presence of the spectators. But what about performance in the presence of the blindfolded subjects? Zajonc's mere presence explanation predicted that subjects in this condition too would show social facilitation. But they didn't; their responses looked like those of the subjects working alone (Cottrell, Wack, Sekerak, & Rittle, 1968). Perhaps it isn't the mere presence of others that leads to social facilitation, but rather it is *knowing that one will be evaluated by other people.*

Cottrell suggested that we are indeed aroused by performing before an audience, but that this drive (1) only occurs when the audience is in a position to evaluate us and (2) is not innate, but a matter of learning with experience that evaluation by others brings rewards and punishments (see Figure 3.2).

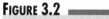

FIGURE 3.2

THE EVALUATION APPREHENSION ACCOUNT OF MERE PRESENCE EFFECTS

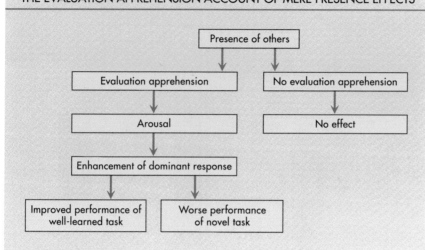

◀ *Social facilitation has been explained by Nickolas Cottrell as resulting from arousal when performing before an audience that is evaluating us.*

This is known as the **evaluation apprehension explanation** and is certainly also a plausible account of the social facilitation phenomenon. But how would a supporter of the mere presence effect reply?

Hazel Markus sharpened the issue. First, Markus agreed with much of Cottrell's argument. She agreed that being evaluated by others is likely to produce drive and social facilitation. But, she reasoned, the question Zajonc raised wasn't whether mere presence is the *only* source of arousal when others are around—no one had said that. The issue was whether the presence of others is *sufficient* to cause arousal (Markus, 1981).

Cottrell's experiment seems to show that mere presence isn't enough to produce arousal, since the group performing with the blindfolded other subjects did not show such an effect compared with the subjects working alone. But, Markus argued, maybe that was because the group described as alone wasn't. After all, subjects in that group thought the experimenter would be aware of their performance; so perhaps *both* groups showed the effect of mere presence. She proposed that Cottrell's experiment, therefore, compared three groups *all of which* were socially facilitated. What was needed to resolve the issue of whether mere presence is sufficient to produce social facilitation was an experiment in which subjects who think no one, not even the experimenter, is watching are compared with people who know they are in the presence of others. Following is an experiment in which the experimenters took special pains to carry out such an unobtrusive test.

Subjects in this experiment, who thought they were there to take part in a study of sensory deprivation, were told that before the experiment could begin, they would be given instructions by a Macintosh computer. To get the instructions, the subjects were to type two things into the Macintosh: their names and a code created by typing the letters of their names in backward order, interspersing ascending digits between each pair of letters. Unbeknownst to the subjects, the computer kept track of how long it took them to

According to Nickolas Cottrell, the presence of others produces arousal

- only if the other people are in a position to evaluate; and

- as a result of learning.

FIGURE 3.3

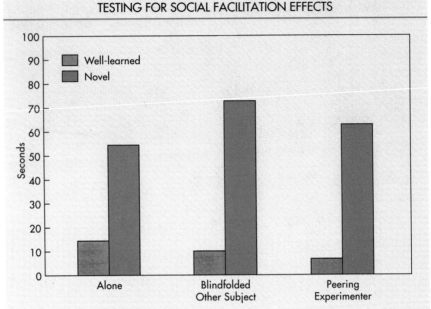

TESTING FOR SOCIAL FACILITATION EFFECTS

▶ *Mean time taken to complete a well-learned and a novel task when alone, in the presence of a blindfolded "other subject," and with an experimenter peering over the subjects' shoulders. (Data from Schmidt, Gilovich, Goore, & Joseph, 1986)*

do each. Typing one's name is surely more practiced than typing it backward and interspersing ascending digits.

The subjects did this in three conditions. In one condition, they were alone (they actually were!). In another, a confederate who was also there, supposedly, for the experiment on sensory deprivation was in the room but wore a blindfold, headphones, and was facing away from the subjects—about as mere a presence as one can arrange. In the third condition, the experimenter peered over the subjects' shoulders as they typed. The results were that the merely present confederate (as well as the peering experimenter) caused the subjects to type their names faster and the code more slowly than they did when alone (see Figure 3.3; Schmidt, Gilovich, Goore, & Joseph, 1986). These results suggest, then, that the mere presence of others *is* enough to produce social facilitation. But this is *not* to say that evaluation apprehension doesn't also lead to social facilitation. Rather, the general pattern of results suggests that evaluating spectators produce even more social facilitation than do merely present others. The expectation of evaluation by others is indeed another social influence on our behavior.

LEADERSHIP

The groups we have observed so far have barely been groups at all; they are really just collections of individuals at a single location. We want to move now to a discussion of more substantial groups and what influences their performance. One common and important, though perhaps not universal, feature of more substantial groups is the presence of a leader, and leaders surely have an influence on how productive groups are. So we focus now on leadership. We want to know: What kinds of people make good leaders—what are the personality traits of good leaders—and how do good leaders lead?

Contingency View of Leadership

The method most commonly used to find personality traits of leaders is, at least conceptually, quite simple. Researchers administer personality tests (measures of traits) to a group of subjects and also gather ratings of those subjects' effectiveness as leaders; the ratings are sometimes gotten from subordinates, sometimes from supervisors or observers, sometimes from peers. Investigators then look for relations (technically correlations) between the measured traits and the effectiveness of the leaders. The hope of such research is to find a single trait (or perhaps small collection of traits) that is consistently related to leadership.

Reviews in the 1940s and 1950s of the scores of studies using this method indicated that there were many correlations to be found between leadership and personality. Indeed, there were too many correlations to be found. That is, in most of the studies, some relationship of a personality variable and leadership effectiveness was found, but (1) within a study these relations were fairly weak, and (2) when one compared one study with another, *different* personality traits were related to leadership (Stogdill, 1948; Mann, 1959).

This state of affairs led to a consensus in the field that there was no single trait that effective leaders shared. Rather, the view was that leadership demanded different traits in different circumstances. This idea, which has dominated research on leadership over the last three decades, has been called the ***contingency view of leadership,*** because it suggests that the traits that make a good leader are contingent on the circumstances the leader faces. Of course, just saying that the traits characterizing a good leader depend on circumstances isn't much of a theory of leadership. What is needed to give

A

B

◄ *(A) Nelson Mandela and (B) Saddam Hussein: two leaders who share charisma but little else.*

such a conception substance is a specification of *which traits* in *which circumstances* lead to effective leadership. Fred Fiedler has spelled out just such a theory.

Fiedler suggests that we look at the matter this way. The crucial issue with regard to what kind of person will make a good leader is how *favorable to the leader* the overall situation is. At one extreme is a situation that is very favorable to the leader, a situation in which the leader has great authority, very positive relationships with the group, and where there is a very well-specified task. It is easy to be a leader in such circumstances. At the other extreme is a situation that is very adverse to any leader, a situation in which the leader has no authority in a group, where the members don't get along with each other or with her, and where there is a poorly specified task. Fiedler has theorized, and amassed a substantial amount of data to show, that at both ends of the dimension—if circumstances are very favorable to the leader or if they are very unfavorable to the leader—a specific sort of person will do best as a leader, but in circumstances in the middle, when circumstances are neither favorable nor unfavorable, a different sort of person will do best. More specifically, the theory proposes that in intermediate circumstances, leaders who are very concerned with the interpersonal relations within a group do better than those with a rigid task focus, while in circumstances at either extreme, task-focused leaders do better (Fiedler, 1964; see also Strube & Garcia, 1981; Peters, Hartke, & Pohlmann, 1985).

Consistency in Leadership

As valuable as Fiedler's contribution has been, recently some researchers have proposed that there is evidence that a trait of leadership does exist, but that we just haven't found it yet. How could one have evidence that there is a trait of leadership lurking without being able to specify what it is? The answer is: through a "round robin" study. In a round robin study, you assemble a group of people and assign them a task. You then look to see who emerges as the leader. Then you change the task and the members of the group, and see who emerges as the leader this time. If it happens that the same people keep emerging as the leader, regardless of task or group composition, then you have reason to believe that *something*, though you know not what, about these people leads to their consistently being leaders.

David Kenny and Stephen Zaccaro have pointed out that through the decades in which researchers have more or less given up on the notion of a leadership trait because they have been not able to find it, there have been a few studies employing a round robin design. And these studies have, by and large, found that the same people emerge as leaders in different groups (Carter & Nixon, 1949; Bell & French, 1950; Borgatta, Bales, & Couch, 1954; Barnlund, 1962). Kenny and Zaccaro concluded that it would be unwise, in the face of this evidence, to give up on the notion that there is a trait (or set of traits) that leaders consistently have (Kenny & Zaccaro, 1983).

A recent study of this sort has shed light on at least one quality valuable in a leader. In this study, subjects participated in four tasks. The tasks were designed to require very different behaviors from a leader if she was to be effective. One task needed someone to structure the task for the group, another demanded that an effective leader be considerate of the members, and so on. The first question was: Would the same people emerge as the leader even though the demands were so different, or would different people emerge as leaders on different tasks?

The answer was that there was considerable—though far from perfect—consistency in who became the leader. This result is consistent with the other round robin studies mentioned above. But this study did turn up some evidence about what made the consistent leaders consistent leaders. The subjects all filled out the self-monitoring scale (see Chapter 6 for a fuller discussion of this scale). Subjects who score high on this scale differ from those who score low in many ways, but one of them is that high scorers tend to be more attentive to, and influenced by, the social demands of the immediate situation; in other words, they tend to be more flexible. And, as you might have guessed, it was the flexible, high-scoring subjects who were more likely to emerge as leaders than were the less flexible, low scorers (Zaccaro, Foti, & Kenny, 1991). So our quest for a trait associated with consistent leadership has reached a rather ironic moment: the one thing a person must consistently be to be a leader is flexible!

Round robin studies suggest that

• the same people emerge as leaders on a variety of tasks in a variety of groups;

• flexibility of personality may be a trait shared by people who consistently emerge as leaders.

SOCIAL LOAFING

Are leaders really necessary? One reason people think they are necessary is that without them, people in groups may shirk their duties—avoid work. Is this belief true, or is it a mere prejudice? Do people in groups tend to loaf more than they should? This question was first raised experimentally by Max Ringelmann.

Ringelmann was an agricultural engineer who was interested in the relative efficiency of farm labor supplied by horses, oxen, machines, and men. In particular, he was curious about their relative abilities at pulling a load horizontally. In one of his experiments, carried out in the 1880s, he had groups of fourteen men pull a load, and he measured the force that they generated. He also measured the force that each of the men could pull when pulling alone. Their mean force when pulling alone was 85.3 kilograms, but their average force when pulling together was only 61.4 kilograms (Kravitz & Martin, 1986). In other words, there was a loss of about 24 kilograms per man (about 50 pounds) when the men pulled as a group. Where did the missing 24 kilograms go?

There are two possibilities. Either the subjects tried less hard because they were part of a group—there were motivational losses—or the 24 kilograms disappeared into coordination losses. Coordination losses in this case would mean that, for example, they didn't all pull at once, so that their efforts didn't quite sum at any one moment to the maximum they were capable of. Or perhaps they pulled in slightly different directions, so that part of their effort was spent pulling against each other rather than against the load they were trying to pull. Ringelmann himself thought that coordination loss, rather than pulling less hard, was the source of the missing force, and so it might have been. But about one hundred years later, researchers using American college students have come to a different conclusion.

In one replication of Ringelmann's original research, 102 male students pulled on a rope either as individuals or in groups of from 2 to 6. As Ringel-

▶ Sure they are pushing hard, but are they going to or from school? Would it matter in terms of social loafing?

FIGURE 3.4

SOCIAL LOAFING

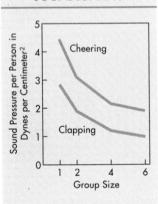

▲ Individual contributions to group clapping and cheering as a function of the number of people in the group. As the number increased, each individual contributed less. (From Latané, Williams, & Harkins, 1979)

mann had found, 2 subjects pulled with an average force 9 percent less than that generated by each subject alone. And 3 subjects pulled with 18 percent less force. Adding additional subjects did not reduce the average contribution further; they continued to pull at about 82 percent of their full capacity. So Ringelmann's result was replicated.

In a further study, however, an attempt was made to determine whether sagging motivation or coordination losses accounted for the decline in performance. The researchers used a clever ruse. In the alone condition, subjects of course pulled alone. In the group condition, they *thought* there were other people pulling, but in fact they were pulling alone there too. The other subjects in their group were actually confederates who held the rope and made it sway a bit, but didn't actually pull on it. Thus, any decrease in force could only be because of a reduction of effort on the part of the subjects who (erroneously) thought they were pulling as part of a group. In fact, there was a decrease in force when subjects thought they were pulling as part of a group (Ingham, Levinger, Graves, & Peckham, 1974). Now this does not mean that there aren't coordination losses when people pull together on a rope, but it does suggest that in addition to any coordination losses, there are also motivational losses.

Rope pulling is a cumbersome experimental procedure, so Bibb Latané introduced an easier one to study the same phenomenon. Latané had subjects clap and cheer either alone or in groups of two or six and found, as had previous experimenters, that being part of a group reduced the effort (in this case, noise) that each person contributed (see Figure 3.4). To distinguish coordination losses from motivational losses, Latané had subjects cheer either alone or in what they *thought* were groups of two or six, in what he called "pseudogroups." Pseudogroups were created by having the subjects wear earphones, so they could not tell that they were the only ones cheering. Latané found that the average sound output per person in a real group of six was only about one-third of the sound the person could produce alone. In pseudogroups of six, each person produced about three-quarters of the sound he produced alone. (The substantial difference between these numbers resulted from coordination loss, in this case the inevitable failure of sound waves to add together perfectly when there is more than one source of sound.)

So again we have a decrease in effort as a consequence of believing that one is part of a group. Latané contributed a new method for studying this phenomenon, and he also gave it a new name, by which it has since become known: **social loafing** (Latané, Williams, & Harkins, 1979). Subsequent research, of which there has been quite a bit, has been directed toward determining just when this social loafing will occur and when it won't.

For one thing, loafing is not confined to tasks like rope pulling or shouting, tasks that require gross physical effort; it can also be found on tasks that require cognitive effort. In one study, individuals, groups of four, or groups of sixteen were assigned to evaluate a poem and an editorial. The subjects reported working harder on their evaluation when they were responsible for it as individuals in contrast to when they were part of a group (Petty, Harkins, Williams, & Latané, 1977).

Loafing isn't, however, an *inevitable* consequence of participating in a group's effort. In another study, subjects once again were asked to produce noise either alone, in groups of two or six, or in pseudogroups of two or six. Once again there were losses in performance when people performed either in groups or in pseudogroups. Social loafing was eliminated, however, when the subjects performed in groups but were told that their individual contributions to the group effort would be monitored (Williams, Harkins, & Latané, 1981; also Kerr & Bruun, 1981; Jackson & Padgett, 1982; Zaccaro, 1984). Subjects seem to loaf only when their efforts are lost in the crowd of the others' efforts.

There is also evidence that people will not loaf if at least *they themselves* have a clear idea of how well they are doing individually in comparison with a social standard even if the experimenter doesn't (Szymanski & Harkins, 1987). And social loafing is reduced if the subjects have a clear standard against which to compare the *group's performance* (Harkins & Szymanski, 1989). So the conditions that maximize loafing are those in which no one knows how much effort each individual is expending, and there is no clear standard against which to compare the group as a whole.

Social loafing is less of a problem on challenging rather than easy tasks. In one experiment, subjects were given a task of generating uses either for a knife or for a detached doorknob. Now it is surely more of a challenge to think of uses for a detached doorknob rather than for a knife. All subjects did the task alone, but some were told that the uses they generated would be combined with those of nine other subjects, and that it would be this joint ten-person product that would be evaluated. Subjects came up with fewer uses for the knife when they thought they were only one of the ten use-generators, demonstrating the social loafing effect once again. But there was no such effect for the doorknob task. On this more challenging task, the subjects worked just as hard whether they thought they were working as individuals or as part of a group (Harkins & Petty, 1982).

Table 3.1

	COMBINATION RULES FOR GROUP PERFORMANCE	
Type	*Description*	*Example*
Additive rule	Individual contributions are added	Tug-of-war
Disjunctive rule	Only best performance in each group matters	Anagram
Conjunctive rule	Only worst performance in each group matters	Convoy of ships
Compensatory rule	Errors cancel out	Unbiased judgments

SOURCE: Adapted from Steiner, 1966.

Combination Rules

Another factor that affects whether subjects will loaf has to do with the ways members' efforts are combined. Ivan Steiner proposed a revealing way to classify tasks in terms of these different combinations (see Table 3.1; Steiner, 1966). A tug-of-war is an excellent example of an **additive** combination **task,** or **rule;** the total force generated by a team is the sum of the individuals' efforts (minus coordination losses). But there are other ways to combine members' efforts.

Imagine doing an anagram as a group. For the group to succeed, it is necessary and sufficient that one person get the right answer; a group with two people who get the right answer will do no better than one in which only one person does. So on a task like this, the group's performance is dependent only on its *best member's* effort. Such a task is called a **disjunctive task.** One can also imagine circumstances in which the group's progress is dependent on its *poorest member's* performance: for example, a convoy of ships can move only as fast as its *slowest* ship. Such a task is called a **conjunctive task.** Finally, there are tasks in which one member's performance can cancel the defects of another's, someone who guesses that a room is hotter than it is cancels (to some degree) an error by someone who guesses that the room is colder than it is. This kind of task is called **compensatory.** Now what do these distinctions have to do with social loafing?

Consider a disjunctive task, one in which only the best member's efforts matter. And imagine that you know you aren't very good at this sort of thing. There really is little point in your trying very hard. And by the same logic, if your group is doing a conjunctive task and you are very good at it, there also isn't much point in your trying hard. In both cases, from the point of view of the group's performance, your efforts are more or less dispensable. (Notice that on additive tasks—like rope pulling—members' efforts are never dispensable.) Given this analysis, we would expect social loafing from people who know themselves to be bad at a task if it is organized disjunctively and from people who know themselves to be very good on a conjunctive task.

In an experiment testing this notion, subjects were given the task of blowing air through a mouthpiece for thirty seconds. The subjects were told to blow as much as they could (without hyperventilating). This somewhat un-

Social loafing does *not* occur (or is reduced) if

- individuals' performances are monitored by a supervisor;

- individuals have clear standards for their own performances;

- individuals have clear standards for the group's performance;

- the task the group is performing is engaging;

- an individual knows she is good at the task *and* the group's payoff is determined by the *best* performance of a group member.

◄ *While in a relay race, team-mates can compensate for each others' performances. In most races, however, a runner is on her own.*

usual task was chosen because subjects were unlikely to have much of an idea about how good they were at it, and because there isn't any skill involved. But before they began the experiment, they were given a fake test of their air-blowing ability. Some of them were told that they were really great air blowers; others were told that they weren't such hot air blowers. (Who was told which was determined randomly.)

All were then told that they would be blowing as part of a group, and that the best group would win a $10 prize. Some of the subjects were told that the way the competition would work was that the only score that mattered was the score of the *best* blower; others were told that which group won the prize depended on the score of the group's *worst* performer. The subjects' scores in this competition were compared to their scores when tested alone. The results were that, as expected, the hot-shot puffers performed up to their real abilities if they thought the prize depended on the best member of the group, but they held back if they thought the prize depended on the group's weakest member. The reverse was true for the subjects who thought they weren't very good at blowing air: these subjects slacked off if they thought the prize depended on the best performer, but they did not if they thought the prize went to the group with the best "worst" performer (Kerr & Bruun, 1983). So whether a person shirks on a group task depends in part on how able she thinks she is relative to others in the group, and on whether the task is disjunctively or conjunctively structured.

Perceptions of how good the *other people* in a group are at performing a task can also affect performance. For example, in one study, subjects were told that they would be working with a partner; they were simply to list all the uses for a knife they could think of. Some subjects were led to believe that their partners were good at this sort of thing; others were led to believe that their partners were bad at this sort of thing. All the subjects were told that it was an additive task—that is, only the total number of uses the two of them came up with would matter. In this circumstance, subjects engaged in **social compensation;** that is, they contributed more uses for the knife when they thought their partner wasn't very good at generating them than when they thought he *was* good (Williams & Karau, 1991).

Social Loafing in a Cross-Cultural Perspective

The research discussed so far was carried out on students in the United States. But the culture of the United States, and the Western world more generally, is notoriously individualistic. Other cultures are less so; would one find social loafing in other cultures?

In some circumstances, at least, the answer seems to be yes. William Gabrenya, for example, has examined the tendency to loaf among grammar school students in Taiwan, and he has found that they too socially loaf on the standard noise-making task (Gabrenya, Latané, & Wang, 1983). These are especially important results because Chinese culture is often thought of as at the opposite extreme from American: Just as American culture is thought of as the prototype of an individualistic culture, Chinese culture is thought of as collectivist, a culture in which people (metaphorically) know that they should pull together and therefore may be expected to literally pull together. (See Chapter 10 for more on this subject.) Still, the noise-making tasks employed in these experiments are meaningless and unimportant. What would happen on a task the participants saw as more diagnostic of their abilities?

In a subsequent study, Gabrenya used a somewhat different task that he told subjects was of greater significance. He found in this study some evidence that Chinese middle school males (though not females) showed evidence of "social striving"—they performed at 108 percent of their individual level when tested working in pairs. They actually worked *more* as part of a group than as individuals. American middle school students and both Chinese and American sixth graders, on the other hand, exhibited social loafing on the same task (Gabrenya, Wang, and Latané, 1985). So in the right culture in the right circumstances, groups may call forth additional effort from individuals. But we have seen evidence of this already.

Social Loafing and Social Facilitation

The research on social facilitation reviewed at the beginning of this chapter suggested that the mere presence of others increases arousal and effort (even if it sometimes disrupts performance). Which effect, social loafing or social facilitation, is true? you might well ask. Well, they both are, I would reply. They are phenomena that emerge under different degrees of group participation. Social facilitation occurs even when interaction is minimal, when people are merely in one another's presence. Social loafing occurs only when an individual's work is merged with the efforts of others. And indeed, one can find evidence of *both* phenomena on the same task depending on how the performance on the task is evaluated (Harkins, 1987; Jackson & Williams, 1985; Sanna, 1992).

GROUP COHESIVENESS

The opening phase of the Second World War was marked by a series of incredible victories by the German army. The Wehrmacht conquered essentially all of continental Europe with a speed that was all but unimaginable. By

December of 1943, all of Western Europe was under the control of the German army, as was essentially all of European Russia. Hitler's troops were by then in the suburbs of Moscow; from their most advanced positions, they could see the spires of the Kremlin. But the army fell ever so slightly short of taking Moscow, and it was forced to spend the winter encamped outside of the city rather than inside it. And the Russian winter exacted an enormous price from Hitler's troops, just as it had in the previous century exacted a terrible price from Napoleon.

In June of 1944, the German army had to fight on two fronts after the successful invasion of Europe by the American, British, and Canadian troops at Normandy. From June 1944 to July 1945, when the war ended, the German army was engaged in a war it was now doomed, and obviously doomed, to lose on two fronts. The amazing and tragic fact is how hard these troops fought in this hopeless effort. It was, of course, a matter of utmost concern to the Allied forces to understand just why Hitler's soldiers fought so tenaciously.

One possible answer is that they fought so hard because of Nazi ideology. The degree to which the average German soldier (and for that matter average German citizen) embraced Nazi ideology is a matter of intense historical interest, and something beyond the scope of our treatment here. But suffice it to say that Allied intelligence did not believe that it was ideology that kept the German soldier fighting. Rather, Allied intelligence believed (based on various data, including interviews with captured German soldiers) that the real source of the German army's will to fight was to be found in the morale and **cohesiveness** of the very smallest units of the army; so long as these units stayed intact, they waged war ferociously. But once the units disintegrated, there was little evidence of isolated individuals' fighting to the death. The soldiers were willing to fight to their death, not so much because of an ideology or for the Fatherland, but *so as not to let their buddies down* (Shills & Janowitz, 1948). So group cohesiveness in real, enduring groups can be a source of motivation rather than something that erodes motivation.

▲ *An all-too-cohesive group (a Nazi rally in Germany under Hitler).*

Factors Affecting Cohesiveness

Why are some groups cohesive while others aren't? Social psychologists have treated group cohesiveness, for the most part, as a matter of the *attractiveness* of a group to its members (or potential members). So what makes groups attractive to people?

ATTRACTIVENESS OF A GROUP

There are many reasons that may contribute to a group's cohesiveness.* One is that members may just like one another. People may like each other for various reasons; this isn't the place to discuss each of them—we will in Chapter 14. For the moment, suffice it to say that personal attraction of one member toward another is one source of group cohesiveness. Another is the prestige that the group may have. Honor societies like Phi Beta Kappa are attractive because just being a member is prestigious. Or a group may help

---

*"Morale" and "*esprit de corps*" are other words sometimes used to refer to what I have been calling cohesiveness. I mean these terms to be interchangeable.

▲ Two exclusive groups. (A) The Beatles (B) The United States Supreme Court.

one achieve other rewards: being a partner in a successful firm is attractive because it provides personal financial rewards. We can also mention factors that detract from cohesiveness; factors that make groups *less* cohesive.

COSTS OF A GROUP

Some costs are the mirror images of the sources of attractiveness. If a group is made up of people you *don't* like, then you will be less attracted to it. Some groups have *negative* prestige; it would be, one supposes, very difficult to start an alumni association for Cell Block 9 of the state prison, because merely being a member of such a group stigmatizes. Some groups impose financial costs—dues, initiation fees, and the like. Just participating in a group involves costs of time and energy. Traveling to and from a group is a cost. And concerning oneself with a group's fate is an emotional cost.

John Thibaut and Harold Kelley called attention to a more subtle cost of being a member of a group, something economists call "opportunity costs"; this is the cost of *not* being a member of an *alternative* group (Thibaut & Kelley, 1959). Thibaut and Kelley argued that whether someone will join or remain in a group depends on what they called the **comparison level for alternatives,** whether the person has the chance of joining an even more attractive group. Thus, for one person a particular group may be very attractive, while to another it may not be, simply because the second person has an even more attractive alternative.

LOYALTY

One final source of group cohesiveness that has not received its share of attention in the social psychological literature is loyalty. **Loyalty** as used here is the sense of obligation that a person has to a group just by virtue of her history with that group. Knowing that one has shared in a group's life, especially in its adversity, leads to a strong sense of obligation toward that group and its members (Sabini & Silver, 1990).

There are, then, a variety of factors that affect group cohesiveness. There are both rewards and costs involved in being part of a group. The rewards increase cohesiveness; the costs reduce it. Another factor to be taken into account is each member's comparison level for alternatives. Finally, loyalty, conceived as a matter of obligation to a group and its members born of a shared history, leads to cohesiveness. But how does it matter whether or not a group is cohesive—what are the consequences of group cohesiveness?

Consequences of Cohesiveness

One consequence of cohesiveness is apparent in every high school clique: cohesiveness leads to uniformity of attitudes, and the more cohesive the group, the more uniform the attitudes. This idea was developed into a more formal statement by Leon Festinger, who proposed that groups exert pressures on their members to conform to group standards, and that these pressures are likely to be especially strong (1) for cohesive groups and (2) about issues of direct relevance to the group. He also proposed that these forces toward uniformity take the form of communication directed toward deviant members aimed at bringing them into line with group standards (Festinger, 1950). These ideas were developed in the course of a field study of developing groups in a married students' housing development at MIT right after the Second World War (see Chapter 14; Festinger, Schachter, & Back, 1950); they were subsequently tested in a series of more controlled, laboratory experiments.

CLASSIC FINDINGS IN SOCIAL PSYCHOLOGY: UNIFORMITY OF ATTITUDES

Stanley Schachter examined how pressures toward uniformity work in a study using the first meeting of college clubs that he had set up just for his experimental purposes. Each club was assigned the task of discussing what should become of Johnny Rocco, a juvenile delinquent, whose life and times the subjects had read about. The options varied from offering him love and understanding to punishing him severely. Into each group Schachter introduced three confederates. One, the "mode," was told to take as his own the group's modal position on the issue—that is, he was to endorse just about what the average person in the group endorsed. Another confederate was assigned the role of "slider"; he was to start out as a deviant from the point of view of the group's average position, but then move steadily toward the mean as the discussion developed. The third was given the role of deviant, and he was told to take a position very different from the group's and to stick to his guns. There were two measures of interest: (1) the pattern of communication to the confederates and (2) the degree to which each of the confederates was accepted by the group.

Communication to the slider, as expected, started at a rather high level, as a consequence of his originally deviant view. But as his opinion came into line with the group's, communication toward him declined. Communication to the deviant, on the other hand, was a matter of how relevant the Johnny Rocco case was to the group. Some of these clubs, Schachter told the subjects, were created in order to give advice to officials who have to deal with people like Johnny Rocco. Others were movie or radio clubs to whom this exercise was of less relevance. For the relevant clubs, communication to the deviant member started at a high level, but then fell off. But for the clubs to whom

Groups tend to be cohesive *if*

- the members like each other;
- being a member of the group confers prestige;
- being a member of the group confers other rewards;
- the costs of being a member of the group are small;
- there are no alternative sources for the rewards that being a member of the group provides.

A   B

▲ (A) The Daughters of the American Revolution—a group with no task whatsoever, but where cohesiveness is the whole point of the group. (B) Buckaroos at a ranch. They are a vanishing breed struggling to maintain their way of life in a changing world.

this discussion had little relevance, communication to the deviant remained at a high level.

The interpretation of this result is made clearer by considering it in light of the results of the other measure of interest: rejection. The mode and slider confederates were not rejected by the group, but the deviant was. And he was especially rejected in the relevant groups. So the drop-off in communication to the deviant seemed to be a matter of the group's giving up on him, rather than of the group's finally deciding to accept him (Schachter, 1951; Schachter, Nuttin, DeMonchaux, Maucorps, Osmer, Duijker, Rommetviet, & Israel, 1954; Mills, 1962; for criticism, see also Emerson, 1954). The groups first tried to bring their deviant member into line, but once that seemed hopeless, they just gave up.

Recently, Arie Kruglanski carried out similar experiments using Israeli Boy and Girl Scouts. He engaged groups of Scouts in discussions about where they would have their summer work camp. He doctored the groups with confederates who argued for the site he knew (from pretests) the Scouts would prefer and confederates who argued for a site he knew they wouldn't like. Thus, he created conformists and deviants. But he also manipulated stress the group faced in two ways. He gave some of the groups deadlines by which they had to reach a decision, and he had the confederates express their views either right before the deadline or well in advance of it. Kruglanski found that groups were substantially more rejecting of a deviant who proposed an undesirable solution right before the deadline than they were to someone proposing the same solution well in advance of the deadline. The stress of a decision deadline amplified the tendency to reject the deviant. Kruglanski also used a different kind of stress—noise—and he found that this stressor too amplified the rejection of a deviant (Kruglanski & Webster, 1991).

CLASSIC FINDINGS IN SOCIAL PSYCHOLOGY: GROUPTHINK

The line of experimental research described above, then, suggests that cohesive groups are likely to reject people who hold deviant opinions, especially when the groups are under stress. But the amount of stress one can produce in an experiment is typically not very great. So to see the effects of severe stress, we have to move outside the laboratory. Irving Janis significantly advanced our understanding of the effects of stress on cohesive groups by doing just that. Janis decided that one place to look for groups under great stress is in Washington. He reasoned that groups of foreign policy advisers to the president are, at least sometimes, under very severe stress. (Those advising President Kennedy about the Cuban missile crisis were, and they knew they were, close to starting a nuclear war—that's stress!) So Janis decided to listen to what the participants in several of these decisions had to say about the process of reaching a decision (Janis, 1972, 1982).

Janis investigated presidential decisions that were clearly foreign policy fiascos: President Kennedy's decision to invade Cuba at the Bay of Pigs, President Truman's decision to send troops into North Korea, the decision of the naval high command at Pearl Harbor that there was no need to make serious provisions for a possible assault by Japan; President Johnson's decision to increase the number of American troops sent to Vietnam, and, last, President Nixon's decision to continue the Watergate coverup. Janis also looked at two decisions that were clearly successful: President Kennedy's decision to blockade Cuba during the Cuban missile crisis and President Truman's decision to rebuild Europe after the Second World War: the Marshall Plan.

The fiascos really were fiascos. Just to take an example, the Bay of Pigs involved an attempted invasion of Cuba by Cuban refugees trained and supplied by the CIA. These refugees were deposited on the beaches of Cuba at the Bay of Pigs, where they were quickly captured by Castro's forces. The upshot of this was a massive humiliation for the United States, which in the end, had to pay a ransom in money and medical supplies to reclaim the refugees. But this much tells you only that the invasion had a very unhappy outcome; it doesn't show that the invasion was a fiasco, something that by virtue of its poor design deserved to fail. The historical record documents that it was that too.

Just to get the feel of what a fiasco it was, consider this. The members of the (newly in place) Kennedy administration assumed that even if the refugees

▼ (A) President Lyndon Johnson's Tuesday Group meeting to advise him about the Vietnam War. (B) Even groupthink cannot conceal the truth forever. President Johnson is pictured here just after being told that the war in Vietnam could not be won. Shortly thereafter, he announced that he would not seek a second term as president and opened negotiations with North Vietnam. But the war would last another six years.

A

B

were captured, there would be no problem for the United States, since it would simply deny any involvement. They assumed that the rest of the world would surely believe this lie. But there really wasn't the slightest chance that the rest of the world was going to believe that the United States wasn't involved in an invasion of Cuba, especially since word of the plan got out before the invasion and was widely reported in the world press. And then there was a matter of geography.

The policymakers who planned the invasion assumed that if the invaders were to face opposition, they would link up with anti-Castro guerrillas in the Sierra Del Escambray Mountains. But even a quick glance at a map of Cuba would have revealed that those mountains were separated from the Bay of Pigs' landing area by eighty miles of swamp! The idea that the invading forces could traverse this swamp was pure fantasy. Thus, the Bay of Pigs invasion was, in Janis's phrase, a perfect failure, and it deserved to be. But how did this happen?

One thing can be ruled out. It wasn't because the Kennedy administration was made up of stupid men. Before joining the administration, Dean Rusk, Kennedy's secretary of state, was the head of the Rockefeller Foundation. Robert McNamara, secretary of defense, had been a professional statistician, an analyst for the air force, and the president of Ford Motors. McGeorge Bundy, a chief adviser, had been dean of arts and sciences at Harvard, and so on. These were all very smart, very distinguished men. So why the fiasco?

Symptoms of Groupthink Janis attributes the faulty decisions to what he has called groupthink, by which he meant a deterioration of mental efficiency, reality testing, and moral judgment that results from ingroup pressures to seek consensus. Groupthink is what happens when the task demands on a decision-making group are overwhelmed by the social demands to reach consensus. Janis believed that there are eight specific symptoms of groupthink; these are given in Table 3.2. Janis has argued that the historical record of the foreign policy fiascos documents many of these symptoms of groupthink; the record for the successes shows fewer symptoms.

TABLE 3.2

THE GROUPTHINK SYNDROME

People suffering from groupthink
1. overestimate the group they are a part of;
2. believe in the inherent morality of the group, regardless of how immoral its plans are;
3. develop group rationalizations for defective policies;
4. rely on stereotypes of their adversary rather than accurate conceptions;
5. suppress rather than express their doubts and reservations about a decision;
6. have the illusory belief that the group is unanimous in its decision when many in fact have doubts and reservations;
7. overtly call upon those who do express criticism to suppress that criticism out of loyalty to the group or its leader;
8. sometimes appoint someone Janis calls a "mindguard," who is in charge of suppressing dissent.

Avoiding Groupthink   What can a president, or any other leader, do to avoid groupthink? Janis has several suggestions. First, it is important to avoid isolation on the part of policymakers. In the Bay of Pigs case, the Kennedy administration was so concerned with secrecy that the people in the government who had the most useful information were prevented from contributing, because they weren't even let in on the plan.

Second, the leader should establish procedures and norms that insure that every side of an issue is aired, and that all are encouraged to express, rather than suppress, their real opinions and fears. The leader must be especially careful not to indicate his own opinion before seeking advice. Advisers who know the position the leader favors are bound to be affected by this knowledge. They may be influenced in their thinking—they may truly come to believe that what the leader wants is the best course—or they may know full well that what the leader wants is wrong, but they may suppress their urge to say so for fear that they will lose the leader's favor (or their jobs). As mentioned in Chapter 2, the first sort of influence has been called internalization; the second is called compliance.

Clark McCauley has reexamined the Janis material and concludes that there is evidence for both internalization and compliance in the historical record. In the Bay of Pigs fiasco, for example, there is ample evidence that some of Kennedy's advisers held their tongues despite their private reservations, but there is no evidence of compliance in the case of the Pearl Harbor disaster (McCauley, 1989).

Further Tests of Groupthink   One test of the utility of a theory like Janis's is whether other researchers can find the same lesson Janis did in the same historical record. Philip Tetlock looked at the public statements of the key policymakers involved in the same fiascos and successes. He examined twelve passages per policymaker for each crisis, and coded each passage for three of the groupthink symptoms. He found that the policymakers involved in fiascos were more *simplistic* in their thinking than those not involved. Second, those Janis said were suffering from groupthink did make more positive statements about the United States (ingroup overvaluation) than did those not suffering from groupthink. Contrary to expectations, however; the groupthinkers did not engage in more negative thinking about their Communist opponents. Tetlock, then, found a good deal of support in the record for Janis's position (Tetlock, 1979).

In a further attempt to demonstrate the utility of the groupthink position, Janis created a master list of international disputes since World War II. Sadly, there were seventy-six of them. These were presented to two experts in political science who were asked to rank the four most serious during the five administrations from Truman to Nixon. These four crises were then rated on seven symptoms of faulty decision making by the investigators. Next, each crisis was rated by both a liberal and a conservative expert for the degree to which the outcome of the crisis was favorable to the United States' interests. Some of the crises were rated by both as having a favorable outcome for the United States (for example, President Eisenhower's decision *not* to send troops to Vietnam); others were rated by both as having a negative effect on U.S. interests (President Nixon's decision to "tilt toward Pakistan" in the Pakistan-Indian war).

The question was: Did the decisions that showed few symptoms of defective thinking also result in the most positive outcomes? The answer was strongly positive. There was a quite strong correlation between the absence of symptoms of faulty decision making and the favorability of the outcome for the United States (Herek, Janis, & Huth, 1987). Sound decision making does seem to pay off in better outcomes.

These studies support the groupthink model in the sense that they suggest that the symptoms of groupthink are more likely to be present in the records of bad foreign policy decisions than they are in the records of good foreign policy decisions. The studies also indicate that groupthink may be a disease that often infects decision makers. But Janis also proposed a particular cause of that disease: a combination of high cohesiveness and stress. Is there evidence for that?

Philip Tetlock carefully examined ten foreign policy decisions, from Neville Chamberlain's decision to appease Hitler to Jimmy Carter's decision to try to rescue the hostages in Iran. Tetlock found that some of these decisions were indeed infected with the syndrome of groupthink, as Janis suggested. The symptoms of groupthink did tend to hang together. But the results did not support Janis in terms of the *causes* of groupthink. There was no evidence that cohesiveness or stress figured as important causes of groupthink. Rather, what seemed important was the behavior of the group leader. Leaders who encouraged open discussion tended to avoid groupthink even in cohesive and stressed groups (McCauley, 1989; Tetlock, Peterson, McGuire, Chang, & Feld, 1992). Groupthink, then, emerges as a syndrome of symptoms, symptoms of a bad climate for making decisions. Groups that see such symptoms developing need, perhaps, to find their way to leaders who will be less inclined to suppress dissent.

THE CONTAGION OF AN EATING DISORDER

The results of studies on uniformity and groupthink tell us something about groups' abilities to affect attitudes and decisions; a recent study by Christian Crandall shows us just how pervasive group influence can be. Crandall in-

Irving Janis argued that groupthink can be reduced by

- avoiding isolation of the group;
- the leader's pressing for the expression of diverse points of view;
- the leader's withholding her own opinion until others have expressed theirs.

vestigated the incidence of bulimia, an eating disorder characterized by binge eating often in association with purging, in a college sorority. Cliques of women within the sorority tended to cluster in the degree to which they binged. A second study using two sororities suggested why cliques clustered. In both sororities, there was a relation between a young woman's score on a binge-eating scale and her popularity with the sorority. In one sorority, the *more* a woman binged, the *more* popular she was; in the other, the most popular members were those intermediate in their binging. In *both* sororities, however, popularity was tied to the group's conception of the *right* degree of binging (Crandall, 1988).

Groups, then, provide people with many satisfactions, and these satisfactions are reasons to join them. But to be a member of a group is to be open to the group's influence. The person who wants to be independent, then, ought to stay clear of groups, especially cohesive ones. But as Emile Durkheim, one of the founding fathers of sociology, discovered, there is an important problem with this isolated way of life: suicide. Durkheim found that people without significant attachments to cohesive familial, religious, or political groups were more likely than those with such connections to commit suicide (Durkheim, 1897/1951). And even if they don't commit suicide, they will surely be lonely.

GROUPS VERSUS INDIVIDUALS

In our discussion of groups so far, I have mentioned several factors that lead to good or poor performance on the part of a group. But there is a fundamental question we haven't addressed yet: Do groups perform better (or worse) than individuals?

Suppose, for example, you were the president of a company and you wanted advice about something, say whether to invest in a new product line. One way to get advice would be to find the most knowledgeable person you could and ask her what to do. Alternatively, you might appoint a committee to discuss the problem and to present you with a group recommendation. Which should you do? Which advice will be better? Whether groups are better problem solvers than individuals has concerned social psychologists from the very beginnings of the field. We shall see, however, that although this question is easy to ask, its simplicity conceals quite a bit of complexity.

Group Judgment and Bias

Let us begin with the simple example of a group judgment patterned after an experiment carried out by Hazel Knight in 1921 (Knight, 1921; cited in Lorge, Fox, Davitz, & Brenner, 1958). Suppose you wanted to know the temperature of a room but lacked a thermometer. You might ask a single person what the temperature was, or you might gather a group of people and let them discuss it. From our discussion of the Sherif experiment in Chapter 2, we have some idea what would happen. Imagine that the true temperature of the room is 72 degrees. We would expect some of the people to start with a guess higher than that, while others would start lower. Over time, the group would converge in its discussion to a point near the mean of the original guesses. The question we now want to ask is: How good would that mean judgment be in comparison with the judgment of a single, randomly chosen individual? The answer is that it would likely be better.

The fact that the group does better than a randomly chosen individual suggests that there are benefits of group discussions. Perhaps the give and take of opinions leads to accurate judgment. But as Knight realized, the results don't really show that. To see why, suppose you came up with a third solution. You simply asked several people to write their answers on a slip of paper individually, and then you averaged those judgments. How would that answer compare with the answer of a single individual? Well, it too would likely be more accurate. But the improvement could hardly be attributed to the benefits of group discussion. Why is this pooled judgment likely to be better?

It is helpful to think about it this way. There are many influences on individuals' judgments of room temperature. One, but only one, is the actual temperature of the room. There are a host of others. Each person's metabolism matters—the faster it is, the warmer the room will seem. Another is the person's history: Eskimos might judge all rooms warmer than people from the tropics. And so on. But if we collect our sample of judges broadly enough, these other factors will be randomly distributed and these random errors (or biases) will cancel one another out—one person will have a fast metabolism, another will have a slow one; the person with the fast metabolism will judge high, but the one with the slow metabolism will judge low. Any procedure that pools their judgments, whether it be group discussion or simply mechanically averaging their answers, will result in an answer closer to the one factor that is influencing *all* of their judgments, the true temperature of the room. Moreover, simple statistical principles dictate that the more judgments we pool, the closer we will come to the true answer. This result yields a methodological and a practical conclusion.

The methodological conclusion is that in order to show that group *discussions* are productive, it is not enough to show that a group's judgment is better than an individual's. One must also show that it is better than the result of mechanically pooling the judgments of the same number of individuals. The practical point is relevant for our executive trying to decide whether to invest in a new product line. If he believes that there are many people he could ask for advice and that each is biased, but that the biases are in different directions, then any procedure he chooses—mechanical averaging or group discussion—is likely to result in a better judgment than he would get by asking a single individual.

But what if he believes that all of the people in his organization share the same bias? Will it help to consult a group? To see the problem, imagine that you can ask only people from the tropics about the temperature of the room. Because of their history, let us assume that they are all biased in the direction of finding rooms cooler than they really are. Will you get a better estimate of the true room temperature by asking large groups of them? The answer is no. Indeed, it has been shown that there are circumstances in which pooling the judgments of people who share a bias is likely to lead to an answer *further* from the truth than you would get by asking just one of them (Einhorn, Hogarth, & Klempmer, 1977). The more people you ask, the more their answers will cancel out one another's *random* biases, but their answers will not cancel out the systematic bias produced by their shared histories. Instead, as the number of people you ask increases, the average answer will converge, but it will not converge toward the truth. It will converge toward their shared bias. Yes, 10,000 Frenchmen *can* be wrong; indeed, they are likely to be wrong about anything that the French in general have a bias about, say the relative merits of French versus California wine. And 20,000 Frenchmen are even more likely to be wrong!

The problems groups have with bias is nicely illustrated in some clever experiments by Garold Stasser and William Titus (Stasser & Titus, 1985, 1987; see also Stasser & Stewart, 1992). In their experiments, groups of subjects are given all of the information they need to solve a problem. In some cases, *each member* of the group has all of the information needed to solve the problem. But in other cases, each member is given only part of the relevant information. Indeed, because the subjects have only part of the information, they are as individuals led to the *wrong* solution; they are given a bias. If the groups were able to get all the information they have collectively onto the table, they could see the right answer. The question was: Could they get the information on the table when each person is misled by the partial information he had? The answer was no, even though they discussed the information and their problem. The groups, like the individuals that composed them, often picked the wrong answer, the one supported by the partial information the individuals had. The mere fact that a group of people discuss some decision is no guarantee that their biases will be overcome.

So imagine now that our executive faces a decision about whether to move the company from one city to another, and he believes that employees in general like living where they do—they are biased against moving. It would do him no good to get advice from a group of employees; indeed it might do him harm. The effect of group discussion is likely to be greater certainty in their shared bias rather than an accurate appraisal of the situation. Group discussion is certainly not a panacea for all of the ills that beset individual judgment.

Group Performance on Cognitive Tasks

There *are* conditions in which groups outperform individuals. To see the conditions under which they do, we need some distinctions drawn by Patrick Laughlin. One kind of task a group might face is deciding where to have dinner. Here, the only criterion for a successful decision is that it maximize the members' satisfaction. The group isn't concerned with finding the *right* answer—there is no right (or wrong) answer to the question: Would you rather have Chinese or Italian food? Let us call such a task a **preference** task.* The group's sole problem (no pun intended) is to combine individual prefer-

---

*Laughlin refers to such tasks as *judgmental,* suggesting that there are no right answers, just judgments to be expressed. But this is a bit confusing. If a group, say a jury, has to judge whether someone did or did not commit a crime, they are asked (and presumably are trying) to get the matter right, not just to express their *preference.* A person might *prefer* that the defendant be innocent but *judge* that he is guilty. Of course, in any particular case the question of whether the defendant is guilty or innocent might be extremely murky, but that is a matter of whether the decision (be it a judgment or an intellectual evaluation) is *demonstrable,* an issue we take up next. So, in any event, I prefer the notion of group preference rather than group judgment for cases in which the group believes there is no right answer.

TABLE 3.3

COMBINATION RULES FOR DIFFERENT TYPES OF PROBLEMS

Type	Characteristic	Combination Rule Used
Preference	No right answer	Majority (or plurality) wins
Intellective demonstrative	Right answer, easily seen, once proposed	Right answer wins if proposed
Nondemonstrative	Right answer, but not easily seen, even once proposed	Right answer wins *if* proposed and endorsed by more than one member

SOURCE: Based on Laughlin, 1988.

ences into a group preference. (See Table 3.3.)

Now consider a problem in geometry. Problems in geometry are ***intellective***—they have a right answer—unlike problems of pure preference. Moreover, questions in geometry, or at least many of them, have answers that are ***demonstrable.*** Someone who thinks she knows the right answer can demonstrate that it *is* the right answer.

Now we need a further distinction, one within the class of demonstrable problems. Consider your favorite riddle. For a riddle to be effective, it must have two properties. First, when you hear it, the answer must be difficult to see. Second, when you hear the answer, it must be immediately, "intuitively" obvious that the answer is right. (Of course, professors of mathematics are notorious for finding the most difficult matters intuitively obvious!) Problems for which the answer (once proposed) is intuitively obvious have been dubbed, among other things, "Ah ha!" problems or "Eureka!" problems. A riddle, or for that matter any joke, falls flat on its face if the right answer isn't immediately and intuitively obvious. So even *within* the class of demonstrable problems, there are matters of degree. Some answers only need be stated for everyone to see them as right; others require more thinking. We can think of demonstrability, then, as a continuum or dimension. Laughlin found that these distinctions between preference and intellective problems, and between intellective problems with demonstrable answers and those without, are important to understanding when groups outperform individuals (Laughlin & Ellis, 1986; Laughlin, 1988; Laughlin, VanderStoep, & Hollingshead, 1991).

Laughlin gave groups of subjects problems of preference, intellective problems with easily demonstrable answers, and problems with solutions that are less easily demonstrated. He then asked this question: How do groups combine the answers all of the members have to arrive at a group answer? More specifically, he wanted to know what *rule* groups used in reaching the final, group answer. Now, by "rule" he did not mean something that the members explicitly followed, one they were conscious of and could articulate. Rather, he was interested in the ***implicit rule*** they followed.

James Davis has developed a procedure called ***social decision scheme analysis*** for inferring such implicit rules. The mathematics of this procedure are somewhat complex, but the basic idea is simple. You ask the members of a group for their initial opinions, then allow them to discuss. As they discuss, from time to time you interrupt them to determine their current positions. Last, you ask for their final, group judgment. The aim is to infer and characterize the simplest rule that would account for how the group got from where it started to where it wound up (Davis, 1973). As we shall see, this technique has been widely applied to chart the progress of juries on their path from the opinions of the individual jurors to a final verdict. For now, our interest is in what rules the groups used in reaching a group answer to the problems Laughlin gave them.

On preference problems, groups simply gave the preference of the majority if there was a majority for a single answer. If there wasn't a majority, then the group went with a plurality (the answer with more support than any other, even if less than a majority of the group preferred it). If there was no plurality, the group was equally likely to pick any outcome. So on preference problems, groups were democratic and egalitarian. But on intellective problems, the groups used different implicit rules.

With the Eureka! problems, the groups acted as if they were following the rule: Truth wins. That is, if anyone in the group proposed the right answer, the groups adopted it. On less demonstrable problems, the groups followed the rule: Truth supported wins, meaning that the group adopted the correct answer if it was proposed and if it was endorsed by other members of the group. The less demonstrable a solution was, the more support it needed for it to emerge as the group's collective answer.

These results suggest this. For problems with clear, immediately obvious solutions, a group will perform as well as its best member, in the sense that it will adopt the correct answer if someone gets it in the first place. But as the issue gets murkier and the solution less clear, the group will be less and less likely to perform as well as its best member.

Groups that must make an ambiguous judgment (low demonstrability) tend to pool information in an egalitarian way, and this is likely to lead to better answers than any one member would give. But the advantage comes from the pooling of judgments rather than from any discussion that might go on; when matters are maximally ambiguous, there's not much that can come from discussion. There is reason to believe too that group discussion is not likely to overcome shared biases; indeed, it might well make matters worse.

We now turn to a particular case of decision making by groups. Juries constitute a group brought together to decide the guilt or innocence of an accused person.

> Groups will perform as well as individuals *when:*
>
> - the individuals in the group do *not* have a shared, systematic bias;
>
> - the problem the group is asked to solve has a correct answer *that can be demonstrated.*

JURY TASK PERFORMANCE

Anglo-American law has one striking central feature: it turns its most critical decisions over to ad hoc groups of amateurs—juries. It is hardly surprising, then, that social psychologists interested in groups have found juries to be an attractive subject for research. Research on jury performance is of substantial practical interest to the legal system and is at the same time a place to sharpen our understanding of how groups in general work. It is with an eye to both of these concerns that we turn to research on how juries work. Such research, however, faces several serious problems.

The first problem is that we don't know the right answer to the problems juries try to solve. In the laboratory, we pose problems to subjects and compare subjects' answers with the right answer. So we must remember that we cannot answer with certainty the very first question that we would like to ask about juries: How well do they do their jobs?

There is also a second problem. Social psychologists would love to know what goes on in jury rooms; we would love to know how juries discuss their cases. The only way to know *that* would be by tape-recording jury discussions. But we can't. In fact, in the 1950s, some researchers, with the permission of the presiding judge, did record a very small number of jury discussions. But although this fact was supposed to be a secret, it became public, resulting in adverse consequences. A congressional investigation was started, the attorney general censured the group that did the taping, and statutes were passed in many states making it plainly illegal to do it again. The intensity of this reaction tells us something about the place of jury trials in American culture; Americans treat them as something approaching the sacred. So, for good or ill, social psychologists are not able to investigate jury decision making processes directly. How, then, can we study the jury?

There are two techniques. One is to interview jurors and judges after a case is over. This is perfectly legal, commonly done by the media and also sometimes done by attorneys on both sides of a case. The second way uses mock juries.

"Mock juries" refers to a wide variety of techniques used to simulate a jury trial. These techniques include some that are very realistic—assembling a group of people who are on jury duty but were not called for a particular case, having them listen to a real trial in the courtroom, and then asking them to enter a room in the court building under the auspices of a bailiff and reach a verdict (although they know, of course, that their verdict won't count). Other techniques are much less realistic—simply giving a group of subjects a written description of the facts of a case and asking them for a verdict, or an opinion as to how much the defendant should be punished. There are many steps between these two extremes; one common practice is to videotape the recreation of a trial, and then ask groups of people to deliberate about it.

It is hard to know how faithfully even the most realistic of these mock juries capture what goes on in a real jury. Even the most realistic of them leave out what is surely the key fact for juries: they know there are real consequences of their decision. And there is evidence that knowing one is making a fateful decision affects how one makes that decision (Wilson & Donnerstein, 1977). Nonetheless, the most realistic of the procedures are probably a fair substitute for studying real juries, but it is probably wise to place less confidence in procedures that are far from realistic.

 CLASSIC FINDINGS IN SOCIAL PSYCHOLOGY: JURIES AND JUDGES

We can't know how well juries do as far as the criterion we really care about—the truth about a crime—is concerned, but we do know something about how juries do compared with judges (see Table 3.4). Harry Kalven Jr.

TABLE 3.4

| Judge Would Have | Jury | | | |
	Acquitted	Convicted	Hung	Total
Acquitted	13.4	2.2	1.1	16.7
Convicted	16.9	62.0	4.4	83.3
Total	30.3	64.2	5.5	100.0

VERDICTS OF JUDGES AND JURIES*

*Percentage of verdicts in 3,576 trials.
SOURCE: Data from Kalven & Zeisel, 1966.

and Hans Zeisel, in the most extensive study of the American jury ever carried out, obtained the jury's verdict in 3,576 criminal trials. They also asked the judge in each case to indicate (while the jury was deliberating) just how he would have found, had he been the one to decide the case. In 13.4 percent of the cases, judge and jury agreed on acquittal, and in 62.0 percent of the cases, judge and jury agreed on conviction. So in just over 75 percent of the cases, judge and jury were in agreement. In only 2.2 percent of the cases, the judge would have acquitted, but the jury convicted. In 16.9 percent of the cases, the reverse was true—the jury acquitted, but the judge would have convicted.

For the most part, then, the judge and jury were in agreement, and when they weren't, it was likely to be because the jury was more lenient. These numbers, by the way, don't add up to 100 percent because of cases where the jury "hung" or the judge could not reach a decision. (A hung jury means that the jury cannot reach agreement. In a criminal case, the prosecution *can* try the defendant again after a hung jury verdict, although often it decides

◄ In the film The Star Chamber, a group of the most powerful members of a community take the jury process into their own hands.

not to.) The evidence in civil cases—where one person sues another—was similar. There, out of a sample of some 4,000 cases, judge and jury agreed in 78 percent of the cases (Kalven & Zeisel, 1966).

Aside from the striking level of agreement between the judges and juries, the other fact that stands out from these data is the tendency for juries to be more *lenient* than judges.

Judges were also invited to give their guess as to *why* they disagreed with their juries. The most common reason they gave was disagreement about interpretation of the evidence. The second most common reason was disagreement about the proper interpretation of the law, and the third was sentiments about the defendant (Kalven & Zeisel, 1966). Of course, we don't know if the judges were right in these guesses, but they suggest three things. First, something fairly obvious: evidence is sometimes difficult to interpret.

The second issue is more complicated, and has to do with the role of the jury. In many jurisdictions (California, for example), judges explicitly tell juries that it is the *judge's* role to interpret the law: to decide what the relevant law is in the case at hand, and to decide which facts are relevant to the verdict. The jury's job is simply to decide what the facts are. A jury in such cases is strictly a "trier of facts." In other states (Maryland, for example), the judge informs the jury that it is the jury's job to interpret the law as well as to decide the relevant facts. The judge's role there is to *assist* the jury in interpreting the law. Despite these explicit differences, Kalven and Zeisel's results suggest that to some degree, juries in all jurisdictions see themselves as interpreters of the law.

Last, the evidence suggests that juries sometimes take personal characteristics of the defendant into account more than judges think they should. Judges believe that juries are too influenced by evidence that the defendant was of good character, a family man, a pillar of the community, and so on. Judges believe that character should come into play, but only at sentencing; they don't believe it should matter as much as it seems to with regard to the verdict. But again, these are the reasons judges *think* jurors differ with them. They may be wrong.

The Kalven and Zeisel research is an important bit of background information because it suggests that juries might not do such a bad job, and it is with that background belief that we should consider the recent history of social psychologists' research on jury processes.

Juries

- in general reach the same verdicts judges would;

- are a bit more lenient than judges would be;

- might take the defendant's personal characteristics into account in deciding guilt more than judges would.

Jury Size and Unanimity

From watching *Perry Mason* or *L.A. Law*, most of us have probably come to believe two things about juries: (1) they have twelve members, and (2) they must reach a unanimous verdict. But actually, neither is true.

It *is* true that since the time of Henry II, the traditional common law jury has had twelve members. But the state of Florida, among others (to save money), has legislated that under certain circumstances a criminal jury can consist of only six. A defendant named Williams was convicted by a six-person jury; he appealed the conviction on the grounds that the Sixth Amendment to the Constitution required an impartial jury, and that a six-person jury was not impartial. In *Williams* v. *Florida* (1970), the U.S. Supreme Court upheld the state statute and the conviction, claiming that six-person juries were "functionally equivalent" to twelve-person juries, that a six-person jury would deliberate just as a twelve-person jury would. The evidence the Court cited in support of this claim was scant, scarcely evidence at all. Many social psychologists felt that the Court was allowing the states to tamper with a system that worked quite well, and that the Court was doing this without real evidence about the effects of the tampering. All of this goaded social psychologists to gather more substantial evidence about differences between six- and twelve-person juries.

In *Apodaca, Cooper, and Madden* v. *Oregon,* the U.S. Supreme Court dealt with the requirement of unanimity in a jury decision. Oregon is one of several states that allow for nonunanimous verdicts in *criminal* cases (numerous states allow them in civil cases). Oregon permits a decision if there is a ten-person majority on a twelve-person jury. The Court held once again that there was no constitutional requirement that a jury's verdict be unanimous. The Court argued that the jury's discussion in a nonunanimous rule case would be just as searching and vigorous as it would be if the jury were operating with a rule of unanimity. Again, the Court's evidence was scant, and this too served as a goad to empirical research. The empirical question here is: Does it matter to a jury's deliberation whether it operates under a unanimous or majority decision rule?

It is worth recalling the questions we would really like to answer: Do six-person juries make *more mistakes* than twelve-person juries? Do juries with majority rather than unanimity rules make more mistakes? But there is no hope of being able to answer these questions directly. The related questions we might be able to address are: Are there *differences* between the verdicts of six- and twelve-person juries? Do juries with unanimous decision rules reach different verdicts from those with majority rules? The Court's argument was that there were *no* differences. If there are differences, then the Court was wrong, and it becomes reasonable to ask whether those differences are *likely to be* in the direction of improved or reduced justice.

◀ *In the film* Twelve Angry Men, *Henry Fonda starts out being the sole juror favoring acquittal but winds up convincing the rest of the jury. A great movie, even though such turn arounds rarely happen in life.*

Initial Juror Opinion and Final Jury Verdicts

A good starting point for this discussion is the movie *Twelve Angry Men*. In this brilliant film, Henry Fonda finds himself part of a twelve-person jury debating a case of first-degree murder. On the initial ballot, we learn that the jury votes eleven to one in favor of conviction; Henry Fonda (luckily for the defendant) is the lone holdout. Inexorably he turns the jury around; by the end of the trial, the jury votes to acquit (unanimously). Those of us who have seen the movie are grateful that (1) he was on the jury at all, and (2) the jury couldn't convict the poor guy without being forced by the unanimity rule to listen to Fonda's arguments. *Twelve Angry Men* reminds us that we want a defendant to be given every chance to establish his innocence, and that a twelve-person jury forced by the unanimity rule to listen to all sides of the issue is in line with that desire. But *Twelve Angry Men* is only a movie. We want to ask: How often does this sort of thing happen?

Kalven and Zeisel were able in 225 cases to interview people who had been jurors, and from these interviews they reconstructed the juries' initial ballots and final verdicts. (All used twelve-person juries and unanimous rules.) These data (see Table 3.5) show that if all of the jurors voted in the same direction on the first ballot, then that decision became the jury verdict. The table also shows that if from one to five jurors voted "guilty," then there was a very good (91 percent) chance of the jury's acquitting, and only a 2 percent chance of the jury's convicting. If, on the other hand, a majority voted to convict on the first ballot, there was an 86 percent chance of the defendant's being convicted and only a 5 percent chance of his being acquitted. These data suggested to Kalven and Zeisel that in real life, if not the movies, most of the work the jury does is done before the first ballot is ever taken. Indeed, the very high likelihood that a jury's verdict will end up corresponding to the initial position of its majority suggested that the case was decided by the time the jury entered the jury room. (At least when there was a majority. There were ten cases where the jury split six to six on the first ballot—three convicted, three acquitted, none hung.)

James Davis, using his social decision scheme approach on mock juries, has argued that regardless of the decision rule the judge assigns the jury, juries act as if they used a "two-thirds, otherwise hang" rule. This rule means that if the jury finds itself with a two-thirds majority in either direction, then those holding out will join the two-thirds, but if there isn't a two-thirds ma-

TABLE 3.5

FIRST BALLOT AND FINAL VERDICT					
	Number of guilty votes on first ballot				
Final verdict	0	1–5	6	7–11	12
Not guilty	100%	91%	50%	5%	—
Hung	—	7%	—	9%	—
Guilty	—	2%	50%	86%	100%
Number of cases	26	41	10	105	43

"IT'S A HUNG JURY, YOUR HONOR. THE EVIDENCE ASIDE, SOME OF US THINK HE LOOKS GUILTY, AND SOME OF US THINK HE DOESN'T LOOK GUILTY."

jority in any direction, then the jury will *tend* to hang (Davis, Kerr, Stasser, Meek, & Holt, 1977). There may be some Henry Fondas in jury rooms, but they are apparently not common. This does not imply, by the way, that jurors don't pay attention to the jury discussion; rather, the evidence suggests that the majority tends to control the nature of the discussion, and the discussion determines the outcome (Tanford & Penrod, 1986).

In light of these data, we should not expect to find large or consistent differences in verdicts between juries with majority and unanimous rules (Davis, 1989). But the Supreme Court made a somewhat different claim about small or nonunanimous juries; the Court claimed that they were the "functional equivalent" of larger and unanimous juries.

The Court's opinion was not only (or even not so much) that different juries reach the same verdict, but that different juries deliberate in the same way. But Charlan Nemeth found in a study of a mock jury that although there were no differences in the verdicts of juries assigned to unanimous and majority rules, there was an important difference in the nature of the juries' deliberations. Unanimous juries' deliberations were characterized by greater conflict than were the deliberations of two-thirds majority juries (Nemeth, 1977). This suggests that juries required to reach unanimous verdicts are more likely to air the issues of the case thoroughly. This is an important finding, because we surely want juries to consider their cases thoroughly. If unanimous verdict requirements help accomplish that end, then they seem worth a certain amount of added expense.

> Jury size and the requirement of unanimity have *not* been shown to have a large effect on verdicts, *but* unanimous requirement juries might discuss cases more thoroughly.

The Death-Qualified Jury

A final question we can ask about juries is how the composition of a jury affects a jury's verdict. To understand how this issue arises in jury trials, we need a bit of legal background. Before a jury trial begins, potential jurors are interviewed to determine their suitability to serve on the jury. This process is called the *voir dire* (truth-telling time). The purpose of the *voir dire* is to be sure that jurors are unbiased—for example, to be sure the defendant's mother isn't on the jury. If a reason that a potential juror might be biased is uncovered during the *voir dire*, the juror is *excluded for cause*. (A limited number of jurors can also be removed simply because one side or the other doesn't want them on the jury.)

As important as this function of the *voir dire* is, it can introduce a difficult problem in certain circumstances, as illustrated by the case of William Witherspoon. Witherspoon was convicted of murder and sentenced to death in Cook County (Chicago), Illinois, in 1960. His jury was **death qualified,** meaning that any potential juror who expressed categorical opposition to the death penalty during the *voir dire* was excused for cause. The logic of such excusals is clear; if a jury person's opposition is categorical, then he might vote to acquit the defendant, not because of the evidence in the case, but because he would not be willing to find a person guilty *no matter the evidence.*

Witherspoon appealed his conviction (eventually) to the U.S. Supreme Court, claiming that the use of a death-qualified jury biased the case against him. Now the issue isn't that his jury was biased in favor of the death penalty for people found guilty; that, of course, is true. But Witherspoon's claim was stronger than that; it was that death-qualified juries are biased against defendants with regard to the question of *guilt or innocence.*

His argument was that, as it happens, people in favor of capital punishment are (on average) biased in favor of the prosecution, while those opposed to capital punishment are biased toward the defendant. Selecting for or against one or two such people is not likely to have much effect on a verdict, but if the whole jury is selected using this criterion, that is another matter. But why should people in favor of the death penalty be pro-prosecution when it comes to guilt or innocence?

One reason is this. There is a well-documented personality characteristic called authoritarianism (about which we shall have quite a lot to say in Chapter 4), which inclines a person to be rigid, conventional, and punitive toward people who deviate from social norms. People high in authoritarianism are likely to favor the death penalty, and conversely, those who favor the death penalty are likely to be high in authoritarianism. Thus, a death-qualified jury is likely to be an authoritarian jury. Now, in addition to being punitive, authoritarians are also likely to be overly swayed by authority—they obey more in the Milgram experiment, for example (see Chapter 2 for a discussion of this experiment). Prosecutors are authorities. Thus, Witherspoon argued, death-qualified juries are authoritarian, and authoritarian juries are likely to be biased in favor of the prosecution.

The Court's majority did not accept Witherspoon's argument; it decided that the empirical evidence was too "tentative" and "fragmentary" to support the Court's overturning the conviction. It upheld his conviction.* But the state of the evidence has changed substantially since 1968, when *Witherspoon* v. *Illinois* was decided. A long series of studies beginning perhaps with one by Herman Mitchell and Donn Byrne has shown that one or another piece of Witherspoon's claim was correct (Mitchell & Byrne, 1973).

A study by Gary Moran and John Comfort illustrates the general finding. Moran and Comfort carried out two studies of jurors who were actually im-

*Since *Witherspoon*, the Court has added quite a bit of complexity to death qualifications.

paneled in felony cases, although not necessarily capital cases. The first study used 282 jurors; the second used 346 jurors. The results indicated that those who favor capital punishment are significantly more likely to be Caucasian, male, married, wealthy, Republican, politically conservative, and authoritarian. Death-qualified juries, then, overrepresent Caucasians, males, married people, and so on, and underrepresent blacks, women, unmarried people, and so on. Thus, there is reason to believe that death-qualified juries are unrepresentative of the population as a whole, and biased toward the prosecution (Moran & Comfort, 1986).

So this leaves us (all of us) in a difficult position. If we exclude from all capital trials jurors who are opposed to the death penalty, we stack the deck for the prosecution. Indeed, Nancy Pennington and Reid Hastie have estimated that 17 percent of all potential jurors are excludable from capital cases based on their opposition to the death penalty. They went on to estimate that such death-qualified jurors are 20 percent more likely to convict a defendant than are other jurors. Based on this assumption, they estimated that 10 percent of defendants would be convicted by a death-qualified jury, but would not have been convicted by a representative jury. So excluding jurors opposed to the death penalty might substantially increase convictions in capital cases (Pennington & Hastie, 1990). We can't conclude from this result that excluding such jurors leads to a 10 percent increase in the number of *innocent* defendants that are convicted; all we can say is that 10 percent more defendants will be convicted who would not be convicted with a randomly selected jury.

Jonathan Freedman has also attempted to estimate the impact of capital punishment on convictions in capital cases. His strategy, however, was to survey jurors who had served on murder cases in Canada (where there is no death penalty). He asked them how their verdicts would have been affected had there been a death penalty. Thirty percent of the jurors reported that they would have been less likely to vote for conviction had there been a death penalty; 3 percent reported they would have been *more* likely to vote for conviction (see Figure 3.5). We don't know whether all 30 percent who would have been less likely to vote for conviction were categorically opposed to capital punishment; some of them may have been willing to impose it in some cases but may have thought that the evidence in the particular case they sat on was strong enough to convict the defendant without the death penalty, but were not willing to convict on the same evidence with the death penalty (Freedman, 1990). In any event, these data suggest that just as excluding jurors opposed to the death penalty may increase conviction rates, not excluding them may substantially reduce conviction rates. This leaves us with a dilemma.

There are two solutions that come to mind. Get rid of the death penalty. Without the specter of the death penalty, there will be no need to death-qualify juries, thus biasing them against defendants, and those opposed to the death penalty will have no reason to hold out against guilty verdicts. Failing this, there is a second solution: use the first twelve people to pass the courthouse door—remove the right to challenge jurors after a *voir dire*. This is, as it happens, how the British assemble juries. If we do this, then there will be some capital trials with jurors opposed to the death penalty. But the jury will not be selected to have *only* people hostile to the death penalty. And a single

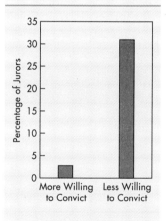

FIGURE 3.5
DEATH-QUALIIFIED JURIES

▲ *Canadian jurors' willingness to convict in a murder case if there were a death penalty in Canada. Many more jurors were less willing to convict than were more willing to convict. (Data from Freedman, 1990)*

person on a jury is unlikely to have a large effect on the verdict. And if she does have an effect, it is simply likely to lead to more hung juries. There are worse things. One worse thing is what we seem to do now: systematically bias juries against defendants in capital cases.

SUMMARY

1. Merely being in the presence of other people has effects on our performance of tasks; the effect is called *social facilitation.* According to Robert Zajonc, the presence of others produces arousal, and arousal *enhances* the performance of simple, well-learned tasks but *detracts* from the performance of complex, novel tasks. The presence of others can also give rise to *evaluation apprehension,* arousal that occurs as a result of knowing that others are in a position to evaluate us.

2. Being part of an ad hoc group may lead to *social loafing,* lessened motivation to perform a physical or cognitive task. This is especially likely to occur when the individual contributions to a task cannot be monitored, the task is simple rather than challenging, an individual thinks she is *good* at a task but thinks that the group's payoff depends on the *worst* member's performance, or an individual thinks she is *poor* at a task and thinks that the group's payoff depends on the *best* member's performance.

3. Group cohesiveness is typically *increased* by attractions that a group offers and *decreased* by costs a group imposes. Loyalty to a group may enhance cohesiveness. Cohesive groups exert pressure on their members to reach a shared consensus. Members of cohesive groups with deviant views are likely to face rejection.

4. Irving Janis has argued that cohesive groups are prone to *groupthink*—a deterioration of mental efficiency, reality testing, and moral judgment that results from pressures toward consensus. Groupthink has been implicated as a cause of a variety of foreign policy fiascos in recent American history.

5. Groups are likely to make better judgments than individuals do *only if* the members do not suffer from a shared systematic bias, and if they are able to get all of the relevant facts on the table.

6. Juries tend to reach the same verdicts that judges would reach. Where they differ from judges, they tend to be more lenient. We do not know who is more accurate.

7. Death-qualified juries—juries from which people opposed to the death penalty have been excluded—are more likely to convict a defendant than would a jury composed of a truly random sample of the population.

CHAPTER 4

Prejudice and Intergroup Conflict

The 1960s were full of dramatic images; they brought us, for one thing, the first nationally televised war. But before this, another drama was played out in the national media and in the national consciousness. This one involved two principal characters, Martin Luther King Jr. and Theophilus Eugene "Bull" Connor. The action took place on the streets of Birmingham, Alabama; its climax came on Good Friday, April 12, 1963. Martin Luther King came to Birmingham to help the blacks of that city win the right to sit at the same lunch counters as whites, to drink from the same water fountains, to use the city's public restrooms. Bull Connor was the city's commissioner of fire, police, and education. The particular form of education he favored was quite distinctive.

Connor's chief educational tool was the police dog, a tool he used relentlessly against King and the other ministers leading the hymn-singing civil rights protestors. The spectacle was horrifying, a confrontation between the dignified, pacifist Martin Luther King and the fat, red-necked, vulgar Bull Connor—a caricature of the Southern sheriff. In the weeks that followed, as the protests continued, police dogs gave way to bombs, and the governor of Alabama, George Wallace, announced that, in defiance of a federal court order, he would refuse to admit two black students to the summer session of the University of Alabama.

For many observers, particularly in the North, Bull Connor served as the symbol of the bigot. Of course, there was something smug in this. For those of us growing up in the North, it was very safe to see Connor and his dogs

A

B

▲ (A) Bull Connor leads uniformed officers during mass arrest at a civil rights demonstration in Birmingham, Alabama, in May 1963. (B) Martin Luther King Jr. in 1965.

in faraway Birmingham as the essence of prejudice. But in truth, prejudice was not then and is not now constrained by regional boundaries.

In 1989 in the Bensonhurst section of Brooklyn, a gang of from ten to thirty bat-wielding white young men attacked four African-American youths who had come to the neighborhood to look at a used car. One of the victims—Yusef Hawkins, age sixteen—was shot to death. His crime? He was suspected of attempting to date the former girlfriend of one of the assailants (Blumenthal, 1989). And who can forget the videotape of Rodney King being beaten by white police officers in Los Angeles? Or the riots in Los Angeles that followed the acquittal in the first trial of these police officers, riots directed in part at Asian merchants? But prejudice involves more than race.

We have seen that the dissolution of the Soviet empire, an event fervently hoped for for decades, has left behind a bitter residue, the residue of "ethnic cleansing." In Northern Ireland, the same relentless terror occurs *within* an ethnic group, fueled by religious differences. And then there is Allen Schindler, a seaman aboard the USS *Belleau Wood.* On October 27, 1992, his beaten and mutilated body was found in a public restroom near Sasebo naval base in Japan. The crime for which he was executed was being gay. There were neither ethnic nor religious differences between him and those who murdered him, just a difference in sexual preference.

Finally, the scope of prejudice—and this chapter—includes hostile or demeaning attitudes toward women. As we all know, women too have been and continue to be targets of discrimination, prejudice, and even violence. There is, unfortunately, no shortage of prejudice in the United States and around the world.

WHAT IS PREJUDICE?

Social scientists have used both "prejudice" and "discrimination" to characterize the treatment of one group at the hands of another. At first blush, these terms seem synonymous. Social scientists have, however, used these terms to draw a distinction: they have used "prejudice" to refer to attitudes, and "discrimination" to refer to behavior.

Discriminatory Behavior

It seems obvious that discriminatory behavior is a consequence of prejudiced attitudes, but this isn't necessarily so. A person may act in a discriminatory way without harboring prejudiced attitudes, and vice versa. We shall consider the relations between attitudes and behavior more fully in Chapter 17; for now, to keep these concepts distinct, consider an example of discrimination without prejudice.

In the 1940s, New York department stores refused to hire African-American sales clerks because, they claimed, customers wouldn't shop in stores with visible African-American help. Some managers said that they themselves had nothing against African-Americans; they just couldn't endanger profits. Some, no doubt, were just giving an easy excuse for their own prejudice, but for others the claim was no doubt true. These managers weren't prejudiced, but they discriminated nonetheless. This sort of discrimination has been called **institutional racism,** since it is a result of institutional pressures rather than a direct result of prejudiced attitudes. Just as we cannot assume that every instance of discrimination results from prejudice, we cannot assume that prejudice always results in discrimination: social pressure, especially legal pressure, can move even the worst bigot to behave. **Discrimination,** then, is unfair treatment regardless of its psychological source. But what exactly is a prejudiced attitude?

Prejudice refers to hostile attitudes.

Discrimination refers to unfair behavior.

Discrimination sometimes, but not always, results from prejudice.

Prejudiced Attitudes

Social psychologists have meant by a prejudiced person someone who believes in the inherent inferiority of some group, or who evaluates people negatively just on the basis of their group identity, or who wishes to avoid or attack someone just on the basis of group membership. **Prejudice,** then, refers to beliefs or evaluations or impulses to act. Psychologists have measured atti-

▼ Prejudice in the form of rigid segregation of the races was a blunt and obvious matter in the South until the civil rights movement of the 1960s.

A

B

tudes by recording people's beliefs about minorities, or by finding out to what extent they endorse segregation (or more hostile acts), or by asking people to evaluate group members. The diversity in meaning and measurement creates a problem, since researchers are measuring different phenomena. But this problem is mitigated by the fact that the various measures are typically correlated to a reasonable degree; that is, people who are prejudiced on one measure are usually prejudiced on other measures as well (Harding, Proshansky, Kutner, & Chin, 1969).

Another concept often encountered in discussions of prejudice is **stereotype.** We shall consider the notion of a stereotype more carefully later, but for now, suffice it to say that "stereotype" refers specifically to *beliefs* about groups, and is used to suggest that these beliefs are inaccurate, difficult to change, and unfavorable. The belief that women are "too emotional" to hold positions of power and responsibility is an example of a stereotype.

Sources of Prejudice

In this chapter, we will examine social psychological research on prejudice of all kinds, on prejudice against Jews, African Americans, women, gays, and so on. Many social psychologists would argue that all of these examples of prejudice have some common psychological core, and for that reason it makes sense to treat them together. But I would prefer to treat that as an open question. So as we discuss the various approaches to prejudice that social psychologists have taken, we should keep in the back of our minds the question: How does this approach help me understand what our various prejudices have in common? Let us return now to Bull Connor.

Where should we begin in trying to understand Bull Connor? Social scientists have departed from three different starting points. One is an obvious fact about him—he was a Southerner; Connor's bigotry, though no doubt extreme, was nonetheless a reflection of the attitudes of a particular region at a particular moment. And at that moment, the South had its own beliefs, values, institutions, patterns of interactions—in short, its own culture. Moreover, Bull Connor as sheriff had a particular role to play in upholding these institutions, in maintaining this culture. To those who see this as the central fact of the drama, it is not Bull Connor the individual who needs to be ex-

▼ *(A) Alabama governor George Wallace standing in the doorway of the University of Alabama to prevent officials of the Justice Department from registering the black students. (B) Vivian Malone, one of the two black students who was enrolled, sitting with white students in class in June 1963 after integration of the university had been accomplished.*

A

B

plained, rather it is the relationship of blacks to whites in Southern culture that is the real issue. Scholars who take the cultural approach to prejudice, then, look for reasons why one culture or group becomes prejudiced against another. The individuals who make up those groups are to be understood in light of that broader, cultural pattern.

Another approach begins with Connor the person; researchers in this tradition have looked for peculiarities in Connor's personality, twisted motives. They see his race hatred as the fundamental fact, or trait, about him and look to his personal experience as the real source of that irrational hatred. Similarly, these scholars would look at the personality traits underlying membership in, for example, the neo-Nazi party, the party that marched through Skokie, Illinois, the predominantly Jewish suburb of Chicago. This tradition calls attention to the fact that prejudice is often associated with conventionality—the Nazis, for example, suppressed all modern art in Germany, seeing it as decadent, and instead glorified art expressing excessively sentimental ideas about German life. Scholars in this tradition would look for the common motivational root of this broader pattern.

A third approach begins with the ideas Connor had, that blacks are inferior, polluting, that even to sit at the same lunch counter with a black is to somehow be demeaned. In this third tradition, *cognition* (belief) is the crucial aspect of prejudice. We shall take up, then, these three approaches to prejudice: (1) as a cultural phenomenon, (2) as a motivational phenomenon, and (3) as a cognitive defect.

THE CULTURAL VIEW

At first, many of us might not accept the notion that Bull Connor became what he became because he was born in the South. On the contrary, our first reaction is to say that he was sick or crazy, to believe that no normal person could do what he did or think what he thought. The natural tendency is to look for some deep flaw *in him*. But this is too easy, and Connor made it even easier; he was in many ways so unattractive a figure that it was easy to see him as pathological. But let us consider the prejudice of a more sympathetic figure: Thomas Jefferson.

Thomas Jefferson is famous, of course, for those stirring words about how self-evident it is that all men are created equal. Thomas Jefferson, more than any other founding father, was the symbol of the rights of the individual. Thomas Jefferson was no shabby caricature of a Southern sheriff. Jefferson had an extraordinary mind. John Kennedy once gave a dinner for American Nobel Prize winners; his toast was to the most distinguished group of minds ever to be assembled in the White House—since Jefferson dined alone. And yet Jefferson held slaves. True, he wasn't very pleased by the idea, and true, he freed them at his death, but the fact remains that this democrat, this glowing mind, was a slave owner. To understand how he could own slaves, the most important thing to understand about him is that he grew up in Virginia. Jefferson is the character the cultural view grasps most fully. But for a cultural view of prejudice to be of any value, it is not enough for it to assert simply that prejudiced people come from prejudiced cultures—that's a truism; it has to tell us where those prejudiced cultures come from. Realistic

▲ *Thomas Jefferson wrote the Declaration of Independence, but he also held slaves. Shown is a fragment of a list of slaves on his Virginia plantation.*

conflict theory, the cultural view we shall discuss in detail, tries to answer that question.

According to realistic conflict theory, competition for material resources leads to

- hierarchical organization;
- increased loyalty to the ingroup;
- derogation of the outgroup;
- biased evaluation of ingroup and outgroup products.

Realistic Conflict Theory

Realistic conflict theory argues that groups become prejudiced toward one another because they are in conflict, conflict over real, tangible, material resources. Theorists in this tradition would point out that Bull Connor's reactions to the civil rights movement were not wholly irrational, although they were wholly immoral. They would suggest that what Connor and the other segregationist politicians were really about was maintaining their political power. The right to have coffee at Woolworth's was important in a symbolic sense, but the real issue of the civil rights movement was the right to vote, the right to political power. According to this view, Connor and his class were reacting to a serious material threat.

More generally, realistic conflict theory claims that in the face of conflict, groups undergo specific changes. First, their relations to their competitors become hostile. They begin to think of the *outgroup* in stereotyped ways; they begin to act toward that outgroup in ways that their own morality would otherwise forbid. A second change involves relations between the individuals and their *ingroup.* Conflict not only produces hostility to the outgroup, but also intensifies loyalty to the ingroup. This pattern of hostility to others and intense loyalty to the ingroup is referred to as **ethnocentrism.** Are these claims true; does material conflict have these effects?

To answer this question, we shall take up three specific studies: (1) an experiment on hostility between groups of campers, the Robbers Cave experiment, (2) research done on the effects of integrating the army during the Second World War, and (3) research on cooperation in the classroom.

CLASSIC FINDINGS IN SOCIAL PSYCHOLOGY: THE ROBBERS CAVE EXPERIMENT

Muzafer Sherif and his collaborators carried out a classic study designed to show that if you randomly assign people to groups and then place those groups in conflict, ethnocentrism will result (Sherif, Harvey, White, Hood, & Sherif, 1961). In particular, Sherif predicted that conflict would produce several phenomena. First, it would lead each group to adopt a hierarchical internal structure. Second, it would produce loyalty to the members of the ingroup and hostility to the outgroup. Third, conflict would cause the ingroup to think of the outgroup in derogatory, stereotypic ways. Finally, it would lead people to overvalue the performance of the ingroup relative to that of the outgroup. But further, Sherif proposed that this hostility would be overcome if, and only if, the two groups found themselves in a situation in which they had a **superordinate goal:** a goal that neither group could reach alone but that they could reach by working together.

THE EXPERIMENT

Sherif created a summer camp in Robbers Cave State Park, Oklahoma. The camp, which lasted about three weeks, took twenty boys, all carefully selected by Sherif to be normal, ordinary boys. Sherif wanted to be sure that if his experiment had the result he thought it would have, it wouldn't be because he had selected campers who were, for example, generally hostile and difficult to get along with. He wanted his subjects to be more or less typical representatives of their age, sex, and class.

Sherif instructed his camp counselors to run the camp as nondirectively as possible: the campers were to be free, within reason, to pick their own activities, to create their own problems, and to find their own solutions to those problems. The idea was to be as sure as possible that whatever happened in the camp was a result of what the boys wanted and not a result of what the counselors imposed.

The experiment began by dividing the boys randomly into two groups and then bringing them to the camp in two separate groups. One group named itself the "Rattlers," the other the "Eagles." In the first stage of the experiment, lasting about a week, the two groups had no contact with each other; in fact, they didn't even know of each other's presence. Each group spent its time in typical camp activities: hiking, swimming, baseball, and so on. Each developed its own leadership and unique rules of behavior. The Rattlers, for example, became a tough-guy group, which, among other things, encouraged cursing; the Eagles, on the other hand, forbade cursing. Toward the end of the first week, the two groups discovered each other. Campers in both groups had the same immediate reaction: "Those kids are invading our baseball diamond!"

To test the key proposition of realistic conflict theory—that conflict over resources leads to prejudice—Sherif introduced material conflict in the second phase of the experiment. He did this in a natural way; he created a tournament. The tournament consisted of a series of athletic events—tugs-of-war, baseball games, and so on. The winning team of each event got points, and at the end of the week, each member of the team with the most points was to receive a prize, a four-blade knife. Sherif hypothesized that this conflict would lead to ingroup cohesiveness and outgroup hostility. And indeed this is what he found.

Counselors' ratings of the status relationships in the two groups confirmed that the leadership hierarchies became more rigid with the introduction of conflict. Another prediction, stereotyping of the outgroup, was demonstrated

▼ *Campers in Sherif's Robbers Cave experiment. (A) The Rattlers and Eagles eye each other warily across the lawn. (B) The two groups pool their efforts to pull the truck out of the mud. (C) The groups mingle after achieving the common goal together.*

A

B

C

in two ways. First, the counselors counted the number of invectives ("pig," for example) that one group hurled at the other. Second, each of the boys rated his own group and the other on six traits: "brave," "tough," "friendly," "sneaky," "smart aleck," and "stinker." Each boy was to say whether all, most, some, a few, or none of the boys in his and the other group had these qualities. There was close agreement; each group believed that the other was made up predominantly of sneaks, smart alecks, and stinkers, while the ingroup consisted of brave, tough, friendly young men. As Sherif expected, conflict led to unfavorable characterization of the outgroup and favorable characterization of the ingroup.

This competitive stage, also as predicted, was marked by overt hostility. Each group raided the other's bunkhouse. Each burned the other's flag. There was constant talk in the air and plans being made for "raids" and "counter-raids."

The third stage of the experiment was designed to show that this friction could be reduced. First, with the idea that simple contact might reduce hostility, the two groups were brought together seven times. As always, the counselors neither stirred up nor quelled hostility. Each of these interactions only escalated the conflict. Quite typically, they ended in a food fight. Mere contact, then, failed dramatically to reduce hostility.

Sherif then arranged for experiences that, according to his theory, *should* reduce conflict; that is, he arranged for the campers to have superordinate goals, goals that neither group could achieve alone but that they could achieve working together. First, he faked a failure of the camp's water supply. The groups responded to this emergency by going off separately to find the source of the problem, but they found themselves converging on the water tank, where the problem lay. They cooperated in fixing it, and, perhaps to their own surprise, got along with each other in the process.

Next, Sherif had a truck (that was to carry their food to a cookout) get stuck in a rut. The Rattlers and Eagles now had a tug-of-war, not against each other, but jointly against the mud holding the truck. Overcoming this shared obstacle, as Sherif predicted, had a dramatic effect in creating a more friendly atmosphere.

Sherif also expected this shared experience to reduce negative stereotyping. He gathered two sorts of data to explore this point. First, the counselors noticed a decline in name calling. Second, he had the campers rate each other on the same trait words they had used earlier. The counselors' impression that stereotyping was reduced was supported by the more formal data: there was a significant reduction in the assignment of unfavorable traits to the other group and a slight reduction in the assignment of positive traits to the ingroup.

Sherif also asked the boys to tell him (in his disguise as the camp handyman) who their friends were. About 70 percent of the friendships were within the ingroup, while 30 percent were between the two groups. While this does show a strong preference for the ingroup, it was a significant reduction from the 93 percent favoritism found at the end of stage 2.

Another indication of the improved relations between the groups came on the ride home from the camp. The boys decided that instead of going home in separate buses, as they had come, they would go home together. Along the way they stopped for lunch. The Rattlers had $5, which they had won in a camp competition, and they could have used this money to pay for their own food. But they decided instead to pay for malteds for all of them—for those in the ingroup and outgroup alike.

VIRTUES OF THE EXPERIMENT

This experiment illustrates the central theme of realistic conflict theory: conflict between groups leads to cohesion within groups and hostility between groups, and cooperation to achieve a common goal is one way to overcome this hostility. Further research suggests that conflict between groups of adults is especially likely to be reduced in acting toward a superordinate goal *if* the two groups involved have distinct roles in helping achieve the shared goal (Deschamps & Brown, 1983; Brown & Wade, 1987). Having distinct roles to play allows each group to maintain its own identity; having a shared goal allows the two groups to interact in less hostile ways within those roles.

▲ *From the film* Lord of the Flies, *a treatment of the violence and brutality adolescent males are capable of.*

Aside from its results, the Robbers Cave experiment has another virtue. Social psychologists have an affection for this experiment, in part, no doubt, because it involves children (albeit *Lord of the Flies* children), but there is another reason. Much of the research social psychologists do has an abstract, "unreal" quality. Experiments are often conducted in laboratories where people are on guard, putting their best foot (or what they take to be their best foot) forward; they often involve strangers who come together for an hour or so with no history of a relationship or potential for future interaction. The dependent variables are sometimes a bit odd from the subject's point of view—checklists or questionnaires—and for that reason, they are difficult to interpret. Sherif's experiment is a brilliant exception; he was very concerned that it be as natural as possible. He wanted not only to illustrate realistic conflict theory, but to do so in a compelling way. The Robbers Cave experiment is a classic study in part because it is a model of a full-bodied realization of a theoretical point.

Limitations of the Experiment   What can we take away from the Robbers Cave experiment? It did demonstrate that conflict over a material reward can produce at least some aspects of ethnocentrism. And it did show that having a superordinate goal can reduce hostility. But we must consider the limitations of the study. The experiment used American boys, who are quite used to competition, but realistic conflict theory is a theory about human nature, not American culture. From this study alone, we cannot tell whether the tendency to express ethnocentrism in the face of conflict is a fact about human nature, or a fact about American culture. Second, the conflict began a tad early. The groups in fact became hostile from the moment they discovered each other, *before Sherif imposed the competition for material goods.* The competition, to be sure, enhanced the hostility, but its rudiments did not have to wait for competition. In recent years, investigators have attempted to specify the minimum conditions for intergroup conflict, and have argued that competition for material goods is not necessary for ethnocentrism to develop.

INTEGRATION OF THE MILITARY

Another important source of evidence on realistic conflict theory can be drawn from a classic survey, *The American Soldier.* This research investigated the attitudes of American soldiers during the Second World War. One piece of that investigation focused on soldiers' reactions to the forced integration of some units of the army.

Until quite late in the war, black units were segregated from white units. But as replacements became scarce, the army began to include black platoons in white companies. White soldiers were now fighting in close proximity to blacks, although the platoons themselves remained of one race.

Given the strong sentiment against it, we might expect that integration sparked conflict between blacks and whites, but it didn't. After integration took place, the reactions of white soldiers and officers were overwhelmingly positive; 96 percent of the white officers reported themselves pleasantly surprised at the result, and 76 percent of the white soldiers involved reported that their attitudes toward blacks had become more positive because of the experience of fighting next to them (Star, Williams, & Stouffer, 1958). As experience accumulated, attitudes became more favorable. These findings support the results of Sherif's experiment.

Soldiers in the Second World War faced an extraordinary shared threat: German guns. And they were successful in overcoming that threat; they won the war. Remember that Sherif found that overcoming a shared obstacle (here, a shared enemy) was a crucial element in reducing prejudice. Further, the official policy of the army and the authority of its officers stood behind the integration; there was a prominent, enforced set of norms in place. Realistic conflict theory holds that prejudice is mediated by the groups of which one is a part, and, moreover, that in times of conflict the allegiance of groups to those who hold authority in those groups will increase. If the officers had not supported the policy or, worse, resisted it, the outcome might have been different.

The military has once again become the focus of American society's struggle over integration. But in the meantime, the country has had an African-American as chairman of the Joint Chiefs of Staff. Indeed, the military now seems to lead the rest of American culture in providing opportunities for black men. Perhaps for this very reason, it is the focus of other civil rights movements as women struggle to occupy combat positions and gay men and lesbians fight for the right to share the risks and rewards of a military career.

COOPERATION IN THE CLASSROOM

Elliot Aronson has experimented with cooperation in the classroom as a way of reducing racial tensions there. Aronson noticed that the typical American classroom is a very competitive place, a place where students compete with each other fiercely to gain esteem in the eyes of their teachers and, therefore, self-esteem. Aronson introduced a different kind of learning environment to some grammar schools in Austin, Texas, in an effort to reduce racial tensions, elevate the self-esteem of minority children, and provide a better learning environment for all concerned. One technique he used, called the **jigsaw classroom,** involves giving small, multiethnic groups a joint task to perform—writing a biography, for example—and giving each member of the group one piece of information they need to do their task, facts about a specific period in the person's life. By structuring the task this way, the groups are forced, like Sherif's campers, to participate together in the pursuit of a superordinate goal. Aronson found, like Sherif, that working together on a superordinate goal reduces hostility and enhances self-esteem and respect for others

(Aronson, 1990; see also Desforges et al., 1991).

Marilyn Brewer and Norman Miller have argued that cooperative interactions are especially likely to lead to reduced intergroup bias if the participants have an interpersonal focus; that is, if they have as one of their goals forming an impression of the individual personalities of the people they are working with (Bettencourt, Brewer, Croak, & Miller, 1991).

Minimal Groups

Henri Tajfel and his associates have pressed the claim suggested in the Robbers Cave experiment that competition is not necessary for the development of favoritism toward insiders; they have argued that merely creating two groups, no matter how haphazardly, is enough to bring about ethnocentrism. To support such a claim, Tajfel constructed what he called **minimal groups.** They are created this way. Subjects (usually numbering four to sixteen, and typically high school or college students) are shown pairs of paintings and asked individually to pick which of the pair they prefer. The paintings are by two modern abstract artists (Paul Klee and Vasily Kandinsky), but they are not labeled. After this, some subjects are told they belong with those who preferred Klee, and others are told they belong with those who preferred Kandinsky. But the subjects are actually assigned to the two groups randomly. So now we have two groups formed randomly, but who believe they were formed on the basis of preference for one modern abstract artist over another. These are the minimal groups. The groups stay minimal because the experimenter instructs subjects not to talk among themselves or with members of the other group.

The point of this manipulation is to establish randomly created groups that are not in conflict but that believe themselves to have been formed on the basis of their preferences between two modern artists, a not very vital matter. Then the object is to show that these groups display at least some aspects of ethnocentrism. If a distinction as trivial as this one is enough to produce discrimination, then surely dividing people on a more serious basis should be too.

A

B

 (A) The Angler *by Paul Klee (1921). (B)* Black Relationship *by Vasily Kandinsky (1924).*

Several sorts of dependent variables have been used to demonstrate ethno-centrism with minimal groups. In some cases, subjects are taken one at a time into a separate room and then asked to say how much two subjects should be paid (by the experimenter) for a subsequent task. They are told only the subjects' code numbers, from which they can infer only that one subject is part of their group while the other is one of the other group (see Tajfel, Billig, Bundy, & Flament, 1971, for an example). Several studies have shown that subjects reward the ingroup person more than the outgroup person. Thus, assigning people to a group just on the basis of what they think is a matter of taste produces ingroup bias.

In other studies, subjects have been asked to rate the members of their own group and the outgroup on personality traits. (They had been told the experiment was about ''first impressions.'') Subjects rated members of their own group more favorably. So the ingroup bias extends to snap judgments about personality (Rabbie & Horowitz, 1969). In other research based on a minimal group procedure, subjects who have been presented with balanced descriptions of favorable and unfavorable behavior from ingroup and out-group members have been found to be biased to recall more favorable behav-iors from ingroup members and more unfavorable behaviors from outgroup members (Howard & Rothbart, 1980). Taken together, then, the minimal group technique has reliably been shown to produce various kinds of bias. Indeed, by 1982, Henri Tajfel was able to locate more than thirty studies that documented ingroup favoritism on a great variety of dependent measures (Tajfel, 1982). Since favoritism in the minimal group situation has by now been well established, recent attention has been directed toward establishing *why* minimal groups produce ingroup favoritism rather than *whether* they do.*

EXPLANATIONS FOR INTERGROUP BIAS

Several different accounts have been offered, but the most promising one, called **social identity theory,** is that subjects overreward those in their own group to enhance their own status (Tajfel & Turner, 1979). The logic is that if all of the best people are in the group I am in, then I must be one of the best people. Groucho Marx once said he wouldn't join a club that would have him as a member, but this ironic view of life doesn't seem to be too pervasive. Most of us would rather inflate the virtues of the groups of which we are members.

If the ingroup discrimination seen in the typical minimal group experi-ment is a consequence of subjects' desires to increase their self-esteem, then we might expect that discriminating in favor of one's ingroup does in fact raise self-esteem. One experiment tested this assumption in a very straight-forward way. Subjects were divided into groups in the usual way (preference

---

*Minimal group procedures produce ingroup favoritism, i.e., they get people to reward mem-bers of the ingroup more than members of the outgroup, or to rate ingroup members more positively. They have not been shown to produce hostility or negativity toward the outgroup. Thus, it is a bit of a stretch to call what is produced in them ethnocentrism. Some psychologists would make that stretch, however, on the grounds that the favoritism shown in minimal groups is the first step toward ethnocentrism.

for Klee or Kandinsky). Half the subjects were then allowed to assign points to their own group and to the outgroup. The other half were asked to read an irrelevant newspaper article. All the subjects were then asked to report on their self-esteem. The results showed that: (1) the subjects who were given the chance to award points indeed showed ingroup bias, and (2) the subjects who were allowed to (and did) express this bias had higher self-esteem than those who were not allowed to allocate points but read a newspaper instead (Oakes & Turner, 1980; see also Lemyre & Smith, 1985).

Other research has found that subjects high on "collective self-esteem"—subjects who think highly of the groups they are in, and who see such groups as contributing in a central way to their identity—are prone to intergroup bias in a minimal group situation. Those with lower collective self-esteem show less bias (Crocker & Luhtanen, 1990).

But there is evidence that especially low collective self-esteem can lead to intergroup bias too. Richard Lalonde, for example, followed a group of male hockey players in their late teens. The hockey team they played for was in last place in a nine-team regional college league in the province of Quebec. (With a two-wins and twenty-eight-losses record, one can be confident they had low collective self-esteem.) The players were asked to rate themselves and the opposing teams on four attributes: aggressive, dirty, skilled, and motivated. As you might guess, the team members could not deny that the other teams were more skilled, aggressive, and motivated than they were—the record spoke too loudly for that. But intergroup bias showed itself in the subjects' rating of how dirty they and the other teams were; the members of this losing team rated the other teams as dirtier players. Thus, they compensated for their inability to assert, with any plausibility, hockey skill by asserting a greater moral virtue. Maybe the other teams *were* dirtier, and there really was no evidence of bias here. This is possible, of course, and it is hard to be objective about which team is dirtier, but the investigator himself watched the games and asked the coaches around the league for their judgment. In the opinion of these experts, this *losing* hockey team was actually one of the dirtiest in the league (Lalonde, 1992)! Thus, if the facts lead one to see one's group as deficient in one (crucial) way, it may be possible to compensate by asserting some great virtue in an altogether different direction.

LIMITS OF INTERGROUP BIAS

There is some evidence that intergroup bias does not *always* occur. What happens, for example, when people have to distribute something aversive? We know that when people distribute rewards, they tend to be biased toward their own even minimal groups. But suppose they are distributing punishments? Are we so easily biased in this circumstance?

In one study, subjects were assigned to two groups in thoroughly minimal ways and were then asked to expose their own and the other group to an annoying, high-pitched blast of noise. In this circumstance, there was no evidence of ingroup favoritism; rather, subjects were scrupulously fair. In another study, however, subjects were told that (1) their group was in the minority (they were led to believe that their group constituted only 20 percent of the experiment, while the outgroup constituted the other 80 percent), and (2) their group had low status in the experiment because the people in it weren't very good at the task at hand. In this circumstance, the subjects were

Minimal groups have been shown to produce

- favoritism in paying the ingroup;

- biased snap judgments of ingroup members;

- biased recall of positive facts about the ingroup and negative facts about the outgroup.

willing to be biased in handing out aversive treatment. In this experiment, then, the minority group subjects in the low-status condition *were* willing to be biased in handing out negative experiences, just as the members of the losing hockey team—a low-status minority in the league—was willing to be biased in handing out negative evaluations (Mummendey et al., 1992).

Bias in favor of ingroup members and against outgroup members may actually be reversed. In particular, it has been proposed that in order to enhance their own status, people will evaluate an *unlikable* member of their own group more negatively than an equally unlikable member of an outgroup, but at the same time (and for the same status-enhancing reason) they will evaluate a *likable* member of the ingroup more positively than an equally likable member of the outgroup. This simultaneous enhancement of the virtues of a well-liked ingroup member and derogation of an inadequate ingroup member has been dubbed the **black-sheep effect** and has been demonstrated in a series of studies (Marques & Yzerbyt, 1988; Marques, Yzerbyt, & Leyens, 1988). The tendency to derogate the black sheep of a group—presumably to show how virtuous the group generally is, how high its standards are—limits the more general tendency to overvalue ingroup members.

Undoubtedly people derive status from their groups, and it makes sense that they would inflate the status of their groups for that reason. Although this feature of groups is left out of realistic conflict theory, it does fit with a well-established fact of racial prejudice: prejudice is highest in the lower socioeconomic groups. Perhaps this is so because so long as African Americans, for example, are seen as racially inferior, then even the lowest-status white can have someone to look down upon. Bull Connor was perhaps protecting not only his own real political power with his police dogs but also his social status and that of the rest of the Southern white lower class. Perhaps the contribution of this research is to remind us that status is a very important motivator of human affairs. We should perhaps expand realistic conflict theory to include status as something over which people compete.

The Cultural View: An Assessment

How well does the cultural approach explain Bull Connor's behavior? It calls attention to some very important things about him, the most important of which is that he was part of a culture that to some degree supported his appalling behavior. And it urges us to see cultures in light of their conflicts, conflicts both at home with their outgroups, in this case blacks, and at a distance with other cultures—here, the North. But Bull Connor wasn't just another Southerner; he was surely an extreme example even of that place and time. The motivational approach, which we now take up, tries to find aspects of his own experience, arising from personal motivation and conflicts, that made him likely to go beyond the typical segregationist.

MOTIVATIONAL APPROACHES

The motivational approach we shall examine owes much to that most controversial genius Sigmund Freud, and his extraordinary notion that human behavior is the product of motivational conflict, motivational conflict of which the person is unaware. The extreme Freudian view, the idea that all that we do—writing a book, reading a book, building a bridge, and so on—is driven by unconscious forces is a bit hard to accept. But Freud began his explorations with a more limited set of phenomena—irrational acts. And the less rational behavior is, the more attractive a Freudian account of it is.

Bull Connor's violent, unreasoned attacks are just the sort of thing that call out for a Freudian account. We want to say of him that it wasn't really Martin Luther King Jr. he wanted to attack, that there must be some deeper reason for his setting the police dogs loose. Birmingham's African Americans must have represented something else to him, and it was the something else that he really hated. The first motivational theory we shall consider, **frustration-aggression theory,** suggests that prejudiced people deep down aren't really trying to attack the overt target of their prejudice, but are really expressing their hostility to something else. Let us see how such an explanation might be worked out in detail.

"I FORESEE THE DAY WHEN RACIAL AND RELIGIOUS DIFFERENCES WILL BE OF NO IMPORTANCE WHATEVER, AND PEOPLE WILL HATE ONE ANOTHER FOR COMPLETELY PERSONAL REASONS."

Frustration-Aggression Theory

Frustration-aggression theory is an offspring not only of Freud, but also of American animal learning theory (it is discussed in more general terms in Chapter 13). Its authors, especially Neal Miller and John Dollard, attempted to take Freudian principles and show that they could be translated into terms developed in the context of research on animal learning. At the same time, they wanted to show that scientifically purified concepts of learning theory could be applied to the understanding of the "real world," to both individual and social problems.

The Freudian idea with which they started was that in the course of socialization, the child is repeatedly frustrated. Waiting to be fed until a parent is ready, learning to control bladder and bowels, and so on are all frustrating. According to Freud, this chronic frustration leads to chronic hostility. The child would like to attack her parents; after all, they are the source of the frustration. But parents are bigger than children, so the child learns that such a response is unwise. Then too the child also loves her parents, making them a doubly inappropriate target. So, the theory goes, the child **displaces** her hostility—onto safer and less-loved targets. Bull Connor, the theory argues, was displacing his frustrations; Martin Luther King Jr. wasn't the real source of his problems, but he was a convenient outlet for Connor's hostility.

EVIDENCE FOR THE THEORY

Carl Hovland and Robert Sears found an inverse correlation between the price of cotton and the number of lynchings of blacks in the South in the period 1882—1930 (as the price of cotton went down, the number of lynchings went up). According to Hovland and Sears, this was because as the price of cotton went down, Southerners became frustrated* (cotton was a very im-

---

*Learning theory had a precise definition for frustration: the blocking of a goal-directed response. And this definition was always invoked in theoretical discussions. But in practice, learning theorists tended to treat all negative events, whether the blocking of a goal-directed response or not, as equivalent. A decline in the price of cotton was certainly a negative event; how it was a frustration in the technical sense is not now and never was clear.

portant part of the economy of the South) and took out their frustration on blacks—safe and available targets (Hovland & Sears, 1940; see Hepworth & West, 1988, for a recent reanalysis). After all, how could they aggress against the real source of frustration—the market price of cotton?

In an experimental study of prejudice and displacement, other investigators asked young male camp counselors (ranging in age from eighteen to twenty) to rate Mexicans and Japanese on several traits. Then these young men were frustrated by being forced to take some tedious tests—instead of going to a show they had expected to see. Further, the tests were rigged to make them fail. Finally, they were asked to rate the ethnic groups again. After the frustration, the counselors used fewer favorable trait terms than they had used before the frustration (Miller & Bugelski, 1948).

How compelling is this evidence? It has one serious drawback. Consider the Miller and Bugelski study. The counselors were not asked to rate groups they liked, so we don't know whether the frustration produced an increase in prejudice specifically or in hostility more generally. If the counselors had also rated their friends less favorably after the frustration, then the effects of the frustration might best be described as putting them in a bad mood.

Does frustration increase prejudice specifically or hostility more generally? Leonard Berkowitz conducted an experiment bearing on this issue. He gave his subjects, female college students, a questionnaire measuring anti-Semitism. He insulted half of them (but not the other half). The subjects were then put to work with "another subject" (actually a confederate). To half of the subjects, the confederate was introduced as Miss Cohen; to the other half, she was introduced as Miss Johnson. After working a while, the subjects were asked to evaluate their partner on several traits. If frustration affects prejudice specifically, the anti-Semitic subjects who were insulted should have become hostile to Miss Cohen but not to Miss Johnson. But if frustration just puts people in a bad mood, then the subjects should have become hostile to the confederate no matter what her name was.

Berkowitz reports that whether the confederate was called Cohen or Johnson had no effect on her ratings by the anti-Semitic subjects (or for that matter by the other subjects). If they had been insulted, anti-Semitic subjects became hostile to the confederate, no matter what her name was. The subjects who were not anti-Semitic reacted in just the other way. They became more positive to the confederate after being insulted, regardless of her name (Berkowitz, 1959). (Remember, it was the experimenter, not the confederate, who insulted the subjects.) The experiment suggests, then, that anti-Semitic subjects become hostile when insulted, but this hostility seems to be general rather than restricted to the target of their prejudice.

AN ASSESSMENT

What, then, does frustration-aggression theory contribute to our understanding of prejudice? What aspects of prejudice does it explain less well? It seems best at explaining when ethnocentrism will be incited—Hitler's popularity rose and fell with the German economy; the worse times were, the more popular he became. But the effects of frustration seem to be general, and therefore the theory seems ill-suited to explain why specific groups are the targets of prejudice. (Why were the Jews Hitler's target?) Further, frustration-aggression theory does not address the other side of the ethnocentrism coin: the glorification of the ingroup. We turn now to another motivational theory, also derived from Freudian thought, the theory of the **authoritarian personality,** which does try to address both sides of the ethnocentrism syndrome.

CLASSIC FINDINGS IN SOCIAL PSYCHOLOGY: THE AUTHORITARIAN PERSONALITY

Theodor W. Adorno, Else Frenkel-Brunswick, Daniel Levinson, and R. Nevitt Sanford (often referred to as the Berkeley group), the authors of *The Authoritarian Personality,* did not have Bull Connor in mind; they had even more horrifying images, an even more malignant example of irrational racial hatred, the Holocaust (Adorno, Frenkel-Brunswick, Levinson, & Sanford, 1950). Thus, the form of prejudice they began with was anti-Semitism. But as we shall see, they came to believe that what they found out about anti-Semitism applied to Bull Connor as well.

The Berkeley group believed that prejudice was related to personality in a specific way: they believed that a person's personality *caused* him to be prejudiced. The distinction between having a personality that is descriptively prejudiced and having a personality that causes prejudice is subtle but important.

The Berkeley group argued that both a prejudiced and a tolerant world view are available to us, and that which each of us adopts depends on aspects of our personality not directly related to prejudice. In particular, as we shall see, a child's early experiences with her parents determine whether or not she will become prejudiced. This is what makes *The Authoritarian Personality* a motivational, Freudian approach. Individuals are seen as driven by unconscious forces created in their own history to seek out specific attitudes, in this case prejudice. Bull Connor's behavior, according to this view, was closely tied to the ways he was treated by his parents. This is a common enough claim in our post-Freudian age, but it is a difficult matter to support such a

A **B**

◀ *Racial violence may result from a syndrome of authoritarianism. (A) Police dogs set loose on civil rights protestors in Birmingham, Alabama, in May 1963. (B) Police dogs being used in Virginia Beach, Virginia, to subdue rioters in September 1989.*

TABLE 4.1

SOME ITEMS FROM THE ANTI-SEMITISM (A-S) SCALE

1. One trouble with Jewish businessmen is that they stick together and connive, so that a Gentile doesn't have a fair chance in competition.
2. Persecution of the Jews would be largely eliminated if the Jews would make really sincere efforts to rid themselves of their harmful and offensive faults.
3. Jewish leaders should encourage Jews to be more inconspicuous, to keep out of professions and activities already overcrowded with Jews, and to keep out of the public notice.
4. I can hardly imagine myself marrying a Jew.
5. The trouble with letting Jews into a nice neighborhood is that they gradually give it a typical Jewish atmosphere.
6. There may be a few exceptions, but in general, Jews are pretty much alike.

SOURCE: Adorno, Frenkel-Brunswick, Levinson, & Sanford, 1950, p. 84.

claim. We turn now to the evidence the Berkeley group gathered to show that personality causes prejudice.

PERSONALITY SCALES

The Berkeley group began their investigation by constructing a questionnaire designed to measure the extent of a person's anti-Semitism. The **Anti-Semitism Scale (A-S Scale)** consisted of a number of statements about Jews; subjects were asked to indicate whether they agreed or disagreed with each. Further, they were to indicate whether their agreement or disagreement was slight, moderate, or strong. Table 4.1 has some of the items from the A-S Scale.

The Berkeley investigators believed that anti-Semitism was only one part of the larger syndrome of ethnocentrism, so they next constructed an **Ethnocentrism Scale (E Scale).** The E Scale probed subjects for their attitudes toward blacks and other minorities, as well as Jews. Adorno and his collaborators selected eighty subjects from the hundreds they had tested on the Ethnocentrism Scale. These eighty subjects were then given in-depth clinical interviews. Forty were picked because they scored very high on the E Scale, and forty because their scores were very low. The hope was that wide-ranging interviews with these extreme groups would highlight any differences there might be in the personalities of prejudiced and unprejudiced people.

From the interviews, with the help of psychoanalytic theory, the researchers constructed a theory of what they called the antidemocratic or prefascist personality, a personality attracted to prejudice. This personality syndrome, they argued, consists of the traits listed in Table 4.2. Evidence for the existence of the syndrome came from a new questionnaire the Berkeley group developed. This scale, called the **California F** (*for fascism*) **Scale,** consisted of items expressing the attitudes thought to comprise the **authoritarian syndrome.** Like the A-S and E Scales, it consisted of statements with which the subjects were to agree or disagree. Some items from this test are presented in Table 4.3.

To show that this broader pattern of personality was related to prejudice,

TABLE 4.2

CLUSTERS OF PERSONALITY TRAITS ON THE F SCALE

Trait	Description
Conventionalism	Rigid adherence to conventional, middle-class values.
Authoritarian submission	Submissive, uncritical attitude toward idealized moral authorities of the ingroup.
Authoritarian aggression	Tendency to be on the lookout for and to condemn, reject, and punish people who violate conventional values.
Anti-intraception	Opposition to the subjective, the imaginative, the tender-minded.
Superstition and stereotypes	The belief in mystical determinants of the individual's fate; the disposition to think in rigid categories.
Power and "toughness"	Preoccupation with the dominance-submission, strong-weak, leader-follower dimension; identification with power figures.
Destructiveness and cynicism	Generalized hostility, vilification of the human.
Projectivity	The disposition to believe that wild and dangerous things go on in the world; the projection outward of unconscious emotional impulses.
Sexual repression	Exaggerated concern with sexual "goings-on."

SOURCE: Adapted from Adorno, Frenkel-Brunswick, Levinson, & Sanford, 1950, pp. 255–57.

TABLE 4.3

SOME ITEMS FROM THE F SCALE

1. Obedience and respect for authority are the most important virtues children should learn.
2. Science has its place, but there are many important things that can never possibly be understood by the human mind.
3. What this country needs most, more than laws and political programs, are a few courageous, tireless, devoted leaders in whom the people can put their faith.
4. No sane, normal, decent person could ever think of hurting a close friend or relative.
5. Sex crimes, such as rape and attacks on children, deserve more than mere imprisonment; such criminals ought to be publicly whipped, or worse.
6. Homosexuals are hardly better than criminals and ought to be severely punished.

SOURCE: Adorno, Frenkel-Brunswick, Levinson, & Sanford, 1950, pp. 255–57.

the Berkeley group gave both the E Scale and the F Scale to the same group of subjects and found a correlation of 0.75. This quite high correlation supports the notion that the syndrome of authoritarianism is indeed related to prejudice. The evidence suggests, then, that prejudice is not found in isolation; it suggests that the Nazis' suppression of modern, unconventional art was related to their anti-Semitism. And it suggests that homosexuals were not on the list of people to be exterminated in the Holocaust by accident.

AUTHORITARIANISM AND THE STATUS QUO

What, one might well ask, is the essence of the authoritarian personality? What holds the syndrome together; what is its psychological core? Some recent evidence provides an interesting perspective on this question. One group of researchers examined changes in the level of authoritarianism in the United States as a function of how much international threat the country has been under. The authors argued that the period 1978–82 was one of high tension between the United States and the then Soviet Union, while the period 1983–87 was a period of lessened threat. And they found on a variety of attitude measures that relate to authoritarianism that the more threat Americans were under, the more authoritarian they were (on average). So one fact to keep in mind is that authoritarianism waxes and wanes with perceived threat from an outgroup—a fact that would please realistic conflict theorists (Dotty, Peterson, & Winter, 1991).

A second bit of evidence comes from studies of authoritarianism and political attitudes in the early 1990s. The evidence suggests that in the United States, authoritarianism is associated with, among other things: a punitive attitude toward people with AIDS, support of very harsh treatment of those dealing in drugs, hostility toward measures designed to protect the environment, opposition to the right to choose an abortion, the belief that the homeless are homeless because they are lazy (Peterson, Doty, & Winter, 1993). Authoritarians, then, are strong supporters of "family values"; they are staunch believers in the American way of life.

What would an authoritarian from another culture be like? Surely he wouldn't be a supporter of the American way of life? Surely authoritarianism isn't just an American idea. In May and June of 1991, right before the popular election of Boris Yeltsin, 163 residents of Moscow were surveyed as to their political attitudes, and they were also administered a version of the authoritarianism scale. The results indicated that the subjects who were high in authoritarianism were also very conservative in the sense that they resisted any change from Communist control of the Soviet Union (McFarland, Ageyev, & Abalakina-Papp, 1992). Now the last thing that American authoritarians are is supporters of communism. Taken together, then, this pattern of results suggests that at the heart of the authoritarian syndrome is a passionate attraction to the status quo and the authority that is seen as maintaining it, along with a strong desire to punish those who are seen as a threat to it. It is this attachment to the status quo, rather than any specific ideology, that runs like a thread through the authoritarian syndrome.

A LAST WORD

The Authoritarian Personality set out to understand the Holocaust. How does it do? It doesn't explain why the Jews were the Nazis' special target. To understand that, we must reach back in Germany's history. It pays to remember that Martin Luther was among the most vicious anti-Semites in history. And authoritarian personality theory doesn't explain why the Holocaust happened

There is substantial evidence that the components of authoritarianism hang together as a syndrome.

The evidence is less clear about the cause of the syndrome.

when it did. This, undoubtedly, had to do with the state of the German economy in the early 1930s, when Hitler became an important political figure. This fact is probably better dealt with by frustration-aggression theory. What *The Authoritarian Personality* does try to explain is why some people but not others were attracted to the Nazi program. Were members of the Nazi party more likely to embody the personality traits encompassed by the authoritarian personality? Were they harshly reared as children? We don't know. Adorno set out to study this very question in Frankfurt, Germany, but he had no choice but to flee Germany before the fury of the Holocaust.

Prejudice and Ambivalence

In the mid-to-late 1960s, the civil rights movement changed from a movement with its primary focus on the South to a movement focused on the North. And this had important implications both for the movement and for researchers interested in understanding prejudice—in the North, the images changed. Prejudice in the South, at least until the mid-1960s, was blunt. The aim of the civil rights movement was equally clear and simple: to overcome this legally endorsed, overt prejudice. Psychological theories of prejudice in those days attempted to account for this direct, unmitigated hostility. But as the movement moved North, it encountered a different climate.

Northerners were not prejudiced in the same way Southerners were; very few believed there should be laws restricting the rights of African Americans to vote, hold jobs, and so forth. But at the same time, Northerners were not, and are not, devoid of prejudice. Theories were needed that captured the kind of prejudice encountered in the North in the 1960s. Many researchers turned for guidance to a classic analysis of American race relations, Gunnar Myrdal's *The American Dilemma* (Myrdal, 1944).

Myrdal, a Swedish social scientist, analyzed American race relations in terms of conflicted motives. He argued that many Americans were hostile toward blacks and believed them to be inferior, but that these same Americans also believed in the American Creed, the notion that all people are free and equal before the law, the notion that all people are entitled to be treated as they themselves deserve, based on their own accomplishments or failures. Myrdal saw with his outsider's eyes that it was too simple to say that white America was hostile toward African Americans, one also had to see the other side. The more complex attitudes of the North and the more covert prejudice in the North required a more subtle analysis. Here too, Freudian thought was fundamental.

EXPLICIT VALUES AND UNDERLYING FEELINGS

A study by Shirley Weitz illustrates both an approach consistent with Myrdal's analysis and the way in which Freudian thinking became useful to an analysis of Northern prejudice. Weitz asked eighty Northern white male undergraduates to fill out a questionnaire measuring sympathy toward blacks. She then asked them to interact with a black fellow subject (actually a confederate). She recorded their interactions and coded the tapes for the friendliness of the white subjects' tone of voice. Some subjects were very sympathetic in their answers on the questionnaire, but they were obviously quite tense in the interaction. This discrepancy, she argued, reflected conflict in

A   B

(A) Children in South Africa as apartheid disintegrated. (B) Adults in South Africa. A new way of life seems harder for the adults than for the children; the children had not as thoroughly learned to hate and fear.

their motives, a conflict between their explicit values and their more implicit feelings (Weitz, 1972). She suggested that her subjects really were sympathetic toward African Americans, but that at the same time they also felt somewhat hostile and afraid. The sympathy was explicit and known to the subjects; the hostility and fear, she argued, were repressed by the subjects, driven from conscious awareness. Weitz proposed that her coding of the tapes picked up these repressed feelings, while the questionnaires reflected the overt values.

These Northern subjects were neither prejudiced nor not prejudiced; they were deeply ambivalent, driven toward both sympathy and hostility. One pole was expressed, conscious, and affirmed; the other was no less real but was denied awareness. This idea of a conflict between an affirmed, conscious belief and a denied, unconscious one owes as much to Freud as the authoritarian personality theory does. But this leads to an obvious question: Which of these two poles can we expect to see expressed in behavior? Should we expect to see these Northern students holding to their expressed values or succumbing to their repressed feelings?

Weitz proposed that *both* attitudes will be expressed in behavior—sometimes one and sometimes the other. And she suggested that which attitude will be expressed depends on circumstances. Specifically, in circumstances in which people have a clear idea of what fairness demands of them, or where they know that particular behaviors can only result from prejudice, they will be likely to act in accord with their explicit beliefs, to act in unprejudiced ways. In other circumstances, however, where standards of conduct are less clear, people will be likely to show their more hostile side. In the South, this distinction was not needed, as letting police dogs loose shows no ambivalence; Bull Connor's behavior does not call for sophisticated theories. But in the North, Weitz proposed, this sort of prejudice was intolerable; it conflicted with overt, expressed values. Therefore the hostile side of Northern attitudes could only be seen in circumstances that were less clear.

Her dependent variable was this. The white subjects were asked to commit themselves to return to the lab to work with a black partner. The amount of time they were willing to commit themselves to was her measure of implicit hostility. Her argument was that how much time a subject *should* commit himself to was unclear; there were no public, objective norms specifying how much a person should give. Lacking this norm, subjects who felt hostile or afraid could sign up for very little time. As she predicted, the amount of time subjects were willing to spend with a black partner related to her codings of how uncomfortable they were talking to a black, and did not relate to how much sympathy they expressed on the questionnaire.

AMBIVALENCE AND RESPONSE AMPLIFICATION

The picture that Weitz's experiments paint is of people acting in a positive way toward blacks when a behavior is likely to be seen as a sign of bigotry, and acting in a hostile way when the issue of bigotry isn't clear (Dutton, 1971; Gaertner, 1975; Gaertner & Dovidio, 1977). This picture suggests that whites, or at least some Northern whites, have a deep-seated hostility toward African Americans, but they are restrained from expressing this by social norms opposing it or their own values inhibiting it. But Irwin Katz and David Glass have argued that this picture leaves something out: the fact that many people feel genuine sympathy toward blacks. The game is really three-handed—there are egalitarian norms and values, feelings of hostility, and feelings of sympathy. In ambiguous circumstances, either the hostility or the sympathy will be expressed. Further, Katz and Glass suggest that the conflict between the sympathy and hostility will show itself in an amplification of whatever response is expressed: that is, in a circumstance where a white is in contact with a black and her sympathy is aroused, she will express more sympathy toward the black than she would toward a white in the same position. On the other hand, if her hostility is aroused, she will express more of that too (Katz & Glass, 1979).

In one experiment designed to illustrate this ambivalence, white undergraduate subjects, after having been given a suitable cover story, read to another subject either a neutral or a very harsh personality description describing that other subject (of course, a confederate). The subjects were told to read it with feeling, as if it were their real impression. Then the subjects who read the negative impression were told that the other subject, who had to leave the experiment early to go on a job interview, had become quite upset on hearing how little the subject thought of him. In half the cases, the confederate was white, and in half the cases black.

On the way out of the experiment, the subject found a note from the confederate asking for help in a psychology experiment he was doing himself as part of a psychology course. (Since all the subjects were recruited from psychology courses, this was not such an astonishing coincidence!) The subjects were asked to help by copying a sample sentence over and over again; the experiment supposedly had to do with changes in handwriting with practice. The dependent variable was how many times the subjects copied the sentence over (see Figure 4.1).

The results showed that the effect of criticism depended on the severity of the criticism and the race of the target. For mild criticism, race mattered little; subjects copied about the same amount for a black or white victim. But the effect was quite different for harsh criticism. Subjects wrote more sentences

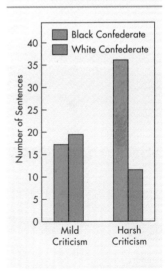

FIGURE 4.1

AMBIVALENCE AND RESPONSE AMPLIFICATION

▲ Sentences written to help a black and a white confederate after having criticized him mildly or severely. (Data from Katz, Glass, Lucido, & Farber, 1979)

for a black who had been victimized than for a white, even though the evaluations were identical (Katz, Glass, Lucido, & Farber, 1979). Criticizing someone led the subjects to become sympathetic toward him, and this sympathy was expressed in helping him out; these white subjects helped the black victim more than the white presumably because the black victim aroused more sympathy. This is one side of the ambivalence-amplification coin.

Other research has illustrated the more pessimistic side, that when the situation is likely to produce hostility, blacks will bear an unfair share of that too (Katz, Glass, & Cohen, 1973). And in yet another study, white subjects in a group were exposed to either a black or a white confederate who caused them to succeed or fail at a task. These white subjects evaluated the black confederate more positively than the white confederate if he was responsible for the team's success, but less favorably than the white confederate if he was responsible for the group's failure. Again we see evidence of amplification of response (Hass et al., 1991; see also Rogers & Prentice-Dunn, 1981, on race as an amplifier of response).

Irwin Katz and Glen Haas have argued that both feelings of sympathy and feelings of hostility toward blacks as a group are rooted in core American values. They have argued, following Myrdal, that one core American value is humanitarianism, but another is the Protestant work ethic. African Americans, they suggest, are perceived by white America as in need of economic help, and this perception engages sympathy connected with humanitarian values; on the other hand, blacks are perceived as not doing enough to help themselves, and this breeds resentment because of the American commitment to the Protestant work ethic. In support of their view, these investigators constructed a scale to measure the degree to which people are committed to humanitarian values and another scale to measure commitment to the Protestant work ethic. They also created scales to measure subjects' attitudes toward blacks.

Katz and Haas found, as they expected, that in a large sample of Northern white college students, those subjects with the greatest attachment to humanitarian values also had the most positive attitudes toward blacks, while those with the greatest commitment to the Protestant work ethic had the most negative attitudes toward blacks. Moreover, in a second study, they found that causing students to think about their humanitarian values made their attitudes toward blacks more positive, while reflecting on the Protestant ethic made them more negative (Katz & Haas, 1988). Thus, the ambivalence that characterizes whites' attitudes toward blacks has its source deep within the values that characterize American life.

AMBIVALENCE RESEARCH CONSIDERED

We have seen in a variety of studies that race doesn't affect behavior in a simple way. One important factor is whether racism is an explicit issue. Northern white liberals would act in a positive way toward blacks if their failure to do so would bespeak racism. But they might not be so positive if their failure couldn't be traced to racism. Moreover, in some cases where racism isn't an explicit issue, whites might be more sympathetic to an African American than they would be to a white under the same circumstances (Crosby, Bromley, &

▲ *Archie Bunker in* All in the Family *epitomized the staunch upholder of the Protestant work ethic, who used it as a club with which to attack blacks and other minorities.*

Ambivalence theory claims that whites' attitudes toward African Americans are *both* hostile *and* sympathetic.

• Which side is expressed depends on circumstances.

• Both reactions tend to be exaggerated when expressed.

Saxe, 1980). This is particularly likely to happen in a face-to-face situation. At the same time, if the situation calls forth hostility, then the black may bear more of that burden. It is this complexity, this ambivalence of motivation, that earlier theories more suitable to explain unalloyed ethnocentrism failed to capture.

The ambivalence approach to prejudice shifts our image away from Bull Connor and toward those of us who sat in smug satisfaction in the North. It brings us closer to the feelings and motives of the United States—North and South—thirty years after the police dogs were set loose on Martin Luther King Jr. But we have not yet considered the third approach to prejudice, the cognitive one.

COGNITIVE APPROACHES

Cognitive approaches to prejudice emphasize that prejudice is fundamentally a matter of belief; the source of Bull Connor's behavior is, in the end, the beliefs he had about blacks. If any of us believed what he believed—that blacks are innately and essentially inferior, that they are by their very existence a danger—we too would act as he acted. Moreover, these cognitive approaches argue that his coming to believe these things is not the result of his peculiar motivation or experience of being harshly disciplined. Rather, cognitive theorists argue that at the root of prejudice is the fact that our memories are fallible and that therefore we are prey to beliefs about groups of people that are not in accord with our experience with those people. Cognitive approaches stress the obvious fact that our interactions with the world, including our interactions with other people, are based on what we think they are like, and sometimes our beliefs are not very faithful records of that world.

What Are Stereotypes?

Research in the cognitive tradition has focused on a particular aspect of prejudice: stereotypes. The notion of stereotypes was introduced to American social science by the political commentator Walter Lippmann in 1922. He was concerned with the fact that in making political decisions, no one, including political leaders, approaches the current situation fresh; we approach it with preconceptions—stereotypes. He argued that these preconceptions have two different problems. First, they are simplifications of the facts. Stereotypes are about classes of people, not particular people, and therefore don't do justice to the individuals who are part of the group. For example, if we have a preconception that a particular ethnic group is pushy, we may avoid that whole group. But this isn't fair to the individuals in the group.

Second, our preconceptions may lead us to misperceive individuals even if we have contact with them; expecting someone to be hostile because he is black may lead us to see hostility in innocuous things that that person does. Stereotypes, then, were seen by Lippmann, and social scientists who followed him, as dangerous because they lead us to be unfair to and misperceive others. Moreover, the fact that a person believed stereotypes to be true was seen as a reliable mark of prejudice.

A   B

▲ (A) From Amos 'n' Andy, a television show from the 1950s that portrayed blacks as naive and generally not very bright. (B) From Martin, a more recent television show that, some think, still trades in stereotypes.

CONTENT OF STEREOTYPES

Early research on stereotypes consisted of demonstrating that subjects indeed had them. The classic method was introduced by Katz and Braly (1933). They asked one hundred Princeton students to indicate the traits that best described nine specified ethnic groups. The subjects agreed that, for example, blacks were superstitious and lazy, Americans (presumably Anglos) were industrious and intelligent, Jews were shrewd and mercenary, and so forth. This technique gives a picture of the content of the stereotypes and the degree to which they are shared.

Two subsequent generations of Princeton students were examined using this method, one in 1951 and another in 1969 (Gilbert, 1951; Karlins, Coffman, & Walters, 1969). The results showed a general trend toward a weakening of consensus and an increase in positive stereotypes of blacks and Jews. Research in this tradition tells us about the content and popularity of stereotypes, but it can't address more interesting questions: Why do stereotypes develop? How are they maintained? More modern research has attempted to answer these questions.

STEREOTYPES AND CORRELATIONS

What do subjects mean when they say a trait is characteristic of some ethnic group? Do they mean that every member has the trait—for example, that every black is lazy? If so, then stereotypes are irrational indeed; it is profoundly unlikely that every member of any ethnic group has any particular trait. And this ought to be obvious from everyday experience and common sense. But perhaps this isn't what the subjects mean when they assigned the traits to ethnic groups.

One investigator asked his subjects (South Africans) to attribute traits to ethnic groups, and then he asked them directly whether they believed that every member of the group had the traits they had just assigned. Only a small minority meant this strong form of stereotypes in assigning the traits (Mann, 1967). A more sensible interpretation of what subjects mean when they assign traits is that they believe that the trait is more likely to be found in that ethnic group than in some other group, or among "people in general." In statistical language, to hold a stereotype is to believe that there is a correlation between being a member of an ethnic group and having certain traits. Given this statistical interpretation of stereotypes, we can rephrase our question: How can people come to believe in, and sustain their belief in, the existence of a correlation between ethnic groups and traits?

Why Do Stereotypes Develop?

Three different accounts have been proposed to explain why stereotypes develop. The first, the **shared distinctiveness account,** is a purely cognitive account; it proposes that the tendency to form stereotypes of people is a natural consequence of the way we process information—all information. In particular, David Hamilton has proposed that a phenomenon well-known in general psychology, the **illusory correlation,** can explain the development and maintenance of stereotypes without needing to posit that we have any motivational biases at all with regard to our thinking about groups of people. The second account also sees stereotypes as a consequence of the way we think about people, but it suggests that stereotyping depends on our having categorized people into ingroups and outgroups. The essence of this account, the **outgroup homogeneity account,** is that once we divide people into ingroups and outgroups, we are likely to form stereotypes of the outgroups. The third account, the **cultural account,** argues that we cannot understand the stereotypes we have of various groups in cognitive terms alone; it suggests that the stereotypes we have are a consequence of the specific way our culture has structured interactions between ingroups and outgroups. According to this view, the history of a culture determines the particular content that various stereotypes have. Let us consider these explanations one at a time.

THE SHARED DISTINCTIVENESS ACCOUNT

Shared distinctiveness is a phenomenon uncovered by Loren and Jean Chapman. They have shown that in certain circumstances, if two distinctive (unusual) events sometimes occur at the same time, people will come to believe that there is a correlation between them—that is, the events not only sometimes go together, they generally go together (Chapman & Chapman, 1967). David Hamilton has extended this notion to stereotypes by arguing that for a white person, both meeting an African American and having an unpleasant interaction are uncommon, distinctive events. According to the logic of shared distinctiveness, because these events are more likely to stand out, whites will perceive a correlation between blacks and unpleasant encounters, even if interactions with blacks are no more likely to be untoward than interactions with whites. This suggests a way that shared distinctiveness could give rise to stereotypes.

To show that this mechanism works with judgments of groups of people, Hamilton carried out an experiment in which he gave subjects a series of statements to read. The statements were all of this sort: "Joe, a member of group A, gave up his seat on the subway to a lady," or "Bob, a member of group B, dropped litter in the subway station." Each statement mentioned someone from group A or B and some mildly positive or negative behavior. There were thirty-nine people mentioned in the set of statements; twenty-six

A

B

▲ *(A) In the 1939 film* Gone with the Wind, *Hattie Mc-Daniel portrayed a stereotypical black mammy, for which she won the best supporting actress Academy Award. (B) In the 1992 film* Passion Fish, *Alfre Woodard plays a nurse who must care for a white paraplegic (Mary McDonell), but their relationship is less stereotypical and more balanced.*

FIGURE 4.2

ILLUSORY CORRELATION WITH JUDGMENTS OF PEOPLE

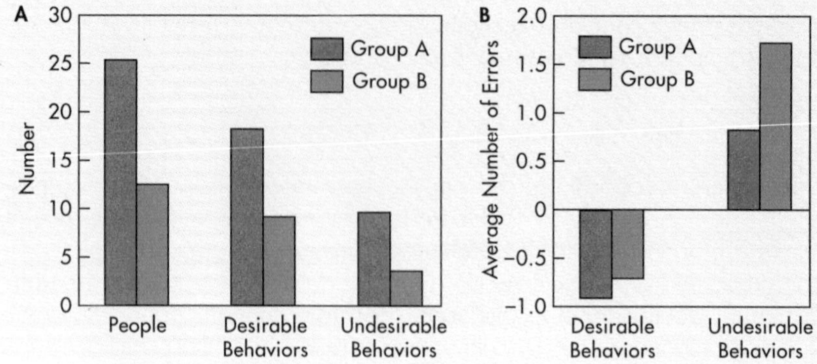

▶ (A) There were twice as many desirable and undesirable behaviors in group A, but there were also twice as many people in group A. (B) Subjects were especially prone to overestimate the number of rare (undesirable) behaviors in the rare (B) group. (Data from Hamilton & Gifford, 1976)

were from group A, and thirteen were from group B. There were also thirty-nine behaviors, twenty-seven moderately positive and twelve moderately undesirable.

The behaviors were paired with the people in this way. There were eight undesirable acts assigned to group A and four to group B; twice as many of the undesirable acts came from group A (see Figure 4.2A). But there were also twice as many people in group A, so there was *no correlation* between group membership and the kind of acts reported. But the investigators predicted that subjects would see a correlation nonetheless between undesirable acts and group membership. In particular, they expected people to overestimate the proportion of undesirable acts committed by people in group B, because in the set they constructed, both membership in group B and committing undesirable acts were rare and hence distinctive. As predicted, when subjects were asked at the end of the session to identify which of the acts came from group B and which from group A, they overassigned the undesirable acts to group B (see Figure 4.2B; Hamilton & Gifford, 1976; see also Spears, van der Pligt, & Eiser, 1985; Spears, van der Pligt, & Eiser, 1986). This research, then, provides some support for the notion that shared distinctiveness can provide an explanation for why minorities (here meant in the literal sense) are seen as having undesirable traits (for detailed accounts of the cognitive mechanisms of the illusion, see Fiedler, 1991; Smith, 1991).

There are, however, reasons to doubt that shared distinctiveness can explain the development of the stereotypes we actually hold. One comes from a study showing that the correlation was formed *only* when the information provided was of low personal relevance to the subjects (Sanbonmatsu, Shavitt, & Sherman, 1991). Another reason is that while the shared distinctiveness model predicts that all minority groups will have as part of their stereotype every uncommon trait, they in fact do not. For example, both being gay and being black are uncommon, so the model predicts that part of the stereotype of blacks is that they are gay. But this isn't so. For that matter, being a genius or a heroine is uncommon, so the model would also predict that the stereotype of blacks includes being heroines and geniuses. Hamilton's model doesn't account for the selectiveness of stereotypes.

A common observation about stereotypes is that we tend to have them about groups of which we ourselves are not members. We tend to have stereotypes about outgroups, not ingroups. The outgroup homogeneity explanation focuses on *why* we have stereotypes of outgroups. To form a stereotype, the argument goes, is to *generalize* from the characteristics of one or a few members of a group to the group as a whole. So the question becomes: Under what circumstances do people generalize from a few examples to a class as a whole? It makes sense to generalize from a few instances to a broader class if (and only if) one believes the class to be homogeneous; that is, if one believes the class is made up of individuals who are pretty much alike. We can explain the fact that we have stereotypes of outgroups (but not ingroups), then, if we assume that people believe that outgroups are generally homogeneous but their ingroups are heterogeneous.

In one study of the outgroup homogeneity effect, students from Princeton University and Rutgers University were shown a videotape of another student making a decision. Some of the subjects were told that the person in the tape was from their own institution; some were told that the person was from the opposite institution. The person on the tape made a decision about which the subjects had no prior expectation: he had to decide to wait alone or with other subjects while the experimenter fixed a piece of broken equipment. The subjects were then asked to estimate the percentage of other people from the same institution who would make the same choice.

The data indicated that subjects generalized more from the behavior of an outgroup member to other outgroup choices than they did from the behavior of an ingroup member to other ingroup choices. So, for example, if the Rutgers subjects saw what they thought was another Rutgers student elect to wait alone, they thought that about 55 percent of other Rutgers students would make the same choice, but if they saw a Princeton student wait alone, they thought that about 70 percent of Princeton students would elect to wait alone—"We're all very different, but those other guys are all alike" (Quattrone & Jones, 1980; see also, Linville, Fischer, & Salovey, 1989; Park & Judd, 1990; Park, Ryan, & Judd, 1992). Subsequent research has suggested that competition between groups—as Sherif suggested—heightens this tendency to see outgroups as homogeneous (Judd & Park, 1988).

Outgroup homogeneity refers to the belief that members of outgroups are pretty much alike. This belief can enhance stereotyping.

There is also reason to believe that we have more complex representations of our ingroups than of outgroups. For example, we can think of more features of ingroup members than outgroup members (Linville & Jones, 1980; Linville, 1982). And we may form more subgroups of our ingroups than of outgroups (Park, Ryan, & Judd, 1992). Finally, we may tend to store information about ingroup members differently from the way we store information about outgroup members; we may store ingroup information by person, while we store outgroup information by activity. So for members of our families, for example, we collect in one "place" in memory all sorts of information about the same person; whereas for people we don't know so well, we collect information by activity. This would lead us to have differentiated perceptions of the people we know well, but less differentiated information about outgroups (Estrum, Carpenter, Sedikides, & Li, 1993).

If it is true that we see outgroups as more homogeneous than ingroups, then it is easy to explain why we are more likely to form stereotypes of outgroups. We saw above that while the idea of shared distinctiveness seems to go some way toward explaining why we form the particular stereotypes of outgroups that we do, it may not be adequate to the task. The outgroup homogeneity notion, on the other hand, highlights the fact that we have outgroup stereotypes without attempting to explain why these stereotypes have the content they do. Let us turn to the cultural account of stereotypes, which seems to do a better job of explaining content.

THE CULTURAL ACCOUNT

Robert LeVine and Donald Campbell suggest that stereotypes depend less on cognitive defects and more on social facts. First, they point out that the stereotype of Jews is the stereotype of urban dwellers held by rural peoples in many parts of the world, and the stereotype that blacks are lazy and superstitious is the stereotype of rural people by urban people. LeVine and Campbell propose that these stereotypes have developed because through the course of their history Jews were forced to live in cities, and in this country (until the First World War) blacks were forced to live in rural areas. They argue that the stereotypes follow from the segregated but different treatments the two groups found at the hands of the majority.

Consider the case of European Jews in more detail. They were forced into cities because they were not allowed to own land. In the cities, they found that their best opportunities were often as merchants. The majority, then, forced Jews into merchant occupations. This meant that interactions between gentiles and Jews were often of the merchant-customer sort. It is hardly surprising that this history of role-constrained interactions would lead to the stereotype that Jews are shrewd and mercenary. Considering that it was illegal in the South to educate slaves, we should not be surprised to find that part of the stereotype of blacks is that they are ignorant (LeVine & Campbell, 1972).

Similarly, as we shall see in Chapter 12, there is a tendency for men and women to emerge as different kinds of leaders; women tend to specialize in being leaders who are sensitive to the social-emotional needs of their groups, while men tend to be more task-focused leaders. But as Alice Eagly has argued, this may well be the result of assignment to these roles by our culture; it is this assignment to roles that makes behavior conform to stereotypes (Eagly & Karau, 1991).

LeVine and Campbell suggest a plausible way for stereotypes to develop, a way that does not rely on cognitive defects. But this still leaves the question: How are they maintained?

How Are Stereotypes Maintained?

The illusory correlation, a phenomenon discovered by cognitive psychologists, has been offered as a mechanism by which stereotypes, once formed, are maintained, even in the face of data that do not support them. The idea is that if people expect there to be a correlation between two things, then even if there isn't, they will see the correlation in the data. This idea is a possible account of the maintenance of stereotypes.

In one experiment, subjects were asked to read twenty-four statements; each statement paired an occupation with two traits. For example, "Mark, a doctor, is wealthy and timid." The sentences were constructed so that each trait was paired an equal number of times with each occupation—there was no correlation. But when asked to pair traits with occupations at the end, subjects showed the effects of their existing stereotypes; for example, they tended to overestimate the number of wealthy doctors in the sample (Hamilton & Rose, 1981; Hamilton, Dugan, & Trolier, 1985).

This research suggests that once stereotypes are formed, they are not easily influenced by data. We can pursue this research one step further and ask: Why do illusory correlations persist in the face of counterevidence? What cognitive mechanisms and defects are involved?

DIFFERENTIAL REMEMBERING AND THE ILLUSORY CORRELATION

Suppose you wanted to calculate the correlation between being wealthy and being a doctor. What information would you need? You would need the number of cases that fit each of the four cells of Table 4.4. The more cases of wealthy doctors and poor nondoctors, the higher the correlation would be. The more cases of poor doctors and wealthy nondoctors, the lower the correlation would be. Now suppose that as you tried to recall all of the cases you had just seen, you tended to forget the poor doctors and the wealthy nondoctors. Because of the differential forgetting, when you got to the point of calculating the correlation, you would err in the direction of perceiving the stereotypical association. Thus, if people tend to forget cases that clash with their stereotypes but remember cases that conform to their stereotypes, they will perceive an illusory correlation. But do people remember stereotype-consistent information better than stereotype-inconsistent information? Many investigators have found just this.

To take one example, one group of experimenters told subjects that they would be given fifty descriptions of behaviors, one at a time. Each description was said to correspond to one man in a particular group. Before they saw the descriptions, some subjects were told that the group was known to be unusually friendly; others were told that the group was unusually intelligent. All subjects were then shown the same fifty descriptions: seventeen were of friendly behaviors, seventeen were of intelligent behaviors, three were of unfriendly behaviors, three were of unintelligent behaviors, and ten were of behaviors that were unrelated to friendliness or intelligence. At the end, subjects were asked to recall how many behaviors of each type they had just seen.

As expected, those subjects who had been told the group was friendly recalled the friendly behaviors, while those who had been told the group was intelligent recalled the intelligent behaviors. Forewarning about the charac-

TABLE 4.4

	ILLUSORY CORRELATION	
	Wealthy	Not Wealthy
M.D.'s	1	2
Not M.D.'s	3	4

teristics of the group, then, enhanced recall for behaviors consistent with the warning (Rothbart, Evans, & Fulero, 1979). We can push this inquiry one last step and ask: Why did subjects recall the confirming instances better? Was it that they encoded these cases in memory better as they read them, or that at the time of recall they found it easier to get the confirming instances out of their memories?

In this experiment, the effect occurred at the point of encoding, as the subjects were read the descriptions. We can tell this because other subjects were told of the groups' characteristics only after they read the individual descriptions, and they did not show the recall bias.

Other research has suggested that there might be bias at the point of recall too. Mark Snyder gave subjects a woman's biography to study. One week later, the same subjects were told a further fact about her: some were told that she was a lesbian, others that she was heterosexual. Then the subjects were given a thirty-six-item multiple-choice test about the woman's life. The answers showed that the subjects tended to recall details of her life that fit their preconceptions. For example, the biography said that she had gone out with boys in high school but that she didn't have a steady boyfriend. Those told that she was a lesbian remembered that she didn't have a steady boyfriend but forgot that she had dated boys; those told she was heterosexual more often forgot that she didn't have a steady boyfriend and remembered that she had gone out with boys. This distortion must have occurred at the point of recall, since the subjects didn't know about her sexual preference at the time they encoded the information (Snyder & Uranowitz, 1978; see Clark & Woll, 1981, however, for a critique of, and failure to replicate, this result).

Differential remembering either because of more effective encoding as information is taken in or because of bias at the time of recall can lead to an illusory correlation, which could account for the persistence of stereotypes. This cognitive defect could account for why we perceive groups as a whole as having characteristics they don't have. But there are other ways that we might hold on to stereotypes even if the evidence gives them a rough time.

Suppose you believe that professors are absent-minded. Now suppose you meet some professors and discover that they aren't absent-minded at all. Does this imply that you will give up your stereotype—if your memory for the present-minded professors is perfect? Well, maybe.

Whether the evidence will upset your stereotype depends on just who the present-minded professors are. One key issue is whether they are in *other ways* typical of their profession. If they are in every other way typical professors, then the data they provide might change your stereotype, but if they are in other ways very atypical, the data might not cause your stereotype to change.

To illustrate the way that stereotype revision depends on the typicality of exemplars, David Wilder conducted an experiment using students from two neighboring colleges. Some were drawn from Rutgers, others from Douglass College. The experiment took advantage of the fact that the women from each college held clear stereotypes about each other: Douglass women saw Rutgers women as much too interested in having a good time to take their studies seriously; Rutgers women saw Douglass women as too conservative—too concerned with their appearance and with their studies to have any fun in life. The experimenter arranged for students from each school to interact, one at a time, with a confederate who was dressed and made up to look like either a typical or an atypical student from the other school. Thus, to appear to be the typical Rutgers student (or the atypical Douglass student), the confederate wore jeans and no makeup and said she hoped that the experiment would be over on time, as she had a party to go to. When she appeared to be a typical Douglass student (or an atypical Rutgers student), she wore a skirt and blouse, pumps, and makeup and announced that she hoped the experiment would be over on time, since she had to study. In half of the cases, the confederate interacted in a pleasant way with the subject; in the other half, she acted in an unpleasant way.

After the interactions, the subjects indicated their attitudes toward women from the rival school. The subjects changed their evaluations of the rival school in a positive direction when they had a pleasant interaction with a *typical* member of the other school. Unpleasant interactions altogether or pleasant interactions with *atypical* members of the other school did not improve attitudes (see Figure 4.3; Wilder, 1984).

Further research by Myron Rothbart suggests the operation of a general cognitive principle here. Rothbart showed subjects collections of geometric objects: rectangles, triangles, ellipses, and so on. Each example was colored. There was no relation between the objects' color and shape; that is, overall the triangles, for example, were red just as often as they were green. There were, however, two kinds of examples of each shape—"good" examples and "bad" examples. Now triangles are an easily defined class of stimuli; if a shape is closed and is made up of three lines and all of them lie in a plane, then it is a triangle. But, apparently, some triangles are "better" examples of "triangle" than others; that is, people judge equilateral triangles (all sides equal) to be better triangles than acute triangles.* And so too for the other shapes:

---

*Just what subjects mean when they say equilateral triangles are better than acute ones is anything but clear. See Armstrong, Gleitman, & Gleitman, 1983, for a witty as well as trenchant consideration of the matter. For our purposes, suffice it to note that in whatever sense, some are reliably judged better than others.

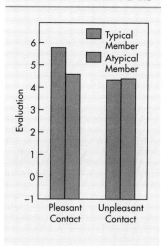

FIGURE 4.3

EVALUATIONS AND TYPICALITY OF EXEMPLARS

▲ *Evaluations of a stereotyped rival college as a result of having had pleasant or unpleasant contact with a typical or atypical student from that college. (Data from Wilder, 1984)* some examples are judged better than others even though all meet the geometric definition of their type.

Rothbart created a stimulus set in which there was a relation between the color of the stimulus and whether the stimulus was a good or bad example of its category. Although a triangle, for example, was no more likely to be green than red, the good examples were more likely to be green, while the bad ones were more often red. The question was: What color were the subjects likely to believe the triangles *in general* were? The data showed that subjects *overestimated* the frequency with which the geometric shapes were the color of their "good" exemplars—triangles were estimated to be mostly green. Thus, the good exemplars of the category were overrepresented in the subjects' recollection of the whole set.

In a second study, the same principle was found to operate with regard to more social stimuli—in this case, fraternity brothers. Subjects were told about the political attitudes of a set of fraternity brothers. Some of the brothers were described as being typical of fraternity men; others were made to seem unusual for men in a fraternity. The question of interest was what impression subjects would form of the political attitudes of members about whom they had been given no information. Consistent with the results from prototypical and atypical triangles, the subjects inferred that the other members of the fraternity had the political attitudes of the typical fraternity brothers (see Figure 4.4; Rothbart & Lewis, 1988).

These results suggest another reason that stereotypes are difficult to overcome. Imagine that people have the belief that stockbrokers are selfish. Now imagine that these same people read about a group of stockbrokers who donate great sums of money and great amounts of their time to the poor. We might imagine that this information would help to erode the stereotype that brokers are selfish. But the evidence discussed here suggests that this might well not happen. Rather, subjects might take the brokers' generosity as *proof* that these brokers are atypical examples of stockbrokers, and hence that their

FIGURE 4.4

PROTOTYPICALITY AND ESTIMATES OF POLITICAL ATTITUDES

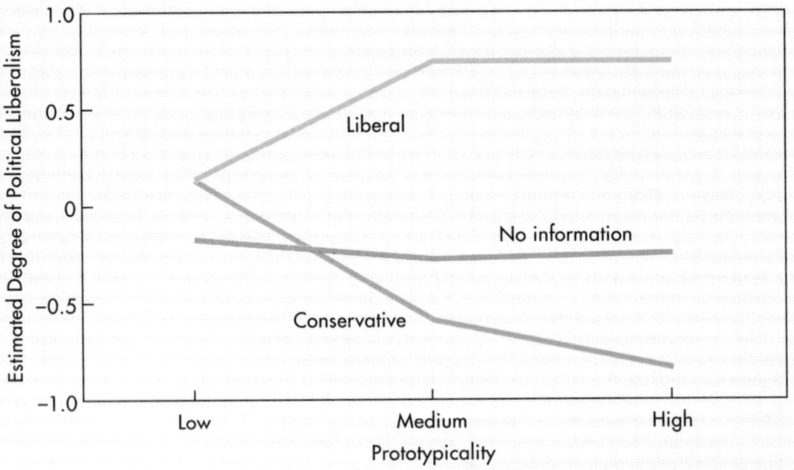

▶ *Estimated liberalism of the stimulus person's fraternity as a function of the stimulus person's political behavior and his typicality as a fraternity member. People generalize more from typical than from atypical members. (From Rothbart & Lewis, 1988)*

behavior isn't very revealing about the behavior of stockbrokers as a whole. The evidence suggests, then, that stereotypes aren't very easily upset when evidence that disconfirms them is concentrated in a few exemplars; for a stereotype to be eroded, it is important that lots of members violate the stereotype—even a little bit—rather than that there be a few dramatic violations (Weber & Crocker, 1983; see Manis, Nelson, & Shedler, 1988, and Johnston & Hewstone, 1992, for a discussion of a similar issue). Our willingness to segregate a few examples out from our general stereotype, to fence them off from the bulk of instances, endows stereotypes with a certain resistance to change.*

Small deviations from a stereotype by many members are more effective in changing stereotypes than are large deviations by a small number of people.

Stereotypes and Cognitive Functioning

So far we have addressed how stereotypes are formed and maintained, but we haven't addressed how stereotypes function, that is, what they do to (or for) our thinking. What role do they play in our mental activity? We especially want to know how stereotypes, beliefs about groups of people, affect our thinking about particular people.

STEREOTYPES AND INDIVIDUALS

Stereotypes are beliefs about kinds of people, but we don't meet, fight with, flirt with, teach, learn from, or hire *kinds of* people; we do all of these things with actual, individual people. How, then, do we use stereotypes in dealing with individuals? In particular, how are our stereotypes related to what we think about particular people? Do we use them *instead* of information about particular people, *in addition to* information about particular people, or perhaps only as a *default* option—something that is used only when other information isn't available?

In one experiment designed to explore these issues, subjects were asked to read what was supposedly a transcript of a conversation between two friends. For some subjects, the conversation was supposedly between Nancy and her friend Susan. For other subjects, the transcript was the same in every way, except that the characters were simply identified as Paul and Mike. For a third group, the characters were simply identified as person A and person B. In the conversation, the two friends talked about what they had been up to in the previous week. One of the friends focused on three difficult situations he (or she) had been involved in. One problem involved being harassed by a rather seedy character while shopping; another involved wanting to cut off a student favored by a professor in order to make a point in class; and the

▲ *Hillary Rodham Clinton at a National Health Care policy meeting. Has she changed our ideas about what a first lady could (or should) be?*

---

*Whether this segregation is rational or not is a tricky issue. Two types of cases can be distinguished. In one type, the evidence for deciding that the exemplar is an odd one is independent of the stereotype. Say you have a stereotype that Americans love football, and you run into an American who doesn't. But you also know that this particular American has lived sixteen of his eighteen years in Europe. In this case, it makes perfect sense not to let the example affect the stereotype. But in the second type of case, your reason for deciding that the example is odd is exactly the fact that it doesn't fit the stereotype. There is surely something circular about holding on to the stereotype by declaring the example odd just because it doesn't fit the stereotype. Such a procedure is suspect. Still, it isn't entirely crazy. You may treat the evidence that the example doesn't fit the stereotype not as proof that the example is odd, but just as suggestive evidence, to be confirmed or disconfirmed by further tests. Whether this is rational or not is too complex a question to be pursued here.

third involved wanting to break into a conversation in order to meet a likable person.

Now each of these situations allowed for an assertive or a passive response. And indeed, half of the subjects in each of the above conditions read about someone who forcibly told the seedy character to bug off, interrupted the teacher's pet, and broke into the conversation to meet the likable person. The other half of the subjects read about more wimpy responses. Regardless of what they had read, the subjects returned to the lab on the next day. On that day, they were asked to recall the behaviors they had read about, predict what the assertive or wimpy protagonist would do in situations they had not read about, and rate the protagonist (target) on twenty masculine and twenty feminine traits.

A third of the subjects were reading about a woman who did something (actually three things) that was quite assertive. But women are stereotypically thought of as passive. What would control these subjects' impressions of the characters: the behaviors or the stereotypes? As it happened, subjects' predictions of the target's behavior in new situations and their ratings on the traits were *unaffected* by the target's gender but strongly affected by the target's behavior. In this study, then, subjects who were given both stereotypes in the form of the target person's gender and information about that particular target's behavior ignored the stereotypes and paid attention only to the behavioral information. In fact, subjects paid so little attention to the gender information that one is led to wonder whether subjects actually knew the stereotype that women are passive. But further conditions in the experiment showed that when *no* behavioral information was given but the target's gender was specified, the subjects based their trait ratings and predictions on the gender stereotypes (Locksley, Borgida, Brekke, & Hepburn, 1980).

Subsequent research suggests that subjects given both behavioral and gender information don't really ignore gender, but neither do they ignore behavior; rather, they seem to act fairly rationally by combining the two sorts of information in predicting behavior or rating traits* (Rasinski, Crocker, & Hastie, 1985; see also Krueger & Rothbart, 1988, on the use of gender information, and Fiske & Neuberg, 1990, for a general model of how people combine categorical information like gender with individual information). Thus, there is some evidence that subjects can be fairly rational in their handling of gender-stereotyped information. Unfortunately, there is evidence that people are less rational in the way they handle these stereotypes in a situation that is far more important to women than having their behavior predicted by undergraduates.

Employment and Jury Decisions

One aspect of gender stereotypes is that we all "know" that there are male jobs and female jobs. It is reasonable to assume that since people involved in hiring employees also know this, they use this information to decide whom to hire for which jobs. Now basing employment decisions on gender infor-

---

*Sixth graders, but apparently not third graders, are able to take account of behavior in making predictions, even when it conflicts with stereotypes (Berndt & Heller, 1986).

mation is morally wrong and illegal in many cases, but the question here is: Is it irrational? It might not be. If we believe that men and women differ in their personality traits, and if we believe that certain traits are desirable in an employee, then it is rational to prefer one gender over the other for a particular job if we have no information about the particular applicants' traits. Thus, gender can play a rational (if illegal) role in hiring decisions if it serves to inform people about the personality traits of applicants. On the other hand, if it affects such judgments *over and above* its effect on trait inferences, then it has an unreasoned as well as illegal effect on hiring.*

To find out how gender information is used, résumés of a bogus job applicant were sent to upper-level managers and business professionals, the kinds of people likely to make real hiring decisions. The résumé was accompanied by a cover letter explaining that the résumé was being sent as part of a study of hiring decisions, but the letter didn't mention gender as a focus of the study. The managers were asked to indicate how likely they were to interview the applicant for three jobs: a gender-neutral job—administrative assistant in a bank; a male sex-typed job—sales manager of a heavy machinery manufacturing company; and a female sex-typed job—dental receptionist/secretary.

There were six different résumés. Half of the managers got a résumé for Kate Norris; half got one for Ken Norris. So gender of the applicants was one of the factors that was varied. But the résumés also contained information designed to affect the managers' inferences about the applicants' traits. One-third of the managers learned that Kate (or Ken) had spent her (his) time doing "masculine" jobs—she (he) had sold sporting goods in a retail store during her (his) summer vacation, worked on a campus grounds maintenance crew, and had been captain of her (his) basketball team. A third of the managers learned that Kate (or Ken) had spent her (his) time doing sex-neutral things—working in a shoe store during the summer. And a third learned that she (he) had held "feminine jobs"—selling jewelry, for example. So, as in the study having to do with trait ratings and behavioral predictions, these subjects had both gender information and diagnostic information available. The question was which would they use to (1) infer the applicant's traits and (2) decide whether to interview her (him).

The managers ignored the gender information and used the information about the person's behavior in inferring traits. So the person who had worked in a sporting goods store, had done grounds maintenance, and was captain of the basketball team was seen as having "masculine" traits, regardless of gender. (When the applicant had engaged in sex-neutral behavior, then gender *did* matter.) And it was also true that the behavioral information affected the probability that the person would be interviewed for the job—the person with a "masculine" history, regardless of gender, was more likely to be interviewed for the sales manager job than the person with the "feminine" history. But gender also mattered when it came to the probability of inter-

▲ *Pictured here is Kristin Baker, the first woman captain of the Corps of Cadets at West Point.*

Gender may influence decisions about hiring over and above its effect on the attribution of job-relevant traits.

---

*The problem of gender stereotypes in business organizations does not, of course, confine itself to the issue of hiring. Belle Raggins and Eric Sundstrom have provided an interesting and detailed account of the broader aspects of the issue of gender and organizations (Raggins & Sundstrom, 1989).

▲ *Fathers can be nurturant too. And they need not give up masculine traits to be so.*

viewing; the woman who had worked in the sporting goods store was *less* likely to be interviewed for the sales manager job than was the man who had the same history.

The results suggest that gender stereotypes have both a rational and an irrational effect on hiring decisions. Their rational impact affects trait inferences; this effect is rational because people believe traits to be associated with gender.* But since in this study gender made a difference in the decision to interview, gender seems still to affect occupational suitability judgments *over and above* its link with traits (Glick, Zion, & Nelson, 1988; see also Futoran & Wyer, 1986; Nelson, Biernat, & Manis, 1990).

As important as hiring decisions are, jury decisions are, perhaps, even more so; it is therefore important to know whether and when jurors' verdicts are influenced by stereotypes. Even more important is knowing how to remove bias. There is evidence from mock jury studies that jurors are more likely to find a black defendant guilty than a white one (given the same facts), especially if the victim was white. But the more encouraging news is that in one study, at least, this tendency was reversed if the jurors were given instructions from the judge that focused their attention on the components of the crime that had to be proved if they were to find the defendant guilty (Pfeifer & Ogloff, 1991). Stereotypes can affect our perceptions of behavior and of character, but that is not to say that they have free reign. We aren't entirely victims of our preconceptions. What actually happens in the world affects our perceptions too! (See Kunda & Sherman-Williams, 1993, for a similar point.)

Stereotypes and Cognitive Stress

Stereotypes are thought of as ways we have of simplifying our cognitive tasks—tasks of storing and recalling information about people. If stereotypes are indeed useful in simplifying our cognitive lives, then it should be true that we rely on them more when we are cognitively busy than when we are less busy. Perhaps when we are less busy, we have the time and inclination to judge people as individuals and less as examples of social groups. Is there evidence that the use of stereotypes increases as people are placed under greater cognitive pressure?

In one study, subjects were asked to form impressions about one, two, or four social groups about whom they were given ten or twenty behavioral episodes in written form. The information was arranged so as to produce a stereotype for each of the groups as the subjects read the behaviors, but there were also some incongruent behaviors included in each set. The question the investigators asked was: How would informational demands on the subjects affect their recall for congruent versus incongruent information? The results were, as predicted, that increasing the informational pressures on the subjects—by giving them more groups and more behaviors—led them to simplify their task by paying less attention to the incongruent—stereotype inconsistent—information (Stangor & Duan, 1991). So in this study, cognitive pres-

---

*They are also right, since (for whatever reason) traits *are* associated with gender. But the questions of accuracy and rationality are quite distinct.

sure added to the tendency to stereotype. Using stereotypes does seem to simplify cognitive life.

Other evidence indicates that stressors of various kinds also lead us to rely more on stereotypes. For example, loud noise (Paulhus, Martin, & Murphy, 1992) and working on another task concurrently (Martell, 1991) have been shown to increase stereotypical thinking.

There is also evidence, however, that as useful as stereotypes might be to the busy mind, there comes a point where we are so busy that even our stereotypes take too much time to use. Daniel Gilbert, for example, used either an Asian or a Caucasian research assistant who asked subjects to complete word fragments. Now the word fragments connected to stereotypes of Asians, e.g., "pol te" (polite) and "s ort" (short). If the presence of the Asian research assistant was enough to activate the subjects' stereotypes, we would expect them to complete the word fragments in the stereotypical manner. And this is just what happened when the subjects had nothing to do except complete the words, but this isn't what happened when subjects had to repeat to themselves an eight-digit number as they did the word task. In *that* condition, the subjects were not likely to complete the words in the stereotypical way. To use Gilbert's metaphor, a wrench is a handy tool for a busy person, but it does you no good if you are too busy to find it. Gilbert also showed in the same study—consistent with the main line of the story I have been telling—that if, however, the subjects did activate their stereotypes, they were more likely to use them when busy (but not too busy) than when not busy (Gilbert & Hixon, 1991).

The Accuracy of Stereotypes

It is attractive to believe that stereotypes are inaccurate. We all know that stereotypical thinking is wrong, and it is reasonable to assume that it is wrong in the sense that it is inaccurate. But are our stereotypes inaccurate?

Let us consider gender stereotypes first. Part of our stereotype of women is that they are nurturant, while men are achieving. Is this true? If what we mean by this is that *all* women are nurturant and *all* men are achieving, then it is surely false. But, as I mentioned above, surely most people do not believe stereotypes in that strong sense. Rather, the standard way to interpret such beliefs is to assume that people believe that women are *more likely to be* nurturant (than men are) and that men are *more likely to be* achievement striving (than women are). Is *this* belief true?

In Chapter 12, I discuss research with the Bem Sex Role Inventory that suggests that women are more likely to report themselves to be nurturant and men are more likely to report themselves to be achievement striving. True, the men and women in these studies may themselves be blinded by stereotypes and hence may be reporting things about themselves that aren't so, but these results suggest, at least, that in this statistical sense, stereotypes might have some kernel of truth. Of course, people might overestimate the degree of difference between men and women, so they might be wrong in degree about gender stereotypes.

What about ethnic stereotypes? Are they accurate? Only two studies have attempted to assess the accuracy of ethnic stereotypes. The first was in 1936, the second in 1978. Why studies that address this obvious question are so rare is a matter we shall comment on below. First the two studies.

In 1936, Robert LaPiere solicited Californians' stereotypes about a small, segregated minority in that state: Armenians. They were the targets of a host of negative characterizations—dishonest, always on welfare, always in trouble with the law, among other things. LaPiere checked these beliefs against official records. He found that Armenians had, on average, no worse credit histories than other Californians—in the eyes of credit bureaus, just the group that takes such matters most seriously. He found that one out of every five hundred Armenians applied for welfare, while one out of every one hundred Californians as a whole applied for welfare. About 1.5 percent of Armenians had been involved with the police; the average for all residents of the state was about 6 percent. According to the official records, then, Armenians conformed to their stereotypes *less well* than did the people who stereotyped them (LaPiere, 1936)!

The more recent study of the accuracy of stereotypes addressed stereotypes of blacks. A variety of subjects (college students, social workers, members of a church choir, union members attending a leadership conference, among others) were asked to estimate the percentage of adult black Americans and the percentage of adult Americans in general who had not completed high school, had been the victims of violent crime, were on welfare, had four or more children. They were also asked what percentage of black and white children were born illegitimate, and what percentage of black and white families had female heads. For most questions, there were differences in the estimates for blacks and Americans as a whole—in that sense, the subjects had stereotypes. But there are government statistics for the same questions, and so, as in the LaPiere study, estimates could be checked against the facts (McCauley & Stitt, 1978; see Judd & Park, 1993, for an excellent discussion of the complexities involved in deciding whether stereotypes are accurate).

It turned out that on about one-half of the measures, the subjects' perceptions of the differences between blacks and Americans as a whole *underestimated* the differences between blacks and whites. Stereotypes may not be so wrong after all.

KNOWING VERSUS USING STEREOTYPES

There is a difference between *knowing* a stereotype and *believing* it. Anyone growing up in American culture is likely to have learned what the stereotypes of various ethnic groups are, and indeed these stereotypes are likely to affect, quite unconsciously, people's processing of information. For example, in one study, white subjects were divided into high- and low-prejudiced groups on the basis of their responses to an attitude questionnaire. Subjects of both sorts were then shown lists of words for very brief intervals. Some of the words were associated with stereotypes of African Americans (none of the words were directly related to hostility); others were neutral. All of the words were displayed for intervals too brief for the subjects to recognize the words; they were told simply to indicate where in the visual field the words occurred— top, down, left, or right.

In a second part of the procedure, the subjects were given vignettes describing characters who acted in ambiguously hostile ways. For example, one was about a race-unspecified Donald who demanded his money back from a

Table 4.5

EVALUATION OF HOSTILITY STEREOTYPE AND ACTIVATION OF STEREOTYPE

Type of Subject	Knowledge of Stereotype	Activated Automatically	Activated Under Controlled Processing
Prejudiced	Yes	Yes	Yes
Unprejudiced	Yes	Yes	No

SOURCE: Based on Devine, 1989.

store clerk immediately after paying. The subjects were then asked to evaluate Donald on a variety of scales. The results showed that Donald was evaluated as more hostile by those subjects—both high and low in prejudice—who had previously been exposed to the black-stereotype-associated words than by those subjects who had been exposed to the neutral words (see Table 4.5). This happened even though the subjects were *unable to say what words they had seen.* Indeed, their guesses as to what words they had seen were correct only 2 percent of the time.

These results suggest that the very brief exposure to the stereotype-associated words activated or primed the subjects' black stereotypes—quite unconsciously. The activation of these stereotypes was too weak for the subjects to be able to report what the words were, but nonetheless, this activation was sufficient to color their judgments of Donald. Moreover, this effect was found for both the prejudiced and unprejudiced groups, suggesting that all of the subjects knew, at least implicitly, stereotypes associated with blacks, and that these stereotypes could affect—beyond their control—their processing of information in an ambiguous case.

In a final part of the study, subjects were asked to list labels they associated with "black Americans." In this consciously controlled procedure, differences did emerge between the labels that the more and less prejudiced subjects listed. The more prejudiced subjects listed more of the unflattering labels that are a part of the stereotypes all white Americans have learned; the less prejudiced subjects didn't (Devine, 1989).

The moral of this research is that all Americans have learned, *know,* the stereotypes associated with various ethnic groups, and these stereotypes are likely to have subtle, unconscious, uncontrollable effects on the way people process information. But this is not to say that everyone is equally prejudiced or racist; differences between people arise in how they use these stereotypes. In the end, the important issue may not be whether stereotypes are true or not, or whether people in some implicit, unconscious sense know them, but in how people use these stereotypes when they do have control, when they are responsible for what they think, say, and do (see Devine et al., 1991, for a discussion of the difference between prejudiced and unprejudiced subjects in these terms).

THE IMMORAL USE OF CORRECT INFORMATION

It is sometimes morally wrong to act on the basis of stereotypes, whether they are accurate or not. It seems that it couldn't be wrong to act on the basis of

> Even if stereotypes are to some degree accurate, it is morally problematic to use them when information about particular people is readily available.

correct beliefs. But it is in some contexts. Consider this example.

On average, blacks have less education than whites. Suppose you are a personnel manager. A black person and a white person apply for the same job. Whom do you hire? If you know nothing about them except their races, and if you believe that having a high school diploma is necessary for the job, then rationality would require that you hire the white. After all, the odds are better that the white has the requisite diploma. Even if the difference was small—say 49 percent of blacks and 51 percent of whites were high school graduates—you would be maximizing your chances if every time there was a job opening you hired the white. Notice that this would lead not to a work force in which 51 percent of the employees were white, but one in which 100 percent were white. Acting rationally, even on accurate information, then, can have intolerable consequences.

The intolerable consequence of employing only whites in this example follows from an important defect in how the accurate information is used. It is relatively easy to tell if a particular person has a high school diploma; as employment manager, you should check in particular cases rather than rely on inferences from admittedly correct group data. This is especially true when, as is the case with blacks, reliance on group data further disadvantages a group that has been discriminated against throughout its history.

THE ATTRIBUTION OF RESPONSIBILITY

There is another way for stereotypes, even if they are accurate, to be involved in unfair thinking. The perception of individuals, or groups of individuals, often involves not only ideas about what traits they have but also assumptions about who is responsible for their having those traits.

Public debate about racial issues in the United States at this time, for example, seems to be over this issue: who is responsible for the current state of black America, and who is responsible for improving it? This may be a far more important issue than whether descriptively the stereotypes are correct. Ethnocentrism may show up not so much in the content of stereotypes as in the assessment of responsibility. For example, in one study, thirty adult Hindus in south India were asked to read one-paragraph descriptions about either another Hindu or a Muslim. The protagonists did something either desirable or undesirable, and the subjects were to give reasons for the acts. The Hindus tended to find reasons that gave other Hindus credit for their positive acts, while finding excuses for their negative acts. On the other hand, they found reason that denied credit for the Muslims' positive acts, but did not find excuses for their negative acts. Bias toward the outgroup may show itself not so much in beliefs as in the allocation of responsibility (Taylor & Jaggi, 1974; see Hewstone, 1990, for a review).

NATURAL KIND THEORY

Let me mention one final possible resolution of the tension between our belief that stereotypical thinking is wrong and the evidence that suggests that stereotypes aren't entirely inaccurate. Perhaps it is a mistake to think of stereotypes as just beliefs about correlations between group membership and other qualities; perhaps there is more to stereotypical thinking than that. This issue has to do with the more general question of what we mean when we make general statements, a time-honored problem of substantial complexity in the field of *semantics* (the subfield of philosophy concerned with the meaning of concepts) and beyond the scope of this chapter, but we can, perhaps, engage it a bit.

Suppose I make a general claim: "Kittens are cute" will do as an example. What claim am I making by asserting that? The straightforward interpretation is that all kittens—each and every one—are cute. This is certainly a strong claim. The problem is that it is as brittle as it is strong; that is, it can be shown to be wrong by producing a single example of a not-cute kitten. We have seen that when it comes to ethnic stereotypes, this doesn't seem to be what people mean. They don't seem to mean that each and every member of a group is anything. Instead, we have been assuming that when people say things like "Kittens are cute," they mean that there is a correlation between being a kitten and being cute; they mean that the average kitten is more likely to be cute than is the average something or other. This is, clearly, a much weaker claim, more difficult to prove wrong. But perhaps it is too weak; perhaps when we say "Kittens are cute," we mean something stronger than that there is a mere correlation between being a kitten and being cute.

Perhaps we mean that it is in the nature of a kitten to be cute; perhaps we mean that the natural thing for a kitten to be is cute. Perhaps we mean that there must be something wrong with any kitten that hasn't expressed its cute nature. (Mind you, I am not claiming that any of this is true; I am merely trying to spell out what we might mean when we assert that kittens are cute.) The notion that general claims like "Kittens are cute" (and what we call stereotypes in the context of thinking about groups of people) are neither universal claims nor claims of mere correlations, but are instead claims about the nature of things, goes by the name of **natural kind theory** in philosophy (see Putnam, 1975). Let us see what we can learn about stereotypes by applying this natural kind view not to kittens but to stereotypes.

Consider gender stereotypes. What does a person mean in saying that women aren't good leaders? If the person means that there is a correlation between being a man and being a good leader, he is correct; that is, there *is* evidence that there is a correlation between being a leader and being a man. But, as it happens, this might well be entirely because men are more likely to be given positions of leadership than women are.

If you believe that general claims are nothing more than claims about correlations, then you can have no complaint about the belief that women aren't good leaders, because all it does is assert the existence of a correlation that happens to be true. But suppose you have a natural kind view of general statements. Then you believe that people who assert that women aren't good leaders are asserting more than a correlation between gender and leadership. Then you think that people are asserting that it is *natural* for men to lead and for women to follow, that there is something wrong with a woman who wants to be a leader, and so on. And if, instead, the fact is that the *only* reason that there is a correlation between leadership and gender is opportunity, then the claim that women aren't good leaders is false even though there is a correlation. In this circumstance, the claim is false because it asserts more than that there is a correlation, and that more that it asserts is false.

So perhaps what we object to about stereotypes *isn't* that they are inaccurate assertions of a correlation; the fact is that stereotypes seem just as objectionable when they capture correlations accurately as when they don't.

Perhaps what we object to about them is their implication that whatever correlations they involve have come about because it is natural, proper, even morally fitting for things to be as they describe. Perhaps we object to other people's stereotypes of us not because they are distorted pictures of how the world is—or not *just* because they are distorted pictures of how the world is—but because they are claims we do not agree with about how the world should be. Perhaps we object even to an "accurate" stereotype because we detect that the person who asserts it means to say more than that there is a correlation of some sort.*

Cognitive Approaches: An Assessment

Cognitive psychology has thus discovered a variety of limitations we have as information processors, and these limitations could lead to the development and maintenance of stereotypes, even if they are inaccurate. But there is at the moment little known about the accuracy of stereotypes. Still, stereotypes can be used in offensive ways, even if they are correct. Last, prejudice may have more to do with the assessment of responsibility for traits than with beliefs about those traits themselves.

WRAP-UP

I promised at the beginning of this chapter to address the question of whether prejudice is all one thing. Is it? From the point of view of realistic conflict theory and its offshoots, all prejudice is a matter of putting others down as a way of enhancing self-esteem; from this point of view, all prejudice shares a core. But the fact that all kinds of prejudice do tend to inflate one's self-esteem doesn't mean that the desire for enhanced self-esteem drives all prejudice—though it is surely a plausible hypothesis. From the point of view of the authoritarian personality, it makes perfect sense that all prejudice has a common core; the common core is, as I have mentioned, an intense attachment to the status quo and the authority that sustains it.

The cognitive perspective has an easy time explaining what all prejudice has in common—stereotypes. But the problem is that in the cognitive view, stereotypes are nothing more than general categories. And general categories are part of all thinking, thinking about minority groups, toasters, cars, tables, and chairs. So this approach collects, perhaps, too much in the same bucket. This is not to say that the cognitive approach to prejudice isn't important, it is just to express my own skepticism that it is the whole story.

*Some theorists have addressed this problem in a different way, arguing that insofar as the only reason for the correlation between gender and leadership is opportunity, then the correlation is spurious because it is accounted for by the third variable of opportunity (Schaller, 1992; Schaller & O'Brien, 1992). But, one imagines, all correlations can be accounted for by some third variable, but not all correlations are spurious. So it must be something about opportunity's accounting for the correlation that makes it spurious, and that, I believe, reduces to a natural kind view.

1. Three different approaches to understanding prejudice have been taken. The *cultural approach* sees the prejudiced individual as a product of a prejudiced culture. The *motivational approach* considers prejudice a consequence of hostile motives, hatred. The *cognitive approach* sees prejudice as an outgrowth of pernicious beliefs about people.

2. *Realistic conflict theory* argues that when groups are in competition for material resources, ingroups will become more cohesive and hostile to the outgroups. This pattern is known as ethnocentrism.

3. Recent research on *minimal groups* suggests that one can create bias toward the ingroup and against the outgroup simply by assigning people to different groups on the basis of something quite arbitrary.

4. Frustration-aggression theory argues that prejudice against some group is a consequence of displaced aggression toward someone (or something) else, someone who has caused frustration.

5. An *authoritarian personality* is someone who in addition to being prejudiced is conventional and hostile toward the unconventional, submissive to authority, hard-headed (as opposed to soft-hearted), superstitious and stereotyped in thinking, preoccupied with being tough, cynical, and overly concerned with other people's sexual misbehavior.

6. *Ambivalence theory* asserts that whites' attitudes toward blacks are made up of both sympathy toward blacks and hostility. There is some evidence that ambivalence can lead to an amplification of whatever response is dominant in some situation. Depending on the circumstance, it can lead to either hostile or helpful responses toward blacks.

7. The cognitive approach toward prejudice argues that prejudice is a result of people's having defective beliefs about the members of other gender, racial, or ethnic groups. These *stereotypes* are beliefs about the essential nature of groups of people, and are used to form impressions of individual members of those groups.

8. Research on stereotypes has focused on two questions: How do stereotypes develop? How are stereotypes maintained? There is substantial evidence that if people have a prior theory that two things are related, they will tend to see a relation between them (in a set of data) even when there is no real relation there. There is also research suggesting that if people encounter a member of a group who does *not* fit their stereotype of the group, they will decide that *for that very reason* the person isn't typical of the group, and they will not revise their impression of the group as a whole.

PART TWO

THE SELF

In this part, we turn our attention from the group to the individual: the self. In Chapter 5, we address the questions: What is it to know a person? How do we come to know someone? Here we consider the self—our own as well as others'—as an object of cognition.

Chapter 6 focuses on the public, external side of the self—how we present our selves to others, our public displays of character. In Chapter 7, we consider the self as something internal and private. Perhaps the most telling internal and private experiences we have are those involving emotion, so here we focus on the experience and expression of emotion.

Finally, cultures surely shape selves, and in Chapter 8, we will look at some specific ways that cultures affect us; we will ask, among other things, whether the very conception Western culture has of a self is specific to the West. As morality is surely an important part of the self, in this chapter we shall also look at moral codes, from a cross-cultural perspective. ■

CHAPTER 5

Person Perception and Social Cognition

obots are a staple of science fiction; consider the enormous popularity of R2D2 and C3PO from the movie *Star Wars.* It is odd they are so popular, since they are, after all, mechanical devices more like refrigerators than people. And no one writes fiction about refrigerators. Surely what makes robots more interesting than refrigerators is that something about robots' (but not refrigerators') behavior leads us to think of them with concepts we usually reserve for people (or other animals). We think of robots as having desires and fears, abilities and weaknesses—in short, personalities. The contrast between robots and refrigerators calls attention to the very special way we think about people as distinct from mechanical objects. It is on this special sort of thinking that we focus in this chapter.

We will investigate two related questions: (1) What do we know about someone when we know him well? and (2) How do we come to know a person? What are the psychological processes involved in coming to know a person?

We begin our discussion of person perception with a paper by Solomon Asch that appeared in 1946. Asch's concern, one that continues to motivate researchers to this day, was with how we form an overall impression of someone. Our knowledge of other people, whether acquired by observing their behavior directly or by hearing about them from others, comes to us more or less piecemeal, but our impressions cohere. If this is so, then we must organize and integrate the information we receive.

To study how impressions cohere, Asch invented a method of investigation, a simple and direct one. Asch read to his subjects a list of personality traits describing one person. He then asked the subjects to write a brief sketch of the person characterized by those traits. Such free-form character sketches are a very interesting kind of information, but they are hard to compile and compare, so Asch also gave each subject a list of eighteen pairs of traits, mostly opposites, and asked him to check off the item of the pair that was "most in accordance with the view he had formed." The free-form essay and especially the trait checklist gave Asch a standardized record of each subject's impression, of his transformation of the data.

CENTRAL AND PERIPHERAL TRAITS

One list of personality traits Asch used was: *intelligent, skillful, industrious, warm, determined, practical,* and *cautious.* Another list was the same with one exception: *cold* replaced *warm.* This small change had large effects. For example, 91 percent of subjects told that the person was *warm* inferred that he was also *generous,* but only 9 percent of the subjects told the person was *cold* inferred that he was *generous.* Substituting *cold* for *warm* affected more than *generous;* it made a difference to another eleven of the eighteen trait pairs. The perception of how warm a person was influenced the way subjects perceived him generally; because of this, Asch called *warm* and *cold* **central traits.**

Some traits were less central. In another study, Asch read this list: *intelligent, skillful, industrious, polite, determined, practical,* and *cautious.* Other subjects heard the same list except that *blunt* replaced *polite.* This substitution too affected subjects' overall impressions; 87 percent of subjects told that the person was *polite* also thought he was *good-natured,* while only 56 percent of those told he was blunt thought him to be *good-natured.* But although switching *polite* and *blunt* had an effect on impressions, it was a much weaker one than varying *warm* and *cold.* The switch affected fewer inferences, and the inferences it did influence were affected less. As Asch put it, whether someone is *polite* or *blunt* is a more peripheral fact about him than whether he is *warm* or *cold.*

DRAWING INFERENCES ABOUT TRAITS

The results of these studies show that we draw inferences about aspects of people's personalities that we do not know directly, that we will *infer* the presence of some traits from our knowledge of others; indeed, some traits, like *warm,* lead to very broad inferences. In other words, our knowledge of people is **structured** by our expectations that various traits go together. These expectations can be thought of as a kind of theory of personality that each of

▲ *Hats can shape impressions too! What sort of impression do you form of him?*

us has and uses in our everyday encounters. Of course, we do not know this theory explicitly. If I ask you to just state what traits go together, you no doubt can't tell me. But the fact that if I give you one trait you will infer another is reason to believe that you have an ***implicit personality theory,*** a theory of how personalities hang together. The Asch studies of impression formation, then, introduce us to the notion that our thinking about people is in terms of a structure, consisting of relations among concepts.

But where do our implicit theories of personality come from? Some theorists believe that we infer that someone is generous if he is warm because *generous* and *warm* are similar in meaning. These theorists argue that our implicit theories of personality are really an illusion foisted upon us by our language (D'Andrade, 1965; Shweder, 1975, 1977, 1980; Shweder & D'Andrade, 1979). Other psychologists propose that the reason people think certain traits go with certain other traits is because those traits *do go* together—there is no illusion about it (Jackson, Chau, & Stricker, 1979). And finally, other theorists argue that language *is* involved in the structure of implicit personality theory, but this does not mean that language is foisting an illusion upon us (Roner & Revelle, 1984; Borkenau, 1986, 1990; Borkenau & Ostendorf, 1987; Weiss & Mendelsohn, 1986; Riemann & Angleitner, 1993). All sides of this debate agree on one thing, the fundamental fact that Asch stressed: our impressions of people *are* organized; there is a structure that underlies our impressions of people.

▲ *Anita Hill and Barbra Streisand receiving awards from the American Civil Liberties Union. Impressions of these women have changed substantially over the years.*

Traits and Behavior

Asch's studies treat traits as the building blocks of our understanding of people. But what are traits, and how do they relate to behavior, at least in the eyes of the perceiver? After all, we don't always know a person's traits the way Asch's subjects did—secondhand; sometimes, at least, we infer them directly from the person's behavior. What rules govern our inferences from the behavior we see? How accurate are we in drawing these inferences?

The inspiration for Asch's work on person perception was Gestalt psychology's insistence that the nature of a whole stimulus is different from the sum of its parts. Fritz Heider's book *The Psychology of Interpersonal Relations* (1958) was also a seminal contribution to social psychology, and it too was written from a Gestaltist perspective. The idea Heider started from is that of object constancy in visual perception. Object constancy has to do with the fact that as we move about in the world, the image that an object casts on our retina (the proximal stimulus) constantly changes. Yet we do not see a changing object (distal stimulus); rather, we see the enduring object through the changing stimulation. Heider argued that our perception of people's personalities was much like this.

The particular behaviors that someone emits constantly change, yet we see an enduring personality behind that changing behavior. We see, as it were, the properties of the person that give rise to the changing behaviors. Traits are, for Heider, the properties that give rise to behavior; they are the fixed ***dispositions*** of a person that we know when we know her well.

We always face a problem in deciding on someone's personality from her behavior. The problem is that behavior never occurs in a vacuum; it is always carried out in some specific situation. So to read a person's character from

Central traits
- lead to inferences about many other traits;
- have strong correlations with many other traits;
- are semantically similar to many other traits.

Peripheral traits
- lead to few inferences about other traits;
- have weak correlations with other traits;
- are semantically different from other traits.

FIGURE 5.1

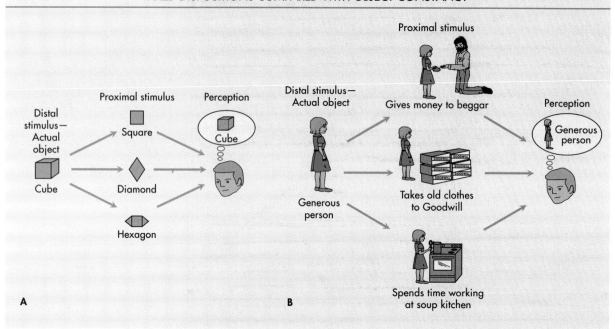

FIXED DISPOSITIONS COMPARED WITH OBJECT CONSTANCY

▲ *Just as we infer the properties of objects from the pattern of light and shadow they cast upon the retina, so too do we form an impression of a person's underlying character from her behavior. (Based on Heider, 1958)*

her behavior, we must interpret that behavior in light of the situation. Some situations, according to Heider, reveal personality; others conceal it. If you watch students taking an exam, you will see that they all look pretty much alike; this situation obscures personality. An intimate dinner is more likely to be revealing. The observer of someone's behavior is always faced, then, with the problem of deciding how the behavior is related to the person's character, and to do this, he must take into account the features of the situation that contributed to the behavior (see Figure 5.1).

ATTRIBUTION THEORY

Two key papers that appeared in the 1960s marked the first stage in the development of Heider's ideas. Both attempted to spell out in more detail how we see through behavior and situations to stable personality. Both presented what have been called ***attribution theories.*** (An ***attribution*** is a belief about the cause of a behavior.) The first paper was by Ned Jones and Keith Davis (1965), who were concerned primarily with inferences about a person's dispositions from her *intentional actions,* the things she does on purpose. They were interested in how observers work backward from overt behavior (and its effects) to the intention of the person acting (called the "actor") and then to the stable dispositions of the person that gave rise to the intention.

Jones and Davis's Correspondent Inference Theory

If each action had a single effect, then we could simply assume that a person's intention in acting was the single effect the action brought about. But typically, actions have many effects. Jones and Davis's article presented a theory, **correspondent inference theory,** that attempted to explain how we reason from actions and effects to intentions and dispositions, given that we are faced with actions that have multiple effects. Consider an example of an action, someone's accepting a particular job. The question we want to answer is: What does her taking it tell us about her, her intentions, and her stable dispositions?

Imagine that Beth accepts a job in San Francisco. Imagine further that the job is as a research immunologist at a prestigious drug company, the job pays very well, Beth's longtime friend, Bob, lives in San Francisco, and Beth just loves the climate and culture of the city. Now suppose you are Bob, and you want to know why Beth took the job; more specifically, you want to know what her taking the job implies with regard to her intentions and stable dispositions toward you. Your problem is difficult; Beth had plenty of reasons to take the job. Thus, your confidence that she took it for any single reason, especially the reason that she wanted to be near you, should be very low.

But suppose instead that you live in Philadelphia. And you know Beth hates Philadelphia. And suppose she took a low-paying job with a company with no prestige in the heart of downtown Philadelphia. Now your confidence that she intended to be near you and that she really does care about you (has stable dispositions toward you) should be much greater. More generally, your confidence in your inferences from someone's behavior to her intentions and dispositions should vary as a function of the number of reasons she had for the behavior. This is one link between behaviors and inferences about intentions (see Figure 5.2).

Jones and Davis were also interested in another aspect of our inferences

▼ *Acts with many positive effects lead to uncertain attributions about the actor's motive; acts with a single positive outcome lead to clearer attributions.*

FIGURE 5.2

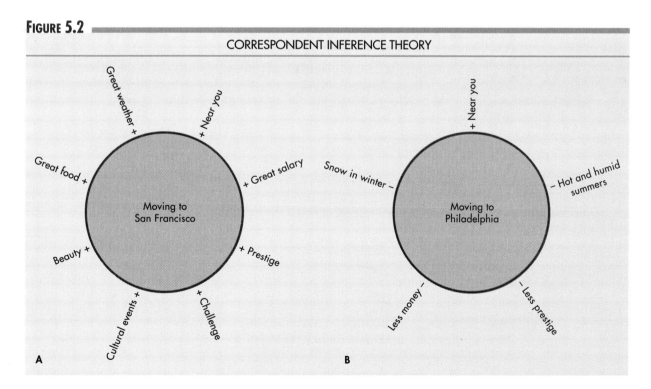

CORRESPONDENT INFERENCE THEORY

Great weather +
+ Near you
Great food +
+ Great salary
Moving to San Francisco
Beauty +
+ Prestige
Cultural events +
+ Challenge

A

Snow in winter −
+ Near you
− Hot and humid summers
Moving to Philadelphia
Less money −
− Less prestige

B

from behavior to dispositions. Suppose you observe Tom giving money to someone on the street, someone shabbily dressed. You might infer that Tom is a generous person. But now suppose on closer examination you notice an element of the scene that had escaped your attention: the shabbily dressed person has a gun. Now your inference to generosity is, presumably, checked. Jones and Davis argue that the reason your inference is checked is that you thought that only some people—generous people—would give this fellow money, but now you know that *anyone* would. Because you know anyone would give him money, you wouldn't make a personalized, *internal* attribution to Tom's particular dispositions. Thus, Jones and Davis were concerned with two issues: (1) How do we decide what someone intended when they acted? and (2) When do we see a person as having especially strong dispositions?

RESEARCH ON JONES AND DAVIS'S THEORY

In one study designed to test the Jones and Davis theory, subjects were told that they were going to hear a tape of a job applicant trying to convince a psychologist of his suitability for a job as either a sailor on a submarine or an astronaut. The applicant was to tell the truth—unless it happened that a lie would be more persuasive! The subjects were told that submariners and astronauts need very different personalities. Submariners spend lots of time together with other people, with no room for privacy. They need outgoing personalities. Astronauts, on the other hand, spend lots of time alone; they need just the reverse personality.

Half the subjects heard the applicant describe himself as very outgoing; half heard him describe himself as a loner. The subjects were asked to say what they thought the applicant was really like (see Figure 5.3), and also say how confident they were in their ratings. Let us consider the submariner applicant. The subjects who heard him describe himself as an extravert didn't take the claim all that seriously. They rated him as moderate on the gregariousness dimension, and they were not very confident in their ratings. Those who heard him say he was a loner, on the other hand, believed him, and were quite confident. Just the reverse happened in the astronaut condition (Jones, Davis, & Gergen, 1961).

Faced with two reasons for the submariner applicant to say he was outgoing—because it was true and because saying it would get him a job—subjects placed little credence in his self-description. But the submariner applicant had only one reason to say he was a loner—it was true—hence, subjects placed great faith in this claim. So this experiment provided support for Jones and Davis's attribution theory.

Kelley's Covariation Theory

Harold Kelley introduced a metaphor of his own to capture the way people perceive behavior (Kelley, 1967, 1971a, 1971b). Kelley argued that in attempting to understand each other, we reason as scientists do. More specifically, like scientists we are concerned with causes, the causes of behavior. And he went on to suggest that we use the methods scientists use to discover these causes.

Imagine we notice Claire laughing at a comedian. According to Kelley, in

FIGURE 5.3

JONES AND DAVIS'S ATTRIBUTION THEORY

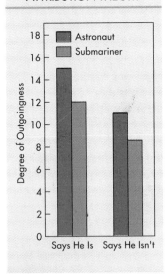

▲ Subjects' ratings of the outgoingness of a job candidate who said he was outgoing and a job candidate who said he was not outgoing. Being outgoing is desirable for a submariner; subjects believed him when he said he wasn't outgoing, but they were skeptical when he said he was outgoing. Outgoingness is undesirable in an astronaut, so the reverse was true. (Data from Jones, Davis, & Gergen, 1961)

trying to understand this behavior and Claire's nature, the first question that occurs to us as lay scientists is: Where is the cause of her behavior? Is the cause of her laughing in her or in the comedian? Kelley argued that we answer this question by relying on a notion fundamental to science: causes **covary** (vary) with effects. The discovery of covariations is an essentially statistical matter. To determine whether *A* causes *B*, we have to compare the frequency with which *B* occurs in the presence of *A* with the frequency with which it occurs in *A*'s absence. Thus, in Claire's case, once we know what her laughing covaries with, we know what caused it. But how do we do this?

Suppose we know that Claire laughs only at this comedian; nothing else makes her laugh. Then we know that her laughing covaries with the comedian, and we should locate the cause of her laughter in the comedian—it is something about him that causes the laughter. Now suppose we also know that Claire laughs whenever the comedian performs; this would lend further confidence that it is the comedian who made her laugh—after all, if she only laughed this once, perhaps it was her mood. A third question is also relevant: How do other people react to the comedian? If everyone else also laughs, this suggests that the comedian really is funny. If no one laughs, this would suggest that he isn't, and that the laughter has more to do with Claire's unique personality than with the comedian's talent (see Figure 5.4).

Our example, then, focuses on three kinds of information people might use to locate the causes of behavior: (1) how close to unique the stimulus is in producing the effect—this is referred to as **distinctiveness information;**

FIGURE 5.4

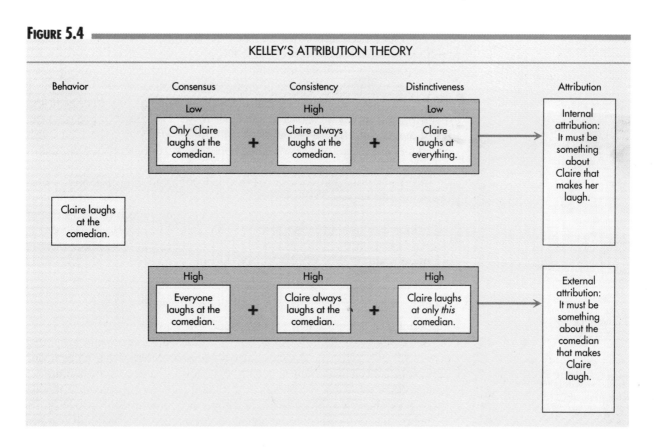

ATTRIBUTION THEORY   **153**

(2) how reliable the stimulus is in producing the reaction from the person—this is called **consistency information;** and (3) whether the stimulus produces the same effect in others—**consensus information.**

Kelley argues that we will infer that behavior is externally caused—produced by the features of the stimulus to which the person is reacting—to the degree that we know that the behavior is high in distinctiveness, high in consistency, and high in consensus. To the degree, on the other hand, that the behavior is low in distinctiveness (Claire laughs at everything) and low in consensus (no one else laughs at this comedian), we will infer that the behavior is internally caused—something about Claire causes her to laugh at the comedian.

The principle of covariation—that causes covary with effects—is the heart of Kelley's theory of how we determine the causes of behavior. But Kelley recognized that we aren't always in a position to apply this principle. Often, for example, we want to determine the cause of a behavior even though we have only a single instance to observe. What do we do then?

CAUSAL SCHEMATA

Kelley suggests that when we have only a single occasion to go by, we must rely on our general knowledge of the kind of situation we are observing to help us locate causes. There are two specific causal models Kelley focused on: a model of **multiple necessary causes** and a model of **multiple sufficient causes.** We use a multiple necessary causal schema when we believe that some effect requires at least two different causes. For example, we believe that for a gun to go off, there must be at least two causes present: the trigger must be pulled, and there must be a bullet in the chamber. These two causes are multiple necessary because both must be present for the effect to occur.

On the other hand, we sometimes believe that causes are multiple sufficient, that the effect will, occur if either of two causes is present. We may believe, for example, that a person will get a particular job if either of the following is true: (1) he is well qualified for it, or (2) a close relative is on the board of directors. These causal schemata, Kelley claims, can assist us with our causal reasoning when we can't apply the sure method of covariation analysis.

Kelley suggests that we use the multiple sufficient causal model to **discount** possible causes. Thus, if we believe that either of two causes is sufficient to cause the behavior, then our inference back from the behavior to *either* of the causes will be weak. If we believe that people give money either because there is a gun on them or because they are generous, and we know there is a gun on them, then we won't believe they are generous.

Jones and Davis's correspondent inference theory
- focuses on intentional behavior;
- attempts to explain how we infer dispositions of the actor from intentional behavior.

Kelley's attribution theory
- focuses on unintended, spontaneous reactions;
- attempts to explain how we decide whether such behaviors are internally or externally caused.

A Comparison of Jones and Davis's Model with Kelley's Model

Jones and Davis and Kelley present models of how ordinary people make inferences about the causes of behavior. The Jones and Davis model is focused on *intentional behavior;* for the most part, it addresses inferences from behavior back to intentions and then dispositions. Kelley's model is focused more on *reactions* (like laughing), behaviors that we don't so much do as have happen to us. Still, there is much the models have in common. Both consider the common-sense interpreter of behavior as attempting, in a rational way, to infer back from what she sees to the unseen dispositions of the actor. And both place great emphasis on discounting, on weakened faith in one cause if others are present. Each in its own way attempts to follow through on the program Fritz Heider launched.

It may not be very surprising to learn that subjects participating in experiments follow the Jones and Davis or Kelley model; indeed, it may seem that they are just being rational. In fact, it might be argued that the Kelley and Jones and Davis models aren't models of what subjects *do* at all, but rather are models of how subjects *ought to* use information. Now these are different matters. **Normative models** tell us what people *should* do. They must be justified by showing how failing to follow them leads to something undesirable. **Descriptive models** tell us how people in fact behave; they are verified by evidence that people's behavior accords with them.

By the late 1960s and early 1970s, situations were discovered in which subjects deviated from the attribution theories we have learned. And the reactions of researchers were quite clear; they saw the subjects as making errors and suffering from biases and illusions. The *models* weren't described as wrong; the *subjects* were described as wrong. There is by now a fair consensus in the field that the models described above are normative models that tell us how people should think about the causes of behavior (as we shall see, however, not everyone agrees that they are the right normative models). As such, they perform an important function: they direct our attention to places where people deviate from what they should do.

The third generation of research in the Heiderian tradition is concerned with when and where people deviate from rational standards in their understanding of other people—why they commit attributional errors. These errors are controversial. There are critics who argue that no errors have in fact been documented. I have gathered these criticisms together in the section following this one, "Attributional Critics." This order reveals best what attribution *theory* is. It isn't, when all is said and done, a theory; rather, it is a perspective and a vocabulary, a way of thinking and talking about people's thinking about other people. And the critics too have a perspective and vocabulary. It is best to see each perspective as a whole, rather than piecemeal.

Descriptive models
• are about how people think or act;

• are shown to be wrong if people do not act as the model says they do.

Normative models
• are about how people *should* think or act;

• are *not* shown to be wrong if people do not act as the model says they should;

• posit that if people do not act as the model says they should, then people are making an error.

Actor-Observer Differences

In 1971, Ned Jones and Richard Nisbett were the first to call attention to a way in which people's thinking deviates from a normative model. Their argument focused on what they claimed were pervasive differences between the way we think about our own actions and the way we think about other people's actions. If there *are* such differences, then we deviate from a normative model in a serious way, for the first requirement of normative, objective action or thought is that it be evenhanded, that it apply in the same way to everyone.

Jones and Nisbett's study begins with an imaginary discussion between a faculty adviser and her graduate student advisee about why the student has made so little progress in his research. The student offers lots of reasons. He claims the research hasn't been done because hundreds of subjects need to be recruited, piles of questionnaires must be reproduced, the right statistical package has to be found, and besides, this is a bad year for doing research because his girlfriend just broke up with him, and so on. In other words, the student offers all sorts of external causes of his lack of progress. But running through the adviser's mind is a different account of why the research hasn't been done—this student just isn't together and he never will be. This imaginary interaction, then, involves an actor, the student, attributing his behavior (or its lack) to external causes and an observer, the adviser, attributing the same behavior to an internal cause, "untogetherness."

Jones and Nisbett suggested that it is ever thus between actors and observers. They proposed that there is a general tendency for people to see their own behavior as externally caused but to see other people's behavior as internally caused. This asymmetry in thinking has been called the **actor-observer difference** in attribution.

In addition to calling attention to this difference, Jones and Nisbett offered some possible reasons for its prevalence. First, as actors, we are primarily attentive to properties of our environment, rather than to our own qualities. It is the environment, after all, that poses challenges and opportunities for us. Because environmental features attract our attention, they figure prominently in our explanations.

Jones and Nisbett suggested a second source of the actor-observer difference, which is that we know much more about ourselves than other people do. Thus, we may believe that what we did in a particular situation was a consequence of specific details of that situation. But other people, who don't know us as well as we know ourselves, may assume that we did what we did because of broad dispositions of our character rather than because of the concrete details.

EXPERIMENTAL RESULTS

In one study conducted as part of research in support of Jones and Nisbett's argument, male college students were asked to write essays—one about why they liked the woman they dated most frequently, and one about why they chose their particular major. Then they wrote two more essays, this time about their best friend's favorite date and major. The investigators coded the essays for kinds of attributions (see Figure 5.5). They found that the subjects made more **situational attributions,** attributions to the external situation, when writing about themselves than when writing about their best friend. They said, for example, that they dated that woman because she was warm, and they chose that major because it was interesting. But when writing about their best friend, they invoked dispositions as often as they invoked situations—he dates her because he likes warm women; he majors in chemistry because *he finds it* interesting. Thus, the explanations they gave for their own behavior differed *in form* from the explanations they gave for their friend's behavior.

In another study, subjects were given twenty trait pairs, *quiet-talkative,* for example. They were told to rate themselves, their best friend, their father, an admired acquaintance, and newscaster Walter Cronkite on these trait pairs. The subjects' options were to rate the person on either one or the other pole

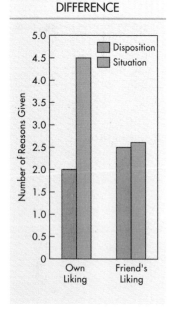

FIGURE 5.5

THE ACTOR-OBSERVER DIFFERENCE

▲ *When asked why they liked their girlfriend, subjects answered predominantly with facts about their girlfriend (situational attribution). When asked why their best friend liked his girlfriend, subjects answered with an equal mix of facts about their friend and facts about their friend's girlfriend (dispositional and situational attributions). (Data from Nisbett, Caputo, Legant, & Marecek, 1973)* (for example, *quiet* or *talkative*) or to say "depends on the situation." Subjects used the "depends on the situation" option more in reference to themselves than to the other people. Nisbett interpreted this result to mean that people see others as being highly consistent in their behavior but realize that they themselves are variable, sensitive to the situation.

In a third study, the experimenter told the subjects that they were there to take part in a study of decision making. To do so, they were to watch carefully as another subject made a decision. There were thus two kinds of subjects: actors who made decisions and observers who watched the actors decide. What the actors had to decide was whether they would volunteer to escort some people around campus on the weekend. The people to be escorted were the spouses of contributors to an institute devoted to the learning difficulties of disadvantaged children. So the actors were given a socially worthy motive to volunteer, and the observes knew it.

The actors were also offered a somewhat less lofty reason—money. Some were offered $.50 per hour for being escorts, others were offered $1.50. Thus, the actors had a decision to make, whether to volunteer, and two reasons to say yes—to help the institute for disadvantaged children and to earn some money. The observers knew of both reasons. Some actors volunteered, some didn't (although each actor knew only what she did, and each observer knew only what the actor he was watching did). Actors and observers were then asked a variety of questions about the decision the actor made, and they were also asked to make a prediction: Would the actor volunteer to canvass for a charity, the United Way?

Observers' predictions of whether the actor would volunteer for the United Way were strongly influenced by whether she had volunteered to be an escort. If the actor volunteered to do one, the observer predicted she would do the other. In other words, the observers inferred the presence of a broad disposition to volunteer for the actors who volunteered, and inferred its absence for the actors who refused. But, in fact, the actors' willingness to volunteer was controlled by something else entirely: how much money they were offered. Most offered $.50 per hour didn't volunteer to escort the visitors; most offered $1.50 per hour did. Since canvassing for the United Way was to be unpaid, it is small wonder that the actors' willingness to volunteer for that was unrelated to whether they volunteered to escort for pay. Here we have a case of observers inferring a broad disposition, while actors actually responded to concrete details of the situation, just the kind of asymmetry Jones and Nisbett described (see Figure 5.6; Nisbett, Caputo, Legant, & Marecek, 1973).

In these three studies, we see examples of people offering or displaying external, environmental reasons for their behavior, while observers offer internal, dispositional reasons for the same behavior. The studies suggest that actors are biased to see their own behavior as caused by the environment, while observers are biased to see it as caused by broad dispositions. The initial evidence, then, was quite supportive of the notion of a systematic difference between actors and observers in the explanation of behavior. How has the claim fared subsequently?

The evidence is really quite mixed. Some studies have continued to find that people see themselves as more variable in their behavior than they believe other people are (Baxter & Goldberg, 1987; Prager & Cutler, 1990).

FIGURE 5.6

INFERRING BROAD DISPOSITIONS

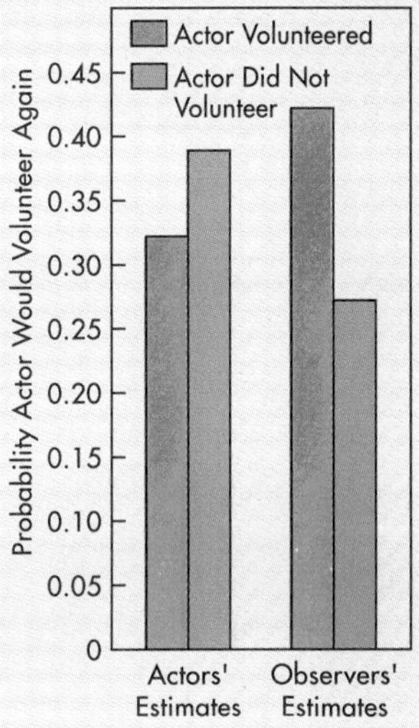

▲ *Actors' and observers' estimates of the probability that an actor would volunteer for a similar task given that she did (or did not) volunteer for the first task. Observers assumed that actors would do what they did the first time. The actors had less strong beliefs, and their predictions were opposite to those of the observers. (Data from Nisbett, Caputo, Legant, & Marecek, 1973)*

Other research has not been as supportive. For example, in one study, investigators asked members of a fraternity to rate themselves and their brothers on a variety of trait scales. The subjects used more trait ratings for themselves than for others—just the reverse of the predicted pattern (Monson, Tanke, & Lund, 1980).

In another study, subjects made attributions to themselves and their spouses. Subjects were less willing to ascribe traits to themselves than to their spouses, again in line with Jones and Nisbett's proposal. But there were several troublesome notes. First, some of the subjects in the study were given a different trait list from the list usually used in such studies; this one was made up of either clearly desirable or clearly undesirable traits. Now the actor-observer difference disappeared; in its place appeared a strong tendency to attribute positive traits to everybody and negative traits to no one. Perhaps, then, there isn't a general bias toward assigning traits to others; perhaps the bias is confined to rather neutral traits.

There was another result in this study. In addition to rating themselves and their spouses, the subjects were asked to assign responsibility to either the situation or the person. Now in the Jones and Nisbett view, behavior is caused either by the situation or by the person. Therefore, we would expect attributions to the situation to be negatively correlated with attributions to the person; if you see the situation as the cause, you shouldn't see the person as responsible, and vice versa. But this isn't how the ratings turned out. There was only a small negative correlation between them ($-.14$). Taken together, these results suggest that there may be attributional differences between self and other, but they call into question what an attribution is (Taylor & Koivumaki, 1976). We will return to these questions when we consider some criticisms of the attributional position.

Jones and Nisbett claimed that there was a pervasive tendency for actors to attribute their behavior to the situation and for observers to attribute it to the actor's dispositions. Is there? Well, it isn't very profitable to debate how widespread something must be to be pervasive. Suffice it to say that there isn't an overwhelming tendency.

SALIENCE

Jones and Nisbett offered another reason for the apparent asymmetry between actor and observer: visual **salience** (the aspects that stand out). After all, it is possible that, for some reason or other, although the actor-observer difference itself is not such a pervasive tendency, the tendency to attribute to causes that are salient, that stand out, is. Indeed, this seems to be exactly so.

Michael Storms, for example, asked subjects to come to a laboratory for a brief "get acquainted" conversation. Two subjects took part in each conversation; an additional two subjects observed. The conversation was also videotaped from two different angles. One camera saw the conversation from a participant (actor's) point of view; the other camera looked at the scene from an observer's point of view. After the conversation, subjects were treated in one of three ways. Some saw a videotape of the conversation made from their own point of view. Other subjects saw a videotape made from the *opposite* point of view—actors saw videotapes from observers' points of view, and vice versa. Control subjects saw no videotapes.

Subjects then filled out a questionnaire that asked them to say to what

FIGURE 5.7

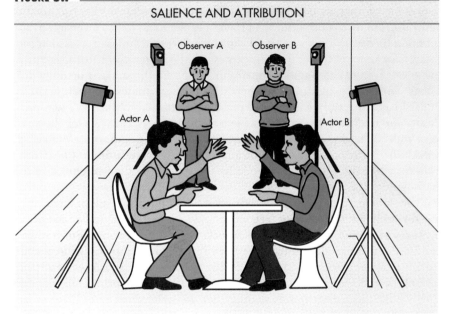

SALIENCE AND ATTRIBUTION

Observer A   Observer B

Actor A   Actor B

◄ *The actor-observer effect was examined by placing cameras behind actors and observers and making videotapes of the actors' conversation from these different vantage points. Those who later watched the videotape made from one of the actor's perspectives showed the actor-observer effect, making situational attributions. Those who watched the videotape made from one of the observer's perspectives made dispositional attributions. (Adapted from Gleitman, 1991, p. 475; data from Storms, 1973)*

degree the actors' behavior was caused by their personalities and to what degree it was caused by the situation. The subjects were also asked how nervous, friendly, talkative, and dominant the actors had been in the conversation. Those subjects who saw no videotape or who saw a videotape made from their own perspective showed the actor-observer effect; actors made greater situational attributions than did observers, and observers made more dispositional attributions than did actors. But subjects who saw the conversation from a new perspective on videotape expressed a new attributional pattern (see Figure 5.7). They made attributions consistent with the perspective *from which the videotape was recorded.* Thus, the subjects' attributions reflected the perspective from which they had most recently seen the conversation (Storms, 1973).

CLASSIC FINDINGS IN SOCIAL PSYCHOLOGY: THE FUNDAMENTAL ATTRIBUTIONAL ERROR

The bias in attributions that has received the greatest amount of attention from researchers was uncovered in a study by Ned Jones, who gave subjects at Duke University some essays to read and asked them to infer the attitude of the essay writer (Jones & Harris, 1967). Half the subjects read a pro-Castro essay; half read an anti-Castro essay. For half the subjects, this was the whole study; all they had to do was characterize the attitude expressed in the essay and attribute it to the writer.

The task was substantially more difficult for the other half. They were told that the essay was part of an exam in a political science course in which the students had been told to write a pro- or anti-Castro essay. These subjects

ATTRIBUTIONAL ERRORS AND BIASES   **159**

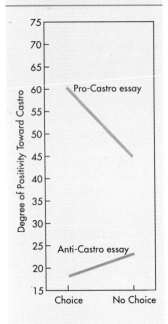

FIGURE 5.8

THE FUNDAMENTAL ATTRIBUTIONAL ERROR

▲ *Subjects' estimates of the essay writer's true attitude toward Castro, as indicated by degree of positivity toward Castro. The subjects reading the pro-Castro essay in the no-choice condition discounted the essay a bit, but not fully. (Data from Jones & Harris, 1967)*

knew the essay writers might have had two reasons for espousing the view they did: because they believed it or because of the professor's instruction (or both). According to both Jones and Davis's version and Kelley's version of attribution theory, the subjects should "discount" the attitudes expressed in the essay; they shouldn't treat them as expressing the writer's real attitudes, since the essays were written under constraint. What did the subjects actually do?

As we should expect, the subjects who thought the essays were written under free choice simply attributed pro-Castro attitudes if the essay was pro-Castro and anti-Castro attitudes if the essay was anti-Castro. As for the subjects who believed the essays were written under constraint, those who read anti-Castro essays assigned the authors very anti-Castro attitudes, nearly as anti-Castro as the attributions made by the readers of the free-choice essay (see Figure 5.8).

The significance of this result, however, is ambiguous. It might mean that the subjects took the essay at face value and assigned to the writer the same attitudes they read. If so, this result reflects a failure to discount. But it might be that the subjects discounted what they read entirely; they may have completely ignored the essay in inferring the writer's attitude. After all, what attitude would they infer if they ignored the essay? A neutral one? No. For they would still have grounds to infer that the writer was anti-Castro. Most of the students at Duke at this time were anti-Castro, and the subjects surely knew it. If the subjects discounted the essay's position, then, they should be thrown back on what they took to be the typical attitude on campus—what we shall call the **base-rate attitude**—in inferring the writer's view. Thus, whether subjects in this condition paid any attention to the essay or not, they would reach the same conclusion—that the writer had anti-Castro attitudes.

The key condition in which to tell whether subjects discounted, then, was the condition in which the subjects knew that the writer wrote a pro-Castro essay under constraint. Here, if the subjects took the behavior at face value, they would assign a pro-Castro attitude; if they ignored the essay, they should attribute negative attitudes. What the subjects in fact did was assign the writer a *somewhat* positive attitude toward Castro, more positive than most students', but less positive than the essay itself.

Ned Jones argued that these results show that subjects made an error. He suggested that in inferring pro-Castro attitudes in this key condition, the subjects were insufficiently sensitive to the situational constraints—being instructed to write a pro-Castro essay—that would have affected the writer. Had the subjects been sufficiently aware of these constraints, they would have ignored the essays and assigned the anti-Castro attitudes that characterized the campus. Lee Ross has dubbed this mistake the **fundamental attributional error,** which we commit when we take behavior closer to its face value than we should (Ross, 1977; Jones, 1979). This error is consistent with the actor-observer difference discussed above. Observers—the essay readers—saw the behavior as internally caused even though the information they were given about how it was written should have led them to see it as externally caused.

In subsequent research, subjects were given an essay about Castro to read that had supposedly been written under constraint. Then, nine months later, they were given another essay supposedly written by the same person, also under constraint, endorsing the opposite position. The question was, what inference would subjects make from this pattern? One might expect that they would finally catch on and decide that the writer was just a wimp who writes whatever he is told to write. But this isn't what they inferred at all. Rather, they concluded that the writer really did hold the (opposite) attitudes expressed in the two essays. Therefore the subjects concluded the only thing they could conclude—that the writer sincerely changed his views about Castro between the first essay and the second (Allison, Mackie, Muller, & Worth, 1993).

INVESTIGATING THE FUNDAMENTAL ATTRIBUTIONAL ERROR

Lee Ross and his colleagues randomly assigned Stanford undergraduates either to make up general knowledge questions or to answer questions other people made up (Ross, Amabile, & Steinmetz, 1977). The subjects making up the questions were told to make them hard but not impossible. As might be expected, the questioners did a good job of stumping those who had to answer. The contestants got a mere four out of ten right; the students who made up the questions also answered them, and, of course, got all ten right. A sample question was: What do the initials W and H stand for in W. H. Auden?

Both groups of subjects were then asked to rate themselves and each other on their general knowledge. Now before we see the results, we should consider this situation more closely. What did the subjects know that would help them with their ratings?

The deck was loaded, of course, in favor of the students who made up the questions. They appeared quite knowledgeable because they knew the answers to some very hard questions. If they had done as well with a *random selection* of hard questions, they would have been very knowledgeable indeed. But, of course, they didn't answer a random set. They answered the least random set you can imagine; they answered just those questions they knew the answers to. The contestants, on the other hand, had the deck loaded *against* them; they were asked to answer questions that the people who made them up thought they couldn't answer. Since all these facts were perfectly obvious to the people asking and the people answering the questions, we might expect both groups to discount the answers, as in the Jones and Harris study, and rate themselves and each other as about as intelligent as the average Stanford student. But they didn't.

The students asking the questions showed a *slight* tendency to see themselves as more knowledgeable than the people answering. There was a much stronger tendency for the people answering to see themselves as significantly less knowledgeable than the average Stanford student, and to rate those who asked the questions as more knowledgeable. Here again we seem to have a failure to discount. The contestants in particular seemed to miss the way the deck was stacked against them and for the questioners. Why the students asking the questions *didn't* show much of a bias is an interesting question. Perhaps they were more aware of the situation, or perhaps they were being modest.

The investigators also made a videotape of a typical session and showed the tape to observers who were asked to rate both parties. These raters didn't see the students having to answer the questions as particularly ignorant, but they did rate the questioners as particularly knowledgeable. Here again we see observers taking behavior more at face value than perhaps they should,

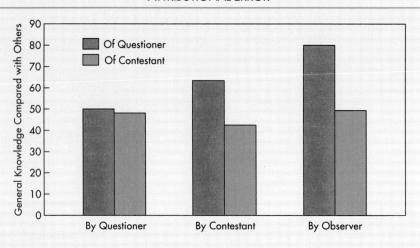

FIGURE 5.9

RATINGS OF GENERAL KNOWLEDGE AND THE FUNDAMENTAL ATTRIBUTIONAL ERROR

▶ Questioners', contestants', and observers' ratings of the questioners' and contestants' general knowledge relative to other students. (Data from Ross, Amabile, & Steinmetz, 1977)

▪▪▪▪▪▪▪▪▪▪▪▪

Subjects are influenced by an essay in inferring the writer's attitudes *unless*

- the writer mentions the constraints she faces in the essay itself; or

- the writer writes an exceptionally weak essay; or

- the writer displays her true attitudes nonverbally; or

- the subjects suspect the writer has an ulterior motive for writing what she wrote.

▪▪▪▪▪▪▪▪▪▪▪▪

another example of the fundamental attributional error (see Figure 5.9).

In the same vein, Arthur Miller gave some subjects, but not others, the results of Stanley Milgram's studies of obedience to malevolent authority (discussed in Chapter 2). In those studies, you will recall, subjects were ordered to shock a protesting victim to 450 volts, and most did. Miller asked his subjects to predict what a specific person would do in this experiment. Subjects who were told the results of the Milgram study did predict that a higher level of shock would be administered than did subjects who were not told of the results, although the difference was small. Thus, subjects were affected by the information about the degree to which Milgram's subjects were constrained, although not to the degree they should have been.

Miller also asked subjects to describe the traits of a person who gave a substantial shock (versus someone who stopped early in the sequence). He found that, as we might expect, subjects were much more negative about the people who gave a strong shock than they were about those who didn't. But he also found that this tendency was not influenced by subjects' knowledge of the results of the Milgram experiment. Thus, subjects' *predictions* were affected by their knowledge of the results, but their *trait inferences* weren't. According to both Kelley's and Jones and Davis's accounts of attribution theory, trait inferences *should* have been affected, so this experiment too represents a failure to use consensus information (Miller, Gillen, Schenker, & Radlove, 1974).

LIMITS OF THE FUNDAMENTAL ATTRIBUTIONAL ERROR

The fundamental attributional error has proven remarkably robust. Several studies have shown that when subjects read essays and are asked to assess the author's attitudes, they are significantly influenced by the direction of the essay even when they know the essay was written under constraint. And this effect happens even when they write an essay against their own attitudes before they judge other subjects' essays and attitudes (Miller, Jones, & Kimbell,

1981). The effect also occurs when the subject knows that the essay writer was given arguments to use by the experimenter (Snyder & Jones, 1974).

But there are cases where the fundamental attributional error is weaker. And these are informative. For example, the essay writer can cause the effect to lessen if *in the essay itself* she mentions that she is writing without free choice (Miller, Baer, & Schonberg, 1979). Or she can write an especially weak essay (Miller, Ashton, & Mishal, 1990). In one study, subjects saw a videotape of someone who had been assigned to read about arguments for or against the right to abortion. The character on the videotape either smiled or grimaced when assigned the essay to read. Subjects used these facial expressions to infer his true beliefs—a smile led them to believe the position he was assigned was his own, a grimace that it wasn't (Fleming & Darley, 1989). So we can signal the fact that we don't really believe what we are saying in more subtle ways than by saying so outright.

Finally, one study probed the fundamental attributional error in something closer to its natural, everyday guise. In this study, subjects read an essay about a controversial topic supposedly written by a student, Rob Taylor, as part of a summer internship program. Some students learned that Rob had been *assigned* to write an essay on a particular side of the issue; some were told Rob was assigned the pro position, others that he was assigned the con. Other students read that Rob had been given a *choice* of which side of the issue to take, but that before writing his essay, Rob had learned that the professor supervising his summer internship (and who would be evaluating him later) had very strong views on the topic. As it happens, Rob's essay corresponded to his supervisor's position. Thus, some subjects read essays by someone who had been instructed to write in a certain direction; others read essays by someone who had an *ulterior motive*—gaining favor with his supervisor—for writing in that direction. What attitude would the subjects attribute to Rob in the two conditions?

Subjects who read that Rob had been assigned a position committed the fundamental attributional error: They attributed to Rob attitudes in the direction of his essay. *But* subjects who thought that Rob had an ulterior motive did not infer that the attitude he expressed was his real one (see Figure 5.10; Fein, Hilton, & Miller, 1990). So this study suggests that people *can* discount someone's behavior in inferring his attitude, and that they will do so in the context in which such issues usually arise—when people say things that they have an ulterior motive for saying.

BASE RATES

Now that we have some sense for the limits of the fundamental attributional error, some sense of *when* it occurs, we are ready to ask *why* it occurs. Suppose you were told that a panel of psychologists had administered personality tests to some successful engineers and lawyers. The psychologists prepared thumbnail sketches of each of the people they interviewed and placed the sketches in a box; there were thirty sketches of engineers and seventy of lawyers in the box. And suppose the psychologist was about to pull one of the sketches out and read it to you, but first he wanted you to guess the odds that it was the sketch of an engineer. You would probably have an easy time with this question; you would likely guess that the probability that it would be an engineer was .3, or the odds were 7 to 3 against its being an engineer.

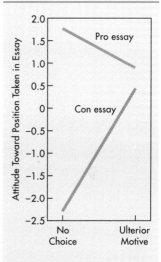

FIGURE 5.10
DISCOUNTING BEHAVIOR IN INFERRING ATTITUDES

▲ *Subjects' estimates of an essay writer's true attitude toward a topic when the subjects knew he wrote with no choice or knew he had an ulterior motive. The subjects virtually ignored the essay when they believed he had an ulterior motive. (Data from Fein, Hilton, & Miller, 1990)*

Now imagine you were read the following description randomly chosen from the box:

> Tom W. is of high intelligence, although lacking in true creativity. He has a need for order and clarity, and for neat and tidy systems in which every detail finds its appropriate place. His writing is rather dull and mechanical, occasionally enlivened by somewhat corny puns and by flashes of imagination of the sci-fi type. He has a strong drive for competence. He seems to have little feel and little sympathy for other people and does not enjoy interacting with others. Self-centered, he nonetheless has a deep moral sense. (Kahneman & Tversky, 1973, p. 238)

What would you guess now? You have two conflicting facts about this sketch. First, it was drawn from a set in which 70 percent were descriptions of lawyers, and second, it sounds a lot like an engineer. Intuitively, it seems that your answer should take account of both facts—the fact that the sample is made up mostly of lawyers, called the ***base rate,*** and the fact that the sketch sounds like that of an engineer, called the ***diagnostic fact.*** So what would you say the odds are? What should you say?

The answer is given in a mathematical formula called ***Bayes's Theorem,*** which tells us how to combine information about base rates with information about particular cases. To use Bayes's Theorem, in addition to the base rate we need to know what is called the ***diagnostic ratio.*** This ratio divides the probability that this particular sketch would be written about an engineer by the probability that it would be written about a lawyer. Thus, the diagnostic ratio tells us how closely associated with being an engineer this sketch is. Bayes's Theorem tells us that we can tell how likely it is that Tom W. is an engineer by multiplying the base rate (70 percent) by the diagnostic ratio. It tells us to treat the two kinds of information—diagnostic and base rate—in an evenhanded fashion.

Ignoring Base-Rate Information   Daniel Kahneman and Amos Tversky have found that when given problems of this sort, subjects pay too little attention to base rates and too much attention to the diagnostic ratio. Thus, they guess that the description is certainly of an engineer, and their guess is almost unaffected by the percentage of lawyer sketches in the box (until the percentage gets to zero). This failing on subjects' part has been called "ignoring the base rates." But what does it have to do with the fundamental attributional error?

Subjects in the Jones and Harris and Ross, Amabile, and Steinmetz studies may also have ignored base rates. In the Jones and Harris study, they may have taken the pro-Castro essay they read as evidence of the writer's real attitudes and paid too little attention to the base rate, the likelihood that any student on that campus was anti-Castro. Similarly, in the Ross study, subjects seemed to overweigh the number of correct answers given, and to ignore the base rates. There is some evidence, then, that the reason people make the fundamental attributional error is that they generally fail to take base rates into account.*

*Why do people fail to take base rates into account? For one thing, it is difficult to use Bayes Theorem. Kahneman and Tversky suggest that as a shortcut, people use the "representativeness heuristic" (shortcut): they judge how likely X is to be A by deciding how similar to a typical A the X is (Kahneman & Tversky, 1972). They ask themselves, for example, how like an engineer Tom W. is. This usually works, but not always.

Using Base-Rate Information   People don't always fail to take base rates into account. Izack Ajzen, for example, asked subjects to estimate a particular other student's grade point average (GPA) on the basis of information about him. The subjects were given data indicating the degree of relation between this information and GPA. For example, some subjects were given information about the relation between IQ and GPA, and then were given the student's IQ. These students used the information they received to predict GPA. But other subjects were given information about a positive relation between family income and GPA, and these students did not use this information in predicting GPA. The difference is that the subjects understood that there was a causal relation between IQ and GPA, but they could see no causal relation between family income and GPA (Ajzen, 1977). There is some evidence that subjects ignore base-rate information when they lack a causal theory because they are suspicious of the accuracy of such base rates (Hinsz, Tindale, Nagao, Davis, & Robertson, 1988; Hinsz & Tindale, 1992). The reason that a causal theory may get subjects to use base rates may be that causal theories convince people that base-rate information is accurate.

In any event, we do sometimes fail to take account of base-rate information, and this failure may lie at the heart of our making the fundamental attributional error when we make it. But what of the cases where we don't make the fundamental attributional error? For example, why don't we make it when faced with a possible ulterior motive? Perhaps it is because we are all used to ignoring the "diagnostic information" in these cases. After all, we all know that we should not treat at face value someone's glowing description of a play her son was in; perhaps in this case, we know enough to rely on base rates.

FIGURE 5.11
EGOCENTRISM AND CONSENSUS

Egocentrism and Consensus

People's troubles with base-rate information, however severe, are not confined to misusing it or failing to use it; some theorists argue that we also misestimate it when we do try to use it, which leads to another attributional failing—*egocentrism.* Consider this study by Lee Ross. He asked subjects to suppose that they were stopped and interviewed about a product in a supermarket. They were to suppose that they said something favorable about the product, and then discovered that they had been videotaped. The question was whether they would be willing to sign a release to have the tape shown on television. In addition to predicting their own behavior, they were also asked to predict what other people would do. People who said they *would* sign the release also said other people would sign it; people who said they *would not* sign the release also said most other people would not (see Figure 5.11).

Other subjects were asked to wear a sign saying "Eat at Joe's"; those willing to wear it predicted others would too, and vice versa (Ross, Green, & House, 1977). Thus, in both studies, subjects assumed that others would do what they themselves would; that is, they misestimated the base rates in the direction of their own behavior.

Ned Jones and Richard Nisbett discussed a possible reason for this egocentric basis: People forget a fundamental distinction, a distinction between qualities of objects and evaluations. Qualities of objects like weight, size, color, and so on are part of the object, external to the observer. Evaluations are not

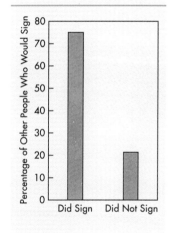

▲ *Subjects' estimates of the percentage of other subjects who would sign a release. Subjects assumed that most other people would do what they did. (Data from Ross, Green, & House, 1977)*

part of the object; they are internal to the observer. This distinction has been obvious to philosophers since the seventeenth century. But, Jones and Nisbett argue, people forget it and naively take their evaluations to be based on qualities of the object too—to be external. Because we assume that our evaluations are external, we assume that other people will make the same evaluations, and therefore we assume that other people will act toward the object the way we do. This "naive realism," as Jones and Nisbett call it, leads to our assuming a false consensus in agreement with our own views (Jones & Nisbett, 1971).

There are other possible accounts of the false consensus effect. For example, our own evaluation of a situation is of course more easily recalled than is someone else's evaluation; it is more *available* to us. And there is reason to believe that we confuse how easy it is to recall something, how available it is, with how common it is (Ross & Sicoly, 1979).

Another reason is more interesting; it has to do with how people construe the choices they are offered. Imagine that you were asked whether you preferred recent movies or older movies, and also what most other people would prefer. So you try to recall both recent and older movies you have seen. You think of a really terrible old movie you rented last week and a great recent movie you just saw. What might you do? You might say that you preferred recent movies—generalizing from the one you remembered—and you might also decide that other people would prefer recent movies to old ones. Now suppose that another subject remembered just the reverse—a really classic old film and a terrible new one. That subject would express a preference for old films, and might imagine others would have the same preference. Thus, we would find a false consensus effect: the subject who prefers the new films thinks others will too, and vice versa. But the effect here is really a consequence of how each person construes those general categories "old films" and "new films." In our example, false consensus happened because the subjects had different instances of these categories in mind. It might be that if the two subjects had the same list of old and new films to focus on, they would agree about which of them most people would prefer, regardless of their own preferences. And, indeed, there is experimental evidence that, as in our example, the false consensus effect is to some degree a consequence of **differential construal**—people's construing the choices they have in different ways (Gilovich, 1990; see also Griffin, Dunning, & Ross, 1990, for a related consequence of differential construal).

Self-Serving Biases in Social Perception

The biases discussed so far have been conceived of by most people as *purely cognitive* biases, errors we make because we are not perfectly adequate information processors. These errors are, in Lee Ross's apt phrase, "shortcomings of the intuitive psychologist" (Ross, 1977). But there is one more bias that has been unearthed in social psychologists' exploration of our thinking about people, and this one is not so obviously just a cognitive bias.

Suppose you overheard an acquaintance of your discussing a low grade he got on an exam. Suppose he said that he didn't do very well because of bad luck, a noisy room, ill health, poor lighting, fatigue, and so on. In other words, he claimed that his exam score poorly reflected his real level of mastery. And suppose that you never heard him claim he did well on an exam because of good luck—in that case, the instructor had simply asked the right questions. You would probably suspect that this fellow was biased in his attributions about the exam. In particular, you would probably suspect that he was **self-serving,** making just those attributions that would make him look best.

A pattern of internal attributions for success and external attributions for failure has often been found in the research literature. (There may be some people who chronically do the reverse—attribute their failures to internal causes and their successes to external causes. As you might imagine, such a pattern of attributions is quite depressing; see Seligman, Abramson, Semmel, & Von Bayer, 1979.) Now the obvious interpretation of this bias is *motivational*; that is, people see themselves as responsible for their successes but not for their failures because they *want* to see themselves that way. But as obvious as this interpretation is, it may not be the right one. Let us see why.

Several critics have argued quite forcefully for a purely cognitive account of the self-serving bias. They argue that people could come to see themselves as responsible for success but not for failure for a variety of nonmotivational, purely cognitive reasons. For example, we typically intend to succeed; we do not intend to fail. And often it is what we intend that determines whether we attribute an act to internal or external causes. Moreover, we often *expect* to succeed, and expected outcomes are more likely to be attributed internally (Miller & Ross, 1975; Nisbett & Ross, 1980). For both of these reasons, merely showing that people are biased in their attributions for success and failure isn't enough to demonstrate a *motivational* bias in attribution.

In one experiment that attempted to rule out these alternative, nonmotivational accounts, subjects were given what they were told was a test of social perceptiveness. After taking the test, they were randomly led to believe they had succeeded or failed. They were then asked for the reasons they had failed, and what they thought of the test. Half the subjects were led to become *ego-involved* in the test; they were told it was a well-substantiated test of social skills. The other subjects had their egos protected; they were told it really wasn't well validated at all. The ego-involved subjects showed much more of

◀ *Jack Haley, Bert Lahr, Frank Morgan, Judy Garland, and Ray Bolger in* The Wizard of Oz. *The Tin Man, Cowardly Lion, and Scarecrow attributed their failures internally and their successes externally. It took the Wizard of Oz with his medals and words to make them realize that respectively they had heart, courage, and brains.*

FIGURE 5.12 ▬▬▬▬

TASK INVOLVEMENT AND ATTRIBUTIONS FOR SUCCESS AND FAILURE

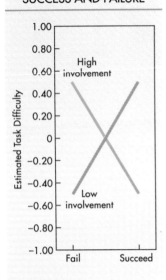

▲ *Ego-involved subjects who failed a test believed it was more difficult than did those who passed. Subjects who were not ego-involved made the reverse attributions. (Data from Miller, 1976)*

the self-serving bias than did those who were not ego-involved. The ego-involved subjects who "failed" made more external attributions about their performance, and said they believed the test was more difficult, than did the subjects who weren't ego-involved. Ego-involved subjects who "succeeded" made fewer external attributions about their performance, and believed the test was easier, than did subjects who weren't ego-involved (see Figure 5.12). This result is difficult to encompass within a purely cognitive view. The cognitive account cannot explain why the ego-involved subjects differed in their attributions from the non-ego-involved subjects (Miller, 1976; see also Kunda, 1987; Mullen & Riordan, 1988; Doherty, Weigold, & Schlenker, 1990; Agostinelli, Sherman, Presson, & Chassin, 1992, in support of the notion that self-serving attributions are motivated as well as cognitive).

Attributing success and failure isn't the only way self-serving biases show themselves. For example, there is evidence that people who admit that they often commit driving violations (speeding, tailgating, and so on) think that other people do so too, while those who don't do these things often think that others are also more careful (Manstead et al., 1992).

As we have seen, there is reason to believe that the false consensus effect can sometimes happen in a perfectly innocent way because of the specific examples of general categories that people happen to think of. But there is also reason to believe that people put differential construals to work for them. In one study, subjects were asked to decide what specific criterion someone must reach to qualify for the possession of a desirable trait—what score do you need on the math SAT, for example, to be considered intelligent? The subjects had also been asked some weeks before what their own SAT scores were. And lo and behold, the lower the subject's SAT, the lower the score he thought a person needed to qualify as intelligent (Dunning & Cohen, 1992; see also Dunning, Perie, & Story, 1991). So the subjects' criteria were geared toward establishing themselves as possessing desirable characteristics. Other research has shown that subjects are better at criticizing ideas they don't believe than ideas they do believe (Ditto & Lopez, 1992; see also Klein & Kunda, 1992).

Experimental evidence is beginning to accumulate, then, to show that people can be self-serving in their biases. But this evidence does not negate Nisbett and Ross's original point. There are, no doubt, occasions in which people are self-serving in their beliefs about themselves and others. But these occasions are probably less common than we imagine; there are many non-motivated, purely cognitive reasons that people may be biased in their beliefs.

So far we have considered biases that arise because people don't take full advantage of the information they have available to them. Subjects don't, for example, use base-rate information enough even when they have it. But there is also evidence that people use shortcuts, **heuristics,** in the way they acquire information in the first place, and these shortcuts too lead to bias. We turn now to what we know about the attributional process itself, and the biases it brings in its wake.

Confirmation Bias

The Kelley model tells us that to understand why someone reacted the way she did to some particular stimulus, we must seek out or recall all we can about that person's previous responses to that stimulus, her previous responses to other stimuli, and other people's responses to that stimulus. This is a lot of information. Perhaps, to save time, we don't go through all of that information processing after all.

CANDIDATE CAUSES AND TESTING HYPOTHESES

Ranald Hansen (1980) has suggested that people follow a simple procedure in thinking about the causes of an event. First, they think of a possible cause, a "candidate cause." Second, they look for evidence that this explanation is true. If this works, they stop. Let us consider this proposal more closely.

Where does the candidate cause come from? Fritz Heider proposed some shortcut rules of thumb. One is that we expect the causes of a person's emotions and opinions to lie in her situation; we look for a stimulus that might have provoked them. Achievements (like winning a race), on the other hand, require the participation of both the world and the person, and simple actions (like greeting a friend) are explained by the actor's intention—these have an internal cause. These simple ideas provide places to look for the causes of various behaviors. And using these rules by themselves leads to no bias. After all, one must come up with hypotheses somehow. But do people treat these guesses as to the cause of a behavior in an evenhanded way? Do they look, as a good scientist should, for evidence both for and against their hypotheses, or are they biased in the way they test these hypotheses? The evidence is that they aren't evenhanded.

In one investigation, subjects were told that they would be interviewing someone, and that it would be their task to determine whether she was an introvert; other subjects were given the same task, but they were to find out if she was an extravert. The subjects were then asked to tell the experimenter which questions they would ask her. The questions they wanted to ask were biased toward confirmation. That is, the subjects testing the hypothesis that she was an introvert asked questions to which the interviewee was likely to answer yes if she was an introvert, questions that could confirm introversion. For example, they asked her, "Do you like intimate get-togethers with a few friends?" But they did not ask questions like "Do you like wild and boisterous parties?" to which extraverts are likely to answer yes. Subjects testing the hypothesis that she was an extravert did just the reverse, asking questions likely to be answered in the affirmative by an extravert, but ignoring questions typical of introverts.

The problem with this strategy is that questions like "Do you like intimate get-togethers with a few friends?" aren't very diagnostic of introversion. It is true that most introverts will answer yes, but so *will many extraverts.* Questions of this sort would reveal *most people* to be introverts. Similarly, the questions subjects asked the person they thought might be an extravert would show most people to be extraverts. Indeed, in one condition, people listened to a subject answering the introvert questions and concluded that he was an introvert, but when he answered (truthfully) the extravert questions, they thought he was an extravert. Thus, this study provides evidence that once subjects hit on a hypothesis, they tend to investigate it in such a way as to confirm it (see Figure 5.13; Snyder & Swann, 1978).

Of course, if hypotheses were taken up in a rational and sensible way, then the fact that we tend to confirm hypotheses wouldn't be likely to lead

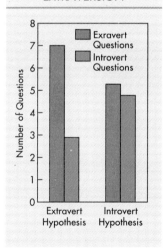

FIGURE 5.13

CONFIRMATION BIAS FOR INTROVERSION AND EXTRAVERSION

▲ *The kind of questions subjects asked depended on the hypothesis they were asked to test. (Data from Snyder & Swann, 1978)*

us to have false beliefs, but there is reason to believe that which hypothesis someone entertains may be subject to all sorts of forces that *aren't* reasonable or sensible. For example, recall the case of Tom W. the engineer/lawyer discussed above. In one follow-up study, some subjects were asked to estimate the probability that Tom was an engineer; others were asked to estimate the probability that he was a lawyer. Since he had to be one or the other, these two probabilities had to sum to 1.0; so asking for one probability is, in effect, asking for the other. Subjects' estimates that Tom was an engineer were higher when they were asked that question directly than when they were asked for the probability that he was a lawyer (Lehman, Krosnick, West, & Li, 1992)! So the exact question we are asked (or think of ourselves) can affect the answer we give. Surely this wouldn't be true if we were perfectly rational.

But it is important not to overstate the case. There is also evidence that people may not be so bad at testing hypotheses after all. In one study, for example, some subjects were again given the task of testing the hypothesis that a person was an introvert; others were to test the hypothesis that he was an extravert. The subjects then interacted with the person. The results indicated that (1) the subjects did *not* select questions in a confirmatory way, and (2) the subjects *were* able to detect whether the person they were interacting with was an introvert or an extravert (Pennington, 1987). Other evidence suggests that an important determinant of whether subjects test hypotheses in a biased way is whether they have a clearly stated alternative hypothesis in mind. If they do, then subjects tend to be relatively unbiased in their hypothesis testing (Trope & Mackie, 1987).

ATTRIBUTIONAL CRITICS

Discussions of how people should, and do, make attributions dominated social psychology in the 1970s; by 1980, at least one thousand articles in the attribution literature had appeared (see Kelley & Michela, 1980). Attribution theory represented a significant advance in our understanding of the way people think about others. Still, attribution theory and its list of biases have not gone without challenge. It is time now to turn to its critics, who have claimed that attribution theory may have seriously misconstrued our thinking about people.

The attributional literature we have been reviewing rests on several assumptions: in ascribing traits to someone, we are reporting a particular internal cause of that person's behavior; the search for the cause of a person's behavior is essentially a statistical matter—we find the cause by determining what covaries with it; and when subjects answer attributional questions, they are simply reporting the upshot of their causal, statistical search. Each of these assumptions has been challenged. And all the challenges have a common starting point: the notion of a cause of behavior.

Consider crossing the street to get a cup of coffee. Attribution theory suggests that we attempt to understand this action by focusing on its causes. So what are they? The problem is, there are so many. One is the presence of the store across the street selling the coffee, another is the green light on the traffic signal, another is the labor of the person who picked the coffee beans, another is the lessons the street crosser got from his parents on how to cross the street—all of these, and infinitely more, are causes of the behavior. The task of finding *the* cause of a person's behavior is hopeless, and the task of finding *all* the causes of a person's behavior is equally hopeless. Many of the criticisms of attribution theory take root because they help specify *which* cause of behavior people care about.

Consider the role of statistical thinking in the specification of the causes of behavior. Statistical reasoning can come into play in deciding which of two (or a few) possible causes is *the* cause of a particular event. But how does the observer of behavior get to the point of deciding between two (or a few) causes? The field must be sharply delimited before statistical reasoning becomes relevant. Critics assert that attribution theorists have paid little attention to how one gets to the point of two (or a few) possible causes. Attribution theorists tend to agree, and suggest that indeed common-sense understandings come into play in narrowing the field to a small set of possible causes. But, they argue, it is still important to see how statistical reasoning is used at that stage (see Kelley, 1971b).

Here the debate tends to end, with each side gracefully conceding that the other side has something to say. Beneath the explicit debate, however, is a rarely stated but often felt conflict, a conflict in which each side mutters (under its breath), "While I concede that your principles come into play, they come into play only in a trivial percentage of the cases. It is *my* principles that do the real explanatory work." This is a particularly difficult issue to resolve, but before trying to resolve it, let us see what the critics have to say about attributional matters.

Social Knowledge Structures

Several theorists have argued that attribution theory takes little account of the fact that our social knowledge is organized and stored in memory in the form of particular structures, and it is these structures that focus attention on possible causes. Roger Schank and Robert Abelson, for example, have called attention to our knowledge of that little piece of the social world, restaurants. There are things that all of us know about restaurants—all restaurants. We all know, for example, that people eat food there, that restaurants have menus, that restaurants charge for their food, that the bill for the food comes after the meal, and so on. It is indeed because we know these facts about restaurants in general that we know what to expect and how to act in a restaurant we have never visited before (Schank & Abelson, 1977).

Schank and Abelson, then, argue that we have stored in our memories **scripts** for many different activities, including going to a restaurant. A script specifies what actions will happen (in general terms) and in what order. It leaves open *slots* to be filled in at the time one goes, for example, to a particular restaurant. The script doesn't specify what a person will order in the restaurant; that is a *variable* that changes from one occasion on which the script is used to another (see Figure 5.14). So scripts are one kind of "knowledge structure" we use to make our way around the social world. Schank and Abelson propose that there are other kinds of knowledge structures, especially plans and goals.

Stephen Read has argued that it is in terms of these structures, in terms of scripts, plans, and goals, that we look for explanations of actions (Read,

Attribution theories assume that
- traits are internal causes of behavior;
- searching for causes is essentially a statistical matter;
- when people answer attributional questions, they are reporting on the fruits of their statistical search.

FIGURE 5.14

SOCIAL SCRIPTS

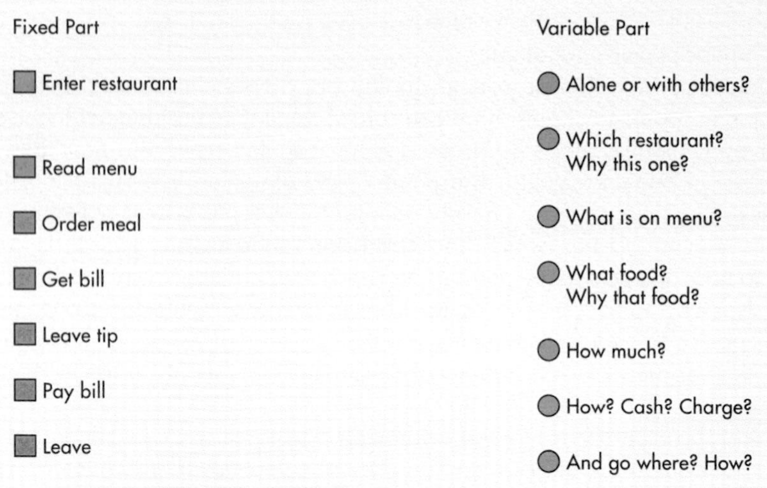

Fixed Part	Variable Part
▪ Enter restaurant	● Alone or with others?
	● Which restaurant? Why this one?
▪ Read menu	
▪ Order meal	● What is on menu?
▪ Get bill	● What food? Why that food?
▪ Leave tip	● How much?
▪ Pay bill	● How? Cash? Charge?
▪ Leave	● And go where? How?

▶ *The fixed and variable parts of a restaurant script.*

1987; see also Hilton & Knibbs, 1988; McGill, 1991; Miller, Taylor, & Buck, 1991). When we search for the causal explanation for some event, we call up our script for that action and focus on the empty slots within it. Explaining the action is a matter of filling in the slot.

Consider again the simple action of crossing the street to get a cup of coffee. Most of the factors listed above that might be called causes of the person's behavior, like the labor of the people picking the coffee beans, aren't specified in anyone's "going to the store" script. That script does, however, contain a slot for the *goal* of the person going to the store—that is, what he wants to buy. To understand someone's going to the store, then, we don't need to know who made whatever is sold there, but we do need to know what the person wants to buy. It is that goal—the person's reason for acting—that is the slot that needs to be filled in in the script, and the explanation that is sought. According to this view, we don't ordinarily bother with covariation information in explaining another person's behavior; we just seek a goal to fill the empty slot.

Social knowledge structures may give us more than slots to be filled, they may provide some answers too. For example, in one study, American subjects were told stories about Soviet citizens who defected to the United States or U. S. citizens who defected to the Soviet Union. Subjects were asked to imagine why these people defected; they answered that the Soviets defected because of problems in the Soviet Union, external causes, while Americans defected because of faults in their own personalities, internal causes. This result shows bias. But a more interesting result was that when subjects were asked a week later to recall the facts about the stories they had read, they tended to make up (confabulate) external reasons for the Soviet defectors and personality reasons for the American defectors (Sedikides & Anderson, 1992). People seem to have a "defector" knowledge structure that assigns different causes for their own and other defectors.

Defecting from one country to another is, whatever else it may be, a goal-directed behavior. It is typically explained by some goal the defector is seeking—for example, personal freedom. Not all behaviors are, however, explained by a person's goal. **Actions**—behaviors under the control of a person's will—*are* typically explained by reference to goals. But behaviors that are not under the control of the will are not explained this way. There are three interesting classes of occurrences—behaviors we can't will. The first includes those behaviors that we typically don't will: slips, reflexes, sneezes, and so on. The second includes spontaneous emotional expressions—blushing, for example. The third includes achievements such as winning a race. This last category is somewhat paradoxical because *running in a race* is surely an action, something within our control (and necessary to winning), but *winning the race* isn't under our control. We can't just win a race because we want to.

Occurrences and actions, then, are quite different sorts of things, and the evidence indicates that they require different sorts of explanations (Zuckerman, 1978; Zuckerman & Feldman, 1984). Actions are typically (though not always) explained by their reasons (goals); occurrences are explained by their causes. Attribution theory, especially as proposed by Harold Kelley, with its focus on causes, is especially suited to the explanation of occurrences—like laughing—rather than actions.

Actions are
• under the control of the actor;

• typically explained by goals rather than causes.

Occurrences are
• not fully under the control of the actor;

• typically explained by causes rather than goals.

Causes and Responsibilities

Some critics of attribution theory have argued that in explaining behavior, we focus on certain classes of causes; in particular, we focus on those causes that help us determine who is *responsible* for the action or occurrence (see Table 5.1). Suppose you didn't do well on a test and were asked why. What might you choose to say: "I lacked ability," picking out an internal cause, or "The test was too hard," specifying an external cause? Now the facts of the matter are clear here. You didn't do well because you lacked ability (the requisite amount), and the test was too hard (too hard for you to do well). As is typically true for a particular result to occur, the right internal cause met the right external cause. Still, there is a difference here in claiming one rather than the other as the cause.

To call the test the cause of your failure is to do more than tell your interrogator something he already knows—that the test was too hard for you. It is to claim that the instructor *is at fault* for your failure. If the test was too hard, not just for you but *in comparison with some reasonable standard*, then you are not at fault for failing. The instructor, of course, is likely to believe that the failure was caused by your lack of ability, meaning not that you

TABLE 5.1

CAUSES AND RESPONSIBILITIES		
	Goal	*Causes of Behavior*
Scientists	Explain events	All causes
Lawyers	Fix responsibility	Legally (morally) relevant causes

lacked the ability to pass the test—that is obvious—but again, that you lacked the ability *in relation to a reasonable standard.* According to this view of attributions, we make them not to locate causes but to fix responsibility. Perhaps in making attributions, then, we aren't lay scientists attempting to specify causes, but rather we are lay lawyers attempting to assess responsibility (Fincham & Jaspers, 1980; Hamilton, 1980; Mehlman & Snyder, 1985; Hilton & Slugoski, 1986; Shaver & Drown, 1986; Sabini & Silver, 1987).

"MAN THE LAWYER"

The "man-the-lawyer" view places the attributional errors in a different light. According to this conception, we are not naturally given to treating each other as a scientist might. To take a predictive, scientific stance toward others might be unnatural, and we might therefore have very little practice at it. If so, then it is hardly surprising that when we are asked to make predictions, we do so poorly.

It is not very difficult to understand why we tend to ignore base rates. Base rates and consensus information aren't very important to *moral* judgments, to judgments involving responsibility; just because lots of people do the wrong thing doesn't make it right. Recall that in the study by Arthur Miller, some subjects were told about the Milgram results, and others weren't. Knowing the results led subjects to change their predictions about what the typical person would do, but it did not change the traits they assigned to someone who obeyed. Perhaps this was because subjects used traits not to (or not just to) make predictions, but also to ascribe moral blame—and moral blame is independent of base rates (Sabini & Silver, 1982).

There is some direct evidence that subjects take a lawyer's (or moralist's) perspective even when they are asked explicitly causal questions. Consider a study by Mark Alicke, in which subjects read a story about John. John, it seems, was driving his car over the speed limit, hit an oil slick at an intersection, and struck a pedestrian, causing fairly severe injuries. Subjects were asked to list one cause of the accident, the one they thought was the primary cause. And they were also asked to indicate how responsible John was for the accident.

Some subjects were told one more fact about the story: John was speeding so he could hide an anniversary present for his parents before they got home. Other subjects were told a different story: John was speeding to hide a vial of cocaine before his parents got home. Surely, from a man-the-scientist perspective, this variation should not matter in what subjects listed as the primary cause of the accident. But it did. John was named as the primary cause more often in the cocaine version than in the anniversary gift version, and he was rated more responsible for the accident in the former version (Alicke, 1992). And surely, though John's reason for speeding may not affect the causal story much, it certainly affects our moral judgment of him. So this study suggests that even when subjects are asked explicitly causal questions, their broader, moral reactions influence the answers they give.

EGOCENTRIC BIAS

The man-the-lawyer view also has a way of dealing with the egocentric bias, our tendency to assume that other people evaluate the world in the same way we do and therefore act in the same way we do. Ned Jones and Richard Nisbett allow that assuming that other people see the world as we do isn't such a bad idea with regard to the physical world. After all, we saw in the Asch studies in Chapter 2 how hard it is on people when they come to imagine that the physical world might *not* be the same for everyone. But Jones and Nisbett argue for a sharp distinction between perceptions and evaluations. Thus, for people to assume that everyone *evaluates* the world in the same way they do is to make a serious mistake. But is there a sharp distinction between evaluations and descriptions?

Suppose every line of this book were either too light to read or blurred. And suppose you said the book was poorly printed, and that therefore no one would want to read it. Now surely saying that the book is badly printed is an evaluation, and expecting people not to want to read it is an expectation about behavior. But would it really be a mistake for you to expect others to evaluate the printing as you do? Probably not. Surely some evaluations are as uncontroversial as our most secure perceptions.

According to the man-the-lawyer view, then, there isn't a sharp, categorical distinction to be drawn between evaluations and descriptions, since it is quite reasonable for people to assume that others will evaluate the world as they do (see Sabini & Silver, 1982, for more on this). This is not to deny that the assumption that others will evaluate the world as we do is sometimes in error, but it is to suggest that when this assumption *is* an error, it is one that follows from our natural attitude, our assumption that there is only one world for all of us. And it is also to suggest that assuming that others evaluate as we do isn't an error *in general.* Indeed, Robyn Dawes has pointed out that it would be irrational indeed to *ignore* one's own actions and reactions in deciding how other people will behave. In Dawes's view, there is no evidence that people give *too much* weight to their own reactions. The evidence so far merely shows that people take account of their own responses in deciding what other people's responses are likely to be (Dawes, 1989).

Pragmatics

The final set of criticisms of attributional approaches we shall consider focuses on the **pragmatics** of question asking and answering. Pragmatics, a field invented by the philosopher John Austin (Austin, 1962), is a subdiscipline of linguistics. In the broadest terms, pragmatics has to do with all that is implicit in the use of language. For example, to illustrate this point, once a term I begin my lecture by announcing something like "I saw Vice-President Gore this morning, and he was sober." My saying this typically gets a laugh—but why? How is my utterance defective?

One defect the statement has is that it is untrue—I have never seen Vice-President Gore, drunk or sober. But that isn't why it draws a laugh. Rather, students laugh because of something *presupposed by* uttering that sentence. In particular, this utterance presupposes that there is something remarkable about Vice-President Gore's being sober. Note that the statement *doesn't claim* explicitly that there is something remarkable about the vice-president's state; the insidious fact is that the utterance carries this implication without having to state it. Pragmatics is the study, then, of the propositions that interactants assume, and are entitled to assume, surround explicit statements.

TABLE 5.2

GRICE'S MAXIMS	
Maxim	Explanation
Relevance maxim	Say only what is relevant.
Quantity maxim	Give only as much detail as the listener needs.
Quality maxim	Say only what you have reason to believe.
Directness maxim	Don't beat around the bush.

The philosopher H. P. Grice developed the work of John Austin by articulating some specific principles that guide utterances in general (and explanations of behavior in particular). Grice argued that speakers typically honor "maxims" of conversation (see Table 5.2). For example, in answering questions, speakers obey the ***quantity maxim,*** which specifies that someone answering a question should reply only with as much detail as the person asking is likely to want. So, some months ago, I badly sprained my ankle, and people would ask me how it was. I replied to these polite and sympathetic questions with a few words. A reply of the sort, "Well, it's okay to walk on, but sharp turns to the right are quite painful, and it is all but impossible for me to walk on sidewalks slanted from right to left . . ." would flagrantly violate the maxim of quantity. But notice that it is just the right answer to the same question from a physician! So Grice's maxims must be interpreted as relative to what the asker wants to know.

Another of Grice's norms, the ***quality maxim,*** says that a speaker should refrain from saying things for which she has no evidence. The ***directness maxim*** has to do with the manner in which an answer is given; it enjoins speakers to answer directly, not to beat around the bush. It is the maxim abused by politicians asked questions they would rather not answer. Finally, Grice proposed a ***relevance maxim,*** which dictates that the answer to a question be relevant to what the speaker already knows and wants to know.

Consider the maxim of relevance in relation to my remark about Al Gore. It is precisely the norm of relevance that the statement violates. After all, there is an infinite number of facts about Al Gore that might be mentioned; the norm of relevance dictates that I mention only those that somehow edify the person hearing my remark. The interesting fact about Grice's maxims is that they not only guide what speakers do, they also serve as rules that auditors use in interpreting what is said to them. Thus, when someone hears me say, "I saw Al Gore this morning in his sober state," the listener is entitled to assume that I am following the maxim of relevance, and thus to conclude that I believe that there is something notable about the vice-president's being sober. It is via interpretation under the maxim of relevance that my utterance implies that Gore is usually not sober, that his being sober this morning is an illuminating remark about him.

Recently, social psychologists have begun to think about attribution research in light of pragmatics (Brown & Van Kleeck, 1989; Hilton, Smith, & Alicke, 1988; Hilton, 1990). After all, the subjects in an attribution experiment are engaged in something like a conversation with the experimenter; it would not be odd if they were to frame their answers, perhaps unconsciously,

---

I say: "I saw Vice-President Gore this morning, and Gore was sober."

Literal meaning: John Sabini saw Vice-President Gore this morning, and Gore was sober.

Relevance maxim: Say only things that are noteworthy.

Listener assumes, therefore: It must be noteworthy that Al Gore is sober.

Conclusion: Gore has a drinking problem.

in light of the principles of pragmatics that they generally apply to their conversations.

Theorists in the attribution tradition have, however, been insensitive to these issues of pragmatics. Consider the fundamental attributional error in light of pragmatics, in particular the maxim of relevance. The experimenter in a study such as we reviewed earlier gives the subject two kinds of information: first, the essay that the person (supposedly) wrote, and then the information that the person was told to write that essay. Now suppose the subject reacts to all of this by saying to herself, "Well, how in the world am I supposed to know what this fellow's attitude is? As far as I can tell, I have no evidence about his real attitude. All I have is this essay he was told to write." But she might then say, "I do, however, know that the experimenter gave me his essay to read. So the experimenter must believe that it is relevant. I guess I had better use it."

If this is the sort of reasoning the subject engages in, then she will attribute an attitude to the essay writer, not because she fails to think about statistics and causality correctly, but because she thinks that the experimenter is following, and expecting her to follow, the norm of relevance. The subject might attribute an attitude in the direction of the essay because she assumes the experimenter gave her the essay to read for a reason. Indeed, if subjects are told that some of the information they are given might be irrelevant (if they are warned that the maxim of relevance might be violated), then they are less willing to attribute attitudes in line with the essay (Wright & Wells, 1988).

Darrin Lehman has gathered data that suggest two things with regard to subjects' tendency to ignore base rates (the attitude of the typical student) in favor of diagnostic information (the attitude expressed in the essay): (1) this happens because experimenters tend to give the base-rate information first and the diagnostic information second, and (2) this "recency" effect (in which the more recent information weighs more heavily) occurs *not* because of the way our memories work, but because subjects assume that the experimenter intends them to rely more on the information he presents last.

CAUSE AND CONSIDERATION

Let us consider another of the attributional biases in light of pragmatic constraints. Recall the Nisbett, Caputo, Legant, and Marecek study discussed above, in which subjects described themselves as attracted to the girl they were going out with by her warmth, but they claimed that their best friend went out with his girlfriend because he liked warm girls. This was taken as evidence that actors make external attributions, attributions to the situation, but observers make internal attributions, attributions to the person's dispositions. But, we might well ask, is there really any difference between the two explanations in terms of the *causes they imply?* Consider the fact that if you are attracted to someone because she is warm, then two things must be true: (1) she must be warm, and (2) you must be attracted to warm women. The superficial form—internal or external—may not mark out a real distinction in how the subjects *think* about the events in question (Ross, 1977; Monson & Snyder, 1977; Sabini & Silver, 1987). But there are reasons to prefer one form to another—pragmatic reasons.

To see this, imagine that you were asked to explain why you did well on

▲ *Is Bill Clinton really that fond of children, or is he just honoring the constraint that political campaigners must seem to like children?*

an exam. You might say, "Oh, it was easy," making an external attribution, or you might say, "Oh, I passed because I am brilliant," making an internal attribution. One only hopes you will answer the first—regardless of your beliefs. You might give the first answer rather than the second, not because you don't believe the second, but because you know that calling yourself brilliant is bragging and likely to cost you some friends.

More generally, to explain your own actions by referring to your own qualities is self-centered. Most of us, at least, learn to inhibit our talking about ourselves, especially with strangers. So there is a reason—a pragmatic reason—to say you go out with a woman because she is warm rather than because you like warm women. The former pays your girlfriend a compliment, the latter calls attention to yourself. The different forms we use to describe ourselves and our friends may reflect something very important—politeness. But it may not reflect fundamental differences in thinking, as attribution theory has it.

Consider now that in the same Nisbett et al. study, the observers were asked the reasons for students' volunteering to escort benefactors of disadvantaged children around the campus. The observers attributed the actors' behavior to altruism, when it was really a matter of their wanting money. Now both wanting money and having altruistic feelings might well be thought of as internal. So it isn't right to describe the observers as having mistakenly attributed the volunteers' behavior to an internal cause. The volunteers did agree because of an internal cause, the desire for money. The observers were mistaken because they attributed the behavior to the *wrong* internal cause.

One obvious difference between altruism and the desire for money is that the former is more flattering than the latter. So given two possible accounts of why the actors volunteered, the observers picked the *more positive* account. Again, considerations of politeness seem to offer a better reason for the subjects' choice of explanations than does a concern with causal accounts.*

There are, then, alternative ways of construing the data that have been collected under the guidance of attribution theory. These alternatives start from fundamentally different premises about the natural concerns and attitudes on which our thinking about people is based. They tend to see attributional data as a reflection not just of our thinking about behavior but also of our attempts to interact with other people in a polite and considerate way. And they see us as more like lawyers than scientists, lawyers who take our evaluations seriously, as objective.

The attributional perspective has two great virtues in its approach to how we understand other people. First, it encompasses much of our thinking in a single framework; it says that we are, at heart, lay scientists, indeed lay statisticians attempting to find the causes of behavior. The fact that so much of our thinking can be encompassed in a single framework is a great advantage in a theory. Second, that perspective has uncovered a variety of ways that

---

*Grice's maxims far from exhaust the rules we follow in using language in everyday life. For a more complete discussion of how these rules might relate to attributional phenomena, see Edwards & Potter, 1993; Fiedler, Semin, & Koppetsch, 1991. I expect that the richness of the constraints on conversation will increasingly impact on attribution theory; I expect that it will be increasingly realized that language isn't just something into which we squeeze our thoughts, but rather is one of the tools we use to think in the first place.

we may go wrong in understanding people's behavior; this too is a great virtue.

Critics of attribution theory, on the other hand, offer a less unified point of view. They argue that what we *say* about why a person did what she did is determined by a wide variety of factors—facts about how our knowledge is organized in terms of scripts, plans, and goals, facts about our desire to affix responsibility, facts about the pragmatic rules that govern conversation. The critics offer, then, in place of a single perspective a diverse collection of particular claims. In general, in science one favors a single coherent framework over a hodgepodge of criticisms. Yet I find myself muttering with the critics. I find myself drawn to alternative explanations of the attributional phenomena, while conceding that statistical reasoning, and the analysis of covariation, surely has its place.

COGNITIVE PROCESSES

So far, we have concentrated on the *structures* of person perception: (1) how traits relate to one another—our implicit theories of personality—and (2) how knowing someone's traits affects our overall evaluation of her. We will now focus on the *processes* of social cognition and perception; that is, *how* we encode, store, recall, and evaluate one another's behavior and personalities.

CLASSIC FINDINGS IN SOCIAL PSYCHOLOGY: PRECONCEPTIONS AND EVALUATIONS

An experiment by Harold Kelley will help us keep in mind just what we would like to understand. The experiment involved the traits *warm* and *cold,* which, you may recall, Asch found to be central, having broad effects on our ascription of other traits to a person (see Figure 5.15).

Kelley told small classes of undergraduates that they would have a guest lecturer they had never met for their next class. He then described the guest

FIGURE 5.15

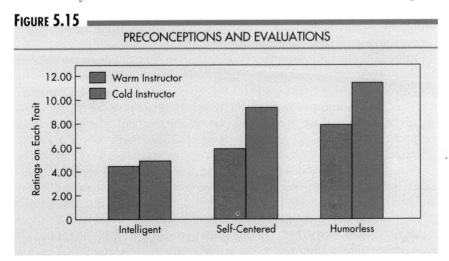

◄ *Subjects told to expect a warm or cold instructor draw different inferences about his traits. Some traits are affected more than others. (Data from Kelley, 1950)*

as rather cold to one class and very warm to the other. In the following session, this instructor lectured to the two classes for about twenty minutes, and he tried to act in the same way in both classes. After the session, the students were asked to evaluate their guest lecturer on a variety of trait scales. They rated the instructor who had been described as warm more positively than they rated the same instructor when he had been described as cold. But the warm-cold manipulation affected different traits to different degrees; "considerate" was affected more than "intelligent," for example. The results showed, then, that subjects' preconceptions about the instructor's traits affected their evaluations of him (Kelley, 1950). Now we want to know *how* the preconceptions affected behavior.

In order to understand how preconceptions affect our understanding of other people, social psychologists have borrowed two kinds of resources from cognitive psychology: concepts and methods. It is broadly true that our current understanding of the world is influenced by two kinds of things: (1) the information that is currently available to us in whatever stimulus we are paying attention to and (2) our general knowledge about the world. What we currently think, see, feel, hear, and so on is a consequence of the joint influence of these two sources. A serious problem for every field of psychology is to specify *how* these two sources come to influence our actual thought. For us to function in the world effectively, the information we already have must be integrated with what we currently see in an orderly and structured way.

Consider, for example, a baseball game. Most people who watch their first baseball game find it boring. There are several reasons for this. It might just be that baseball is boring. But against this hypothesis is the fact that millions of people enjoy it quite a lot. So let us see if there aren't reasons why newcomers might find it boring even though experienced fans don't.

For one thing, new viewers just don't know, quite literally, what to look for. To the fan, even on the most routine play, the field is alive with patterned action. The experienced viewer can see, for example, how the defensive players are adjusting on each pitch to the particular circumstances of the game. The true fan knows, for example, that if there is a man on first, she should look to see what the first baseman does to hold him on, and, not so obviously, what the second baseman does to compensate for what the first baseman is doing. And how the second baseman and the shortstop are cooperating on setting up a double play, and so on. So the fan knows where to direct her attention to see all that there is to see.

There is a second difference between the fan and the first-time viewer. Even if someone whispered what to look for in the ear of the new-comer, he still wouldn't be able to integrate all the information. That is, he wouldn't appreciate the meaning of the individual facts in relation to the overall strategy of the game, and the particular tactics of the moment. These actions on the part of the various players, even if he could see them, would look like individual acts rather than elements of a coherent plan.

And there is a third difference. For the lifelong fan, the current circumstance evokes memories of games gone by, of other circumstances like this one, of what other teams did, or might have done, or didn't do. And a great part of the pleasure of the game comes from this sort of evocation. So there are three, at least, ways that experience matters: (1) it controls attention, (2) it integrates information, and (3) it guides memory. It is handy to have a

There is a lot going on all at once in this photo. The fan can see it; others can't.

term to refer to these three effects of experience, and there have been several candidates proposed: *script, template, construct,* and *schema* are examples. I shall use **schema** (plural **schemata**) to refer to these effects of experience.

Now to get back to our problem of understanding people, the obvious step is to assume that traits function as schemata. That is, to assume that the reason that the subjects in Kelley's experiment saw the "warm" lecturer as warm was because having been told he was warm, they (1) directed their attention to aspects of his behavior that are evidence of warmth, (2) saw his underlying warmth as explaining a variety of his behaviors, and (3) preferentially recalled behaviors they interpreted as warm in reaching an overall evaluation of him. The research we shall review gives further substance to this notion that traits function as schemata.

Cognitive schemata
• control attention;
• integrate information;
• guide which memories are activated.

Activation of Schemata

In one study, the investigators gave subjects a list of adjectives to learn. The adjectives were supposed to be descriptive of a fictional character. There were four kinds of lists. One list created the impression that the character was an introvert; it included adjectives such as *hesitant, oversensitive, bashful,* and so on. There were also adjectives on the list not relevant to introversion, for example *lucky* and *modern.* Another list included adjectives that described an extravert. Examples of these were *entertaining, impulsive, friendly,* and so on. There were adjectives on this list too that were irrelevant to introversion or extraversion. The other two lists contained neither introvert nor extravert adjectives.

In the second phase of the experiment, the subjects were given new lists of adjectives and asked to say which of them they had been given in the previous phase of the experiment. This sort of task is called a **recognition memory task** to distinguish it from a **recall memory task,** in which subjects are simply asked to write down the words they have seen. The lists that

COGNITIVE PROCESSES   **181**

FIGURE 5.16

TRAITS AND MEMORY

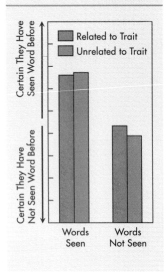

▲ Subjects' certainty that they had (or had not) seen a word before depended on whether a relevant schema had been activated. Subjects were somewhat less willing to reject a word if it was related to an activated schema. (Data from Cantor & Mischel, 1977)

In the presence of a newly forming schema, information *incongruent* with the schema is favored in memory.

In the presence of a well-established schema, information *consistent* with the schema is favored in memory.

subjects were now given included some adjectives they had seen and some they hadn't seen. Among those they hadn't seen before, some were descriptive of introverts and some descriptive of extraverts. The critical result was that subjects who had been exposed to the introvert list were less sure they hadn't seen the new introvert adjectives, while subjects who had been exposed to the extravert list were less sure they hadn't seen the new extravert adjectives (see Figure 5.16). Thus, each group was influenced toward believing they had seen adjectives they hadn't, and they made this mistake especially about adjectives that were consistent with those they had seen (Cantor & Mischel, 1977). (Words subjects think they have seen, but haven't, are called **intrusions**.) How can we account for these data?

The authors of this study argue that when the subjects saw a list including several introvert adjectives, they thought of the person as an introvert—in technical language, their "introvert" schema was activated. When they were later to recall what they had seen, they answered by asking themselves whether the adjectives were consistent with this activated schema. The consistent intrusions were part of the activated schema (even though they weren't on the earlier list), so the subjects remembered, quite mistakenly, having seen them before. The incoming information served to awaken their schema, and once it had been awakened, it was the schema they used rather than the input information. Notice that the subjects weren't told that the character was an introvert (or extravert) explicitly; this impression was created by giving them the particular adjectives that are part of this higher-order schema. In fact, other subjects *were* told explicitly that the subject was an introvert or an extravert in addition to being given the particular adjectives, but there weren't any differences on the recall test between those who were explicitly cued in this way and those whose schemata were activated just by the specific adjectives. Thus, it isn't necessary to invoke the name associated with a schema to activate it for cognitive processing.

This study activated a schema associated with a trait, but traits aren't the only schemata we use in thinking about people. Further research has shown that we have schemata corresponding to our "significant others"—people who are (or have been) important in our lives. Thus, we have stored away as a schema all sorts of information about our best friend—facts about his life, traits, background, physical features, and so on. The evidence indicates that if we meet someone who in some way (or more likely in several ways) resembles him, our best-friend schema will be activated, and we are likely to ascribe to this new person features that are true of our best friend but that we have no reason to believe of this person we just met. Facts about the people we know well, then, serve—as traits do—to organize our memories and cause us to "fill in" missing facts about people who resemble them (Anderson & Cole, 1990).

SENSITIVITY TO INCONGRUENT MATERIAL

An activated schema can cause people to accept things they haven't seen but that are consistent with the schema. But it can also have the reverse effect; the activation of a schema can cause people to be particularly sensitive to *incongruent* material. Thus, if you believe that someone is an introvert, you may also be quite good at remembering particularly *extraverted* things she has done. You aren't likely to *intrude* extraverted material, but if you are told

FIGURE 5.17

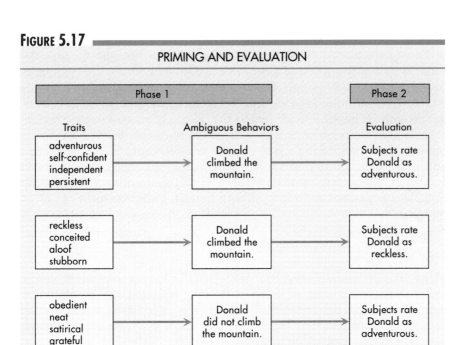

◄ *The design of an experiment to show how schemata can affect cognitive processing at the point where the behavior is first encountered.*

of extravert-like behavior of someone you think is an introvert, it will certainly stick out in your mind (Hastie & Kumar, 1979).

When will your memory favor consistent information, and when will it favor inconsistent information? The answer is not entirely clear, but some theorists believe that the key issue is whether you have already stored a clear impression of the person, or whether your impression is still forming. The evidence at the moment suggests that when you are *forming* and testing your impression of someone, then behaviors that are *incongruent* with your overall impressions are better recalled, but once you have a firm impression, the advantage goes to *congruent* behaviors (Higgins & Bargh, 1987; Stangor & Ruble, 1989). So once a schema is activated, depending on a variety of factors, both consistent and inconsistent behaviors may be highlighted, but in any case, behavior that is *irrelevant to the schema* is easily forgotten. Activated schemata, however, consistently act to filter out irrelevant instances.

PRIMING OF SCHEMATA

The studies discussed so far have focused on schemata's effects on memory, but whether or not a schema has been activated can also have effects earlier in cognitive processing, at the point of interpreting behavior in the first instance. These effects can happen even when the original activation of the schema has nothing to do with the behavior.

For example, in one investigation (see Figure 5.17), subjects were exposed to matched pairs of trait words. Some subjects, for example, were shown *reckless*, while others were shown *adventurous*. In a second phase of the experiment, which the subjects were told was unconnected with the first, the subjects read a description of a behavior by Donald that was construable as reckless or adventurous. Subjects were then asked to rate Donald's behavior on a reckless-adventurous scale. The results indicated that the subjects' evaluation of the behavior was affected by the prior activation of the appropriate schema; that is, the subjects who saw *reckless* rated the specific behavior as more reckless than did those subjects who saw *adventurous*. In technical language, the ***priming*** of their reckless schema made it *available* to them, and led them to interpret the ambiguous behavior in those terms even though the initial activation had nothing to do with Donald. Thus, schemata can affect interpretation as well as memory (see Higgins, Rholes, & Jones, 1977; Srull & Wyer, 1979).

CHRONIC ACTIVATION

Many psychologists have argued that people differ in which of their schemata are chronically activated, or are close to being activated. George Alexander Kelly, for example, proposed that the central way in which we differ from one another is in just which schemata (or to use his word, ''constructs'') we use to interpret the world. Some research has addressed the role of chronically activated schemata in memory and interpretation (Kelly, 1955).

In one study, students were asked to list characteristics of people they liked, disliked, frequently encountered, and so on. One group of students wrote down *inconsiderate* or *selfish* as the first trait on the list about people they knew, while others did not mention those traits. The subjects who mentioned *inconsiderate* spontaneously were assumed to have that trait as a chronically active schema. Those that didn't mention it were assumed not to have it as a chronically active schema. The subjects were later told about the behavior of a person and asked to write down the one word that best described him. The key description was ''He monopolized the telephone where he lived.'' It was constructed by the investigators to be an ambiguous description, applying to someone who was both talkative and inconsiderate. The question was: How would the two types of subjects interpret it? The results showed that those who had *inconsiderate* as a chronically active category saw the specific, ambiguous behavior as inconsiderate, while those who did not have *inconsiderate* chronically active did not interpret the behavior that way (Bargh, Lombardi, & Higgins, 1988).

Encoding Behavior

What controls which schemata are activated by a particular behavior? One answer seems to be traits closely related to the behavior. In one study, for example, subjects were given eighteen sentences describing behaviors and told to memorize them. In a recall task, the subjects were given cues to the sentences. One kind of cue was the name of a trait related to the behavior described by a sentence. This recall cue was effective in enhancing subjects' recall of the behaviors (Winter & Uleman, 1984; Winter, Uleman, & Cunniff, 1985). But it is well known by cognitive psychologists that cues enhance memory if, and only if, they are in the same terms as the terms in which the subject originally *encoded* the material. Thus, the fact that traits helped subjects recall behaviors is evidence that the behaviors were stored in terms of traits in the first place (see also Bassili & Smith, 1986; Newman & Uleman, 1990; D'Agostino, 1991). There is evidence, then, that even without special instruction, subjects encode the behavior they see in terms of traits.

"WITH ALL I'VE LEARNED ABOUT PSYCHOLOGY RECENTLY, ESTABLISHING WHO'S NAUGHTY AND WHO'S NICE IS NOT AS SIMPLE AS IT USED TO BE."

But people may also encode behavior in other terms. In one study, for example, subjects were given a description of a person to read, and they were told to read the material so that they could pass on a general impression of the person to another subject. Other subjects weren't told anything about passing on their impressions. Now all the subjects were asked to write out their impressions. The subjects who expected to pass on their impressions used more traits than those not forewarned. In a second experiment, some subjects were told that they would be communicating their impression in words, others were told that they would be communicating in the form of a line drawing. But again, they were all asked for their impressions in words. Those expecting to use words all along used more traits in describing the person they read about (Hoffman, Mischel, & Baer, 1984). Thus, we are especially likely to think in terms of traits when we intend to communicate our impressions in words and when we have more practice using traits (Smith, Stewart, & Buttram, 1992; Bassili, 1993).

In another study, using a similar method, subjects were instructed either to form an impression about the person described in a vignette, or to think about whether something about the person or something about the situation caused the behavior. The subjects were then given vignettes describing a behavior; for example, "The carpenter approached the lost tourists to offer directions." And along with these behavioral descriptions they were also given information leading to the assumption that the behavior was either characteristic of the person, "The carpenter often approaches lost tourists," or characteristic of the situation, "Many other people who saw the lost tourists approached them." Finally, the subjects were asked to complete some word fragments, h—pf–l, for example. The question was: Would priming with the behavioral vignettes speed completion of word fragments that were semantically related to the traits implicated by the behaviors? For example, would the description of the carpenter's behavior speed the subject's seeing that the above fragment is *helpful?* If so, then priming with the behavior activates the related trait.

A second question focused on the attributional information. Most social psychologists think of traits as broad dispositions of a person. If so, then we might expect that the behavioral descriptions would activate the semantically related trait word if and only if the attributional information suggested that the particular behavior was part of a broad disposition of the person. Thus, we might expect that the carpenter's behavior would prime *helpful* if and only if the accompanying information suggested that helpfulness was a general trait of the carpenter.

That is what we might expect, but it wasn't what happened. Rather, the behavioral descriptions primed the related trait word regardless of whether the accompanying information made it seem as if the behavior were characteristic of the situation or of the person (Bassili, 1989). The suggestion of these data is, then, that trait concepts are essentially abstract characterizations of behavior that can also sometimes, but only sometimes, be used to characterize people as well. These data also suggest that although we may spontaneously think of *behavior* in terms of traits, we don't necessarily think of *people* in terms of traits.

In one study, subjects were given different purposes for their descriptions. Some were told to describe someone as if they were trying to enable the listener to pick her out of a crowd in Grand Central Station; others were told to describe her so that the listener would know what it was like to live around her. As you might imagine, those given the first instruction used physical descriptors, whereas those given the second instruction used trait words (Fiske & Cox, 1979). Thus, although we have a predilection for traits, we are also flexible information processors.

We have seen that priming and the purposes we have in learning information can affect the impressions we form of people. A natural question to ask is: Which is stronger? Are we mostly the victims of passive priming, such that just hearing a trait word has powerful effects on our memories, effects that we can tune just a bit depending on our purposes at the moment? Or is the reverse true? Is the way that we store information mostly affected by our purposes at the moment, while priming has just a small effect? It is difficult to quantify these effects, or to answer this question in general. There has, however, been one experiment that provides us with some sense of the relative power of these effects.

In this study, subjects were told that they would be given information about a person, and that they would then be asked to communicate their overall impression of the person to another subject. Some subjects were led to believe they would be giving their impression to someone who liked the person they would hear about. Others thought they would be giving their impression to someone who didn't like that person. A third group of subjects thought they would be communicating to someone who had a neutral impression. Past research suggests that such instructions should induce subjects to move both their public, expressed evaluations and their private memories in the direction of their target's opinion. In addition to this manipulation, some of each kind of subject also had their memories primed with either positive or negative trait words before seeing descriptions of ambiguous material. Now the question was this: Which effect would dominate? Would the priming affect recall of the ambiguous behavior more than the target's opinion, or vice versa?

The results were that priming mattered, but only for the subjects who thought they would be communicating to someone with a neutral opinion. Priming had no effect when subjects thought they would be communicating to someone with a positive or negative opinion. The target's opinion had such a strong effect that it swamped the effect of the priming manipulation (Sedikides, 1990). These data suggest, then, that our purposes in encoding information have a greater effect than does the fortuitous priming of traits. We aren't all that victimized by randomly hearing this or that trait word.

The Organization and Representation of Impressions

Solomon Asch, you will recall, asked his subjects to form an impression of a person described by a few traits. Perhaps the fact that impressed him most about his subjects' impressions was that they were unified. Subjects seemed to form an overall impression of a person rather than just remember a list of traits. This fact has an interesting relation to the way our memories work. Recent research has thrown much light on this fact first uncovered by Asch.

IMPRESSIONS AND MEMORY

Several investigators have given subjects lists of traits or behaviors and later asked for recall of these lists. Often the subjects have been asked either to memorize the list or form an impression of the person described by the traits. Ironically, the consistent finding is that recall for specific traits or behavior is better when subjects attempt to form a unified impression than it is when they explicitly attempt to memorize (Hamilton, Katz, & Leirer, 1980; Srull, 1983; Klein & Loftus, 1990). It seems that attempting to form a general impression of someone is a very good way to store information about her so that it can later be retrieved. There is also reason to believe that forming a general impression of someone is just what subjects do when they are given information about someone and told that they will shortly be interacting with that person. Apparently, "anticipated interaction" or "general impression" instructions lead to superior memory because both kinds of instructions lead subjects to think about the information more, and especially to attempt to understand inconsistencies, and thus to form stronger associations among the individual bits of data (Gordon & Wyer, 1987; Devine, Sedikides, & Fuhrman, 1989; see Klein & Loftus, 1990, for a different but related account of why general impression instructions enhance recall).

OVERALL IMPRESSIONS AND RECALL OF SPECIFIC FACTS

How is our overall evaluation of a person related to the specific facts we can recall about her? We might expect that they would be consistent, that the facts we can recall about someone justify or explain our overall evaluations. But perhaps this simple idea isn't true. I have had the experience of being

◀ From Rashoman, *the classic film depicting how different the same event can look when seen from different points of view. Minoru Chiaki* (left,) *Kichijro Veda* (center), *and Takashi Shimura* (right) *represent three different schools of thought, depicting wavering spiritual hope, cynical disbelief, and practical reformation.*

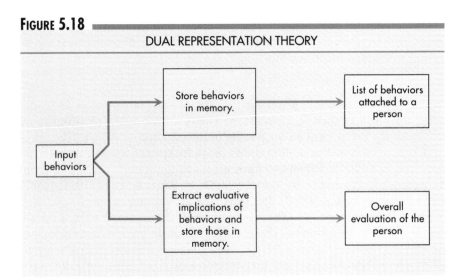

FIGURE 5.18

DUAL REPRESENTATION THEORY

Input behaviors

Store behaviors in memory.

List of behaviors attached to a person

Extract evaluative implications of behaviors and store those in memory.

Overall evaluation of the person

▶ *According to the dual representation view, when we learn of a person's behavior, we (1) store it in memory and (2) use it to update our overall evaluation of the person.*

asked what I think of someone, and then being asked why. Often I have been tongue-tied at such moments, able to think of very little about the person to justify my reaction. In this regard at least, I am not very different from everyone else; the research literature also suggests that people's memories and overall evaluations are often out of alignment. Why?

Explanations of this phenomenon focus on what is often called **dual representation** theory. The basic idea of dual representation theory is that when we form an overall impression of someone—either because of instructions in an experiment or naturally because of the expectation of interaction—we extract the implications of the behavior we see at the same time that we store the behavior itself in memory (see Figure 5.18). Thus, if we see someone do something terribly selfish, we will both store (remember) a generally dim view of the person and store in memory the specific behavior (see Srull & Wyer, 1989, for an elaboration of the model).

In the jargon of computer talk, we form our general evaluations "on line." As we learn new information about a person, we do two things with it: (1) we update our general impression, and (2) we store that behavior in memory too. As experience with the person grows, we may begin to forget certain specific behaviors, but those behaviors continue to have an impact on our overall impression because they affected the starting point of our overall evaluation. Such a model of our memory for people suggests that early information will have a greater impact on overall evaluations, a primacy effect, but that later information will have a greater impact on specific behavior recall, a recency effect.

A variety of experimental techniques have been used to explore these ideas. One technique relies on varying the "set" (goal or purpose) of the subjects, telling them to read a list of behavioral descriptions about someone and asking them either to form an overall impression of the person or simply to try to comprehend the individual behaviors (see Figure 5.19). At the end of one such experiment, both sorts of subjects were asked for their recall of the behaviors and their overall evaluations. Subjects given the "overall impression set" were expected to form an evaluation "on line"—as they read

FIGURE 5.19

"SET" AND OVERALL EVALUATIONS

Subjects given "overall impression set." →

Subjects try to remember list of behaviors. → Subjects forget some behaviors.

Subjects form general evaluation. → Forgotten behaviors still influence general evaluation.

A Disjunction between overall evaluation and behaviors recalled.

Subjects given "comprehension set." → Subjects remember some behaviors. → Subjects forget some behaviors. → Subjects form general evaluation based only on remembered behaviors.

B No disjunction between overall evaluation and behaviors recalled.

◀ *Disjunction between overall evaluations and recall of specific behaviors will occur when subjects are initially given an "overall impression set." Such disjunction does not occur when subjects are initially given a "comprehension set" and form their overall evaluation at the end of the experiment. (Based on Lichtenstein & Srull, 1987)*

each behavior—and therefore to reveal a disjunction (disconnection) between their overall evaluations and their specific recall. The "comprehension set" subjects, on the other hand, were expected to form their overall evaluation of the person only at the end of the experiment and therefore to base it on the behaviors they recalled. They were expected *not* to show the expected disjunction between recall and overall evaluation. And this is just what happened (Lichtenstein & Srull, 1987).

A second technique involves giving subjects information about someone, and then telling them that specific pieces of information are in error and should be disregarded. The question is: How will the disregarded information affect overall evaluations? If impressions are formed "on line," then it should be quite difficult to remove the effect of information they have already heard because this information will have been incorporated into their overall evaluation. The best that subjects can do when told to disregard information is to "adjust" their current evaluation. So if subjects are told to disregard positive information, they can and do adjust their current evaluation downward, and if they are told to disregard negative information, they can adjust their impression upward. But how much should they adjust? By precisely the amount that the original information mattered. The problem is that they may not (and the evidence suggests they do not) know just how much each piece of information affected them. Therefore, adjustments are likely to be crude at best. And, as a result, the impressions after trying to disregard information are not really what they would have been had the subjects never heard the information in the first place (Wyer & Budesheim, 1987).

There is evidence that dual representation theory describes our self-knowledge too. Suppose I asked you how creative you were. How would you answer? I mean, how would you go about answering? One thing you might do is think of specific behaviors you have performed that displayed creativity. If this is how you go about answering my question, then you should be very fast at answering if just before I asked you how creative you were I had asked you to think of a creative behavior you had performed. After all, if such a memory had just been evoked, you should be quick to evoke it again. But experimental evidence shows that evoking specific behavioral instances of a trait does *not* speed up the answering of a general question about subjects' traits (Klein, Loftus, & Plog, 1992). On the other hand, asking subjects to describe how they typically behave when exemplifying a trait does speed up the subjects' general judgments of themselves (Klein, Loftus, & Sherman, 1993). This evidence suggests that we keep track of summary judgments of our standing on (some, at least) traits separate from behaviors we have performed that embody those traits.

The technique used to document dual representation theory bears a striking resemblance to the television series *L.A. Law.* In courtrooms, or at least courtrooms on television, lawyers are forever saying things to juries they know are inadmissible, and judges are forever telling juries to "disregard that last remark." The experimental evidence we have just reviewed suggests that juries really can't disregard what they have already heard. But lawyers may not be getting away with as much as this evidence suggests. Studies using mock juries—groups of subjects told to act as if they were a jury—have shown that subjects *can* disregard evidence they have heard *in reaching a verdict.* Apparently, getting people to think as they would if they were jurors enables them to "erase" the effects of information they later learn they should ignore (Schul & Manzury, 1990). Why this is so is not clear. Perhaps it is because jurors are asked to reach a verdict about the guilt or innocence of a defendant *with regard to a specific act* rather than to form a general evaluation of the defendant.

SUMMARY

1. On learning that someone has specific traits, we spontaneously infer the presence of other traits. This indicates that we have an *implicit personality theory.* Some traits are central to our conception of personality; they lead to many inferences about other traits. Other, peripheral, traits lead to few inferences.

2. *Attribution theories* are about how we draw inferences from a person's behavior to the traits that account for that behavior. Ned Jones and Keith Davis's *correspondent inference theory* applies centrally to intentional actions and specifies that our inferences about the reasons for a person's behavior become less certain as we discover more reasons the person might have had for acting.

3. Harold Kelley's covariation theory applies centrally to spontaneous reactions like laughing rather than intentional actions. It claims that on observing a person's behavior in response to some object, we typically ask ourselves: Was that behavior caused by the object (externally caused) or by some feature of the person (internally caused)?

4. Attribution theorists claim to have discovered several biases in how people reason about behavior. For example, people are said to believe that their own actions are externally caused while believing that other people's behavior is internally caused. The *fundamental attributional error*, is the tendency to accept behavior as indicative of an actor's real attitudes—even when we know the person was acting under constraint. People do not make this error when the actor makes the fact of acting under constraint explicit, or when the constraints take the form of ulterior motives. The fundamental attributional error has been explained as a consequence of people's failure to take account *of base rates.*

5. People have been found to assume that other people will behave in the same way they do or will evaluate things in the same way they do (*egocentrism bias*). People have also been found to be *self-serving* in making external attributions for their failures but internal attributions for their successes. Finally, people have been shown to test hypotheses in a way that is biased toward finding evidence that confirms the hypothesis they are testing.

6. Critics of attribution theory have raised several objections to its focus on causal explanations. (1) There is an infinite set of causes of any behavior, thus it would be a hopeless and frustrating task to search for *all* of the causes of behavior. People use social knowledge frames to narrow their search for causes. Once the search has been narrowed, there may not be much room for the operation of attributional processes. (2) People are often far more interested in knowing who is responsible for something than they are in simply knowing who caused it. (3) People may answer questions about why someone did something in an external vs. internal way more for reasons of politeness than because of fundamental facts about how we perceive ourselves and others.

7. Cognitive schemata are theoretical entities that cognitive psychologists use to help us understand how attention is controlled, information is integrated, and (c) memory is guided. Traits function as schemata.

8. *Dual representation theory* claims that when we learn facts about a person, we use this information in two distinct ways: we update our general evaluation of that person, and we store the specific behavioral facts. If we decide that we were wrong about a certain behavior, we can "erase" it from our representation of the person's behaviors, but it is more difficult to undo the impact the behavior had on our general impression.

CHAPTER 6

Self-Presentation

This chapter has a focus only slightly removed from that of Chapter 5. There we noted that people inevitably form impressions of the personalities of the people they encounter. In understanding how we form those impressions, we stressed the ways our thinking about people is like our understanding of the rest of the things in the world: rocks, stars, trees, hurricanes, and so on. But left out of that discussion was a crucial way in which our knowledge of people is different from our knowledge of hurricanes. We can be confident that, for all of their perversity, hurricanes aren't deliberately trying to make a specific impression on us. But matters are different with our fellow humans. We all know that there are times when we attempt to impress someone in a specific way. For example, we deliberately try to get the person interviewing us for a job to think we have just the qualities she wants in a new employee. And we have every reason to suspect that other people do this to us as well. The focus of this chapter is on social psychological thinking about how people attempt to control the impressions other people form of them, a topic often referred to as ***self-presentation,*** or ***impression management.*** Impression management, as we shall see, might also be called attribution management, since what is often at issue is the attributions others make about us.

This chapter also cuts close to the self. Perhaps it seems natural to think of the self in terms of private, internal experience; we tend to think of our selves in terms of our emotions, desires, and values. But there is a tradition of thought about the self, one most closely identified in this century with George Herbert Mead and Charles Horton Cooley, that stresses the way in which our knowledge of our selves is a reflection of others' opinions of us (Cooley, 1902/1964; Mead, 1934/1962). For thinkers in this tradition, having a self of a certain sort means primarily to act in a certain way in a public arena. And therefore our knowledge of our selves comes from what goes on in that arena. Their view leads to the idea that the self is more something we accomplish than something we all have inside that we merely need to express. For example, the most important aspect of a great artist's self is her being a great artist; this is a matter of public accomplishment, not private experience. Not many of us are great artists. Still, a vital part of many people's selves is being a loving, caring parent or spouse. Being those too is at least in part a matter of actually doing things for the people we care about rather than having private, internal feelings about them. So it is not entirely foreign to us to think of the self as something that goes on outside, in the social world.

GOFFMAN'S APPROACH TO SELF-PRESENTATION

We begin our discussion of self-presentation with the work of a sociologist, Erving Goffman. In a fascinating series of papers and books, Goffman let us see how common, important, and subtle self-presentation is (1955, 1956, 1959). The most comprehensive statement of Goffman's position is in his *Presentation of Self in Everyday Life* (1959), so it is there that we start.

Impression Management and Identity

Goffman begins his discussion in this book with some truisms. First, how people treat us depends on what they think of us, on who they think we are. Second, since the way people treat us depends on their impression of us, it is in our interest to influence what other people think of us. Third, one important way we can affect what others think of us is through our behavior; therefore, it is in our interest to arrange our behavior so that people draw the conclusions we want them to about who we are. One way Goffman introduces the notion of self-presentation, then, is through self-interest: by pointing out that it is in people's interest to manage the impressions others form of them.

There is another way Goffman introduces the idea of self-presentation; this way of thinking is less obvious but perhaps more profound. It starts with the idea that the way we behave toward people depends, at least in part, on the *definition of the situation* in which we interact with them. Needless to say, the way a professor treats students in a lecture hall (and the way they treat the professor) is crucially influenced by their shared understanding that this is a lecture. And notice that its being a lecture depends on the social roles of the parties involved—a lecture needs a lecturer and an audience. After all, the same hall is just a maintenance problem to other people in the university. So the nature of the situation depends on the *social identities* of the parties involved.

Now this matter of identities is subtle. In part it is a formal matter, a case of the person's being entitled by an institution to play a specific **social role**— my students certainly hope that I have been appointed by the university as a professor! But Goffman argues that more than a formal role is involved in sustaining the definition of the situation. For example, a professor is expected to be knowledgeable about his subject matter. Beyond that, he is supposed to be generally educated and smart—in some vague, everyday sense. He should

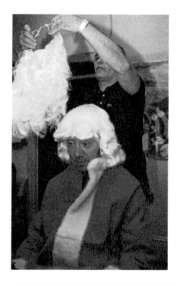

▲ *In Goffman's words, we are "backstage" with Santa Claus; this person was or will be playing the role of Santa Claus.*

▲ *What impression does he want to project?*

Impression management is *obviously* important to people who are pretending to be what they aren't. It is less obviously, but equally, important to people who want to be treated as they really are.

be concerned, at least to some degree, about his students and their welfare generally. And, of course, he is expected to be an adult, in control of his emotions, impulses, and body. Goffman suggests that there are demands on students as well. Students should be smart too; smart enough for college. They should also be interested in the material, willing to work hard to get a grade, and so on.

From the point of view of managing the social interaction that goes on in a classroom, it isn't very important whether any of this is true or whether anyone actually *believes* these things. I know as an instructor that some of my students aren't in the least interested in what I am saying. I know that interest waxes and wanes, and that at any given moment there is as much waning going on as there is waxing. But regardless of what I believe, if I am to continue as a lecturer, I must *act as if* my students care about the material, even if I don't believe it. And they must act as if it were true too. Students who look attentive but are in fact daydreaming are a problem, an educational problem, but students who display their lack of interest by reading the newspaper are in addition a social problem. So Goffman argues that social interactions are governed and made intelligible by the parties involved implicitly agreeing to treat each other as if they had certain identities; he refers to this implicit contract as a **working consensus.**

There are *two* reasons, then, why while lecturing, the instructor might try to create and sustain the impression that he is a reasonable facsimile of a professor. One is so that students will treat him as he wishes to be treated. The other is that insofar as instructor and students are to interact in the classroom, there must be at least a working consensus that the instructor actually has all of those properties professors are supposed to have. If social interactions are to run along smoothly, those involved had better not give any evidence that they are *not* the people required by the working consensus. And, similarly, there are at least two reasons for students not to read the newspaper in class. One is that the instructor might flunk them, but the other is so as not to disrupt the class by violating the working consensus.

Impression Management and Embarrassment

Goffman's treatment of impression management calls attention to embarrassment as a link between our emotions and our self-presentations. Although the emotion of embarrassment was mentioned before in our discussion of social influence (Chapter 2), it is in the context of self-presentation that we should consider embarrassment directly.

LOSS OF ESTEEM

Goffman's writings have spawned two quite different theories of embarrassment. The first was developed by André Modigliani. Modigliani suggested that people become embarrassed when they suddenly lose self-esteem. And, he argued, the typical cause of suddenly losing self-esteem is losing esteem in the eyes of another. This conception of embarrassment ties our emotions to our self-presentation via our self-esteem. It says, following Mead, that our sense of our own worth is intimately connected to what others think of us, and that if we fail to impress others, we will lose esteem in our own eyes and become embarrassed.

In a series of studies, Modigliani arranged for subjects to fail a task (impossible anagrams) either in private or public. Some subjects were told that the anagrams were very difficult, but they were also told that the other subjects working on the anagrams wouldn't know that. He found that public failure on the anagrams did lead to a loss of self-esteem and embarrassment, even when the subjects knew they were very hard (Modigliani, 1968, 1971). But there is reason to believe that failure in others' eyes isn't the whole story of embarrassment, and that a loss of *esteem in one's own eyes* isn't necessary for embarrassment to occur.

FIVE DISTINGUISHED PROFESSORS, EACH TRYING TO LOOK LIKE A MORE DISTINGUISHED PROFESSOR THAN THE OTHER FOUR

INTERACTION

As part of a social psychology graduate seminar my fellow students and I were told to get on a New York City subway and do something very simple. We were to approach seated passengers and say to them, "Excuse me, may I have your seat?" There are two interesting things about this experiment (Milgram & Sabini, 1978). First, most of the time you get a seat, and second, it is horribly embarrassing to do. Really, it is just terrible. Sometimes we would get up in front of people and freeze; we were sometimes not able to squeeze the words out. Now I am sure we looked weird in the eyes of the other riders, but there was no reason for us to lose esteem in our own eyes. *We knew we weren't crazy.* We knew we were doing it so as not to fail the course! But we were extremely embarrassed. So our embarrassment here also suggests that a loss of self-esteem isn't necessary for embarrassment to occur.

In light of these results, Jerry Parrott, Maury Silver, and I (1988) proposed an account of embarrassment that removes any connection between embarrassment and esteem (self- or in the eyes of others). This account is based on Goffman's second approach to impression management, one that is less concerned with esteem than with continuing the interaction. To illustrate this theory, we gave subjects three scenarios to read and asked them how embarrassed they would be in each. One scenario involved asking someone of the opposite sex out on a date and receiving the reply "Ah, I'm not very good at this, but *no.*" Most subjects reported that they would feel quite embarrassed if this happened to them. Every theory of embarrassment predicts that (1) in such an event, one loses self-esteem, (2) one becomes acutely aware of one's lack of esteem in the eyes of the person one is asking out, and (3) it is hard to know what to say next.

But in another scenario, the person replied, "I'd love to go out with you, but I'm involved with someone else." Subjects reported that this would be less embarrassing. This might be because (1) it is less hard on self-esteem, (2) it doesn't give evidence that the other person thinks little of you, or (3) it makes it easier to continue with the interaction.

In the third scenario, before asking out the other person (the target), the protagonist asked the target's best friend whether the target was involved with someone else, and the best friend reassured the protagonist that there was no one else. Nonetheless, the target replied, "I'd love to go out with you, but I'm involved with someone else." The subjects reported that this would be less embarrassing than the flat-out, unembellished, sincere, direct turndown. But why? It wasn't because they were spared a loss of esteem in the eyes of the person they asked out. They knew just how little she thought of them; they knew the "someone else" was just an excuse. And, indeed, when asked about

FIGURE 6.1

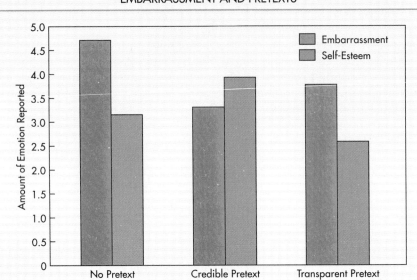

EMBARRASSMENT AND PRETEXTS

▶ *The effects on self-esteem and embarrassment of being turned down for a date with no pretext, with a credible pretext, and with a pretext subjects knew to be false. The transparently false pretext saved embarrassment but did not prevent loss of self-esteem. (Data from Parrott, Sabini, & Silver, 1988)*

self-esteem, subjects reported that this condition lowered their self-esteem to a point below that produced by the flat turndown (see Figure 6.1).

So even though in such a condition people's esteem in the eyes of another is revealed to be very low, and their self-esteem goes with it, they aren't so embarrassed. We argued that this is because, regardless of what happens to esteem, the working consensus isn't cracked. Even though they privately both knew it wasn't true, the protagonist and target could still save face and interact with each other as if they were both desirable, date-worthy creatures (Parrott, Sabini, & Silver, 1988). After all, it is exactly to avoid embarrassment that we invent pretexts like this, even transparently false ones. Still, this research involved subjects' reports about how they *would* feel in the relevant situation, which isn't the same as asking people who are actually in the situation how they feel. Further experimental evidence is needed to decide just what circumstances produce embarrassment. (See Miller, 1992, for a contrary view of embarrassment and Leary, Britt, Cutlip, & Templeton, 1992, for a discussion of the determinants of blushing.)

CONSEQUENCES OF EMBARRASSMENT

Embarrassing incidents have a variety of effects. For one thing, they give rise to the typical displays or signs of embarrassment. People who are embarrassed avoid eye contact (Modigliani, 1971; Edelmann & Hampson, 1979). They also give off more general signs of distress—speech disturbances (stuttering, for example) and bodily movements (shaking, for example) (Edelmann & Hampson, 1979).

Another consequence of embarrassment is the attempt to restore the situation (or at least one's identity), to engage in what Goffman calls "facework." Think what happens, for example, if you trip on the sidewalk—for no reason. What do you do? I know what I do; I turn around and stare at the sidewalk as if *it* were at fault for my clumsiness. In so doing, I am announcing to anyone who happens to be looking that I am not the sort of person who trips unless there is something wrong with the sidewalk; I am restoring my face (see Brown, 1968, 1970, and Brown & Garland, 1971, for experimental examples of facework).

The most common way embarrassment makes its presence known in the social world is by virtue of what people will do to *avoid* it in the first place. In Chapter 2, we reviewed studies that involve the fear of embarrassment. We saw that people will deny the clear evidence of their senses (the Asch experiment), obey an authority to insane limits (the Milgram experiment), fail to respond to another in distress, and even fail to act in the face of danger to themselves out of fear of embarrassment (the Latané and Darley experiments). These are experimental results, but presumably they mirror facts in the real world. One place that the effects of fear of embarrassment have been documented in the real world is in the domain of adolescent contraceptive use. A cliché of the movies and television is that it is terribly embarrassing for adolescents to purchase condoms. Unfortunately, it is more than a cliché; it really is embarrassing. Unwanted pregnancy and AIDS may be the costs that some people pay rather than face embarrassment (Herold, 1981).

The How of Self-Presentation: Performances

The motives people have for self-presentation and the emotions they feel when such attempts fail take up only a small part of Goffman's work. For the most part, he is concerned not with the *why* of self-presentation but with the *how*. After all, to present one-self as one wishes, one must not only be motivated to do so, one must also stage a performance that projects the right impression (Leary & Kowalski, 1990).

SETS AND PROPS

A theatrical performance takes place on a stage, and while the whole world surely isn't a stage, the whole world does share certain crucial features with stages. The theater makes use of sets and props, which orient the audience to the action that will follow and, more important for our purposes, inform the audience about the characters that will appear in the play. Goffman proposes that we too in our everyday lives make use of settings and props. The kind of house someone lives in, for example, says something about who he is. Is it a mansion? A hovel? A middle-class, suburban, single-family dwelling, a dorm room, an urban apartment? These background elements of our everyday lives announce to all who see them something about the kinds of people we are and the kinds of things we care about.

When we move into a new home, it may strike us as cold, inhuman. We want to populate it with ''personal touches,'' reminders of the people we know, the art we appreciate, the music we like, the trips we have taken. These ''props'' too announce to anyone who sees them something of who we are, what we care about. Thus, as inhabitants of a set, we can use it to inform ''audiences'' about our selves, and as audiences, we ''read'' a set to make inferences about the person who constructed it.

Settings and props are resources to announce a character, but every re-

"WELL, JUST DON'T THINK ABOUT THOSE YOU ARE WHAT YOU DRIVE COMMERCIALS."

▲ To what degree does taking on the superficial aspects of a role facilitate acquiring the deeper ones?

source comes at a cost. What are the costs? One is obvious. Having a nice house costs money in the first place. And upkeep is expensive. Paint wears out; upholstery fades and frays; china chips and cracks. Worse yet, some of the pitfalls are entirely beyond your control—the neighborhood may go downhill.

TEAMS

The typical play involves more than one character. And the interactions among the characters are a very important, perhaps the most important, way each character communicates to the audience just who she is. Goffman argues that in everyday life too, we often put on performances of our own characters in collaboration with other people, who help us project our identities. Goffman calls these groups of people with whom we perform "teams."

A thoroughly respectable middle-class family who has just purchased and furnished their home will typically use their new setting to communicate who they are, not as lone individuals but as a family. And when the family "has company," each member will have to count on the others to play their roles. This is both a resource and a source of danger. Just as we draw inferences about people from the settings they appear in, so too do we draw inferences from the people they associate with. We know something about a person if we know her spouse, children, family, friends, and co-workers. And we learn quite a lot about a person from the ways her friends treat her.

Actually, we may learn two different things from how someone's friends treat her. First, we may learn something about who she is. If her friends treat her as smart, organized, and generally competent, we have some reason to believe she is all of these things. But, second, even if she *isn't* all of these things, we know that she is likely to be someone who *expects to be treated as* someone who is all of these things. So even if her friends have a distorted picture of her, they probably don't have a distorted picture of how they should treat her in order to get along with her.

Chapter 5 discussed how we come to know what people are really like. But Goffman focuses our attention on how people expect to be treated. He reminds us that for many purposes in our everyday lives, it isn't important for us to know who someone really is. What is important to know is the kind of person she takes herself to be or at least is willing to be treated as. Perhaps we do want to know who our very closest friends really are, but Goffman suggests that it is unnecessary (and perhaps even undesirable) to know who most of the people we interact with really are. It is sufficient to have an untroubled relationship with them, to know what character they are portraying.

There are costs to being team players, however. One problem with teammates is that just as we can shine in the reflected glory of their accomplishments—parents proudly display the awards their children have won and show off the good manners they have taught them—we must also pay the price of their failures. A criminal's family will pay a price in shame if he is caught. Smaller infractions exact a smaller cost. So one cost of being a member of a team rather than a one-man show is that we pay a price for the misbehavior of another person.

Another problem has to do with coordination. Take the owners of a jewelry store in a small community as an example. Suppose the price they charged a customer had to do, in part, with how good a customer he was; not unreasonably, they charged their best customers less than they charged people they didn't know. But they acted as if they were giving everyone the best possible price. Now to make all of this work, they could not just label the articles with prices. The customers had to ask them the price of the watch or ring they were interested in. And this led to a problem of coordination.

Suppose a customer asked one owner, Kathy, how much a watch cost, but then shopped some more before taking it to the other owner, Harry, to be rung up. What would Harry charge? It wouldn't look right to ask the customer, and he couldn't tell from the article itself, and it would look very bad if he charged more or less than Kathy had asked for. To avoid this, the owners used a code. Harry would ask Kathy not for the price of the watch but for its code number. Kathy would answer with a number that told Harry how much markup she had already asked for. From this he could figure out what she had told the customer.

Harry and Kathy were engaged, then, in a bit of self-presentational work; they were presenting themselves as selling their goods at the same, rock-bottom, discount price for all customers. To sustain this appearance, they needed to coordinate their efforts, *and to conceal the fact that they were coordinating them.* This communication requires effort, attention, and memory, and leads to the danger that it will break down. Spy stories, with their appealing tales of such problems and near-misses, convey this danger well.

APPEARANCE AND MANNER

One source of information about our character that is always available, at least in face-to-face interaction, is our appearance and manner. Our gender, age, and physical attractiveness are always available as a source of inference. (See Chapter 14 for some of the inferences we draw from these aspects of a person.) We can, to some degree, alter the way we look, but only to some degree. So for the most part, we must, like any actor or actress, work within what we have been given in putting on performances.

The clothes we wear announce much about us. The fabrics, color, and cut we choose tell about our taste and our social class. Rarely do we choose

▲ *Madonna over time. Same person, very different personae.*

our clothes so as to announce these things; rather, part of our socialization—by our family and later our peers—teaches us to like (and think we look good in) certain sorts of clothes. But regardless of why we wear what we wear, they comment on who we are.

How we talk announces volumes too. First, there is the matter of accent. None of us thinks we have an accent in our native tongue. But people with an ear for this sort of thing can place where someone grew up from a very small sample of what she says. And, it is said, the trained listener to British conversation can locate the speaker not just geographically but, perhaps more important, in social class.

Then there is the matter of what a person chooses to say. A friend of mine once asked me if I had learned to say "indeed" (as a way of agreeing with what someone just said, as a substitute for "right") in order to be a professor. As I listened to others, I noticed that no one but professors use "indeed" this way (though everyone understands it). This mildly Victorian way of speaking announces one's occupation. Jargon of every sort serves the same function. In fact, some people treat a disparagement of their field's jargon as a rejection of them personally. So various aspects of the way one speaks announce who one is.

Self-Presentation and Faking

Goffman's approach to the social life is a powerful and interesting one. But it is also a view that has attracted criticism. The criticisms, for the most part, center around Goffman's treatment of the self in such an "external" way. Because he argues that when in social interaction *one of our concerns* is with self-presentation, some readers take him to be implying that we are all fakes, that we are constantly trying to convince other people that we are something we aren't. But this isn't the right way to understand Goffman. An example may clarify these matters.

Consider two people. One of them, Mary, is a good friend of yours. She really is. The other, Diane, isn't really your friend, but she is pretending to be one (for some reason). Now the difference between a real friend and a fake friend is an important one; you would surely want to be able to tell them apart. Goffman, it is true, isn't immediately concerned with this difference; rather, he is concerned with what Mary and Diane *have in common.* His focus is on what Mary and Diane will both have to do in order to communicate to you that they are your friends. Both of them, for example, will have to convince you that they think about you, that they are concerned about your feelings and welfare. Both will, then, be engaged in self-presentation. To be sure, one of the selves that is presented is a fraud and the other is real, but that is a different issue. Goffman's claim that we engage in self-presentation is not a way of saying that we are fakes; rather, it is a way of saying that facts that aren't communicated are of no social significance.

But there is still something that sticks in the craw about Goffman's perspective. Perhaps it is the strong belief in our culture that authentic people, people who really are what they seem to be, have no need of artifice. They just do whatever comes naturally, and by doing what comes naturally, they express who they really are. Therefore, to the degree that someone engages in self-presentation, it must be because he is a fraud. It is this idea that Goff-

THE COME-AS-YOU-WISH-YOU-WERE PARTY

man does reject. He rejects it as a romanticized view of how life really is.

Let us return to Mary, your true friend. Suppose you call Mary up to talk to her about some problem you are having. The cultural ideal suggests that since Mary really is your friend, if she just acts as she feels, she will communicate her friendship to you. But Goffman asks us to look at this situation more closely and realistically. It might be true, Goffman agrees, that when you call her, she can just act as she feels and express friendship. But what if she is tired, or has a headache, or is concerned about some problem of her own, or is very excited about a date she has that night, or is engrossed in a television program? Goffman reminds us that if she is in one of those states when you call, and if she expresses what she feels, you will not have the sense that she is much of a friend (she wouldn't *be* much of a friend either). Even though she really is your friend, she will at this moment have to work at communicating to you that it is true. She will have to suppress her own concerns and attend to yours.

Thought about closely, this idea that we will succeed in expressing ourselves to others simply by acting out our feelings at every moment is untenable. It is untenable because our feelings are too unstable, too easily affected by fairly trivial matters—for example, how tired we are. The spy must discipline herself to mislead other people about who she is; the rest of us must discipline ourselves to inform people about who we really are.

Techniques of impression management are as important to the person who would communicate who he really is as they are to the con man. There is evidence that people want *both* to present themselves to others in a favorable light and to communicate to others what they consider to be a true view of themselves.

In one experiment, a subject interacted with three confederates. After their interaction, each of the confederates provided the subject with feedback about his impression of the subject. One of the confederates made a quite positive appraisal of the subject with regard to an aspect of the self the subject herself thought was good, say intellectual ability; this confederate made no mention of what the subject thought was a weak aspect of her abilities, say social skills.* So this confederate offered the subject *self-enhancing* (positive) feedback

In conveying a self, people can make use of (among other things)
- props,
- sets,
- teammates,
- manners,
- appearance.

*What aspect of her self the subject thought was strong or weak was determined in a pretest.

that was also *self-verifying* in that it corresponded to what the subject herself thought. Another of the confederates gave the subject feedback that was positive about an aspect of the self the subject thought was quite weak (self-enhancing, but not self-verifying). Finally, the third confederate offered negative feedback about an aspect of the self the subject too thought was quite weak. The question was: Which confederate would the subject choose to interact with in a second session?

Subjects preferred, as we might expect, the confederate who praised an aspect of the self the subject herself thought was praiseworthy—the self-enhancing, self-verifying confederate. But which confederate was the second choice? Was it the confederate who praised or the confederate who criticized what the subject herself thought was a negative aspect of her self? The results were that the subject preferred to interact with the confederate who criticized, who saw her weaknesses as they really were, rather than the confederate who didn't see the weakness (Swann, Pelham, & Krull, 1989). This evidence suggests that we like to present a favorable impression of what we ourselves consider to be our strengths, but we are more comfortable interacting with someone who perceives our weaknesses as they really are—at least when nothing material hangs in the balance. We certainly don't want an employment interviewer to see our weaknesses if we think her perceptiveness will cost us a job!

STRATEGIES OF SELF-PRESENTATION

Ned Jones and his collaborators have developed the self-presentational view by focusing on some specific ways that a person might present herself (see Table 6.1). Or, to put it another way, they have focused on some strategies we use to get other people to make just the attributions about us that we want them to. This discussion develops one line of Goffman's thinking: that self-presentation is in the service of gaining power over other people (Jones & Pittman, 1982).

Ingratiation and Self-Promotion

One strategy of self-presentation involves ***ingratiation.*** Ingratiation is a matter of illicitly making oneself likable in another's eyes. Ingratiators must, of

TABLE 6.1

SELF-PRESENTATION STRATEGIES		
Strategy	*Technique*	*Aim*
Ingratiation	Flatter and agree	To be seen as likable
Self-promotion	Brag	To be seen as competent
Intimidation	Threaten	To be seen as dangerous
Exemplification	Brag and gossip	To be seen as morally pure
Supplication	Beseech	To be seen as weak

SOURCE: Jones & Pittman, 1982.

course, conceal the real aim of their activity or it will backfire, making the person undesirable in the eyes of his target. Jones articulates several common ways that a person might try to accomplish the goal of looking desirable to another.

One way is simply to agree with what other people think. Another is to praise your target's accomplishments, personality, and so on. A third way is to do favors for the person you want to please. But these strategies require subtlety to succeed; pushed too far, they give away their purpose. And they have one further problem. The target of ingratiating behavior is often easier to fool than observers are. After all, we tend to think that our opinions are correct (if we didn't, why would we hold them?). Because we believe our opinions are correct, we're not terribly suspicious of the motives of people who agree with us. But people who don't share our opinions do have reasons to be suspicious of people who agree with us. Thus, a further difficulty the ingratiator faces is that while he may enhance his position in the eyes of his target, he may with the same behavior *lower* his position in the eyes of an audience. As is so often true in life, knowing how to ingratiate is dependent on knowing how much is too much.

Jones argues that **self-promotion** is another self-presentational strategy, similar to ingratiation. But while the ingratiator tries to be seen as likable, the self-promoter tries to be seen as *competent.* Applicants for professional or graduate schools, for example, may *want* to show the interviewer that they are likable, but they *must* demonstrate that they are competent. More generally, ingratiation is a strategy we might use to get other people to like us, while self-promotion is aimed at getting other people to respect us. The most compelling way to self-promote is to demonstrate the competence we want to be seen as having. It would be crazy to doubt, for example, that Arnold Palmer and Jack Nicklaus in their prime were competent at golf. Millions of people saw them demonstrate competence. But much of the time we must give the impression of competence in less direct ways, which makes self-promotion a difficult strategy to carry out.

In one experiment designed to illustrate the relative difficulty of self-promotion over ingratiation, the experimenters asked pairs of undergraduates who didn't know one another to have two conversations. When the subjects arrived for the first session, they were asked to carry on a twenty-minute conversation. The alleged purpose was to study "conversation syntax"; the

▼ *In the film* Zelig, *Woody Allen is Zelig, a chameleon all of whose self-presentations are fake.*

subjects were told that their conversation would be video- and audiotaped. They were then asked to come back a week later for a second conversation. Between the sessions, the experimenter took one member of each pair aside and made her a confederate. The experimenter told her that in the next session, she should either make the other subject like her as much as possible, or get the other subject to regard her as extremely competent. Thus, in some conversations, one member of the pair was instructed to be ingratiating, while in others, one member was told to be self-promoting. Half of the newly enlisted confederates were given the whole week to think about how to do this; the other half were given only a few minutes.

By and large, the ingratiators were modestly successful; they did get their partners to like them, although so did control subjects given no instructions. But the self-promoters failed. They were liked less and thought less competent than were the control partners or the ingratiating partners. Further, the ingratiators who had only a few minutes did as well as those who had a week; and the self-promoters who had a week did as badly as those who had only a few minutes. Apparently, we know well how to ingratiate, but we are not so practiced at self-promotion (Godfrey, Lord, & Jones, 1986).

Intimidation and Exemplification

Another way of gaining power over someone is by convincing him that you are dangerous. Convincing people that you can and will cause them trouble if they don't do what you want them to is aptly labeled by Jones as **intimidation.** Intimidation has its dangers too. The first is that someone will call your bluff. Intimidators had better be prepared to follow through on their threats. And second, people don't much like intimidators. We typically associate with them at all only if there are other reasons to do so, such as being the intimidator's spouse, child, or colleague. But none of these bonds is indissoluble. Spouses can divorce, children can move out, and colleagues can take other jobs. So the intimidator must be accurate in calculating just how strong these other bonds are.

Another strategy to achieve interpersonal influence is by what Jones calls **exemplification.** Exemplification consists in portraying integrity and moral worthiness. The exemplifier is a kind of self-promoter, but the self-promoter projects competence, while the exemplifier projects purity of character. This strategy also has its dangers. The exemplifier, like any self-promoter, risks being found out as less than he appears to be—that is, as a hypocrite. In one rather complex experiment, subjects were shown an "interview" in which a confederate described himself in one of two ways. One self-description was of a "pragmatist," a person who was willing to cut moral corners to get ahead in life. In the other tape, the confederate described himself as someone who would never cut moral corners—that is, as an exemplifier. After seeing these tapes, subjects rated the person on a variety of adjectives descriptive of character. They then learned a further fact about the target: he had cheated in a subsequent part of the experiment to avoid getting electric shocks. Finally, they rated the character again.

In this experiment, subjects were presented with someone who was a self-professed corner-cutter and another fellow who was a self-declared paragon, both of whom had cheated when tempted. How were the impressions the subjects formed of them affected by the news of their having cheated? Both characters were downgraded, but in different ways. The pragmatist was seen as exploitative and devious, while the exemplifier was seen as a hypocrite and self-deluded (Gilbert & Jones, 1986). (The subjects apparently saw the exemplifier's interview as sincere—motivated not to impress the interviewer so much as to impress himself.) There was also a hint in the data that the pragmatist made the subjects angry, while the hypocrite made the subjects feel pity for his self-delusions.

Supplication and Self-Handicapping

A final strategy is **supplication,** making oneself seem weak and dependent. Supplication works because there are widespread norms in Western culture that say needy people should be taken care of. But supplication too has its costs. For one thing, weak people are rarely able to insure that others will live up to those norms, and for another, weakness isn't very attractive.

A tactic related to supplication that has received quite a bit of attention has been labeled **self-handicapping.** Handicaps are things we all, for the most part, would like to avoid. But there are occasions, some have argued, when people might actually seek them out. Imagine that you were about to be evaluated on some task, and you were unsure that you would be able to do well. A handicap would have two advantages. First, if you failed, it would provide you with an excuse for your failure. And second, if you succeeded, it would make your success seem even greater.*

Now if your concern is with looking to others as if you are handicapped, then the advantage comes not from *having* the handicap but from seeming to have one. It is commonly observed that not very good golfers will loudly announce a variety of aches and pains that are sure to interfere with their game, even before they have taken their first shot. But if your concern is not with what other people think of you but with what you think of yourself, then the advantage comes from actually acquiring the handicap (Leary & Shepperd, 1986). In particular, Ned Jones has suggested that people may drink alcohol for such a reason; if a person fails at something because he drinks, then he can console himself with the thought that if he hadn't been drinking, he surely would have succeeded, and if he succeeds, then he *really* must be talented (Jones & Berglas, 1978).

In an experiment designed to be analogous to a situation that might lead people to drink, the experimenters gave subjects a set of problems to solve and then gave them feedback on their performance. All the subjects were told that they had done very well compared with other subjects. Some subjects were given rather simple problems, so they actually solved them and could take the feedback as indicative of their real abilities. Others, however, had worked on what were in fact insoluble problems. So for them, the feedback seemed less convincing. All were told that they would then be asked to solve another set of similar problems. The subjects who had solved the easy prob-

> Self-handicaps
> • enhance the value of success;
> • reduce the cost of failure.

*Indeed, different people may self-handicap for each of these reasons. People with high self-esteem may handicap to enhance their accomplishments, while people with low self-esteem may do so to protect themselves from failure (Tice, 1991).

FIGURE 6.2

SELF-HANDICAPPING

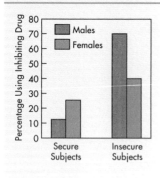

▲ The percentage of male and female subjects using performance-inhibiting drugs varied according to whether the subjects were secure or insecure. Male subjects in particular were likely to take a performance-inhibiting drug (such as alcohol) if they believed they were unlikely to live up to standards that had been set for them. (Data from Berglas & Jones, 1978)

lems felt reasonably secure in their ability to do well. But the subjects who had been given the insoluble problems felt much less secure.

Both groups were told that the experiment had to do with the effects of certain drugs on performance and that two drugs were under investigation. One drug was thought to enhance performance; the other was thought to interfere with it. The subjects were then allowed to choose the drug (and dose) they wanted to try (something one would never do in a real experiment on drugs!). Further, some subjects were led to believe that the experimenter would know how well they did on the second task, while others were told that the experimenter would not know how well they had done.

The investigators believed that the subjects who were confident they would do well on the second half would take the performance-*enhancing* drug, while the less confident subjects would prefer the performance-*inhibiting* drug, such as alcohol. The performance inhibitor would serve as a self-handicap, protecting the subjects from a loss of self-esteem. The results confirmed the investigators' predictions, although more strongly for males than females. The insecure subjects took the performance-inhibiting drugs; they self-handicapped (see Figure 6.2). Moreover, the subjects who thought the experimenter would not know the results of their performance self-handicapped just as much as those who thought the experimenter would know the results, suggesting that the subjects were trying to protect their esteem in their own eyes rather than their esteem in the eyes of the experimenter (Berglas & Jones, 1978).

Other investigators have found, however, that when the experimenter not only doesn't know the test results, as in this study, but also apparently won't know which drug the subject has taken, then subjects do not self-handicap. So it is at the moment unclear whether self-handicapping is a matter of fooling oneself or fooling others (Kolditz & Arkin, 1982). Probably both occur, and it is probably also true, as the king of Siam in *The King and I* remarked, that fooling others is an excellent way of fooling oneself. In any event, subsequent research has extended the reach of the notion of self-handicapping in several directions.

Some investigators have focused on people's willingness to report a variety of psychological problems as a way of taking on the appearance, at least, of having a handicap. Hypochondriacs have been shown to report more physical complaints if these complaints serve as an excuse for poor performance than they do if they believe the complaints will not be a good excuse (Smith, Snyder, & Perkins, 1983). Students who complain of great anxiety about tests complain more when they are about to take a test that has been portrayed as sensitive to disruption by anxiety than they do if it has been portrayed as insensitive to such disruption (Smith, Snyder, & Handelsman, 1982). And shy male (but not female) students used reports of anxiety to self-handicap on a test of social intelligence (Snyder, Smith, Augelli, & Ingram, 1985).

Robert Arkin and James Shepperd have uncovered a related strategy: enhancing the performance of a competitor. Suppose you imagined that your performance at some task would be compared with the performance of someone else, and you were offered the chance—as were subjects in one experiment—to give your competitor an advantage or give him a handicap. Which would you do? Giving him a handicap makes you more likely to do well relative to him, but (publicly) giving him an advantage works like giving yourself a handicap; it will make your success sweeter, should you win, and it will make your failure less bitter (though more likely). Arkin and Shepperd have found that in such circumstances, subjects, especially male subjects, will enhance the performance of a competitor (Shepperd & Arkin, 1991).

DOES SELF-HANDICAPPING WORK?

In the long run, self-handicapping certainly doesn't solve one's problems. But does it work in the short run? Do observers who witness the handicapping react the way the handicapper thinks they will?

Consider a study in which subjects were told that John received an A, C, or F on a history exam, and they saw a videotape in which John either accepted or turned down an invitation to go to a movie the night before the exam. What effect did the information about John's going to the movie (the handicap) have on subjects' impressions of him? As the handicapper might hope, going to the movie did make him seem smarter in the face of poor performance on the test (smarter than he would have seemed if he had stayed home and studied). But that was only half the story; the self-handicapping John was also rated less positively on other, motivational traits, such as how concerned he was with his school work (Luginbuhl & Palmer, 1991). So by self-handicapping, John leaped from the frying pan of low ability to the fire of a weak character. Self-handicapping confers an advantage in the short run *only* if John would rather be seen as lazy than stupid—that seems to be the sort of trade-off the self-handicapper makes.

Basking and Blasting

The strategies of impression management discussed so far are rather direct; they involve making oneself seem desirable, in one or another sense, by advertising, or at least defending, one's virtues. Robert Cialdini has exposed two indirect techniques of impression management. One technique Cialdini refers to as **basking in reflected glory.** This technique was illustrated in a simple and clever way in a study in which the investigators simply counted the number of students wearing clothing with university logos on the Mondays following either victories or failures of the college football team. As predicted, the number of decals was greater on Mondays following a victory than on Mondays following a defeat (Cialdini, Levy, Herman, Koslowski, & Petty, 1976).

In a subsequent study, students were called on the phone and given a "test of campus knowledge." Randomly, some were told they had failed; others were told they had succeeded. These fake results were designed to make the students feel secure or insecure about their standing on the campus. The same students were then asked to report on the most recent football game. Overall the students tended to use "we" when reporting about victories—"We scored a touchdown in the last seconds." But they used "they" when reporting about their team's defeats—"They fumbled on the five-yard line." And this tendency was especially strong among subjects who had just *failed* the campus events test (Cialdini & Richardson, 1980). So the subjects were especially likely to bask in the reflected glory of the football team by talking as if they were a unit when they felt insecure.

People will sometimes use even the most trivial linkages to connect them-

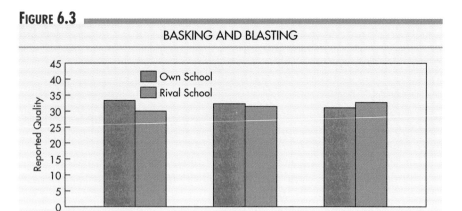

FIGURE 6.3

BASKING AND BLASTING

▶ *Subjects who thought they had failed a test were especially likely to point out virtues of their own university and flaws in a rival university. They did this to restore self-esteem. (Data from Cialdini & Richardson, 1980)*

selves to someone with desirable attributes. In one study, subjects learned that "another subject" they were participating with had the same birthday they did. Some subjects also learned that this other subject did very well on a test; others learned he did quite badly. In a second phase of the experiment, subjects were given an opportunity to announce this "coincidence." The subjects who thought the other subject had done well took the opportunity to mention it, while those who thought he hadn't done well failed to mention it (Cialdini & De Nicholas, 1989). So mere association with a successful person is treated as a way of enhancing self-presentation. Paul Rozin has pointed out that people will try to shake hands with a respected person and avoid shaking hands with a disrespected person, as if some bit of the person's essence were transferred to them by even this most trivial contact (Rozin, Millman, & Nemeroff, 1986).

Blasting, another indirect technique isolated by Cialdini, was documented this way. Students at the University of Arizona were stopped on campus and given a "creativity test." Since no one knows what should be on such a test, it was easy to tell some people (randomly) that they succeeded and others that they failed. Students were then asked to describe their own school and their across-state rival, Arizona State. The positive comments made about their own school and the negative comments made about the other school were counted. Positive comments about their school were basking; negative comments about the other school were blasting (see Figure 6.3). Both blasting and basking were enhanced by failure on the creativity test (Cialdini & Richardson, 1980).

Impression Management and Self-Deception

Because people read our characters from our behavior, we cannot help but give off impressions of who we are in all we do. Perhaps because we need a stable sense of who we are in order to interact, and certainly because at times it is crucial for our broader interests, we sometimes arrange things in order to give just the right impression of who we are. This does suggest that all the world is a stage. But it doesn't mean that the characters we present on that

stage are different from the characters we really are. It means that once on the stage, we are compelled to perform *some* character.

We have seen that should we be interested in projecting a character in order to advance our own interests, there are several strategies open to us: ingratiation, self-promotion, and so on. We may even find it useful to project a character with a handicap. And where direct action fails, indirection—basking and blasting—may serve.

Finally, these studies call attention to the ways we may engage in impression management not to impress others, but to impress ourselves. We care, it seems, not just about what others think of us, but also about what we think of ourselves. And this can lead us to enhance our esteem in our own eyes. If this strategy works, then we will wind up with a view of ourselves (a *sincere* view) that is different from what is true of us, and we will be mired in self-deception. Self-deception is an important reason to be wary of the notion of the self as something internal, as a matter of sincerity. If we really want to know who someone is, even ourselves, we want to know more than what a person thinks of herself; we want to know what the person will do when a real public test arrives. Solomon knew better than to rely on sincerity in deciding which woman really loved the child.

INNER AND OUTER FOCUS OF ATTENTION

The notion of impression management leads us to imagine that people typically keep track of two different sorts of things: (1) what they really think, believe, feel, care about, and (2) what other people would prefer they thought, believed, felt, or cared about. This idea leads immediately to a metaphor based on the self as an object in physical space. Using this metaphor, we can imagine the real facts about a person to be inside him, whereas the demands that others make of him are outside him. Thus, any act can be conceived as having its sources either inside the person (if it truly reflects the person's beliefs) or outside him (if it reflects instead what others want of him).

Subjects who conformed to the majority in the Asch experiment, and in so doing betrayed their senses, can be thought of as "outer directed," responding to the other subjects. Subjects who stuck to their guns can be thought of as "inner directed." So too for subjects who either obeyed or disobeyed in the Milgram experiment. So "inner and outer" is a convenient metaphor for thinking of these matters. Of course, it is *literally* true that your behavior must in the end have to do with the action of your central nervous system, something inside you, and the environment, something outside you. (But these two forces conspire equally for both conformers and nonconformers. Conformers are guided by what others think—something about the world—but nonconformers are guided by the length of lines, something else about the world.) There are behaviors that are literally internally caused—writhing in pain if your appendix bursts—and those that are externally caused: falling to the ground under the influence of gravity. These are of little interest to a psychologist (although they are of great interest to a physician and physicist, respectively). Behaviors that psychologists are interested in are caused by the interplay of things outside the skin (stimuli) and things inside the skin (the central nervous system). So all behavior, whether reflective of the true or a fake self, has sources both inside the skin and outside it. Still, thinking of the self as the "inner" cause of behavior and things alien to the self as "outer" may be useful. Several different, though related, lines of social-psychological research take off from this metaphor.

Objective Self-Awareness

Robert Wicklund has proposed one way of developing the metaphor. His proposal has its roots in the writing of George Herbert Mead, one of the turn-of-the-century founders of American sociology and social psychology. Mead proposed that our notion that people have a self is ambiguous and that it might be better to think of people as having two selves. First, there is the "I," the active self, the self that engages the world. It is made up of a person's desires, values, beliefs, and so on. But we humans, and perhaps other organisms, are able to reflect on our selves. That is, we can come to know ourselves as others see us. This self that we know by reflection, our public or social self, Mead called the "me."

When we are engrossed by some activity—solving a puzzle, for example—the "I" attends to the world and acts. In cases of total engrossment, there is no attention paid to the impression this "I" is casting; there is no awareness of the "me." But at other moments, and never more so than in embarrassment, the "me" becomes the center of attention. We become acutely aware of ourselves as creatures who can be seen and assessed by others. Adam and Eve, before the regrettable incident with the apple, were said to have had no such knowledge; they simply *were*—they satisfied their desires. But after the fall, they became self-conscious. They became aware, for example, that they were naked. They became capable of shame. In Mead's language, they developed "me"s.

Wicklund claimed that becoming aware of oneself as the object of ap-

▲ *Adam and Eve, self-conscious and none too happy about it. (Masaccio,* The Expulsion from Eden, *Alinan/Art Resource)*

praisal produces a special psychological state, the state of **objective self-awareness.** The state of self-focused attention happens from time to time in everyday life, often as the result of other people's attention. Wicklund (with his collaborators) developed a variety of laboratory techniques designed to make subjects objectively self-aware, that is, aware of themselves as the focus of attention. Putting a subject in front of a mirror, videotaping, and audio-taping are all techniques that involve focusing the subject's attention on her self. Wicklund proposed that making someone aware of her self calls her attention to her self in relation to her standards. Objective self-awareness is a matter of being aware of how well (or ill) we live up to our own moral, aesthetic, and other standards (Wicklund, 1975a). Much of the research inspired by Wicklund's theory has examined the relation between objective self-awareness and living up to behavioral standards.

Objective self-awareness involves focusing on ourselves as we think others see us.

OBJECTIVE SELF-AWARENESS AND STANDARDS

As one example of such work, consider an experiment by Charles Carver. Carver selected twenty subjects to be in an experiment in which (the subjects thought) a learner would be taught material through punishment in the form of electric shocks. The subjects were selected for the experiment because on a prior screening questionnaire they expressed either a very favorable or very unfavorable attitude toward using punishment to teach people things. Thus, half the subjects had strong personal beliefs in favor of punishment; half had strong personal beliefs against it. The subjects were shown a machine that was capable of administering five levels of shock. Some subjects faced a mirror; others did not. The results were that subjects who faced the mirror shocked in accordance with their own beliefs about punishment, but those who did not face the mirror did not act in accord with their own beliefs. In other words, in the mirror condition, there was a *correlation* between the subjects' beliefs about punishment and how much shock they gave. Absent the mirror, there was no such correlation. This result is in support of the notion that being reminded of ourselves as objects of appraisal triggers a concern with our standards of behavior and induces us to live up to those standards (Carver, 1975).

◀ *The first inklings of objective self-awareness?*

This same general idea has been supported in other studies using very different standards. For example, in another investigation, dieters who were made to feel that their eating was the object of the experimenter's attention ate less than did dieters who were not made self-aware (Polivy, Herman, Hackett, & Kuleshnyk, 1986). There are, however, difficulties with the notion that objective self-awareness makes us live up to our standards.

Commonly in life, there are different standards that apply in the same situation, and living up to one standard conflicts with living up to others. The problem, then, is *which standards* will become salient when a person focuses on herself as an object.

In one study, smokers who wanted to smoke less were assigned a task either while facing a mirror or while not facing a mirror. The experimenters watched them through a one-way mirror, and noted how many cigarettes they smoked, how many puffs they took, and how many times they flicked ashes. The results indicated that the mirror slightly *increased* the number of cigarettes the subjects smoked. Now if objective self-awareness makes subjects more attentive to the standards they apply to their own behavior, then it should have *decreased* the number of cigarettes they smoked, since they all wanted to smoke less (Liebling, Seiler, & Shaver, 1974).

Wicklund has replied that this experiment is not really an embarrassment to his theory because, among other things, we don't know whether the mirror focused attention on that particular standard, the one connected with cigarette smoking (Wicklund, 1975b). Fair enough. But as the investigators who carried out the cigarette experiment countered, the theory of objective self-awareness isn't terribly useful if it can't specify *which* standards become salient (Liebling, Seiler, & Shaver, 1975). The notion that self-consciousness focuses attention on standards, then, is a seriously incomplete theory.

Self-Consciousness and Motivation

One interpretation of the above result is that self-focused attention increases subjects' motivation or, as it is sometimes called, drive. Increases in motivation have several effects, but one well-documented effect is to increase the probability that subjects will engage in well-practiced habits. For smokers, puffing and flicking are well-learned habits, and these did increase. So in addition to calling attention to standards, self-focused attention may increase motivation to do whatever one is doing.

Increasing motivation often enhances performance on a task, but it can sometimes interfere with performance. Indeed, a well-known law of general psychology, the Yerkes-Dodson Law, claims that for very complex tasks, as motivation increases, performance falls off (see Gleitman, 1991). This law, in combination with the results of the previous experiment, suggests that there should be cases where self-focused attention interferes with performance.

Roy Baumeister has provided evidence that this is indeed so. Baumeister looked at the performance of the home team in game seven of any World Series (see Figure 6.4). Now a little background for those of you who aren't baseball fans. The World Series is the end-of-the-season contest to determine

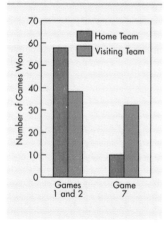

FIGURE 6.4

SELF-CONSCIOUSNESS AND MOTIVATION

▲ *Games won by the home and visiting teams in the World Series vary according to which game is being played. Overall, the home team has a distinct advantage, but in the seventh game, when the championship is on the line, the visitors have the advantage. (Data from Baumeister & Steinhilber, 1984)*

the team that is ethnocentrically known as the World Champion. The World Series is a best-of-seven competition, so there are as many games as are needed for one team or the other to win four. Thus, in many seasons, there is no seventh game, and in those seasons where there is, it is because each team has won three of the six previous games.

For a variety of practical reasons, there is a home-field advantage in baseball; for example, the home team knows the nuances of the field better, and the team has been selected with just those nuances in mind. And, indeed, in general, the home team tends to win more than it loses. Consistent with this, the home team tends to win the sixth game of the World Series. But the surprising fact (surprising at least to baseball fans) is that the home team tends to *lose* the seventh game (Baumeister & Steinhilber, 1984; Heaton & Sigall, 1989).

To see why, let us consider what it is like to be playing baseball in the seventh game. The players on both sides face enormous pressure. This is the ultimate accomplishment of their profession; all of the nation's sportswriters are focused on everything they do, and there is added pressure for the home team. Typically there are many more fans of the home team than there are of the visiting team. And the fans' cheering, applauding, and chanting will be exquisitely tied to the momentary fortunes of the home team. If anything leads to self-consciousness, this should. Baumeister interprets the fact that the home team tends to lose the seventh game (and to make more fielding errors!) as evidence that this pressure exceeds optimal levels and interferes with performance (causes the home team to "choke," in the none-to-polite language of sports). (See also Davis & Harvey, 1992, on drive and choking in baseball; see Chapter 3 on social facilitation theory.)

We have seen, then, that objective self-awareness can call attention to a person's internalized standards and lead him to act in accord with what he believes. But it also seems to be able to increase motivation. Increased motivation can have both facilitating and disruptive effects, depending on how well-practiced the behavior is and on how high the final level of motivation is. One major difficulty with the theory is that the manipulations that have been used to explore it—mirrors, video cameras, and so on—call attention directly to the most superficial aspect of the self, appearance, and indirectly to, one supposes, all other aspects of the self. Thus, whenever there is a wide variety of standards that might be called into prominence by the manipulations, it is hard to say just which standards will be made salient.

Self-Awareness as a Personality Trait

The concept of objective self-awareness as developed by Wicklund was meant to refer to a transient state of mind that all of us find ourselves in from time to time. But a second line of work developed from the inner-outer metaphor begins with the idea that being self-conscious might be a personality trait. That is, perhaps some people are chronically self-conscious, while other people are chronically un-self-conscious.

To investigate this possibility, Alan Fenigstein, Michael Scheier, and Alan Buss (1975) constructed a questionnaire (called the Self-Consciousness Scale) with thirty-eight questions or, as they are more commonly called, items. The items related to a variety of aspects of self-consciousness: concern with one's feelings, a preoccupation with past, present, or future behavior, a concern with one's appearance, a concern with one's regard in the eyes of others, and so on. This questionnaire was given to two hundred undergraduates, who were asked to indicate the degree to which each item was true of them. The responses were then subjected to a statistical procedure called **factor analysis.** Factors are clusters of items that people tend to answer in the same way—they tend to either agree or disagree with all the items of the cluster.* It is usually safe to assume that if there are distinct factors, there are distinct phenomena underlying them (the reverse inference—if there aren't distinct factors, then there aren't distinct phenomena—is much less assured). The analysis revealed three distinct factors.

One factor is called **private self-consciousness,** and it included items that referred to being attentive to one's real feelings; for example, one item was "I reflect about myself a lot." A second factor has been called **public self-consciousness** and relates to a concern with oneself as a social object (what Wicklund calls objective self-awareness). An example of an item on this scale was "I'm concerned about what other people think of me." The third factor is called **social anxiety** and refers to the tendency to become upset by social attention; a sample item was "I feel very anxious when I speak in front of a group."

The factor analysis also revealed that although these three ways of being self-conscious are distinct from one another, they are also related to some degree; that is, the factors themselves are modestly correlated. There is some tendency for those who are publicly self-conscious to be privately self-conscious and socially anxious as well. These results suggest, then, that there are three ways of being self-conscious, and that people differ in the degree to which they are chronically self-conscious in each way (Fenigstein, Scheier, & Buss, 1975; see also Britt, 1992). (These results are for American college students. It isn't necessarily true that the same structure would emerge for other samples, and there is some evidence that the same structure indeed *does not* emerge for other subjects; see Piliavin & Charny, 1988.)

Although both privately and publicly self-aware subjects are in some sense attentive to themselves, their different ways of being self-attentive should lead to different sorts of behavior, and there is evidence to support this. Subjects high in public self-awareness, for example, are *more* likely than those low in public self-awareness to go along with a group, even when the group is obviously wrong. Those high in private self-awareness are *less* likely than those low in private self-awareness to go along with a group (Froming & Carver, 1981). Public self-awareness, then, is related to susceptibility to social pressure.

Private self-awareness has also been linked to the degree to which people disclose the facts of their emotional lives to their romantic partners. And degree of self-disclosure has been linked to satisfaction in such relationships (Franzoi, Davis, & Young, 1985). Thus, privately self-aware people are not only attentive to their emotional lives, they are willing to share them with others too.

Aspects of self-consciousness
- Private self-consciousness
- Public self-consciousness
- Social anxiety

*Technically, cluster analysis and factor analysis are different techniques, but nonetheless, they are closely related. For our purposes, it is useful to think of factor analysis as uncovering clusters.

Mark Snyder has developed the most prominent extension of Goffman's approach. He has suggested that some people engage in impression management, while others don't. Some people control their behavior by paying attention to their inner (real) selves; others pay attention to the impressions they are creating. Snyder refers to people who pay great attention to the impressions they are giving as **self-monitors.***

To demonstrate that self-monitoring is an interesting way in which people differ from one another, Snyder generated forty-one self-descriptive statements related to the five ways he thought high self-monitors differ from low self-monitors (see Table 6.2). Here are the five ways he thought they differed, along with an example of a statement related to each. High self-monitors are (1) concerned with the social appropriateness of their self-presentations ("At parties and social gatherings, I attempt to do or say things that others will like"); (2) attentive to what other people are doing as guides to their own self-expression ("When I am uncertain how to act in social situations, I look to the behavior of others for cues"); (3) able to control and modify their self-presentation and self-expressions ("I can look anyone in the eye and tell a lie with a straight face [if for a right end]"); (4) willing to use this ability in specific situations ("I may deceive people by being friendly when I really dislike them"); (5) less consistent in their social behavior from situation to situation ("In different situations and with different people, I often act like very

TABLE 6.2

HIGH SELF-MONITORS RELATIVE TO LOW SELF-MONITORS

High Self-Monitors	Low Self-Monitors
1. Concerned with the social appropriateness of their self-presentations.	1. Not concerned with what other people think it is appropriate to do.
2. Attentive to what others are doing as a guide to their own self-expressions.	2. Attentive to their inner selves; not concerned with what others are doing.
3. Able to control their self-expressions.	3. Not concerned with controlling their self-expressions.
4. Willing to control their self-expressions in social situations.	4. Not willing to control their self-expressions in social situations.
5. Inconsistent in their self-presentations from situation to situation.	5. Consistent in their self-presentations from situation to situation.

SOURCE: Based on Snyder, 1974, 1979.

*This name is a bit confusing. One might think of self-monitors as people who pay a great deal of attention to their *real selves* (what they really think, and so on) in social interactions, but this isn't the way Snyder named the distinction. Self-monitors, then, are people who pay *less* attention to their real selves but more attention to their projected selves.

different persons"). The items were given to roughly two hundred undergraduates who were asked to indicate whether each statement was true.

The responses to twenty-five of the items hung together. That is, for these items, it was more or less the case that people who said that one item was true also said that the others were true. These twenty-five items became the Self-Monitoring Scale. Showing that the items of a proposed scale hung together is a very important first step in the construction of a psychological test or scale. If the items hang together, then it is likely that they all reflect a single underlying trait. If they don't hang together, then they might not be reflecting a single underlying trait. If a scale hangs together perfectly (which would mean that if a subject answered one question "yes," then he answered all questions "yes"), then it is said to be perfectly **reliable.** The reliability of a scale, then, tells us the degree to which a scale measures *some one thing.*

The Self-Monitoring Scale in this original study hung together fairly well, but hardly perfectly. This tells us that it is a measuring instrument, but an imperfect one. A highly reliable scale measures *something.* But having a scale that measures something isn't very useful; one wants a scale that measures what one set out to measure.

Establishing that the scale measures what one says it measures is a matter of establishing the **validity** of the scale, showing that people's scores on a scale fit in with other things we know about them in the way that the concept that led to the development of the scale suggests. A scale that produces scores that make sense in this way is said to have **construct validity.** Snyder conducted several studies to show that the Self-Monitoring Scale was valid in this way.

First, he asked sixteen fraternity brothers to rate each other on five self-monitoring traits. If the Self-Monitoring Scale measures what it says it measures, then the ratings of one of the fraternity brothers by the other brothers should correlate with the answers that brother gave about himself. They did.

If self-monitoring involves the ability to project a self, whether the true one or not, then stage actors should score higher on the scale than do people who are not used to performing on stages. They do. Snyder's original work with the Self-Monitoring Scale showed, then, that the scale was, at least to some degree, reliable and valid (Snyder, 1974, 1979). High self-monitors do look like people who were well described by Goffman; low self-monitors look like people who, for one reason or another, are not well described by Goffman.

Self-Monitoring and Conformity

Snyder, his collaborators, and several independent investigators have extended our understanding of differences between high and low self-monitors in several interesting directions. In one study, subjects were asked in a group to discuss what advice they would give to a hypothetical person facing a difficult trade-off between a safe but not very well-paying and more risky but better-paying job. Before the discussion, they had indicated the degree of risk they personally favored, and they were asked the same question after the discussion. Some subjects were told that their discussions would be videotaped; others were not. Snyder predicted (and found) that high self-monitoring subjects would shift their opinions more than low self-monitoring subjects

FIGURE 6.5

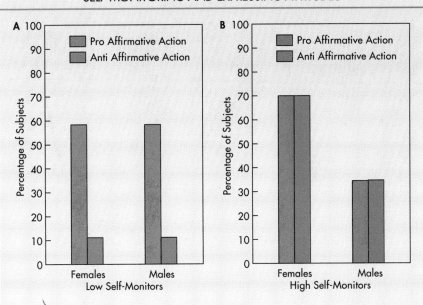

SELF-MONITORING AND EXPRESSING ATTITUDES

A Low Self-Monitors
Pro Affirmative Action / Anti Affirmative Action
(Percentage of Subjects; Females, Males)

B High Self-Monitors
Pro Affirmative Action / Anti Affirmative Action
(Percentage of Subjects; Females, Males)

◄ *(A) Low self-monitors' willingness to be part of a discussion on affirmative action varied in both men and women based on what their attitudes toward affirmative action were.*
(B) High self-monitors' willingness to participate in a discussion group on affirmative action did not depend on their attitudes toward affirmative action. Women acted as if they thought there was something in it for them to join, so they did, regardless of their attitudes. Men, on the other hand, didn't join regardless of their attitudes. (Data from Snyder & Kandzierski, 1982)

when they thought they *weren't* being videotaped, but that just the reverse would be true if they thought they *were* being videotaped. The idea is that self-monitors want to be liked by members of the group, but they also don't want to be seen as wimps by the people who will be seeing the videotape. Therefore, when the camera is on, they hold firm; but when the camera is off, they give in. Low self-monitors, one is invited to believe, are unaffected by the presence of the camera; they change their mind (or don't) based on the rational force of the discussion (Snyder & Monson, 1975).

In another study mining the same vein, male and female subjects were asked to join a discussion group having to do with affirmative action toward women. The investigators had previously ascertained the subjects' attitudes toward affirmative action. The authors predicted that low self-monitoring subjects would join or avoid the group depending upon their attitudes toward affirmative action. Those in favor would join; those against wouldn't. The prediction was based on the assumption that low self-monitoring people view social situations as occasions to express their true attitudes. Thus, they pick the situations they will enter based on whether those situations allow them to express their attitudes. The results concurred (see Figure 6.5A). Low self-monitors either joined or refused to join depending on their attitudes toward affirmative action. But what did the high self-monitors do?

The male high self-monitors (by and large) didn't join the group, but the females did—*regardless of their attitudes toward affirmative action* (see Figure 6.5B). High self-monitors, apparently, weren't very concerned with expressing their attitudes. Rather, it seems that male high self-monitoring subjects decided that groups discussing affirmative action just weren't places for men, no matter their attitudes, so they didn't join. High self-monitoring females agreed that such groups were for women and did join, again regardless of

▶ *Are witnesses' behaviors in-fluenced by their knowing they are on television? Would it matter if they are high or low self-monitors?*

their attitudes. So for high self-monitors, attitudes were of no relevance (Snyder & Kandzierski, 1982).

There are other ways in which having attitudes is a different matter for high and low self-monitors. As we shall see in Chapter 16, if you induce some people in subtle ways to endorse some belief they don't really have, they are likely to be taken in by their own lie. That is, they are likely to move their own opinion in the direction of the position they endorsed; the point is to make themselves look less like liars in their own eyes. This general phenom-enon is known as "reducing cognitive dissonance," and I shall have more to say about it later. But for now, suffice it to say that high self-monitors seem less inclined to dissonance. If you induce high self-monitors to endorse an opinion they don't have, they do not distort their beliefs to make themselves look good in their own eyes. They lie, but apparently they know they are willing to lie, so they don't engage in self-deception to cover their deception of others. Self-monitors are people, the results suggest, who know they are willing to manipulate others (Snyder & Tanke, 1976; Paulhus, 1982).

The results we have seen so far suggest that high self-monitors differ from low self-monitors in some important ways that are closely related to the con-cept of self-monitoring as described by Snyder. The differences indicate that low self-monitors are people who are attentive to their real beliefs; they are straightforward people who tell you what they think. There are attractive and not so attractive aspects of being a low self-monitor. The low self-monitor's honesty is, of course, appealing. That honesty, reliability, and trustworthiness are desirable in our friends hardly needs to be pointed out. The less appealing aspect of being a low self-monitor is the suggestion that they are bulls in social china shops. Honesty is nice, but tact isn't so bad either. We don't need (and we certainly don't want) honesty from our friends all the time. We want our friends to know, without our having to tell them, just when we want the truth and just when we don't. Certainly the high self-monitor is a better bet for the diplomatic corps.

Self-Monitoring and Relationships

Recent research has looked at the different ways that high and low self-monitors have relationships with other people.

FRIENDSHIPS

High self-monitors tend to have a variety of people they do different things with. Low self-monitors, on the other hand, tend to prefer to do a wide range of things with a smaller group of friends. High self-monitors prefer "specialists" as activity partners; low self-monitors prefer their close friends, regardless of whether those friends are well suited to the activity (Snyder, Gangestad, & Simpson, 1983).

ROMANTIC RELATIONSHIPS

As you might expect, high and low self-monitors have different kinds of romantic relationships as well as different kinds of friendships. High self-monitors form *shallower* dating relationships than do low self-monitors. Specifically, high self-monitors prefer different dates for different activities, rather than a single "steady" date. They also date more people (twice as many dating partners according to one study; see Snyder & Simpson, 1984).

High self-monitors have also been shown to be more concerned with the physical appearance of their partners than are low self-monitors. In one study, high and low self-monitoring men who were not involved romantically were given personality descriptions and photos of potential dates. The high self-monitors took more time looking at the pictures (and less time at the personality descriptions) than did the low self-monitors; they also said appearance was more important (high self-monitors do lack self-deception). They were, it might be added, no more attractive than low self-monitors.

In a second study, high and low male self-monitors were asked to make choices between women with desirable appearances but undesirable personalities and women with the reverse qualities. The low self-monitors chose the date with the desirable personality and the less desirable appearance; the high self-monitors did the reverse (Snyder, Berscheid, & Glick, 1985).

High self-monitors engage in more casual sex than do low self-monitors. In one study (conducted before the threat of AIDS was so obvious), high self-monitors said they had had more sexual partners and more one-night stands, planned to have more sexual partners, and endorsed the idea that people *should* have more partners (Snyder, Simpson, & Gangestad, 1986). You might imagine, given all of this, that extremely high self-monitors aren't particularly well adjusted; they're not. But then again, neither are extremely low self-monitors. In fact, as is true of so many things in life, there is some evidence that people intermediate in self-monitoring are better adjusted than those at either extreme (Miller & Thayer, 1988).

Support for the Self-Monitoring Scale

Self-monitoring is an idea that looks a good deal like public self-awareness, and indeed, people who score high on one scale on average, score high on the other (Fenigstein, 1979). Both high self-monitors and those high in public self-awareness are attentive to the impressions they make on others; low self-monitors and those high in private self-awareness, on the other hand, are attentive to their internal states. (Note that these two approaches differ in that for Snyder, you are focused either on the impressions you make or on the real self. But the Self-Awareness Scale does not force such a dichotomy; it allows you to be highly attentive to one or the other, but it also allows you to be attentive to both or neither.)

Early research with the Self-Monitoring Scale was directed toward establishing the construct validity of the scale (showing that the scale measures what it sets out to measure), and such research met with a good deal of success—actors are higher than their audience on the Self-Monitoring Scale; high self-monitors impress their fraternity brothers as high self-monitors. More recent research has told us more about the social lives of high vs. low self-monitors. The scale has been shown to relate to broad aspects of social life, well beyond the concept as originally conceived. The upshot of that research is that high self-monitors seem to have shallower relationships than do low self-monitors.

Criticisms of the Self-Monitoring Scale

As successful as self-monitoring research has been, it also has its critics. The criticisms of the scale and of its successes are intimately related. From the start, there has been a certain amount of complexity, perhaps ambiguity, in the conception of just who self-monitors are. One can approach this question from either a conceptual or an empirical direction. Let's try the conceptual direction first.

SELF-MONITORING: A MATTER OF SOCIAL SKILLS?

Perhaps the real difference between low and high self-monitors is that high self-monitors are better at figuring out how to behave in a way that leads other people to like them. Perhaps this is the *only* difference between high and low self-monitors. In support of this view, there is evidence that the Self-Monitoring Scale correlates with other measures of social skills (Furnham & Capon, 1983).

Ned Jones showed subjects videotapes of two people interacting, and they seemed to be getting along quite well, agreeing with each other about most things. Some subjects were told that one of the interactants had been offered money if he got the other fellow to like him; others were not given this information. All subjects were then asked to rate the agreeable fellow on the videotape. The subjects were divided into high and low self-monitors. High and low self-monitors differed in the way they rated the fellow on the tape.

The high self-monitors who *didn't* know that the person in the tape was being paid to be ingratiating liked him a lot. But the high self-monitors who *did* know liked him much less. Thus, for subjects high in self-monitoring, whether the fellow on the tape was being paid to be likable or not strongly affected their ratings of his personality. But the low self-monitors didn't react this way. They were much less sensitive to the information about whether the fellow was being paid. They liked the agreeable person better than the disagreeable person, paid or not (Jones & Baumeister, 1976). This is an odd result.

It seems obvious to me, at least, that not differentiating between someone being paid to be agreeable and someone who is agreeable without being paid just isn't bright. The low self-monitors seemed to be missing something that a socially perceptive person would certainly pick up. So there is some reason to believe that low self-monitors are people who lack social skills. But can that be all there is to self-monitoring? Could the Self-Monitoring Scale be nothing but a social skills test? After all, as we saw earlier, there is evidence that high and low self-monitors differ in ways that are much broader than just social skills; they seem to differ in motivation and values.

This is actually a quite subtle matter. Could differences in relationships arise just from differences in social skills? The answer is yes. Suppose there are equal numbers of shallow people (people who prefer shallow sexual relationships, for example) among the high and low self-monitors, and suppose that the high self-monitors are just more socially skilled than the low self-monitors. Now let us also suppose that socially skilled people are more successful in getting other people to have the kinds of relationships with them that they want. The upshot of these assumptions is that high self-monitors would, on average, have more casual relationships even though they didn't have greater *desires* for such relationships. Thus, even though self-monitoring may have consequences that extend beyond having well-developed social skills, these consequences may all be the result of differences in social skills. Further work is needed to clarify whether the Self-Monitoring Scale is simply an implicit measure of social skills.

EMPIRICAL CRITICISMS

Some critics have relied on factor analysis of the Self-Monitoring Scale to suggest that it may obscure important differences between people. The logic of such analyses is that if a scale measures just one thing, then there shouldn't be any factors (clusters) within the scale. The presence of factors within the scale indicates that there are separate traits concealed by it. Several investigators, for example, have found that there are three factors lurking within the Self-Monitoring Scale. One has to do with acting ability, another involves "other directedness" (being concerned with other people's evaluations of self), and the last has to do with extraversion or sociability (Briggs, Cheek, & Buss, 1980; Gabrenya & Arkin, 1980; Lennox & Wolfe, 1984). These factor analyses suggest that we would do better to abandon the notion of self-monitoring and focus instead on these various components; they suggest that the Self-Monitoring Scale is an imperfect instrument because it measures not one thing but several.

Snyder has argued in reply to these criticisms that although there are subfactors within the Self-Monitoring Scale, the scale nonetheless measures a single underlying trait. Indeed, he has argued that this single trait is controlled *by a single gene.* This conclusion is based on sophisticated statistical analyses of responses to the scale. Further, on the basis of this analysis, Snyder has revised the original twenty-five-item scale, removing a few items that do not relate to what he believes to be the single underlying trait (Gangestad & Snyder, 1985). Nevertheless, there is still evidence that even the revised Self-

▲ *Michael Jackson keeping up appearances in a difficult situation. Here he addresses his audience live from his Neverland Ranch, responding to allegations that he sexually molested at least one child.*

Monitoring Scale contains two factors, one having to do with performing in public, the second with other directedness (Briggs & Cheek, 1988).

There can be little doubt that the Self-Monitoring Scale measures something that has widespread implications for people's social relationships. And these implications seem to have to do with how willing people are to submerge their values, motives, and beliefs in favor of what will make them popular at the moment. It is also clear that the differences between high and low self-monitors have broad implications. And this is the virtue of the scale. What is not so clear is just what self-monitoring is, and why it is related to all the things it is, empirically, supposed to be related to. But we can be certain that further research will address these issues.

WRAP-UP

We have, in this chapter, focused on impression management, the idea that people intentionally act in such a way as to get other people to form the right impression of them. We reviewed social psychological thinking guided by this notion. We looked at some of the strategies that people attempting to engage in impression management might use, and some of the pitfalls that such a strategy might involve.

In the last section, we looked at some research directed by the notion that people differ in the degree to which they use impression management. High self-monitors (or publicly self-conscious people) do seem to differ substantially from those low in self-monitoring or low in public self-awareness. But in considering this idea of the self, we have been forced to contrast it with the other, more intuitive idea of the self, the self as something private and inside. In Chapter 7, we will turn the tables and face squarely one aspect of this inner self: emotions. As we shall see, however, we will be forced also to look outward at the world.

SUMMARY

1. According to Erving Goffman, there are two reasons why people attempt to control the impressions other people form of them. First, it is often in our interest to get people to form a particular impression of us. Second, our ability to interact in a coherent, intelligible way depends on our having a shared conception of the nature of the situation, and that in turn depends on a shared conception of the identities of the participants.

2. Failed attempts at impression management often result in embarrassment. Embarrassment often accompanies a loss of esteem—either in our own eyes or in the eyes of others. But it may also result simply from being unable to continue with our performance, regardless of the impact of this failure on esteem.

3. In presenting ourselves as a certain sort of person, we make use of the setting in which we live and the objects we have around us. How other people treat us—our teammates—is an important clue to our identity, as are our appearance and manner.

4. Ned Jones pointed to specific ways we may attempt to gain power over others by manipulating their impressions of us. *Ingratiation* involves getting people to like us by being agreeable. *Self-promotion* involves getting people to admire our competence by advertising our accomplishments. *Intimidation* is a matter of getting people to fear us by seeming dangerous. *Exemplification* is a matter of displaying our moral virtue to get people to respect us. And *supplication* involves getting people to take pity on us by seeming weak.

5. Having a handicap can make a failure seem excusable and a success seem all the greater. People, therefore, sometimes *self-handicap*—arrange to have a handicap to enhance their self-presentation.

6. Robert Wicklund has proposed that actors performing a task must pay attention *either* to the task itself or to themselves as performers. Paying attention to oneself as performer, *objective self-awareness*, can call attention to one's internalized standards for performing the task. Thus, focusing on self can bring a person's behavior into line with his standards. Self-focused attention can also affect one's motivation to perform a task, sometimes leading to motivation that is so intense that it detracts from performance.

8. Mark Snyder has developed a scale that attempts to measure the degree to which people are high or low in *self-monitoring*. High self-monitors are relatively more (1) concerned with the appropriateness of their social presentations, (2) attentive to others' behavior as a guide to their own, (3) able to control their performances, (4) willing to use this ability, and (5) inconsistent in their behavior. In addition, high self-monitors have been found to have more shallow social relationships than do low self-monitors. The reason is not yet established.

CHAPTER 7

Emotion: Experience and Expression

In Chapter 6, we considered the self from the point of view of public action, but in doing so, we also had our eye on the relation between public action and private beliefs. In this chapter, we will reverse perspective and focus on emotion, one important component of the self as privately experienced. As we shall see, however, to do justice to emotion, we are forced to keep in mind the broader, public, social world in which emotion is expressed. In this chapter, then, we will examine what social psychologists have learned about the experience and expression of emotion.*

THE JAMES-LANGE THEORY

American psychological theorizing about emotion begins, as does so much of American psychology, with William James (James 1890/1950). James developed his analysis of the emotions by asking us to think about a concrete emotional episode. The question he wanted his analysis of the episode to answer was: What element of this experience makes it the emotion it is? To see what he had in mind, let us follow his discussion.

*We will *not* be able to cover all that is known about emotion. Our concern is with emotion as it is important to social psychology; thus, we will be slighting much that has been learned about, for example, the neural underpinnings of emotion.

Suppose you were walking along a path, and you were to see, suddenly, through a clearing, a bear. You might well become afraid and run away. Along with your running away, James says, your perception of the bear would produce something else too, what he called "bodily changes"—sensations you would feel, especially the knotting of your stomach, pounding of your heart, and so on (see Figure 7.1). What James wanted to know was: Which of the things that happens here *is* the emotion?

He started with your perception of the bear, and asked whether *that* was the emotion. But he argued that your perceiving the bear can't itself be the emotion because you could, after all, perceive a bear but not be afraid. And if this is possible, then there must be something other than the perception of the bear that makes this fear. That something that distinguishes merely perceiving a bear from being afraid of the bear is your *reaction to the bear.* Your reaction to the bear, then, *IS* the fear. James proposes that though common sense would describe you as reacting as you did *because* you were afraid, you would do better to think of yourself as being afraid *because* of your reaction! Again, James wants to stress that it is your *reaction* that constitutes the emotion, not your merely noticing that there is a bear out there.

To take another example, think of being in love. What constitutes your being in love? Certainly not perceiving the person you love. Lots of people can have the same perception of the person you love and not feel the same way about your beloved. Rather, what constitutes your being in love is your reaction to that person. Let us return to your encounter with the bear.

James says that your reaction to the bear *IS* your fear. But your reaction to the bear, remember, had two components—running away and the knotting of your stomach. Which is the emotion? James rejects the running away as a necessary component of your fear, because there are cases in which we have all felt emotions, even strong ones, without doing anything at all. After all, if seeing the bear made you paralyzed with fear, you would certainly still be afraid, but you wouldn't be running away. So overt behavior cannot be a

▲ *William James.*

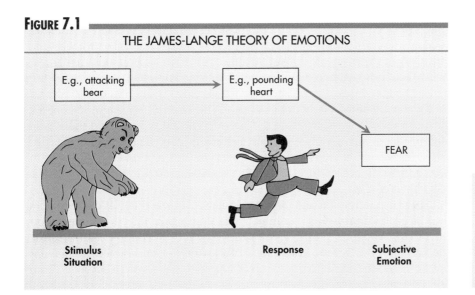

◀ *According to William James, seeing a bear leads to two things: (1) bodily changes and (2) running away. The perception of the first is the emotion. (Adapted from Gleitman, 1991)*

necessary component of emotional experience, although it looks like a good candidate.

James concludes that the only viable candidate left for the emotion is the *experience* of "bodily changes." The one thing that must be present for us to experience an emotion is some set of bodily changes. Strip those away, James says, and all that is left is cool, passionless, emotionless perception. James might have identified your fear solely with your bodily changes, but he didn't. The reason is that bodily changes (emotions) could occur without your noticing them. James would not allow that, for to him emotions were elements of experience first and foremost. To him, the notion of an unexperienced emotion simply made no sense. So James instead argued that it is *your perception of bodily changes* that *is* your emotion (James, 1890/1950).

If the emotions *are* the perception of bodily changes, and since there are many different emotions we can feel, there must be many different bodily changes we can perceive; each one must correspond to a different emotion. Fear must be different from anger, and they must both differ from love by virtue of our experiencing different bodily changes in each. James, then, raises the issue of how we know our emotions, and he answers it: by introspecting on our bodily states. Each emotion word we have is the name of a different bodily state. These different states are in the typical case *caused by* specific events in the world—bears lead to fear, our beloved to love. And these same circumstances also give rise to overt behaviors. But the external events and the overt behaviors are not themselves part of the emotional experience. The only things that are intrinsic to the experience of emotions are the perceptions of bodily changes.

There is much to be said for James's view. For one thing, it makes a good deal of evolutionary sense. Common sense says that first there is emotion, then there is action. But if you are to survive your encounter with the bear, the very first thing you should do is run away, not experience the emotion of fear. Emotions are a luxury for creatures; action pays off in survival. There is good sense in designing the creature to act first and reflect later.

According to William James, the *perception* of bodily changes is the emotion. Thus, for James, emotions can never go unnoticed.

James's view also corresponds to experiences I have had, and other people have reported. Some of us have faced a situation that might well have resulted in our death. And the experience was for me, at least, one not of terror but of a certain uncanny calm. I recall, and others have recalled, becoming afraid only *after* the danger had passed. What we would describe as fear or terror did, as James suggested, happen only on reflection. So James's view of the emotions makes a good deal of sense. Notice also that it makes of emotion something completely internal and private—a churning stomach is something only its possessor can perceive.

But James's theory also has certain problems. For one thing, James was vague about just what these bodily changes are. Carl Lange, a physiologist and a contemporary of James, offered a concrete proposal for just what the physiological changes are that constitute the bases for the emotions. He proposed that it was changes in the viscera (or what we would now call the ***autonomic nervous system***) that are the bases of the emotions.

There is good sense here too. Consider fear for a moment. What does it feel like to be afraid, really afraid? We feel our stomach tensing, our heart pounding, and our hands trembling. These are all effects of activation of the ***sympathetic nervous system,*** part of the autonomic nervous system, which is a specific neural pathway that has diffuse effects throughout the body (see Figure 7.2 on page 228). The result of arousal of this pathway is to prepare us to fight or flee. When this neural network is activated, our pulse speeds up, our blood pressure rises, sending more oxygenated blood to the parts of our body crucial for intense activity. Our digestive system turns off—facing a hungry bear is no time to be digesting food, lest one become food. The liver secretes vitamin K, which aids clotting—just in case the bear is a bit successful. And there are a myriad of other physiological changes (some of which we can sense, some of which we can't) that prepare us for our encounter. The view that the emotions consist in the recognition of activation of the viscera has come to be known as the James-Lange theory of emotion. It is this theory that has set the agenda for much research on emotion.

COGNITION-AROUSAL THEORY

The James-Lange theory was almost immediately criticized by Walter Cannon, who was also a contemporary of James and the major early investigator of the sympathetic nervous system. (Indeed, it was Cannon who called attention to the sympathetic system as the "fight or flight" system.) Cannon argued that the sympathetic nervous system isn't a very likely candidate for the emotions for two important reasons. First, its time course isn't the time course of emotion. It responds too slowly to underlie emotion, and it remains activated for too long. Second, this visceral system is too undifferentiated to constitute the basis of the large number of emotions we can feel. The sympathetic nervous system is, to put it bluntly, on or off, and while this might be enough to explain how we feel fear, how can such a simple system account for love, or melancholy, or awe? This controversy set in motion a great deal of empirical research on the nature of emotion and especially the differences among the emotions.

FIGURE 7.2

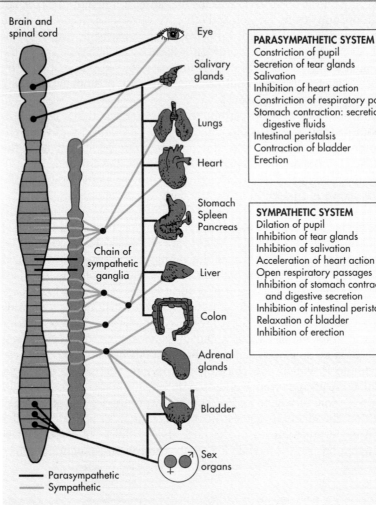

THE AUTONOMIC NERVOUS SYSTEM

PARASYMPATHETIC SYSTEM
Constriction of pupil
Secretion of tear glands
Salivation
Inhibition of heart action
Constriction of respiratory passages
Stomach contraction: secretion of
    digestive fluids
Intestinal peristalsis
Contraction of bladder
Erection

SYMPATHETIC SYSTEM
Dilation of pupil
Inhibition of tear glands
Inhibition of salivation
Acceleration of heart action
Open respiratory passages
Inhibition of stomach contraction
    and digestive secretion
Inhibition of intestinal peristalsis
Relaxation of bladder
Inhibition of erection

▶ *The autonomic nervous system consists of both the parasympathetic nervous system and the sympathetic nervous system. The sympathetic nervous system is aroused during a variety of emotions, including fear and anger. (From Gleitman, 1991)*

The Sympathetic Nervous System and Emotion

It is useful to think about the relation between knowledge of arousal of the sympathetic nervous system and emotion in terms of three distinct questions: (1) Is knowledge of arousal of the sympathetic nervous system *necessary* to the experience of emotion? (2) Is knowledge of arousal of the sympathetic nervous system *sufficient* for the experience of emotion? (3) Does knowledge of arousal of the sympathetic nervous system *in any way* relate to the intensity of emotion? As we shall see, these questions have quite different answers.

NECESSITY OF AROUSAL

If we must know that our sympathetic nervous system is aroused in order to experience emotion, or to put it in its more usual form, if we need *feedback from* our sympathetic nervous system to experience emotion, then people who cannot receive feedback from their sympathetic nervous system as a result of spinal cord injuries should not experience emotion at all. There have been two studies of the emotional lives of people who have sustained such injuries. The results of these two studies are in less than perfect agreement, but it seems safe to say that patients without autonomic feedback *do* experience strong emotions. Indeed, many subjects reported that their most intense experiences of fear and love occurred *after* the trauma that severed their spinal cord (Chwalisz, Diener, & Gallagher, 1988). This evidence suggests, then, that autonomic feedback isn't necessary to the experience of emotion. But is it sufficient to produce emotion?

SUFFICIENCY OF AUTONOMIC FEEDBACK FOR EMOTION

Marañon (1924) injected subjects with adrenaline, a neurotransmitter active in the sympathetic system. Subjects so injected became physiologically aroused. If sympathetic arousal is sufficient for emotion, these subjects should have become emotional—which emotion they should have experienced is difficult to say, but that they should have experienced some emotion is clear.

Most of Marañon's subjects reported nothing approaching an emotional episode; they simply reported various physiological symptoms. But about one-third of the subjects reported what they described as "as if" emotions; they said they felt as if they were angry, for example, but they weren't really angry. The result of this simple experiment, then, suggests that arousal isn't sufficient to produce emotion, but the "as if" description is tantalizing. It suggests that arousal produces something close to emotion. The question is: What is the missing element? This suggestion was followed up in one of the most famous of psychological experiments, the Schachter and Singer experiment (1962).

The evidence suggests that arousal of the sympathetic nervous system

- is *not* necessary for the experience of emotion;

- is *not* sufficient for the experience of emotion;

- *may* affect the intensity of the experience of emotion.

CLASSIC FINDINGS IN SOCIAL PSYCHOLOGY: THE SCHACHTER AND SINGER EXPERIMENT

Stanley Schachter and Jerome Singer offered a theory about the nature of emotion that gives a place to arousal but also explains why it isn't sufficient to produce emotion. Their idea was that emotions are an amalgam of physiological states and beliefs about the causes of those states. To be afraid, for example, is to be physiologically aroused and to believe that the arousal was caused by your perceiving some danger. Schachter and Singer argued that the reason that Marañon's subjects did not feel emotions, or felt "as if" emotions, was that although they experienced the typical symptoms of emotion, they knew that those symptoms were drug induced rather than induced by some circumstance typically provocative of emotion. Schachter and Singer argued that arousal was necessary to produce the experience, but not sufficient to produce it. How could one test such a theory?

The trick is to produce arousal by administering adrenaline or its synthetic equivalent, epinephrine, without the subjects' knowing that the drug was the source of the arousal. There are several ways of doing this. One is to give subjects the drug without their knowing they have gotten any drug at all. And Schachter and Singer did consider such things as pumping adrenaline into the air supply of a lab room! But in the end they gave up on such ideas and settled for giving subjects the adrenaline in such a way that they knew they had gotten a drug, but did not know *that the drug produced arousal.*

PROCEDURE OF THE EXPERIMENT

Schachter and Singer recruited male college students for what they were told was an experiment about the effects of a certain vitamin, Suproxin, on vision. They were told that they would be given the Suproxin, be asked to wait a while as it took effect, and then have their vision tested. If the subject agreed to be in the experiment, he was given an injection.

The design of the experiment was rather complex, and is illustrated in Table 7.1. As you can see, some subjects—those in cells a and b—actually received an injection of salt water, a **placebo,** something that has no effects. The remaining subjects in the experiment were given injections of epinephrine. Giving some subjects epinephrine and others salt water is an effective way to test one component of the theory—the claim that arousal has an effect on emotion. But how can one test for the cognitive component? The answer lies in the other things the experimenter did to the subjects in addition to giving them injections.

First, as the table shows, some subjects were told about the effects of epinephrine. They were told that their hands would start to shake, their hearts would pound, and their faces might become warm and flushed; these are the real side effects of epinephrine. These subjects were like Marañon's in that they would be experiencing arousal, and they knew it would be caused by a drug. The expectation was that these informed subjects would not experience emotion, or, at most, they would experience "as if" emotion.

Other subjects were simply not told about any side effects from the Suproxin (uninformed subjects); the experimenters hoped that these subjects would not see a connection between the drug they had been given and their arousal. There was, of course, the possibility that they would figure out on their own that their physiological state was drug induced, so a third condition was created. This last group of subjects was *misinformed* about the side effects; they were told that the Suproxin might produce headache, numbness of the

TABLE 7.1

PREDICTED RESULTS FOR SCHACHTER AND SINGER EXPERIMENT		
	Euphoria	*Anger*
Placebo	a	b
	No emotion	No emotion
Epinephrine-informed	c	d
	Little emotion	Little emotion
Epinephrine-uninformed	e	f
	Euphoria	Anger
Epinephrine-misinformed	g	
	Euphoria	Not run

SOURCE: Based on Schachter & Singer, 1962.

feet, and so on. These are *not* effects of epinephrine. The point of including this manipulation was to distract them from the real side effects of the drug by having them look for effects that wouldn't be there.

Let us review the experiment and its logic so far. Because some subjects were injected with epinephrine and others weren't, some subjects were more aroused than others. If arousal is a component of emotion, then the aroused subjects should have been more emotional than the control (placebo) subjects. Among those subjects given epinephrine, there were some who *knew* that their arousal was a product of the drug, the epinephrine-informed subjects. The experiment for these subjects was essentially a replication of the Marañon experiment. To the degree that cognition is a component of emotion, these subjects should *not have experienced emotion.*

There were also other subjects, the epinephrine-uninformed and the epinephrine-misinformed subjects, who the experimenters hoped did not attribute their arousal to the drug, and hence who should have experienced emotion. But which emotion? Schachter and Singer proposed that *which* emotion would depend on what exactly the subject thought caused the arousal. If this is true, then by getting the subjects to have different ideas about what caused their arousal, it should be possible to get them to experience different emotions. So Schachter and Singer set out to give them different ideas about what caused their arousal.

Recall that the subjects were told that they would have to wait for the drug to take effect before their vision could be tested. The experimenters filled this interval with events that subjects could plausibly believe were the real source of their arousal. The hope was that the uninformed and misinformed subjects would see these events as the source of their arousal, and hence would experience the appropriate (different) emotions.

Some subjects waited in a room that was filled with what can only be described as junk. Also in the room with them was the experimenter's confederate, supposedly another subject waiting to have his vision tested. The confederate did his best to engage the subject in playing with the junk. He played a mock game of basketball using paper cups and a wastepaper basket, he made paper airplanes to throw around the room, he wadded up bits of paper and shot them with a slingshot made from a rubber band, and he fooled around with a hula hoop. (It was 1961 or so, and the hula hoop had just replaced the Davy Crockett cap as America's favorite fad.) All of this was designed to get the subject to attribute his arousal to the fooling around. If the subjects did attribute their arousal to these antics, Schachter and Singer expected them to experience the appropriate emotion, euphoria. (Euphoria is a bit much; I doubt anyone would be made euphoric by a hula hoop. Perhaps mirthful is a better description.)

Other subjects (these were just from the uninformed group) were also asked to wait with an experimental accomplice, but they filled out a lengthy questionnaire, as did the accomplice. The questionnaire proceeded from the annoying to the insulting. Early questions asked tedious things like: What are the foods you eat in a typical day? What childhood diseases have you had and at what age? Later questions listed things like "Seems to need psychiatric care," "Does not bathe or wash regularly," and asked subjects to mention for which member of their immediate family each seemed most appropriate. A later question asked subjects how many times a week they had sexual intercourse. And the very last question asked them: "With how many men (other than your father) has your mother had extramarital relationships? 4 and under _____; 5–9 _____; 10 and over _____."

At various points, the confederate snapped out his frustration and then anger. As you have probably guessed, this condition was created to induce the subject to see his arousal as being the consequence of being first annoyed and then insulted. Schachter and Singer expected the uninformed subjects in this condition to see themselves as (and to be) angry.

We have, then, the seven conditions of the experiment shown in Table 7.1. The control subjects, since they received no epinephrine, should have experienced no (or relatively little) emotion. Similarly, the epinephrine-informed subjects in both the euphoria and anger conditions should have experienced little emotion, not because they weren't aroused, but because they knew their arousal was produced by the drug. The uninformed and misinformed subjects in the euphoria condition were expected to be euphoric, and the subjects in the uninformed anger condition were expected to become angry.*

The dependent variable in the experiment, the subjects' emotional state, was measured in two ways: (1) the subjects were simply asked to report what emotion they felt, and (2) there were observers stationed behind a one-way mirror who observed the subjects' behavior. Any sign that the subject was joining in with the confederate in the euphoria condition was scored as evidence of euphoria, and any displays of anger were scored as evidence of anger.

RESULTS OF THE EXPERIMENT

The Schachter and Singer experiment was one of the most influential in social psychology. You might infer from this that its results were especially clear. Unfortunately, this is far from true. The results, all in all, were rather equivocal.

First, let us look at the euphoria condition. Recall that the investigators used two measures of the subjects' mood: their answers to scales asking them to report their moods, and their behavior as coded by observers behind a one-way mirror. On the self-report scales, the subjects who were told that the Suproxin shot would produce arousal reported the least euphoria (see Table 7.2). The placebo, uninformed, and misinformed subjects reported more, and an essentially equal amount. This pattern of results also showed up on the behavioral measure (see Table 7.3). How do these results square with Schachter and Singer's predictions?

Schachter and Singer's theory predicts that the subjects informed that their arousal was due to a drug should not have been very emotional, so the fact that the epinephrine-informed group was less aroused than the others is encouraging. What is not so encouraging for their theory is that the placebo group was almost as emotional as were the misinformed and uninformed groups. The physiological component of Schachter and Singer's theory led them to predict that the placebo group, having received no epinephrine, should have been *less* emotional than those receiving epinephrine. Still, as Schachter and Singer pointed out, there was nothing about the placebo that

---

*The misinformed anger condition was not run.

TABLE 7.2

SELF-REPORTED EMOTION IN THE SCHACHTER AND SINGER EXPERIMENT

	Euphoria	Anger*
Placebo	1.61	1.63
Epinephrine-informed	0.98	1.91
Epinephrine-uninformed	1.78	1.39
Epinephrine-misinformed	1.90	NA

*The numbers indicate the degree of happiness minus the degree of irritation, so increasing numbers indicate greater happiness and less anger.

NA: Not applicable, as this condition was not run.

SOURCE: Data from Schachter & Singer, 1962.

TABLE 7.3

BEHAVIORAL MEASURES OF EMOTION IN THE SCHACHTER AND SINGER EXPERIMENT

	Euphoria	Anger
Placebo	16.0	0.79
Epinephrine-informed	12.7	−0.18
Epinephrine-uninformed	18.3	2.28
Epinephrine-misinformed	22.6	NA

NA: Not applicable, as this condition was not run.

The numbers represent ratings of the degree to which subjects engaged in euphoric or angry behavior as rated by an observer through a one-way mirror. Higher numbers indicate euphoria or anger.

SOURCE: Data from Schachter & Singer, 1962.

prevented arousal, and it is reasonable to argue that the circumstances made the subjects *aroused enough* to experience emotion. So within the euphoria conditions, there was some support for the theory. Was there support within the anger conditions?

On the self-report scales, the epinephrine-informed subjects were only slightly less irritated than those in the placebo or epinephrine-uninformed groups. There are three points that must be made about this result. First, the self-report scale score was formed by asking the subjects how happy they were and how irritated they were. Their scores on the irritation scale were subtracted from their scores on the happiness scale. The result was that the epinephrine-informed group had *higher* scores on this measure than did the other two groups. Schachter and Singer interpreted this result to mean that these subjects were *less* angry than subjects in the other groups, which is a reasonable interpretation. Second, this result was quite small and statistically unreliable. But third, Schachter and Singer had an explanation for the weakness of the result. Whom would the subjects be angry with? The experimenter was the obvious target. But Schachter and Singer argued that *all* these subjects were undergraduates and participating in the experiment as part of a

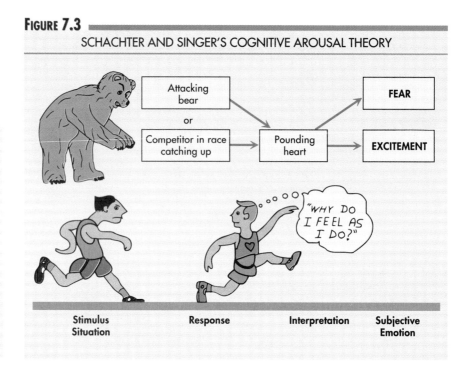

FIGURE 7.3

SCHACHTER AND SINGER'S COGNITIVE AROUSAL THEORY

▶ *According to Schachter and Singer, emotion is a product of both physiological arousal and an interpretation of that arousal. Both an attacking bear and a competitor catching up in a race will lead to the response of running and a pounding heart, but the nature of the emotion experienced (here, fear or excitement) will depend on what the subject interprets as the source of the emotion. (Adapted from Gleitman, 1991)*

requirement for their introductory psychology course. As a result, they may have been reluctant to express anger at the experimenter for fear that word would leak back to their instructor.

Results on the behavioral measures were more comforting. The epinephrine-informed subjects did engage in the fewest angry behaviors; the epinephrine-uninformed subjects engaged in the most angry behaviors; the placebo subjects were intermediate. This is just the order of results that Schachter and Singer had predicted.

Schachter and Singer theorized that emotion is a product of physiological arousal plus an interpretation of that arousal. They believed that the degree of arousal explains the intensity of the emotion; the nature of the interpretation accounts for the nature of the emotion (see Figure 7.3). The results more or less supported Schachter and Singer's predictions, but they were not as strong as one might like. It is true that where the results failed, Schachter and Singer had an explanation after the fact for the failure. But such after-the-fact, or ***post hoc,*** explanations are a poor substitute for successful predictions.

REPLICATIONS OF SCHACHTER AND SINGER

Even though Schachter and Singer's experiment had rather weak results, their theory took, and continues to occupy, a central place in psychological thinking about emotion. Indeed, the weakness of the experiment's results became a bit of an embarrassment to social psychologists who in their own work were constantly referring to the experiment. This embarrassment finally led to two attempts to replicate the experiment. To make the embarrassment deeper, the replications failed! In both cases, the results of the experiment did not support Schachter and Singer (Marshall & Zimbardo, 1979; Maslach, 1979). Still, Schachter and Singer replied (with considerable justification) that both replications were technically flawed, and that therefore the failure to replicate was uninformative about the underlying theory (Schachter & Singer, 1979). But, once again, explaining away failures is a poor substitute for success.

TRANSFER OF AROUSAL

What we have seen of Schachter and Singer's theory so far leaves mysterious just why the theory has been so influential. One reason is the success of an idea close to Schachter and Singer's. This is research guided by the notion of **transfer of arousal,** the idea that arousal produced by one stimulus can be transferred to another.

Dolf Zillmann has developed a line of research involving anger and transfer of arousal. In these experiments, subjects are insulted by a confederate and are then given an opportunity to take revenge. But between the insult and the revenge, the subjects do something else. Some do something boring— threading buttons on a wire. Others do something arousing—riding a stationary bicycle, for example. In these experiments, the subjects who do something arousing between the insult and revenge retaliate *more* than do those who do something boring (Zillmann, 1971; Martin, Harlow, & Strack, 1992; see Chapter 13 for details). Zillmann proposes that the degree of retaliation is a measure of the subject's anger, and that the subject's anger is a product of two sources—the insult and the bicycle riding. But, Zillmann argues, the subject misattributes the arousal produced by the bike riding to the insult, and because of this misattribution, becomes excessively angry and overretaliates. In this experiment, as in the Schachter and Singer experiment, the subject's eventual emotional state is affected by arousal produced by something other than the source of the emotion; this effect is called **emotion transfer.** Zillmann (and others) have replicated this effect in a substantial number of experiments, and other experimenters have shown similar results for sexual attraction (Dutton & Aron, 1974; see Chapter 15).

These experiments, although different from Schachter and Singer's in the source of arousal they use, are guided by the same fundamental notion: that emotion is an amalgam of physiological arousal and an interpretation of its cause. So this line of successful experiments provides support for the general line of thinking begun by Schachter and Singer. The difficulties with the Schachter and Singer experiment and the attempts to replicate it may have to do more with the problems involved in producing arousal using drugs than with any weakness of the underlying conception. In any event, the success of the transfer of arousal studies is one reason for the prominence of the Schachter and Singer notion, even with the weak results Schachter and Singer found.

There is substantial evidence that arousal produced by one emotion can intensify the experience of a second emotion produced while the person is still aroused from the first emotion. This is called transfer of arousal.

COMPLEX NATURE OF EMOTIONS

There is, perhaps, a more fundamental reason for the popularity of the Schachter and Singer theory—it answers Cannon's challenge to the James-Lange theory. The sympathetic nervous system seems to be important to the experience of emotion because the symptoms of strong emotion are manifestations of sympathetic arousal. Further, the sympathetic nervous system can be aroused *in degree.* So the degree to which it is aroused seems to be a natural way to interpret the degree to which a person feels a particular emotion. But, as Cannon saw, something more differentiated than the sympathetic nervous system is needed to account for the complexity and subtlety of the emotions. Cognition, in the form of appraisals of one's environment, surely has this property.* For many psychologists, there *must* be a cognitive aspect of emotion to account for its wondrous complexity (see Averill, 1980; Sabini & Silver, 1982; Mandler, 1984; Smith & Ellsworth, 1985, 1987; Easterling & Leventhal, 1989; Tesser, 1990; Roseman, Spindel, & Lose, 1990). Thus, despite the weakness of Schachter and Singer's results, their central claim—that emotions involve a cognitive element in addition to a bodily component—has taken hold. (Recently, however, Paul Ekman developed evidence that suggests that there might be unique patterns of sympathetic activity associated with each emotion, and that these patterns are cross-culturally universal [Levenson, Ekman, Heider, & Friesen, 1992]. If these results stand up, they may cause a substantial reappraisal of the Schachter and Singer position.)

There is quite a shift from James's view of the emotions to Schachter and Singer's. By locating the emotions in our internal state, James made our emotions: (1) something we can know with perfect certainty—after all, we surely know if our stomach is knotted—and (2) something private and personal. But according to Schachter and Singer's view, we can be wrong about what emotion we are experiencing; that is, we can be wrong about what produced our arousal. There is an aspect of our emotions that isn't private and personal, but rather is in the world—the circumstances that produced the arousal. But before accepting Schachter and Singer's account of the emotion, we should consider one other place people have looked for the information that might distinguish among our emotions: our facial expressions.

FACIAL EXPRESSION AND EMOTION

People's faces are fascinating. And they are fascinating to social psychologists for much the same reason they are to the rest of us: their magnificent expressiveness. Indeed, the human face is richly supplied with muscles and nerves that have no obvious function other than the creation of expressions. This state of affairs leads someone given to thinking in terms of evolution to suppose that human facial expressions are the product of natural selection (evolution). Charles Darwin thought in terms of evolution, and he was the first to look at facial expressions as something we humans have inherited from our ancestors.

Darwin made two very fruitful suggestions about facial expressions (Darwin, 1872/1965). First, he suggested that facial expressions have evolved

*There is another candidate for the differentiated element in emotion: response readiness. Recently Nico Frijda proposed that emotions can be distinguished by the actions that each emotion disposes toward (Frijda, Kuipers, & ter Schure, 1989). Anger, for example, involves a readiness to seek revenge; shame, a readiness to hide. Future research may well find that a readiness to act should join the amalgamation of appraisal and arousal.

from facial actions that once were directly useful in terms of survival. The facial expression we show in anger, for example, was once a part of what our ancestors did in attacking an antagonist with their teeth (see Figure 7.4). But Darwin further argued that because of the frequent association between the states of mind that provoked the facial movements and those movements themselves, these facial expressions began to appear whenever the organism entered the corresponding state of mind. This he called the **principle of serviceable associated habits.** Thus, Darwin proposed that facial expressions are inherited, and that they are windows onto the soul of emotion—they are direct, mechanical expressions of our state of mind.*

Second, Darwin suggested that facial expressions act back on the emotional states that typically produce them. He suggested that expressing emotion through the face intensifies the experience of the emotion. This idea, now called the **facial feedback hypothesis,** has become prominent in the recent literature.

In this section, we shall first look at Darwin's legacy for the study of emotion and then turn to a more general discussion of facial and other non-verbal expressions.

FIGURE 7.4

EMOTION IN THE BABOON

▲ *Darwin proposed that facial expressions evolved from facial actions that were directly useful for survival.*

CLASSIC FINDINGS IN SOCIAL PSYCHOLOGY: UNIVERSALITY OF EMOTIONAL EXPRESSIONS

Darwin argued that the way to tell whether facial expressions are innate is to ask whether they are universal. That is, if people in every human culture express emotions with the same facial movements, then we have some reason to assume that these facial expressions are innate. Darwin issued a challenge to empirical investigators to answer this question. Without doubt, Paul Ekman is the scientist most deeply involved in responding to the challenge.

Ekman's approach to the issue was to assemble pictures of several faces showing six emotions: happiness, sadness, disgust, anger, surprise, and fear (see Figure 7.5 on page 238). These pictures were then shown to subjects in a variety of cultures; the subjects were asked to report the expressions the faces showed. The first cross-cultural study involved subjects from the United States, Brazil, Chile, Argentina, and Japan. The results indicated a remarkable degree of consensus about which faces went with which emotions. There can be no doubt that the results support Darwin's and Ekman's view that the facial expressions of emotion are universal and innate. But there was a problem with the study. As different as these cultures are, they are all modern, literate cultures. Perhaps people from these cultures all have the same idea of what facial expressions go with what emotions, not because they share the same human genes, but because they all see the same movies and television

*Darwin was a Lamarckian; that is, he believed that because anger and certain expressions have been associated in the life of a particular individual, this association will be passed on to his descendants. This was a perfectly reasonable position for Darwin to take; its implausibility could not be known until much more became known about the mechanism of evolution—genetics. Modern theorists accept the notion of the inheritance of facial expression without accepting the Lamarckian path of inheritance.

FIGURE 7.5

EKMAN'S SIX
FUNDAMENTAL EMOTIONS

▼ *Facial expressions of emotion are (A) happiness, (B) surprise, (C) sadness, (D) anger, (E) disgust, and (F) fear. (From Ekman & Friesen, 1975)*

A

B

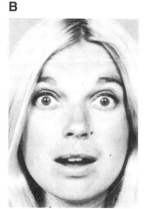

C

D

E

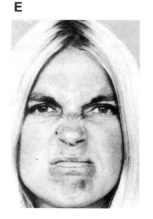

F

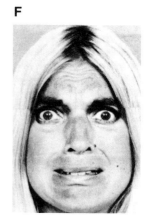

shows! These cultures are different, to be sure, but they also have substantial influences on each other (see Table 7.4).

To overcome this objection, Ekman and his collaborators obtained judgments of the emotions displayed in these pictures from members of a preliterate culture, the Fore of New Guinea. Until fourteen years before the Ekman study, no one from this cultural group had had any contact whatsoever with outsiders. By the time of the study, some members of the culture had had contact with Westerners, but many had not. Ekman focused on people from the Fore culture who had seen no movies, spoke neither English nor Pidgin, had never lived in a Western settlement or worked for Caucasians. The subjects, then, were about as far as one can get from Western culture while remaining on the planet. Again, there was a startling degree of agreement about the faces shown in the pictures. The sole failure of agreement was over the distinction between fear and surprise; Westerners and these preliterate subjects disagree about which is which. But even here it is worth noting that these expressions are often associated in our everyday experience—rarely is a person afraid without being surprised.

In a follow-up study, videotapes of New Guinean subjects displaying emotions were shown to American college students, who correctly identified which emotion was being expressed (Ekman, 1973). These results provide powerful support for the view that the match between facial expressions and emotions is universal, at least for a subset of emotions. And if the matches are universal, then it is reasonable to suppose that they are innate.

This finding has been extended in two ways. First, Ekman and others have added to the list of cultures that recognize one another's facial expressions. The list now includes Italy, Scotland, Estonia, Greece, Germany, Hong Kong, Sumatra, and Turkey (Ekman et al., 1987). Second, there seem to be other universals. Contempt, for example, apparently has a universal, innate expression (Ekman & Friesen, 1986). And I. Eibl-Eibesfeldt has found what he believes to be a universal gesture, although it probably is not part of an emotion display.

Eibl-Eibesfeldt has recorded on film the public life of a variety of cultures using a very clever device: a camera that films from the side of its lens. It does *not* record what goes on in front of it; rather it records what is going on to

TABLE 7.4

CROSS-CULTURAL EVIDENCE FOR UNIVERSAL EMOTIONAL EXPRESSIONS

	Percentage of People Correctly Identifying Emotion from Photograph					
Culture	Happiness	Disgust	Surprise	Sadness	Anger	Fear
United States (N = 99)	97	92	95	84	67	85
Brazil (N = 40)	95	97	87	59	90	67
Chile (N = 119)	95	92	93	88	94	68
Argentina (N = 168)	98	92	95	78	90	54
Japan (N = 29)	100	90	100	62	90	66

SOURCE: Ekman, 1973.
N = number of subjects.

the side. The people being filmed, then, are typically unsuspecting. Using this device, Eibl-Eibesfeldt has documented what he calls an "eyebrow flash" in many cultures, from France to Samoa; the eyebrow flash is a raising of the eyebrows that lasts for about one-sixth of a second, and is seen when two

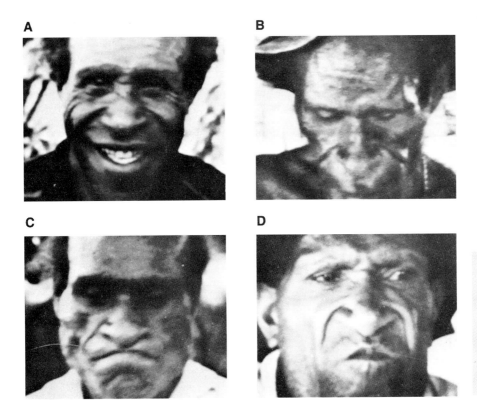

A

B

C

D

◀ New Guinea tribesmen portray their reactions to various scenarios. (A) "Your friend has come, and you are happy." (B) "Your child has died." (C) "You are angry and about to fight." (D) "You see a dead pig that has been lying there for a long time."

people who know each other well meet and greet (see Figure 7.6). This display, however, is probably best seen not as a display of emotion, but rather as a ritual of greeting (Eibl-Eibesfeldt, 1972).

Eibl-Eibesfeldt has also made another important observation relevant to the universality of nonverbal expressions. He pointed out that deaf and blind children show the same expressions that sighted and hearing children do. (Of course, they respond to different stimuli, but the point is that the patterns of facial expressions they show are much the same as those of sighted and hearing children.) How could they have learned these expressions? Perhaps by touch. But there are children whose mothers took the drug Thalidomide during pregnancy and who as a result were born with multiple birth defects. Some of them were born deaf, blind, and without hands and arms, so they had nothing to touch with. They too showed the same expressions and gestures (Eibl-Eibesfeldt, 1972).

FIGURE 7.6

A UNIVERSAL GESTURE

▶ *The eyebrow flash is a universal expressive gesture of greeting. Each example shows a person at the beginning of the interaction, when the eyebrows are still lowered; and during the greeting, when the eyebrows are raised to their maximum. (A and B) French; (C and D) Balinese; (E and F) Papuan (Huri tribe). (From Eibl-Eibesfeldt, 1972)*

We are in a position now to give a provisional answer to Darwin's question. Yes, the facial expressions associated with some emotions seem to be universal and innate. This might seem to imply that people from every culture give off these facial expressions every time they experience the corresponding emotion; the discussion does *not* imply this, and people don't.

Display Rules

Stereotypically, people from Mediterranean cultures are expressive, while Asians are inscrutable. How could this be true if facial expressions are innate?

Ekman answers that each culture passes on to its members, as an item of socialization, rules about when and where emotions are to be expressed; he calls these rules ***display rules.*** So one reason that people may differ in their degree of expressiveness is that the cultures they come from differ in their display rules. Japanese culture, for example, lays great stress on suppressing emotional displays, including facial displays of emotion. Ekman argues, however, that when Japanese people display emotion, they do so with the same expression Westerners do. Further, he has demonstrated this experimentally.

Ekman studied twenty-five subjects from Wadesa University in Tokyo and twenty-five from the University of California at Berkeley. At both locations, an experimenter from the subjects' own culture explained to them that they were to be part of an experiment on physiological responses to stress. To accomplish this, the experimenter hooked the subjects up to electrodes to monitor their heart rates and other physiological indices. The experimenter explained that to produce stress, they would be shown a very stressful film, designed to elicit anxiety and disgust. Then the experimenter left the room and turned on first a neutral film and then the stressful film. Unbeknownst to the subjects, the experimenter also switched on a video camera recording the subjects' facial expressions. After the subjects watched for a bit, the experimenter returned and interviewed them about their emotional reactions to the film. The subjects' facial expressions were recorded during this phase of the experiment too.

The videotapes were coded using a very sophisticated coding system designed to pick up any hint of facial expression. The results of the coding revealed that the Japanese and American subjects' facial expressions *while they were alone in the room* were highly similar, but that they were substan-

Display rules are social rules about what emotional expressions should be displayed in which circumstances.

▼ *Are men allowed to cry, especially policemen? Apparently our display rules allow for such expressions if you are with the mounted police and your horse has just been put out of its misery after having been hit by a drunk driver.*

A

B

tially different while they were talking to the experimenter. In this circumstance, the American subjects continued to give off facial expressions that were quite negative, while the Japanese subjects' facial expressions became positive. The Japanese subjects had been trained from childhood on that displaying an emotion like disgust while in public, and for that matter while speaking to a figure of respect—a scientist—was extremely impolite, and must therefore be suppressed. The results of this study, then, indicate that American and Japanese expressions of emotion are really quite similar, but that the Japanese have learned to suppress expressions of emotion (Ekman, 1973). The Japanese, by the way, also don't show the eyebrow flash. They do, however, recognize it when they see it, and they recognize it as part of a greeting. They just find it brazen!

One of Darwin's ideas has worked out. There is reason to believe that the facial expressions of emotion are innate. What about Darwin's other ideas: that facial expressions are direct, mechanical signs of internal states, and the facial feedback hypothesis? How have these ideas fared? Let us turn first to the facial feedback hypothesis.

Facial Feedback

Darwin proposed that allowing the face to express an emotion intensifies the experience of the emotion, while suppressing the expression inhibits it (Darwin, 1872/1965). And William James was certainly of the view that any expression of emotion made the emotion more intense (James, 1890/1950). This idea has been labeled the ***facial feedback hypothesis.*** Actually, there are two versions of the facial feedback hypothesis, what we shall call the "strong" and the "weak" versions.

The strong version of the hypothesis is the idea that the expression on one's face can determine the *quality* (kind) as well as the intensity of an emotion. The weak version proposes that the expression on one's face can

▼ *Some positive emotional expressions: (A) the thrill of victory in a basketball game and (B) the pleasure of sharing a secret joke.*

A

B

affect the *intensity* but not the quality of an emotional reaction. These two views are importantly different.

Recall that the line of thought originating with Cannon and culminating in the Schachter and Singer experiment suggests that feedback from arousal of the autonomic nervous system is too diffuse to provide information about *which* emotion you are feeling. Therefore, this information must be found elsewhere. Recall that Schachter and Singer proposed that the place to look is in the environment, the world that produced the arousal. They claimed that a person knows what emotion she is feeling by examining the environment for the likely cause of her arousal. According to this view, the emotions are discriminated by the environmental causes of arousal.

There is also another place we might look for the information as to which emotion we are feeling: our own faces. Since the face has a rich collection of muscles and nerves, the face—unlike the sympathetic nervous system—is a possible source of discriminating information about which emotion we are feeling. This conjecture is given added support by the finding that the facial expressions of the basic emotions, at least, are universal and innate. The face, then, might play the role that Schachter and Singer assign to the environment: letting us know which emotion we are feeling. What, then, do we know about the facial feedback hypothesis?

NECESSITY AND SUFFICIENCY OF FACIAL EXPRESSIONS

Roger Tourangeau and Phoebe Ellsworth set out to answer whether facial expressions were (1) necessary or (2) sufficient to the experience of emotion. To do this, they carried out a straightforward experiment.

They asked subjects to look at three sorts of films: fear inducing, sadness inducing, and neutral. While they watched, subjects watching each sort of film were also asked to place their faces in one of three expressions: a fearful expression, a sad expression, a neutral expression. Other subjects were given no instructions about their faces. Thus, some subjects set their faces in the pose *appropriate* to the emotion induced by the films, but others had their faces in poses *inappropriate* to the emotions induced by the films. Surely, if the facial feedback hypothesis were true in the strong form, the subjects in appropriate poses should have experienced stronger emotions than those experienced by subjects whose faces and movies were mismatched. Did they?

The results of the experiment were quite dramatic. Although the nature of the films had a strong effect on the subjects' emotional experiences (and on their physiological responses), their facial expressions had *no effect* (see Table 7.5). It didn't matter what the subjects were doing with their faces. These results—on the face of it, so to speak—are damaging to the facial feedback hypothesis in any form (Tourangeau & Ellsworth, 1979).

The publication of the Tourangeau and Ellsworth experiment provoked a variety of responses; most were designed to rescue some version of the facial feedback hypothesis. Some of the criticisms were methodological, arguing that the subjects in the study probably didn't really have their faces in the positions natural to their spontaneous expressions of emotion (Hager & Ekman, 1981; Izard, 1981; Tomkins, 1981). Ellsworth and Tourangeau replied that their study, like every study, was less than perfect, but that it nonetheless provided strong grounds to doubt the necessity and sufficiency of facial expression in the experience of emotion (Ellsworth & Tourangeau, 1981).

TABLE 7.5

SELF-REPORTED EMOTION AND THE FACIAL FEEDBACK HYPOTHESIS

Stimuli	Facial Pose			
	Fear	Sad	Neutral	Uninstructed
Fear	6.0	7.5	7.8	4.6
Sad	3.3	3.2	3.9	3.6
Neutral	3.3	2.1	2.3	2.5

Note: The numbers represent emotional intensity. The rows differ from each other substantially, but the columns don't, indicating that what the subjects were seeing mattered to their emotional state, but their facial expressions did not.

SOURCE: Data from Tourangeau & Ellsworth, 1979.

FACIAL EXPRESSIONS AND INTENSITY OF EMOTIONS

A central problem in research on the facial feedback hypothesis is that to test the theory, the experimenter must get the subject to pose a facial expression, but she must do this *without tipping the subject off* as to the purpose of the study. This is a difficult challenge, and the lingering suspicion that it hasn't been met clouds interpretation of the experimental results.

One group of investigators has dealt with the problem of posing facial expressions in a clever and compelling way. They invited subjects to a lab, and told them that the experiment had to do with problems newly handicapped people had in doing familiar tasks in novel ways. People who become paralyzed, for example, have to find new ways of writing. Some people paralyzed in their dominant hand must use their nondominant hand; others have to learn to write by holding pens in their mouths, and so on. Thus, in this experiment, the subjects were asked to use magic markers to write, but without using their normal writing hands.

Some subjects were asked to use their nondominant hand. Others were instructed to hold the markers in their teeth, without letting their lips touch the marker. Still others were asked to hold the markers in their lips without letting their teeth touch the marker. The particular task the subjects were to do was to rate the funniness of some cartoons. Now you may be wondering what in the world this somewhat bizarre task has to do with the facial feedback hypothesis. And that is exactly the point. It is very unlikely that the subjects saw any relation between what they were told to do and the facial feedback hypothesis.

Try to hold a pen in your mouth with your lips, but not your teeth. If you do this right, your face will be forced into something approximating a frown. Now if you try it the other way, with your teeth but not your lips, you will produce a smile (see Figure 7.7). So some subjects were asked to rate the funniness of a cartoon without any manipulation of their mouths (the nondominant hand group); others were asked to do it while frowning; others, while smiling. The results were that smiling enhanced the funniness, and frowning reduced it—in support of the facial feedback hypothesis.

In a second study, the experimenters drew a distinction between the sub-

The evidence suggests that facial expressions are *neither* necessary nor sufficient for the experience of emotion. Facial expressions may affect the *intensity* of experienced emotion.

FIGURE 7.7

PROCEDURE TO TEST FACIAL FEEDBACK HYPOTHESIS

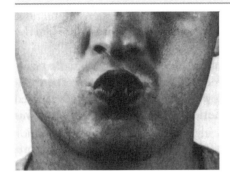 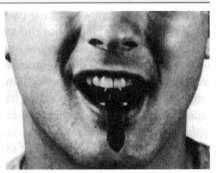

◀ *In the experiment testing the facial feedback hypothesis, holding a magic marker with teeth but not lips produced a smile; holding it with lips but not teeth produced a frown. (From Strack, Martin, & Stepper, 1988)*

jects' evaluation of how funny the cartoons were (in an objective sense) and how amused the subjects were by the cartoons. The interesting result was that the subjects' ratings of the objective funniness of the cartoons were *unaffected* by whether they held the pen in their lips or in their teeth, but their ratings of how *amused* they were by the cartoons *were* affected (Strack, Martin, & Stepper, 1988). This study has done the best job of meeting the challenge of manipulating subjects' facial expressions without the subjects' being aware that their expressions are the focus of the investigation, and it has found evidence that feedback from the face provides some information as to the *intensity* of affective response. It provides, then, fairly strong support for the weak version of the facial feedback hypothesis—the view that facial feedback informs about the intensity, although not the quality, of emotional experience.

Fritz Strack has suggested that facial expressions aren't the only way we use the parts of our bodies we have some control over to inform ourselves about (and modulate) our emotional states. Employing another clever ruse, Strack told subjects that they were to take part in a study of ergonomics and that, therefore, they would perform the rest of the experiment in a specific posture. Some subjects carried out the experiment in an upright, sitting position—an ordinary pose. But other subjects were told to sit up especially straight, and still other subjects were told to slump. Subjects performed an achievement task and were then told that they had succeeded at the task. The question was, would their postures affect the amount of pride they felt in their accomplishment? Would the subjects in the upright posture feel more pride than would the slumped subjects? The answer was yes. So not only may it be true that pride makes one hold one's head up high, but holding one's head up high may intensify feelings of pride (Stepper & Strack, 1993).

EVOLUTION AND FACIAL EXPRESSION

Paul Ekman, as we have seen, has provided important evidence that some human facial expressions are universal and innate. This leads us to wonder why they are innate; where they have come from. There are two answers to this question, both of which can be traced back to Darwin.

"YOU MEAN YOUR BIG SMILE IS BOTTLED-UP AGGRESSION? MINE IS BOTTLED-UP HOSTILITY."

Readout and Social Communications Views

One answer we have already seen: the principle of serviceable associated habits. This is the general idea that the reason there are specific facial expressions associated with specific emotions is that there are specific behavior patterns associated with specific motives. Thus, Darwin argued that the reason our faces look the way they do when we are angry is that our ancestors' putting their faces in this pose was a preliminary to attacking an enemy with their teeth. Darwin suggested that because of the history of association between the mental state of aggression and this facial pose, there is now a mechanical connection between anger and certain facial expressions. The expressions, as the jargon has it, provide a direct "readout" of people's emotional states; this is the ***direct readout*** view.

There is another possible answer to the question of how facial expressions came to be innate, articulated by Sir Julian Huxley. His position is that facial expressions evolved as "displays," that is, ritualized expressions to others of an organism's internal state (Huxley, 1914, 1966). According to this ***social communications view,*** facial expressions evolved because of their social function. This approach makes it easier to understand why facial expressions are where they are. It isn't important that we see our facial expressions; it is important that *others* see them.

The direct readout and social communications views converge on the idea that our facial expressions are inherited from our ancestors, but they also have points at which they disagree. To see the issue clearly, consider goose bumps. When we get cold, we do what many species do when they are cold, we pilo-erect—our body hairs stand on end. This turns out to be a useful thing for birds to do to get warmer; humans have so little body hair left, however, that it is a perfectly ludicrous thing for us to do, but that is neither here nor there. The point is that goose bumps provide a "readout" of our internal state, our temperature. But goose bumps did not evolve *in order* to express our internal state. Further, the presence of goose bumps is *not* sensitive to our social situation; they arise whether we are alone or in the presence of others, whether it is in our interest to let others know that we are cold or not. The readout view of facial expressions sees them as like goose bumps in their linkage to internal states.

Now let us look at the social communications view. If facial expressions have evolved from social communications among other primates, then we would expect them to be sensitive to social circumstance. After all, it is not in an animal's interest simply to broadcast its internal state. For one thing, it is a waste of energy to broadcast anything when alone. For another, it may be in an organism's interest to conceal its internal state, or even to broadcast a state that isn't there. In any event, if human facial expressions have evolved from primate communications, then we would expect them to be sensitive at least to the grossest social features of the current setting—we wouldn't expect people to do much in the way of giving facial expressions when they are alone. This is a difficult matter to resolve in the laboratory, since subjects may well believe they are always being witnessed by an experimenter. But it is a question ripe for field research.

Robert Kraut and Robert Johnston have addressed this question in a natural environment of at least some humans: bowling alleys. Kraut and John-

The social communications theory of emotional expressions proposes that emotional expressions evolved because of the way they serve to influence the behavior of other organisms.

The direct readout view of emotional expressions proposes that they evolved in some other way, and that spontaneous emotional expressions always signal the actual emotional state of the organism.

ston focused on smiles, and they wanted to know just when it is that we smile while bowling. The readout view suggests that we smile whenever we are happy; but the social communications view suggests, at the very least, that we don't smile when it is perfectly useless to—when no one is looking at us.

First the investigators looked at bowlers bowling alone. Bowlers who are alone can score strikes or spares, happy events, but they cannot engage in social communication. The readout approach predicts that lone bowlers will smile in these cases; the social communications view predicts they won't. They didn't.

In a second study, the investigators stationed observers at the back of the alleys and watched thirty-four bowlers roll 116 balls. The question was: When would bowlers who had rolled good balls smile? While facing down the alley after a good roll, or when they turned to face their friends?

These results too were strongly in favor of the social communications interpretation. Smiling was unrelated to how well the bowlers bowled. On the other hand, bowlers were nine times more likely to smile while facing their friends than when facing down the alley (see Figure 7.8). The overall results of this study strongly support the social communications view of human smiling; they suggest that features of a person's social situation have a powerful effect on their facial expressions, and they are troublesome for the readout view (Kraut & Johnston, 1979; see also Gilbert, Fridlund, & Sabini, 1987, on facial expressions and social context).* But surely it is true that we *sometimes* smile when alone, even though we may smile alone less than we do when with others. How can a social communications view of facial expressions handle those cases?

One strategy has been proposed by Alan Fridlund. Fridlund has noted, as have many before him, that even when we are alone, we are sometimes in something like a social interaction; we are in a "pseudointeraction." For example, remembering a conversation we have just had is a lot like being in a conversation, and rehearsing a conversation we are about to have is, perhaps, even more like being in a conversation. So, Fridlund suggests, some smiling while alone may well be the result of such pseudointeractions.

To give this account weight, Fridlund conducted an experiment based on these ideas. He asked male and female subjects to watch a pleasant videotape under one of four circumstances. Some subjects were simply alone in a room watching. But other subjects came to the lab with a friend. Of those subjects, some watched the tape and thought their friend was down the hall doing another task, others thought their friend was in a different room watching the same tape, and still others watched together with their friend in the same room. These four circumstances varied from complete privacy (alone) to complete sociality (same room with their friend). The other two conditions were intermediate in the degree to which they were social.

Fridlund monitored the electrical activity in the muscles that controlled some of the subjects' facial expressions while they watched the videotape and was, therefore, able to record precisely how much smiling the subjects did. He also asked the subjects to indicate how pleasant they found the videotape.

*These results are difficult from the point of view of a display rules account too. It is not clear that there are display rules in our culture that would lead a solitary bowler to suppress a smile on getting a strike.

▲ *Regardless of where this ball winds up, we are unlikely to see a facial expression until the bowler turns around to face other people.*

FIGURE 7.8

THE SOCIAL COMMUNICATIONS VIEW OF FACIAL EXPRESSIONS

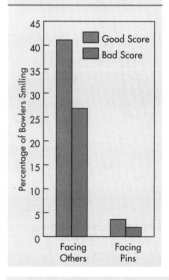

▲ *Smiling from bowlers while facing the pins or other people with a good or bad score. Score mattered little, but few bowlers smiled while facing the pins. (Data from Kraut & Johnston, 1979)*

The direct readout view might expect a correlation between how pleasant the subjects found the tape and how much smiling they did. The social communications view would expect that pleasantness ratings would not relate to smiling, but that the conditions under which the subjects watched the tape would affect smiling. Specifically, it would predict that those with a friend in the room would smile most, those with a friend down the hall watching the same tape would smile next most, those with a friend otherwise engaged would be next, and those alone would smile least. In this study, at least, there was no correlation between rating of pleasantness and degree of smiling, but the social conditions produced smiling in just the order predicted by the social communications view (see Figure 7.9; Fridlund, 1991). And this lends substance to the idea that solitary smiling may be, perhaps to a large degree, in response to pseudointeractions.

It would be rash, however, to conclude that the conversation between the social communication and direct readout supporters is over. Not at all. For one thing, Paul Ekman has suggested that Fridlund measured the wrong electrical activity to detect spontaneous smiles (Frank, Ekman, & Friesen, 1993). And perhaps this is so; it will take time to sort that question out. Stay tuned.

The Fridlund study suggests that facial expressions are at least intensified in the presence of other people. But this is not to deny the essential point of the display rules idea—that we sometimes suppress our facial expressions precisely because we are in the presence of other people. So, for example, Ross Buck has assigned subjects to look at slides depicting sexual, picturesque, or unpleasant scenes alone or in the presence of strangers or friends. The results were that the presence of friends seemed to enhance facial expressions for sexual scenes, but inhibit expressions for unpleasant ones. The presence of

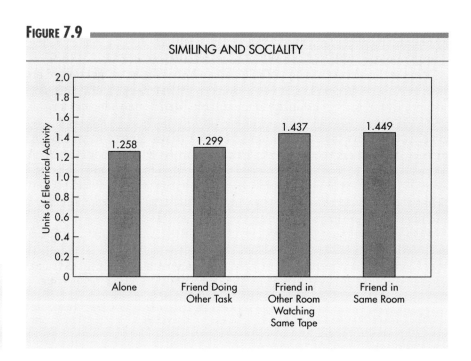

FIGURE 7.9

▶ *Electrical activity in the muscles controlling smiles increases as the circumstances become more social. (Data from Fridlund, 1991).*

strangers, on the other hand, seemed to inhibit all expressions (Buck, Loslow, Murphy, & Costanzo, 1992). And, as we might expect, the presence of other people can certainly cause us to suppress displays of happiness at success—when our success is in competition with those other people, who failed (Friedman & Miller-Herringer, 1991). In the neighborhood in which I grew up, the failure to modulate your glee at besting your friends in sports was likely to cost you your friends—or your teeth! So the fact that the presence of other people may *in some circumstances* intensify the inclination to display a facial expression does *not* deny that the presence of other people *in other circumstances* may cause us to suppress those selfsame expressions.

▲ *A child's facial expression. Children's faces are even better suited to give off expressions than are adults'.*

The Detection of Deception

Our everyday experiences with emotion and its expression suggest that emotional expression isn't *entirely* under our control, that there is some truth to the direct readout view. After all, it takes a good deal of experience and self-discipline *not* to give away one's hand when playing poker (Yardley, 1957). Is it possible to reconcile the apparent fact that emotional expression isn't entirely under our control with a social communications point of view? Let us consider signaling systems from an evolutionary point of view in more detail.

SIGNALING SYSTEMS

Suppose you were designing a signaling system to express a creature's internal state. And suppose you were concerned only with the interests of the creature giving off the signals. What would you have the system communicate?

Suppose you designed it like goose bumps, to always reflect the creature's internal state honestly. As mentioned above, there is a problem with such a system. There might be occasions in which it is in the creature's interests to give off a false signal, to mislead her competitors. To solve this problem, you need to bring the signaling system under the creature's control, to allow her to, as it were, say whatever was in her interest to say, whether true or false. From the signaler's point of view, that communication system is best that says only what the signaler wants it to say. But such a system suffers from its own problem.

Consider the matter now from the point of view of the recipient of the signals. If the system only signals what the signaler wants, then why would anyone trust it? Communications systems evolve facing this tension between the signaler's interests and the recipient's interests. If they are too well shaped to the signaler's interests, they risk being abused by signalers and, in the evolutionary long run, being ignored by recipients. For a signal system to endure, it must serve the interests of both signalers and recipients.

Some signal systems that primates use *are* under the control of the signaler. Human language is one such system. But other primates have them too. Robert Seyfarth and Dorothy Cheney, for example, have demonstrated a complex system of calls given off by vervet monkeys that serve a variety of social functions, including warning other members of the approach of a troop of predators. These signals do seem to be under the control of the signaler. But if a monkey repeatedly gives off a false signal, like the boy who cried wolf, the signaler will find his call ignored (Seyfarth, Cheney, & Marler, 1980; Cheney & Seyfarth, 1988).

One way, then, to deal with the inevitable conflict of interest between signaler and recipient is for the recipients to be able to learn to ignore the signals of unreliable senders. But this solution takes a lot of doing. First, it can only work in species that have rather stable social relations. If most of the signals one receives are from strangers one will never meet again, then the communications system can't be protected in this way. And it requires that the organisms have the cognitive capacity to recognize individuals.

The other solution is to give the signaler only partial control over the signals she emits, to build the system so that it "leaks" information about the sender's real state of affairs even when she is trying to conceal it or trying to send a deceptive message. A leaky system, one neither entirely under the signaler's control nor one that is entirely out of the signaler's control, is a compromise between the interests of sender and receiver.*

THE FACE AND CONCEALING EMOTIONS

Now, what about the human face? Is it a leaky system? Recent work suggests that the face does leak our true emotions; the fake smiles we present when trying to conceal other emotions *can* be distinguished from real smiles, at least by carefully trained observers. Paul Ekman has shown that coders using his Facial Affect Coding System can distinguish "masking smiles" from authentic smiles at better than chance levels (Ekman, Friesen, & O'Sullivan, 1988). But such coding takes quite a bit of time and can only be done while watching and rewatching videotapes of smiles; thus, it is of little help to poker players!

*The general question of how leaky a system has to be is an issue beyond the scope of this book. See Dawkins and Krebs (1978) for a fascinating discussion.

▶ *Poker faces.*

If you are going to play poker, you should not let your opponents place electrodes on your face; there is evidence that the underlying neural activity at specific locations in the face can provide a precise record of your affective response to stimuli (see Cacioppo, Petty, Losch, & Kim, 1986; Cacioppo, Martzke, Petty, & Tassinary, 1988; Cacioppo, Bush, & Tassinary, 1992).

This evidence suggests that despite our best efforts to conceal emotional expressions, they are registered on the face. But it does not mean that under ordinary circumstances we can detect real emotion in the face. Indeed, there is evidence that we are not very good at this.

In one study, Ekman and Wallace Friesen had the dean of a nursing school recruit sixteen beginning female nursing students for a study of deceptive communication. They told the nurses that an important skill they would need in their profession was the ability to conceal their emotional reactions from patients and their families. After all, no one needs a nurse who reacts with horror to what might be horrible facts; nurses need to be reassuring no matter the facts. The students were also told that experienced nurses do very well at concealing their feelings. Thus, the subjects were led to believe that the study was an important one, related to their chosen career.

The nurses watched four films and were interviewed about their feelings afterward. Two of the films depicted pleasant scenes, but two were medical training films that showed amputations and the treatment of severe burns. The nurses were instructed to be honest in reporting their feelings about the pleasant films and *one* of the stressful films, but they were told to lie and act as if they found the other stressful film quite pleasant. In other words, for one of the films, they were asked to substitute the portrayal of emotions they didn't feel for the emotion they did feel. The interviews were videotaped, and master tapes of the sixteen subjects' interviews were shown to judges. Some judges saw a tape of the subjects' faces but not their bodies; others saw a tape of their bodies but not their faces. The judges were told that some of the interviews were deceptive and some were honest; they were asked to judge which was which.

The judges were more accurate in classifying deceptive interviews when they saw the bodies than when they saw the faces. The judges were, however, equally accurate in classifying honest interviews regardless of the tape they saw. Why the judges did better at detecting deception with the tapes of the bodies than with the tapes of the faces was answered by the nurses who were filmed.

The nurses were interviewed about what they were paying attention to during the deceptive interviews. And they reported, as the authors expected, that they were trying very hard to control their faces when they were attempting to be deceptive. They were less concerned about their bodies. So these nurses believed that their faces would leak their true emotions and, therefore, worked hard to control them. The results indicated that although the face is a source of information about what a person is feeling, it is not a good place to look to detect deception precisely because people know their faces display cues of deception and therefore attempt to control them when they want to be deceiving (see Figure 7.10). On the other hand, people pay less attention to the movements their bodies and legs are making (squirming, for example) during deception, so the body turns out to be a better place to

FIGURE 7.10
DETECTING DECEPTION

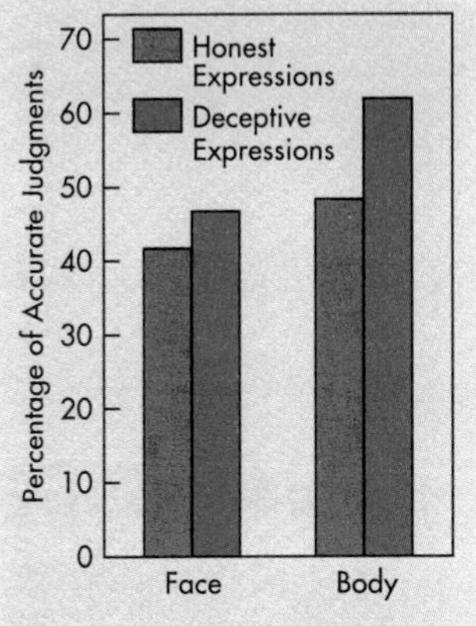

▲ Accuracy of detecting deceptive and honest bodies and faces. Watch the body to find a liar. (Data from Ekman & Friesen, 1974)

look for cues of deception (Ekman & Friesen, 1974). The face and body aren't, however, the only places to look for cues of deception; a person's tone of voice may also give him away.

DETECTING DECEPTION VERSUS DETECTING WHAT IS BEING CONCEALED

There is a difference, of course, between detecting that a person is concealing his feelings and detecting what those real feelings are. Research has found that accuracy at detecting *that* deception has occurred is substantially better than accuracy at detecting *what* the person's true feelings are. Research has also found that people who are particularly good at detecting the presence of concealed feelings are not especially good at discerning just what the real feelings are (DePaulo & Rosenthal, 1979).

In one study, experienced salespeople were videotaped making "pitches" for various items. In some cases, they made their pitch for a consumer item they actually liked; in other cases, they made a pitch for an item they didn't like. Undergraduate subjects viewed these videotapes and attempted to ferret out the salespeople's actual attitudes. The results suggested that the subjects were not entirely taken in by the pitches they saw; they assumed that the attitudes expressed were not the same as the salespeople's real attitudes. But the subjects were not able to tell which items the salespeople actually liked and which they didn't (DePaulo & DePaulo, 1989). The results suggest, therefore, that with experience we can become able to conceal deceptive cues—conceal them well enough, at least, to deceive the average consumer.

GENDER AND NONVERBAL CUES

Lore has it that women are more intuitive than men, and one interpretation we might give this is that women are better than men at reading other people's nonverbal expressions. Judith Hall, in her review of seventy-five published papers on the topic, concluded that about this, at least, the lore is correct. In controlled studies of the phenomenon, there is a massive superiority for women over men in terms of accuracy at reading (decoding) other people's expressions. This superiority holds up whether men or women are giving off (encoding) the messages (Hall, 1978).

Hall's review considers all studies in which men were compared with women at reading nonverbal expressions. But suppose we look *only* at studies in which deception is going on. Are women better than men at detecting leaky cues? The answer seems to be no. Women are better than men at interpreting open, unconcealed expressions of feelings, but they are no better (or worse) than men at detecting concealed, leaked affect (Rosenthal & DePaulo, 1979).

Why might women be better than men at reading facial expressions? Sara Snodgrass has suggested that this is a consequence of the fact that women have in general occupied inferior positions to men in our culture, and people in a subordinate position had better be sensitive to the states of mind of their superiors. It is less important that superiors be sensitive to their subordinates. And, indeed, in an experiment in which men and women were arbitrarily assigned to be superior or subordinate and then interacted for an hour or so, the results indicated that there were no differences between men and women in their emotional sensitivity. But it was true that subordinates, regardless of gender, were more sensitive than were superiors (Snodgrass, 1992).

Faces are more expressive than other parts of the body, but they may not be the best place to look to detect deception, because people know they should control their faces when they are being deceptive.

At least in laboratory settings, people perform at better than chance levels in detecting deception from nonverbal cues. But, if the truth be told, we are not in general astonishingly better than chance at detecting deception. In the competition between people as senders, who want to control their expressions, and people as receivers, who want to discern the truth beneath the control, there is a *slight* edge to the receivers (Zuckerman, DePaulo, & Rosenthal, 1981). An evolutionary perspective is comfortable with this finding. A strong advantage to receivers would undermine the system by giving the evolutionary edge to unexpressive senders, but a strong edge to senders would also undermine the system by leading receivers to ignore expressions altogether. Communications systems require a balance of the interests of senders and receivers.

WRAP-UP: WILLIAM JAMES REVISITED

We began our discussion of emotion with William James's view that the perception of bodily changes *IS* the emotion we feel. How does this position fare in light of what we have learned in this chapter?

First, we looked at visceral feedback, the James-Lange position. We found that, as Cannon proposed, feedback from the sympathetic nervous system is too undifferentiated to provide information about *which* emotion is being experienced. Results from the Schachter and Singer experiment and, perhaps more important, from a large number of studies of transfer of arousal all suggest that people cannot tell just from the state of the sympathetic nervous system which emotion they are feeling. Recent studies of subjects without (or with restricted) feedback from their sympathetic nervous systems indicate that such feedback isn't *necessary* for the experience of emotion. Marañon's findings, in addition to results from Schachter and Singer's informed subjects, suggest that feedback from the sympathetic nervous system also isn't *sufficient* to produce the experience of emotion. The results of the transfer of arousal studies, however, indicate that such feedback may modulate the *intensity* of the emotion.

Our attention then turned to facial expression. There is evidence that the pairing of facial expressions and emotions felt is (at least for some emotions) universal and likely innate. Facial expressions are, unlike visceral reactions, quite differentiated, and therefore might provide evidence about the kind of emotion felt. But the evidence is that subjects don't use facial expressions to infer their emotions. There is evidence, however, that they use their facial expressions to infer the *intensity* of emotions felt. Thus, the story for facial expressions is quite like the story for visceral feedback.

But where does this leave us? How are we to answer the two questions that William James raised: (1) What are the emotions, and (2) How do people know *which* emotion they are feeling? Let me suggest a modified Jamesian view of the emotions and an answer to how we know our emotions. First, emotions are complex mental states, including, at least, visceral changes, facial expressions, and overt behavior. It is too simple to think that emotions are any one of these. These complex states are set in motion by appraisals of the environment.

Now, how do we come to know our own emotional states? We know our emotions by inferring what these complex states are from their expressions and from the circumstances in which they occur. (James favored the former, Schachter and Singer the latter; perhaps both positions capture part of the truth.) Some manifestations of emotion—visceral changes and facial expressions—are particularly good sources of information about the intensity of an emotion. Other sources of information—external circumstances (and overt behavior)—are particularly good sources of information about the quality of the emotion.

There are two ways of thinking about facial expressions of emotion. One way considers facial expressions as tightly bound to emotional experience. In this view, facial expressions evolved so we could experience (or perhaps know) emotional states. The other view considers facial expressions as having evolved to signal to others. In that view, facial expressions are not unrelated to our mental states. But neither are they as connected to our mental states as the facial feedback hypothesis would have it. Rather, facial expressions are one, but only one, source of evidence for other people (and ourselves) as to what our mental states are. They evolved to serve (exclusively) neither the purposes of the sender of facial expressions nor the purposes of the perceiver of those expressions. They are leaky signals, a compromise of the interests of sender and receiver.

SUMMARY

1. William James offered a theory of what the emotions are: perceptions of the bodily states provoked by some stimulus. Carl Lange offered a more specific version of James's theory, claiming that the relevant bodily state is the sympathetic nervous system.

2. Evidence from people who have suffered the severing of their spinal cords suggests that the perception of arousal of the sympathetic nervous system *isn't* necessary to emotion. Other evidence, gathered by injecting people with adrenaline, suggests that sympathetic arousal isn't sufficient for the experience of emotion either. The degree of sympathetic arousal may, however, affect the intensity of experience of emotion.

3. Schachter and Singer proposed that people experience emotion when they are aroused and when they interpret that arousal to be the result of an appropriate source. The data from their experiment weakly supported their claims. Further support for their theory, however, comes from studies of *transfer of arousal,* in which the arousal produced by one stimulus is transferred to another.

4. Darwin proposed that the facial expressions of emotion are evolved and hence innate, and that expressing emotions in one's face tends to intensify that emotion—the *facial feedback hypothesis.* There is substantial evidence to support the first of these claims. People from a variety of cultures have been shown to express and interpret emotions similarly. And although there is little evidence that facial expression can modify the *kind* of emotion we experience, there is some evidence that it can affect the intensity of the emotions we feel.

5. Darwinian thinking leads us to wonder why facial expressions are innate. One answer is that they provide a direct "readout" of an organism's emotional state—the *direct readout view.* Another is that facial expressions serve as a way for organisms to communicate to one another what their motivations and intentions are—the *social communications view.*

6. Although the face is a rich source of information about someone, it is also true that we all know that other people watch our faces to detect our true emotions, and hence we are circumspect with our facial expressions. We are often better able to detect deception by focusing on other people's bodies rather than on their faces because people pay less attention to controlling their bodies.

CHAPTER 8

The Self in Cultural Perspective

Social psychologists have many reasons to be interested in cultures and the differences among them. For one thing, social psychologists sometimes claim (or at least fail to disclaim) that the principles they discover are universal, applying to all of humankind. But often these claims have been tested only on American college sophomores. Many social psychologists have taken the discipline to task for this myopia (see, for example, Gergen, 1974; Jahoda, 1988; Pepitone & Triandis, 1988; Sharon & Amir, 1988). For this reason, if no other, social psychologists have become increasingly interested in cultural differences.

Throughout this text, I have tried to keep track of research from other cultures, and have tried to include such research in the discussions of particular phenomena. But the focus so far has been on specific phenomena, such as prejudice, and not on culture. In those chapters, culture is an important character but does not play the leading role. In this chapter, however, we want to focus directly on cultural influences on our psychology. More specifically, our concern will be with cultures and the selves of the people who live in those cultures.* Here, culture takes (or at least shares) center stage. The other leading character in this chapter is the self—our basic, rock-bottom conception of what a person is.

*Some authors distinguish the concept of the self from the concept of a person. But I will use "self" and "person" interchangeably.

256

To begin, I should offer an explicit conception of the self. But as many writers who have marched (or blundered) into this area have warned, the self is a very slippery topic. Nonetheless I make the following suggestion: our modern, Western conception of the self is that each of us has a self; each of us is a bounded entity. Each of us, moreover, is an example of three different kinds of things bound into that single entity. First, each person is a body, a physical, mechanical object in time and space. But the self is more than a body. The body somehow or other is intimately connected to the second element of the self, the subject of conscious experiences—we see, feel, dream, are in pain, have emotions, and so on. And third, we are responsible for our actions; we are, in the main, responsible for what our bodies do—we are moral agents. In our Western conception of the self each of us is a synthesis of these three different kinds of things.

This conception of the self isn't explicit in the minds of every member of Western culture. Far from it. Rather, it is implicit. For example, the notion that we are moral agents responsible for our behavior is implicit in the fact that we punish each other for transgressions, or at least we praise and blame each other. And the very concepts of praise and blame involve the notion of responsibility. Likewise, we saw in Chapter 2 (in the discussion of the Asch experiments on conformity) that people become upset if other people in their presence seem to be having—unaccountably—experiences different from theirs. Again, our sense that we share experiences is usually implicit; it becomes focal only under special circumstances.

Exactly how and why these three elements of the self hang together are classically imponderable. How a mechanical object like a body can have experiences is one version of the famous mind-body problem. And how a mechanical object can be responsible for its actions is one version of the classic problem of freedom of the will. I certainly will not try to resolve these issues here. It is enough that we understand that the self is related to the body, experience, and moral action. This, I propose, is our rock-bottom conception of what a person (any person) is.

People also, of course, have beliefs about themselves as particular individuals; that is, beliefs about their individual qualities. These beliefs are often called the **self-concept.** We have beliefs, for example, about whether we are tall or short, skinny or fat, smart or dumb, graceful or clumsy, generous or cheap, and so on.* But our focus in this chapter is not on people's conceptions of individuals (see Chapter 5 for that); rather, it is on our culture's concept of a self (or person), every self or person.

You have been introduced to one of the main characters of this chapter—the self; let me now introduce you to the other—culture. Definitions of culture tend to weave back and forth between the concrete and specific (but superficial) and the abstract and vague (but useless). As I favor the latter, the definition I offer is the vague idea that cultures are ways of living. Cultures

▲ Jeune Chevalier dans un Paysage *by Vittore Carpaccio. A gentleman who certainly seems to have a fully developed sense of self.*

The Western conception of the self is composed of

• a body;

• a subject of experience;

• a moral agent.

*I hasten to add that *some* of our beliefs about ourselves are true, but *some* are surely false. So the self-concept should not be confused with our individual self—the sum of all that is true of us.

▶ *A woman painting her portrait and in so doing giving testimony to the importance she attaches to her own appearance, a very Western idea.*

include both patterns of actual behavior and understandings of norms—ideas about how people ought to behave. Cultures are typically associated with languages and political entities. And cultures have no sharp boundaries. I will refer, indeed I have already referred, to Western culture. But what exactly is Western culture? Is it how people live and think they should live on Fifth Avenue in Manhattan? On the Champs-Élysées in Paris? In a village in Sicily? Did the people living in all of these places in 1700 live in Western culture, or was that a different culture? Suffice it for our purposes to admit that cultures have fuzzy boundaries, but also to recognize that people living in Manhattan, Paris, and Sicily now are closer to people who lived there in 1700 than any of these places is to a Tibetan village.

CULTURE AND THE SELF

Now that we have met the two main characters of our chapter, the next question is: How do they relate to one another? The first thing to note is that there has been great change in this relationship over the ages in Western culture, and that there are important differences from one culture to the next in how individuals relate to their cultures. One important dimension on which Western culture has varied over time and existing cultures currently vary is what is called ***individualism-collectivism.*** This distinction is quite complex, but it is easiest, perhaps, to begin to understand in its historical, political guise. So let us consult a bit of history.

The Individual and the State

At Runnymede in 1215, an extraordinary political event occurred. King John of England agreed to sign the Magna Carta—under substantial duress, to be sure. The Magna Carta granted to the king's feudal barons certain rights, which the king committed himself to honor. King John promised, for example, not to incarcerate his barons without a trial. Thus, some would argue, was the notion of individual rights born in the West.

In Philadelphia more than five hundred years later, other extraordinary political events took place. In particular, the people of the to-become United States first declared themselves as having unalienable rights endowed upon them by their Creator (in the Declaration of Independence), and then (in the Constitution) undertook to start up a new country. Shortly thereafter, these same citizens adopted the Bill of Rights, in which the people of the United States imposed limits on what the government could do to them. This Bill of Rights covered some of the same ground as did the Magna Carta; for example, both assert the idea that the government shouldn't arrest people without a trial. But for all their similarity, the Magna Carta and the American documents are radically different. And the way they are different bears on how selves relate to collectivities.

In the Magna Carta, the state—in the person of the king—conferred rights on individuals. True, the king did this only under duress, but the fact remains that it was seen as true that it was the king's place to confer rights on his subjects because the state was prior to the individuals who composed it. But in Philadelphia five centuries later, a very different idea had emerged.* The Declaration of Independence asserts that individuals have rights regardless of what the state does. Further, it is the place of the people to impose limits on what the government might do because individuals are prior to the state.

So there are two very different *political* ideas that have enjoyed wide currency in Western culture. One idea is that individuals are subservient to, in a way creations of, the larger collectivity. The other is that collectivities are subservient to and the creations of individuals. The notion that the individual is fundamental and powerful and the object of ultimate value is called ***individualism;*** the reverse notion that some social group larger than the individual—in this case, the state—is fundamental, powerful, and of ultimate value is called ***collectivism.***

To be sure, collectivist cultures may or may not place great emphasis on the *state* as an entity more important than the individual. For many cultures—China, for example—it is the family that occupies the position of supreme importance; indeed, the state in traditional China is of little significance (as is religion). For others, it might be a religious entity that is supremely important. But the point is that in collectivist cultures, the individual's interests are strictly subordinated to the interests of *some* broader social entity.

SOCIAL RAMIFICATIONS OF COLLECTIVISM AND INDIVIDUALISM

This distinction between collectivism and individualism is seen by many social scientists as a crucial one that characterizes not only different historical periods of Western culture, but also existing cultures. I have so far spoken of the distinction as a political one, and indeed it is. But there is a richer difference, one with a much broader scope than the political arena alone (Markus & Kitayama, 1991).

In individualist cultures, the individual and her emotions, needs, abilities, and desires are important relative to the needs of larger social groups. In collectivist cultures, social groups are more important.

*The "Glorious Revolution" of 1688, which placed the same emphasis on the individual, preceded—substantially—the American Revolution.

► The Adoration of the Magi. *This brilliant painting stands at the very edge of the Renaissance. It is a collaboration of Fra Angelico, a pre-Renaissance figure, and Fra Fillippo Lippi, an early Renaissance figure.*

To get an idea of this scope, let us look more closely at the beginnings of the emergence of individualism in Western culture. In 1487, Filippino Lippi, an Italian Renaissance master, signed a contract to paint frescoes. The unusual feature of the contract was that it specified that Lippi himself would do the painting—"all in his own hand," as the contract put it (rather than assigning an assistant to do the work; see Baxandall, 1972). The extraordinary thing is that anyone cared who actually did the painting.

Contracts with painters before this time specified lots of things—the size of the painting, how much gold would be in it, how much ultramarine (a color made from a rare and expensive pigment), and so on—but they *didn't* specify the individual who would do the painting. All of that changed in the Renaissance; it changed because the idea gained currency that artists are affected by (and some times afflicted by) genius. Heretofore, painters were craftsmen who were to make the painting look like the other paintings of the period. But from the Renaissance on, a different attitude takes hold. The artist is to make his work distinctive. Art should reveal the self of the artist; it is now supposed to be original, not derivative. These ideas have had much broader currency than with Italian Renaissance painters, even if the ideas first arose there. We seem now to feel this way about everybody, not just artists.

Part of Western culture's celebration of individualism is to see the individual as unique, and to encourage each person to develop her uniqueness. We value self-expression independently of our opinion of what is expressed by the self. We place great value on the innovative and the creative. We prize the expression of emotion, and we care that people are authentic, sincere, spontaneous. And, perhaps most important, we value individual accomplishment. These are aspects of individualism that Anglo-American culture has developed to an extreme degree. (See Hui, 1988, for a scale intended to measure this construct, and Triandis et al., 1988, for further development of the distinction.)

Geert Hofstede surveyed the employees of a major international corporation, IBM, in sixty-seven countries (see Figure 8.1). The survey tapped, among other things, the personal and social values of the employees. His results indicated that subjects from the United States, Australia, Britain, Canada, and the Netherlands were the most individualist. Subjects from Taiwan, Peru, Pakistan, Colombia, and Venezuela were the least (Hofstede, 1980/1984).

For those of us brought up in the West, individualist ideas seem obvious, natural, uniquely human; for that reason, if no other, it is important to understand that other cultures have different ideas about how individuals' selves should relate to the collectivity. In many other cultures, especially, though

FIGURE 8.1

INDIVIDUALISM AND COLLECTIVISM AMONG EMPLOYEES OF IBM AROUND THE WORLD

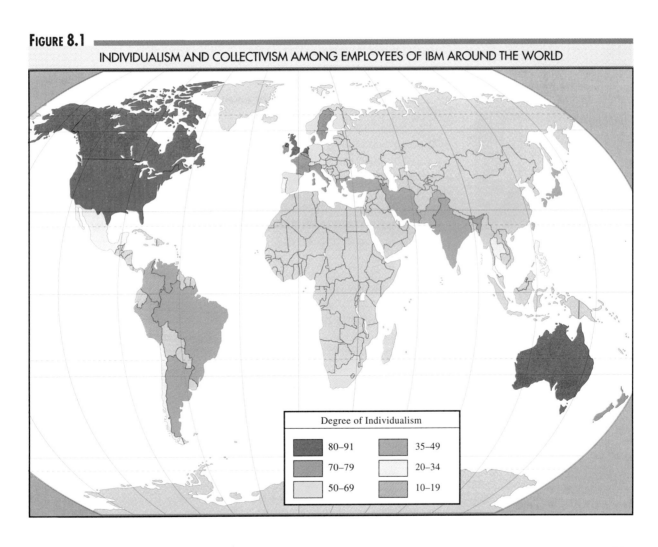

Degree of Individualism

80–91	35–49
70–79	20–34
50–69	10–19

▲ *(A) Bonnie Blair and (B) Dan Jansen are allowed, or even required, to display their emotions about having won Olympic gold medals. Westerners seem to insist on ever more dramatic displays from their athletes.*

not exclusively, Asian and African cultures, the individual is urged *not* to express himself, but to be a proper part of the group, especially the family. Not all cultures value creativity in art; many of them prize workmanship— Egyptian art was essentially static for a millennium. Not all cultures teach their people to express themselves. If you go to an American psychoanalyst, you will be instructed to get in touch with and express your emotions. If you consult a Japanese therapist, one who practices Morita therapy, you will be helped to suppress your emotions and impulses; you will be taught discipline (Weisz, Rothbaum, & Blackburn, 1984). Similarly, Steve Derné tells us that the Hindu men he interviewed from the city of Bernares did not see their true selves as expressed in their emotions; they saw themselves as expressing their truest, most important selves when fulfilling the social roles their lives as-signed them (Derne, 1992; see also Potter, 1988, on the irrelevance of emo-tion to serious action in Chinese life).

INDIVIDUALISM AND MORAL AUTHORITY

Long before the American revolutionaries asserted the political authority of the individual over the state, Martin Luther led a revolution every bit as important, one that asserted the moral authority of the individual against not the state but the Catholic Church. The Catholic Church has a distinct view of the relation of each individual to God: there is no direct path for the indi-vidual to God or salvation; salvation is to be found by being part of the church. And it is the church that will explain God's will (and law) to the individual. The individual is significant only as part of the church. It was all of this that Luther and Protestantism rejected.*

Protestantism asserts that the individual can and should have a direct relation to God; the individual must figure out for herself what is right and wrong. The only moral authority in the world is the moral authority of in-dividual consciences. So individualism exerts a pervasive influence on how we see ourselves as relating to the collectivities of which our society consists. (I do not deal here with one absolutely vital way that individualism affects our culture—its impact on family life. This is discussed in detail in Chapter 15.)

COLLECTIVIST CURRENTS IN WESTERN CULTURE

I have presented ways in which Western culture is individualist—and it is— but it is also easy to get carried away with this idea. To restore some sense of balance, it is perhaps worth recalling that in the Second World War, col-lectivist Japan and the individualist United States went to war. And the United States won because, among other things, millions of Americans were willing to put their lives on the line for their country. Surely Americans understand loyalty as a virtue and betrayal as a vice. And though it is true that Americans celebrate individual achievement, it is also true that even Americans find bragging about oneself offensive—though it is less offensive, perhaps, to brag

*Although it is fashionable in the social psychology literature to refer to individualism as the ideology of Western culture, it is important to bear in mind that the Catholic Church has not abandoned its collectivist notions about the relation of the individual to the larger group. So individualist better characterizes the predominantly Protestant northwest of Europe than it does the predominantly Catholic south and east.

about one's family. And Americans do admire people who sacrifice their own desires to take care of family or friends. Indeed, it might be said that Western culture has a well-developed appreciation of individualism and its virtues, but also an appreciation of collectivist virtues like loyalty.

We in the West seem capable of other collectivist emotions as well. Surely patriotic events can produce intense emotions. So too can sporting events. Soccer matches in the individualist West have, after all, resulted in riots. And many Americans of the right age recall the defeat of the 1980 Soviet hockey team by the American hockey team during the winter Olympics—an event combining patriotism and sports—as one of the most emotional experiences of their lives. So perhaps we Westerners aren't individualist instead of being collectivist; perhaps we are individualist *and* collectivist. Perhaps the fact is that Western culture is under tension and flux in resolving these two opposing themes in the relation of the self to others. Still, there can be little doubt that individualism is more developed in the West than in most of the rest of the world.

Is the Self Itself a Culturally Relative Idea?

The difference between individualist and collectivist ideas about how selves and societies are related has led some scholars to wonder whether the Western conception of the self isn't itself just a Western idea. Maybe the very notion that each of us is a bounded entity (an entity that relates to other entities, to be sure, but still a bounded entity) is exclusively Western. The notion that the Western conception of a person is an idea whose legitimacy is relative to the culture alone was first proposed, perhaps, by Marcel Mauss in an influential essay published in 1938 (Mauss, 1938/1985). And it has been advanced more recently by both anthropologists—Clifford Geertz, for example—and psychologists such as Richard Shweder, Hazel Markus, and Shinobu Kitayama (Geertz, 1974; Shweder & Bourne, 1982; Markus & Kitayama, 1991). We will follow the story as it was developed by Shweder.

India is a collectivist culture. Indeed, collectivism goes rather far in Indian metaphysics. According to this belief, although the world appears to be made up of a variety of things, this variety is really an illusion. The wise person is able to perceive through the variety to the fact that there is really only one existing thing in the world (*brahman*). The task of the wise person is to meditate away the apparent multiplicity and get to the essential oneness of the universe (Bharati, 1985). Actually, this idea is not as far from traditional Western thought as it might seem. There is, for example, a Catholic doctrine—the doctrine of the Mystical Body of Christ—that teaches that all baptized people become one with each other and Christ.

But these are both metaphysical notions, and the question is: Do these doctrines affect the way people think about themselves in everyday life, in the practical realms of everyday affairs, or are these ideas that are taken seriously only in the right frame of mind? Shweder argues that the "holism" or collectivism of Indian culture does lead Indians to think of themselves and each other in fundamentally different ways than Westerners do. He suggests that the notion of an individual, bounded self sharply set off from its context is a Western idea, not one present in Indian culture.

FIGURE 8.2

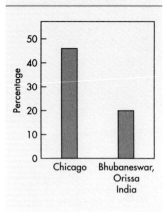

SUBJECTS' USE
OF TRAIT TERMS

▲ *Percentage of descriptions of a person that are general (trait terms) in the United States and India. (Data from Shweder & Bourne, 1982)*

To show this, Shweder carried out a simple study in the United States and in India. He asked people in both countries to describe several acquaintances. Simply put, American subjects tended to use trait terms where Indians tended to speak in terms of behaviors. Thus, an American would say, "She is friendly," whereas an Indian would mention concrete behavior—"She brings cakes to my family on festival days." Or an American would say, "He is cheap," whereas an Indian would say, "He has trouble giving things to his family"; or instead of saying he is kind, an Indian might say, "Whoever becomes his friend he will remember forever and always help him out of his troubles." It is important to note two things: (1) Indians do use trait words, they just don't do so as much as Americans do, and (2) the difference is substantial; about 50 percent of American descriptions were in terms of abstract, context-free trait terms, while only about 20 percent of Indian accounts were of that sort (see Figure 8.2; Shweder & Bourne, 1982).

Shweder argues that the reason the Indian subjects say what they do is that they think holistically; they do not separate the individual from her context in offering descriptions. In short, they do not have the individualist conception of self that Westerners have.

Well, perhaps. But when Texas governor Ann Richards used behavioral, contextual, concrete language to characterize George Bush—she said he was born with a silver foot in his mouth—she didn't do that because she lacked a conception of Bush as a discrete, bounded self or entity. She did it because she knew that a very effective way of painting a picture of a person is by mentioning a particular behavior, a behavior carefully selected to stand for a broader class. In this case, she summoned up two classes by mixing her metaphors so nicely! Perhaps Shweder's Indian subjects are like Governor Richards; indeed, "Whoever becomes his friend he will remember forever and always help him out of his troubles" seems quite vivid to me. So maybe the Indian subjects have simply found a different, more powerful, more poetic way to allude to traits. It would be rash to impute a different concept of the self on the basis of this sort of evidence. And, actually, there is another problem with the evidence.

Why should holism lead people to use behavioral rather than trait descriptions? The claim is that Hindu (among other) subjects don't distinguish a person from the background circumstances in which he acts. But the Indian subjects seemed to have no trouble distinguishing the friend who needs help from the one who offers it; so they must be making a distinction after all. There is no evidence that they perceive some amorphous, undifferentiated help-needing/help-giving.

The evidence, nonetheless, is that people from India and other cultures tend to rely less on broad traits in describing people than Westerners do (see also, Miller, 1984, 1986, 1987; Bond & Cheung, 1983; Cousins, 1989). But the precise significance of this difference is not yet clear. Perhaps it indicates a very different conception of self in such cultures, but perhaps it doesn't. (See also Kumagai & Kumagai, 1986, for a caution against exaggerating the differences.) It seems safer at this point to believe that though cultures have different ideas or ideologies about how selves should relate to collectivities, they share the same idea about what the selves actually are.

Differences in self-presentation, however, are substantial. In one study, Chinese subjects from Hong Kong watched a confederate who performed either well or poorly on an intellectual task. The competent person was *not* liked better than the incompetent person. American studies have found that competent people *are* liked better than incompetent people (see Chapter 14; Bond, Leung, & Wan, 1982). Presenting oneself as competent might lose friends and influence people in the wrong way in China.

How, then, does culture affect us, and especially, how does culture affect those aspects of our behavior and feelings that come closest to our sense of ourselves? We will take up three specific versions of this question. First, we will ask about culture's effects on what and how we eat. The self is, among other things, a body, and food and eating have obvious and crucial connections to the body. Then we will turn to the self as subject of experience; in particular, the experience of emotion. We will ask whether people experience the same emotions the world over. And finally, we will look at culture and morality to see what prospects there are for uncovering a universal moral code.

FOOD AND CULTURE

I start with food because eating is a fundamental transaction between the self qua body at least and the environment. It is *one* activity in which our biology and our cultures rub up against one another. Thus, it is an example (but only one) of how the bodily self is integrated into a culture.

Cultural Versus Biological Constraints on Diet

Just what eating has to do with the *body* is, in rough outline, quite clear: if you don't eat, there is no body. Because of this close connection to survival, one might imagine that the job of understanding how, what, when, where, and why we eat belongs to a biologist rather than to a psychologist (or anthropologist). But there is much more to eating than biology.

Consider that, as Elisabeth Rozin says, in every culture people eat something, but in no culture do people eat everything. That is, in no culture do people eat all of the things that are *biologically* fitting for them to eat (E. Rozin, 1982). For example, Rozin points out that the bushmen of Botswana in the northwest corner of the Kalahari Desert face droughts every two to three years. Each drought brings with it a severe restriction in foodstuff, yet of the 223 species of animals in the area, only 54 are considered by them to be edible.

Or consider American culture. I did not have, and I suspect few of my Western readers had, insects for breakfast. This is not for biological reasons. Insects are a perfectly fine protein source and are, indeed, consumed in some cultures. But not mine. I also did not eat the family cats for breakfast—indeed, I fed them breakfast, though they too are perfectly fine sources of the nutrients we need. I didn't forgo the insects and the cats for biological reasons; I did so for cultural reasons.

Mechanisms of Cultural Constraint

Let us look more closely at some mechanisms by which culture affects transactions between the self and the environment.

▲ *The Egyptians thought that cats were gods; some people believe that cats still think that. While cats aren't thought of by Westerners as food, they have a close connection to food as they made the development of cities possible by protecting the cities' food supplies from rodents.*

COGNITION AND CULTURE

In an illuminating work on the nature of culture, Peter Berger and Thomas Luckmann make some important points about how culture affects us. They point out, for example, that the first and perhaps most important way culture affects us is by defining the range of things that will ever occur to us. The first and perhaps most important reason that I didn't eat insects for breakfast is that it never occurred to me. It would have occurred to me had I been raised in a different culture (Berger and Luckmann, 1967; see also D'Andrade, 1984). But culture reaches deeper than that.

AFFECT AND CULTURE

When I think of eating insects for breakfast, something else happens. I find the idea disgusting; the thought of it is literally nauseating. The disgust that this nausea is part of, as Paul Rozin has argued, is a specific and differentiated emotion. It is not just a matter of rejecting the substance as food—I would reject paper as food too, but I don't find the thought of chewing on it disgusting. (When my cats chew on paper, I find that annoying or cute—depending on what paper they are chewing on—but not disgusting.) And I don't eat brussels sprouts, not because I find them disgusting but because I just don't like them. So there are all sorts of ways of rejecting potential sources of food; disgust is one particular way we come to reject food (P. Rozin & Fallon, 1987). But disgust at eating insects is not a human universal. Somehow, my culture hooked up my disgust reaction with the thought of eating insects. And more generally, cultures link emotions with the stimuli that trigger them. We shall return to this point in detail below.

CULTURE, BIOLOGY, AND HUMAN NATURE

Berger and Luckmann make a further point about culture, a point that my disgust at eating insects illustrates. Although it is true that disgust at eating insects is not a cultural universal, it *feels* like it is. Gagging at the thought of eating a roach is so spontaneous and natural, so immediate and so powerful, that we can be seduced into believing that it must be so for everybody everywhere. It must be a biological, immutable fact not about our culture and others but about human nature. Berger and Luckmann point out that cultural facts *typically* appear to cultural insiders to be not cultural facts but rather "natural" facts, facts about biology, human nature. It just isn't always true that things that seems spontaneous, natural, unforced, and uncalculated are also uninfluenced by culture.

Why are we so easily shaped by culture when it comes to diet? Is it possible, that is, for us to understand in biological terms why culture plays such a heavy role in human food selection? Perhaps we can.

THE GENERALIST'S DILEMMA

Paul Rozin has pointed out that species that can (biologically speaking) eat many different things—species like humans and rats—face a serious problem: lots of things in the wide world are poisonous! This isn't a problem for species that are genetically programmed to eat a narrow diet. They simply eat what they are wired to eat and avoid being poisoned that way. But we are wired to eat a wide variety of things; how do we avoid killing ourselves? How do rats do it?

It is, unfortunately, surprisingly hard to poison a rat. One reason is that rats are innately *neophobic* in their taste preference; that is, they dislike new tastes. But if hungry enough, they will overcome their neophobia to eat small amounts of new things. Thus, they tend to introduce new tastes, and therefore new foods, into their diets only gradually; they sample small amounts (often sub-fatal amounts) of new foods and avoid eating lethal doses until they have established that the substance is not dangerous. Might humans too be neophobic? If so, then it would account for the fact that we eat so little of what is available to us. We eat, perhaps, only what tastes good to us, and only things that we have been exposed to by our parents will taste good to us.* Indirect evidence comes from the way that cultures treat new foods.

Elisabeth Rozin suggests that cultures introduce new foods just as you might expect neophobics to. They make use of characteristic tastes (E. Rozin & P. Rozin, 1981; E. Rozin, 1982). A signature of Chinese cooking, for example, is soy sauce, ginger, and rice wine. A signature of southern Italian cooking is olive oil, garlic, tomatoes, and pungent cheeses. Were Italians to begin to eat insects, we would expect them to do so by preparing them with a little olive oil and garlic. By marking a new food with an old taste, the new food becomes familiar, acceptable, comfortable, safe. In this way, culture overcomes neophobia; in this way, cultures can make new foods tasty to old palates.

FOOD TABOOS

Another way that culture affects what we eat is via food taboos. Food taboos aren't part of daily experience for many Western people. Indeed, there are pockets of Western culture that seem to have no food taboos, in which people may eat whatever they like so long as what they eat is culturally defined as food. You may not eat insects or the family cat, but those aren't thought of as food. Of course, you also may refrain from eating certain foods on pragmatic grounds—fat and salt are bad for your health—but there is no moral issue about it. But many cultures do have food taboos. Indian Brahmans, for example, are vegetarian, and for them, eating meat is a profound moral transgression. People may develop an aversion to a tabooed food, or they may even find the thought of eating such a food disgusting, but the point is that whether they find the food disgusting or appetizing, they may not eat it. They must refrain from eating it for another reason. Cultures, then, tend to "moralize" food. Taboos are one way, but there are others.

FOOD AND STATUS

In Brahman households, who gets served what and in what order is a moral-political matter having to do with status and power. For example, better quality foods and earlier serving are the right of the relatives of the husband; wives' relatives receive lesser food later (Appadurai, 1981). In Western culture too, food is used to mark off status and power. Serving someone lobster, caviar, and champagne makes a different statement from serving hot dogs and beans. Though just what that statement is a subtle matter. Hot dogs and beans on a ceremonial occasion isn't a very good sign, but on a less

*One would expect children's and parents' food preferences to be highly correlated. But they aren't (P. Rozin, 1991). This poses a problem to anyone who wants to understand how we acquire food preferences.

ceremonial occasion it may signal intimacy rather than disrespect. And it is no insult to serve someone your third best wine so long as he doesn't know it is your third best wine.

So there is no question that Westerners use food to mark status. Sharing a meal with someone is clearly a way of conferring a certain status on that person. If you have dinner with your real estate agent, you are saying, or she is saying, that your relationship isn't all business. Finally, it is perhaps worth noting in this context, where the moral and the gustatory run together, that the central Christian ritual is the commemoration of a meal. Clearly, though eating is surely a biological matter, it is also, and just as fundamentally, a cultural matter.

Let me recount one more story of cultural influence on eating, this one designed to raise questions about the origins of cuisine.

Adaptation and Cuisine

In parts of Mexico and other Latin American cultures, corn tortillas are a staple of the native diet. Tortillas are made from corn that has been turned into a flour. But before the corn becomes flour, it is boiled with lime (not the citrus fruit, but calcium hydroxide). As it happens, boiling corn with lime is a very good thing to do from a nutritional point of view. Solomon Katz has discovered that preparing the corn in this way (1) introduces needed calcium into the diet, (2) increases the availability of certain B complex vitamins, and (3) alters the ratio of amino acids in the corn to make it a more complete or balanced source of protein (Katz, Heidiger, & Valleroy, 1974). (This is so even though boiling with lime actually reduces the total amount of protein in the corn.) But the question is: Is the fact that it is good for people to boil their corn with lime somehow connected with the fact that they do it? And if so, how?

One way these two facts *might* be connected is that the Mexicans under-stand that it is good for them from a nutritional point of view to treat their

▶ *Mexican children enjoying tortillas.*

corn with lime, and it is because they understand this that they boil it. But this is probably not so. Paul Rozin asked some residents of a traditional Mexican village why they use lime in preparing the flour for tortillas. The villagers said they did it because it made it easier for them to roll out and handle the tortillas; they believed that the lime treatment softened the corn. Rozin asked his informants to make tortillas from untreated corn; it was indeed more difficult to crush the corn into cornmeal, and the tortillas were more brittle (P. Rozin, 1982). So it seems that though the treatment of the corn with lime is in fact a health boon, it is done for entirely other reasons: because (1) that is, no doubt, how the people of the village learned to do it from the previous generation, and (2) if they deviated from this procedure, it would cause them certain cooking problems.

This example should teach us a lesson, which is that even though some cultural practice is biologically beneficial (has ***adaptive significance,*** in technical language), this does not imply that the biological benefit is in any way connected with why people do it. Until Solomon Katz investigated the matter, no one *knew* that there was adaptive significance, so the natives who were for generation after generation boiling their corn with lime certainly didn't do it because they knew about the health effects. It is highly unlikely that there is a direct connection between the behavior and its desirable consequences.

CULTURAL EVOLUTION?

The health effects of the lime *might* account for the adoption of the practice indirectly. Imagine that once upon a time there were two villages in Mexico quite close to one another. In one, for some reason—perhaps because it made it easier to press the flour—the villagers boiled their corn with lime. In the other, they didn't. The people who lived in the first village grew bigger, stronger, and more resistant to disease because they had better nutrition, and they eventually took over their neighboring village. They either killed the original residents, or perhaps taught them to boil their corn with lime to make better tortillas. In this way, the practice of boiling corn with lime spread because of its health effects, but it spread without anyone's understanding the nutritional effects.

This story is an example of ***cultural evolution***—some practice that arose by accident but was significant in terms of survival of the culture. In this story, the practice spread *because* of its survival value. The basic notion of cultural evolution (as of biological evolution) is that cultural practices come into being by random generation and then the selective retention of those random variations that have survival values. (See Chapter 9 for more on evolution and how it works in the biological arena.) We do not know whether Mexicans came to boil their corn with lime this way, but it is certainly one possibility.

Insofar as a practice spreads because of its survival value, it is an element of evolution. This is so *whether or not* anyone is aware of the survival value.

EMOTION

What, when, and with whom we eat is clearly a cultural matter and is clearly connected to the body. And the body has some, though it isn't known exactly what, connection to the self. But as we turn now to the relations among the self, emotion, and culture, what is clear and what isn't reverses: it seems more obvious that our emotions have to do with the self than does what we eat, but it also seems less than obvious just how culture matters to the emotions. The waters we are about to enter here are a bit choppy!

We need a conception of emotion to start with. Perhaps the most popular current conception of emotion, first proposed by Stanley Schachter and Jerome Singer (see Chapter 7), is that emotions consist of two conjoined elements: (1) physiological arousal and (2) a hypothesis about what caused that arousal. In their theory, all emotions share the same physiological arousal; emotions are differentiated, then, by their causes. But let us see just what that means.

Imagine that I find myself in a state of arousal and hypothesize that it is because of the approach of a buzzing bee that seems intent on landing on my face. Call this emotion event one. Now imagine I become aroused because I hear on the radio that the Dow-Jones Industrial Average is down nine hundred points and still sinking. (Imagine further that I own enough stocks to care about a crash!) Call this emotion event two. In both cases, I think I could fairly be described as afraid. But what do these two events have in common?

One popular answer is that the two events share the same *feeling*. And this leads to the idea that if I were to introspect on my immediate feelings during these two episodes, I would be able to identify the same element. But the thing I am likely to be focused on if I introspect is physiological arousal. These experiences of tightness in the stomach, pounding in the ears, and so on might be quite intense—depending on how close the bee is and how much money I have in the market. But they are *not* what make the events experiences of *fear*, though they may be what make them experiences of emotion. What makes them specifically *fear* is that in both cases, I hypothesized that my arousal was caused by an imminent danger.

Cognition, Emotion, and Culture

If you think of emotions as primarily internal feelings, then the question of the effect of culture on emotions is conceptually simple but practically difficult to answer, because it has to do with whether people from different cultures have the same internal feelings when in the same emotional state. But if you think of the emotions in a more cognitive way, as involving beliefs about the world, then though cross-cultural questions about emotion become more complex, we don't have to crawl into each other's skin to answer them (though Paul Ekman and his colleagues have begun to gather evidence of cross-cultural similarity in physiological response during emotional experience; see Levenson, Ekman, Heider, & Friesen, 1992).

With a (partially) cognitive conception of the emotions, the cross-cultural question we can ask is: Do the same stimuli trigger emotional events from one culture to another? Once we raise this question, however, we come face to face with a serious conceptual problem, the problem of level of abstractness.

At some level of concreteness, the answer to our question has to be no. Consider: among the Ifaluk, a culture in the Solomon Islands we will meet shortly, stock market crashes do not cause fear. They don't have stock markets. So no one ever hypothesizes, "I must be aroused because of the Dow-Jones Industrial Average's losing nine hundred points." But there certainly

▲ *The universal human smile.*

are dangers in Ifaluk, and if by fear we mean arousal triggered by the perception of danger, then there is fear on Ifaluk. So the sensible question about the cross-cultural prevalence of emotion has to do not with *concrete* triggers of arousal, but with more abstract categories. What we want to know is: Do the same categories of events trigger the same bodily responses across the cultural world?

DIMENSIONS OF EMOTION-TRIGGERING COGNITIONS

To address this question, it is helpful to organize the categories of cognitions that might trigger an emotion into a small set of dimensions along which the categories differ. Various dimensions have been proposed. There is, for example, one set offered by Craig Smith and Phoebe Ellsworth (Smith & Ellsworth, 1985), who argued that events are appraised along eight particular dimensions: pleasant (or unpleasant), attention getting (or not), controllable (or not), certain to happen (or not), obstacle to a goal (or not), requiring great effort to overcome (or not), legitimate (or not), and things one is responsible for (or not).

Stock market crashes (and fear-provoking stimuli more generally) are unpleasant, attention getting, uncontrollable, and obstacles to goals, and they vary among themselves in how inevitable and legitimate they are as well as whether one is responsible for them. Do the same dimensions capture emotional experience all over the world, or are these just the dimensions that capture emotional experience for Americans?

One set of investigators asked college students from the United States, Japan, People's Republic of China, and Hong Kong to reflect on specific emotional episodes. Then the students were asked to rate those episodes on the eight dimensions that Smith and Ellsworth articulated (plus two more, how able the subject thought he was to cope with the event, and how appropriate the subject thought it was to have those feelings in that situation). The subjects were also asked to indicate which emotions each episode triggered. Different emotions were assigned different ratings on the ten dimensions. Had it not been so, if all of the emotions had received the same ratings, then the dimensions would not be doing a very good job of capturing differences among the emotions! Did the patterns of appraisal differ from culture to culture?

The answer to this is *not* a categorical yes or no. Indeed, there were differences among the cultures. And there were bigger differences on some dimensions than others—there was more agreement about pleasantness, for example, than about who was responsible for what. But *by and large,* the same dimensions were mapped onto the same emotions across these four cultures (Mauro, Sato, & Tucker, 1992). This result suggests that emotional experience does *not* vary wildly from one culture to the next. This is not to say that emotions are identical, either—the Chinese were more likely to take pride in events that were beyond their control than were the Americans. Still, the results of this study, among others, suggest a less than resounding conclusion: appraisals of emotion-eliciting circumstances are fairly similar from one culture to the next (see Mesquita & Frijda, 1992, for a review; see also Matsumoto, Kudoh, Scherer, & Wallbott, 1988; Russell, Lewicka, & Niit, 1989; Stipek, Weiner, & Li, 1989).

The abstract dimensions of the triggers of emotion seem to be more or less the same from one culture to another. The concrete triggers of emotion vary substantially.

Emotion Terms in Different Cultures

A different approach to the study of emotion cross-culturally focuses on the names of emotions. Do the languages of the world all have names for the same emotions? This approach invokes the problem of translation: how do we know that the words (emotion labels) are translated correctly? Typically, someone who speaks both languages fluently translates a questionnaire from one language, say English, to the other, say Japanese; then another bilingual speaker translates it back into English (a procedure called **back translation,** in the jargon). If the back-translated English matches the original, then one has a successful translation. It may not, however, be a *perfect* translation.

It may be that there is no perfect translation from one language into another, but that both the original translator and the back translator did the best they could; the original translator found the closest Japanese equivalent of the English word, and the back translator found the closest English equivalent of that Japanese word. If the back translation worked, these tasks converged, but there might still be no perfect (or even very good) translation from one language to another. Indeed, there are those who argue that there are emotion words for which there are no perfect translations into some languages.

Anna Wierzbicka, for example, claims that Polish has no word for "disgust" (Wierzbicka, 1986). And Catherine Lutz claims that English has no word for *fago*, a commonly felt emotion on the Micronesian island of Ifaluk (Lutz, 1988). *Fago* is a complex emotion involving compassion, love, and sadness in relationships in which one person is dependent on another (parent and child, for example); it does not occur among equals (sisters, for example). One never feels more *fago* than when one's mother dies. Does this mean that Polish people don't experience disgust? Do Americans experience *fago* (but not know it)? After all, what we really want to know about is emotional experience cross-culturally; emotion words are just a tool.

As James Russell has pointed out in his careful review of this literature, languages are more than single words. I don't know whether it is possible to describe the experience of disgust to a native Polish speaker using more than one Polish word, but I suspect it is. I think I understand Lutz's description of *fago*, even though English has no single word for it. So, though it is true that the emotion words do not match up perfectly, it does seem that one can more long-windedly translate from one language to another using more complex phrases. Though I must admit that I am not sure of this. There is, for example, an emotion that is a common part of Japanese culture, one called *amae. Amae* is a matter of wanting to feel dependent, cared for, and accepted by a superior. It is apparently a central experience in Japanese culture (Doi, 1973). This is not a central emotion in the West, but it isn't entirely alien either.

One is left, again, with the conclusion that the emotional lives of people in other cultures are fairly similar to ours, but there are emotions in other cultures, such as *fago* or *amae*, that seem to be made up of familiar elements arranged in different ways. The cross-cultural evidence suggests, then, that our emotional lives are close enough that we can at least understand one another.

DIFFERENCES IN WHAT IS LEXICALIZED

As we have seen, cultures do differ in which emotions are **lexicalized,** or referred to by a single word. That may matter in some ways. People may more readily tend to think of themselves or others as experiencing an emotion that has been lexicalized. And how we think of ourselves in terms of our emotions may, à la Schachter and Singer, steer our emotional experiences. To return to a point made earlier, one way that cultures surely differ is in the concrete triggers of emotional experience. It is worth pausing for a moment to get a feel for what these differences are like.

DIFFERENCES IN CONCRETE TRIGGERS OF EMOTION

As I mentioned above, no one on Ifaluk suffers from a fear of a stock market crash. Conversely, on Tahiti, people suffer from *mehameha*, a kind of fear provoked by seeing a ghost (Levy, 1973). Those of us in cultures without ghosts are also in cultures without *mehameha*. Consider what happened to Catherine Lutz.

Lutz reports that when she arrived among the Ifaluk, she was offered two choices. She could sleep in the same room as the other members of her adoptive Ifaluk family, or she could have her own hut. The Ifaluk would never for a moment consider this as a serious choice. For them, sleeping alone in a room by oneself is a crazy idea, bound to result in terrible loneliness. It would be the sort of experience for which one would be entitled to *fago* from one's parents. But they knew that crazy Westerners had different ideas. Lutz took the separate hut.

One evening she awoke screaming because a man who was not a member of her adoptive family had entered her hut. She was terrified, concerned, as any American woman might be, with the threat of rape. Her family came running when they heard her, and burst out laughing. It seems that in such a circumstance, men are just not dangerous on Ifaluk, and no native would be afraid (Lutz, 1988).

Westerners understand loneliness, but sleeping alone isn't (usually) enough to provoke it. On Ifaluk, danger is understood, but a man's entering a woman's room at night isn't enough to provoke it. At an abstract level, the emotions are the same, but at the concrete level, they differ. It is important to appreciate both the similarities and differences.

Emotions and Self-Presentation

Finally, emotions may play different roles in self-presentation and self-understanding in different cultures. For example, both among the Ifaluk and among Americans, one way people judge another person and understand themselves is through their emotional lives. But the emotions are somewhat different. Lutz reports that on Ifaluk, men are willing to report that they are frightened in a variety of circumstances—for example, sleeping alone. American men, I would suggest, would conceal such a fear were they to feel it. Ifaluk men wish to portray themselves as harmless and innocent in certain ways; American men are, perhaps, more concerned to display themselves as "tough." American men, therefore, are more willing to report anger than are Ifaluk men (again, I am not commenting here on differences in experience, just on what is expressed). In both Ifaluk and the United States, in any event, people dramatize their emotions in the belief that which emotion they experience where is telling about their true nature.

We now come to the third element of the self, the self as moral actor. Perhaps the most important thing to say about morality in cross-cultural perspective is that no one (to my knowledge) denies that morality *itself* is universal: there are no cultures without a moral system. If we examine the ethnographic record, we discover that different cultures have different moral codes, just as they have different languages. And just as native languages seem natural, inevitable, and uniquely human to native speakers, so too do moral codes seem natural, inevitable, and uniquely human to native "livers." The problem is that *everyone* feels that the way his people live is the right way. But everyone can't be right; it can't be true that everybody has a different way of life, yet each is the uniquely human way to live. So we are left wondering: What is the right way to live?

Cultural Relativism

One resolution to this dilemma is the position known as ***cultural relativism,*** the belief that all cultural systems, all moral codes, are equally valid. It is the belief that there is no *one* right way to live; rather, each culture offers its own, equally good way to live. Cultural relativism is often combined with a view called ***social constructivism,*** the view that cultures and moral systems are constructed by humans and are therefore, in an important sense, arbitrary.

For relativists and social constructivists, questions of right and wrong (and truth and falsity) are strictly internal to a particular culture; that is, one can ask, "For Americans, is it all right to lie, cheat, and steal?" and one can answer, "No." But one cannot ask, "Is it all right for any human to lie, cheat, and steal?" because for the relativist, all moral questions are relative to some culture's code.*

Relativism has two very attractive features. It spares us the difficulty of deciding which culture's moral code is the right one. For the relativist, there is no right one. We are free to follow any code we like, just as we are free to speak any language we like. Second, relativism seems to argue for tolerance of other cultures, and we are certainly uncomfortable with the view that we should impose our way of life on poeple in other cultures, or theirs on us.

The relativist argument for tolerance goes something like, "Since no culture has an exclusive grasp of moral right and wrong, no culture has the right to impose its morality on another. We ought to live in mutual respect for one another's moral systems. It would be capricious and arbitrary to decide, as Aristotle did, that one's own moral position is the right one." So relativism is always a popular way to deal with the apparent differences among cultures. But relativism is not so clearly an argument for tolerance.

---

*Interestingly, Peter Berger, the father of American social constructivism, pointed out in *A Rumor of Angels* (1969) that there is no necessary connection between the idea that morality is socially constructed and the idea that all moral positions are equally valid. After all, the practice of medicine is also socially constructed, but it really is true that penicillin works better to cure infections than does blowing across a chicken's wing three times.

The problem is that relativism has a well-developed capacity to chop off the branch it is sitting on. One rejoinder to the relativist arguing for tolerance is: Is the belief that we should be tolerant of others *itself* simply a belief in some specific culture? If so, what right do you have to inflict it on people in other cultures who might believe that they should make sure that everybody follows the one, right moral code? Relative to the Athenian code, there was only one right way to live, the Athenian way! The relativist has, it seems, no grounds to urge relativism on others.

Moral Universalism

So relativism is not the perfect solution to the problem of apparent moral diversity. What other options are there? One possible solution is that the apparent differences among cultures are only superficial; perhaps there is *more deeply* a universal morality that all cultures subscribe to. This is a very attractive position. For one thing, if we could locate a demand for tolerance in that deeper moral code, then we really could urge it on everybody! The problem is, how do we demonstrate that there is such a code? How do we find it?

One approach to this problem is developmental. It seems clear to people that children are born without a moral code, but somehow acquire it, at least in rudimentary form, by about age seven. And children acquire exactly the moral code of the culture they live in. Perhaps understanding how children acquire morality will tell us something about what is universal and what is local in moral thinking. The most influential figure in the study of the development of moral thought over the last twenty years was Lawrence Kohlberg. So we start with his ideas about moral development. As we shall see, Kohlberg proposed that certain aspects of morality are universal, and he advanced substantial evidence to support that idea.

CLASSIC FINDINGS IN SOCIAL PSYCHOLOGY: KOHLBERG'S THEORY OF MORAL DEVELOPMENT

Kohlberg argued that moral development was really a matter of cognitive development, the development of the ability to think. He proposed that as the child becomes more sophisticated in her thinking, she inevitably becomes more sophisticated in her moral thinking too. In particular, Kohlberg, following Jean Piaget, argued that thinking about a situation or an action in a moral way was a matter of taking the right perspective. He suggested that the young child is egocentric in the sense that she naturally sees her actions strictly from the perspective of her own pleasure or pain. But, Kohlberg said, as she matures, she takes broader and broader perspectives. First she comes to see her action from the societal perspective; she can see what other people in her own culture think of her. And then she comes to view herself and her behavior from a "universal" perspective, from the point of view of abstract rules or principles.

Kohlberg's Stages   Kohlberg, again following Piaget, argued that this development of perspective on one's own behavior occurs in stages. That is, the path of moral development is in every culture and always the same, moving through these stages in an invariant order. He argued that there is no back-sliding; once at a certain stage, one never moves backward—barring cognitively catastrophic events like schizophrenia. But, he suggests, one need not make it all the way through these stages; individuals (and cultures) may differ in which stages they get through.

There are three Kohlbergian stages.* During the first stage, called **preconventional,** the child cannot distinguish right from wrong in terms of what is pleasant or unpleasant for the child. The child during this stage is the perfect egoist confusing his own pleasure with moral right and wrong. During the second stage, the **conventional** stage, the child sees morality not as a matter of his own pleasure but as a matter of living up to the expectations of society and its authorities. During this stage, the child has a broader perspective on his behavior; he can conceive of it from the perspective of a particular culture. In the final stage, the **postconventional** phase, the adolescent comes to understand that morality is really a matter of being guided by objective, impartial, formal principles (Kohlberg & Kramer, 1969; Kohlberg & Hersh, 1977). These principles constitute a formal, abstract perspective on one's behavior. Kohlberg, then, identifies morality not with a specific content, but with formal principles.

Kohlberg argues that children's moral understanding matures by passing through these stages in order. Though people from different cultures may stop at different stages, moral development in all cultures will occur in a fixed order; there will be no stage skipping or backsliding. Moreover, Kohlberg argues that because a view of morality as a matter of abstract principles comes last in development, it is the right moral position (Kohlberg, 1971).

If Kohlberg is correct, then there is at least something that is universal in moral codes cross-culturally—the order of the stages moral thought passes through. Kohlberg, then, holds out the hope for some manner of moral universality against the claims of radical relativism. But his claims are empirical, and they must be examined empirically.

Kohlberg's Method Kohlberg investigated moral development by interviewing children and adults about some hypothetical moral dilemmas. The most famous of these dilemmas has to do with Hans. Hans has a wife who is dying of cancer. In the town where Hans and his wife live, there is a druggist who just happens to have a drug that can cure her. But the druggist, like one of those giant pharmaceutical houses Hillary Clinton wants to tame, won't give Hans the drug unless Hans pays a lot of money, money he doesn't have. So the question is: What should Hans do? Should he steal the drug and save his wife's life, or let her die? And why?

The subjects' answers to the second question, not the first, are crucial for Kohlberg. For Kohlberg, whether a subject thinks that Hans should steal the drug or not has *no* bearing on his level of moral development; the crucial issue is the reasons the subject gives to justify the decision. A child, for example, who answered that Hans should take the drug because he would feel very sad if his wife died would be scored at the lowest level (stage 1, precon-

According to Lawrence Kohlberg, there is a fixed progression of moral thought through three stages: preconventional, conventional, postconventional.

*Each is split into two substages; so there are often six stages referred to. For our purposes, we need not distinguish the substages.

ventional), as would a child who said Hans should let his wife die because otherwise he would be arrested and go to jail, where he would feel bad. Someone who said, "The law is the law; it is sad indeed, but she has to die," would be scored stage 2 (conventional), as would someone who said, "He should steal the drug because otherwise he will let down his mother-in-law, who is surely expecting him to." And finally, "He should steal the drug because life is more important than money," and "Life without liberty is meaningless. Liberty implies private property. He must not steal," are the last, most mature, most developed responses (stage 3, postconventional).

EVIDENCE ON THE UNIVERSALITY OF KOHLBERG'S STAGES

Kohlberg's initial work on the development of morality involved samples of middle-class, urban boys from the United States, Taiwan, and Mexico, as well as from two isolated villages in Turkey and Yucatán (Kohlberg & Kramer, 1969). In all samples, the dominant trend was for progression from preconventional to conventional to postconventional stages; so the order in which people moved was as Kohlberg had predicted. There was, again as Kohlberg had expected, little evidence of backsliding. There certainly were, however, cultural differences in how rapidly development progressed and in the percentage of subjects who made it to the highest stages of development (see also Turiel, Edwards, & Kohlberg, 1978; Nisan & Kohlberg, 1982; Snarey, Reimer, & Kohlberg, 1985). Subjects from isolated villages, for example, were less likely to reach postconventional stages than those from urban settings.

A recent review uncovered forty-five cultures in which Kohlbergian research has been conducted, and while this is hardly an exhaustive sample of the world's known cultures, it isn't a matter of American middle-class college sophomores either. The hypotheses of invariant movement through stages and an absence of stage skipping and backsliding were well supported by the data in this review (Snarey, 1985). So at the level of the data, development does seem to be characterized as the development of increasingly broad perspectives on people's own behavior. But there are questions that can be raised about the interpretation of those data.

CRITICISM OF KOHLBERG

One concern we might have is that the Kohlberg method depends—perhaps too much—on the reasons subjects give for their moral decisions, rather than on the moral decisions themselves. It does seem that the reasons become more sophisticated as one moves through the stages. ("Exactly," Kohlberg might say, "moral development *is* cognitive development.") But the problem is that maybe what Kohlberg's method measures is children's increasing *verbal* sophistication, not their increasing *moral* sophistication. Maybe what Kohlberg is seeing is children's increasing ability to justify their moral decisions, not their increasing ability to come to those moral decisions in a thoughtful way. There have been other, less methodological critiques as well.

Gilligan's Critique of Kohlberg In a very influential book, Carol Gilligan argued that the Kohlbergian focus on impersonal, abstract rules and values grasped by the individual (somehow) may characterize how morality is thought about by men, but it isn't how women think about morality. Gilligan proposed that on the standard Kohlbergian moral measures, women turn up as less morally developed than men, but this, she argued, is because women speak about morality in a "different voice." Their moral voices, she argued, have to do not with rules and values but—though she didn't put it this way—with more collectivist notions. In her terms, women's morality is concerned not with following rules, but with caring for people. Men follow an ethic of rules, justice, and fairness; women are more concerned with taking care of people with whom they have a relationship (Gilligan, 1982).

Gilligan's claims have proven very popular; they seem to ring true to people even though there aren't a lot of data in support of them (Brabeck, 1983; Walker, 1984; Thoma, 1986; Smetana, Killen, & Turiel, 1991). In fact, some studies have found just the reverse of what Gilligan proposed. For example, Don Ernst asked men and women what they would think of a person who violated a rule—cheating on an exam, for example—to benefit themselves or to benefit a friend. The results were that men approved of violating a rule to benefit a friend, but not to benefit themselves. Women found breaking the rule reprehensible whether to benefit self or a friend (Ernst, 1990). Gilligan would have predicted, perhaps, the reverse result. On the other hand, the Ernst study used questionnaires rather than in-depth interviews, as Gilligan used. But on still a third hand, some of the results Gilligan reported were drawn from a study of women about to seek an abortion, and if there is any topic on which we might expect to find gender differences, it would be that one. In any event, Gilligan has certainly called attention to caring for people to whom we are related as an aspect of morality neglected, perhaps, by Kohlberg.

Caring versus Duty Cross-culturally Joan Miller has argued that the real cleavage over morality isn't between men and women in the West, but rather between people in individualist and collectivist cultures. Miller suggests that Indian culture, for example, places greater stress than Western culture does on obligations to care for other people. To show this, she asked subjects from New Haven, Connecticut, and Hindu subjects from Mysore, India, what they thought of someone who failed to respond to another person's need. Some subjects were told about a failure to respond to a life-threatening need, others to a moderate need, and still others to a minor need. And some subjects were told that the needy person was a stranger to the person who ignored the need, others were told that the needy person was a best friend, and still others were told that the person who ignored the need was a parent of the needy person.

In this study, American subjects saw parents as morally obliged to respond to moderate or serious needs of their children, and to life-threatening needs of friends or strangers. They did *not* see the protagonist as obliged to respond to the moderate or minor needs of strangers or friends, or the minor needs of their children (see Figure 8.3). Indians saw the protagonist as morally obliged (though in different degrees) to respond to all of the needs (Miller, Bersoff, & Harwood, 1990).

In another study, Miller, like Ernst, asked subjects—again from India and the United States—what a person should do when faced with a conflict between an obligation to someone the person had a relationship with and a general moral obligation. For example, subjects were asked to imagine that they were in Los Angeles and had their best friend's wedding ring, and they were supposed to deliver it to him in San Francisco but they don't have money

FIGURE 8.3

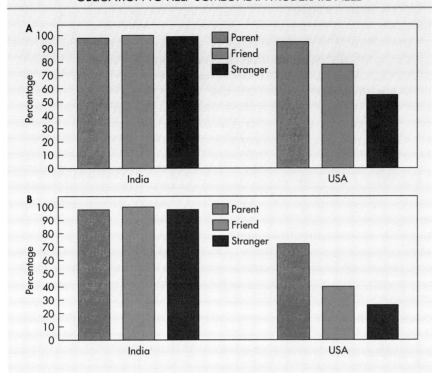

OBLIGATION TO HELP SOMEONE IN MODERATE NEED

◀ (A) Percentage of subjects from India and the United States who believed that a person has an objective obligation to help someone in moderate need. In some cases the person in need was a child of the potential help giver, in others the person was a friend, and in yet others the person was a stranger. (B) Percentage of subjects from India and the United States who believed that people have a right to intervene if a parent, friend, or stranger does not help someone in moderate need. (Data from Miller, Bersoff, & Harwood, 1990)

for the train ticket. The dilemma was: Should he steal the ticket from another passenger? Endorsing the idea that the person ought to steal the ticket favors the interpersonal choice over the demands of impersonal justice; the reverse choice sacrifices the interpersonal obligation to the concern for justice. The results were that about 40 percent of the choices made by subjects in the United States favored the interpersonal choice over the demands of justice, but about 80 percent of Hindu choices were in that direction (Miller & Bersoff, 1992). Here is evidence that Hindu subjects place greater stress on the demands that grow out of relationships rather than on the demands of abstract justice.

Miller's research turned up another interesting difference between American and Hindu subjects. Hindu subjects thought that if a certain choice was the right one for the person in the story to take, then it would also be morally right to force the person to perform that act (or to forcibly prevent the person from doing a wrong act). By and large, then, Indian subjects saw moral requirements as enforceable by anyone who chose to get involved. But American subjects had a different view. Though they thought the story protagonist had an objective, moral obligation to perform a certain act—say, steal the train ticket—they didn't think that anyone had the right to make the person do it. So they saw a distinction between what was morally right and wrong and what was enforceable. One more characteristic of our individualist culture, then, is our strong inhibition against intervening in what we see as other people's right to make moral decisions and undertake the actions that follow from them, even when we think that other people are wrong in those decisions.

The Gilligan/Miller critique suggests that Kohlberg's moral theorizing is too dependent on abstract principles and not dependent enough on the caring for one another that we do in specific relationships, in what is sometimes called **beneficence.** Miller, in particular, argues that Kohlberg misses this other aspect of morality because he is too thoroughly embedded in Western individualist culture. We shall return to these issues, but for now, let us raise a third criticism of the Kohlbergian scheme.

The Content of Moral Rules

Suppose we agree that in the end, morality is a matter of formal principles of having the right perspective on one's behavior. Still, are these *sufficient* constraints to produce any (let alone the right) moral code? Perhaps Kohlberg uncovered *necessary* constraints on a valid, universal morality, but perhaps these constraints aren't sufficient to identify a moral code entirely.

Consider the principle that we be indifferent as to which flavor ice cream we eat. That is, I suppose, an abstract principle, and it is hard to see how we would get in trouble if everyone followed it. But is it part of our moral system? Does anyone think it immoral to prefer chocolate to vanilla? Why wouldn't you endorse this principle as a moral rule? It is a perfectly good abstract principle. Presumably your sense that this principle has nothing to do with morality would stop you. Morality just doesn't have to do with preferences among ice cream flavors. It seems that the Kohlbergian formal approach needs at least to be supplemented if it is to be an adequate account of what the moral principles are.* The principles need specific *contents;* they need to come closer to consequentialism, which *does* take account of contents. Perhaps, as the consequentialist insists, morality is about what is good for people.

TURIEL'S THEORY

Eliot Turiel and his colleagues Larry Nucci and Judith Smetana have taken the view that one of the resources that children of all cultures bring to the task of learning morality is their innate understanding that morality has to do with specific contents; specifically, they understand that moral rules have to do with physical harm, injustice, or the denial of someone's rights. Thus, an immoral action is one that physically harms someone, does an injustice to someone, or denies someone his rights (Turiel, 1977). If Turiel is correct, then the child can reject the ice cream flavor indifference principle as a candidate moral rule because it doesn't involve the right sort of content; it doesn't have to do with rights, justice, or harm.

But what about the rule that sons not eat chicken immediately after their fathers' death? This is a moral rule in India; why wouldn't an Indian child reject it as a possible moral rule? How does that involve harm, injustice, or rights?

*The same criticism can be launched against the ethical system of Kant. Kant too roots morality in thought conceived of as formal principles. (See Wolff, 1974, for a charming account of Kant's ethical system.)

Supernatural Beliefs   Turiel would argue that such examples involve one of two things: supernatural beliefs or conventions. The Indians who believe that a firstborn son in mourning should not eat a chicken also believe that if he *does* eat a chicken at the wrong moment, then his father's soul will find no peace through eternity. Thus, the chicken eating *does* involve harm to the father. To be sure, there is a difference in moral judgment and behavior between the Indians and Westerners, but it arises not because of a difference in moral code, but because of a difference in beliefs about a matter of fact: whether a father's soul will wander the world restlessly for eternity because of his son's chicken eating. If we believed *that,* we wouldn't eat chicken either! So some differences in moral practices throughout the world depend on such differences in supernatural belief. But perhaps other differences have to do with conventions.

Conventions   Turiel, following the philosopher Lewis (1969), argues that some of the rules of American culture—drive on the right side of the road, use the salad fork for salad, the word "no" means what the word "no" means—are conventional rules rather than moral rules, and that even children appreciate the difference. What are conventions?

Conventions, Lewis proposed, have at least three features. First, they are only binding on those who are part of the community, and they can be changed by mutual agreement of the parties involved. Thus, if everyone in America agreed to drive on the left side of the road, they *could.* If we all decided that "yes" would mean "no" from now on (and vice versa), then "yes" would mean "no" from now on (and vice versa). Other kinds of laws or rules cannot be changed this way. For example, Newton's laws of physics do not succumb to democratic pleadings: even if we all got together and decided that rocks will in the future fall up, they won't. Physical laws aren't conventions. Even if we all decided that the sum of the angles of a triangle would henceforth add up to 150 degrees instead of 180 degrees, they won't—the laws of mathematics aren't conventions. And even if we all decided that it was okay to kill our fathers, it wouldn't be. Morality isn't a matter of convention. So conventions are unique in that we all understand that they could be changed by mutual consent.

Second, conventional rules can also be made context dependent—it is okay to wear pajamas to bed, but not to school. Finally, conventional rules may apply to some people only: those over twenty-one may drink alcohol. There are, then, three ways at least that conventions differ from morality.

Turiel claims that children know these differences too, at least implicitly. And they know that conventional rules and moral rules are also justified differently. Moral rules, he argues, are justified by appeal to the harm, injustice, or deprivation of rights that occurs when they are violated; conventional rules are justified by the social disorganization that would occur if they were violated—where would we be if people decided willy-nilly to drive on the left or right as the spirit moved them!

To demonstrate that children can distinguish conventional from moral rules, Turiel presented child subjects with the violation of a rule—a child steals a pen—and he asked his subjects a series of questions. The questions were designed to get at children's ideas about who made the rule against stealing, who should punish the child, how serious the transgression is, and whether the rule could be changed if everybody got together and decided to change it. These questions were designed, then, to see whether children can distinguish those that are conventions from those that are moral rules. The subjects were also asked why the act was good or bad, in order to see if they appreciated that moral rules are justified by appeal to harm and conventions to disorganization.

The typical finding in Turiel's study and others is that children do see moral rules as different from conventional ones in that moral rules cannot be altered by agreement and are justified by appeal to harm. And this result has shown up among American, Korean, and Ijo children (Nigeria), among others (Weston & Turiel, 1980; Song, Smetana, & Kim, 1987; Hollos, Leis, & Turiel, 1986). These distinctions show up at around age six, just when children are usually thought to begin to be capable of moral thought.

Interestingly, children can distinguish the moral from the conventional even when the moral transgression is a minor one, such as stealing an eraser, and the conventional transgression is major, such as wearing pajamas to school. And even if they think that someone would *prefer* to perform the minor moral violation, they say that the person *should* prefer to perform the conventional transgression (see Figure 8.4; Tisak & Turiel, 1988). Children as young as four make such distinctions about both real transgressions they have witnessed and hypothetical examples presented to them (Nucci & Nucci, 1982; Smetana, Schlagman, & Adams, 1993). One of the kinds of violations children see as conventional, it seems, is cross-gender behavior. For example, in one sample of five-to-thirteen-year-olds, for a boy to wear a skirt was seen as a conventional, not moral, violation (Stoddart & Turiel, 1985). There is substantial evidence, then, to support Turiel's claims about the differences between convention and morality, and about their differing connections to harm.

DO ALL IMMORAL ACTS INVOLVE HARM?

There are also some data that are not so consistent with Turiel's position. In one study, affluent and poor adults and children in Philadelphia, Pórto Alegre,

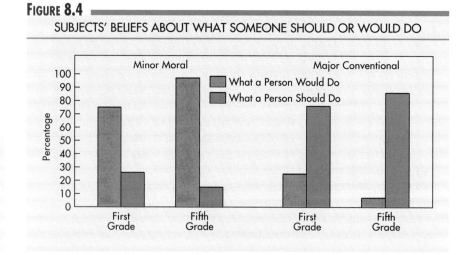

FIGURE 8.4

SUBJECTS' BELIEFS ABOUT WHAT SOMEONE SHOULD OR WOULD DO

▶ *Percentage of subjects in the first and fifth grade indicating what a person* should *and* would *do if given a choice between a minor moral and major conventional violation. (Data from Tisak & Turiel, 1988)*

Brazil (a wealthy and developed part of the country), and Recife, Brazil (a much less wealthy and developed part of the country), were interviewed about their reactions to a variety of behaviors that involved violations, but that did not seem to involve harm. For example, one story had to do with a woman who cleaned her bathroom with a flag from her country, another involved eating a dog, another was about a brother and sister who kissed passionately when no one was around, and yet another had to do with having sex with a chicken (this story was given to the adults only). These stories were designed to exemplify actions that though harmless were either disrespectful of authority or disgusting. The question was: Would subjects "moralize" these acts, or, as Turiel would claim, would they detect the absence of harm and place them on the conventional side of the ledger?

The results were that upper-class residents of all cultures saw the events as harmless and, therefore, not moral. But lower-class subjects from both Philadelphia and Brazil saw them as having the features Turiel identifies with moral judgments (Haidt, Koller, & Dias, 1993). The authors suggest that harm is too narrow a base to build all of the world's morality on. They argue instead, following Richard Shweder (in press), that worldwide there is more to morality than harm alone. Shweder proposes that Turiel's exclusive focus on harm and rights is just a Western idea and that this exclusive focus is connected with some singular notions that people in the West have about the self. It is possible that the overdevelopment of individualism in the West is related to Westerners' focus on morality as having to do with harm, rights, and justice.

Universalism or an Anything-Goes Relativism?

We began the discussion of morality in cross-cultural perspective by asking whether we are forced to relativism, the idea that right and wrong are relative to culture in something like the way that fouls and penalties are relative to the game being played. We saw that Kohlberg might have uncovered universals, and might therefore have its finger on *necessary* conditions for anything we would agree is a moral system. But it seems that Kohlberg's scheme is not *sufficient* to define what is or is not a moral code. One possibility, à la Turiel, is to add to the Kohlbergian formal principles the idea that morality has to do with a particular content—with harm, rights, or justice. But that runs afoul of two kinds of examples: (1) obligations to care for people with whom we have relationships (collectivist duties) and (2) actions that do not seem to involve harm, but that people find disgusting or disrespectful. Can we admit those examples to a moral scheme without agreeing to relativism?

COLLECTIVISM AND KOHLBERG

First, one might ask, is the obligation to care for those close to us really foreign to a Kohlbergian morality? It is true that the notion that Hans should steal the drug from the druggist and save his wife because he has strong, warm feelings for his wife is not the kind of abstract principle that Kohlberg sees as underlying morality. It relies too much on personal, subjective feelings; morality is built of sterner stuff for Kohlberg. But the principle that husbands should try to save their wives' lives, regardless of their feelings, is the kind of principle that Kohlberg should respect. It is, it seems to me, universalizable.

Caring obligations do *not* pose a threat to a Kohlbergian scheme. More generally, perhaps, collectivist demands do not pose a threat to a Kohlbergian system.

But what about acts that people find disgusting or disrespectful but involve no harm? Are they moral transgressions? If so, can we have a conception of morality broad enough to incorporate an injunction not to have sex with a chicken but narrow enough to avoid an "anything goes" relativism?

Three Moral Rhetorics   Richard Shweder thinks we can. He has argued that there are three *and only three* "moral rhetorics," or sets of moral ideas (Shweder, in press). One moral rhetoric has to do with harm, rights, and justice. It is the one Kohlberg, Turiel, and for that matter consequentialists are most comfortable with. It is the moral code, Shweder says, that the individualist West likes to think is the only legitimate one. The second rhetoric surrounds collectivism; it has to do with taking care of people with whom we have relationships. As I have said, I don't see this as antithetical to the first. The third, which we take up now, has to do with sanctity and purity, with ideas like pollution, respect, and disgust.

Pollution and the Self   Pollution is an important idea in many cultures, though not a prominent one in Western culture. The idea is that contact with certain substances—including people—leaves a person dirty, not just in a physical sense, but spiritually or morally dirty. The polluted person becomes unfit for participation in the community because he can contaminate others. A person who is polluted by contact with the wrong person or substance becomes unfit or unclean, not worthy of our respect. In the West, we don't make much of this idea, though it isn't entirely foreign to us either.

In a chapter entitled "Excremental Assault," Terrence Des Pres wrote powerfully of concentration camp life in Nazi Germany. The most profound degradation the inmates suffered came from being forced into contact with excrement—their own and others'—by the worse than primitive facilities for sanitation (Des Pres, 1976; compare Solzhenitsyn, 1973, on the excremental assault in Stalin's camps). Excremental contact is certainly a Westerner's most vivid experience of contamination and pollution. Incest is perhaps another idea we understand as polluting, as making a person unclean.

Shweder argues that pollution rules and taboos constitute a moral rhetoric quite distinct from the other two. Are pollution ideas moral, or are they of some other kind? There is a good reason to think of pollution and contamination in moral terms: contamination results in a lowering of the self in the eyes of others and in one's own eyes. A person guilty of incest is surely lowered, and a person who wants to have sex with a chicken seems diminished. Moral infractions do that too. But there are differences between moral infractions and contaminations.

The questions of choice and knowledge are crucial to moral judgments. It is unfair to *blame* somebody for something he had no control over or didn't know about. But pollution judgments don't work that way. A person is polluted by contact with something contaminating whether he had control over the contact or not. Oedipus puts his eyes out because he committed incest with his mother, Jocasta, but Oedipus didn't know he was committing incest. But that doesn't matter; the fact of his having committed incest is what tor-

Richard Shweder believes that there are three and only three moral rhetorics:

• a rhetoric of harm, rights, and justice;

• a rhetoric of caring;

• a rhetoric of pollution.

tures him regardless of what he knew. So the logic of pollution works differently from the logic of moral judgments.

In fact, pollution judgments seem to follow the logic of aesthetic judgments. Consider the judgment that someone is beautiful or smart (or ugly or stupid). These judgments elevate or lower a person in our eyes, and they are qualities that are beyond a person's control—no one chooses to be stupid. But I would *not* want to call these judgments moral, precisely because being beautiful or smart is not under a person's control. True, as Ervin Goffman has pointed out, there are many ways in which the judgment that a person is deformed is like the judgment that he is evil—in both cases, he is likely to be shunned—but considering someone deformed isn't really a moral judgment. It is, I suggest, an aesthetic judgment (see Sabini and Silver, 1987). Still, I must agree with Shweder that these judgments surrounding pollution are judgments about the worth of a self. So although there are reasons to see the rhetoric of contamination and pollution as a separate domain of the assessment of the self, the fact remains that if we broaden our view and include all judgments about the self, we may find, as Shweder suggested, that there are three and only three rhetorics about the self.

UNIVERSAL PRINCIPLES?

Maybe, after all, if we combine the formal principles offered by Kohlberg with the substantive constraints proposed by Turiel, we can constrain the play of moral judgments the world over. And maybe it will prove possible to split off judgments of selves connected to pollution and respect as either a separate sphere of moral judgment or as a different kind of judgment altogether. Perhaps taken together, we can avoid relativism and therefore find serious reasons to respect one another.

Beneath the obvious cultural differences in judgments of the self, perhaps there are universal principles to be found. Perhaps all cultures' moral codes really are in the form of abstract principles that imply a certain sort of perspective on one's own self and action, and all of the world's moral codes do involve harm, rights, and justice—though other judgments of the self involve pollution, contamination, and disgust. Perhaps the apparent violation of these principles does have to do with conventions or supernatural beliefs. Perhaps.

WRAP-UP

There can be no doubt that which culture a person is born into will have a large impact on her behavior throughout her life. Even with so biologically relevant a behavior as eating, culture makes itself felt. And clearly, at some level of concreteness, our emotional lives are profoundly affected by culture. The question is: Is there also a level of abstractness at which our emotional lives are also similar from culture to culture?

Perhaps this is a glass-half-full versus half-empty question, a matter of burden of proof, and some believe that the burden lies with those who would argue *for* cultural differences, while others feel that the burden lies with those who would argue *against* cultural differences. Perhaps people differ not so much in their interpretation of the evidence as they do in their starting assumptions.

Moral universalism is, I believe, a viable possibility. Some have been frustrated by our inability to pin down just what that universalism dictates, even after centuries of trying. But I have the contrary view—what's a few centuries?

SUMMARY

1. The conception of a self implicit in Western thought includes a body, a subject of experience, and a moral agent.

2. One important dimension along which cultures vary is the dimension of individualism-collectivism. *Individualism* is the idea that individuals, especially their thoughts, feelings, rights, interests, achievements, and points of view are more important than larger social entities. *Collectivism* is the reverse belief. Cultures that have emerged from Europe's northwest tend to be the most individualistic.

3. Some scholars believe that the very notion of a self is a Western idea, but the evidence isn't as yet overwhelming.

4. Culture has an enormous impact on what people eat and what they don't eat. Culture affects not only our eating behavior but also our thoughts and emotions connected to food. Some cultural practices might have emerged because they led to positive consequences for the culture. This is called *cultural evolution*.

5. At some level of abstractness, emotions seem to be pretty much the same from one culture to another, but what concrete events trigger which emotions varies from one culture to another.

6. Lawrence Kohlberg argued that in every culture, people pass through the same stages of moral development in the same order. The empirical evidence is, by and large, supportive of Kohlberg's position. Carol Gilligan has argued that Kohlberg's system describes men's morality, that women have a different morality. But there is little empirical support for her position.

7. Joan Miller has argued that Kohlberg's moral scheme is really only part of the picture, that collectivist cultures have somewhat different moral views; their morality has less to do with formal principles than with demands to care for others. Eliot Turiel has argued that morality has to do with specific contents—rights, harm, and justice.

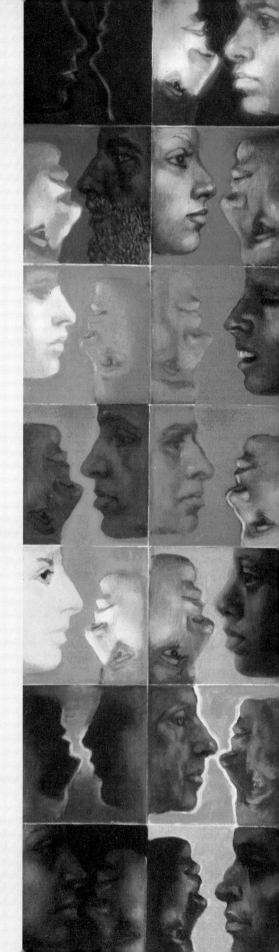

PART THREE

THE SOCIAL MOTIVES

One sense in which we are social creatures is that we have motives that are inherently social—they involve other creatures like ourselves. In this part, we consider some of these social motives.

We begin with perhaps the most encouraging fact about us as a social species: we can act altruistically toward others, and we can be fair to other people. In Chapters 9 and 10, we consider possible sources and ramifications of our propensity to act fairly.

Humans seem to have a special ability not shared by other earthly creatures (or perhaps shared only by our closest primate relatives)—we can act toward another person in anticipation of how that person will act back. In other words, we can manipulate each other. In

Chapter 11, we consider such manipulative actions, or strategic interactions. In the final section of that chapter, we ask whether, and under what circumstances, such individual motivation can be harnessed for the greater social good.

Next we deal with sexual desire. In Chapter 12, we ask how evolution and culture have shaped us to have the sexual proclivities we have.

Unfortunately, no treatment of human social motives would be complete without a consideration of hostility. So in Chapter 13, we consider where aggression comes from and how it is modulated. ■

CHAPTER 9

Altruism

On October 17, 1989, at about 5:00 in the evening, the San Francisco Bay area quivered from an earthquake. The quake set off a variety of natural disasters: fires in the Marina District, the collapse of a section of the Bay Bridge, and the loss of electrical power and light throughout the region. Along with these natural disasters came a predictable set of social ills, especially reports of looting in the dark, unprotected San Francisco streets. But the worst disaster from the quake occurred in Oakland, where the top deck of the Nimitz Highway collapsed onto the lower level, trapping an (at the time) unknown number of commuters in the rubble.

The collapse of the Nimitz Highway on the border of a residential section of Oakland also triggered some predictable social behavior. Residents picked their way into the rubble to try to release trapped strangers. Doing this was truly heroic. The highway was still quivering from aftershocks; it was impossible for the rescuers not to realize that their actions were exposing them to the risk of being killed themselves. The following day, television reporters descended on the area to interview people who had tried to help. In one interview, the reporter asked a fellow who had climbed onto the Nimitz why he had done it. The interviewee seemed a bit bewildered by the question, but replied by stating the obvious: "There might have been people in there who needed my help."

Heroic actions, like those in Oakland, cause us to reflect on altruism, one motive that is related to our ability to consider others' interests as well as our own. Altruism—and more broadly helping behavior—is the concern of this chapter. And then we shall look at the social psychology of receiving help, at conditions that favor or oppose people's seeking help from others. Altruism is a pro-social sentiment that is a crucial element of our psychology.

A   B

▲ (A) A section of the Anaheim
stadium damaged during the
Los Angeles earthquake in
1993. (B) A woman being res-
cued during the earthquake.

THE CONCEPT OF ALTRUISM

Altruism involves behavior intended to help others. It is doing something for someone else, like trying to rescue earthquake victims, with no benefit to oneself, often with the possibility of risk to oneself. But does altruism really exist at all? Do people really ever act for the sake of others, or are they really acting selfishly, even when they seem to be doing things for others? There are several reasons for doubting whether altruism exists.

The first reason is, perhaps, everyday observation. We are all familiar with cases in which someone acts as if he were doing us a favor, but we later learn that self-interest lies behind the "favor." We have every reason to believe that those nice people who call us up to tell us we have won a free vacation somewhere are actually involved in making money for themselves rather than doing us a wonderful favor. Or consider the salesperson who offers to take you to lunch; she is really more interested in selling her goods and earning a commission than in the intrinsic satisfaction of providing you with a nice lunch. Examples like these in which someone does something for us in the hopes of later gaining a **material benefit**—money, for example, but also fame, power, status, sex—are cases in which self-interest is masquerading as altruism. And because such actions are (relatively) common, we may wonder whether all apparent acts of altruism aren't similarly motivated by a concealed, material self-interest. Let us call the view that all seemingly altruistic acts are really material self-interest in disguise **vulgar cynicism.**

Actually, vulgar cynicism isn't all that plausible. It is hard to believe that the rescuers at the Nimitz hoped to gain something material from rescuing people from the highway or, more precisely, that the reason they did what they did was that they hoped to get something out of it valuable enough to justify the risk they were taking. In judging whether an act is altruistic, what matters is what the actor believes about the outcome of her act. It might be argued that the rescuers at the Nimitz *thought* they would gain some material good—perhaps the chance to write their story of heroism and sell it to a publisher. But this isn't very plausible. It is hard to imagine that these heroes

Vulgar cynicism is the view that all apparent altruism is motivated by a desire for material reward.

Subtle cynicism is the view that all apparent altruism is motivated by the desire for psychological reward.

really thought their chances for gain justified their actions. So vulgar cynicism isn't a very good reason to believe that people are not altruistic.

There are other reasons to doubt the existence of altruism. One is evolutionary thinking about behavior. But in order to understand why evolution seems to forbid altruism, we need to understand how natural selection works. After we have grasped this, we can ask how it relates to altruism, and whether anyone is really ever altruistic.

Natural Selection

Consider British moths. Once upon a time, one species of moths was mostly white. Their white color camouflaged them from predators when the moths lighted on the white bark of trees. But then came the Industrial Revolution, and with it air pollution darkening the trees, buildings, and so forth. Now the moths' white color, rather than being a camouflage, became prominent, attracting the attention of predators. If this were all there were to the story, we would not expect to find many moths left in England. But it isn't; it is just the starting point for natural selection.

Although the moths were white, some were whiter than others; there was, in other words, some **variability** in color. Moreover, this variability was genetically determined; that is, the offspring of lighter moths were, on average, lighter than the offspring of darker moths. Because there was variability in color, some moths did better than others at escaping their predators; the darker the moth, the more successful it was at avoiding being eaten. And since once a moth has been eaten it is unable to reproduce, the darker the moth, the more likely it was to have offspring. The darkening of the trees provided a **reproductive advantage** to the darker moths relative to the lighter moths. Thus, because the lightest moths had fewer offspring, the average color of a British moth grew darker with each generation. To be sure, the change from one generation to the next was small, but over a sufficient number of generations, this gradual, cumulative effect added up to a signifi-

FIGURE 9.1

NATURAL SELECTION AND
REPRODUCTIVE
ADVANTAGE

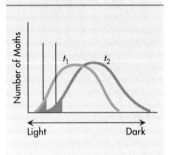

▲ *A graph of the distribution of moth colors at time 1 (t_1) and after the backgrounds began to darken (t_2). The shaded area under each curve indicates moths that did not reproduce. In each generation, the lightest moths lost to their darker relatives in the competition to reproduce. Thus, the distribution moved slowly to the right.*

cant change in the typical color of moths: the originally white British moths evolved into black British moths (see Figure 9.1; see Kettlewell, 1973).

Notice that this evolution worked without any hint of purposiveness—the white moths didn't *try* to become darker. Nor did they, for the good of their species, decide to have darker offspring. These aren't the mechanisms of evolution. Rather, evolution worked by conferring selective reproductive advantage on some members of the population and a corresponding selective disadvantage on others. Note too that had all of the moths been of precisely the same color to start with, there could have been no evolution; there would have been no way for the environment to confer selective advantage for color. And even if there had been differences in color, had they been caused by something not genetically transmitted—say, differences in diet caused by differing availability of nutrients in different locations—there couldn't have been evolution either. Evolution requires that some members of the species do better than others, and that this differential success be linked to their genes.

SURVIVAL OF THE FITTEST

The moth example suggests that natural selection provides for the survival of the fittest. But fittest for what? The obvious answer is survival itself; after all, the darker moths were more suited to survive than the lighter ones. But survival isn't exactly what evolution is about. To see why, consider the praying mantis.

Praying mantises, at least in some circumstances, have a very odd sex life. The female of the species is an aggressive sort that preys on small insects that come her way. As it happens, a male praying mantis is also a good bit smaller than a female. Thus, sad to say, the sight of a male puts the female more in a mood for lunch than romance. But there is a problem here: Where do new praying mantises come from? The answer is that natural selection has given the male a strategy to allow him to procreate with these dangerous females. His strategy is simple, if lacking in heroism: He sneaks up on her and tries to mount her before he attracts her attention—and her appetite. But his stealth can work only so far; once the male has mounted, the female can hardly fail to notice his presence, and then she bites his head off.* One might expect this dramatic greeting to inhibit the effectiveness of his attempts to inseminate her, but it doesn't. It so happens that the mantis mates *more* effectively without a head than with one. (Losing one's head—for the praying mantis, as for other species—is more a goad than a deterrent to sexual passion.)

This behavior on both the male's and female's part is tightly controlled by their genes. But suppose a male praying mantis were born with a genetic mutation that caused him to lack any sexual desire. Such a mantis would surely survive longer than his brothers who led more passionate lives; he would be more fit to *survive* than they would. But would natural selection use this mutation? Would a new species of chaste praying mantises now evolve? Hardly. Because the fellow with the mutation would never mate, he could not pass on his mutant gene to the next generation. As fit as he might

*As it happens, this pattern of behavior may occur only in conditions of captivity and when the female is virtually starved (Liske & Davis, 1984). But these details don't interfere with the point of the story for our purposes.

be to survive, he would be magnificently unfit to reproduce. So while natural selection operates to select the fittest, fittest doesn't mean the longest lived; it means the genes most fit to reproduce themselves.

Any gene that encourages an individual to have viable offspring will be represented in the next generation; a gene that detracts from an organism's reproducing will be rare (comparatively) in the next generation. Looked at this way, natural selection has to do with competition, but not competition between species and their predators. The competition is *between members of the same species* to produce offspring.

ADAPTATION

Let us return to our British moths. When we left them, they had darkened and were nicely camouflaged against the pollution-darkened trees. But the British once again pulled the rug out from under them: they cleaned up their air. Now the dark moths were well adapted, *but to an environment that no longer existed.* Darker color now conferred a selective disadvantage. And this illustrates another general point about evolution: natural selection prepares a species, but it prepares it for the environment its ancestors faced, *not necessarily the environment it will face.* Natural selection has no foresight; it prepares us not for what the future will bring, but for what the past has brought. (Still, as we should expect, the blind forces of evolution went back to work on the moths; they have now returned, with the unpolluted air, to their original color.)

Altruism and Evolution: Selfish Genes and Altruistic Individuals

There is an evolutionary puzzle about altruism, one that Darwin appreciated. Imagine two members of some species, Chris and Pat. Imagine that Chris has a gene that leads her to act altruistically, an "altruism" gene. But Pat has instead a "nonaltruism" gene. Who is likely to bear more offspring in the end? Whose genes are likely to predominate in subsequent generations, Chris's or Pat's? Pat will have for her use the resources she can provide herself *plus* the resources that Chris gives her; Chris, on the other hand, has the resources she can provide for herself *less* the resources she gives away to Pat. It would seem that Pat must in the long haul do better than Chris, and therefore it will be the selfish Pat's genes that will take over the species rather than the altruistic Chris's.

Because natural selection works, for the most part, via competition between members of the same species, it seems that natural selection must lead to selfish individuals. This suggests that we couldn't be a species with altruistic motives because evolution wouldn't allow it. But in fact, students of animal behavior have documented numerous cases of altruism.* It is worth under-

---

*When we speak of altruism in the human case, we mean behavior *intended* to help another. Scholars interested in animal behavior use the term more broadly to refer to behavior that usually helps another creature *whether intended to do so or not.* Because the human concept of altruism applies only to behavior motivated to help another, it may seem beside the point to consider cases in which an animal benefits another without this motivation. But the puzzle of altruism from an evolutionary point of view does not depend on whether altruistic behavior is intended as such or not, and the resolution of the puzzle in the case of unintended behavior also applies to intentional, motivated helping of another.

standing how evolution can account for altruism, not so much to "prove" that evolution made us altruistic, but rather to see why it doesn't rule out the possibility that we are.

INCLUSIVE FITNESS

One particularly prevalent case of altruism occurs between parents and children; in many species of birds, for example, a parent will issue an alarm call if a predator comes near a child. The call both warns the child to flee and attracts the attention of the predator to the parent. In this act of altruism, a parent actually risks its life for its child. How can natural selection account for this pattern of behavior?

W. D. Hamilton contributed the crucial conceptual advance that led to an evolutionary understanding of this kind of altruism (Hamilton, 1964). Hamilton pointed out that selection works on the level of the *gene*, not the *organism*. Thus, though risking one's life for one's child may be a foolhardy move from the point of view of the individual's survival, it isn't necessarily self-defeating from the point of view of one's genes. Let us work the example through in more detail.

Imagine that Chris and Pat are both mothers. Chris has a gene that leads her to risk her life for her child, but Pat doesn't. Whose genes will win out in the long run? If a predator attacks one of Pat's children, let us assume that the child will be destroyed. But if the predator attacks Chris's children, her child might not be destroyed, though Chris might. The answer to whose genes will win out in the long run depends on the degree of risk Chris assumes for her child. To simplify matters, let us assume that there is no chance that the predator will get both Chris and her child. Further, let us assume that Chris's child also possesses this altruism gene. If Chris is successful in saving both her own life and her child's, then there will be two copies of the gene around. And eventually Chris's altruism gene will dominate the population, will become part of the species' biological heritage. If Chris's strategy fails, however, and she is eaten by the predator, there is still one copy of her gene around— her child's. It seems, then, that this altruism gene can't lose. If Pat's child is attacked by a predator, there will be only one copy of her nonaltruism gene, but if Chris's child is attacked, there will be at least one and possibly two copies of the altruism gene left.

But matters are not quite this simple. Remember that in many species, including humans, parents share only half their genes with their children. Thus, Chris's child has only a 50 percent chance of inheriting her altruism gene; if Chris dies for her child, there is really only a 50 percent chance that there will still be an altruism gene left. The fact of our sharing only 50 percent of our genes with our children tips the odds back toward Pat's nonaltruism gene. But not all the way back. Chris will maximize the probability of passing on her genes if she accepts the risk of her life for her child, when and only when that risk is less than 50 percent. In the long run, a parent who accepts this limited risk will pass on more genes than a parent who never risks her life. The probability of dying in this heroic act must be weighed against the probability of sharing the altruism gene with one's child.

This argument can be extended to account for altruism for people other than one's child. What risks would it be best for an organism to take for a nephew? The probability that Chris will share a particular gene with a

▲ *A killdeer, a small American bird, feigning injury and keeping predators away from its nest.*

"GO RIGHT AHEAD. I KNOW YOU'RE BRED TO BE MEAN AND VICIOUS, JUST AS I'm BRED TO BE ALTRUISTIC."

nephew is 25 percent; thus, her altruism gene will do better than Pat's non-altruism gene if it leads Chris to take less than 25 percent risks for nephews. The general point here is that altruism genes can survive just insofar as they lead their bearers to take risks in proportion to the degree of relatedness between them and the beneficiary of their altruism. This, in very simplified form, is Hamilton's notion of **inclusive fitness**—in judging the fitness of a gene, one must look at the gene's effects not only on the organism that possesses it, but also on all of the organism's relatives. Note that this implies that for even the most distant relative, it pays to act altruistically if there is *no* risk to oneself. It pays to throw a lifesaver even to a ninth cousin, though plunging in to save a drowning relative is something better reserved for closer kin.*

This explanation can account for altruism only among organisms that are genetically related. Can we account for an altruism offered more broadly, altruism to strangers trapped on the Nimitz Highway?

RECIPROCAL ALTRUISM

Robert Trivers has provided an account of how altruism can extend beyond the family circle (Trivers, 1971). Imagine that you see someone drowning, someone not genetically related to you, and you have a lifesaver at hand. Could evolution give you a gene that causes you to throw it? On the face of it, it couldn't because there will always be some cost to you in throwing the life preserver, though the cost may be trivial. For example, there is always a cost in time. And you might slip and fall in yourself. Finally, you and this other person compete for resources, and to save him is to increase the number of competitors for resources; that isn't in your interest—individual or genetic.

There is a circumstance in which you might profit. Suppose you knew that you would be in the same boat at some later date and that he would then reciprocate, saving you. In this case, it is in both of your interests for you to save him. But we rarely know that we will be in the same situation or that our benefactor will save us. What is in your genetic interest in this case? The answer depends on the cost to you in saving him, the benefit you would gain if he were to save you, the probability that you will need his help, and the probability that he would reciprocate should the opportunity arise. In this example, the cost to you is so low that the benefits needn't be very great for you to advantage yourself in saving him. As the costs to you increase, the benefits you are likely to receive in return must also increase for it to be in your genetic interest to save him. Reciprocal altruism, then, can account for altruism, if only a relatively riskless altruism, beyond genetic relations.

This analysis, however, must face the problem of cheating. Suppose a population has a gene that leads the people to be altruistic, even to people who are not genetically related. Now suppose that a particular member of the species has a genetic mutation that causes him *not* to act altruistically, to be a "cheater." Whose genes will win out in the long run, the altruist's or the cheater's? Regrettably, the cheater's genes will survive because the

▲ *A ground squirrel giving an alarm call at the sight of a predator. Such alarm call giving is common among animal species.*

*This model is oversimplified in many ways. For example, a mother should take account of her own age. If she is young and has many chances to reproduce, the balance tips toward saving herself; if she is past reproductive age, the balance tips the other way. See Dawkins, 1976, for a lucid discussion of the complexity.

cheater will profit from other's altruism but not incur the cost of his own. In technical language, a gene that leads organisms to be altruistic to everyone is not an ***evolutionarily stable strategy*** (ESS); it is a genetic variation that will not survive in the long run. Reciprocal altruism seems to be a dead end, since it isn't a stable adaptation. But Trivers has provided a path back from the dead end.

Imagine that the same gene that leads us to act altruistically also leads us to punish people who don't reciprocate. This gene might become a stable variation because, although cheaters would profit from others' altruism, they would suffer the cost involved in being punished. Trivers goes beyond this analysis to speculate, provocatively, that humans are just such a species, that we have genes that dispose us to act altruistically and that also dispose us to punish people who don't, and especially people who don't reciprocate altruism (Trivers, 1971). In Trivers's favor, it is true that we don't like someone who fails to throw a lifesaver to a drowning person, and we like even less someone who fails to throw a lifesaver to save someone who had thrown a lifesaver to save him! Trivers proposes that our urges to act altruistically have the same genetic source as our urges to punish people who don't, and especially people who are ungrateful enough not to reciprocate altruism. We are a species inclined to throw lifesavers, and we are a species inclined to become angry with people who don't reciprocate.

This solution to the problem of cheating on altruism is not necessarily the right one, the one that our genes have taken. It involves speculation about our genetic past. It is important to understand this sort of explanation, not because it is correct, but to appreciate that there is a variety of ways in which natural selection might be compatible with our disposition to act altruistically, and to appreciate some of the logic of an evolutionary account. The point is that we cannot dismiss the presence of human altruism, even toward strangers, on evolutionary grounds. Indeed, evolutionary arguments point in just the reverse direction, suggesting that we may well be a species that has been shaped by evolution to behave altruistically. We have seen, then, that neither

Altruism as a stable phenomenon can evolve *only* if there is a way to prevent those without the altruism gene from cheating, from taking advantage of the kindness of strangers without reciprocating.

A   B   C

vulgar cynicism nor evolution provides good reasons to dismiss the possibility of real, authentic human altruism. But there is a third kind of argument that might be used to refute the possibility of human altruism, a view I shall call subtle cynicism.

▲ (A) A Little League coach; (B) a teacher with his student; (C) a veterinarian with a patient. All of these people are acting for the good of others, but each is doing so as part of his or her job. Is this, or to what degree is this, altruism?

Subtle Cynicism

Vulgar cynicism is the view that all apparent acts of altruism are secretly motivated by the hope of material gain for the "altruistic" person and are therefore not really altruistic. **Subtle cynicism** shares the view that all apparently altruistic acts are motivated not by the hope of material gain—money, for example—but rather by the hope of another type of gain, a psychological gain. The logic of subtle cynicism is that when people appear to be acting to help others, they are in fact motivated by the belief that helping others will do something desirable for them, something psychological, *and* that it is the desire for this psychological benefit that actually motivates them. This approach holds either that helping people provides people with pleasure or that failing to help people provides pain and that people help others simply in order to provide themselves this pleasure, or to avoid this pain. The rescuers at the Nimitz Highway, according to this view, did what they did either because they would have suffered some great pain in simply walking away from the disaster—shame, perhaps—or they expected to experience some great pleasure rescuing victims. Thus, the rescuers were actually spurred by the selfish motives of avoiding pain or gaining pleasure; they weren't acting altruistically (see Batson, 1987, for a thorough discussion and critique of this approach).

Now, while vulgar cynicism was easy to dismiss, subtle cynicism isn't so easy to dismiss. It is difficult to know what lurked in the hearts of the Nimitz rescuers; perhaps they did act to avoid pain or gain pleasure. To give substance to the subtle cynicism position, it is necessary to show that helping other people either avoids pain or provides pleasure. But merely showing this is *not* enough to substantiate subtle cynicism. Subtle cynicism further argues that *were it not for the pleasure or the pain*, people wouldn't perform altruistic

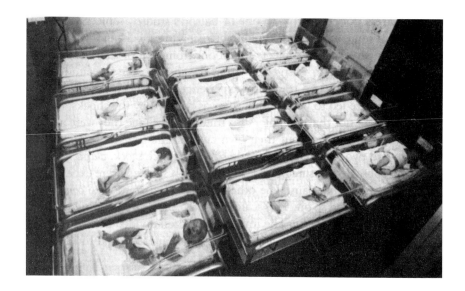

acts. So the first question we ask is: Is there reason to believe that helping other people reduces pain or provides pleasure? Yes, there is.

DISTRESS AT ANOTHER'S DISTRESS

Some evidence that helping others can reduce pain appears in the first hours of life. In one study, the investigator played audiotapes for sixty-six-to-seventy-two-hour-old infants. The tapes included the sound of another infant's cries as well as white noise of an equivalent loudness. The infants cried to the sound of another infant crying; they cried much less to the equally loud white noise even though monitoring of the infants' physiological responses suggested that the noise aroused them as much as did the cries (Simner, 1971). Further research has shown that even younger infants, thirty-four hours old, also cry to the sound of another infant's cries (Sagi & Hoffman, 1976). These data suggest that we are innately disposed to become distressed at certain cues of another's distress.*

The fact that we experience distress at another's distress means that relieving another's distress might relieve our own. If your crying makes me uncomfortable, then I can relieve my own discomfort by removing whatever is making you cry. If relieving another's distress is motivating, then we ought to learn a response faster if it relieves someone's distress than if it doesn't.

In one study demonstrating this effect, subjects were told that they were to observe and evaluate another subject's performance. The "other subject" was, they were told, being shocked while performing a perceptual-motor task (which the subjects were to evaluate). The subjects were to record their evaluation by pushing a sequence of buttons. For some subjects, the other person's shock stopped as soon as they pushed the buttons; for others, it didn't. (Ac-

---

*These data don't quite show that there is an innate disposition to become distressed at cues of another's distress. Even infants of this age can be classically conditioned, and they may have associated the sound of *their own* cries with their own hunger, thirst, pain, and so on. Perhaps the sound of another infant's cries are enough like their own to evoke classically conditioned distress.

tually, there was no shock; the other person was an experimental accomplice pretending she was being shocked.) Subjects who thought that their behavior shut off their fellow subject's pain learned the sequence of buttons faster than those whose behavior didn't stop the other person's pain (Weiss, Boyer, Lombardo, & Stitch, 1973). Terminating another's pain, then, is reinforcing in part because it relieves one's own distress.

In another experiment, subjects in one condition thought they stopped a confederate's shock by solving an interpersonal problem. They did so faster than did subjects whose solutions did not turn the shock off. The two groups, on the other hand, became equally aroused to the other person's pain. Just seeing another in pain, then, produces arousal, while being able to terminate that pain motivates learning (Geer & Jermecky, 1973). This evidence suggests that part of the subtle cynic's claim is correct; relieving another's distress can reduce our own. But the cynic claims that the apparent altruist relieves another's pain *only* in order to reduce her own. This is a difficult issue to resolve. But several experimenters have devoted considerable ingenuity to trying to resolve it.

EMPATHY AND REDUCING DISTRESS

Empathy involves an understanding of and compassion for another's distress.* C. Daniel Batson has invented an experimental technique that attempts to measure this intrinsic concern for a victim's distress and to disentangle distress from empathy. In one of Batson's studies, subjects watched a videotape of someone who appeared to be receiving shock, and who was very upset by the shock. The subjects found out from one of the victim's comments that her problem wasn't really that the shocks were so painful; rather, it was that she had had a traumatic experience with shock as a child. Thus, the subjects were led to believe that she was terrified by the shocks, but that the shocks were not that painful. After they saw this tape, they were asked to fill out a questionnaire about their own current emotional state. The questionnaire had two subscales. One scale listed words like *shock, alarm, fear,* and so on; this subscale measured the degree to which subjects were experiencing distress at the victim's pain. The other subscale had words like *compassion, concern, warmth,* and so on, and measured the degree to which subjects were experiencing empathy. The investigators then divided the subjects into two groups: those experiencing more distress than empathy, and those experiencing more empathy than distress.

Half of each group were then told that they would watch as the victim received another series of shocks. But they were offered an option; they could switch places with the victim. As expected, a substantial number of both those experiencing vicarious distress and those experiencing empathy agreed to take the victim's place.

The other half of each group, however, were told that they would *not* be

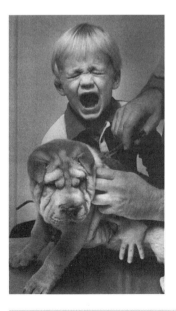

▲ *Distress at another's distress.*

*Terminology in this domain is far from settled. Some would refer to understanding another's distress and being motivated to relieve it as *sympathy* and reserve the term "empathy" for cases in which one not only understands and cares about another's distress but also shares it. It is also possible to share another person's negative state but not be motivated to fix it—an empathy without sympathy. (See Wispe, 1986, and Eisenberg, 1991, for an interesting discussion of these distinctions.)

FIGURE 9.2

INFLUENCE OF DISTRESS
OR EMPATHY ON HELPING

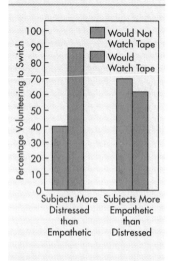

▲ *Percentage of subjects willing to trade places with the woman being shocked varied according to whether or not they could escape from watching her being shocked. Subjects driven by distress and those driven by empathy volunteered to switch places with the woman if they had to continue to watch her being shocked. Only empathetic subjects switched places if they didn't have to continue to watch. (Data from Batson, O'Quinn, Fultz, Vanderplas, & Isen, 1983)*

■■■■■■■■■■■

Distress at another person's distress can motivate helping that person in order to relieve one's own aversive state.

Empathy involves wanting to help another person independent of one's own psychological state.

■■■■■■■■■■■

seeing the rest of the victim's trials; then these subjects too were offered the option of volunteering to switch places. The researchers predicted that subjects experiencing predominantly their own distress at the victim's distress would *not* be willing to switch in this condition, since their own distress would be relieved anyway; they weren't going to have to watch her pain anymore. The subjects experiencing empathy, on the other hand, *were* expected to volunteer. Since these subjects were concerned about the victim's terror, not their own distress, the fact that they wouldn't have to watch her shouldn't matter. They should act altruistically whether they would see the victim or not. And this is what happened (see Figure 9.2).

For subjects who were experiencing distress at another's distress, a crucial fact determining whether they would switch places was whether they would have to watch the victim's pain again; for those experiencing empathy, whether they were to watch or not didn't matter (Batson, O'Quinn, Fultz, Vanderplas, & Isen, 1983). This result has been replicated several times by Batson and his colleagues, suggesting that empathy and distress at another's distress may really be distinct, and that empathy in the sense of a concern with another's distress, independent of one's own distress, may motivate altruistic behavior (Batson, 1987; Batson, Fultz, & Schoenrade, 1987). These results are evidence against one form of subtle cynicism. They suggest that the "empathy" subjects, at least, helped the victim for reasons other than relieving their own distress.

Some social psychologists, especially Robert Cialdini and his associates, believe that even empathetic helping is not quite as unselfish as it looks. The reason for the skepticism is that a substantial body of evidence, which we shall review shortly, shows that helping other people improves a bad mood **(negative state relief)**. Cialdini has argued with regard to the Batson experiment that (1) empathizing with the person receiving the shock puts the subjects in a bad mood, (2) helping the victim removes the subjects' bad moods, (3) the subjects know that helping will improve their moods, and (4) they therefore help the victim in order to improve *their own* moods.

To show this, Cialdini conducted an experiment in which some female subjects saw the standard "painful shock" experiment under instructions to empathize with the victim. As expected, these subjects experienced bad moods. Some of the subjects were then offered the opportunity to help, and they did. But for others, a rewarding experience was interposed between their witnessing the victim's being shocked and their being given the chance to help. Some of these subjects were praised for their social competence; others were given money. Cialdini argued that the rewarded subjects should already have had their bad moods relieved (by the interposed rewarding experience). He predicted that even though they empathized with the victim, they wouldn't take the shocks for the victim. And this is just what happened. The empathetic subjects who had *not* had their bad moods relieved by the interposed reinforcement helped the victim more than did subjects not instructed to empathize, but those who had had their moods relieved *did not* help more than the less empathetic subjects. The results of this study suggest that empathy motivates helping only because it involves first getting into a bad mood on seeing another's distress, and then improving that mood by helping.

A second experiment suggested that subjects in an empathetic state would help only if they thought that helping would improve their mood (see Figure

9.3). Cialdini gave subjects a placebo (a sugar pill masquerading as a real drug) and then exposed them to an empathy-arousing appeal for help. Some of the subjects were told that the drug would make the moods they were in very unstable; others were told that the drug would make their moods very stable—for the duration of the experiment, nothing they could do would alter their moods. Thus, some subjects were led to believe that helping might improve their moods; others were led to believe that helping would be of no use to them in improving their moods. The subjects in the unstable condition helped; those in the stable condition helped less. These results taken together support subtle cynicism; they suggest that empathy motivates helping *only* *because* empathizing with someone in distress causes one to become sad, and the helping is done strictly to improve *one's own mood* (Manucia, Baumann, & Cialdini, 1984; Cialdini, Schaller, Houlihan, Arps, Fultz, & Beaman, 1987).

Daniel Batson has answered this debunking explanation of empathy. He carried out an experiment based on this logic: if empathy produces helping only because the helper hopes to improve her own mood, then empathetic subjects *will not* help if they believe their moods will be relieved whether they help or not. Batson argued that if helping is for the sake of improving one's mood, then people should be no more willing to help if they know their mood will improve no matter what they do than people are willing to shovel the snow off their sidewalks if they think the sun will be out soon and melt the snow anyway. If helping is not to improve their own moods, it must really be motivated by a desire to help the victim for her own sake.

To show this, Batson exposed subjects to an empathetic helping appeal. Before they had a chance to help, he told the subjects that they would— whether they helped or not—be shown a film that improved people's moods. Batson argued that if empathetic helping is egocentric, as Cialdini claimed, then the subjects expecting their mood to be lifted anyway would not help. But if helping is truly selfless, then mood elevation or not, they would help. The subjects expecting the mood elevator helped the victim as Batson had expected (Batson, Batson, Griffitt, Barrientos, Brandt, Sprengelmeyer, & Bayly, 1989).*

The Batson and Cialdini experiments point in opposite directions with regard to subtle cynicism. The Cialdini experiment suggests that empathetic helping is done in order to improve one's own mood; the Batson experiment suggests that people will help even if they don't need to improve their moods. Further data may well settle the matter. The research so far has surely sharpened and narrowed the issue, even if it has left it unresolved. In the interim, there are several points worth considering.

First, it is difficult to establish experimentally that something *doesn't* exist. Even if the data from laboratory experiments fail to verify the existence of a truly unselfish altruistic motive, this doesn't *prove* that the rescuers at the Nimitz were acting for subtly selfish reasons. Perhaps in the face of true tragedy, motives are evoked that are not evoked in the laboratory.

Second, subtle cynicism isn't all that cynical. Consider what life would be

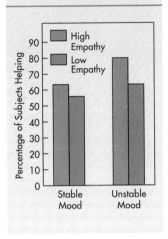

FIGURE 9.3

HELPING TO IMPROVE MOOD

▲ *Percentage of high and low empathy subjects willing to switch places with a victim (1) when they thought their moods could change and (2) when they thought their moods had been fixed in place. (Data from Cialdini, Schaller, Houlihan, Arps, Fultz, & Beaman, 1987)*

*See also Dovidio, Allen, & Schroeder, 1990, for other reasons to doubt that the negative state relief model is all there is to altruism. Also see Smith, Keating, & Shotland, 1989, and Batson, Batson, Slingsby, Harrell, Peekna, & Todd, 1991, for a related skirmish about whether feedback from the victim is necessary to produce altruism.

like if vulgar cynicism were true. Life would really be quite depressing. We would know that no matter what appearances were, people were always out to benefit themselves materially. We would be well advised to watch our backs because we could be sure that lurking behind every seemingly selfless act was a bill to be paid later. This is the portrait of a very cold life. But let us consider life if subtle cynicism were true. Suppose it is true that the only reason someone does something for us is that seeing us pleased pleases them. There is much less reason for fear here. In this world, we need not constantly check our backs in the face of seemingly generous acts. True, the person who is acting generously toward us is also getting some pleasure out of it, but why begrudge the generous person the pleasure her generosity brings her? We needn't fear that such a person is secretly out to get us; she has received in the very fact of seeing us pleased the payment she requires for her generosity. If this is the world we inhabit, life isn't so cold after all.

Finally, it is possible to get carried away with one's cynicism. It might be true that people do good acts for others in order to receive the reward of knowing they did the right thing. Does this fact, if it is a fact, show that their altruism is fake? Not necessarily. Suppose this special reward can be gotten no other way. This isn't like mood elevation—something that can come from a drink, seeing a funny movie, making money, and so on; it is a special sort of reward that comes uniquely from doing the right thing. And suppose in the end that people who do good for others do it just because they receive this moral reward. I would argue that doing good in order to receive this special reward is acting altruistically. Conceding that the point is controversial, I would argue that demanding that the true altruist act without even this motive is tantamount to claiming that the true altruist must do good for others for *no reason*. But acting for no reason isn't altruism; it is a kind of insanity.

Thus, I would say this. Insofar as people act to achieve some material reward, they are surely not acting altruistically. Insofar as people help others in order to relieve their pain or improve their moods and insofar as they would

▶ Mr. Joe Zanca was driving home when he noticed a brush fire and stopped to help the firefighter. But would he have stopped in a different mood?

just as soon improve their moods by getting money, watching a movie, and so on (as seems true of the subjects in the Cialdini experiments), then they aren't acting altruistically either. But if they help others to gain for themselves the sense that they have done the right thing, that they are moral people, and insofar as there is no other way that they would accept to produce this feeling, then they have acted altruistically. So far, I, at least, have not been persuaded that people never act for just this reason.

Attributional Determinants of the Helping Emotions

The research discussed so far suggests that empathy is one cause of helping behavior. And it is not unreasonable to assume that there are other emotions too that might move us to help—sympathy, pity, and so on. On the other hand, quite different emotions might get in the way of helping someone in need; we are hardly likely to help someone we are angry with. So the question naturally arises: What determines *which* emotion we are likely to feel on hearing of another's need? Bernard Weiner has offered one answer: that our **causal attributions** about why people need help and what they have done to help themselves determine our emotional reactions to their need, and those emotions in turn determine whether we will help them (Weiner, 1980).

In one study, subjects read a scenario describing a student who was having trouble in school. The subjects then learned of the cause of her trouble. Some subjects read that she missed a lot of classes because she had been out of town with her friends having fun; others read that she unexpectedly had to go home; others were given no reason for her missing class; and finally, other subjects read that she had had an accident and had been hospitalized. The investigator argued that these causes vary in how controllable they are; going out of town to have fun is more controllable than having an accident and breaking your leg. The subjects were asked to indicate what emotion the scenario evoked in them and also to indicate how likely they would be to help the person described in the scenario. The finding was, as we might expect, that neediness caused by less controllable causes evoked greater empathy than neediness produced by controllable causes, and that greater empathy produced a greater willingness to help (Betancourt, 1990).

In this study, then, the controllability of the cause of the trouble determined empathy. But we should probably not be too literal in our understanding of what "controllable" means. Being hit by a car as you cross a street is an uncontrollable cause of having a broken leg—though even here, you could have decided not to cross. But imagine that you read about a student who missed an exam because she learned that her brother was terribly ill and needed to go to the emergency room, so she took him. Quite literally, she could have decided not to go to the hospital; her going was in some sense controllable. But still we would feel empathetic toward her; we would feel anger at her instructor if he refused to give the student a make-up test. In this case, the cause of the student's trouble is controllable, but the key point is that it is also justifiable.

Thus, there are two questions we ask about the cause of a person's trouble: Is the cause controllable, and was it justifiable?* These two issues are also

*See Chapter 16 for more on this in the context of cognitive dissonance.

deeply related to our judgments of the moral worth of an act. So it is probably reasonable to assume that any factor that affects our judgment of the moral worth of people and their acts will also affect our emotional reactions to them, and our willingness to help them.

Sometimes too we care not only about how people have gotten themselves into a fix, but also what they have done to get themselves out of it. In one study, for example, subjects read about a student who fell behind in class (because of not working, despite working very hard, or because of illness) and who then either worked hard to catch up, did no work to catch up, or became sick and couldn't catch up. The subjects' willingness to help the student was strongly affected by whether he tried to dig himself out of the hole he was in regardless of how he got there in the first place (Karasawa, 1981)! So even if your being in a fix is blameless, you are unlikely to evoke much empathy unless you make reasonable effort to help yourself out of the ditch. Responsibility, both for the cause of a problem and also for the solution, has a powerful effect on our empathy. And we might suspect that a person's moral worth more generally affects our empathy and altruism.

Perspective Taking and Empathy

A second determinant of whether we will feel empathy toward someone is the "point of view" we take toward a person's problem. For example, in the study mentioned above in which a student fell behind in school because of a trip out of town with friends, an accident, and so on, half of the subjects were told that as they read the scenario, they were to try to take the perspective of the person interviewed in the story, to feel as that person would feel. The other half of the subjects were told to try to be as "objective as possible" in reading it. The subjects given the first instruction were more empathetic toward the student and were more willing to help than were subjects given the second instruction (Betancourt, 1980; see also Macrae & Milne, 1992). Thus, taking the person's perspective or point of view affected the readers' emotional states and altruism. And surely the more general point is correct—if we want people to feel empathetic toward us, we first have to get them to see things from our point of view.

Two points, perhaps, should be made about this: (1) seeing the world from another's point of view is quite an achievement in cognitive terms, and (2) the notion of taking another's perspective is not so much a description as it is a metaphor—a useful and evocative metaphor, but still a metaphor. Perhaps future research will analyze the metaphor (see Sabini & Silver, 1982, for a start).

Empathy depends on whether

• the cause of the person's neediness is controllable;

• the cause of his neediness is justifiable;

• he has tried to reduce his neediness;

• one takes his point of view.

THE DEVELOPMENT OF EMPATHY

However the debates about the nature of altruism come out, all parties agree that empathy, being concerned about another's distress, is distinct from distress at another's distress—simply being placed in an unpleasant state because one is confronting cues associated with another's distress. Infants in the nursery who cry at the sound of another infant's crying surely do not realize that there is another person there who is unhappy, much less do they actually care about that other person's discomfort. They are simply responding to innately aversive cues. This leads us to ask: How does real empathy develop? And, in particular, is there a developmental connection between empathy and distress at another's distress?

We don't know the answer to these questions entirely, but we do have some idea of what the answer might be. Martin Hoffman has brought together some pieces of the puzzle (Hoffman, 1975, 1981). One plausible answer to both questions is that distress at another's distress is a necessary starting point for the development of empathy. Perhaps if people didn't experience distress at another's distress, they would never come to experience empathy. One aspect of this primitive distress is, after all, that it compels attention to another's distress. But what more is required of a person for her to experience empathy?

Overcoming Egocentrism

To care about another's experiences, we first have to be able to understand those experiences. This ability seems to develop later than we might think. In fact, the great developmental psychologist Jean Piaget argued that until roughly seven years of age, children are not capable of seeing the world as another sees it (Piaget & Inhelder, 1956). Children *literally* can't see the world as another sees it. In one investigation, Piaget showed children a model of a mountaintop; as they looked at it, they were shown a teddy bear placed at various points around the perimeter of the model. They were then asked to pick from a group of photos the one that best matched the view that the teddy bear had of the model (see Figure 9.4). Children to age four couldn't even understand the question; children from ages four to seven tended to pick the picture that depicted their own view of the model. Piaget believed that until children could overcome this perceptual egocentrism, they couldn't overcome other kinds of egocentrism—for example, considering another person's needs, desires, and feelings.

One might imagine from this that children below the age of seven don't display much empathy, but they do. Recent research suggests that Piaget's conception of egocentrism isn't quite correct. We can distinguish various sorts of egocentrism in addition to inability to take another's visual perspective. Another kind of egocentrism is cognitive. In one study, children were presented with eight pictures in a particular order and asked to tell a story about them. They were then told that a friend of theirs would be shown four of the eight pictures, and they were asked to tell the story their friend would. Here the child had to overcome egocentrism in the sense that she had to ignore information she had, since her friend would not have this information. She had to "see" the story as her friend would, but here the "see" is a metaphor. Thus, it seems that children can overcome egocentrism earlier than Piaget thought, which may be why they can be altruistic earlier (Hoffman, 1975).

There is evidence that performance on various sorts of egocentrism tasks does correlate with altruism for young children from about ages three to six, but that it doesn't correlate with altruism for older children (Grusec, 1981). This suggests that overcoming egocentrism is related to the development of altruism, but that it is only one component. At tender ages, some of the children who have overcome egocentrism act altruistically, while some don't,

FIGURE 9.4

PIAGET'S THREE-MOUNTAIN TEST FOR PERCEPTUAL EGOCENTRISM

▲ The child is asked to pick the picture that best matches the view the teddy bear would have of the scene from its vantage point of the model. (Adapted from Gleitman, 1991)

▲ Siblings comforting each other, and perhaps learning to be more broadly empathetic in the process.

depending on these other components; none of the children, on the other hand, who *haven't* overcome egocentrism act altruistically. This would result in a correlation between perspective-taking ability and altruism in young children. When we look at older children, however, we find that all of them have overcome egocentrism enough to be altruistic. Therefore, whether or not they act altruistically depends only on the other components, and thus there is no correlation between perspective taking and altruism. But what are these other factors that contribute to empathy?

Socializing Altruistic Behavior

It is not enough to know what another is experiencing to do something about it. One must also care about what that other person is experiencing. Part of becoming altruistic is developing the motive to help others. What accounts for this?

One important factor seems to be how affectionate parents are with their children (Hoffman, 1975). Another factor is whether parents discipline their children by explaining the natural connection between their behavior and the feelings of others (Hoffman, 1975; Zahn-Waxler, Radke-Yarrow, & King, 1979). A third factor seems to be how much parents explicitly value altruism (Hoffman, 1975). Another important variable is "modeling." Children may respond with generosity if they see someone else, particularly an adult, respond with generosity (Bryan & Walbek, 1970). A final factor worth noting is how people respond to a child when she is generous.

In one study, children were induced to act generously by watching an adult model act generously. Some children were told, after their generous act, that they must be the kind of child who is very generous; others were told that they gave in order to live up to the model's expectations. Children told that they were generous gave more later when the model wasn't there than did the children who were told they gave out of a desire to live up to the model's expectations (see Figure 9.5; Grusec, Kuczynski, Rushton, & Simutis, 1978). The suggestion of this study is that it is important for parents to use

FIGURE 9.5

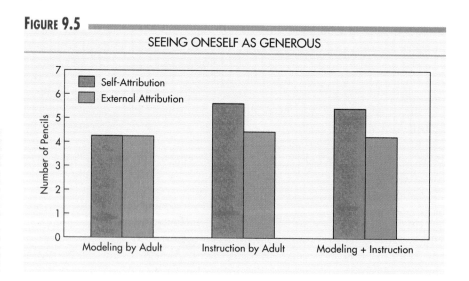

▶ *Children's willingness to share pencils with another child was affected by whether they perceived themselves as sharing to please an adult model or because of a self-attribution of being a generous person. (Data from Grusec, Kuczynski, Rushton, & Simutis, 1978)*

whatever techniques they can to get their children to be generous, but they must also lead their children to believe that they are being generous out of their own impulses.

The literature on moods and altruism is of interest for two reasons: it sheds light on altruism, and it sheds light on moods. We shall try to be attentive to both. Moods seem to come in two types, good and bad. We take up good moods first.

Good Moods and Altruism

In one representative study of moods and altruism, teachers in a suburban school system were asked to perform a perceptual-motor task. Some were told that they had done well; others were told they had not. To make sure the subjects didn't take their success or failure lightly, they were told that the task was a good measure of how creative they were in general. After they got the good or bad news, they met a confederate who put a collection can for a local charity in front of them. The dependent variable was the amount of money the subjects contributed. Subjects who were told they had succeeded, and hence thought they were creative, contributed more money than did the subjects who thought they had displayed a lack of creativity (Isen, 1970). The successful subjects' good mood facilitated their generosity.

Other studies have induced good moods in a wide variety of ways. One investigator looked at the relation of weather to generosity. In one study, he asked pedestrians to stop and answer questions for a survey and found that the number of questions they were willing to answer depended on how sunny it was. In another study, he looked at the relation between sunshine and tipping in a restaurant (see Table 9.1). There was a small but significant positive correlation; the sunnier it was, the bigger the tips patrons left (Cunningham, 1979).

With refreshing regularity, investigators find that anything that puts people in a good mood enhances their generosity. But why? More specifically, does a good mood affect altruism by intensifying either empathy or distress at another's distress, the two motives for altruism we have already learned?

The answer to this question is far from clear, but "No" would be an

▲ *From the film* Miracle on 34th Street, *in which Kris Kringle (played by Edmund Gwenn) truly believed he was Santa Claus. Did he believe he was Santa Claus and give to others to make himself feel good, or did he give to others because he felt good?*

TABLE 9.1

CORRELATIONS OF WEATHER AND GENEROSITY

Correlation of	Weather and Tips
Amount of sunshine	0.23
Temperature	0.03
Humidity	0.17

SOURCE: Data from Cunningham, 1979.

Audrey Hepburn campaigns for the United Nations Children's Fund (UNICEF).

Good moods

• increase helpfulness;

• increase self-indulgence;

• enhance attentiveness to the world;

• enhance the aversiveness of aversive outcomes.

informed guess. The experiments that have investigated distress at another's distress and empathy have exposed subjects to cues of another's pain to arouse these motives. Experiments on mood and helping have typically solicited helpful acts, but *not* by exposing people to another's distress. Thus, there is no reason to implicate distress at another's distress in these studies. And it is a bit far-fetched to see empathy as the heart of the matter. It is hard to see the amount of tip one leaves as resulting from empathy for the waiter. Further evidence comes from studies that have examined in just what ways subjects are willing to be helpful when in a good mood.

In one such study, subjects were either given cookies while studying in the library, or they weren't. Then they were asked by someone other than the cookie donor to help them with an experiment by serving as a confederate. In one condition, the subjects were told they would have to *help* the real subject with some task; in another condition, they were to *hinder* the real subject. Being given a cookie increased subjects' willingness to volunteer to be the confederate if that involved helping, but not if it involved hindering (Isen & Levin, 1972).

In another study, subjects found a dime in a pay phone and were then asked to participate in an experiment in which they had to read sentences that described pleasant or unpleasant happenings.* The subjects who had found a dime were more likely than control subjects who hadn't found a dime to read the positive sentences for the experimenter, but they were *less* likely to read the negative sentences (Isen & Simmonds, 1978). Finally, a study of 221 salespeople in a retail chain found that being in a good mood at work was related to the salespeople's willingness to do extra work to help others (George, 1991).

Good moods enhance altruism, but apparently only if the altruism will sustain their good moods. Subjects are *less willing* to do things that will wreck their good moods. Now what does that mean about good moods and our motives in helping others?

In one study, third grade children were put into good, bad, or neutral moods by remembering experiences that made them happy or sad or had no affective implications. They were then told to help themselves to some candy. Children in both the good and bad moods exhibited self-gratification, helping themselves to more candy than did those in the neutral mood. Later, they were given twenty-five pennies and offered the opportunity to contribute some of their money to poor children. Children in good moods gave more money to charity than did those in either a bad or a neutral mood. Thus, good moods enhance self-gratification *and* generosity; bad moods increase self-gratification alone. The suggestion that self-gratification and generosity go together is further supported by the finding that there was a positive correlation between the amount of candy children in the good mood took and the number of pennies they gave away. There was no such correlation in the bad or neutral moods (Rosenhan, Underwood, & Moore, 1974; see also Baumann, Cialdini, & Kenrick, 1981).

People in good moods do lots of things that enhance their pleasure; one of those things is being generous to others. This account rests on two assumptions: (1) we are endowed with motives to provide each other with plea-

*In those days, long since departed, a dime bought a local call, even in Philadelphia.

sure, and (2) the effect of good moods on altruism is mediated by the desire to seek pleasure, including the pleasure of being generous to others. But good moods might enhance generosity in another way too.

In one of the reports mentioned above (Isen & Levin, 1972), subjects either succeeded or failed at a task. Subsequently a confederate passed through the room they were waiting in carrying an armful of books, which the confederate then dropped to the floor. The primary dependent variable was whether the subjects helped pick up the books. As you might expect, those who had succeeded on the task did so more often than those who had failed. But a subsidiary measure was how much the subjects remembered about the confederate and her behavior before dropping the books. The subjects in a good mood remembered more than those in a bad mood. What this suggests is that being in a good mood seems to enhance attention, seems to make one take in more about the world. Bad moods, on the other hand, seem to restrict attention. This shouldn't surprise us. One of the effects of a sunny, spring day or of being in love—two famous sources of good moods—seems to be an openness to experience, an attentiveness to the world around us.

It has also been shown that people in good moods will only help if the helping doesn't expose them to aversive cues. Is there a more general mechanism that can account for this? To answer this question, recent research on the cognitive effects of good moods has looked at subjects' willingness to gamble when in good moods. This research has found that good moods induce caution, that people in good moods are especially aware of and sensitive to the possibility of losing money, and perhaps to aversive conditions generally (Isen, 1987; Isen, Nygren, & Ashby, 1988). Subjects who are in good moods, then, are unwilling to help if this will expose them to aversive cues. This is best seen as just one manifestation of a more general fact: people in good moods find aversive things even more aversive than they would if they weren't in a good mood.

▲ A blind man begs on a streetcorner. Why do people give? To avoid feeling guilty? In order to feel good about themselves? To avoid distress at having to look at this pathetic scene? Or just because they believe it is the right thing to do?

Bad Moods and Altruism

A variety of kinds of bad moods has also been studied. Oddly enough, in adults, bad moods do not have the reverse effect of good moods. In fact, at least in some studies, bad moods have been shown to *increase* altruism just as good moods do. For example, guilt has been shown to increase helping, and that helping is *not* confined to the victim of the act that induced the guilt in the first place (Carlsmith & Gross, 1969; Koneçni, 1972). Just as guilt increases altruism, confession, which presumably relieves guilt, reduces it. In one clever study, Catholics were solicited for donations to the March of Dimes either on the way into confession or on the way out (see Figure 9.6). More people gave money on the way in than on the way out (Harris, Benson, & Hall, 1975). Embarrassment, another unpleasant state, also enhances helping, as does thinking about unpleasant events (Apsler, 1975; Daumann, Cialdini, & Kenrick, 1981).

Why should bad moods increase altruistic action? One hint comes from a study in which subjects were made to feel guilty about upsetting a set of computer cards. The subjects were then solicited for a favor. But between being made to feel guilty and being solicited for the favor, some subjects were either complimented or unexpectedly paid, while other subjects had neither

FIGURE 9.6
BAD MOODS AND ALTRUISM

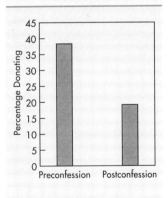

▲ Percentage of Catholic subjects donating money to a charity before and after confession. Guilt seems to lead to altruism. (Data from Harris, Benson, & Hall, 1975)

of these positive events happen to them. In keeping with the bad-moods-lead-to-altruism pattern, the subjects who were made to feel guilty agreed to do the favor more than those who had not been made to feel guilty. But this effect was abolished in those subjects who were paid or complimented. Apparently, to a person in a bad mood, being praised, being paid, and doing someone else a favor are all apparently substitutable for one another (Cialdini, Darby, & Vincent, 1973).

Another hint about why bad moods stimulate altruism comes from studies of bad moods in children. Children don't seem to show enhanced altruism when in bad moods (though, remember, they do show enhanced altruism when they are in good moods). One explanation for this has been offered by Robert Cialdini and his associates (Cialdini & Kenrick, 1976). Cialdini argues that the reason adults are particularly helpful when in bad moods is that helping relieves their bad moods. But it doesn't relieve the bad moods of children. This is because the connection between helping others and improvement of mood is acquired in the course of socialization (Aronfreed, 1970). Children, being imperfectly socialized, haven't established this connection. But this reasoning conflicts with the finding that children who are in good moods do help more than those in bad moods, and this suggests that they do find helping others rewarding. Can we resolve this discrepancy? Perhaps.

In a series of studies, David Rosenhan and his associates have shown that where one focuses one's attention affects the relation between mood and helping (Rosenhan, Salovey, Karylowski, & Hargis, 1981). In particular, they have found that subjects who hear about another's misfortune but are encouraged to focus on their own feelings do *not* help more than those in a control group not in a bad mood. But those who focus on the feelings of the person experiencing the misfortune *do* help more (Thompson, Cowan, & Rosenhan, 1980; Rosenhan, Salovey, & Hargis, 1981; Carlson & Miller, 1987). Rosenhan concludes from this that focusing attention on the self when a person is in a bad mood inhibits helping.

Perhaps we can reconcile these various results. It may be that (1) being generous to others is innately reinforcing, (2) good moods direct attention to the world, but (3) the natural tendency when in a bad mood is to dwell on one's own state. Because of this last fact, children who are in bad moods don't act helpfully. If they were to act helpfully, they would see that it would improve their moods. But children often don't know what's best for them. Perhaps with age, socialization, and experience, one learns to pay attention to others when in a bad mood in order, among other things, to derive the reinforcing effects of being helpful. This account preserves the innately reinforcing properties of helping others, which the data about good moods seem to demand, and also explains the fact that children don't help when they are in bad moods. They would help if they knew what was good for them, and they will learn eventually that trying to be good to others is one way to overcome their bad moods.

ALTRUISM AND DOING THE RIGHT THING

One reason, surely, for helping others is the perception that helping other people is the right thing to do. There are social norms that dictate that helping others is important. In this section, we will look at the complexities involved in answering the question: When do people respond to social norms instructing them to help others?

As several authors have pointed out, one problem with norms is that they are necessarily abstract, that is, they cover a wide range of diverse cases. And it is therefore difficult to decide how to apply them in specific cases (Latané & Darley, 1970; Schwartz & Howard, 1981; Sabini & Silver, 1982). For instance, we all know that people ought to give to charity, but how much? And to which charity? Because these questions must be answered before people can apply their general norms to particular cases, it is difficult to predict behavior in a specific case from a knowledge of the norms a person holds. This problem does not imply, however, that there is something wrong with the notion of social norms; rather, it is a direct consequence of norms' being abstract. In any domain that involves abstract rules, there is always a problem in specifying how those rules are to be applied to specific cases. Every student of the law or physics knows that it is easy to learn the laws involved; the difficult thing is to know how to apply them in concrete cases.

So how do people figure out how to apply social norms regarding helping? Chapter 2 discussed research on helping in emergencies as an example of social influence. There we saw that people tend to look to other people *in the same situation* to decide what to do. Because we are dependent on each other in this way, we can by our mere inaction cause others to define the situation inappropriately or, what amounts to the same thing, to apply social norms to the situation in the wrong way. Ironically, however, we can sometimes induce other people to act appropriately precisely by acting inappropriately; *violating* a social norm can, in some circumstances, lead other people to follow it.

Paying Attention to a Norm

In one experiment, for example, as subjects neared a parking lot, they passed a confederate who did one of three things. He either simply passed them by (control condition), he picked up a piece of litter, or he dropped a piece of litter (one of those bags from a fast-food restaurant). In half the cases, the experimenters had carefully set the stage for this little drama by carefully cleaning up the area (except for the offending piece of litter); in the other half, they had just as carefully made a thorough mess of the area. Thus, subjects in a clear or littered environment saw someone pass by, clean up litter, or create litter. Once the subjects reached their cars in the lot, they found a handbill advertising "Automotive Safety Week" on their windshields. The question was: What would subjects do with this piece of paper itching to become litter? More specifically, how would the little drama they had just witnessed affect what they did with the paper?

The answer is that, as you might expect, the subjects who saw the confederate pick up the fast-food bag were less likely to litter with the handbill than were the control subjects who saw the confederate simply walk by. Witnessing the confederate follow the norm of making the world a cleaner place made norms against littering salient, whether the parking lot was clean or dirty. But what about the subjects who saw the confederate add to the mess; how would they react? Well, especially in the clean parking lot, those

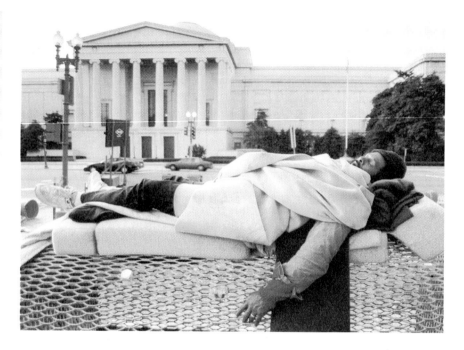

▶ *A homeless person ten blocks from the White House. Recently, a homeless person froze to death right outside the Housing and Urban Development Agency (HUD) in Washington. There are so many homeless people in our cities, we may fail to see any one of them.*

subjects too were *less* likely to litter than were the control subjects. The confederate's littering called attention in the clean environment to norms against littering (Reno, Cialdini, & Kallgren, 1993).

In the circumstance of this experiment, it was apparently quite easy to get subjects to pay attention to the drama of the littering norm. It isn't always so easy to get people to pay attention to the proper norm.

Failure to Pay Attention to the Victim

In surely the most ironic study in the social psychology literature, John Darley and C. Daniel Batson recruited seminary students to give a lecture. Half of them were to talk on problems in the modern ministry. The others were to speak on the meaning of the "Good Samaritan" parable. The volunteers were sent to one building to fill out some preliminary questionnaires; then they were sent to another building to give their talk. Some were told that they were late and should hurry to the next building; others were told there was no rush. Along their path, they met someone lying on the ground in need of aid; 63 percent of the seminarians who had plenty of time stopped to help while only 10 percent who were late stopped to help. And remember that half of them were on their way to talk about the parable of the Good Samaritan! Apparently the instructions from the experimenter produced "tunnel vision," preventing the subjects from seeing that they should help (and seeing the relevance of the Good Samaritan parable, about which they were thinking, to their immediate situation) (Darley & Batson, 1973).*

*Anthony Greenwald has reanalyzed the Darley and Batson data and shown that overall those subjects on the way to give the Good Samaritan sermon *were* more likely to help than those not on the way. But the point remains that a surprising number of the seminarians thinking about the Good Samaritan *didn't* help (Greenwald, 1975).

Reducing Ambiguity and Focusing Responsibility

Lance Shotland has conducted a series of experiments designed to determine just what someone needing help might do to get it. In particular, he asked what any woman who is being attacked by a man ought to do. In one study, subjects saw a man drag a woman into a room of a college office building. Then from behind the door, the students heard the sounds of an attack. In some conditions, the subjects just heard the attack; in other conditions, the victim attempted to attract aid in various ways. In some cases, she blew a police whistle; in others, she yelled, "Fire!"; and in others, she yelled, "Help, rape!" About 40 percent of the subjects (both men and women) aided the victim. Most of them did so not directly—confronting the attacker—but indirectly, by going for aid. More of the subjects exposed to the "Help, rape!" message went for aid than did those exposed to the other messages (Shotland & Stebbins, 1980). Shouting "Fire!" or blowing the police whistle may well have confused the subjects, adding to rather than reducing ambiguity. But when victims reduce ambiguity, they can provoke aid.*

One key to getting aid when you need it, then, is reducing ambiguity about what exactly is happening. Another key is focusing responsibility on who exactly should provide the aid. In one experiment conducted at Jones Beach, a popular New York City beach, an experimenter placed a blanket on the sand, and on the blanket he placed a radio. After a while he got up and asked someone on an adjacent blanket one of two things: "Do you have a light?" or "Excuse me, I'm going to the boardwalk for a few minutes; would you watch my things?" Then the experimenter's confederate acted as if he were stealing the radio. Only four of the twenty subjects who had been asked for a light intervened to stop the thief. But nineteen of the twenty subjects who had been asked to watch the victim's things did so (see Figure 9.7).

The same procedure was used in a Manhattan cafeteria. A woman in her early twenties put down a suitcase and asked someone nearby either for a light or to watch her things. Then a confederate took the suitcase. All eight of the people asked to watch her things intervened. Only one of the eight asked for a light did so (Moriarty, 1975). Similar effects have been reported in a college library; 77 percent of subjects intervened against a thief stealing something left on a library table when the victim had asked the subject to watch the items left behind; only 48 percent intervened without being asked to watch (Shaffer, Rogel, & Hendrick, 1975).

If you had been asked to explain why people in New York don't intervene against thieves before you knew of these results, you would probably have said that it was because they are afraid of violence. But note that in these studies, there are high rates of intervention despite fear of violence. Knowing that one has been made responsible to another is sufficient to overcome that fear, even for "alienated" New Yorkers.

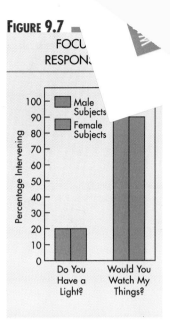

FIGURE 9.7
FOCU
RESPON.

▲ *Percentage of subjects who intervened to stop a thief at Jones Beach, New York, varied according to whether the subjects felt they had a responsibility to stop the thief. Asking subjects to "watch my things" proved very effective, although certainly not by reducing fear of the thief. (Data from Moriarty, 1975)*

---

*Yelling "Fire!" is a technique frequently urged on women in such a circumstance. The logic is that people who would not get involved in stopping a rapist out of fear of being attacked themselves would nonetheless be willing to summon help if they thought there was a fire. As we can see, this is *not* the best advice.

Some people are more likely to help than others. We will now examine some data about personalities, backgrounds, and self-esteem to get a sense of who is likely to help.

Helping in Emergencies and Personality

In the context of their studies of bystander intervention (see Chapter 2), Bibb Latané and John Darley wondered if the personalities of those who helped differed from the personalities of those who did not. To try to find out, they administered a variety of personality measures to their subjects and looked for correlations between these measures and the propensity to help. The search was disappointing; none of the personality measures predicted helping. But more recent research has found one aspect of personality that *does* predict whether someone will help. Both male and female subjects who reported having stereotypical male traits—aggressiveness, dominance, and so on—were *less likely* to help than those who did not report having these traits (Siem & Spence, 1986; Tice & Baumeister, 1985). Apparently having these "masculine" traits involves seeing oneself as the sort of person who is always poised and cool, and that gets in the way of offering help in an emergency.

Urban-Rural Differences

Latané and Darley's attempt to distinguish between subjects who did and did not help turned up one interesting difference; subjects raised in cities were less likely to help than those raised in rural areas. Subsequent research has followed up this finding in several ways. In one study, Paul Amato assessed the willingness of rural and urban Australians to engage in a wide variety of

▶ *Some helping, at least, follows from a deep moral conviction. Mother Theresa, who has devoted her life to helping the poor of Calcutta and the world, prays here in front of the Gandhi memorial in New Delhi.*

helping behaviors ranging from the trivial, writing down your favorite color for a student in a psychology class, to the serious—helping a person who collapses on the street. Across this variety of requests to help, people in cities were less likely to help than those in less urban areas (Amato, 1986).

More generally, the evidence seems clear that one is less likely to receive help in a city than in a rural or suburban area. It is *not* as clear that being raised in a city has the permanent effect of suppressing the willingness to help. Rather, it seems that where the help is requested has a much greater effect on whether it will be received than does where the targets of the request were raised. People at the moment in a city help others less than people in rural areas regardless of their backgrounds (Steblay, 1987).

Why cities inhibit helping is less clear. Perhaps it is because, as Stanley Milgram suggested, in cities people face constant appeals for their time, money, and attention. Under such circumstances, turning a deaf ear to such requests serves as a defense against "cognitive overload" from the barrage of demands (Milgram, 1970).

Reactions of the Person in Need of Help

Receiving help you need from someone in a position to give it is a blessing, but not an unmixed one. One reason the blessing is mixed is that by the very fact of helping you, the person giving the help advertises her superiority. Thus, receiving help can be a blow to one's self-esteem (Fisher, Nadler, & Whitcher-Alagna, 1982; Nadler & Fisher, 1986). Getting help can also affect how one is thought of by others. In one study, subjects read about people who sought psychological help after having been victims of a flood. The subjects were asked for their impressions of these victims' character. People who suffered substantially from the flood were *not* denigrated for seeking professional, psychological help. But victims who didn't suffer much objectively were looked upon as inadequate for seeking help (Yates, 1992).

In some cases—where someone is having an epileptic seizure, for example—there can be little doubt that the benefit of asking for help out-weighs the burden. But in other cases, people might well prefer to muddle through on their own to spare their self-esteem than to get help and the lowering of esteem that goes with it. And potential help givers, sensitive to this fact, might be inhibited from offering help in order to spare the person's feelings. This idea has generated a substantial body of research addressed to the question of when people seek help and when other people offer it.

In one investigation, Israeli high school students were gathered for a study of personality, problem solving, and interpersonal judgment. When they arrived at the lab, they first filled out a questionnaire measuring their self-esteem, and answered questions about a variety of attitudes (toward premarital sex, the Arab-Israeli conflict, and so on). Then they were asked to solve a series of anagrams. Half of the subjects were told that performance on the anagram task had no relation to important things like their intelligence or creativity, but the other half were told that anagram performance was a good measure of these traits. They performed the anagram task with a same-sex partner, and they were told that during the anagram task they could ask their partner for help if they wished. But before they began, they were shown the attitude questionnaire that their partner had (supposedly) filled out. For half of the subjects, their partner's form (actually made up by the experimenter) made it seem that their partner was very like them; for the other half, the form indicated that their partner was not at all like them. Now all of this was stage setting. The question of interest was this: Under what circumstances would the subjects ask for help, and under what circumstances would they rather do it themselves?

The self-esteem view of help seeking suggests that subjects would be *less* likely to ask for help from a partner who was very like them (someone it would be natural to compare themselves with), and especially when the task was described as a measure of something important to their self-esteem— creativity and intelligence. We might also expect this inhibition to be greatest among subjects who were high on self-esteem rather than those who had little self-esteem to lose. The results were consistent with this view: high self-esteem subjects avoided asking for help when the task seemed important and when their partner was very like them (Nadler, 1987).

Receiving help, however, isn't always a blow to one's esteem; the loss of esteem has been found to be lessened if the help seeker believes that at some future point she will be able to reciprocate the help giving. Boys and girls in one study were found to be more likely to ask for help if they thought they would be in a position to give help later in the study (Nadler, Mayseless, Peri, & Chemerinski, 1985).

There are ways of getting help that do not involve admitting to anyone that you need it, and when this is possible, we should expect people to be more willing to ask for help. One investigator assigned subjects a difficult cognitive task to be done on the computer and told them that they could, if they got stuck, ask for help. For some subjects, the help was to come from the experimenter's assistant; for others, the help was to come from the computer itself in complete privacy. As we might expect, people preferred to ask the computer for help rather than the experimenter's assistant (Karabenick & Knapp, 1988). One often hears about the ways that computer technology may be a threat to people's privacy, but computers also have the potential to enhance privacy, especially for people seeking the kind of help computers can provide.

Asking for help lessens esteem in the help giver's eyes as well as in one's own; thus, we might expect that people would be especially reluctant to ask for help from someone whom they want to impress. In line with this hypothesis, other research has shown that people are more reluctant to ask for help from a physically attractive person than from a less attractive person, especially if they expect to interact with that person later (Nadler, 1980). This tendency has been demonstrated for both sexes if the potential help giver is of the same sex. If the help is to come from someone of the opposite sex, then men prefer to ask for help from the unattractive person, but women are more likely to seek help from an attractive male (see Figure 9.8; Nadler, Shapira, & Ben-Itzhak, 1982). Apparently, in keeping with traditional sex roles, men believe that acting in a dependent way toward an attractive woman will cost them esteem in her eyes, but women believe that asking for help from an attractive male will not make them look unattractive to the male—in fact, it might enhance their attractiveness.

There is one further cost involved in making one's needs known to others. Suppose you let on that you are in need of help, and someone offers you that

FIGURE 9.8

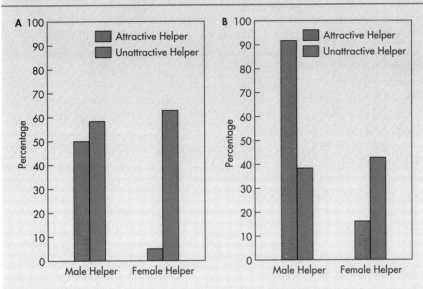

SEEKING HELP AND SELF-ESTEEM

◀ *(A) Percentage of male subjects seeking help from an attractive or unattractive male or female. Men avoided seeking help from an attractive female, presumably because they believed it would make them look unattractive in her eyes. (B) Percentage of female subjects seeking help from an attractive or unattractive male or female. Women were especially likely to seek help from an attractive male, presumably because they believed it would make them look more attractive in his eyes. (Data from Nadler, Shapira, & Ben-Itzhak, 1982)*

help, but for one reason or another you decide not to accept it—perhaps you think it is bad advice. How will the person feel who has had her offer of help rejected? One study exploring this issue showed that subjects had a dim view of someone who was in obvious need of assistance but who had declined that aid when it was offered (Rosen, Mickler, & Collins, 1987). It may well be, as Benjamin Franklin proposed, that a good way to get someone to be attracted to you is by having that person do *you* a favor, but an excellent way to get someone to dislike you is by letting them offer a favor that you then decline.

If asking for help can lessen one's esteem, then giving help can enhance it, especially if the help is ineffective. To illustrate this, in one study, subjects were asked to do a task modeled on the television game Password, the aim of which is to use clues your partner gives you in order to guess a word your partner has been shown. The experimenter told some of the subjects that their performance was related to their general intelligence; he told other subjects to treat the task as a game. In some cases, the subjects played Password with a partner who was a stranger; in other cases, their partner was a friend. Now, the game was structured so that the partner giving the clues could give a good clue that made guessing the word easy or a hard one that made it unlikely. The partners gave harder clues when they thought the task was a measure of IQ than when they thought it was just a game. Moreover, when they thought it was an IQ test, friends gave each other *harder* clues than strangers did, but when it was just a game, friends gave each other *easier* clues. At least in this study, the friends were happy enough to be helpful when the game didn't mean much, but they certainly didn't want to help their friends show them up when the game was a measure of IQ (Tesser & Smith, 1980).

People are more likely to seek help

• if they have *low* self-esteem;

• if they don't have to admit to someone that they need it;

• if the help giver is an *unattractive* member of the same sex.

The question of whether there really is any such thing as altruism is hotly debated in the professional literature of social psychology. But long before there were social psychologists, it was debated by philosophers—both professionals and those who crop up in dorm rooms late at night after a few beers. Have social psychologists resolved this debate? Probably not. Have they contributed to it in a productive way? Yes. The debate as recounted in this chapter is, I think, more precise, more concrete, and more sensible for the intervention of experimental social psychologists.

Evolutionary biology has also contributed to a clarification of the issue. The notion that our propensity to become angry with and aggressive toward cheaters may be an intrinsic part of human nature is, I believe, an important idea. The notion that much altruism is born of emotion is also an important one, so long as it is balanced by a recognition that people also sometimes act altruistically despite their emotional states. Emotions are important, but duty is too.

Finally, it is important for both potential help getters and help givers to be aware of the costs of receiving help, *not* because they should in every circumstance deter people from seeking help, but because by being aware of them one can weigh them carefully. One can recognize that there is a cost in asking for help, and one can ask whether that cost, realistically considered, is worth the help. One can ask this too, of course, about the help one offers.

SUMMARY

1. Altruism—behavior motivated by the desire to help others—seems to be contrary to the very notion of natural selection, but it isn't. W. D. Hamilton has pointed out, for example, that altruism on behalf of kin is consistent, within limits, with natural selection. Altruism toward one's kin has been explained by the notion of *inclusive fitness.*

2. Robert Trivers has offered explanations of how altruism for strangers can be explained by natural selection. Altruism can evolve by natural selection if and only if that altruism is directed only toward other organisms who also have an altruism gene.

3. *Subtle cynicism* is the view that people seem to act altruistically, but they are really being selfish—not because they are receiving some material reward in return for their action but because they are receiving some psychological reward. For example, people might relieve others' pain only because in so doing they also end their own distress. The experimental evidence is currently mixed on the question of whether relieving one's own distress is the only reason people act in an apparently altruistic manner.

4. The development of altruism requires that children (1) become able to understand the world from another's point of view and (2) come to care about the experiences another person is having.

5. Both good and bad moods enhance altruism. Good moods enhance altruism for both adults and children, and only if the altruistic act leaves people in contact with cues likely to sustain their moods. Good moods also enhance

self-gratification. Bad moods enhance altruism only for adults, not children, and restrict people's focus so they sometimes miss opportunities to help.

6. Much of the time that people help one another it is because they think it is the right thing to do, rather than because they are gripped by an urge to help. But in order for people to help others, they must (1) perceive the situation as one in which help is required and (2) see themselves as responsible to help.

7. Personality differences between people who help in emergencies and those who don't seem not to be terribly important or strong. On the other hand, there does seem to be one strong predictor of whether someone will help in an emergency: someone who grew up in or is currently in a city (or both) is substantially less likely to help than someone who was brought up in or (and) is currently in a less urban area. Where one is now matters more than where one was brought up.

8. People sometimes avoid help, even when they need it. One reason is that receiving help seems to place a person in an inferior position to that of the person giving help.

CHAPTER 10

Justice

Experiments discussed in Chapter 9 called upon people to help other people in need, to sacrifice their own concerns for the welfare of others. The willingness to sacrifice one's own interests altruistically is an important component of moral action; being kind, considerate, and generous are key moral injunctions we all recognize (even though we may not always follow them). But such impulses are not all there is to morality. Another moral principle, at least as important, is the injunction to be fair or just. Kindness and fairness are not at all the same thing.

Imagine that you were in charge of selecting students to be admitted to a university, and suppose that one of the applicants called you up and explained how much she wanted to be admitted and how much it would mean to her parents. Hearing such appeals leads to an urge to help the person out. In such a position, you really want to give the applicant what she wants, to act empathetically. But as powerful as the impulse to help is, there is another consideration: fairness. If you admit this student, then you must deny another student because places are limited in number. And you ask yourself: Is it fair to admit this student? Is it fair to the student who will not be admitted? In this case, a concern with fairness, justice, or equity directly conflicts with altruistic impulses. (Notice, by the way, that *selfishness* doesn't come into play on either side.) Altruism and empathy are moral sentiments connected with our concerns for other people; fairness and justice are equally selfless, equally moral sentiments.

There are two kinds of issues connected with justice or fairness. First, in a particular case, what is the solution that is fair to all parties? This is an issue of **substantive** or, as it is often called, **distributive** justice. Consider a

320

criminal trial. Surely we would all agree that the just outcome is that the guilty person (and only the guilty person) be punished for the crime. The criminal justice system concerns itself with finding out just who the guilty party is—that is what the system is about. But the famous icon of justice reminds us that justice is blind, meaning that our legal system, like all human institutions, is not omniscient. It is subject to error; it can mistake the guilty for the innocent and, worse, the innocent for the guilty. In light of the fallibility of our system of justice, substantive justice requires that we do the best we can knowing that we are blind, that we administer justice with a set of procedures that are themselves fair. *How* a decision to punish (or reward) ought to be made is an issue of **procedural** justice. In the first section of this chapter, we shall consider what social psychologists have learned about people's thinking about substantive justice; in the following section, we shall consider people's thinking about procedural justice.

Distributive (substantive) justice has to do with whether the outcome of a case is fair to all parties.

Procedural justice has to do with whether a fair procedure is used.

Fair procedures should lead to fair outcomes *on average*, but certainly not in every case.

EQUITY THEORY

So what is the fair way to distribute rewards? Stacey Adams called attention to one particular notion of fairness, one he called **equity.** Equity, Adams argued, exists when each person's benefits from being in a group—his outputs relative to his inputs—are equal to other people's outputs *relative to their inputs* (Adams, 1965).* If five people work at a task, and one works for six hours and gets $30 while another works for two hours and gets $10, and *if the only relevant inputs are the number of hours worked*, then equity exists because each has received $5 per hour. Notice that equity is not *equality;* one

*See also Walster, Berscheid, and Walster (1973) for further developments of equity theory. Much of the work inspired by this development of the theory has to do with equity in close relationships, which is discussed in Chapter 15.

person received more than the other, but this is, according to Adams, equitable, since their outputs relative to their inputs are equal. Note further that an *equal* distribution of pay, with each person getting $20, would not be *equitable,* since the ratios of outputs to inputs would not be equal. Paying people an equal hourly rate is one obvious way of producing equity, but it only works if the single relevant input is number of hours worked.

Experimental Evidence

Adams argued that (1) people are motivated to insure that equity exists among those who share inputs and outputs, and (2) people take account of more than number of hours worked in calculating equity. To demonstrate these claims, Adams conducted an experiment in which subjects were "hired" for a proofreading task. But before the subjects began, some were told that they were qualified to be paid the usual rate for proofreading—a certain amount per page. Others were told that they were not qualified to be paid the usual rate but that they would be paid that amount anyway. A third group of subjects were told that because they were not qualified, they would be paid less than the usual rate. Adams reasoned that such instructions would create a sense of inequity in the second group, and that they would therefore be motivated to restore equity. The other two groups, he suggested, would see themselves as getting what they deserved, and therefore they would find the arrangement equitable.

How could the "overpaid" subjects in the second condition restore equity? One thing people who perceive themselves as overpaid often can do is work *faster,* get more done in a given period of time. But this wouldn't work here, since they were paid by the page; the faster they worked, the more money they would get, and that would just make the inequity worse. But what they could do is work harder, more carefully. So Adams predicted that the overpaid subjects in the second group would make *fewer* errors on their proofreading task than would the fairly paid workers in the other two groups. And this is just what happened, supporting both of Adams's claims (Adams, 1965).

Problems for Equity Theory

Equity theory really consists of two distinct claims. The first is motivational—that people, or at least American college students, have a genuine motive to produce equity. The second is cognitive—that the equity formula is an adequate account of people's thinking about substantive justice. There is ample evidence from laboratory studies, as well as everyday life, that in some circumstances and to some degree, people are motivated to produce equity. This is not to say that equity is the only motive people have when dividing resources (no one wants to deny that greed too exists), but it is to claim that the restoration of justice is a real, independent motive.

The second claim, that the equity formula accounts for people's sense of fair division, is more problematic. Subsequent research has uncovered at least four difficulties with this claim: (1) gender differences in the allocation of rewards, (2) the problem of abilities as an input, (3) the problem of determining a standard of reference for deciding what is fair, (4) the problem of

▲ *Once her siblings wake up, this child will learn a lot about the allocation of resources.*

whether to consider needs in deciding what is fair, and (5) the problem of differential mobility. As we shall see, the first of these is more of an apparent than a real problem, but the other four will give us insight into where equity theory is incomplete as a theory of people's sense of fairness or justice, and will teach us just how subtle the notion of fairness is.

GENDER DIFFERENCES IN THE ALLOCATION OF REWARDS

Gerald Leventhal asked male and female subjects who had performed a task to divide a reward between themselves and a same-sex partner. Some of the subjects were told that their performance was superior to their partner's, others that their performance was inferior. The male subjects acted more or less in accord with equity theory; they took more than half the reward when they thought their performance was superior but less than half when they thought their performance was inferior. The female subjects, on the other hand, did not follow equity theory's predictions; women who thought their performance was superior took approximately half the reward, and those with inferior performance took much less than half (Leventhal & Lane, 1970). These results, and a substantial number of similar results, suggest that men differ from women in their adherence to equity theory. When women are superior in performance (or when acting as an uninvolved, third-party allocator), they veer away from an *equitable* distribution of rewards toward an *equal* distribution; they prefer equality to equity. Does this mean that women have a fundamentally different sense of what fairness is?

One explanation for the gender differences in allocation relies on the idea that it isn't that men and women have different ideas about what fairness is; rather, men and women characteristically have different goals they are attempting to accomplish with their allocations, and their different strategies follow from their different goals.

An experiment by Jayne Stake lends support to this position. Stake told male and female subjects that they were to take the part of a manager in a business simulation. As manager, they were to allocate bonuses and pay raises. They were asked how they would allocate these resources under three different goals: (1) to reward fairly, (2) to maximize productivity, and (3) to make the workers' relationships with one another as positive as possible. The people to whom they allocated the bonuses and raises varied both in how much they produced and in their abilities. The results indicated that subjects of both genders rewarded according to each "worker's" output when asked to reward fairly. But they tended toward equality and away from equity when they wanted to make the interpersonal relationships as positive as possible. (Disparities in the amount of reward that people receive, no matter if fairly deserved, tend to produce divisiveness; equal rewards lessen divisive comparison.)* And when they were to maximize productivity, they rewarded on the basis of capability (Stake, 1983).

This result suggests that one reason that women in other studies turn

---

*In support of the relationship-furthering nature of equal divisions, several experimenters have found that people allocate *equally* (or closer to equally) when they expect future interactions with the people they are allocating for more than when they don't expect such interactions (Shapiro, 1975; Sagan, Pondel, & Wittig, 1981; Major & Adams, 1983).

Problems for equity theory:

- Are there gender differences in reward allocations?
- Are abilities inputs?
- What standards should be used to decide fairness?
- Do needs matter?
- Does differential mobility matter?

toward equality more than men do is that they characteristically care more about maintaining warm relationships among members of the group. Men, on the other hand, characteristically act as if they were attempting to maximize productivity. One account, then, of the typical gender difference found in allocation studies relies on the traditional roles assigned to men and women; women are traditionally seen as more concerned with interpersonal relationships, and men are seen as being more concerned with achievement. There are circumstances, however, that alter these allocation strategies. One study found that although female subjects deviated toward equality while men allocated equitably *when allocations were public*, when allocations were private—no one would know how the allocator allocated—the gender difference reversed: men rewarded equally, while women allocated equitably (see Figure 10.1; Kidder, Bellettirie, & Cohn, 1977; see Major & Adams, 1983, for a partial replication). The investigators believe that men and women in this study followed the traditional gender roles in public, but rebelled against them when dividing privately.

The research we have reviewed so far suggests that women's preference for equal versus equitable allocations does *not* reflect fundamental differences in the way men and women construe fairness. Rather, these observed differences seem to implicate (1) differences in the goals that men and women have when facing an allocation task—men may be more concerned than women with stimulating productivity, and women may be more concerned than men with maintaining comfortable intragroup relations; and (2) men and women trying to live up to traditional gender roles in public. It seems that the gender differences do not pose a fundamental problem for equity theory; they do suggest that equity isn't the *only* motive we have when allocating.

ABILITY AND EQUITY

The second problem equity theory faces is how to count abilities in dividing resources. Adams found that subjects saw themselves as owing extra effort if they were deficient in the ability needed for his proofreading task. This suggests that abilities count along with effort when deciding on what a person's inputs are; the more of one you bring to a task, the less of the other you must display. But abilities don't always count as an input. In one study, Leventhal told subjects that they would be taking part in a study by the Psychology Department, in cooperation with the Physical Education Department, in which athletes would be paid for their performance on a high jump. But the experimenter further explained that the department was unsure of the fairest way to pay the participants; after all, the jumpers could differ in several ways. Some would jump higher than others. But some would be taller than others to start with. Then again, some would exert more effort in jumping. Finally, some of the athletes were to be given special, useful training about how to jump, while others would not get that training. The question was how much to take each of these factors into account in allocating rewards for the high jump. To answer this, subjects were given descriptions of sixteen combinations of these various factors (how high the person jumped, how tall he was, whether he was trained, and so on) and asked to assign what they thought was fair pay.

One way to think about this is that pay should be on the basis of perfor-

FIGURE 10.1
EQUITY OR EQUALITY?

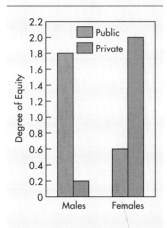

▲ *The degree to which men and women in public and private followed equity rather than equality in dividing rewards. (Data from Kidder, Bellettirie, & Cohn, 1977)*

mance, period. If the subjects thought this way, then they should have varied their payoff strictly on the basis of height jumped. But the subjects didn't do that; they allocated rewards in a much more complex manner. For two people who jumped equally high, they gave the one *without* training more reward than the one with training. Again, holding height jumped constant, they gave the person who exerted more effort more reward than the one who exerted less effort. The shorter person got more reward than the taller person (Leventhal & Michaels, 1971). Thus, certain characteristics of the person—height and training, for example—counted against the reward he was to receive for a given performance.

In the Adams study described above, subjects who thought they lacked the ability to proofread well saw themselves as owing the experimenter something for paying them at the rate he would have paid a competent proofreader. In equity terms, they saw ability as a relevant input factor in determining equitable output. In line with such thinking, we might think of height as something that contributes to a person's ability to jump high. In the context of a high jump, we might pay the taller person *more*, since he brings more ability to the task. But these subjects paid the taller person *less*; they penalized him for being constitutionally able to jump high. (Note that in both studies, effort counted as an input.) What does this inconsistency mean?

Let us step back from the laboratory studies for a moment and consider real rewards in our society. First, we would probably all agree that if everyone were born with equal potential and equal opportunity to develop that potential, then fairness would dictate that people be paid strictly in line with their accomplishments. In such a utopia, ultimate performance seems to be strictly a matter of how much a person applies himself, strictly a matter of quality of character. But in the real world this isn't how things are.

I simply cannot hit a golf ball as well as Jack Nicklaus; to some degree, this is because I have not applied myself to this task as hard as he has, but I also suspect (and all those who have watched me play suspect) that it is partly a matter of innate ability, or the lack thereof. Most of us would agree that he should be paid more for golfing than I should, even though his superior ability is in part a matter of his genetic endowment. So we do to some degree see it as fair that people receive more for the application of special skills, so long as there is substantial effort involved in developing those skills. But we seem to be made uneasy by athletes, for example, who earn huge sums of money with little apparent effort. Babe Ruth was a baseball player (perhaps the most talented ever) who accomplished an enormous amount, seemingly without any discipline—personal or professional. Surely baseball fans admired his talent, and surely they thought he should be well paid, but there was some resentment about the fact that one year he earned more than the president of the United States. And surely now there is even more resentment that some athletes earn ten times as much as the president. Thus, to some degree, we do treat sheer talent as an input that must be matched by a corresponding output for equity to exist. But as the experiment we have just reviewed suggests, talent (unlike effort) is also something that we think makes a person *less* deserving of reward—holding accomplishment constant. To be a complete account of judgments of distributive justice, equity theory must also be an account of how we treat ability.

CLASSIC FINDINGS IN SOCIAL PSYCHOLOGY: RELATIVE DEPRIVATION THEORY

During the Second World War, Samuel Stouffer and his associates conducted research for the United States army directed at understanding sources of soldiers' discontent with army life. A surprising finding of this research had to do with soldiers' dissatisfaction with their chances for promotion. As it happened, soldiers in the air corps were much less satisfied with their chances to advance than were those in the military police (MP). This would be perfectly easy to understand and encompass within equity theory if objectively the air corps offered relatively slow advancement while the military police offered a rapid rise to the top, but actually the circumstances where closer to the reverse. The air corps soldier got promoted at a fair pace, while MPs' chances for promotion were among the worst in the army (Stouffer, Suchman, DeVinney, Star, & Williams, 1949).

Stouffer argued that the paradoxical situation arose because each soldier judged how well he was doing relative to other people in his unit; thus, soldiers who didn't advance very fast in units with rapid promotion felt deprived, while soldiers who didn't advance in units with slower overall promotion rates felt relatively less deprived. These results called attention to the fact that whether someone feels deprived or not doesn't depend so much on how well he is doing absolutely (or in the broadest possible perspective) as it does on how well he is doing relative to the group he compares himself with, his **reference group.** This general notion goes under the rubric of ***relative deprivation theory.*** Relative deprivation theory helps us understand the simple fact that American workers are among the best paid in the world, yet some of them feel deprived—unfairly paid. This is, no doubt, because their reference group isn't all of the other workers in the world, but rather their neighbors and other people like themselves in background, experience, and education who they may see as better paid.

Relative deprivation theory has been used by sociologists, historians, and political scientists to explain a wide variety of phenomena including, for example, revolutions of rising expectations—the notion that revolutions often do *not* occur when conditions are at their worst, but rather when circumstances have begun to improve. It is when people begin to see improvement, especially in their neighbor's lot, that they find their current state unacceptable and are moved to rebellion (Davies, 1962).

Social psychologists too have contributed to the development of relative deprivation theory by attempting to articulate in greater detail just when people feel resentment about their failure to possess something. Faye Crosby has argued, for example, that people feel such resentment when they fail to have something they want and (1) they see that similar other people have it, (2) they feel entitled to possess it, (3) they think that it is feasible to possess it, and (4) they do not blame themselves for their failure to possess it (Crosby, 1976). In one study designed to test these notions, subjects read vignettes about someone who was deprived of something she wanted—an A in a course, for example. The conditions Crosby hypothesized to contribute to a sense of resentment were varied in the scenarios, and the subjects were asked to indicate how much resentment the main character would feel.

Some of the results were consistent with Crosby's theorizing: resentment was higher when the future feasibility of obtaining the desired outcome was high, when the character felt entitled to the outcome, and when a better-off comparison person was present (see Figure 10.2). But other results were not as expected: the subjects attributed *greater* resentment when the person blamed herself for the failure to obtain the outcome than when she didn't. We might have expected the reverse result, that people would feel more re-

FIGURE 10.2

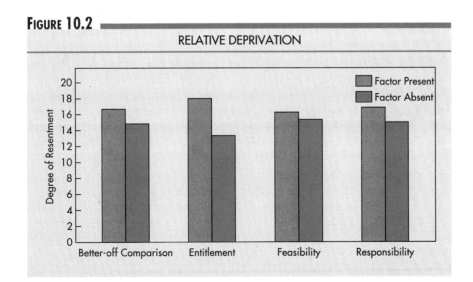

sentment if they *weren't* responsible. Why the results were reversed is unclear (Bernstein & Crosby, 1980). In any event, the study did demonstrate some of the theoretically interesting links between actual deprivation and a person's sense of resentment for her deprivation.

Crosby's account goes some way in filling in the gap in relative deprivation theory and therefore in helping us to apply equity theory; it gives us a more worked-out picture of just when people will perceive their situation as inequitable. But it relies on notions like entitlement; it says that people will feel more resentment if they don't have something they feel entitled to than if they don't have something they don't feel entitled to. But it is a dangerous thing for equity theory to make use of a notion like entitlement; after all, equity theory is supposed to tell us when people act as if the distribution of rewards is unfair—when they believe they have less than they are entitled to. It won't do, therefore, for equity theory to invoke a notion like entitlement, since it is exactly entitlement that equity theory is meant to explain.* Relative deprivation theory, then, is probably best seen not as a way to flesh out equity theory, but as a theory about the kinds of things a complete theory of equity will also have to explain—which people make up a person's reference groups, under what circumstances people see themselves as entitled to things, and so on.

Some recent research in relative deprivation theory has linked the experience of resentment to some recent thinking in cognitive psychology generally, in an attempt to bridge these gaps. Perhaps general facts about human cognition can help to answer some of these questions.

Daniel Kahneman and Amos Tversky have called attention to a simple fact of our experience, especially our experience of misfortune. Imagine that it is important for you to catch a plane that leaves at 9:30, but that because of a traffic jam you arrive at the airport at 9:31, and, amazingly enough, the plane left precisely on time. You almost made it, and you are likely to torment yourself with thoughts about "If only I had left a minute earlier." Now imagine that you arrived not a minute late, but forty-five minutes late. Here you are less likely to torment yourself with "If only I had . . ." Or imagine that in preparing for an exam in a course, you came across some material in your notes that was quite difficult and somewhat tangential to the main emphasis of the course, so you decided to skip it. But the next day, to your chagrin, you find that material figuring prominently on the exam. So you don't do very well. Now compare this with a case in which you missed the class because you were sick when the material was covered, so you never saw any hint of it. Again it is likely in the first case that you would say to yourself, "If only I had . . . ," but in the second, you would not. Kahneman and Tversky have suggested that there are specially negative emotions, greater disappointments, connected to cases where one "almost" achieves something. Why do these thoughts arise in one case but not another?

In the case of the missed plane, there is a clear sense in which you almost caught it. But what about the material you didn't study? We might want to say you "almost" studied it, but in what sense did you almost study it? Kahneman and Tversky argue that what drives the sense of "almost" in both

▲ *Matt Bahr kicking the winning field goal for the New York Giants at the Super Bowl in January 1991. Later in the game, Scott Norwood had a chance to kick a field goal for the Buffalo Bills, which would have caused Buffalo to win, but he missed. Did the Buffalo players and their fans feel especially bad about losing because they came so close to winning?*

*In fairness to Crosby, she did not see herself as attempting to fill in gaps in equity theory by developing relative deprivation theory. I have placed her work in that context.

cases is that it is *easy to imagine* having caught the plane and *easy to imagine* having made the opposite decision when you saw the difficult material (Kahneman & Tversky, 1982; Kahneman & Varey, 1990; Macrae, 1992). Their claim is that we use how much work we have to do to imagine something as a measure of how close reality came to the state we are imagining. (Kahneman and Tversky have dubbed this idea the **simulation heuristic.**) It isn't clear just what "easier to imagine" means here. Is it really easier to imagine leaving one minute earlier than forty-five minutes earlier? But in any event, the phenomenon of increased disappointment when you almost achieve something you desire—however the "almost" should be taken—seems real enough and bears on the notion of relative deprivation.

In one experiment, some subjects were told that there was a chance of earning a bonus for participating in an experiment. After the first round of the experiment, they were led to believe that based on their performance so far, they were unlikely to earn the bonus. But half of the subjects were told about an alternative procedure that was used for other subjects. They were also told that given their performance on the first round, had they been in the other group, they *would have* received the bonus. Other subjects were not told of the alternative procedure. The results indicated greater discontent among the subjects who were told about the more lenient alternative procedure (see Figure 10.3; Folger, Rosenfield, Rheaume, & Martin, 1983; Cropanzano & Folger, 1989). They no doubt said to themselves, "If only I had been assigned to the other condition . . . ," and that led to their greater discontent with their lot. (The effect does not occur, as we might expect, if a justification is offered for the use of the procedure that caused them to lose the bonus; see Folger, Rosenfield, & Robinson, 1983; Folger & Martin, 1986.) So the "relative" in relative deprivation must also take into account other ways the world "almost" turned out but didn't. Apparently we feel deprived if other people like ourselves do better, and if, in some sense, we ourselves almost did better.

This line of work on the cognitive underpinnings of relative deprivation theory may shed some light on the questions that remain for equity theory. It may help us understand just when people will feel that they have been treated inequitably; perhaps our sense of inequity is tied not only to the inputs we contributed and the outcomes we received, but also to the outcomes we *might* have received under a different allocation rule. And perhaps this *might-have-received* notion can be rooted in the way our minds work. But I strongly doubt that such work linking equity and relative deprivation to cognitive processing will fill in all of the gaps in the equity picture. There remains the difficult problem of specifying in each concrete circumstance just what group is the person's reference group, and just what way the world might have turned out. Indeed, there is reason to believe that people simultaneously compare their outcomes against several different standards (Rice, Phillips, & McFarlin, 1990).

THE PROBLEM OF NEED

A strict interpretation of equity theory pays no attention to the outcomes that a person needs. As I introduced it, equity theory has to do with balancing outcomes with inputs; there is no place in such a formula for the notion of individual need. But clearly we do see needs as mattering in some cases.

Imagine a nurse in a hospital with two of his patients. One is very sick,

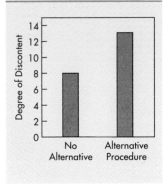

FIGURE 10.3

RELATIVE DEPRIVATION AND ALMOST DOING BETTER

▲ *The degree of discontent among subjects who expected not to receive a reward varied based on whether they had been informed of another procedure (not in force) under which they would have received the reward. (Data from Folger, Rosenfield, Rheaume, & Martin, 1983)*

much in need of attention or she will die; the other isn't sick at all and doesn't need much attention. Suppose the second person claimed, "I am paying the same room fee that she is, so I should get just as much attention as she does. You're tending to her respirator while my toe itches, and that isn't fair!" Surely we would see such a person as crazy. Attention from the medical staff in a hospital must be based, at least in part, on the amount of attention that each person needs. And there is also experimental evidence that people do pay attention to individual need in a task in which subjects are to allocate rewards to a group (Elliott & Meeker, 1986). Indeed, recent evidence suggests that subjects can be quite exquisite in distinguishing between what a person needs and what she *thinks* she needs. And in the same studies, people have been shown to take taste into account too; subjects are willing to give a person who appreciates something more of it than they will give to someone who doesn't (Bar-Hillel & Yaari, 1993).

But we don't always take account of need or taste in deciding what is fair. Some companies during the 1950s had a policy of firing women if they got married. The logic was that married women needed their jobs less than unmarried women did. And one justification that was given to pay women less than men *for the same job* was that women needed the money less than men did! Surely today we believe that people should be paid the same if they do the same job. So it seems that we sometimes take need into account in allocating resources, and we sometimes don't. Equity theory cannot be a complete theory of allocation without saying just when we take need into account and just when we don't.

DIFFERENTIAL MOBILITY

There is an emerging social problem tangled up with our sense of equity—the problem of **differential mobility.** To see the problem, suppose you had two employees who performed equally well. But imagine that for one reason or another, one of them could easily relocate to another city if the opportunity arose, while the other would find this difficult. (One might be married to a professional with a practice in your area; practices are very hard to move.) Now imagine that the mobile employee comes to you and reports that he got a job offer in another city at a higher rate of pay; will you match the offer? Would you do the same for the immobile employee who you know could not take the other offer? Would it be fair to pay the mobile person more? In a survey of two hundred employees in one locale, Caryl Rusbult found that employees do perceive mobility as affecting pay—more mobile people get paid more—and that this effect on pay is unfair (Rusbult, Campbell, & Price, 1990; also Rusbult, Insko, Lin, & Smith, 1990). But, of course, it might not look that unfair to mobile employees. And even if it does, it is hard to imagine someone turning down a better offer elsewhere because it would be unfair to co-workers at her former job!

Dual-career couples certainly face this problem more than single-earner families. It will be interesting to see how our culture works this problem out.

Equity Theory and Culture

Equity theory began with the assumption that people are motivated to produce equity, to equalize outcomes relative to inputs. Evidence was then gathered to show that people will act, at some cost to themselves, so as to produce equity. But the theory has run into a collection of problems. First there is the problem of abilities—are they inputs or aren't they? Then there is the problem of relative deprivation—what group do I compare myself with in determining whether my outcomes are in line? Then we saw the problem of needs—do they count? Finally, there is the problem of whether it is fair for organizations to take advantage of the fact that some employees have more job mobility than others. What do these problems suggest?

One suggestion is that people do indeed have a general and abstract notion of equity; they do believe that rewards should reflect inputs, but that this notion can be interpreted in a variety of different ways. So what do people do in specific cases? Perhaps unaided, there isn't much people can do; perhaps all they can do is recognize the legitimacy of various points of view. But people don't come to *most* of the circumstances they face in everyday life unaided; they come armed with their culture's conceptions about what to do in specific circumstances to help them out. We all know that the nurse in our example ought to allocate his effort based on his patients' needs. We all know that although we might take how hard a student tried into account in assigning a grade, we would never downgrade a student's perfect performance just because she found the material easy. And we all know that regardless of how equity works out in the larger world, we shouldn't give twin children different allowances.

Of course, these common cultural understandings may fail us when we come up against novel circumstances. But even here culture can help in the form of common law. American culture's common law—that body of our laws that hasn't been passed by legislatures as statutes, but rather is the codification of traditions—dictates what equity is in many cases that the layman doesn't understand. To be sure, some arcane legal principles may seem arbitrary, but even arbitrary principles may be better than no principles as a basis to predict the outcomes of our actions.

PROCEDURAL JUSTICE

We have seen some of the factors that affect people's judgments about whether a division of rewards is fair. Questions of fairness can also be addressed to the procedure by which a decision is reached. John Thibaut and his associates launched an extensive program of research designed to explore the basis of people's judgments about the fairness of procedures designed to settle disputes.

The jumping-off point for Thibaut's exploration is the distinction between the two different legal systems in use in the Western world. One system, used in the United States and Great Britain, is **adversarial,** meaning that the two sides to a dispute (criminal or civil) have the primary responsibility for finding and presenting evidence in support of their cases; the judge plays a more passive role, insuring that the two sides play by the legal rules. The judge (or jury) plays the central role in deciding the case, but the actual process of the trial—the decision as to what evidence to present and in what order to present it—is largely determined by the two sides.

But in much of Western Europe, legal proceedings do not follow an adversarial model; rather, it is the judge (with the assistance of investigators) who is primarily responsible for investigating the matter under dispute and presenting the evidence. This form of procedure is often called **inquisitorial.** Thibaut and his group concerned themselves first with the question of which procedure strikes people as fair.

In one study, American college students were solicited for a business simulation. They were to play the role of the president of one of two competing advertising companies. Each company also had a "creative director" (played by a confederate) who was to dream up new names for products. The two advertising companies were to compete for a $5 prize, determined by who made up the most names. Partway into the simulation, the presidents were told that the company they were competing against had charged them with plagiarizing names, and a "trial" would be held, with the winner of the trial taking the $5 prize.

Some of the presidents were led to believe that their creative directors were certainly innocent; some were led to believe that their directors were certainly guilty; and others were led to believe that their directors *might* have engaged in espionage. So the manipulation of the subjects' beliefs about guilt or innocence constituted one variable in the mock trials.

The way the trial was conducted constituted another variable. In some cases, the subjects were told that each side could select an attorney to represent it to the mock court; the roles of attorneys were played by law school students. In other cases, the subjects were told that there would be a single investigator appointed by the court to present evidence on both sides. A mock judge (also played by a law student) delivered either a guilty or an innocent verdict. Finally, other subjects served as uninvolved observers of the mock trial.

The point of these extensive theatrics was to determine how fair the involved (guilty, innocent, or unsure) subjects and observers would rate the trial under the adversarial and inquisitorial rules with guilty and innocent verdicts. The results were that both the participating and observing subjects rated the proceedings as more fair and satisfying under the adversarial than under the inquisitorial rules; they also saw the adversarial proceedings as preserving a greater degree of dignity for all of the participants. This preference was found among all groups of subjects—those who thought their creative directors were guilty, those who thought they weren't guilty, and those who weren't sure—and it was true regardless of whether the subjects were *judged* guilty or innocent. As you might suspect, however, subjects were also more satisfied with an innocent rather than guilty verdict, especially if they knew they were innocent (see Figure 10.4; Walker, LaTour, Lind, & Thibaut, 1974; Lind, Kurtz, Musante, Walker, & Thibaut, 1980).

The preference for adversarial procedures is not too surprising; the subjects, after all, were American college students used to adversarial proceedings. Somewhat more surprising is a finding from another, similar study in which subjects from the United States, Britain, France, and Germany rated adversarial proceedings as more fair than inquisitorial ones; this finding held for the subjects from France and Germany who were *not* used to such procedures as well as for the subjects from the United States and Britain who were (Lind, Erickson, Friedland, & Dickenberger, 1978). The preference for

In an adversarial legal system, each side presents the case from one point of view; neither side is expected to be impartial.

In an inquisitorial legal system, neither side presents a case; the case is presented by the judge, who is expected to be impartial.

FIGURE 10.4

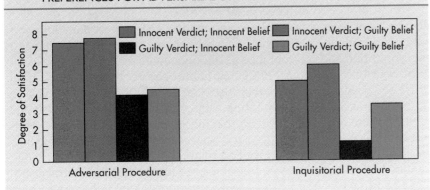

PREFERENCES FOR ADVERSARIAL OR INQUISITORIAL PROCEDURES

◀ *Subjects' satisfaction with adversarial and inquisitorial procedures depended on whether they were found guilty or innocent, and whether they believed themselves to be guilty or innocent. (Data from Walker, La-Tour, Lind, & Thibaut, 1974)*

adversarial proceedings does not seem to extend to non-Western, less individualistic subjects; in one study, students from the United States and ethnically Chinese students from Hong Kong judged an adversarial and nonadversarial technique to resolve a dispute. As in previous studies, the American subjects preferred the adversarial procedure. Chinese students, however, showed no consistent preference (Leung & Lind, 1986).*

Further research using questionnaires distributed to undergraduates as well as passengers waiting for their flights to depart (people who have little to do but fill out questionnaires) suggests that the unpopularity of inquisitorial procedures can be relieved, however, if both sides are allowed at least to testify on their own behalf (as is often true in European proceedings) and if there is the right of appeal from an unfavorable verdict (Sheppard, 1985). But being able to speak one's mind isn't the *only* determinant of whether a procedure is judged as fair. In on study, a random sample of residents of Chicago were interviewed about their experiences with legal authorities—the police, for example. The interviews revealed that there were three key determinants of whether the citizens saw their interactions with the police as procedurally fair. They were prepared to see the proceedings as fair if and only if they saw the person they dealt with as neutral, trustworthy, and treating them with respect. To the degree that they saw the public officials as biased, corrupt, or out to demean them, they did not see the procedures as fair (Tyler, 1989).

The pattern of results we have reviewed suggests that people can see a procedure as fair even when they do not believe the outcome was correct so long as they have some measure of control over the *process* by which the decision is reached. In particular, they will treat a procedure as fair if they have a reasonable chance of getting their side of the story before the person (or persons, in the case of a jury) who will make the decision, and if they see the decision maker as unbiased. Now we can return to the finding, mentioned above, that Chinese students did *not* prefer an adversarial procedure. This may have been because Chinese students didn't care as much as American students about having control over the process of presenting their case, or it

People see procedures as fair when they believe

• they had a chance to get their side of the story told;

• the decision maker was impartial.

They see such procedures as fair even when the outcome isn't.

*See Chapter 8 for more on the distinction between individualist and collectivist cultures.

may have been for another reason, a reason that highlights the drawbacks of an adversarial procedure.

For all of its virtues, adversarial procedures are divisive—by their very nature. They inevitably involve confrontation and competition. American culture tolerates, even encourages competition and confrontation; it tends to see competition and confrontation as the engines of progress—economic, political, scientific, and so on. But Chinese culture stresses the good of the group above the good of the individual; it stresses harmony and group solidarity (Leung & Lind, 1986; see also Leung, Bond, Carment, Krishnan, & Liebrand, 1990).* These are just the values that adversarial procedures erode. Thus, just as we saw that culture plays a crucial role with regard to judgments of substantive equity, so too do we find that culture, and the different values various cultures stress, plays a crucial role in judgments of procedural justice. (See Chapter 8 for a more extensive discussion of culture and morality.)

Procedural Justice and Organizational Goals

In discussing distributive justice, we saw that people asked to promote positive intragroup relations favor equality over equity. But considerations of procedural justice matter to intragroup relations too. Indeed in one survey of managers of both for-profit and nonprofit organizations, the respondents claimed that they were more concerned with procedural fairness than substantive fairness in order to promote a positive atmosphere in their organizations (Tyler & Griffin, 1991; see also Brockner, DeWitt, Grover, & Reed, 1990). Managers who were particularly concerned with positive interpersonal relations were also concerned with letting their employees have a sense that they had control over the decision-making process (if not the outcome). They also placed stress on their own competence and on being polite toward, and showing respect for, the rights of employees. Managers who were less concerned with interpersonal relations (and more concerned with output) were also concerned with procedural fairness, but they tended to see that as having less to do with ceding control and being respectful and more to do with being (and appearing to be) neutral in the sense of unbiased. There is good reason then for managers to be concerned about appearing to be fair, since there is evidence that an employee's sense that the organization she works for uses fair procedures has a substantial effect on her attitudes toward and performance in the organization (Konovsky & Cropanzano, 1991).

BELIEF IN A JUST WORLD

We began this section by looking at research that shows that people are motivated to produce equitable outcomes. We close this section with a discussion of some research that points to what happens when people's desire to live in a just world gets out of hand.

---

*It is easy to let these ideas become caricatures. American culture certainly doesn't *always* encourage confrontation and competition. There are certainly cases where people are expected to put the group's interest ahead of individuals' interests. But this shouldn't obscure the point that there are important differences in the degree to which cultures allow competition and confrontation.

Melvin Lerner and Carolyn Simmons conducted an experiment in which undergraduate women came to a laboratory to take part in a study that they thought was about the perception of emotional cues. When they arrived, they met an experimental accomplice posing as another subject. This other subject was supposedly there to be in a study on human learning. Before the study began, the subjects rated themselves on a variety of scales relating to their own social attractiveness.

The subjects were then ushered into a room with a one-way mirror looking into a room with electrodes, shock generators, and so on. They were told that military officers and businessmen were interested in being able to tell just how much emotional stress their subordinates were suffering, but that very little was known about cues of emotional distress. To gather data about this, the subjects were asked to observe the "other subject" they had seen earlier as she took part in the "learning experiment." They were told, "Your job will be to observe closely the emotional state of the worker and to watch for cues which indicate her state of arousal" (Lerner & Simmons, 1966).

The subjects then saw a ten-minute videotape of the other subject suffering as she received shock for giving wrong answers. After seeing the tape, some of the subjects were told that the experiment was half over; they would see another ten minutes of the learning experiment. Other subjects were told that they could express their opinions as to whether the other subject would continue to be punished for incorrect responses, rewarded for correct responses, or be in a control condition where neither would happen. All but one of these subjects voted for her now to be rewarded; that subject voted for the control condition. Thus, the subjects responded to her suffering with sympathy. The subjects were then asked to rate her on two sets of scales: the same scales they had previously rated themselves on and scales measuring their impressions of how desirable she was as a potential friend.

The subjects who thought that the victim would continue to be shocked rated her as less desirable than they rated themselves at the beginning of the experiment, and rated her as less desirable than did the subjects who thought she was now going to be rewarded. Seeing the victim suffer and knowing that she would continue to suffer led the subjects to devalue and derogate her rather than (or at least in addition to) feeling sympathy for her. But why should seeing someone suffer lead subjects to derogate her?

The investigators interpreted the results by arguing that we would all like to believe that the world is just, that by and large people get what they deserve. We want to believe this because to realize that it isn't true makes much of our behavior pointless. What point is there, for example, in studying for exams if they aren't fair? The investigators argued that the sight of someone suffering *who hasn't done anything to deserve it* calls this belief in a just world into question. To preserve their belief in a just world, the subjects decided that although the victim hadn't done anything to deserve that particular suffering, she was a generally undesirable person who, in that sense, deserved to suffer. When subjects could, on the other hand, give her some compen-

Lt. Col. Ed Seiler amid a pile of victims at Landsberg Concentration Camp. He is addressing two hundred civilians who were forced to witness this cruelty. How much would one have to blame the victims to make this world seem just?

sation for her suffering (by assigning her to the reward condition), they had no such need to derogate her, since some degree of justice was restored. This claim, referred to as the ***just world hypothesis,*** suggests that seeing a victim suffer, in addition to arousing selfless impulses to help her, may also arouse more selfish impulses to preserve our own sense of an orderly, predictable, fair world (Lerner & Simmons, 1966).

There was another result in this experiment, which may point to another source of victim derogation. In some conditions, subjects thought that the experiment was over when they filled out their ratings. In those conditions, the subjects derogated the victim (in comparison with the reward condition), but they did so *less* than the subjects who thought they would see another ten minutes of her suffering. As we learned in Chapter 9, seeing someone else suffer causes distress *in the witness,* and in part the subjects may have been blaming the victim for causing their own distress, especially in the condition where they thought their own distress would continue. This is irrational, of course; the victim did *cause* this secondary distress, but she was surely not to blame for it. But people in emotional states often have irrational feelings, so this shouldn't surprise us.

Limitations of the Just World Hypothesis

Since the publication of the Lerner and Simmons article, there have been a variety of criticisms of the just world hypothesis, a variety of attempts to explain the data in other ways or to limit the applicability of the theory. These accounts agree that we sometimes derogate victims; what they disagree about is whether this is because of our believing in a just world. It is best, perhaps, to consider them not so much as alternatives to Lerner's theory as they are suggestions of additional ways we come to derogate victims.

RESPONSIBLITY FOR THE INJUSTICE

One group of researchers has argued that we engage in victim derogation when we feel, rationally or irrationally, that we are responsible for the victim's situation. Thus, the argument goes, it isn't all victims we derogate, it is the ones we feel we have harmed (Cialdini, Kenrick, & Hoering, 1976). The idea is that we derogate victims because if the victims are unworthy in some way, then we need not seem so guilty, even in our own eyes—the victims deserved whatever trouble they got. (By linking victim derogation to responsibility, this school of thought makes victim derogation a kind of cognitive dissonance; see Chapter 16 for more on dissonance theory.)

SHARED FATE

Another approach, advanced by Lerner himself, suggests that we don't derogate victims unless we believe that the same thing that happened to them might happen to us; that is, unless we believe that we have a **shared fate,** as it is called technically, with the victim. (See Lerner & Miller, 1978, but also Chaiken & Darley, 1973, for some contrary data.) This idea is that East Coast residents can feel unalloyed sympathy toward victims of a San Francisco earthquake, since earthquakes are rare on the East Coast. But people living in Los Angeles, who are afraid the same thing might happen to them, are likely to have more complex feelings. On the one hand, they too will feel sympathy. But on the other, the fear that they too might become victims of a quake might lead them to feel, not that the earthquake was the fault of people living in San Francisco, but that *getting caught in the quake* was the victims' own fault! This account is close to the just world account, but it is more of a "just neighborhood" account, since it assumes that people are only concerned about justice when the victimization is close to home.

Perhaps it seems that given the murky state of the literature, it isn't worth paying much attention to the just world hypothesis, but this would be a mistake. There probably is a real phenomenon of victim derogation, and it can have important consequences in the real world. Let us look at one example.

Victim Derogation and Rape

Many commentators have pointed to the sad fact that women who are victims of rape must bear, along with physical and emotional pain at the hands of the rapist, a second burden: the knowledge that other people often see them as in part responsible for their fate. This tendency to heap gratuitous blame on the victim is easily understood as a manifestation of the just world phenomenon. Women certainly don't want to believe that they will be raped, and men don't want to believe that it could happen to women they care about. Perhaps to preserve the belief that it won't happen, all of us would rather believe that women who are raped somehow bring it upon themselves.

This interpretation is supported in one study in which subjects were given a description of a rape in which there was no evidence that the victim was at fault. The subjects were asked, however, to indicate the degree to which they thought the victim was at fault. They were also asked to assign a prison sentence to the rapist. Some subjects were told that the victim was a virgin; others were told that she was married; others, that she was divorced. (Pretest had established that the subjects considered virgins the most "respectable," married women next most respectable, and divorced women least respectable—the study was carried out in the early 1970s.) A prediction that can be

People may derogate victims

- because they want to see the world as fair;

- because they blame the victim for their own distress at hearing about the victimization;

- because they feel responsible themselves for causing the victimization;

- because they want to believe that they won't themselves be victimized.

▲ *Jodie Foster as a rape victim in the film* The Accused. *In the film, as often happens to real rape victims, she is blamed for her own rape.*

drawn from the just world hypothesis is that the more respectable the person is, the more subjects will blame her for the rape. Since justice is served either by finding the person as a whole undesirable or finding that she is responsible for the act, the more respectable on the whole she is, the more responsible for the act she must be. As expected, the subjects assigned less blame to the divorced woman than to the married woman or the virgin. The subjects also, however, sentenced the rapist to the longest sentence when he was described as having raped the virgin. Thus, it was for the crime they found most horrifying that they most blamed the victim (Jones & Aronson, 1973).

WRAP-UP

Equity theory makes two claims. One is that people are motivated to produce equity, even when it doesn't help them—indeed, even when it costs them. And I think there can be no doubt that this is true. To be sure, people often prefer to take things for themselves rather than to produce equity, and they even offer equity concerns as a mask for what is really greed. But these undeniable facts should not lead to excessive cynicism—we are still able to, and often do, care about equity.

The other claim of equity theory is that its formula captures people's sense of what fairness is. This may be so, but a bit of pushing and shoving must be done to make it so; for example, just the right other people must be considered when deciding whether the equity ratio is sustained. Perhaps, then, equity theory isn't so much a substantive theory as it is a framework within which to raise questions and sharpen issues. *That* kind of theory is important in science and in the intellectual world more generally.

People care about procedures. Especially in American culture, in which "rights" seem to be the cornerstone of our civic lives, people care passionately that the proper procedures are followed in reaching decisions. So much of our sense of fairness is bound up in our sense of the right procedure. Would it be rude to ask whether we might be *too* concerned with procedural justice, with our rights to fair treatment?

Finally, the just world hypothesis suggests that our dedication to fairness can lead to some very undesirable results. Our unwillingness to tolerate the perception of unfairness can lead us to insult the already injured by blaming the victim for his unfortunate situation. This is surely a tendency—as understandable as it might be—that we need to resist.

SUMMARY

1. Social psychologists have been concerned with two kinds of justice: substantive and procedural. Substantive justice has to do with whether people get what they deserve. Procedural justice has to do with whether the procedures used to determine who is guilty and who is innocent are fair.

2. Equity theory claims that people are motivated to produce equity conceived of as equal ratios of outputs to inputs. Five problems for equity theory have received research attention. (1) Women prefer equality to equity. (2) People are not consistent in deciding whether ability is a relevant input. (3) Just

what *standard* one should apply in deciding what is fair is not clear. (4) It is not clear how (or how much) to count needs in deciding what is fair. (5) Some employees can easily relocate to another city, while others can't.

3. Westerners seem to see *adversarial* procedures such as our legal system as fair. But non-Western students do not prefer such systems, presumably because adversarial systems are inherently divisive.

4. Melvin Lerner has argued that people find it so important to believe that they live in a just world that when they are confronted by a case of apparently flagrant injustice, they distort matters so as to see the victim as deserving her fate. There is evidence that rape victims, for example, are victimized in this way.

CHAPTER 11

Strategic Interaction

In this chapter, we will focus on situations in which people have conflicting interests. Consider, as an example, the seller and buyer of a house. The seller wants to make as much as she can from the sale; the buyer wants to pay as little as possible. And these goals are in conflict. The more the seller makes, the more the buyer loses. In the typical case, the buyer and seller will negotiate over the final price. The seller will list the house at some price, and the buyer will make a counteroffer, an opening bid. The buyer's aim in making his bid, of course, is to make the lowest offer the seller will accept. Or if, as is typical, the seller will not accept that first offer, then the buyer's aim is to get the seller to lower her asking price in response to the offer. Their negotiation is an example of a *strategic interaction,* an interaction in which each party aims to influence the other to behave in a way that is favorable to his or her own interest.

Strategic interactions are marked by two features: (1) there is a conflict of interest between two or more people, and (2) each person's actions are designed so as to affect the future behavior of the other. Situations of this general sort are common. The most obvious examples are cases of economic competition, like that between buyer and seller, but arms negotiators too operate in such circumstances, as do couples engaged in flirtation. So research in this area is of rather general interest.

Before we begin our review of the research, however, let us look at the methods that are typically used. Much of the research involves what are often called *experimental games,* or *simulations.* An experimental game involves creating a conflict of interest and the possibility of mutual influence, and then assigning subjects the task of making as much as possible for themselves under the rules of the game. Typically, subjects play these games for "points" or a small amount of money—a few dollars, perhaps. In simulations, subjects are asked to pretend that they are bargaining for larger sums, but there is no real money involved. The investigators are interested in what people do when there is something of real significance involved—for example, in what arms negotiators or labor negotiators do. The question is: Can the results from simulations and games be generalized to cases of more interest?

This is a controversial matter. Most social psychologists would argue that one cannot generalize *directly* from behavior in these games to cases where more is involved. But many investigators believe that experiments of this sort are valuable nonetheless. They would argue that precisely by removing the influence of really large sums, one can see the principles of behavior that are inherent to strategic interaction, principles that follow from the two features of strategic interaction already mentioned: competition and the possibility of future influence. They would argue that those principles can be generalized to more important cases. Consider an analogy.

Physicists attempting to understand the behavior of real mechanical systems often analyze them by first considering an idealized version of such a system. They begin by analyzing the behavior of a system of pulleys, levers, and weights while *ignoring the effect of friction.* This is not because physicists haven't heard about or don't believe in friction. Rather, the frictionless case is easier to analyze and understand than one with friction. They know that to understand the system fully, friction will have to be added back in later. But they believe that even without friction, something important can be understood—the effects of gravity, say.

Similarly, proponents of gaming research argue that important principles of strategic interaction can be grasped without considering the effect that adding real sums of money, or other desirable goals, would have. So some social psychologists would argue that the gaming research to be reported here is as useful to social psychology as frictionless pulleys are to physics. But others would argue that this analogy really doesn't hold. They would argue that by removing the friction—subjects' knowledge that something important hangs on their decisions—gaming research removes exactly the most important aspect of competitive situations as they unfold in the real world.

There seems to be merit on both sides of the issue. On the one hand, it does seem right that people's behavior depends in a strong way on what is at stake. People often just aren't very engaged by trivial sums; on the other hand, I have seen friends of mine become quite enraged over a Monopoly game played for nothing more than play money. In the long run, the issue can only be resolved by comparing what goes on in high pressure circumstances with what happens in the laboratory. For now, let us see what has been discovered about strategic interaction in the laboratory.

▲ *(A) and (B) From* In the Line of Fire, *in which Clint Eastwood and John Malkovich engage in strategic interactions to determine whether the president of the United States lives, or is assassinated.*

BARGAINING

Right now, as it happens, I am buying a house. Buying a house, unlike buying a can of peas, involves direct, purely competitive bargaining between buyer and seller. By purely competitive bargaining, I mean that every dollar I as buyer save is a dollar less that the seller makes. Our economic interests are perfectly and inversely correlated. Home buying and car buying are two situations in our society where many people bargain in this explicit way. But there are other instances. Labor unions have an interest in getting their members the highest possible hourly rate; management has an interest in the lowest rate. Social psychologists have been concerned with just how people bargain in such purely competitive situations.

First a word about fairness or equity is in order. In this chapter, we shall start by ignoring considerations of fairness in bargaining. This isn't because people are unconcerned with being fair, but because (1) it was discussed in some detail in Chapter 10, and (2) even if the seller and I are concerned about fairness in our transactions, it is hard to see how to translate that concern into action. What, after all, is the fair price for a house?

A starting point is: How much have other houses in the neighborhood sold for? But this is only a starting point. Perhaps prices have been rising since the last similar house was sold, so shouldn't the price go up? Or down if prices have been falling? But by how much? Even if we knew the answer to these questions, would this really tell us the fair price? After all, houses are investments. Shouldn't the fair price add to the price at which the seller bought it some fair return on his money over the years he has held it? But suppose I bought it at that price and then had to sell it right away to someone less concerned with fairness. Is it fair that I take a loss if I couldn't sell it for as much, or make a huge profit if I sold it for much more? Perhaps ours would be a better society if we worried about all of this, but this isn't what we do. Rather, we act as if it were the seller's responsibility to be sure he doesn't sell it for less than is fair, and my responsibility to be sure I don't buy it for more than is fair by whatever standards we think best. What typically *doesn't* happen is that we come together to reason about what the fair price is.

But this doesn't mean that even in this transaction fairness is irrelevant. We are both obliged to bargain in good faith. I am obliged not to waste the seller's time by making an offer I have no intention of following through on, and he has an ethical obligation not to waste my time if he doesn't really intend to sell. He is also obliged not to conceal defects of the house he knows to be there, and indeed, if he does, he is guilty of fraud. So even in this exchange, morality matters, but there is still one aspect of the situation, the final price, that is handled by bargaining rather than by trying to reach a consensus about the fair price.

The typical house buyer and the typical house seller are strangers to each other. Purely competitive bargaining is most likely to take place between strangers. If I were buying a house from my mother, I would be obliged to consider a whole range of things I would not consider in buying from a stranger. With my mother, fairness would play a stronger role, as would our relative financial conditions, and so on. Indeed, it seems to be true that outside of games and sports, explicit, unadulterated competition is confined to strangers.

Research on bargaining started, wisely, with the simplest possible bargaining situation; as the research developed, complexity was added. We too shall start simple. Here's what simple means.

Imagine that the bargaining is between two parties only: each seller has only one potential buyer to sell to, and each buyer has only one potential seller to buy from. The buyer and seller have dual monopolies, or **duopolies.** Further, imagine that there is only one issue being bargained over: price.

"OK, WE'RE BOTH WEARING OUR MIRROR SUNGLASSES. NO ONE HAS THE UPPER HAND. NOW, LET'S NEGOTIATE."

Later we shall look at cases in which there are several issues in the same deal, as is usually true with labor negotiations. Imagine now that each party is bargaining for herself rather than as a representative of a group; we shall later see what being a representative does to bargaining. And finally, imagine that there are no third parties; further on in the chapter, we shall look at what happens when mediators and arbitrators are added.

Duopoly Bargaining

So here you are out to buy a house. Let us see how we can characterize the situation, psychologically, for you and the seller. First, what do you know? As the buyer, you know what the seller listed the house for; this is, as it were, the seller's *initial offer* to you. You also probably have some idea of a limit as to how much you are willing to spend. This number goes by a variety of names: *resistance point* and *limit* are two of the common ones. You can assume that the seller has a limit lower than which he will not go, but you do *not* know *what* it is. Now, if his limit is higher than yours, that is, if the lowest price he will sell at is higher than the highest price you will buy at, there cannot be a deal between you. But if his limit is lower than yours, there can be a deal, and the deal will happen at some point in the interval between his limit and yours (see Figure 11.1). The task for you is to find the bottom of that range, and for him to find the top of that range. So now we have set the stage for the action. What do you do?

Your immediate, strategic problem is to make an offer in response to his asking price. What should that offer be? You want to make it as low as possible, so why not try $1? But this would be ridiculous. Obviously he would come back with his asking price. You want to make an offer instead that will induce him to make a counteroffer that is a concession from his asking price.

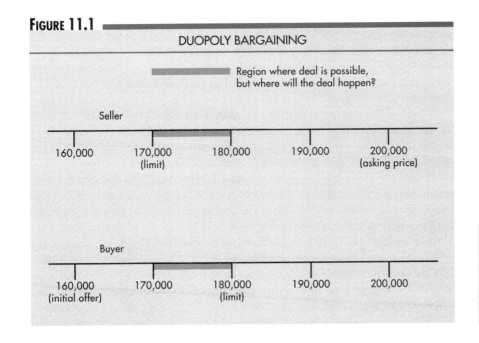

FIGURE 11.1

DUOPOLY BARGAINING

Region where deal is possible, but where will the deal happen?

Seller

160,000   170,000   180,000   190,000   200,000
             (limit)   (asking price)

Buyer

160,000   170,000   180,000   190,000   200,000
(initial offer)   (limit)

◀ *One example of duopoly bargaining is selling and buying a house. In a duopoly, there will only be a deal if the two participants' range of acceptable prices overlap.*

And your offer should be well below your limit, an offer that gives you room to respond to any concession he makes with a concession of your own. So let us assume that you make an offer $20,000 below your limit, and he responds by making a concession, by shaving $10,000 from his asking price. Now what should you do? Should you match his concession by going up $10,000 in an effort to encourage even more concessions from him, should you hold firm at your last offer, or should you perhaps make a concession of $5,000, half of the concession he made, to convince him that you are close to your limit?

First note that there is no best, rational answer independent of the effect your counteroffer will have on him. So your counteroffer should be based on some assumption about how your bargaining partner will respond to your offer. What assumption should you make to minimize your cost?

LEVEL OF ASPIRATION

The first empirical evidence came from some experiments by Sidney Siegel and Lawrence Fouraker. Their experiments involved pairs of subjects (students in an economics course). Half were asked to imagine themselves buyers; half were to imagine themselves sellers (of some product). Their task was to bargain over the price they would buy (or sell) the product at, and the quantity of the product they would buy (or sell). They were given tables showing them their profits for various levels of price and quantity. As you might expect, as the price went up, the profit for the seller increased, and as the price went down, the profit for the buyer increased. (These profits, by the way, were real, amounting to a few dollars, which the subjects could take home with them.)

The results of some preliminary experiments suggested to the investigators that how much profit someone made bargaining depended on her **level of aspiration (LOA).** A level of aspiration is the profit someone thinks is just adequate. If she makes less than her LOA, she will feel that she has failed; if she makes more, she will feel that she has succeeded. A seller's level of aspiration, then, is neither her opening offer nor her limit. Her opening offer exceeds her level of aspiration—she doesn't really expect to get that, and she won't feel bad if she doesn't. It is not her limit either; if she only gets her limit, she will feel like a failure. Siegel and Fouraker went on to propose that the bargainer with the higher level of aspiration for profits would be the one who made the greatest profit.

To show that higher levels of aspiration were associated with higher profits, the experimenters told subjects that after their bargaining session, they would have a chance to double their profits, but in order to participate in the second phase, they had to exceed a certain profit on the first phase. Some subjects were given a low cutoff, others a higher one. This cutoff point was assumed to affect the subjects' level of aspiration, since below that they could not enter the second phase and no doubt would feel like failures. In some bargaining sessions, both buyer and seller had low LOAs; in others, they were both given high LOAs; in half of the sessions, one had a high LOA, while the other had a low LOA. The results showed that the bargainer with the higher level of aspiration made more money. Now what does this have to do with deciding what counteroffer to make to the seller's opening offer when you are trying to buy a house?

Siegel and Fouraker argued, based on their data, that the opening offer

> Making concessions in the face of other people's demands raises their level of aspiration, the minimum outcome they will find acceptable.

you make back to your partner and any concessions you make to her concessions will affect her level of aspiration. In particular, they argued that making a high initial offer and reciprocating her concessions would have the effect of increasing her level of aspiration. And from your point of view, that is a bad idea, because as her level of aspirations increases, her bargaining will get tougher, and her profit will rise (Siegel & Fouraker, 1960). So Siegel and Fouraker recommend a tough bargaining strategy. If you are buying, start low and go up very slowly; if you are selling, start high and go down very slowly. Subsequent research has found a substantial amount of support for the recommendation that a tough bargaining strategy lowers one's opponent's level of aspiration and leads to a more favorable outcome for oneself (Chertkoff & Conley, 1967; Komorita & Brenner, 1968; Yukl, 1974a,b). But there are some limits as to how tough one should be.

RECIPROCITY

Sociologist Alvin Gouldner has called attention to the importance in our culture of reciprocity (Gouldner, 1960). We expect others to reciprocate the good deeds we do for them, and we are hardly surprised if other people are annoyed when we don't reciprocate the good deeds they do for us. The implications of this norm were studied in two investigations by Sam Komorita. In these experiments, subjects were told to act as if they were bargaining over the price to be paid for a used appliance. They thought they were bargaining with another subject, but in fact they were bargaining with the experimenter (negotiations proceeded in the form of notes passed back and forth). In some conditions, the experimenter matched the concessions that the subject made, but in other conditions, the experimenter did not reciprocate concessions. The results indicated that the experimenter did better for himself when he reciprocated subjects' concessions than when he ignored them. And this was especially true when playing against very competitive subjects; they, in particular, seemed to resent the absence of a concession in return for their own

◀ A "potlatch" ceremony, a celebration of reciprocity.

and would make no further concessions (Esser & Komorita, 1975; Komorita & Esser, 1975). What does *not* pay is making bigger concessions than one's opponent made in an effort to reward concession making. That seems to raise the opponent's level of aspiration and lead to a worse outcome for oneself (Bateman, 1980).

As we shall have occasion to note again in a different context, people are induced to cooperate by treating them in a *contingent* way, by more or less matching their cooperative moves. Matching concessions leads to being perceived, as Komorita has characterized it, as "tough but fair," and this seems to be the best policy, especially when coupled with a tough initial offer (Lawler & MacMurray, 1980; McGillicuddy, Pruitt, & Syna, 1984).

DOORS IN THE FACE

The power of reciprocity as a norm has been demonstrated in the "real world" in a clever set of experiments by Robert Cialdini. Cialdini sent teams of confederates out to approach subjects and ask them to do a rather large favor: spend two hours a week for two years being a big brother or big sister to some juveniles in need of such aid. No one agreed to do it; the confederates had, as it were, the doors closed in their faces. But the confederates had a second request. They asked the subjects if they would be willing to spend two hours just once taking the same kids to the zoo. About 50 percent agreed to this small request. But other groups were asked the small request without the first request; only about half as many agreed (see Figure 11.2).

There are many ways to account for this result. Perhaps it is a perceptual contrast; perhaps the small request seems smaller after hearing the first one. Cialdini thought that wasn't the right explanation; he thought that the small request after the large one was seen as a concession by the bargainer, and that it therefore evoked a counterconcession from the subjects. How to tell?

Well, if it is a perceptual effect, then it shouldn't matter whether the same person made both requests. But if it is a matter of a bargaining concession, then we should see the enhanced compliance with the second request *only* if the two requests come from the same person. And that's what happens (Cial-

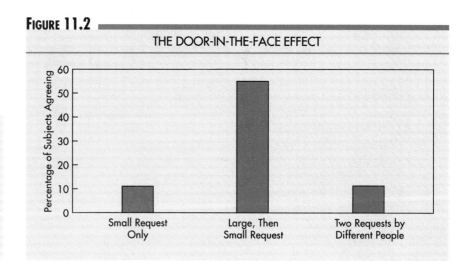

FIGURE 11.2

► *People are more willing to give in to a small request if they have just been asked (and refused) a large request, but only if the two requests come from the same person. (Data from Cialdini, Vincent, Lewis, Catalan, Wheeler, & Darby, 1975)*

THE DOOR-IN-THE-FACE EFFECT

dini, Vincent, Lewis, Catalan, Wheeler, & Darby, 1975). So reciprocity governs bargaining even when the bargaining is implicit (see Dillard et al., 1991, for a discussion of the door-in-the-face phenomenon and its possible explanations).

Cialdini has argued that our sense of fairness in mutual concession making extends even to persuasion. If someone succeeds in persuading you of something, then he will feel an obligation to succumb to you, should you try to persuade him. To show that, Cialdini had subjects in an experiment answer a questionnaire about their attitudes toward issues of current interest. Then he had a subject make arguments against a confederate's position, and in one condition, the confederate moved his position closer to the subject's. In another condition, the confederate did not move. Thus, the subject was led to believe he had persuaded (to some degree) the confederate or that he hadn't moved the confederate at all.

In the next phase of the experiment, the tables were turned, and the confederate got to make arguments against the subject. Cialdini predicted (and found) that confederates who seemed to move toward the subject's position were themselves more persuasive. Cialdini interprets this to mean that subjects "repaid" the confederate for being persuaded by returning the compliment. This compliance, however, was in public only *unless* the confederate actually did make strong arguments for his position (Cialdini, Green, & Rusch, 1992). (But it is important to note that equally cogent arguments from nonyielding confederates were not persuasive.)

INFORMATION ABOUT OPPONENTS' PROFITS

In the experiments discussed so far, the subjects did *not* know their opponents' profits from a settlement at any particular price; to be sure, they knew that as their profits declined, their opponents' profits increased, but they did not know at any particular price what their opponents' profits were relative to their own. This is a reasonable representation of the home buyer's situation, as it is of many negotiations. But suppose you are negotiating with a used car salesman over the price of a car, and you know what he paid for it, and what it cost him to fix it up. How does that affect your negotiations? Information about your opponent's profit can either by symmetrical (both parties know each other's profits) or asymmetrical (one party knows profits for both, the other knows only his own).

Thomas Schelling advanced an ironic hypothesis about what would happen in the asymmetrical information condition. He proposed that knowledge is weakness. He reasoned that people will not try to make more on a transaction than the person they are bargaining against. Thus, if they know what their partner will make, they will feel constrained not to try to get more. The person who *doesn't* know what his partner is making, however, will be free to bargain as hard as he can (Schelling, 1960).

In one condition of their experiments, Siegel and Fouraker created asymmetric information and found some tentative support for Schelling's suggestion. They found that when someone who was informed both about his own profits and his partner's bargained with someone who knew only his own profits, the incompletely informed subject made more money. But subsequent research using a similar method found a different pattern of results.

In this experiment, subjects were told to imagine that they were used car dealers. They had, they were told, a "mongoose" sedan on their lot that had cost them $2,500. Another dealer had a customer for a mongoose, but no car. The subject who had the mongoose was to bargain over price with the one who needed a mongoose. (Actually, all of the subjects played the mongoose seller; the experimenter played the mongoose buyer.) In some cases, the subjects knew that the customer would pay the other dealer $3,500 for the car; in other cases, they did not know what the customer would pay. The experimenter, who played the role of Colonial, the other dealer, made a very low initial offer to some subjects, $2,615, but he made a quite favorable offer to other subjects, $3,050. The question was: How would these initial offers affect the negotiations for subjects who *knew* Colonial's profit and for those who *didn't know* Colonial's profit?

Whether Colonial made a high or low initial offer affected the price at which the transaction was closed when the subjects did not know Colonial's profit. But when they did know Colonial's profit, the initial offer was of no consequence for the price they settled on. When the subjects did not know their opponent's profits, in line with our general discussion, a tough opening bid from their opponent lowered the subjects' level of aspiration, whereas a weak opening bid raised it (see Figure 11.3). But there were no effects of opening bid on subjects who knew their opponent's profit (Liebert, Smith, Hill, & Keiffer, 1968). These subjects knew what to aspire to, independent of the opponent's offer—an even split of the profits.

These results suggest that ignorance is not always weakness, and that toughness in negotiations isn't nearly so effective when your opponent is fully informed about where the fair settlement point is. This does not imply, however, that ignorance is *always* strength. If you are bargaining with someone, and for some reason you have an unreasonably high expectation for your own profit, then knowing the other person's profits will tend to moderate your expectations; in this case, information produces weakness. But if your expectations are too low, then information will enhance your expectations and lead to a better outcome for you (Hamner & Harnett, 1975).

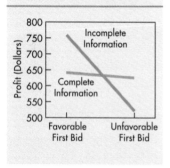

FIGURE 11.3

BARGAINING AND KNOWLEDGE OF OPPONENT'S PROFITS

▲ *Profit from a bargain varied according to the opponent's opening bid and whether the subject knew the other side's profits. When the subject did not know the other side's profits, he tended to use the other subject's opening bid as a guide to his own behavior. But if he knew the other side's profits, his opponent's opening bid mattered much less. (Data from Liebert, Smith, Hill, & Keiffer, 1968)*

Integrative Bargaining

The bargains we have looked at thus far have been ones in which the bargaining is strictly and purely competitive: every dollar a seller gains the buyer loses, and vice versa. But sometimes when people bargain, there are some better and some worse agreements for *both* parties. Under what circumstances will bargainers find jointly beneficial solutions that do well for both parties, and under what circumstances will they not (always assuming that there is such a solution)?

In one experiment, the investigator, Dean Pruitt, had subjects bargain over the price of three commodities: iron, sulfur, and coal. The buyer and seller were given tables showing their profit for each commodity as a function of price. The tables showed that iron was profitable for the buyer to buy, while coal was profitable for the seller to sell. It was of course true that the buyer made the greatest profit by making a deal for *each* commodity at the lowest possible price, and the seller made the greatest profit by selling each commodity at the highest possible price, but their payoff tables indicated that the buyer should care more about the price of iron than coal or sulfur, while the seller should care more about coal. Thus, they could maximize their *joint* profit if the buyer made concessions on coal, while the seller made concessions on iron. A simple compromise in which they opted for moderate levels on each commodity would serve both of them less well than this optimizing solution. But each bargainer saw only her own tables, so at the beginning of the session, they did not know about the asymmetries in the commodities or the possibility of mutually gratifying deals. The question is, then, under what circumstances would they find the optimizing solution?

Pruitt hypothesized that three factors were important. First, to reach an optimizing bargain, called **integrative,** the bargainers had to have the right orientation to their task—a problem-solving orientation. To show this, Pruitt told some subjects to adopt an individualistic approach—not to be concerned with the other fellow's profit and instead to pay attention only to their own profit. He told other subjects to approach the bargaining with a problem-solving posture, that their task was to find the best *overall* solution. Another factor Pruitt thought important was how motivated the bargainers were to work at finding the optimal solution. A mediocre compromise was easy to find; the optimizing one was harder. To motivate some of his subjects, Pruitt told them that they were expected to make $2,300 profit, an amount that *could not* be achieved through a simple compromise. Others were told that they were expected to make only $2,000, which *could* be achieved through an easy compromise. Finally, Pruitt believed that an important determinant of success would be whether the bargainers truthfully revealed their payoffs to each other. If they knew each other's payoff, they would have an easier time finding the mutually profitable solution. To see if this was true, Pruitt told some subjects that they were allowed to lie about their payoffs, that bluffing was okay, and that they could *not* show their profit sheets to each other. Other subjects were told that the experimenter wouldn't let them lie to each other about their profit structures.

The results showed clear support for Pruitt's hypothesis about the subjects' orientation. Having a problem-solving orientation rather than an individu-

An integrative outcome is one that maximizes outcome for both parties involved. It is possible when there is more than one issue involved in a bargain, and when the two parties are primarily concerned with *different* issues. Thus, each party can make concessions on the issue he cares about less than the other party.

alistic one facilitated their finding the integrative solution. Motivation also mattered; pairs of bargainers who were more motivated reached better solutions. Finally, the truth-in-bargaining manipulation produced effects in the expected direction: those forced to be honest did better, but the result was not statistically reliable.

These experimental results give us a clue about the circumstances under which bargainers will find integrative solutions. But *how* do they find these integrative solutions? Pruitt coded the behaviors of the bargainers to see if he could discern how they reached the integrative solutions. He found that the problem-solving orientation (as compared with the individualistic orientation) led to more truthful exchanges, more proposals for a general approach to the bargaining, more statements of concern about the other bargainer, less use of pressure tactics, and the proposal of a greater variety of possible solutions. And he found that the use of these tactics generally, no matter who used them, led to better solutions (Pruitt & Lewis, 1975).

Reflecting on these results leads to some perhaps useful domestic advice. If two people are going to divide up the unpleasant chores that any household requires, there are a variety of ways this might be done. One is by each person's deciding to do half of every chore. This is a simple solution, and it is what we might expect if they bargain contentiously, each concerned with his own advantage. But if they approach their division of labor with a different orientation, one in which they try to optimize their *joint* satisfaction, they are likely to find that their preferences for household chores, fortunately, are not identical; maybe one hates to do dishes more than the other, who in turn hates more to shop for food. Having been honest with themselves and each other, they have now found the basis of a deal, one that leaves each with the task he doesn't mind so much. The key point, however, is that such integrative solutions will not automatically happen. They will happen only if the two parties adopt the right approach and work at it.

Further research has given us additional insights into integrative bargaining. One study suggests that bargainers should have specific bargaining goals and fairly high levels of aspiration for the outcome of the bargaining. Nonspecific goals lead to compromise solutions, and if aspirations on the part of both parties are very low, then the bargainers are not likely to reach optimal solutions (Huber & Neale, 1987). Another study turned up two factors that affect the likelihood of a jointly profitable settlement. Time pressure interferes with finding integrative solutions; it tends to lead to compromises. And if there are many issues to be settled (as there are in labor negotiations, disarmament talks, and negotiations about how the housework gets done), settling issues one at a time is less useful than settling them together. Working on all of the issues at once allows for "logrolling," in which each party concedes on issues more important to the other (Yukl, Malone, Hayslip, & Pamin, 1978; see also Mannix, Thompson, & Bazerman, 1989).

Of particular relevance to domestic bargaining are some findings about the expectation of future cooperative interaction. When bargainers have high aspirations and are very motivated, then the expectation for future cooperative interaction with the same person leads to reduced contentiousness and joint benefit. But when aspirations are low and people aren't very motivated, then the expectation of future interaction leads to particularly poor joint outcomes—people don't work very hard at finding joint solutions (Ben-Yoav &

Integrative solutions are likely to occur if

- bargainers have a problem-solving orientation;

- bargainers are highly motivated to find the optimal solution;

- bargainers truthfully reveal their costs and profits;

- bargainers have specific rather than vague bargaining goals;

- bargainers are *not* under time pressure;

- issues are bundled, rather than taken up one at a time;

- bargainers are *not* face to face.

Pruitt, 1984a). So a cooperative orientation doesn't inevitably lead to high joint benefit; it must be coupled with high expectations.

Sometimes it is best to bargain over the phone. There is evidence that, especially when people aren't in a good mood, face-to-face bargaining leads to the use of contentious tactics, but the imposition of a visual barrier reduces contentiousness and improves joint payoff (Carnevale & Isen, 1986). So having a face-to-face bargaining session while angry at your partner is a poor idea; better to wait until one is less angry to decide who should take out the garbage. Finally, experience matters. Recent research shows that experienced negotiators reach better agreements than naive negotiators (Thompson, 1990).

Oligopoly Bargaining

The experiments we have reviewed so far have all involved bargaining in a duopoly—one seller and one buyer who must make a deal with each other. But our economic system relies on the notion of a free market in which if buyer and seller don't agree, they are free to bargain with other buyers and sellers. Indeed, our antimonopoly statutes are specifically designed to prevent monopolies. What happens when people bargain in the context of a free market?

OPENING STRATEGIES

In one study, subjects took the part of an economy car buyer. They played against four "dealers," all selling the same car. The dealers were assigned a variety of different strategies to use in making offers to the buyers; some dealers used "tough" opening strategies, others used "soft" opening strategies. The buyers were constrained to negotiate with each dealer at least once; then they were free to negotiate with whichever dealer they chose. The results indicated that dealers who used soft opening strategies (made concessions to the buyer that were $20 greater than the buyers' concessions) reached more deals and made more money per customer than did those dealers who used tougher strategies (did not match concessions) (Esser, 1989; Esser, Carillo, Scheel, & Walker, 1990). So although a tough strategy may work best in duopoly bargaining, it doesn't work best when buyers are free to deal with other sellers.

FRAMING EFFECTS

Another study in which lots of buyers and sellers came together and were free to deal with whomever they wished turned up one fairly obvious and one quite subtle condition in which bargainers reached integrative solutions. The expected result was that experienced bargainers did better than novices. The subtle effect had to do with how the bargain was "framed" for the subjects.

Buyers and sellers in this game were negotiating about the sale of a single commodity. But the profit to each was presented as a function of three factors: delivery time, discount terms, and financing terms. Delivery time mattered most to buyers; financing terms meant most to sellers. So there was the possibility of an integrative solution. The framing manipulation had to do with how each of these factors were presented to the subjects. Some subjects (positively framed) received tables showing how their *profits* would vary as a

▲ *Lot and his daughters leaving the corrupt city of Sodom. In the biblical story, Abraham bargained with God to save the people of Sodom and Gomorrah, trying to convince God not to destroy these cities if there existed even one righteous man within their bounds. (Albrecht Dürer,* Lot and His Daughters*)*

function of these three factors. But other subjects (negatively framed) were told that their *expenses* would vary as a function of these factors. The subjects who got the profit information were induced to think of the bargaining as a place where they would surely make money; the question to be settled was just how much. The money they would make varied between $0 and $8,000 (fictitious, of course—the experimenters weren't rich). The subjects who got the expenses information, on the other hand, were induced to think of the bargain as a place where they could only lose money (relative to the maximum $8,000 they could make); and the amount they could lose varied between 0 and 8,000 imaginary dollars.

Consider a labor negotiation between the management of a profitable company and a union. Within some economic limits, there are two ways of thinking about the cost of labor to management. One way is to think that the company will make money no matter where the contract is settled, but the lower the contract, the more profit it will make. So every dollar labor gets is *one less dollar* of profit. The other way is to think that the company could make a certain profit if labor were free, and every dollar management pays to labor is a dollar out of their pockets. These two ways of thinking come, in the economic end, to the same thing, but people might react differently to each. And the subjects in the experiment did respond differently. Positively framed bargaining led to more deals, and more profitable deals, than did negatively framed bargaining (Bazerman, Magliozzi, & Neale, 1985). The investigators noted that this result dovetails nicely with some more general results in cognitive psychology.

Daniel Kahneman and Amos Tversky have found that people treat gains and losses in different ways. Consider the following choice: Would you prefer to receive $3,000 or an 80 percent chance of winning $4,000? Most subjects prefer the sure $3,000; within limits, they prefer a *certain* smaller amount to a chance at a larger amount. But suppose you were convicted of a crime and the judge gave you the following choice. Either pay $3,000 or rely on chance, with the judge putting ten balls numbered 0 to 9 in a hat and pulling one; if

0 or 1 comes out, you will pay nothing, but if a number from 2 to 9 comes out, you will pay $4,000. Most subjects prefer to take the chance, rather than pay the sure thing. The general finding is that people prefer sure things to gambles when they can make money, but they prefer gambles to sure things when they will lose money. They are risk *averse* for profit and risk *seeking* for losses (Kahneman & Tversky, 1979). The finding that bargainers treat profits and losses differently, even though they are economically equivalent, seems to be part of a more general fact about our psychology having to do with how we frame decisions.

Negotiations Among Representatives

Thus far, our cast of characters in the bargaining situation has been small; only bargainers have been involved. But often bargaining involves an expanded cast. It is not uncommon for people to bargain not just for themselves, but for some group they represent—their constituency. Labor unions and management, for example, often employ specialists in negotiations to represent their side. Arms negotiators aren't negotiating for themselves but for the nations they represent. The cast of characters in a negotiation can also be expanded in another direction. Often there are third parties involved in attempting to resolve conflict between the principals. Such third parties can involve themselves in two ways. Mediators may consult with both parties to facilitate an agreement, or arbitrators may, by mutual agreement of the parties, impose a settlement. Judges, family therapists, and ombudsmen are often called upon to intervene in disputes in one or another of these ways.

How does the presence of an expanded cast affect negotiation? First, we will look at negotiations between representatives of constituencies, and then we will examine the influences of third parties.

BARGAINING AS A REPRESENTATIVE OF A CONSTITUENCY

One common finding is that people bargain harder when they bargain for a constituent than they do when they bargain for themselves; though, as you might imagine, this doesn't happen if the negotiator's constituent urges co-

"ANOTHER SETBACK — THE MEDIATORS JUST WENT OUT ON STRIKE."

operation with the other negotiator (Benton & Druckman, 1974; Wall, 1976). Apparently, even if a negotiator were inclined to be conciliatory, loyalty to the group she represents would lead to her being somewhat tougher. This effect is especially so if the negotiator is part of the group she is negotiating for, rather than an outsider brought in just to do the negotiating (Breaugh & Klimoski, 1981).

Negotiators are usually under conflicting social pressures. One source of pressure is the constituents they are negotiating for, but negotiators are also involved in social interaction with the person they are negotiating against. The negotiator's job is to balance these pressures. Research by Dean Pruitt and Peter Carnevale suggests that balancing is particularly difficult while being observed by constituents. Their research showed that subjects who were being observed by constituents bargained in a more hostile way and reached less favorable outcomes than when bargaining in isolation from constituents (Carnevale, Pruitt, & Britton, 1979).

Further research suggests that this intensification of bargaining is likely when the constituents doing the observing are men; being observed by female constituents led negotiations to be less contentious, regardless of the sex of the negotiators. Presumably, this is a result of the negotiating subjects' beliefs about their constituents' expectations as to how they, the negotiators, should behave (Pruitt, Carnevale, Forcey, & Van Slyck, 1986). Consistent with this interpretation, negotiators of both sexes negotiated less cooperatively when they were negotiating *for* female constituents—a kind of chivalry. Negotiators, then, are sensitive to what they think their constituents demand. But their behavior is also shaped by their relationship with their counterpart negotiators. The results of one study suggest that accountability to one's constituents increases aggressive behavior and lowers joint payoff when negotiators do *not* expect future cooperative interactions with their counterpart negotiator, but accountability to constituents reduces contentiousness and increases joint profit when future cooperative interaction is expected (Ben-Yoav & Pruitt, 1984b).

Another factor affecting the aggressiveness with which third parties negotiate is how clearly they understand the position of the party they are negotiating *for*. The more ambiguity there is in the real position of the person they are negotiating for, the more aggressive they are in their own negotiating (Lax & Sebenius, 1991). So if you hire someone to buy a house for you, do *not* make it perfectly clear just how much you are willing to spend, if you want your agent to negotiate hard for you.

THIRD-PARTY INTERVENTION

Third parties can become involved in disputes in a variety of ways, but two are particularly common. One is as a mediator. **Mediators** have no power to impose a settlement on the two parties involved. **Arbitrators,** on the other hand, can impose a settlement. Arbitrators are commonly used to settle labor disputes when the possibility of a strike is too damaging to the public good. In several states, police and firefighters are precluded by law from striking. The law provides, instead, that disputes involving these crucial employees be submitted to a panel for binding arbitration: arbitrators agreeable to both sides determine what a fair settlement is, and their decision is binding on both parties.

One variant on binding arbitration is called ***final offer arbitration.*** In this arrangement, each side submits its final offer to an arbitrator, who may then choose *one or the other*, whichever one strikes her as fairer, but she cannot compromise them. The idea here is to force both sides to be reasonable in their final offer; if one side is unreasonable, it faces the likely prospect that the other side's offer will be accepted. This type of arbitration is used by several jurisdictions to settle municipal labor disputes and by baseball to settle contract disputes. It was also used in a very famous trial.

Socrates was indicted for corrupting the young, for teaching them not to believe in the gods their parents believed in. Socrates was indicted, in short, for un-Athenian activities. The trial was a close one, with a vote, as near as we can tell, of about 280 in favor of conviction and 220 for acquittal. But an

Mediators have no power to impose a solution; they can only recommend settlements.

Arbitrators have the power to impose a settlement.

In final offer arbitration, the arbitrator must impose one or the other of the party's proposed settlements; she cannot impose a compromise.

◄ *Jacques Louis David's* The Death of Socrates.

Athenian trial had two phases. In the first, the jury decided guilt or innocence; in the second, it decided the penalty. Athens used final offer arbitration to decide penalties. Each side submitted a proposed penalty, and the jury was constrained to pick one or the other.

Socrates's accusers proposed death for his penalty. Socrates, always impudent, first proposed that his penalty be free meals for the rest of his life at the *prytaneion,* a place of honor. Plato tried to talk some sense into Socrates, urging that he propose a more respectful penalty, so Socrates suggested one mina—a small sum of money. By first proposing an honor and then a trivial fine, Socrates was deliberately insulting the jury, and in the end he backed off, offering thirty mina, a more respectful fine. But though the jury might have accepted this amount (which Plato and others were willing to pay on his behalf) had he offered it from the start, after his facetious offers, they weren't willing to accept it. A larger number voted for the death penalty than the number that voted to convict him (Stone, 1988). Most negotiators don't have to pay in hemlock for not taking final offer arbitration seriously, but most do have to pay.

NONZERO SUM CONFLICTS

We began our study of competition with purely competitive bargaining—cases in which the interests of the two parties are perfectly and inversely related. Such situations are called ***zero sum,*** or ***constant sum.*** Situations in which cooperation between players can bring rewards to both are called ***nonzero sum,*** because the sum of one person's loss and another's gains need not be zero. In the remainder of this chapter, we shall focus on nonzero sum situations.

Decision Theory

In a zero sum game, the total profit for the two parties is a fixed amount, so the more one wins, the more the other loses.

In a nonzero sum game, the total profit for the two parties is *not* a fixed amount, so some outcomes are better for *both* parties than are other outcomes.

The most prominent, and some would say most interesting, nonzero sum situation has its origins in a scholarly discipline called, variously, game theory, decision theory, or utility theory. I will refer to it as ***decision theory,*** since this seems to be the least misleading name.

Decision theory was inaugurated by a seminal book by John Von Neumann and Oskar Morgenstern first published in 1944. Decision theory is a tool for analyzing situations in which a person faces a nontrivial decision. Nontrivial decisions are those that involve either (1) a conflict between positive and negative aspects of a situation—I would love to eat another piece of that dessert, but a single slice has 1,000 calories, or (2) uncertainty—I know I might make a fortune if I invest in your new company to make small, inexpensive kitchen gadgets, but I might also lose my shirt.

Decision theory is designed to help decision makers decide how to act so as to maximize their long-run satisfaction with their decisions.* As a simple

*Decision theory does *not* tell someone what goals she ought to pursue. This is often a source of confusion because discussions of decision theory are often carried on in the context of wagers having money as their payoff. But this is merely a convenience; decision theory is about how to maximize one's goals no matter what they are. Decision theory does *not*, by the way, demand selfishness. From the point of view of decision theory, altruists are people who have other people's welfare as one of their own goals, and decision theory aims to help them maximize that.

example, decision theory tells us *not* to bet on the daily number in a state lottery if we wish to make money. If there are 1,000 numbers in the daily numbers game, each number will hit, on average, once every 1,000 days. A thousand bets will cost $1,000 (if it is a $1 lottery). But when we hit, the state pays off at only 600 to 1. So on average, we are down $400 for every 1,000 bets. The daily number is a savings account that pays something like −40 percent interest!

THE PRISONER'S DILEMMA SITUATION

For many situations, decision theory is a guide to action. But there is one famous nonzero sum situation in which decision theory cannot help much. The situation was first described by A. W. Tucker, and is called the **prisoner's dilemma.** Here is the anecdote Tucker used to introduce it (see Luce & Raiffa, 1957).

Imagine that a district attorney has called in two suspects because he is sure that they are guilty of robbery, but he can't prove it. So he takes each aside and tells him, "Look, I know you're guilty of armed robbery, but I can't prove it. So here's what I'm going to do. If you confess to armed robbery and implicate your partner, I will convict both of you, but I will get you a short sentence for turning state's evidence, say three months. Your partner will get twenty years. But I warn you, I'm going to make the same offer to your partner, so make up your mind fast. By the way, if you both confess, then I'll recommend ten years for each of you. Now if neither of you confesses, I will get both of you for some charge I can trump up, maybe possession of stolen goods, and you will both get one year." Now he calls the suspect's partner in and says exactly the same thing.

Many terms have been used to characterize the prisoner's dilemma; "fiendish" and "diabolical" are two of them; "ironic" is another.* It is important to appreciate what is so diabolical about it, but it takes a while for this quality to sink it. Let's explore it a little.

Table 11.1 shows the prisoner's dilemma situation in the way it is usually represented, as a four-cell matrix. Each cell represents some combination of

TABLE 11.1

PAYOFF MATRIX FOR THE PRISONERS' DILEMMA

		Prisoner 2	
		Cooperate (Refuse to confess)	Defect (Confess)
Prisoner 1	Cooperate (Refuse to confess)	1 year for prisoner 1 1 year for prisoner 2	20 years for prisoner 1 3 months for prisoner 2
	Defect (Confess)	3 months for prisoner 1 20 years for prisoner 2	10 years for prisoner 1 10 years for prisoner 2

*In fact, one reason, I believe, for the immense popularity of the prisoner's dilemma as a topic of study is just this irony. There is something aesthetic about it.

choices by the two prisoners. "Defect" means to defect from the prisoners' conspiracy; that is, to confess. "Cooperate" means to cooperate with each other (not the D.A.!) by refusing to confess. The numbers in each cell indicate the payoff for the two prisoners if they make that decision. The cell in the top left corner, for example, shows one year for each prisoner if neither confesses, and the one in the bottom right shows that each will get ten years if they both confess. The bottom left cell shows that if prisoner 1 confesses but prisoner 2 doesn't, then prisoner 1 gets three months but prisoner 2 gets twenty years; while the top right entry shows the reversed payoffs if prisoner 2 confesses but prisoner 1 doesn't.

Notice that four numbers characterize the prisoner's dilemma. They are often referred to as R, which is the reward for mutual cooperation (here one year); P, the punishment for mutual defection from their conspiracy (ten years); S, the sucker's payoff—what happens to the person who doesn't defect if the other one does (twenty years); and T, the temptation to defect (three months).*

Each prisoner faces a decision between two choices; one is to cooperate, the other is to defect from their partnership. If they both make the cooperative decision, then they will each get a short sentence—one year. Between them, then, they will do two years if they both cooperate, and that is the smallest sum in any cell of the matrix. So from the point of view of their *collective* good, they should cooperate with each other.

But what about from the point of view of each individual considering only his own good? Prisoner 1 might say to himself, "Obviously, what I should do depends on what my partner Frank is going to do. I don't know what he is going to do, but let's suppose he defects. What would be my best move there?" If you look down column 2 of the table (where prisoner 2 defects), it becomes clear that prisoner 1 should defect, because then he gets ten years rather than twenty years. So the answer for prisoner 1 is: if prisoner 2 defects, then prisoner 1 does best by defecting too. Now prisoner 1 says to himself, "What if Frank cooperates, then what should I do?" To answer this, look down column 1. Here the answer is also clear. If prisoner 2 is going to cooperate, then prisoner 1 does better by *defecting;* he gets only three months rather than one year. So though prisoner 1 doesn't know what prisoner 2 will do, this really doesn't matter. *No matter what prisoner 2 does, prisoner 1 is better off confessing.*

What is the logic of the situation from prisoner 2's point of view? The payoffs are symmetric, so exactly the same answers inevitably occur to prisoner 2. Thus, each prisoner is led by the logic of his situation and a concern for his own hide to confess! This is what's diabolical—individual rationality leads both prisoners to confess, which is a much worse payoff for them collectively (and individually) than they would have gotten had they not confessed.

Imagine you are facing a series of prisoner's dilemma decisions. If you are playing with different people on every trial, the same logic applies to each trial, and you should always defect. But suppose you are going to be playing

*Certain two-by-two matrices represent prisoner's dilemma situations; others don't. What makes a payoff matrix a prisoner's dilemma is that T (being the only one to defect) is the best a person can do, while S (being the only one to cooperate) is the worst, and R (the reward for mutual cooperation) is better than P (the punishment for mutual defection). Other relations among the elements aren't prisoner's dilemmas.

again and again with the same person. Now what should you do? There is a new element added by repeated play, the chance to use your response on this trial to affect your opponent's responses on future trials. Perhaps by cooperating on the first trial, you will be able to induce your partner to cooperate on subsequent trials, and if that happens, then maybe cooperation isn't doomed. Extended play with a single partner seems to allow hope of cooperation. Luce and Raiffa thought that they themselves wouldn't defect on every trial over extended play, and that people in general would come to cooperate over extended play. In the last thirty years, there have been literally hundreds of experiments conducted to answer the question of how subjects actually play the prisoner's dilemma game.

WHAT PEOPLE DO IN A PRISONER'S DILEMMA

In the typical prisoner's dilemma game as played in the laboratory, subjects are shown a payoff matrix, like that in Table 11.1. Rather than years in jail, the payoff is in the form of points the subjects earn on each trial. Usually these points can be traded at the end of the experiment for small sums of money, and often the subjects don't know as they play just what the conversion rate from points to money will be.

On each trial, the subjects are asked to indicate what move they would like to make. After both have picked a move, the experimenter informs them of their opponent's choice, which tells them their payoff. They continue trial after trial with the same partner. Do subjects learn to cooperate?

No, they don't. The typical result for repeated trials up to, say, fifty is that subjects start off with a low level of mutual cooperation, less than 50 percent, and then they become *less* cooperative as play continues. Indeed, by the end of the trials, the typical pair of players find themselves "locked in" to repeated mutual defections, either in retaliation for previous defections or out of fear of future defections (see Minas, Scodel, Marlowe, & Rawson, 1960, for a typical result). If play continues beyond this point, and some heroic subjects have played up to three hundred trials, cooperation does tend to rebound a bit, but it still typically remains in the 20 to 40 percent range (Oskamp & Perlman, 1965). There is, by the way, no consistent pattern of gender differences in degree of cooperation in the prisoner's dilemma (Hartman, 1980).

This low level of cooperation is depressing. For one thing, one can think, as social scientists have, of the arms race between the United States and the former Soviet Union as an instance of a prisoner's dilemma. Mutual cooperation in the form of arms reductions would have rewarded both sides with reduced arms expenditures. But both sides found *unilateral* reductions the worst outcome (one side plays cooperate, the other side plays defect), so both sides until recently competed by spending more money for arms. The threat of economic and political ruin, it seems, was needed to slow down this hideous race. Partly for these reasons, many social psychologists have conducted research attempting to determine whether there might be strategies in repeated play that would induce cooperation from one's opponent.

Pacifism   Perhaps the first cooperation-inducing strategy that occurs to you is a "pacifist" strategy, one of always cooperating, no matter what your partner does. The simple and sad fact about a pacifist strategy is that it invites exploitation (Shure, Meeker, & Hansford, 1965). There are ethical reasons to endorse pacifism; but you shouldn't endorse it in the naive belief that you will not be exploited.

Another strategy, which has received a lot of attention of late, is an extremely simple one called ***Tit for Tat*** (TFT). To play Tit for Tat, you simply do unto the other subject as she has most recently done unto you; that is, if your opponent has cooperated on the previous move, then cooperate on the next one, and if she defected, then defect. Tit for Tat has the obvious appeal of simplicity. It also induces cooperation. In several studies, it has been found that if a subject, thinking he is playing against another subject, plays against an experimenter who plays TFT, the subject will respond with substantial cooperation. The general trend seems to be that a strategy that is *contingently* cooperative elicits more cooperation than one that is relentlessly cooperative, or, for that matter, relentlessly uncooperative (Sermat & Gregovich, 1966; Oskamp, 1971). Reciprocating strategies like Tit for Tat are especially effective at inducing cooperation if you announce that this is just what you are doing (Lindskold, Walters, & Koutsourais, 1983; Lindskold, Han, & Betz, 1986).

Robert Axelrod has done some interesting and illuminating further research on Tit for Tat. Axelrod invited psychologists, economists, game theorists, and so on to submit strategies for a prisoner's dilemma for a computer "tournament." In the tournament, each strategy would play against each other strategy (and against itself) for two hundred moves. Each strategy would be allowed to keep track of its own moves and its opponent's moves, so it had the history of the interactions with its current partner to base current moves on. The question to be answered was which strategy was the "best one" in the sense that it would amass the greatest number of points. (Remember, there is no best strategy absolutely, because there is no best strategy independent of one's opponent's strategy.)

Fourteen entries were submitted. Some were quite complex, building models of their opponents' psychology and so on. The simplest, Tit for Tat, was

▼ *(A) President Richard Nixon and Soviet general secretary Leonid Brezhnev sign the Nuclear Arms Limitation Treaty in May 1972. (B) Secretary of State George Shultz and Soviet foreign minister Eduard Shevardnadze sign documents at the Geneva Summit on arms limitation in November 1985; President Ronald Reagan and Soviet leader Mikhail Gorbachev look on.*

A

B

submitted by Anatol Rapoport. Rapoport's version involved cooperating on the first move, and then doing whatever one's opponent did on the previous move. It also won the tournament. Now this doesn't prove that Tit for Tat is *the* best strategy to play against every possible opponent—there is no single best strategy to play against *every* opponent. But Tit for Tat was the best point getter in this case (Axelrod, 1980a).

Axelrod then called for a second round of the tournament; this time the entrants knew that Tit for Tat had won the previous round, so they were gunning for it. Sixty-two entries were submitted in the second round. The simplest entry, Tit for Tat, won again (Axelrod, 1980b, 1984)!

Axelrod looked at the relatively successful strategies and the relatively unsuccessful ones, and he picked out some patterns that seemed to distinguish them. He presented what he learned in the form of advice for the prisoner's dilemma player. Here it is, just in case you and a partner are arrested for armed robbery.

For one thing, be "nice." By being nice, Axelrod meant *don't be the first to defect*. Tit for Tat is a prototypically nice strategy, since it cooperates on the first move, and defects only if its partner defects.

Another rule is: Don't be envious. Don't worry about how many points your opponent is gaining. Tit for Tat never tries to beat a particular opponent. Indeed, there is a potent irony in Tit for Tat winning the tournaments, since it never won a competition against a single other strategy *head to head*. It *can't* win a competition head to head, because in a prisoner's dilemma game, you can only do better than your opponent on a given trial if you defect while your opponent cooperates. But Tit for Tat will only defect with its opponent cooperating if on some previous trial it cooperated while its opponent defected; thus, the best Tit for Tat can do is come out even.

The third rule is: Reciprocate both cooperation and defection. Pacifist strategies that entirely fail to reciprocate defections get exploited; strategies that don't reciprocate cooperation don't take enough advantage of the opportunities for mutual profit from cooperation. Tit for Tat returns both in kind. So these rules, all followed closely by Tit for Tat, led to high scores in the tournament.

Sam Komorita has suggested a fourth rule on the basis of his own computer simulations. He has pointed out that it is important that the player reciprocate both defection and cooperation immediately rather than with a delay. Delaying punishment or forgiveness robs it of its ability to induce cooperation.

Tit for Tat does have its weaknesses, however. In the computer tournament, there was no problem with mistaken execution of a strategy. But suppose you were playing Tit for Tat, and so was your opponent. Imagine that on the first nine moves you both cooperated, but that on the tenth move you meant to be cooperative, and you thought you were, but you actually and accidentally played "defect" instead—maybe you pressed the wrong button. Or suppose that your opponent misperceived your last move. Then what would happen? Well, on the eleventh move, your opponent would play defect back at you in response to your accidental defect on the tenth move. Since your opponent, however, played cooperate on the tenth move, you would play cooperate on the eleventh move. But on move twelve, you would defect in response to your opponent's defect on move eleven, and so it would go till

Tit for Tat (TFT):

- Cooperate on first move.
- Don't be envious
- Do whatever your opponent did on the last.

FIGURE 11.4

TIT FOR TAT

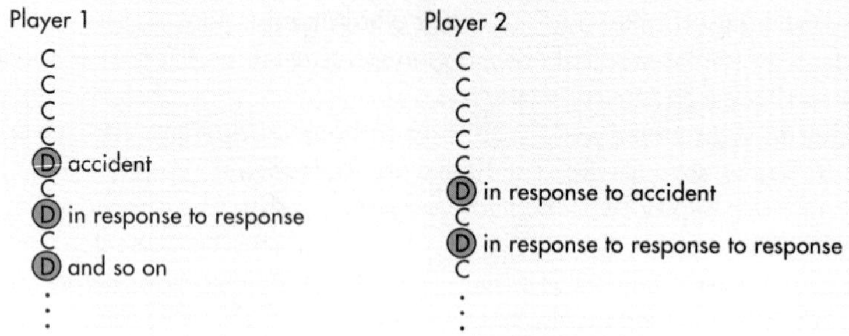

Player 1

C
C
C
C
(D) accident
C
(D) in response to response
C
(D) and so on
⋮

Player 2

C
C
C
C
C
(D) in response to accident
C
(D) in response to response to response
C
⋮

▶ *A single accidental defect response will reverberate forever if both sides play Tit for Tat.*

the end of time (see Figure 11.4; Molander, 1985). (Note that the players know what their opponent did in the previous round, but not in the current round.) Tit for Tat is a relatively forgiving strategy; it holds an exploitative move against you for only one round. But even it may be too unforgiving; it seems wiser to throw in an additional cooperative move once in a while to see whether your opponent's lack of cooperation was a consequence of an accident or misperception.

Indeed in a more recent tournament, a bit of "noise" was added to responses. That is to say, the tournament directors added a bit of cooperation or competition to each contestant's response.* Thus, a competitive response was now ambiguous; it could have come about because of the competitor's deliberate attempt to compete, or because on that trial the tournament director's program added competitiveness. In this "noisy" tournament, Tit for Tat didn't do very well; it was too unforgiving. A program called "Nice and Forgiving" won; Nice and Forgiving was more generous to its opponent that Tit for Tat is. Nice would be maximally cooperative so long as it saw 80 percent cooperation over the last series of trials. In other words, it allowed its opponent to chisel a bit (20 percent) just in case the chiseling was noise (Bendor, Kramer, & Stout, 1991). So there is now computer simulation evidence in support of Axelrod's claims that a strategy nicer than Tit for Tat might be a better strategy in a noisy world.

The suggestion that Tit for Tat, or some close relative, is the best strategy to play in prisoner's dilemmas converges with the finding from studies of bargaining that matching concessions is the best strategy in a bargaining situation. We also saw that players who match concessions are perceived as tough but fair. A similar result appears in the prisoner's dilemma literature— players playing Tit for Tat are seen as intelligent, strong, and fair (McClintock & Liebrand, 1988). This is a rather remarkable convergence. Research in this tradition has *not* been concerned to investigate subjects' moral thinking or behavior. It has been concerned instead with how people react to purely competitive or nonzero sum situations, yet it converges on the idea that, at least in the context of *repeated rounds played with the same partner*, the equitable

---

*In this tournament, unlike the standard prisoner's dilemma format, cooperation and competition weren't all or none on each trial; each player could be *more or less* cooperative.

solution is also the most effective, and that acting equitably gains one quite positive characterizations from one's opponents. Perhaps this shouldn't surprise us. Moral categories are part of the way we look at the world; they affect the way we respond to other people, and they surely affect what we think of people.

Game theory, based on individual rationality, can offer little guidance about what to do on repeated plays of a prisoner's dilemma, but the evidence *suggests* that (1) people tend to compete with one another rather than cooperate, and thereby fail to maximize their outcomes, and (2) if you want to succeed in a nonzero sum situation like the prisoner's dilemma, *if you will be playing repeatedly with the same partner*, it is best to adopt a Tit for Tat strategy, responding to your partner's cooperation with cooperation and to his competition with defection. Research on Tit for Tat gives us hope that cooperation might be possible in a nonzero sum game.

The high level of mutual defection found in the typical prisoner's dilemma study is disturbing; it makes it seem as if the structure of the payoffs gets the subjects to act in self-defeating ways. But this conclusion follows only if the subjects are trying to do what the experimenter tells them to do, amass points. Suppose instead that the subjects are trying to "win" the game, in the sense of getting more points than their opponents—or at least avoid losing the game by getting fewer points than their opponents. If *that* is their goal, then the mutually cooperative choice has nothing to recommend itself, and the fact that subjects settle into mutual defection says no more than that subjects do the obviously rational thing when given the opportunity.

Experimenters in the prisoner's dilemma tradition usually try to head this off by telling subjects that they should amass as many points for themselves as possible, and they often pay the subjects in proportion to their points. But still, the amount of money involved is usually quite small, so earning money has typically not been a very potent motive.* And it is reasonable to assume that the subjects in these experiments have lots of experience playing card, board, or more athletic games for points; in many games, the number of points one gets is meaningless except in relation to the number of points one's opponent gets. Perhaps despite the experimenter's instructions, subjects convert the boring experience of playing trial after trial of the prisoner's dilemma game into a less boring, maximizing-the-differences game, in which the aim is to get more points than one's opponent. And if their aim is to do that, then defecting is the rational thing for them to do.

Tragedy of the Commons

A biologist, Garrett Hardin, in a widely read article called attention to an obscure pamphlet published in 1833 by an amateur mathematician named William Forster Lloyd. In it, Lloyd discussed the following scenario. Imagine a small town with a town commons, an area of pasture on which all of the

*Attempts to determine what happens when subjects play for larger amounts of money have, unfortunately, yielded inconsistent results. Some studies have found significant effects of the amount of reward on game-playing behavior (Gallo, 1966; McClintock & McNeel, 1966; Gallo & Seposh, 1971). Others have not found such effects (Willis & Joseph, 1959; Wrightsman, 1966).

townspeople's cattle are allowed to graze. Imagine that for centuries the townspeople have been grazing their cattle on the commons without problem; the commons has been able to grow enough grass to support all of their cattle and then some. But one day there is a great medical discovery, and a disease that had been killing off many of the cattle is cured. The immediate effect of the discovery is wonderful for the town. First the herdsmen and then the rest of the town prosper. But there is a second effect of the new medical treatment that isn't so wonderful—the commons begins to die. The townspeople hadn't realized it, but the commons had been able to support their herds because the number of cattle had been held in check by the disease. Once the disease was cured, restraint on the number of cattle was lifted, and the cattle overgrazed the commons.

What if such a scenario were really to unfold? Wouldn't people see it happening and stop adding cattle before the commons was killed off? Lloyd and Hardin suggested that they well might not. The reason they might not rests in the logic of the situation as it presents itself to each person in the town. Suppose someone asks himself whether he should add an animal to his herd. He knows that there are two effects of such an addition: (1) he will achieve a profit equal to the value of an animal, and (2) he will suffer a loss caused by the declining ability of the commons to support cattle. But this cost is not borne by him alone; it is borne by the whole community of herdsmen. And so long as the commons is able to support any cattle at all, the cost *to him* of an additional animal, because it is only his share of the cost of overgrazing, will be less than the profit he makes from the animal—which, of course, is all his. This logic will apply until the cost of adding an animal is the death of all of the town's animals, including his, but by that time the commons will be too far gone to survive.

Now the same logic applies to every herdsman. Every herdsman will realize that by adding an animal to his herd, he will increase his wealth substantially while decreasing the total wealth of the community a bit. So each

▶ *The commons as painted by C. M. Giddings in his* Cleveland Public Square.

herdsman increases his herd by one, and then two, and so on. As Hardin says, "Ruin is the destination toward which all men rush; each pursuing his own best interest in a society that believes in the freedom of the commons. Freedom in a commons brings ruin to all" (Hardin, 1968).

Hardin and Lloyd saw in the parable of the commons the heart of some of the most difficult problems our world faces: overpopulation, pollution. The trap posed by this logic is, sadly, of importance to all of us. But why is it of relevance to this chapter, at this point?

The reason is that the **tragedy of the commons,** or, as it is often called, a **social trap** or a **social dilemma,** has a payoff structure that can well be thought of as an n-person prisoner's dilemma game—a prisoner's dilemma game played by any number of people more than two. The tragedy of the commons is the generalized case of a situation of **mixed motives,** one in which it is to a person's advantage both to cooperate and to compete. It is like the prisoner's dilemma in that if everyone cooperates by keeping their herds down, then all will enjoy modest success. If you, and you alone, were to have a large herd, then you would do very well compared with the others, who would do somewhat less well than if you cooperated. But if you all failed to cooperate, then collectively your cattle would not prosper as well as they would if you all cooperated.* There has been quite a lot of research on cases in which groups of people manage to preserve, or fail to preserve, a common good.

In a social dilemma, a prisoner's dilemma involving more than two people, everyone suffers if each person attempts to maximize his individual gain.

COMMUNICATION AND THE N-PERSON PRISONER'S DILEMMA

One factor found to influence the degree to which people cooperate in the *two-person* prisoner's dilemma game is whether they get to talk to one another. The typical finding is that subjects cooperate more, and do better collectively, if they have a chance to talk (Deutsch, 1960). Robyn Dawes was interested in whether this was so for the n-person version as well, and if so, what was important about communicating. To find out, Dawes designed the following experiment.

Subjects met in groups of eight. Each subject had the choice of defecting or cooperating. If a subject cooperated, he got $2.50; if he defected, he got $12, but each member of the group (including himself) was fined $1.50. Thus, each subject had an $8.50 motive to defect. But, alas, if all eight subjects defected, then each subject would get $12 but be fined 8 × $1.50 and come out with nothing. Before deciding what to do, groups of subjects did one of four things. Some groups worked silently on an unrelated task. Other groups had a "get acquainted" discussion but were not allowed to discuss the decision that confronted them. Still other groups met and discussed their dilemma. A final group of subjects discussed their dilemma and took a nonbinding roll-call vote about what they would do.

---

*The situation in which if you all fail to cooperate the commons dies *isn't* a generalized prisoner's dilemma game. In the prisoner's dilemma, mutual defection isn't the worse possible outcome for either player. There is a two-person game called "chicken" (patterned after the children's game), in which the double-defect outcome is worse for both parties than is the outcome for the prisoner who doesn't confess though his partner does. The arms race resembles the two-person prisoner's dilemma game in structure. Nuclear war is certainly "chicken," since a launch by both sides is the worst thing that could possibly happen. The tragedy of the commons is really an n-person "chicken."

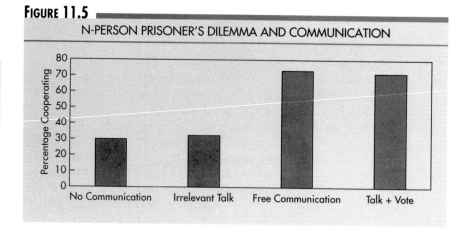

FIGURE 11.5

N-PERSON PRISONER'S DILEMMA AND COMMUNICATION

(Bar chart y-axis: Percentage Cooperating, 0 to 80; x-axis categories: No Communication, Irrelevant Talk, Free Communication, Talk + Vote)

► *Percentage of subjects cooperating in an n-person prisoner's dilemma game varies as a function of their communication possibilities. Talking leads to enhanced cooperation, but only if subjects can talk about their upcoming responses. (Data from Dawes, McTavish, & Shaklee, 1977)*

In the no communication and irrelevant communication conditions, about 30 percent of the subjects made the cooperative decision (see Figure 11.5). In the relevant communication and relevant communication plus vote conditions, about 70 percent of the subjects cooperated. So the chance to discuss the dilemma had a strong effect. But this wasn't because having a chance to talk created a sense of being part of a group, or made the subjects feel that the other people in the group were real human beings. The irrelevant discussion probably did all of those, but it didn't induce cooperation. The communication that worked was a discussion of the problem itself with or without a vote (Dawes, McTavish, & Shaklee, 1977).

The two results of the Dawes experiment—that not everybody defects, even without discussion, and that discussion helps—are the general trends in n-person-prisoner's-dilemma-like games. But why does discussion help? We don't know the complete answer, but a further experiment, also by Dawes, suggests that what is crucial about discussions is the opportunity to make promises. Promises, even unenforceable ones, lead to trust, and trust leads to cooperation (Orbell, van de Kragt, & Dawes, 1988). This isn't to say of course, that promises lead to *perfect* cooperation. In the experiment discussed above, if there was a nonbinding vote after the discussion, virtually every subject said he would cooperate. But even after saying this, a few subjects defected. Still, most didn't, and that is the important fact from the point of view of society as a whole. The commons will survive with a few cheats, so long as most people aren't.

IDENTIFIABILITY AND CHOICE

The research on social traps we have explored so far has looked at cases where people make a *single* decision to cooperate or defect. But our long-term conservation problems, like air pollution, involve repeated trials. One decides every day whether to pollute the environment by driving to work rather than by taking public transport. What happens in social dilemmas with repeated trials? A variety of factors have been found to be important.

One variable that has received considerable attention is the identifiability (rather than anonymity) of the person making the decision. In one experiment, groups of four players played a version of the prisoner's dilemma. In half of the groups, the subjects were introduced to each other before the game, and the choices they made on each trial were known by the other members of their group; in the other half, the subjects did not see each other before playing the game or while they played the game, and their decisions on each trial were not made known to one another. The more anonymous groups cooperated less (Fox & Guyer, 1978). This study suggests that public decisions made as part of groups that know one another, at least slightly, are more cooperative than private, anonymous choices. Other research, however, has *not* found such effects (Jerdee & Rosen, 1974; Jorgenson & Papciak, 1981). Still, one suspects that at least in stable communities, exploitation is much more difficult in public than in private.

STRUCTURAL SOLUTIONS

In his article on the commons dilemma, Hardin was not optimistic about individual restraint as a solution to problems of conservation; in fact, he believed that individual restraint was doomed to fail. One reason is this. Imagine two companies in the Midwest that produce small, plastic kitchen gadgets. Suppose they have equal shares of the market. One installs expensive equipment to scrub the sulphur out of its waste gasses; the other doesn't (and produces acid rain in the Northeast and Canada). By virtue of the additional cost of scrubbing its waste, the socially minded company will have higher costs to make its gadgets. This must result in lower profits. The likely outcome is that the polluting company will expand, while the socially responsible company will grow smaller. The polluter will eventually drive the socially minded company out of business.

Hardin suggested that the pollution problem can only be solved by the imposition of a penalty for resource exploitation (presumably by the government). This penalty could take several forms. One would be a law with criminal penalties for pollution. Another would be a tax on pollution; the tax would have to exceed the economic advantage from pollution. Another possibility is to allow people damaged by a company's pollution to sue for damages. But the question is: Will people be willing to give up their access to a public good (the air) and support the imposition of control?

Some experiments suggests that people will be willing to give up their unfettered right to exploit the environment under certain conditions. In one experiment, subjects in groups of six (some American, some Dutch) were told that there was a resource pool of 300 units. On each trial, each member of the group could take from the pool (harvest) from 1 to 10 units. At the end of each trial, the number of units they took would be subtracted from the number the trial started with. The pool would then be "replenished" (simulating the regrowth of the commons). Replenishment was a matter of multiplying the remaining units in the pool by some fixed factor—about 1.1—and then a new trial would begin.

The subjects were told that their aim should be to harvest as much as possible, but also maintain the pool at its starting size. (At this replenishment rate, an average harvest per subject of 4.5 units would result in the pool's maintaining a constant size.) There was one constraint, however: the pool could never exceed the original 300 units. (If you relax this constraint, the game is transformed into a much more nerve-racking one.) The game continued for ten trials. The subjects were also told that one group in the exper-

Structural solutions may solve social dilemmas, but they are difficult to put in place in a culture like America's, which stresses the rights of individuals.

FIGURE 11.6

STRUCTURAL SOLUTIONS
TO N-PERSON PRISONER'S
DILEMMAS

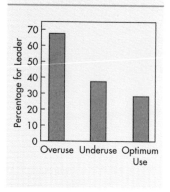

▲ *The percentage of subjects voting for a leader to apportion resources varies as a function of the subjects' perceptions of their management of the resource. When subjects believe they are overusing the resource, they will vote for a leader. (Data from Messick, Wilke, Brewer, Kramer, Zemke, & Lui, 1983)*

iment would be selected at random, and that the members of that group would receive additional payment of 10 cents for each unit they had harvested.

Subjects were given feedback about how much was being harvested from the pool by their group as a whole, and by each member. But the feedback was false. Some groups were told that they were harvesting at an average rate *below* the optimal 4.5 units; others were told they were harvesting at just about the optimal rate; and some groups were told that they were overharvesting—wearing the pool out. After ten trials, subjects were given the option of abandoning free access to the pool; for the remainder of the experiment, they could elect a leader who would assign harvests to each member. The results were that a majority of subjects in the overuse condition, but only the overuse condition, voted to appoint such a leader (see Figure 11.6; Messick, Wilke, Brewer, Kramer, Zemke, & Lui, 1983). Further research has been fairly consistent in supporting the idea that as subjects perceive the resource as being depleted, they will give up free access in favor of some system that controls individual use (Rutte & Wilke, 1984; Samuelson, Messick, Rutte, & Wilke, 1984; Samuelson & Messick, 1986; Yamagishi, 1986; Samuelson, 1991).

Tit for Tat and its close relatives have been proposed as the best practical solution to the two-person prisoner's dilemma. Can Tit for Tat work in the n-person game? On the face of it, it doesn't seem so. One problem is that in the n-person game, defecting in response to another player's defection punishes not only the defector on the previous trial but any cooperators on that trial too. Still, Sam Komorita has shown that in a six-person game, if one or two (simulated) players played Tit for Tat, then the other (real) subjects were more likely to cooperate than if there were no simulated reciprocator. And two simulated reciprocators led to more cooperation than did one (Komorita, Parks, & Hulbert, 1992). So if one can (somehow) get a "critical mass" of players to play Tit for Tat, one may be able to induce cooperation even in the n-person game. Structural solutions, on the other hand, do not need to recruit a critical mass of reciprocators.

People may not, however, be very willing in everyday life to support structural reforms. Jon Baron has shown that subjects often object to proposals for new laws to solve resource problems even when the subjects agree that the new laws would make things better for the society as a whole. So, for example, subjects might oppose a law that limited how much a person could collect after certain minor car accidents because such a law restricted people's right to sue, even though such a law, the subjects agreed, would lower car insurance costs for everybody (Baron & Jurney, 1993). The notion of rights is deeply entrenched in our political consciousness, and I am not suggesting it shouldn't be. But it is important to realize that rights get in the way of solving problems, and it would not be wise to have too many rights that get in the way of too many solutions.

THE PUBLIC GOODS PROBLEM

The commons dilemma raises the question of whether, and under what circumstances, people will restrain their consumption of some shared resource in order to preserve it. But there is another situation in which the same conflict between individual and collective good arises. In this version of the problem, the question isn't whether people will use up a public good at their own profit, but whether people will provide a public good at their own cost.

A public good is one that every member of the community can use. Roads, sewers, bridges, public schools, parks, tennis courts, and so on are public goods if all comers may use them regardless of who has contributed to their construction. Goods and services provided by governments (so long as there are no fees for use) are public goods. Some public goods, like roads, are also public investments that pay off in increased economic activity, which is of use to the community as a whole.

Giving blood is an example of the provision of a public good (blood goes to those who need it, rather than to those who have provided it) in which the decision to contribute is made by individuals rather than by the government. Consider the decision of whether or not to donate blood. Donating blood involves some cost and is inconvenient and somewhat unpleasant (though not massively unpleasant, and there is *no* chance of getting AIDS by *donating* blood). The Red Cross will make blood available to you if you need it whether you have donated blood previously or not. Thus, there is a strong temptation for each individual to "let George do it." The willingness to use a public good, but not to contribute to it, has been called the ***free-rider problem.*** But if everyone "free rides," there will be no blood for anyone. What do people do when faced with the question of providing public goods?

One series of experiments looked at a situation in which people had a choice of investing in a public or a private good. Investing in a private good paid off for the investor alone. Investing in a public good, like building new roads, paid off for all members of the group whether they invested or not. One hypothesis about such a choice was that people would invest nothing at all in the public good; this is the radical free-rider hypothesis. Fortunately, this isn't what happened. Subjects did invest *some* of their money in the public good. But they invested substantially less than the amount needed to maximize the profit to the group as a whole (Marwell & Ames, 1979, 1980). Just as in the commons dilemma, where people in general *take* more than they should, in public good problems, the finding is that people *give* less than they should. But in both cases, the picture isn't entirely bleak; on the whole, people don't take as much as they *could,* nor do they give as little as they *could.* We have seen this result before. In cooperative groups, like a tug-of-war, people don't entirely stop pulling, but they do pull less than the maximum they could pull (see Chapter 3).

Some problems, like pollution, can be framed as a commons dilemma problem: Will people restrain themselves from using up too much air? Or they can be framed as a public goods problem: Will people contribute to solutions to air pollution? Does it matter how the problem is framed? There is reason to believe from two-person decomposed prisoner's dilemma games that how a problem is framed matters, and there are similar results with group problems. There is evidence that people manage resources better when the management of the resources relies on *taking less* rather than *giving more* (Fleishman, 1980; Brewer & Kramer, 1986; but see McDaniel & Sistrunk, 1991, and Aquino, Steisel, & Kay, 1992, for contrary results). And in one experiment where the format didn't matter in terms of how much people profited, subjects were more willing to give up control over the decision as to how much they could take than over the decision as to how much they should give (Rutte, Wilke, & Messick, 1987). If the situation allows, policymakers

WHEN YOU GIVE BLOOD YOU GIVE ANOTHER BIRTHDAY, ANOTHER DATE, ANOTHER DANCE, ANOTHER LAUGH, ANOTHER HUG, ANOTHER CHANCE.

American Red Cross
PLEASE GIVE BLOOD.

▲ *So long as a few people give blood, there will be enough for those who need it. Thus, most people "free ride." But if everyone* were *a free rider, there would be no blood for anyone.*

are well advised to present the issue as having to do with control over the use of resources, rather than control over contributions.

Finally, in a simulation rich with political reverberations, investigators found that the initial distribution of resources affected how willing people were to cooperate in solving resource dilemma problems. People were more willing to be cooperative in solving a dilemma if resources were equally distributed in the first place (Aquino, Steisel, & Kay, 1992). An unequal distribution of resources made everyone—"rich" and "poor" alike—unwilling to cooperate, but for different reasons. The rich refused to cooperate out of fear that by cooperating they were being suckers; the poor wouldn't cooperate because they saw their contribution as too small to matter anyway.

Coalitions

The formation of coalitions is the final problem of nonzero sum situations that we shall consider. The problem of coalition formation arises when there is some prize up for grabs, but no one person has enough resources to win it. To capture the prize, some group will have to form and pool their resources. Then the problem becomes one of splitting the payoff.

Presidential nominating conventions are an example. It sometimes happens that no candidate comes to the convention with sufficient delegates to be elected. So candidates will have to make a deal to pool their delegates in favor of one of them. But the candidate who offers delegates to another will want a share of the prize—usually participation in a new administration. The problem researchers address is: Which coalitions will form, and how will they divide their spoils?

Modern interest in coalitions seems to have been sparked by an irony uncovered by sociologist Georg Simmel (Simmel, 1908/1950). Simmel was interested in the unique sociology of the triad (groups of three people). As part of his general treatment of triads, he noted that they sometimes gave rise to coalitions of two against one. Simmel didn't claim that triads *inevitably*

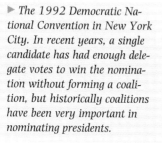

▶ *The 1992 Democratic National Convention in New York City. In recent years, a single candidate has had enough delegate votes to win the nomination without forming a coalition, but historically coalitions have been very important in nominating presidents.*

divide into a coalition of two against one, but he pointed out that they often do. About this he was surely right. Research on overcrowding in college dormitories, for example, reveals that a major determinant of satisfaction with three-person rooms is whether they divide into coalitions of two against one or not. As you might imagine, the odd person out is not a very happy person (Reddy, Baum, & Fleming, 1981).

The irony that Simmel discovered is known as **_tertius gaudens,_** which literally means "third who enjoys," and has to do with the following situation. Imagine that you are a candidate for your party's nomination for president, and you have 48 percent of the delegates you need. Suppose that another candidate also has 48 percent of the delegates, and a third candidate has the remaining 4 percent. Suppose you go in search of a deal in which the person you make the deal with will give you delegates, and in return you will do something for her. Now with whom do you think you will make your deal? The other person with 48 percent of the delegates, or the person with 4 percent?

The notion of _tertius gaudens_ suggests that you will prefer to deal with the person with 4 percent. The reason is that if you make a deal with the candidate who has as many delegates as you, she is going to want an equal share of the "spoils" of victory. The person with 4 percent, on the other hand, will not be in a position to be so demanding. The ironic upshot of this reasoning is that "weakness is strength"; you (or your 48 percent opponent) will either win the nomination or be excluded from a winning coalition, but the 4 percent person is sure to be in the winning coalition. Indeed, imagine that one candidate has 48 percent, another has 30 percent, and the third has 22 percent. This line of argument suggests that the person with the 48 percent is the one who will be excluded in favor of the more closely matched other two! Great strength is great weakness.

One theory of coalition formation, **_minimum resource theory,_** follows from this way of thinking (Gamson, 1964). Minimum resource theory claims two things: (1) of the possible coalitions that might form, that coalition will form with the minimum amount of resources needed to win, and (2) the rewards of winning will be divided by the coalition members in _proportion_ to the resources they have brought to the coalition. Some initial laboratory tests of minimum resource theory using triads were supportive (Vinacke & Arkoff, 1957), and it is also true that in European parliamentary governments, the number of parliamentary ministries that a party controls (the spoils) is directly proportional to the number of seats in the parliament that the party controls (Browne & Franklin, 1973).

Minimum resource theory has also been criticized. Harold Kelley argued that it only _seems_ as if strength is weakness. He suggested that if you think about it a bit, you will see that in the case where one candidate has 48 percent of the delegates, another has 30 percent, and the third has 22 percent, the three candidates actually have _equal_ power; not equal resources but equal power. The reason is that with the three people involved (call them _A_, _B_, and _C_), there are three winning combinations that can form—_A_ and _B_, _B_ and _C_, and _A_ and _C_. Each candidate has the ability to participate in two of the three; each person has equal _pivotal_ power. Kelley suggested that with repeated exposure to this type of game, the subjects would see that they have equal power, that the difference in their resources is a red herring and has no

bearing on how resources ought to be divided. And Kelley conducted an experiment in which he found, as he expected, that with experience, strength
is no longer weakness (Kelley & Arrowood, 1960).

The generalization of Kelley's reasoning to cases in which there are more
than three people is called **minimum power theory** and it holds that the
real power a person has (and the division of the spoils he is entitled to) depends
on the number of coalitions that are winning coalitions with him, but losing
coalitions without him (divided by the total number of coalitions possible)
(Shapley & Shubik, 1954). Both minimum resource theory and minimum
power theory do better than chance at predicting which coalitions will form
and at predicting how a coalition's winnings will be divided in experimental
games. But in absolute terms, neither theory is adequate. In response to this
situation, various more complex theories of coalition formation have been
advanced, principally by Sam Komorita.

Both minimum resource theory and minimum power theory assume that
a coalition's earnings will be divided equitably and that which coalition someone decides to join depends on where her equitable share of a coalition will
be largest. Each person, these theories assume, will choose to join that coalition that (equitably) gives her the largest share. Which coalition forms,
therefore, depends on which coalition can (equitably) hand out the largest
shares to the largest number. The two theories differ, however, as to what
equity consists of. Minimum resource theory sees equity as distribution in
proportion to resources; minimum power theory sees it in terms of distribution
in proportion to pivotal power.

There is still another way to think about coalition formation. Suppose on
one trial, some coalition forms and divides its resources equitably. Further
suppose that someone is left out of the winning coalition. That person gets
nothing. He will be motivated, on the next trial, to make an offer to one (or
more) of the members of the previously winning coalition to form a new

coalition, and he will be motivated to offer the other person more than could be gotten from an equitable distribution (in either sense). After all, if he doesn't do this, he gets nothing.

So as experience with these situations grows, players will be inclined to *bargain* over which coalitions they will be members of. **Bargaining theory** claims that the initial coalitions that form will be governed by people's attempts to maximize their payoff within the constraints of equity. It further assumes that neither a distribution in terms of resources nor a distribution in terms of power will characterize this initial distribution. Rather, some point midway between them will control initial distributions. But bargaining theory claims that as experience grows, equity will matter less to coalition formations, and bargaining in a strictly competitive sense will matter more—because of the willingness of excluded members to bargain. So bargaining theory splits the difference between minimum power theory and minimum resource theory for early rounds. It predicts that bargaining will ensue after these rounds, and that the stable formation that coalitions will achieve will be determined by the formation that maximizes outcome *independent* of considerations of equity (Komorita & Chertkoff, 1973).

Bargaining theory is an advance over earlier theories in that it takes account of the dynamics of bargaining over repeated trials. And it specifies the nature of those changes over time. Both bargaining theory and its newer, improved version, **equal excess theory,** show great promise in accounting for the data they are held responsible to: data about which coalitions will form and how they will divide their spoils (Komorita, 1979). A final model, called **weighted probability theory,** takes account of the fact that smaller coalitions are easier to form and maintain than large ones (Komorita, 1974).

The history of research on coalition formation shows a clear progression from simple theories based on quite plausible assumptions to more complex models with higher aspirations: models that hope to not only account for which coalitions will form but even give an account of the bargaining process that produces winning coalitions (see Komorita, 1984, for a review).

WRAP-UP

In this chapter, we considered situations involving strategic interactions, in which two (or more) parties have conflicting interests and in which each party can affect the other's future behavior with her current behavior. In some cases—bargaining over the price of a house, or a car, or wages—one party's gains are the other's losses. So the combined payoff for both parties is fixed; the only question is how much of the total payoff each gets. Such situations are called zero or constant sum.

Other situations are more complex because the total payoff the parties involved can receive is *not* fixed (nonzero sum). If all participants cooperate, they may jointly gain more than they will by competing. But these situations often involve mixed motives.

In the prisoner's dilemma situation, for example, if the two parties cooperate on all trials, they will maximize their joint payoff. But this desirable outcome can come about *only* if each party is willing to cooperate. A person may fail to cooperate on a given trial for two different reasons: he may want

▲ *Diego Rivera's* Detroit Industry *shows the strategic interactions involved when people
work together as well as when
they are in conflict.*

to exploit his partner, or he may be afraid that if he cooperates, his partner
will exploit him. Thus, both greed and fear may lead to a lack of cooperation.
Consider the reaction of someone who notices that his partner has refused to
cooperate on the previous trial. What inference can he draw about his partner's motive? Well, it isn't clear. His partner may have failed to cooperate
either out of greed or fear. Because of this ambiguity, the optimal strategy is
unclear.

There is reason to believe, however, that in both bargaining and prisoner's
dilemma situations, a person is best off by portraying himself as tough but
fair. In the case of bargaining, this involves being a tough bargainer, but one
who matches concessions, at least in frequency. In the case of repeated plays
of the prisoner's dilemma situation, it involves playing Tit for Tat—matching
cooperative moves with cooperative moves and punishments with punishments.

Many of the problems we currently face—overpopulation, air pollution,
recycling—can be thought of as an n-person prisoner's dilemma situation.
Consider recycling. Recycling is a bit of a bother. And if no one else recycles,
then there will be no real benefit to the environment of one person's recycling.
On the other hand, there would be a tremendous benefit to the environment
if *everyone* recycled. (It is also true that not much harm would befall the
environment if everyone but you recycled.) In such situations, Tit for Tat isn't
possible because an uncooperative response punishes everyone, whether they
cooperate or not. Such situations seem to require structural solutions—laws
requiring recycling. And people seem to be willing to enact such solutions if
they perceive the environment as endangered. It is unlikely that goodwill
alone will be enough in such situations to bring about the most desirable
solution.

SUMMARY

1. *Strategic interactions* are situations in which (1) two or more people have
   wholly (or partially) conflicting goals, and (2) each person acts so as to affect
   the future behavior of the other.

2. When bargaining, how much a person is likely to make depends on her *level of aspiration*, how much she believes she must make to do an adequate job of bargaining. Tough bargaining strategies lower her opponent's level of aspiration, and therefore are more profitable than soft bargaining strategies.

3. In order to reach a jointly optimal bargain, bargainers should (1) have the right, problem-solving, orientation to their task, (2) be strongly motivated to work hard to find an optimal solution, (3) truthfully reveal their profit structure to their opponent, (4) have specific (rather than vague) bargaining goals, (5) have an adequate amount of time in which to bargain, (6) work on all issues at once, rather than one at a time, and (7) bargain at a distance rather than face to face.

4. People who bargain as a representative of others tend to bargain harder than people who bargain for themselves. People who bargain on behalf of others are often able to work more effectively if their constituents are not aware of their every move.

5. Third parties can become involved in conflicts either as mediators or arbitrators. *Arbitrators* can impose a settlement; mediators have no such power. *Mediators* must be seen as impartial to be effective.

6. Situations in which the total profit all parties can make is fixed are called *zero sum* or *constant sum*. Situations in which the total profit all parties can make is determined by the parties' behavior are called *nonzero sum*.

7. The *prisoner's dilemma situation* is one in which two players will optimize their joint payoff if they both cooperate. At least in the single-game case, however, individual rationality dictates that each player defect rather than cooperate.

8. When people play prisoner's dilemma games with the same partner repeatedly, they tend to find themselves locked into repeated trials of mutual defection.

9. There is no single "best" strategy to play in repeated-play prisoner's dilemmas, since the outcome depends on what one's partner does. Computer simulations suggest, however, that *Tit for Tat*—cooperating on the first move and then doing whatever one's partner did on the previous move—is the most successful strategy.

10. The *tragedy of the commons* is essentially an n-person prisoner's dilemma game in which if all cooperate, all prosper; if all defect, all are destroyed; and if some cooperate and some defect, the defectors prosper. Many current problems—air pollution, overpopulation, resource depletion—can be modeled as n-person prisoner's dilemmas.

11. Being identifiable and making promises to cooperate enhance cooperation in an n-person prisoner's dilemma. But in the end, structural solutions—governmental regulation, for example—are needed in a tragedy of the commons situation.

12. A variety of models have been proposed to predict how coalitions will form in a situation in which no one person has sufficient resources to gain some reward but groups of people can band together to take the prize. Modern theories attempt to explain not only which coalitions will form, but also the process by which they form.

CHAPTER **12**

Sex and Gender

This chapter has two topics; the first is sexual behavior and attitudes. We shall examine sexual behavior from two points of view: from the perspective of culture and from the perspective of evolution. Our aim will be to understand the influences that each has had on our sexual proclivities.

The second topic is gender. That we humans come in two types, male and female, is a biological fact. This biological fact necessitates that we play different roles in reproduction. But cultures elaborate on this fundamental reproductive difference in many ways, assigning men and women to quite different places in our social worlds even when that assignment has nothing to do with reproduction. The second part of this chapter, then, deals with the psychological aspects of the different social roles that men and women are assigned to.

SEXUAL BEHAVIOR IN CULTURAL PERSPECTIVE

There can be little doubt that our culture has profound effects on our sexual attitudes and behavior. To see just how powerful these effects are, we shall look at how sex is handled in two island cultures. One is an Irish folk community, the other is Polynesian. I have selected these cultures because they represent extremes of the ways cultures treat sex.

Sex on Inis Beag

John Messenger's (1971) report on the Irish island he called Inis Beag paints a rather bleak picture. The dominant theme of people's feelings about sex is

376

anxiety and guilt. Sex is rarely discussed, and never discussed with children or, for that matter, adolescents. Sex is seen as a duty for women to endure, rather than as a pleasure to be pursued. Female orgasm is unheard of, let alone experienced, by most of the women. And some of the women who have heard of it think it quite deviant. The men, while undoubtedly enjoying intercourse and reaching orgasm, are worried about sex too, seeing it as a physically debilitating strain. Masturbation is reported to be common, but premarital and extramarital intercourse are unheard of. Even marital intercourse is restricted, with little foreplay or variation in position. Moreover, intercourse between husband and wife is accomplished while partially dressed.

Culture on Inis Beag, then, restricts and limits whatever sexual potential our biology gives us. But the culture and its people survive; this degree of restriction may be unpleasant, but it is not impossible for humans.

Sex Among the Mangaians

The Mangaians represent a very different way to live (Marshall, 1971). On Mangaia, when a boy reaches puberty, he is circumcised by an expert. But the expert is knowledgeable in more than the requisite surgery. He also is charged with instructing the boy in sexual technique, in particular how to bring his partner to orgasm several times before ejaculating. And this lecture material is supplemented with a laboratory course. After the incision has healed, the young fellow is turned over to an experienced woman who, along with ministering to his medical needs, completes his instruction on ways of satisfying women. It is important that the boy learn these lessons well, because if he fails to perform adequately, his sexual partners will make sure that he gains a reputation as an inept lover. Females are schooled by other females in sexual matters; little could come as a surprise here.

Premarital intercourse is typical. Needless to say, there is a lot of pregnancy out of marriage among the Mangaians, but this is not a matter of shame for them, nor is there much pressure for the woman to marry the father of the child.

Sexual attractiveness on the part of Mangaian women has to do *not only* with their physical appearance but also with their sexual behavior; the more active a woman is during intercourse, the more she is appreciated by the male. Female genitalia are considered to be attractive, and women are thought to vary in how attractive their genitalia are. Mangaian men have no interest in female breasts, something they take to be of interest only to nursing infants.

Marital sex is considerd to be the prerogative of the male, since men are thought to want it more than women. The Mangaian husband reports that he expects to have intercourse each night in his twenties, though he begins to miss nights as he ages (compared with an average rate of 2.8 times a week for men in their twenties in the American sample reported by Alfred Kinsey in 1948).

Extramarital intercourse is not condoned among the Mangaians, but exceptions are made. If a man or a woman is away from the island for an extended period of time, then it is considered natural and acceptable for his or her partner to find another partner, though women are believed to be able to wait longer than men.

Sex among the Mangaians, then, is a very different matter than it is among the people of Inis Beag. Mangaian mores encourages sexual experience, especially for the young, and men and women are explicitly trained in carrying it out. This too is a way for humankind to treat its sexuality.

Sexual Scripts in Present-Day America

It is easy to see *how* sexuality is socialized on Mangaia; it is a matter of explicit training, as learning arithmetic is for Westerners. How our own Western culture socializes us is less clear. To be sure, parents, teachers, and clergy have an obvious and explicit hand. But we also learn from peers, television, movies, and so on. In any event, we all learn a lot about how to be sexual independent of our own experience. To document this, one pair of investigators gave heterosexual college students fifteen descriptions of sexual acts ranging from kissing on the lips to genital sex, and asked them to put the acts in the order they occur in a typical sexual encounter. The results showed that the subjects were in strong, although not perfect, agreement about the order in which the acts occurred.

Why did the subjects agree as to the order of the various activities? One plausible answer is that they simply ranked the acts from least to most arousing; they assumed that in the typical encounter, people do the least arousing things first and then move up a ladder of arousal. But other subjects were asked to rate each of the actions in terms of how arousing it was. The results showed that the various actions were *not* ordered in this way; in some cases, less arousing acts followed more arousing acts (Geer & Broussard, 1990).* The results suggest that socialization has (somehow) given each of us a ***sexual script,*** an ordered sequence of behaviors that we know to enact in a sexual encounter (Gagnon & Simon, 1973).

*The temporal order was closer to one of increasing arousal from the male's point of view than from the female's, but even for the males the order was not determined entirely by arousal.

Sexual Revolution

Culture, as we have seen, exerts powerful effects on people's sexual behavior through sexual norms and mores. In this section, we want to consider Western culture in historical perspective and see if we can understand why some, at least, of its sexual norms changed in response to a variety of influences. My aim here is to convince you that it is possible to do more than say that culture affects behavior; we can also try to understand *why* culture affects behavior in the ways it does. I also hope to convince you that cultural norms can be affected by all sorts of cultural elements.

You have probably heard a rumor that in the late 1960s and early 1970s, there was a sexual revolution in Western culture. Just what changed during this period? Was it a revolution? Why did it happen? What is the current state of the revolution—has there been a counterrevolution? To appreciate these questions, it is useful to return for a moment to the prerevolutionary days of the 1950s.

"LOOK AT THE WAY SHE'S APPROACHING HIM. I'D SAY THERE'S A SEXUAL REVOLUTION GOING ON."

SEXUAL STANDARDS

To oversimplify dramatically, in the 1950s, there was a fairly clear official standard of sexuality in Western culture. Sexual intercourse was something to be confined to marriage. Men and women were expected to be virgins until their wedding night. Evidence of deviation from this standard was seen as shameful. But this was only the "official" standard. In fact, it was a double standard that was far more tolerant of deviation by men than by women. In the movies of the times, Doris Day and Rock Hudson were both expected to save themselves for marriage, but Rock Hudson's constant attempts to seduce Doris Day just showed that he was a "real" man—perhaps something of a cad, but not a "fallen" man. There were, however, no movies in which Doris Day attempted to seduce Rock Hudson; audiences simply would not have tolerated a heroine who tried to seduce a reluctant male.

The standard was also official in the sense that substantial numbers of men and women deviated from it. In his study of sexual behavior in the 1930s

◀ *Doris Day and Rock Hudson in the film* Lover Come Back *(1962). While the lovers could declare their love for each other, in the movies of the early sixties, sex was still generally left for after marriage.*

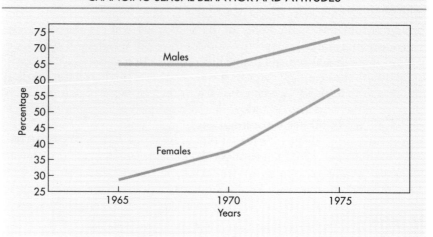

FIGURE 12.1

CHANGING SEXUAL BEHAVIOR AND ATTITUDES

▶ *Percentage of sexually expe-rienced male and female stu-dents at one college from 1965 to 1975. Sexual experience in-creased during the period, but mostly for females. (Data from King, Balswick, & Robinson, 1977)*

and 1940s, Alfred Kinsey found that about half of the female subjects and a much larger percentage of the male subjects were *not* virgins at the time of marriage. So this standard was, even before the sexual revolution, being widely violated. Still, it was a standard of sorts. What happened to all of this during the 1960s and 1970s?

Literally scores of studies have been published documenting changes in sexual behavior and standards during this period. Although the details vary from study to study, depending on the samples used, the broad picture is consistent from one sample to another. We will look at just one study to illustrate the general trends. This study surveyed undergraduates in a Southern university about their sexual behavior and attitudes in 1965, 1970, and 1975 (see Figure 12.1). In this sample, 65 percent of the unmarried men in 1965 had experienced sexual intercourse, while about 29 percent of the women had. By 1975, the corresponding figures were 74 percent of the men and 57 percent of the women (King, Balswick, & Robinson, 1977). So in terms of premarital sexual behavior, there was a slight increase for the men and a much larger increase for the women. The rates tended to converge at the higher, male rate. So if there was a sexual revolution *in behavior,* it was a revolution primarily in the behavior of women rather than of men.

What about standards for behavior? In 1965 in this sample, 33 percent of the men thought that premarital sexual intercourse was immoral; 70 per-cent of the women thought so. By 1975, only about 20 percent of the men and women believed this. Again, there was a change in attitudes, a change toward greater permissiveness among the men and an even greater change among the women. Moreover, from 1965 to 1975, both men and women became more permissive in their attitudes toward premarital intercourse; their behavior reflected this permissiveness.

What about the double standard? Did it change? In this same study, the subjects were asked how they felt about a man who had had intercourse with "a great many women" and a woman who had had intercourse with "a great many men" (see Figure 12.2). In 1965, 35 percent of the men thought that a man with a great deal of experience was immoral, and 42 percent of the

FIGURE 12.2

ATTITUDES TOWARD SEXUALLY EXPERIENCED MEN AND WOMEN

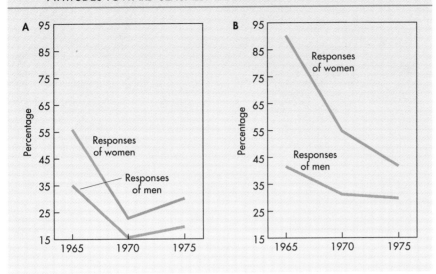

◀ (A) Percentage of male and female subjects who judged that a man with many partners is immoral. There was a substantial decline through the period of the "sexual revolution."
(B) Percentage of male and female subjects who judged that a woman with many partners is immoral. The decline through the period of the sexual revolution was much greater than it was for men. But even so, by 1975, slightly more men and women judged a woman with many partners immoral than judged a man immoral. (Data from Robinson & Jedlicka, 1982)

men thought that a woman who had had such experience was immoral. So there was some evidence that men were, as a group, harsher toward experienced women than toward experienced men. Women, however, were far harsher in their attitudes toward women than men. Again in 1965, 56 percent thought that a man with a great deal of experience was immoral, while 91 percent thought that a woman with such experience was immoral.

By 1975, sexual standards had become less discriminatory against women. By then, only about 20 percent of the men thought that such a man was immoral, while about 28 percent thought that such a woman was immoral. There was a much greater change in standards among women. By 1975, 30 percent of the women thought an experienced man was immoral, and 41 percent thought an experienced woman was immoral. These data suggest that, at least with regard to attitudes toward promiscuity, by 1975 fewer men and women held double standards; both men and women had become much more tolerant.

The general picture that emerges from these and other data is of a general increase in permissiveness toward premarital sexual intercourse, and some erosion of the double standard. But this is not to say that there remained no standard of sexual behavior. Rather, what seemed to emerge during this period was a collection of different standards. Some members of this generation held on to the notion that any sexual intercourse before marriage was wrong. Others believed in "permissiveness with affection"; the idea that sex was permissible in the context of a loving relationship, regardless of whether the partners intended to marry (Reiss, 1966). The fact that the data show less tolerance for a great deal of experience than for intercourse before marriage per se is consistent with this view. Other members of the generation had yet more permissive standards, holding that sex was proper so long as no one was hurt or exploited. Although these standards differ from one another, it is important to see that they are all standards; the question that college stu-

The sexual revolution

• began around 1900;

• was primarily a revolution in the behavior of women;

• involved a convergence of standards for men and women to the previous standard for men.

▶ *What you can talk about in situation comedy is one barometer of the sexual revolution, at least at the level of talk, if not behavior. (A) Paul Reiser and Helen Hunt can talk quite openly about their sex life on* Mad About You. *But (B) Lucy and Desi in* I Love Lucy, *one can be sure, did not discuss sex on television.*

A   **B**

dents in the 1965–75 period seemed to ask themselves was not so much "Should there be standards of sexual behavior?" as it was "What should the standards of sexual behavior be?"

There is another sense in which sexual standards changed. These standards had to do not so much with what people did or thought right, but what they talked about, read about, saw on television and in films. Perhaps one example will suffice to give a sense of what has happened. It is not unusual these days to see men and women in bed together on network television. In the 1950s, no such thing was allowed. On *The Dick Van Dyke Show* during the late 1950s, the (married) stars were never shown in bed discussing the day's events. In fact, it was not even possible to suggest that they might do this. The set that contained their bedroom clearly showed twin beds, as if to suggest that they never actually shared a bed. (It was left to the viewers' imagination to figure out where their son came from.) And there was no Dr. Ruth of the 1950s!

HISTORICAL TRENDS

Do these changes add up to a sexual revolution? To answer this, we need some perspective, and the Kinsey data provide it. What Kinsey's data suggest is that the trend toward increasing sexual permissiveness began much earlier than 1960; in fact, it began with the generation born about 1900. If there was a revolution, the revoluntary vanguard consisted of the men and women born at the turn of the century who achieved maturity during the "flapper" era of the 1920s. So the changes in sexual attitudes and behavior that came to great prominence in the 1960s continued a historical trend that began much earlier as a rebellion against the Victorian, more restrictive, era. But this is not to say that change didn't accelerate during the 1960s. Why did it accelerate then?

CAUSES OF THE SEXUAL REVOLUTION

An enormous number of factors have been proposed to explain the changes in attitudes seen in the 1960s. Which of them was key is difficult to answer, and more the job of a cultural historian than a social psychologist. But perhaps we can at least take a brief look at some of the prominent hypotheses, just to get a sense of the kinds of cultural influences that might affect sexual standards.

Penicillin and Venereal Disease   The question we want to ask is: Why were the men and women who came to sexual maturity around 1960 more permissive in their sexual standards and behavior than the generations that preceded them? Well, for one thing, penicillin was discovered as this generation was being born; this discovery meant that syphilis no longer threatened a horrible death as a possible consequence of intercourse. Thus, the "baby boomers," born just after the Second World War, were the first generation to come to sexual maturity without real fear of venereal disease. And, as we might expect, this generation tended to see the fear of venereal disease as a not very important reason to refrain from intercourse (Jedlicka & Robinson, 1987). (Obviously, the discovery of AIDS in the mid-1980s has had the effect of reinstating fear of disease as a reason to abstain from sex.)

Contraceptives   A second influence on the sexual behavior of the baby boomers was the invention in 1960 of the first contraceptive pill and at about the same time of the intrauterine device (IUD). Although there had been reasonably effective contraception available before this, the birth control pill and the IUD were more effective, and they were the first means of contraception that were "intercourse independent," in that they did not require action at the time of intercourse. The availability of effective contraception, and the subsequent legalization of abortion, reduced the fear that an unwanted pregnancy would disrupt lives. But of late, the safety of both the IUD and the contraceptive pill have become controversial, and the legal status of abortion uncertain.

Female Marriage Squeeze   A third possible influence on sexual behavior for baby boomers may have been the "female marriage squeeze." The female marriage squeeze refers to a simple demographic fact. Men prefer younger wives, while women prefer older husbands. Consider, in this light, the situation of women born in 1947 at the beginning of the baby boom. When they reached the age at which they might have been expected to marry, in 1969, they were looking for men who were about two years older than they were—men born in 1945. But 1945 was still during World War II, and there weren't many boys (or girls) born in that year; thus, there were fewer men born in 1945 than women born in 1947. Women born in 1947 were "squeezed" when it came to finding marriage partners, and the problem persisted *so long as the birthrate continued to rise.*

This unavailability of men has been hypothesized to have had widespread effects on American culture. One consequence may have been the women's liberation movement; another may have been an increase in permissiveness toward premarital intercourse, especially an increase for women (Heer & Grossbard-Shechtman, 1981). But the interesting fact is that when the birthrate *falls,* as it did after the baby boom in the 1960s, a "male marriage squeeze" results; that is, women coming to age from the early 1980s on found an *oversupply* of appropriately aged men to marry. One might expect this state of affairs to lead to a decline in premarital sexual permissiveness.

▲ *(A) The "flappers"in the twenties were as upsetting to their parents as (B) youths of the sixties were to theirs.*

A

B

C

▲ Our changing sexual attitudes are mirrored in our changing tolerance for bodily displays at the beach. People in bathing suits in (A) the 1880s, (B) the 1890s, and (C) the 1990s.

▪▪▪▪▪▪▪▪▪▪▪▪▪▪

The sexual revolution of the 1960s may have been accelerated by

• the discovery of a cure for syphilis;

• the development of the IUD and the birth control bill;

• the marriage squeeze;

• the baby boom.

▪▪▪▪▪▪▪▪▪▪▪▪▪▪

Socialization of Baby Boomers   The last factor to be considered in the sexual revolution is the simple fact of the baby boom. Every culture faces the problem of socializing its young, of instilling, among other things, the culture's sexual standards. The baby boom posed quite a problem for the culture. There was suddenly a huge number of young people to be socialized. In a variety of ways, the dramatic increase in numbers of young people strained the resources of the culture—baby boom children, just as one example, faced chronically overcrowded classrooms. One consequence of this state of affairs is that parents and teachers—key socializing agents—may have been less able to cope with the demands placed on them. This might be expected to lead to a generation able and eager to challenge the culture's strictures in general, and its sexual standards in particular. And this seems to be just what happened; there can be little doubt that the baby boom generation challenged the culture's norms. But as the birthrate falls, the socializing agents of the culture are less stressed, and one might expect them to be more effective. One might expect this to lead to a less rebellious generation, which seems to have happened.

We see, then, that many of the forces that may well have set the sexual revolution in motion have reversed themselves. The reversal of these forces might be expected to produce a sexual counterrevolution. Has there been a sexual counterrevolution?

Counterrevolution?

For some reason, counterrevolutions are not as interesting to document as revolutions are. Although there were scores of studies documenting changes in attitudes and behavior during the 1960s and 1970s, there have been relatively few studies examining changes in attitudes and behavior during the 1980s. There are, however, a few reports that suggest that there may have been changes in post-baby-boom attitudes and behavior. One study, for example, documented that over half of the sexually active students in the survey had altered their sexual behavior out of concern about AIDS and that about 15 percent of the students who were not sexually active reported that fear of AIDS had prevented them from becoming sexually active. What is not so clear from the results of this survey is whether concern about AIDS had affected their behavior, or just their reports of their attitudes about engaging in sexual activity (Carroll, 1988; Baldwin, Whiteley, & Baldwin, 1990). Still the study does indicate that college students are at least aware of an AIDS risk related to sexual behavior.

Other research has indicated that even before the risk of AIDS became so prominent, there was a decline in sexual activity among college students. One study surveyed college women about their sexual behavior in the academic year 1983–84 (see Figure 12.3). Women at the same college had previously been surveyed in 1973–74 and 1978–79. In the early 1970s, about 35 percent of the women surveyed were sexually active; in the late 1970s, this number had risen to about 50 percent; by the early 1980s, the percentage had declined again to 37 percent (Gerrard, 1987). Comparable data were not collected about college men.

Changes in sexual attitudes have also been documented. Recall the studies done in 1965, 1970, and 1975 in a Southern university; this same university was surveyed once again in 1980. The data showed a continuing, but slight, increase in sexual behavior for both men and women. By 1980, 77 percent of the men (compared with 74 percent in 1975) and 64 percent of the women (compared with 57 percent in 1975) had had intercourse, so permissiveness in this sense was still on the rise. But attitudes seemed to reverse themselves. By 1980, 27 percent of the men and 39 percent of the women (compared with 20 percent and 30 percent in 1975) thought that a man who had sexual intercourse with many partners was immoral. And 42 percent of the men and 50 percent of the women (compared with 29 percent and 41 percent in 1975) thought that a woman who had sexual intercourse with a great many men was immoral.

So we see in these data a trend toward less permissiveness, at least in attitudes toward promiscuity, and an increase in the number of men and women holding a double standard—judging a promiscuous woman more harshly than a promiscuous man (Robinson & Jedlicka, 1982; Robinson, Ziss, Ganza, Katz, & Robinson, 1991). Other research too has documented a double standard in the sense of harsher judgments of a woman than of a man, not because she has had sexual intercourse per se, but because she had had sexual intercourse at an early age, or in the context of a casual relationship (Sprecher, McKinney, & Orbuch, 1987).

Taken together, such data as we have suggest that there is something of a sexual counterrevolution currently happening in American culture. The sexual revolution and counterrevolution, however, did not happen in a vacuum; they happened in the cultural context of a variety of potent factors, some of them technological—the invention of antibiotics and contraceptives—and others demographic, the baby boom and the attendant marriage squeeze.

Just as culture, with all its complexities and interrelations, provides one context within which we should see our sexual behavior, so too does evolution provide another equally important context we must be sensitive to. Our sexual desires are part of our biology, and that biology has a long evolutionary history; so it is reasonable to imagine that our genes, and through them evolution, have also had an impact on our sexuality. The question we ask now is: Has evolution affected our sexual desires and behavior? And if so, how?

FIGURE 12.3

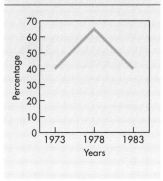

CHANGES IN FEMALE
SEXUAL ACTIVITY

▲ *The percentage of sexually active female students at one college changed between 1973 and 1978, and then again between 1978 and 1983. There seems to have been something of a sexual counterrevolution in the latter period. (Data from Gerrard, 1987)*

All four possible causes of the sexual revolution of the 1960s have reversed; there seems to be a counterrevolution in progress.

One fact about evolution and sex is clear. Evolution, through our genes, has determined the structure of our reproductive *equipment.* But some scholars argue that evolution has shaped more than just our bodies; they argue that our evolutionary past influences our sexual desires and behavior too. This is a controversial claim, for two different reasons.

The first reason is purely scientific. Evolutionary claims are very difficult to test. Evolution is about history; it is about how something came to be. But we obviously cannot do experiments to verify the history of sexual behavior in our own and related species. So the best we can do is draw inferences about how our species' sexuality evolved from evidence about our own and other species' sexual behavior. These inferences are often more tenuous than inferences we draw on the basis of experimental evidence.

The second reason is political. Evolutionary thinkers have, by and large, focused on differences between men and women in their sexual proclivities, and argued that to some degree these differences are innate. And this idea is politically controversial. It is easy to see why.

Aristotle declared, "We should look upon the female state as being, as it were, a deformity." And this thesis was not just a biological theory of interest to scholars, but rather was a foundation for the treatment of women in Athens. In the "golden age" of Greece, in the first flowering of our notions of political equality, women were systematically excluded from "serious" life. They were confined, like slaves, to the household, and to the absolute control of first their fathers and then their husbands. This pattern of political subjugation, justified by a biological thesis of innate inferiority, has not been, of course, confined to Greece; we live with it too. Because political inferiority has typically been justified by notions of innate differences, there is good reason to be wary of claims about genetic differences between the sexes.

Despite its controversy, however, one cannot turn one's back on the evidence for evolutionary differences; evolution is too powerful an approach to a basic understanding of ourselves to ignore. A better strategy is to appreciate the limits of evolutionary arguments; in particular, to see why evolution is not a justification for political inequality, and to realize that claims about innate differences need not suggest inferiority.

Our guides for this exploration of evolutionary differences are two interesting and provocative books and one recent and provocative article that have brought evolution and human sexual behavior together in a single frame. The books are *Sex, Evolution and Behavior* (1978) by Martin Daly and Margo Wilson and *The Evolution of Human Sexual Behavior* (1979) by Donald Symons. The article is by David Buss and David Schmitt (Buss & Schmitt, 1993). The strategy I shall follow is first to present the logic of the evolutionary point of view without worrying about whether it is the correct explanation of human sexual behavior. Once we understand what evolution has to say, then we can look at such data as there are about human sexual behavior, and ask whether these data are consistent with that evolutionary point of view. That is, that evolution is responsible (to some degree) for our sexual desires will be treated as a *hypothesis;* we will want to know whether the data are consistent with that hypothesis.

Sexual Reproduction and the Sexes

To gain perspective on how men might be different from women, we first look at how and why males of other species are different from females in their sexual behavior. To do that, we first need to be clear about what, in its most fundamental biological sense, it is to be a male or a female.

Humans, and many other species, reproduce sexually by the male's depositing sperm inside the body of a female. Other species use other means; for example, in many species of fish, the female expels eggs, and the male expels sperm over the eggs. Thus, fertilization takes place outside the bodies of the parents. But for all of the differences in how it is accomplished, the constant in sexual reproduction is that it is achieved through the combination of genetic material from two parents. But what distinguishes the male contributor to this production from the female? There is one fundamental criterion by which we can distinguish males from females: males produce sperm, and females produce ova (eggs).

Ova are much larger than sperm because in addition to genetic material, they contain the nutrition needed by the zygote, which is the product of the union of the sperm and ovum (see Figure 12.4). Thus, a female invests more of her nutritional resources to make an egg than a male does to make a sperm. Because they are more "expensive" to make, in many species females produce far fewer eggs than males do sperm. Consider this. The human female is born with about 4,000 ova. At roughly one-month intervals, one ovum will "ripen" and become ready for fertilization. In a reproductive span of roughly twenty-five years, then, a woman will produce about 270 ripe ova. In contrast, the human male produces millions of sperm *per day*. And he will continue to produce them from puberty to death. The differentiation of the sexes, then, begins with the fact that mothers invest much more in the next generation from the start; genetic roles may be symmetric, but reproductive roles certainly aren't!

ASYMMETRY IN PARENTAL INVESTMENT

In fish, the necessary asymmetry in reproductive roles ends at the production of sperm and ova. Since fertilization occurs outside the body, if further nurturance is to occur, there is no particular reason why it should be the female who provides it. And in some species—for example, the sea horse—it is the male, not the female, who cares for the young. But in species that accomplish fertilization inside the body, it is the female who must take the next step and care for the young until they are ready to face the world. Hens accomplish this by preparing the eggshell, which will protect the newly created chicks. But in humans, this care is within the mother's body for another nine months. And then in mammals, including humans, the female produces milk to continue her nurturance of the young. In mammals in particular, then, there is a further asymmetry in the contribution of males and females to the next generation.

Another way to look at this asymmetry in parental investment is in terms of the interval between one conception and the opportunity for another. A woman who has conceived cannot conceive again for at least the nine months she is pregnant, and usually for a longer period if she nurses her infant. A man who conceives a child on Tuesday can quite possibly conceive another

FIGURE 12.4
SPERM AND OVUM

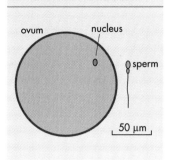

▲ *Mammalian ovum (egg) and sperm, drawn to the same scale. Note how much larger the ovum is than the sperm. (From Daly & Wilson, 1978)*

on the same day, and certainly can within a few days (with a different mate, of course). Thus, a female ties up much more of her reproductive life with each conception than a males does.

SEXUAL BEHAVIOR AND ASYMMETRY IN INVESTMENT

Given this fundamental asymmetry, what implications can we derive about sexual behavior? Suppose a female horse conceives with a male horse that possesses really undesirable genes, genes that will lead to the death of their foal before reaching reproductive age; she has invested a significant fraction of her reproductive life with this foal who will not contribute genes to the next generation. A female who chooses her mate with more care, on the other hand, will be more likely to have offspring that themselves reproduce, and therefore will be more likely to pass on her genes to subsequent generations. In other words, natural selection favors the development of females who are selective in their mates; females who aren't selective lose the reproductive competition to those who are.

Now consider the situation for the male. Although the male too should exercise some care about his mate, the cost to him of a poor match is much lower. He has not invested nearly as great a portion of his reproductive life in any particular match. In fact, mating on a given day, even with the worst possible mate, will give him at least some chance to pass on his genes, while mating with no one gives him no chance. What does this fundamental difference in investment suggest about the mating patterns of males and females? The answer is simple: evolution should foster choosy females and ardent, less discriminating males.

Because it is usually in the genetic advantage of a male to mate with *any* female, females usually don't have the problem of enticing ardent males to mate with them. But males do have a problem enticing choosy females. It is a male's job to convince the female that of all her available options, *he* is the one she should pick. Males are competing with each other for the opportunity to mate with females, and especially the most desirable females. Thus, as a general rule, the animal kingdom is populated by males who woo females, and females who select the most desirable suitor. (An important exception, however, is the sea horse species, where it is the males who care for the young, and the males who are thus more selective.) Our model so far, then, specifies male competition for females and female selectivity from among available males.

ASYMMETRY IN KNOWLEDGE OF OFFSPRING

There is a second asymmetry between males and females. A male who invests time and energy in the care of *his* young will be more likely to contribute genes to successive generations. But a male who invests time and energy in *another male's* young suffers from a double genetic disadvantage. First, he is not giving his own young the care that would advantage them, thereby putting them at a competitive disadvantage. And second, he *is* giving another male's genes that care, thus further disadvantaging his own. Males who cared for no young would do better by their genes. The same is true for females, but females always know which children they conceived. Natural selection, then, should favor males who make sure that the young they care for are theirs.

Males and females differ in their reproductive roles in that

- females invest more in each offspring;
- maternity is certain, paternity is uncertain.

We have found two fundamental differences between males and females in species like ours. First, the female investment in time and energy is greater at every stage than is the male's. Second, females always know which young are theirs, but males don't. But how does all of this matter with regard to differences in sexual behavior? To address this question, we shall look at several different kinds of data related to human sexual behavior. Let us start with what is known about human marriage from a cross-cultural perspective.

Cross-Cultural Evidence

What kind of marital relations should we expect humans to have? What do the asymmetries between males and females in terms of parental investment predict in terms of human bonding? Because it is in the interest of the male to mate with as many females as possible, one would expect men to want to have multiple mates. In contrast, according to this line of reasoning, we would expect females to find the best mate and have all of their young with him. Second, because men can't be sure if a child is theirs, they should be very careful that the females whose young they care for do not have other mates. But because women *can* be sure that any child they care for is theirs, they should be bothered less if the father of their children is involved with other females. This suggests that both men and women can accept a marital arrangement in which males have multiple wives *(polygyny)*, but men should not be happy with, or women attracted to, one in which wives have multiple husbands *(polyandry)*. What is the evidence on this point?

POLYGYNY AND POLYANDRY

Information on marital arrangements cross-culturally is drawn from a review of the anthropological evidence by Clellan Ford and Frank Beach (1951), who examined the evidence on sexual behavior in 190 cultures (see Figure 12.5). In the 185 cultures for which evidence was available, about 16 percent were, as Western culture is, formally monogamous; that is, each person was allowed only one mate. This is not to say, of course, that no one in these other cultures had extramarital affairs, but it does mean that in this minority of cultures, monogamy was the official standard. In the remaining 84 percent of the cultures, men were allowed, indeed encouraged, to have multiple wives. According to Ford and Beach, there were only two societies in which polyandry, the marriage of a female with multiple males, was the approved form: the Marquesans of Polynesia and the Toda of India. But Robert Suggs has disputed the claim for polyandry among the Marquesans; so of the 185 cultures in Ford and Beach's sample, there may be only one society officially allowing polyandry. And that case is special.

Among the Toda, the most common form of polyandry is one in which a woman marries a husband and his youngest brother (Marshall & Suggs, 1971). Since a male is genetically related to his brother's children, although not as strongly as to his own, it follows from an evolutionary view that if a man were to tolerate any other mate for his wife, he should tolerate his brother. A male who takes care of his brother's children is not as genetically

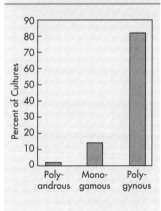

FIGURE 12.5
MARITAL ARRANGEMENTS CROSS-CULTURALLY

▲ *Most of the world's cultures endorse polygyny. (Data from Ford & Beach, 1951)*

A

B

▲ (A) A polygamist with four wives and seven children. (B) Royston Potter, another polygamist, with his two wives and six of his seven children. Polygyny has existed (and exists now) even in Western culture.

disadvantaged as one who takes care of an unrelated male's children. So the facts of human marriage are reasonably consistent with evolutionary theorizing; polygyny is a much more common (the most common) form of human marriage than polyandry (the least common).

NORMS ABOUT VIRGINITY

A further consequence of male concern with the paternity of their children follows. Men should want their wives to be virgins when they marry, but wives shouldn't care whether their husbands are. Now what about the data? There are some cultures in which the virginity of neither partner is a matter of concern, and some that insist that both partners be virgins. There are many that insist on female virginity but not male virginity, but there are *no* cultures that insist on male virginity but not female virginity. Again there is evidence that the asymmetry in reproductive roles shows up in cultural norms about sexual behavior (Ford & Beach, 1951; see also the more recent survey by Buss, 1989).

AGE AND STATUS PREFERENCE IN MATES

Assume for the moment that evolution has caused males to be sexually attracted to just those women who are likely to be good at bearing and taking care of their children. If this is true, whom should a male look for? First he should be attracted to women who have reached the age of fertility; mating with a woman who is not yet fertile will not be of any use. How can a male tell if a female has reached fertility?

Estrogen, produced by the female at puberty, has an obvious effect on the female form. The development of breasts and widening of the hips is a good clue that a female has begun ovulating. So we should expect that males will be attracted by these signs of fertility. It will come as no surprise that men are attracted by these secondary sexual characteristics.

Women also reach an age when they cease being fertile, and if evolution has acted on males to cause them to be attracted to fertile women, then men should also be attracted to relatively young women within the population of women who have reached maturity. Indeed, the younger a woman is, the longer she is likely to live to care for their offspring. Thus, we should expect men to be most attracted sexually to young, but post-pubescent women.

Now let us look at the situation from the female's point of view. Pre-pubescent males are of no more use to a female (in terms of reproduction) than pre-pubescent females are to males. So we should expect women too not to be attracted to males until they have begun to show signs of sexual maturity. But there is no age at which males *cease* being able to reproduce; sperm are produced throughout a man's life. So being relatively older is not as big a drawback in a male.

Females, though, if they are to pass on their genes, ought to select males who will provide them and their offspring with resources. What is less clear is just what traits a female ought to look for in a male to maximize her chances of finding a good resource provider. Perhaps in a hunter-gatherer society, she should look for physical strength and agility. The peak development of these traits in males, it seems, is not to be found in adolescence. Rather, these traits are likely to be found somewhat later in a male's life. This reasoning suggests that there will be a difference between men and women in their age preferences for the ideal mate. Men will prefer younger women, but women will prefer somewhat older men—handy how it all works out!

David Buss has investigated age preferences in ideal mates in a sample of thirty-seven cultures across the world. In each sample, the men queried preferred, on average, women who were younger than they were. And in each sample, women preferred men who were slightly older than they were (Buss, 1989). So the data support the view that men prefer younger women, while women prefer older men. It must be said that the samples that Buss used were *not* a random sample of all the cultures of the world; still, these data do provide some support for the view that evolution has acted on our desires with regard to the ages of the preferred partner. (See also South, 1991, for confirmation of the age preference difference in a random sample of American households.)

Buss also reasoned that women should be attracted to males who possess traits that make them good resource providers. Thus, he expected women to be attracted to men who were industrious and ambitious, traits likely to lead to the providing of resources. And, indeed, Buss found that in all but one sample, women were attracted to men with these traits more than men were to women with these traits (Spain was the exception). American college students too were asked to rate people in terms of desirability as marriage partners. Each subject rated people who varied in physical attractiveness and socioeconomic status. Both men and women preferred attractive to unattractive people as potential marriage partners. And both preferred high- to low-status partners. But social status had a substantially larger effect on women's ratings than it did on men's. Further, a high status but only moderately attractive man was as attractive to women as a highly attractive but only moderately successful man—status compensated for attractiveness. But this same trade-off did not occur when men were picking a partner. They clearly preferred the highly attractive but lower-status person (Townsend & Levy, 1990).

Alan Feingold has conducted a meta-analysis that examined the results of thirty-four studies of what men and women find desirable in a partner. Some of these studies relied on questionnaires. Questionnaire studies are quite valuable, but they present a problem: subjects know what is being asked of them and may answer questions in line with what they think the investigator wants to hear—or they themselves want to believe. So to supplement these

▲ *Elizabeth Taylor and Larry Fortensky after their wedding. Their marriage is a rare example of an older, attractive woman marrying a younger man without wealth or status.*

findings, investigators sometimes use personal ads in newspapers. These ads provide another window on what men and women desire in a partner, one that is, perhaps, more likely to be honest than are questionnaire responses.

Feingold's review revealed a consistent pattern of results: on both questionnaires and in the ads they place in papers, women place much more stress on characteristics that make people "good providers." Thus, women, more than men, want partners who are ambitious, intelligent, and of high socioeconomic status (Feingold, 1992; also South, 1991). Of course, this might be for nonevolutionary reasons; it might be because women have fewer resources of their own and hence need to acquire them through their partners.

David Buss has examined this issue in the following way. We can rank cultures by the degree to which men and women differ in resources. We might expect that those cultures with the biggest disparity in resources would also be the cultures with the greatest disparity in the degree to which men and women value ambitiousness. But there was no evidence that this is true (Buss & Schmitt, 1993). Still, it might be that in no culture do women have sufficient resources to make them indifferent to their partners' ambitiousness.

Douglas Kenrick has proposed that dominance is a trait that is linked to the provision of resources, and hence it ought to be a trait that women find attractive in a male. To see if this is true, at least for American college students, he showed college men and women silent videotapes of someone of the opposite sex acting in a dominant or submissive way. He then asked the subjects to rate the taped character for sexual attractiveness and desirability as a date (see Figure 12.6). Whether the man in the tape acted in a dominant or submissive way affected the women's ratings; they preferred the dominant to the submissive male. But dominance had no effect on the men's ratings; they liked the submissive female just as much as the dominant one (Sadalla, Kenrick, & Vershure, 1987).

These data suggest that the behavioral traits women find attractive in a male might be determined by evolutionary forces. But there is a caveat. In

FIGURE 12.6

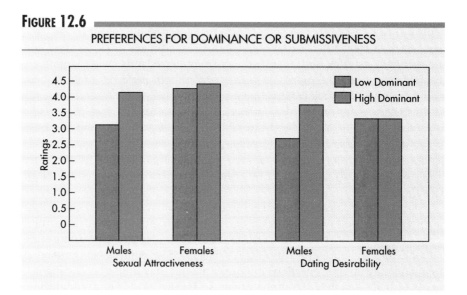

▶ Ratings of dominant and submissive males and females on sexual attractiveness and dating desirability. The ratings were done by students of the opposite sex who saw a dominant or submissive act. (Data from Sadalla, Kenrick, & Vershure, 1987)

one survey of American college women, the subjects indicated that they cared more about kindness in a potential mate than they did about any other trait, including industriousness and ambition (Buss & Barnes, 1986); there is no clear evolutionary reason this should be so. Still, the data are consistent with the view that evolution has had some influence on gender differences in our preferences for mates.

CLASSIC FINDINGS IN SOCIAL PSYCHOLOGY: DIFFERENCES IN SEXUAL BEHAVIOR

It is relatively easy to find out what cultures tell people to do about sex; it is much harder to discover what people actually do. In almost all cultures, sex is private. For the most part, we have to be content with what people say they do, rather than with observations of what they really do. The first, and in most ways still the best, investigation into what people *say* they do in the area of sexual behavior is one we have already encountered. It was carried out by Alfred Kinsey and his associates (Kinsey, Pomeroy, & Martin, 1948; Kinsey, Pomeroy, Martin, & Gebhard, 1953). William Masters and Virginia Johnson have observed and recorded the *actual* behavior of a reasonably small number of people, and we also shall have occasion to refer to their research at various points (Masters & Johnson, 1966).

DIFFERENCES IN PREMARITAL AND EXTRAMARITAL SEX

If men are interested in having multiple mates and women aren't, then we should expect more men to have had premarital and extramarital sexual experience than women. What are the data? Roughly 50 percent of the women Kinsey interviewed had had premarital intercourse, the majority with one partner, often their fiancés. For men, on the other hand, 98 percent of those with only a grammar school education, 85 percent of those who had gone on to high school but no further, and 68 percent of those who had attended college had had premarital intercourse. (Kinsey's sample of women was too skewed to enable him to break down his data for them in the same way.)

When we turn to extramarital relations, we again find greater experience for men, with approximately 50 percent of men having had extramarital relations as opposed to about 25 percent of women (by age forty in both cases). More recent surveys, including a random sample of American adolescents from thirteen to nineteen years old, are fully in support of Kinsey's data, showing higher levels of premarital and extramarital sexual behavior for men than women (Sorenson, 1972; Hunt, 1974). The survey evidence, then, is consistent in confirming the evolutionary picture of ardent males and selective females.

We might also expect that men and women would differ in what they find attractive in dating partners. And these differences might not be the same as their preferences in marriage partners (see Buss and Schmitt, 1993). There is evidence, for example, that both men and women find a person who has had little sexual experience more desirable as a marriage partner than one with more sexual experience—both men and women want faithful marriage partners. But when it comes to casual dates, the genders diverge. Women prefer men with moderate sexual experience; men prefer women with lots of sexual experience (Sprecher, McKinney, & Orbuch, 1991; see also Clark, 1990).

SEXUAL BEHAVIOR OF GAY MEN AND LESBIANS

Another kind of evidence about greater variety seeking by men than women is found in the sexual behavior of gay men and lesbians. Symons (1979) argues that when we look at gay men and lesbians, we get a better picture of male and female sexual desire than we do when we look at heterosexuals. Symons suggests that heterosexual patterns are a compromise between male and female sexual patterns, between the natural proclivities of the two partners. He argues that homosexual patterns, on the other hand, represent each gender's pattern unalloyed.

Gay men and lesbians, like heterosexual men and women in Western culture, place great emphasis on the desire to form stable, exclusive relationships. But there is, nonetheless, a profound difference in their success in doing just that. One study of the sexual behavior of 151 lesbians and 581 gay men in Germany (a study carried out before AIDS terrorized the gay community) found that the typical lesbian had had sexual relations with two partners. The typical gay man, on the other hand, had had sexual relations with sixteen partners. Only 1 percent of the lesbians had had sex with more than ten partners, while 61 percent of the gay men had (Schäfer, 1977).* John Gagnon argues that data like these simply show that lesbians have learned, just like their heterosexual sisters, that women should be faithful; that long before sexual preference arises, women learn that to be a proper woman is to restrict one's sexual experience (Gagnon, 1977). Still, it is at least as likely that the reason that lesbians and heterosexual women are so similar is because both are, in the end, women. In any event, these data are consistent with the evolutionary hypothesis that men are more likely to seek multiple sexual partners than are women.

Differences in Sexual Desire and Arousal

If evolution has influenced our sexual behavior, it has done so by acting not on behavior directly but on some psychological mechanism that causes that behavior (the proximate mechanism). Presumably, it has acted on our sexual desires—on our propensity to become sexually aroused in response to sexual stimuli. Let us look now at data closer to the proximate mechanisms we might expect evolution to have affected, at what we know about gender differences in sexual arousal.

*There is some evidence that the threat of AIDS has caused gay men to reduce the number of their sexual partners (Siegel, Bauman, Christ, & Krown, 1988). But the reduction, tragically, may not be adequate. There is evidence that the very horribleness of the threat of AIDS may itself lead people at risk to deny the threat, and fail to modify their behavior enough to minimize that risk (Bauman & Siegel, 1987). There is some reason to believe, by the way, that the best way to minimize risk is to restrict the number of one's partners and, most important, to use condoms (Reiss & Leik, 1989).

One difference between men and women that Kinsey turned up might provide insight into gender differences in the mechanisms of sexual arousal. Kinsey found that 14 percent of his female respondents reported having been sexually aroused by erotic stories, while the corresponding figure for men was 47 percent, even though most men and women had been exposed to such material at one time or another. This finding suggested that the proximate mechanism that accounts for men's greater variety seeking is that males are simply more easily aroused by sexual stimuli. Aside from Kinsey's data, there are other reasons to believe that women are less aroused by erotica than are men.

A quick look at the magazine rack of a local campus store revealed approximately sixty different magazines catering to males' desires to look at nude women. There was one magazine with male nudes—*Playgirl.* There was once a second magazine featuring nude males, *Viva,* but it removed the nudes because of a lack of readership. This suggests that males are more likely to seek our visual sexual stimulation. In fact, the National Commission on Pornography found that 50 percent of American males had seen a pornographic movie at least once, while 14 percent of women had (Technical Report, U. S. Commission on Pornography, nd). But as neat as this theory is, the evidence has turned against it.

Since the early 1970s, investigators have looked at the ways that men and women actually respond to erotica. In such studies, subjects are shown erotic slides or movies, or they listen to or read erotic written material. After exposure, the subjects, and the control groups who have been shown nonerotic material, are asked to report how sexually aroused they are. They are also often asked to report sensations specifically related to sexual arousal—for example, erection in males and vaginal lubrication in females. Finally, in some studies, subjects are asked to report their sexual behavior for the day or two before seeing the erotica and a day or two after.

The original experimental studies reported that men were, as Kinsey had claimed, slightly more aroused than women (see Schmidt, 1975, for a review). But subsequent research has not supported this finding. Recent results indicate that women are aroused as much as men; they report physical sensations to the same degree men do, and both men and women are affected in their sexual behavior outside the lab in the same way. Specifically, both men and women are likely to increase their rate of sexual behavior, whatever that is, in response to the erotica. Thus, men and women who typically masturbate will tend to do so more, often incorporating what they have seen into their fantasies, and men and women with regular sexual partners will tend to engage in slightly more coitus (Mosher & Abramson, 1977). Women do, however, report more negative affect—guilt, for example—while watching erotica, although they also show physiological signs of becoming aroused (Morokoff, 1985). Perhaps this accounts for why women don't seek out erotica even though they are aroused by it.

There is another way to square the data with Kinsey's original claim. Perhaps it is true that *on average,* men are more attracted to and aroused by sexually explicit material than are women, but that there are *some* women who are just as aroused by erotica as are men. If we could expose randomly selected groups of men and women to erotica, we would expect the men to respond more (on average) than the women (on average). But we can't randomly select the subjects for our studies. Rather, we must, for ethical reasons, rely on people who volunteer. Suppose the women (and men) who volunteer for such studies in the first place are just those people who find erotica appealing. Now our studies would measure the attractiveness of erotica not to the average man or woman but to the selected group that finds it appealing. In these subgroups, we shouldn't expect gender differences in arousability, precisely because the subjects have "self-selected" themselves either into or out of the study based on their attraction to erotica. The question of whether research on erotica has been fatally compromised in this way is not settled, but there is some evidence that women in general are less likely to volunteer for studies of erotica, and that the women who do volunteer may be the most experienced sexually (Kenrick, Stringfield, Wagenhals, Dahl, & Ransdell, 1980; Wolchik, Sprecher, & Lisi, 1983; Wolchik, Braver, & Jensen, 1985; Nirenberg, Wincze, Bansal, Liepman, Engle-Friedman, & Begin, 1991).

Kinsey's claims about female relative nonresponsiveness to erotica dovetails nicely with both evolutionary arguments for and substantial data for greater variety seeking among males. And they also correspond to casual observation of the amount of male-oriented versus female-oriented erotica. Perhaps the experimental studies of erotica notwithstanding, men are, on average, more easily aroused.

MALE-FEMALE DIFFERENCES IN MASTURBATION

Perhaps the best data about gender differences in sexuality are data about masturbation. Masturbation requires no partner and is typically done in private; since it is so convenient and private, it is likely to be the "purest" indicator of an individual's sexual arousability. What do the data tell us?

Kinsey found that 96 percent of his males who had completed college, 95 percent of those who had stopped at high school, and 89 percent of those who had completed grammar school had masturbated to orgasm. The corresponding rates for females were roughly 60 percent, 59 percent, and 34 percent. But there might be all kinds of reasons for this difference. For one thing, signs of sexual arousal are far more obvious to boys than they are to girls; it is just easier for boys to figure out how to masturbate than it is for girls. So the numbers of men and women who masturbate may reflect knowledge rather than desire.

But we can also ask about the *frequency* of masturbation among men and women who *do* masturbate. In the Kinsey data, the median rate of masturbation among unmarried women was 0.3 to 0.4 times per week, roughly between once every three weeks and every other week. The male rate was between 0.4 and 1.8 times per week, roughly between once every other week and twice a week. Again we find a higher rate for men, suggesting greater arousability. (See Leitenberg, Detzer, & Srebink, 1993. Some investigators have, however, found evidence for differences in the proportions of males and females seventeen to thirty years old who masturbate, but no differences in the frequency with which those who masturbate do so; see Arafat & Cotton, 1974.) Still, the bulk of the evidence from studies of masturbation suggests that men do masturbate more than women, and this suggests that men are more easily sexually aroused than women.

Finally, in an effort to study the effects of sexual deprivation on sexual desire, Barry Singer solicited thousands of students to participate in a study of sexual behavior. The study required that subjects (1) keep a diary of feelings of sexual arousal and (2) abstain from all sexual activity for one month. Almost three hundred women, about 10 percent of those solicited, volunteered, but only fifteen men volunteered. The women who volunteered had no difficulty completing the study; only six of the fifteen men completed the abstinence study! Singer also asked college men and women who were not abstaining to report on how frequently sexual thoughts interfered with their studying. Women reported that this infrequently happened; men, that it happened quite frequently (Singer, 1985). This too suggests the pattern evolution predicts: ardent males, choosy females.

Perspectives on Genetic Influences

We have focused on the possible evolutionary and thus genetic roots of human sexual behavior. This discussion should be seen in perspective, the perspective of human morality, politics, and happiness. It is easy to *mis*understand evolution and to confuse it with matters not of its concern.

One common way to misunderstand natural selection is to believe that because something has a genetic basis, it is unchangeable. This isn't true. Certain tastes—for example, caffeine, alcohol, nicotine, and chili pepper—are, some evidence suggests, innately aversive. On the other hand, we are shaped to dote on sugar. But one or another of the very substances that are innately aversive is enjoyed by a large majority of the earth's population. And some of us, as we experience a variety of cuisines, lose our taste for sweets. Genes aren't destiny. Who we are at any moment is always a product of our genetic endowment along with our experience. To be sure, there are some genetic influences that can't be changed, at least at the moment. If someone is unfortunate enough to have genes that cause Huntington's chorea, an inherited, progressive degeneration of the nervous system that shows itself at roughly age forty, he will succumb. There is no environmental influence we now know of that can alter this fate. But we have no reason to believe that sexual desire holds us on as short a leash, and indeed cross-cultural evidence suggests, to the contrary, that we can shape our own motives and behavior.

EVOLUTION AND MORALITY

Given that we can, at least to some degree, shape our culture, how *should* we? Should we model our social and political institutions to fit evolution? Does evolution provide a moral guide for our political decisions? There is no reason to think so. Just because a certain practice is "natural," in the sense of being shaped by evolution, is no reason to believe it moral. We know, for example, that in some primate species, males destroy other males' young, yet none of us would want to suggest *this* as an acceptable moral canon. To confuse facts about nature with moral facts is a famous fallacy called by philosophers the "naturalistic fallacy." The difficult fact for us to face as humans is that we cannot find an external anchoring for our morality in the natural world.

So too with gender differences. The political relations between men and women must be decided by the morality we follow, not by our genes. The ennobling thing about humans, after all, is not that we can live in accordance

▲ *Warren Beatty portrayed a modern-day Don Juan in the 1968 movie* Shampoo.

with our evolutionary past (horses do that quite well), but that we can choose our way of life.

EVOLUTION AND HAPPINESS

Evolution doesn't tell us how we *must* live, or how we *should* live (in a moral sense), but doesn't it tell us how we will be happiest living? No, it doesn't do that either. Evolution does not select for happiness. There is no reason to assume that the happiest creatures are those with the greatest reproductive success, and it is only reproductive success that evolution detects. Our genes impel us, insofar as they impel us, to their ends, not ours. If reproductive advantage leaves us miserable, this is of no concern to evolution. Even if it is true that evolution has shaped males to be variety seeking, this is no reason to suppose that men who succumb to this temptation, become Don Juans, will be the happiest. Don Juan isn't a very appealing character. The double standard may be "natural" in some sense, but that does not imply it is inevitable, moral, or what will make us happiest.

EVOLUTIONARY MYSTERIES

We have seen that evolution provides one perspective from which we can view our sexuality, and that some of the facts of human sexuality seem to be consistent with that view. But there are other facts of our sexuality that seem mysterious from that perspective. Let us take a look at one of them.

Homosexuality

If evolution, and thus reproduction, has shaped our sexual desires, then homosexuality is a profound mystery. Surely evolution should have led us to be attracted to people with whom we can reproduce. Yet Kinsey found that about 10 percent of the males in his sample considered themselves to be exclusively homosexual, and perhaps half of that percentage of the women did. (One recent survey found that 1 percent of males report being exclusively gay [Billy, Tanfer, Grady, & Klepinger, 1993].) Why, then, are some people sexually attracted to other people with whom most emphatically they cannot reproduce? Is it *possible* that there is a gene that disposes people who have it to be gay?

On the face of it, it would seem that there could not be a gene for homosexuality, since being gay should surely lead one to have fewer offspring than being heterosexual. But, oddly enough, it is *possible* that homosexuality is genetically determined. To see how, consider sickle-cell anemia, a very dangerous, life-threatening disorder that does have a genetic basis. How could a gene for this condition evolve?

The answer is that the gene responsible for this condition is recessive. You will have the disorder *only if* you inherit the gene from both parents. But if you inherit the gene from only one parent (and a non-sickle-cell gene from the other) then you gain something important in terms of reproductive success: resistance to malaria (see Figure 12.7). The sickle-cell gene, then, has two effects. One is beneficial—resistance to malaria; the other is destructive—sickle-cell anemia. The gene will survive in the gene pool so long as its ben-

FIGURE 12.7

RECESSIVE GENES AND BENEFICIAL EFFECTS

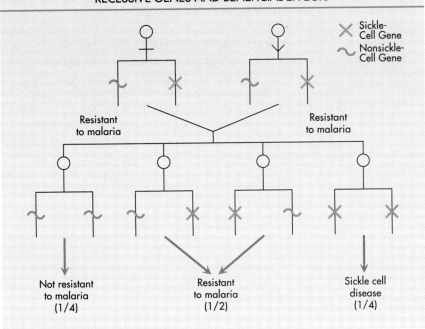

X Sickle-Cell Gene
~ Nonsickle-Cell Gene

Resistant to malaria

Resistant to malaria

Not resistant to malaria (1/4)

Resistant to malaria (1/2)

Sickle cell disease (1/4)

◄ People who have the sickle-cell gene (X) on one chromosome but not on its mate (~) are resistant to malaria but do not suffer from sickle-cell disease. Assume the mating of a man and a woman, each of whom has this desirable pattern. Each of their offspring will receive (randomly) either the sickle-cell gene or the non-sickle-cell gene from each parent. Thus, one-quarter of the offspring will receive the non-sickle-cell gene from the mother and the non-sickle-cell gene from the father; these offspring will not be protected from malaria. One-quarter will receive the non-sickle-cell gene from Mom but the sickle-cell gene from Dad; one-quarter will receive the sickle-cell gene from Mom but the non-sickle-cell gene from Dad; in both cases, these offspring (like their parents) will have resistance to malaria. But one-quarter of the offspring will receive the sickle-cell gene from both parents; they will suffer from sickle-cell anemia.

eficial effect outweighs (on average among those who have it) its destructive effect.

The same logic can be applied to homosexuality—without in the slightest implying that it is a disorder. Perhaps there is a gene that has more than one effect. Suppose that in the context of certain genes, it disposes its bearer to be homosexual, but in the context of other genes, it disposes its bearer to be heterosexual and also confers some other reproductive advantage. Such a gene could evolve and endure.

Is there any direct evidence that there is a genetic basis for homosexuality? One way to assess whether some trait has a genetic basis is by asking about identical twins. Identical twins are called that because they are identical in their genetic makeup; the twins are the product of a single fertilized ovum (a zygote), which splits in half shortly after conception and becomes two genetically identical individuals. Such twins are also called *monozygotic* (MZ for short). Nonidentical twins, on the other hand, occur when two ova are fertilized during the same period. In this case, two ova are fertilized by two different sperm; thus, nonidentical twins, called *dizygotic* (DZ for short), are no more alike genetically than are siblings born at different times. Now if a trait is entirely determined by a person's genes, then identical twins must share that trait (they must be *concordant* for that trait, in technical language). For example, identical twins are 100 percent concordant for eye color.

But the reverse inference cannot be made. That is, just because identical twins are concordant on a trait does not imply that the trait is genetically determined. For the most part, for example, identical twin infants are concordant for street address—they live at the same address. But this does not imply that street address is genetically determined. Rather, it illustrates another way that identical twins are similar to each other: for the most part, they grow up in similar environments. But dizygotic twins also grow up in similar environments (for the most part). And if you accept the premise that the environments for monozygotic twins are no more similar in relevant ways than are the environments for dizygotic twins, then you should accept the idea that the difference between the concordance rate for MZ twins and DZ twins is a measure of the degree to which a trait is determined by genes.*

Michael Bailey and Richard Pillard have recently gathered substantial data on the concordance rates for MZ and DZ male and female twins. In one study of males, the concordance rates for homosexuality among MZ twins was 52 percent; among DZ twins, it was 22 percent; and among adopted siblings it was 11 percent (Bailey & Pillard, 1991). (Adopted siblings may be no more related genetically than any two humans, but they share similar environments.) A similar study of women found that 48 percent of MZ twin pairs were concordant, 16 percent of dizygotic twins were concordant, but only 6 percent of adoptive siblings were (Bailey, Pillard, Neale, & Agyei, 1993; see also Buhrich, Bailey, & Martin, 1991; Whitam, Diamond, & Martin, 1993). These data suggest substantial influence of genes on sexual orientation. But they also indicate that there is room for environmental influence too. The concordance rate for homosexuality even among identical twins was, after all, far from 100 percent.

ENVIRONMENTAL INFLUENCES

How and when, one might ask, does the environment affect sexual orientation? The short answer is: We don't know. A longer answer is that although we don't know when or where sexual orientation is determined, we can point to two likely suspects: the intrauterine environment and puberty. During both periods of life, the sexual hormones are quite active shaping our primary and secondary sexual characteristics, and it would not be surprising if our sexual proclivities were also being shaped then too. (For more detail, see Money & Ehrhardt, 1972; Hines, 1982; Ellis & Ames, 1987, on intrauterine influences; and Storms, 1981, on a mechanism at puberty that might be important.)

In any event, what is clear is that some account is needed to explain sexual object choice. Not just to explain why some of us are gay and others not, but also to explain why some of us come to prefer blonds and others brunettes, why some of us are moved by square jaws and others not, and so on. Even if genes play a role in determining sexual object choice, so too must the environment, and how they mesh is the central question.

PSYCHOLOGICAL GENDER DIFFERENCES

The focus of the chapter now changes. Natural selection is closely tied to reproduction. And reproduction is, obviously, closely tied to sexual behavior.

---

*Technically, the measure of the degree to which a trait is genetically determined is called the *heritability* of the trait. The heritability of a trait is a number from 0 to 1. A heritability of 0 means that the trait (or, more properly, the variance in the trait) is determined not at all by genes; a heritability of 1 means that the trait is entirely determined by genes.

Thus, it would not be terribly surprising if it were true that evolution has had some influence on the different sexual proclivities of men and women. But Western culture, and indeed all cultures, elaborates on reproductive differences between men and women. For example, although times are changing, it is still true that men are tremendously overrepresented in positions of power; although there are women in Congress, for example, there surely isn't an equal distribution of men and women in Congress. Why is this true? One answer might be that men and women are simply different in their psychologies, and that in light of these psychological differences, it *must* be true that men and women occupy different social positions. Another answer relies on the notion of ***social roles,*** the idea that men and women are assigned different places in the social world regardless of the basic similarities in their psychologies. We will consider these ideas in turn.

Are men and women fundamentally different in their psychologies? The most comprehensive review of differences between men and women revealed two surprising facts. First, convincing evidence of differences between men and women tested in the controlled environment of the laboratory were found in only four areas: verbal ability, mathematical ability, visual-spatial ability, and aggression (Maccoby & Jacklin, 1974). So the differences between the genders are rather narrow. Second, they aren't very large. Consider mathematical performance, for example.

Differences in Mathematical Ability

The fairly consistent finding in the research literature is that males do better than females on standardized tests of mathematical performance. But this finding must be qualified in several significant ways: (1) the differences do not appear reliably until junior high school age; (2) the differences appear *only* on standardized tests; if anything, girls do better than boys in high school mathematics courses; (3) the average difference *between* girls and boys seems to be only about 10 percent of the total difference in performance *within* each gender; (4) there is evidence that the gap is narrowing (Kimball, 1989).

Why these differences exist at all is controversial. There may be a genetic basis for them. Or different ways of socializing boys and girls may account for the differences, with boys being encouraged to perform in mathematics in ways that girls aren't. Probably both genes and environment contribute (Benbow, 1988). But regardless of their source, the differences are small.

Differences in Verbal Ability

Just as junior high school boys outperform girls on mathematical tests, junior high school girls outperform boys on verbal tests. But these differences seem to be even smaller than the differences in mathematical ability, and the evidence is that even this difference is disappearing (Hyde & Linn, 1988). Thus, recent evidence suggests that whatever differences there are between men and women in their abilities are small, and growing smaller.

This pattern may come as a surprise. One reason might be that people's self-evaluations are based on their gender expectations as well as their performance. For example, in one study, male and female subjects were asked to perform a "masculine" task (take a quiz on political and sports figures), a

▲ *Do gender stereotypes affect the ways this child is taught and the expectations we have for him?*

"feminine" task (a quiz on film stars and fashions), and a variety of neutral tasks. The results were complex. First, the men expected to and did do better on the masculine task; women expected to and did do better on the stars and fashion task. But the key point is that the subjects' self-evaluations *overesti-mated* the gender differences on these tasks; men, for example, expected to do better on the masculine tasks than they actually did. This overestimation occurred primarily on tasks that were ambiguous, and it happened especially for the male subjects (Beyer, 1990). Thus, we have evidence that our expectations about performance differences between males and females may well exaggerate whatever differences there are.

Mothers can make matters worse. In another study of the determinants of children's perceptions of their performance, 1,500 mothers and their eleven-to-twelve-year-old children were asked about the children's ability in the math, sports, and social domains. The results indicated that though the mothers' assessments of their children's performance were, of course, affected by their children's performance, they were also affected by their children's gender and the mothers' gender stereotypes. And there was evidence that the mothers' perceptions of their children's abilities affected their children's perceptions of their own abilities (Jacobs & Eccles, 1992). So in these two studies, we have evidence that both mothers and children succumb to gender stereotypes about performance, and that these stereotypes affect their perception of the children's abilities. The upshot of this is that whatever differences do exist are exaggerated.

Teachers too have their stereotypes. For example, twenty teachers were asked to teach a male and a female student two different lessons. One lesson was on a "masculine" subject (mechanics); the other was on a more "feminine" subject (how Latin has affected English). The teachers were videotaped during their lesson, and the tapes were rated for positive and negative behaviors. The teachers displayed a pattern of more positive behavior and less negative behavior toward the student whose gender was "appropriate" to the lesson (Hechtman & Rosenthal, 1991). Again, this result suggests that teachers exaggerate gender differences on tasks. This pattern might have a particularly corrosive effect on females' performance, since there is some evidence that women's self-evaluations are more dependent on other people's evaluations of them than are men's self-evaluations (Roberts, 1991). In light of all of this, there is little surprise in our surprise that gender differences in ability seem to be small and getting smaller.

GENDER ROLES

One place to start thinking about gender roles is with a very influential view of American life proposed in the 1950s by sociologist Talcott Parsons (1955). For Parsons, the family, like all groups, has two kinds of tasks: the task of accomplishing things—making money—and the task of tending to the social-emotional needs of its members. According to Parsons, these tasks are assigned for the most part to different specialists within the family. The father makes the money; the mother keeps the family together as a social-emotional unit. These two tasks, the argument goes, require different sorts of personalities.

The task-oriented leader—the father—had better be dominant, assertive, and in general "tough" to make it in the world. The mother, on the other hand, must be warm, caring, loyal, and willing to sacrifice her own desires for those of the group. So, the argument goes, families—like all organizations—need to recruit personnel who have been trained to possess just these qualities. Who is to do this training? The answer is the family itself. Not only should the American family be made up of fathers with "masculine" orientations toward the world and women with "feminine" ones, but the American family should also be well suited to train children to become the mothers and fathers of their own families.

Socialization and Gender Roles

Parsons argued that the family by and large succeeded in socializing girls to grow up with the right personalities to become ideal mothers and socializing boys to become ideal fathers. Parsons accepted psychoanalysis, the theory of human development proposed by Freud, as the mechanism by which this socialization was to be accomplished.* The American family was seen in the 1950s as both expressing and creating this division of labor by gender.

It is important to understand just what this socialization was to accomplish. It was first to lead to the development of men and women who were prepared to act in their respective ways as the adults in their own families. But that wasn't enough. It was also important that the developing little girls and boys see this division of personalities by sex as *natural.* Boys were not only to become breadwinners, but to see it as fitting and proper that they

---

*The details of how this socialization was to occur are (1) terribly complex, (2) not generally accepted by psychologists now, and (3) not going to be discussed further by me.

◀ *A scene from* Father Knows Best. *As the title suggests, in this popular television series of the 1950s, father worked outside the home and knew everything; mother mostly prepared meals and dried tears.*

grow up to be breadwinners. Girls were to become mothers and distinctly *not* breadwinners, and they were to see that as natural and proper. Socialization was to produce people who not only played out their assigned roles in the family, but did so without any sense of coercion or loss; men and women were to see their playing out their assigned roles as the "natural" unfolding of their personalities. Indeed, boys and girls were to be socialized to become adults who thought that men and women who *didn't* play their assigned parts were defective. The traditional stereotypes about male and female traits served to justify and rationalize the sexual division of labor (Hoffman & Hurst, 1990).

There is no question that at least in a limited sense, these patterns of socialization work. For example, Alice Eagly has reviewed the literature of the emergence and effectiveness of leadership as it relates to gender. She found that in initially leaderless groups, men *did* emerge as leaders more often than women did, especially in short-term groups that did not require extensive social interaction (Eagly & Karau, 1991). And men were evaluated as better leaders, at least under a narrow set of circumstances—when leadership was especially directive and authoritarian (Eagly, Makhijani, & Klonsky, 1992). Eagly attributed these results to the different gender roles or personality types that men and women are assigned to, just the roles that Parsons articulated.

In the 1950s, assignment to these personality types on the basis of biological sex was not something to be accomplished once and for all in childhood; rather, we were to find even in adulthood that serious deviation from our assigned roles would be met with social pressure to conform. In such a world, it was natural and obvious that companies paid women less than men for exactly the same job—after all, he had a family to support—or even fired women who married; what did she need a job for, she had a husband!

The psychological wisdom of the day tended to endorse this sociological view. The psychological wisdom too saw human nature as composed of two fundamentally different kinds of personalities—masculine ones and feminine ones. Masculinity and femininity could be thought of as the two ends of the personality spectrum. Moreover, the psychology of the time saw "feminine" women and "masculine" men as adjusted and normal, while women with achievement strivings and men with social-emotional needs were seen as abnormal and pathological.

Changing Gender Concepts

Well, times have changed. No doubt the most important change is political. We no longer see it as even vaguely justifiable to pay women less than men for doing the same task—let alone to fire a woman because she marries. This does not mean, however, that we do in fact pay women the same amount we pay men; one typical study found, for example, that recent female graduates with an MBA (master of business administration) were paid about $2,700 *less* than their male counterparts (Frieze, Olson, & Good, 1990). And this is not because women do not negotiate as aggressively as men do. In at least one study, they did, and still received 1.6 percent lower salaries than men did (Gerhart & Rynes, 1991). Although this difference may seem small, the effect of a small difference in starting salary can *over the course of a career* be huge, since raises are typically thought of as a percentage of starting salary. Still, American culture will no longer tolerate *overt*, blatant discrimination by

▲ *Women are still the ones to become pregnant, but our ideas about what jobs women can hold, even when pregnant, have certainly changed.*

gender. But the changes have been broader than merely political and economic.

Today, we—and here I mean we as a culture—tend to regard the view that males and females will "naturally" grow up to have different personalities not as a biological fact but as a stereotype, an oversimplified and probably inaccurate picture of the way things are. Psychologists have participated in the breaking up of this traditional picture.*

In the traditional picture we have been painting, it was natural to think of masculinity and femininity as opposites, to imagine that people were one or the other, or perhaps less crudely, that there was a single *dimension* that stretched from femininity on one end to masculinity on the other. Men, it was expected, would cluster toward one end of the dimension, while women would cluster at the other. But this idea has come under strong challenge.

In the early 1970s, Sandra Bem as well as Janet Spence and Robert Helmreich proposed that the notion of a single dimension of masculinity-femininity misdescribed what people are like. Rather, they proposed that the traits that we call masculine, the ones that make for a good breadwinner (assertiveness, for example) and those we call feminine (nurturance, for example) are really quite independent of one another. That is, there is no reason a person can't be *both* nurturant and assertive, or *neither* nurturant nor assertive. The proposal, then, was that the traditional Parsonian picture was wrong by assuming that if someone was socialized to have the qualities a breadwinner needed, then she couldn't also be socialized to have the qualities a social-emotional linchpin needed.

Sociology and psychology of the 1950s assumed that

- each family (like any small group) needed a task-oriented leader and a socio-emotional leader;

- men were by their nature the former and women were by their nature the latter;

- men with "feminine traits" were unhappy, and women with "masculine" traits were unhappy.

Measuring Masculinity and Femininity

To demonstrate that masculinity and femininity involve independent sets of traits, Bem developed the Bem Sex Role Inventory (BSRI), and Spence and Helmreich developed the Personal Attributes Questionnaire (PAQ). These two instruments are similar, although they differ in the details of the logic that guided their construction. We shall look in detail first at how the BSRI was constructed, and how it is related to the notion of psychological androgyny, and then we shall consider the Spence and Helmreich questionnaire.

THE BEM SEX ROLE INVENTORY

Sandra Bem began by making a list of two hundred personality traits that were positive in social value and struck her as either masculine or feminine in tone. Samples of undergraduate subjects were then asked to rate the items in terms of how desirable they would be "for a man" or "for a woman." Bem looked for items that distinguished men from women—she looked for traits that her subjects thought of as more desirable for one gender than the other. Twenty traits considered to be more desirable in a man—for example, being independent—were collected as a masculinity scale; twenty that were considered more desirable in a woman—being nurturant, for example—made up the femininity scale; twenty items that did not differentiate the sexes were

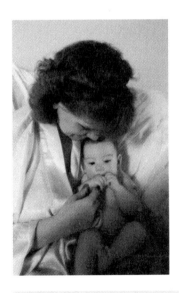

▲ *A woman being nurturant toward a child.*

---

*One measure of the breakup comes from a review of the differences between the way little boys and little girls are now being socialized. A meta-analysis of 172 studies recently found only small differences in the way boys and girls are treated (Lytton & Romney, 1991).

included as filler items. Notice that this method of constructing the scales starts with differences in the culture's **normative** conceptions—our ideas of what men and women *should* be like—not with data about what men and women *are* like.

Roughly one thousand college students were then given these scales and asked to rate the degree to which each trait *was a correct description of themselves*. If there is a single dimension, and if these self-reports about traits were accurate, then those who described themselves as having masculine traits should *not* also have described themselves as having feminine traits. There should be a strong *negative* correlation between the masculine and feminine scales. But in fact, the data revealed small correlations between the scales. For men, there was a small *positive* correlation (+0.11); for women, there was a small negative correlation (−0.14). These data suggest that masculinity and femininity *are* independent dimensions, that a person may be high on *both* scales or low on both scales.

The data further suggest that the division of personalities into masculine and feminine is too simple. There are actually four types: (1) masculine people, who have lots of the masculine traits and few of the feminine ones; (2) feminine people, who possess many feminine traits and few masculine ones; (3) androgynous people, who have *both* masculine and feminine traits; and (4) undifferentiated people, who possess *neither* of these kinds of traits. Now, as it happened, these four types were not evenly divided by gender in the Bem study. As you might expect, there were more masculine men than women and more feminine women than men. This is just to say that gender role socialization does work to some degree; our culture does succeed, to some degree, in assigning personality traits by gender (Bem, 1974).

THE PERSONAL ATTRIBUTES QUESTIONNAIRE

The Spence-Helmreich PAQ was developed with the aid of judges, and also uses separate masculinity and femininity scales. But there is one central difference between it and the BSRI: the judges in this case were asked to select positively valued traits that were more "typical" of a man than a woman, and vice versa. So from the start, the Spence-Helmreich instrument revolved around male-female differences that people think exist, rather than the differences that they think *ought* to exist.*

Spence and Helmreich also asked subjects to indicate the degree to which each of the traits was descriptive of themselves, and they looked for differences between the sexes on the two scales and at correlations between the sexes on the two scales. Like Bem, Spence and Helmreich found differences between the sexes, which confirmed their judges' beliefs that there are more masculine men than women and more feminine women than men, and like Bem, they found only slight correlations between the scales (in this case, weakly positive), again confirming the independence of masculinity and femininity (Spence, Helmreich, & Stapp, 1974).

What can we conclude from these studies? In one way, both scales confirm our stereotypes about men and women. They show that men and women do differ (or at least say they differ) on just those traits we would expect them to

*Richard Lippa has advanced a reliable measure of masculinity and femininity, one also based on empirical differences between men and women (Lippa and Connelly, 1990; Lippa, 1991).

differ on. Where these two lines of research challenge our traditional conceptions is in our sense of naturalness about all of this. If it were somehow natural for men to be masculine and women to be feminine, then we should expect the two measures to be tightly and negatively linked—for those scoring high in one to score low in another—and that isn't true. Parsons was apparently wrong in arguing that socialization must produce either masculine or feminine people. It *doesn't* produce just these two types.

Masculinity, Femininity, and Adjustment

What of the idea that masculine men and feminine women are "well-adjusted," while men with feminine and women with masculine traits are somehow pathological? Sandra Bem challenged that idea too, arguing that the best-adjusted people weren't feminine women and masculine men, but people of both genders who had both sets of traits. These androgynous people, she argued, would be best able to deal in a flexible way with whatever demands their lives placed on them; they could call on the tough, masculine traits when those were needed, and the more social-emotional, feminine traits when those qualities were desirable (Bem, 1975).

Research on the relations among gender, psychological traits, and adjustment has led to clear and consistent results. The results favor Bem. Both men and women who describe themselves as possessing masculine, achievement-oriented traits have higher self-esteem (a widely used measure of adjustment) than those who lack these traits. And both men and women who describe themselves as having feminine, nurturant traits are better off than those who do not (Whitley, 1983; Marsh, Antill, & Cunningham, 1987; see also O'Heron & Orlofsky, 1990). It is, then, both possible and desirable to have children who can become *both* achievement-oriented and nurturant.

Some studies of the effect of masculinity and femininity have found that though having both masculine and feminine traits predicts better adjustment for both men and women, it is more important for both men and women to possess masculine traits than to possess feminine traits. Indeed, in some studies, the beneficial effect of having masculine traits has been nine times as great as that of having feminine traits (Lubinski, Tellegen, & Butcher, 1981, 1983; see also Aubé and Koestner, 1992, on the greater importance of masculine traits). One interpretation of these results is that though American culture values both achievement and nurturance, it places much greater stress on achievement and assertiveness, the masculine traits, than it does on expressiveness and nurturance, the feminine traits. Still, one wonders whether there might not be a male bias in the conception of adjustment that leads to this difference. Some theorists believe that masculine self-esteem and adjustment are tied to independence and difference from others, while feminine self-esteem is tied to connection to others (Josephs, Markus, & Tafarodi, 1992; see also Marsh and Byrne, 1991, on the notion that self-esteem is a complex concept with both masculine and feminine aspects). The Parsonian ideas return!

The BSRI and PAQ are psychological inventories that ask people to report on their traits; it is reasonable to ask of all such self-report measures whether they reflect the traits the subjects actually have, or just the traits the subjects

For both men and women, possessing masculine *and* feminine traits is related to being well-adjusted.

▶ (A) "Drag Queens" play with our conceptions of gender stereotypes, as does (B) k.d. lang, who performs in her characteristically androgynous attire.

A   B

think (or wish) they had. In other words, we want to know whether the scales really do differentiate subjects in terms of their relevant behavior.

By now there is quite a bit of evidence that the BSRI and the PAQ do distinguish between subjects in relevant ways. One study examined subjects' willingness to do things that were gender inappropriate. In this study, **sex-typed** (masculine men and feminine women), **androgynous,** and **cross-sex-typed** (males with higher femininity than masculinity scores and females with the reverse pattern) subjects were told that the experimenters needed pictures of them performing a variety of activities (for another study). The subjects were given fifteen pairs of activities and were asked to pick one from each pair that they would be willing to be photographed doing. They were to be paid a variable amount of money, depending on their choices.

Some of the choices pitted a gender-neutral activity (peeling an orange, for example) against a masculine sex-typed activity (baiting a fishhook). Others involved a choice between a neutral activity and a feminine sex-typed one—preparing baby formula, for example. Still others were choices between neutral actions. In all of the cases involving gender-typed activities, it was the gender-*inappropriate* activity that paid more—males would receive more for making the formula, women more for baiting the hooks. Thus, the subjects' desire to make money was pitted against their desire to avoid doing things typical of the opposite gender. The investigators expected the androgynous and cross-sex-typed subjects to be more willing to perform the gender-inappropriate (but more profitable) activities than the sex-typed subjects. The experimenters' expectations were confirmed (see Figure 12.8). Moreover, as expected, the sex-typed subjects felt worse about performing the gender-inappropriate actions when they were forced to (Bem & Lenney, 1976).

In another study, pairs made up of one man and one woman interacted with one another. Some pairs were made up of an androgynous man and an androgynous woman. Others consisted of two sex-typed partners, that is, a man high on the masculinity scale but low on the femininity scale and a woman high on the femininity scale but low on the masculinity scale. If these scales are valid, then we should expect that the men would have dominated the interactions more in the sex-typed pairs, and so they did. In contrast, at least in the right circumstance, the androgynous men and women shared

FIGURE 12.8

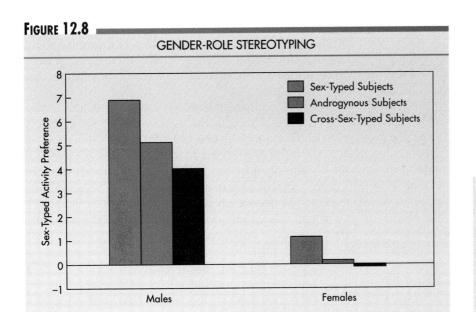

GENDER-ROLE STEREOTYPING

◄ *Gender stereotypical activity preferences for sex-typed, androgynous, and cross-sex-typed subjects. Sex-typed subjects (especially males) were more stereotypical in their preferences than other categories of subjects. (Data from Bem & Lenney, 1976)*

leadership in the course of their interactions (Porter, Geis, Cooper, & Newman, 1985). Results like these suggest that the scales really do measure differences relevant to our conceptions of femininity and masculinity.

You may be wondering just what the "right circumstance" was in the experiment above. In this study, men and women shared leadership if (and only if) just before beginning their discussion they privately filled out a scale called the Attitudes Toward Women Scale, which assesses the degree to which people have traditional or egalitarian attitudes toward women (Spence & Helmreich, 1978). The androgynous subjects who had recently expressed their attitudes toward women acted in an egalitarian way. But androgynous subjects who had not recently thought about these issues acted in a traditional, sex-typed way, with the male dominating the conversation. This result suggests that the same people who are androgynous—possess both masculine and feminine traits—have liberal attitudes toward women.

WRAP-UP

We humans are the product of our genes and our environments. Perhaps the best way to think of this is to conceive of our genes as placing our behavior on a leash—we cannot become creatures our genes will not let us become. The question, then, with regard to any behavior is: How long is the leash by which our genes hold us?

This will depend on the kind of behavior in question. In particular, it will depend on how relevant to reproduction the behavior is. Because of its obvious connection to reproduction, then, we might expect the leash for sexual behavior to be fairly short. It is hard to quantify just how long the leash is, but the evidence we have considered on cultural differences in sexual behavior suggests it isn't all that short—there is plenty of room for culture to play a role. The historical changes we have seen recently in sexual standards and behavior also suggest that the leash is a long one. Still, there do seem to be some differences between men and women in their sexual proclivities that *might* be traced back to our genes.

Western culture elaborates on these differences, with the result that men and women are assigned different roles in the social world. We saw that in Talcott Parsons's view of the family, the two tasks that each family needed done—achievement in the world and tending to the family's social-emotional needs—were sharply distinguished by gender. Men were required to make the money; women were required to take care of the family. These role assignments within the family both took advantage of and produced distinctive personalities. So it was the family that was the focus and source of gender role stereotypes. What is the case with families now?

The thrust of the evidence is that although marriages have become more egalitarian in recent years, it is still true that the mother has the primary responsibility for child care. As Sandra Bem puts it, it is still the mother the school will call if her child is sick (Bem, 1984). With regard to the tensions between careers and families, there seems still to be an "unequal egalitarianism" (Wetherell, Stiven, & Potter, 1987; see Chapter 15 for more on this topic).

SUMMARY

1. Cultures differ to a substantial degree in the sexual standards and attitudes they inculcate.

2. Western culture has recently undergone substantial change in these attitudes—the *sexual revolution.* For the most part, the sexual revolution consisted in a change in sexual standards and behavior for *women.*

3. Females (of most species) invest more in their offspring and are certain who their offspring are, while males cannot be certain. In general, males might be expected to be more sexually ardent, while females might be expected to be more selective. A variety of data about human sexuality are consistent with this expectation.

4. *Homosexuality* is a major puzzle from the point of view of evolutionary theory, since gay men and lesbian women would be expected to have fewer offspring than heterosexual men and women. It is possible, however, that homosexuality *does* have a genetic basis.

5. Culture takes the fundamental, biological differences between men and women and elaborates on them to create gender roles. In the traditional view, men were seen as having those traits needed for achievement, while women were seen as having traits needed to provide nurturance.

6. In the traditional view, men who had masculine traits and women who had feminine traits were seen as adjusted, while men with feminine traits and women with masculine traits were expected to be maladjusted. Recent evidence suggests that men and women who possess *both* sets of traits are actually better adjusted.

CHAPTER 13

Aggression

It is not surprising that social psychologists have been concerned about aggression. We live in a century marked by two world wars, and with the knowledge that a next one would be the last. Closer to our everyday lives, fear of street violence undermines our sense of security and sours our appreciation of our great cities. It is natural that psychologists want to be able to help control our all too obvious propensity for violence. In this chapter, we shall review social psychologists' thinking about aggression.

WHAT IS AGGRESSION?

In order to proceed, we need a conception of what aggression is and some distinctions among types of aggression. Social psychologists usually include under "aggression" only actions *intended* to harm another. Accidentally hurting someone else is *not* aggression. Within the domain of intentional actions, two types can be distinguished. One type, often called **impulsive** or **emotional aggression,** includes actions in which the aim of the act is to cause harm to its victim. Punching someone in the nose who has insulted you is an example of impulsive aggression. The other type has been called **instrumental aggression,** which includes intentional actions that harm another but that are aimed at something other than harming the victim. A mugger who stabs someone to get her money is engaged in instrumental aggression because harming the victim isn't the mugger's aim; his aim is getting the money.

We will not focus on instrumental aggression in this chapter. This is not because instrumental aggression doesn't display an interesting psychology; it does. But the interesting question about instrumental aggression isn't "Why is the person motivated to commit the aggression?" That is fairly obvious; his motivation is the money. The interesting question is "Why isn't the person inhibited from committing the aggression?" And that is a question about the person's morality, not his aggressive motives.

ANIMAL AGGRESSION

Types of aggressive motivation:

- predatory
- inter-male
- sex-related
- maternal
- danger-induced
- irritable

Our primary focus in this chapter will be on impulsive aggression—action motivated by a desire to harm another. The sheer prevalence of aggression in the human record has led thinkers throughout the ages to speculate about the origins of these dark human urges. Some, especially Freud, have even argued that we have an instinct for aggression. The notion is that we have inherited this instinct from our predatory, evolutionary predecessors. But this idea isn't faithful to the facts about aggression in other species. In particular, it misses the important fact that there isn't *one* kind of aggression manifest in other species, but rather several different kinds. Most have nothing to do with predation. These distinctive types of aggression are marked by different behavioral manifestations, different triggering stimuli, and different neural and hormonal underpinnings. In order to keep human aggression in perspective, then, we shall first take a look at the various kinds of aggression prevalent in the animal world: predatory, inter-male, sex-related, maternal, danger-induced, and irritable.

Predatory Aggression

Many species of animals hunt for their living. We humans, in our "natural habitat," probably did. And a predator pouncing on its prey exemplifies intentional harm doing.* Predatory aggression is simple and clear in one way: there's no mystery about its evolutionary significance—if you make your living by hunting, then you had better be equipped by your genes to do it. Because of the simplicity and obviousness of this aggression, it is tempting to see it as the *only* form of aggression—to imagine, for example, that when animals attack members of their own species, they are just revealing their predatory instincts against their own species. But virtually all researchers on animal aggression agree that predatory aggression is *not* the only form.

One reason to distinguish predatory aggression from other kinds is that the behavior of a predator after its prey is strikingly different from that of the same animal aroused in a different way. Observe a cat stalking a mouse. First, she lowers her back close to the ground; silently and with unequaled grace she slinks near her prey, and then ruthlessly and explosively she launches a lethal attack on her target, typically severing the mouse's neck with a single bite. This is a very business-like response to the problem of earning a living.

*If you wanted to press the point, you might argue that predatory aggression is really just "instrumental" aggression. After all, the hungry tiger has no more concern for her prey than a bank robber does for his victim. But we cover predatory aggression here because it is traditionally seen as a kind of aggression, and because it is useful to consider other sorts of aggression in relation to it. A similar caveat applies to maternal aggression, which we will come to shortly. See Lysak, Rule, & Dobbs, 1989, on various ways to define aggression.

◄ (A) A predator in the wild and (B) a household predator.

Cats, even the ones we keep as pets, have been shaped by their evolutionary past to be extremely effective predators.

But cats also show a kind of attack that has been referred to as emotional or enraged. This kind is elicited when a cat is threatened or in pain. In this state, the cat loses much of the economy of motion that typifies her predatory behavior: She attacks by lashing out with her paws rather than by an almost surgical attack with her teeth. An enraged cat, as opposed to a cat stalking a mouse, is *piloerect;* that is, her fur stands on end, which is a sign of arousal of the sympathetic nervous system, a symptom of emotion in humans. And she hisses, a foolish thing to do if she were stalking a mouse. These differences in response suggest that there are different neural systems involved in predatory attack and rage.

John Flynn and his collaborators at Yale have provided strong evidence to support this distinction. In these now-classic experiments, the investigators stimulated an area of the brain called the *lateral hypothalamus;* in response, the cat offered her typical prey-stalking behavior, and killed with a sharp bite through the neck. Moreover, a cat stimulated in this way preferred to attack a rat rather than the experimenter. But if a different area of the brain, the *medial hypothalamus,* was stimulated, the cat showed cat rage— it attacked with its claws, hissed, and preferred to attack the experimenter rather than a rat. So there are at least two different ways that a cat attacks something, and they are served by different areas of the cat brain (Wasman & Flynn, 1962; Levinson & Flynn, 1965). This convergence of behavioral and neural evidence suggests that it is important to distinguish predatory aggression from other attacks. As we shall see, there is good reason to distinguish several more subtypes of aggression.

Inter-Male Aggression

In many species, males fight each other more often than females fight each other. Typically, the male young in these species (and this includes humans) play in a more rough-and-tumble way than do females, and both aggression between adult males and the rough-and-tumble play of the young are related to testosterone, the male sex hormone. For these reasons, we refer to this kind of aggression as inter-male aggression, but this does not imply that it is altogether absent among females; it isn't.

One evolutionary reason for inter-male aggression was discussed in Chapter 12: males compete for access to females, while females less often compete for access to males. Competition for females among males is typically intense, while competition for males by females is typically weaker. There seems, then, to be evolutionary pressure for the development of inter-male aggression. This leads us to suspect that there is a distinct inter-male form of aggression.

This suspicion would be strengthened if there were a specific form of behavior used in inter-male aggression. And many investigators have reported just that. Niko Tinbergen has observed, for example, that male deer fight each other by lowering their majestic antlers and charging. But when these same deer fight anything but another male deer, they use their front hooves. The magnificent antlers seem to have evolved in the service of inter-male aggression (Tinbergen, 1953). From the imposing appearance of the deer antlers, one might suppose that they are especially lethal, but just the reverse is true. In fact, it is commonly observed that inter-male aggression in many species is *less* lethal than other forms of aggression (Lorenz, 1966; Moyer, 1976). This fact too leads us to suspect that inter-male aggression is a special form of aggression.

Sex-Related Aggression

Freud and many subsequent theorists have proposed an intimate connection between sexual arousal and aggression. Observation of the behavior of other species suggests this, since in some species the behavior of a courting male looks very much like his behavior when attacking another male; that is, the behavioral components of courtship are like the components of aggression. (This "aggression," though, rarely leads to injury. German ethologist Konrad Lorenz argues that this is because the female engages in gestures that limit the male's aggression.) A further reason to suppose a link between sexual arousal and aggression is that testosterone, the male sex hormone, leads to both increased sexual desire among males (and females) of many species (including humans) and to an increase in a variety of forms of aggression (see Money & Ehrhardt, 1972, on testosterone and human sexual behavior and aggression, and Brownson & Desjardines, 1971, on testosterone and aggression in other mammals). As we shall see, there is a growing research literature on sex and aggression in humans. We shall turn to that research later as we consider human experimental research on aggression.

It is important to distinguish this form of aggression from inter-male aggression. Inter-male aggression is sex-related, in the sense that the establishment of a territory or of high rank in a dominance hierarchy leads to opportunities to mate. Thus, the final payoff, to some degree, for inter-male aggression is the opportunity to have sex. But while sex may be the ultimate payoff of inter-male aggression, it doesn't depend on sexual arousal or the presence of sexual stimuli. There is a difference between the ultimate payoff of an act and the stimulus conditions that elicit it. The term ***sex-related aggression*** is reserved for aggression stimulated by sexual stimuli.

Maternal Aggression

In most mammalian species, a mother will attack anything that seems to her to threaten her young. This ***maternal aggression*** is released only if the mother is in the hormonal state associated with having recently given birth, and if she is in sight of her young. Indeed, most cases of attacks on humans by bears in national parks are a result of the humans coming between the mother bear and her young.

Maternal aggression has not received much attention from social psychologists, probably because it isn't much of a social problem. We support mothers who protect their children; we wouldn't want to eliminate that instinct. Indeed, we probably wouldn't even want to say that a mother who defended her child from attack was engaged in aggression at all. In ordinary

◀ Grizzly bears. The mother bear will show maternal aggression if something (or someone) comes between her and her cubs.

usage, we reserve the term "aggression" for unjustified attacks, and we usually consider the defense of one's child justified.

There seems to be good reason to distinguish each of the four types of aggression discussed so far—predatory, inter-male, sex-related, and maternal—from each other. But as we turn now to the last two types—danger-induced aggression and irritable aggression—the grounds are shakier. It is not quite so clear that these really are two rather than one kind of aggression. But provisionally it seems worth distinguishing them.

Danger-Induced Aggression

An animal that perceives itself as in danger may emit a variety of responses. Probably the most common is to flee. If it can't flee, then it may freeze in place or offer an **appeasement gesture,** some behavior that turns off the attacker's aggression. (Children who yell "uncle" are a clear example.) But if escape fails, the animal will attack the threat (Moyer, 1976). This is an important point for wild animal trainers; one thing you never want to do when training a tiger is to come between it and its escape route. If it perceives you as a threat, it is likely to want to flee, but if it can't flee, it is likely (like a cornered rat) to turn on you, an outcome you wouldn't want to encourage.

Danger-induced aggression can clearly be distinguished from predatory aggression. As mentioned before, a cat attacking its prey does so in an efficient, quiet, controlled way, without signs of sympathetic nervous system arousal, but a cat facing danger hisses, shows signs of arousal, and attacks in a different way. Self-defensive aggression, unlike inter-male, sex-related, or maternal aggression, is just as common in both sexes in most species.

The evolutionary significance of self-defensive aggression is clear: if the choice is fight or die, then it is clearly in the animal's genetic advantage to fight. But it is also important to remember that fleeing a predator one can escape is likely to pay off even better in terms of reproductive advantage. And for species preyed on by predators whose attack tendencies are stimulated only by moving targets, freezing or feigning death may work just as well as attacking, so they do; animals have no pride in the face of predators.

Irritable Aggression

Irritable or **annoyance aggression** is aggression released by a variety of disparate stimuli that have little in common except that they annoy. For example, if rats are subjected to electric shock, they will rear up and assume an attack posture and attack another rat or even an inanimate object. And while being shocked, they will even work to provide themselves with an object to attack (Azrin, Hutchinson, & Sallery, 1964; Azrin, Hutchinson, & McLauglin, 1965). Other aversive conditions besides shock will produce this sort of attack. Such frustration, as we shall see, is of particular relevance to the research on human aggression.

Irritable aggression is similar in many ways to self-defensive aggression—they both involve sympathetic nervous system arousal; they both occur in both sexes; they are both, in some sense, a response to an attack. The major difference seems to be that self-defensive aggression is usually preceded by attempts to flee, while annoyance aggression isn't.

▲ Irritable aggression.

We have seen that it is a bit naive to think of humans as having inherited an aggressive, predatory instinct from our evolutionary predecessors. And this leads us to ask: Which of these six kinds of aggression is the precursor to human aggression or anger? The answer depends on which kind of human aggression one has in mind. Probably none of them is a precursor to instrumental aggression, aggressing against someone just to get something he has. Rather, social psychologists have been concerned with impulsive aggression, which is probably best thought of as aggression born of anger (Berkowitz, 1974). So our question is: What are the precursors to anger?

Aggression as Response to Transgression

We begin our review of social psychologists' investigation into the roots of human anger with two opposed theories (see Figure 13.1). The first one is exceedingly traditional, cognitive, and rooted in the notion that anger is the result of being attacked. It suggests that anger is at its heart something quite reasonable, if not entirely rational. The second is a more modern theory with its origins in the psychoanalyst's couch and the animal learning laboratory. It suggests that anger is blind, brute, irrational, and never reasonable.

THE ARISTOTELIAN ACCOUNT

The traditional account is Aristotle's. Aristotle argued that the source of human anger is the perception of insult; people are moved to harm another just when they perceive (rightly or wrongly) that the other person has insulted them (*The Rhetoric*, Book 2). According to this view, anger is a response to an assessment of the environment, a rather abstract assessment that a transgression has occurred, so in that sense it is cognitive. This view also sees anger as an essentially social phenomenon in the sense that it is sensitive to social norms. The very notion of a transgression implies social standards. Further, since Aristotle saw anger as essentially directed toward revenge for injustice, he saw anger as a pro-social emotion, serving to maintain the social

FIGURE 13.1

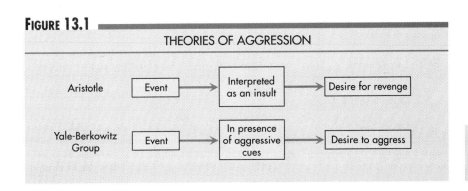

THEORIES OF AGGRESSION

Aristotle: Event → Interpreted as an insult → Desire for revenge

Yale-Berkowitz Group: Event → In presence of aggressive cues → Desire to aggress

◀ *The Aristotelian and Yale accounts of the nature of aggression.*

order by punishing those who transgressed against it.* Some current social psychologists still essentially accept this Aristotelian account (Averill, 1982; Sabini & Silver, 1982).

THE FREUD-YALE ACCOUNT

A different view of anger was developed by a group of Yale psychologists who were interested in bringing Freudian insights together with animal learning theory's rigorous, experimental methods. Freud argued that socialization inevitably involved frustration. Having to wait to be fed until Mommy is free, having to wait to empty one's bladder or bowels until in the appropriate place, and so on all involve **frustration,** the blocking or inhibition of a response. According to Freud's account, these frustrating experiences lead to a reservoir of aggression that is released by future frustrations (Freud, 1933). The Yale group's attempt to make this claim rigorous was also informed by evidence that, as we have seen, frustrated animals tend to attack whatever is handy. These two lines of evidence led John Dollard and his colleagues to a bold claim: "The occurrence of aggressive behavior always presupposes the existence of frustration and, contrariwise, the existence of frustration always leads to some form of aggression" (Dollard, Miller, Doob, Mowrer, & Sears, 1939).†

"I HEARD IT'S HARMFUL FOR A PERSON TO KEEP HIS HOSTILITY BOTTLED UP, SO I FIRED EVERYBODY."

The Freud-Yale view is very different from Aristotle's. According to the Freud-Yale view, anger is essentially a blind, irrational response to frustration. Proponents of the **frustration-aggression theory** argued that because of the way we are innately wired, we respond to the frustration of our desires with the impulse to commit aggression regardless of whether that aggression will remove the frustration and regardless of the moral legitimacy of the frustrating person's action. Because anger is blind, it is a threat to, rather than support of, the social order. Which theory is correct?

One aspect of the Yale group's theory is fairly widely conceded to be too strong. Surely *some* aggression is purely instrumental, not involving impulses stirred up by frustration. So many modern theorists would allow that only *some* aggression is connected to frustration. But the issue of whether *all* aggression was the result of frustration wasn't the bone of contention between the Yale group and the Aristotelians; the bone of contention was whether frustration was a *sufficient* cause of anger. Let us see how the evidence has gone on that score.

CLASSIC FINDINGS IN SOCIAL PSYCHOLOGY: DOES FRUSTRATION ALWAYS LEAD TO AGGRESSION?

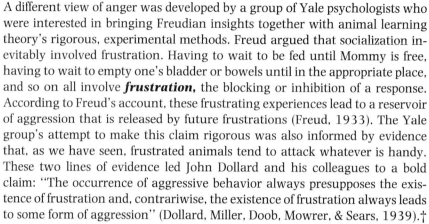

The Yale group amassed considerable evidence for its claim; some of it is reported in Chapter 4. Here I mention only one study. In this study, subjects

---

*This is not to say that Aristotle didn't think that anger could get out of hand. Indeed, Aristotle thought *everything* could get out of hand.

†Yale psychology was also wedded to the behaviorism of the day; hence, it avoided a notion like "anger" and spoke only of "aggression." Although the Yale view should have been called the frustration-anger hypothesis, it is known as the frustration-aggression hypothesis. So we will follow the Yale group's nomenclature in talking of frustration aggression; but we really mean to be talking (as they did) about frustration anger.

were asked to imagine themselves in sixteen frustrating situations and asked how they would feel. In one situation, for example, subjects imagined they were waiting for a bus, and the bus driver passed by the bus stop, thus frustrating the people waiting to get on. The subjects reported that in this and the other fifteen situations they would feel angry (Doob & Sears, 1939). And this supports the frustration-aggression hypothesis.

JUSTIFIED AND UNJUSTIFIED FRUSTRATION — *people much less angry with justified frustration than unjustified.*

The frustration-aggression hypothesis also lines up with common sense; most of us have had the experience of lashing out at someone, or even something—a car that won't start—because we have been frustrated. The frustration-aggression hypothesis captures this intuition, and it has received substantial experimental support (Berkowitz, 1989). But there has always been another set of studies that point away from frustration as the usual cause of human anger, and away from annoyance aggression as the animal analogue of human anger. Consider a study by Nicholas Pastore.

Nicholas Pastore noted something about all of the situations that Doob and Sears used in their investigation; they all involved not only frustration but *unjustified* frustration (Pastore, 1952). Pastore argued that it wasn't being frustrated that made subjects angry; it was being illegitimately frustrated. The waiting passengers weren't only frustrated; they were *transgressed* against. And this suggests that the bus driver's reason for passing the waiting customers by would affect how angry the passengers would become.

To show this, Pastore constructed sixteen new descriptions. Each contained the same frustration as one in the original set, except that now the frustration was *justified.* The rewritten version of the bus incident, for example, claimed that the bus said ''garage'' on its side, indicating that it was out of service. Pastore found that people reported much less anger when the situation described a justified frustration (see Figure 13.2). Pastore's data suggest, then, that it isn't frustration per se that arouses anger; rather, our anger turns on whether or not we perceive the frustration as justified. And therefore it depends on, among other things, the intent of the frustrating agent and the social norms governing the frustration (Kane, Joseph, & Tedeschi, 1976; Dyck & Rule, 1978; Ferguson & Rule, 1983).* And some experimenters have found, contrary to the Yale group's hypothesis, that people will become aggressive *only* if the aggression relieves that frustration; that is, only in cases in which the aggression is a *rational* response to the frustration (Buss, 1966).

Finally, there is evidence that mitigating information can reduce retaliation in return for an insult. **Mitigating information** is information about the occurrence of a transgression that suggests that the offender is not as bad a person as she otherwise might seem. Mitigating information is one example of what Ewing Goffman has called **remedial exchanges.** Other examples of remedial exchanges are justifications, excuses, and apologies (Goffman, 1971). **Jusifications** are claims that one did the right thing in light of the circumstances; ''Yes, I did push you to the ground, and yes, pushing people

---

*Kenneth Dodge has data that suggest that boys who are chronically in trouble with their teachers and peers get into such trouble for aggressive action in part because they *fail* to distinguish between intentional and accidental harm doing. They are aggressive because they perceive unintentional acts as intentional, and then retaliate (Dodge & Crick, 1990).

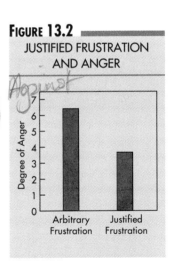

FIGURE 13.2
JUSTIFIED FRUSTRATION AND ANGER

▲ *Self-report of how angry subjects would become in the presence of arbitrary and justified frustration. (Data from Pastore, 1952)*

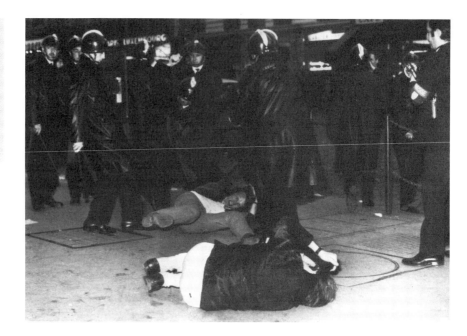

▶ *Police everywhere claim the right to use some measure of force in doing their job. Although their use of force within limits is justified, here they have overstepped their justification in their severe beating of this student demonstrator in Paris in May 1968.*

to the ground is wrong. But there was a sniper over there taking aim at you." **Excuses** claim that the person who did the wrong thing *couldn't have done otherwise.* "I know we were supposed to meet yesterday, but I was, at the time, in a coma." Last, **apologies** concede that one did the wrong thing, but that one promises to reform, to become a better person.

In one experiment, for example, an experimenter rudely and unfairly bawled out subjects. But the subjects then learned that the experimenter had acted so rudely because he was a graduate student and had a midterm exam coming up that he was very worried about. This information, while not excusing his behavior, at least made it seem less hostile. In some circumstances, such information reduced retaliation (Kremer & Stephens, 1983). But it does not reduce frustration.* This line of evidence supports Aristotle against the Freud-Yale group.

But the Yale group probably never intended to claim that frustration inevitably produced aggressive behavior; rather, they wanted to claim that frustration led to the *desire*, or the impulse to hurt someone. Most of us most of the time do not just act out our impulses. The Yale group would argue that on seeing the bus pass them by, Pastore's bus riders would become angry, but on recognizing that it was legitimate for the bus to pass them, they would suppress their anger and *not* engage in overt aggressive actions (Berkowitz, 1989). (They might also argue that being passed by the bus is frustrating, and discovering that the bus was *not* out of service is also frustrating. So in the not-out-of-service case, there are two frustrations rather than one.) These

*Two points to note. First, this experiment (like most investigating human aggression) relies, as Aristotle suggested, on insults—not frustration—to produce anger. Second, whether mitigations will reduce anger depends on their timing, among other things. Several studies have shown that mitigating information presented *before* the insult, or at least right after it, reduces anger better than mitigating information presented later (Zillman & Cantor, 1976; Kremer & Stephens, 1983; Johnson & Rule, 1986).

rejoinders hold on to the view that frustration gives rise to the impulse to inflict pain, but they agree that aggressive behavior isn't the inevitable result of those impulses.* So where do we stand?

Both the Aristotelians and the young Turks from Yale would argue that a central case of anger is one in which someone does something to you, something that you perceive as wrong. Aristotle would claim that this is because that's just the way we are; we are built to respond to transgression with anger. The Yalians would argue that this does happen, but for a different reason: the transgressions involve frustrations, and frustrations (blindly) give rise to anger.

AVERSIVE STATES AND ANGER

The Aristotelians have difficulty with the results of experiments like one carried out by Leonard Berkowitz. In this experiment, the subjects were told, under an experimental pretext, to keep their hands in water as they evaluated (by administering rewards and punishments) the work of another subject (actually a confederate). The subjects were run in two conditions; in one, they kept their hands in tepid water; in the other, they kept them in quite cold—6 degrees centigrade—water. Some subjects in each condition were told that punishment would help the other subject (the confederate); others were told that punishment would hurt her. In the punishment-hurts condition, the subjects with their hands in cold water punished the confederate more (and rewarded her less) than the subjects with their hands in tepid water (see Figure 13.3). In other words, the subjects who were in some pain reacted to the confederate in a less pleasant way than those who weren't in pain. They also reported feeling more irritated and annoyed than those with their hands in tepid water (Berkowitz, Cochran, & Embree, 1981). All of this is true, note, even though the confederate was in no way *responsible* for the subject's pain. Because the subjects were punishing someone in no way responsible for their pain, results like this one support the Yale group's anger-is-blind conception against Aristotelians.

But Berkowitz has also gathered data of some comfort to Aristotelians. He had found that aversive states do give rise to thoughts of punishment and transgression (Berkowitz, 1982, 1984, 1989; Berkowitz & Heimer, 1989). So perhaps the reason that aversive states lead to aggression is that they cause people to perceive themselves as having been transgressed.

In a similar vein, Roy Baumeister asked subjects to describe an incident in which someone really angered them (victims' stories), or to describe an incident in which they really angered someone else (perpetrators' stories). He found that victims tended to see the provoking event as arbitrary, gratuitous, or incomprehensible, harking back to Pastore's studies. Perpetrators, not surprisingly, had different views. About half of the perpetrators' stories depicted the incident as justified, or if not justified, then something over which they had no control (excusable); thus, about half of the perpetrator stories accepted no blame. *All* of the victim stories attributed blame to the perpetrator. Thus, Baumeister found some evidence that both victims and perpetrators—at least

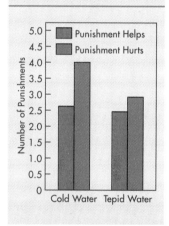

FIGURE 13.3

AVERSIVE STATES AND THE EXPRESSION OF ANGER

▲ *Punishment delivered by a subject acting as a supervisor to a subordinate varied based on whether the supervisor had her hand in cold or tepid water and on whether she believed that the punishment would help or hinder the subordinate. The pain from the cold water led the supervisor to deliver more punishment. (Data from Berkowitz, Cochran, & Embree, 1981)*

---

*Remember that we are talking here about whether frustration is a sufficient condition for aggression, not about whether frustration increases aggression provoked by, for example, insult. We will come back to this second question below.

in retrospect—construe their episodes of anger in moral terms (Baumeister, Stillwell, & Wotman, 1990; see also Betancourt & Blair, 1992, and Paquin, 1992).

These results on the face of it suggest an important role for moral cognitions in the genesis of anger and aggression. But Berkowitz has argued that these moral cognitions are *not* the cause of anger and aggression. Rather, aversive events give rise to angry, hostile, aggressive impulses by *blind association*, but these events also have a second, independent consequence: moralistic thoughts. The moralistic thoughts, then, aren't for Berkowitz *causes* of the aggressive impulses; they are mere (noncausal) *accompaniments* of episodes of anger. They are what are technically called **epiphenomena.**

There is a third possibility. The moralistic thoughts may be after-the-fact justifications for the victims' anger. They may be ideas the victims will use to explain to other people, and themselves, why they are so angry. All parties agree that punishment and transgression are related to anger and aggression; the remaining questions are about just how they are related.

The Modulation of Anger

We have so far asked only about the conditions that stimulate anger in the first place. But there is a substantial amount of research directed to the broader question of the conditions that increase or decrease the amount of aggression displayed or the amount of anger felt. The first modulator we will consider is frustration itself.

FRUSTRATION AND DEGREE OF ANGER

To examine the effects of frustration on anger, subjects in one study were told that they were to solicit pledges for a charity over the phone. Half of the subjects were told that they would receive 10¢ for each pledge; the others were told they would receive $1. Presumably the $1 group would be more frustrated when someone turned them down than would the 10¢ group. In addition, half of the subjects were told that the list of people they were calling was known to have a 10 to 15 percent probability of responding to such solicitations; the others were told that their list could be expected to yield a 60 to 65 percent success rate. This led half of the subjects to expect to succeed and the other half to expect to fail.

When a subject called a number from the list, she reached a confederate; the confederate always turned the solicitor down, but he did so in one of three ways. To one-third of the subjects, the confederate claimed that he wouldn't give because charities are a "rip-off." The subjects saw this, as they were supposed to, as an illegitimate frustration. In another third of the cases, the confederate claimed that he always gave to charities, but that he had just been laid off and couldn't right now. This the subjects saw as a justified frustration. When the remaining subjects called, the confederate led them to believe that while he usually gave to charity, he wouldn't give to this one, and he gave the impression that it was the subject's fault that he wouldn't contribute. This made the subjects feel that their being frustrated was their own fault.

This experiment varied (1) the degree to which the subject was frustrated by the confederate's turning him down, (2) the degree to which the turndown was expected, and (3) the reason for the turn-down. The aim was to find which of these affected the subject's anger. Anger was measured in a variety of clever and unobtrusive ways. For example, the experimenter measured the force with which the subject gently hung up or slammed down the phone.

As we might expect from the Pastore result, the subjects led to believe that it was the confederate's fault that he didn't contribute expressed the greatest anger, while subjects led to believe it was their own fault expressed the least anger. The legitimate frustration condition was between them. But, illustrating the role of frustration, whether the subjects lost $1 or 10¢ also mattered; subjects who lost $1 became angrier than those who lost 10¢, and those who expected to succeed were angrier at being turned down than those who expected to fail (Kulik & Brown, 1979). The results of this study suggest that whether frustration per se instigates aggression, the degree to which one is frustrated can affect the degree to which one becomes angry. To return to the example of the customers waiting for a bus, we might well expect that they will become much more angry at being passed up by the driver for no good reason if they are trying to get to a job interview for which they are already late than if they have plenty of time to get somewhere it isn't very important to be.

CUES ASSOCIATED WITH AGGRESSION AND ANGER

Leonard Berkowitz has, in line with his associationist position, argued for a second situational factor that modulates the degree of aggression expressed. He has argued that aggression is more likely to be expressed in the presence of cues associated with aggression. In one study illustrating this claim, subjects were given a chance to retaliate against a confederate who had insulted them by administering shock in a "learning experiment," but before they got their chance, they watched a movie. Half saw a prizefight film, *Champion*, in which Kirk Douglas is savagely beaten; the other subjects saw a film without aggressive content. The subjects who saw the prizefight film shocked the confederate more than did subjects who saw the neutral film (Berkowitz, 1965). In a subsequent study, all of the subjects saw *Champion*, but the name of the confederate was varied: in some cases, he was given the name Kirk or Kelley, the name of the character Kirk Douglas played; in other conditions, he was given names unassociated with the movie. In support of Berkowitz's claim, subjects used more shock against the confederate when he had a name associated with the character in the film (Geen & Berkowitz, 1966).

In the most famous study of this series, Berkowitz included cues associated with aggression in a rather dramatic way—he put a .38 caliber revolver and a twelve-gauge shotgun next to the shock machine. In other conditions, the subjects found either a badminton racket or nothing. The subjects were told that these things had been left there by someone else! Subjects who found the artillery shocked more than did those who didn't—the **weapons effect**— again in support of Berkowitz's claim (Berkowitz & LePage, 1967). But does all of this show that aggressive cues increase the tendency to act aggressively because of their associations with aggressive behavior?

To appreciate the criticisms raised against this work, we first have to be clear about what Berkowitz's claim is and what it isn't. His claim is couched in the tradition and language of learning theory: these cues are supposed to

affect aggression in an unreasoned way. But there is another way that they might affect aggression. The subject might figure out that the presence of these odd objects (or the coincidence of the matching of the names) means that the experimenter intends them to be aggressive; or the subject might, not unreasonably, conclude that the experimenter is the kind of person who approves of aggression, given his taste in movies and his appreciation of decor. Now if the cues lead to aggression in these ways, then the experiments demonstrate not so much that subjects are led to aggress by cues associated with aggression as that subjects aggress more when they think an authority wants them to. Thus, before we accept the Berkowitz interpretation, we have to be sure that subjects didn't figure out what was going on, and act accordingly.

In several studies of the weapons effect and studies of the impact of aggressive cues more generally, investigators have asked subjects *after the experiment was over* to indicate what they thought the experimenter's hypothesis was. In these investigations subjects could be divided into those who were suspicious of the experimental procedure and those who weren't. Michael Carlson has recently reviewed this literature, asking whether the weapons effect shows up only among the suspicious subjects or more generally. His conclusion is that the presence of aggressive cues *does* facilitate aggression but *only* among subjects who are *not* suspicious. In fact, suspicious subjects show *less* aggression in the presence of aggressive cues, as if they see through the experimental procedure and decide *not* to cooperate (Carlson, Marcus-Newhall, & Miller, 1990).

These data do not utterly settle the matter. After all, it might be argued that the subjects who *admitted* they were suspicious in the post-experimental interview were just uncooperative subjects. Perhaps they did see through the experimenter's hypothesis and decided to display their uncooperativeness with the experimenter in two different ways: (1) they acted in a way to refute the hypothesis—they suppressed aggression in the presence of the weapon, and (2) they uncooperatively told the experimenter of their suspicions, thus tainting their data. Perhaps the "unsuspicious" subjects weren't unsuspicious after all. Perhaps they were just more cooperative, and cooperated by *not* reporting their suspicions *and* by acting in an aggressive way in the presence of aggressive cues. So it is still possible to argue against the weapons effect, even in the face of the evidence. But it probably isn't wise to continue the argument.

Still, it is important to keep in mind that subjects are likely to treat details of the experimental setting as having been placed there deliberately by the experimenter in order to have some specific effect on them. They don't treat things they find in the lab as we do seashells at the seashore—as consequences of nature unassisted, or unedited by human intentions. When cues have no natural, plausible connection to the experiment, as may have been true of the weapons, we should expect subjects to be suspicious at the least. And they may therefore try to figure out what the experimenter is up to. But insofar as the experimenter gives the subjects a chance to reveal their suspicions in a post-experimental interview, it is reasonable to assume that they will take the opportunity to express their suspicions—if for no other reason than their delight in being able to show the experimenter that they outwitted her.

CLASSIC FINDINGS IN SOCIAL PSYCHOLOGY: THE TRANSFER OF AROUSAL

Dolf Zillmann (1971) has accepted the evidence that aggressive cues enhance aggression, but he has proposed a quite different account of *how* they do so. Zillmann has argued that along with being associated with aggression, many of the stimuli used in these studies have another characteristic: they are arousing. Consider the study showing that seeing *Champion* enhanced aggression. Zillmann has proposed that *Champion* was more arousing than the control film, and that the arousal produced by the film transferred to the subjects' anger, thus accounting for the higher levels of retaliation by those who saw *Champion.* This logic implies that if they had seen another film that aroused them even more, they would have used even more shock, even if that other film had no cues associated with aggression.

To test this, Zillmann used the standard technique of having a confederate shock subjects, under a suitable pretext, and then allowed the subjects to retaliate. But before that, they got to see one of three films. One was an educational film, another was *Champion,* and the third was an erotic film showing tender foreplay. Pretest showed that the erotic film was the most arousing (caused the greatest increase in blood pressure), *Champion* was the next most arousing, and the educational film, as you might expect, was the least arousing. According to Berkowitz's theory, *Champion* should have produced the highest level of retaliation, since it had the most cues associated with aggression. But in Zillmann's ***transfer of arousal*** view, the erotic film should have produced the greatest retaliation. It did (see Figure 13.4).

One might argue, though, that even though the erotic film didn't contain cues associated with aggression, it didn't exert its effect through the transfer

▲ *Sports are arousing, and their being so may enhance the impulse to retaliate against a real (or imagined) insult. (In this particular case, self-control did not win out over impulse.)*

FIGURE 13.4

TRANSFER OF AROUSAL AND AGGRESSION

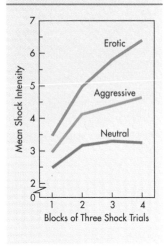

▲ *Mean shock intensity delivered to an insulting confederate depended on the film subjects watched between the insult and the retaliation. Even though the erotic film had no aggressive cues, it led to the highest levels of retaliation. (From Zillmann, 1971)*

of arousal either. Perhaps seeing the erotic film aroused the subjects sexually, and this arousal, which the subjects were in no position to relieve, was frustrating; perhaps it was this frustration that enhanced aggression.

Zillmann repeated the experiment using a different kind of arousal. While they were waiting to retaliate, Zillmann had subjects either ride an exercycle, which producs physiological arousal, or do something that doesn't produce arousal. Again the subjects who rode the exercycle retaliated more (Zillmann, Johnson, & Day, 1974). But how does this transfer of arousal work?

Drive Versus Interpretation Accounts One interpretation gives drive a direct role. According to this interpretation, extraneous arousal "energizes" behavior; it makes one do whatever one happens to be doing more intensely. This view is supported by a good bit of common sense. It does seem that when aroused, we do what we're doing more intensely, just as when tired, we do things less intensely. But this isn't the interpretation Zillmann gave the transfer of arousal effect. His explanation derived from the work of Stanley Schachter and Jerome Singer (1962).

These investigators (whose experiment is discussed in greater detail in Chapter 7) claimed that arousal affects emotion in an indirect way. When people are aroused, they try to figure out what the cause of that arousal is, and then act according to their interpretation. If someone thinks she is aroused because she has been insulted, she will retaliate; if she thinks she is aroused because of an attractive male, she might have sexual fantasies; if she thinks she is aroused, on the other hand, because of a drug she took, then she won't experience any emotion.

Zillmann applied this general notion to the enhancement of retaliation through extraneous arousal. He suggested that when the subjects get a chance to retaliate, they know they are aroused, but their problem is in deciding why. On the one hand, they know they were insulted or shocked, which might be the source of their arousal; on the other hand, they know that they rode an exercycle, which might also be the source of their arousal. Their problem is to decide *how much* of their arousal is due to the insult. Zillmann argued that this is a difficult question, and that subjects are therefore likely to attribute at least some of the arousal from the exercise to the confederate's behavior, and therefore they "overretaliate." (See Chapter 12 for a similar account of the transfer of arousal from fear to sex.)

In further experiments, Zillmann went on to pit these two accounts of the transfer of arousal effects against each other. In one particularly elegant study, Zillmann examined the time course of the overretaliation effect. He argued that at the moment the subject gets off the exercycle, his arousal is highest. But it is also at that moment that he should realize most clearly that it is due to the exercise. Zillmann predicted that subjects allowed to retaliate *then* would *not* overretaliate.[*] And the data supported him. (Note that ac-

---

[*]Another test of whether the interposed activity increases aggression by introducing arousal is by having a confederate treat the subject especially *nicely* at the beginning of the experiment and giving the subjects a chance to reward the confederate at the end. Violent films interposed between the nice treatment and the opportunity to reward, by producing arousal, ought to lead the subjects to reward the confederate more compared with subjects who were exposed to a neutral (or no) film. Violent films *did* increase rewarding of the confederate in one experiment (Mueller, Donnerstein, & Hallam, 1983).

cording to the direct drive account, the subject's knowledge of why he was aroused wouldn't matter, and that since his drive would be highest at that moment, he should retaliate most then.)

Zillmann further argued that as time goes on, arousal decreases, but the source of arousal grows less clear. How fast arousal dissipates depends on how physically fit a subject is. Fit people experience a very rapid decline in arousal, but subjects who are out of shape experience a much slower decline. Zillmann predicted that if he allowed his subjects to rest before giving them a chance to retaliate, those who were well-conditioned would not overretaliate, since they would no longer be aroused. Subjects who were out of shape, on the other hand, would overretaliate, because they would still be aroused. And this is just what happened (see Figure 13.5). The transfer of arousal story looks very neat; it nicely corresponds to the data. But the evidence is not quite that comforting, and the theory is not quite that simple.

AVERSIVE STATES AND AGGRESSION

In the 1960s, the American public became familiar with the notion of the "long, hot summer," which referred to the propensity for riots, especially race riots, to break out during the hottest, most uncomfortable days of the summer. This observation leads one to suspect that violence increases as a function of temperature, at least at the upper reaches of temperature, where increases are aversive.

Several investigators have pursued this idea by examining the relationship between the incidence of violent crime and temperature. In one study, Craig Anderson looked at the relations between FBI crime statistics for both violent and nonviolent crime as a function of season of the year for the ten-year period from 1971 to 1980. The results indicated that violent crime was significantly more common in the second and third (hot) quarters of the year than in the first and fourth (cool) quarters. Nonviolent crime was also related to season, but substantially less so. Further, the relation between season and crime rate was found to be stronger for cities with hotter summers (Anderson, 1987). The exact shape of the relationship between the temperature and violence is a matter of substantial debate, but all sides agree that the relationship is positive. What is under dispute is whether the relationship is linear or curvilinear (Anderson & DeNeve, 1992; Bell, 1992; Reifman, Larrick, & Fein, 1991). Other research has shown that levels of atmospheric ozone, a reasonable measure of the degree of air pollution generally, are also related

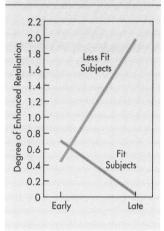

FIGURE 13.5

TIME COURSE OF THE OVER-RETALIATION EFFECT

▲ *Retaliation for an insult immediately after exercise and later for fit and less fit subjects. Retaliation right after exercise was low, perhaps because it was clear to subjects why they were physiologically aroused then. Unfit subjects remained aroused and overretaliated later; fit subjects were no longer aroused later. (Data from Zillmann, Johnson, & Day, 1974)*

▼ *(A) 1967 riot in Detroit, Michigan, (B) 1964 riot in Brooklyn, New York, (C) 1966 riot in Chicago, Illinois.*

A

B

C

to the amount of violent crime in an area (Rotton & Frey, 1985). And Dolf Zillmann has shown that exposure to aversive erotica, films of sado-masochism and bestiality, enhances aggression by males toward other males (Zillmann, Bryant, & Carveth, 1981).

Just why the aversive states produced by hot temperatures, air pollution, and disturbing erotica increase violence is not known, but two hypotheses currently seem to be favored. One is the idea that these states produce arousal directly, and that subjects transfer that arousal to aggression; the other is in line with the modern frustration-aggression hypothesis. Perhaps being in an aversive state gives rise to ideas associated with violence through a process of association (Anderson, 1989). But regardless of *why* there is an association between aversive states and degree of aggression, there is substantial evidence that there is a relation between them.

We have found, then, a variety of factors that can increase the propensity to violence, whatever its source. All of these factors seem to involve aversive states and arousal. Just how aversive states and states of heightened arousal matter is not, at the moment, settled.

Arousal may "transfer" from one source to another. Aversive states of all kinds may intensify aggression via transfer of arousal.

SEXUAL AGGRESSION

Rape is, of course, an example of aggression. It is a form of aggression that 15 percent of the college women in one American sample had suffered. Another 12 percent had experienced a failed attempt (Koss, 1992). In this section, we will review evidence that has been collected about the determinants of this particular form of aggression.

Date Rape

Some rape occurs when women are attacked by strangers. But there is reason to believe that much of the unwanted sexual activity that women are exposed to comes not from strangers but from men they know (Muren, Perot, & Byrne, 1989). Many rapes, then, occur in the context of a dating relationship, and are known as ***date rape.***

Although rape is clearly an example of aggression, it also involves sexual motivations. Whether a given instance of rape is motivated by the desire to have sex with the victim, the desire to hurt or humiliate her, or the desire to demonstrate power over her is difficult to determine. (That it is intentional, counternormative harm doing *doesn't* depend on its motivation; therefore, its motivation is quite irrelevant to whether it is aggression.) One study attempted to determine the motivations of undergraduate men who admitted to having forced a woman they were dating to have sex with them. To gain some understanding of the motivations and attitudes of these men, the investigator interviewed 71 men who admitted to date rape, and compared their responses with those of 227 undergraduate men who did not admit to rape.

In every case of date rape reported by these men, the rape followed a bout of intense sexual activity, certainly suggesting a role for sexual arousal and perhaps frustration in the genesis of date rape. The date rapists, on the other hand, didn't seem to be men who were *chronically* sexually frustrated; indeed, they were on average *more* sexually active than the control group of nonrap-

Roughly 25 percent of the women in one college sample had been the victim of an attempt at date rape.

ing undergraduate males. The evidence, however, also suggests that although these rapists were more sexually active than the average male, they also desired sex more frequently than the average male did, so relative to their own desires, they may have seen themselves, however unreasonably, as deprived. This suggests that sexual desire does play a role in date rape.

But the date rapists' attitudes toward women and sex also seemed to play an important role. The date rapists had a history of generally ignoring moral bounds in their attempts to get women to have sex with them (see Table 13.1). So not only did they use force on at least one occasion, they also admitted to using fraud of all sorts on other occasions—including, for example, telling women they loved them when they didn't. Moreover, they believed that their peers would approve of such deceit, and indeed they reported experiencing substantial peer pressure toward sexual conquests. The picture that emerges from the data is that date rapists simply don't take women's rights to control their own bodies seriously, at least when it comes to sex (Kanin, 1985). Neither do they believe that their peers expect them to take women's rights seriously.

Other research suggests that sexually aggressive men tend to have aggressive personalities in general and that they also tend to have a history of sexual promiscuity. It is the combination of high levels of both that has been implicated in the genesis of aggression against women (Malamuth, Sockloskie, Koss, & Tanaka, 1991). And still other research has revealed that men's general attitudes toward women are related to their attitudes toward date rape. The finding is that men with *old-fashioned* attitudes toward women and their role in society are *more* tolerant of date rape than are men with less conservative attitudes (Check & Malamuth, 1983; Shotland & Goodstein, 1983; Sigelman, Berry, & Wiles, 1984; Muehlenhard, Friedman, & Thomas, 1985; Fisher, 1986; Koralewski & Conger, 1992).

There is also reason to believe that people in general are more tolerant of date rape than they are of stranger rape. In one study, the investigators presented simulated newspaper accounts of a rape to 650 subjects. In some ac-

▲ *In the film* Thelma and Louise, *Thelma and Louise, played by Geena Davis and Susan Sarandon, respond to an attempted rape with violence. Justified violence? Certainly mitigated.*

TABLE 13.1

METHODS SELF-REPORTED DATE RAPISTS USED (ON OTHER OCCASIONS) TO MANIPULATE WOMEN TO HAVE SEX WITH THEM (COMPARED WITH CONTROLS WHO HAD NOT ADMITTED TO DATE RAPE)

	Rapists (N = 71)	Controls (N = 227)
Attempt to intoxicate female with alcohol	76*	23†
Falsely profess love	86	25
Falsely promise "pinning," engagement, or marriage	46	6
Threaten to terminate relationship	31	7
Threaten to leave female stranded	9	0

* 28 percent also involved marijuana.

† 19 percent also involved marijuana.

SOURCE: From Kanin, 1985.

counts, the rapist and victim were described as strangers; in other accounts, the victim and attacker were described as dating; in the final set of accounts, they were described as dating and as having had prior consensual sexual intercourse. The subjects were asked to read the accounts and answer a variety of questions designed to measure how seriously they took the crime: How long should the rapist's sentence be? How much was the *victim* to blame?

Overall, the women subjects judged the rape as more serious than the men did. But subjects of both sexes judged the crime as less serious if the victim and rapist knew each other. It is important to realize that the law takes no account of acquaintance and its degree in defining rape. Forcing someone to have sex is rape whether the person is known or not. But this study suggests that these subjects, and especially male subjects, tended to let the rapist off easier if he was acquainted with the victim (L'Armand & Pepitone, 1982).

RAPE MYTHS AND AGGRESSION AGAINST WOMEN

Researchers have isolated another possible cause of male aggression against women. In one study, sixty-five male and fifty female undergraduate students were asked to sign up for a study that involved watching commercial films. Half of the men and half of the women saw two films, *Swept Away* (1975) and *The Getaway* (1972). The first centers around an upper-class woman who is shipwrecked on an island with a crew member of the ship on which she had been sailing. She had treated him in the haughty way she saw befitting their class differences while they were aboard ship, but once on the island he forces her to have sex with him, which she eventually enjoys. Thus, it depicts rape, but rape that the woman eventually enjoys. The second film stars Steve McQueen as a very macho man who physically abuses women, but the women he abuses become attached to him. The other half of the subjects saw *A Man and a Woman* (1966) and *Hooper* (1978), both of which are "tender"— if not sentimental—depictions of romantic attachment.

Several days later, a class in which these students were enrolled filled out questionnaires about their attitudes toward rape and interpersonal violence, especially violence against women. The class was a large one, so there was no reason for the subjects to connect the films they saw with the questionnaires they were asked to fill out. The women who had not seen any of the films were less accepting of rape and violence against women than were the men who had not seen the films. Seeing *Swept Away* and *The Getaway* increased this difference; it made the men more accepting of rape and the women less so. Watching the romantic films had no effect on these attitudes.

▶ *(A) Ali MacGraw and Steve McQueen in the violent film* The Getaway. *(B) Sally Field and Burt Reynolds in the romantic film* Hooper.

A

B

Thus, seeing depictions in movies of women who had been forced to have sex led male subjects to become more accepting of rape (Malamuth & Check, 1981). This study suggests that there is a danger posed by pornography that depicts women enjoying rape. The danger is that men will come to condone rape out of the false belief that it is what women want.

A second study related to men's beliefs that women are attracted to rape used sexual arousal as a dependent variable. In this study, male and female subjects read depictions of either mutually consenting sex or rape. In some depictions, although the woman in the story experienced pain in being raped, she also eventually experienced orgasm; in others, she did not. The male subjects exposed to the pain plus orgasm story reported being as aroused as were the subjects exposed to the other stories. Female subjects, on the other hand, were more aroused by the consenting sex (Malamuth, Hein, & Feshbach, 1980).

These two studies taken together suggest that men are aroused by depictions of sex mixed with aggression, and that seeing depictions of such sex leads men to become more tolerant of rape, while it has just the reverse effect on women. Together they lend little support to the belief that women secretly desire being raped, but they do suggest that men are easily convinced that this is true.

THE IMMEDIATE CONTEXT AND THE PERCEPTION OF DATE RAPE

Several details of the immediate context have been shown to affect subjects' perceptions of whether or not an instance of intercourse is rape. For example, in one study, subjects read about a date between Lee and Diane, who had known each other for about six months. Lee picked Diane up at her apartment; they went to a movie, and then Lee suggested that they return to his apartment to listen to some music. Diane said okay. When they arrived, Lee put on some music and poured some wine. The moment became, as is its wont, more passionate. Kissing and fondling followed, and Diane was clearly enjoying it. But a point was reached beyond which she did not wish to go. And she repeatedly told Lee to stop, at one point slapping him across the face. But despite her repeated protests and persistent struggles, intercourse occurred. The subjects were asked, among other things, to decide whether the incident was a rape. (It was without question rape by legal definition.)

Some subjects were told at the beginning of the scenario that Lee and Diane had never had intercourse with each other before this evening; others were told that they had had intercourse once before; and still others were told that they had had intercourse ten times before. The question was: How would the couple's sexual history affect the perception of rape? The answer was that if Lee and Diane had had intercourse ten times before, then the incident was less likely to be perceived as a rape than if they had never engaged in intercourse or had only done so once (Shotland & Goodstein, 1992). Apparently subjects believed that by consenting to intercourse ten times in the past, Lee and Diane had entered into a "social contract" to do so again this evening. But I repeat, legally, insofar as Diane did not consent on this occasion, Lee engaged in rape. Nonetheless, the interesting result is that the mere repetition of a pattern of intercourse ten times was enough to lead subjects to see the partners as having rights with regard to each other (Shotland & Goodstein, 1992).

Other research using similar methods has found that the earlier in a sexual

- A history of having had intercourse with someone,

- waiting until late in a sexual encounter to protest,

- having had an expensive date,

- having agreed to go to a man's apartment, and

- having asked the man out

all reduce the odds that a woman will be seen as having been raped by a date even though she rejects his sexual advances. None of these factors has legal or moral relevance.

encounter that a woman protests a man's advances, the more likely the encounter will be perceived as rape, and the more violent the male is, the more likely the event will be perceived as rape (Shotland & Goodstein, 1983). Still other research has suggested that if the male has invested money in the date, his forced sex is less likely to be perceived as rape; that if the woman agrees to go to the man's apartment, she lessens the likelihood that he will be perceived as having raped her; and finally, that she is less likely to be perceived as having been raped if she asks him out rather than the other way around (Muehlenhard, Friedman, & Thomas, 1985; Jenkins & Dambrot, 1987). Again, the factors have no legal (or moral) relevance, but they do affect subjects' perception of what is and is not date rape.

Male Jealousy and Aggression

The sexually related aggression discussed so far has involved sexual arousal and aggression, but there is another way that sex and aggression are commingled: in assaults against one's partner provoked by sexual jealousy. Martin Daly and Margo Wilson have assembled an impressive amount of data from Western culture as well as others showing that (1) a substantial proportion of all murders involve one partner killing the other, and (2) the most common cause of such murders is one partner's belief that the other has been sexually unfaithful (Daly & Wilson, 1988). The data further suggest an interesting gender difference in these cases, which Daly and Wilson interpret within an evolutionary framework.

Murder is more likely to be the result of a wife's infidelity than a husband's. Now this is *not* because men are more likely to kill their wives than women are to kill their husbands; in fact, recent data suggest that, at least in the United States, wives are just as likely to kill their husbands. The data suggest, however, that when a wife kills her husband, it is because her husband is threatening her, and she kills him to protect herself. But the common reason that he is threatening her is that he believes, rightly or wrongly, that she has been unfaithful. So even in cases in which she kills him, the ultimate source of the murder is her real or fancied infidelity.

Why is infidelity on a wife's part so provocative? This is a difficult question to address. It is surely true that American culture, at least until recently, has been tolerant of men who killed because of their wives' infidelity. Indeed, Daly and Wilson point out that until 1974, the Texas penal code held that if a husband caught another man having sex with his wife and he killed the interloper on the spot, that was to be considered justifiable homicide, and the husband was not to be subjected to any criminal penalty whatever. Wives weren't similarly allowed to kill their husbands' lovers. This Texas law is an extreme example, but as Daly and Wilson point out, it is not at all unusual for the law to treat such murders in a less severe way than it treats other homicides. So perhaps our culture simply allows men to become provoked more than it allows women to become provoked.

But Daly and Wilson believe that lurking behind this cultural fact is a biological, evolutionary fact. As we saw in Chapter 12, there are profound reproductive asymmetries between men and women. One of these asymmetries is that women always know which children are theirs, but men cannot know this unless they can be sure that their sexual partners are exclusively

▲ *(A) The Piano (1993) and (B) What's Love Got to Do with It? (1993). Two views of the manipulation and violence all too common in male-female relationships.*

their sexual partners. A male who is not sure that his partner is faithful ru
the risk of providing resources for a child who is not his; women run no su
risk. Therefore, the argument goes, men are disposed by their genes to re
violently to their partners' infidelity, but women are less disposed to react tl
way. The data on marital homicide are at least consistent with this evo
tionary account.

We have so far looked at the various motives that underlie aggression
therefore the instigation to aggression, and some factors that affect the deg
of aggression expressed. But there is an aspect we have not yet touched upon:
how learning affects the expression of aggression.

Learning How to Aggress

An infant knows how to have a temper tantrum, to flail about, cry, and so
forth. But it doesn't know how to throw a knife, shoot a gun, or construct a
cutting remark. In one study that illustrates how children learn to aggress,
children were shown—on film, in a cartoon, or live—someone attacking a
"Bobo" doll in novel ways; they saw the "model" beat the doll on the head
with a mallet, fling it into the air, kick it across the room, and pummel it with
balls. Subsequently, the children displayed these same behaviors against the
doll. Of course, it is stretching a point to call whatever one does to a Bobo
doll aggression, but the study does show that children learn how to do things,
including aggress, by **modeling,** watching the behavior of other people (Bandura, Ross, & Ross, 1963a, 1963b).

For a culture to survive, children must learn more than how to aggress;
they must learn *when* to aggress. And more important, they must learn when
not to aggress and *how much* to aggress, given the circumstances. So we turn
first to what psychologists have had to say about how this is learned, and
then to features in the immediate situation that seem to subvert people's usual
restraint against aggression.

▼ *Children watch an adult
strike a rubber "Bobo" doll
with a mallet, and then they
strike it too.*

Learning Not to Express Aggression

One inhibition against expressing aggression and thereby harming others is the moral code we all share; in fact, the injunction not to harm others seems to be the central element of our moral code. Since this is so, a discussion of learning not to aggress is part of a broader discussion of how we become moral actors.

One reason not to hurt someone is that one will be punished for it. And it is no doubt true that one reason children eventually stop picking on their brothers and sisters is because someone bigger than both of them stops them. But punishing children for aggressing can have a paradoxical effect, for reasons we shall soon see.

MODELING

When learning theory was the dominant theory in psychology, it was popular to assume that an organism could learn only from its own experience; that is, it could learn to do or not do things only by being rewarded or punished. But in a series of experiments, Albert Bandura and his colleagues showed that children could learn to do or not to do things vicariously—by seeing the consequences for other people who do them. In one experiment, children saw a model physically attack and harass another child. Some of the children saw the aggressive model punished for his behavior; others saw him get away with it. A control group saw a model involved in vigorous but nonaggressive play.

In a posttest, the children were allowed to play with a Bobo doll. The results indicated that seeing the aggressive model increased the amount of "aggression" that the children showed toward the doll, and this was particularly true for those children who saw the model go unpunished for his aggression. Thus, these children learned not just how to aggress, but that it was proper to aggress (Bandura, Ross, & Ross, 1963a, 1963b). Watching other people aggress may, then, lead to the disinhibition of aggression. And this points to the paradox with regard to punishing children for aggressing.

▶ *(A) A child who is punished then (B) punishes her doll—learning aggression from aggression?*

A

B

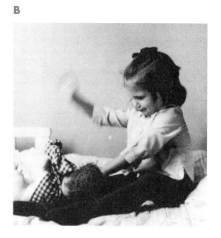

Punishing a child indeed acts to inhibit the behavior for which the child was punished, but punishment, if done in the wrong way, can have another effect: it can provide a model of aggression that encourages aggression. In one study, for example, parents were interviewed to assess the techniques they used to control their children, and then their children were observed in nursery school play. The degree to which parents used **arbitrary power,** that is, disciplined children without giving reasons for that discipline, at home was positively related to the degree to which the children displayed hostility at school. Parents who used arbitrary power, and thus were authoritarian in controlling their children's aggression at home, apparently taught the children two things: (1) not to aggress at home (through direct punishment) and (2) that acting in a hostile way was an appropriate way to get what one wants (through modeling) (Hoffman, 1960).

The extreme form of this dual effect is seen in child abuse. In one study, the family backgrounds of thirty-four abused children were investigated. The results indicated that in over one-half of the cases, the parents had grown up in families in which they themselves, their siblings, or one of their parents was subjected to physical abuse (Silver, Dublin, & Laurie, 1969). These data don't quite show that witnessing or being the victim of abuse increases the likelihood of abusing a child. We don't know how many parents who *don't* abuse their children grew up in homes where abuse is common; but it is reasonable to assume that the figure is less than 50 percent. Nor do we know how many children who are abused *don't* abuse their own children. Still, these data are a reason to believe that abused children abuse their own children, and that growing up around physical abuse lessens inhibitions against using physical aggression. Nonetheless, this evidence is somewhat indirect, and some scholars argue that we really don't know yet whether "abuse begets abuse" (Widom, 1989, 1991; DiLalla & Gottesman, 1991; Alexander, Moore, & Alexander, 1991).

Television and Responses to Aggression

There is experimental evidence that suggests what kind of aggression witnessed by children might lower their inhibitions against engaging in it. In one study, children from eight to ten years old were shown excerpts from one of two television shows—*S.W.A.T.*, a police show replete with physical aggression, or a show with no aggression. After they had seen the show, the experimenter left the room, asking the children to keep an eye on some preschoolers by watching them through a television monitor. The children saw a videotape of these preschoolers getting into a fight that ended in physical aggression. While this was going on, the subjects were hooked up to a device that monitored their state of physiological arousal. The children who had just seen *S.W.A.T.* became less aroused at the sight of the "real" fight than did those who had seen the control tape. Seeing this violent show apparently reduced the children's emotional response to real violence (Thomas, Horton, Lippincott, & Drabman, 1977). The emotional response we have to another person who is being hurt is presumably one of the things that inhibits us from aggressing against them.

A second finding from the same study is also important in understanding how the modeling of aggression affects our behavior. The children were also asked about the television they usually watched. The shows were coded for the amount of aggression they typically contained. Physiological arousal to the fight by the preschoolers was then related to the amount of aggression the subjects typically watch at home. The more aggressive television they watched, as a percentage of the total amount they watched, the *less* aroused they became at the fight. This result was substantial for the children who had not just seen *S.W.A.T.* (Cline, Croft, & Courrier, 1973). One way, then, that watching aggression can lead to aggression is by making us unresponsive to real aggression when we see it.

MODELING AND JUSTIFIED AGGRESSION

One might imagine that whether children imitate the aggression they see on television would depend on whether the aggression was justified or not. One might imagine that seeing *unjustified* aggression would enhance aggression, but that watching *justified* aggression wouldn't. But quite the reverse seems true. Subjects in one study were attacked and insulted by a confederate. They then watched aggression on television. In some cases, the aggression was presented as justified—the good guy used aggression against the bad guy. In other cases, the bad guy started the aggression. The subjects then had a chance to retaliate. The subjects who saw the justified aggression retaliated more than those who saw the unjustified aggression (Meyer, 1972).

DOES VIEWING VIOLENCE ON TELEVISION CAUSE AGGRESSION?

Laboratory results like those we have been reviewing have led social scientists and politicians to cast a jaundiced eye on the television programs that the networks expose us to. The question these investigations have addressed is: Does watching aggressive television lead to aggression on the part of the viewers, as the laboratory research on aggression suggests?

The debate on this question is complex. Unfortunately, despite decades of research effort, it is not yet settled. One aspect of the issue seems clear: there is a relation between the amount of aggressive television that children watch and the degree to which they are themselves aggressive (see Gerbner & Gross, 1976; Fenigstein, 1979; Geen, 1983, for reviews). But many studies show *correlations* betwen exposure to television aggression and aggression, but they do not show the *causal* relations. They do not tell us whether watching aggression on television leads to aggressive behavior, whether being disposed to aggressive behavior leads to watching aggressive television, or whether some third factor causes both a disposition to aggress and an attraction to aggressive television.

There is reason to believe both that the arousal of aggressive urges leads to a preference for watching aggressive material and that watching aggressive material leads to a disposition to act aggressively. One investigator asked subjects to engage in aggressive fantasies, nonaggressive fantasies, or no fantasies. The subjects were then asked to select the film they would like to watch. Those who had engaged in aggressive fantasies were more likely than those in the other groups to select an aggressive film (Fenigstein, 1979). Aggressive urges may, then, lead to a desire to see aggression portrayed.

There are several experimental studies exploring the effects of watching aggressive material on aggressive urges. One study was of Belgian children

▲ *A member of a S.W.A.T. team from the television show of that name.*

"I LOVE THE WHOLE THING. IN FACT, ONE DAY I'M GOING TO TAKE UP EITHER ANIMATED CARTOONING OR VIOLENCE."

who had gotten into trouble with the court, their schools, or their parents, and who had been sent to what might be called reform schools. In one of these schools, researchers had intervened by showing all of the boys in two "cottages" a commercial, aggressive film every night for a week; the boys in two other cottages saw control films. Observers then coded the children's behavior for a variety of types of acts outside of the film-viewing setting. Stark differences between those in the various cottages were found both on the level of interpersonal aggression and on the level of aggression toward inanimate objects. Those who watched the aggressive films were clearly more aggressive (Leyens, Camino, Parke, & Berkowitz, 1975).

Other, similar studies, however, have found no relation between diets of televised violence and real violence; some studies have even found that the more violence children are shown, the *less* aggressive they are in real life. In light of this conflicting evidence, the debate continues as to whether violence on television actually causes violent behavior in children (see Freedman, 1984, 1986; Friedrich-Cofer & Huston, 1986; Phillips, 1986; Wood, Wong, & Chochese, 1991).

Recently American culture has introduced a new way to expose children to violence: the video game. Already a small research literature has begun to develop around the question of whether watching violent video games causes aggression in children (Anderson & Ford, 1986; Cooper & Mackie, 1986; Schutte, Malouffe, Post-Gordon, & Rodasta, 1988). As will probably come as no surprise, the results are conflicting, with some studies showing an increase in children's aggression following violent video games, while others do not.

Laboratory studies suggest a causal link between seeing aggression on television and behaving violently, but field studies have been less than convincing. Violence does *not* seem to enhance the popularity of shows.

AGGRESSION AND POPULARITY OF TELEVISION SHOWS

Whether the plethora of television shows that show good guys attacking bad guys are dangerous or not, they are certainly an aesthetic blight. One wonders why, in the face of their possible danger and certain ugliness, they persist. Presumably because network programmers believe aggression enhances the popularity of television shows. But does it?

What would happen if one correlated the degree of aggression contained in television shows with their popularity? Would it be true that the more violent, the more popular? One pair of investigators did just that; they took sixty-two episodes of eleven television shows and coded them for acts of aggression, then they correlated these with their popularity ratings. The result was a correlation of 0.05 (for all intents and purposes, 0). They also took one of the more violent shows, *Police Woman,* and edited it. One version left the violence in; the other removed it. They showed these two versions to University of Illinois undergraduates and asked them how well they liked them. There was almost no difference in liking (Diener & DeFour, 1978). There is no reason to believe, then, that aggression actually improves even the popularity of television shows. Contrary to the usual explanation, the "vast wasteland" of television may be so despite, and not because of, viewers' tastes.

TELEVISED VIOLENCE AND REAL-WORLD EFFECTS

We have seen that there are many laboratory demonstrations that televised violence can lead to aggression. Yet field research designed to tell us whether television leads to aggression in the broader social world is equivocal. Why?

There are several possible reasons. For one thing, laboratory experiments typically look for immediate, short-term effects. So perhaps the effects of watching television are quite short-lived; long-enough-lived to be detected in the experimental session, but not long-enough-lived to be found in everyday life. More generally, laboratory experiments are usually set up to find whatever effects are there to be found. They are usually designed to be as sensitive as possible to even very small effects; perhaps the effects of television viewing are large enough to be detected by the sensitive instrument of the laboratory experiment in a controlled environment in which all other influences are minimized, but not large enough to be found in the field.

TELEVISION AND COVETOUSNESS

Although the bulk of the literature on the effects of televised violence has focused on its effects on children, there is one interesting study that has looked at the effects of television on rates of violent crime. This study looked at what happened to the crime rate when television was introduced into the United States. The question was: Did the crime rate go up because of the introduction of television?

This question would be unanswerable were it not for a fluke in the way television entered American culture. Suppose the whole of the United States had received television at the same time, and suppose the crime rate had increased after its introduction. This would *not* show that the introduction of television *caused* the increase in the crime rate; perhaps something else happened at the same time to cause the increase. But, as it happens, just as television was being introduced, the Federal Communications Commission ordered a freeze on the issuance of new licenses from late 1949 to mid-1952. Some parts of the country got television before the freeze, while others got it after.

Because of this fluke, one can ask whether there were increases in violence in those areas where television was just being introduced relative to areas where it had not yet been introduced, and relative to areas where it had long since been introduced. (It is important to note that violence has been a mainstay of television right from the start, so there is every chance of detecting its impact early.) The data (FBI Crime Statistics) suggest that the introduction of television was *not* associated with an increase in *violent* crime. Areas just getting television didn't experience a sudden increase in violent crime as a consequence of the depiction of violence on television. But, interestingly, the introduction of television *was* associated with an increase in thefts (Hennigan, Del Rosario, Heath, Cook, Wharton, & Calder, 1982). Why should the introduction of television have led to an increase not in violent crime but in thefts?

Hennigan et al. suspect that the real effect of television viewing on the American public was to expose people of the middle and lower classes to the lifestyles of the upper classes. This window onto a life of luxury led not so much to aggression as it did to the desire to have the material things other people seemed to have. And this increase in desire led people to use whatever means they had available, legal or not, to acquire it. It is important to note that people's exposure to what they didn't have is an *accidental consequence* of the propensity to depict the upper middle class and upper class rather than the lower class on television, but there is nothing accidental about television commercials. Commercials are constructed for no purpose other than to get people to want what they don't have. This evidence suggests that although television may not have a role after all in stimulating *impulsive aggression*, it may be quite a bit more potent at stimulating *instrumental aggression*.

Our review of aggression so far has had a peculiarly individualistic slant, peculiar for a text in social psychology at least. We have looked at various influences on the individual's tendency to engage in violence without giving attention to the social context of much of the world's aggression. Now it is time to correct that imbalance, to consider the influence of the social situation on an individual's inclination to aggression.

CLASSIC FINDINGS IN SOCIAL PSYCHOLOGY: DEINDIVIDUATION AND AGGRESSION

Gustav Le Bon called attention to being a member of a mob as one situation likely to lead to a breakdown of restraint against aggression (Le Bon, 1896). Our own century has witnessed too many instances of mob violence, from *Kristallnacht*—the riot organized by the Nazis to destroy German Jewish businesses, synagogues, and homes—to the riots in Watts, Harlem, and Newark in response to white racism in the 1960s. Social psychologists have attempted to articulate the factors that promote this disinhibition.

Leon Festinger, Albert Pepitone, and Theodore Newcomb introduced the notion of **deindividuation** as one factor likely to lead to mob violence (Festinger, Pepitone, & Newcomb, 1952). They argued that the key to deindividuation is anonymity; what usually stops us from expressing aggression is a sense of being, and being treated as, an individual, but when we are a member of an anonymous group, we lose this sense. They also suggested that being, in their words "submerged" in a group makes the group attractive to us, that we sometimes seek out the experience of being lost in a mob. And surely part of the attraction of going to a football game to root for our team is this sense of being submerged (and it should be pointed out that riots against officials have broken out in the aftermath of just such events).

To demonstrate the aggression-liberating effects of being lost in a group, the investigators conducted an experiment in which groups of undergraduates were told that a national survey of undergraduates had revealed that 87 percent had deep-seated feelings of hatred toward one or both of their parents. These survey results were, of course, fictional. The subjects were asked to discuss their feelings in relation to these results. (Students might be expected simply to deny these feelings, but the experimenters had an almost fiendish psychoanalytic solution to that problem: they said that the survey also revealed that just those people who most resisted the idea that they hated their parents were the people who did so most!)

Coders rated the discussions that ensued for expressions of hostility toward parents. They also attempted to construct a measure of the degree to which the groups were deindividuating. This measure was constructed by asking the students which members of the groups made which particular comments; the number of comments that were misidentified served as a measure of the degree of anonymity in the group. The investigators found a relation between the number of errors made and the number of hostile comments made—the less well the members knew each other, the more hostile they seemed to be. There was also a weak correlation between how anonymous the groups were and how attractive they were to the people in them, as the investigators proposed.

Philip Zimbardo further explored features of a situation that led to the disinhibition of aggression through deindividuation. In addition to anonymity, he called attention to, among other things: loss of a sense of responsibility, physiological arousal, intense sensory stimulation, and being in a novel situation. To illustrate these effects, he conducted a rather dramatic experiment.

Undergraduate women were brought to a lab in a group, asked to wear very loose-fitting lab coats (disguising their individualizing clothes) and hoods covering their faces. Other subjects were given large name tags to wear. The

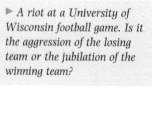

▶ *A riot at a University of Wisconsin football game. Is it the aggression of the losing team or the jubilation of the winning team?*

◄ Aggression isn't the only, or even the most common, emotion experienced in war.

subjects were then asked to evaluate someone they saw being interviewed. The evaluation was to be rather forceful—they were to shock the poor female undergraduate being interviewed. The dependent variable was the amount of shock given. To reduce the sense of responsibility the "deindividuated" subjects felt, they were also told that the experimenter couldn't tell which members in the group gave which level of shock.

The results supported Zimbardo's claims. The deindividuated subjects gave more shock than did those for whom personal identity and personal responsibility were stressed. Moreover, the study showed another interesting effect. Some groups of subjects saw a nice, sweet, pleasant woman being interviewed; other groups saw a rather obnoxious interviewee. The subjects that saw themselves as responsible for their actions shocked the obnoxious woman more than the nice one, but the deindividuated subjects shocked both equally (Zimbardo, 1969). This deindividuation not only released, in the sense of intensifying, the subjects' hostility; it made it indiscriminate.

The studies on deindividuation mentioned so far have all involved subjects acutely aware that they were in a laboratory. But one study looked at deindividuation in a natural setting, at children who had gone out trick-or-treating. As the subjects came to the door, they found a bowl of candy and a bowl of money. They were told to take one piece of candy. Then the experimenter, posing as the home owner, left them alone, while an experimental assistant, unbeknownst to the children, observed them. Some children arrived in groups; others arrived alone. On some occasions, the experimenter asked the children for their names, and on some occasions, she didn't. In some cases, the experimenter appointed one of the children to be in charge of making sure the children took only one piece of candy, and in some cases, she didn't (in all cases, it was the smallest of the children she put in charge).

As we might expect, children in a group cheated—took extra candy or

▲ Kids in Halloween garb may show deindividuation. This child may be more likely to cheat when his or her identity is hidden by a mask and costume.

money—more than children who were alone. Children cheated more if the experimenter had not asked their names. They cheated most when all of these things were true and *someone else* was responsible (Diener, Fraser, Beaman, & Kelem, 1976).

Leon Mann has investigated crowd aggression of another kind. He has examined cases in which crowds of onlookers have "baited" people who were threatening suicide—cases in which crowds have, for example, *encouraged* people to jump from buildings. The evidence, drawn from newspaper accounts, suggests that such incidents tend to happen in conditions that heighten anonymity: in darkness (rather than during daylight), with large crowds (rather than relatively small crowds), and when the crowd is neither very close to the victim—so the individuals can be seen by the victim—nor so far away as to make the crowd's behavior irrelevant to the victim (Mann, 1981).

Our discussion of aggression so far has, curiously, left out the most prevalent form of aggression, aggression in an institutional context. I began this chapter by mentioning that this has been a very violent century—25 million dead in the Second World War alone. The bulk of the aggression in this century, then, has been inflicted by people acting as part of some institution, the army for example. What can social psychologists say about that aggression? The most important research is covered in Chapter 2; here, I can only refer the reader back to the discussion in that chapter of the studies of obedience to authority by Milgram and of prison violence by Zimbardo.

WRAP-UP

Our review suggests that it is an intrinsic part of human nature to experience aggressive urges. The reason for this is simple. We care about things. We care about our own lives, our children, our sense of our selves. When we perceive that these things are being attacked, we experience the urge to attack back. Sometimes we perceive attacks where there aren't any, or we attack back too strongly because we are frustrated or aroused in some other way. In these ways, we are less than rational, less than adequate perceivers of the world. And this no doubt is one source of our wrongdoing. On the other hand, we learn to inhibit aggression. Unfortunately, this learning isn't perfect; sometimes our desires overwhelm our inhibitions, and surely this is a sad fact about us. Moreover, some circumstances are remarkably able to subvert whatever moral notions we have learned. And this is a profound danger. In the end, it is probably wrong to ask if we are good or bad. It is important to remember that we aren't perfect, and some of the ways we aren't.

SUMMARY

1. Aggression refers to action intended to harm another. *Impulsive aggression* is done with the aim of harming another. *Instrumental aggression* is done in order to accomplish another end.

2. There are six different kinds of aggression known in the animal world. *Predatory aggression* is directed toward killing something one feeds on. *Inter-male*

aggression is between members of the same species over control of resources, especially potential mates. *Sex-related aggression* is displayed by males while in the presence of females. *Maternal aggression* is directed by mothers toward defending their offspring. Aggression in response to danger is called *danger-induced aggression.* A variety of annoyances sometimes give rise to a tendency to aggress; this kind of aggression is called *irritable aggression.*

3. These different kinds of aggression can be distinguished by one of the following: the circumstances that provoke them, the hormones that control them, the neural circuits involved in their expression and the form the overt behavior takes, and the evolutionary role that each plays.

4. Two opposed views of the nature of human anger have been proposed. One, descended from Aristotle, sees anger as a response to insult. The other, descended from Yale learning theory and psychoanalysis—the *frustration-aggression hypothesis*—sees anger as essentially blind and irrational, a response to frustration. The dispute is over the role that cognition plays in the genesis of anger.

5. One factor increasing the intensity of an angry response is the kind of frustration itself, and whether it is perceived as justified. Cues associated with aggression have also been shown to intensify aggressive responses. And, people who have been aroused from some source irrelevant to the source of their anger will express more anger than those who have not previously been aroused.

6. One study has found that date rapists have generally exploitative attitudes toward women and that they believe that their friends too share these attitudes.

7. The most common cause of intrafamilial homicide is male jealousy at female infidelity—real or imagined.

8. Learning plays a role in aggression. We learn *how* to aggress, but we also learn—sometimes through modeling—when it is appropriate to engage in aggression, and we may even learn what emotional reactions to have to aggression. It is not clear whether television violence causes real aggression. There is evidence, however, that television has led to an increase in nonviolent crimes of avarice—burglaries.

9. Much of the violence of the twentieth century has occurred in the context of social institutions. One way institutions foster violence is by producing *deindividuation*—a weakened sense of personal responsibility for one's aggressive actions.

PART FOUR

ENDURING RELATIONSHIPS

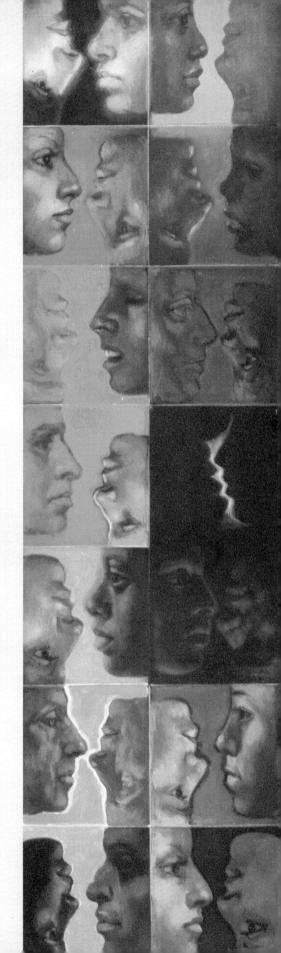

The earlier parts of this book have dealt with the basic forces that shape our social lives; in the final two parts, we consider how these forces come together to create those lives. In this part, we consider enduring relationships. In Chapter 14, we ask the questions: What attracts one person to another in the first place? Why do people like the particular people they like?

Our social lives, fortunately, are made up of something more stable, firmer than our momentary likes and dislikes of other people. They are made up, in part, of enduring relationships. In Chapter 15, we look at such relationships—especially romantic ones. We ask: What accounts for their stability and success? And also: Why do some relationships end in breakup or divorce? ■

CHAPTER 14

Interpersonal Attraction

Thereis no fact of our social lives more obvious than that we like some people more than others. Not so obvious is just why we are attracted to these people. In this chapter, we will ask, and in part answer, the question: What are the determinants of interpersonal attraction?

PROPINQUITY

Propinquity, or physical proximity to others, has a significant effect on attraction. We begin with a study that took advantage of a unique opportunity to investigate the effects of propinquity on interpersonal attraction.

CLASSIC FINDINGS IN SOCIAL PSYCHOLOGY: WESTGATE

From 1942 to 1945, most college-age men were fighting a war rather than enrolling in college, but when the war ended, the GIs fortunate enough to return wanted to pick up their civilian lives. These GIs were unlike the usual freshmen; they were older, many were married, and they were busy creating what later became known as the "baby boom." Among the problems they caused was a tremendous demand for housing on campuses. MIT responded to this demand by constructing the Westgate Housing Complex for married graduate students.

447

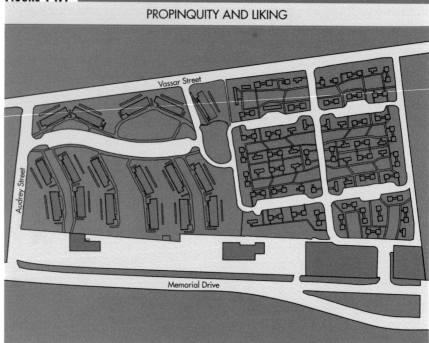

FIGURE 14.1

PROPINQUITY AND LIKING

▶ *This site plan of Westgate and Westgate West shows how isolated the two complexes were from other residential areas. To the north and west, they were next to a wall of factories, warehouses, and trucking garages; to the south, they were next to a highway and the Charles River; to the east, they were next to athletic fields. This isolation from the larger community meant that they could be studied as self-contained units. (From Festinger, Schachter, & Back, 1950)*

Westgate consisted of 100 prefabricated single-family houses. In the spring of 1946, 100 families moved into these houses. About a year later, a second, similar project, Westgate West, consisting of 170 apartments, was also occupied. Westgate and Westgate West consisted, then, of about 250 young families, total strangers to one another with no shared history, in a housing community fairly isolated from any other residential areas (see Figure 14.1). Obviously, friendships would develop, and the question was: What would determine who became friends with whom?* To answer the question,

FIGURE 14.2

THE LAYOUT OF THE WESTGATE APARTMENTS

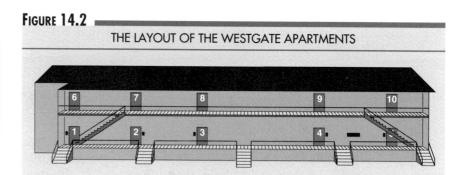

▶ *This schematic diagram of a Westgate West apartment building shows the two floors of the building, with five apartments on each floor. Two stairways, one at each end of the building, connected the two floors. (From Festinger, Schachter, & Back, 1950)*

*Actually, there were several questions. One question had to do with the social pressures that would develop in such a setting; this was discussed in Chapter 3. Here we focus on the determinants of friendship formation.

Leon Festinger, Stanley Schachter, and Kurt Back interviewed the residents of the two complexes and asked them to name the people they saw the most socially. One factor stood out as the most important determinant of friendship choices: physical distance.

Consider Westgate West. Figure 14.2 is a schematic rendering of one of the 17 Westgate West apartment buildings. There were 10 apartments in a building, 5 to a floor. And there were 17 such buildings. Because of their layout in the complex as a whole, there were 272 pairs of adjoining apartments. Thus, there were 272 possibilities for next-door neighbors to socialize with each other; 41 percent of these opportunities were exercised—41 percent of the next-door neighbors socialized with one another. There were 204 socializing opportunities provided by families just two doors down, but only 22.5 percent of these chances were taken. So whether two families were immediately adjacent or just two doors down mattered in terms of whether the families would develop friendships. As for opportunities to socialize with people at opposite ends of a floor, only 10.3 percent of these opportunities were pursued. Figure 14.3 shows the effect of distance on proportion of options taken.

FIGURE 14.3

EFFECTS OF LOCATION ON SOCIALIZING

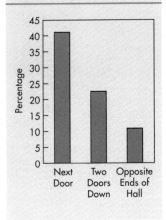

▲ Percentage of opportunities to make friends varied as a function of location. People were twice as likely to make friends with their next-door neighbors as they were to make friends with the people just two doors down. (From Festinger, Schachter, & Back, 1950)

Functional Distance and Liking

In the Westgate study, it wasn't exactly physical distance that mattered; what mattered was what the authors called **functional distance**, the way the layout of the space affected the probabilities that people would casually bump into one another. Figure 14.4 shows the layout of the Westgate single-family houses. Each of the complexes was laid out in the form of a U. All of the houses except those along the short segment of the U opened onto the courtyard. The houses along the short segment opened onto streets that ran through the complex. Residents of houses along the long segments were likely to bump into one another as they came into or left the complex, or as they sat out on their lawns. But the residents of the short segments weren't as likely to bump into their neighbors—though they were physically close to them. These families lived at greater functional distance and, as a consequence, had fewer than half as many friends as did the people living in the long segments. Similarly, the residents of the Westgate West apartments who lived at the foot of stairs connecting the two floors were more likely to have friends on other floors than were other residents.

◄ Schematic drawing of the arrangement of the single-family houses in the Westgate complex. Note that all of the houses except those on the ends opened onto a shared courtyard; the end houses faced onto the street. Those who lived in the end houses were less likely to bump into their neighbors and hence lived at greater functional distance from those whose houses faced onto the courtyard. (From Festinger, Schachter, & Back, 1950)

FIGURE 14.4

FUNCTIONAL DISTANCE

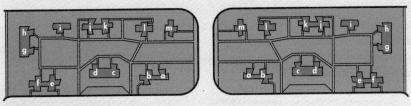

► *Westgate.*

In general terms, the finding that people are more likely to become friends with people close at hand than people far away is obvious. Of course it is true that I am more likely to become friends with someone living in Philadelphia than someone in Rome! But what is interesting about the results here is the incredibly small scale over which this general principle works. In the Westgate West apartment complex, for example, only twenty-two feet separated the doors of the apartments. But the added twenty-two feet needed to reach someone two doors away rather than someone next door roughly halved the odds that friendships would develop.

In a subsequent, similar study of friendship choices among male students in a freshman dorm, closeness of dorm rooms on a hall predicted friendship choice even though the travel time from one dorm room door to another was two seconds (Priest & Sawyer, 1967). And, to take the matter to its extreme, two studies have looked at classes in which students were assigned seats alphabetically; these studies found that alphabetical adjacency—and therefore adjacency in seating—was a substantial predictor of friendship choice (Byrne & Buehler, 1955; Segal, 1974).

Propinquity matters to friendships, and it even matters to spouse selection. In the first of several studies on the effects of propinquity on marriage, James Bossard examined five thousand marriage licenses from Philadelphia issued in the first five months of 1931, and coded the distance between the addresses listed by the prospective bride and groom. About 13 percent of the couples listed the same address—this result probably *doesn't* reflect the effects of propinquity on marriage partner selection, but rather the fact that even in 1931 substantial numbers of people were cohabitating before marriage. Of more importance was the result that about one-third of the couples listed addresses within five blocks of one another, which probably does reflect the effect of propinquity (Bossard, 1932).*

*In a city, people who live close to one another are also likely to be similar in terms of social class, religion, and ethnic group, so the finding that people who marry other people physically

Propinquity and Disliking

The effect of propinquity on attraction has been described as almost mechanical because of the regularity with which it shows up. But it isn't quite mechanical. Investigators have looked at a suburban development. They found, consistent with all we have seen, that the probability of friendship choice was an inverse, linear function of distance. But they also found an even closer relation between *dislike* and distance: when residents were asked to mention the people that they *disliked,* they also reported people who lived close by. Indeed, disliked people were even more likely to live close at hand than were liked people (Ebbesen, Kjos, & Koneçni, 1976; see also Paquin, 1992). The authors attributed this effect to "environmental spoiling." Your neighbors are better able than anyone else to spoil *your* environment by having loud parties late at night, letting their crabgrass grow, letting their garbage pile up, and the thousand other ways neighbors can get on one another's nerves. So, though it is true that propinquity typically leads to liking, it doesn't *always* lead to liking.

> Propinquity leads to the formation of relationships, both friendly and hostile.

CLASSIC FINDINGS IN SOCIAL PSYCHOLOGY: MERE EXPOSURE

The Eiffel Tower is one of the world's most admired structures, especially by Parisians who see it as the central icon of their city. But it was not always loved; as Albert Harrison points out, when the tower was completed in 1889, it was far more loathed than loved (Harrison, 1977). Indeed, in 1900, there was a substantial movement to tear the ugly thing down. What happened to change people's attitudes?

The simplest possibility is that the more exposure people have to something—a building, another person, a school of art (Impressionism too was immediately loathed)—the more people will like it. If so, that would help account for the effects of functional distance on liking, since functional distance is related to exposure. Robert Zajonc has proposed just this principle—that mere exposure to something leads to liking that thing.

Zajonc advanced several sorts of evidence on the effect of ***mere exposure.*** First, he had subjects rate 154 pairs of English antonyms, indicating which of the poles of the pairs had the more desirable meaning. He then consulted a source, the Thorndike-Lorge list, which indicates the relative frequency with which English words are used in print. He found that for the overwhelming majority of the pairs, the more frequently used member was the more desirable one—*able,* for example, occurs about four times more often in English prose than does *unable,* and clearly it is better to be able than unable.

> Repeated exposure to people tends to lead to liking.

To explore the relation beween exposure and liking further, Zajonc made up words the subjects had surely never seen before—*Ikititaf, afworbu,* and *saricick.* He told the subjects that the stimuli were Turkish words, and that the study was about how people pronounce foreign words. Then he flashed

---

close may reflect the operation of these factors as well. The best evidence at the moment suggests that *both* propinquity and segregation by group contribute to this finding (Morgan, 1981).

FIGURE 14.5

RELATION OF EXPOSURE AND LIKING

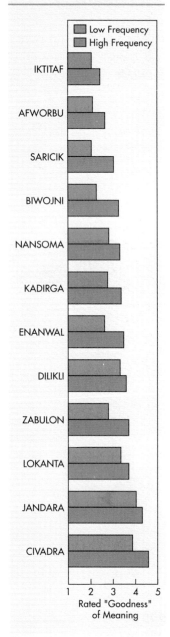

each word to subjects 0, 1, 2, 5, 10, or 25 times and had them pronounce the word. Last, he told them that each was a Turkish adjective, and he realized that guessing the actual meanings of the words might be difficult, so he would ask them only to guess how good or bad the words' meanings were. He found that the more often the subjects had seen the words, the better they thought their referent (see Figure 14.5).

One plausible reason for this is that the more often the subjects pronounced a word, the easier it became to pronounce it, and they might be rating ease of pronouncing it. So, to control for that, Zajonc showed another group of subjects figures that look to the untrained eye like Chinese calligraphy and asked them to do no more than look at them. He exposed each of the figures for only about two seconds and found once again that the more often the subjects saw them, the better they thought the words' meanings were (Zajonc, 1968).

A further study brings us closer to mere exposure and liking for people. In this study, the investigators used four women as stimuli. Ms. *A* dressed as an undergraduate and attended fifteen sessions of a lecture course. For each lecture, she arrived before the class began, walked down the aisle of the lecture hall, and sat at the front where the other students could see her. Ms. *B* did the same thing, but she attended only ten lectures; Ms. *C* came to class only five times, and Ms. *D* never showed up. At the end of the term, the students in the class were shown slides of each of the women and were asked to indicate how familiar they found her, how attractive they found her, and how similar to them they believed she was.

The number of times the person attended class was only weakly related to judgments of familiarity. But the number of classes attended had a bigger impact on attraction and similarity. (Pretesting showed that students who had never seen the women before rated them as about equal on all of these measures.) Thus, apparently, the mere presence of these women in class affected their attractiveness and perceived similarity to the students (we will see why this should be so below), even though familiarity was only barely affected (Moreland & Beach, 1992).

The evidence suggests that merely being exposed to a stimulus—be it the Eiffel Tower or another subject—leads to enhanced liking. Indeed, there have been about two hundred experimental tests of the exposure-leads-to-liking hypothesis over the last twenty years, and there is little room left to doubt the hypothesis (Bornstein, 1989). Still, is it fair to ask if it is *always* true that repeated exposure leads to liking?

It doesn't seem to be true that hearing the same song over and over because the record is stuck leads us to want to hear it yet again. And indeed, there is evidence that the relationship between exposure and liking is shaped like an inverse U; exposure leads to liking up to a point, but beyond that point, it becomes really quite aversive—boring (Zajonc, Shaver, Tavris, & Van Kreveld, 1972; see also Bornstein, Kale, & Cornell, 1990). So while it has often been observed that repeated exposure to unusual music or art is required before one grows to like it (Krugman, 1943), literally repeating the same song over and over will not enhance liking. Also, one wonders whether truly aversive stimuli—like the smell of a neighbor's rotting garbage—will ever be liked. Still, the evidence is that if you don't hate a stimulus to begin with and you aren't exposed to it too often, the more often you are exposed to it, the more

A

B

▲ *(A) Claude Monet's* Impression, Sunrise, *the painting from which the movement got its (at the time, derogatory) name. (B) The Eiffel Tower. Initial loathing was followed by worldwide popularity.*

you will come to like it. It is reasonable to suppose that the MIT graduate students in the Westgate complex found each other and their degree of exposure to each other well within these limits.*

SIMILARITY

Fritz Heider proposed that there is a human tendency to prefer cognitive balance to cognitive imbalance (Heider, 1958). Consider for a moment two people, *A* and *B*, and something toward which they have some attitude—perhaps another person, a political issue, or a set of values. Some of the relations among these three elements, Heider said, are balanced. If *A* likes *B* and *B* likes *A* and they both have favorable (or unfavorable) attitudes toward something, then they are in a balanced state (see Figure 14.6 on page 454). If they like each other but have *opposite* attitudes toward something, then the state is imbalanced. Just what balance is has never been entirely clear, but it seems that one can tell if a triad is balanced by assigning a + to the "liking" relationship and a − to the disliking relationship and then multiplying the signs of the relationships together. If the outcome is a +, then the relationships are balanced; if the outcome is a −, then they are unbalanced.

Heider proposed that our psychology presses us to create balance, or at

*We might want to know *why* exposure leads to liking. This is less clear, but explanations tend to implicate *response competition*. The idea is that when we are first exposed to any stimulus, we have a variety of different responses to it, and this is unpleasant and frustrating. As exposures increase, however, our response tendencies settle down to a single response, and this is more pleasant (Harrison, 1968). The interested reader is invited to consult Albert Harrison's interesting review article for more detail (Harrison, 1977).

FIGURE 14.6

SOME EXAMPLES OF BALANCED AND UNBALANCED TRIADS

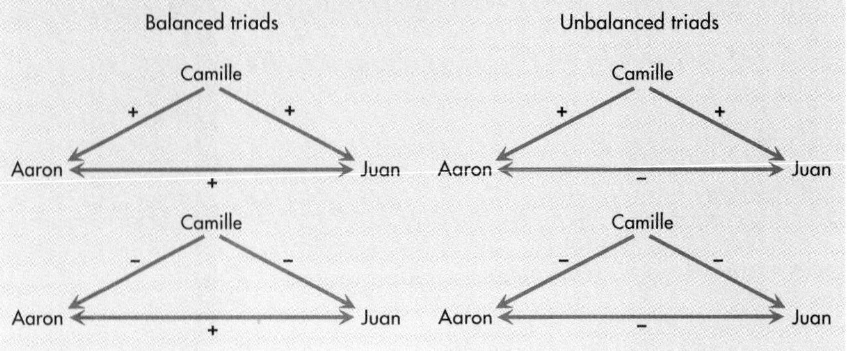

▶ *Some balanced and unbalanced triads.*

least the perception of balance. From this idea, two propositions about interpersonal attraction follow: (1) if we like someone, then we should prefer to see her as sharing our attitudes, and (2) we should like people who share our attitudes.

Similarity of Attitudes and Attraction

Theodore Newcomb set out to explore these ideas in the context of an extraordinary experiment. Newcomb contacted students who were transferring into the University of Michigan for their sophomore year in 1954 and 1955. He offered to allow them to live for free in a house he had acquired for one semester in return for their giving him up to five hours each week to participate in research. Each year, seventeen men (the capacity of the house) took him up on the offer. The research strategy Newcomb followed was to assess the subjects' attitudes toward a variety of issues before they arrived and their attitudes over the course of the semester. He also asked them to report as the semester went on how attracted they were to each of the other members of the house. This strategy gave Newcomb the chance to explore the development of relationships among people who were utter strangers to each other at the outset.

What Newcomb expected to find was that the first of the propositions derived from Heider's position would dominate interpersonal attraction at the beginning of the semester, but that the second would dominate later on. That is, he expected to find that people who were attracted to each other early on (for whatever reason) would *perceive themselves* as having similar attitudes toward a variety of issues (and toward other members of the house), but that much of this perceived agreement would be illusory rather than real. It would happen not because people who had similar attitudes were attracted to each other—there wouldn't be time yet for people to learn each other's attitudes— but because people attracted to each other, want to see themselves as having similar attitudes. But, he predicted, as the subjects had a chance to interact with one another and learn each other's real attitudes, attraction would be grounded in real agreement rather than illusory agreement.

"NO MORE 'SAME AGE, SAME PROFESSION, SAME INCOME GUYS. THE LAST ONE WAS SO COMPETITIVE WITH ME, HE WANTED TO KILL ME."

The results were by and large as he expected. Early in the semester, the subjects who were attracted to each other *perceived themselves* to be in agreement both about values and issues and about their attitudes toward the other men in the house, but this agreement was more imagined than real. Toward the end of the semester, on the other hand, their attraction toward one another depended on real agreement (Newcomb, 1961). Newcomb's research, then, suggested that attitude similarity is one key determinant of attraction.

Donn Byrne followed Newcomb's idea up in an extensive research program. One contribution Byrne made was the development of a simpler laboratory method for investigating attraction and similarity. The method has become known as the **bogus stranger technique.** An early study illustrates how it works.

Byrne first administered an attitude scale that consisted of twenty-six topics ranging from those very important to subjects (God and premarital sex, for example) to less important issues (Western movies and television programs). The subjects were to indicate their attitudes toward each topic on seven-point scales. Two weeks later, the subjects were falsely informed that they were now in a study on how well people can predict other people's behavior. In order to make these predictions, they were told that they would be given the attitude scales filled out by another subject. In fact, they were given a fake scale, filled out by the experimenter. The scale showed that the "other subject" had either highly similar or highly dissimilar attitudes to their own. They were then asked a series of questions about this "other subject."

First, they were asked for their personal feelings toward the "stranger," and how much they would like to work with this person. They were also asked to evaluate the person as to his intelligence, knowledge of current events, morality, and adjustment. The results clearly supported the similarity-leads-to-attraction hypothesis. The subjects liked the similar person more than the dissimilar one, they wanted to work with the similar person more, and they evaluated the similar other more favorably (Byrne, 1961). This

FIGURE 14.7

LIKING AND SIMILARITY OF ECONOMIC STATUS

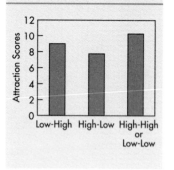

▲ *Attraction to a stranger of similar or dissimilar economic status. The results are typical of manipulations of similarity-dissimilarity of all sorts. (Data from Byrne, Clore, & Worchel, 1966)*

■■■■■■■■■■■■

Similarity in beliefs, personality, interests, economic status, and so on typically leads to attraction.

■■■■■■■■■■■■

study, then, supported the idea that similarity leads to attraction, introduced a new, simple method of investigation, and showed that similarity also leads to enhanced evaluation.

Byrne and his colleagues, using the "bogus stranger" technique, have shown that the relation between similarity and liking extends well beyond attitudes. For example, if subjects fill out a personality scale and are then given a scale filled out by a bogus other subject, they will like the bogus other who is similar to them in personality; if they fill out a scale indicating how much money they have to spend and receive responses from a bogus stranger on that scale, they will like the person more if he has a similar economic position (see Figure 14.7; Byrne, Clore, & Worchel, 1966; Byrne, Griffith, & Stefaniak, 1967). Indeed, it would be no exaggeration to claim that the positive relation between similarity and attraction is both the broadest and most reliable finding in social psychology. (As we shall see, however, though it is broad, it is *not* universal; there are circumstances in which similarity does *not* lead to liking.)

Explanations for Relation of Similarity and Attraction

In addition to introducing a method and extending the range of the similarity-attraction claim, Byrne also proposed an explanation for why it happens. He has argued that the reason we are attracted to similar other people is that similarity is reinforcing. Consider attitudes. Just what an attitude is is a matter of some difficulty (see Chapter 16), but suffice it to say that an attitude includes a belief about what is true, or about what is morally right to do. If you have a negative attitude toward someone—for example, you believe that he is obnoxious—then you think you are right about his obnoxiousness, and you believe he shouldn't be invited to intimate dinner parties. Byrne suggests that interacting with other people who have the same attitude toward him that you do will be rewarding because it will sustain your view of this obnoxiousness; interacting with people who like him, on the other hand, will call your view into question. Byrne argues that having one's view of the world sustained gives rise to positive affect, while having one's view of the world attacked gives rise to negative affect (Byrne & Nelson, 1965). Small wonder, then, that we like to hang around with people who agree with us!

Envy and Self-Esteem Maintenance Even though similarity typically leads to attraction, it can lead to something else too: envy. The English language has imposed a burden on those of us who study envy. Time was when "envy" and "jealousy" were used to refer to two different concepts. Now, it seems, "envy" has all but dropped out of the language. But still there is at least one context where envy and jealousy can be kept distinct. If a woman shoots her husband because she finds him in bed with another woman—that's jealousy, not envy! Jealousy has to do with intrusions upon romantic (or other exclusive) relationships; envy has to do with why Cain slew Abel.*

---

*It is Iago, not Othello, who is consumed with envy. Othello, not Iago, is consumed with jealousy. Even if you don't agree with this use of language, the point is that Iago is consumed by his impotent fury at Othello's accomplishments. But Othello is the one consumed by rage over betrayal; these are different, no matter what words one uses.

Cain, you may recall, slew Abel because Abel's sacrifice was found more pleasing by the Lord. So envy has to do with rage at another's accomplishment, accomplishment that makes you look bad. The envious person, I have argued (Sabini & Silver, 1982), reacts to accomplishments that make him look bad by undercutting the person who accomplished something. This is, of course, not the only way to react to a friend's accomplishment. You might congratulate her, become depressed at the recognition of your own failure and her success, or attempt to enhance your own public stature by basking in the reflected glory of her accomplishment by stressing the way the two of you are a unit (Cialdini, Borden, Thorne, Walker, Freedman, & Sloan, 1976). What determines which reaction a person will have?

One factor surely has to do with the domain of life in which the other person has received acclaim. The further it is from something you see as important to yourself, the easier it is to congratulate. It is easy for me to congratulate someone on his golf shots, since golf isn't my life; it is even easier for me to congratulate someone on her brilliant play at bridge, since I don't know the first thing about bridge. Congratulating someone on the point she made in a seminar *is* harder, since, after all, attending seminars is part of my life.

Friendship is a delicate matter. Abraham Tesser has gathered evidence that students pick as friends other students who overall are about as accomplished as they are, but whose accomplishments are in different domains (see Figure 14.8). This maximizes their chances to celebrate each other's accomplishments while staying away from envy (Tesser, Campbell, & Smith, 1984; Tesser, Pilkington, & McIntosh, 1989). And he has shown that eminent male scientists' relationships with their fathers were closer the further the father's work was from the son's field of accomplishment (Tesser, 1980). Differences are sometimes to be preferred to similarity.

SIMILARITY AND INFERRED EVALUATION

Elliot Aronson proposed that we like people who are similar to us because we expect them to like us, and we tend to like people who we believe like us. To gather evidence, Aronson conducted an experiment in which subjects interacted with a confederate; in half the cases, the confederate agreed with the subject, while in the other cases, he disagreed. After their interaction, the

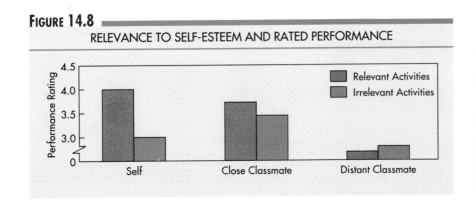

FIGURE 14.8

RELEVANCE TO SELF-ESTEEM AND RATED PERFORMANCE

◄ *Student ratings of self, close classmate, and distant classmate on activities relevant (or irrelevant) to their self-esteem. They tend to see themselves as better than their close friends on relevant activities, but worse than their close friends on irrelevant activities. (From Tesser, Campbell, & Smith, 1984)*

FIGURE 14.9

SIMILARITY AND INFERRED
EVALUATION

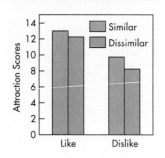

▲ *Attraction to a subject who likes you (or doesn't) and is similar (or dissimilar) to you. Similarity matters little if you know whether the person will like you. (Data from Aronson & Worchel, 1966)*

▲ *The marriage of Tom Thumb and Lavinia Warren.*

confederate was asked to write a brief description of his reaction to the subject. In half of the cases, the confederate indicated that he liked the subject; in the other half, he indicated that he didn't. Then the subjects were shown these descriptions, and they were asked to evaluate the confederate.

As you might expect, subjects who thought the confederate liked them liked the confederate, and they didn't like the confederate who didn't like them. Moreover, if the confederate liked them, then they liked the confederate *whether their attitudes were similar or dissimilar,* and if the confederate didn't like them, they disliked him regardless of his attitudes (see Figure 14.9; Aronson & Worchel, 1966). These results suggest that information about a person's attitudes is redundant once we know that she likes us; once we know *that,* we don't care about her attitudes. More recent research has been consistent in showing that believing that someone will like us leads to our liking her, although the research is *not* consistent about whether *all* of the effect of similarity on attraction is a result of inferred liking (Insko, Thompson, Stroebe, Shaud, Pinner, & Layton, 1973; Touhey, 1975; Condon & Crano, 1988). In any event, one way that similarity leads to liking seems to be by giving rise to the inference that a similar person will like us more than a dissimilar person will.

SIMILARITY AS FACILITATING INTERACTION

Deborah Davis has suggested another way in which attitude similarity may affect attraction. The positions we have seen so far suggest that the more important an issue is to you, then the more another's similarity to you on that issue will affect attraction. But Davis suggests that it isn't an issue's importance that determines whether similarity will affect attraction; rather, it is whether being similar on that issue will affect interpersonal interactions.

Imagine that you love going to rock concerts, and you have very discriminating taste. Whether someone shares your taste might well matter to your interactions with her; shared taste will lead to shared pleasures. You may also have religious beliefs that are very important to you, much more important than your taste in rock music. But these religious beliefs may not matter much to how you interact with a friend who doesn't share them. The question is: Whom will you be attracted to more, the person who shares your taste in rock music but is of a different religion, or the person who is of the same religion but likes only Mozart? Davis predicts the first; Byrne predicts the second.

To answer the question, Davis carried out an experiment in which subjects rated their attraction to people who agreed or disagreed with them on various attitudes. They also rated each attitude for importance and for the degree to which the attitudes would be important in everyday interaction. She found, in support of her theory, that importance to interaction rather than importance in general mattered to attraction (Davis, 1981).

We have, then, three theories about how similarity leads to liking. One implicates positive affect connected with similar others and negative affect associated with dissimilar others. The second theory suggests that we like similar other people because we expect them to like us. The third proposes that similarity matters because (and only because) that similarity will affect interaction. Which is right? Well, probably they all are; probably each contributes to the overall relation.

I mentioned above that though the relation between similarity and attraction was reliable and broad, it was not universal. When doesn't similarity breed liking?

Similarity and Discrediting Traits

There is some evidence that if someone has an undesirable trait, then we will like him better if he is dissimilar to us rather than similar. In one study, half of the subjects interacted with a confederate who was introduced as similar to them on certain personality tests. To the other subjects, she was presented as being dissimilar. With half of each kind of subject, the confederate acted in a pleasant way; with the other half, she was rude and generally obnoxious. The subjects were then asked to rate their experimental partner for the degree to which they liked her.

Not surprisingly, the subjects liked the pleasant confederate more than the obnoxious one. And in line with all we have seen so far, the subjects liked the similar pleasant person more than the dissimilar pleasant person. But matters were different for the obnoxious confederate. The subjects liked the obnoxious *dissimilar* confederate more than the obnoxious similar confederate (well, actually, they disliked her less) (Taylor & Mettee, 1971). A similar pattern of results was found in a study in which a partner was presented as emotionally disturbed or normal; normal partners were liked more if they were similar, but emotionally disturbed partners were disliked less if they were dissimilar (Novak & Lerner, 1968).

Although these (and other) findings are exceptions to the rule that similarity leads to attraction, they do not embarrass the explanations of *why* similarity usually leads to attraction. They are readily compatible with Byrne's view. If it is reinforcing to find ourselves in agreement with most people, and we are therefore attracted to similar people, it should be anything but rewarding to see ourselves as similar to an obnoxious person, and we should (and do) find ourselves repelled by such similarity. And these findings fit with a somewhat enlarged conception of balance theory.

■■■■■■■■■■■
Similarity may lead to attraction because

- learning of similarity in beliefs is reinforcing;
- similarity leads to the expectation of liking;
- similarity leads to easier, smoother social interaction.

■■■■■■■■■■■

EVALUATION

It is hard to like someone who we know thinks little of us. It is far easier to appreciate someone who appreciates us. And indeed, there is experimental evidence that people like other people who evaluate them positively rather than negatively, whether the evaluations are deserved or not (Skolnick, 1971).

Patterning of Evaluation and Attraction

Elliot Aronson has suggested that the temporal *patterning* of evaluation is crucial in determining attraction. In particular, he has proposed that we are particularly attracted to someone who at first has a negative view of us, a view that then becomes positive.

To investigate this, Aronson created an experimental situation in which subjects were exposed to four patterns of evaluation by "another subject"—

FIGURE 14.10

LIKING AND PATTERNS OF FEEDBACK

Liking

8
7
6
5
4
3
2
1
0

Always Positive | Negative, Then Positive | Always Negative | Positive, Then Negative

▶ *Liking for people varied as a function of the kinds of feedback they gave. The subjects liked the person most who at first gave them negative feedback but then became positive toward them. (Data from Aronson & Linder)*

actually a confederate. (To enhance credibility, through elaborate staging, the subjects "overheard" these evaluations delivered directly to the investigator rather than to themselves.) The four patterns were (1) positive from the first and remained positive throughout the session, (2) an initially negative reaction that then became positive, (3) relentlessly negative evaluations, and (4) an initial positive reaction that then became negative. The results were, as Aronson expected, that the "other subject" who was first negative and then became positive was the most attractive partner; the continuously positive partner was next most attractive; the initially positive but then negative evaluator was the least attractive (see Figure 14.10; Aronson & Linder, 1965).

These results suggest that we are more responsive to compliments from new acquaintances than we are to the same compliments from people we know well. And if this is so, then loyalty seems in great danger. But things may not be as bad as they seem. There is evidence that people prefer the newfound admirer to the steady admirer *only* when they are presented with the two patterns of feedback one after the other; if they are presented with both patterns at the same time, subjects prefer the constant admirer to the newfound admirer (Berscheid, Brothen, & Graziano, 1976).

Ingratiation and Attraction

Although letting on that you think highly of someone is a good way to get that person to like you, there is sometimes a problem with this strategy. The tricky circumstance is when you are in some way or other dependent upon the person you are evaluating and are seen as an ingratiator. Ned Jones demonstrated the problem with ingratiation, deliberately and covertly getting someone to like you, in several experiments.

In one experiment, subjects interacted with a confederate who was instructed to be either hyper-agreeable with the subject, or respectful but autonomous. In some cases, the subjects were informed that the confederate

▪▪▪▪▪▪▪▪▪▪

Positive evaluations are reinforcing (so long as they are not ingratiation), but their *pattern* as well as magnitude determines how reinforcing they are.

▪▪▪▪▪▪▪▪▪▪

had been instructed to be spontaneous; in other cases, they were told that he had been instructed to be attraction seeking. The point of this was to convince some subjects that the person they were interacting with was behaving in a spontaneous way, while leading others to believe that he had an ulterior reason to be attractive to them. The subjects who thought that the confederate was spontaneous had no reason to suspect that he would be ingratiating, but the other subjects should have been led to at least wonder about this. How would the suspicion of ingratiation affect the subjects' perceptions of the confederate?

The results showed that the agreeable confederate was liked more when the subjects were told that he had been instructed to be spontaneous. The subjects apparently "took off points" from the agreeable confederate when his agreeableness could be seen as a strategy to be attractive. The autonomous confederate, on the other hand, was liked *more* when the subjects thought he had been instructed to be attractive; apparently his being autonomous even though he was instructed to be attractive earned him "extra credit" for remaining independent in the face of pressure to ingratiate (see Figure 14.11; Jones, Stires, Shaver, & Harris, 1968).*

In a further experiment, subjects were confronted with a positive, negative, or mixed evaluation from someone who was either dependent on them or not. The evaluations were either accurate or not. As we might expect, in general, the subjects liked the evaluator more if her evaluations were positive than if they were negative or mixed. They also liked the evaluator more if her evaluations were accurate than if they were inaccurate. In this experiment, subjects did not take off points for positive evaluations of them from a confederate who was dependent on them, but they did give extra credit—they evaluated the confederate more favorably—if she gave a negative evaluation when she was dependent on them (Drachman, DeCarufel, & Insko, 1978). At least within the conditions explored in these experiments, then, although being dependent on someone makes it *hard* to compliment her without being seen as insincere and therefore undercutting your evaluation, it isn't impossible. Although points are sometimes taken off, you still get at least partial credit. And to some degree, negatively evaluating someone upon whom you are dependent can sometimes earn you extra credit.

Competence and Attraction

At the heart of the similarity-attraction relation in any of its guises is the idea that we are attracted to people who can provide us with rewards. If this is so, then we should certainly find competence attractive, since competent people are more likely to bring rewards than are incompetent people—unless, of course, we are betting against them! But the member of a group with the best ideas is often not the best-liked member. Elliot Aronson suggested that one

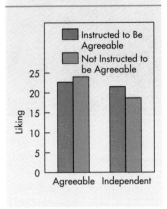

FIGURE 14.11

AGREEABLENESS AND
AUTONOMY

▲ *Liking for someone the subjects knew was instructed to be agreeable or not as a function of whether he agreed with or was independent from the subject. (Data from Jones, Stires, Shaver, & Harris, 1968)*

*The interactions with the subjects were videotaped and shown to other subjects. These observers were asked, among other things, to predict the real subjects' evaluations. They expected the real subjects to see the agreeable, instructed-to-be-attractive confederate as more insincere than the subjects actually saw him. It was apparently harder for the targets of the ingratiation to attribute ingratiation than it was for these uninvolved observers. On the other hand, the observers did not predict the "extra credit" effect; they expected the target subjects to be less attracted than they were in the case where the confederate was autonomous.

▲ *Lieutenant Columbo from the television series* Columbo. *The terribly popular character seems to be attractive to his audience in part because of his fumbling and disheveled manner—but he always gets his man or woman.*

FIGURE 14.12

COMPETENCE AND ATTRACTION

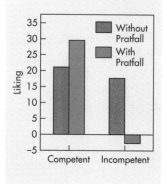

▲ *Attraction to a competent or incompetent person with or without a pratfall. The competent person's attractiveness was enhanced by the pratfall; the incompetent person's attractiveness was reduced. (Data from Aronson, Willerman, & Floyd, 1966)*

reason for this might be that people of great intellectual gift are seen as "too good," austere, inhuman. Aronson set out to show that though competence is preferred to incompetence, what is really attractive is competence in a human package.

To show this, Aronson had subjects listen to a tape that they were told was of a student trying out for *College Bowl*, a television show that was like *Jeopardy* except that it was played by teams of subjects drawn from the same college. They heard either a very competent fellow or someone more mediocre. The competent fellow got 92 percent of the questions right. During an interview, he (modestly) allowed as how during high school he had been an honor student, editor of the yearbook, and on the track team—quite a package. The more mediocre fellow (actually the same confederate) got only 30 percent of the answers and said he had gotten average grades during high school, had been a proofreader on the yearbook, and had tried out for but failed to make the track team—quite mediocre.

The subjects who heard these tapes liked the competent fellow slightly more than the mediocre fellow. But two other groups of subjects heard exactly the same tapes with an addition. The addition consisted of the candidate's saying, "Oh my goodness, I've spilled coffee all over my new suit!" along with the sound of chairs being pushed back from what must have been the soaked and dripping table, and the inevitable clatter as all concerned tried to mop up the mess. How did this pratfall affect subjects' attraction to the candidate?

The pratfall caused attraction to the competent fellow to soar (see Figure 14.12). It increased by 50 percent. But no such advantage of clumsiness accrued to the mediocre fellow; in fact, his attractiveness *declined* by 100 percent (Aronson, Willerman, & Floyd, 1966). Apparently the spilled coffee, though it marred the competent person's suit, enhanced his overall aura; but for the mediocre fellow, it was simply the last straw, dooming his self-presentation.

Subsequent research has asked whether everybody reacts this way. The subjects in these studies saw a competent and mediocre applicant for the position of ombudsman, this time on videotape. Again, half of the subjects saw the regrettable incident with the coffee cup. But this time before the subjects saw the tapes, they filled out a questionnaire measuring their own self-esteem. On the basis of the questionnaire, the subjects were divided into low, moderate, and high self-esteem groups. In this version, the spilled coffee had no effect on the subjects' evaluation of the mediocre applicant—they didn't like him, but they liked him no less for his mess. But the three kinds of subjects responded differently to the competent but clumsy fellow. The subjects who were intermediate in self-esteem liked the fellow more when he spilled the coffee. But both the high and low self-esteem subjects downgraded the competent fellow for his pratfall. The reasons for this downgrading may be different in the two groups. The investigators speculated that the low self-esteem subjects were looking for a "perfect hero," which the competent fellow seemed to be until he made such a mess of himself. The high self-esteem subjects, on the other hand, may not have found the competent fellow intimidating; they may have found him quite like themselves. The pratfall showed that he wasn't like them after all—he didn't really have the "right stuff" (Helmreich, Aronson, & LeFan, 1970).

We now turn to the most obvious source of attraction: physical appearance. Physical attractiveness is important to us in selecting someone to be sexually involved with, but as we shall see, its effects are much broader than that.

Attractiveness and Culture

Are there universal standards of physical attractiveness? The answer seems to be yes, but these universals are only a small part of the ideal cultures impose. According to a review of the cross-cultural evidence by Clellan Ford and Frank Beach, cleanliness was a universal—no culture prefers dirty people. Another standard might be the state of the complexion; many diseases manifest themselves in an unhealthy complexion, so it would not be odd that people find others with unattractive complexions unattractive. Ford and Beach mention another universal, which one hesitates to mention—plumpness in women (Ford & Beach, 1951). One hesitates to mention it because American culture, at the moment, is on a thin craze, attested to by the number of diet books in the stores. But a quick glance at a Renoir or Rubens painting shows that past cultures have had a taste for plump women. Probably no culture, including American, prefers actually emaciated people.

What about facial beauty? Are there universal standards here? Michael Cunningham reasoned that there might be. As we saw in Chapter 12, men should find youth attractive in a sexual partner, although there is no reason for women to find youth attractive in a partner. If this is so, then facial features associated with youth should be attractive to males. There is a set of features referred to as "neotenous" by ethologists because these are features that babies, puppies, infant monkeys, and so on have, but that the adults of

▼ *Some less-svelte attractive women: (A) Peter Paul Rubens's* The Three Graces, *(B) Auguste Renoir's* Diana, *and (C) Paul Gauguin's* The Moon and the Earth

A

B

C

these species don't. These features make the young of many species "cute" to us, and probably to adults of these same other species—although it is hard to tell what a golden retriever finds cute! Neotenous features include larger foreheads, larger eyes, wider-set eyes, smaller noses and chins, and so on.

To determine whether these features make a face attractive, Cunningham presented pictures of Miss Universe contestants as well as pictures of women drawn from college yearbooks to male American college students and asked them to judge how attractive the faces were. He also measured the physical parameters of the faces related to neoteny—distance between the eyes, size of the nose, for example. Cunningham found, as he expected, that measures of how neotenous the faces were predicted how much the subjects liked the faces, lending some support to the idea that neotenous features are attractive to American men, at least.* And since some of these women were selected by members of their own cultures to represent them in the Miss Universe contest, it is reasonable to assume they were attractive to native audiences also. So perhaps neoteny is universally attractive (Cunningham, 1986).

Cunningham believes that evolutionary theory can also predict what features women find attractive in men. He proposes that women too should be attracted to neotenous features, because such features will stimulate nurturative feelings; but women should also be attracted by facial signs of sexual maturity and dominance, and should be attracted to men who seem to be of high social status but who also seem to be friendly, approachable. He found (using U.S. samples of undergraduates) that neither the most mature nor the most neotenous faces were most attractive; rather, faces intermediate in neoteny were most attractive. A big smile, prominent cheekbones (a maturity sign), and high-status clothing were attractive to women (Cunningham, 1990). It is important to know whether the facial findings generalize to other cultures.

It would certainly be a mistake to imagine that our judgments of what is attractive are closely linked to "survival value" or to what we think has survival value. Take suntans, for example. The facts seem to be that exposure to the sun can lead to skin cancer many years later. Thus, suntans are a sign of danger. This is especially true in Australia, which has lots of sun and fair-skinned people, and where two out of three Australians are likely to develop some form of skin cancer in their lives. Nonetheless, when a sample of high school students from Victoria, Australia, were asked to judge the attractiveness and healthiness of people shown to them by picture, they rated the stimuli with moderate tans as most attractive and most healthy, even though untanned skin is healthier (Broadstock, Borland, Gason, 1992). (During the Victorian era, pale skin was strongly valued; how we came to admire suntans I cannot tell you.) So one cannot always assume that what is attractive is also healthy.

Whatever limits there are on what a culture finds attractive are quite broad. Within these limits, people are free to prefer blonds or redheads, dark bodies or pale bodies, blue eyes or brown. Some cultures even engage in deliberate scarring of the body or tremendous augmentation of the lips to enhance attractiveness. After all, none of these things makes much of a dif-

▲ *Facial scarring enhances attractiveness in some cultures.*

*Some facial signs of "maturity" also predicted attractiveness; high cheekbones, for example, are distinctly not features of young members of any species, but they do attract American men.

ference in terms of survival, so there would be no reason to expect uniformity. Still, regardless of whether the standards are universal, each culture has some objective standards for what is attractive, standards that competent people within the culture know. How does it matter in Western culture how physically attractive you are?

Attractiveness and Dating

We all know that physical attractiveness plays a role in romantic relationships. But just *how important* is it? After all, if asked to mention the qualities we find attractive in another person, we might mention shared interests, personality, intelligence, sense of humor, and so on. How much, among all of these other influences, does physical attractiveness matter?

One investigation directly addressed this question. Students at a large Midwestern university were solicited to attend a "computer dance" at which they were to be matched by computer with a partner for the evening; 664 subjects attended. Each had filled out a series of questionnaires in advance, supposedly to allow the computer to match each partner with an appropriate date. The experimenters collected all of this information and analyzed it very quickly; that is, they ignored it. Instead, they matched the partners randomly under one constraint: they made sure the man was taller than the woman. Filling out the forms in advance did play an important role in the experiment, however; it gave the experimenters a chance to rate the subjects on physical attractiveness.

The dance began at 8:00. At 10:30 there was an intermission, and the experimenters rounded up all but five couples to give them rating forms to fill out asking how much they liked their date, how eager they were to ask him or her out again, how attractive they found their date, how attractive they thought their date found them, and so forth. The main focus of investigation was: How well would the experimenters' ratings of the physical attractiveness of the dates correspond to how attracted their partners were? After all, if personality, intelligence, and so on are important, then we should expect that the correspondence would not be very high. But in fact there was a substantial correlation (0.44) between how attractive the experimenters rated the *female* member of a pair and how much her partner liked her, and a slightly lower correlation with how much he wanted to go out with her again. But what about the other way around? There was a 0.36 correlation between how attractive the experimenters found him and how much his partner liked him. So for both sexes, physical attractiveness mattered quite a lot.

When we use the subjects' own ratings of their partners' attractiveness, the correlations are even higher. There was a 0.78 correlation between how attractive males found their date and how much they liked her, and a 0.69 correlation for women (Walster, Aronson, Abrams, & Rottman, 1966).

It is not clear which rating is the better measure of the real relation between physical attractiveness and liking. On the one hand, the partners for the dance had a much better chance to look at their dates than did the experimenters, who made their ratings at a glance. Further, the experimenters' ratings were made when the subjects weren't dressed up, and physical attractiveness depends, in part, on makeup, clothes, and so forth. On the other hand, there may be a distortion in the partners' ratings of physical attractiveness based on how appealing their partners' personalities were. The correlation between the participants' judgments of physical attractiveness and liking could mean *either* that they liked their dates because they found them physically attractive, or that they found them physically attractive because they liked them. Probably both processes work. Thus, in the end the experimenters' ratings of physical attractiveness, which were obviously unbiased by personality, probably represented an *underestimate* of the effect of pure physical attractiveness, while the subjects' ratings probably reflected an *overestimate.*

Somewhat more surprising than the fact that physical attractiveness mattered so much is the fact that other things, which one might expect to matter, didn't. For example, the experimenters knew the subjects' rank in high school, a crude measure of intelligence. Although students typically say that they want their dates to be intelligent, this measure didn't correlate at all with liking. One personality variable we might expect to correlate, introversion, didn't matter either. The *only thing* that the experimenters could detect that *did* matter was physical attractiveness. Indeed, similar research has indicated that even attitude similarity doesn't matter in the context of a brief dating relationship (Curran, 1973; Kleck & Rubenstein, 1975). Though as it happens, there is also evidence that people are likely to assume that physically attractive other people are more similar to them in attitudes and personality than are physically less attractive people (Mashman, 1978; Marks, Miller, & Maruyama, 1981; Marks & Miller, 1982).

The finding that the physical attractiveness of a romantic partner matters more to men than it does to women has been repeated using a variety of different procedures. The result has emerged in studies in which people are directly asked what is important to them. It has emerged from studies in which the personal ads found in newspapers are coded for what people are seeking. It has also shown up in studies that correlate how many dates people say they have had over a fixed period of time with judgments of how attractive they are, and so on (Feingold, 1990). It is a very robust finding.

The results supporting the imperiousness of physical attractiveness should be interpreted with caution, however. For one thing, we can't be sure that other variables are not affecting our perception of who is physically attractive. Suppose attractive people happen to have some other desirable quality unattractive people don't. Then part of the correlation between attractiveness and liking could be due to that associated quality. As we shall see, this is a real problem in assessing the impact of physical attractiveness per se. But the results raise another question: How does physical attractiveness matter in longer-term relationships?

The Matching Hypothesis

If we imagine, plausibly enough, that people want to date, and for that matter marry, the most attractive person they can find, then we should expect that couples will be roughly matched on physical attractiveness. This is a simple consequence of market forces. If Tom is moderately attractive and he tries to date Maria, who is stunning, then she is likely to turn him down, and he is likely to continue to be turned down until he finds someone about as attractive as he is. And similarly for Maria. Matching for attractiveness may happen, as with Tom, either because people aim too high and are put in their place,

Romantically involved couples tend to be matched in physical attractiveness.

or because they have a conception of how high they dare aim and hence find their place with fewer hard knocks. In any event, we should expect a rough matching in physical attractiveness between established couples. And this is just what has been found (Murstein, 1972; Feingold, 1988). (See Aron, 1988; Kalick & Hamilton, 1986, 1988, for some interesting computer modeling of matching; and Folkes, 1982, for some insight about how it happens in a dating service.)

Does physical attractiveness continue to matter once married? Are people married to attractive people happier? One investigation found that husbands' reported satisfaction with their marriage was reliably, though modestly, related to their perception of their wives' attractiveness and to their perception of how attractive *their wives found them.* But wives' satisfaction was unrelated to their perception of their husbands' attractiveness or their perception of how attractive their husbands found them (Murstein & Christy, 1976).

In light of the discussion in Chapter 12 about men and physical attractiveness, we shouldn't be surprised that men who perceive their wives as attractive are happier than those who don't. What is a bit surprising is the fact that women's satisfaction with their marriages is *unaffected* by whether they think their husbands find them attractive. Why this should be so is a question worth pursuing.

Attractiveness and Same-Gender Relationships

There is evidence that physical attractiveness affects same-gender relationships too. One study focused on one-gender dorms. The investigators rated high school yearbook photos of students, and related those judgments to the subjects' dating popularity and popularity with their dorm-mates. There *was* a relation between rated attractiveness and popularity with the other people in the dorm. But it showed that life isn't a bed of roses for attractive people either. In fact, the *most* attractive men and women were the most likely to be *rejected* by their dorm-mates. Slightly less attractive men and women were most likely to be accepted. The fate of the least attractive people was not rejection, but isolation. Their dorm-mates neither liked them nor disliked them. Attractive people are salient. Apparently the most attractive people create envy among their same-sex peers, while slightly less attractive people are more accepted (Krebs & Adinolfi, 1975).

Attractiveness and Task Evaluation

Several studies have shown that how attractive a person is can affect how highly that person's work is thought of. For example, in one study, male subjects were asked to evaluate an essay. Attached to the essay was a picture of either an attractive or unattractive female, supposedly the author. Half of the subjects received a very good essay, and half a poor one. The subjects' judgments of the essay were, to be sure, affected by its quality, but they were also affected by how attractive they thought the author was (Landy & Sigall, 1974). Using a similar method, investigators have shown that the evaluation of an employment applicant and the evaluation of a child's transgression can be affected by physical attractiveness (Dion, 1972; Dipboye, Fromkin, & Wiback, 1975). In general, attractive people are evaluated more positively. So physical attractiveness can have effects on how a person is treated that range beyond the dating situation. Why?

AN ATTRACTIVENESS STEREOTYPE?

Several investigators have found that people attribute more positive qualities to attractive people than to unattractive people. For example, Karen Dion, Ellen Berscheid, and Elaine (Hatfield) Walster (1972) asked subjects to rate people on sets of personality traits—based on their pictures alone. They found generally more favorable ratings of the attractive people of both genders. Results of this sort suggest that some part of the preferential treatment that attractive people receive is a result of other people's beliefs about them. They suggest that there is an "attractiveness stereotype" that might in part explain why attractive people are treated better than unattractive people. Evidence that people ascribe desirable traits to attractive people leads us to ask: Are they right? Are attractive people nicer than unattractive people?

ATTRACTIVENESS AND SOCIAL SKILLS

There is some evidence that attractive people *are* different in one way from unattractive people—they are more socially skilled. In one study, subjects talked to each other over the phone and then rated the social skills of their unseen partner. These ratings were correlated with the *experimenters'* ratings of the partners' physical attractiveness. The correlations were modest but reliable, suggesting that to some degree, attractive men and women *are* more socially skilled (Goldman & Lewis, 1977). It is not hard to see why. Physically attractive people have more practice exercising their social skills, especially with members of the opposite sex, and seem to be rewarded for their exercise with more rewarding interactions, both with members of their own sex and with members of the opposite sex (Reis, Nezlek, & Wheeler, 1980; Reis, Wheeler, Spiegel, Kernis, Nezlek, & Perri, 1982; Feingold, 1992).

These results are one reason we shouldn't leap to the conclusion that the subjects in the computer dating study mentioned above were only concerned with physical attractiveness. As Marc Cook (1981) and Rom Harré (1981) have pointed out, attracting a member of the opposite sex is a skilled performance; indeed some have suggested that flirtation is a bit of an art (Sabini & Silver, 1982). And if the skills needed for these performances are correlated with physical attractiveness, then there are two different reasons why physically attractive people are liked by their partners.

A lifetime of being thought attractive may well lead to the development of an attractive personality, but there is evidence that if the person you are interacting with here and now thinks you are attractive, that too can bring out a more attractive personality. In one study, male subjects were randomly paired with female subjects for a ten-minute phone call. The males were given a picture that they were told was of their phone partner. In fact, it wasn't. Half of the subjects received a picture of an attractive woman, and the others were given a picture of an unattractive woman, independent of the real attractiveness of their partner. The phone calls were recorded, and judges rated the *women's* behavior in terms of self-confidence, warmth, and outgoingness—without seeing them, or the pictures that were supposedly of them.

There were substantial differences favoring the women the men *thought* were attractive (Snyder, Tanke, & Berscheid, 1977). The women who were interacting with men who thought they were physically attractive were more outgoing, self-confident, and so on. Subsequent research has shown that men too respond with a more desirable personalty to being treated like an attractive person (Andersen & Bem, 1981). Being treated as attractive by someone brings out the most sociable in us; being perceived as physically attractive can have effects in even a ten-minute interaction.

Again, we shouldn't, however, overstate the importance of physical attractiveness on our perception of others. One study, for example, looked at the relationship between the physical attractiveness of people arrested for various crimes and the fines and bail amounts they were assigned by a judge. Physical attractiveness mattered, but only for defendants accused of misdemeanors—minor offenses. Attractiveness did not matter for those accused of felonies—serious crimes (Downs & Lyons, 1991). The more general finding seems to be that physical attractiveness does have a substantial impact on perceptions of social competence, a bit of an effect on perceptions of intellectual competence, but no effect on judgments of integrity (Eagly, Ashmore, Makhijani, & Longo, 1991). Since there are relations between physical attractiveness and social skills, the stereotype that surrounds attractiveness seems to have more than a small grain of truth; if anything, it is an exaggeration of what is true rather than an illusion.

CLASSIC FINDINGS IN SOCIAL PSYCHOLOGY: ANXIETY AND AFFILIATION

Thus far, we have treated attractiveness, the degree to which people want to interact with someone, as if it were a characteristic of a person, a characteristic that depends on other aspects—what the person looks like, for example. But sometimes being an attractive interaction partner is a matter of being in the right place at the right time with the right partner.

Stanley Schachter investigated one situational determinant of the desire to interact with others. When female undergraduates he had recruited arrived at the appointed laboratory, they were greeted by a serious-looking gentleman wearing, among other things, horn-rimmed glasses and a white lab coat with a stethoscope dangling from its pocket. He introduced himself as Dr. Gregor

Zilstein of the Medical School's Departments of Neurology and Psychiatry. He told them that they were there to take part in an experiment on the physiological effects of electric shock. He went on to explain that for such research to be of importance to humanity, the shocks would have to be, and here he was quite candid, intense. He explained that they would be hooked up to a shock generator—an impressive device placed just behind him. The special equipment would record their blood pressure, pulse, and so on as it delivered the shocks. He did, however, assure them that though the shocks would be quite painful, they would cause no permanent damage.

He next told them there would be a ten-minute delay while the equipment was prepared. They were free to spend the ten minutes in some comfortable rooms with easy chairs, books, and magazines. But perhaps some of them might wish to wait along with other subjects rather than alone. So he asked them to indicate which they preferred—to wait alone or with other subjects also waiting to be shocked. Then he said that it had occurred to him that they might wish not to participate in the experiment after all (though then they would receive no extra credit toward their course grade); so he asked them to indicate whether they would like to withdraw from the experiment. About 20 percent of the subjects took him up on this offer.

The experimental drama was designed to produce anxiety, to which, I am sure you will agree, it was admirably suited. The point was to determine whether anxiety affects whether people prefer to be alone or with others. To test this, a control group that was *not* anxious (or at least less anxious) was needed. ''Dr. Zilstein'' told these other subjects just what he told the anxious group, except that he said the shock would not be painful. It would be more like a tickle or tingle than anything one would call pain. These subjects were, as one might imagine, less anxious about the experiment, and none asked to leave.*

The question was whether being anxious affected whether subjects preferred to wait alone or with others. It did (see Figure 14.13). Twenty out of thirty-two subjects in the high-anxiety condition preferred to wait with others, while only ten of thirty subjects in the low-anxiety condition did so (Schachter, 1959). *Why* did the anxious subjects want to wait with other subjects?

Perhaps they just wanted to be distracted by having someone to talk to, or perhaps they thought that just being with another person would calm them down. To see if this was so, Schachter performed a variation on his experiment. The good doctor again told some subjects they could wait either alone or with other people in the experiment. But he gave other subjects a different choice. They could wait either alone or with other students who weren't in the experiment but were in the building waiting to see their advisers. The anxious subjects, as it happened, were *not* interested in waiting with these other students who were not in the experiment. As Schachter put it, misery loves company, but only miserable company. It seems that just having another person there wasn't what the subjects wanted—the nonanxious students waiting for their advisers could have provided those benefits.

*No subjects were in fact given any shocks—mild or severe.

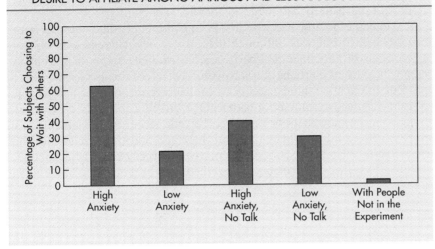

FIGURE 14.13

DESIRE TO AFFILIATE AMONG ANXIOUS AND LESS ANXIOUS SUBJECTS

◀ *The desire to be with other people depends on how anxious one is and who those other people are. (Data from Schachter, 1959)*

The anxious subjects must have wanted something that only other subjects in the same state they were in could give them. What?

Perhaps they wanted to compare notes about the shock they were facing. To test this hypothesis, Dr. Zilstein told a new batch of subjects that if they chose to wait with other subjects, they would not be allowed to discuss the experiment, shock, or anything like that. If the anxious subjects wanted to have company in order to compare notes, then they shouldn't have been interested in this company any more than they would be interested in the nonsubject students. But they were; the anxious subjects preferred to have fellow subjects as company even under these strictures, rather than be alone.

So it seems that it wasn't a specific desire to discuss the experiment that motivated them. Indeed, the anxious subjects were more eager to wait with others even in a further condition in which they were told they wouldn't be allowed to talk at all. This is really quite mysterious. The anxious subjects wanted to be with other people, but only other people facing the same stress, and they wanted to be with *those* people even if they weren't allowed to talk to them. What could they have hoped to get out of being with others without talking to them?

Schachter proposed that the subjects wanted to wait with others so long as they could do one thing: compare their *reactions* to the shock with the other subjects' reactions. This, he suggested, they could do even if they couldn't talk to one another; they could at least *see* each other's nonverbal expressions. Schachter argued that his pattern of results was consistent with the idea that people have a need to compare themselves with other people to determine whether their reactions are aberrant or normal, and that this desire for social comparison is a sufficient condition for wanting to affiliate while anxious (Schachter, 1959).

Further analysis of the data revealed an interesting pattern. First-born children (including only children) behaved differently from later-born children: (1) the first-borns and onlies were made more anxious by Dr. Zilstein than were the later-borns, and (2) holding anxiety constant, it was *only* the first-borns and onlies who wanted to affiliate while anxious. Later-born children didn't particularly care whether they had company or not.

It is difficult to know just why first-born children are different from later-born children in this way, although there are surely differences in the way they are raised. Parents of first-borns are, for example, more anxious about being good parents; perhaps this is why first-borns are themselves more anxious. But on the other hand, parents are probably more attentive to their first-born child, and they may do a better job of calming the child down while anxious. So perhaps first-born children become more used to having their anxiety reduced through affiliation. But there are many other differences between first-born and later-born children; we don't really know which of them is crucial in terms of producing these differences in desire to affiliate while anxious.

Follow-up Research

Subsequent research following up on Schachter's has by and large supported the view that subjects who are made fearful of an impending event want company (Gerard & Rabbie, 1961; Sarnoff & Zimbardo, 1961; Gerard, 1963; Zimbardo & Formica, 1963). And this seems especially true when subjects are uncertain about the nature of their own reaction. In one experiment, for example, subjects were given caffeine (a stimulant) but were told that it was a painkiller; others were given either a placebo, which they were told was a painkiller, or caffeine and told it was a stimulant. They were then allowed to be either in an experiment alone or with others. The subjects given the caffeine but told it was an analgesic were especially likely to want to be with others, presumably because they were confused about why they were now feeling aroused and wanted to compare their reactions with other subjects' reactions (Mills & Mintz, 1972).

There are also limits to the Schachter effect. One has to do with embarrassment. Although subjects facing pain prefer to wait with others, those facing embarrassment don't. Subjects expecting to have to suck on babies' pacifiers, bottles, and breast shields in front of the experimenter, for example, prefer to wait alone (Sarnoff & Zimbardo, 1961; Buck & Parke, 1972). And if they are going to affiliate, they prefer to do it with people who are *not* in the same embarrassed state (Firestone, Kaplan, & Russell, 1973). Nonetheless, at least in laboratory studies, the Schachter results have generally been replicated. Matters are different outside the laboratory.

Affiliation in Real-Life Anxiety-Producing Situations

Laboratory experiments, for obvious ethical reasons, have two limitations: (1) the level of anxiety that can be induced is modest, and (2) the subjects must know they can escape if they choose. But there are circumstances in life where neither is true. Do people facing greater stressors they cannot escape prefer to be with other people who face the same stress so they can compare reactions?

In one study, three hundred women who came to a hospital in Tel Aviv

TABLE 14.1

PREOPERATIVE ROOMMATE PREFERENCES AMONG CORONARY-ARTERY
BYPASS GRAFT PATIENTS AS A FUNCTION OF ANXIETY LEVEL

| | | Preoperative Roommate Preference | | |
		Preoperative Heart	Postoperative Heart	Total
Preoperative	Low	5	22	27
Anxiety	High	7	20	27
	Total	12	42	

Note: Cell entries represent number of patients. Both high- and low-anxiety patients preferred to have as a roommate a patient who survived the surgery rather than someone like themselves waiting for surgery. Reassurance seemed to matter more to them than social comparison.
SOURCE: Kulik & Mahler, 1989.

to give birth were asked whether they would prefer to be with other women also about to deliver, or alone. And they were asked what they would want to talk about if they were with other women. Most of the mothers-to-be wanted to be alone. And if they were to be with someone, they wanted to talk about anything but giving birth, anything that would distract them. They seemed quite uninterested in comparing their emotional states with other women in the same situation (Rofé & Lewin, 1986).

In a further study, seventy men who were about to undergo major, life-threatening surgery (coronary artery bypass graft—CABG) were asked whether they would like to room with someone in the same state they were—about to undergo CABG surgery—or someone who had already had the surgery and was in a very different emotional state. The majority of the patients preferred to be with someone who had already gone through the surgery and was now recuperating (see Table 14.1; Kulik & Mahler, 1989). These patients too were not very interested in comparing their current emotional state with that of other poeple facing the same situation. Rather, they seemed attracted to the reassurance and perhaps practical advice that someone who had *survived* what they were facing could give them. Apparently, then, though comparing one's emotional state with others is one reason we may affiliate when anxious, it isn't the only reason. When anxiety is severe and the situation is unavoidable, other motives dominate.

> Anxiety can lead to the desire to affiliate in order to compare emotional reactions, but when the anxiety is severe, people may prefer reassurance to the opportunity to compare emotional reactions with others in the same boat.

Being with Others and Anxiety

One further issue dangles from the Schachter experiment. The line of work we have reviewed so far asks whether and why anxious subjects want to affiliate or be alone. But it tells us nothing about what happens to people who *do* affiliate or wait alone while anxious. Lawrence Wrightsman pursued this issue in an experiment in which he threatened subjects not with shock, but

FIGURE 14.14

CHANGES IN ANXIETY
LEVEL WITH CONTACT

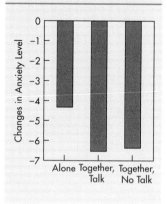

▲ *Changes in anxiety level depended on how subjects waited for the second part of the experiment. Anxiety levels dropped with the passage of time whether people waited alone or with others. (It dropped more for those waiting with others only among first-borns.) (Data from Wrightsman, 1960)*

with a series of injections of glucose (or insulin) to change their blood sugar levels dramatically (supposedly to study the cognitive consequences of such gyrations). The subjects (both males and females) were randomly assigned to wait alone for the injections, to wait with four other subjects but without talking to them, or to wait with four others while being allowed to talk. The question here was: What effect would these manipulations have on the subjects' anxiety?

First, all subjects' anxiety levels dropped as they waited, whether they waited alone or with others (see Figure 14.14). And for the average subject, the degree to which anxiety dropped was *not* related to whether they waited with others or alone. But waiting with others *did* produce a greater drop in anxiety for *first-born and only children*. This result dovetails nicely with Schachter's. First-born and only children want to affiliate while anxious, and well they should, because for them and only for them, affiliating reduces anxiety.

A second result also dovetails nicely with Schachter's. For all subjects, regardless of birth order, waiting with other subjects produced a "homogenization" of anxiety. That is, the four-person groups who waited together were closer together in their levels of anxiety *after they waited* than they had been *before* they waited. Schachter proposed that people wanted to wait with others to compare their emotional states. This result suggests that they *did* compare their emotional states, and as a consequence, their levels of anxiety converged (Wrightsman, 1960).

Anxiety, then, leads at least first-born and only children to want to be with others. And at least part of the reason for this is a desire to compare their emotional states with other people's. For first-borns and onlies, waiting with others tends to reduce anxiety. For people in general, regardless of birth order, being with others tends to bring people's level of anxiety closer together.

WRAP-UP

Why are people attracted to each other? The natural inclination is to imagine that we are attracted to (or repulsed by) people because of their personalities. And this is certainly true. But it leaves out the important role chance plays: we can only be attracted toward people we interact with, and to some degree, whom we interact with is a matter of chance. As the Westgate study showed, we rarely pick our neighbors, but once someone has become a neighbor, it is likely we will develop either an attraction for him or a repulsion.

A substantial body of research shows that—within limits—merely being exposed to something again and again tends to produce attraction to it. And this may be one reason that we come to like our neighbors. Of course, being exposed to someone again and again also allows us to get to know that person, so it may not be exposure per se that matters, it may just be that exposure allows for knowledge to develop.

What can we find out about someone that leads us to like her? One thing is that she is similar to us. Similarity—on almost any dimension—leads to liking, probably for a variety of reasons. For one thing, we like having our attitudes and opinions confirmed by others; for another, it is easier to interact with people who are like us than with people who are different from us.

We also like people who think a lot of us, especially people who once didn't but now do. So agreeing with people is one way to get them to like us. But some care must be exercised in using this strategy, for if we are caught using it, we will be seen as ingratiators and the strategy will backfire—cause us to be disliked.

Competence is also attractive. Competent people are liked better than incompetent people, especially if the competent people have foibles—little flaws that endear them to us. To be well liked, reveal your strengths, but don't hide innocent failings.

Being physically attractive leads to liking too, and not just by people of the opposite gender. Physically attractive people are seen as having a large variety of attractive traits, and there is some reason to believe they may in fact be more socially skilled than less attractive people.

Finally, anxious people (or at least anxious first-born and only children) find other people who are anxious about the same thing attractive—at least in the sense of being desirable people to interact with. First-born and only children like to compare their emotional states with other people's, and they also tend to be made less anxious by being in the presence of other people in a similar state. But, the evidence suggests, really anxious people, such as people facing life-threatening surgery, prefer to be with others who can reassure them that all will be well rather than with people who are also anxious.

Attraction sometimes, at least, is the first step in the development of enduring relationshps. So thinking about attraction and its sources leads us to wonder about the social psychology of relationships. That topic is saved for the next chapter.

SUMMARY

1. People are more likely to like people they live close to than people they live farther from. And this is true even over very short distances. Living close to someone also increases the likelihood that you will come to dislike her intensely.

2. People seem to like anything they are exposed to over and over better and better—the *mere exposure* effect.

3. People tend to like people who are similar to them (and to think that people they like are similar to them). Several accounts of why this is true have been proposed. (1) People like to have their opinions and attitudes agreed with. (2) People assume that others who are similar to them will like them, and we like people who like us. (3) It is easier to interact with people who agree with us.

4. We like people who think well of us, especially people who once thought little of us but now think highly of us. But we don't like people who we think are agreeing with us just to get us to like them.

5. Competent people are liked better than incompetent people. Competent people with foibles are liked better than competent people without foibles, but incompetent people with foibles are liked even less than incompetent people without foibles.

6. Cultures vary quite a bit in their standards of physical attractiveness; they vary both from culture to culture and from time to time within a single culture. Still, there may be some universals. There is some reason to believe, for example, that a youthful appearance of a woman is everywhere attractive to men.

7. Physical attractiveness affects how we are seen by others above and beyond its effect on dating desirability. Physically attractive people are seen as having more desirable social traits than unattractive people, and there may be a grain of truth in this.

8. Anxious first-born and only children seem to want to be with other people who are anxious about the same threat. The reason seems to be a need to compare their emotional states with others'. But really anxious people seem to prefer to be with people who can reassure them that they will be all right rather than with people with whom they can compare their emotional states. Finally, being with other anxious people seems to calm anxious first-borns and onlies.

CHAPTER 15

Relationships

It need hardly be said that friendship and love are of immense importance to a happy life. Indeed, it would be hard to overestimate their importance. So it isn't surprising that social psychologists have devoted considerable attention to the phenomena of relationship development, maintenance, and dissolution. We begin our discussion of relationships by considering friendship.

What do we know about friendship? What is a friend? In Western culture, we don't have a ceremony to create a friend—though Freud used to give out special rings to those ever so temporarily in his good graces. As a consequence, we don't have very clear demarcations between acquaintances, associates, colleagues, and, as we say, true friends. But even though "friend" isn't a concept with clear boundaries, it would be foolish to deny that some people are our friends and others aren't. But, then, by what criterion (or criteria) do we decide someone is a friend?

What Is a Friend?

Paul Wright suggests that the degree to which two acquaintances make their plans, decisions, and activities dependent upon one another is the degree to which they are friends. And surely this is part of the story, though it can't be the whole story, since con men make their plans dependent on the activity of their "pigeons," and they aren't friends. So another piece of friendship has

477

▶ *Charlie and Bill, who have been friends for over sixty years, enjoy a joke together.*

to do with caring about another's welfare; part of what it is to be a friend is to take another's interests as your interests.

Wright has also specified some of the virtues that friendship offers. Friends, he suggests, provide at least three sorts of things to each other: (1) stimulation, (2) various material benefits, as well as useful information, and (3) ego support (Wright, 1969). And this certainly seems like a reasonable, tentative list.

Recently, psychologists have studied friendship because of accumulating evidence that "social support" (which includes relationships with one's friends, spouse, and relatives) is associated with better physical and psychological well-being. This evidence suggests that social support has this beneficial effect for two different reasons: (1) as Emile Durkheim was the first to note, being integrated into a social network is a good thing, quite independent of how hard one's life is in other ways (Durkheim, 1897/1951), and (2) friendship "buffers" one against a wide variety of stressors that intrude on one's life (Cohen & Wills, 1985).

Just how social support is related to the reduction of the impact of stressors is currently under dispute—and, more important, under investigation (see, for example, Quittner, Glueckauf, & Jackson, 1990, and Kessler, Kendler, Heath, Neale, & Eaves, 1992). The evidence shows that having a rich network of social support leads to lessened psychological and physiological reactions to stress (Uchino, Kiecolt-Glaser, & Cacioppo, 1992). But, and this is a rather large but, there is also evidence that some stressors (chronic household crowding, floods) can erode the very social support that reduced the stress (Lepore, Evans, & Schneider, 1991; Kaniasty & Norris, 1993).

It is desirable to have friends. But how do friendships develop? What is the process of developing a friendship? We certainly don't know all of the answers to these questions, but part of the answer is surely that friendships develop as people reveal themselves to one another. How, why, and when people reveal themselves is treated by social psychologists under the term "self-disclosure." Let us see what we know about how people disclose themselves to one another.

Self-Disclosure

Self-disclosure is the revealing of private aspects of the self, including experiences, desires, fears, fantasies, and so on, to other people. A substantial body of research indicates that lonely people are also people who fail to disclose themselves to other people (Chelune, Sultan, & Williams, 1980; Berg & Peplau, 1982; Fanzoi & Davis, 1985; Davis & Fanzoi, 1986). Indeed, Sydney Jourard, who introduced the study of self-disclosure, saw the absence of self-disclosure (or an excess of self-disclosure) as implicated in a wide variety of mental ills (Jourard, 1971). The management of self-disclosure and intimacy is a topic well worth a closer look.

SELF-DISCLOSURE AND RECIPROCITY

In one of the earliest studies of self-disclosure, Jourard asked the eight faculty members of a newly formed School of Nursing to indicate how much each person had disclosed to each other member, and how much she had been disclosed to by each other member. He found that two measures of self-disclosure were correlated. The more intimate information someone had disclosed *to* someone else, the more that person had disclosed back (Jourard, 1959). Jourard also found, not surprisingly, that the greater the degree of self-disclosure between pairs of faculty members, the more they liked one another. Research on self-disclosure has focused, in the main, on these two aspects: reciprocity and liking for the discloser. These results lead us to ask: What accounts for this pattern of self-disclosure and liking? To develop an answer, many investigators moved the study of self-disclosure into the laboratory.

In one experiment, groups of four undergraduate women were brought together. After ten minutes of "get acquainted" conversation, each subject indicated how much she liked each other subject. Then the subjects were told that they would continue to interact by exchanging notes. To do this, they were each given a list of seven questions about themselves; the questions ranged from the superficial to the quite intimate. On each of ten trials, every subject sent a note to every other subject answering one of the seven questions. Finally, after the ten trials, the subjects again indicated how much they liked one another.

The intimacy of the question the subjects answered on the first trial was positively related to how much the subjects liked each other at the end of the ten-minute session; thus, initial disclosures to one another were related to initial liking of one another. The investigators also examined how liking grew during the interaction; the results showed that the more a subject had been *disclosed to* by another subject, the more she liked that other subject (see Figure 15.1 on page 480). Finally, the data showed that the more a subject was disclosed to by another subject, the more she disclosed back to that subject (Worthy, Gary, & Kahn, 1969). The experiment, then, in a laboratory session beginning with strangers, and again using female subjects, found essentially the same pattern of results Jourard had found in his field study.

The investigators interpreted the results in terms of the notion of reci-

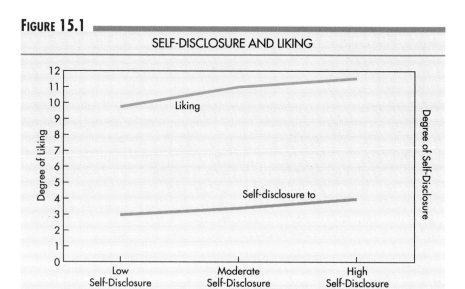

FIGURE 15.1

SELF-DISCLOSURE AND LIKING

▶ *Liking of and disclosure to a low, moderate, and high self-disclosing other person. (Data from Worthy, Gary, & Kahn, 1969)*

procity. As they saw it, disclosing oneself to another is a way of giving that other person something valuable—a reward. Being rewarded by someone makes you like her, so being disclosed to produces liking. Last, they suggested that subjects also follow a "norm of reciprocity." Alvin Gouldner has proposed that the most basic social norm in our culture is to return to someone as he has given to us (Gouldner, 1960). The norm of reciprocity accounts for why the self-disclosures from one subject to another are in balance with the disclosures back.

GENDER DIFFERENCES IN SELF-DISCLOSURE

The discussion of self-disclosure so far, you may have noticed, has been about women. Are the dynamics of self-disclosure different for men? In one study, male subjects were asked to interact with someone they thought was another subject but who was actually a confederate. The subjects were told—correctly, as it happens—that the study was about the organization of interaction. They were to take turns speaking; it was arranged that the confederate spoke first in all cases. For half the subjects, the confederate spoke about a superficial topic; for the other half, he spoke about a more intimate topic. The results of interest had to do with whether the subjects would reciprocate intimacy, and whether they would like the more intimate confederate more. The answer to the first question was yes, but to the second, no (Ehrlich & Graeven, 1971). These results suggest that men too understand that reciprocity applies to exchanges of personal information. But the results also suggest that being disclosed to is not as rewarding to men as it is to women, or perhaps that self-disclosures from men aren't as rewarding as those from women.

This difference between men and women in patterns of self-disclosure is consistent with several other findings about men. Several studies have asked men and women to report on the number and kinds of friendships they have with other men or other women. The consistent finding is that men typically

■■■■■■■■■■■■
Self-disclosures tend to be reciprocated at least in part because people understand that they *should* reciprocate.
■■■■■■■■■■■■

report having as many friends or even more friends than women do, but the quality of those relationships is different. To oversimplify dramatically, for men, friendship is a matter of *doing things together;* for women, friendship is a matter of *talking to one another about intimate matters* (Caldwell & Peplau, 1982; Reis, Senchak, & Solomon, 1985). For men, a round of golf with a buddy in which nothing more intimate than what club is best to use for this shot seems to be a satisfying bit of their friendship; for women, spending hours with a friend without exchanging anything more intimate than that doesn't seem like something one does with a friend—or worse, seems like something one would only do if one were terribly angry with a friend (Helgeson, Shaver, & Dyer, 1987).

Each gender finds the other's friendships somewhat enigmatic. Presumably these differences have their roots in socialization. Men are brought up to conceal intimate facts about themselves—at least from other men; women are brought up to reveal themselves. Exactly how this works is unclear. Perhaps men's reluctance to reveal weaknesses to other men has to do with their being trained to compete with one another (revealing weaknesses gives away strategic advantages), or perhaps women are just better listeners; indeed, men disclose more to women than they do to other men (Komarovsky, 1974). There is also reason to believe that self-disclosing men are seen as maladjusted, whereas women who engage in the same disclosure are not (Derlega & Chaiken, 1976).

It is important to note, though, that we are speaking here of matters of degree, not kind. There is more overlap than difference in men's and women's conceptions of intimacy (Helgeson, Shaver, & Dyer, 1987). And though the finding that women disclose more than men is reliable, the magnitude of the effect is fairly small (Dindia & Allen, 1992). Men *do,* for example, know more

◀ *John Sloan's* Sunday, Women Drying Their Hair.

Self-disclosure is *not* the only way to reciprocate self-disclosures. Other displays of intimacy may also serve to honor the norm of reciprocity.

about their friends' thoughts and feelings than they do about strangers' (Stinson & Ickes, 1992). And there are women who behave in the way typical for men, and vice versa.

For women too, there can be too much self-disclosure. In one study, undergraduate women were asked to rate how much they would like someone who engaged in low, moderate, or high self-disclosure. The high self-disclosing person was described as someone who would tell a stranger about her greatest romantic disappointments, her preferred method of birth control, and the greatest problem she had faced during the previous year. The subjects liked the moderate self-discloser more than the low self-discloser, but they liked the high self-discloser *less* than the moderate one. For women, there are limits as to how much one should disclose to another early in a relationship (Cozby, 1972). Those limits are probably different than they are for men, but there are still limits.

RECIPROCITY AND EXPRESSIONS OF CONCERN

I have stressed so far that the norm of reciprocity leads people—men and women—to return intimacy for intimacy out of respect for the norm of reciprocity, if for no other reason. In the research discussed so far, subjects have been required to return communications about themselves for communications directed to them from and about another person. So their problem is simply to select the appropriate level of intimacy to return. But in everyday life, there are many ways of responding to another's self-disclosure.

John Berg and Richard Archer have gathered evidence to suggest that one may meet the demands of reciprocity without returning any information about oneself, be it intimate or superficial. In one study, they gave subjects a description of an interaction between two women. Some subjects read of an interaction in which one of the women disclosed some intimate information; others read of a less intimate disclosure. They then read that in return, the other woman replied with an intimate disclosure, a less intimate disclosure, an expression of sympathy and concern and no disclosure, concern plus nonintimate disclosure, or concern with highly intimate disclosure. The subjects were asked to say how attracted they were to the person who made the response. The subjects were most attracted to the woman who replied simply with sympathy and concern (Berg & Archer, 1982).

So though the norm of reciprocity operates, what it seems to demand is that we return some expression of concern and regard for another's self-disclosure. A similarly intimate self-disclosure is one way to do that, but there are other, even more desirable ways. After all, there is nothing particularly attractive about an interaction in which you reveal some problem you are having only to have that met by a reply in which the other person reveals an even worse problem, as if he were trying to one-up you with problems!

Loneliness

Our discussion of friendship wouldn't be complete without a glance at loneliness. Loneliness is a significant problem with social relationships. Indeed, some investigators have suggested that as many as one-quarter of the population at any given moment feel intensely lonely (Russell, Peplau, & Cutrona, 1980).

▲ A cowboy and his dog.

TABLE 15.1

THE UCLA LONELINESS SCALE

Statement	Never	Rarely	Sometimes	Often
1. I feel in tune with the people around me.*	1	2	3	4
2. I lack companionship.	1	2	3	4
3. There is no one I can turn to.	1	2	3	4
4. I do not feel alone.*	1	2	3	4
5. I feel part of a group of friends.*	1	2	3	4
6. I have a lot in common with the people around me.*	1	2	3	4
7. I am no longer close to anyone.	1	2	3	4
8. My interests and ideas are not shared by those around me.	1	2	3	4
9. I am an outgoing person.*	1	2	3	4
10. There are people I feel close to.*	1	2	3	4
11. I feel left out.	1	2	3	4
12. My social relationships are superficial.	1	2	3	4
13. No one really knows me well.	1	2	3	4
14. I feel isolated from others.	1	2	3	4
15. I can find companionship when I want it.*	1	2	3	4
16. There are people who really understand me.*	1	2	3	4
17. I am unhappy being so withdrawn.	1	2	3	4
18. People are around me but not with me.	1	2	3	4
19. There are people I can talk to.*	1	2	3	4
20. There are people I can turn to.*	1	2	3	4

Note: The total score is the sum of all twenty items.
* Item should be reversed (i.e., 1 = 4, 2 = 3, 3 = 2, 4 = 1) before scoring.
SOURCE: Russell, Peplau, & Cutrona, 1980.

The UCLA Loneliness Scale has been designed to identify lonely people. The scale consists of twenty descriptions of experiences and asks people to indicate how often they have these feelings (see Table 15.1). Among these twenty items, there seem to be two fundamental aspects of loneliness: (1) lacking friends, referred to as **social loneliness,** and (2) having friends, but finding those friendships superficial, unsatisfying, referred to as **emotional loneliness** (Williams & Solano, 1983; Russell, Cutrona, Rose, & Yurko, 1984). Being lonely, then, is a matter either of having failed to develop friendships, or finding that the friendships one has developed are emotionally unsatisfying.

There is some evidence that there are gender differences in the relation of loneliness to self-disclosure. For men, loneliness seems to be associated with an absence of self-disclosure to women. But not disclosing themselves to other men seems not to be so important for men. Rather, having a dense network of friends seems important to men. For women, on the other hand, failing to disclose oneself to a man or to other women leads to loneliness, and the density of a friendship network seems less important (Solano, Batten, & Parish, 1982; Stokes & Levin, 1986).

Now that we know what loneliness is, we would like to know what causes it. The full answer to this question is not yet understood, but some partial

answers are known. One study examined male and female roommate pairs. Each subject filled out the UCLA Loneliness Scale, as well as a set of questionnaires that measure how skilled the roommates are in a variety of social situations. The subjects were also asked to evaluate their roommates on a variety of adjectives, and they were asked to indicate their evaluation of people in general. Last, they were given a questionnaire designed to tap the degree to which they had what are traditionally thought of as "masculine" and "feminine" traits (see Chapter 12 for a discussion of these traits).

The results indicated that the lonely subjects (compared with the not-lonely subjects) lacked social skills, had a jaundiced view of people in general—and their roommates in particular—and had fewer of the traits traditionally thought to be masculine and the traits traditionally thought to be feminine (Wittenberg & Reis, 1986). Whether negativity toward other people is a cause or effect of loneliness is unclear, but it is not surprising that it and a lack of social skills (or at least a lack of confidence in one's social skills) are associated with loneliness.

ROMANTIC LOVE

Some relationships, often beginning with friendship, reach, as we all know, the state of romantic love. It is with no small trepidation that a poor textbook writer ventures into this topic, the province of dramatists, poets, lyricists, screenplay writers, and so many adolescent fantasies. But no discussion of relationships, at least in Western culture, would be adequate without it. So we turn now to a consideration of what romantic love is in Western culture, and to the factors that foster and inhibit it.

What Is Romantic Love?

There seem to be some features of the experience of romantic love that are a necessary part of it, while there are others that often but need not always accompany it. One necessary feature is surely sexual attraction; it would be odd to report being romantically in love with someone without experiencing sexual excitement. Though such excitement waxes and wanes, still it must sometimes be present for us to identify our state as romantic love. But there is more to romantic love, of course, than sexual attraction.

FEATURES OF ROMANTIC LOVE

Zick Rubin (1970) attempted to find further features of romantic love, as distinct from mere liking, by constructing "loving scales," questionnaires about couples' feelings toward each other. Each person was to fill out the scales with regard to someone they were in love with and also with regard to an opposite-sex, "platonic" friend. Three features distinguished responses about romantic lovers from those about friends: there was more expression of affiliative and dependency needs toward romantic lovers, there was a greater predisposition to help romantic lovers, and there was greater absorption in and sense of exclusiveness with a romantic lover. As behavioral validation of these scales, Rubin observed the pairs in interaction with each other and recorded how much eye contact they made. The couples that declared themselves to be lovers spent longer looking into each other's eyes than did those who claimed to be just friends. While the finding that lovers look into each other's eyes is hardly surprising, it does lend validity to the scales.

Further, in one study, 231 dating college couples were followed for a period of two years. Of these, 103 couples broke up during the study, while the remainder either married or were still dating by the end of the study. A subject's score on the loving scale predicted, to some degree, whether he or she would still be in a relationship with the other person two years later. More specifically, it was the woman's loving for her partner, more than the man's loving for her, that predicted whether the couple would still be together (Hill, Rubin, & Peplau, 1976).

Perhaps inspired by Rubin's success in measuring romantic love, several other theorists have contributed their own conceptions of love. Each adds something to our picture of romance. Robert Sternberg, for example, places romantic love in the context of other kinds of love (Sternberg, 1986). He argues that all kinds of love can be thought of as being made up of three elements: passion, intimacy, and commitment. For Sternberg, in the troubadour tradition, **romantic love** consists of passion and intimacy but not commitment. (For Elaine Hatfield too, intimacy and passion are the cornerstones of romantic love; see Hatfield & Sprecher, 1986). **Companionate love,** on the other hand, has commitment and intimacy but no passion. What Sternberg calls **consummate love** includes all three. Other theorists have turned to our primate cousins for inspiration about the nature of human romantic attachment.

According to Rubin's loving scale, people who are in love

- express more dependency and affiliative needs toward their lover than toward a friend;

- are more likely to help a lover than a friend.

Romantic Love and Attachment

As noted by the British psychiatrist John Bowlby, the young of many species of primates (including humans) are born too unfinished to ensure their own survival very long without the caring attention of an adult. So natural selection has provided our young with mechanisms to help gain the attention and physical closeness of adults (Bowlby, 1973). Very young infants can, of course, do very little. But they can cry when distressed and gurgle, coo, nuzzle, and so on when happy. Their crying is very motivating to caregivers to approach the infant to do something to relieve the distress, and the cooing, gurgling, and nuzzling are powerfully reinforcing to keep adults doing whatever they are doing. Thus, even the youngest infants have *some* ability to affect how far adults wander from them.

Toddlers can do more to control their proximity to adults. They can toddle to or away from the relevant adult, more directly affecting proximity. According to attachment theorists, these attachment behaviors—cooing, crying, approaching, and avoiding—are one kind of manifestation of an innately given attachment system. But attachment also consists of emotional bonds that are formed between caregiver and child. These bonds are another, equally important aspect of attachment, and are made obvious in the sadness that the child feels when a caregiver leaves and his delight at the caregiver's return.

Attachment Styles in Children   Not all caregivers respond in the same way to infants, and how they respond affects the nature of the attachment that is formed. Specifically, Mary Ainsworth (and her co-workers) has observed that infants whose caregivers reliably respond to their distress cries tend to form **secure attachments.** Securely attached toddlers, she notes, use their caregivers as "home bases" for exploring the world. So a securely attached child in a novel environment but in the presence of someone she is attached to will explore that novel environment with occasional glances back toward Mom or Dad or whoever to be sure that all is well. The child is able to feel secure in her attachment to the caregiver even though they are not currently in contact. The security of the attachment liberates the child's curiosity.

But if the caregiver has a history of being inconsistent in response to the child, sometimes forcing affection on the child, sometimes rebuffing it, then the child will form an **anxious** or **ambivalent attachment** style rather than a secure one. In a novel situation, such children are anxious or angry; they explore the world less and cry more. Finally, a caregiver who is consistently rejecting will produce a child who has an **avoidant attachment** style. Such a child will actively avoid its caregiver in a strange situation and, in general, detach from the caregiver (Ainsworth et al., 1978).

Along with these emotional and behavioral consequences of how caregivers treat infants come cognitive consequences. Bowlby argued that the child develops out of these early social interactions what he called **working models.** That is, the child forms an idea (or schema) of (1) what caregivers are like and (2) what the self is like. The secure child comes to believe that the world of human attachments is a pretty good place, one in which other people can be counted on to, among other things, respond to distress with comfort. And such a child comes to see herself as a lovable person. The less securely attached child, on the other hand, comes to see the world as a harsher place and the self as a less desirable object of other people's regard (Bowlby, 1973).

Attachment Styles in Adults   Recently Cindy Hazan and Phillip Shaver have argued that the adult phenomenon of romantic love is deeply tied to these

Children and adult romantic partners express an attachment style. The three styles that have been discovered are

• secure attachment;

• anxious/ambivalent attachment;

• avoidant attachment.

attachment processes. They suggest that romantic love *is* an adult manifestation of the same emotional and behavioral mechanisms that are obvious in the toddler and that romantic love taps into the selfsame working models the adult formed long ago as a child (Hazen & Shaver, 1987).

As a first step in showing the continuity between adult romantic love and childhood attachment, Hazan and Shaver placed an ad in a local newspaper asking readers to answer a questionnaire about their adult romantic relationships and their childhood attachments to their parents. The investigators analyzed about six hundred responses from the newspaper readers—who were, apparently, quite eager to answer these questions. The subjects' romantic relationships were classified into secure, anxious, or avoidant, based on their answer to the question: Which of the following best describes your feelings? What followed was a description of three types of romantic relationships; each was an adult version of the childhood attachment styles uncovered by developmental researchers (see Table 15.2).

The results indicated that (1) the frequencies of adult romantic "styles" were similar to the frequencies of attachment styles found by infant researchers—as they should be if adult attachments are merely reinvocations of childhood ones, and (2) the subjects who reported having the most secure romantic attachments were also those who had had the kind of relationships with their parents likely to produce securely attached children; i.e., the relationships were affectionate, caring, and reliable (Hazan & Shaver, 1987). This study, then, provided some evidence that parent-child relationships can affect the quality of adult romantic relationships in a way that is consistent with the idea that the same attachment mechanisms, including cognitive models, that influence infant-caregiver relationships also influence relationships between romantic partners.

More recent research has in general been supportive both of the idea that there are different styles of romantic attachment that to some degree mirror those found between children and caregivers and the idea that early experi-

TABLE 15.2

ADULT ATTACHMENT TYPES

Question: Which of the following best describes your feelings?

Secure: I find it relatively easy to get close to others and am comfortable depending on them and having them depend on me. I don't often worry about being abandoned or about someone getting too close to me.

Avoidant: I am somewhat uncomfortable being close to others; I find it difficult to trust them completely, difficult to allow myself to depend on them. I am nervous when anyone gets too close, and often, love partners want me to be more intimate than I feel comfortable being.

Anxious/Ambivalent: I find that others are reluctant to get as close as I would like. I often worry that my partner doesn't really love me or won't want to stay with me. I want to merge completely with another person, and this desire sometimes scares people away.

ence plays an important role in shaping these adult experiences (Simpson, 1990; Feeney & Noller, 1991; Carnelley & Janoff-Bulman, 1992; Cohn et al., 1992). There is some (encouraging) evidence, though, that except for gross parental deprivation, adult experiences can compensate for unfortunate childhoods (Parker, Barrett, & Hickie, 1992). Apparently, working models can be revised.

ROMANTIC LOVE AS AN ADVENTURE

Georg Simmel (1911/1971) treated romantic love, the "affair," in his sensitive essay on the adventurer. And, indeed, that is the way romantic love entered Western culture, with the myth of the knight on the white horse slaying dragons to capture the heart, if not the hand, of his lady fair. As an adventure, romantic love is like climbing Mount Everest or running rapids. What elements does it share with these other adventures?

For one thing, it is cut off from everyday life—as Simmel puts it, from the continuity of one's life. True, romantic lovers often do things together that, unlike climbing Everest, are quite mundane. But they are done in a way that transforms and enchants them. Our routines are interrupted by the accompaniment of our lover, interrupted though not frustrated. We find our life taking new contours under her influence. The lover and the mountain climber both find themselves living for the moment; they find their attention drawn to the here and now. In our more sober moments, we are aware of how what we do now relates to our future.

Simmel points to another feature of the experience of romantic love: it has continuity, internal sense, its pieces fit together. In these ways, he likens love to a work of art, which is also a transformation of our usual experience, but

▶ *Sir Edward Burne-Jones's* The Baleful Head. *Romantic love as an adventure.*

◄ *Companionate love.*

also one with internal continuity. Lovers delight in finding the ways that their life together flows in a necessary way from their unique personalities and experiences.

Simmel points to one more aspect of romantic love. Love, like gambling, combines elements of chance and skill. One of the reasons we find the idea of assigned marriages so repulsive is because we think of marriage and love in terms of an epiphany, a discovery of something unexpected and delightful. But at the same time, there is a sense of accomplishment in love, perhaps of conquest. At least there is if the love is returned; unrequited love produces a different set of feelings for both the pursuer and the pursued (Baumeister, Wotman, & Stillwell, 1993).

But all of this must wane. Eventually the lives we construct with our newfound love become our everyday lives. Enduring relationships transform themselves into the frame of our lives, rather than an excursion from our lives. We can flee from our everyday lives to the special world in the arms of our lover only so long as our lover isn't part of our everyday lives. This is what the troubadours knew full well. It is one thing to slay an occasional dragon for one's lady fair; but even dragon slaying can become a job just like any other. The basic elements of romantic love—arousal, novelty, a focus on the moment, discovery—cannot be perpetually reexperienced, no more than one can perpetually rediscover the beauty of the New York skyline, at least if one lives there.

WHAT ENDURES OVER TIME?

Romantic love may well be ephemeral, and we may, in a literal sense, grow disenchanted with our lover, but none of this should suggest that enduring relationships between people are impossible. Long-standing relationships have their own virtues. For one thing, there is by definition a shared history, which provides a source of memories unique to the relationship. For another, the conversion of discovery and invention, characteristic of romantic love, into routines provides security and a background for the further elaboration of our lives. And if the overvaluation of the object must wane, a concern and caring about the real person behind the image grows. Loyalty replaces passion as the governing sentiment, perhaps, but our sense of loyalty to another and theirs to us is as compelling an experience in its way as passion is in another. Romantic love is, to be sure, a delicious experience, but by itself not one around which a life can be built. Still, it is such a delicious experience that it is worth asking just how it is created. What features foster the development of romantic love?

The Enhancement of Romantic Love

One factor, to be sure, is physical attractiveness. But what others are there? Ellen Berscheid and Elaine (Hatfield) Walster (1974) have proposed that romantic love will grow when people become aroused in each other's presence *and* interpret this arousal as being due to attraction to the other person. In claiming this, they are applying Schachter and Singer's (1962) general theory of emotion, discussed in detail in Chapter 7, to the specific emotion of romantic love.

CLASSIC FINDINGS IN SOCIAL PSYCHOLOGY: PHYSIOLOGICAL AROUSAL AND ROMANTIC LOVE

Donald Dutton and Arthur Aron (1974) carried out an intriguing experiment based on this proposition. There are two bridges over the Capilano River near Vancouver, British Columbia. One, the Capilano Canyon Suspension Bridge, is quite famous, and for good reason. It is a suspension bridge 5 feet wide and 450 feet long, spanning a 230-foot drop over white-water rapids. The bridge wobbles, sways, tilts, and gives every impression of pitching anyone on it into the rapids below. The other is much more substantial, provides little in the

▶ *The Capilano Suspension Bridge, a tourist stop near Vancouver, British Columbia.*

way of an amusement park ride, and spans a mere 10-foot drop into a small stream. So much for the setting.

Dutton and Aron had an attractive female research assistant stop men as they crossed each bridge and ask them to write some imaginative stories in response to some pictures. She also told them that they could get the results of her scoring of the stories, if they wanted, by calling her. When on the dangerous bridge, she identified herself as Gloria; when on the other, she called herself Donna.

The experimenters proposed that the men crossing the dangerous bridge would be quite aroused, and that on encountering the attractive assistant, they would not be able to tell how much of their arousal was caused by the bridge and how much by Gloria. To the degree that they thought it was Gloria making their hearts go pitter-patter, they should have become romantically, or at least sexually, attracted to her. The men crossing the other bridge, while they might have found Donna quite attractive, would have had no reason to become attached to her aside from her intrinsic charm.

Thus, the experimenters predicted two results: (1) that the men crossing the rickety bridge would include more sexual imagery in their stories than would men crossing the more secure bridge, and (2) that they would also be more likely to call for the results of the study, as a pretext, presumably, for making a date with Gloria. Both hypotheses were confirmed (see Figure 15.2).

Dutton and Aron interpret this result by claiming that the men aroused by their perilous crossing attributed their arousal, at least in part, to Gloria. But other interpretations are possible. Perhaps the danger itself made the men think about sex; perhaps there was no confusion about the source of arousal. To check this, the investigators had a male assistant ask for the stories on the two bridges. In this case, no differences were found. So attribution of the arousal to an accustomed target of sexual arousal is necessary for the expression of sexual imagery.

FIGURE 15.2

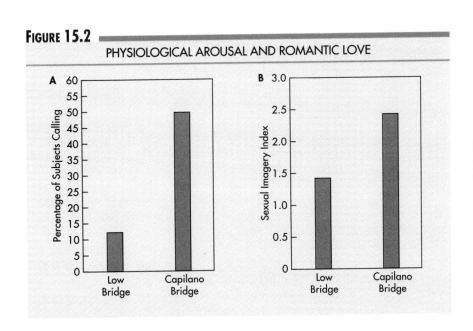

PHYSIOLOGICAL AROUSAL AND ROMANTIC LOVE

◀ (A) Percentage of male subjects calling the experimenter when they had met her on the low bridge or the Capilano Canyon Suspension Bridge.
(B) Amount of sexual imagery included in stories by male subjects who met the confederate on the low bridge or the suspension bridge. (Data from Dutton & Aron, 1974)

Another possible interpretation involves the fact that the suspension bridge is quite famous and attracts vacationers to the area specifically to experience crossing it. The other bridge is part of a park frequented by local families. Perhaps the men crossing the dangerous bridge were just generally more adventurous, and in particular sexually adventurous, and that is why they included more sexual imagery and made more calls to Gloria. To control for this possibility, the experimenters repeated the experiment, this time using only the dangerous bridge. Half of the men were asked for stories as they crossed, while the other half were solicited *after* they had crossed and calmed down. As the experimenters predicted, the sexual imagery and phone calls were stimulated only when Gloria asked for the stories *as* the men crossed.

Finally, Dutton and Aron conducted a laboratory experiment along the same lines. This time they threatened half the male subjects with strong electric shock, while half were to get "weak shock that some people describe as an enjoyable tingle." While they waited for their shock, the subjects met a female confederate posing as another subject. Subjects were asked how much they would like to date her and how much they would like to kiss her. As predicted, men expecting strong shock were more interested in her than those expecting weak shock.

These results and their interpretation are a bit controversial. First off, some investigators, though they have repeated the experiment in as detailed a way as they could, have failed to find the same result. They speculate that the reason was that in fear-producing circumstances, subjects were fully aware that it wasn't the presence of Gloria that was making their hearts go pitter-patter. If subjects don't misattribute their arousal, they shouldn't experience enhanced attraction (Kenrick, Cialdini, & Linder, 1979). But if the subjects didn't misattribute fear in the Dutton and Aron experiment, then why the enhanced attraction to Gloria?

Douglas Kenrick and Robert Cialdini have proposed that a different mechanism underlies the Dutton and Aron phenomenon. They point out that there is experimental evidence that in some circumstances, the presence of other people tends to calm anxious people. So, they suggest, the reason that the subjects may have liked Gloria so much is not that they mistakenly thought she stirred them up but that she in fact calmed them down. The subjects came to associate her with a reduction in anxiety and fear, and that is why they liked her (Kenrick & Cialdini, 1977). But there is yet more to the story.

In one experiment, male subjects' arousal was manipulated by having them run in place for either fifteen seconds or two minutes. As soon as the exercise was completed, the subjects looked at a videotape of a woman (supposedly to be used in another study). In one condition, the woman in the tape wore form-fitting attractive clothes, her face and hair were made up attractively, and she delivered her speech in an animated way. In the other condition, she was less attractive—her makeup was less well done, her head was covered with a scarf, her clothes were baggy, and as a final nice touch, she had the sniffles. Now the results.

When rating the attractive woman, the subjects who had just exercised rated her higher than those who had not. This fits the misattribution account if we believe the subjects weren't aware that their arousal was in part caused by the exercise. Of course, their physiological states were also returning to normal as they looked at her—just because they were no longer exercising—

▲ *Amusement parks are good places for dates because they produce arousal.*

FIGURE 15.3

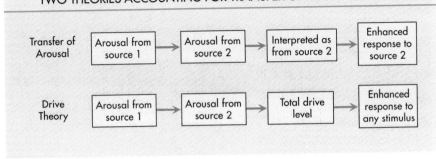

TWO THEORIES ACCOUNTING FOR TRANSFER OF AROUSAL EFFECTS

so perhaps they liked her not because of misattribution, but because she was associated with an increasingly normal and relaxed physiological state.

What about when the woman was made to look unattractive? Here the aroused subjects rated her as *less* attractive than the unaroused subjects did (White, Fishbein, & Rutstein, 1981). How can we interpret this result? If being associated with a physiological state that is returning to normal leads to enhanced attraction, then the stimulus should have been seen as *more*, not less, attractive by the subjects who had just exercised. So we seem to be thrown back on a misattribution account. But does that really work? It has always seemed to me that it made fair sense for subjects to say to themselves, "Well, I'm aroused; I guess it's because she's so attractive." But I have never found compelling, "Well, I'm aroused; I guess it's because she's so *unattrac-tive!*" The misattribution account doesn't seem to work so well either.

Douglas Kenrick has proposed another account and some data that bear on the misattribution of arousal directly (see Figure 15.3). Kenrick carried out two experiments; one involved the arousal of fear, the other exercise. They again involved the rating of a female confederate by male subjects. But in some conditions, the subjects' attention was either directed to the real source of their arousal before they rated the female confederate or it wasn't. Now according to the misattribution view, calling attention to the real source of arousal ought to destroy the enhanced attraction with arousal effect. But it didn't. So now how do we account for the enhanced attraction?

Kenrick believes that arousal simply directly facilitates any reaction the subject is having to the confederate (Allen, Kenrick, Linder, & McCall, 1989). A rather general finding within the psychology of animal learning is that increasing an organism's drive (or arousal) level will intensify its responses *regardless of what they are.* This effect has nothing whatsoever to do with what the animal thinks is causing the arousal; it is just a mechanical, blind effect of the arousal. Perhaps it is this that accounted for Gloria's enhanced attrac-tiveness.

The lesson to be learned is that taking your date to an exciting place is a bit risky. If she is likely to find you attractive in the first place, then such a strategy is likely to enhance your attractiveness in her eyes. But if she is likely to find you unattractive . . .

▶ Of course, sexual arousal plays a role in romantic love too—it isn't entirely a consequence of displaced arousal!

SEXUAL AROUSAL

One source of arousal likely to contribute to romantic love is, of course, sexual arousal. But the question remains: Is it sexual arousal satisifed or sexual arousal thwarted that contributes to romantic attachment? Is the person who plays hard to get more likely to inflame, or the one who gives in? Freud wrote, "Some obstacle is necessary to swell the tide of libido to its height, and at all periods of history whenever natural barriers in the way of satisfaction have not sufficed, mankind has erected conventional ones in order to enjoy love" (Freud, 1922/1976). Some investigators have found that men are more attracted, contrary to Freud's claim, to the person who gives in. They have argued that the optimal strategy to attract another is to appear to be hard to get for *other people*, but to succumb easily to the person you are trying to attract.

PREMARITAL ROMANTIC RELATIONSHIPS

Romantic attraction may be a fleeting thing, but sometimes it leads to more enduring relationships. We turn now to "significant relationships" between men and women. What makes them endure, and what makes them fall apart?

Time was when there was a substantial scholarly literature about dating. But of late, interest in this topic seems to have declined. One undergraduate informant has suggested to me that this is because people don't exactly date anymore. Rather, they "hang out" together, often as part of a larger group, until they find themselves in a "relationship" with someone in the group. There have been, however, a few studies of customers of dating services. One question these studies addressed is: Who gets asked out? One study looked at the characteristics of the most and least active daters in a service of 450 customers. As will probably come as no surprise, younger, more attractive women tended to be asked out more than older, less attractive women. Physical attractiveness also had an effect on whether men were asked out, but social status also played a role for men (though not for women) (Green, Buchanan, & Heuer, 1984). The bulk of research on paths to marriage focuses, however, on a later point in the process, once a relationship has formed, and asks about factors that determine its course.

Relationship Stability

Some evidence on the stability of premarital relationships comes from a study of college-age couples followed for two years. The degree to which the partners were similar in various ways was associated with whether the couples stayed together. The more similar the students were in age, physical attractiveness, College Board scores, and educational aspirations, the more likely they were to stay together for the two years of the study (Hill, Rubin, & Peplau, 1976).

The same study examined the couples' behavior and feelings about sex. One finding, consistent with what we learned about sexual behavior in Chapter 12, is that it was the women who by and large determined whether (and if so when) the couple began to have sex. The observed pattern fit the notion of the ardent male and the selective female. For example, the male's religious beliefs did *not* predict whether the couple were sexually intimate, but the female's beliefs did—Catholic women were less likely to be having sex than were other women. Finally, the study found that being sexually intimate neither contributed to nor detracted from the couples' overall satisfaction with their relationship or with the odds that they would still be together after two years (Peplau, Rubin, & Hill, 1977). More recent research has found, however, that whether a relationship was sexual predicted whether it would endure over three months (Simpson, 1987).

EXCHANGE AND EQUITY

Much of the more recent research on the stability of premarital relationships has taken advantage of a framework drawn from ***exchange theory.*** Exchange theory treats relationships as a matter of the exchange of "goods" and "costs." It proposes that people attempt to maximize the goods they receive and minimize the costs they pay in their relationships. These rewards and costs are seen as relative in two ways: (1) relative to what each partner has come to expect out of relationships in general and (2) relative to the rewards and costs they could find in some particular other relationship.

There are several natural reactions one might have to exchange theory. One reaction is to find it a bit repulsive. At least at first blush, exchange theory seems to reduce our closest friendships and romantic attachments to the same sort of arrangement we have with our grocer, dry cleaner, and used-car salesman. And, we want to say, *my* friendships aren't like this! An exchange theorist is wont to reply that of course our relationships with our family and friends are different from those with our butcher, baker, and candlestick maker. But the way they differ is in the *content* of what is exchanged. In a marriage, the argument goes, we exchange many things, but among them are surely affection, approval, and intimacies. None of these will set even the most meager steak loose from the butcher.

Exchange theory proposes that people attempt to maximize their rewards in relationships. But some researchers have suggested that instead, people attempt to achieve equity in relationships. Equity is achieved when each partner derives (roughly) the same degree of reward relative to cost (see Chapter 10 for more on equity theory). The notion here is that people who are involved

Exchange theory predicts that people are happiest when they are getting the most reinforcement out of a relationship.

Equity theory predicts that people are happiest when they are getting roughly the same reinforcement as their partner.

FIGURE 15.4

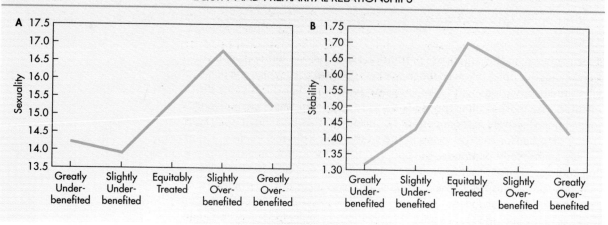

EQUITY AND PREMARITAL RELATIONSHIPS

▲ *(A) The sexuality of premarital relationships depended on how equitably the subjects believed they were treated. Relationships were likely to be sexual if subjects believed they were slightly overbenefited.*
(B) The stability of premarital relationships depended on how equitably subjects believed they were treated. The relationships perceived as equitable were the most stable. (Data from Walster, Walster, & Traupmann, 1978)

in equitable relationships will suffer unpleasant emotions that will get in the way of their satisfaction. People who gain *less* than their partners—underbenefited partners—will experience anger or resentment; people who gain *more* than their partners—overbenefited partners—will experience guilt (Walster, Walster, & Berscheid, 1978). Neither is much fun.

In one study investigating equity in relationships, students who were dating someone in particular were asked a variety of questions about their relationships. To assess equity, the investigators simply asked the subjects to indicate on an eight-point scale the following: how much they contributed to their relationship, how much their partner contributed, how much they got out of their relationship, and how much their partner got out of it. In addition, the subjects were asked about how sexual their relationship was, and how likely they thought their relationship was to endure. Three and one-half months later, the subjects were surveyed again to determine whether the relationship had endured.

One finding was that greatly underbenefited and overbenefited partners were likely to avoid sex in their relationships (see Figure 15.4A). And subjects in equitable relationships were more likely to expect their relationships to endure (see Figure 15.4B). They were right: the more equitable relationships were much more likely to endure for the three and one-half months of the study (Walster, Walster, & Traupmann, 1978). And there is evidence that equity matters to satisfaction for married couples too (Van Ypern & Buunk, 1990). Other research examining the equity theory idea has verified that the emotions people experience in relationships are related to equity and inequity (Sprecher, 1986).

Although there is evidence that people are happier in equitable versus inequitable relationships, the question remains as to *how much* equity per se matters. After all, a relationship may be equitable because neither partner has much committed to the relationship. Such a relationship is equitable, but not very rewarding. One can also imagine relationships in which people gain immense satisfactions (and considerable costs), but their partners gain even more. Such a relationship is inequitable, but does it really matter much if the satisfactions are so great?

Several recent studies followed relationships of undergraduates for various periods of time and asked them about the rewards and costs of their relationships. The general thrust of this research is that though equity per se matters in terms of stability, it matters only a bit in comparison with the absolute level of reward. By and large, relationships that provide substantial satisfactions are stable, even if somewhat inequitable, and relationships that don't provide much in the way of satisfaction, even if equitable, are not stable (Michaels, Edwards, & Acock, 1984; Cate, Lloyd, & Henton, 1985; Cate, Lloyd, & Long, 1988).

INVESTMENT IN A RELATIONSHIP

Caryl Rusbult has argued that rewards and costs contribute to the degree to which people are *satisfied* with relationships, but other factors in addition to satisfaction contribute to how *committed* to a relationship people are (Rusbult, 1983). One factor is the availability of alternatives; the better the deal a person can get elsewhere, Rusbult argues, the less committed that person will be to a particular relationship. But there is one more factor: how much a person has already invested in the relationship. Recently the exchange model has been altered to take into account this additional factor.

Investment in a relationship is a complex matter. In part, it is a matter of emotion invested, in part a matter of shared history, in part a matter of habits—well-practiced ways of getting along. All of these make it difficult to decide to leave a relationship. Rusbult argues that the degree to which one is invested in a relationship will determine how committed one is to that relationship, over and above how satisfied one is.

In one study, Rusbult followed thirty-four undergraduates and their relationships for the course of an academic year. She found, as she expected, that changes in satisfaction and commitment to their relationships were related to changes in rewards received. The more rewards increased, the more satisfaction and commitment increased. Changes in costs of the relationship, on the other hand, had little impact on changes in satisfaction and commitment. If the satisfactions available from other relationships declined—someone else you might go out with became involved with someone else and unavailable—then commitment to the original relationship increased.

All of this is consistent with exchange theory. But Rusbult also found that increases in investment led to increased commitment (Rusbult, 1983; see Kurdek, 1991, 1992, on the usefulness of the investment model for understanding gay and lesbian relationships as well as heterosexual ones). Similarly, the duration of a relationship has been found to predict its stability *independent of the satisfactions the relationship provides,* and duration is at least one measure of degree of investment (Simpson, 1987). And investment has been shown to predict college students' continued enrollment in their colleges (Hatcher, Kryter, Prus, & Fitzgerald, 1992). The fact that investment leads to commitment raises an interesting question: Should it? Is it rational for people to consider how much they have invested in something in deciding whether to continue to invest?

Certainly in the extreme, it would be an error. If you have not committed yourself to stay in a relationship and it has deteriorated to the point where it provides no satisfactions and lots of costs, and if there are alternatives for you, then it would be a bit crazy to stay. But the issue is: Does it make sense to count the degree to which you have invested in a relationship *even a little* in deciding whether to stay? Perhaps it does. One reason is that continuity in one's life is probably worth something. There is something ugly about living a life in which one changes one's friends with the ease with which one changes one's socks. And then too, what is the alternative? A life in which one constantly weighs the options available to determine if one could do better elsewhere. This doesn't seem like a very happy way to live. So counting degree of investment in a relationship *to some degree* may not be irrational at all (Sabini & Silver, 1989).

NEED SATISFACTION DEPENDENCE

Other research has focused on people's "comparison level for alternatives" in their relationships. If a person can satisfy some important need in a relationship and has no other alternative source of that need satisfaction, then the person is said to be **need satisfaction dependent** in the relationship. In two studies of undergraduates' relationships, Caryl Rusbult found that measures of need satisfaction dependency in a relationship are good predictors of whether people will decide to end those relationships; not surprisingly, people who are dependent on particular relationships for the satisfaction of important needs are less willing to break up than those who aren't (Rusbult, 1992).

COMMUNAL RELATIONSHIPS AND EXCHANGE

Some theorists have suggested that it is a mistake to view intimate relationships in the context of exchange theory. Margaret Clark and Judson Mills, for example, have argued that some relationships, which they call **communal,** are not structured along the lines of exchange at all (Clark & Mills, 1979). Consider a family meal. It would be odd indeed for children to pay for their food. And it wouldn't matter much whether the way they paid was in money or approval—imagine a family in which a child had to offer five bits of approval per carrot! Rather, Clark and Mills suggest, families and other communal relationships are organized according to the rule that people are to be given *what they need.* In exchange relationships, the argument goes, people get what they pay for, but in communal relationships, they are given whatever they need.

In one experiment designed to illustrate this distinction, male subjects (one at a time) were brought together with an attractive female confederate, Paula. Each subject was told that he and Paula would be doing an experiment together, and they would receive a joint payment, depending on how much work they did. It was up to them to decide how to split it. What they had to do was locate sequences of numbers embedded in a fifteen-row-by-twenty-six-column matrix; their pay depended on how many sequences they found. The confederate had the first turn at this rather boring task. While Paula worked, the subject was removed from the room and given some information about her. Some subjects learned that Paula was single, new to the university, and had volunteered to participate in the experiment in the hopes of making friends. Other subjects learned that she was married and participating in the experiment because it was interesting and could be scheduled at a convenient time for her husband to pick her up.

The point of this manipulation was to influence the kind of relationship the subjects might have hoped to achieve with Paula. The experimenters hoped that the subjects would want to develop a romantic—or at least friendly—relationship with the single, there-to-make-friends Paula, but they expected the subjects with the there-to-be-picked-up-by-her-husband Paula to have no such aspirations. Therefore, they expected the first group of subjects to try to structure their relationship with Paula in a communal (all for one and one for all) way, but the second group of subjects to structure their relationship along more exchange-driven lines. What were the results?

When the subjects returned to the lab, they found that Paula had circled with a marker the sequences of numbers she had found in the matrix. It was now the subject's turn. The behavior of interest was very subtle. What color ink would the subject choose to circle the sequences he found? If he chose the *same* color Paula had used, then they were destined to have a communal relationship—at least for the duration of the experiment—since there would be no way for them to distinguish his inputs from hers, and hence no way to apportion pay on the basis of their relative contributions. But if he chose a *different* color, then it would be possible to pay each according to their contributions.

As expected, only about 10 percent of the subjects who thought they could create a communal relationship with Paula chose different colors, while about 90 percent of those who thought she was married did (see Figure 15.5). In subsequent studies, Clark showed that pairs of friends who came to the lab together also chose to use different-colored inks less than did pairs of strangers, further supporting the notion that in communal relationships, people do not keep track of inputs in the way that exchange and equity theories say they must (Clark, 1984).

Other, similar research has suggested that, as Clark and Mills claimed, people *do* keep track of other people's *needs* when they desire (or have) a communal relationship, but that people in a communal relationship (friends) tend not to keep track of others' contributions (Clark, Mills, & Powell, 1986; Clark, Mills, & Corcoran, 1989). Clark and Mills argue that exchange theory has too narrow a conception of human relationships; there is no denying that *some* of our relationships are organized by exchange, but not all of them.

Alan Fiske joins Clark and Mills in arguing that not all relationships are exchange relationships. But his theorizing, based on observations in other cultures as well as Western, suggests that there aren't two but rather four sorts of relationships one can have (see Table 15.3 on page 500; Fiske, 1990). One type is exchange; another is communal. A third is a relationship ordered by strict equality. In such a relationship, people do not receive from others as they need, as in communal, nor do they receive in proportion to their inputs, as in exchange; they receive exactly as everyone else receives. Voting in our system of government is arranged this way: one person, one vote. People don't get more votes because they work harder, nor do they get more because they need them. Last, relationships may be arranged by authority. In authority relationships, one person orders; others follow those orders. The followers may, perhaps, *replace* the authority and install another one, but that is another matter.

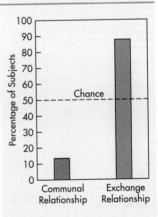

FIGURE 15.5

COMMUNAL RELATIONSHIPS AND EXCHANGE

▲ *Percentage of subjects choosing a distinctive color pen was a function of relationship type. Subjects were less interested in keeping track of inputs in communal relationships. (From Clark, 1984)*

TABLE 15.3

	TYPES OF RELATIONSHIPS	
Type	Distribution Rule	Example
Exchange	Free market.	Selling a car
Communal	Take as much as you need.	Thanksgiving dinner
Equality matching	Everyone gets the same amount.	Dividing 3 doughnuts among 3 children
Authority	Leaders give orders; followers follow.	Parents and children in a supermarket

SOURCE: Based on Fiske, 1990.

Interestingly, Fiske argues that these four types of relationships can (and do) occur with the very same people. A mother might, for example, give her daughter as much food as she needs but also contract with her to mow the lawn at a fixed rate, order her to clean up her room, and split the one remaining candy bar with her right down the middle. So these ways of organizing the social allocations of rewards and costs don't characterize *relationships* so much as they characterize activities *within* relationships. Eating is organized communally, lawn mowing in an exchange way, and so on.

So what are we to make of these criticisms of exchange theory? An exchange theorist might argue this way. Say what you will about communal relationships and the like, the data show that when you come down to it, people leave relationships when their rewards sink, and especially if they think they can do better elsewhere. The hard fact is there are no communal relationships according to exchange theory.

But wait; parents don't abandon their sick children because sick children use up more resources than they contribute. So at least there are some relationships in the world that are more than exchange. What about romantic relationships; are these all just exchange?

The data do suggest that people's decisions to remain in or leave relationships are, at least to some degree, governed by exchange considerations, but this does not imply that people enter them with the intention of having exchange relationships. Perhaps people often enter relationships, be they romantic or friendship, with the aim of having communal relationships, however they may turn out. And perhaps the divorce rate suggests that even marriages aren't communal in that people do at some point decide to leave. But the implications of the divorce rate are not that clear. Fiske, for example, points out that even though in communal relationships one gets as one needs, this does not mean that communal relationships cannot be dissolved. Various sorts of abuses lead to the dissolution of a communal relationship; so the fact that people can be driven to divorce does not imply that their relationship is an exchange relationship. And, finally, one might suppose that in most relationships, people are willing to be underbenefited (relative to the benefits the other person derives or relative to some other standard) *to some degree* and for *some period of time*, but not limitlessly.

An exchange theorist might argue that this position is no different from hers except in degree. Ah, but the degree matters. Suppose you and a friend alternate taking each other out to dinner. One week you pay; one week he pays. You might try to insure that the bills are exactly equal from one week to the next—you spent $51.04 last week, he must spend the same amount this week. Or you might just seek rough parity, rough enough to be sure no one is being exploited. Admittedly, there is nothing but a matter of degree separating these two schemes, but they are nonetheless quite different in their degree of pettiness. And perhaps one objection people might have to exchange theory is just that, the pettiness of the picture it paints of all of our relationships.

Cohabitation

Love and marriage, as we all know, go together rather commonly. There are three principal questions we will address about marriage: (1) Who marries whom—how do people select spouses? (2) How do people come to get married? (3) What distinguishes happy from unhappy marriages? But before we look at marriage, we should pause briefly to examine something else that love leads to: *cohabitation*, living together before marriage.

As mentioned in the previous chapter, even in the 1930s, a significant number of couples applying for marriage licenses listed the same address on their application, so even then living together before marriage was not unheard of. Since then, the incidence of couples' living together without being married has substantially increased. Evidence about its increasing prevalence comes from several sources. One source is the U.S. Census Bureau. Census Bureau surveys indicate that in 1975, there were about 900,000 unmarried couples living together in the United States. By 1980, this number had nearly doubled to 1.6 million; by 1981, there were 1.8 million couples. These numbers suggest that about 4 percent of all couples living together were unmarried. About half of the people involved in these relationships had never been married, while the other half had been married at least once (Spanier, 1983). Unmarried cohabitation is surely a phenomenon of increasing significance. Why has it increased of late?

One reason is surely that it has become more socially acceptable over the last few decades. Another possible cause is that the average age at marriage has increased, as has the age at which people bear their first child (leaving open the possibility of other relationships before marriage and childbearing) (Spanier, 1983). What implication does the increase in cohabitation have for marriage in the United States?

One place to look for an answer to this question is the National Survey of Families and Households (NSFH). This survey, conducted in 1987–88, involved 13,017 households carefully selected to represent the families and households of the United States. About 1,000 of the respondents had at some point in their lives cohabited. Results from this survey indicate that the percentage of people in the United States who marry by age 25 has been in sharp decline since 1950. For example, 72 percent of the people in the survey who reached age 25 around 1970 were married by that age, but only 55 percent of those reaching age 25 around 1985 were married by then. Perhaps this decline is because people cohabit at younger ages instead of marrying and thus tend to marry later. Indeed, if one includes cohabitors and married people, the decline from 1970 to 1985 in numbers of people forming unions by age 25 is only about 8 percent (Bumpass, Sweet, & Cherlin, 1991). Thus, there is some reason to believe that cohabitation has come to take the place of marriage during young adulthood.

Similarly, rates of remarriage after divorce have recently declined (a decline of about 16 percent from 1970 to 1980), but the percentage of divorced people forming a new union actually increased slightly in the same period. So, again, cohabitation is compensating during phases of people's lives.

This does not mean that those who are cohabiting intend never to marry (or remarry). Results from the same survey of households indicated that about 80 percent of cohabitors intend to marry one day, and most intend to marry their cohabitational partner (Bumpass, Sweet, & Cherlin, 1991; Risman, Hill, Rubin, & Peplau, 1981). Cohabitation is seen as something one does during certain phases of one's life, rather than a substitute for marriage. And the evidence suggests that people are right about this; cohabitations do tend to be short-lived. Ninety percent end either in marriage or break up within five years. Cohabitation, then, isn't a substitute for marriage.

Are the marriages of people who have cohabited with each other happier or less happy than the marriages of people who haven't cohabited? One might expect that cohabitation would lead to better marriages on the grounds that it would allow couples that aren't suitable to discover that fact early and not get married in the first place. Cohabitation might be expected to work like a "trial marriage," weeding out the marriages that are better off never blooming. Unfortunately, it doesn't seem to work that way.

The evidence, again from the NSFH, is that marriages preceded by cohabitation are *less* stable and happy than those not preceded by cohabitation (DeMaris & Rao, 1992; Thompson & Colella, 1992; see also DeMaris & Leslie, 1984). And the longer a couple had cohabited before marriage, the worse things were for that couple. Why is this? There are many possibilities.

One possibility is something of a statistical one. The longer it has been since a person got married, the more likely it is that she has also been divorced (this *must* be so). Well, cohabitors have been married longer than they seem; they should, as it were, get credit for the time they were cohabiting. But the evidence is that even adjusting for this, cohabitors still have poorer marriages (DeMaris & Rao, 1992).

Another reasonable hypothesis is that people who cohabit are less conventional in their attitudes toward marriage, and these unconventional attitudes don't lead to very high marital satisfaction. Thus, it isn't the cohabitation per se but rather the unconventionality of the people who are willing to cohabit that leads to their poorer marriages. This is a perfectly sensible idea, but the survey of American families also asked the respondents to indicate their attitudes toward families. And it was true that cohabitors tended to have less conventional attitudes. But these differences in attitudes did *not* seem to account for the differences in marital satisfaction (DeMaris & MacDonald, 1993). So at the moment, we do not know why cohabitors have weaker marriages, but they seem to.*

Cohabitation before marriage is associated with less happy and less stable marriages.

---

*People will not, for some reason, tolerate a direct, experimental approach to this problem, one in which half of the couples to be married next year are randomly assigned to cohabit this year while the other half aren't allowed to.

Who Chooses Whom?

How do people select their mate from the vast number of candidates out there in the world? Sometimes in life (and even in this book) when you ask a simple question, you get a complex answer, but sometimes when you ask a complex question, you get a simple answer. Here goes: people marry those who are similar to themselves.

CLASSIC FINDINGS IN SOCIAL PSYCHOLOGY: HOMOGAMY

The tendency to marry people like oneself is called **homogamy.** It has perhaps best been documented in research by Ernest Burgess and Paul Wallin (1953). Burgess and Wallin distributed 6,000 questionnaires to college students in a variety of courses throughout the Chicago area. The students were asked to give the questionnaires to engaged couples. Questionnaires were returned by about 1,200 couples; the responses from the first 1,000 received were retained for the study, and 226 of these couples were interviewed before marriage. About three to five years after they married—850 of the original 1,000 engaged couples married—these couples were again sent questionnaires; 666 returned them, and 124 of these couples were reinterviewed.

Burgess and Wallin asked subjects about eighty-eight traits or characteristics, and then calculated the degree to which the couples were similar on each trait compared with the amount of similarity on the trait found in *random* pairings of the participants. After all, couples are very, very similar in the number of eyes they have, but this is hardly because people select mates on that basis. Rather, it is because we are all similar on that trait, which implies that *randomly* matched pairs would also be similar. Thus, the relevant question is: Were the engaged couples more similar on the self-reported traits than were randomly paired couples from the same sample?

The answer was massively yes. On *none* of the eighty-eight traits were

couples significantly likely to be more *different* than chance would predict. On sixty-six of the traits, there was evidence of homogamy—a greater than chance degree of similarity between the engaged couples (see Table 15.4). What were the couples similar in?

Burgess and Wallin divided the traits they studied into three kinds: social, physical, and personality. Social characteristics (there were forty-seven) included such things as religion (which religion, degree of participation, and so

TABLE 15.4

SIMILARITY OF ENGAGED COUPLES

Characteristic	Similarity Index
Religious Affiliation and Behavior	
Religious affiliation	2.14
Church attendance	1.69
Church membership	1.43
Social Habits	
Drinking alcohol (never, rarely, occasionally, etc.)	1.81
Leisure time preferences	1.29
# of friends of opposite sex	1.10
Conceptions of Marriage	
Wife should work	1.64
# of children desired	1.42
Wife should keep her own name	1.19
Courtship Behavior	
Age began dating	1.55
# of people each has gone steady with	1.27
Previously engaged (or not)	1.10
Family Background	
Urban, rural, suburban, etc.	1.49
Education of parents	1.37
Parents' social status	1.24
Physical Characteristics	
Physical attractiveness	1.20
Weight	1.08
Family Relationships	
Attachment to siblings	1.15
Ratings of happiness of parents' marriage	1.14
Attachment to parents	1.11
Psychological Characteristics	
Feelings easily hurt	1.13
Leader of social events	1.11
Stage fright	1.10

Note: The degree to which 1,000 engaged men and women resembled each other. A similarity index of 1.00 means that the couples are no more alike than they would be if they had married another member of the study chosen by chance. A number greater than 1.00 means that they are more similar than that.

SOURCE: Data from Burgess & Wallin, 1953.

on), family background (parents' social class), age at which the partners began dating, number of people they had gone steady with, conceptions of marriage (whether partner should work after marriage, number of children desired), drinking and smoking habits, leisure time preferences, number of friends of the same and opposite sex, attitudes toward parents, and so on. Homogamy was found on all but four of these. The greatest degree of homogamy was found for religion. People were more than twice as likely to be engaged to someone of the same religion as chance would predict; the couples' parents tended to be of the same social class; men who began dating early tended to be engaged to women who began dating early; men who never drank tended to be married to women who never drank; and so on for a wide variety of traits.

Six physical characteristics were studied. On five of them, couples tended to match. Tall men married tall women; fat men married fat women; people in good health were engaged to other people in good health; and so on. As mentioned before, there was also matching on physical attractiveness—as self-reported.

The couples were asked about forty-two personality characteristics. It was here that the evidence for homogamy was weakest, both in the sense that a significant degree of homogamy was found on only fourteen of the forty-two traits, and in the sense that even on those fourteen traits, the degree of homogamy was not very great. (The couples' reports of their behavior suggested that they were similar in whether they often daydreamed, were likely to be the leaders at social affairs, were likely to experience stage fright, and so on.) But still, there were no reversals—no cases in which opposites attracted.*

The tendency to homogamy is not restricted to heterosexual couples. In one study of married heterosexual couples, cohabiting heterosexual couples, and gay and lesbian couples, the tendency to homogamy was found to be greatest among lesbian couples (Kurdek & Schmitt, 1987).

The tendency to pick a spouse who is similar to oneself has an interesting consequence: stability of personality over time. If two introverted people marry, they are likely to provide an introverted environment for each other, thus reinforcing each other's preferences. Had one married an extravert, some personality change in an extraverted direction might have resulted. Thus, one contribution to the stability of adult personality over time may be our tendency to marry people like ourselves (Caspi & Herbener, 1990).

Other research has found a tendency toward similarity between married partners on a host of other variables. Husbands and wives have been found to be similar in political attitudes, and to *think* that they are even more similar than they are (Byrne & Blaylock, 1963). Couples also tend to be similar in intelligence (Richardson, 1939). And couples are generally of the same age, though they do not tend to be *exactly* the same age. Rather, husbands tend to be about two years older than wives if both are marrying for the first time

▲ *A man and his opossum.*

*The Burgess and Wallin study, by looking at engaged rather than already married couples, shows that homogamy exists at the point of choice of a mate. Other studies that have found that husbands and wives resemble each other are open to the plausible interpretation that marriage *produces* similarity, that the longer people are married, the more alike they become. That no doubt happens too. In fact, Robert Zajonc has shown that couples who have been married for twenty-five years *look* more alike than they did when they were first married (Zajonc, Adelmann, Murphy, & Niedenthal, 1987).

(Bytheway, 1981). Partners also tend to be matched on a personality variable called "sensation seeking." People who are high on this trait tend to like things like jumping out of planes—with a parachute, of course—more than people who are low on this trait (Lesnik-Oberstein & Cohen, 1984).

Recently David Buss asked each member of ninety-three married couples to report the frequencies with which they engaged in eight hundred behaviors related to eight interpersonal categories—introverted and extraverted, for example. The results showed substantial interspouse correlations for specific acts, including acts where one might not expect to find correlations, such as passivity in sexual encounters (Buss, 1984). The evidence for similarity in marital choices, then, is massive.

COMPLEMENTARITY OF NEEDS

Some investigators believe that similarity does not tell the whole story in mate selection. In particular, Robert Winch has argued that couples also select each other to be complementary, rather than similar, on certain personality needs. For example, people high in **nurturance**—the desire to take care of other people—tend to marry people who are high in **succorance,** the desire to be taken care of. The notion of complementarity of needs is perfectly sensible; it would only make sense for people who like to take care of others to match up with people who like to be taken care of. But are people that sensible?

Winch closely examined twenty-five couples in an effort to determine each person's pattern of needs. Each subject was assessed in regard to twelve needs and general traits. Partners' scores were then intercorrelated. The results suggested to Winch that assertive people, for example, tend to marry more passive people (Winch, 1955; Winch, Ktanes, & Ktanes, 1955). But subsequent research has not, in the main, supported Winch's view. Most research on need patterns in married couples has found either no relation, or similarity (Katz, Glucksberg, & Krauss, 1960; Schellenberg & Bee, 1960; Murstein, 1961; Tharp, 1963; Levinger, 1964; Antill, 1983). As sensible as it might be for people with complementary needs to pair up, the bulk of the evidence suggests they don't. Rather, the evidence suggests that people marry other people like themselves.

Similarity, not complementarity, predicts attraction.

MARRIAGE

For many of us, a happy marriage is one of life's great satisfactions. Indeed, marriage is associated with both physical and psychological well-being (Burman & Margolin, 1992; Lee, Seccombe, & Shehan, 1991). Married people seem to have fewer physical problems and survive longer once diagnosed with serious physical disorders than do people who were never married or who were divorced. *Why* this is so is much less clear. One answer might be that being married provides emotional support that lessens the severity of physical ailments. Another is that spouses help each other make lifestyle changes that contribute to health. Another possibility is that people who marry are on average physically and psychologically healthier to begin with than people who do not marry, so healthy people marry (or stay married), while less healthy people stay single (or divorce). To the degree that this is true and

"I'M SORRY, BUT I'M WAITING FOR MR. RIGHT."

accounts for the association between marriage and well-being, there is no *causal* relationship between marriage and longevity.

To see if such a "self-selection into marriage" mechanism might account for the association between marriage and well-being, one study followed nine thousand unmarried Norwegians for a two- to four-year period. The subjects were assessed for physical and psychological well-being at the start of the study, and this assessment predicted which of them would marry: the subjects who were healthier at the start were more likely to marry. There was no evidence *in this study* that marriage had a causal effect on well-being (Mastekaasa, 1992). On the other hand, it might take more than two to four years for such causal mechanisms to become apparent. Thus, we are left for the moment with a clear association between marriage and well-being, but without a clear understanding of the causal mechanism for the association.

Perhaps the most obvious question about marriage is: Why do people marry? And the answer seems clear. Because the two parties involved are in love with each other. It seems clear to us that there is a natural connection between romantic love and marriage. And, indeed, there is a connection between the two *in Western culture at this moment.* But it is worthwhile to begin our discussion of marriage by putting this connection in cultural and historical perspective. Western culture is so taken with the idea that romantic love ought to be the basis for marriage that it is easy to believe that romantic love, like marriage, is a human universal, which it isn't, rather than a particular cultural development, which it is.

Love and Marriage in Sixteenth-Century England

Lawrence Stone points out that Western culture has three related beliefs about marriage:

> The first is that there is a clear dichotomy between marriage for interest, meaning money, status, or power, and marriage for affect, meaning love, friendship, or sexual attraction; and that the first is morally reprehensible. . . . The second modern preconception is that sexual intercourse unaccompanied by an emotional re-

lationship is immoral, and that marriage for interest is therefore a form of prostitution. The third is that personal autonomy, the pursuit by the individual of his or her own happiness, is paramount, a claim justified by the theory that it in fact contributes to the well being of the group. (Stone, 1979, p. 70)

He goes on to point out that these three notions were foreign to the sixteenth century.*

True, the notion of romantic love existed in the sixteenth century (Stone in fact sees it as an invention of the twelfth century), but it was not seen then as a reasonable ground for marriage. Marriage in sixteenth-century England was, as it still is in much of the world, arranged by the families of the bride and groom in order to solidify and extend their social standing and power. The married couple were expected to make the best of the arranged situation, and they usually did—not because romantic love developed over the course of their marriage, but because they didn't expect it to, and were not disappointed when it didn't. According to Stone, modern audiences see Romeo and Juliet in a different light than did the audiences for whom it was written. We see them as hero and heroine giving, in the end, their lives for their love rather than marrying the partners picked for them by their families. Elizabethan audiences, Stone claims, were likely to sympathize with their plight, but in the end to see them as fools attempting to build a life around the ephemeral experience of love.

Romeo and Juliet would be unintelligible to members of some cultures, like the Mangaians whom we met in Chapter 12, for not only do they not see romantic love as the basis of marriage, they don't even have a concept of romantic love at all (see Chapter 7). Husbands and wives in that culture are expected, of course, to be intimate in the sense of enjoying sex together, and raise their children together, but they are not expected to have the kind of intimacy *we* expect husbands and wives to share.

There are two points to keep in mind, then, as we discuss romantic love. First, it is not a human universal. Second, at its inception in Western culture, in the twelfth century, it was not seen as having anything to do with marriage. Indeed in the troubadour myths, where it began, it was specifically an emotion experienced by two people married to *others;* it was an explicitly extramarital delight. How this extramarital emotion came to be melded with marriage and child care is a fascinating story, well told by Stone, but beyond the scope of this discussion. For now, let us see how our conception of marriage has changed over this historical period.

Changing Conceptions of Marriage and the Family

In the long historical view, there has been a steady progression in the institution of marriage. The nature of this change has been toward marriages based upon companionship. To see what this is in contrast to, let us return

---

*There has been measurable change in attitudes about this even over the last twenty years. In the late 1960s, William Kephart asked Philadelphia college men and women, "If a boy (girl) had all the other qualities you desired, would you marry this person if you were not in love with him (her)?" Sixty-five percent of the men answered a flat no; only about 25 percent of the women answered no (Kephart, 1967). A similar survey in 1984 revealed that now 86 percent of the men said no, as did 80 percent of the women (Simpson, Campbell, & Berscheid, 1986).

to the world of the *Donna Reed Show* as seen through the eyes of a contemporary sociologist, Talcott Parsons (Parsons, 1955). For Parsons, the nuclear family was a small group, much like other small groups. As such, it fulfilled two distinctly different needs: **expressive** (symbolic and emotional) needs and **instrumental** (pragmatic) needs. These two functions were nicely assigned to the two adults in the nuclear family: the woman got the social-emotional functions, the man got the instrumental tasks. So the woman stayed home and took care of the house and socializing the children while the man went out and earned money (see Chapter 12). And they lived happily ever after. But something has gone wrong in this script. What?

Well, the script was never exactly right. Even in the early 1950s, there were significant numbers of women who were living with their husbands and working outside of the home. And many more of them had worked outside the home during the Second World War. (In the 1950s, women knew they *could* be riveters because they *had* been riveters.)

Some have argued that another contributor to the changes in the American family wrought over the last thirty years has been the "marriage squeeze." In the early 1950s, women were marrying men who were about two years older than they were. But consider what happened in, say, 1967. In that year, the women who reached prime marriage age—about age twenty—were looking for men about two years older than they were. But men two years older than these women would have to have been born in 1945. Because of the Second World War, there weren't many men born in 1945. Thus, beginning in 1957 and lasting until the birthrate produced by the baby boom stabilized, as Marcia Guttentag and Paul Secord put it, there were *too many women.* Such a sexual imbalance can have many effects. Guttentag and Secord discuss in particular how it led women to question the place in society to which they had been assigned (Guttentag & Secord, 1983).

The *Donna Reed Show* script was just not consistent with the direction that the family had been heading for centuries—toward less differentiation in roles, greater equality, and greater companionship rather than complementarity within marriages. So the American marriage has been under various pressures. The degree to which each factor has contributed is difficult to determine; the task of determining it is surely to be left to historians. For our purposes here, suffice it to note that marriages have changed, and research questions addressed to them have also changed.

▲ *Murphy Brown,* a doubly untraditional mom. She is a professional and a single mother.

Marital Satisfaction

What, then, in our era leads to satisfied marriages? What does modern research have to say on this score?

SELF-DISCLOSURE

One example of a current concern of research that would surprise someone born fifty years ago has to do with the relation of self-disclosure to marital satisfaction. If marriage is solely a matter of the man as breadwinner and the woman as homemaker, then self-disclosure seems to be beside the point. But if marriage is about companionship, and companionship is a matter of, among other things, the exchange of concerns, then we might expect the degree to which couples disclose to each other to be related to how satisfied they are.

▲ *Steve Martin and Kimberly Williams in* Father of the Bride. *A wedding as traditional as they come.*

And this is just what has been found (Hendrick, 1981; Hansen & Schuldt, 1984; Franzoi, Davis, & Young, 1985). Moreover, couples discrepant in degree of self-disclosure also seem to be less satisfied (Davidson, Balswick, & Halverson, 1983).

SEX-ROLE ATTITUDES

A traditional way of thinking about marital satisfaction is that marriages are happy if the members of the couples each fulfill their assigned sex roles. And, indeed, this approach seemed to do better than any other in predicting marital success through the mid-1960s (Tharp, 1963). But what is true now?

As we saw in Chapter 12, several researchers—especially Sandra Bem as well as Janet Spence and Robert Helmreich—have developed measures of the degree to which people adhere to traditional sex roles. In Donna Reed's day, we would expect that traditional men and women had the most satisfying marriages, but these scales didn't exist then, so we don't know which marriages were the happiest. But there *is* evidence about what is true now. The evidence seems to be that traditional couples are *not* the most satisfied at the moment, though neither are they the least satisfied.

In one study of 331 military couples from U.S. and European bases, there was little relation between the partners' sex-role attitudes and their marital satisfaction, *except that* couples in which the man held traditional attitudes but the woman held more modern attitudes proved to be the least satisfied (Bowen & Orthner, 1983). Other research has suggested that the degree to which marriages (and enduring relationships among gay men and women) are satisfying has to do with the degree to which both partners report themselves as having both "masculine" and "feminine" traits (Antill, 1983; Kurdek & Schmitt, 1986a, 1986b; Zammichieli, Gilroy, & Sherman, 1988). It is not, in other words, the degree to which couples see themselves as being complementary in role and personality that predicts marital satisfaction, but rather the degree to which they see themselves as similar. So we have more suggestive evidence that satisfaction in modern marriages is a matter of emotional expression and companionship.

CHILDREN

For a time, the conventional wisdom was that the longer people were married, the less satisfied they were with their marriages. But more recent research suggests that this is not true, that the relation of marital satisfaction to how long the marriage has lasted is shaped like a U—satisfaction first falls and then rises (see Figure 15.6; Renne, 1970; Figley, 1973; Ryder, 1973; Rollins & Cannon, 1974; Glenn & McLanahan, 1982). Why is the function U-shaped?

A closer look at the pattern of the data suggests that marital satisfaction begins a sharp decline with the birth of the first child, and it begins to rise again just when the last-born child leaves home. The evidence, then, is that children are hard on marriages. Note that this evidence was obtained by asking people how satisfied they were with their marriages, and noting the relation of the marital satisfaction curve to the birth and dispatching from the home of children. This was *not* found out by asking people whether having children was a source of satisfaction to them, or whether having children was a source of satisfaction in the marriage. People generally answer that children

FIGURE 15.6

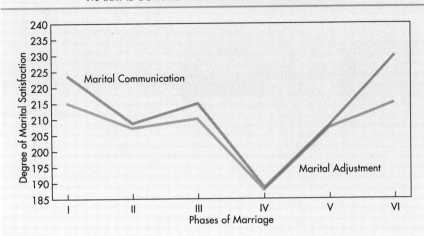

MARITAL COMMUNICATION AND ADJUSTMENT

Marital Communication

Marital Adjustment

Degree of Marital Satisfaction

Phases of Marriage

◀ *The low point of marital communication and adjustment over the phases of a marriage is reached just as the last child prepares to leave the home (phase IV). Once the children have left, both communication and adjustment improve strikingly. (Data from Figley, 1973)*

are a source of satisfaction (Luckey & Bain, 1970). But children are also responsible for a substantial decline in marital satisfaction.

Why do children bring such a decline? One piece of the answer seems to be that wives claim that their husbands aren't paying enough attention to them once a child has been born. Wives resent this loss of companionship. But why are wives complaining that their husbands aren't paying attention to them? Perhaps the answer can be gleaned from a study of 106 married faculty women at Northwestern University. The study asked faculty women to report on the number of hours they and their husbands devoted to their careers, housework, and child care. The results should be seen in light of the fact that these women, like most married women, worked outside the home. And like many married women who work, they were strongly committed to both their careers and their marriages. Several interesting facts emerged.

First, husbands and wives without children spent an equal amount of time devoted to their careers—about 56 hours per week. But the wives spent almost three times as much time on household work—18.4 versus 6.3 hours per week. What happened when a child was born? The average husband's commitment of time to his career actually slightly increased with the birth of a child; the average husband now spent 57.9 hours working toward his career. But the wife's contribution declined to 48.5 hours per week. So the birth of a child places pressure on the wife's but not the husband's career. When we look at husbands' contributions to housework and child care, a different picture emerges. Husbands' contributions in these areas increased from 6.3 hours per week to 20.6 hours per week. But wives' contributions increased from 18.4 to 59.7 hours per week. So what is the picture here?

The picture is that even before a child is born, the wife is doing more than her share of housework, but this probably isn't a major source of tension, since in absolute terms she is not contributing that many more hours. And she is able to contribute an essentially equal number of hours to her profession. But the birth of the child changes all of this. Her husband does increase

MARRIAGE **511**

FIGURE 15.7

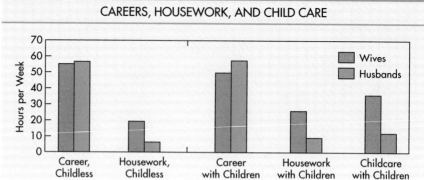

CAREERS, HOUSEWORK, AND CHILD CARE

▶ *Hours devoted to career, housework, and child care among female faculty members and their husbands varied according to whether the couples were childless or had children. (Data from Yogev, 1981)*

his contribution to housework, but this lags far behind the contribution that the wife makes. And this added time the husband contributes does *not* come out of the time he spends on his profession. Rather, one suspects, the added time is removed from the time he would have spent socializing with his wife. For the wife, the birth of a child requires a large increase in the time she must contribute to her housekeeping and child care, this time *does* come out of her career time, and she probably faces the loss of companionship from her husband. Her husband, on the other hand, may find it hard to understand why she is complaining, since he too is spending all of those extra hours doing housework (see Figure 15.7; Yogev, 1981).

Subsequent research has verified various pieces of this picture in larger, more representative samples. One study demonstrated that a marital partner's satisfaction is related to the division of labor in the family (Yogev & Brett, 1985). And it has been shown in much larger, more representative samples that the more the division of labor turns toward traditionalism after the birth of a child, the less satisfied wives are (Belsky, Lang, & Huston, 1986; Ruble, Fleming, Hackel, & Stangor, 1988).

George Vaillant has challenged the finding that marital satisfaction follows a U shape; he has found that husbands' marital satisfaction is quite stable over the course of marriages, and that wives' satisfaction declines but that the decline is quite modest (Vaillant & Vaillant, 1993). There are at least two differences between Vaillant's study and those that turned up the U-shaped function; either difference might account for the difference in results. For one thing, studies that found the U shape typically asked people to *recall* their degree of marital satisfaction at various points in their marriages, whereas Vaillant's data were assembled by following subjects over a forty-year period and asking them about their level of satisfaction at the moment. Indeed, when Vaillant asked his subjects to *recall* how happy they had been, he too found U-shaped curves; so perhaps the U shape is a trick of memory!

But Vaillant's study differed from the typical study in another way also. His subjects were 268 Harvard College males who were sophomores from 1938 to 1942. They were among the best off people in the country; they were hardly a random sample of the economic spectrum. Perhaps their economic position buffered them from many of the stresses of child rearing.

Other research based on a random sample of the U.S. population, consisting of 2,034 men and women, suggested that the number of children couples have detracts from the amount of time husbands and wives spend in joint activity (White, 1983). Thus, anything that detracts from the amount of companionship that husbands and wives are able to provide each other will detract from marital satisfaction.

Results from the National Survey of Families and Households confirm this picture. First, the average wife in the survey performed 42.04 hours per week of household labor, while the average husband performed 12.23 hours. So wives certainly still do most of the housework. Second, wives' perception of the fairness of the division of labor was fairly strongly related to the degree to which their husbands participated in women's work (cleaning, cooking, and so on) rather than to the degree to which husbands performed male tasks (mowing the lawn, making repairs). Wives' perception of fairness was also connected to how appreciated they thought their work was by their husbands (Blair & Johnson, 1992).

POWER

There is something distasteful about discussing *power* in intimate relationships; we are more comfortable thinking of marriages (or any other companionate relationships) as places where power doesn't intrude. But in even the best of marriages, the two parties involved will not agree about every decision that they must make—somehow they must decide where they will spend Thanksgiving. Power has to do with how the partners try to make their own preference the one that wins. Two questions about marital power arise: (1) How do the partners exercise power? and (2) How is marital satisfaction related to how the partners express power?

Time was when both questions had a simple answer for most marriages. Men were acknowledged to have power, so they exercised it directly. Women, given their place in society generally, exercised power indirectly—by supplication or manipulation. And marriages were happiest when men were the decision makers. But women are moving into positions of power in the world at large (though they are still far from holding equal power). Has this change at the societal level affected power in the marriage?

A recent survey of the tactics that men and women use in intimate relationships looked at several factors in relation to the use of "strong" power tactics (bullying and autocratic decision making) and "weak" power tactics (supplication and manipulation). The data consisted of reports by the partners of the sorts of influence they used in their relationships. There were several findings.

Being more dependent than one's partner led to greater use of weak tactics: the member of the couple who earned less and who saw himself or herself as less physically attractive (and hence less "marketable") tended to use weak tactics regardless of gender. But in addition to this fact and regardless of these factors, wives used weak tactics to a greater degree than did husbands. This leads one to think that something about being a woman, perhaps women's place in society, leads to these tactics regardless of the partners' relative marketability in the particular relationship. But the study also included gay male and lesbian couples, and the finding that emerged was that the use of weak tactics depended not so much on the gender of the person exercising power as it did on the gender of the *target* of the tactics. Men and women used weak tactics on men. Heterosexual women and gay men used these tactics more than did heterosexual men and lesbian women. Thus, either there is something that heterosexual women and gay men share that leads them to use such tactics, or there is something about being a man that leads men and women to use these tactics on them (Howard, Blumstein, & Schwartz, 1986).

Now the second question: How does the division of power affect marital satisfaction? The trend from a considerable number of studies is fairly clear: egalitarian marriages where power is fairly evenly divided are the happiest. But perfect symmetry with regard to power has not been achieved. Marriages in which the husband is dominant are happier than marriages in which the wife is dominant. Also, coercion on the part of either partner is not associated with happy marriages (Gray-Little & Burks, 1983). With regard to power, marriage is in transition from an older, institutional form in which the husband provided and decided to a newer form characterized by companionship. The pattern of results suggests that men and women are happiest in companionate marriages. But if the marriage is not to be companionate, then it had better be traditional—the man holds power—rather than the reverse.

BEHAVIOR EXCHANGE

Whatever the ultimate sources of marital satisfaction and dissatisfaction may be, they have their effects on marriages because they affect *behavior* between husbands and wives. It is in their behavior that we find the final cause of marital satisfaction and dissatisfaction. For this reason, many scholars of the family have examined the behavior of happy and unhappy couples to see how this happiness or unhappiness is in the end generated.

In one study, distressed and nondistressed couples (obtained by advertising for subjects with happy and unhappy marriages) were studied in two ways. First, the couples were asked to keep records of things that they each did that pleased and displeased the other person in their everyday lives. Second, these couples were brought into a laboratory, and their behavior during a discussion (rigged to involve conflict) was observed.

The investigators expected that distressed couples would differ from the happy couples in their everyday interactions. In particular, they thought that the distressed partners would rely more on aversive control as opposed to positive control over each other's behavior—they would punish each other more (for behavior they didn't like) and reward each other less (for behavior they did like). These expectations were supported by the data. In addition, the results suggested that distressed couples simply avoided each other more than nondistressed couples did (Birchler, Weiss, & Vincent, 1975). These distressed couples had created marital lives that were indeed aversive.

Subsequent research has supported the notion that distressed and nondistressed couples differ in the amount of pleasing versus displeasing behavior they engage in. In one study, subjects were asked to record positive and negative behaviors, and they were also asked to report on a daily basis how satisfied they were with their marriages. Aside from documenting the preponderance of negative events in the marriage, the study revealed that distressed couples were more *reactive* to events of the day in judging their marital satisfaction; what happened on *that particular day* had a greater effect for them

FIGURE 15.8

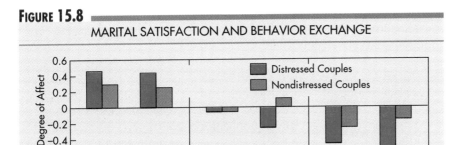

MARITAL SATISFACTION AND BEHAVIOR EXCHANGE

◀ Reactivity to positive, neutral, and negative events varied among distressed and nondistressed couples. Distressed husbands and wives were more reactive. (Data from Jacobson, Follette, & McDonald, 1982)

on how happy they were with their marriages (see Figure 15.8; Jacobson, Follette, & McDonald, 1982). This result suggests that the preponderance of negative events is especially troublesome for distressed couples. They had, as it were, spent their accumulated goodwill that could have helped them get through the bad times of daily life. They could not, as the nondistressed couples could, think of their satisfaction in the marriage in terms of the long haul; their satisfaction was based to a greater degree on what their spouses had done for them lately—very lately.

Communication in Distressed Versus Nondistressed Couples   There is a further problem besetting distressed couples—they seem not to communicate very well. In one study, John Gottman asked distressed and nondistressed couples to discuss problems they were having in their marriages. As they interacted, they were asked to indicate how positive in tone (versus hostile) they intended each of their messages to be. They also indicated how they "took" their partner's messages. The results suggested that the distressed and nondistressed couples did not differ in how they *intended* their messages. But they did differ in how they *interpreted* their partner's messages. The distressed couples interpreted their partner's messages to be significantly more negative than did the nondistressed couples (Gottman, Notarius, Markman, Blank, Yoppi, & Rubin, 1976). So in addition to actually emitting fewer positive and more negative behaviors and responding to those behaviors more, distressed couples seem also to suffer from a "communication deficit" that leads them to see each other's behavior in a more negative light than it was intended.

Further support for the communication deficit model comes from studies in which couples were asked to communicate specific, standardized affective messages to each other; the recipients were then asked to "decode" the affect intended. In some studies, the partners were asked to read standardized affectively ambiguous messages to each other, but to communicate a particular affect using nonverbal means—tone of voice, for example. In other studies, one member looked at slides producing various affective reactions; the partner's nonverbal reactions to the slides were videotaped, and the partner was asked to assess the emotion his or her partner was experiencing. The general thrust of these studies was that distressed couples were less accurate in detecting emotional reactions through these nonverbal means (Noller, 1980; Sabatelli, Buck, & Dreyer, 1980; Gottman & Porterfield, 1981; Gaelick, Bodenhausen, & Wyer, 1985; Noller & Gallois, 1986).

Physiological and Affective Reciprocity A final line of research has examined self-reported affect and physiological changes during naturalistic communications among distressed and nondistressed couples. Couples in these studies were asked to have a discussion about problem areas both partners thought were important to their marriage. As they talked, various measures—including their pulse rates, their skin conductance (thought to relate to general arousal), and simply how much they squirmed in their seats—were continuously recorded, and their conversations were videotaped. After the conversations were over, the subjects were asked to review the tapes (separately) and to indicate just what they were feeling at each moment. An analysis of these measures suggested that distressed couples (relative to nondistressed) showed (1) greater negative affect, (2) greater negative affect reciprocity—if one partner began to experience unpleasant feelings, then the other partner would too shortly thereafter, and (3) greater physiological linkage—if one partner became aroused, then the other did too (Levenson & Gottman, 1983).

Some of these same couples were followed up three years later, and the *change* in their marital satisfaction over the three years was well predicted by the amount of arousal they had experienced at the initial testing (Levenson & Gottman, 1985; see also Gottman & Levenson, 1992; and also Halford, Hahlweg, & Dunne, 1990, for cross-cultural evidence). The conclusion these results point to is that distressed couples are anything but indifferent to each other. Rather, their relationships look like springs that are too tightly coiled. Each partner is hyper-responsive to what the other says, and negative affect especially reverberates through their interactions.*

ATTRIBUTIONS AND MARITAL DISCORD

Chapter 5 discussed the view that our perceptions of another person, while based in the end on his behavior, are dependent on whether we see that behavior as something the other person is *responsible* for, or something he cannot control. And further, our impression is dependent on whether we see the behavior as revealing something enduring about the person, or something transient—a mood, for example. Differences between distressed and nondistressed couples in this domain have also been found.

The pattern of results that emerges from this research is that nondistressed couples have a more benign, generous attributional pattern than do distressed couples. In several studies, partners were asked to make attributions for specific behavior on the part of their spouses. Blaming the partner for marital conflicts was typical of distressed couples (Madden & Janoff-Bulman, 1981). In another study, distressed couples were found to see their partners' *negative* behaviors as characteristic of them, while nondistressed couples saw their partners' *positive* behaviors as flowing from their partners' personalities (Ja-

*In Chapter 11 in the context of the discussion of the prisoner's dilemma game, we saw the unfortunate consequences for any stable relationship in which the two partners exchange Tit for Tat. The trouble is that Tit for Tat has trouble forgiving transgressions. Here, in a very different context, with very different measures, we see another manifestation of this difficulty.

cobson, McDonald, Follette, & Berley, 1985). In yet another study, distressed couples were inclined to make more generous attributions for their own behavior than for their partners', while nondistressed couples showed just the reverse pattern, making more generous attributions for their partners' than for their own (Fincham, Beach, & Baucom, 1987; see Bradbury & Fincham, 1990, for a review).

Spouses who make negative attributions for their partners' behaviors have been shown to engage in less effective problem solving with their spouses and to reciprocate negative behavior more than spouses who make more generous attributions (Bradbury & Fincham, 1992). And making negative attributions for a partner's behavior has been shown to predict changes in marital satisfaction one year later; so negative attributions don't simply reflect the current state of marital satisfaction of the couple (Fincham & Bradbury, 1993).

This research has not, however, as yet indicated whether the less generous attributions characteristic of distressed marriages are true or illusory. After all, if partners in a marriage *are* engaging in undesirable behavior, then it would be no surprise that the partners would make negative attributions, and that marital satisfaction would decline. On the other hand, it might be true that marital satisfaction declines because the partners begin to interpret each other's behavior in a more negative light, even though it has *in fact* become no more negative. If attributions become more negative even though there have been no real changes in behavior, then the tendency to make negative attributions is a real cause of marital distress, and the next (and so far unanswered) question is: Why do couples change the way they interpret their partners' behavior?

A glimmer of light has been shed on this issue by a study in which couples were probed to determine the attributions they spontaneously made in their daily lives. Distressed husbands in one study were shown to make *more* attributions for their wives' behavior than did husbands in happier marriages (Holtzworth-Munroe & Jacobson, 1985). Apparently, in happy marriages, couples worry less about why their partners do what they do; in unhappy marriages, there is simply a greater desire, and perhaps need, to analyze each other's behavior. Perhaps once we start looking for reasons for someone's behavior, we are likely to turn up negative ones.

Caryl Rusbult has called attention to what she calls "accommodation" in happy marriages. Accommodation refers to the tendency to withhold reciprocating when one's partner has done something potentially destructive to the relationship. It has to do with *not* getting even. The ability to accommodate has been shown to relate to the partners' ability to see things from each other's perspective, and the willingness to accommodate has been shown to relate to how committed to the relationship the partners are (Rusbult, Verette, Whitney, Slovik, & Lipkus, 1991). So perhaps one of the keys to a successful marriage is forbearance. Perhaps couples find themselves in the worst trouble when neither partner has the cognitive and characterological wherewithal to leave bad enough alone!

MARITAL DISTRESS: A REVIEW

The research we have reviewed here paints a consistent picture of the distressed marriage. Distressed marriages seem to spiral ever downward. Distressed couples exhibit more negative behavior toward one another; they un-

Both happy and unhappy couples engage in attempting to control each other's behavior, but people in unhappy marriages

- use aversive rather than positive control;

- are more reactive to what happens on a particular day;

- interpret each other's remarks in a more negative way;

- are more responsive physiologically to each other's emotional state;

- make more negative attributions about the causes of each other's behavior.

derstand each other's intentions less well (and less positively); their negative states become coupled, even physiologically; and they simply are less generous in interpreting each other's behavior. Couples willing to volunteer for research, at least, are not indifferent to each other; rather, they seem locked into relationships they cannot improve. Of course, this may be true *only* for couples willing to participate in research. There may be other couples for whom distress is more a matter of indifference to one another than of interlocking negativity.

DIVORCE

The final topic we will consider is divorce. Of course, marital dissatisfaction is a major cause of divorce, but it isn't true that all unhappy marriages end in divorce—some stay together for the sake of the children, or for religious or other reasons. In any event, we will begin by looking at certain demographic and societal factors that have been shown to relate to divorce. Then we will consider marital stability and instability from the perspective of the individual. Finally, we will ask about the institution of marriage itself.

Social Factors: Recent Trends in the Divorce Rate

Demographic and societal factors have produced a trend toward more divorces (Bloom, Asher, & White, 1978). Changes in society and in individuals' attitudes have been used to explain both the general trend and the particulars of who divorces and who doesn't.

The divorce rate has increased substantially over time. In 1867 (the first year for which we have such data), there were 0.3 divorces per 1,000 people in the United States; in 1979, the divorce rate rose to 5.3 per 1,000 people (see Figure 15.9 to get an idea of the even higher rate of divorce among young people, here women between the ages of twenty-five and twenty-nine). This is an absolutely huge increase. (What is not so commonly known is that the divorce rate *declined* slightly from 1979 to 1985, to 5.0; Glick & Lin, 1986.) Why the huge increase? Several factors have been suggested. One is increased

FIGURE 15.9

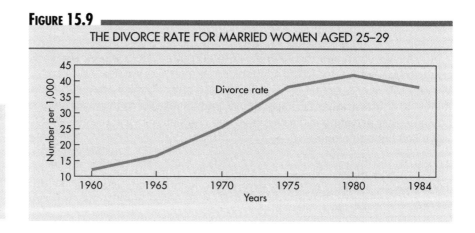

THE DIVORCE RATE FOR MARRIED WOMEN AGED 25–29

▶ *The divorce rate per 1,000 women aged twenty-five to twenty-nine from 1960 to 1984. The divorce rate rose sharply from 1960 to 1980, but then began to fall a bit. (Data from Glick & Lin, 1986)*

urbanization over that period; we have changed from a primarily rural, agrarian society to a primarily urban society. The place of women in society has also changed. Most married women now work outside the home (Atkinson & Huston, 1984), which provides women with a source of income independent of their husbands'. People are also living longer. It has been pointed out that marriages today last about as long as they did in the Middle Ages; the difference is that then they ended in death rather than divorce (Stone, 1977).

Attitudes toward divorce have also changed sharply, even over the more recent period of the last forty years. In the 1950s, Nelson Rockefeller was a popular governor of New York who kept running for, and failing to win, the Republican nomination for president. Speculation was that he could never be elected president because he was divorced; Ronald Reagan's divorce was certainly a nonissue in his campaigns. Most states have now "liberalized" their divorce laws, allowing for some form of "no-fault" divorce. Divorce has gotten remarkably easier over the years.

There are also features of a society as a whole that have been related to the rate of divorce. One study, for example, compared the divorce rate in sixty-six countries. Certain features of a society were predictive of how many marriages ended in divorce. For example, the gender ratio mattered: the more women relative to men in the society, the *higher* the divorce rate. The level of economic development of the society also mattered: the very poorest and very richest societies had the *highest* divorce rates; countries intermediate in economic development had lower rates—Ecuador and Thailand are examples of such intermediate nations. And finally, the degree to which women were part of the labor force mattered: as women entered the labor force, divorce first declined, but then increased. So countries, like the United States, with very high levels of women's participation in the labor force have very high levels of divorce (Trent & South, 1989). Changes in the divorce rate have been attributed to each of these factors; the degree to which each is important is difficult, if not impossible, to tell.

Individual Factors: Who Divorces?

The variables we have looked at so far are *social* variables that relate to the rate of divorce. We now turn to the *individual* variables that relate to the likelihood that a person will divorce. Demographers have shed further light on divorce by asking: Who divorces?

Race is an important predictor of divorce. Blacks divorce at a rate roughly one and one-half times the rate for whites (Glenn & Supanic, 1984). Why this is so is unclear.

Age at first marriage is also a well-documented predictor. Those married before age twenty have a substantially higher divorce rate than those who marry later. The divorce rate declines with age at first marriage until about twenty-six for men and twenty-three for women. Beyond that point, age does not seem to matter much. Exactly why age at marriage matters is not known, but there are at least two possibilities: young people are (on average) worse at *being* spouses than are older people, or young people are worse at *picking* spouses than are older people. The evidence at the moment seems to favor the former over the latter hypothesis (Booth & Edwards, 1985).

Jews divorce less than do Catholics, who divorce slightly less than do Protestants; those without religion divorce most often. Frequency of attendance at church services is also related to divorce; the more frequently one attends, the less likely one is to divorce. Religion, especially the more traditional (and conservative) Jewish and Catholic religions, both fosters a conservative way of life supportive of marriage and provides barriers against divorce.

A final variable that has been shown to relate to divorce is whether the partners finish whatever educational institution they have entered. In general, the more educated a couple are, the *less* likely they are to divorce, but this relationship breaks down for people who fail to complete a level of education. So though people with one, two, or three years of college education are more educated than those with no college education, they are *more* likely to divorce than those with no college experience. This phenomenon, called the "Glick" effect (after Paul Glick, the demographer who discovered it), has been interpreted as indicating that the same people who lack the persistence to finish an education program they have begun also lack the persistence needed to stay married.

These correlates of divorce have, for the most part, been found in data collected by the U.S. Census Bureau; as such, they have a special status—census data are surely the most extensive and accurate data that social scientists have to work with. But psychologists have also collected data—for more than fifty years—on sources of marital stability. Let us look now at the question of divorce from the viewpoint of the individual considering whether or not to divorce. We will try to understand the various demographic factors as they impinge on the lives of individuals deciding whether to stay married or divorce.

George Levinger reviewed the research literature on divorce in 1965. His discussion is in terms of what factors lead to marriages that stay together. Table 15.5 is reproduced from that article. As you can see, the table is organized in terms of categories derived from exchange theory. The first column lists variables that provide rewards for the partners of the marriage. The table tells us that there is evidence that marital stability increases with the degree of esteem the partners have for each other, the degree to which the partners provide companionship for one another, and the degree of sexual enjoyment the couples experience. Stability also increases with the husband's income, education, and occupational prestige. These are all associated with resources for the couple to provide itself with satisfactions of various sorts. Couples who own a home are more stable, perhaps because home owning is satisfying.

Last, the table indicates that similarity in religion, education, and age are predictive of stable marriages. (Though there is some recent evidence that similarity in age may *not* matter to stability; Vera, Berardo, & Berardo, 1985.) We saw earlier that people tend to choose to marry people who are similar to them, and apparently this is a good idea, since similarity also leads to stability. Levinger interprets these findings by suggesting that such similarities lead to greater ease of communication and, therefore, satisfaction.

The second column lists what Levinger calls **barrier strengths,** forces that oppose dissolution of the marriage rather than enhance the attractiveness of the marriage. These are the costs of breaking up. The last column lists potential sources of satisfaction outside of the marriage; the presence of these

TABLE 15.5

FACTORS DIFFERENTIATING STABLE FROM UNSTABLE MARRIAGES

Sources of Attraction	Sources of Barrier Strength	Sources of Alternate Attraction

Affectional rewards:
  Esteem for spouse
  Desire for companionship
  Sexual enjoyment
	Feelings of obligation:
	  To dependent children
	  To marital bond
		Affectional rewards:
		  Preferred alternate sex partner
		  Disjunctive social relations
		  Opposing religious affiliations

Socioeconomic rewards:
  Husband's income
  Home ownership
  Husband's education
  Husband's occupation
	Moral prescriptions:
	  Proscriptive religion
	  Joint church attendance
		Economic rewards:
		  Wife's opportunity for independent
		    income

Similarity in social status:
  Religion
  Education
  Age
	External pressures:
	  Primary group affiliations
	  Community stigma—rural-urban
	  Legal and economic bars	

SOURCE: Levinger, 1965.

factors leads to marital instability rather than stability. Two of these factors warrant comment.

The category **disjunctive social relations** has to do with whether the husband and wife share their outside relationships or have separate relationships, with the wife visiting her relatives and having her friends, and the husband visiting his relatives and his friends.

The last entry in the table is the wife's opportunity for independent income—her education, occupation, and so on. We have seen that the husbands' incomes lead to marital stability, but the evidence was that wives' incomes lead to marital *instability*, a result also found when we compare rates of divorce from one country to another. The idea here is that a wife's ability to be independent lessens the propensity for her to be forced to remain in a marriage, and thus lessens stability. And in the extreme, there is evidence that wives who are repeatedly physically abused by their husbands are more likely to leave the marriage if they are able to support themselves and their children than if they are not (Gelles, 1976; Strube & Barbour, 1983, 1984).

Recently, E. Lowell Kelly published a forty-five-year follow-up study of 278 couples who became engaged between 1935 and 1938. One can be fairly certain that the couples that were still together after forty-five years were not now going to divorce! This study found that the men in these couples who were more neurotic, less in control of their impulses, and who had had extensive premarital sexual contact, both with the woman they married and with other women, were less likely to have had stable marriages. The pattern for women was essentially the same; however, for women, the degree to which their families of origin were conflicted and tense also predicted the breakup of their marriages. Being unneurotic and conventional predicted marital stability for these men and women (Kelly & Conley, 1987).

The Kelly study represents a rare opportunity to look at the fate of couples followed for the whole of their married lives. But one must remember that these couples were made up of men and women born around 1915. One wonders if the same results would be found with marriages formed today.

And the same question arises with regard to the Levinger review of marital stability. It was, after all, written in 1965, describing research begun around 1930. One is forced to wonder whether this research describes marriages as they exist *now*, or whether it is really about marriage as it currently exists only in reruns of the *Donna Reed Show*—with a wife who stays home and bakes all day while the husband goes off to work (and makes all of the important decisions and functions as the disciplinarian not only of the two children but also of his wife, Donna). The last twenty-five years have been marked by dramatic changes in our conception of the place of women in the family and the world; the American marriage has surely changed because of this. Are these factors still related to marital stability? Probably they are. More recent reviews continue to implicate these same variables in relation to marital satisfaction and stability (Spanier & Lewis, 1980).

One recent study that followed 222 newlywed couples over a five-year period found that four sorts of variables differentiated the 64 couples that split up from the 158 couples that were still together. Two of them have been called distal, because they existed before the marriage. The first sort was demographic—age, income, and education. As has been found before, low incomes, for example, predicted dissolution. The second kind of predictor was the personalities of the partners; once again, neuroticism on the part of one or both partners was a risk factor for divorce.

The other types of variables were called proximal, because they were presumably the more immediate causes of the breakups, and they were the way that the distal factors manifested themselves. The variables focused on by exchange theory and its offspring (satisfaction, cost, investment, comparison level for alternatives, and so on) are one class of such proximal variables, and they were shown to predict stability. The final risk factor had to do with discrepancies between the two partners in their degree of dependence on the relationship. The larger the difference between the two partners, the less stable their relationships were. This recent study, then, suggests that the variables that social scientists have focused on for several decades are still predictive of marital success or failure (Kurdek, 1993).

Divorce and the Institution of Marriage

Does the high rate of divorce in American society, regardless of its cause, mean that marriage is less important to people than it used to be? Is marriage a dying institution? There is good reason to think that the statistics on divorce mean nothing of the sort. For one thing, most divorced people remarry. For example, for those people who were age sixty-five to seventy-four in 1980, 80 percent of those whose first marriages had ended in divorce remarried by 1980. More of them will remarry by the time they die (Glick & Lin, 1986).*

Marrying again after divorce is fair evidence of how important marriage is. In fact, it might be argued that the increase in the divorce rate is evidence

*For much of the period during which the divorce rate climbed, so did the remarriage rate. Of late, the remarriage rate has declined, however, especially among women (Glick & Lin, 1986).

that marriage is *increasingly* important to people, so important that they are willing to incur the costs of divorcing to free themselves from unhappy marriages.

In this chapter, we have repeatedly switched our focus back and forth between culture and the individual. Relationships—especially marriage and parenthood, but also friendship—are central elements of Western society. To a large measure, to understand Western culture is to understand the relationships it includes. But relationships must also be lived out by individuals. For families to endure and function, the psychology of individuals must articulate with the cultural demands on relationships. And as I have pointed out, with regard to these fundamental relationships, Western culture is in flux. Changes in culture place strains on our relationships. So perhaps it is appropriate to speculate here about some changes that seem to be happening, and the kinds of tensions they seem to be producing. That is where the irony lies.

One change I have noted in this chapter (and in others) is the increasing emphasis Western culture places on the individual. We live in a culture in which the individual and his satisfaction in life is of paramount importance. This must produce strains on relationships because all relationships involve the attempt to satisfy the needs and desires of more than one person, and it could hardly be expected that two people will always have their desires in perfect synchrony. A symptom of this tension is our divorce rate.

But having said this, I must now remind you of the other half of the paradox. Just as the divorce rate may be a measure of how important people feel individual satisfaction is, the remarriage rate is an indication of how important people feel marriage is. We have much less evidence about friendship, but I suspect that the demands on us to achieve individual satisfaction also cause strains on friendships, just as they do on marriages. (Demographers don't keep track of broken friendships the way they do of divorces, so we don't really know.) But at the same time, the very emphasis that social scientists place on understanding friendships suggests that friendship too is of increasing importance in Western culture.

The fix we find ourselves in seems to be that we increasingly value individual satisfaction—which strains relationships—but we also believe that strong and enduring relationships are essential to individual satisfaction. I wish I knew how all of this will work out. But I don't. All I can say is that there is no master plan somewhere that we can consult to learn how to solve this problem; all we can do is live our lives and our relationships. The overall solution, if there is one, will be found in the experiences of the individuals who make up a culture.

SUMMARY

1. Friendship consists in a willingness to make one's plans and projects dependent on the plans and projects of another person. It also involves an active concern for another person's well-being.

2. Self-disclosure is a key element of friendship. People's self-disclosures to one another have been shown to honor the norm of reciprocity. Further, women tend to like people who disclose intimate matters to them. Men seem to prefer people who are less extreme in their self-disclosures.

3. There may be two forms of loneliness: social loneliness, an absence of friends, and emotional loneliness, an absence of self-disclosure within one's friendships.

4. Romantic love is enhanced by any factor that increases physiological arousal. Why this is so is unclear; it might be because arousal simply increases *any* response tendency, or it might be because people can confuse arousal from another source with arousal from romance—in the right circumstance.

5. Exchange theory and equity theory have both been applied to the study of premarital relationship stability. They differ in their assumptions about what relationships work best. Exchange theory claims that people try to maximize their individual rewards in relationships; equity theory claims that people attempt to achieve equal (or equitable) rewards in relationships. The evidence suggests that both play a role. Rewarding equitable relationships last longer than less rewarding equitable ones. The degree of investment people have made in a relationship also predicts the relationship's stability.

6. Cohabitation in the United States has increased dramatically in the last twenty years. For many people, cohabitation isn't a substitute for marriage; it is a step along the way to marriage.

7. People tend to select as mates other people who are similar to them in social background, physical appearance, and, to a lesser degree, psychological traits. There is some slight evidence that people also select partners who have needs that are complementary to their own.

8. The notion that romantic love should be the foundation of marriage seems to have entered Western culture around the seventeenth century. Our notion of marriage continues to change away from the older conception that marriage was an essentially economic matter to a newer conception that the primary function of marriage is to provide companionship for the marital partners. Change in this direction has been accelerated by Western culture's recent reassessment of the role of women in the family and in the broader society.

9. Several researchers have asked about the sources of marital satisfaction at a behavioral or cognitive level. There is evidence that distressed couples rely more than nondistressed couples on aversive control rather than positive reinforcement. Distressed couples also seem to be more reactive to particular events; less able to take a longer view of their relationship. Other evidence indicates that distressed couples are less good at communicating with each other and are more physiologically responsive to each other. Finally, distressed couples are more inclined to blame each other for bad events and to withhold credit from each other for positive events than are happy couples.

10. Divorce can be thought of as a consequence of two kinds of factors: factors that reduce satisfaction in a marriage and factors that make it easier to leave a marriage. For example, the divorce rate seems to decline as the husband's income increases, but rise as a wife's income rises. This may be because although the wife's added income increases the quality of life, it also makes it easier for her to leave the marriage, since she is less likely to be dependent on her husband for social support.

PART FIVE
ATTITUDES

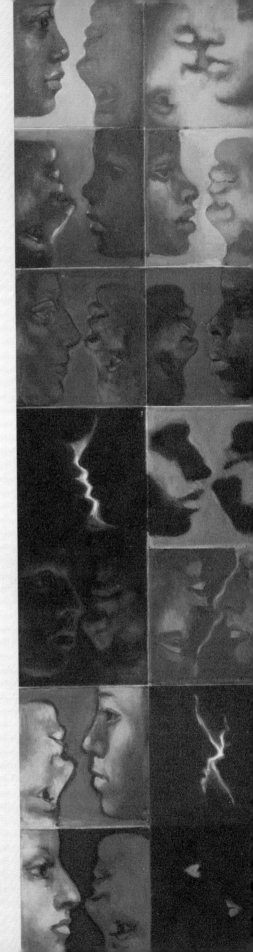

When a voter enters the booth, she is faced with a choice, a choice about what lever to pull. There are many determinants of which lever she will pull. The groups of which she is a part will matter. The emotions she might feel about one or another candidate matter. Her motives matter too; she might vote the ways she does because she thinks her vote will help promote a kind or just society. The enduring relationships she has will affect how she feels about politics, as they will affect how she feels about most things. All of these influences will act on our voter to produce her current attitudes toward the candidates. Attitudes, then, can be thought of as the representation of many of the social forces that have acted on a person to make her what she is. This part is devoted to the study of attitudes.

In Chapter 16, we consider where attitudes come from and how they are changed. As important as attitudes are in determining behavior, they are not the only determinants of behavior. In Chapter 17, we try to find a theoretical place for attitudes by asking how they relate to other sources of behavior. ∎

CHAPTER 16
Attitudes and Attitude Change

merican sports broadcasters love to set up cameras in bars in the hometowns of the two teams playing a big game, say the Super Bowl. The cameras lie in wait for a "big play." What the cameras catch is a cliché: pleased expressions, wild cheering, and rhythmic chants in one bar, and sullen silence in the other. I have borrowed this cliché to illustrate roughly the same point that impresses broadcasters: the same event can provoke quite different responses from different people. In everyday conversation, we might account for this difference by saying that the crowds in the two bars have different *attitudes* toward the big play—supporters of one team find it a great boon; the other team's fans see it as a disaster. It is because of these different attitudes that the people in the two bars react so differently. Attitudes are used to explain why people react to events, people, policies, the way they do. So what are attitudes?

WHAT ARE ATTITUDES?

Traditionally **attitudes** have been defined as involving beliefs, feelings, and dispositions to act. But recently theorists seem to be moving toward a conception of attitudes as evaluations that are related in complex ways to beliefs, feelings, and actions. This newer approach allows the question of the relation of attitudes to behavior, for example, to be an empirical rather than definitional issue (see Chapter 17). Thus, attitudes today are simply seen as evaluations of "objects" (Fazio, Sanbonmatsu, Powell, & Kardes, 1986; Pratkanis & Greenwald, 1989; Judd, Drake, Downing, & Kasnick, 1991; see also Tesser & Shaffer, 1990).

Objects include people, actions, events, cities, policies, foods—in short, anything that can be evaluated. Different objects are evaluated in different ways: you might think that a particular person would make a good president, but you probably don't think that cherries jubilee would make a good—or bad—president, and most of us wouldn't expect Bill Clinton to make a very tasty dessert. Nonetheless, it makes sense to talk about having positive or negative evaluations of all manner of objects, so long as we understand that a positive evaluation of something means an evaluation of it as a good example of whatever it is—to have a positive attitude toward Bill Clinton is to evaluate him as a president, not as a dessert.

The Psychological Functions of Attitudes

Attitudes can be thought of as having three distinct functions: (1) they help define social groups, (2) they help establish our identities, and (3) they guide our thinking and behavior (Schlenker, 1982; Pratkanis & Greenwald, 1989).

To illustrate the first function: what holds the cheering fans in the bar together as a convivial group is precisely their shared attitude toward their team and its fortunes. Of course, the group in the bar isn't a very important group; it is likely to exist only so long as the game lasts. But more important attitudes are implicated in more important groups. Their shared attitude toward abortion, for example, is all that holds a pro-choice (or pro-life) organization together. Indeed, there may be nothing that holds American culture together except for shared attitudes toward central values—political and personal liberty.

A second, closely related function of attitudes is self-definition. Just as a crucial element of some social groups is a set of attitudes, so too are attitudes central elements in people's conception of themselves. Who was Thomas Jefferson without his attitudes toward tyranny and justice? Who is Nelson Mandela without his attitudes toward apartheid?

Last, attitudes are important elements of people's individual, cognitive lives; they affect the way people think, feel, and act. It is just because our bar patrons have the attitudes they do that they direct their attention so intently to the television at key moments, think about the good and bad events that might transpire, cheer, pat each other on the back, and buy all manner of trinkets associated with their team.

To understand attitudes, and research about attitudes, one must have in mind two distinct points of view: attitudes as social entities and attitudes as individual, cognitive entities. Because attitudes are poised on the cusp of the individual and the social, because they link individual cognition to social participation, it is not at all surprising that for many social psychologists, understanding attitudes—how they are formed and how they function—is the central problem of social psychology.

Attitudes function to

- help define social groups;

- help individuals establish their identities;

- help guide our thinking and behavior.

◄ *Pro-choice and pro-life demonstrators meet. Their attitudes toward this political issue guide their behavior in demonstrating.*

Attitudes and Associationism

Social psychologists in the 1930s, who wanted to understand the formation or change of attitudes were drawn to animal learning theory as an inspiration. Indeed, in that period, learning theory was the most fertile source of explanation for all psychological phenomena. If the truth be told, "learning theory" is a bit of a misnomer since there were quite a number of learning theories. Still, these theories shared a common, central assumption: that learning (conceived broadly as the acquisition of a motor skill, knowledge, an attitude, and so on) is simply a matter of association. Specifically with regard to attitudes, learning theory held that if you have had positive experiences (reinforcement) associated with some person, place, or thing, you will have a positive attitude toward it, and conversely, to the degree that you have had negative experiences (punishment), you will have a negative attitude. **Associationism** implied that no matter how much you believe that, for example, your political attitudes are the result of reasoning, of examining the evidence, of considering things from other people's point of view, the fact is that they are really the result of associations between those attitudes and rewards.

The association between your attitudes and rewards might be somewhat indirect. Suppose your parents held very conservative views. If you received appropriate reinforcement from them, then you too would come to have conservative views; the rewards associated with your parents would come to be associated with their political views. The details of how the various learning theories explained all of this varied from one to another and were complex and sophisticated, but for our purposes, the present oversimplification will do. The point is that learning theories suggest that the formation of attitudes is a process devoid of reasoning, of cognition. (See Cacioppo, Marshall-Goodell, Tassinary, & Petty, 1992, for an example of research in this tradition.) Political attitudes, in particular, are therefore seen as essentially irrational.

Irving Lorge carried out a careful and direct experiment to illustrate the irrationality of attitudes. His method was quite elegant. Subjects read some statements about political issues, the most famous of which is "I hold it that a little rebellion, now and then, is a good thing, and as necessary in the political world as storms are in the physical." Each quote was attributed to some famous political figure; in this case, Thomas Jefferson. The subjects were asked to express their degree of agreement or disagreement with each statement. When they completed this task, they were then asked to say how much they respected a group of political figures, including those to whom the quotes had been attributed, and some to whom no quotes had been attributed.

At a second session, the subjects were shown the quotes again, and again asked to state their degree of agreement or disagreement. But there was one change: this time the attributions of the quotes were different; for example, the above quote was attributed not to Jefferson but to Lenin, the father of the Russian Revolution. Lorge found that the subjects' degree of agreement with the quotations was dependent on who they thought wrote them; the same quote attributed to Jefferson won significant assent but was soundly disagreed with when attributed to Lenin (Lorge, 1936). Moreover, the amount of change between the two exposures was related to the differences in prestige between the two alleged authors—a quote originally ascribed to a low-prestige figure gained acceptance if it was attributed to a high-prestige figure the second time around, and the degree to which it improved was roughly proportional to the difference in prestige of the two figures. (The above quote, by the way, is from Jefferson.)

To Lorge, this clearly showed the blind way in which we respond to political statements. After all, the subjects received literally the same stimulus on both occasions. If they were being rational, if they were responding to the content of the statement, then shouldn't they have given the same response no matter who they thought its author was? If an instructor marked the exact same test with two different grades, depending on whose paper he thought it was, we would surely suspect an irrational bias. The Lorge demonstration seems very compelling, and it makes sense of so much of what we see on television. Why do advertisers pay extraordinary sums to have athletes, movie stars, or stunning models hold up their product? Isn't it so that the positive feelings associated with these people will transfer to the product? But as compelling as the demonstration was, Solomon Asch wasn't persuaded.

ASCH'S REANALYSIS

In a brilliant rejoinder to Lorge's demonstration, Asch set out to show that the subjects weren't acting irrationally, by association. His rejoinder had two components: (1) he reanalyzed Lorge's original data, calling attention to some important details that hadn't been noticed, and (2) he carried out an experiment of his own using a slightly different procedure.

Asch's rejoinder rested on one important claim: although it looks as if the subjects were responding to the identical stimuli in the two cases, they

▲ *How much do celebrities such as Cher get paid to endorse a product?*

weren't. He argued that changing the author changed the stimulus. Subjects weren't responding just to the words on the paper but to what they took the author to *mean* by those words. And although the words stayed the same, the subjects understood them to mean quite different things depending on who said them. So in Asch's view, the ascription of author affected subjects' agreement, not by transferring prestige via association, but by giving the subjects new information about the quotes. The information about the author formed a context within which the subjects interpreted the literal words.

There are two questions we can ask of Asch's interpretation of Lorge's results. First, is it true? What evidence is there that subjects interpreted the statements differently depending on their authors? And second, if it is so, is it rational? *Should* subjects have interpreted the quotes differently depending on their author? We take these questions up in order.

One bit of evidence came from Lorge's own original data. If authorship affected interpretation, then those statements that were most ambiguous should be affected most by the change in authorship; statements that were clear should be affected less. After all, "August 11, 1982, was a Wednesday" means the same thing no matter who said it. So Asch divided the statements Lorge used into two groups: ambiguous and clear. Then he looked at how each group was affected by the change in authorship. He found that the interpretation of the statements that seemed ambiguous changed significantly more depending on the author than did those that were clearer. This lends some support to Asch's claim that the subjects' attitudes were affected by new information.

But Asch also provided much more direct support. He repeated Lorge's procedure with subjects of his own (college students) and asked them not only to state their degree of agreement or disagreement but also to write down what they thought the quotes meant. Asch found systematic differences in interpretation depending on the presumptive author. For example, when the quote about rebellion was attributed to Lenin, subjects took it to be advocating violent revolution, like the Russian Revolution. When the quote was attributed to Jefferson, subjects took it to mean changes in political party or political ideas. Since the subjects were probably comfortable with the idea of changing political party and uncomfortable with the idea of armed insurrection, we can see why their ratings changed depending on the author (Asch, 1948).

With this and additional evidence, Asch made a compelling case. He showed that Lorge's experiment doesn't really illustrate the operation of blind association. Instead, it reminds us of the general point Gestalt psychologists including Asch stressed: that our perceptions, emotions, and interpretations are to the total stimulus field (the Gestalt), not just to any single element of the picture.

What can we take away from the Lorge-Asch controversy? Lorge began with the assumption that attitudes, evaluations, are merely blind associations between attitude objects, the political statements, and good or bad feelings, feelings the subjects had toward their supposed authors. Watching television suggests that there is much to be said for this view; so many commercials seem to consist of nothing but ways to get us to associate some product—a brand of cola—with something or someone we already have some positive feeling toward, a rock star or an athlete. But Asch's position has the opposite premise, that some of our attitudes are richly cognitive—are connected with

> ■■■■■■■■■■■■■
> The fact that people change their attitudes toward some remark depending on who said it may be rational, since who said something often affects what something means.
> ■■■■■■■■■■■■■

important beliefs and our reasoning about those beliefs. No doubt neither point of view is correct about *all* attitudes; probably all of us have some attitudes of each sort.

One way to characterize subjects' responses to the stimuli they faced in the Lorge and Asch studies is that they tried to make sense of the quotations they read by interpreting them in a way that was consistent with whatever else they knew about the supposed authors of the quotes. Cognition and consistency are deeply tied. To think about something is to struggle with the problem of bringing all that one knows into alignment, to make it all consistent.

It would not be an exaggeration to say that no idea in social psychology has been more fruitful than the proposal that attitudes are linked, that one idea or *cognition* affects the way we respond to other ideas. This idea took its most influential form in the hands of Fritz Heider (1946).

Balance Theory

Heider argued that there is a psychological force that impels people to make their cognitions (beliefs) about a given object (or group of linked objects) balanced. That is, we are compelled to be consistent in our beliefs and ideas—if you like Jose, Jose likes Melissa, and you like Melissa, your attitudes are said to be balanced; you are exhibiting **cognitive consistency.** But if you don't like Jose but still like Melissa, then your attitudes are said to be unbalanced. Heider argued that in the unbalanced case, you will feel some pressure either to like Jose better or Melissa less. Unbalanced attitudes, like twisted coat hangers, Heider said, are unstable, difficult to maintain. One kind of evidence for this comes from the learning of balanced and unbalanced structures. For example, balanced structures are easier to learn than unbalanced structures. If I give you a list of people and a list of the relations among those people, you will find it easier to remember the lists if the relations are balanced (De Soto, 1960).

Heider's introduction of this notion stimulated several theorists to develop it further (Osgood & Tannenbaum, 1955; Rosenberg, 1960; Crockett, 1982; Abelson, 1983; Insko, 1984). The most influential development came at the extraordinarily talented hands of Leon Festinger (1957). His particular statement of the notion, along with the experiments he, his students, and his associates conducted, profoundly influenced a generation of social psychologists and stimulated thirty-eight years (to date) of experiments. We shall examine this idea in some detail.

 ## CLASSIC FINDINGS IN SOCIAL PSYCHOLOGY: THE ORIGINAL COGNITIVE DISSONANCE THEORY

Festinger's version of Heider's cognitive consistency notion, called **cognitive dissonance theory,** claimed that when people have in mind two or more psychologically inconsistent cognitions (beliefs), they experience a state of arousal that is unpleasant and that they will try to reduce by altering one or more of the cognitions. Let us reflect on this idea a moment, to see what was exciting about it.

To see cognitive dissonance theory in perspective, we must look at it in relation to the dominant notions of the time in psychology in general. One goes back at least to the British empiricist philosopher David Hume. He argued that reason was always the slave of passion; that is, that thinking always occurs under the press of desire, or, in the language of the learning theory of the 1950s, in the train of some drive. This idea is simple enough—if a rat is hungry, its cognitions relevant to food are activated; if it is thirsty, its water-relevant notions come to the fore. But Festinger turned the idea around; he argued that relations between ideas—specifically their psychological inconsistency—give rise themselves to drive. Thus, reason isn't always the slave of the passions; at times, reason can give rise to its own passions.

Second, Festinger's claim gave greater substance to Heider's balance notion. It specified just what the force toward balance was: an unpleasant state of arousal. The notion of a force, after all, is a *metaphor* drawn from the language of physics; unpleasant arousal is a *description* in the language of psychology.

A third important feature of Festinger's theory is that it seems to say that we try to be rational. After all, one test of the rationality of a set of beliefs is their internal consistency. If you believe that the town of Harrison is in Missouri and that your aunt lives in Harrison but she lives in Texas, something is wrong with your system of beliefs. They are inconsistent; they can't all be true. Further, we know this even though we don't know where your aunt lives or where Harrison is; we know the system is defective without knowing anything about the empirical world, and this implies that your thoughts are not just wrong but irrational. Festinger's theory seems to claim that when people recognize their irrationality, they are uncomfortable and try to bring their thoughts back into rational alignment.

Curiously, what really attracted attention about cognitive dissonance theory was not that it took account of the fact that humans try to be rational, but that the experiments it provoked were almost always designed to show how irrational we are. We turn now to a few of the most important experiments carried out under the cognitive dissonance banner. Part of the charm of the theory, and one of its great defects as originally stated, is in how widely and cleverly it can be applied; to appreciate the theory and understand why a generation of researchers flocked to it, we have to see how it was applied in concrete experiments.

EFFECTS OF INITIATIONS

Elliot Aronson and Judson Mills carried out an experiment on the effects of initiation. On the face of it, the experiment seems to have nothing to do with cognitive dissonance, but Aronson and Mills were able to interpret the theory to explain the results. Rather than tell you at the beginning how to look at the experiment in dissonance terms, let me describe the experiment, and then we'll see how dissonance theory relates to it.

The experiment involved three treatments: severe initiation, mild initiation, and a control condition with no initiation. In all cases, female under-

Cognitive dissonance theory:

• Psychologically inconsistent ideas in mind

cause

• an aversive drive state, which

causes

• distortion of beliefs to reduce psychological inconsistency and drive.

graduates volunteered for the experiment under the ruse that it involved joining a discussion group on sex. When they arrived, the experimenter (a male) told them that some people are just not able to discuss this topic freely, so he had developed a screening test to see which people would be able to participate. The screening test involved reading some standardized material to him. Subjects who became too upset at this would not be allowed to enter the discussion group. What happened next depended on which treatment the subject received.

In the control condition, the subject was asked simply to read a list of not very embarrassing words, which of course she did without problem, so she was told that she passed. In the mild condition, however, the words were mildly embarrassing—*prostitute, petting, virgin,* for example. (This was the 1950s, when television censors would not allow programs on the air if they used the words *virgin* or *pregnant,* among others!) All of these subjects also passed. The subjects in the severe condition were also given a list of twelve words, but these included the most obscene words you can think of. In addition, they had to read some very explicit material describing sexual intercourse. All of the subjects in this condition too were told they passed the screening test. The point was to make the subjects differ in the degree to which they had to suffer to get into the sex discussion group, in something like the way fraternities make pledges suffer.

Once a subject passed this "hurdle," she was told that she could join the discussion group. The experimenter said, however, that the group had been formed the week before, and at that time the members had been given a reading assignment. Since the subject hadn't done the assignment, she couldn't participate this week; she would join them next week. But since she was there, she could at least listen in on this week's discussion. The subject was led off to a cubicle with a set of earphones, which she was told hooked up to a mike in the room where the discussion was going on. Actually it was hooked up to a tape recording of a discussion the experimenters had carefully scripted.

The subjects then heard a discussion that Aronson and Mills described this way: "The participants spoke dryly and haltingly on secondary sex behavior in the lower animals, inadvertently contradicted themselves and one another, mumbled several non sequiturs, started sentences that they never finished, hemmed, hawed, and in general conducted one of the most worthless and uninteresting discussions imaginable" (Aronson & Mills, 1959, p. 79). After listening to this conversation, the subjects rated the discussion and the participants on several scales indicating how worthwhile they thought the discussion was. The results showed that the group that had gotten the severe initiation reported the discussion to be significantly better than did those exposed to no or mild initiations (see Figure 16.1). Fraternities are wise, after all, in subjecting pledges to humiliation; it makes members think the fraternities are more desirable once they get in. But what does this have to do with cognitive dissonance theory?

COGNITIONS INVOLVED IN DISSONANCE

Aronson and Mills reasoned this way. Let's focus on the harsh initiation group and consider the cognitions (beliefs) these subjects had at the end of the experiment. One was "This discussion was really worthless." Another was "I

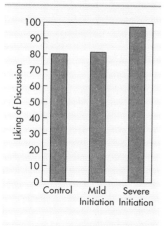

FIGURE 16.1

COGNITIVE DISSONANCE AND THE EFFECTS OF INITIATIONS

▲ *Ratings of the quality of the discussion in the Aronson and Mills experiment as a function of the severity of initiation. (Data from Aronson & Mills, 1959)*

went through a very embarrassing initiation in order to get into it." Aronson and Mills claimed that these beliefs were psychologically inconsistent. This inconsistency gave rise to a state of discomfort. To relieve the discomfort, the subjects had to alter one of the cognitions. Although the theory doesn't specify which of the cognitions the subjects would alter, apparently the subjects changed their belief about how worthwhile the discussion was.

But, Aronson and Mills argued, the belief that the discussion was worthless is *not* psychologically inconsistent with the belief that the initiation was innocuous, so the control group had no dissonance and therefore no need to distort. Thus, the harsh initiation subjects altered their belief that the discussion was worthless, while the control group didn't. (The results for the mild initiation group were intermediate between the control and harsh groups.)

PROBLEMS WITH A DISSONANCE ACCOUNT

The experiment seems clear enough, but the explanation is a bit unsatisfying. Part of the problem is the notion of "psychologically inconsistent." There is surely nothing *logically inconsistent* about believing that you went through a harsh initiation to get into a worthless group; that just makes you a fool. But Aronson and Mills assure us that these two beliefs are psychologically inconsistent. One wants to know what precisely that means and how to tell whether two beliefs are psychologically inconsistent. By the end of the 1960s, the clamor to define psychological inconsistency had become quite loud, and we now know better what it means. But to tell you that now would be to get ahead of the story.

There is another problem with the explanation. Even if we accept that the subjects in the harsh initiation condition did experience dissonance and did want to alter one of their cognitions, why did they alter their belief about the worthwhileness of the discussion group? Why didn't they decide the initiation wasn't so bad after all? The first major critique of dissonance theory raised these objections and suggested a variety of other interpretations of the Aronson and Mills experiment (Chapanis & Chapanis, 1964). It suggested, just to mention one plausible alternative interpretation, that the harsh initiation group liked the discussion better not because of dissonance, but because after going through the initiation, they were expecting the discussion to be terribly embarrassing too. They were so relieved to find that they would not have to discuss the intimate details of their sexual experiences in the graphic language used in the initiation that they found the discussion just fine.

But other research has taken care of this alternative explanation, and a half dozen or so others (Gerard & Mathewson, 1966). In one such follow-up experiment, the subjects' initiation was a physically painful experience (electric shock). These subjects too showed the dissonance effect, although they had no more reason to expect the discussion to be embarrassing than did the other groups. One of the surprising things about dissonance theory is that the experiments done in its spirit always seem to have a bundle of alternative explanations, or methodological deficiencies, yet the theory survives them all.

So the particular problems with the Aronson and Mills experiment didn't seriously damage it. The general problems of defining psychological inconsistency and deciding which cognition will change lingered on. But before we get back to those, we turn to another dissonance experiment.

Cognitions involved in the Aronson and Mills experiment:

1. That discussion was very boring.

2. I went through a very embarrassing initiation to get into it.

⇒Psychological inconsistency

⇒Distortion of #1

But

1. That discussion was very boring.

2. I went through a mildly embarrassing initiation to get into it.

⇒No psychological inconsistency

⇒No distortion

This experiment, also by Elliot Aronson, this time with Merrill Carlsmith (Aronson & Carlsmith, 1963), is important not only because it illustrates dissonance theory but for another, deeper reason. Perhaps the most important question about the development of children is: How do children become moral actors? How do they internalize, come to see as their own, the standards of the society in which they are raised? All sorts of standards that we as adults recognize, ranging from rules of courtesy to deep moral commands like not harming another, are originally impositions from outside. How do we come not only to follow them, or feel guilty when we don't, but to see them no longer as impositions placed on us by someone else? Learning theory had an answer to this.

The argument was that the essential element in the internalization of norms is punishment. Children are punished for doing wrong, and this punishment has two results: (1) it makes the child less likely to do wrong again, and (2) cues associated with the punishment situation come (perhaps via classical conditioning) to give rise to an unpleasant emotional state independent of the punishment; this unpleasant state we call guilt. To be concrete, Jimmy reaches into a cookie jar; his mother punishes him. The next time Jimmy is near the cookies, he doesn't reach. But if he even thinks about reaching, he will begin to feel the way he felt when he was punished. This feeling he will learn to call guilt. As we shall see, the Aronson and Carlsmith experiment contradicted this story, or at least provided an important revision of it. As before, let us consider the experiment and then how dissonance theory interprets it.

Experimental Procedures   The Aronson and Carlsmith experiment used twenty-two four-year-old children. An experimenter met with them at a nursery school and showed them five toys they could play with. The experimenter asked them to compare the toys two at a time. In this way, the experimenter was able to tell which toy was each child's second favorite. Then he said that he would have to leave for a while, but he would be right back. He told them that while he was gone, they could play with any of the toys except X, where X was whatever their second favorite was. Now, half of the subjects (all were run one at a time) were told that if they played with X, the experimenter would be annoyed. The other half were told that he would become very angry. "I would have to take all of my toys and go home and never come back again. . . . If you played with X, I would think you were a baby." So half of the subjects were mildly threatened for playing with the toys, and half were more severely threatened.

Then the experimenter left the room for ten minutes, and the subject was surreptitiously observed while the experimenter was gone. None of the children played with the forbidden toy. When the experimenter returned, he again asked the children to rate the five toys, and found that for the children he had severely threatened, there was no decrease in their liking for the forbidden toy. But the children only mildly threatened now liked it *less* than they did before (see Figure 16.2A and B). The implication of this for the internalization of morality is that severe punishment may indeed keep children from doing what you don't want them to, but they will still be tempted to do it. Mild punishment, ideally just enough to keep them from doing it, on

FIGURE 16.2

DISSONANCE AND INTERNALIZATION OF NORMS

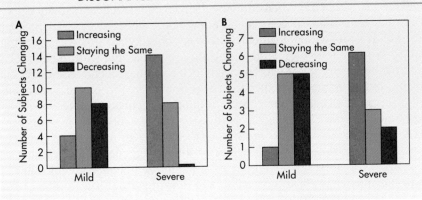

(A) Number of subjects increasing, decreasing, or leaving unchanged their immediate preference for their second favorite toy as a function of the severity of threat causing them not to play with it. (B) Number of subjects increasing, decreasing, or leaving unchanged their preference for their second favorite toy forty-five days after not playing with it. (Data from Aronson & Carlsmith, 1963)

the other hand, will also dissipate the temptation to transgress. Since in socializing a child we not only want her to give up doing the things we don't want her to do but we also want her to give up wanting to do them, counterintuitively, mild threat is superior to severe threat. But what does all of this have to do with dissonance theory?

Cognitions Involved in Dissonance   Aronson and Carlsmith turn to the cognitions the children have after they have resisted playing with the toys. Both groups believe "That was my almost favorite." Both groups believe "I didn't play with it." The severe group also believes "If I had played with it, the experimenter would have been very angry with me and picked up his toys and gone home." Aronson and Mills claim that this set of cognitions is psychologically consistent; the cognitions make sense. The mild group shares the first two beliefs, but not the third. Those in the mild group believe instead "Had I played with it, the experimenter would have been annoyed." Aronson and Carlsmith claim that this set is psychologically inconsistent; it makes no sense. Thus, the severe threat group had no need to alter cognitions, while the mild threat group did.*

Cognitive dissonance says, then, that if you can get someone to resist temptation with just a little threat, dissonance will insure that they will delude themselves into believing that they weren't really tempted in the first place. But if you browbeat them into submission, there will be no dissonance, no delusion. We have some of the same problems with this experiment that we had with the previous one. Why did this cognition change, why not one of the others, and why are those cognitions psychologically inconsistent? But before we address these points we take up our last and the most famous of the dissonance experiments.

FORCED COMPLIANCE AND DISSONANCE

Subjects in an experiment by Leon Festinger and Merrill Carlsmith (Festinger & Carlsmith, 1959) (students at Stanford who were required to take part in

*There is some evidence that this result may vary from social class to social class and culture to culture; the reason for this is not yet clear (Clemencé, 1990).

research) signed up for a two-hour experiment on "measures of perfor-mance." When they arrived at the lab, the experimenter put them to work loading spools on a tray, then dumping them off and then loading them again. They did this thrilling task for about a half hour, while the experimenter sat there with a stopwatch, grunted, and took notes. When this was over, the subject was given a board with forty-eight pegs on it, and was asked to turn each a quarter turn to the left. This went on for another half hour. For subjects in the control group, the experiment was now over. But on their way out, the experimenter asked them to go to another room to be interviewed by someone from the Psychology Department who was collecting data on sub-jects' evaluations of experiments. In the other room, the interviewer (actually part of the experiment, but who didn't know which condition each subject was in) asked questions about the experiment, including how enjoyable it was, how much they learned from it, and how important it was.

Aside from this control group, there were two other groups, whose ex-perience was a little different. After they finished turning the pegs, the exper-imenter had a little chat with them. He told them that the experiment was about how performance at tasks of the sort they had just completed varies as a function of what subjects expect the task to be like. He told them that although they had been given no expectation before the experiment, other subjects would be told in advance that the task was really interesting or really dull. The point, he said, was to see how people with different expectations do in their performance. (None of this was true.) Then he went on to explain in a fumbling, embarrassed manner that to create the impression that the ex-periment is interesting, the experimenters use a research assistant who poses as a subject. This research assistant tells the real subject that he just finished the experiment and that it was fun, intriguing, and so on. But, the experi-menter continued, we have this problem. You see, the next subject is waiting outside right now, and the research assistant hasn't shown up. So we were thinking that maybe we could pay you to go out and tell her that it's really interesting. Then, once we've trained you, you could be on call, and if this ever happened again, we could call on you.

So the experimenter brought the subject into the experiment, and induced him to lie to the next subject (actually a confederate). Subjects in one group were paid $1, and those in another $20, for telling the "next subject" the lie that the experiment was interesting. Then the experimenter rehearsed the subject in the spiel he was to give the next subject. Once he was up to snuff, the experimenter took him out and released him on the confederate, and most subjects indeed delivered their spiel about how interesting the experiment was. When they finished, they too were interviewed by someone from the Psychology Department about the experiment; they too were asked how in-teresting they found the experiment to be (and, by the way, they were induced to give back the money they got).

In summary, there were three groups: a control group, a group paid $1 to tell the next subject the experiment was interesting, and a group paid $20 to do the same. One more detail before we get to the results. The experiment used seventy-one subjects, but eleven had to be discarded. Some refused to take the bribe, or took the money and then told the other subject the truth; others were just suspicious of the experiment.

EXPERIMENTAL RESULTS

The important result had to do with how interesting the subjects said the experiment was to the "interviewer from the Psychology Department." In particular, Festinger and Carlsmith were interested in how being paid $1 versus $20 to say this really tedious experiment was interesting would affect their perceptions of how interesting it was. Learning theory might predict that the more the subjects were paid, the more interesting they would think the experiment was. But Festinger predicted, and found, just the reverse. The $20 group reported the experiment to be slightly less interesting than did the control group. But the $1 group found it to be significantly *more* interesting (see Figure 16.3). Those paid less, not more, to lie came to believe their lie. How does dissonance theory explain this result?

Festinger and Carlsmith said that at the end of the experiment (focus just on the $1 and $20 groups), both groups had the cognitions "The experiment is really boring; and I told someone else it was fun and intriguing." And both had one more relevant cognition: "I was paid X dollars to say it was interesting." Festinger and Carlsmith claim that for the group paid $20, these cognitions weren't psychologically inconsistent. True, the subjects knew they lied, but they also knew they lied for $20, a considerable amount of money in 1958. Apparently, the subjects knew they had a price, and it was no more than $20. But the $1 group believed they lied for $1, and that was just too hard for them to swallow; it was psychologically inconsistent, gave rise to dissonance, and led them to alter their belief about how interesting the experiment was—so they wouldn't see themselves as $1 liars. Again dissonance theory was able to predict a counterintuitive result.

But there is another plausible interpretation of the results. Perhaps, for some reason or other, the $1 group did a better job of telling the confederate it was interesting. Indeed, perhaps they did such a good job that they convinced themselves. But Festinger and Carlsmith ruled this out by having judges, blind to the amount of money the subjects had been paid, rate the subjects' performance at convincing the confederate. If anything, $20 was better, although the difference was quite small. So again the dissonance interpretation survives.

DEFINING PSYCHOLOGICAL INCONSISTENCY

We have looked at a small sample of the hundreds of experiments that were carried out under the aegis of cognitive dissonance theory. The success of the theory was in stimulating research, in producing findings that were surprising, that conflicted with our intuitions about what people would believe and do. But by 1969, little had been done to solve the two difficult problems at the heart of the theory: specifying just what psychologically inconsistent meant and specifying which cognitions would undergo distortion. Both of these problems have since been addressed, but addressing them fundamentally altered cognitive dissonance theory.

Perhaps a solution to the problem of defining psychological inconsistency has occurred to you. The solution seems straightforward. Look, you might say, there is this phenomenon that involves distortions in belief. This phenomenon is real enough; it shows up in all sorts of places. So why don't we just let the data decide whether two cognitions are inconsistent? We'll simply

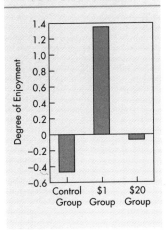

FIGURE 16.3

FORCED COMPLIANCE AND DISSONANCE

▲ *Degree of enjoyment of the experimental task as a function of how much the subject was paid to tell the "next subject" it was fun. (Data from Festinger & Carlsmith, 1959)*

Cognitions involved in the Festinger and Carlsmith experiment:

1. That experiment was very boring.

2. I told the next subject it was great fun.

3. I was paid $1 to tell her that.

⇒Psychological inconsistency

⇒Distortion of #1

But

1. That experiment was very boring.

2. I told the next subject it was great fun.

3. I was paid $20 to tell her that.

⇒No psychological inconsistency

⇒No distortion

say that two cognitions are psychologically inconsistent whenever holding both of them in mind leads to distortion. Thus, the issue of psychological inconsistency becomes an empirical matter, to be decided by the evidence. Something like this solution was taken. But this is a very dangerous course.

It is dangerous because it takes cognitive dissonance theory out of the realm of testable theories. If there is an independent way to specify psychological inconsistency, then we can test the claim that it gives rise to distortion by giving people cognitions that meet the specifications and then seeing whether the distortions arise. If they don't, then the theory is wrong. But if we turn the whole matter around and say that cognitions are inconsistent only if they give rise to distortions, then there is no way for the theory to be shown wrong, to be falsified.

A theory of this sort is called circular or tautological. And being tautological is a dangerous flaw in a scientific theory. But, oddly enough, as long as one is aware of the danger, tautological theories can be productive; indeed, some philosophers of science have pointed out that much of classical physics, surely a productive science, had that oddly circular quality. The important point, though, is that once the data have decided what psychological inconsistency is, the theory may look very different than it started out to look. And this is just what happened.

Elliot Aronson made a fruitful suggestion about how to define psychological inconsistency; he suggested on the basis of the data that it was most clearly present when some important aspect of the person's self was involved in one of the cognitions (Aronson, 1969). In other words, people become aroused, uncomfortable, and prone to distort when they have in mind cognitions that are unflattering about their selves, their character, their nature. In specific, Aronson suggested that people distort when they see themselves as acting stupidly or immorally (Aronson, Chase, Helmreich, & Ruhnke, 1981).

This fits the data I have presented so far. In the Aronson and Carlsmith and Aronson and Mills experiments, the dissonance-experiencing subjects may have seen themselves as fools for giving up the chance to play with a toy they liked so much in the one case, and for going through such a difficult initiation to get into a worthless discussion group in the other. In the Festinger and Carlsmith experiment, subjects may well have felt guilty about lying to someone about the experiment. But how can we test this notion that psychological inconsistency is really a matter of having unflattering ideas about oneself?

To do so, we have to specify the conditions under which doing something reflects on a person's self or character. Erving Goffman, following and expanding upon the philosophical analysis of John Austin, articulated some of the conditions under which a person's self is tainted by her behavior (Austin, 1970; Goffman, 1971). Goffman begins by considering the ways that a person can get out of the negative implications for self of an act she shouldn't have performed. One way is to offer an ***excuse.*** According to Goffman, an excuse is a claim that she "couldn't have done otherwise." For example, if you claim you couldn't come to class because you were in a coma at the time, you are offering an excuse. Another way of avoiding the negative implications of your act would be by offering a ***justification.*** A justification concedes that you were indeed in control of your action, but claims that in light of the circumstances, what you did was the right thing to do. Saying you couldn't make class because you were taking your brother to the hospital is a justification. Our negative acts reflect badly on us insofar as we lack excuses or justifications.

A third aspect of our action, one that also bears on our moral worth, is the magnitude of the wrong we have done. It is one thing to be guilty of snubbing someone; it's quite another to be guilty of killing him. So we now have three features of acts relating to their implications for our selves: (1) the degree to which we had control of them (had a choice about them), (2) the degree to which our actions were justified, and (3) the magnitude of the consequences of our acts.

UNDERSTANDING PSYCHOLOGICAL INCONSISTENCY

If what produces the distortions in the cognitive dissonance studies is the fact that some cognitions have negative implications for our selves, then the distortions should be related to the same factors that affect responsibility (Collins & Hoyt, 1972). In the late 1960s and 1970s, research on cognitive dissonance showed that these factors do indeed affect the dissonance phenomenon.

Dissonance and Choice

One experiment highlighted the role of choice in dissonance arousal. At the time, a North Carolina law was being discussed that forbade Communists and anyone who had ever taken the Fifth Amendment from speaking on college campuses. Since such a law is in clear violation of commonly accepted standards of freedom of speech, as well as of intellectual freedom, it was quite unpopular on North Carolinian campuses. Experimenters attempted, successfully, to get students to write essays in favor of the law, and offered to pay them either $.50 or $2.50 for their essays. (It is remarkably simple to get students to write essays that diverge from their own opinions. The typical technique is to tell them that you are, say, writing a report on the issue, and that you need opinions pro and con, and that you have found that the best way to get such opinions is to ask people to write pro and con essays. Then you tell them that you have enough con essays, but that you still need some pro essays, so would they mind writing one?)

In some conditions, the experimenters stressed the subjects' freedom to refuse to write the essay; in other cases, the experimenters didn't stress this. The experimenters predicted and found the dissonance effect, that is, when the subjects' free choice was stressed, the group paid $.50 changed their attitude, became more favorable toward the law, but the group paid $2.50 didn't. In the condition that did not stress free choice, neither group changed its view (Linder, Cooper, & Jones, 1967).

These results suggest that insofar as the subjects' freedom to participate or not is salient, they will suffer the dissonance effect, but if that freedom is not salient, they won't. (Needless to say, the subjects in all conditions were in fact free to write or not write the essay, but the subjects in the high-choice condition had that pointed out to them.) This experiment illustrates the effect of free choice, the first of the conditions underlying moral judgments, on the dissonance effect.

MAGNITUDE OF HARM DOING AND DISSONANCE

Other experiments have addressed the issue of the amount of harm done as a determinant of the dissonance effect. In another study, subjects were induced to write essays favoring the legalization of marijuana (which the subjects opposed). Some subjects were told that the essays would be shown to groups that were already committed (either in favor or against legalization); other subjects were told that the essays would be shown to groups that had not yet made up their mind. Subjects were offered either a large or small payment for their essay. The experimenters predicted a dissonance effect for the subjects who thought an uncommitted group would see the essay, but no such effect if they thought that an already committed group would. And this is just what they found—the group offered little reward and whose essays were to be seen by the uncommitted groups changed their attitudes toward legalization; the others didn't (see Figure 16.4).

The interpretation is that when the subjects thought they were writing to a committed group, they didn't expect their essay to have any effect anyway, so they experienced no dissonance, but when they wrote for an uncommitted group, they expected their essay to cause harm. So the magnitude of the harm actually done affects the action of dissonance (Nel, Helmreich, & Aronson, 1969). Indeed, in a recent experiment, subjects were led to believe that an essay they wrote that was in line with their real beliefs would cause someone harm; they subsequently changed their attitudes too (Scher & Cooper, 1989).

Other researchers have extended the analysis of the role of harm doing in dissonance arousal. To understand it, we have to consider more closely the role of the magnitude of the harm done in our moral judgments. At first glance, it seems that in everyday thinking, people are only responsible for the harm they do that *they know will follow from their actions;* after all, if I plug in my electric coffeepot and thereby cause a power failure in the neighborhood, and because of that someone's refrigerator stops and their food spoils, I am not responsible. I couldn't foresee that my act would result in that damage.

But, on the other hand, consider this: my university library once had a fine system for overdue books that worked this way. If you had a book overdue, the fine was a dime per day (this was several years ago). But if someone wanted that book, the fine jumped to a quarter a day. Now you might say the system was unfair. After all, a person keeping the book out doesn't know whether someone else will want it or not; he can't foresee the harm he is doing. But let's look more closely. We generally hold people responsible not just for the harm they foresee, but for the harm that is *foreseeable,* that is, for the harm that they should know *might* happen as a result of their acts. The damage I did to someone's food by plugging in my coffeepot was not only unforeseen, but *unforeseeable.*

So we can divide the consequences of our actions into three categories: the consequences we foresee, the consequences that are foreseeable but not foreseen, and those that are unforeseeable. In one experiment, subjects were induced to write a counterattitudinal essay. Some of the subjects were led to believe that their essay *could not* do any harm; others were given information

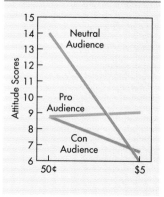

FIGURE 16.4

DISSONANCE AND THE AUDIENCE FOR A LIE

▲ *Attitude change in the direction of an unpopular view as a function of the amount paid to lie and the audience for the lie. (From Nel, Helmreich, & Aronson, 1969)*

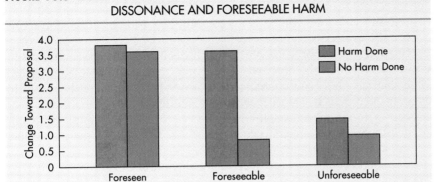

FIGURE 16.5

DISSONANCE AND FORESEEABLE HARM

◀ *Attitude change toward an unpopular position as a function of knowledge of the harm done. (Data from Goethals, Cooper, & Naficy, 1979)*

that implied that their essay *might* cause harm; and a third group was told that their essay *would* do harm. Thus, harm was unforeseeable by the first group, foreseeable by the second, and foreseen by the third. After they had written their essays, all of the subjects were told that their essay (in favor of increasing the size of the incoming class) would do harm because it would be shown to the university admissions committee. The investigators proposed that the dissonance effect would occur both for foreseen and foreseeable but not for unforeseeable consequences, and that is just what they found (see Figure 16.5; Goethals, Cooper, & Naficy, 1979).

Dissonance and Self-Worth

Dissonance research has found that the dissonance effect follows principles we identify with moral reasoning: people distort their perceptions or attitudes in just those circumstances where we would hold them responsible for their acts. But morality isn't the whole story of dissonance, for several reasons. First, recall that the dissonance effect occurs, typically, only in the small reward conditions of the experiments discussed above. When subjects were paid more, they apparently didn't succumb to dissonance (or didn't succumb as much). Second, in the Aronson and Mills and Aronson and Carlsmith experiments, subjects showed dissonance after doing something that they might think was foolish, but what they did was certainly not immoral. These findings focus our attention on something a bit broader than morality: ***self-worth.*** Perhaps subjects respond with distortion whenever their behavior seems to have negative implications for their sense of self-worth, whether for moral or other reasons.

Now harming another person is hard on one's self-worth, so a self-worth account can easily accommodate the findings that harm doing leads to dissonance. But being foolish or stupid also is an affront to one's worth, so a self-worth account can accommodate those findings too. To make the self-worth account work, though, one has to believe that in the studies we have reviewed, subjects who lied for $.50 suffered a greater threat to their sense of self-worth than did those who lied for $2.50! I find that a bit hard to believe. On the other hand, I find it hard to believe that subjects differentiate at all between the $2.50 and $.50 conditions, but there is lots of evidence that they distort in the $.50 case but not in the $2.50 case. Since they do distinguish them, I am willing to accept that they distinguish them in terms of their self-worth.

The notion that our sense of self-worth lies behind the dissonance result is also consistent with some recent research. In a study by Claude Stelee, some subjects were given a chance to affirm values that were important to them in the time between their writing a counterattitudinal essay and their answering an attitude questionnaire; other subjects did not get to affirm values. The subjects who got to affirm values (to **self-affirm**) did *not* display dissonance; those who were not able to affirm values did show the dissonance effect. Somehow affirming a worthy self made it less important to deny that one had lied (Steele & Liu, 1983; see also Sherman & Gorkin, 1980; Steele & Liu, 1981; Lydon & Zanna, 1990).

In some recent research by Elliot Aronson, people were *not* induced to harm other peple, but they were induced to seem like hypocrites. In one experiment, for example, some subjects were induced to urge other people to take shorter showers—the research was carried out at a swimming pool in California during the recent drought. (Other subjects were not induced in this way.) They were then reminded that they themselves sometimes wasted water while showering (others were not reminded). The question was: How long would the subjects themselves shower? The answer was that subjects who were made to feel like hypocrites—those who had chided others about long showers *and* who had been reminded of their own long, wasteful, languorous showers—took shorter showers than did those who had not been made to feel like hypocrites (Dickerson, Thibodeau, Aronson, & Miller, 1992; see also Thibodeau & Aronson, 1992, for a review, and Aronson, 1992, for a general discussion). Feeling like a hypocrite, even though it didn't harm anyone, was enough to trigger dissonance. Apparently, shorter showers could be expected to cleanse the self as well as the body.

Dissonance Theory Reconsidered

Empirical research has, then, answered the question: When are two cognitions dissonant? But, as I warned, the answer dramatically changes the nature of dissonance theory.

Dissonance theory started out by claiming that formal properties of cognitions, that is, whether they are consistent or not, can give rise to motivation *independent of the content of those cognitions.* But it ends up saying something quite different—that whether dissonance will occur or not depends on the specific *content* of the cognitions. It occurs when the self is involved in some important way. Dissonance theory is no longer about how important we find it to have consistent cognitions; it is about how important it is for us to think well of ourselves.

This is something people have long believed. Well before the decades of dissonance research, we knew that people like to think well of themselves. Freud, for example, called attention to the fact that people often *rationalize* their acts. They try to make acts that are either silly or evil look sensible or moral. In its original form, dissonance theory seemed to claim that this rationalization was just one expression of a more general phenomenon—that people want to be consistent in their thinking. If that were true, then dissonance theory would provide an *explanation* of rationalization in the sense that it would show that rationalization is just a part of a more general phenomenon. But since the dissonance phenomenon is more or less restricted to those cases where Freud would talk of rationalization, it isn't a more general theory, nor is it an explanation. Dissonance turns out to be the same as rationalization. Dissonance theory hasn't, as was first thought, discovered a new phenomenon; it has verified in experimentally rigorous ways one we have known about for quite a while.

The overlap between dissonance and rationalization is quite tight. For one thing, rationalization, Freud thought, worked only if the rationalizer was unaware that he was doing it. You can't, the argument went, knowingly deceive yourself. Well, in one study, the investigators had subjects write an essay in favor of higher tuition under conditions in which the fact that they could choose to write or not to write the essay was made salient (a control group wrote without such saliency). Some of the high-choice subjects after they wrote the essay were encouraged to feel and express any feelings of guilt and anxiety; other high-choice subjects were told that having such feelings was rare and a sign of poor mental health; finally, some high-choice subjects were told nothing at all about their feelings. The results were that the subjects who were encouraged to express their feelings showed the least distortion of their attitudes; their attitudes were closest to the low-choice control group (Pyzczynki, Greenberg, Solomon, Sideris, & Stubing, 1992). Rationalization, it seems, occurs only where you can't see it!

Whether we call it rationalization or dissonance, it is a tremendously important fact about us. The fact that we—unconsciously—distort our perceptions and attitudes so as to make ourselves look good, perhaps in our own eyes, is something that it would be dangerous for us to forget.

> Dissonance theory began life as a theory about how the formal relations among cognitions produced motivation regardless of the content of those cognitions, but the evidence suggests that dissonance occurs *only* if a particular content, the self, is involved in a particular way.

ALTERNATIVES TO DISSONANCE THEORY

Dissonance theory's account of its results has not gone unchallenged over the years; one important challenge came from a radical behaviorist perspective and was advanced by Daryl Bem (Bem, 1965). Bem's challenge to dissonance theory has prodded the further development of the theory.

Self-Perception Theory

Bem developed his ***self-perception theory*** by raising a basic question: How do people know their own attitudes? This question seems a bit odd. The immediate response we might want to give is: "I don't know how I know my attitudes, I just do!" If really pressed, we might say that we just introspect, "look inward" to discover our attitudes. But Bem, working in the tradition of behaviorism (which is skeptical about introspection), rejected this answer and proposed that people come to know their own attitudes in a different way.

Bem first asked how we know *other people's* attitudes. The answer to that has to be through their behavior (counting what people say about themselves as a kind of behavior); after all, we can't introspect on another's attitudes. Bem went on to argue that we know *our own* attitudes in much the same way, that is, by observing our own behavior.

On first hearing, the idea that we infer our attitudes from our behavior sounds distinctly perverse. To undersand it, we have to see why it *sounds* perverse and then see why it is actually quite reasonable. One reason it sounds odd is because we have attitudes toward lots of things we have never experienced, and we know it. Suppose I asked you, "What is your attitude about taking a shower with an alligator?" Presumably, you would have a rather dim view of such an admittedly exciting prospect. But, also presumably, few of you have actually experienced such an encounter. And Bem seems to be saying that lacking suitable experience, having never behaved toward an alligator in the shower, you don't know what your attitude is. But he isn't really saying *that!*

Bem would argue that while you may not have had much experience bathing with alligators, nonetheless, you have had experience with other dangers. Your knowledge of how you would react to an alligator in the tub is a generalization based on your experience with other dangerous things. So Bem is not suggesting that we must actually have had experience with a particular object to know our attitude toward it, but he is claiming that when we haven't had direct experience, we determine our attitude by comparing and contrasting the attitude object with things we have had experience with. And this isn't so unreasonable after all.

THE DISSONANCE RESULTS

Bem looked at the cognitive dissonance findings through the filter provided by his notion of how we know our own attitudes. He focused his attention on the Festinger and Carlsmith experiment, in which subjects who were paid $20 to deceive "another subject" didn't distort their attitude in line with their deception, but those paid only $1 did. Bem claimed that when the subjects were asked how much they liked the experiment, they didn't *compare* their attitude toward the experiment with what they said about it, as dissonance theory claims, but rather, *for the first time,* they tried to figure out what their attitude was. How were they to do that?

Bem argues that they examined their behavior in regard to the experiment. The $20 subjects found that they had said it was interesting, and that was one relevant fact, but they also recalled that they had been paid $20 for saying so. Bem claims that the subjects concluded from these facts that the experiment must not have been very interesting; after all, why would the experimenter have paid them so much money to say the experiment was interesting if it really was interesting? Bem suggests that the subjects looked at the situation just as someone would who was asked about *someone else's* attitude. If we were told that someone else was paid a lot of money to say something, we probably wouldn't believe that the person really believed what he said.

Bem applied the same logic to the $1 group. Here the question is: What would you believe about the real beliefs of someone paid only $1 to say something? You would probably infer that she really did believe it; you usually can't buy much of a lie for only $1. So Bem argues that the $1 group inferred that they found the experiment interesting from the fact that they said so for so little money.

SELF-PERCEPTION THEORY VERSUS DISSONANCE THEORY

Notice the differences between Bem's self-perception account and dissonance theory's account. Bem sees the result in the $1 group as a rational inference from the data; dissonance theory sees it as the product of distortion. Bem does not need to postulate an unpleasant state of arousal to explain the results, but dissonance theory does. How can we tell which theory offers a better account of the data? Since Bem assumes that subjects in the experiment inferred their attitudes from their behavior in much the same way that they would infer another person's attitudes from her behavior, the first thing he had to show was that other people who knew the subjects' behavior would infer that the $1 group really did find the experiment interesting, while people who knew of the $20 group's behavior wouldn't infer that they found it interesting.

To do this, Bem simply described the behavior of the $20 group to subjects and asked them to guess the $20 group's attitudes, and he described the $1 group's behavior to other subjects and asked them to guess the $1 group's attitudes. As predicted, the subjects inferred that the $1 group's attitudes were more positive than the $20 group's. This shows that the subjects in the Festinger and Carlsmith experiment *would have* reached the conclusion they did about their own attitudes if they had taken the perspective of someone else and examined their own actions (Bem, 1965). But it doesn't yet show that they *did* take an outsider's view. We need other evidence to accept Bem's account over the dissonance account.

DECIDING BETWEEN BEM'S ACCOUNT AND DISSONANCE

Two different kinds of evidence have been brought to bear on the debate between Bem and the dissonance theorists. One way to approach the problem is to ask whether the circumstances that produce the distortions characteristic of the dissonance experiment also produce arousal. The dissonance account suggests that they will; Bem's account doesn't. The evidence on this point is now fairly clear; dissonance-arousing circumstances *do*, as Festinger suggested, produce arousal (Gaes, Melburg, & Tedeschi, 1972; Pallak & Pittman, 1972; Croyle & Cooper, 1983; Elkin & Leippe, 1986). Moreover, drugs that produce additional arousal enhance the dissonance effect, while sedatives, including alcohol, reduce it (Cooper, Zanna, & Taves, 1978; Steele, Southwick, & Critchlow, 1981).

The second kind of evidence documents the impact of arousal in a somewhat less direct, but important way. To appreciate this evidence, we have to ask what role the arousal plays in the distortions characteristic of dissonance. One role was proposed by Festinger. He argued that the arousal intrinsic to

According to self-perception theory:

- Attitudes are inferred from behavior.

- Attitudes in dissonance groups are rationally inferred.

- There is no drive state (arousal) involved in dissonance.

According to cognitive dissonance theory:

- Attitudes are directly known.

- Attitudes in dissonance groups are distortions.

- Drive states (arousal) are necessarily a part of dissonance.

FIGURE 16.6

COGNITIVE DISSONANCE AND AVERSIVE DRIVE IN THE ORIGINAL
AND REVISED THEORIES

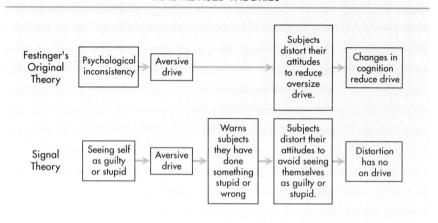

dissonance was aversive (causing "aversive drive"), and that subjects responded by reducing the inconsistent cognitions so as to remove the dissonance. But other theorists have assigned the arousal a less direct role. They have argued that the arousal in dissonance serves as a *signal* that the person has done something wrong. It isn't the arousal per se that produces the distortion; rather, the arousal simply informs the subject that he has done something wrong. The subject distorts because he doesn't want to face this fact (see Figure 16.6).

A way to determine if this is the right account is to tell subjects that their arousal *doesn't* mean they have done something wrong. But how could we do this? One clever technique relies on **misattribution.** In misattribution studies, subjects are given a drug to take, and they are told the drug produces arousal. Actually the drug is a **placebo,** an inert substance, but the subjects are led to believe it causes arousal. Thus, when the subjects experience arousal (actually dissonance arousal), they believe it is a consequence not of their misbehavior but of the drug. Believing this, they have no reason to distort.* This line of thinking suggests that subjects who have been given placebos that they are told will produce arousal will *not* show dissonance effects, while similarly treated subjects without the placebo will. A substantial line of experiments has found just this (Fazio, Zanna, & Cooper, 1977; Higgins, Rhodewalt, & Zanna, 1979). Thus, the evidence is that there is arousal involved in dissonance, but it isn't the arousal per se that produces the distortions; it is the subjects' beliefs about what has produced that arousal.

Further evidence on the role of arousal in the dissonance phenomena comes from a study in which arousal was tracked *after* the subjects had expressed their attitudes. Recall that in the original Festinger formulation, sub-

---

*This way of thinking about the arousal is consistent with the results of the Schachter and Singer experiment. In that experiment, and in the transfer of arousal studies spawned by it, arousal plays a role in emotion in part by triggering a search for the cause of the arousal. The cause that is hit on will determine the natural history of the emotional experience.

jects distort their beliefs in order to remove the aversive arousal. If this is true, then we should expect that the expression of distorted beliefs should in fact reduce arousal. To determine this, subjects were asked (under high- or low-choice circumstances) to write an essay in favor of imposing a $15 parking fee on campus—a very unpopular proposal. The subjects were then asked to express their attitudes while their physiological arousal was measured. As expected, the subjects in the high- (but not low-) choice condition showed attitude change in favor of the parking fee, but contrary to expectations, expressing these distorted attitudes did *not* reduce arousal.

In a follow-up study, all subjects wrote counterattitudinal essays under conditions of high choice. Some of the subjects were subsequently given the chance to express their attitudes; others were given no such chance. One would expect that the subjects who were allowed to express their (distorted) attitudes would show a faster reduction of arousal than would the subjects who were not given the opportunity, but quite the reverse happened. In fact, the subjects who did express their distorted attitudes remained aroused longer (Elkin & Leippe, 1986). These results suggest that the distortion that is part of the dissonance phenomenon does *not* occur in order to reduce aversive arousal.* Rather, they suggest that the arousal simply serves as a signal that the person experiencing dissonance has done something sleazy. The distortion occurs to ''undo'' that sleaziness quite independent of the arousal that signals its presence.

Let us sum up the evidence we have seen so far on the debate between Bem and the dissonance theorists. The evidence suggests that: (1) the circumstances that produce dissonance *do* produce some drive state (arousal), and (2) this drive state doesn't directly produce the attitude change involved in dissonance; rather, it serves as a cue, suggesting that the subject has done something wrong. These facts about dissonance are not encompassed by Bem's interpretation, since he sees the ''dissonance results'' as the result of a dispassionate, rational inference of one's attitudes from one's behaviors. So where does this leave us with regard to Bem's argument about how we know our own attitudes, and his solution to the attitude-behavior discrepancy?

The fact that subjects experience arousal in dissonance-evoking circumstances suggests that they knew their behavior was inconsistent with their real beliefs. Apparently finding ourselves aroused is a hint that we have done something wrong. This cue, combined with a knowledge of our own behavior and a knowledge of our own initial attitudes (perhaps known by generalization as Bem suggests), is enough to lead us to distort our views. On the whole, then, this evidence supports the dissonance view rather than Bem's self-perception interpretation. But there is evidence for Bem's account of at least some attitude change from investigation of a different phenomenon: intrinsic motivation.

INTRINSIC MOTIVATION

Dissonance theory seems to explain what happens to our attitudes when we are induced to act in a way that contradicts them, but what, if anything,

---

*Of course, it might be that subjects distort their beliefs in order to remove the arousal, but the distortion just doesn't work. But then why would they bother to distort their beliefs the next time they were experiencing dissonance?

happens to our attitudes if we are induced to act *in accord* with them? Suppose you were paid to do something you like doing anyway; would that affect your attitude toward the activity? Dissonance theory, at least in its original form, would make no prediction, since it has to do with what happens to people when they act in an inconsistent way, but self-perception theory does make a prediction. Self-perception theory looks at the situation this way. Before you were paid to do the activity—say, play chess—if you were asked whether you liked it, you would, if you're a chess player, say yes. The reason is that in reviewing your behavior, you would notice that you played it a lot, although you got nothing tangible out of it.

But once you are paid to play, the situation is different. Now as you look back at your behavior, the matter is less clear. Perhaps you are playing only to get the money, perhaps you don't really like to play after all. So self-perception theory suggests that rewarding people for doing what they initially enjoyed doing will sap their intrinsic interest, converting the activity from a pleasure to a chore. And there is a good deal of evidence to support this view.

Mark Lepper and his associates have shown this interest-sapping effect of reward in a series of studies with children. In one study, children were given something to do they enjoyed: working on some puzzles. Some of the subjects were told that they would be rewarded for working on them, while the others were promised no such reward. At the end of the session, however, both groups were rewarded with an opportunity to play with some attractive toys. Thus, both groups were rewarded, but one was rewarded for working on the puzzles, while for the other group, the reward had nothing to do with the puzzles.

The measure of interest to the experimenters was whether, and for how long, the children would play with the puzzles later, when promised no reward. The researchers observed the children's behavior with the puzzles (in a different context) one to three weeks later and found that the children who had been rewarded for working on the puzzles now played with them less than those who had made no such deal (see Figure 16.7). So being "paid" to work on the puzzles robbed it of its intrinsic fun; in the words of the experimenters, it "turned play into work" (Lepper & Greene, 1975).

One reason that paying people may sap motivation is very much in the spirit of self-perception accounts. Perhaps by paying people to do things, we give the impression that those things are difficult, tedious, and generally unpleasant. And the more we pay, the more tedious they seem (Freedman, Cunningham, & Krismer, 1992).

REWARDS FOR EXCELLENCE AS INTRINSIC MOTIVATORS

Rewarding people for doing things they enjoy doing anyway doesn't always sap intrinsic motivation. Rewarding people for *good* performance on a task, rather than just paying them to do it regardless of quality, is *less* likely to reduce intrinsic motivation (Ryan, Mims, & Koestner, 1983). To explain these results, Edward Deci and Richard Ryan have proposed what they call **cognitive evaluation theory** (Deci & Ryan, 1980). This theory proposes that rewards have two aspects: (1) they have the effect of controlling behavior, and (2) they provide feedback about competence. If you pay someone to do a task and what he is paid is independent of how well or poorly he does it, then your reward has only a controlling function, and the recipient will see

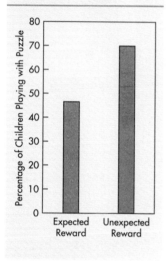

the reward as an attempt to control his behavior. He will see his behavior as externally controlled rather than as intrinsically motivated. But rewards that are contingent on excellent performance in addition to controlling behavior also serve as feedback about the person's competence. Coming to see oneself as competent, the theory suggests, *enhances* intrinsic motivation.

Thus, the same reward can have two different and opposite effects. Whether the controlling or informational aspect is made salient will determine which effect predominates and whether intrinsic motivation is increased or decreased (see Enzle & Anderson, 1993).

In one study, subjects were rewarded for their performance on a psychological test in which they had to find figures embedded in a kind of camouflage. For some subjects, the experimenter used language that stressed his expectations that the subject do the task well and the subject's obligation to try hard; this language heightened the controlling aspect of the reward. For other subjects, the language stressed competence feedback. They were told how well they did but without stress on the experimenter's expectations. These changes in language affected whether the subjects continued to do the puzzles for no reward when they were later left alone with some unsolved puzzles. The subjects instructed with competence language were more likely to return to the puzzles on their own than were the subjects instructed with the controlling information (Ryan, Mims, & Koestner, 1983).

Research on intrinsic motivation, then, in line with Bem's position, suggests that seeing oneself as doing something for extrinsic reward can erode intrinsic motivation. People do seem to act as if they said to themselves: "If someone is paying me to do something, then I guess I don't really want to do it for its own sake." There is other research too that supports self-perception theory as an account of some behavior; that research is connected with the "foot-in-the-door phenomenon."

THE FOOT-IN-THE-DOOR PHENOMENON

Suppose you wanted to convince someone to let a survey team of six people come into his house for two hours so that the team could inventory all of the household products he used. How would you go about getting his permission? You might pay him a lot of money. But there is a cheaper way to induce people to put up with this major inconvenience. You could just ask them to do it for free. Jonathan Freedman and Scott Fraser did just that with thirty-six residents of Palo Alto, California, and eight people agreed. So just asking people is cheap but time consuming, since only about 22 percent accede to the request.

But there is a way to make your request more effective. As the experimenters found out, you can call up the householder a couple of days in advance and ask him a few innocuous questions, such as "What brand of soap do you use?" You can then call back a couple of days later and ask for the larger favor. The experimenters found that 50 percent of the subjects approached with the small request first later agreed to the larger, disruptive request. This technique of asking a small favor first and then a larger one is well-known among salespeople as the ***foot-in-the-door technique,*** evoking the notion that once you get your foot in the customer's door with a small request, you can use the opening you have created to wedge your whole body through.

Rewarding people for their performance has two effects:

- It controls their behavior.

- It informs them how well they have done.

The first erodes intrinsic motivation; the second doesn't.

As interesting as this effect is, there was a second experiment that proved even more interesting. In this experiment, some subjects were approached by an experimenter who identified herself as a representative of a California group trying to promote safe driving. The subjects were asked if they would be willing to let the group install a huge billboard-like sign in their front yards reading "Drive Carefully." The subjects were shown a picture of a house with just such a huge sign in the front yard; the sign was badly lettered, and so large that it largely obscured the front of the house. As you might imagine, fewer than 20 percent of the subjects agreed.

But in another condition, an experimenter asked the subjects if they would be willing to put a very small—three-inch square—sign in their windows that said "Be a Safe Driver." Many more subjects agreed with this modest request. As you have probably guessed, this simple request was followed up about two weeks later with the more dramatic request for the billboard space. And now 76 percent of the subjects agreed (see Figure 16.8). This is, once again, the foot-in-the-door phenomenon.

But there was another condition. Before being asked about the billboard, these subjects were asked to put in their windows not a safe driving sign, but a little sign saying "Keep California Beautiful." Then two weeks later, they were approached by a *different* experimenter from a different group asking them to put the safe driving billboard on their lawn. These subjects, then, had been approached with a request for a small favor before the big request, but the two requests were from different people (one a male, one a female) and had to do with unrelated causes. Still, 47 percent of the subjects agreed to the larger request (Freedman & Fraser, 1966). Why?

The authors speculated that self-perception might be an answer. Perhaps the subjects, having agreed to the first request, came to see themselves as "the sort of person who does this sort of thing"; this would lead to their agreeing to the second request. The change in self-perception was hypothe-

FIGURE 16.8

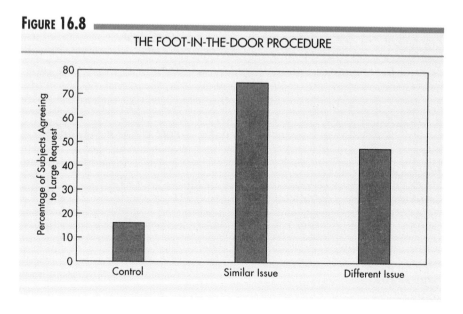

THE FOOT-IN-THE-DOOR PROCEDURE

▶ Percentage of subjects agreeing to a request as a function of the kind of request they had previously been exposed to. The foot-in-the-door worked better when the second, larger request was similar in terms of issue to the first request. But even when the second request was different, well over twice as many subjects complied with it as complied when no first request was made at all. (Data from Freedman & Fraser, 1966) sized as the bridge between the two otherwise unrelated requests. Subsequent research using foot-in-the-door procedures has by and large confirmed the speculation that changes in self-perception account for the transfer of agreement across changes in requests (DeJong, 1979). And one group of researchers has gathered evidence that seven-year-old children (but not five-year-old children) are susceptible to foot-in-the-door manipulations, apparently because it is only at that age that children begin to appreciate stability of personality (Eisenberg, Cialdini, McCreath, & Shell, 1987).

Daryl Bem proposed self-perception theory as an alternative to dissonance theory, as a simpler account of the same phenomena. But the history of the research we have just reviewed suggests that he was wrong about that. The evidence suggests that when people are somehow induced to do things that they at least retrospectively see as stupid or immoral, they do experience an unpleasant state of arousal. This unpleasant state triggers distortion designed to make themselves seem less stupid or sleazy. But this does not mean that self-perception theory is useless. In fact, self-perception theory has proven to be quite useful in accounting for attitude changes when people are induced to do things they might have done anyway—playing with Magic Markers, for example. The conflict between dissonance theory and self-perception theory has given way to a truce, in which the domain of attitude change has been partitioned into the territory of dissonance theory, when behavior flies in the face of attitudes, and the territory of self-perception theory, when attitudes and behavior are in closer approximation (see Figure 16.9; Fazio, Zanna, & Cooper, 1977; see also Schlenker & Trudeau, 1990).

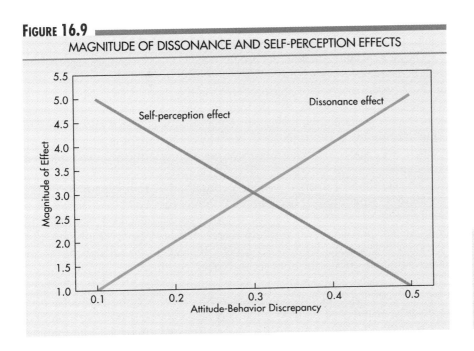

FIGURE 16.9

MAGNITUDE OF DISSONANCE AND SELF-PERCEPTION EFFECTS

Self-perception effect

Dissonance effect

Magnitude of Effect

Attitude-Behavior Discrepancy

◀ *Dissonance effects grow and self-perception effects shrink as the discrepancy between attitude and behavior increases. (Based on Fazio, Zanna, & Cooper, 1977)*

Further Challenges to Cognitive Dissonance Theory

As useful and robust as cognitive dissonance theory has proven to be, it has repeatedly faced challenges either in the form of failures to find phenomena that dissonance theory predicted would occur or in the form of alternative theories that claim to be able to explain the same phenomena that dissonance theory explains. These controversies, however, have been far from sterile; each has contributed to a better understanding of just what dissonance is, and when it will appear. We will now consider two such problems, one of each type. The first has to do with a phenomenon that dissonance expected to find but for several decades could not find, and the second is a rival interpretation of the dissonance phenomenon.

SELECTIVE ATTENTION

One of the original claims of dissonance theory was that people were motivated by dissonance to avoid information inconsistent with their beliefs, but, oddly enough, a great deal of early work on dissonance theory found this not to be so. A study by Norm Feather illustrates this failure.

Feather gave smokers and nonsmokers lists of articles they might be given to read, and asked them to select from the list those they wanted to read. Some were given lists with a title suggesting the article would provide evidence for a link between lung cancer and smoking, and others were given the same lists except that the crucial article provided evidence that there wasn't a link. (This research was carried out before the evidence was overwhelming.)

Dissonance theory suggests that smokers would want to read the "no-link" article *more* than would nonsmokers, while they would want to read the "there is a link" article *less* than nonsmokers. But the results of this study and of most of the others in the literature showed instead that smokers were *more* interested in *both* articles than nonsmokers (Feather, 1963). Most of the early research on selective exposure found, as Feather did, no evidence of it (see Brock & Balloun, 1967, however, for an exception).

The general failure to find that people avoided information discrepant from their behavior led early reviewers of the literature to conclude that dissonance does not produce selective exposure (Freedman & Sears, 1965). This is not to say that selective exposure to information consistent with one's own views doesn't exist in the world; rather, the suggestion was that it has nothing to do with dissonance. Let us pause to see why people might mostly come into contact with material supporting their preexisting attitudes, even without dissonance.

Consider this. If you are a politically conservative, young, up-and-coming stockbroker, what are you likely to read? Surely the *Wall Street Journal*. You have to read the *Wall Street Journal*, or other periodicals like it, if you are to do your job. But what will you find there? Articles that favor conservative economic policies that tend to advantage the well-off, or articles that favor policies that advantage the not very well-off at cost to those who own stocks? This doesn't seem hard to answer. Thus, our Wall Street broker is likely to come into contact with material that supports his own views, without trying to do so very much at all (Freedman & Sears, 1965). So selective attention can result even without much of a motive to avoid discrepant information.

Still, the failure to find motivated selective exposure effects was something of an embarrassment to dissonance theory, an embarrassment that has recently been lessened.

Dieter Frey has argued that selective exposure effects may occur only under certain circumstances (Frey, 1986). For one thing, people need *not* avoid information contrary to their views if they believe they can easily refute the opposing information; in fact, being able to refute a contrary view might even enhance one's initial attitude. Indeed, Feather found that cigarette smokers perceived the articles claiming that smoking was bad for them as particularly weak; perhaps they didn't avoid them because they thought they would be able to argue effectively against them. One way that you can expect to be able to refute an argument is if you have already heard the argument and successfully refuted it before. Perhaps Feather's smokers believed that they had heard all of the arguments before.

There is another case in which you might not avoid contrary information—when you haven't yet made up your mind. If you are about to make a decision, then it is in your interest to gather as much relevant information as you have the energy to think about. But once you have made what you believe to be an *irrevocable* decision, then there is no utility in gathering new information, and information contrary to the decision you have made may give rise to the pain of dissonance. So Frey has argued that selectively avoiding contrary information should occur only for information that seems (on the face of it) credible and persuasive, and *after* an irrevocable decision has been made.

In a substantial series of experiments, Frey demonstrated motivated selective exposure under just these circumstances (Frey, 1981, 1986; Frey & Rosch, 1984). It now seems that dissonance *can* lead us to look for facts and arguments that support our views and decisions in those circumstances where the information is likely to have impact, and where it is unlikely to be useful in terms of revising our course of action—just where dissonance theory might expect it to occur.

People selectively avoid information to contradict their behavior when

- the information is new;
- the information is credible;
- they are irrevocably committed to their path of action.

DISSONANCE AND SELF-PRESENTATION

The current view of dissonance theory, at least as it applies to the large number of experiments that have gotten people to argue against what they truly believe, is that people experience dissonance because they *see themselves* as having done something sleazy. In order to make themselves look less sleazy in their own eyes, it is argued, they distort their true beliefs to move them closer to what they argued for. But James Tedeschi has suggested that in the traditional dissonance experiment, the subject does report beliefs different from the ones she truly has, but not, as dissonance has it, so that she will look less sleazy in *her own* eyes, but rather so that she will look less sleazy in the eyes of the experimenter (Tedeschi, Schlenker, & Bonoma, 1971).

Tedeschi bases his argument on the view, discussed in some detail in Chapter 6, that people want to create a favorable impression in the eyes of others. They want to do so because it is typically in their interest to create such an impression—people are nicer to us if they think we are deserving rather than sleazy. Consider the subject in a typical dissonance experiment in this light. The subject knows that the experimenter knows that she has argued against something that is unpopular on her campus; she is likely to believe, therefore, that the experimenter thinks she isn't a person of much character. What can she do to improve the experimenter's opinion of her? She can pretend that the opinions she expressed, no matter how atypical for a student, are nonetheless her real opinions. Thus, when she fills out the questionnaire at the end, she lies—not to herself, but to the experimenter.

This line of argument has much in common with a dissonance account. The crucial difference is in whom the subject is pretending to. According to the dissonance view, the subject is pretending to herself; according to the self-presentational view, she is pretending to the experimenter. How can we tell which is the better account?

One way is by using a technique called the "bogus pipeline." The bogus pipeline consists of sophisticated-looking equipment with electrodes that are attached to the subject at various points. Subjects are told that the equipment is a very accurate lie detector—actually quite a bit of staging is used to convince them of this. Subjects are then put through a standard dissonance procedure in which they argue against a position they believe (with free choice and for little money) and are asked about their attitudes while hooked up to the machine. If the dissonance phenomenon were *wholly* a matter of self-presentation to the experimenter, then we would expect no attitude change while hooked up to the machine, because the subjects would expect the experimenter to find out that they were lying—again—and that would make them look *even worse* in the experimenter's eyes. On the other hand, if the attitude change produced by dissonance is sincere, then it should show up even with the bogus pipeline.

The results from an experiment using this procedure indicated that even with the bogus pipeline, subjects *do show some attitude change*, indicating that the distortion in the dissonance procedure is, at least in part, to convince themselves that they weren't sleazes (see Figure 16.10; Paulhus, 1982). Nonetheless the degree of attitude change found in this study was less than that shown by another group of subjects who indicated their final attitude in the standard way, which suggests that some part of the typical attitude change found in a dissonance procedure *is* the result of self-presentational concerns.

A second technique used to address the differences between the dissonance and self-presentational accounts varied the attractiveness of the experimenter. In one condition, dissonance was induced by an experimenter who was rude and unpleasant; in another condition, the experimenter was friendly and pleasant. If the dissonance effect were a matter of self-presentation, then we should expect it to occur to a greater degree with the pleasant experimenter than with the rude one—subjects should have been more eager to impress the attractive person than the unattractive one. But in fact, there was just as much dissonance displayed with the unfriendly as with the friendly experimenter (Rosenfeld, Giacalone, & Tedeschi, 1984). The results of these studies suggest that although self-presentational concerns play a part in the attitude change typically seen in dissonance studies, there is still evidence for a true self-deceptive (rather than other-deceptive) dissonance effect. Dissonance theory has withstood this challenge as well.

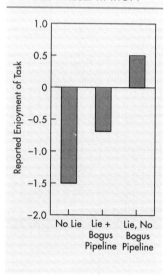

FIGURE 16.10

DISSONANCE AND SELF-PRESENTATION

▲ *Reported enjoyment of a boring task in a control group, a group that lied to another subject and reported enjoyment using a bogus pipeline, and a group that lied and reported enjoyment using paper and pencil measure. Some of the distortion in the typical dissonance experiment was probably due to self-presentation to the experimenter. But some of it wasn't. (Data from Paulhus, 1982)*

Cognitive Consistency and Schemata

What has become of consistency theory, the idea that people tend to make their cognitions fall in line? A version of consistency theory with regard to attitudes survives in a limited form.

Abraham Tesser argues that one *can* see the operation of a tendency toward consistency simply by asking people to think about something toward which they have attitudes. In thinking about things toward which you have an attitude, Tesser claims, you will alter your thinking so as to make it more *evaluatively consistent.* Imagine that you have a generally positive attitude toward someone, but you can also think of some things you don't appreciate about him. Suppose Bill is a good friend, funny, kind, and helpful, but he is, if the truth be told, cheap. Tesser claims that if you think about him, you will tend to: (1) find new positive things to think about him—you will suddenly remember how smart he is, (2) lose (forget) the negative things—forget about the cheap birthday present he got you, or (3) reintepret some negative things so they're not so negative after all—decide it wasn't really that cheap after all. Because of these mechanisms toward consistency, thinking about some attitude object should produce **attitude polarization**—if your attitude is initially positive, it should become more positive; if it is negative, it should become more negative (Tesser, 1978).

To demonstrate such thought-induced attitude polarization, subjects have simply been asked to think about some attitude object for various lengths of time; at the end of the period, their attitudes are sampled, and the degree to which they are polarized is sampled. The general finding is that the longer one thinks about something, the more extreme one's attitudes become (Tesser & Conlee, 1975).

So far, the attitude polarization phenomenon seems just like the cognitive consistency theory with which dissonance began. But an important constraint to the theory has been added fairly recently. Tesser now believes that the tendency toward consistency is due not to motivational factors, but to the operation of cognitive schemata.*

Schemata are organized representations of knowledge. So, for example, you probably have a "restaurant schema"—a fairly organized idea about what goes on in restaurants. Your schema for restaurants includes your knowledge that food is served in restaurants, that restaurants have menus from which you choose what you want to eat, that people wait on you there, that you should tip them, and that you have to pay the bill—unlike your parents' kitchen. Schemata serve various cognitive functions. For one thing, they are a guide to your actions in a restaurant—using your schema, you know you should read the menu, pick something to eat, tell the waiter what you want, and so on. For another thing, they order your memories about examples that fit under the schema. If you think about particular restaurants you have been in, you are likely to remember the features of those restaurants that are salient in your general restaurant schema, such as the food served, the service, and so on, but you are unlikely to remember details of the experience that are not salient in your general schema—the kind of typeface

*Singular schema. See Chapter 5 for more on cognitive schemata.

the menu is printed in (unless there is something really extraordinary about the type).

People differ in the degree to which their particular schemata are organized, articulated, and detailed. A restaurant owner, for example, will have a much more developed restaurant schema than you or I have. Tesser believes that the degree to which attitudes will polarize with thought depends on the degree to which the thinker has a detailed schema for the attitude object. He believes that thinking about something under the guidance of a detailed schema will lead someone to make inferences about elements of the object that are evaluatively consistent with each other. Thus, Tesser invokes a kind of consistency notion to account for attitude polarization, but he argues that consistency works *locally* within schemata rather than on all of one's thinking as a whole, as dissonance theory had it. Consider our restaurant again.

Tesser suggests that if you had a bad meal in a restaurant but were impressed with the service, as you reflect upon your experience later, you wil tend to recall the service as being worse than it was. Because both service and food are salient elements of your restaurant schema, reflection will bring these elements into evaluative alignment. But if someone invites you to invest in the building in which the restaurant is housed, then you will think about the restaurant in a different way, using a different schema, and the bad meal you had there should not "leak" into your assessment of the restaurant as a real estate investment.

If schemata are responsible for attitude polarization, then we should expect that people who have well-developed schemata about some attitude object should show greater attitude polarization than people who have less-developed schemata. To test this notion, Tesser showed male and female subjects videotaped examples of women's fashions and football plays and asked them to rate each. The subjects were then either distracted for 90 seconds or given the 90 seconds to think about what they had seen. He predicted, and found, that men would show attitude polarization if they were allowed to think about the football plays, but that men would not show polarization after thinking about the fashions (see Figure 16.11). He expected, and found, the reverse result from women—thinking about fashion caused them to polarize on the fashions, but thinking about football plays did not cause polar-

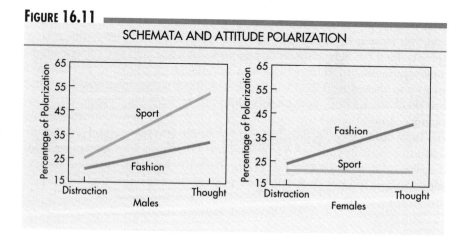

FIGURE 16.11

SCHEMATA AND ATTITUDE POLARIZATION

▶ Attitude polarization as a function of thought versus distraction, stimulus (fashion versus football), and gender of the subject. (From Tesser & Leone, 1977) ization about football (Tesser & Leone, 1977). Tesser accounted for these effects by claiming that on average, women have more developed schemata about women's fashions, while men, again on average, have more developed schemata about football.

Other investigators selected subjects who had either well-developed or less-developed schemata about capital punishment and censorship. The subjects then wrote essays about each topic. Writing the essays led to attitude polarization *only* for the subjects who had consistent and articulated schemata about these issues. Moreover, the essays revealed, in line with Tesser's claims, that the subjects with articulated schemata became polarized in their attitudes; when they revealed inconsistent ideas (maybe capital punishment isn't much of a deterrent), they also generated counterarguments against those ideas (perhaps capital punishment is a good idea even if it isn't a deterrent) (Chaiken & Yates, 1985).

Thinking about an issue doesn't *always* lead to polarization of attitudes. In one study, subjects were asked to think about six topics that involved conflicting values. For example, one issue was: Should public park lands be opened to mining and exploration in order to promote economic growth and prosperity? This issue involves two values. One value is beauty, the other is economic well-being. The subjects had been asked before reading this question to rate each of these values in importance to them. Now for some subjects, there was no real conflict here; subjects who placed no value on beauty and great value on economic well-being should have found this choice easy, as would those who placed no value on economic well-being and great value on beauty. But those who valued each equally should have found themselves in conflict. The investigators predicted, and found, that thinking about the issue did *not* produce polarization for the conflicted subjects, but it *did* polarize the subjects who found the topic easy and conflict free (Liberman & Chaiken, 1991).

This research documenting and exploring the mechanisms for attitude polarization is a return to the notion of attitude consistency that spawned the original formulation of dissonance theory. But this return to consistency differs from the original statement by suggesting that people can live with evaluative inconsistency in their thinking so long as the inconsistency doesn't reside within the same schema—we can live with the idea that a great university is located in a terrible part of town more easily than with the idea that a great university has terrible teachers.

Thinking about things may increase the extremity of an attitude toward it by allowing you to

- discover new attitude-consistent information;

- forget attitude-inconsistent information;

- reinterpret inconsistent information as consistent information.

PERSUASION

Our discussion so far has focused on the internal dynamics of attitudes—the way they change in response to thinking or behavior that is relevant to them. But a key way that attitudes change is in response to attempts at persuasion. Our focus shifts now to people's responses to attempts to persuade them to change their attitudes.

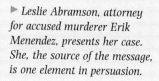
Components of Persuasion

One of the earliest and most influential programs of research on attitudes was developed immediately after the Second World War at Yale University under the leadership of Carl Hovland. The research program was an outgrowth of Hovland's research for the army during the war; the army was interested in measuring and improving its enlisted men's morale. As Hovland worked on this project, he became impressed by how little of a scientific, experimental nature was known about the effects of various methods of attitude change. After the war, he established a working group at Yale (including, among others, Irving Janis, Harold Kelley, and Herbert Kelman) devoted to the systematic, scientific analysis of attempts to persuade, to change people's attitudes.

Hovland and his colleagues attacked the problem of persuasion in something like the way we might approach the workings of an electronic system, say a stereo. If we wanted to know how a stereo worked, the first thing we might do is analyze it into components: CD player, amplifier, speakers, and listener. The Hovland group analyzed the components of persuasion in a similar, straightforward, commonsensical way; it considered the system to be made up of a **source** of the persuasive message, a **medium** in which the message is expressed, a **message,** and the **target** of the message.

Having analyzed a stereo into components, what might someone do next? If she had some theoretical understanding of the system, she could rely on that to provide further guidance. But Hovland didn't have much of a theory of attitude change to begin with, so he had to start from scratch. What might someone do in such a case? She might tinker; she might change things about the various components of the system to see how that affected its performance. And that is more or less how the Yale group proceeded. The group tried to determine how variations in the nature of the source, medium, message, or target affected the degree of attitude change produced by a particular persuasion attempt. But to say that the Yale group was starting from scratch is a bit of an overstatement.

▶ *Leslie Abramson, attorney for accused murderer Erik Menendez, presents her case. She, the source of the message, is one element in persuasion.*

TABLE 16.1

KINDS OF ATTITUDE CHANGE		
Type of Attitude Change	Depends on Surveillance	Persuasion Based on
Internalization	No	Belief in claims
Identification	No	Admiration
Compliance	Yes	Reward or punishment

SOURCE: Adapted from Kelman, 1958.

The Yale group started with two different hunches about what would make a difference: learning theory and common sense. While Hovland was at Yale, he fell under the influence of Clark Hull, the decade's most important animal learning theorist, who had developed a learning theory compatible with the Hovland group's approach. To see how these two sources of suggestions merge, we shall consider in some detail the Yale group's analysis of one component in the system—the source.

SOURCE CHARACTERISTICS

What characteristics of a person make her likely to be effective in persuading you to do or believe something? Herbert Kelman (1958) argued that this depends on the kind of persuasion involved (see Table 16.1). One kind of persuasion involves getting you really to believe the claims the source is making; this kind he called ***internalization.*** At its best, education is internalization. Another kind of persuasion comes about not because you believe the claims the source makes, but because you like the person or want to be like the person saying those things. This kind of persuasion Kelman called ***identification.***

Last, we can be persuaded to do something not because we believe it is right, but because the person who wants us to do it will either reward us for doing it or punish us for not doing it. This kind of persuasion (which really has little to do with attitude change) Kelman called ***compliance.*** A gun held to someone's head produces great compliance, but little in the way of internalization. So far, we have relied on common sense rather than on formal theory. But we can go further in our analysis of source characteristics.

It seems obvious that the three different sorts of persuasion rely on different source characteristics—to be effective at extracting compliance, one had better have power; to arouse identification, being attractive (in one sense or another) is important; and to produce internalization, one had better be credible. Indeed, we can further analyze the notions of credibility, attractiveness, and power. We shall focus a bit on credibility.

Credibility To think about what it is to be credible, it is best to consider what makes us suspicious of what someone says. Two reasons to discount what someone says are (1) that we believe the person doesn't know what he is talking about, and (2) although we believe the person knows what he is talking about, we don't believe that he is telling us the truth—he has a reason

Leonardo says:

"Hey, dudes!
Don't forget your helmet when
you head out for a bike ride!"

HEAD OUT WITH A BIKE HELMET

TEENAGE MUTANT NINJA TURTLES

NEW YORK STATE DEPARTMENT OF HEALTH

A bike helmet protects your head from falls and bumps.
So be safe while you're having fun.
Wear your helmet every time you ride your bike.

▲ *Getting people to identify with the source can help persuade.*

to lie. The Yale group made this point by saying that credibility is composed of expertise and trustworthiness. Again, this analysis is commonsensical.

Much of the research in the Yale tradition involved the systematic exploration and documentation of these rather obvious points. But as obvious as these points are, they are probably only roughly correct. So the Yale group was concerned to find their limits, cases where these simple principles failed. When these principles fail, matters get more interesting. At such moments, the Yale group tended to call upon its other source—learning theory.

The Sleeper Effect   The Yale group called on learning theory to resolve an anomalous effect known as the "sleeper effect" (Hovland, Lumsdaine, & Sheffield, 1949; Hovland & Weiss, 1951). The sleeper effect was discovered in the course of Hovland's research for the army. The War Department had prepared seven half-hour films called the *Why We Fight* series. They were designed to communicate to soldiers something of the history of the events that led up to the war, to convince them of how difficult it would be to defeat the Nazis, and to instill confidence in the abilities of our own troops and our allies. Hovland's aim was to determine how effective the films were both in communicating information about the war and in affecting morale. The particular film he focused on was the fourth in the series and was called *Battle of Britain*, a documentary about the heroic response of the Royal Air Force and the British people to Germany's saturation bombing of British cities. Britain's successful resistance against this onslaught was one turning point of the war.

One question Hovland asked was: How long do the effects of the film endure? To find out, Hovland and his associates administered a questionnaire related to the film to four groups of subjects. One group was given the questionnaire five days after seeing the film; a control group, which had not seen the film, received the questionnaire at the same time. The other two groups received the questionnaire roughly nine weeks later; again, one group had seen the film, and the other hadn't. The difference between the film group and the control group at five days showed the short-term effect of the film; the difference between the film and control groups at nine weeks showed the (relatively) long-term effects. The *difference between these differences* showed the effect of time on whatever attitude change the film produced.

Common sense suggests that over time, the effect of the film would wane—both because of the simple passage of time and because of all the experiences related to the war that had taken place in the nine-week interval. And this is indeed what Hovland found for some of the items on the questionnaire, but curiously, some of the items produced *more* attitude change at nine weeks than at five days. This enhanced, delayed effect is called the **sleeper effect.** Hovland offered some hypotheses about why the sleeper effect occurred. He proposed that the effect might depend on the credibility of the source. He suggested that high-credibility sources might have a large effect at first, but their impact would decline with time; low-credibility sources, on the other hand, would be expected to have little impact at first, but their impact might increase with time. Hovland and Weiss followed up this possibility in a more controlled study.

They presented subjects with four messages meant to be persuasive—for example, that antihistamines ought to be sold without prescription. The messages were attributed either to a high-credibility source, *The New England*

Journal of Biology and Medicine, or a low-credibility source, a mass circulation, monthly pictorial magazine. As expected, the high-prestige source had more impact on attitudes immediately after exposure, but when the subjects were tested again four weeks later, the high-credibility source had lost influence and the low-credibility source had gained influence. Now why might this occur?

One possibility is that when the subjects hear the original message, they are influenced by two cues: (1) the message itself, which tends to move their attitudes toward the position taken by the source, and (2) the credibility of the source. At the time the subjects first hear the message, these two cues are associated. In the high-credibility case, this second associated cue enhances the effect of the message; in the low-credibility case, this second cue suppresses the effect. If these two cues become disassociated over time—that is, subjects remember the message and the source, but forget the connection between them—then the message from the high-credibility source will lose its extra advantage, and the message from the low-credibility source will no longer be suppressed by the source cue. Figure 16.12 shows the effects of time on the two conditions. This disassociation of message from source could account for the sleeper effect.

The logic of the Yale group's research is clear in this example. It begins with a commonsensical analysis of the phenomenon, demonstrates that this obvious assumption (high-credibility sources are more influential than low-) is more or less true, looks for cases where it isn't true, and then seeks an explanation for those cases in some more formal, less commonsensical theory, in this case learning theory.

The Hovland and Weiss report stimulated much discussion and research on the sleeper effect for a while. But in 1974, a paper entitled "Is It Time to Put the Sleeper Effect to Rest?" appeared reporting seven experiments de-

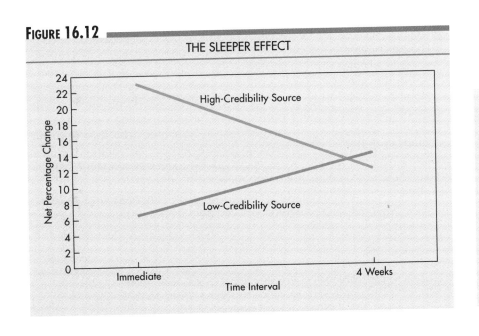

FIGURE 16.12

THE SLEEPER EFFECT

◄ *Immediately after hearing a message, subjects are more likely to agree with the position of the high-credibility source and less likely to agree with the low-credibility source. Over time, however, the message becomes dissociated from its source, leading to less agreement with the high-credibility source and more agreement with the low-credibility source. (From Hovland & Weiss, 1951)* signed to test for a sleeper effect. None showed it (Gillig & Greenwald, 1974).* It now appears, however, that the sleeper effect was only resting. Anthony Greenwald has reported a series of sixteen experiments that have closed in on just when one can expect to find a sleeper effect. According to Greenwald, the sleeper effect will occur if (1) subjects are presented with a message, (2) they note the evidence in favor of the claim ("scientific evidence"), (3) they are then given information that completely discounts the credibility of the message (it was prepared by someone in the public relations department of a tobacco company), and (4) they then immediately rate the trustworthiness of the source. Under these conditions, although subjects are likely to completely dismiss the message immediately, they will over time be at least slightly persuaded by the message. Greenwald goes on to argue that the sleeper effect occurs because subjects are unable to integrate the message and its source in memory (Pratkanis, Greenwald, Leippe, & Baumgardner, 1988).

The sleeper effect may account for something I, at least, find puzzling. Sometimes, usually after an environmental disaster, a "company spokesperson" dismisses the event with an explanation, but it seems to me that no one could possibly believe the explanation, given the obvious vested interest of the person saying it. I wonder, "Why would they bother to say such things?" Perhaps they say such things because, although their claim is immediately dismissed, it comes to have some impact via a sleeper effect. In any event, the sleeper effect is one nonobvious legacy turned up by the Yale group.

FEAR AND PERSUASION

Irving Janis, another member of the Yale group, raised this question: Suppose you want to get someone to do something to improve his health by convincing him of the dangers of not doing so. What is the best strategy to use? Common sense suggests that the more afraid you make people, the more effective the message will be, especially if you inform them of a reliable way to avoid these dangers. (Needless to say, there is a difference between convincing someone that he ought to do something and getting him to do it, but that is a matter we shall take up in the next chapter.) Janis set out to determine whether this bit of common sense is true by conducting a controlled experiment.

The experimenters exposed three different groups of subjects to a presentation designed to get them to take better care of their teeth. The presentations differed in the degree of fear that they aroused. The most arousing personalized the appeal, stressing all of the terrible and painful things that can happen to you as a result of inadequate oral hygiene, including showing slides depicting in gruesome color the perils of not brushing. The least arousing appeal set forth the same facts in more neutral terms. The results were quite a shock to common sense. The *minimal* appeal worked better at getting people to go to the dentist and made subjects more resistant to the counterclaim that dental care was not terribly important. The investigators attempted to account for this reversal in language derived from learning theory.

The sleeper effect will occur if

- subjects are presented with a message;
- they notice evidence in favor of the message;
- they are given information attacking the credibility of the source of the evidence;
- they immediately rate the trustworthiness of the source.

*Actually, a distinction can be drawn between an *absolute sleeper effect*, meaning that a message from a source of low credibility actually gains impact with time, and a *relative sleeper effect*, meaning that while a message from a highly credible source loses impact over time, a message from a less credible source *doesn't lose impact*. The experiments reported here did not find an absolute sleeper effect, but they did find a relative sleeper effect.

They claimed, in line with Hull's position, that in order to reinforce a desired behavior with a fear appeal, you first have to arouse fear, but that in itself does not produce the desired behavior. The desirable behavior is reinforced only when that drive is reduced, since according to Hull, it is the reduction of drive that produces reinforcement. The authors argued that the most emotional appeal arouses drive that is not relieved by the recommendations at the end of the message, and since this drive is still present at the end, the behavior recommended is not reinforced. The low-fear condition, on the other hand, although it arouses less drive, nonetheless is more effective because all of the drive it arouses is relieved.

Janis went on to suggest that the unrelieved arousal in the high-fear condition is aversive, so the subjects relieve it not by going to the dentist, but by ignoring the whole issue. As Freud would put it, they defend themselves against the anxiety-arousing idea by denial. In this way, Janis was able to take the commonsensical view that arousing fear motivates people, show that it doesn't work if the fear arousal is too great, and then explain why it doesn't work in terms that are compatible both with the learning theory of the day and with Freudian observations (Janis & Feshbach, 1953).

Unfortunately for Janis's hypothesis, Leventhal (1970) has pointed out that the twenty or so subsequent studies on this issue have not found the inverse relation between fear arousal and attitude change. Rather, they have typically found that the more fear is aroused, the more effective the message. Further research has produced a better understanding of just when fear-arousing messages will be effective.

Ronald Rogers has argued (and gathered evidence for the claim) that there are four conditions that determine whether a fear appeal will work. For such a message to work, it must convince the target that (1) the danger is serious, (2) the dangerous outcome is also quite probable, (3) the response recommended to avoid the danger will work, and (4) the target is *able* to make the recommended response (Maddux & Rogers, 1983; see also Beck & Lund, 1981). Thus, to convince someone to stop smoking, you have to convince her that the danger of smoking is severe (lung cancer, heart disease), the odds of contracting one of these disorders if she continues to smoke are high, the odds will be substantially reduced by quitting, and crucially, she is able to quit smoking.

Similarly, there is evidence that fear appeals combined with information that one can do something about the danger have been shown to cause residents of the Los Angeles area to take steps to prepare for an earthquake (Mullis & Lippa, 1990; see Gleicher & Petty, 1992, for a possible mechanism for this effect). Under these conditions, fear appeals can motivate important behavioral changes. The first two elements convince a person that it is wise to change; the second two reassure the person that change can happen and therefore remove some of the negative consequences of fear arousal.

YALE GROUP RESEARCH IN RETROSPECT

How are we to assess the Yale approach with hindsight's acuity? What of enduring value did it produce? Perhaps two things. First, it raised many of the issues that theorists of attitude change still concern themselves with. How credibility affects persuasion, for example, is still an ongoing research issue. Second, it was a model for the attempt to link facts about individual psychology to facts about attitude change. Over the years, learning theory has waned in importance, and cognitive approaches have become ascendant. With this change has come a corresponding shift from learning theory attempts to account for attitude change to cognitive attempts. But Yale group research provides the example of careful, controlled experiments designed to solve these problems. Now it is time for us to consider these more modern, cognitive approaches to persuasion.

COGNITION AND PERSUASION

The central proposition of cognitive approaches to persuasion is that whether a message persuades someone depends upon how the target processes the message and in particular on his cognitive responses to the message (Eagly & Chaiken, 1984). The development of this approach to attitude change first occurred in the context of research on the effect of distraction on attitude change. We will follow that history.

DISTRACTION AND PERSUASION

Research on the effects of distraction on persuasion developed from an experiment by Leon Festinger (Allyn & Festinger, 1961). The investigators were interested in whether being prepared to hear a message designed to change your opinion affected the amount of attitude change the message produced. To find out, they exposed some Palo Alto high school students to a message arguing that teenagers not be allowed to get driver's licenses—a message students certainly disagreed with. The subjects were divided into two groups: one group was told about the message in advance and told to focus on the content of the talk; the others were told that they were to focus not on the message or the topic but on the speaker's personality.

Oddly, there was greater attitude change in the group told to focus on the speaker's personality than in the group told to focus on the message. In a subsequent study, Festinger suggested that this effect might occur because the personality instruction distracted subjects from the content of the message (Festinger & Maccoby, 1964). So he set out to test the hypothesis that distraction enhances persuasion.

He showed groups of fraternity brothers a film in which the audio track was of a speaker advocating the abolition of fraternities—about as unlikely a message-audience combination as one could imagine. Half of the subjects saw the film with the visual part matched, showing the speaker delivering the message. But for the other half, the visual part was a cartoon called "Day of the Painter," which was apparently quite humorous and engaging. There was some evidence that the group shown the cartoon visual was more persuaded than the group shown the visual of the person delivering the message. So these two studies taken together suggest that distracting someone from a message they are not likely to agree with improves persuasion. But why?

One interpretation takes us back to learning theory. It suggests that the cartoon was a pleasant, reinforcing stimulus, and that the attitude change was a result of pairing the message with this pleasant stimulus. To show this, one experimenter carried out an experiment in which either junk food or a noxious odor was paired with a persuasive message. He found that the food increased the amount of attitude change the message produced (compared with attitude change in a control group not given the food), but the noxious odor had no effect. He argued that the pleasant snack was associated with the message, and that this association produced the attitude change.

There is an obvious interpretation of this result that doesn't rely on association in quite the blind way that learning theory meant it (Janis, Kaye, & Kirschner, 1965). Perhaps the subjects were just pleased to be given the snack, and therefore thought the experimenter was a nice guy and, because they liked him, answered his questions as if they were persuaded by his message. But Janis ruled this out. He was careful to lead the subjects to believe that the source of the message was not the donor of the snacks. So if this effect worked by association, it was of the blind sort, relying on simple association between the snack and the message, not on what giving the snack said about the character of the source.

◀ *Members of Congress, the Cabinet, the Supreme Court, and the diplomatic corps listen to President Bill Clinton deliver his State of the Union Address. What did they remember about it? The substance or the style?*

But problems quickly developed for this interpretation. For one thing, Philip Zimbardo has found that even quite unpleasant distractions increase persuasion. It is hard to encompass such a result in a learning theory framework (Zimbardo & Ebbesen, 1970; Zimbardo, Snyder, Thomas, Gold, & Gurwitz, 1970). So how are we to understand the enhancement that comes from distraction? Timothy Brock has proposed a solution that depends on what he takes to be subjects' normal cognitive response to a message that is opposed to their view. He argues that if subjects are not distracted, they will produce counterarguments to a message they disagree with, but that when they are distracted, they cannot counterargue. Distraction works, he suggests, by altering subjects' cognitive responses to a persuasive message. He offers several kinds of support for this claim (Petty & Brock, 1981).

First, although the distraction effect has been found for a variety of topics and distractions, it is most clear when the topics are important—for example, the abolition of fraternities when presented to fraternity members or proposals to increase tuition when presented to students. These are just the sorts of topics about which subjects should be eager and prepared to offer counterarguments. Second, the effect does not occur when the subject's attention is directed primarily to the *distraction*; in this case, attending to the distraction prevents them from understanding the message.

There are other experimental results that show more directly that distraction works by inhibiting counterarguing. In one study, subjects listened to an argument that tuition be increased from $150 to $300. While they listened, they also were supposed to watch a panel of lights and call out the numbers of the flashing lights. The number of flashes per minute was varied from none to twenty-four per minute, thus creating no, low, or high distraction. After they heard the message, the subjects were asked to state their current belief about tuition and to list their thoughts about the tuition message as they heard it. The lists were then scored for the total number of counterarguments by judges who did not know which condition the subjects were in. As the experimenters expected, the number of counterarguments decreased with increasing distraction, and the amount of persuasion the message produced went up as distraction increased (see Figure 16.13). These results suggest that as distraction increases, counterarguments decrease, and for that reason, persuasion is enhanced (Osterhouse & Brock, 1970).

This research on the effects of distraction on persuasion suggests that at least under the no-distraction condition, persuasion is a rational matter. Whether a person is persuaded or not depends on how weighty the arguments for a point of view are compared with the weight of the counterarguments. If the first are weightier, we are persuaded; if the second have more weight, we aren't. Asch would be happy with such a view—attitude change is essentially rational—but Lorge wouldn't because it gives no place to less rational influences on attitude change. More recently, attitude theorists have attempted to redress this balance by recognizing the place that both rational and less rational influences have in attitude change.

CENTRAL VERSUS PERIPHERAL ROUTES TO ATTITUDE CHANGE

Richard Petty and John Cacioppo have proposed in their **elaboration likelihood model** that there are two different "routes to persuasion"—two different ways to persuade someone. One route they call **central;** if a persuasive

FIGURE 16.13

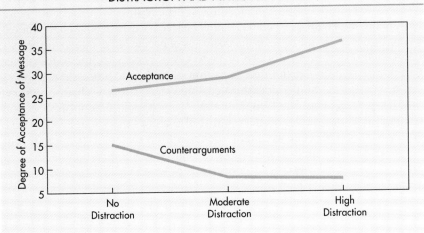

DISTRACTION AND ATTITUDE CHANGE

Amount of counterarguing and attitude change as a function of the degree of distraction. The more distracted subjects are, the less counterarguing they do and the more persuaded they are. (Data from Osterhouse & Brock, 1970)

message is processed via the central route, the target works hard at evaluating the message. To process a message via the central route, we carefully consider the message, check it for consistency with what we already know about the topic, generate counterarguments, compare the arguments with the counterarguments, and reach an overall conclusion.

But Petty and Cacioppo have proposed another route to persuasion, one they call the ***peripheral route.*** Petty and Cacioppo argue that we all want our attitudes to be true; we all want our evaluations of the world to be in good contact with that world. And we know that the best way to achieve that contact between our evaluations and the world is by systematic processing of (thoughts about) all that we learn. But, they argue, this processing takes a lot of time and is a lot of work. We are rarely willing to deploy all of our cognitive resources (and as much time as we have) to systematic analysis; we mostly process persuasive messages—television commercials, for example—less carefully, via peripheral routes (Petty & Cacioppo, 1986).

The notion of processing via peripheral routes covers any way in which a stimulus can affect our attitudes by some means *other* than systematic thought. Peripheral persuasion includes such things as conditioned associations (favored by Lorge) but also other, more cognitive processes that are less thorough than central persuasion.

Shelly Chaiken has focused attention on one cognitive, but peripheral, route to persuasion: heuristics. It is common in cognitive psychology to draw a distinction between an algorithm and a heuristic. Both are rules we might use to solve a problem, but they are different kinds of rule. An ***algorithm*** is a rule that, if followed exactly, must yield the correct answer—the way we are taught to do long division is an example of an algorithm. ***Heuristics*** are, on the other hand, rules of thumb; they are rules that often give the right answer, but that sometimes don't. "People marry other people who are like themselves" is, as we saw in Chapter 15, a good heuristic. If you were making bets about who would marry whom and you followed this rule, you would make a lot of money, but you would surely not get every case right.

Central route to persuasion for important issues

- is carefully reasoned;

- uses algorithms;

- depends on quality of the arguments;

Peripheral route to persuasion for less important issues

- is less carefully reasoned;

- uses heuristics;

- depends on superficial aspects (e.g., attractiveness of source, source prestige).

Chaiken has argued that one way we can be persuaded of something via a peripheral route is by using cognitive heuristics (Chaiken, 1980; Eagly & Chaiken, 1984). Here are some examples of heuristics: Experts know what they are talking about; politicians I usually agree with are right about political issues; I am likely to agree with the positions of people I like. Chaiken suggests that sometimes we use rules like these to assess persuasive messages rather than use more arduous and time-consuming systematic processing.

The central- versus peripheral-processing view of attitude change is promising because it allows us to agree with Asch that attitude formation and change are often rational matters, but it also allows us to agree with Lorge (and with much of what we might conclude from watching television) that they also are sometimes less than fully cognitive. For this approach to be useful, however, we need (1) a conception of when people will use central, or systematic (vs. peripheral), processing and (2) a way to tell which processing is being used. A study by Chaiken illustrates both.

Chaiken claims that one determinant of whether people will use systematic (central) or peripheral processing is how much people care about the issue. Chaiken argues that if people are very involved in an issue, then they will process a message centrally; if they are less involved, they will process it peripherally. To illustrate this, she conducted a study in which subjects were told that they were to take part in a two-session experiment. They were told that during the first session, their opinions about a variety of matters would be solicited; during the second session (which was actually never held), they would be interviewed in depth about one of the issues, and then they would participate in a group discussion. Some of the subjects were told that at the second session, they would discuss students' sleep habits; others were told that they would discuss changing from a semester to a trimester system. The purpose of this instruction was to insure that some subjects would be more involved with the sleep habits issue than the trimester issue, while others would be more involved with the trimester than the sleep habits issue. The experimenter assumed that having to discuss a topic during the second session would increase issue involvement.

After these instructions, the subjects were told that they would hear an interview (like the one they were to have in the second session). The interview was with a university administrator rather than with another student. This "interview" was a way for the experimenter to introduce a persuasive message into the experiment. The interview consisted of an argument on the part of the administrator either for moving to the trimester system (unpopular with students) or for the view that people should sleep less than eight hours each night (also unpopular). For some subjects, the interview they heard was on the same topic they expected to discuss at the second session; for others, it was on the opposite topic. Because of the match (or mismatch) of topics, some of the subjects should have been highly involved in the interview; other subjects should have been much less involved. This manipulation, then, created more and less involved subjects who listened to the persuasive message.

The interview came in four versions. Some of the versions made the administrator out to be a likable fellow; others made him out to be a quite unlikable guy. (In all versions, he was portrayed as being new to the university, and he was asked about how he found it. In the likable versions, he explained that he found the undergraduates to be mature and reasonable; in the other cases, he explained that he found them to be immature and unreasonable.) In addition, in some versions of the interview, he gave six arguments for his position; in other cases, he gave two. These various versions of the interview were designed to include one difference that should matter to subjects engaged in systematic issue processing—the number of arguments included in the interview. Other versions included a variation that should matter to those engaged in peripheral, heuristic processing—the likability of the communicator.

Chaiken proposed that for the subjects who expected to discuss the same topic at the next session, the number of arguments presented should affect how persuaded they were by the message, while whether the communicator was likable shouldn't. She predicted that for those who were less involved, the likability of the communicator should matter, but the number of arguments shouldn't. To find out if this was so, the subjects were asked their final opinion about the topic they had heard discussed both immediately after the experiment and ten days later. Their opinions on these occasions were compared with their initial opinions to determine the degree to which the messages produced attitude change.

The results were in line with the author's expectations. For the high-involvement subjects, degree of attitude change was affected by the number of arguments in the message, but not by the likability of the communicator; for the low-involvement subjects, the likability of the communicator mattered, but the quality of his arguments didn't (see Figure 16.14; Chaiken, 1980; see also Chen, Reardon, Rea, & Moore, 1992).

This experiment, then, articulates one factor—issue involvement—that affects whether information is processed centrally or peripherally, and it gives us a way to determine whether the information is being processed centrally or peripherally. If information is being *centrally processed*, then degree of attitude change should be affected by features of the argument that are rationally connected to its persuasiveness—the number and quality of arguments, for example. If the information is being *peripherally processed*, it should be unaffected by these factors, but it should be affected by more peripheral, less rational cues—the likability of the communicator, for example.

Using similar methods, Richard Petty and John Cacioppo have addressed an issue first raised by the Yale group: communicator expertise. They exposed high- or low-involvement subjects to strong or weak arguments from a credible or not credible source. They found that subjects who were not involved in the topic were influenced by source credibility, while those who were involved were affected by the strength of the arguments (Petty, Cacioppo, & Goldman, 1981). Thus, once again, a feature that should matter to rational, systematic message processing—argument quality—was shown to affect highly involved subjects, while a cue that should matter to peripheral processing—source expertise—was shown to matter to less-involved subjects.*

The number of arguments someone presents for a position is sometimes

*The same cue might be used in either a systematic or peripheral way. Consider expertise, for example. The fact that your doctor, presumably an expert in such matters, tells you to do something for your health is a perfectly rational reason to do it. Even a systematic processor must count expertise as a reason to have one's attitude affected. But, as is true in this study, when an expert offers the reasons for her opinion, then the systematic, rational processor has better evidence than simple expertise, and he must use this better evidence.

FIGURE 16.14
SOURCE ATTRACTIVENESS
AND PERSUASION

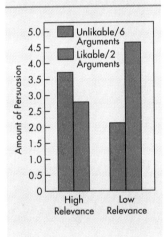

▲ *Persuasion and source attractiveness as a function of the relevance (importance) of the issue. Superficial aspects such as source attractiveness mattered more for unimportant issues. (Data from Chaiken, 1980)*

a cue that is relevant to a heuristic processor. To show this, in one experiment, subjects either highly involved or less involved in an issue heard either six or three arguments against their attitudes. Three of the arguments were strong, but three were weak. The uninvolved subjects were affected by the *number* of arguments presented, but not their quality; the more involved subjects were affected by the quality of the arguments, but not their number (Petty & Cacioppo, 1984). Thus, the number of arguments can be used as a peripheral cue in a heuristic that says the more arguments that can be advanced for a position, the more valid it is.

Whether the audience for a message reacts favorably to a message is another cue as to the quality of a message. It too ought to be, and has been shown to be, a determinant of attitude change for less, but not more, involved subjects (Axsom, Yates, & Chaiken, 1987).

One further determinant of how a persuasive message is processed is intrinsic to the message. Messages with incongruent elements invoke systematic processing, even when the persuasive message isn't very important to the subject (Maheswaran & Chaiken, 1991). So if you want to slip something past someone who doesn't care much about the issue, try to be consistent, at least; inconsistency sometimes sticks out like a sore thumb and invokes close scrutiny.

The research we have just reviewed lends support to the notion that under certain conditions, people process information in a systematic way, while in other conditions, they process it in a more peripheral, less systematic way. And it has been shown that different factors account for the amount of attitude change induced by a message, depending on whether it has been processed in a systematic or peripheral way. One factor is subjects' involvement in the issue. And involvement in the issue has itself been varied in two ways: in some studies, issue involvement has been high or low because of the relation of the issue to subjects' everyday lives (e.g., comprehensive exams to be instituted this year or in the next decade); in other studies, involvement has been varied by assigning subjects (or not assigning them) to discuss the topic later with someone else.*

INFLUENCES OF MODE OF INFORMATION PROCESSING

Research of late has turned toward other factors that affect which sort of information processing someone engages in. In one study, subjects first expressed their attitudes toward measures to reduce acid rain. Some were then put in a good mood by being told that they would be in a lottery to win an extra $2; others were not. All subjects were then given a persuasive message to read about acid rain prevention. Some of the subjects in each condition were given a limited amount of time to read the message; others were given unlimited time. Some messages were strong; others were weak. The results showed that under limited exposure conditions, the subjects who were *not* put in a good mood were affected by the quality of the messages; they were persuaded more by strong than by weak messages. But those in the time limit

*There is some evidence that only the first sort of involvement—called issue involvement—actually induces systematic information processing. Causing subjects to believe that they will later have to discuss the topic (called response involvement) sometimes induces primarily self-presentational concerns and peripheral processing (Leippe & Elkin, 1987; see also Johnson & Eagly, 1989, 1990; Petty & Cacioppo, 1990).

condition and in a good mood were *unaffected* by message quality, suggesting peripheral, heuristic processing. Under unlimited exposure, however, good mood subjects chose to expose themselves to the message longer than did neutral mood subjects (suggesting that they were thinking about it longer), and they too showed evidence of systematic processing (Mackie & Worth, 1989). This evidence suggests that good moods make it more difficult to process messages systematically.

Other research suggests that subjects in good moods pay less attention to variables, such as argument strength, that are associated with systematic processing than do subjects who are in poor or neutral moods (Bless, Bohner, Schwarz, & Strack, 1990; Bless, Mackie, & Schwarz, 1992; DeBono, 1992). The propensity for people in good moods to process information in a lazy way can, however, be overcome by instructions, so heuristic information processing in good moods isn't inevitable. It is just what happens when people are left to their own devices (Petty, Schumann, Richman, & Strathman, 1993).

Another factor that can affect the kind of information processing a person does is the social context of the attitude change. Chapter 3 discussed social loafing, the idea that if a group is assigned a task, each member of the group will exert less effort than she would have had she been assigned the task alone. This effect has been extended to the domain of attitude formation. In one study, subjects were led to believe that they alone or as part of a group of fifteen people were to evaluate a male graduate student in terms of his suitability as a clinical psychologist. They then saw a videotape of a female undergraduate being interviewed by the graduate student about a phobia she wanted to cure. Some subjects heard an interview suggesting that the graduate student was good at this task; others saw a tape suggesting he wouldn't be very good. The evidence—listings of the thoughts subjects had about the evaluators as well as their final evaluations—suggested that subjects engaged in systematic processing when they evaluated alone, but peripheral processing when they were part of a group (see Figure 16.15; Petty, Harkins, & Williams, 1980).

FIGURE 16.15

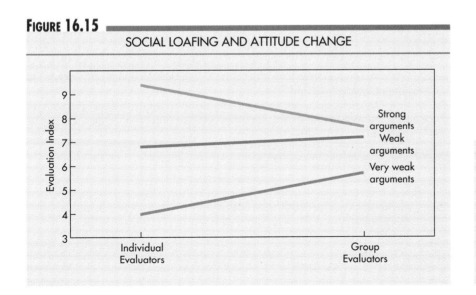

SOCIAL LOAFING AND ATTITUDE CHANGE

◀ *Evaluations varied according to the quality of the stimulus (weak or strong arguments) and whether the person doing the evaluating was alone or in a group. Social loafing was seen even in the attitude domain. (From Perry, Harkins, & Williams, 1980)*

Finally, the form of a communication itself can affect the way it is processed. There is evidence that introducing a persuasive message with a rhetorical question is a good strategy for inducing attitude change if—and only if—good arguments follow. Subjects in one study were more persuaded by, and generated more favorable responses to, a strong message if it was preceded by a rhetorical question, but they were *less* persuaded by a weak argument preceded by such a question (Burnkrant & Howard, 1984; see also Howard, 1990, for other approaches to rhetorical questions).

WRAP-UP

Most of the research discussed in this chapter has focused on what people have had to say about some attitude object. It is indeed true that people often express their attitudes by saying them out loud. This leads us to wonder about how attitudes conceived as evaluations people are willing to express to a researcher are related to more substantive behavior. For example, how do people's attitudes toward seat belts relate to whether they actually wear them? After all, if attitudes are just evaluations people endorse on researchers' questionnaires, they aren't of much interest. There have been times in the history of social psychology when researchers seemed simply to assume that attitudes are reflected in behavior, and there have been other periods when researchers seemed to assume that expressed attitudes had nothing at all to do with behavior. As we shall see, neither view is correct. Attitudes do relate to behavior, but they do so in a rather complex way. In any event, the question of whether attitudes relate to behavior is so important that I have saved it for a chapter of its own, the next one.

SUMMARY

1. Attitudes are evaluations of things—of attitude objects. Attitudes (1) help define social groups, (2) help us establish our identities, and (3) help guide our thinking and behavior.

2. One determinant of our attitudes is the desire for *cognitive consistency*, or balance. *Cognitive dissonance theory* is one development, by Leon Festinger, of this idea that people seek out balance. Cognitive dissonance theory in its original form held that when people have in mind two or more psychologically inconsistent ideas, they fall into an aversive drive state, the state of dissonance arousal. In order to gain relief from this state, people alter one or more of the inconsistent cognitions.

3. The need for consistency has been held accountable for a variety of irrational responses.

4. As successful as dissonance theory was empirically, it had an important weakness, the somewhat obscure notion of psychological inconsistency. Experimental research has suggested that people distort their beliefs when they assert something they don't believe and (1) it was clear they did so under free choice, (2) there were negative consequences of their actions, (3) these negative consequences were foreseeable from the start, and (4) they were offered only a very small inducement to lie. This pattern of results suggests

that at heart, dissonance has to do with not wanting to feel cheap and either stupid or guilty.

5. There have been several challenges to dissonance theory. One, from Daryl Bem, called *self-perception theory*, holds that subjects in dissonance experiments do not distort their views because of their behavior; they infer their attitudes from their behavior in the first place. Thus, when people find they have endorsed a position for a very small amount of money, they infer that they must have believed the position, but if they were paid a lot of money to endorse it, they infer that they didn't believe it.

6. One difference between the dissonance account and Bem's self-perception theory is that self-perception theory does not predict the presence of arousal associated with dissonance. But research has demonstrated that dissonance-provoking circumstances *do* produce arousal, arousal that serves as a signal to remind people that they have done something wrong.

7. Bem's self-perception account has proven more useful in understanding what happens to people's attitudes when they are offered an inducement to do something they *would want to do anyway.*

8. Dissonance theory suggests that people should avoid information inconsistent with their views, but seek out information consistent with their views. Early attempts to demonstrate such *selective exposure* failed. But more recently, researchers have found evidence that people will avoid unpleasant information, but only if (1) they believe they cannot refute the uncomfortable argument, and (2) they are irrevocably committed to their way of thinking or behaving.

9. Abraham Tesser has found that merely thinking about an attitude object tends to polarize one's attitude toward it—making it more positive if it is positive and more negative if it is negative. Tesser relates this to the notion that our knowledge of the world is organized in the form of *schemata*, and that schemata tend toward evaluative consistency.

10. In general, more credible sources—more expert and more trustworthy sources—tend to be more persuasive than less credible ones. But there is some evidence for a *sleeper effect;* that is, a persuasive communication from a noncredible source may have little or no immediate impact, but with the passage of time, it may actually grow in persuasiveness.

11. A central tenet of modern cognitive approaches to persuasion is that whether a person is persuaded by a message depends to a significant degree on how the target of the message *processes* the message—on whether the target, for example, produces counterarguments. Distraction sometimes increases the impact of a message because it prevents people from counterarguing against the message.

12. One important difference in how we process persuasive messages involves whether we systematically and carefully weigh arguments for and against the message, or think about the issue less carefully or peripherally. If the topic of a persuasive message is important to us, we are likely to think about it carefully; if the topic is less important, we are likely to devote less effort to processing the message. Different aspects of a message are likely to affect its persuasiveness, depending on whether we are processing it carefully or carelessly. For example, the quality of arguments will matter if we are carefully processing a message. But if we are only inattentively processing, then other cues—like the attractiveness of the speaker—will become important.

CHAPTER 17

Attitudes and Behavior

Between 1930 and 1932, Robert LaPiere toured the country with a young Chinese couple. LaPiere described them as "personable, charming, and quick to win the admiration and respect of those they had the opportunity to become intimate with." They visited 66 hotels, auto camps, and tourist homes, and ate in 184 restaurants and cafés. None of this is remarkable. What is remarkable is that this was a time of very strong prejudice in the United States against Asians. The prejudice was so extreme that many establishments had a policy against serving Asians. Yet LaPiere and this particular couple were denied service only once.

To document the anti-Asian prejudice that was rampant, about six months after their visit, LaPiere mailed questionnaires to all 250 of the establishments they had visited, and asked whether they would serve Asians. About 50 percent answered the questionnaire. Roughly 90 percent of those responding claimed that they would not serve Asians (LaPiere, 1934). This study called attention to a wide discrepancy between the merchants' self-reported attitudes about serving Asians in general and their actual behavior when confronted with a particular Asian couple. This breach between attitudes and behavior was troublesome to social psychologists for two reasons.

First, there is a general consensus in the field that the aim of psychological research and theorizing is to predict behavior, especially morally and socially significant behavior. But it is very difficult (for both ethical and pragmatic reasons) to carry out research on significant behavior; thus, researchers often instead aim their research at predicting subjects' self-reported attitudes, assuming that these reports of attitudes are a proxy for behavior. If attitudes do not predict behavior, then of what importance is this research?

Second, and more substantive, if self-reported attitudes are not just a proxy for behavior, then how do they relate to behavior? The LaPiere study suggests that there is a real need for theory and research that explores the mechanism by which attitudes affect behavior insofar as they do.

These two issues form the agenda for this chapter. We will follow three perspectives on the relation between attitudes and behavior. The first approach takes attitudes to be *one*, but only one, source of behavior; it articulates the relations among attitudes, norms, intentions, evaluations, and behavior. This discussion will lead us into a broader consideration of human rationality (and its limits). The second approach argues that some attitudes are predictive of behavior but others aren't, and it attempts to distinguish between the two. This discussion will take us into a consideration of *how* attitudes might affect behavior. The third approach argues that attitudes and behavior are consistent, but only for certain sorts of people.

But first we need to satisfy ourselves that there is something worth discussing, that the LaPiere study wasn't a fluke. Perhaps there was something special about it that upset the usual relation between subjects' professed attitudes and their behavior. But there wasn't. In fact, in his thorough review of the research that existed by 1969, Allan Wicker concluded, "The present review provides little evidence to support the postulated existence of stable, underlying attitudes within the individual which influence both his verbal expressions and his actions" (Wicker, 1969, p. 75).

The LaPiere finding, rather than being a fluke, was characteristic of the extant research. Gloom prevailed among attitude researchers; indeed, there followed a period of about five years during which social psychologists all but abandoned research on attitudes. We turn now to the story of how and why attitudes, like the prodigal son, were welcomed back into the psychological family.

THE RECONSTRUCTION OF ATTITUDES

Martin Fishbein and Icek Ajzen prepared the welcoming party for attitudes in two ways. First they offered a cogent criticism of the literature that purported to show that attitudes did not predict behavior. Second, and more important, they proposed a substantive theory of how attitudes relate to other psychological variables in predicting behavior (Fishbein & Ajzen, 1974, 1975). The methodological criticism focused on the problem of generality.

The Problem of Generality

The Fishbein and Ajzen reconstruction of the study of attitudes began with an important observation. They pointed out that attitude measures usually ask about people's feelings about a broad class of people, events, objects, and so on. The LaPiere letter, for example, asked about attitudes toward Asians in general. Behavioral tests of attitudes, on the other hand, are typically in response to a single stimulus, in the LaPiere case one particular Asian couple. Fishbein and Ajzen argued that what research of this sort showed was not that attitudes don't predict behavior but that *general* attitudes don't predict *specific* behaviors. They claimed that higher correlations between attitudes and behavior would be found if measures of general attitudes were correlated

▶ *Paul Cézanne's* Le Grands Baigneuses. *People might have different attitudes toward paintings of nudes in general and toward this particular painting of nudes.*

not with single acts but with broad classes of behavior. And symmetrically, if one wanted to predict single acts, then one would have to ask about people's attitudes toward performing those particular acts. To see the logic of this, let's consider a concrete example.

Suppose we had a measure of people's general attitude toward losing weight, and we wanted to know if that attitude related to their weight-losing behavior. What behavior should we look at? There are many different specific ways of losing weight. A person might skip meals, give up snacks, drink diet soda, give up alcoholic beverages, exercise, pass up desserts, and so on. To lose weight, you have to do some of these, but not all of them. Thus, we wouldn't expect people with positive attitudes toward weight loss to do all of them; moreover, even people who aren't trying to lose weight might do some of them. Both of these facts will lower the correlation between weight loss attitudes and weight loss behavior. So even if we had a very good measure of attitude toward weight loss, we shouldn't expect it to relate very well to any one of these behaviors.

On the other hand, the more of these behaviors you do, the more likely you are to lose weight. If we made up a composite score by adding up all of the behaviors related to weight loss, we would expect people who had a more favorable attitude toward weight loss to have a higher composite score. We should expect a higher correlation between attitudes toward weight loss in general and a composite score than between attitudes toward weight loss and any one of the specific behaviors involved. But if we wanted to predict who would do one specific weight loss behavior, such as exercise, we would do better to ask about people's attitudes toward that behavior in particular rather than asking about general attitudes toward weight loss. Several investigators have found just this sort of result.

What Behavior Is Predicted?

In one study, women of child-bearing age were asked their attitudes toward birth control and whether they were using a birth control pill. The correlation between being in favor of birth control and actually using the pill was very low, 0.05, suggesting little relation between attitude and behavior. But there are a variety of ways of practicing birth control, so the investigators also asked them about their more specific attitude toward using birth control pills. The correlation between this specific attitude and their reported use of the pill was a much more respectable 0.71. Thus, when the attitude question and the behavioral measure were at the same level of generality, there was a substantial correlation.

In a second study, subjects were asked their attitudes toward religion, church, and attending church. They were also asked whether they had attended church the preceding Sunday. The correlation between their attitudes toward religion and their actually attending church was a low 0.18. But the correlation between going to church and their attitude toward attending church was 0.65 (Jaccard, King, & Pomazal, 1977). The results of this study and numerous others suggest that attitudes can be predictive of behavior, but only when the attitudes solicited and the behaviors predicted are at similar levels of generality (Katz, 1982). The gloom about the lack of relation between attitudes and behavior may have been premature.

Fishbein and Ajzen argued that for attitudes to predict behavior, you have to ask about a person's attitude toward a specific behavior. This suggests that LaPiere might have received a different response to his letter had he been specific: Would you serve a well-dressed Asian couple accompanied by a Westerner?

But there is a problem with this way of solving the attitude-behavior problem. The idea that there is a specific attitude accompanying each specific behavior severely undercuts the utility of the attitude concept (Rokeach, 1960). The concept of attitude was invoked in the first place because investigators believed that although there was an infinite variety of behaviors that a person could engage in, there was also a rather limited set of attitudes that could be used to predict those behaviors. If it turns out that attitudes do predict behavior but that there is an infinite set of attitudes that you need to know to predict the behaviors, then there is little reason to invoke the concept of attitudes in the first place. One way around this problem is with a theory of attitudes that allows you to predict attitudes from a smaller set of variables. Fortunately, Fishbein and Ajzen have given us that too.

General attitudes predict aggregated behavior; specific attitudes predict specific behaviors.

▲ *Different attitudes toward poverty and about giving to homeless people would guide our actions toward these men.*

THE MODEL OF REASONED ACTION

Fishbein and Ajzen developed the ***model of reasoned action*** to explain the relation of attitudes to behavior. It starts with the notion that people act *rationally* and places the concept of attitudes within that framework. Fishbein and Ajzen argue that the immediate psychological determinant of behavior is not a person's attitude toward the target of his act but rather his intention to perform that act. Within certain limits, we could predict what a person will do perfectly if we knew her intentions. Fishbein and Ajzen attempt to conquer the problem of predicting behavior by dividing it. They introduce the notion of intentions as the immediate antecedent of behavior, and then introduce attitudes as one, but only one, predictor of intentions. We now need to ask how attitudes relate to intentions in their theory. But before we do, we should examine the limits that Fishbein and Ajzen impose on the degree to which intentions predict behavior.

One limitation comes from the fact that we have to be careful about what we call a behavior. For example, passing an examination, although related to behavior, is not itself a behavior; it is something accomplished by behavior. For someone to pass an exam, not only must he engage in behavior designed to achieve that end, those efforts must be successful. The intention to pass an exam may not correlate perfectly with passing the exam because some people, no matter how well intended, lack the required talent. Similarly, intentions to have children won't perfectly predict who has children, both because some couples are unable to have children and because no method of birth control, save abstinence, is foolproof.

To take a different limitation, one's intentions to be greedy should hardly be expected to predict greedy acts, since few people set out to try to be greedy; they typically set out to get all that they can within the limits of propriety, but sometimes they overstep these limits (Sabini & Silver, 1982). Being greedy, like being successful on an exam, isn't a behavior; it is a characterization of behavior in relation to some standard. The Fishbein and Ajzen claim that intentions perfectly predict behavior is only so for descriptions of behavior that do not involve living up to standards that the person may not be able to meet.

Another limitation has to do with time. If time elapses between the measurement of intention and the act, there may be a failure to correlate because intentions have changed in the interim. If you ask people in September whom they intend to vote for and then ask in November whom they voted for, you may find disparity. But this may be because further information about the candidates has come to light, and intentions have changed. Still, within these limits Fishbein and Ajzen argue that intentions perfectly predict behavior. Now we can ask: Where do intentions come from, and how do they relate to attitudes?

Attitudes and Intentions

The model of reasoned action holds that intentions are a consequence of two elements of a person's psychology: attitudes toward performing an act and "subjective norms" with regard to the act. **Subjective norms** about performing an act are people's perceptions of what other people important to their lives think they should do. The model of reasoned action proposes that there are two (and only two) determinants of a person's intentions: (1) her attitude toward performing an act and (2) her perceptions of what other people important in her life think she should do (subjective norms) (see Figure 17.1).

The model does not specify how much each component will matter in the prediction of particular intentions; it assumes that how much each matters

FIGURE 17.1

THE MODEL OF
REASONED ACTION

Attitudes toward the act

Intentions toward behavior

Subjective norms

▲ According to the model of reasoned action, attitudes toward the act and subjective norms determine intentions toward an act.

will vary from act to act (and perhaps from person to person). The natural question that arises now is: Where do these components come from? Let us consider attitudes first.

THE ORIGINS OF ATTITUDES

Fishbein and Ajzen take a particularly rational stance toward the formation of attitudes. They argue that a person's attitudes toward performing an act are themselves a consequence of two things: (1) her estimate of the consequences of performing the act and (2) her evaluation of those consequences. So to predict whether someone will have a positive attitude toward, say, voting for a particular candidate, we have to know what she thinks all the consequences of voting for that candidate are, and how she evaluates those consequences (see Figure 17.2). We can press the issue one step further and ask: Where do the evaluations come from? Fishbein and Ajzen do not discuss this point explicitly, but we can extend the model of reasoned action to fill this in.

Attitudes and Drives   One source of attitudes toward acts is the drives we have as humans. Why does a hungry person evaluate eating highly? Because he is hungry; his physiology is so constructed that when he hasn't eaten for a while, he is driven to find eating highly attractive. And so too for the sources of our other biological drives. So one source of attitudes toward acts is our innate, biological equipment.

Attitudes and Values   Suppose someone opposed capital punishment; she had a negative attitude toward executing people convicted of murder. And we asked why. To which she replied, "Because it is wrong to take a life." Now we might ask her: "Why is it wrong to take a life?" Suppose she replied, "It just is!" She could offer no further reason for believing that it is wrong. Preserving human life is for her something bedrock, something that needs no further justification. She might be able to tell you how she came to believe that—

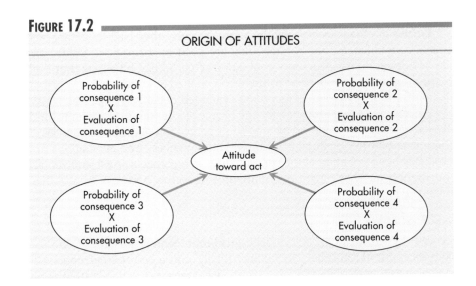

FIGURE 17.2

ORIGIN OF ATTITUDES

◀ *The attitude toward an act is determined by the consequences of the act and evaluations of the act.*

because she was brought up that way—but such a *causal account* of how she came to value life is not a *justification* for believing this. It is just an explanation of how she came to believe this. For her, preserving life is an end in itself.

A different kind of goal, called **contingent goal,** is valuable only because it leads to other goals. Suppose we asked someone why he wanted to increase the defense budget, and he said, "To deter the Russians and head off a nuclear conflict." "Heading off a nuclear conflict" may be an end in itself, but increasing the defense budget isn't—if you could convince him either that we don't need to increase the defense budget to deter the Russians, or that increasing the defense budget won't deter them, then he wouldn't be in favor of increasing the defense budget. Contingent goals are only worth pursuing if they lead to something else that is desirable.

Values are goals that people have, not because they lead to further, desirable consequences, but because they are good in themselves. Values are like biological drives, sources of evaluation of particular acts. Acts that lead to the attainment of important values are evaluated positively, while acts that detract from their accomplishment are evaluated negatively.

We have seen that attitudes are one source of intentions. Attitudes toward acts are themselves produced by a person's perception of the consequences of those acts and her evaluation of those consequences. And evaluations are produced by the relation of the consequences to a person's drives and values. But there is another source of intentions—subjective norms. Why are they included?

SUBJECTIVE NORMS

George Herbert Mead (1934/1974) argued that "significant others" are the sources of our moral beliefs. By taking into account a person's perceptions of significant other people's attitudes, the model of reasoned action is attempting

FIGURE 17.3

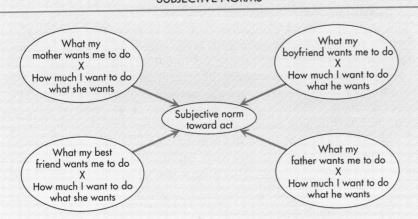

SUBJECTIVE NORMS

What my mother wants me to do
X
How much I want to do what she wants

What my boyfriend wants me to do
X
How much I want to do what he wants

Subjective norm toward act

What my best friend wants me to do
X
How much I want to do what she wants

What my father wants me to do
X
How much I want to do what he wants

◀ *The subjective norms with regard to an act depend on what other people think about a person's doing it, and the importance of these other people in the person's life.*

to incorporate moral concerns as an independent determinant of intentions—independent of a person's attitudes. The model argues that in forming an intention to do some act, you are influenced by your own attitudes as well as by your perception of significant others' attitudes toward that act—you may have a positive attitude toward say, taking drugs, but you also know that other people you care about will disapprove (see Figure 17.3). The degree to which your perceptions of other people's attitudes affect your intentions also depends on how motivated you are to comply with those people's attitudes.

In support of their model, Fishbein and Ajzen report several studies of a variety of different behaviors, ranging from voting for political candidates to family planning. The method of this research is to collect several pieces of data on the same subjects: (1) a measure of their intent to perform a given act, (2) a subsequent report of whether they did or didn't perform the act, (3)

◀ *To what extent does advertising influence attitudes?*

a measure of their salient beliefs about the consequences of the act, (4) a measure of their evaluations of those consequences, (5) a measure of their perceptions of what significant others think they should do, and (6) a measure of how motivated they are to please those significant others. The model is a success if behavior is correlated with behavioral intent, and if behavioral intent is itself correlated with measures 3 to 6 (Fishbein & Ajzen, 1975).

Many studies have demonstrated the general success of the Fishbein-Ajzen reconstruction of attitudes (for reviews, see Cialdini, Petty, & Cacioppo, 1981; Cooper & Croyle, 1984; Chaiken & Stagnor, 1987). The general success of the model has three implications: (1) the model does a good job of predicting behavior—which may be important in some contexts, (2) people are more or less rational in their attitudes and behavior, and (3) research on attitudes is not as pointless as some feared in the wake of the LaPiere and Wicker findings.

Individual Limitations on Reasoned Action

Although the model of reasoned action has generally been successful, it is not perfectly predictive, and where it fails to be predictive can inform us about limits of rational action, a topic of considerable interest in its own right.

PREVIOUS BEHAVIOR

A colleague of mine once proposed his first law of human behavior: "The best predictor of what person A will do in situation X is what person A has done in situation X before." On the face of it, there is nothing inconsistent between this "law" and the model of reasoned action. Take using seat belts, for example. The model of reasoned action says that a person on his way to work on Tuesday morning will decide to use a seat belt or not based on his assessment of consequences and his opinion of his significant others' desires. Now what about on Wednesday; will he do the same thing or a different thing? At least with regard to seat belt use, it is unlikely that new relevant information will have occurred to him in the course of one day. So it is likely that the same considerations will lead to the same conclusion on the following day. Thus, stability from day to day is to be expected from the perspective of the model of reasoned action. But one might ask: Is our ability to predict someone's behavior on a given occasion improved by adding to the variables specified in the model of reasoned action information about what he did in the same circumstances previously (see Figure 17.4)?

Several studies have investigated this question. In one study, subjects were asked about their attitudes toward seat belt use, their subjective norms, and their intentions with regard to using seat belts. But they were also asked about how frequently they had used seat belts in the past. One month later, they were again asked these questions, and about their seat belt use in the intervening month. The results indicated, as the model of reasoned action proposed, that seat belt use during the month was predicted by behavioral intentions, and behavioral intentions were also predicted by subjective norms and attitudes. But whether someone used seat belts was also affected by whether he habitually used them, and this ability of past habits to predict was *in addition to* the predictive power offered by the variables the model specifies (Wittenbraker, Gibbs, & Kahle, 1983; Budd, North, & Spencer, 1984; Sutton & Hallett, 1989). The finding that past behavior helps predict current

FIGURE 17.4

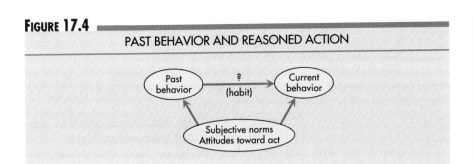

PAST BEHAVIOR AND REASONED ACTION

◀ *Attitudes toward an act determine current intentions and most likely past intentions toward the act. Thus, past behavior and current behavior are likely to be correlated. But past behavior has a correlation with current behavior over and above the correlation proposed by the model of reasoned action.*

behavior when added to the model of reasoned action has been found for several different kinds of behavior: studying for course work, exercise, and dating (Bentler & Speckart, 1981), attending college classes (Fredricks & Dossett, 1983), and blood donating (Bagozzi, 1981). What is the moral of this story?

The simple conclusion is that habits limit the likelihood that we will act rationally. But a bit more needs to be said. A colleague of mine always answers his office phone by giving his name. Is this rational or habit? The answer is both. There is no opposition in this case between what reason dictates and his well-established habits; it is a perfectly rational way to answer the phone, and it is his habitual way. Indeed, we accomplish much by rationally organizing our habits. But the fact remains that *sometimes* habits get in the way of doing what we know to be the rational thing to do.

EMOTIONS

Emotions play a role *within* the model of reasoned action. Imagine that someone asks you your evaluation of the action of burning down your house. You are likely to have a strong negative reaction to such a proposal, and there is nothing irrational about that. Your emotional reaction here is rooted in your values concerning having a home. In general, emotions can be incorporated within the model of reasoned action by admitting them as determinants of evaluation. But do emotions play an additional role? Might there be occasions on which someone computes what the model of reasoned action dictates, decides what to do, but then does something else anyway—for emotional reasons (see Figure 17.5)?

FIGURE 17.5

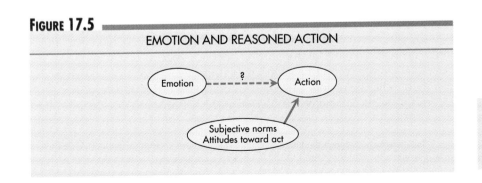

EMOTION AND REASONED ACTION

◀ *Reason determines emotions and behavior. Emotion also seems to affect behavior over and above the impact of reason.*

William Fisher investigated this question in the context of condom use. Fisher asked sexually active undergraduate men to indicate the various variables included in the Fishbein and Ajzen model—their perceptions of the consequences of condom use, their evaluations of those consequences, and so on. But in addition, he also asked them to fill out an erotophobia-erotophilia scale, which tries to get at their emotional reactions to sex. Of these subjects, 44 who had sexual intercourse during the following month were asked to indicate whether they had used condoms during that intercourse.

The results indicated that the elements of the Fishbein-Ajzen model predicted which of these men used condoms during intercourse. But the erotophilia-erotophobia scale *also* predicted whether they used condoms. The men who had more positive attitudes toward sex were more likely to use condoms than were the men with more negative attitudes, and this predictive power of the erotophobia-erotophilia scale was *over and above* the prediction provided by the Fishbein and Ajzen model (Fisher, 1984).

Or, put the other way, men with negative emotional reactions to sex used condoms even less often than their own attitudes toward condoms would predict. Further research indicates that subjects with negative emotional reactions to sex may have difficulty remembering information about contraceptives, which might account to some degree for their failing to use them (Gerrard, Kurylo, & Reis, 1991). Another emotion that sometimes gets in the way of a rational relation between attitudes, norms, and behavior is embarrassment. *One* reason that adolescents don't use condoms to prevent pregnancy and sexually transmitted diseases is their fear of embarrassment at buying condoms (Pleck, Sonenstein, & Ku, 1991; see Morrison, 1989, for a different result with female subjects). Just as habits can sometimes get in the way of our doing what is rational, so too can emotional reactions affect our behavior in a way that is discrepant with the dictates of reason.

PERCEIVED BEHAVIORAL CONTROL

Icek Ajzen has added an element to the model of reasoned action, which has to do with circumstances in which a person may not see himself as able to carry out an action that he knows to be rational. Consider again deciding to lose weight. Suppose a person believes that he would be better off if he lost weight, and believes that his significant others think he should lose weight. Will he form the intention to lose weight? According to the model of reasoned action, he will. But he might not if he doesn't believe he is *capable* of carrying out the behaviors required to lose weight.* Ajzen suggests that the model of reasoned action needs to take into account the degree to which the person believes that he *can* carry out the desired action. Data supporting the view that the perception that one will succeed in a behavior plan can affect intentions have been found for weight loss, performance of a screening test for colorectal cancer, voting behavior, dental hygiene, alcohol drinking, and a variety of other behaviors (Ajzen, 1987; McCaul, O'Neil, & Glasgow, 1988; DeVellis, Blalock, & Sandler, 1990; Netemeyer & Burton, 1990; Beale & Man-

*I have already discussed the fact that even if he *does* form such an intention, he might not be able to carry the intention out. But the issue here is not whether he will succeed in carrying out his intention; the issue is whether he will form such an intention in the first place.

stead, 1991; Madden, Ellen, & Ajzen, 1992; Schlegel, d'Avernas, Zanna, DeCourville, & Manske, 1992).

We have found, then, three limits on the model of rational action. People can be expected to be less than rational in their intentions and behavior (1) when their habits oppose reason, (2) when their emotions get in the way, and (3) when they do not believe that they are capable of doing what reason dictates. There is a fourth limit on the model of reasoned action, but it arises not because we are irrational, but because we are moral.

MORALITY

The model of reasoned action also provides a place for morality as a determinant of action. Actually, it provides two places. First, moral concerns may affect our evaluation of consequences; we may evaluate a course of action as having negative consequences because we find those consequences morally abhorrent. And second, Fishbein and Ajzen follow Mead in taking our perception of other people's perceptions of what we should do as a kind of moral judgment.* But even if Mead is right and our moral norms come, in the first instance, from what other people expect of us, this does not imply that what we currently think is the moral thing to do is what we currently think other people expect us to do.

It is perfectly possible, for example, that we learn a set of moral norms from our parents, but that once we have acquired those principles, we can use those principles to reach conclusions different from those our parents reach. After all, we learn our language from our parents (or someone), but we are not confined to uttering the sentences we have heard our parents (or whoever) utter. We may come to have moral beliefs that are independent of our perceptions of others' expectations about us. And these moral judgments may affect our behavior independently of the variables proposed by Fishbein and Ajzen (see Figure 17.6).

One study examined subjects' attitudes toward being a transplant donor. They asked the subjects to indicate both their own views of the moral aspect of this and what the subjects thought their significant others would think. The investigators found that both factors were important. But the subjects' own moral views were more important in predicting attitudes. This evidence suggests that our moral views are, at least sometimes and to some degree, independent of our significant others' views.

The investigators didn't just examine attitudes, though. They also gave subjects an opportunity to donate bone marrow rather than an organ. (Donating bone marrow is a procedure more like giving blood than donating a kidney in that the body replaces the missing marrow, although it is considerably more painful than donating blood.) Actually donating bone marrow did correlate with subjects' expressed intentions. Thus, the effects of a subject's moral view did penetrate to behavior (Schwartz & Tessler, 1972). Subsequent research on a variety of topics including the use of condoms to prevent AIDS has lent support to the idea that subjects' perception of the right thing for them to do influences their behavior in addition to the variables proposed in the Fishbein and Ajzen model (Gorsuch & Ortberg, 1983; Pagel & Davidson, 1984; Budd & Spencer, 1985).

*Freud too saw morality as absorbed from our parents.

FIGURE 17.6

MORALITY AND REASONED ACTION

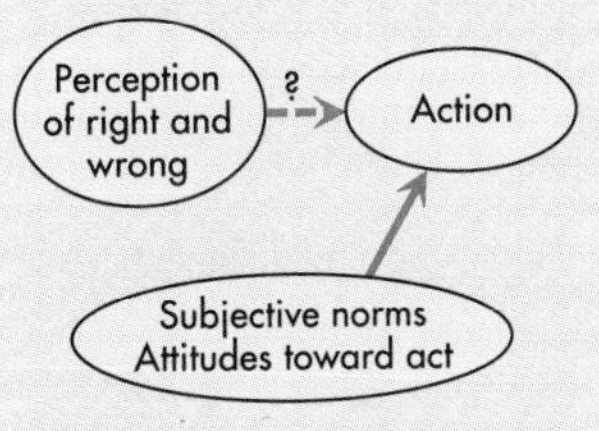

▲ A person's conception of the morality of an act—over and above what she thinks others think is moral—can affect her intentions toward the act.

Social Influence and Reasoned Action

The four limits on the model of reasoned action that we have considered so far all arise from the way we are constructed as individuals, but there are other irrational influences on our behavior that are more deeply social in nature.

MODELING

The model of reasoned action suggests that people are influenced by other people, but it allows for such influence in only one specific way: we are influenced by what others expect us to do. But is this the only source of social influence? The evidence suggests it isn't.

▲ *Roy Carruthers's* Three Smokers. *Is smoking still "cool"? Is that one reason people start to smoke?*

Consider cigarette smoking—surely an irrational behavior. The model of reasoned action suggests that young people would be influenced by whether their parents (and their peers) approved of their smoking. In one test of this model, large samples of primary school and college-age subjects were asked about the components of the Fishbein and Ajzen model. But they were also asked whether their parents smoked. The results indicated that perceived parental approval of the children's smoking had *no* effect on the children's behavior, but *whether their parents smoked did affect whether the children smoked* (Grube, Morgan, & McGree, 1986; see also Melby, Conger, Conger, & Lorenz, 1993). The subjects in these studies, then, cared much less about what they thought their parents approved of than what their parents did.

The research described so far has been conducted with the explicit intention of testing the model of reasoned action. Investigators have measured the variables specified by the model and some other variable in addition—say, past behavior. They have then asked whether these other variables predict behavior over and above the variables specified by the model. But there is a great deal of research discussed in other chapters of this book that also goes to the issue of the rationality of attitudes and behavior. And while it was not conducted with an eye toward explicitly testing the model of reasoned action, it does bear on the issue of whether we are wholly rational creatures. Let us review a bit of that work in the current context.

SOCIAL INFLUENCE THROUGH IMMEDIATE SOCIAL PRESSURE

Chapter 2 discussed the Milgram studies of obedience to destructive authority. In that experiment, subjects were ordered by an authority to deliver what they thought were dangerous and painful shocks to a protesting victim in the guise of an experiment on learning (Milgram, 1974). Some of the reasons I offered for subjects' obedience find a place in the Fishbein-Ajzen model.

It is no doubt true that the value the subjects placed on science contributed to their obedience. But there is at least one important source of obedience that is not well handled by the model of reasoned action. When people not involved with the experiment were asked what they would do were they ordered to deliver the shocks, they said quite certainly that they would stop. This intention probably *does* reflect the variables included in the Fishbein-Ajzen model. But the subjects' actual behavior was different; the majority obeyed the experimenter to the extraordinary limits he set.

Why are people so wrong about what they would do? Perhaps in figuring out what we would do in such a situation, we implicitly use the model of reasoned action. We ask ourselves what the consequences of obeying are and how we evaluate them. We ask ourselves how our significant others would expect us to act. And from this, we conclude that we would stop. But when actually in the situation, we face a social force not covered by the model. Just what this social force is, is difficult to say. Chapter 2 discussed the possibilities. Suffice it here to note that face-to-face interaction with someone seems to bring into play a set of influences on our behavior that we sometimes do not take full account of in forming intentions.

COGNITIVE DISSONANCE

As a final limitation on the model of reasoned action, we should remind ourselves about cognitive dissonance. Cognitive dissonance, as we saw in Chapter 16, is a name for the finding that if you get people to act in a way that is contrary to their real attitudes for a trivial reward, they will come to alter their attitudes in the direction of their action. The phenomenon of cognitive dissonance poses two problems for the model of reasoned action.

One problem is the simple fact that one can get people to do things that are against their better judgment in the first place. If behavior were all that rational, then one wonders how the dissonance procedures could work. But as suggested in Chapter 16, this probably has to do with the same sorts of situational forces evident in the Milgram experiment. In all likelihood, the dissonance phenomenon is possible because people can be subtly manipulated into doing things they genuinely don't want to do.

The second problem is that, as a myriad of experiments have found, once a person has been manipulated into acting in a way contrary to her attitudes, she will unconsciously *distort her attitudes* to square with her behavior. And this implies that sometimes at least, attitudes are themselves irrationally formed. They can be the product of distortion and irrational whether or not

▲ Urging behavior changes based on the effects of behavior on significant others.

they are related to perceived consequences and evaluation; perhaps dissonance leads people to distort those too. In other words, for an attitude to be rational, it isn't enough for it to relate to perceived consequences and their evaluation. The perception of consequences and their evaluation must *themselves* be rational. Even if attitudes formed by dissonance have the right relations to perceived consequences and evaluations, they are not rational because those perceptions of consequences and evaluations themselves are the product of self-deception and distortion.

Reasoned Action: A Review

The model of reasoned action indeed showed that attitudes could be used to predict behavior. It also showed how attitudes could be combined with other psychological states—for example, subjective norms—to predict behavior, and it suggested how attitudes themselves were formed from perceived consequences and behavior. The model has been shown over and over to predict behavior with a more than fair degree of success. But the model does have its limits. Habits can interfere; emotions too can deflect people from rationality; and someone's belief that he will not be able to carry out some behavioral intention may keep him from forming the rational intention in the first place. We also saw that the model may fail to take a person's moral views fully into account. Finally, we noticed that modeling, social influence, and cognitive dissonance may also be instances of deviations from rationality—whether or not they are encompassed by the model of reasoned action.

WHEN DO ATTITUDES PREDICT BEHAVIOR?

Let us turn now to the second approach to the problem of consistency between attitudes and behavior, the idea that whether people are consistent in their behavior and attitudes depends on the nature of the attitudes involved. This discussion will take us into a related question: How do attitudes guide behavior?

Directly and Indirectly Formed Attitudes

Perhaps the most striking thing about attitudes is how good we humans are at forming them. We have all manner of attitudes, including attitudes about things we have no experience with. For example, a person may have a negative attitude about skydiving even though he has never actually jumped out of a plane. This suggests that one important distinction we can draw is between attitudes that are based on direct experience and attitudes that aren't.

Attitudes that aren't based on direct experience are likely to be based on *inferences* about how we would react were we to encounter the attitude object. Presumably these inferences are based on our assessment of how some experience is similar to (and different from) other experiences we have had. We can decide that something is similar to something else we didn't like (or did like) and on that basis form an attitude toward it. But we may be wrong about what the crucial similarity is. Attitudes based on direct experience, on the other hand, are less inferential and hence less likely to be wrong. This way of thinking leads to the hypothesis that attitudes based on direct experience are more likely to be predictive of behavior than attitudes that don't reflect direct experience. This is, in a way, a corollary of my colleague's first law, that the best predictor of what a person will do in a particular situation is what that person has already done in that situation. If we think of a person's self-reports about her attitudes as predictors of what she will do, then we ought to trust those reports most when they are based on the person's own experience.

Russell Fazio and Mark Zanna conducted a series of experiments to document the difference between attitudes based on direct experience and those that are more inferential. In one study, the investigators asked their subjects to indicate their attitudes toward participating in psychological research. They also asked them to indicate how many psychological experiments they had *already* been involved in, and to indicate how many future experiments they were willing to volunteer for. The results showed that the more experiments the subjects had already been in, the stronger was the correlation between their attitudes toward research and their willingness to be in future experiments (Fazio & Zanna, 1978). The attitudes of those who had not participated were glib, poorly related to their behavior; the attitudes of those with experience were better rooted in that experience and more predictive of their behavior.

Fazio and Zanna have taken this finding two steps further. In the first step, they argue that attitudes based on experience are better predictors of behaviors because they are *stronger* than attitudes that are more indirectly formed; they are clearer, held more confidently, and more resistant to attack than are indirectly formed attitudes.

The second step is to root these differences in the way that attitudes guide behavior; that is, in information-processing differences between directly and indirectly formed attitudes. Fazio and Zanna have argued that (1) we have more information about objects with which we have direct experience; (2) when we learn about an attitude object from someone else, that other person may be more salient to us than the facts about the attitude object, but when we learn our attitudes directly, our own behavior is salient; and (3) directly formed attitudes are more *accessible* from memory than are indirectly formed

> Attitudes based on direct experience are more likely to predict behavior than are those based on inferences.

attitudes (Fazio & Zanna, 1981). Recently, research attention has been focused on the heightened accessibility from memory of attitudes from direct experience.

Attitude Accessibility

For attitudes to affect behavior, they must somehow be stored in memory, and they must be accessed from memory at the time of the behavior. So if our attitude toward a particular activity is to affect our behavior with regard to that activity, that attitude must somehow become active in our mind at the time we perform the behavior. The attitude need not be explicitly recalled, but the attitude must at least be *implicitly* activated. The program of research we will now review attempts to establish two points: (1) attitudes based on direct experience are more readily accessed from memory than are attitudes formed indirectly, and (2) such differences in accessibility might account for the fact that directly formed attitudes better relate to behavior. As we shall see, this program of research relies heavily on techniques cognitive psychologists have developed for measuring the degree to which memories are implicitly active in mental life.

ACCESSIBILITY THROUGH RELATED SOLICITATION

In one investigation, subjects were exposed to a series of intellectual puzzles. Some of the subjects were allowed to try the puzzles themselves, while others saw only a videotaped description of someone else working on the puzzles. In the second phase of the experiment, the subjects were given five positive and five negative evaluative adjectives and asked to respond with a "yes" or "no," depending on whether the adjectives described their attitude toward each puzzle. The result of interest *wasn't* the quality of the attitudes the subjects had toward the puzzles; rather it was the *speed* with which the subjects registered their attitudes. The finding was that subjects who had direct experience with the puzzles recorded their attitudes faster than did subjects with indirectly formed attitudes (see Figure 17.7A). Speed of response is one traditional measure used by cognitive psychologists to assess accessibility.

A second experiment examined another factor that we might expect to affect the accessibility of an attitude: the number of times an attitude has been expressed. In this experiment, all of the subjects had indirect exposure to the puzzles. Some of them simply indicated their attitudes toward the puzzles on a form; others were asked to indicate their attitudes on the form and then copy their responses onto two other forms. Thus, some subjects expressed their attitudes once, while others did so three times. Finally, the subjects were given the same timed response task described above. As expected, the subjects who expressed their attitudes three times were faster in responding the final time than were subjects who had had only one previous opportunity to express their attitudes (see Figure 17.7B).

The final question addressed by this investigation was whether enhanced accessibility would lead to a better fit between attitudes and behavior. To determine this, subjects were led to express their attitude toward the puzzles either one or three times; they were then given the puzzles in a "free play" period and told that they could work on them or not as they chose. The results showed that there was a stronger correlation between the subjects' attitudes toward particular puzzles and whether they worked on them for those subjects who had expressed their attitudes three times than for subjects who had expressed their attitudes only once. Apparently, greater attitude accessibility can lead to a tighter correspondence between attitudes and behavior (Fazio, Chen, McDonel, & Sherman, 1982). One reason seems to be that repeated expression leads to increased extremity of attitudes, and extremity leads to accessibility (Downing, Judd, & Brauer, 1992).

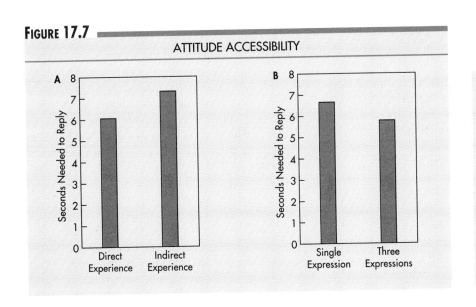

FIGURE 17.7

ATTITUDE ACCESSIBILITY

◀ (A) How long it takes to express an attitude (latency) as a function of the kind of experience one has had with the attitude object. Direct experience leads to faster expression of the attitude. (B) Latency of attitude response as a function of the number of times one has expressed the attitude. Repeated expression leads to faster expression of the attitude. (Data from Fazio, Chen, McDonel, & Sherman, 1982)

In the studies we have examined so far, subjects' attitudes toward attitude objects were solicited by the experimenter. But if attitudes are to guide behavior, then mere exposure to the attitude object would have to be enough to activate the attitude. Suppose someone invites you to play golf. You *might* explicitly ask yourself: What is my attitude toward golf? and then be guided by your response. But more typically, you wouldn't *explicitly* ask yourself that question. So if your attitude toward golf is to have a role in your decision as to whether or not to play, it must be because the mere mention of the word activates the attitude. And if direct experience makes attitudes more accessible, then direct experience should activate attitudes in this implicit sense better than indirect attitudes do.

Russell Fazio asked whether mere exposure to attitude objects is enough—without explicit solicitation—to activate attitudes, and whether such activation is stronger for directly experienced attitudes. The challenge in such research was to find a way to determine whether an attitude had been activated without directly asking subjects for their attitudes. After all, the technique we have seen so far for assessing whether attitudes have been activated—response time to an attitude solicitation—relies on direct probing. How can we determine whether attitudes have been activated wthout direct inquiry?

The answer that Fazio gave relies on another well-explored technique of cognitive psychology—***priming.*** The idea behind priming is that when some element of mental life like an attitude is activated, that activation spreads to other *associated* ideas, so they too become (temporarily) activated. Fazio combined these ideas in a rather complex experiment.

All of the subjects in the experiment were exposed to the intellectual puzzles used in some of the experiments described above. One-third of the subjects experienced them directly; one-third experienced them indirectly and expressed their attitudes three times; and one-third experienced them indirectly and expressed their attitudes only once. One group had relatively accessible attitudes because of direct exposure; one group had relatively accessible attitudes because of repeated expression; and one group had relatively inaccessible attitudes.

In another phase of the experiment, subjects of each type were exposed to either a puzzle they liked (had a positive attitude toward) or a puzzle they didn't like (had a negative attitude toward). In this second phase, they were not asked to express their attitude toward the puzzle, but after exposure, they were asked to give their impression about why someone named Ted had volunteered to be in an experiment. The story they were told about Ted was ambiguous, leaving room to attribute positive (altruistic) or less positive (to earn money) reasons for Ted's behavior. The question of interest was: Would prior exposure to the negative or positive attitude object affect the subjects' explanations for Ted's behavior?

For subjects who had direct experience with the puzzles and for subjects who repeatedly expressed their attitudes (but not for those with only one expression of an indirect attitude), the reasons given for Ted's behavior varied with how positively they evaluated the puzzle they had just been exposed to (see Figure 17.8). Those subjects who had been exposed to attractive puzzles

FIGURE 17.8

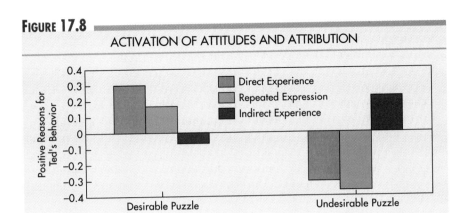

ACTIVATION OF ATTITUDES AND ATTRIBUTION

◄ *Attributions for a person's behavior as a function of whether subjects had just had positive or negative attitudes primed. Subjects who had just had positive attitudes toward a puzzle primed were more likely to see the protagonist of a story as having positive reasons for acting than were subjects who had just had negative attitudes primed. (Data from Fazio, Powell, & Herr, 1983)*

attributed positive reasons for Ted's behavior; those exposed to unattractive puzzles attributed negative reasons (Fazio, Powell, & Herr, 1983).

The logic of the result is this. Consider subjects with positive and accessible attitudes toward the puzzle. When they are exposed to it, their positive attitude toward the puzzle is activated. This activation spreads to other things they have positive attitudes toward—here, altruism. When they are now asked to attribute reasons for Ted's (ambiguous) behavior, they first think of positive reasons, and give them as the reason for Ted's behavior. For subjects with negative and accessible attitudes, the same mechanism works, but this time their negative attitude toward the puzzle "primes" other (relatively) negative attitudes—toward volunteering for money—so they offer this reason. Finally, for subjects with inaccessible attitudes, exposure to the puzzle does *not* activate their attitudes, so there is no priming, and the reasons they give for Ted's behavior are unrelated to whether the puzzle they just did was positive or negative. These results and other similar findings suggest, then, that mere exposure to an attitude object is enough to activate accessible attitudes (Fazio, Sanbonmatsu, Powell, & Kardes, 1986).

Another study in this line of research examined the relations among attitude accessibility, perceptions, and behavior in a more realistic setting. In the summer of 1984, residents of Bloomington, Indiana, were asked about their attitudes toward Walter Mondale and Ronald Reagan. How long it took them to respond to the attitude questions was also monitored, as a measure of attitude accessibility. Months later, these same subjects were asked about their perceptions of who had performed better in the nationally televised debate beween Mondale and Reagan, and also about their perceptions of the debate between the vice-presidential candidates, George Bush and Geraldine Ferraro. Finally, after the election, the subjects were asked whom they had voted for.

As the investigators expected, subjects with accessible attitudes (as measured in the first phase) had positive perceptions of how the candidate they favored performed in the debate, and they also voted for that candidate. These accessible attitudes affected perception of the debate and were consistent with their behavior in voting. For subjects with less accessible attitudes, these relations were weaker; they were less likely to perceive their candidate as having won the debate and were less likely to vote in line with their initial attitudes (Fazio & Williams, 1986).

Other experiments have developed evidence that priming can affect attitudes by affecting which dimensions are salient when the attitude object is being evaluated. In one experiment, subjects were first asked to learn the association between words and colors. The words either had to do with foreign policy (*diplomat,* for example) or with the economy (*fiscal*). In a second, supposedly unrelated, experiment, subjects were asked to evaluate a political candidate on the basis of some information about the candidate's background with regard to foreign affairs and economics. Some of the information was positive, and some was negative. The first part of the experiment was intended to prime (activate) economic concerns for some subjects and foreign affairs concerns for others.

The investigators expected that which concerns were primed in the first part of the experiment would affect which sort of information (foreign affairs or the economy) would have greater impact on subjects' overall evaluations of the candidates in the second part of the experiment. And that is just what happened (Sherman, Mackie, & Driscoll, 1990).

These results bring together the themes we have been exploring. Direct experience and repeated expression are two factors that affect attitude accessibility. And accessible attitudes influence perception and also guide behavior. Inaccessible attitudes play a less active role in mental life, and therefore they do not have these effects on perception or behavior.

Reflecting on One's Attitudes

If attitude accessibility affects the degree to which attitudes and behavior are consistent, then we should expect that reflectng on one's attitudes will *increase* the degree of correspondence between attitudes and behavior. But there is evidence that this isn't always so. In one study, for example, subjects were asked about their relationship with the person they were dating. Some were asked just for an overall (global) evaluation of their relationship; others were asked to analyze just what was good or bad about their relationship before expressing their global attitudes. About nine months later, the subjects were contacted and asked whether their relationship was still intact. The (somewhat surprising) result was that the global attitudes given by the subjects who had first analyzed the good and bad aspects were substantially *worse* predictors of whether the relationship endured than were the global attitudes of those who had not first analyzed their relationship (Wilson, Dunn, Bybee, Hyman, & Rotondo, 1984). Why does this happen?

Part of the answer seems to be that some of our attitudes are more "cognitively driven" than others. Cognitively driven attitudes are those that are formed by a relatively explicit consideration of the merits of the attitude object. Consider *Consumer Reports,* a magazine that carefully analyzes the merits and demerits of any consumer good it reviews. If you read their review of, say, life insurance policies, you are likely to be driven by the analysis to have attitudes toward the various kinds of life insurance that are on the market. Given the fact that your attitude toward life insurance policies was formed in this way, if you reflect on your attitudes right before you talk to the insurance salesman, you are likely to behave in a way that is consistent with your attitudes.

But most of us do not enter into relationships in this way. Most of us simply find ourselves attracted to a particular other person. Our attitude toward that person surely wasn't formed by explicitly listing his features (physical and otherwise), evaluating those features one at a time, weighing the features, and then summing them to form a composite judgment. We probably found ourselves just attracted to this person. But what happens when we are asked to reflect on the features of a life insurance policy or our relationship?

In the case of the life insurance policy, you may have the list of features on which to evaluate policies readily in mind. Reminding yourself of these features can bring your behavior in line with the same features that determined your attitude in the first place. But when you reflect on your relationship, you may feel frustrated. You may not know what to say; you do not have in mind any such list of features. You think you *should* have such a list, so you construct one. But the list is likely to be guided not by what attracted you to the person in the first place, but by your theory of what you think *should* affect whom you get involved with. When asked about your overall attitude toward the person, you are likely to base your attitude on this hastily constructed list of features that you think should matter. The problem is that your real attitude probably wasn't based on this list in the first place, and neither is your subsequent behavior likely to be based on it. Your subsequent behavior is likely to be affected by exactly the same factors that produced your attraction in the first place.

If your attitude was formed by an explicit consideration of features in the first place, then reflecting on those reasons should bring behavior and attitudes into alignment. But if your attitude wasn't formed by such explicit consideration, then reflection should lead to the construction of a largely irrelevant new attitude that should be at variance with your behavior. Several experiments have found just this sort of result. Reflecting on the reasons for one's attitudes can increase attitude-behavior consistency if the attitude was formed in a reasonably explicit way, but it can reduce consistency if the attitude was formed in a less explicit way (Millar & Tesser, 1986). Further, reflecting on globally formed attitudes has been shown to influence reported attitudes without affecting subsequent behavior, thus reducing attitude-behavior consistency (Wilson, Dunn, Kraft, & Lisle, 1989). And if reflection does affect behavior, it may affect it deleteriously by causing people to base their decisions on the wrong criteria (Wilson & Schooler, 1991; Wilson, Lisle, Schooler, Hodges, Klaaren, & LaFleur, 1993).

How much experience you have with an attitude object also affects whether thinking about it will disrupt the relation between attitudes and behavior. If you have a lot of experience, you have probably already thought about it, and therefore thinking about it again will not prove so disruptive. There is evidence that if you have been involved in a relationship for a relatively long period, then reflecting on the reasons you are involved will *not* prove confusing. The disruptive effects of reflection seem to be confined to couples who haven't been involved with each other for very long (Wilson, Kraft, & Dunn, 1989; see Hixon and Swann, 1993, on the consequences of reflecting on the self).

Attitudes formed by analyzing the attitude object are likely to be accessible to reflection. For these attitudes, reflection on the attitude will enhance the predictability from attitudes to behavior. If attitudes are formed without analysis, then introspection is likely to distort the relationship between attitudes and behavior.

What can we say about attitudes formed without an explicit list? Does cognition play no role whatever in the formation of these attitudes? Some psychologists would argue that we form many of our attitudes without any cognitive mediation; affect itself drives these attitudes (Zajonc, 1980). But other psychologists claim that the formation of even these attitudes—like those toward the people with whom we have relationships—involves the recognition of features of the attitude object; the recognition of these features produces the affect and attitude. Indeed Chapter 14 discusses what some of these features are. According to this view, there is cognition involved in the formation even of such global attitudes; the problem is that this cognition is implicit and unconscious. Hence it is inaccessible to reflection, although it guides behavior (Parrott & Sabini, 1989).

Mindlessness

We began this chapter with a review of the LaPiere study demonstrating a startling lack of relationship between attitudes and behavior. Our discussion has taken us in the direction of showing that the situation isn't as gloomy as it first appeared. Often, when you ask people about their attitudes in the proper way, the response you get *does* predict behavior. We have also looked at cognitive mechanisms that might account for the relations between attitudes and behavior. But this is not to say that our behavior is *always* responsive to the information in the environment that is relevant to our attitudes. In particular, Ellen Langer has argued that often in social interactions, we behave mindlessly, running off a "script" of the interaction without paying much attention to the details of the current situation. Consider this experiment.

Langer had experimenters approach people in line (the subjects) to use a Xerox machine and ask if they could cut into the line ahead of them. Some of the experimenters said they had twenty pages to copy; others said they had only five. Some in each condition simply said, "Excuse me, I have five (twenty) pages. May I use the Xerox machine?" Others gave a reason for breaking in: "Excuse me, I have five (twenty) pages. May I use the Xerox machine because I'm in a rush?" Of those asked the large favor with no reason attached, 24 percent honored the request. Somewhat more people honored the large request when a reason was attached (42 percent). When the favor was small, more people in both conditions honored the request (60 percent vs. 94 percent). This is in line with what we might expect if subjects were acting on their attitudes; they were more willing to honor a small than a large request, and they were more willing to accede to the request if a reason was offered than if it was not.

Langer also had her experimenters give "placebic" information as a reason to do the favor. These experimenters said "Excuse me, I have five (twenty) pages. May I use the Xerox machine because I have to make copies?" Now there is something a bit crazy and surely redundant about this request. Of course they have copies to make; why else would they want to use the Xerox machine? This placebic information added nothing in the way of information. Of the subjects asked for the large favor, 24 percent agreed, the same percent that agreed with no reason attached. But in the small favor condition, the

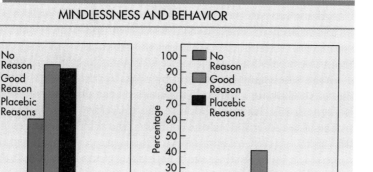

FIGURE 17.9

MINDLESSNESS AND BEHAVIOR

◄ *Proportion of subjects acceding to a small request (xeroxing five pages) or a larger request (xeroxing twenty pages) when no, valid, or placebic (senseless) reasons were offered for the request. Placebic reasons work well for trivial requests, but not for larger ones. People seem to process small requests mindlessly. (Data from Langer, Blank, & Chanowitz, 1978)*

placebic information worked about as well as the real information; 93 percent agreed to the favor (see Figure 17.9; Langer, Blank, & Chanowitz, 1978).

The fact that 93 percent agreed with the placebic information while 60 percent agreed with no information simply can't be because subjects have a more positive attitude toward requests that include utterly useless information. Rather, it seems that subjects in the condition with little cost involved simply responded to the *form* of the request without paying much attention to the details. This result is controversial; others have not found the same result with similar manipulations (Folkes, 1985; see Langer, Chanowitz, & Blank, 1985, for a reply). But the main point of the experiment can hardly be denied. We often respond in social interaction in a reasonably thoughtless, inattentive way. We follow scripts of socially acceptable behavior without much concern for the details of the particular circumstance. And when this happens, we should hardly expect attitudes and behavior to be closely connected. (See Langer, 1989, for some other consequences of mindlessness.)

INDIVIDUAL DIFFERENCES

There is a final perspective on the relation between attitudes and behavior. From this perspective, whether a person's attitudes and behavior correspond depends in part on the personality of the individual. Much of the research has focused on a particular dimension of individual differences called ***self-monitoring.*** As we saw in Chapter 6, Mark Snyder introduced the notion of self-monitoring as an aspect of personality. To summarize briefly, ***high self-monitors*** are people who are attentive to, and often try to influence, other people's perceptions of them; they are inclined to behave in the way that others would like them to behave. They are therefore often less responsive to their own attitudes. ***Low self-monitors*** are less attentive to other people's impressions of them, and less inclined to influence them or live up to other people's expectations. They are therefore often more responsive to their own attitudes. One might expect that attitudes and behaviors are differently related in high and low self-monitors. Just how they are different is a bit complex.

In one study by Mark Snyder, subjects' attitudes toward affirmative action were measured, and their scores on the self-monitoring scale were assessed. About two weeks later, subjects were brought to a lab and given the "facts" about a fictitious lawsuit brought by a Ms. Harrison against the University of Maine. The lawsuit alleged that there had been discrimination based on gender against Ms. Harrison because the university had hired a Mr. Sullivan instead of Ms. Harrison. In one condition, the subjects were given the relevant facts of the case (the résumés of Ms. Harrison and Mr. Sullivan, among other things). They were told to study both sides of the case, weigh the facts carefully, and reach a verdict. In this condition, the subjects' attitudes toward affirmative action did *not* predict the verdict given by either the high or low self-monitors. Nothing about the circumstances here made general attitudes toward affirmative action salient or relevant. Like real jurors, the subjects were induced to leave their own attitudes behind and focus on the law and the facts.

But in another condition, before they were exposed to the court case, the subjects were given three minutes to reflect on their own attitudes toward affirmative action. Thus, their attitudes were made more accessible. In this condition, the subjects' attitudes toward affirmative action *did* relate to their verdict, and this effect was substantially stronger for the low than the high self-monitors.

In a final condition, the judges "charge" to the jurors explicitly told them to consider their attitudes about affirmative action in reaching a verdict. In this condition, attitudes and verdict were actually more strongly related for the high self-monitors—when the social situation dictated that they take their attitudes into account in behaving, they certainly did (Snyder & Kendzierski, 1982). These results suggest that low self-monitors are more likely to act on their attitudes when their attitudes are salient (though not explicitly made relevant) than are high self-monitors (see Figure 17.10).

FIGURE 17.10

RELATION OF ATTITUDES AND BEHAVIOR FOR HIGH AND LOW SELF-MONITORS

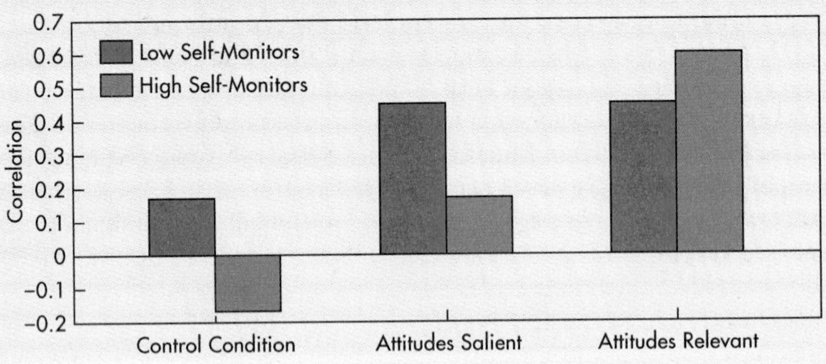

▶ The relation of attitudes to behavior for high and low self-monitors under control conditions, when attitudes were made salient (but not relevant) and when they were both relevant and salient. Attitudes and behavior correlated for high self-monitors only if it was made clear that they should be related. (Data from Snyder & Kendzierski, 1972)

Other research has examined personality and the relation between attitudes and behavior in the context of the Fishbein and Ajzen model of reasoned action. Recall that the model implicates two factors in the formation of an intention to behave in a certain way: the person's own attitude toward the behavior and the person's perception of what others expect him to do. In one investigation, the subjects' own attitudes about how much time they should study and their perceptions of how much they thought others expected them to study were measured. The students were also asked to indicate how much time they actually did spend studying.

Two personality measures were collected on each subject. The first was their self-monitoring score. The second was the degree to which they were "privately self-conscious." **Private self-consciousness** has to do with how much attention one pays to one's own attitudes. Private self-consciousness is akin to self-monitoring; both low self-monitors and high private self-conscious subjects are likely to be attentive to their own attitudes. But they are not the same concept. Low self-monitors not only pay attention to their own attitudes, they are also motivated to respond to those attitudes.*

The investigators expected high attitude-behavior correlations in only one group of subjects: those high in private self-consciousness and low in self-monitoring. Only among these subjects are their attitudes salient, and they are inclined to do what their attitudes dictate. Those high in private self-consciousness and also high in self-monitoring should find their own attitudes salient, but they should also be motivated to do what others think they should do. Those low in private self-consciousness, on the other hand, shouldn't follow their own attitudes regardless of their self-monitoring score, because their own attitudes aren't very salient. The results supported this analysis (Miller & Grusch, 1986). This result dovetails nicely with the results of the Snyder study; it once again suggests that for low self-monitors, attitudes will predict behavior if their attitudes are salient. Taken together, the two studies suggest that attitudes can be salient either because something about the situation makes them salient, or because the subjects' personality (private self-consciousness) makes their attitudes chronically salient.

Another study asked whether low self-monitors differed from high self-monitors because low self-monitors were more likely to see their attitudes as relevant to the formation of their intentions or because low self-monitors were more likely to behave in line with their intentions once formed. In this study, subjects' attitudes, intentions, and subsequent behaviors with regard to two behavioral domains were assessed: voting in the next election and smoking marijuana. Their self-monitoring scores were also assessed. The results indicated that there were no differences between high and low self-monitors in the correspondence between attitudes and behavioral intentions; the difference arose in the degree to which the subject carried out those intentions. Low self-monitors were more likely to act in accord with their intentions. High self-monitors were apparently distracted by their social sensitivity from carrying out their own intentions (Ajzen, Timko, & White, 1982).

*As you might guess, there is a correlation between self-consciousness scores and self-monitoring scores. Low self-monitors are also likely to be high in private self-consciousness. But the correlation isn't perfect. There are some people who are low in private self-consciousness but also low in self-monitoring, and others who are high in both.

We began our discussion of the relation between attitudes and behavior with the LaPiere study, which found a substantial discrepancy between the subjects' attitudes and their behavior. What can we now say about that discrepancy?

The first point to make is that there may not have been a very good match between the attitude question the subjects were asked and the behavior that was measured. The merchants were asked about their willingness to serve Asians in general; but they weren't confronted with Asians in general. They were confronted with a middle-class Asian couple in the company of a Western professor. Perhaps the actual stimulus was far from the stereotype the merchants considered when expressing their attitudes (see Lord, Lepper, & Mackie, 1984, on the impact of stereotypicality).

Second, even though attitudes may be one source of behavior, they aren't the only source. People are also responsive to what they perceive others think they should do, along with their own moral sense of what they should do; perhaps the merchants were responding to these factors. Or perhaps they just served the couple out of habit.

Third, attitudes can only be expected to influence behavior when those attitudes are accessible at the time of acting. Maybe the subjects simply mindlessly carried out their accustomed social script without paying any attention to their attitudes. And perhaps merchants, at least when they are engaged in their business, are high self-monitors—inattentive to their own feelings, paying more attention to others' demands on them. In any event, the literature we have reviewed here suggests that, the LaPiere study notwithstanding, even if attitudes don't *always* predict behavior, they often do. The question research is now addressing is not whether attitudes affect behavior, but rather: Just when and how do attitudes affect behavior?

SUMMARY

1. It is reasonable to believe that a person's attitude toward something will predict behavior toward that thing. But some studies that have looked for relations between attitudes and behavior have failed to find them.

2. Martin Fishbein and Icek Ajzen argue that attitudes can be used to predict behavior but only when the attitudes measured and the behavior to be predicted are at the same level of generality. General attitudes predict behavior in general; specific attitudes predict specific behaviors.

3. The *model of reasoned action* specifies that it is *intentions* that predict behavior most directly; *attitudes* predict behavior less directly by influencing intentions.

4. The model proposes that intentions with regard to an act are determined not only by attitudes but by *subjective norms* with regard to the act—by what we think significant other people expect us to do with regard to the act.

5. Fishbein and Ajzen also argue that we form attitudes toward an action by attempting to determine all of the consequences of that action and then evaluating those consequences.

6. The model of reasoned action has proven successful in predicting people's behavior. But it has also been found to have limitations. One is that what people have done in the past also has an influence on their behavior *over* and *above* the dictates of rationality. Another comes from emotion; sometimes people know what they ought to do, but cannot get themselves to do it for emotional reasons. A third has to do with people's sense of whether they are *able* to do what they know they should do. A fourth occurs because people sometimes have moral views that are independent of what they think other people think they should do.

7. There are also limitations of the model that arise from social reasons. First, people may imitate the behavior of other people who are significant in their lives, even when they don't believe that such imitation is rational. Second, social influence through social pressure may affect behavior directly. Finally, cognitive dissonance is a well-established, irrational source of influence on attitudes.

8. Attitudes based on direct, recent, and repeated experience with an attitude object are more likely to predict behavior than are attitudes based on less recent, less frequent, or less direct experience. One reason may be that attitudes based on direct, recent experience are more accessible, that is, they come to mind more quickly and easily.

9. Though one might expect that reflecting on one's atittudes toward something would lead to their being a better predictor of behavior, there is some evidence that reflecting on one's attitudes can actually lead to their being worse predictors of behavior.

10. People differ in the degree to which their attitudes predict their behavior. Low self-monitors' attitudes predict their behavior better than do high self-monitors' attitudes, at least when their attitudes are salient, though not explicitly relevant. For privately self-conscious people, their own attitudes are chronically more salient than are attitudes of people who are not privately self-conscious.

GLOSSARY

absolute value The magnitude of a number disregarding its sign. Thus the numbers −0.2 and +0.2 both have the absolute value +0.2.

actor-observer difference The observation that actors tend to attribute their behavior to circumstances while observers tend to attribute it to the actor's personality.

adaptive significance The utility of something from the point of view of survival.

additive task A task in which the group's performance is simply the sum of the members' performances minus coordination losses. A tug of war is an example.

ad hoc group A group created to perform in a single, time-limited function. Such groups go out of existence once their task is completed.

adversarial legal system A system like our legal system in which each side, under the guidance of an attorney, has the chance to present its side of the case. This system can be contrasted with an inquisitorial system—used on the continent of Europe—in which the judge has the responsibility of overseeing the investigation.

algorithm A rule that if followed perfectly will always yield the right answer. Algorithms may be contrasted with heuristics, rules that usually, but not always, work.

altruism The propensity to act in such a way as to help others.

ambivalence response amplification A theory that prejudice against blacks, especially in the North, is a consequence of ambivalent attitudes on the part of whites, and that this ambivalence leads both to enhanced helpfulness toward blacks and enhanced hostility. Whether helpfulness or hostility will be expressed in a particular case depends on the details of the situation.

androgyny (psychological androgyny) Having both masculine and feminine traits.

Anti-Semitism scale (A-S scale) A questionnaire consisting of a number of statements about Jews that is designed to measure the extent of a person's anti-Semitism.

apology A remedial exchange in which one admits that one did wrong, claims that one now sees it as wrong, and promises not to do it again. *See also* remedial exchange.

appeasement gesture A behavior of a threatened organism that turns off the attacker's aggression.

arbitrary power The authority parents exercise when they discipline children without an explanation of reasons for that discipline. Children of parents who use arbitrary power tend to display more hostility at school.

arbitrator Someone empowered to impose a settlement on the various parties to a negotiation. Arbitrators may be contrasted with mediators, who have no such power.

asymmetry in parental investment The notion that in many species females contribute more to the nurturance of the young than do males. Some theorists believe that the asymmetry in parental investment produces sex differences in sexual behavior and desires.

attitude An evaluation of a person, place, or thing—any attitude object. Attitudes are thought to be a determinant of feeling and behavior.

attitude accessibility The speed with which an attitude can be brought into consciousness. Relatively more accessible attitudes are thought to have more of an impact on behavior than are less accessible attitudes.

attitude polarization The thought-induced increase in intensity of a particular attitude. This positive or negative polarization is a result of our desire for cognitive consistency.

attribution A belief about the cause of a behavior.

attribution theories Theories about how we see through behavior and situations to stable personality.

authoritarianism A personality syndrome characterized by a rigid adherence to conventional rules. Authoritarianism has been shown to be associated with prejudice and ethnocentrism. Authoritarianism is measured by the F. Scale. *See also* ethnocentrism, prejudice.

authoritarian personality A syndrome that results from a passionate attraction to the status quo and the authority that is seen as maintaining it, along with a strong desire to punish those who are seen to threaten it.

autokinetic effect An optical illusion in which sources of light seem to move even though they are really stationary. The autokinetic effect was used by Muzafer Sherif to illustrate social influence.

autonomic nervous system A system in the body consisting of two sub-systems: the sympathetic nervous system (active when an organism faces danger) and the parasympathetic nervous system (active when the organism is safe). Some theories of emotion treat arousal of the sympathetic nervous system as necessary or sufficient for the experience of emotion.

back translation The second round of language translation used to determine the validity of a cross-cultural questionnaire. For example, a bilingual speaker translates a questionnaire from English to Japanese, and then someone else translates it back to English. If this version matches the original, then the translation is successful.

bargaining theory A theory that claims that coalitions will form initially so as to produce equity, but that eventually coalitions will be formed so as to be midway between those called for by minimum power theory and minimum resource theory.

barrier strengths The forces that oppose dissolution of a marriage rather than enhance the attractiveness of a marriage; in other words, the costs of breaking up.

base-rate information Information about the prevalence of some characteristic in some population of people. Base-rate information can be contrasted with diagnostic information. *See also* diagnostic information.

basking (in reflected glory) A self-presentational strategy in which one enhances one's own self-esteem by attempting to identify oneself with a successful group or person.

Bayes's Theorem A normative model of how we should combine base-rate information with diagnostic information in reasoning about something in particular. *See also* base-rate information, diagnostic information, normative model.

Bem Sex-Role Inventory (BSRI) A scale created by Sandra Bem used to determine whether a person is sex-typed, cross-sex-typed, androgynous, or undifferentiated, closely related to the Personal Attributes Questionnaire. *See also* androgyny, cross-sex-typed, Personal Attributes Questionnaire, sex-typed, undifferentiated.

beneficence The caring for one another that is found in specific relationships.

black-sheep effect The simultaneous enhancement of the virtues of a well-liked ingroup member and derogation of an inadequate ingroup member, presumably to show the virtue and high standards of the rest of the group.

blasting A self-presentational strategy in which one attempts to enhance one's own esteem by derogating one's competitors.

blind experiment An experiment conducted in such a way that the subjects do not know the experimental hypothesis. In a double-blind experiment, the experimental staff is unaware of which group each subject is in.

bogus stranger technique An experimental technique used to investigate attraction and similarity in which subjects are asked to evaluate a fictitious person from attitude scales that have actually been filled out by the experimenter. Subjects tend to like a person with attitudes similar to their own more than a person with dissimilar attitudes.

brainstorming A technique for stimulating the production of creative ideas. Brainstorming instructions stress that people should mention any idea that occurs to them. Ideas are criticized in a later phase.

bystander intervention research Research aimed at determining when people will intervene in an emergency to help someone, typically a stranger, in trouble.

California F. Scale A questionnaire that consists of items expressing the attitudes thought to compose the authoritarian syndrome. Evidence from this scale supports the existence of a personality attracted to prejudice.

causal attributions Explanations of behavior.

causal schema A model of how some effect might be caused. *See also* multiple necessary causal schema, multiple sufficient causal schema.

centralization The degree to which a group funnels information through one (or a few) communication channels.

central route to persuasion Persuasion that works by engaging a subject thoughtfully. Central persuasion relies on algorithms (rather than heuristics) and produces enduring attitude change. *See also* algorithm, heuristic.

central trait A trait richly connected by inferences to other traits; "warm" is a central trait. Central traits can be contrasted with peripheral traits, which are not very connected to other traits; "polite" is a peripheral trait.

co-actors People who perform the same task independent of each other, but in each other's presence.

coalition A subgroup of some larger group that bands together to reach some goal (and divide the reward) they cannot reach individually.

coercive power The ability to get others to do what you want them to because you can punish them.

cognitive consistency The desire to be consistent in our beliefs. We feel pressure to change our attitudes when they are unbalanced in order to maintain this consistency.

cognitive dissonance theory In its original form, the theory that claimed that when people have in mind two psychologically inconsistent ideas they will experience a state of aversive arousal. The theory goes on to claim that in order to relieve that state they will distort one (or more) of the ideas so as to reduce the psychological inconsistency and reduce the drive state. In its more modern form, the theory relies less on the notion of psychological inconsistency; it now claims that when people do things that make them look stupid or guilty in their own eyes they distort in order to look less stupid or guilty.

cognitive evaluation theory The theory that rewards for task performance both control behavior and provide feedback about competence. An emphasis on the controlling aspect will decrease intrinsic motivation while an emphasis on competence will increase intrinsic motivation.

cohesiveness The state of being a close-knit group as defined by the sum of the attractions of a group to its members.

collectivism The notion that some social group larger

than the individual is fundamental, powerful, and of ultimate value.

communal relationship Relationships that are not structured according to exchange theory, but rather according to the principle that everyone gets what he or she needs. Families are, or at least ideally are, communal relationships.

companionate love According to some theorists, a love that consists of commitment and intimacy but not passion.

comparison level for alternatives According to John Thibaut and Harold Kelley, one determinant of the attractiveness of a group to its members is the attractiveness of other groups to which the members might belong.

compensatory task A task on which group members' errors tend to cancel each other.

compliance Conforming to a group's expectations out of fear of punishment or hope of reward. Compliance is likely only when the group can observe the individual's behavior. *See also* conformity.

confederates Peole who pose as subjects but are actually accomplices of the experimenter.

confirmation bias Testing an hypothesis in such a way that it will seem to be true even if it isn't.

conformity Bringing one's behavior into alignment with a group's expectations. May be because of normative or informational influence. *See also* informational influence, normative influence.

conjunctive task A task in which a group's performance is equal to the performance of the group's worst member.

consensus information Information about how most people react to some stimulus. Consensus information is one determinant of whether people make personal or entity attributions for behavior. *See also* attribution.

consistency information Information about whether a person consistently reacts to some stimulus in a particular way, or only reacted that way on one occasion. Consistency information is one determinant of whether people make personal or entity attributions for behavior.

conspecifics Members of the same species.

constant sum conflict *See* zero-sum conflict.

construct validity A scale is said to have construct validity if measurements taken with it fit together with measurements of other quantities in theoretically sensible ways.

consummate love According to some theorists, a love that consists of commitment, intimacy, and passion.

contingency theory of leadership The view that the traits that make someone a good leader depend on (are contingent upon) a variety of specific circumstances in the leadership situation; thus this view denies that there is a trait of leadership, or that there are traits that all and only leaders have. Fred Fiedler's model is the most prominent example of a contingency theory of leadership.

contingent goals Goals people pursue *only* because they lead to the accomplishment of further goals.

control group A group that is *not* exposed to an experimental treatment. Comparing the outcomes for the control and experimental groups allows one to infer the effect(s) of the experimental treatment.

conventional stage In Kohlberg's theory, the second stage of moral development in which the child sees morality not as a matter of his or her own pleasure but as a matter of living up to the expectations of society and its authorities. The child now has a broader perspective on his or her behavior and can conceive of it from the perspective of a particular culture.

coordination losses Losses resulting from the fact that a group may accomplish less than the sum of the abilities of its members, not because of a loss of motivation, but because unless efforts are perfectly coordinated, there will be some waste of effort.

correlational method A method of research that looks for the relations between two variables without manipulating either variable (as opposed to the experimental method, which always involves manipulating at least one variable).

correlation coefficient A measure of how closely two variables are related. Correlation coefficients do not indicate which (if either) of the two variables is *causing* the other to vary.

correspondent inference theory The theory by Ned Jones and Keith Davis that inferences from behaviors to the intentions that guided them are affected by the number of desirable consequences of the action. The more desirable consequences there are, the less certain the inferences are.

covariation theory The theory, proposed by Harold Kelley, that attributions follow the logic of covariation of cause and effect. People make attributions to behaviors depending on what covaries with the behavior.

cross-sex-typed (individual) A man with feminine but without masculine traits, or a woman with masculine but without feminine traits.

cultural account An explanation of stereotype development that argues that stereotypes are a consequence of the specific way cultures structure interactions between ingroups and outgroups.

cultural evolution The notion that cultures change because individuals happen upon new ways of doing things. Some of those new ways are beneficial in terms of the survival of the culture; others are not. The beneficial changes are retained; those that aren't die out.

cultural relativism The belief that all cultural systems and moral codes are equally valid.

danger-induced aggression Aggression against something that poses a danger to an organism, especially likely if escape is blocked.

date rape Rape that occurs in the context of a dating relationship.

death-qualified jury A jury from which anyone opposed to the death penalty on principle has been excluded. Many states use death-qualified juries in capital cases. Death-qualified juries may be more likely to convict people of crimes than are randomly selected juries.

decision scheme analysis Mathematical techniques used to determine what implicit rule a group has used to combine its members' original opinions into a final group opinion.

decision theory A discipline devoted to articulating what the rational action to take is, given the existing pay-off structure.

decomposed prisoners' dilemma A payoff structure similar to a prisoners' dilemma, but one in which it is easier to determine a player's motives from his or her decisions. Such a payoff structure typically removes the mixed motive component of the prisoners' dilemma. *See also* prisoners' dilemma.

deindividuation A State that exists when one is treated anonymously, as part of a group rather than as an individual. Aggression is disinhibited in a state of deindividuation.

demonstrative tasks A task that has a right answer that can be proven or demonstrated (also called *Eureka* or *Ah ha tasks*).

dependent variable A variable that might be affected by manipulating the independent variable.

descriptive theory A theory that tells us what someone will do. A descriptive theory is contrasted with a normative theory, which tells us what they should do.

devil's advocate An official appointed by the Catholic Church to find and report any facts that discredit a candidate for sainthood. The devil's advocate destroys the unanimity of a group and liberates people to express their true opinions. Used more generally to refer to anyone who performs this role.

diagnostic information Information about the characteristics of some particular person. Diagnostic information is contrasted with base-rate information. *See also* base-rate information.

differential mobility The extent to which people are able to relocate, as in employees who are asked to move to different cities. It is often a differentiating characteristic that affects one's opportunities, complicating the notion of social equity.

diffusion of responsibility The belief among members of a group that *someone* should help a person in need, but without an understanding of who *in specific* should help. Diffusion of responsibility has been used as an account of people's failure to intervene in bystander inter-

vention experiments. *See also* bystander intervention research.

direct effect The impact of a minority on the immediate, public behavior of the majority.

directness maxim According to Grice, the principle that enjoins a speaker to answer a question directly.

direct readout view The view of emotional expressions that proposes that a mechanical connection has evolved between certain facial expressions and emotions. According to this view, spontaneous emotional expressions always signal the actual emotional state of the organism.

discounting Weakening an inference from a behavior to a possible cause before one believes that the behavior fits a multiple sufficient causal schema. *See also* multiple sufficient causal schema.

discrimination Behavior that unfairly penalizes someone for being a member of a particular group (regardless of the cause of the behavior).

disjunctive social relations The extent to which a husband and wife have separate outside relationships. These potential sources of satisfaction can lead to marital instability.

disjunctive task A task in which the group's performance is equal to the performance of the group's best member.

displacement In frustration-aggression theory, the act of transferring hostility onto safer targets.

display rules Cultural rules about what emotions to express in which circumstances.

disposition An aspect of personality.

distinctiveness information Information about whether a person reacts in the same way to a large range of stimuli, or is discriminating. Distinctiveness information is one determinant of whether someone makes an entity of personal attribution for behavior.

distraction account An explanation of the social facilitation phenomenon that relies on the idea that the presence of other people is distracting; distraction leads to increased motivation to perform to counteract the distraction. The sum of the increased motivation and the distraction leads to enhanced performance on easy tasks but decreased performance on difficult tasks.

distress at another's distress A phenomenon occurring because people, with infants, become distressed themselves at encountering certain distress cues from others; crying is an example of such a cue. Distress at another's distress can lead people to help another so as to terminate *their own* distress.

distributive justice *See* substantive justice.

dizygotic A term for nonidentical twins that are the product of two ova that are fertilized by two different sperm.

dominance hierarchy A relatively stable arrangement of members of a species such that each member attacks those below it in the hierarchy, while none attacks those above. In most real species hierarchies are not quite this orderly. Dominance hierarchies limit and control inter-male aggression. *See also* inter-male aggression.

double standard   A person (or culture) is said to have a double standard if it believes that the standards for appropriate conduct—especially sexual conduct—are different for men and women.

dramaturgic perspective   The idea that people are commonly involved in projecting a particular image of themselves (whether a true or false image); identified with the sociologist Erving Goffman.

dual representation theory   The notion that when we form an impression of a person we separately store our overall evaluation of that person and the behaviors on which the evaluation is based. In time we can forget the behaviors while recalling the evaluation, leading to evaluations for which we cannot offer a justification.

duopoly   A situation in which there is but one buyer and one seller for a particular commodity.

egocentric attributional error   A person's mistakenly believing that other people will react to some situation as he or she would.

egocentrism   According to developmental psychologist Jean Piaget, a child's inability to understand how the world looks from another person's point of view.

elaboration likelihood model   The theory that there are two different ways to persuade someone, by either the central or the peripheral route. *See also* central route to persuasion, peripheral route to persuasion.

emotional aggression   *See* impulsive aggression.

emotional loneliness   Loneliness that is felt even though one has friends because one's friendships are superficial and unsatisfying. It may be distinguished from social loneliness in which one does not have friends.

empathetic embarrassment   Embarrassment experienced for someone else who has failed in social interaction. One need not oneself be interacting with this other person to experience empathetic embarrassment. May be distinguished from secondary embarrassment. *See also* secondary embarrassment.

empathy   Understanding of, and compassion for, another's distress.

encoding   Storing information in memory.

entity attribution   The belief that a behavior was caused by some particular external circumstance.

epiphenomenon   Something that accompanies a behavior but does not cause it.

equal excess theory   A newer version of bargaining theory that is built on data about which coalitions will form and how they will divide their spoils.

equity theory   The claim that people are motivated to achieve equity among members of a group where *equity* has the specific meaning that the ratio of output to input for each member of the group is the same.

ethnocentrism   Prejudice in favor of one's own group.

Ethnocentrism Scale (E Scale)   A questionnaire that probes subjects for their attitudes toward foreigners.

evaluation apprehension   An explanation for social facilitation that relies on the notion that when in the presence of others we become concerned with succeeding or failing at a task. This enhanced concern produces enhanced drive, which leads to enhanced performance on well-learned tasks and degraded performance on novel tasks.

evolutionary stable strategy (ESS)   A way of acting that can survive in the long run even through there are "cheaters."

exchange theory   The notion that people attempt in their relationships to maximize the "goods" they receive and minimize the "costs" they pay. Exchange theory may be contrasted with equity theory, which suggests that people attempt to achieve equity with their partners.

excuse   A remedial exchange in which one shows that one *couldn't* have done other than one did.

exemplification   A self-presentational strategy in which one presents oneself as morally righteous.

experiment   A research technique, widely used by social psychologists, that is particularly well suited to answering causal questions. In an experiment an independent variable is manipulated to determine what effect the manipulation has on the dependent variable.

experimental games   Methods used to study strategic interaction, in which subjects play games involving conflicts of interest for points or a small amount of money.

experimental group   A group exposed to an experimental treatment (as opposed to a control group). Comparing the outcomes for the control and experimental groups allows one to infer the effect(s) of the experimental treatment.

experimenter bias   Anything an experimenter does to influence the results of the experiment illegitimately. Experimenters usually, for one reason or another, would like the experiment to come out in a particular way; thus they must be careful not to exhibit experimenter bias, whether deliberate or inadvertent.

facial feedback hypothesis   The theory that the expression one has on one's face can produce (or modulate) the experience of emotion.

factor analysis   A method of interpreting test questionnaire results in which clusters of related items (or factors) are analyzed to reveal the underlying phenomenon.

female marriage squeeze   The state of affairs of there being more women of marriage age than males; there was a female marriage squeeze during much of the sexual revolution.

final offer arbitration   A form of dispute settlement in which an arbitrator imposes a settlement, but the arbitrator is constrained to pick one or the other of the final offers made by the parties to the dispute. The arbitrator may *not* compromise between the final offers. *See also* arbitrator.

foot-in-the-door technique   The technique commonly used by salespeople (and occasionally used by experimenters) in which one asks a small favor before asking a large favor. People who accede to the small favor first are likely to accede to the larger favor later.

forced compliance   An experimental technique in which people are induced to assert positions at variance with what they really believe. This technique is commonly used to study cognitive dissonance. See also cognitive dissonance.

free-rider problem   The willingness to use a public good but not to contribute to it.

frustration   The blocking of a response.

frustration-aggression hypothesis   The theory that all agression is a consequence of frustration and that all frustration produces agression.

functional distance   In attraction theory, a distance between residences that takes into account how far apart the two residences are, but also takes into account the arrangement of space as it has an impact on the probabilities that people will interact with each other.

fundamental attributional error   The notion that we tend to attribute behavior to people's personality when we shouldn't—the claim that we tend to accept behavior at face value when we shouldn't.

generalization   The application of the findings of research to people or situations other than those that were studied in the research.

Glick effect   The observation that although the more educated a person is, the *less* likely he or she is to divorce, that people who begin an educational program—college, for example—but don't finish it are *more* likely to divorce than are people who don't start it.

Grice's maxims   Pragmatic principles uncovered by the philosopher Paul Grice. His maxims are typically used both by speakers in constructing their utterances and by listeners in interpreting what they hear. *See also* pragmatics.

group polarization   The observation that groups often adopt positions *more extreme* than the mean of their members' views before the group discusses an issue. Group polarization is the successor theory to risky shift. *See also* risky shift.

group selection   The now largely out-of-favor notion that evolution occurs by competition *between species*, that is, that a variety of species emerge, some are successful and endure, while others become extinct. This notion may be contrasted with the currently more-favored view that evolution works by competition *among members of the same species.*

groupthink   A term coined by Irving Janis to refer to the deterioration of mental efficiency, reality testing, and moral judgment that results from an excessive desire to reach consensus.

heuristic   A rule of thumb, that is, a rule that usually works but doesn't always. Heuristics should be contrasted with algorithms, rules that are guaranteed to work.

high self-monitors   People who are attentive to, and often try to influence, other people's perceptions of them. They are inclined to behave in the way that others would like them to behave and are therefore often less responsive to their own attitudes.

homogamy   The tendency to marry people like oneself. Americans have been shown to be homogamous on a wide variety of traits.

hung jury   A jury that cannot achieve the required degree of consensus as to a verdict (usually unanimity).

hypothesis   A proposition that is being tested in an experiment.

identity (personal)   The set of all attributions correctly made to a person.

illusory correlation   An error that occurs because people tend to perceive correlations where they expect them to be even if they are not there. The illusory correlation has been offered as an account of the maintenance of stereotypes.

implicit personality theory   A theory that we use in everyday encounters about how personality traits are related.

implicit rule   In group decision making, the unconscious and unspoken rule that people follow to reach a collaborative answer.

impression management   *See* self-presentation.

impulsive aggression   Action intended to cause harm to another just for the sake of causing that harm (also called *emotional aggression*).

inclusive fitness   The notion that any gene will endure if it leads its bearer to have more offspring than will other members of the population without the gene. This notion has been used to explain the evolution of altruism toward genetically related members of the population.

independent variable   The variable that an experimenter manipulates directly.

individualism   The notion that the individual is fundamental, powerful, and of ultimate value.

inferred evaluation   The evaluation someone infers that another person will have of him or her; the inference is often based on similarity.

informational influence   Influence exerted by groups

because members take what other members of the group believe to be evidence about what is true of the world.

ingratiation   A self-presentational strategy of attempting in an illicit way to get someone to like you so as to induce that person to treat you in a way that is desirable to you.

inquisitorial system   A system like the one used on the continent of Europe in which a single, neutral third party (the judge) controls the investigation and presentation of each case. May be contrasted with a legal system like the Anglo-American one, called adversarial, in which each side gets to present its case.

institutional racism   Discrimination that is a result of institutional pressures rather than a direct result of prejudiced attitudes.

instrumental aggression   Intentional action that will foreseeably harm another, but that is designed to achieve some end other than that harm. Killing a bank guard to rob a bank, for example.

integrative bargaining   Bargaining in a context in which the parties' interests do not entirely conflict so there are some outcomes that are better than others at satisfying both parties.

intellective tasks   Tasks with right answers.

inter-male aggression   Aggression among members of the same species. It is more common among males, though not confined to males, and it is regulated by testosterone, the "male hormone."

internalization   Conforming to a group's expectations because one is convinced the group is correct. Taking the group's views or expectations and making them one's own. Internalized influence will be displayed by individuals even when they cannot be observed by the group.

intimidation   A self-presentational strategy in which one presents oneself as dangerous in an effort to coerce others into treating one in a desired way.

intrusions   In a recognition memory task, items that subjects believe they have seen but that were in fact never presented.

investment effects   The amount people feel they have already invested in a relationship and the influence that has on their decision whether to stay in or to leave the relationship.

irritable aggression   Aggression produced by some unpleasant stimulus (electric shock, for example) to which an animal is exposed.

James-Lange theory   A theory developed by William James and Carl Lange that the emotions consist in the perception of *bodily changes* in response to a stimulus.

jigsaw classroom   A technique of teaching in which the students are given the information they need to solve problems, but only by pooling the information each has. This technique, developed by Elliot Aronson, has been used to reduce hostility among grammar school students by forcing them to cooperate with each other.

justification   A remedial exchange in which one claims that although one's action *looks* wrong, in light of the context it was in fact correct and what anyone would have done.

just world hypothesis   The claim that people want to believe that the world is just and as a consequence distort their perceptions to make the world seem that way. The just world hypothesis has been used to explain victim derogation, blaming the victims of some misfortune for their problem.

K selected species   A species, like humans, in which only a few children are born to each female, but in which many of the young who are born reach sexual maturity. K selected species may be contrasted to r selected species.

latent effect   The impact of a minority on the delayed, private behavior of the majority.

lateral hypothalamus (cat's)   A portion of the brain that, when stimulated, leads a cat to enact prey-stalking behavior.

leakage   The notion that although people can to some degree control their emotional experience, this control is limited and, therefore, some measure of spontaneous reaction is displayed.

level of aspiration (LOA)   In bargaining, the minimum profit a person can make and feel that he or she has been a success.

lexicalized   Phenomena that are referred to by a single word are said to be lexicalized.

limit   The lowest price a seller will sell at and the highest price a buyer will buy at; also called *resistance point*.

low self-monitors   People who are less attentive to other people's impressions of them, less inclined to live up to other people's expectations, and often more responsive to their own attitudes.

loyalty   The sense of obligation that a person has to a group solely by virtue of his or her history with that group.

male marriage squeeze   The state of affairs of there being more marriage-age men than women available. In the last decade or so there has been a male marriage squeeze in the United States.

matching hypothesis   The idea that the two members of a romantic couple are typically about equal (matched) in terms of physical attractiveness.

material benefit   Something concrete that can be gained by acting in one's own self-interest.

maternal aggression   Aggression by a mother against animals that come too near her young.

medial hypothalamus (cat's)   A portion of the cat brain that, when stimulated, triggers rage on the part of the cat.

mediator   Someone who attempts to help the parties to a negotiation reach a settlement, but who has no authority to impose one. Mediators may be contrasted to arbitrators, who do have the authority to impose a settlement.

medium   In persuasion, the way in which a message is expressed.

mere presence explanation   An explanation of the social facilitation phenomenon. It holds that the mere presence of other people produces increased drive, which has been shown in animal laboratories to enhance performance on well-learned tasks and inhibit performance on novel tasks.

meta-analysis   The combination of results from several studies into a single analysis in order to determine whether a phenomenon is real (in the face of conflicting results).

minimal group   A group selected from a larger collection of people using some trivial criterion. Members of minimal groups are typically not allowed to speak with one another. Minimal groups are groups in only the most meager sense.

minimum power theory   This theory holds that the proportion of resources a person will receive from a successful coalition depends on the number of coalitions that are winning with her but losing without her.

minimum resource theory   A theory that claims that in a situation in which several coalitions *might* form, the coalition will form that has the *minimum resources necessary* to achieve the goal. The theory also claims that the reward will be divided within the coalition in proportion to the amount of resources the parties contributed to the coalition.

minority influence   Influence exhibited by a minority on the majority of a group.

misattribution   An experimental technique in which subjects take a placebo that they are told will produce a certain effect, such as arousal. When subjects then experience arousal, they will believe it is a consequence of the drug and not their own behavior.

mitigation   A remedial exchange in which one concedes that one did wrong, but claims that is wasn't as evil a wrong as it seemed, in light of circumstances.

mixed motive game   A game in which two or more different motives—fear and greed, for example—would lead to the same response. The prisoners' dilemma is an example.

modeling   A way in which children learn how to do things, such as aggress, by watching the behavior of other people.

model of reasoned action   The theory of how attitudes relate to other psychological variables in predicting behavior. The model states that measures of general attitudes are correlated not with single acts but with broad classes of behavior. *See also* subjective norms.

monogamy   A system of marriage in which each male and female has only one spouse. Our culture, like a minority of the world's cultures, is monogamous.

monozygotic   A term for twins that are genetically identical and are the product of a single fertilized ovum that splits in half shortly after conception.

moral drift   An example of group extremity shift seen in the Zimbardo prison experiment; moral drift occurs when people who object to the immorality of others fail to express their views.

multiple necessary causes   According to Kelley, the schema we use to locate the causes of a particular effect when we believe that it requires at least two different causes.

multiple sufficient causes   According to Kelley, the schema we use if we believe that a particular effect will occur if either of two causes is present.

natural kind theory   The idea that general terms refer to essences or natures rather than to statistical entities.

natural selection   The theory proposed by Charles Darwin that species emerge because some members of a population have better reproductive success than do others. Eventually a new species emerges that is characterized by the genetically determined traits of the successful reproducers.

need complementarity   The notion that people tend to marry people who have opposite needs from their own—for example, a dominant person marrying a submissive person. There is, however, very little evidence in favor of this idea; instead, people tend to be homogamous.

negative state relief   The notion that acting altruistically toward another person can alleviate the distressing aspects of a bad mood.

non-zero sum conflict   A conflict in which the total payoff is not fixed, but is determined by the behavior of the parties in conflict. Contrasted with a zero-sum, conflict. *See also* zero-sum conflict.

norm   A common, shared standard.

normative influence   Influence groups exert because members are afraid of the consequences of violating the group's expectations.

normative model   A model of how something *should* be; normative models should be contrasted with descriptive models, which are models of how things are.

normative theory   A theory of what people should do.

n-person prisoners' dilemma   *See* tragedy of the commons.

nurturance   The desire to take care of other people.

obedience   Bringing one's behavior in line with the commands of authority.

objective self-awareness Becoming aware of oneself as an object of perception by other people. According to Robert Wicklund, becoming self-aware inevitably leads to distress because one inevitably finds undesirable aspects of oneself.

oligopoly The circumstance in which there are many buyers and many sellers for a particular commodity.

outgroup homogeneity The idea that we tend to see groups of which we are *not* a part as more homogeneous than we see groups of which we are a part. Outgroup homogeneity has been offered as an account of the *development* of stereotypes.

paralinguistic cues Aspects of spoken language that are independent of the meaning of that which is communicated—tone of voice, for example.

parasympathetic nervous system *See* autonomic nervous system.

peripheral route to persuasion Persuasion that relies on heuristics (speaker's expertise, number of arguments) rather than algorithms (content of arguments). Persuasion via the peripheral route is not very thoughtful and is not likely to be internalized.

peripheral trait A trait that is not very connected by inferences to other traits; "polite" is a peripheral trait. Peripheral traits can be contrasted with central traits, which are richly connected by inference to other traits; "warm" is a central trait. *See also* central trait.

Personal Attributes Questionnaire (PAQ) A scale developed by Janet Spence and Robert Helmreich to measure the degree to which a person has certain masculine traits (achievement traits) and certain feminine traits (nurturative), closely related to the BSRI. *See also* Bem Sex-Role Inventory.

personal attribution The belief that a behavior has been caused by something in the actor's personality.

persuasive argument theory An explanation for the risky shift and group polarization; it holds that groups are extreme because they are effective at mobilizing all of the arguments in favor of the better, more rational alternatives.

piloerect (state) A sign of arousal of the sympathetic nervous system in which hair or fur stands on end.

placebo An inactive substance given to subjects who think it is a real drug.

pluralistic ignorance A state of affairs in which a group of people misinterprets each other's perceptions and uses that misinterpretation as evidence about the world. Pluralistic ignorance has been used to account for why people fail to help strangers in bystander intervention experiments.

polarization The extremism that results from group discussions, producing more risky or more conservative behavior.

polyandry A system of marriages in which women are encouraged to have multiple husbands. Few cultures are polyandrous.

polygyny A system of marriages in which men are encouraged to have multiple wives. Most cultures are polygynous.

postconventional stage In Kohlberg's theory, the final stage of moral development in which the adolescent comes to understand that morality is really a matter of being guided by objective, impartial, formal principles.

post hoc An after-the-fact explanation of a failure or mistake.

pragmatics A discipline devoted to the study of the implicit aspects of language use.

preconventional stage In Kohlberg's theory, the first stage of moral development in which the child cannot distinguish his or her own pleasure from moral right or wrong.

predatory aggression Aggression by an animal on another animal that will be food for the first.

preference task A task with no right answer—for example, picking Chinese or Italian food.

prejudice An unreasonable, hostile attitude toward some group of people.

primary groups Groups in which each member is personally known to each of the other members, and which the members, at least on occasion, meet face-to-face.

priming Activating some schema (concept). Primed schemata tend to have a greater impact than they would had they not been primed.

principle of serviceable associated habits A proposal advanced by Charles Darwin that the facial expressions characteristic of emotions evolved because those expressions became associated with the emotions because they were once pragmatically useful movements.

prisoners' dilemma A particular structure of reward facing two or more players. One consequence of such a structure is that the most rational thing for each party to do (considered individually) will *not* lead to the best total outcome for all of the parties.

private self-consciousness The personality trait of being chronically attentive to the private aspects of one's self—one's thoughts, beliefs, and values, for example.

procedural justice A justice that is concerned with whether the process by which a decision has been made is fair; may be distinguished from substantive (or distributive) justice, which is concerned with whether the outcome of a decision is fair.

propinquity Physical closeness.

prototype A best exemplar of some concept. Some theorists believe that our concepts are stored in the form of prototypes.

proximate mechanism The actual biological mechanism that has emerged to enable an organism to achieve reproductive success. The desire to have sex is an example of a proximate mechanism by which reproduction is accomplished.

public self-consciousness The personality trait of being chronically aware of the public aspect of one's self—physical appearance, for example.

quality maxim According to Grice, the principle that specifies that a speaker should say only what he or she has reason to believe.

quantity maxim According to Grice, the principle that specifies that someone answering a question should reply only with as much detail as the listener needs.

random assignment The absolutely crucial element of an experiment; assigning subjects to conditions whereby each subject is equally likely to be assigned to each condition. The subjects especially must not be allowed to decide for themselves which condition they will be in.

readout theory of emotional expression The notion that emotional expressions are perfect reflections of emotional state independent of social circumstances.

realistic conflict theory The notion that hostility between groups is typically the result of conflict between the groups for some real, material resource.

recall memory task A memory task in which the subject must produce the stimuli he or she has seen before. It is contrasted with a recognition memory task, in which the subject must simply recognize whether he or she has seen some item before.

reciprocal altruism The notion that altruism can be the product of evolution if there is a gene that leads one to be altruistic only to those who also have the gene—and, hence, who would reciprocate the altruism.

recognition memory task A memory task in which the subject must simply recognize whether he or she has seen some item before. It is contrasted with a recall memory task, in which a subject must produce the stimuli he or she has seen before.

reference group A group to which a particular person compares himself or herself. The comparison might be in terms of rewards, or attitudes, or beauty, and so on.

referent power The ability to get others to do what you want them to do because they like you, respect you, and want to be like you.

relative deprivation theory The idea that people feel deprived, not because of the absolute level of reward they are receiving, or because of the relationship of outcome to input, but because of the relation of their rewards to the rewards of other people to whom they compare themselves.

reliable (scale) A measuring instrument—a personality scale, for example—is said to be reliable if it is measuring something consistently. Reliability may be distinguished from validity; validity has to do with whether the scale measures what it claims to measure.

remedial exchange An attempt by a putative transgressor to show that he or she shouldn't be thought ill of (or very ill of) despite the apparent transgression. Examples of remedial exchanges are excuses, justifications, apologies, and mitigations. *See also* apology, excuse, justification, mitigation.

reproductive advantage Something confers reproductive advantage to the degree that an organism with it will reproduce more than an organism without it. Traits, behaviors, physical structures, genes, abilities, desires, and so on can all be said to confer reproductive advantage.

resistance point *See* limit.

retrieval Recalling information from memory.

risky shift The observation that groups often adopt a riskier position after a group discussion than the mean of the group members' position before the discussion.

romantic love According to some theorists, a love that consists of passion and intimacy but not commitment.

r selected species Species, like most species of fish, in which very many young are produced but few of the young reach sexual maturity. These r selected species may be contrasted to K selected species.

saturation The degree to which a communication channel is *overloaded* with information.

Schachter and Singer theory of emotion A theory developed by Stanley Schachter and Jerome Singer that emotion consists in the experience of sympathetic nervous system arousal along with a hypothesis (cognition) of the source of that arousal.

schema (plural schemata) An organization of knowledge. Schemata guide interpretation, help control attention, and affect memory encoding and retrieval.

script An organized structure of knowledge that includes information about the invariant aspect of some situation—for example, all restaurants serve food—and has slots for variables that apply to specific restaurants—for example, how expensive a particular restaurant is.

secondary embarrassment Embarrassment experienced when *someone one is interacting with* fails to carry out the interaction. May be distinguished from empathetic embarrassment. *See also* empathetic embarrassment.

secure attachment The type of attachment in which children use their caregivers as home bases for the exploration of novel environments.

selective attention Paying attention only to those facts that are supportive of one's behavior.

self-concept The set of beliefs that people have about their own individual qualities.

self-disclosure Revealing private facts about oneself to others.

self-handicapping A self-presentational strategy in

which one purposefully takes on a handicap—drinking alcohol, for example—in an effort to save self-esteem by using the handicap to excuse failure and make success seem all the greater.

self-monitoring A personality trait. Those high in self-monitoring tend to behave in whatever way seems socially appropriate in a particular situation, regardless of how the behavior relates to one's true beliefs. Those low in the trait tend to be inattentive to what is socially appropriate and tend, instead, to act in accord with their beliefs and values.

self-perception theory A theory, advanced by Daryl Bem, that people infer their attitudes from their behavior.

self-presentation Acting in such a way as to present an image of oneself as a certain sort of person. The certain sort of person might or might not be who one really is. (Also called *impression management.*)

self-promotion A self-presentational strategy in which one attempts to present oneself as a *competent* person.

self-serving attributional error Erroneously believing that one's own failures are externally caused while one's successes are internally caused, especially when one does not show the same pattern with regard to other people's successes and failures.

sex-related aggression Aggression by males of a species against members of the same species (typically other males) stimulated by the presence of females.

sex-typed (individual) A male with masculine but without feminine traits, or a woman with feminine but without masculine traits.

sexual revolution The liberalization of sexual behavior and standards that occurred during the 1960s and 1970s in the Western world.

sexual script A culturally shared understanding of the process by which a sexual encounter should occur.

shared distinctiveness A possible explanation for the *development* of stereotypes. According to this account, stereotypes develop because we tend to imagine that rare events that happen together occasionally are actually correlated.

shared fate The likelihood that what happened to a victim will happen to us. According to Lerner, a belief in a shared fate may encourage the derogation of victims.

simulation heuristic Refers to the idea that our thinking and emotions are affected by outcomes that did not happen, but *might have* happened. The theory suggests that the easier it is to imagine something happening, the more likely it is that that state of affairs will affect our thinking or feelings.

simulations *See* experimental games.

situational attributions The beliefs that a particular behavior is caused by the external situation rather than by personality disposition.

sleeper effect The notion that a message from an un-reliable or not very credible source may have little persuasive effect at first, but may come to increase in persuasiveness as time goes on because the source is forgotten while the message is retained.

social communications theory of emotional expression The view that emotional expressions are shaped by social circumstance; they are produced in response to the nature of the audience.

social comparison theory A theory proposed by Leon Festinger suggesting that people: (a) compare their opinions to other people's opinions in order to determine what is true, and (b) compare themselves to other people to determine how worthy they are. This theory has been used to explain the risky shift and group polarization.

social compensation When solving a problem, the greater contribution of people who believe that their partners are *not* good at the task, compared to the contribution of people who believe that their partners *are* good at the task.

social constructivism The view that cultures and moral systems are constructed by humans.

social decision scheme analysis A procedure developed by James Davis to infer implicit rules, in which group members are asked their initial opinions and rechecked throughout the experiment. A characterization can then be made of the simplest rule that accounts for the final decision.

social dilemma *See* tragedy of the commons.

social facilitation The phenomenon wherein the presence of other people tends to enhance people's performance on well-learned tasks and inhibit performance on new, poorly learned tasks. A variety of explanations including mere presence have been offered for the social facilitation phenomenon. *See also* distraction account, mere presence explanation, social monitoring explanation.

social identity theory The notion that one reason people are biased toward their own groups is that people want the groups of which they are members to be the best as a way of enhancing their own self-esteem.

social impact theory A theory advanced by Bibb Latané arguing that the amount of influence that a group exerts is a function of the number of people in the group raised to a negative exponent.

social loafing The fact that when groups of people work on a task, they tend to work less hard than they would if they were working alone—at least under certain circumstances.

social loneliness Social isolation, lacking friends. Social loneliness may be distinguished from emotional loneliness, wherein one has friends, but the relationships are superficial and unsatisfying.

social monitoring explanation An explanation offered for the social facilitation phenomenon; it suggests that social facilitation occurs only when audiences are out of sight of the actor and the actor must actively monitor the audience.

social role   A specific position that helps determine the way people will behave and how others will respond to them.

social trap   *See* tragedy of the commons.

source   The origin of a persuasive message whose characteristics, such as power and credibility, help determine whether the persuasion is successful.

stereotype   A belief about a group of people. Some theorists would add that the belief must be false to be a stereotype; others would claim that the belief must also be hostile. The term was coined in the 1920s by Walter Lippmann.

strategic interaction   An interaction between two or more people who have at least partially conflicting interests and in which a person can influence another person's future behavior through their own current behavior.

subjective norms   According to the model of reasoned action, a person's perceptions of what others who are important in their lives think they should do. These norms, along with a person's attitudes toward performing an act, will determine the person's intentions.

subjects   The people (or other organisms) who take part in experiments.

substantive justice   Justice concerned with whether the outcome of a decision about distributing resources is fair in a particular case; also called *distributive justice*. Substantive justice may be distinguished from procedural justice, which has to do with whether the *process* of reaching a decision has been fair, regardless of the outcome.

subtle cynicism   The notion that all acts of altruism are performed in order to avoid an unpleasant, or produce a pleasant, psychological state in the actor.

succorance   The desire to be taken care of by another.

sunk cost fallacy   The mistake of continuing to invest in something because of how much one has already invested in it.

supplication   A self-presentational strategy in which you present yourself as a dependent and needy person in an effort to get others to take care of you.

sympathetic nervous system   *See* autonomic nervous system.

target   People to whom a persuasive message is directed. The characteristics of this audience help determine whether the persuasion is successful.

team   People with whom one cooperates in projecting a certain image of the selves involved.

territoriality   An arrangement found in some species in which members of the species (typically males) defend a plot of land against incursions from males of the same species (or other species that feed on the same resources).

Territoriality is a way in which inter-male aggression is limited and controlled.

tertius gaudens   The notion that in some cases, the weakest group can have the most power. For example, a small minority in an election can have significant power when it decides to which larger groups it will donate its votes.

tit for tat (TFT)   A strategy of cooperating on the first move of a repeated trial prisoners' dilemma game and then reciprocating one's partner's immediately previous move on every subsequent move.

tragedy of the commons   A situation, like the prisoners' dilemma, in which the most rational response from each individual will *not* produce the best outcome for a group of people. (Also called *n-person prisoners' dilemma*, or *social trap*, or *social dilemma*.)

transfer of arousal   A phenomenon in which arousal produced by some source—an emotion, a drug, exercise, for example—increases the intensity of a second emotion.

uncertainty of paternity   The fact that females, but not males, can be certain of which young are theirs. Uncertainty of paternity is seen by some as accounting for differences in sexual behavior and desire between males and females.

undifferentiated (personality)   Someone who has neither masculine nor feminine traits.

validity (of a scale)   A measuring instrument—a personality scale for example—is valid if it measures what it claims it measures. Validity may be distinguished from reliability—the property of measuring something, even if not what the scale claims to measure.

values   Goals that people have because these goals are good in themselves, not because they lead to further desirable consequences.

victim derogation   Blaming the victim of a misfortune for his or her plight. It may be a consequence of wanting to believe the world is just. *See also* just world hypothesis.

voire dire   Literally translated as "truth telling time," a time in which a jury panel is questioned by the judge and, in some cases, the attorneys to determine if there is a reason the jurors should be excluded from the jury.

vulgar cynicism   The notion that all acts of apparent altruism are actually aimed at advancing the actor's own *material* interest.

weapons effect   In Berkowitz's experiments on aggression, the tendency for subject to administer more shocks when a gun was left next to the shock machine. This effect supports the theory that aggressive cues increase the tendency to act aggressively because of their associations with aggressive behavior.

weighted probability theory A theory of coalition formation derivative from bargaining theory, but also taking into account the fact that smaller coalitions are easier to form than larger ones.

working consensus The implicit contract that governs social interaction, in which the parties involved agree to treat each other as if they had certain identities.

working models The ideas that children develop about what caregivers are like and what the self is like. A securely attached child will have more optimistic working models than a less securely attached child.

zero sum conflict A conflict in which the total payoff to the parties in conflict is fixed so that the only issue is how much of the payoff goes to which party (also called *constant sum conflict*). Zero-sum conflicts contrast to non-zero sum conflict. *See also* non-zero sum conflict.

REFERENCES

Abelson, R. P. (1983). Whatever became of consistency theory? *Personality and Social Psychology Bulletin, 9,* 37–54.

Adams, J. S. (1965). Inequity in social exchange. In L. Berkowitz (Ed.), *Advances in experimental social psychology* (Vol. 2, pp. 267–299). New York: Academic Press.

Adorno, T. W., Frenkel-Brunswick, E., Levinson, D. J., & Sanford, R. N. (1950). *The authoritarian personality.* New York: Harper & Row.

Agostinelli, G., Sherman, S. J., Presson, C. G., & Chassin, L. (1992). Self-protection and self-enhancement biases in estimates of population prevalence. *Personality and Social Psychology Bulletin, 18,* 631–642.

Ainsworth, M. D. S., Blehar, M. C., Waters, E., & Wall, S. (1978). *Patterns of attachment: A psychological study of the strange situation.* Hillsdale, N.J.: Erlbaum.

Ajzen, I. (1977). Intuitive theories of events and the effects of base-rate information on prediction. *Journal of Personality and Social Psychology, 35,* 303–314.

Ajzen, I. (1987). Attitudes, traits, and actions: Dispositional prediction of behavior in personality and social psychology. In L. Berkowitz (Ed.), *Advances in experimental social psychology* (Vol. 20, pp. 1–63). New York: Academic Press.

Ajzen, I., Timko, C., & White, J. B. (1982). Self-monitoring and the attitude behavior relation. *Journal of Personality and Social Psychology, 42,* 426–435.

Alexander, C. N., Jr., Zucker, L. G., & Brody, C. L. (1970). Experimental expectations and autokinetic experiences: Consistency theories and judgmental convergence. *Sociometry, 33,* 108–122.

Alexander, P. C., Moore, S., & Alexander, E. R. III (1991). What is transmitted in the intergenerational transmission of violence? *Journal of Marriage and the Family, 53,* 657–668.

Alicke, M. D. (1992). Culpable causation. *Journal of Personality and Social Psychology, 63,* 368–378.

Allen, J. B., Kenrick, D. T., Linder, D. E., & McCall, M. A. (1989). Arousal and attraction: A response-facilitation alternative to misattribution and negative-reinforcement models. *Journal of Personality and Social Psychology, 57,* 261–270.

Allen, V. L. (1965a). Situational factors in conformity. In L. Berkowitz (Ed.), *Advances in experimental social psychology,* (Vol. 2, pp. 133–175). New York: Academic Press.

Allen, V. L. (1965b). Conformity and the role of the deviant. *Journal of Personality, 33,* 584–597.

Allen, V. L. (1975). Social support for non-conformity. In L. Berkowitz (Ed.), *Advances in experimental social psychology* (Vol. 8, pp. 1–43). New York: Academic Press.

Allen, V. L., & Levine, J. M. (1969). Consensus and conformity. *Journal of Experimental Social Psychology, 5,* 389–399.

Allen, V. L., & Levine, J. M. (1971). Social support and conformity: The role of independent assessment of reality. *Journal of Experimental Social Psychology, 7,* 48–58.

Allison, S. T., Mackie, D. M., Muller, M. M., & Worth, L. T. (1993). Sequential correspondence biases and perceptions of change: The Castro studies revisited. *Personality and Social Psychology Bulletin, 19,* 151–157.

Allyn, J., & Festinger, L. (1961). The effectiveness of unanticipated persuasive communications. *Journal of Abnormal and Social Psychology, 62,* 35–40.

Amato, P. R. (1986). Emotional arousal and helping behavior in a real-life emergency. *Journal of Applied Social Psychology, 16,* 663–641.

Amir, Y., & Sharon, I. (1987). Are social psychological laws cross-culturally valid? Special Issue: The generalization of social psychological laws and theories across cultures. *Journal of Cross-Cultural Psychology. 18,* 383–470.

Anderson, C. A. (1987). Temperature and aggression: Effects on quarterly, yearly, and city rates of violent and nonviolent crime. *Journal of Personality and Social Psychology, 52,* 1161–1173.

Anderson, C. A. (1989). Temperature and aggression: Ubiquitous effects of heat on occurrence of human violence. *Psychological Bulletin, 106,* 74–96.

Anderson, C. A., & Ford, C. M. (1986). Affect of the game player: Short-term effects of highly and mildly aggressive video games. *Personality and Social Psychology Bulletin, 12,* 390–402.

Anderson, S. M., & Bem, S. L. (1981). Sex typing and androgyny in dyadic interaction: Individual differences in responsiveness to physical attractiveness. *Journal of Personality and Social Psychology, 41,* 74–86.

Anderson, S. M., & Cole, S. W. (1990). ''Do I know you?'': The role of significant others in general social perception. *Journal of Personality and Social Psychology, 59,* 384–399.

Anderson, C. A., & DeNeve, K. M. (1992). Temperature, aggression, and the negative affect escape model. *Psychological Bulletin, 111,* 347–351.

Antill, J. K. (1983). Sex role complementarity versus

similarity in married couples. *Journal of Personality and Social Psychology, 45*, 145–155.

Appadurai, A. (1981). Gastro-politics in Hindu South Asia. *American Ethnologist, 8*, 494–511.

Apsler, R. (1975). Effects of embarrassment on behavior toward others. *Journal of Personality and Social Psychology, 32*, 145–153.

Aquino, K., Steisel, V., & Kay, A. (1992). The effects of resource distribution, voice, and decision framing on the provision of public goods. *Journal of Conflict Resolution, 36*, 665–687.

Arafat, I. S., & Cotton, W. L. (1974). Masturbation practices of males and females. *Journal of Sex Research, 10*, 293–307.

Arendt, H. (1965). *Eichmann in Jerusalem: A report on the banality of evil* (rev. ed.). New York: Viking Press.

Argyle, M., & Dean, J. (1965). Eye contact, distance and affiliation. *Sociometry, 28*, 289–304.

Armstrong, S. L., Gleitman, L. R., & Gleitman, H. (1983). What some concepts might not be. *Cognition, 13*, 263–308.

Aron, A. (1988). The matching hypothesis reconsidered again: Comment on Kalick and Hamilton. *Journal of Personality and Social Psychology, 54*, 441–446.

Aronfreed, J. (1970). The socialization of altruistic and sympathetic behavior: Some theoretical and experimental analyses. In J. Macauley & L. Berkowitz (Eds.), *Altruism and helping behavior* (pp. 103–126). New York: Academic Press.

Aronson, E. (1969). The theory of cognitive dissonance: A current perspective. In L. Berkowitz, (Ed.), *Advances in experimental social psychology* (Vol. 4, pp. 1–34). New York: Academic Press.

Aronson, E. (1990). Applying social psychology to desegregation and energy conservation. *Personality and Social Psychology Bulletin, 16*, 118–132.

Aronson, E. (1992). The return of the repressed: Dissonance theory makes a comeback. *Psychological Inquiry, 3*, 303–311.

Aronson, E., & Carlsmith, J. M. (1963). Effect of the severity of threat on the devaluation of a forbidden behavior. *Journal of Abnormal and Social Psychology, 66*, 584–588.

Aronson, E., Chase, T., Helmreich, R., & Ruhnke, R. (1981). Feeling stupid and feeling guilty—Two aspects of the self-concept which mediate dissonance arousal in a communication situation. In E. Aronson (Ed.), *Readings about the social animal*. San Francisco: Freedman.

Aronson, E., & Linder, D. (1965). Gain and loss of esteem as determinants of interpersonal attractiveness. *Journal of Experimental Social Psychology, 1*, 156–171.

Aronson, E., & Mills, J. (1959). The effect of severity of initiation on liking for a group. *Journal of Abnormal and Social Psychology, 59*, 177–181.

Aronson, E., Willerman, B., & Floyd, J. (1966). The effect of a pratfall on increasing interpersonal attractiveness. *Psychonomic Science, 4*, 227–228.

Aronson, E., & Worchel, P. (1966). Similarity versus liking as determinants of interpersonal attractiveness. *Psychonomic Science, 5*, 157–158.

Asch, S. E. (1946). Forming impressions of personality. *Journal of Abnormal and Social Psychology, 41*, 258–290.

Asch, S. E. (1948). The doctrine of suggestion, prestige and imitation in social psychology. *Psychological Review, 55*, 250–276.

Asch, S. (1952). *Social psychology*. New York: Prentice-Hall.

Asch, S. (1956). Studies of independence and conformity: A minority of one against a unanimous majority. *Psychological Monographs, 70*, (Whole No. 416).

Atkinson, J., & Huston, T. L. (1984). Sex role orientation and division of labor early in marriage. *Journal of Personality and Social Psychology, 46*, 330–345.

Aubé, J., & Koestner, R. (1992). Gender characteristics and adjustment: A longitudinal study. *Journal of Personality and Social Psychology, 63*, 485–493.

Austin, J. L. (1962). How to do things with words. In *J. L. Austin: Philosophical papers*. Oxford: Oxford University Press.

Austin, J. L. (1970). A plea for excuses. In *J. L. Austin: Philosophical papers*. Oxford: Oxford University Press.

Averill, J. R. (1980). A constructivist view of emotion. In R. Plutchik & H. Kellerman (Eds.), *Theories of emotion*. New York: Academic Press.

Averill, J. (1982). *Anger and aggression*. New York: Springer-Verlag.

Axelrod, R. (1980a). Effective choice in the Prisoner's Dilemma. *Journal of Conflict Resolution, 24*, 3–25.

Axelrod, R. (1980b). More effective choice in the Prisoner's Dilemma. *Journal of Conflict Resolution, 24*, 379–403.

Axelrod, R. (1984). *The evolution of cooperation*. New York: Basic Books.

Axsom, D., Yates, S., & Chaiken, S. (1987). Audience response as a heuristic cue in persuasion. *Journal of Personality and Social Psychology, 53*, 30–40.

Azrin, N. H., Hutchinson, R. R., & McLaughlin, R. (1965). The opportunity for aggression as an operant reinforcer during aversive stimulation. *Journal of the Experimental Analysis of Behavior, 8*, 171–180.

Azrin, N. H., Hutchinson, R. R., & Sallery, R. D. (1964). Pain-aggression toward inanimate objects. *Journal for the Experimental Analysis of Behavior, 7*, 228–229.

Babcock, M. K. (1988). Embarrassment: A window on the self. *Journal for the Theory of Social Behaviour, 18*, 459–483.

Back, K. W. (1951). Influence through social communication. *Journal of Abnormal and Social Psychology, 46,* 9–23.

Bagozzi, R. P. (1981). Attitudes, intentions, and behavior: A test of some key hypotheses. *Journal of Personality and Social Psychology, 41,* 607–627.

Bailey, J. M., Pillard, R. C., Neale, M. C., & Agyei, Y. (1993). Heritable factors influence sexual orientation in women. *Archives of General Psychiatry, 50,* 217–223.

Baldwin, J. I., Whiteley, S., & Baldwin, J. D. (1990). Changing AIDS- and fertility-related behavior: The effectiveness of sexual education. *Journal of Sex Research, 27,* 245–262.

Bandura, A., Ross, D., & Ross, S. A. (1963a). Imitation of film-mediated aggressive models. *Journal of Abnormal and Social Psychology, 66,* 3–11.

Bandura, A., Ross, D., & Ross, S. A. (1963b). Vicarious reinforcement and imitative learning. *Journal of Abnormal and Social Psychology, 67,* 601–607.

Bargh, J. A., Lombardi, W. J., & Higgins, E. T. (1988). Automaticity of chronically accessible constructs in person X situation effects on person perception: It's just a matter of time. *Journal of Personality and Social Psychology, 55,* 599–605.

Bar-Hillel & Yaari, M. (1993). Judgments of distributive justice. In Mellers, B. A. & Baron, J. (Eds.) *Psychological perspectives on justice.* Cambridge: Cambridge University Press.

Barnlund, D. C. (1962). Consistency of emergent leadership in groups with changing tasks and members. *Speech Monographs, 29,* 45–52.

Baron, J., & Jurney, J. (1993). Norms against voting for coerced reform. *Journal of Personality and Social Psychology, 64,* 347–355.

Baron, R. S., Moore, D., & Sanders, G. S. (1978). Distraction as a source of drive in social facilitation research. *Journal of Personality and Social Psychology, 36,* 816–824.

Baron, R. S., Roper, G., & Baron, P. H. (1974). Group discussion and the stingy shift. *Journal of Personality and Social Psychology, 30,* 538–545.

Bartholomew, K., & Horowitz, L. M. (1991). Attachment styles among young adults: A test of a four-category model. *Journal of Personality and Social Psychology, 61,* 226–244.

Bassili, J. N. (1989). Trait encoding in behavior identification and dispositional inference. *Personality and Social Psychology Bulletin, 15,* 285–296.

Bassili, J. N. (1993). Procedural efficiency and the spontaneity of trait inference. *Personality and Social Psychology Bulletin, 19,* 200–205.

Bassili, J. N., & Smith, M. C. (1986). On the spontaneity of trait attribution: Converging evidence for the role of cognitive strategy, *50,* 239–245.

Bateman, T. S. (1980). Contingent concession strategies in dyadic bargaining. *Organizational Behavior and Human Performance, 26,* 212–221.

Batson, C. D. (1987). Prosocial motivation: Is it ever truly altruistic? L. Berkowitz (Ed.), *Advances in experimental social psychology,* (Vol. 20, pp. 65–122). New York: Academic Press.

Batson, C. D., Batson, J. G., Griffitt, C. A., Barrientos, S., Brandt, J. R., Sprengelmeyer, P., & Bayly, M. J. (1989). Negative-state relief and the empathy-altruism hypothesis. *Journal of Personality and Social Psychology, 56,* 922–933.

Batson, C. D., Batson, J. G., Slingsby, J. K., Harrell, K. L., Peekna, H. M., & Todd, R. M. (1991). Empathic joy and the empathy-altruism hypothesis. *Journal of Personality and Social Psychology, 61,* 413–426.

Batson, C. D., Fultz, J., & Schoenrade, P. A. (1987). Distress and empathy: Two qualitatively distinct vicarious emotions with different motivational consequences. *Journal of Personality, 55,* 19–39.

Batson, C. D., O'Quinn, K., Fultz, J., Vanderplas, M., & Isen, A. M. (1983). Influence of self-reported distress and empathy on egoistic versus altruistic motivation to help. *Journal of Personality and Social Psychology, 45,* 706–718.

Bauman, L. J., & Siegel, K. (1987). Misperception among gay men of the risk for AIDS associated with their sexual behavior. *Journal of Applied Social Psychology, 17,* 329–350.

Baumann, D. J., Cialdini, R. B., & Kenrick, D. (1981). Altruism as hedonism: Helping and self-gratification as equivalent responses. *Journal of Personality and Social Psychology, 40,* 1039–1046.

Baumeister, R. F. (1987). How the self became a problem: A psychological review of historical research. *Journal of Personality and Social Psychology, 52,* 163–176.

Baumeister, R. F., & Steinhilber, A. (1984). Paradoxical effects of supportive audiences on performance under pressure: The home field disadvantage in sports championships. *Journal of Personality and Social Psychology, 47,* 85–93.

Baumeister, R. F., Stillwell, A., & Wotman, S. R. (1990). Victim and perpetrator accounts of interpersonal conflict: Autobiographical narratives about anger. *Journal of Personality and Social Psychology, 59,* 994–1005.

Baumeister, R. F., Wotman, S. R., & Stillwell, A. M. (1993). Unrequited love: On heartbreak, anger, guilt, scriptlessness, and humiliation. *Journal of Personality and Social Psychology, 64,* 377–394.

Baumrind, D. (1964). Some thoughts on the ethics of research: After reading Milgram's behavioral study of obedience. *American Psychologist, 19,* 421–423.

Bavelas, A. (1948). A mathematical structure for group structures. *Applied Anthropology, 7,* 16–30.

Baxandall, M. (1972). *Painting and experience in fifteenth-century Italy.* Oxford: Oxford University Press.

Baxter, T. L., & Goldberg, L. R. (1987). Perceived behavioral consistency underlying trait attributions to oneself and another: An extension of the actor-observer effect. *Personality and Social Psychology Bulletin, 13,* 437–447.

Bazerman, M. H., Magliozzi, T., & Neale, M. A. (1985). Integrative bargaining in a competitive market. *Organizational Behavior and Human Decision Processes, 35*, 294–313.

Beale, D. A., & Manstead, A. S. R. (1991). Predicting mothers' intentions to limit frequency of infants' sugar intake: Testing the theory of planned behavior. *Journal of Applied Social Psychology, 21*, 409–431.

Beck, K. H., & Lund, A. K. (1981). The effects of health threat seriousness and personal efficacy upon intentions and behavior. *Journal of Applied Social Psychology, 11*, 401–415.

Bell, G. B., & French, R. L. (1950). Consistency of individual leadership position in small groups of varying membership. *Journal of Abnormal and Social Psychology, 45*, 764–767.

Bell, P. A. (1992). In defense of the negative affect escape model of heat and aggression. *Psychological Bulletin, 111*, 342–346.

Belsky, J., Lang, M., & Huston, T. L. (1986). Sex typing and division of labor as determinants of marital change across the transition to parenthood. *Journal of Personality and Social Psychology, 50*, 517–522.

Bem, D. (1965). An experimental analysis of self-persuasion. *Journal of Experimental Social Psychology, 1*, 199–218.

Bem, S. L. (1974). The measurement of psychological androgyny. *Journal of Consulting and Clinical Psychology, 42*, 155–162.

Bem, S. L. (1975). Sex role adaptability: One consequence of psychological androgyny. *Journal of Personality and Social Psychology, 31*, 634–643.

Bem, S. L., & Lenney, E. (1976). Sex typing and the avoidance of cross-sex behavior. *Journal of Personality and Social Psychology, 33*, 48–54.

Benbow, C. P. (1988). Sex differences in mathematical reasoning ability in intellectually talented preadolescents: Their nature, effects, and possible causes. *Behavioral and Brain Sciences, 11*, 169–232.

Bendor, J., Kramer, R. M., & Stout, S. (1991). When in doubt . . . : Cooperation in a noisy prisoner's dilemma. *Journal of Conflict Resolution, 35*, 691–719.

Bentler, P. M., & Speckart, G. (1981). Attitudes "cause" behavior: A structural equation analysis. *Journal of Personality and Social Psychology, 40*, 226–238.

Benton, A. A., & Druckman, D. (1974). Constituent's bargaining orientation and intergroup negotiations. *Journal of Applied Social Psychology, 4*, 141–150.

Ben-Yoav, O., & Pruitt, D. G. (1984a). Accountability to constituents: A two-edged sword. *Organizational Behavior and Human Performance, 34*, 283–295.

Ben-Yoav, O., & Pruitt, D. G. (1984b). Resistance to yielding and the expectation of cooperative future interaction in negotiation. *Journal of Experimental Social Psychology, 20*, 323–335.

Berg, J. H., & Archer, R. L. (1982). Responses to self-disclosure and interaction goals. *Journal of Experimental Social Psychology, 18*, 501–512.

Berg, J. H., & Peplau, L. A. (1982). Loneliness: The relationship of self-disclosure and androgyny. *Personality and Social Psychology Bulletin, 8*, 624–630.

Berger, P. (1969). *A rumor of angels.* New York: Doubleday.

Berger, P., & Luckmann, T. (1967) *The social construction of reality.* New York: Anchor.

Berger, S. M., Carli, L. C., Garcia, R., & Brady, J. J., Jr. (1982). Audience effects in anticipatory learning: A comparison of drive and practice-inhibition analyses. *Journal of Personality and Social Psychology, 42*, 478–486.

Berger, S. M., Hampton, K. L., Carli, L. L., Grandmaison, P. S., Sadow, J. S., Donath, C. H., & Herschlag, L. R. (1981). Audience-induced inhibition of practice during learning. *Journal of Personality and Social Psychology, 40*, 479–491.

Berglas, S., & Jones, E. E. (1978). Drug choice as a self-handicapping strategy in response to noncontingent success. *Journal of Personality and Social Psychology, 36*, 405–417.

Berkowitz, L. (1959). Anti-Semitism and the displacement of aggression. *Journal of Abnormal and Social Psychology, 59*, 182–187.

Berkowitz, L. (1965). Some aspects of observed aggression. *Journal of Personality and Social Psychology, 2*, 359–369.

Berkowitz, L. (1974). Some determinants of impulsive aggression: The role of mediated associations with reinforcements of aggression. *Psychological Review, 81*, 165–176.

Berkowitz, L. (1982). Aversive conditions as stimuli to aggression. In L. Berkowitz (Ed.), *Advances in experimental social psychology* (Vol. 15, pp. 249–288). New York: Academic Press.

Berkowitz, L. (1984). Some effects of thoughts on anti- and prosocial influences of media events: A cognitive-neoassociation analysis. *Psychological Bulletin, 95*, 410–427.

Berkowitz, L. (1989). Frustration-aggression hypothesis: Examination and reformulation. *Psychological Bulletin, 106*, 59–73.

Berkowitz, L., Cochran, S. T., & Embree, M. C. (1981). Physical pain and the goal of aversively stimulated aggression. *Journal of Personality and Social Psychology, 40*, 687–700.

Berkowitz, L., & Heimer, K. (1989). On the construction of the anger of experience: Aversive events and negative priming in the formation of feelings. In L. Berkowitz (Ed.), *Advances in experimental social psychology* (Vol. 22, pp. 1–37). New York: Academic Press.

Berkowitz, L., & LePage, A. (1967). Weapons as aggression-eliciting stimuli. *Journal of Personality and Social Psychology*, 7, 202–207.

Berndt, T. J., & Heller, K. A. (1986). Gender stereotypes and social inferences: A developmental study. *Journal of Personality and Social Psychology*, 50, 889–898.

Bernstein, M., & Crosby, F. (1980). An empirical examination of relative deprivation theory. *Journal of Experimental Social Psychology*, 16, 442–456.

Berscheid, E., Brothen, T., & Graziano, W. (1976). Gain-loss theory and the "law of infidelity": Mr. Doting versus the admiring stranger. *Journal of Personality and Social Psychology*, 33, 709–718.

Berscheid, E., & Walster, W. (1974). A little bit about love. In T. L. Huston (Ed.), *Foundations of interpersonal attraction*. New York: Academic Press.

Betancourt, H., & Blair, I. (1992). A cognition (attribution)-emotion model of violence in conflict situations. *Personality and Social Psychology Bulletin*, 18, 343–350.

Bettencourt, B. A., Brewer, M. B., Croak, M. R., & Miller, N. (1992). Cooperation and the reduction of intergroup bias: The role of reward structure and social orientation. *Journal of Experimental Social Psychology*, 28, 301–319.

Beyer, S. (1990). Gender differences in the accuracy of self-evaluations of performance. *Journal of Personality and Social Psychology*, 59, 960–970.

Bharati, A. (1985). The self in Hindu thought and action. In A. J. Marsella, G. DeVos, & F. L. K. Hsu, eds. *Culture and self: Asian and Western perspectives*. New York: Tavistock Publications (185–230).

Billy, J. O. G., Tanfer, K., Grady, W. R., & Klepinger, D. H. (1993). The sexual behavior of men in the United States. *Family Planning Perspectives*, 25, 52–60.

Birchler, G. R., Weiss, R. L., & Vincent, J. P. (1975). Multimethod analysis of social reinforcement exchange between maritally distressed and nondistressed spouse and stranger dyads. *Journal of Personality and Social Psychology*, 31, 349–360.

Blair, S. L., & Johnson, M. P. (1992). Wives' perceptions of the fairness of the division of household labor: The intersection of housework and ideology. *Journal of Marriage and the Family*, 54, 570–581.

Bless, H., Bohner, G., Schwarz, N., & Strack, F. (1990). Mood and persuasion: A cognitive response analysis. *Personality and Social Psychology Bulletin*, 16, 331–345.

Bless, H., Mackie, D. M., & Schwarz, N. (1992). Mood effects on attitude judgments: Independent effects of mood before and after message elaboration. *Journal of Personality and Social Psychology*, 63, 585–595.

Blascovich, J., Ginsburg, G. P., & Veach, T. L. (1975). A pluralistic explanation of choice shifts on the risk dimension. *Journal of Personality and Social Psychology*, 31, 422–429.

Bloom, B. L., Asher, S. J., & White, S. W. (1978). Marital disruption as a stressor: A review and analysis. *Psychological Bulletin*, 85, 867–894.

Blumenthal, R. (1989). Police search for 18-year-old in killing of Brooklyn youth. *New York Times*, August 26, 1989.

Bodenhausen, G. V., & Wyer, R. S., Jr. (1985). Effects of stereotypes on decision making and information-processing strategies. *Journal of Personality and Social Psychology*, 48, 267–282.

Bond, C. F., Jr. (1982). Social facilitation: A self-presentational view. *Journal of Personality and Social Psychology*, 42, 1042–1050.

Bond, C. F., Jr., & Titus, L. J. (1983). Social facilitation: A meta analysis of 241 studies. *Psychological Bulletin*, 94, 265–292.

Bond, M. H., & Cheung, T.-S. (1983). College students' spontaneous self-concept: The effect of culture among respondents in Hong Kong, Japan, and the United States. *Journal of Cross-Cultural Psychology*, 14, 153–171.

Booth, A., & Edwards, J. N. (1985). Age at marriage and marital instability. *Journal of Marriage and the Family*, 47, 67–75.

Borgatta, E. F., Bales, R. F., & Couch, E. S. (1954). Some findings relevant to the great man theory of leadership. *American Sociological Review*, 19, 755–759.

Borkenau, P. (1986). Toward an understanding of trait interrelations: Acts as instances for several traits. *Journal of Personality and Social Psychology*, 51, 371–381.

Borkenau, P. (1990). Traits as ideal-based and goal-derived social categories. *Journal of Personality and Social Psychology*, 58, 381–396.

Borkenau, P., & Ostendorf, F. (1987). Fact and fiction in implicit personality theory. *Journal of Personality*, 55, 415–443.

Bornstein, R. F. (1989). Exposure and affect: Overview and meta-analysis of research, 1968–1987. *Psychological Bulletin*, 106, 265–289.

Bornstein, R. F., Kale, A. R., & Cornell, K. R. (1990). Boredom as a limiting condition on the mere exposure effect. *Journal of Personality and Social Psychology*, 58, 791–800.

Bossard, J. (1932). Residential propinquity as a factor in marriage selection. *American Journal of Sociology*, 38, 219–224.

Bouchard, T. J., Jr., & Hare, M. (1970). Size, performance, and potential in brainstorming groups. *Journal of Applied Psychology*, 54, 51–55.

Bowen, G. L., & Orthner, D. K. (1983). Sex-role congruency and marital quality. *Journal of Marriage and the Family*, 45, 223–230.

Bowlby, J. (1973). *Attachment and loss: Volume 2: Separation: Anxiety and anger*. New York: Basic Books.

Boyd, B., & Wandersman, A. (1991). Predicting undergraduate condom use with the Fishbein and Ajzen and the

Triandis attitude-behavior models: Implications for public health interventions. *Journal of Applied Social Psychology, 21*, 1810–1830.

Brabeck, M. (1983). Moral judgment: Theory and research on differences between males and females. *Developmental Review, 3*, 274–291.

Bradbury, T. N., & Fincham, F. D. (1990). Attributions in marriage: Review and critique. *Psychological Bulletin, 107*, 3–33.

Bradbury, T. N., & Fincham, F. D. (1992). Attributions and behavior in marital interaction. *Journal of Personality and Social Psychology, 63*, 613–628.

Breaugh, J. A., & Klimoski, R. J. (1981). Social forces in negotiation simulations. *Personality and Social Psychology Bulletin, 7*, 290–295.

Brewer, M. B., & Kramer, R. M. (1986). Choice behavior in social dilemma: Effects of social identity, group size, and decision framing. *Journal of Personality and Social Psychology, 50*, 543–549.

Briggs, S. R., Cheek, J. M., & Buss, A. H. (1980). An analysis of the self-monitoring scale. *Journal of Personality and Social Psychology, 38*, 679–686.

Briggs, S. R., & Cheek, J. M. (1988). On the nature of self-monitoring: Problems with assessment, problems with validity. *Journal of Personality and Social Psychology, 54*, 663–678.

Britt, T. W. (1992). The self-consciousness scale: On the stability of the three-factor structure. *Personality and Social Psychology Bulletin, 18*, 748–755.

Broadstock, M., Borland, R., & Gason, R. (1992). Effects of suntan on judgements of healthiness and attractiveness by adolescents. *Journal of Applied Social Psychology, 22*, 157–172.

Brock, T. C., & Balloun, J. L. (1967). Behavioral receptivity to dissonant information. *Journal of Personality and Social Psychology, 6*, 413–428.

Brockner, J., DeWitt, R. L., Grover, S., & Reed, T. (1990). When it is especially important to explain why: Factors affecting the relationship between managers' explanations of a layoff and survivors' reactions to the layoff. *Journal of Experimental Social Psychology, 26*, 389–407.

Brown, B. R. (1968). The effects of need to maintain face on interpersonal bargaining. *Journal of Experimental Social Psychology, 4*, 107–122.

Brown, B. R. (1970). Face-saving following experimentally induced embarrassment. *Journal of Experimental Social Psychology, 6*, 255–271.

Brown, B. R., & Garland, H. (1971). The effect of incompetency, audience acquaintanceship, and anticipated evaluative feedback on face-saving behavior. *Journal of Experimental Social Psychology, 7*, 490–502.

Brown, R. (1965). *Social psychology.* New York: Free Press.

Brown, R. (1974). Further comment on the risky shift. *American Psychologist, 29*, 468–470.

Brown, R., & Van Kleeck, M. H. (1989). Enough said: Three principles of explanation. *Journal of Personality and Social Psychology, 57*, 590–604.

Brown, R., & Wade, G. (1987). Superordinate goals and intergroup behaviour: The effect of role ambiguity and status on intergroup attitudes and task performance. *European Journal of Social Psychology, 17*, 131–142.

Browne, E. C., & Franklin, M. N. (1973). Aspects of coalition payoffs in European parliamentary democracies. *American Political Science Review, 67*, 453–469.

Brownson, F. H., & Desjardines, C. (1971). In B. E. Eleftherion and J. P. Scott (Eds.), *Symposium: The physiology of aggression and defeat.* New York: Plenum Press.

Bryan, J. H., & Walbek, N. H. (1970). Preaching and practicing generosity: Children's actions and reactions. *Child Development, 41*, 329–353.

Buck, R. (1980). Nonverbal behavior and the theory of emotion: The facial feedback hypothesis. *Journal of Personality and Social Psychology, 38*, 811–824.

Buck, R., Loslow, J. I., Murphy, M. M., & Costanzo, P. (1992). Social facilitation and inhibition of emotional expression and communication. *Journal of Personality and Social Psychology, 63*, 962–968.

Buck, R., Miller, R. E., & Caul, W. F. (1974). Sex, personality, and physiological variables in the communication of affect via facial expression. *Journal of Personality and Social Psychology, 30*, 587–596.

Buck, R. W., & Parke, R. D. (1978). Behavioral and physiological response to the presence of a friendly or neutral person in two types of stressful situations. *Journal of Personality and Social Psychology, 24*, 143–153.

Buck, R. W., Savin, V. J., Miller, R. E., & Caul, W. F. (1972). Communication of affect through facial expressions in humans. *Journal of Personality and Social Psychology, 23*, 362–371.

Budd, R. J., North, D., & Spencer, C. (1984). Understanding seat-belt use: A test of Bentler and Speckart's extension of the "theory of reasoned action." *European Journal of Social Psychology, 14*, 69–78.

Budd, R. J., & Spencer, C. P. (1985). Exploring the role of personal normative beliefs in the theory of reasoned action: The problem of discriminating between alternative path models. *European Journal of Social Psychology, 15*, 299–313.

Buhrich, N., Bailey, J. M., & Martin, N. G. (1991). Sexual orientation, sexual identity, and sex-dimorphic behaviors in male twins. *Behavior Genetics, 21*, 75–96.

Bumpass, L. L., Sweet, J. A., & Cherlin, A. (1991). The role of cohabitation in declining rates of marriage. *Journal of Marriage and the Family, 53*, 913–927.

Burgess, E. W., & Wallin, P. (1953). *Engagement and marriage.* Philadelphia: Lippincott.

Burman, B., & Margolin, G. (1992). Analysis of the association between marital relationships and health problems: An interactional perspective. *Psychological Bulletin, 112*, 39–63.

Burnkrant, R. E., & Howard, D. J. (1984). Effects of the use of introductory rhetorical questions versus statements on information processing. *Journal of Personality and Social Psychology, 47*, 1218–1230.

Burnstein, E., Vinokur, A., & Trope, Y. (1973). Interpersonal comparison versus persuasive argumentation: A more direct test of alternative explanations for group induced shifts in individual choice. *Journal of Experimental Social Psychology, 9*, 236–245.

Buss, A. H. (1966). Instrumentality of aggression, feedback, and frustration as determinants of physical aggression. *Journal of Personality and Social Psychology, 3*, 153–162.

Buss, D. M. (1981). Sex differences in the evaluation and performance of dominant acts. *Journal of Personality and Social Psychology, 40*, 147–154.

Buss, D. M. (1984). Toward a psychology of person-environment (PE) correlation: The role of spouse selection. *Journal of Personality and Social Psychology, 47*, 361–377.

Buss, D. M. (1989). Sex differences in human mate preferences: Evolutionary hypotheses tested in 37 cultures. *Behavioral and Brain Sciences, 12*, 1–49.

Buss, D. M., & Schmitt, D. P. (1993). Sexual strategies theory: An evolutionary perspective on human mating. *Psychological Review, 100*, 204–232.

Buss, D. M., & Barnes, M. L. (1986). Preferences in human mate selection. *Journal of Personality and Social Psychology, 50*, 559–570.

Byrne, D. (1961). Interpersonal attraction and attitude similarity. *Journal of Abnormal and Social Psychology, 62*, 713–715.

Byrne, D., & Blaylock, B. (1963). Similarity and assumed similarity between husbands and wives. *Journal of Abnormal and Social Psychology, 67*, 636–640.

Byrne, D. & Buehler, J. A. (1955). A note on the influence of propinquity upon acquaintanceships. *Journal of Abnormal and Social Psychology, 51*, 147–148.

Byrne, D., Clore, G. L., & Worchel, P. (1966). The effect of economic similarity-dissimilarity on interpersonal attraction. *Journal of Personality and Social Psychology, 4*, 220–224.

Byrne, D., Griffith, W., & Stefaniak, D. (1967). Attraction and similarity of personality characteristics. *Journal of Personality and Social Psychology, 5*, 82–90.

Byrne, D., & Nelson, D. (1964). Attraction as a function of attitude similarity-dissimilarity: The effect of topic importance. *Psychonomic Science, 1*, 93–94.

Bytheway, W. R. (1981). The variation with age of age differences in marriage. *Journal of Marriage and the Family, 43*, 923–927.

Cacioppo, J. T., Bush, L. K., & Tassinary, L. G. (1992). Microexpressive facial actions as a function of affective stimuli: Replication and extension. *Personality and Social Psychology Bulletin, 18*, 515–526.

Cacioppo, J. T., Martzke, J. S., Petty, R. E., & Tassinary, L. G. (1988). Specific forms of EMG response index emotions during an interview: From Darwin to the continuous flow hypothesis of affect-laden information processing. *Journal of Personality and Social Psychology, 54*, 592–604.

Cacioppo, J. T., Petty, R. E., Losch, M. E., & Kim, H. S. (1986). Electromyographic activity over facial muscle regions can differentiate the valence and intensity of affective reactions. *Journal of Personality and Social Psychology, 50*, 260–268.

Caldwell, M. A., & Peplau, L. A. (1982). Sex differences in same-sex friendships. *Sex Roles, 8*, 721–731.

Campbell, D. T., & McCandless, B. R. (1951). Ethnocentrism, xenophobia, and personality. *Human Relations, 4*, 185–192.

Campbell, J. D., & Fairey, P. J. (1989). Informational and normative routes to conformity: The effect of faction size as a function of norm extremity and attention to the stimulus. *Journal of Personality and Social Psychology, 57*, 457–468.

Campbell, J. D., Tesser, A., & Fairey, P. J. (1986). Conformity and attention to the stimulus: Some temporal and contextual dynamics. *Journal of Personality and Social Psychology, 51*, 315–324.

Cantor, N., & Mischel, W. (1977). Traits as prototypes: Effects on recognition memory. *Journal of Personality and Social Psychology, 35*, 38–48.

Carlsmith, J. M., & Gross, A. E. (1969). Some effects of guilt on compliance. *Journal of Personality and Social Psychology, 11*, 232–239.

Carlson, M., Marcus-Newhall, A., & Miller, N. (1990). Effects of situational aggression cues: A quantitative review. *Journal of Personality and Social Psychology, 58*, 622–633.

Carlson, M., & Miller, N. (1987). Explanation of the relation between negative mood and helping. *Psychological Bulletin, 102*, 91–108.

Carnelley, K. B., & Janoff-Bulman, R. (1992). Optimism about love relationships: General vs. specific lessons from one's personal experience. *Journal of Social and Personal Relationships, 9*, 5–20.

Carnevale, P. J. D., & Isen, A. (1986). The influence of positive affect and visual access on the discovery of integrative solutions in bilateral negotiations. *Organizational Behavior and Human Decision Processes, 37*, 1–13.

Carnevale, P. J. D., Pruitt, D. G., & Britton, S. D. (1979). Looking tough: The negotiator under constituent surveillance. *Personality and Social Psychology Bulletin, 5*, 118–121.

Carroll, L. (1988). Concern with AIDS and the sexual

behavior of college students. *Journal of Marriage and the Family, 50,* 405–411.

Carter, L. F., & Nixon, M. (1949). An investigation of the relationship between four criteria of leadership ability for three different tasks. *Journal of Psychology, 27,* 245–261.

Cartwright, D. (1971). Risk taking by individuals and groups: An assessment of research employing choice dilemmas. *Journal of Personality and Social Psychology, 20,* 361–378.

Carver, C. S. (1975). Physical aggression as a function of objective self-awareness and attitudes toward punishment. *Journal of Experimental Social Psychology, 11,* 510–519.

Caspi, A., & Herbener, E. S. (1990). Continuity and change: Assortative marriage and the consistency of personality in adulthood. *Journal of Personality and Social Psychology, 58,* 250–258.

Cate, R. M., Lloyd, S. A., Henton, J. M. (1985). The effect of equity, equality, and reward level on the stability of students' premarital relationships. *Journal of Social Psychology, 125,* 715–725.

Cate, R. M., Lloyd, S. A., & Long, E. (1988). The role of rewards and fairness in developing premarital relationships. *Journal of Marriage and the Family, 50,* 443–452.

Chaiken, A. L., & Darley, J. M. (1973). Victim or perpetrator?: Defensive attribution of responsibility and the need for order and justice. *Journal of Personality and Social Psychology, 25,* 268–275.

Chaiken, S. (1980). Heuristic versus systematic information processing and the use of source versus message cues in persuasion. *Journal of Personality and Social Psychology, 39,* 752–766.

Chaiken, S., & Stagnor, C. (1987). Attitudes and attitude change. *Annual Review of Psychology, 38,* 575–630.

Chaiken, S., & Yates, S. (1985). Affective-cognitive consistency and thought-induced attitude polarization. *Journal of Personality and Social Psychology, 49,* 1470–1481.

Chapanis, N. P., & Chapanis, A. (1964). Cognitive dissonance: Five years later. *Psychological Bulletin, 61,* 1–22.

Chapman, L. J., & Chapman, J. P. (1967). Genesis of popular but erroneous psychodiagnostic observations. *Journal of Abnormal and Social Psychology, 72,* 193–204.

Check, J. V. P., & Malamuth, N. M. (1983). Sex role stereotyping and reactions to depictions of stranger versus acquaintance rape. *Journal of Personality and Social Psychology, 45,* 344–356.

Chelune, G. J., Sultan, F. E., & Williams, C. L. (1980). Loneliness, self-disclosure, and interpersonal effectiveness. *Journal of Counseling Psychology, 27,* 462–468.

Cheney, D. L., & Seyfarth, R. M. (1988). Assessment of meaning and the detection of unreliable signals by vervet monkeys. *Animal Behaviour, 36,* 477–486.

Chen, H. C., Reardon, R., Rea, C., & Moore, D. J. (1992). Forewarning of content and involvement: Consequences for persuasion and resistance to persuasion. *Journal of Experimental Social Psychology, 28,* 523–541.

Chertkoff, J. M., & Conley, M. (1967). Opening offer and frequency of concession as bargaining strategies. *Journal of Personality and Social Psychology, 7,* 181–185.

Chwalisz, K., Diener, E., & Gallagher, D. (1988). Autonomic arousal feedback and emotional experience: Evidence from the spinal cord injured. *Journal of Personality and Social Psychology, 54,* 820–828.

Cialdini, R. B., Darby, B. L., & Vincent, J. E. (1973). Transgression and altruism: A case for hedonism. *Journal of Experimental Social Psychology, 9,* 502–516.

Cialdini, R. B., & De Nicholas, M. E. (1989). Self-presentation by association. *Journal of Personality and Social Psychology, 57,* 626–631.

Cialdini, R. B., Green, B. L., & Rusch, A. J. (1992). When tactical pronouncements of change become real change: The case of reciprocal persuasion. *Journal of Personality and Social Psychology, 63,* 30–40.

Cialdini, R. B., & Kenrick, D. T. (1976). Altruism as hedonism: A social development perspective on the relationship of negative mood state and helping. *Journal of Personality and Social Psychology, 34,* 907–914.

Cialdini, R. B., Kenrick, D. T., & Hoerig, J. H. (1976). Victim derogation in the Lerner paradigm: Just world or just justification? *Journal of Personality and Social Psychology, 33,* 719–724.

Cialdini, R. B., Levy, A., Herman, C. P., Kozlowski, L. T., & Petty, R. E. (1976). Elastic shifts of opinion: Determinants of direction and durability. *Journal of Personality and Social Psychology, 34,* 663–672.

Cialdini, R. B., Petty, R. E., & Cacioppo, J. T. (1981). Attitudes and attitude change. *Annual Review of Psychology, 32,* 357–404.

Cialdini, R. B., & Richardson, K. D. (1980). Two indirect tactics of image management: Basking and blasting. *Journal of Personality and Social Psychology, 39,* 406–415.

Cialdini, R. B., Schaller, M., Houlihan, D., Arps, K., Fultz, J., & Beaman, A. L. (1987). Empathy-based helping: Is it selflessly or selfishly motivated? *Journal of Personality and Social Psychology, 52,* 749–758.

Cialdini, R. B., Vincent, J. E., Lewis, S. K., Catalan, J., Wheeler, D., & Darby, B. L. (1975). Reciprocal concessions procedure for inducing compliance: The door-in-the-face technique. *Journal of Personality and Social Psychology, 31,* 206–215.

Clark, L. F., & Woll, S. B. (1981). Stereotype biases: A reconstructive analysis of their role in reconstructive memory. *Journal of Personality and Social Psychology, 41,* 1064–1072.

Clark, M. S. (1984). Record keeping in two types of relationships. *Journal of Personality and Social Psychology, 47,* 549–557.

Clark, M. S., & Mills, J. (1979). Interpersonal attraction

in exchange and communal relationships. *Journal of Personality and Social Psychology, 37*, 12–24.

Clark, M. S., Mills, J., & Corcoran, D. M. (1989). Keeping track of needs and inputs of friends and strangers. *Personality and Social Psychology Bulletin, 15*, 533–542.

Clark, M. S., Mills, J., & Powell, M. C. (1986). Keeping track of needs in communal and exchange relationships. *Journal of Personality and Social Psychology, 51*, 333–338.

Clark, M. S., & Taraban, C. (1991). Reactions to and willingness to express emotion in communal and exchange relationships. *Journal of Experimental Social Psychology, 27*, 324–336.

Clark, R. D. III. (1990). The impact of AIDS on gender differences in willingness to engage in casual sex. *Journal of Applied Social Psychology, 20*, 771–782.

Clark, R. D. III (1990). Minority influence: The role of argument refutation of the majority position and social support for the minority position. *European Journal of Social Psychology, 20*, 489–497.

Clémencé, A. (1990). Effect of social-class belonging on the cognitive dissonance resulting from threat severity. *European Journal of Social Psychology, 20*, 525–529.

Cline, V. B., Croft, R. G., & Courrier, S. (1973). Desensitization of children to television violence. *Journal of Personality and Social Psychology, 27*, 360–365.

Cohen, S., & Wills, T. A. (1985). Stress, social support and the buffering hypothesis. *Psychological Bulletin, 98*, 310–357.

Cohn, D. A., Silver, D. H., Cowan, C. P., Cowan, P. A., & Pearson, J. (1992). Working models of childhood attachment and couple relationships. *Journal of Family Issues, 13*, 432–449.

Collins, B. E., & Hoyt, M. F. (1972). Personal responsibility-for-consequences: An integration and extension of the "forced compliance" literature. *Journal of Experimental Social Psychology, 8*, 558–593.

Condon, J. W., & Crano, W. D. (1988). Inferred evaluation and the relation between attitude similarity and interpersonal attraction. *Journal of Personality and Social Psychology, 54*, 789–797.

Cook, M. (1981). Social skill and human sexual attraction. In M. Cook (Ed.), *The bases of human sexual attraction.* London: Academic Press.

Cooley, C. H. (1902/1964). *Human nature and the social order.* New York: Schocken. (First published 1902 by Scribner and Sons, New York.)

Cooper, J., & Croyle, R. T. (1984). Attitudes and attitude change. *Annual Review of Psychology, 35*, 395–426.

Cooper, J., & Mackie, D. (1986). Video games and aggression in children. *Journal of Applied Social Psychology, 16*, 726–744.

Cooper, J., Zanna, M. P., & Taves, P. A. (1978). Arousal as a necessary condition for attitude change following induced compliance. *Journal of Personality and Social Psychology, 36*, 1101–1106.

Cottrell, N. B., Wack, D. L., Sekerak, G. J., & Rittle, R. H. (1968). Social facilitation of dominant responses by the presence of an audience and the mere presence of others. *Journal of Personality and Social Psychology, 9*, 245–250.

Cousins, S. D. (1989). Culture and self-perception in Japan and the United States. *Journal of Personality and Social Psychology, 56*, 124–131.

Cozby, P. (1972). Self-disclosure, reciprocity and liking. *Sociometry, 35*, 151–160.

Crandall, C. S. (1988). Social contagion of binge eating. *Journal of Personality and Social Psychology, 55*, 588–598.

Crocker, J., & Luhtanen, R. (1990). Collective self-esteem and ingroup bias. *Journal of Personality and Social Psychology, 58*, 60–67.

Crockett, W. H. (1982). Balance, agreement, and positivity in the cognition of small social structures. In L. Berkowitz (Ed.), *Advances in experimental social psychology* (Vol. 15, pp. 1–57). New York: Academic Press.

Cropanzano, R., & Folger, R. (1989). Referent cognitions and task decision autonomy: Beyond equity theory. *Journal of Applied Psychology, 74*, 293–299.

Crosby, F. (1976). A model of egoistical relative deprivation. *Psychological Review, 83*, 85–113.

Crosby, F., Bromley, S., & Saxe, L. (1980). Recent unobtrusive studies of black and white discrimination and prejudice: A literature review. *Psychological Bulletin, 87*, 546–563.

Croyle, R. T., & Cooper, J. (1983). Dissonance arousal: Physiological evidence. *Journal of Personality and Social Psychology, 45*, 782–791.

Crutchfield, R. S. (1955). Conformity and character. *American Psychologist, 10*, 191–198.

Cunningham, M. R. (1979). Weather, mood, and helping behavior: Quasi-experiments with the sunshine Samaritan. *Journal of Personality and Social Psychology, 37*, 1947–1956.

Cunningham, M. R. (1986). Measuring the physical in physical attractiveness: Quasi-experiments on the sociobiology of female facial beauty. *Journal of Personality and Social Psychology, 50*, 925–935.

Cunningham, M. R, Barbee, A. P., & Pike, C. L. (1990). What do women want? Facialmetric assessment of multiple motives in the perception of male facial physical attractiveness. *Journal of Personality and Social Psychology, 59*, 61–72.

Curran, J. P. (1973). Examination of various interpersonal attraction principles in the dating dyad. *Journal of Experimental Research in Personality, 6*, 346–356.

Daly, M., & Wilson, M. (1988). *Homicide.* New York: Aldine De Gruyter.

D'Agostino, P. R. (1991). Spontaneous trait inferences:

Effects of recognition instructions and subliminal priming on recognition performance. *Personality and Social Psychology Bulletin, 17,* 70–77.

Dahlbäck, O. (1990). The social value of risk taking. *European Journal of Social Psychology, 20,* 531–535.

D'Andrade, R. G. (1965). Trait psychology and componential analysis. *American Anthropologist, 67,* 215–228.

D'Andrade, R. G. (1984). Cultural meaning systems. In R. A. Shweder & R. A. LeVine, (Eds.) *Culture theory: Essays on mind, self, and emotion.* New York: Cambridge University Press (88–119).

Darley, J., & Batson, C. D. (1973). "From Jerusalem to Jerricho": A study of situational and dispositional variables in helping behavior. *Journal of Personality and Social Psychology, 27,* 100–108.

Darley, J. M., & Latané, B. (1968). Bystander intervention in emergencies: Diffusion of responsibility. *Journal of Personality and Social Psychology, 8,* 377–383.

Darwin, C. (1872/1965). *The expression of emotions in man and animals.* Chicago: University of Chicago Press.

Daumann, D. J., Cialdini, R. B., & Kenrick, D. T. (1981). Altruism as hedonism: Helping and self-gratification as equivalent responses. *Journal of Personality and Social Psychology, 40,* 1039–1046.

Davidson, B., Balswick, J., & Halverson, C. (1983). Affective self-disclosure and marital adjustment: A test of equity theory. *Journal of Marriage and the Family, 45,* 93–102.

Davies, J. C. (1962). Toward a theory of revolution. *American Sociological Review, 27,* 5–19.

Davis, M. H., & Harvey, J. C. (1992). Declines in major league batting performance as a function of game pressure: A drive theory analysis. *Journal of Applied Social Psychology, 22,* 714–735.

Davis, D. (1981). Implications for interaction versus effectance as mediators of the similarity-attraction relationship. *Journal of Experimental Social Psychology, 17,* 96–116.

Davis, J. H. (1973). Group decision and social interaction: A theory of social decision schemes. *Psychological Review, 80,* 97–125.

Davis, J. H. (1989). Psychology and the law: The last 15 years. *Journal of Applied Social Psychology, 19,* 199–230.

Davis, J. H., Kerr, N. L., Stasser, G., Meek, D. & Holt, R. (1977). Victim consequences, sentence severity, and decision processes in mock juries. *Organizational Behavior and Human Performance, 18,* 346–365.

Davis, M. H., & Franzoi, S. L. (1986). Adolescent loneliness, self-disclosure, and private self-consciousness: A longitudinal investigation. *Journal of Personality and Social Psychology, 51,* 595–608.

Dawes, R. M., McTavish, J., & Shaklee, H. (1977). Behavior, communication, and assumptions about other people's behavior in a commons dilemma situation. *Journal of Personality and Social Psychology, 35,* 1–11.

Dawes, R. N. (1989). Statistical criteria for establishing a truly false consensus effect. *Journal of Experimental Social Psychology, 25,* 1–17.

Dawkins, R. (1976). *The selfish gene.* London: Oxford University Press.

Dawkins, R., & Krebs, J. R. (1978). Animal signals: Information or manipulations? In J. R. Krebs & N. B. Davies (Eds.), *Behavioral ecology: An evolutionary approach.* Oxford: Blackwell Scientific Publications.

DeBono, K. G. (1992). Pleasant scents and persuasion: An information processing approach. *Journal of Applied Social Psychology, 22,* 910–919.

Deci, E. L., & Ryan, R. M. (1980). In L. Berkowitz (Ed.), The empirical exploration of intrinsic motivational processes. *Advances in experimental social psychology* (Vol. 13, pp. 39–80). New York: Academic Press.

DeMaris, A., & Leslie, G. R. (1984). Cohabitation with the future spouse: Its influence upon marital satisfaction and communication. *Journal of Marriage and the Family, 46,* 77–84.

DeMaris, A., & MacDonald, W. (1993). Premarital cohabitation and marital instability: A test of the unconventionality hypothesis. *Journal of Marriage and the Family, 55,* 399–407.

DeMaris, A., & Rao, K. V. (1992). Premarital cohabitation and subsequent marital stability in the United States: A reassessment. *Journal of Marriage and the Family, 54,* 178–190.

DeJong, W. (1979). An examination of the self-perception mediation of the foot-in-the-door effect. *Journal of Personality and Social Psychology, 37,* 2221–2239.

DePaulo, P. J., & DePaulo, B. M. (1989). Can deception by salespersons and customers be detected through nonverbal behavioral cues? *Journal of Applied Social Psychology, 19,* 1552–1577.

DePaulo, B. M., & Rosenthal, R. (1979). Telling lies. *Journal of Personality and Social Psychology, 37,* 1713–1722.

Derlega, V., & Chaikin, A. L. (1976). Norms affecting self-disclosure in men and women. *Journal of Consulting and Clinical Psychology, 44,* 376–380.

Derné, S. (1992). Beyond institutional and impulsive conceptions of self: Family structure and socially anchored real self. *Ethos, 20,* 259–288.

Deschamps, J.-C., & Brown, R. (1983). Superordinate goals and intergroup conflict. *British Journal of Social Psychology, 22,* 189–195.

Desforges, D. M., Lord, C. G., Ramsey, S. L., Mason, J. A., Van Leeuwen, M. D., West, S. C., & Lepper, M. R. (1991). Effects of structured cooperative contact on changing negative attitudes toward stereotyped social groups. *Journal of Personality and Social Psychology, 60,* 531–544.

Des Pres, T. (1976). *The survivors: An anatomy of the death camps.* New York: Oxford University Press.

De Soto, C. B. (1960). Learning a social structure. *Journal of Abnormal and Social Psychology, 60,* 417–421.

Deutsch, M. (1960). The effect of motivational orientation upon trust and suspicion. *Human Relations, 13,* 123–139.

Deutsch, M., & Gerard, H. B. (1955). A study of normative and informational social influence upon individual judgment. *Journal of Abnormal and Social Psychology, 51,* 629–636.

DeVellis, B. M., Blalock, S. J., & Sandler, R. S. (1990). Predicting participation in cancer screening: The role of perceived behavioral control. *Journal of Applied Social Psychology, 20,* 639–660.

Devine, P. G. (1989). Stereotypes and prejudice: Their automatic and controlled components. *Journal of Personality and Social Psychology, 56,* 5–18.

Devine, P. G., Hirt, E. R., & Gehrke, E. M. (1990). Diagnostic and confirmation strategies in trait hypothesis testing. *Journal of Personality and Social Psychology, 58,* 952–963.

Devine, P. G., Monteith, M. J., Zuwerink, J. R., & Elliot, A. J. (1991). Prejudice with and without compunction. *Journal of Personality and Social Psychology, 60,* 817–830.

Devine, P. G., Sedikides, C., & Fuhrman, R. W. (1989). Goals in social information processing: The case of anticipated interaction. *Journal of Personality and Social Psychology, 56,* 680–690.

Dickerson, C. A., Thibodeau, R., Aronson, E., & Miller, D. (1992). Using cognitive dissonance to encourage water conservation. *Journal of Applied Social Psychology, 22,* 841–854.

Diehl, M., & Stroebe, W. (1987). Productivity loss in brainstorming groups: Toward the solution of a riddle. *Journal of Personality and Social Psychology, 53,* 497–509.

Diehl, M., & Stroebe, W. (1991). Productivity loss in idea-generating groups: Tracking down the blocking effect. *Journal of Personality and Social Psychology, 61,* 392–403.

Diener, E., & DeFour, E. (1978). Does television violence enhance program popularity? *Journal of Personality and Social Psychology, 36,* 333–341.

Diener, E., Fraser, S. C., Beaman, A. L., & Kelem, R. T. (1976). Effects of deindividuation variables on stealing among Halloween trick-or-treaters. *Journal of Personality and Social Psychology, 33,* 178–183.

DiLalla, L. F., & Gottesman, I. I. (1991). Biological and genetic contributors to violence—Widom's untold tale. *Psychological Bulletin, 109,* 125–129.

Dindia, K., & Allen, M. (1992). Sex differences in self-disclosure: A meta-analysis. *Psychological Bulletin, 112,* 106–124.

Dion, K. (1972). Physical attractiveness and evaluation of children's transgressions. *Journal of Personality and Social Psychology, 24,* 207–213.

Dion, K., Berscheid, E., & Walster, E. (1972). What is beautiful is good. *Journal of Personality and Social Psychology, 24,* 285–290.

Dipboye, R. L., Fromkin, H. L., & Wiback. (1975). Relative importance of applicant sex, attractiveness, and scholastic standing in evaluation of job applicant resumes. *Journal of Applied Psychology, 60,* 39–43.

Ditto, P. H., & Lopez, D. F. (1992). Motivated skepticism: Use of differential decision criteria for preferred and nonpreferred conclusions. *Journal of Personality and Social Psychology, 63,* 568–584.

Dodge, K. A., & Crick, N. R. (1990). Social information-processing bases of aggressive behavior in children. *Personality and Social Psychology Bulletin, 16,* 8–22.

Doherty, K., Weigold, M. P., & Schlenker, B. R. (1990). Self-serving interpretations of motives. *Personality and Social Psychology Bulletin, 16,* 485–495.

Doi, T. (tr. J. Beste) (1973). *The anatomy of dependence.* Tokyo: Kodansha.

Doise, W. (1969). Intergroup relations and polarization of individual and collective judgments. *Journal of Personality and Social Psychology, 12,* 136–143.

Dollard, J., Miller, N. E., Doob, L. W., Mowrer, O. H., & Sears, R. R. (1939). *Frustration and aggression.* New Haven: Yale University Press.

Doob, L. W., & Sears, R. S. (1939). Factors determining substitute behavior and the overt expression of aggression. *Journal of Abnormal and Social Psychology, 34,* 293–313.

Doty, R. M., Peterson, B. E., & Winter, D. G. (1991). Threat and authoritarianism in the United States, 1978–1987. *Journal of Personality and Social Psychology, 61,* 629–640.

Dovidio, J. F., Allen, J. L., & Schroeder, D. A. (1990). Specificity of empathy-induced helping: Evidence for altruistic motivation. *Journal of Personality and Social Psychology, 59,* 249–260.

Downing, J. W., Judd, C. M., & Brauer, M. (1992). Effects of repeated expressions of attitude extremity. *Journal of Personality and Social Psychology, 63,* 17–29.

Downs, A. C., & Lyons, P. M. (1991). Natural observations of the links between attractiveness and initial legal judgments. *Personality and Social Psychology Bulletin, 17,* 541–547.

Drachman, D., DeCarufel, A., & Insko, C. A. (1978). The extra credit effect in interpersonal attraction. *Journal of Experimental Social Psychology, 14,* 458–465.

Drigotas, S. M., & Rusbult, C. E. (1992). Should I stay or should I go? A dependence model of breakups. *Journal of Personality and Social Psychology, 62,* 62–87.

Dunning, D., & Cohen, G. L. (1992). Egocentric definitions of traits and abilities in social judgment. *Journal of Personality and Social Psychology, 63,* 341–355.

Dunning, D., Perie, M., & Story, A. L. (1991). Self-serving prototypes of social categories. *Journal of Personality and Social Psychology, 61,* 957–968.

Durkheim, E. (1897/1951). *Suicide.* New York: The Free Press.

Dutton, D. G. (1971). Reactions of restauranteurs to blacks and whites violating restaurant dress requirements. *Canadian Journal of Behavioral Science, 3,* 298–302.

Dutton, D. G., & Aron, A. P. (1974). Some evidence for heightened sexual attraction under conditions of high anxiety. *Journal of Personality and Social Psychology, 30,* 510–517.

Dyck, R. J., & Rule, B. G. (1978). Effect on retaliation of causal attributions concerning attack. *Journal of Personality and Social Psychology, 36,* 521–529.

Eager, J., & Smith, M. B. (1952). A note on the validity of Sanford's Authoritarian-Equalitarian Scale. *Journal of Abnormal and Social Psychology, 47,* 265–267.

Eagly, A. H. (1983). Gender and social influence: A social psychological analysis. *American Psychologist, 38,* 971–981.

Eagly, A. H., Ashmore, R. D., Makhijani, M. G., & Longo, L. C. (1991). What is beautiful is good, but . . . : A meta-analytic review of research on the physical attractiveness stereotype. *Psychological Bulletin, 110,* 109–128.

Eagly, A. H., & Carli, L. L. (1981). Sex of researchers and sex-typed communication as determinants of sex differences in influenceability: A meta-analysis of social influence. *Psychological Bulletin, 90,* 1–20.

Eagly, A. H., & Chaiken, S. (1984). Cognitive theories of persuasion. In L. Berkowitz (Ed.), *Advances in experimental social psychology* (Vol. 17, pp. 267–359). New York: Academic Press.

Eagly, A. H., & Chrvala, C. (1986). Sex differences in conformity: Status and gender role interpretations. *Psychology of Women Quarterly, 10,* 203–220.

Eagly, A. H., & Karau, S. J. (1991). Gender and the emergence of leaders: A meta-analysis. *Journal of Personality and Social Psychology, 60,* 685–710.

Eagly, A. H., Makhijani, M. G., & Klonsky, B. G. (1992). Gender and the evaluation of leaders: A meta-analysis. *Psychological Bulletin, 111,* 3–22.

Eagly, A. H., Wood, W., & Fishbaugh, L. (1981). Sex differences in conformity: Surveillance by the group as a determinant of male conformity. *Journal of Personality and Social Psychology, 40,* 384–394.

Easterling, D. V., & Leventhal, H. (1989). Contribution of concrete cognition to emotion: Neutral symptoms as elicitors of worry about cancer. *Journal of Applied Psychology, 74,* 787–796.

Ebbesen, E. B., Kjos, G. L., & Konecni, V. J. (1976). Spatial ecology: Its effect on choice of friends and enemies. *Journal of Experimental Social Psychology, 12,* 505–518.

Edelmann, R. J., & Hampson, S. E. (1979). Changes in nonverbal behaviour during embarrassment. *British Journal of Social and Clinical Psychology, 18,* 385–390.

Edwards, D., & Potter, J. (1993). Language and causation: A discursive action model of description and attribution. *Psychological Review, 100,* 23–41.

Ehrlich, H. J., & Graven, D. B. (1971). Reciprocal self-disclosure in a dyad. *Journal of Experimental Social Psychology, 7,* 389–400.

Eibl-Eibesfeldt, I. (1972). Similarities and differences between cultures in expressive movements. In R. Hinde (Ed.), *Non-verbal communication.* Cambridge: Cambridge University Press.

Einhorn, H. J., Hogarth, R. M., & Klempner, E. (1977). Quality of group judgment. *Psychological Bulletin, 84,* 158–172.

Eisenberg, N. (1991). Meta-analytic contributions to the literature on prosocial behavior. *Personality and Social Psychology Bulletin, 17,* 273–282.

Eisenberg, N., Cialdini, R. B., McCreath, H., & Shell, R. (1987). Consistency based compliance: When and why do children become vulnerable. *Journal of Personality and Social Psychology, 52,* 1174–1181.

Ekman, P. (1973). Cross-cultural studies of facial expression. In P. Ekman (Ed.), *Darwin and facial expression.* New York: Academic Press.

Ekman, P., & Friesen, W. V. (1974). Detecting deception from the body or face. *Journal of Personality and Social Psychology, 29,* 288–298.

Ekman, P., & Friesen, W. V. (1982). Felt, false, and miserable smiles. *Journal of Nonverbal Behavior, 6,* 238–252.

Ekman, P., & Friesen, W. (1986). A new pan-cultural facial expression of emotion. *Motivation and Emotion, 10,* 159–168.

Ekman, P., Friesen, W. V., & O'Sullivan, M. (1988). Smiles while lying. *Journal of Personality and Social Psychology, 54,* 414–420.

Ekman, P., Friesen, W. V., O'Sullivan, M., Chan, A., Diacoyanni-Tarlatzis, I., Heider, K., Krause, R., LeCompte, W. A., Pitcairn, T., Ricci-Bitti, P. E., Scherer, K., Tomita, M., & Tzavaras, A. (1987). Universals and cultural differences in the judgments of facial expressions of emotions. *Journal of Personality and Social Psychology, 53,* 712–717.

Elkin, R. A., & Leippe, M. R. (1986). Physiological arousal, dissonance, and attitude change: Evidence for a dissonance-arousal link and a "Don't remind me" effect. *Journal of Personality and Social Psychology, 51,* 55–65.

Elliott, G. C., & Meeker, B. F. (1986). Achieving fairness in the face of competing concerns: The different effects of individual and group characteristics. *Journal of Personality and Social Psychology, 50,* 754–760.

Ellis, L., & Ames, M. A. (1987). Neurohormonal functioning and sexual orientation: A theory of homosexuality-heterosexuality. *Psychological Bulletin, 101,* 233–258.

Ellsworth, P., & Tourangeau, R. (1981). On our failure to disconfirm what nobody ever said. *Journal of Personality and Social Psychology, 40,* 363–369.

Emerson, R. M. (1954). Deviation and rejection: An experimental replication. *American Sociological Review, 19,* 688–693.

Enzle, M. E., & Anderson, S. C. (1993). Surveillant intentions and intrinsic motivation. *Journal of Personality and Social Psychology, 64,* 257–266.

Ernst, D. (1990). *Sex differences in moral judgment.* Unpublished Ph.D. dissertation. University of Pennsylvania.

Esser, J. K. (1989). Agreement pressure and opponent strategies in oligopoly bargaining. *Personality and Social Psychology Bulletin, 15,* 596–603.

Esser, J. K., Calvillo, M. J., Scheel, M. R., & Walker, J. L. (1990). Oligopoly bargaining: Effects of agreement pressure and opponent strategies. *Journal of Applied Social Psychology, 20,* 1256–1271.

Esser, J. K., & Komorita, S. S. (1975). Reciprocity and concession making in bargaining. *Journal of Personality and Social Psychology, 31,* 864–872.

Fazio, R. H., Chen, J.-M., McDonel, E. C., & Sherman, S. J. (1982). Attitude accessibility, attitude-behavior consistency, and the strength of the object-evaluation association. *Journal of Experimental Social Psychology, 18,* 339–357.

Fazio, R. H., Powell, M. C., & Herr, P. M. (1983). Toward a process model of the attitude-behavior relation: Accessing one's attitude upon mere observation of the attitude object. *Journal of Personality and Social Psychology, 44,* 723–735.

Fazio, R. H., Sanbonmatsu, D. M., Powell, M. C., & Kardes, F. R. (1986). On the automatic activation of attitudes. *Journal of Personality and Social Psychology, 50,* 229–238.

Fazio, R. H., & Williams, C. J. (1986). Attitude accessibility as a moderator of the attitude-perception and attitude-behavior relations: An investigation of the 1984 presidential election. *Journal of Personality and Social Psychology, 51,* 505–514.

Fazio, R. H., & Zanna, M. P. (1978). Attitudinal qualities relating to the strength of the attitude-behavior relationship. *Journal of Experimental Social Psychology, 14,* 398–408.

Fazio, R. H., & Zanna, M. (1981). Direct experience and attitude-behavior consistency. In L. Berkowitz (Ed.), *Advances in experimental social psychology* (Vol. 14, pp. 161–202). New York: Academic Press.

Fazio, R. H., Zanna, M., & Cooper, J. (1977). Dissonance and self-perception: An integrative view of each theory's proper domain of application. *Journal of Experimental Social Psychology, 13,* 464–479.

Feather, N. T. (1963). Cognitive dissonance, sensitivity, and evaluation. *Journal of Abnormal and Social Psychology, 66,* 157–163.

Feeney, J. A., & Noller, P. (1991). Attachment style and verbal descriptions of romantic partners. *Journal of Social and Personal Relationships, 8,* 187–215.

Fein, S., Hilton, J. L., & Miller, D. T. (1990). Suspicion of ulterior motivation and the correspondence bias. *Journal of Personality and Social Psychology, 58,* 753–764.

Feingold, A. (1988). Matching for attractiveness in romantic partners and same-sex friends: A meta-analysis and theoretical critique. *Psychological Bulletin, 104,* 226–35.

Feingold, A. (1990). Gender differences in effects of physical attractiveness on romantic attraction: A comparison across five research paradigms. *Journal of Personality and Social Psychology, 59,* 981–993.

Fenigstein, A. (1979a). Does aggression cause a preference for viewing media violence? *Journal of Personality and Social Psychology, 37,* 2307–2317.

Fenigstein, A. (1979b). Self-consciousness, self-attention, and social interaction. *Journal of Personality and Social Psychology, 37,* 75–86.

Fenigstein, A., Scheier, M. F., & Buss, A. H. (1975). Public and private self-consciousness: Assessment and theory. *Journal of Consulting and Clinical Psychology, 43,* 522–527.

Ferguson, D. A., & Vidmar, N. (1971). Effects of group discussion on estimates of culturally appropriate risk levels. *Journal of Personality and Social Psychology, 20,* 436–445.

Ferguson, T. J., & Rule, B. G. (1983). An attributional perspective on anger and aggression. In R. G. Geen & E. I. Donnerstein (Eds.), *Aggression: Theoretical and empirical reviews* (Vol. 1, pp. 41–74). New York: Academic Press.

Festinger, L. (1950). Informal social communication. *Psychological Review, 57,* 271–282.

Festinger, L. (1954). A theory of social comparison processes. *Human Relations, 7,* 117–140.

Festinger, L. (1957). *A theory of cognitive dissonance.* Stanford: Stanford University Press.

Festinger, L., & Carlsmith, J. M. (1959). Cognitive consequences of forced compliance. *Journal of Abnormal and Social Psychology, 58,* 203–210.

Festinger, L., & Maccoby, N. (1964). On resistance to persuasive communications. *Journal of Abnormal and Social Psychology, 68,* 359–366.

Festinger, L., Pepitone, A., & Newcomb, T. (1952). Some consequences of de-individuation in a group. *Journal of Abnormal and Social Psychology, 47,* 382–389.

Festinger, L., Schachter, S., & Back, K. (1950). *Social pressures in informal groups.* Stanford: Stanford University Press.

Fiedler, F. E. (1964). A contingency model of leadership effectiveness. In L. Berkowitz (Ed.), *Advances in experimental social psychology* (Vol. 1, pp. 149–190). New York: Academic Press.

Fiedler, K. (1991). The tricky nature of skewed frequency tables: An information loss account of distinctiveness-based illusory correlations. *Journal of Personality and Social Psychology, 60,* 24–36.

Fiedler, K., Semin, G. R., & Koppetsch, C. (1991). Language use and attributional biases in close personal relationships. *Personality and Social Psychology Bulletin, 17,* 147–155.

Figley, C. R. (1973). Child density and the marital relationship. *Journal of Marriage and the Family, 35,* 272–282.

Fincham, F. D., Beach, S. R., & Baucom, D. H. (1987). Attribution processes in distressed and nondistressed couples: Self-partner attribution differences. *Journal of Personality and Social Psychology, 52,* 739–748.

Fincham, F. D., & Bradbury, T. N. (1993). Marital satisfaction, depression, and attributions: A longitudinal analysis. *Journal of Personality and Social Psychology, 64,* 442–452.

Fincham, F. D., & Jaspers, J. M. (1980). Attribution of responsibility: From man the scientist to man as lawyer. In L. Berkowitz (Ed.), *Advances in experimental social psychology* (Vol. 13, pp. 81–138). New York: Academic Press.

Firestone, I. J., Kaplan, K. J., & Russell, J. C. (1973). Anxiety, fear, and affiliation with similar state versus dissimilar state others: Misery sometimes loves miserable company. *Journal of Personality and Social Psychology, 26,* 409–414.

Fishbein, M., & Ajzen, I. (1974). Attitudes toward objects as predictors of single and multiple behavioral criteria. *Psychological Review, 81,* 59–74.

Fishbein, M., & Ajzen, I. (1975). *Belief, attitude, intention, behavior: An introduction to theory and research.* Reading, MA: Addison Wesley.

Fisher, G. J. (1986). College student attitudes toward forcible date rape: I. Cognitive predictors. *Archives of Sexual Behavior, 15,* 457–466.

Fisher, J. D., Nadler, A., & Whitcher-Alagna, S. (1982). Recipient reactions to aid. *Psychological Bulletin, 91,* 27–54.

Fisher, W. A. (1984). Predicting contraceptive behavior among university men: The role of emotions and behavioral intentions. *Journal of Applied Social Psychology, 14,* 104–123.

Fiske, A. P. (1990). *Structures of social life: The four elementary forms of human relations.* New York: The Free Press.

Fiske, S. T., & Cox, M. G. (1979) Person concepts: The effect of target familiarity and descriptive purpose on the process of describing others, *Journal of Personality, 47,* 136–161.

Fiske, S. T., & Neuberg, S. L. (1990). A continuum of impression formation, from category-based to individuating processes: Influences of information and motivation on attention and interpretation. In M. Zanna (Ed.), *Advances in experimental social psychology* (Vol. 23). New York: Academic Press.

Fleishman, J. A. (1980). Collective action as helping behavior: Effects of responsibility diffusion on contributions to a public good. *Journal of Personality and Social Psychology, 38,* 629–637.

Fleming, J. H., & Darley, J. M. (1989). Perceiving choice and constraint: The effects of contextual and behavioral cues on attitude attribution. *Journal of Personality and Social Psychology, 56,* 27–40.

Folger, R., & Martin, C. (1986). Relative deprivation and referent cognitions: Distributive and procedural justice effects. *Journal of Experimental Social Psychology, 22,* 531–546.

Folger, R., Rosenfield, D., Rheaume, K., & Martin, C. (1983). Relative deprivation and referent cognitions. *Journal of Experimental Social Psychology, 19,* 172–184.

Folger, R., Rosenfield, D., & Robinson, T. (1983). Relative deprivation and procedural justifications. *Journal of Personality and Social Psychology, 45,* 268–273.

Folkes, V. S. (1982). Forming relationships and the matching hypothesis. *Personality and Social Psychology Bulletin, 8,* 631–636.

Folkes, V. S. (1985). Mindlessness or mindfulness: A partial replication and extension of Langer, Blank, and Chanowitz. *Journal of Personality and Social Psychology Bulletin, 48,* 600–604.

Ford, C. S., & Beach, F. A. (1951). *Patterns of sexual behavior.* New York: Harper & Row.

Fox, J., & Guyer, M. (1978) "Public" choice and cooperation in N-person prisoner's dilemma. *Journal of Conflict Resolution, 22,* 468–481.

Frank, M. G., Ekman, P., & Friesen, W. V. (1993). Behavioral markers and recognizability of the smile of enjoyment. *Journal of Personality and Social Psychology, 64,* 83–93.

Franzoi, S. L., & Davis, M. H. (1985). Adolescent self-disclosure and loneliness: Private self-consciousness and parental influences. *Journal of Personality and Social Psychology, 48,* 768–780.

Franzoi, S. L., Davis, M. H., & Young, R. D. (1985). The effects of private self-consciousness and perspective taking on satisfaction in close relationships. *Journal of Personality and Social Psychology, 48,* 1584–1594.

Fredricks, A. J., & Dossett, D. L. (1983). Attitude-behavior relations: A comparison of the Fishbein-Ajzen and the Bentler-Speckart models. *Journal of Personality and Social Psychology, 45,* 501–512.

Freedman, J. L., Cunningham, J. A., & Krismer, K. (1992). Inferred values and the reverse-incentive effect in induced compliance. *Journal of Personality and Social Psychology, 62,* 357–368.

Freedman, J. L. (1984). Effect of television violence on aggressiveness. *Psychological Bulletin, 96,* 227–246.

Freedman, J. L. (1986). Television violence and aggression: A rejoinder. *Psychological Bulletin, 100,* 372–378.

Freedman, J. (1990). The effect of capital punishment on jurors' willingness to convict. *Journal of Applied Social Psychology, 20,* 465–477.

Freedman, J. L., & Fraser, S. C. (1966). Compliance

without pressure: The foot-in-the-door technique. *Journal of Personality and Social Psychology, 4,* 195–202.

Freedman, J. L., & Sears, D. O. (1965). Selective exposure. In L. Berkowitz (Ed.), *Advances in experimental social psychology* (Vol. 2, 57–97). New York: Academic Press.

Freidrich-Cofer, L., & Huston, A. C. (1986). Television violence and aggression: The debate continues. *Psychological Bulletin, 100,* 364–371.

Freud, S. (1922/1976). *Group psychology and the analysis of the ego.* In J. Strachey (Trans. and Ed.), *The complete psychological works* (Vol. 18). New York: Norton.

Freud, S. (1933/1976). *New introductory lectures on psychoanalysis.* In J. Strachey (Trans. and Ed.), *The complete psychological works* (Vol. 22). New York: Norton.

Frey, D. (1981). Postdecisional preference for decision-relevant information as a function of the competence of its source and the degree of familiarity with this information. *Journal of Experimental Social Psychology, 17,* 51–67.

Frey, D. (1986). Recent research on selective exposure to information. In L. Berkowitz (Ed.), *Advances in experimental social psychology* (Vol. 19, pp. 41–80). New York: Academic Press.

Frey, D., & Rosch, M. (1984). Information seeking after decisions: The roles of novelty of information and decision reversibility. *Personality and Social Psychology Bulletin, 10,* 91–98.

Fridlund, A. J. (1991). Sociality of solitary smiling: Potentiation by an implicit audience. *Journal of Personality and Social Psychology, 60,* 229–240.

Friedman, H. S., & Miller-Herringer, T. (1991). Nonverbal display of emotion in public and in private: Self-monitoring, personality, and expressive cues. *Journal of Personality and Social Psychology, 61,* 766–775.

Friend, R., Rafferty, Y., & Bramel, D. (1990). A puzzling misinterpretation of the Asch "conformity" study. *European Journal of Social Psychology, 20,* 29–44.

Frieze, I. H., Olson, J. E., & Good, D. C. (1990). Perceived and actual discrimination in the salaries of male and female managers. *Journal of Applied Social Psychology, 20,* 46–67.

Frijda, N. H., Kuipers, P., & ter Schure, E. (1989). Relations among emotion, appraisal, and emotional action readiness. *Journal of Personality and Social Psychology, 57,* 212–228.

Froming, W. J., & Carver, C. S. (1981). Divergent influences of private and public self-consciousness in a compliance paradigm. *Journal of Research in Personality, 15,* 159–171.

Furnham, A., & Capon, M. (1983). Social skills and self-monitoring processes. *Personality and Individual Differences, 4,* 171–178.

Futoran, G. C., & Wyer, R. S., Jr. (1986). The effects of traits and gender stereotypes on occupational suitability judgments and the recall of judgment-relevant information. *Journal of Experimental Social Psychology, 22,* 475–503.

Gabrenya, W. K., Jr., & Arkin, R. M. (1980). Self-monitoring scale: Factor structure and correlates. *Personality and Social Psychology Bulletin, 6,* 13–22.

Gabrenya, W. K. Jr., Latané, B., & Wang, Y.-E. (1983). Social loafing in cross-cultural perspective: Chinese on Taiwan. *Journal of Cross-Cultural Psychology, 14,* 368–384.

Gabrenya, W. K. Jr., Wang, Y.-E., & Latané, B. (1985). Social loafing on an optimizing task: Cross-cultural differences among Chinese and Americans. *Journal of Cross-Cultural Psychology, 16,* 223–242.

Gaelick, L., Bodenhausen, G. V., & Wyer, R. S., Jr. (1985). Emotional communication in close relationships. *Journal of Personality and Social Psychology, 49,* 1246–1265.

Gaertner, S. L. (1975). The role of racial attitudes in helping behavior. *The Journal of Social Psychology, 97,* 95–101.

Gaertner, S. L., & Dovidio, J. F. (1977). The subtlety of white racism, arousal, and helping behavior. *Journal of Personality and Social Psychology, 35,* 691–707.

Gaes, G. G., Melburg, V., & Tedeschi, J. T. (1986). A study examining the arousal properties of the forced compliance situation. *Journal of Experimental Social Psychology, 22,* 136–147.

Gagnon, J. H. (1977). *Human sexualities.* Glenview, IL: Scott, Foresman.

Gagnon, J. H., & Simon, W. (1973). *Sexual conduct: The social sources of human sexuality.* Chicago: Aldine.

Gallo, P. S. (1966). Effects of increased incentives upon the use of threat in bargaining. *Journal of Personality and Social Psychology, 4,* 14–20.

Gallo, P. S., Jr. & Seposh, J. (1971). Effects of incentive magnitude on cooperation in the Prisoner's Dilemma game: A reply to Gumpert, Deutsch, and Epstein. *Journal of Personality and Social Psychology, 19,* 42–46.

Gallupe, R. B., Bastianutti, L. M., & Cooper, W. H. (1991). Unblocking brainstorms. *Journal of Applied Psychology, 76,* 137–142.

Gamson, W. A. (1964). Experimental studies of coalition formation. In L. Berkowitz (Ed.), *Advances in experimental social psychology* (Vol. 1, pp. 81–147). New York: Academic Press.

Gamson, W. A., Fireman, B., & Rytina, S. (1982). *Encounters with unjust authority.* Homewood, IL: Dorsey Press.

Gangestad, S., & Snyder, M. (1985). "To carve nature at its joints": On the existence of discrete classes in personality. *Psychological Review, 92,* 317–349.

Geen, R. G. (1983). Aggression and television violence. In R. G. Geen & E. I. Donnerstein (Eds.), *Aggression: Theoretical and empirical reviews* (Vol. 2, pp. 103–125). New York: Academic Press

Geen, R., & Berkowitz, L. (1966). Name-mediated aggressive cue properties. *Journal of Personality, 34,* 456–465.

Geer, J. H., & Broussard, D. B. (1990). Scaling heterosexual behavior and arousal: Consistency and sex differences. *Journal of Personality and Social Psychology, 58,* 664–671.

Geer, J. H., & Jarmecky, L. (1973). The effect of being responsible for reducing another's pain on subjects' response and arousal. *Journal of Personality and Social Psychology, 26,* 232–237.

Geertz, C. (1973). *The interpretation of cultures: Selected essays.* New York: Basic Books.

Geertz, C. (1975). On the nature of anthropological understanding. *American Scientist, 63,* 47–53.

Gelles, R. J. (1976). Abused wives: Why do they stay? *Journal of Marriage and the Family, 38,* 659–668.

Gerard, H. B. (1963). Emotional uncertainty and social comparison. *Journal of Abnormal and Social Psychology, 66,* 568–573.

George, J. M. (1991). State or trait: Effects of positive mood on prosocial behaviors at work. *Journal of Applied Psychology, 76,* 299–307.

Gerard, H. B., & Mathewson, G. C. (1966). The effects of severity of initiation on liking for a group: A replication. *Journal of Experimental Social Psychology, 2,* 278–287.

Gerard, H. B., & Rabbie, J. M. (1961). Fear and social comparison. *Journal of Abnormal and Social Psychology, 62,* 586–592.

Gerbner, G., & Gross, L. (1976). Living with television: The violence profile. *Journal of Communications, 26,* 173–199.

Gergen, K. (1973). Social psychology as history. *Journal of Personality and Social Psychology, 26,* 309–320.

Gerhart, B., & Rynes, S. (1991). Determinants and consequences of salary negotiations by male and female MBA graduates. *Journal of Applied Psychology, 76,* 256–262.

Gerrard, M. (1982). Sex, sex guilt, and contraceptive use. *Journal of Personality and Social Psychology, 42,* 153–158.

Gerrard, M. (1987). Sex, sex guilt, and contraceptive use revisited: The 1980s. *Journal of Personality and Social Psychology, 52,* 975–980.

Gerrard, M., Kurylo, M., & Reis, T. (1991). Self-esteem, erotophobia, and retention of contraceptive and AIDS information in the classroom. *Journal of Applied Social Psychology, 21,* 368–379.

Gilbert, A. N., Fridlund, A. J., & Sabini, J. (1987). Hedonic and social determinants of facial displays to odors. *Chemical Senses, 12,* 353–355.

Gilbert, D. T., & Hixon, J. G. (1991). The trouble of thinking: Activation and application of stereotypic beliefs. *Journal of Personality and Social Psychology, 60,* 509–517.

Gilbert, D. T., & Jones, E. E. (1986). Exemplification: The self-presentation of moral character. *Journal of Personality, 54,* 593–615.

Gilbert, G. M. (1951). Stereotype persistence and change among college students. *Journal of Abnormal and Social Psychology, 46,* 245–254.

Gillig, P. M., & Greenwald, A. G. (1974). Is it time to lay the sleeper effect to rest? *Journal of Personality and Social Psychology, 29,* 132–139.

Gilligan, C. (1982). *In a different voice.* Cambridge, Mass.: Harvard University Press.

Gilovich, T. (1990). Differential construal and the false consensus effect. *Journal of Personality and Social Psychology, 59,* 623–634.

Gleicher, F., & Petty, R. E. (1992). Expectations of reassurance influence the nature of fear-stimulated attitude change. *Journal of Experimental Social Psychology, 28,* 86–100.

Gleitman, H. (1991). *Psychology,* 3rd ed. New York: Norton.

Glenn, N. D., & McLanahan, S. (1982). Children and marital happiness: A further specification of the relationship. *Journal of Marriage and the Family, 44,* 63–72.

Glenn, N. D., & Supanic, M. (1984). Social and demographic correlates of divorce and separation in the United States: An update and reconsideration. *Journal of Marriage and the Family, 46,* 563–576.

Glick, P., DeMorest, J. A., & Hotze, C. A. (1988). Self-monitoring and beliefs about partner compatibility in romantic relationships. *Personality and Social Psychology Bulletin, 14,* 485–494.

Glick, P., Zion, C., & Nelson, C. (1988). What mediates sex discrimination in hiring decisions? *Journal of Personality and Social Psychology, 55,* 178–186.

Glick, R. C., & Lin, S.-L. (1986). Recent changes in divorce and remarriage. *Journal of Marriage and the Family, 48,* 737–747.

Godfrey, D. K., Jones, E. E., & Lord, C. G. (1986). Self-promotion is not ingratiation. *Journal of Personality and Social Psychology, 50,* 106–115.

Goethals, G. R., Cooper, J., & Naficy, A. (1979). Role of foreseen, foreseeable, and unforeseeable behavioral consequences in the arousal of cognitive dissonance. *Journal of Personality and Social Psychology, 37,* 1179–1185.

Goffman, E. (1955). On facework. *Psychiatry, 18,* 213–231.

Goffman, E. (1956). Embarrassment and social organization. *American Journal of Sociology, 62,* 264–271.

Goffman, E. (1959). *The presentation of self in everyday life.* New York: Doubleday Anchor.

Goffman, E. (1971). *Relations in public.* New York: Harper & Row.

Goldman, W., & Lewis, P. (1977). Evidence that the physically attractive are more socially skillful. *Journal of Experimental Social Psychology, 13,* 125–130.

Goode, E., & Haber, L. (1977). Sexual correlates of homosexual experience: An exploratory study of college women. *Journal of Sex Research, 13,* 12–21.

Gordon, S. E., Wyer, R. S., Jr. (1987). Person memory: Category-set-size effects on the recall of a person's behavior.

Journal of Personality and Social Psychology, 53, 648–662.

Gorenflo, D. W., & Crano, W. D. (1989). Judgmental subjectivity/objectivity and locus of choice in social comparison. *Journal of Personality and Social Psychology, 57,* 605–614.

Gorsuch, R. L., & Ortberg, J. (1983). Moral obligation and attitudes: Their relation to behavioral intentions. *Journal of Personality and Social Psychology, 44,* 1025–1028.

Gottman, J. M., & Levenson, R. W. (1992). Marital processes predictive of later dissolution: Behavior, physiology, and health. *Journal of Personality and Social Psychology, 63,* 221–233.

Gottman, J., Notarius, C., Markman, H., Blank, S., Yoppi, B., & Rubin, M. E. (1976). Behavior exchange theory and marital decision making. *Journal of Personality and Social Psychology, 34,* 14–23.

Gottman, J. M., & Porterfield, A. L. (1981). Communicative competence in the non-verbal behavior of married couples. *Journal of Marriage and the Family, 43,* 817–824.

Gouldner, A. W. (1960). The norm of reciprocity: A preliminary statement. *American Sociological Review, 25,* 161–178.

Gray-Little, B., & Burks, N. (1983). Power and satisfaction in marriage: A review and critique. *Psychological Bulletin, 93,* 513–538.

Green, S. K., Buchanan, D. D., & Heuer, S. K. (1984). Winners, losers, and choosers: A field investigation of dating initiation. *Personality and Social Psychology Bulletin, 10,* 502–511.

Greenwald, A. G. (1975). Does the Good Samaritan parable increase helping? A comment on Darley and Batson's no-effect conclusion. *Journal of Personality and Social Psychology, 32,* 578–583.

Griffin, D. W., Dunning, D., & Ross, L. (1990). The role of construal processes in overconfident predictions about the self and others. *Journal of Personality and Social Psychology, 59,* 1128–1139.

Grube, J. W., Morgan, M., & McGree, S. T. (1986). Attitudes and normative beliefs as predictors of smoking intentions and behaviours: A test of three models. *British Journal of Social Psychology, 25,* 81–93.

Grusec, J. E. (1981). Socialization processes and the development of altruism. In J.-P. Rushton & R. M. Sorrentino (Eds.), *Altruism and helping behavior.* Hillsdale, NJ: Erlbaum.

Grusec, J. E., Kuczynski, L., Rushton, J.-P., & Simutis, Z. M. (1978). Modeling, direct instruction, and attributions: Effects on altruism. *Developmental Psychology, 14,* 51–57.

Guerin, B. (1986). Mere presence effects in humans: A review. *Journal of Experimental Social Psychology, 22,* 38–77.

Guerin, B., & Innes, J. M. (1982). Social facilitation and social monitoring: A new look at Zajonc's mere presence hypothesis. *British Journal of Social Psychology, 21,* 7–18.

Guttentag, M., & Secord, P. F. (1983). *Too many women?* Beverly Hills, CA: Sage.

Gwartney-Gibbs, P. A. (1986). The institutionalization of premarital cohabitation: Estimates from marriage license applications, 1970 and 1980. *Journal of Marriage and the Family, 48,* 423–434.

Hager, J. C., & Ekman, P. (1981). Methodological problems in Tourangeau & Ellsworth's study of facial expression and experience of emotion. *Journal of Personality and Social Psychology, 40,* 358–362.

Haidt, J., Koller, S. H., & Dias, M. G. (1993). Affect, culture, and morality; or, Is it wrong to eat your dog? *Journal of Personality and Social Psychology, 65,* 613–628.

Halford, W. K., Hahlweg, K., & Dunne, M. (1990). The cross-cultural consistency of marital communication associated with marital distress. *Journal of Marriage and the Family, 52,* 487–500.

Hall, E. (1966). *The hidden dimension.* Garden City, NY: Doubleday.

Hall, J. A. (1978). Gender effects in decoding nonverbal cues. *Psychological Bulletin, 85,* 845–857.

Hamilton, D. L., Dugan, P. M., & Trolier, T. K. (1985). The formation of stereotypic beliefs: Further evidence for distinctiveness-based illusory correlations. *Journal of Personality and Social Psychology, 48,* 5–17.

Hamilton, D. L., & Gifford, R. K. (1976). Illusory correlations in interpersonal perception: A cognitive basis of stereotypic judgments. *Journal of Experimental Social Psychology, 12,* 392–407.

Hamilton, D. L., Katz, L. B., & Leirer, V. O. (1980). Cognitive representation of personality impressions: Organizational processes in first impression formation. *Journal of Personality and Social Psychology, 39,* 1050–1063.

Hamilton, D. L., & Rose, T. L. (1981). Illusory correlation and the maintenance of stereotypic beliefs. *Journal of Personality and Social Psychology, 39,* 832–845.

Hamilton, V. L. (1978). Obedience and responsibility: A jury simulation. *Journal of Personality and Social Psychology, 36,* 126–146.

Hamilton, V. L. (1980). Intuitive psychologist or intuitive lawyer? Alternative models of the attribution process. *Journal of Personality and Social Psychology, 39,* 767–772.

Hamilton, V. L. (1986). Chains of command: Responsibility attribution in hierarchies. *Journal of Applied Social Psychology, 16,* 188–198.

Hamilton, W. D. (1964). The genetical theory of social behavior (I & II). *Journal of Theoretical Biology, 7,* 1–16; 17–32.

Hamner, W. C., & Harnett, D. L. (1975). The effects of information and aspiration level on bargaining behavior. *Journal of Experimental Social Psychology, 11,* 329–342.

Hansen, J. E., & Schuldt, W. J. (1984). Marital self-disclosure and marital satisfaction. *Journal of Marriage and the Family, 46,* 923–926.

Hansen, R. D. (1980). Commensense attribution. *Journal of Personality and Social Psychology, 39,* 996–1009.

Hansen, R. D., & Donoghue, J. M. (1977). The power of consensus: Information derived from one's own and others' behavior. *Journal of Personality and Social Psychology, 35,* 294–302.

Hardin, G. (1968). The tragedy of the commons. *Science, 162,* 1243–1248.

Harding, J., Proshansky, H., Kutner, B., & Chin, I. (1969). Prejudice and ethnic relations. In G. Lindzey & E. Aronson (Eds.), *Handbook of social psychology* (Vol. 5). Reading, MA: Addison-Wesley.

Harkins, S. G. (1987). Social loafing and social facilitation. *Journal of Experimental Social Psychology, 23,* 1–18.

Harkins, S. G., & Petty, R. E. (1982). Effects of task difficulty and task uniqueness on social loafing. *Journal of Personality and Social Psychology, 43,* 1214–1229.

Harkins, S. G., & Szymanski, K. (1989). Social loafing and group evaluation. *Journal of Personality and Social Psychology, 56,* 934–941.

Harré, R. (1981). The dramaturgy of sexual relations. In M. Cook (Ed.), *The bases of human sexual attraction.* London: Academic Press.

Harré, R. (1984). *Personal being.* Cambridge, Mass.: Harvard University Press.

Harris, M. B., Benson, S. M., & Hall, C. L. (1975). The effects of confession on altruism. *Journal of Social Psychology, 96,* 187–192.

Harrison, A. A. (1968). Response competition, frequency, exploratory behavior, and liking. *Journal of Personality and Social Psychology, 9,* 363–368.

Harrison, A. A. (1977). Mere exposure. In L. Berkowitz (Ed.), *Advances in experimental social psychology* (Vol. 10, pp. 39–83). New York: Academic Press.

Hartman, E. A. (1980). Motivational bases of sex differences in choice behavior. *Journal of Conflict Resolution, 24,* 455–475.

Hass, R. G., Katz, I., Rizzo, N., Bailey, J., & Eisenstadt, D. (1991). Cross-racial appraisal as related to attitude ambivalence and cognitive complexity. *Personality and Social Psychology Bulletin, 17,* 83–92.

Hastie, R., & Kumar, P. A. (1979). Person memory: Personality traits as organizing principles in memory for behaviors. *Journal of Personality and Social Psychology, 37,* 25–38.

Hatcher, L., Kryter, K., Prus, J. S., & Fitzgerald, V. (1992). Predicting college student satisfaction, commitment, and attrition from investment model constructs. *Journal of Applied Social Psychology, 22,* 1273–1296.

Hatfield, E., & Sprecher, S. (1986). Measuring passionate love in intimate relationships. *Journal of Adolescence, 9,* 383–410.

Hazan, C., & Shaver, P. R. (1990). Love and work: An attachment-theoretical perspective. *Journal of Personality and Social Psychology, 59,* 270–280.

Heaton, A. W., & Sigall, H. (1989). The "championship choke" revisited: The role of fear of acquiring a negative identity. *Journal of Applied Social Psychology, 19,* 1019–1033.

Hechtman, S. B., & Rosenthal, R. (1991). Teacher gender and nonverbal behavior in the teaching of gender-stereotyped materials. *Journal of Applied Social Psychology, 21,* 446–459.

Heer, D. M., & Grossbard-Schechtman, A. (1981). The impact of the female marriage squeeze and the contraceptive revolution on sex roles and the women's liberation movement in the United States: 1960–1975. *Journal of Marriage and the Family, 43,* 49–65.

Heider, F. (1946). Attitudes and cognitive organization. *Journal of Psychology, 21,* 107–112.

Heider, F. (1958). *The psychology of interpersonal relations.* New York: Wiley.

Helgeson, V. S., Shaver, P., Dyer, M. (1987). Prototypes on intimacy and distance in same-sex and opposite-sex relationships. *Journal of Personality and Social Psychology, 4,* 195–233.

Hendrick, S. S. (1981). Self-disclosure and marital satisfaction. *Journal of Personality and Social Psychology, 40,* 1150–1159.

Helmreich, R., Aronson, E., & LeFan, J. (1970). To err is humanizing—sometimes: Effects of self-esteem, competence and a pratt-fall on interpersonal attraction. *Journal of Personality and Social Psychology, 16,* 259–264.

Hennigan, K. M., Del Rosario, M. L., Heath, L., Cook, T. D., Wharton, J. D., & Calder, B. J. (1982). Impact of the introduction of television on crime in the United States: Empirical findings and theoretical implications. *Journal of Personality and Social Psychology, 42,* 461–477.

Hensley, T. R., & Griffin, G. W. (1986). Victims of groupthink: The Kent State University Board of Trustees and the 1977 gymnasium controversy. *Journal of Conflict Resolution, 30,* 497–531.

Hepworth, J. T., & West, S. G. (1988). Lynchings and the economy: A time-series reanalysis of Hovland and Sears (1940). *Journal of Personality and Social Psychology, 55,* 239–247.

Herek, G. M., Janis, I. L., & Huth, P. (1987). Decision making during international crises: Is quality of process related to outcome? *Journal of Conflict Resolution, 31,* 203–226.

Herold, E. S. (1981). Contraceptive embarrassment and contraceptive behaviour among young single women. *Journal of Youth and Adolescence, 10,* 233–242.

Hewstone, M. (1990). The "ultimate attribution error"? A review of the literature on intergroup causal attribution. *European Journal of Social Psychology, 20,* 311–335.

Higgins, E. T., & Bargh, J. A. (1987). Social cognition and social perception. *Annual Review of Psychology, 38,* 369–425.

Higgins, E. T., Rhodewalt, F., & Zanna, M. P. (1979). Dissonance motivation: Its nature, persistence, and reinstatement. *Journal of Experimental Social Psychology, 15,* 16–34.

Higgins, E. T., Rholes, W. S., & Jones, C. R. (1977). Category accessibility and impression formation. *Journal of Experimental Social Psychology, 13,* 141–154.

Hill, C. T., Rubin, Z., & Peplau, L. A. (1976). Breakups before marriage: The end of 103 affairs. *Journal of Social Issues, 32,* 147–168.

Hilton, D. J. (1990). Conversational processes and causal explanations. *Psychological Bulletin, 107,* 65–81.

Hilton, D. J., & Knibbs, C. S. (1988). The knowledge-structure and inductivist strategies in causal attribution: A direct comparison. *European Journal of Social Psychology, 18,* 79–92.

Hilton, D. J., & Slugoski, B. R. (1986). Knowledge-based causal attributions: Abnormal conditions focus model. *Psychological Review, 93,* 75–88.

Hilton, D. J., Smith, R. H., & Alicke, M. D. (1988). Knowledge-based information acquisition: Norms and the functions of consensus information. *Journal of Personality and Social Psychology, 55,* 530–540.

Hinde, R. A. (1974). *Biological bases of human social behavior.* New York: McGraw-Hill.

Hines, M. (1982). Prenatal gonadal hormones and sex differences in human behavior. *Psychological Bulletin, 92,* 56–80.

Hinsz, V. B., & Tindale, R. S. (1992). Ambiguity and human versus technological sources of information in judgments involving base rate and individuating information. *Journal of Applied Social Psychology, 22,* 973–997.

Hinsz, V. B., Tindale, R. S., Nagao, D. H., Davis, J. H., & Robertson, B. A. (1988). The influence of the accuracy of individuating information on the use of base rate information in probability judgment. *Journal of Experimental Social Psychology, 24,* 127–145.

Hixon, J. G., & Swann, W. B., Jr. (1993). When does introspection bear fruit? Self-reflection, self-insight, and interpersonal choices. *Journal of Personality and Social Psychology, 64,* 35–43.

Hoffman, C., & Hurst, N. (1990). Gender stereotypes: Perception or rationalization? *Journal of Personality and Social Psychology, 58,* 197–208.

Hoffman, C., Mischel, W., & Baer, J. S. (1984). Language and person cognition: Effects of communication set on trait attribution. *Journal of Personality and Social Psychology, 46,* 1029–1043.

Hoffman, M. L. (1960). Power assertion by the parent and its impact on the child. *Child Development, 31,* 129–143.

Hoffman, M. L. (1975). Developmental synthesis of affect and cognition and its implications for altruistic motivation. *Developmental Psychology, 11,* 607–622.

Hoffman, M. L. (1981). Is altruism part of human nature? *Journal of Personality and Social Psychology, 40,* 121–137.

Hofstede, G. (1980/1984). *Culture's consequences* (abridged edition). Newbury Park, CA: Sage.

Hollos, M., Leis, P. E., & Turiel, E. (1986). Social reasoning in Ijo children and adolescents in Nigerian communities. *Journal of Cross Cultural Psychology, 17,* 352–374.

Holtzworth-Munroe, A., & Jacobson, N. S. (1985). Causal attributions of married couples: When do they search for causes? What do they conclude when they do? *Journal of Personality and Social Psychology, 48,* 1398–1412.

Homans, G. (1961). *Social behavior: Its elementary forms.* New York: Harcourt, Brace and World.

Horowitz, I. A. (1980). Juror selection: A comparison of two methods in several criminal cases. *Journal of Applied Social Psychology, 10,* 86–99.

Hovland, C. I., Lumsdaine, A. A., & Sheffield, F. D. (1949). *Experiments on mass communication.* Princeton: Princeton University Press.

Hovland, C. I., & Sears, R. (1940). Minor studies in aggression: VI Correlation of lynchings with economic indices. *Journal of Psychology, 9,* 301–310.

Hovland, C. I., & Weiss, W. (1951). The influence of source credibility on communication effectiveness. *Public Opinion Quarterly, 15,* 635–650.

Howard, D. J. (1990). Rhetorical question effects on message processing and persuasion: The role of information availability and the elicitation of judgment. *Journal of Experimental Social Psychology, 26,* 217–239.

Howard, J. W., & Rothbart, M. (1980). Social categorization and memory for in-group and out-group behavior. *Journal of Personality and Social Psychology, 38,* 301–310.

Huber, V. L., & Neale, M. A. (1987). Effects of self- and competitor goals on performance in an interdependent bargaining task. *Journal of Applied Psychology, 72,* 197–203.

Hui, C. H. (1988). Measurement of individualism-collectivism. *Journal of Research in Personality, 22,* 17–36.

Hunt, M. (1974). *Sexual behavior in the 1970s.* Chicago, IL: Playboy Press.

Huxley, J. S. (1914). The courtship-habits of the Great Crested Grebe *(podiceps cristatus)* with an addition to the theory of sexual selection. *Proceedings of the Zoological Society of London, 35,* 491–562.

Huxley, J. S. (1966). Introduction to "A discussion on ritualization of behaviour in animals and man." *Philosophical Transactions of the Royal Society of London,* Series B, *251,* 249–271.

Hyde, J. S., & Linn, M. C. (1988). Gender differences in verbal ability: A meta-analysis. *Psychological Bulletin, 104,* 53–69.

Hyman, H. H., & Sheatsley, P. B. (1954). "The Authoritarian Personality": A methodological critique. In R. Christie & M. Jahoda (Eds.), *Studies in the scope and method of "The Authoritarian Personality."* Glencoe, IL: The Free Press.

Ingham, A., Levinger, G., Graves, J., & Peckham, V. (1974). The Ringlemann effect: Studies of group size and group performance. *Journal of Experimental Social Psychology, 10,* 371–384.

Insko, C. A. (1984). Balance theory, the Jordan paradigm, and the Wiest tetrahedron. In L. Berkowitz (Ed.), *Advances in experimental social psychology* (Vol. 18, pp. 89–140). New York: Academic Press.

Insko, C. A., Thompson, V. D., Stroebe, W., Shaud, K. F., Pliner, B. E., & Layton, B. D. (1973). Implied evaluation and the similarity-attraction effect. *Journal of Personality and Social Psychology, 25,* 297–308.

Isen, A. M. (1970). Success, failure, attention, and reactions to others: The warm glow of success. *Journal of Personality and Social Psychology, 15,* 294–301.

Isen, A. M. (1987). Positive affect, cognitive processes, and social behavior. L. Berkowitz (Ed.), *Advances in experimental social psychology.* (Vol. 20, pp. 203–253). New York: Academic Press.

Isen, A. M., & Levin, P. F. (1972). Effect of feeling good on helping: Cookies and kindness. *Journal of Personality and Social Psychology, 21,* 384–388.

Isen, A. M., Nygren, T. E., & Ashby, F. G. (1988). Influence of positive affect on the subjective utility of gains and losses: It is just not worth the risk. *Journal of Personality and Social Psychology, 55,* 710–717.

Isen, A. M., & Simmonds, S. F. (1978). The effects of feeling good on a helping task that is incompatible with a good mood. *Social Psychology Quarterly, 41,* 345–349.

Isenberg, D. J. (1986). Group polarization: A critical review and meta-analysis. *Journal of Personality and Social Psychology, 50,* 1141–1151.

Izard, C. E. (1981). Differential emotions theory and the facial feedback hypothesis of emotion activation: Comments on Tourangeau and Ellsworth's "The role of facial response in the experience of emotion." *Journal of Personality and Social Psychology, 40,* 350–354.

Jaccard, J., King, G. W., & Pomazal, R. (1977). Attitudes and behavior: An analysis of specificity of attitudinal predictors. *Human Relations, 30,* 817–824.

Jackson, D. N., Chau, D. W., & Stricker, L. J. (1979). Implicit personality theory: Is it illusory? *Journal of Personality, 47,* 1–10.

Jackson, J. M., & Latané, B. (1981). All alone in front of all those people: Stage fright as a function of number and type of co-performers and audience. *Journal of Personality and Social Psychology, 40,* 73–85.

Jackson, J. M., & Padgett, V. R. (1982). With a little help from my friend: Social loafing and the Lennon-McCartney songs. *Personality and Social Psychology Bulletin, 8,* 672–677.

Jackson, J. M., & Williams, K. D. (1985). Social loafing on difficult tasks: Working collectively can improve performance. *Journal of Personality and Social Psychology, 49,* 937–942.

Jacobs, J. E., & Eccles, J. S. (1992). The impact of mothers' gender-role stereotypic beliefs on mothers' and children's ability perceptions. *Journal of Personality and Social Psychology, 63,* 932–944.

Jacobson, N. S., Follette, W. C., & McDonald, D. W. (1982). Reactivity to positive and negative behavior in distressed and nondistressed married couples. *Journal of Consulting and Clinical Psychology, 50,* 706–714.

Jacobson, N. S., McDonald, D. W., Follette, W. C., & Berley, R. A. (1985). Attributional processes in distressed and nondistressed married couples. *Cognitive Therapy and Research, 9,* 35–50.

Jahoda, G. (1988). J'accuse. In M. H. Bond, (Ed.), *The cross-cultural challenge to social psychology.* (86–95) Newbury Park, CA: Sage.

Jahoda, M. (1959). Conformity and independence. *Human Relations, 12,* 99–120.

James, W. (1890/1950). *Principles of psychology* (Vol. II). New York: Holt.

Janis, I. L. (1972). *Victims of groupthink.* Boston: Houghton Mifflin Co.

Janis, I. L. (1982). *Groupthink: Psychological studies of policy decisions and fiascoes* (2nd ed.) Boston: Houghton Mifflin Co.

Janis, I. L., & Feshbach, S. (1953). Effects of fear-arousing communications. *Journal of Abnormal and Social Psychology, 48,* 78–92.

Janis, I. L., Kaye, D., & Kirschner, P. (1965). Facilitating effects of "eating-while-reading" on responsiveness to persuasive communications. *Journal of Personality and Social Psychology, 1,* 181–186.

Jedlicka, D., & Robinson, I. E. (1987). Fear of venereal disease and other perceived restraints on the occurrence of premarital coitus. *The Journal of Sex Research, 23,* 391–396.

Jellison, J. M., & Riskind, J. (1970). A social comparison of abilities interpretation of risk-taking behavior. *Journal of Personality and Social Psychology, 15,* 375–390.

Jenkins, M. J., & Dambrot, F. H. (1987). The attribution of date rape: Observers' attitudes and sexual experiences and the dating situation. *Journal of Applied Social Psychology, 17,* 875–895.

Jerdee, T. H., & Rosen, B. (1974). Effects of opportunity to communicate and visibility of individual decisions on behavior in the common interest. *Journal of Applied Psychology, 59,* 712–716.

Johnson, B. T., & Eagly, A. H. (1989). Effects of involvement on persuasion: A meta-analysis. *Psychological Bulletin, 106,* 290–314.

Johnson, B. T., & Eagly, A. H. (1990). Involvement and persuasion: Types, traditions, and the evidence. *Psychological Bulletin, 107,* 375–384.

Johnson, K. (1989). A new generation of racism is seen. *New York Times,* August 27, 1989, p. 1.

Johnson, T. E., & Rule, B. G. (1986). Mitigating circumstance information, censure, and aggression. *Journal of Personality and Social Psychology, 50,* 537–542.

Johnston, L., & Hewstone, M. (1992). Cognitive models of stereotype change: 3. Subtyping and the perceived typicality of disconfirming group members. *Journal of Experimental Social Psychology, 28,* 360–386.

Jones, C., & Aronson, E. (1973). Attribution of fault to a rape victim as a function of respectability of the victim. *Journal of Personality and Social Psychology, 26,* 415–419.

Jones, E. E. (1979). The rocky road from acts to dispositions. *American Psychologist, 34,* 107–117.

Jones, E. E., & Baumeister, R. (1976). The self-monitor looks at the ingratiator. *Journal of Personality, 44,* 654–674.

Jones, E. E., & Berglas, S. (1978). Control of attributions about the self through self-handicapping strategies: The appeal of alcohol and the role of underachievement. *Personality and Social Psychology Bulletin, 4,* 200–206.

Jones, E. E., & Davis, K. E. (1965). From acts to dispositions: The attribution process in person perception. In L. Berkowitz (Ed.), *Advances in experimental social psychology* (Vol. 7, pp. 219–266). New York: Academic Press.

Jones, E. E., Davis, K. E., & Gergen, K. J. (1961). Role playing variations and their informational value for person perception. *Journal of Abnormal and Social Psychology, 63,* 302–310.

Jones, E. E., & Harris, V. A. (1967). The attribution of attitudes. *Journal of Experimental Social Psychology, 3,* 1–24.

Jones, E. E., & Nisbett, R. E. (1971). The actor and the observer: divergent perceptions of the causes of behavior. In E. E. Jones, D. Kanouse, H. H. Kelley, R. E. Nisbett, S. Valins, & B. Weiner (Eds.), *Attribution: Perceiving the causes of behavior.* New York: General Learning Press.

Jones, E. E., & Pittman, T. S. (1982). Toward a general theory of strategic self-presentation. In J. Suls (Ed.), *Psychological perspectives on the self* (Vol. 1) Hillsdale, NJ: Erlbaum.

Jones, E. E., Stires, L. K., Shaver, K. G., & Harris, V. A. (1968). Evaluation of an ingratiator by target persons and bystanders. *Journal of Personality, 36,* 349–385.

Jorgenson, D. O., & Papciak, A. S. (1981). The effects of communication, resource feedback, and identifiability on behavior in a simulated commons. *Journal of Experimental Social Psychology, 17,* 373–385.

Josephs, R. A., Markus, H. R., & Tafarodi, R. W. (1992). Gender and self-esteem. *Journal of Personality and Social Psychology, 63,* 391–402.

Jourard, S. M. (1959). Self-disclosure and other cathexis. *Journal of Abnormal and Social Psychology, 59,* 428–431.

Jourard, S. (1971). *The transparent self.* New York: Van Nostrand.

Judd, C. M., Drake, R. A., Downing, J. W., & Krosnick, J. A. (1991). Some dynamic properties of attitude structures: Context-induced response facilitation and polarization. *Journal of Personality and Social Psychology, 60,* 193–202.

Judd, C. M., & Park, B. (1988). Out-group homogeneity: Judgments of variability at the individual and group levels. *Journal of Personality and Social Psychology, 54,* 778–788.

Judd, C. M., & Park, B. (1993). Definition and assessment of accuracy in social stereotypes. *Psychological Review, 100,* 109–128.

Judd, C. M., Ryan, C. S., & Park, B. (1991). Accuracy in the judgment of in-group and out-group variability. *Journal of Personality and Social Psychology, 61,* 366–379.

Kahneman, D., & Tversky, A. (1972). Subjective probability: A judgment of representativeness. *Cognitive Psychology, 3,* 430–454.

Kahneman, D., & Tversky, A. (1973). On the psychology of prediction. *Psychological Review, 80,* 237–251.

Kahneman, D., & Tversky, A. (1979). Prospect theory: An analysis of decision under risk. *Econometrica, 47,* 263–291.

Kahneman, D., & Tversky, A. (1982). The simulation heuristic. In D. Kahneman, P. Slovic, & A. Tversky (Eds.), *Judgment under uncertainty: Heuristics and biases* (pp. 201–208). New York: Cambridge University Press.

Kahneman, D., & Varey, C. A. (1990). Propensities and counterfactuals: The loser that almost won. *Journal of Personality and Social Psychology, 59,* 1101–1110.

Kalick, S. M., & Hamilton, T. E. III (1986). The matching hypothesis reexamined. *Journal of Personality and Social Psychology, 51,* 673–682.

Kalick, S. M., & Hamilton, T. E. III (1988). Closer look at a matching simulation: Reply to Aron. *Journal of Personality and Social Psychology, 54,* 447–451.

Kalven, H., Jr., & Zeisel, H. (1966). *The American jury.* Boston: Little Brown.

Kane, T. R., Joseph, J. M., & Tedeschi, J. T. (1976). Person perception and the Berkowitz paradigm for the study of aggression. *Journal of Personality and Social Psychology, 33,* 663–673.

Kaniasty, K., & Norris, F. H. (1993). A test of the social support deterioration model in the context of natural disaster. *Journal of Personality and Social Psychology, 64,* 395–408.

Kanin, E. J. (1985). Date rapists: Differential sexual socialization and relative deprivation. *Archives of Sexual Behavior, 14,* 219–231.

Karabenick, S. A., & Knapp, J. R. (1988). Effects of computer privacy on help-seeking. *Journal of Applied Social Psychology, 18,* 461–472.

Karlins, M., Coffman, T. L., & Walters, G. (1969). On the fading of social stereotypes: Studies in three generations of college students. *Journal of Personality and Social Psychology, 13,* 1–16.

Katz, D., & Braly, K. W. (1933). Racial stereotypes of one hundred college students. *Journal of Abnormal and Social Psychology, 28,* 280–290.

Katz, I., & Glass, D. C. (1979). An ambivalence-amplification theory of behavior toward the stigmatized. In W. G. Austin & S. Worchel (Eds.), *The social psychology of intergroup relations.* Monterey, CA: Brooks/Cole.

Katz, I., Glass, D. C., & Cohen, S. (1973). Ambivalence, guilt, and the scapegoating of minority group victims. *Journal of Experimental Social Psychology, 9,* 423–436.

Katz, I., Glass, D. C., Lucido, D., & Farber, J. (1979). Harm-doing and victim's racial or orthopedic stigma as determinants of helping behavior. *Journal of Personality, 47,* 340–364.

Katz, I., Glucksberg, S., & Krauss, R. (1960). Need satisfaction and Edwards PPS scores in married couples. *Journal of Consulting Psychology, 24,* 205–208.

Katz, I., & Hass, R. G. (1988). Racial ambivalence and American value conflict: Correlational and priming studies of dual cognitive structures. *Journal of Personality and Social Psychology, 55,* 893–905.

Katz, J. (1982). The impact of time proximity and level of generality on attitude-behavior consistency. *Journal of Applied Social Psychology, 12,* 151–168.

Katz, S. H., Heidiger, M. L., & Valleroy, L. Z. (1974). Traditional maize-processing techniques in the New World. *Science, 184,* 765–773.

Kelley, H. H. (1950). The warm-cold variable in first impressions of persons. *Journal of Personality, 18,* 431–439.

Kelley, H. H. (1967). Attribution theory in social psychology. In D. Levine (Ed.), *Nebraska Symposium on Motivation* (Vol. 15, pp. 192–240). Lincoln, NE: University of Nebraska Press.

Kelley, H. H. (1971a). Attribution in social interaction. In E. E. Jones, D. Kanouse, H. H. Kelley, R. E. Nisbett, S. Valins, & B. Weiner (Eds.), *Attribution: Perceiving the causes of behavior.* New York: General Learning Press.

Kelley, H. H. (1971b). Causal schemata and the attribution process. In E. E. Jones, D. Kanouse, H. H. Kelley, R. E. Nisbett, S. Valins, & B. Weiner (Eds.), *Attribution: Perceiving the causes of behavior.* New York: General Learning Press.

Kelley, H. H., & Arrowood, A. J. (1960). Coalitions in the triad: Critique and experiment. *Sociometry, 23,* 231–244.

Kelley, H. H., & Michela, J. L. (1980). Attribution theory and research. *Annual Review of Psychology, 31,* 457–501.

Kelly, E. L., & Conley, J. J. (1987). Personality and compatibility: A prospective analysis of marital stability and marital satisfaction. *Journal of Personality and Social Psychology, 52,* 27–40.

Kelly, G. A. (1955). *The psychology of personal constructs.* New York: Norton.

Kenny, D. A., & Zaccaro, S. J. (1983). An estimate of variance due to traits in leadership. *Journal of Applied Psychology, 68,* 678–685.

Kenrick, D. T., & Cialdini, R. B. (1977). Romantic attachment: Misattribution versus reinforcement explanations. *Journal of Personality and Social Psychology, 35,* 381–391.

Kenrick, D. T., Cialdini, R. B., & Linder, D. E. (1979). Misattribution under fear-producing circumstances: Four failures to replicate. *Personality and Social Psychology Bulletin, 5,* 329–334.

Kenrick, D. T., Stringfield, D. O., Wagenhals, W. L., Dahl, R. H., & Ransdell, H. J. (1980). Sex differences, androgyny, and approach responses to erotica: A new variation on the Old Volunteer Problem. *Journal of Personality and Social Psychology, 38,* 517–524.

Kephart, W. M. (1967). Some correlates of romantic love. *Journal of Marriage and the Family, 29,* 470–474.

Kerber, K. W., & Singleton, R., Jr. (1984). Trait and situational attributions in a naturalistic setting: Familiarity, liking, and attributional validity. *Journal of Personality, 52,* 205–219.

Kerr, N. L., & Brunn, S. E. (1981). Ringelmann revisited: Alternative explanations for the social loafing effect. *Personality and Social Psychology Bulletin, 7,* 224–231.

Kerr, N. L., & Brunn, S. (1983). Dispensibility of member effort and group motivation loss: Free-rider effects. *Journal of Personality and Social Psychology, 44,* 78–94.

Kerr, N. L., & Huang, J. Y. (1986). Jury verdicts: How much difference does one juror make? *Personality and Social Psychology Bulletin, 12,* 325–343.

Kessler, R., Kendler, K., Heath, A., Neale, M. (1992). Social support, depressed mood, and adjustment to stress: A genetic epidemiologic investigation. *Journal of Personality and Social Psychology, 62,* 257–272.

Kidder, L. H., Bellettirie, G., & Cohn, E. S. (1977). Secret ambitions and public performances: The effect of anonymity on reward allocation made by men and women. *Journal of Personality and Social Psychology, 13,* 70–80.

Kilham, W., & Mann, L. (1974). Level of destructive obedience as a function of transmitter and executant roles in the Milgram obedience paradigm. *Journal of Personality and Social Psychology, 29,* 696–702.

Kimball, M. M. (1989). A new perspective on women's math achievement. *Psychological Bulletin, 105,* 198–214.

King, K., Balswick, J. O., & Robinson, I. E. (1977). The continuing premarital sexual revolution among college females. *Journal of Marriage and the Family, 39,* 455–459.

Kinsey, A. C., Pomeroy, W. B., & Martin, C. E. (1948). *Sexual behavior in the human male.* Philadelphia: Saunders.

Kinsey, A. C., Pomeroy, W. B., Martin, C. E., & Gebhard, P. H. (1953). *Sexual behavior in the human female.* Philadelphia: Saunders.

Klayman, J., & Ha, Y.-W. (1987). Confirmation, disconfirmation, and information in hypothesis testing. *Psychological Review, 94,* 211–228.

Kleck, R. E., & Rubenstein, C. (1975). Physical attractiveness, perceived attitude similarity, and interpersonal attraction in opposite-sex encounter. *Journal of Personality and Social Psychology, 31,* 107–114.

Klein, S. B., & Loftus, J. (1990). Rethinking the role of organization in person memory: An independent trace storage model. *Journal of Personality and Social Psychology, 59,* 400–410.

Klein, S. B., Loftus, J., & Sherman, J. W. (1993). The role of summary and specific behavioral memories in trait judgments about the self. *Journal of Personality and Social Psychology, 19,* 305–311.

Klein, W. M., & Kunda, Z. (1992). Motivated person perception: Constructing justifications for desired beliefs. *Journal of Experimental Social Psychology, 28,* 145–168.

Kohlberg, L. (1971). From is to ought: How to commit the naturalistic fallacy and get away with it in the study of moral development. In T. Mischel, (Ed.), *Cognitive development and epistemology.* New York: Academic Press.

Kohlberg, L., & Hersh, R. H. (1977). Moral development: A review of the theory. *Theory into Practice, 16,* 53–59.

Kohlberg, L., & Kramer, R. (1969). Continuities and discontinuities in childhood and adult moral development. *Human Development, 12,* 93–120.

Kolditz, T. A., & Arkin, R. M. (1982). An impression management interpretation of the self-handicapping strategy. *Journal of Personality and Social Psychology, 43,* 492–502.

Komarovsky, M. (1974). Patterns of self-disclosure of male undergraduates. *Journal of Marriage and the Family, 36,* 677–686.

Komorita, S. S. (1974). A weighted probability model of coalition formation. *Psychological Review, 81,* 242–256.

Komorita, S. S. (1979). An equal excess model of coalition formation. *Behavioral Science, 24,* 369–381.

Komorita, S. S. (1984). Coalition bargaining. In L. Berkowitz (Ed.), *Advances in experimental social psychology* (Vol. 18). New York: Academic Press.

Komorita, S. S., & Brenner, A. (1968). Bargaining and concession making under bilateral monopoly. *Journal of Personality and Social Psychology, 9,* 15–20.

Komorita, S. S., & Chertkoff, J. M., (1973). A bargaining theory of coalition formation. *Psychological Review, 80,* 149–162.

Komorita, S. S., & Esser, J. K. (1975). Frequency of reciprocated concessions in bargaining. *Journal of Personality and Social Psychology, 32,* 699–705.

Komorita, S. S., Hilty, J. A., & Parks, C. D. (1991). Reciprocity and cooperation in social dilemmas. *Journal of Conflict Resolution, 35,* 494–518.

Komorita, S. S., Parks, C. D., & Hulbert, L. G. (1992). Reciprocity and the induction of cooperation in social dilemmas. *Journal of Personality and Social Psychology, 62,* 607–617.

Konecni, V. J. (1972). Some effects of guilt on compliance: A field replication. *Journal of Personality and Social Psychology, 23,* 30–32.

Konovsky, M. A., & Cropanzano, R. (1991). Perceived fairness of employee drug testing as a predictor of employee attitudes and job performance. *Journal of Applied Psychology, 76,* 698–707.

Koralewski, M. A., & Conger, J. C. (1992). The assessment of social skills among sexually coercive college males. *The Journal of Sex Research, 29,* 169–188.

Koss, M. P. (1992). Defending date rape. *Journal of Interpersonal Violence, 7,* 121–126.

Kraut, R. E., & Johnston, R. E. (1979). Social and emotional messages of smiling: An ethological approach. *Journal of Personality and Social Psychology, 37,* 1539–1553.

Kravitz, D. A., & Martin, B. (1986). Ringelmann rediscovered: The original article. *Journal of Personality and Social Psychology, 50,* 936–941.

Krebs, D., & Adinolfi, A. A. (1975). Physical attractiveness, social relations, and personality style. *Journal of Personality and Social Psychology, 31,* 245–253.

Kremer, J. F., & Stephens, L. (1983). Attributions and arousal as mediators of mitigation's effect on retaliation. *Journal of Personality and Social Psychology, 45,* 335–343.

Krosnick, J. A., Li, F., & Lehman, D. R. (1990). Conversational conventions, order of information acquisition, and the effect of base rates and individuating information on social judgments. *Journal of Personality and Social Psychology, 59,* 1140–1152.

Krueger, J., & Rothbart, M. (1988). Use of categorical and individuating information in making inferences about personality. *Journal of Personality and Social Psychology, 55,* 187–195.

Kruglanski, A. W., & Webster, D. M. (1991). Group members' reactions to opinion deviates and conformists at varying degrees of proximity to decision deadline and of environmental noise. *Journal of Personality and Social Psychology, 61,* 212–225.

Krugman, H. E. (1943). Affective response to music as a function of familiarity. *Journal of Abnormal and Social Psychology, 38,* 388–392.

Kulik, J. A., & Brown, R. (1979). Frustration, attribution of blame, and aggression. *Journal of Experimental Social Psychology, 15,* 183–194.

Kulik, J. A., & Mahler, H. I. M. (1989). Stress and affiliation in a hospital setting: Preoperative roommate preferences. *Personality and Social Psychology Bulletin, 15,* 183–193.

Kumagai, H. A., & Kumagai, A. K. (1986). The hidden "I" in amae: "Passive love" and Japanese social perception. *Ethos, 14,* 305–320.

Kunda, Z. (1987). Motivated inference: Self-serving generation and evaluation of causal theories. *Journal of Personality and Social Psychology, 53,* 636–647.

Kunda, Z., & Sherman-Williams, B. (1993). Stereotypes and the construal of individuating information. *Personality and Social Psychology Bulletin, 19,* 90–99.

Kurdek, L. A. (1991). Correlates of relationship satisfaction in cohabiting gay and lesbian couples: Integration of contextual, investment, and problem-solving models. *Journal of Personality and Social Psychology, 61,* 910–922.

Kurdek, L. A. (1992). Relationship stability and relationship satisfaction in cohabiting gay and lesbian couples: A prospective longitudinal test of the contextual and interdependence models. *Journal of Personality and Social Psychology, 9,* 125–142.

Kurdek, L. A. (1993). Predicting marital dissolution: A five-year prospective longitudinal study of newlywed couples. *Journal of Personality and Social Psychology, 64,* 221–242.

Kurdek, L. A., & Schmitt, J. P. (1986a). Interaction of sex role self-concept with relationship quality and relationship beliefs in married, heterosexual cohabiting, gay, and lesbian couples. *Journal of Personality and Social Psychology, 51,* 365–370.

Kurdek, L. A., & Schmitt, J. P. (1986b). Relationship quality of partners in heterosexual married, heterosexual cohabiting, and gay and lesbian relationships. *Journal of Personality and Social Psychology, 51,* 711–720.

Kurdek, L. A., & Schmitt, J. P. (1987). Partner homogamy in married, heterosexual cohabiting, gay, and lesbian couples. *The Journal of Sex Research, 23,* 212–232.

Lalonde, R. N. (1992). The dynamics of group differentiation in the face of defeat. *Personality and Social Psychology Bulletin, 18,* 336–342.

Lamm, H., & Trommsdorff, G. (1973). Group versus individual performance on tasks requiring ideational proficiency (brainstorming): A review. *European Journal of Social Psychology, 3,* 361–388.

Landy, D., & Sigall, H. (1974). Beauty is talent: Task evaluation as a function of the performer's physical attractiveness. *Journal of Personality and Social Psychology, 29,* 299–304.

Langer, E. J. (1989). Minding matters: The consequences of mindlessness-mindfulness. In L. Berkowitz (Ed.), *Advances in experimental social psychology.* (Vol. 22, pp. 137–173). New York: Academic Press.

Langer, E., Blank, A., & Chanowitz, B. (1978). The mindlessness of ostensibly thoughtful action. *Journal of Personality and Social Psychology, 36,* 635–642.

Langer, E. J., Chanowitz, B., & Blank, A. (1985). Mindlessness-mindfulness in perspective: A reply to Valerie Folkes. *Journal of Personality and Social Psychology, 48,* 605–607.

LaPiere, R. T. (1934). Attitudes vs. actions. *Social Forces, 13,* 203–237.

LaPiere, R. T. (1936). Type-rationalizations of group antipathy. *Social Forces, 15,* 232–237.

L'Armand, K., & Pepitone, A. (1982). Judgments of rape: A study of victim-rapist relationship and victim sexual history. *Personality and Social Psychology Bulletin, 8,* 134–139.

Latané, B. (1981). The psychology of social impact. *American Psychologist, 36,* 343–356.

Latané, B., & Darley, J. M. (1968). Group inhibition of bystander intervention in emergencies. *Journal of Personality and Social Psychology, 10,* 215–221.

Latané, B., & Harkins, S. (1976). Cross-modality matches suggest anticipatory stage fright as a multiplicative power function of audience size and status. *Perception & Psychophysics, 20,* 482–488.

Latané, B., Williams, K., & Harkins, S. (1979). Many hands make light the work: The causes and consequences of social loafing. *Journal of Personality and Social Psychology, 37,* 822–832.

Latané, B., & Wolf, S. (1981). The social impact of majorities and minorities. *Psychological Review, 88,* 438–453.

LaTour, S. (1978). Determinants of participant and observer satisfaction with adversary and inquisitorial modes of adjudication. *Journal of Personality and Social Psychology, 36,* 1531–1545.

Laughlin, P. R. (1988). Collective induction: Group performance, social combination processes, and mutual majority and minority influence. *Journal of Personality and Social Psychology, 54,* 254–267.

Laughlin, P. R., & Earley, P. C. (1982). Social combination models, persuasive argument theory, social comparison theory, and choice shift. *Journal of Personality and Social Psychology, 42,* 273–280.

Laughlin, P. R., & Ellis, A. L. (1986). Demonstrability and social combination processes on mathematical intellective tasks. *Journal of Experimental Social Psychology, 22,* 177–189.

Laughlin, P. R., VanderStoep, S. W., & Hollingshead, A. B. (1991). Collective versus individual induction: Recognition of truth, rejection of error, and collective information processing. *Journal of Personality and Social Psychology, 61,* 50–67.

Lawler, E. J., & MacMurray, B. K. (1980). Bargaining toughness: A qualification of level-of-aspiration and reciprocity hypotheses. *Journal of Applied Social Psychology, 10,* 416–430.

Lax, D. A., & Sebenius, J. K. (1991). Negotiating through an agent. *Journal of Conflict Resolution, 35,* 474–493.

Leary, M. R., Britt, T. W., Cutlip, W. D. II, & Templeton, J. L. (1992). Social blushing. *Psychological Bulletin, 112,* 446–460.

Leary, M. R., & Kowalski, R. M. (1990). Impression management: A literature review. *Psychological Bulletin, 107,* 34–47.

Leary, M. R., & Meadows, S. Predictors, elicitors, and concomitants of social blushing. *Journal of Personality and Social Psychology, 60,* 254–262.

Leary, M. R., & Shepperd, J. A. (1986). Behavioral self-handicaps versus self-reported handicaps: A conceptual note. *Journal of Personality and Social Psychology, 51,* 1265–1268.

Leavitt, H. J. (1951). Some effects of certain communication patterns on group performance. *Journal of Abnormal and Social Psychology, 46,* 38–50.

Le Bon, G. (1896). *The crowd.* London: Ernest Benn.

Lee, G. R., Seccombe, K., & Shehan, C. L. (1991). Marital status and personal happiness: An analysis of trend data. *Journal of Personality and Social Psychology, 53,* 839–844.

Lehman, D. R., Krosnick, J. A., West, R. L., & Li, F. (1992). The focus of judgment effect: A question-wording effect due to hypothesis confirmation bias. *Personality and Social Psychology Bulletin, 18,* 690–699.

Leippe, M. R., & Elkin, R. A. (1987). When motives clash: Issue involvement and response involvement as determinants of persuasion. *Journal of Personality and Social Psychology, 52,* 269–278.

Leitenberg, H., Detzer, M. J., & Srebnik, D. (1993). Gender differences in masturbation and the relation of masturbation experience in preadolescence and/or early adolescence to sexual behavior and sexual adjustment in young adulthood. *Archives of Sexual Behavior, 22,* 87–98.

Lemyre, L., & Smith, P. M. (1985). Intergroup discrimination and self-esteem in the minimal group paradigm. *Journal of Personality and Social Psychology, 49,* 660–670.

Lennox, R. D., & Wolfe, R. N. (1984). Revision of the self-monitoring scale. *Journal of Personality and Social Psychology, 46,* 1349–1364.

Lepore, S. J., Evans, G. W., & Schneider, M. L. (1991). Dynamic role of social support in the link between chronic stress and psychological distress. *Journal of Personality and Social Psychology, 61,* 899–909.

Lepper, M. R., & Greene, D. (1975). Turning play into work: Effects of adult surveillance and extrinsic rewards on children's intrinsic motivation. *Journal of Personality and Social Psychology, 31,* 479–486.

Leung, K., Bond, M. H., Carment, D. W., Krishnan, L.,

& Liebrand, W. B. G. (1990). Effects of cultural femininity on preference for methods of conflict processing: A cross-cultural study. *Journal of Experimental Social Psychology, 26,* 373–388.

Leventhal, H. (1970). Findings and theory in the study of fear communications. In L. Berkowitz (Ed.), *Advances in experimental social psychology* (Vol. 5, pp. 119–186). New York: Academic Press.

Lerner, M. J., & Miller, D. T. (1978). Just world research and the attribution process: Looking back and ahead. *Psychological Bulletin, 85,* 1030–1051.

Lerner, M. J., & Simmons, C. H. (1966). Observer's reaction to the "innocent victim": Compassion or rejection. *Journal of Personality and Social Psychology, 4,* 203–210.

Lesnik-Oberstein, M., & Cohen, L. (1984). Cognitive style, sensation seeking, and assortative mating. *Journal of Personality and Social Psychology, 46,* 112–117.

Leung, K., & Lind, E. A. (1986). Procedural justice and culture: Effects of culture, gender, and investigator status on procedural preferences. *Journal of Personality and Social Psychology, 50,* 1134–1140.

Levenson, R. W., Ekman, P., Heider, K., & Friesen, W. V. (1992). Emotion and autonomic nervous system activity in the Minangkabau of West Sumatra. *Journal of Personality and Social Psychology, 62,* 972–988.

Levenson, R. W., & Gottman, J. M. (1983). Marital interaction: Physiological linkage and affective exchange. *Journal of Personality and Social Psychology, 45,* 587–597.

Levenson, R. W., & Gottman, J. M. (1985). Physiological and affective predictors of change in relationship satisfaction. *Journal of Personality and Social Psychology, 49,* 85–94.

Leventhal, G. S., & Lane, D. W. (1970). Sex, age, and equity behavior. *Journal of Personality and Social Psychology, 15,* 312–316.

Leventhal, G. S., & Michaels, J. W. (1971). Locus of cause and equity motivation as determinants of reward allocation. *Journal of Personality and Social Psychology, 17,* 229–235.

LeVine, R. A., & Campbell, D. T. (1972). *Ethnocentrism.* New York: Wiley.

Levinger, G. (1964). Note on need complementarity in marriage. *Psychological Bulletin, 61,* 153–157.

Levinger, G. (1965). Marital cohesiveness and dissolution: An integrative review. *Journal of Marriage and the Family, 27,* 19–28.

Levinger, G., & Schneider, D. J. (1969). Test of the "risk as a value" hypothesis. *Journal of Personality and Social Psychology, 11,* 165–169.

Levison, P. K., & Flynn, J. P. (1965). The objects attacked by cats during stimulation of the hypothalmus. *Animal Behavior, 13,* 217–220.

Levy, R. I. (1973). *Tahitians.* Chicago: University of Chicago Press.

Lewis, D. K. (1969). *Convention: A philosophical study.* Cambridge, Mass.: Harvard University Press.

Leyens, J.-P., Camino, L., Parke, R. D., & Berkowitz, L. (1975). Effects of movie violence on aggression in a field setting as a function of group dynamics and cohesiveness. *Journal of Personality and Social Psychology, 32,* 346–360.

Liberman, A., & Chaiken, S. (1991). Value conflict and thought-induced attitude change. *Journal of Experimental Social Psychology, 27,* 203–216.

Lichtenstein, M., & Srull, T. K. (1987). Processing objectives as a determinant of the relationship between recall and judgment. *Journal of Experimental Social Psychology, 23,* 93–118.

Liebert, R. M., Smith, W. P., Hill, J. H., & Keiffer, M. (1968). The effects of information and magnitude of initial offer on interpersonal negotiation. *Journal of Experimental Social Psychology, 4,* 431–441.

Liebling, B. A., Seiler, M., & Shaver, P. (1974). Self-awareness and cigarette-smoking behavior. *Journal of Experimental Social Psychology, 10,* 325–332.

Liebling, B. A., Seiler, M., & Shaver, P. (1975). Unsolved problems for self-awareness theory: A reply to Wicklund. *Journal of Experimental Social Psychology, 11,* 82–85.

Lind, E. A., Erickson, B. E., Friedland, N., & Dickenberger, M. (1978). Reactions to procedural models for adjudicative conflict resolution. *Journal of Conflict Resolution, 22,* 318–341.

Lind, E. A., Kurtz, S., Musante, L., Walker, L., & Thibaut, J. W. (1980). Procedure and outcome effects on reactions to ajudicated resolution conflicts of interest. *Journal of Personality and Social Psychology, 39,* 643–653.

Linder, D. E., Cooper, J., & Jones, E. E. (1967). Decision freedom as a determinant of the role of incentive magnitude in attitude change. *Journal of Personality and Social Psychology, 6,* 245–254.

Lindskold, S., Han, G., & Betz, B. (1986). The essential elements of communication in the GRIT strategy. *Personality and Social Psychology Bulletin, 12,* 179–186.

Lindskold, S., Walters, P. S., & Koutsourais, H. (1983). Cooperators, competitors, and response to GRIT. *Journal of Conflict Resolution, 27,* 521–532.

Linville, P. W. (1982). The complexity-extremity effect and age-based stereotyping. *Journal of Personality and Social Psychology, 42,* 193–211.

Linville, P. W., Fischer, G. W., & Salovey, P. (1989). Perceived distributions of the characteristics of in-group and out-group members: Empirical evidence and a computer simulation. *Journal of Personality and Social Psychology, 57,* 165–188.

Linville, P. W., & Jones, E. E. (1980). Polarized appraisals of out-group members. *Journal of Personality and Social Psychology, 38,* 689–703.

Lippa, R., & Connelly, S. (1990). Gender diagnosticity: A new Bayesian approach to gender-related individual differences. *Journal of Personality and Social Psychology, 59,* 1051–1065.

Lippman, W. (1922). *Public opinion.* New York: Harcourt, Brace and Co.

Liske, E., & Davis, W. J. (1984). Sexual behavior of the Chinese praying mantis. *Animal Behavior, 32,* 916–918.

Locksley, A., Borgida, E., Brekke, N., & Hepburn, C. (1980). Sex stereotypes and social judgment. *Journal of Personality and Social Psychology, 39,* 821–831.

Loftus, E. F. (1979). *Eyewitness testimony.* Cambridge, MA: Harvard University Press.

Lord, C. G., Lepper, M. R., & Mackie, D. (1984). Attitude prototypes as determinants of attitude-behavior consistency. *Journal of Personality and Social Psychology, 46,* 1254–1266.

Lorge, I. (1936). Prestige, suggestion and attitudes. *Journal of Social Psychology, 7,* 386–402.

Lorge, I., Fox, D., Davitz, J., & Brenner, M. (1958). A survey of studies contrasting the quality of group performance and individual performance, 1920–1957. *Psychological Bulletin, 55,* 337–372.

Lubinski, D., Tellegen, A., & Butcher, J. N. (1981). The relationship between androgyny and subjective indicators of emotional well-being. *Journal of Personality and Social Psychology, 40,* 722–730.

Lubinski, D., Tellegen, A., & Butcher, J. N. (1983). Masculinity, femininity, and androgyny viewed and assessed as distinct concepts. *Journal of Personality and Social Psychology, 44,* 428–439.

Luce, R. D., & Raiffa, H. (1957). *Games and decisions.* New York: Wiley.

Luckey, E. B., & Bain, J. K. (1970). Children: A factor in marital satisfaction. *Journal of Marriage and the Family, 32,* 43–44.

Luginbuhl, J., & Palmer, R. (1991). Impression management aspects of self-handicapping: Positive and negative effects. *Personality and Social Psychology Bulletin, 17,* 655–662.

Lutz, C. (1988). *Unnatural emotions.* Chicago: University of Chicago Press.

Lydon, J. E., & Zanna, M. P. (1990). Commitment in the face of adversity: A value-affirmation approach. *Journal of Personality and Social Psychology, 58,* 1040–1047.

Lysak, H., Rule, B. G., & Dobbs, A. R. (1989). Conceptions of aggression: prototype or defining features? *Personality and Social Psychology Bulletin, 15,* 233–243.

Lytton, H., & Romney, D. M. (1991). Parents' differential socialization of boys and girls: A meta-analysis. *Psychological Bulletin, 109,* 267–296.

Maass, A., & Clark, R. D. III (1983). Internalization versus compliance: Different processes underlying minority influence and conformity. *European Journal of Social Psychology, 13,* 197–215.

Maass, A., & Clark, R. D. III (1984). Hidden impact of minorities: Fifteen years of minority influence research. *Psychological Bulletin, 95*, 428–450.

Maccoby, E. E., & Jacklin, C. N. (1974). *The psychology of sex differences.* Stanford: Stanford University Press.

MacIntyre, A. (1966). *A short history of ethics.* New York: Colliers.

Mackie, D. M. (1987). Systematic and non-systematic processing of majority and minority persuasive communication. *Journal of Personality and Social Psychology, 53*, 41–52.

Mackie, D. M., & Worth, L. T. (1989). Processing deficits and the mediation of positive affect in persuasion. *Journal of Personality and Social Psychology, 57*, 27–40.

Macrae, C. N., & Milne, A. B. (1992). A curry for your thoughts: Empathic effects on counterfactual thinking. *Personality and Social Psychology Bulletin, 18*, 625–630.

Macrae, C. N. (1992). A tale of two curries: Counterfactual thinking and accident-related judgments. *Personality and Social Psychology Bulletin, 18*, 84–87.

Madden, M. E., & Janoff-Bulman, R. (1981). Blame, control and marital satisfaction: Wives' attributions for conflict in marriage. *Journal of Marriage and the Family, 43*, 663–674.

Madden, T. J., Ellen, P. S., & Ajzen, I. (1992). A comparison of the theory of planned behavior and the theory of reasoned action. *Personality and Social Psychology Bulletin, 18*, 3–9.

Maddux, J. E., & Rogers, R. W. (1983). Protection motivation and self-efficacy: A revised theory of fear appeals and attitude change. *Journal of Experimental Social Psychology, 19*, 469–479.

Madsen, D. B. (1978). Issue importance and group choice shifts: A persuasive arguments approach. *Journal of Personality and Social Psychology, 36*, 1118–1127.

Maheswaran, D., & Chaiken, S. (1991). Promoting systematic processing in low-motivation settings: Effects of incongruent information on processing and judgment. *Journal of Personality and Social Psychology, 61*, 13–25.

Major, B., & Adams, J. B. (1983). Role of gender, interpersonal orientation, and self-presentation in distributive-justice behavior. *Journal of Personality and Social Psychology, 45*, 598–608.

Malamuth, N. M., & Check, J. V. P. (1981). The effects of mass media exposure on acceptance of violence against women: A field experiment. *Journal of Research in Personality, 15*, 436–446.

Malamuth, N. M., Heim, M., & Feshbach, S. (1980). The sexual responsiveness of college students to rape depictions: Inhibitory and disinhibitory effects. *Journal of Personality and Social Psychology, 38*, 399–408.

Malamuth, N. M., Sockloskie, R. J., Koss, M. P., Tanaka, J. S. (1991). Characteristics of aggressors against women: Testing a model using a national sample of college students. *Journal of Consulting and Clinical Psychology, 59*, 670–681.

Mandler, G. (1984). *Mind and body.* New York: Norton.

Manis, M., Dovalina, I., Avis, N. E., & Cardoze, S. (1980). Base rates can affect individual predictions. *Journal of Personality and Social Psychology, 38*, 231–248.

Manis, M., Nelson, T. E., & Shedler, J. (1988). Stereotypes and social judgment: Extremity, assimilation, and contrast. *Journal of Personality and Social Psychology, 55*, 28–36.

Mann, J. W. (1967). Inconsistent thinking about group and individual. *The Journal of Social Psychology, 71*, 235–245.

Mann, L. (1981). The baiting crowd in episodes of threatened suicide. *Journal of Personality and Social Psychology, 41*, 703–709.

Mann, R. D. (1959). A review of the relationship between personality and performance in small groups. *Psychological Bulletin, 56*, 241–270.

Manning, F. J., & Fullerton, T. D. (1988). Health and well-being in highly cohesive units of the U.S. Army. *Journal of Applied Social Psychology, 18*, 503–519.

Mannix, E. A., Thompson, L. L., & Bazerman, M. H. (1989). Negotiation in small groups. *Journal of Applied Psychology, 74*, 508–517.

Manstead, A. S. R., Parker, D., Stradling, S. G., Reason, J. T., Baxter, J. S. (1992). Perceived consensus in estimates of the prevalence of driving errors and violations. *Journal of Applied Social Psychology, 22*, 509–530.

Manstead, A. S. R., & Semin, G. R. (1980). Social facilitation effects: Mere enhancement of dominant responses? *British Journal of Social and Clinical Psychology, 19*, 119–136.

Mantell, D. M., & Panzarella, R. (1976). Obedience and responsibility. *British Journal of Social and Clinical Psychology, 15*, 239–245.

Manucia, G. K., Baumann, D. J., & Cialdini, R. B. (1984). Mood influences on helping: Direct effects or side effects? *Journal of Personality and Social Psychology, 46*, 357–364.

Marañon, G. (1924). Contribution à l'étude de l'action émotive de l'adrenaline. *Revue Française d'Endocrinologie, 2*, 301–325.

Marks, G., & Miller, N. (1982). Target attractiveness as a reaction to assumed attitude similarity. *Personality and Social Psychology Bulletin, 8*, 728–735.

Marks, G., & Miller, N. (1987). Ten years of research on the false-consensus effect: An empirical and theoretical review. *Psychological Bulletin, 102*, 72–90.

Marks, G., Miller, N., & Maruyama, G. (1981). Effect of targets' physical attractiveness on assumptions of similarity. *Journal of Personality and Social Psychology, 41*, 198–206.

Markus, H. (1978). The effect of mere presence on social

facilitation: An unobtrusive test. *Journal of Experimental Social Psychology, 14,* 389–397.

Markus, H. (1981). The drive for integration: Some comments. *Journal of Experimental Social Psychology, 17,* 257–261.

Markus, H. R., & Kitayama, S. (1991). Culture and the self: Implications for cognition, emotion, and motivation. *Psychological Review, 98,* 224–253.

Marques, J. M., Yzerbyt, V. Y., & Leyens, J.-P. (1988). The "black sheep effect": Extremity of judgment toward in-group members as a function of group identification. *European Journal of Social Psychology, 18,* 1–16.

Marques, J. M., & Yzerbyt, V. Y. (1988). The black sheep effect: Judgmental extremity toward ingroup members in inter- and intra-group situations. *European Journal of Social Psychology, 18,* 287–292.

Marsh, H. W., Antill, J. K., & Cunningham, J. D. (1987). Masculinity, femininity and androgyny: Relations to self-esteem and social desirability. *Journal of Personality, 55,* 661–683.

Marsh, H. W., & Byrne, B. M. (1991). Differentiated additive androgyny model: Relations between masculinity, femininity, and multiple dimensions of self-concept. *Journal of Personality and Social Psychology, 61,* 811–828.

Marshall, D. S. (1971). Sexual behavior on Mangaia. In D. Marshall & R. Suggs (Eds.), *Human sexual behavior: Variations in the ethnographic spectrum.* New York: Basic Books.

Marshall, G. D. & Zimbardo, P. G. (1979). Affective consequences of inadequately explained arousal. *Journal of Personality and Social Psychology, 37,* 970–988.

Martell, R. F. (1991). Sex bias at work: The effects of attentional and memory demands on performance ratings of men and women. *Journal of Applied Social Psychology, 21,* 1939–1960.

Martin, L. L., Harlow, T. F., & Strack, F. (1992). The role of bodily sensations in the evaluation of social events. *Personality and Social Psychology Bulletin, 18,* 412–419.

Marwell, G., & Ames, R. E. (1979). Experiments on provision of public goods. I. Resources, interest, group size, and the free-rider problem. *American Journal of Sociology, 84,* 1335–1360.

Marwell, G., & Ames, R. E. (1980). Experiments on the provision of public goods. II. Provision points, stakes, experience, and the free-rider problem. *American Journal of Sociology, 85,* 926–937.

Mashman, R. C. (1978). The effects of physical attractiveness on the perception of attitude similarity. *Journal of Social Psychology, 106,* 103–110.

Maslach, C. (1979). Negative emotional biasing of unexplained arousal. *Journal of Personality and Social Psychology, 37,* 953–969.

Maslach, C., Santee, R. T., & Wade, C. (1987). Individuation, gender role and dissent: Personality mediators of situational forces. *Journal of Personality and Social Psychology, 53,* 1088–1093.

Mastekaasa, A. (1992). Marriage and psychological well-being: Some evidence on selection into marriage. *Journal of Marriage and the Family, 54,* 901–911.

Masters, W. H., & Johnson, V. E. (1966). *Human sexual response.* Boston: Little, Brown.

Matsumoto, D., Kudoh, T., Scherer, K., & Wallbott, H. (1988). Antecedents of and reactions to emotions in the United States and Japan. *Journal of Cross Cultural Psychology, 19,* 267–286.

Mauro, R., Sato, K., & Tucker, J. (1992). The role of appraisal in human emotions: A cross-cultural study. *Journal of Personality and Social Psychology, 62,* 301–317.

Mauss, M. (1938/1985). A category of the human mind: The notion of person: The notion of self. (Tr. W. D. Halls.) In M. Carrithers, S. Collins, & S. Lukes, (Eds.), *The category of the person (1–25).* Cambridge: Cambridge University Press.

McArthur, L. A. (1972). The how and what of why: Some determinants and consequences of causal attribution. *Journal of Personality and Social Psychology, 22,* 171–193.

McArthur, L. Z. (1976). The lesser influence of consensus than distinctiveness information on causal attributions: A test of the person-thing hypothesis. *Journal of Personality and Social Psychology, 33,* 733–742.

McArthur, L. Z., & Post, D. L. (1977). Figural emphasis and person perception. *Journal of Experimental Social Psychology, 13,* 520–533.

McCaul, K. D., O'Neil, H. K., & Glasgow, R. E. (1988). Predicting the performance of dental hygiene behaviors: An examination of the Fishbein and Ajzen model and self-efficacy expectations. *Journal of Applied Social Psychology, 18,* 114–128.

McCauley, C. (1989). The nature of social influence in groupthink: Compliance and internalization. *Journal of Personality and Social Psychology, 57,* 250–260.

McCauley, C., & Stitt, C. L. (1978). An individual and quantitative measure of stereotypes. *Journal of Personality and Social Psychology, 36,* 929–940.

McCauley, C., Stitt, C. L., Woods, K., & Lipton, D. (1973). Group shift to caution at the race track. *Journal of Experimental Social Psychology, 9,* 80–86.

McClintock, C. G., & Liebrand, W. B. G. (1988). Role of interdependence structure, individual value orientation, and another's strategy in social decision making: A transformational analysis. *Journal of Personality and Social Psychology, 55,* 396–409.

McDaniel, W. C., & Sistrunk, F. (1991). Management dilemmas and decisions: Impact of framing and anticipated responses. *Journal of Conflict Resolution, 35,* 21–42.

McFadden, R. D. (1986). Black man dies after beating by whites in Queens. *New York Times,* December 21, 1986, 1.

McFarland, S. G., Ageyev, V. S., & Abalakina-Papp, M. A. (1992). Authoritarianism in the former Soviet Union. *Journal of Personality and Social Psychology, 63,* 1004–1010.

McGill, A. L. (1991). Conjunctive explanations: Accounting for events that differ from several norms. *Journal of Experimental Social Psychology, 27,* 527–549.

McGillicuddy, N. B., Pruitt, D. G., & Syna, H. (1984). Perceptions of firmness and strength in negotiation. *Personality and Social Psychology Bulletin, 10,* 402–409.

McGuire, T. W., Kiesler, S., & Siegel, J. (1987). Groups and computer-mediated discussion effects in risk decision making. *Journal of Personality and Social Psychology, 52,* 917–930.

Mead, G. H. (1934/1962). *Mind, self, & society.* Chicago: University of Chicago Press. (First published 1934)

Mehlman, R. C., & Snyder, C. R. (1985). Excuse theory: A test of the self-protective role of attributions. *Journal of Personality and Social Psychology, 49,* 994–1001.

Melby, J. N., Conger, R. D., Conger, K. J., & Lorenz, F. O. (1993). Effects of parental behavior on tobacco use by young male adolescents. *Journal of Marriage and the Family, 55,* 439–454.

Mesquita, B., & Frijda, N. H. (1992). Cultural variations in emotions: A review. *Psychological Bulletin, 112,* 179–204.

Messenger, J. C. (1971). Sex and repression in an Irish folk community. In D. Marshall & R. Suggs (Eds.), *Human sexual behavior: Variations in the ethnographic spectrum.* New York: Basic Books.

Messick, D. M., Wilke, H., Brewer, M. B., Kramer, R. M., Zemke, P. E., & Lui, L. (1983). Individual adaptations and structural change as solutions to social dilemmas. *Journal of Personality and Social Psychology, 44,* 294–309.

Meyer, T. P. (1972). Effects of viewing justified and unjustified real film violence on aggressive behavior. *Journal of Personality and Social Psychology, 23,* 21–29.

Michaels, J. W., Edwards, J. N., Acock, A. C. (1984). Satisfaction in intimate relationships as a function of inequality, inequity, and outcomes. *Social Psychology Quarterly, 47,* 347–357.

Middleton, R. (1976). Regional differences in prejudice. *American Sociological Review, 41,* 94–117.

Milgram, S. (1961). Nationality and conformity. *Scientific American, 205,* 45–51. (Reprinted in Milgram, S. *The individual in a social world: Essays and experiments,* Reading, MA: Addison Wesley)

Milgram, S. (1963). Behavioral study of obedience. *Journal of Abnormal and Social Psychology, 67,* 371–378.

Milgram, S. (1964). Group pressure and action against a person. *Journal of Abnormal and Social Psychology, 69,* 137–143.

Milgram, S. (1965a). *Obedience* (A filmed report). New York: New York University Film Library.

Milgram, S. (1965b). Some conditions of obedience and disobedience to authority. *Human Relations, 18,* 57–76.

Milgram, S. (1970). The experience of living in cities. *Science, 167,* 1461–1468.

Milgram, S. (1974). *Obedience to authority.* New York: Harper & Row.

Milgram, S., & Sabini, J. (1978). On maintaining urban norms. In A. Baum, J. E. Singer, & S. Valins (Eds.), *Advances in environmental psychology* (Vol. 1). Hillsdale, NJ: Erlbaum.

Millar, M. G., & Tesser, A. (1986). Effects of affective and cognitive focus on the attitude-behavior relation. *Journal of Personality and Social Psychology, 51,* 270–276.

Miller, A. G., Ashton, W., & Mishal, M. (1990). Beliefs concerning the features of constrained behavior: A basis for the fundamental attribution error. *Journal of Personality and Social Psychology, 59,* 635–650.

Miller, A. G., Baer, R., & Schonberg, P. (1979). The bias phenomenon in attitude attribution: Actor and observer perspectives. *Journal of Personality and Social Psychology, 37,* 1421–1431.

Miller, A. G., Gillen, B., Schenker, C., & Radlove, S. (1974). The prediction and perception of obedience to authority. *Journal of Personality, 42,* 23–42.

Miller, A. G., Jones, E. E., & Kimbell, S. (1981). A robust attribution error in the personality domain. *Journal of Experimental Social Psychology, 17,* 587–600.

Miller, D. T. (1976). Ego involvement and attributions for success and failure. *Journal of Personality and Social Psychology, 34,* 901–906.

Miller, D. T., & Ross, M. (1975). Self-serving biases in the attribution of causality: Fact or fiction? *Psychological Bulletin, 82,* 213–225.

Miller, D. T., Taylor, B., & Buck, M. L. (1991). Gender gaps: Who needs to be explained? *Journal of Personality and Social Psychology, 61,* 5–12.

Miller, J. G. (1984). Culture and the development of everyday social explanation. *Journal of Personality and Social Psychology, 46,* 961–978.

Miller, J. G. (1986). Early cross-cultural commonalities in social explanation. *Developmental Psychology, 22,* 514–520.

Miller, J. G. (1987). Cultural influences on the development of conceptual differentiation in person description. *British Journal of Developmental Psychology, 5,* 309–319.

Miller, J. G., Bersoff, D. M. (1992). Culture and moral judgment: How are conflicts between justice and interpersonal responsibilities resolved? *Journal of Personality and Social Psychology, 62,* 541–554.

Miller, J. G., Bersoff, D. M., & Harwood, R. L. (1990). Perceptions of social responsibilities in India and in the United States: Moral imperatives or personal decisions? *Journal of Personality and Social Psychology, 58,* 33–47.

Miller, L. C., & Cox, C. L. (1982). For appearances' sake:

Public self-consciousness and make-up use. *Personality and Social Psychology Bulletin, 8,* 748–751.

Miller, L. E., & Grush, J. E. (1986). Individual differences in attitudinal versus normative determination of behavior. *Journal of Experimental Social Psychology, 22,* 190–202.

Miller, M. L., & Thayer, J. F. (1988). On the nature of self-monitoring: Relationships with adjustment and identity. *Personality and Social Psychology Bulletin, 14,* 544–553.

Miller, N. E., & Bugelski, R. (1948). Minor studies in aggression: The influence of frustrations imposed by the in-group on attitudes expressed towards out-groups. *Journal of Psychology, 25,* 437–442.

Miller, R. S. (1987). Empathic embarrassment: Situational and personal determinants of reactions to the embarrassment of another. *Journal of Personality and Social Psychology, 53,* 1061–1069.

Miller, R. S. (1992). The nature and severity of self-reported embarrassing circumstances. *Personality and Social Psychology Bulletin, 18,* 190–198.

Mills, J., & Mintz, D. M. (1972). Effects of unexplained arousal on affiliation. *Journal of Personality and Social Psychology, 24,* 11–14.

Mills, T. M. (1962). A sleeper variable in small groups research: The experimenter. *Pacific Sociological Review, 5,* 21–28.

Milton, G. A. (1965). Enthusiasm vs. effectiveness in group and individual problem solving. *Psychological Reports, 16,* 1197–1201.

Minas, J. S., Scodel, A., Marlowe, D., & Rawson, H. (1960). Some descriptive aspects of two-person non-zero sum games: II. *Journal of Conflict Resolution, 4,* 193–197.

Mitchell, H. E., & Byrne, D. (1973). The defendant's dilemma: Effects of jurors' attitudes and authoritarianism on judicial decisions. *Journal of Personality and Social Psychology, 25,* 123–129.

Modigliani, A. (1968). Embarrassment and embarrassibility. *Sociometry, 31,* 313–326.

Modigliani, A. (1971). Embarrassment, facework, and eye contact: Testing a theory of embarrassment. *Journal of Personality and Social Psychology, 17,* 15–24.

Molander, P. (1985). The optimal level of generosity in a selfish, uncertain environment. *Journal of Conflict Resolution, 29,* 611–618.

Money, J., & Ehrhardt, A. A. (1972). *Man & woman, boy & girl.* Baltimore: The Johns Hopkins University Press.

Monson, T. C., & Snyder, M. (1977). Actors, observers, and the attribution process: Toward a reconceptualization. *Journal of Experimental Social Psychology, 13,* 89–111.

Monson, T. C., Tanke, E. D., & Lund, J. (1980). Determinants of social perception in a naturalistic setting. *Journal of Research in Personality, 14,* 104–120.

Moran, G., & Comfort, J. C. (1986). Neither "tentative" nor "fragmentary": Verdict preference of impaneled felony jurors as a function of attitude toward capital punishment. *Journal of Applied Psychology, 71,* 146–155.

Moreland, R. L., & Beach, S. R. (1992). Exposure effects in the classroom: The development of affinity among students. *Journal of Experimental Social Psychology, 28,* 255–276.

Morgan, B. S. (1981). A contribution to the debate on homogamy, propinquity, and segregation. *Journal of Marriage and the Family, 43,* 909–921.

Morgan, C. P., & Aram, J. D. (1975). The preponderance of arguments in the risky shift phenomenon. *Journal of Experimental Social Psychology, 11,* 25–34.

Moriarty, T. (1975). Crime, commitment, and the responsive bystander: Two field experiments. *Journal of Personality and Social Psychology, 31,* 370–376.

Morokoff, P. J. (1985). Effects of sex guilt, repression, sexual "arousability," and sexual experience on female sexual arousal during erotica and fantasy. *Journal of Personality and Social Psychology, 49,* 177–187.

Morrison, D. M. (1989). Predicting contraceptive efficacy: A discriminant analysis of three groups of adolescent women. *Journal of Applied Social Psychology, 19,* 1431–1452.

Moscovici, S., Lage, E., & Naffrechoux, M. (1969). Influences of a consistent minority on the responses of a majority in a color perception task. *Sociometry, 32,* 365–380.

Moscovici, S., & Zavalloni, M. (1969). The group as a polarizer of attitudes. *Journal of Personality and Social Psychology, 12,* 125–135.

Mosher, D., & Abramson, P. (1977). Subjective sexual arousal to films of masturbation. *Journal of Consulting and Clinical Psychology, 45,* 796–807.

Mosher, D. L., & Scodel, A. (1960). A study of the relationship between ethnocentrism in children and the ethnocentrism and authoritarian rearing practices of their mothers. *Child Development, 31,* 369–376.

Moyer, K. E. (1976). *The psychology of aggression.* New York: Harper & Row.

Mueller, C. W., Donnerstein, E., & Hallam, J. (1983). Violent films and prosocial behavior. *Personality and Social Psychology Bulletin, 9,* 83–89.

Mugny, G. (1985). Direct and indirect influences in the Asch paradigm: Effect of "valid" or "denied" information. *European Journal of Social Psychology, 15,* 457–461.

Muehlenhard, C. L., Friedman, D. E., & Thomas, C. M. (1985). Is date rape justifiable? The effects of dating activity, who initiated, who paid, and men's attitudes toward women. *Psychology of Women Quarterly, 9,* 297–310.

Mullen, B. (1985). Strength and immediacy of sources: A meta-analytic evaluation of the forgotten elements of social impact theory. *Journal of Personality and Social Psychology, 48,* 1458–1466.

Mullen, B., Driskell, J. E., & Smith, C. (1989). Availability and social projection: The effects of sequence of measurement and wording of question on estimates of consensus. *Personality and Social Psychology Bulletin, 15*, 84–90.

Mullen, B., & Riordan, C. A. (1988). Self-serving attributions for performance in naturalistic settings: A meta-analytic review. *Journal of Applied Social Psychology, 18*, 3–22.

Mullis, J.-P., & Lippa, R. (1990). Behavioral change in earthquake preparedness due to negative threat appeals: A test of protective motivation theory. *Journal of Applied Social Psychology, 20*, 619–638.

Mummendey, A., Simon, B., Dietze, C., Grünert, M., Haeger, G., Kessler, S., Lettgen, S., & Schäferhoff, S. (1992). Categorization is not enough: Intergroup discrimination in negative outcome allocation. *Journal of Experimental Social Psychology, 28*, 125–144.

Muren, S. K., Perot, A., & Byrne, D. (1989). Coping with unwanted sexual activity: Normative responses, situational determinants, and individual differences. *The Journal of Sex Research, 26*, 85–106.

Murstein, B. I. (1961). The complimentary need satisfaction hypothesis in newlyweds and middle-aged married couples. *Journal of Abnormal and Social Psychology, 63*, 194–197.

Murstein, B. I. (1972). Physical attractiveness and marital choice. *Journal of Personality and Social Psychology, 22*, 8–12.

Murstein, B. I., & Christy, P. (1976). Physical attractiveness and marriage adjustment in middle-aged couples. *Journal of Personality and Social Psychology, 34*, 537–542.

Myers, D. G., & Bach, P. J. (1974). Discussion effects on militarism-pacifism: A test of the group polarization hypothesis. *Journal of Personality and Social Psychology, 30*, 741–747.

Myers, D. G., & Bishop, G. D. (1971). Enhancement of dominant attitudes in group discussion. *Journal of Personality and Social Psychology, 20*, 386–391.

Myrdal, G. (1944). *An American dilemma.* New York: Harper.

Nadler, A. (1980). "Good looks do not help": Effects of helper's physical attractiveness and expectations for future interaction on help-seeking behavior. *Personality and Social Psychology Bulletin, 6*, 378–383.

Nadler, A. (1987). Determinants of help seeking behaviour: The effects of helper's similarity, task centrality and recipient's self-esteem. *European Journal of Social Psychology, 17*, 57–67.

Nadler, A., & Fisher, J. D. (1986). The role of threat to self-esteem and perceived control in recipient reaction to help: Theory development and empirical validation. In L. Berkowitz (Ed.), *Advances in experimental social psychology* (Vol. 19, pp. 81–122). New York: Academic Press.

Nadler, A., Mayseless, O., Peri, N., & Chemerinski, A. (1985). Effects of opportunity to reciprocate and self-esteem on help-seeking behavior. *Journal of Personality, 53*, 23–35.

Nadler, A., Shapira, R., & Ben-Itzhak, S. (1982). Good looks may help: Effects of helper's physical attractiveness and sex of helper on males' and females' help-seeking behavior. *Journal of Personality and Social Psychology, 42*, 90–99.

Nel, E., Helmreich, R., & Aronson, E. (1969). Opinion change in the advocate as a function of the persuasibility of his audience: A clarification of the meaning of dissonance. *Journal of Personality and Social Psychology, 12*, 117–124.

Nelson, T. E., Biernat, M. R., & Manis, M. (1990). Everyday base rates (sex stereotypes): Potent and resilient. *Journal of Personality and Social Psychology, 59*, 664–675.

Nemeth, C. (1977). Interactions between jurors as a function of majority vs. unanimity decision rules. *Journal of Applied Social Psychology, 7*, 38–56.

Nemeth, C. (1986). Differential contributions of majority and minority influence. *Psychological Review, 93*, 23–32.

Nemeth, C., & Chiles, C. (1988). Modelling courage: The role of dissent in fostering independence. *European Journal of Social Psychology, 18*, 275–280.

Nemeth, C., Mayseless, O., Sherman, J., & Brown, Y. (1990). Exposure to dissent and recall of information. *Journal of Personality and Social Psychology, 58*, 429–437.

Nemeth, C., Swedlund, M., & Kanki, B. (1974). Patterning of the minority's response and their influence on the majority. *European Journal of Social Psychology, 4*, 53–64.

Nemeth, C., & Wachtler, J. (1973). Consistency and modification of judgment. *Journal of Experimental Social Psychology, 9*, 65–79.

Nemeth, C., & Wachtler, J. (1983). Creative problem solving as a result of majority versus minority influence. *European Journal of Social Psychology, 13*, 45–55.

Netemeyer, R. G., & Burton, S. (1990). Examining the relationships between voting behavior, intention, perceived behavioral control, and expectation. *Journal of Applied Social Psychology, 20*, 661–680.

Newcomb, T. (1961). *The acquaintance process.* New York: Holt, Rinehart and Winston.

Newman, L. S., & Uleman, J. S. (1990). Assimilation and contrast effects in spontaneous trait inference. *Personality and Social Psychological Bulletin, 16*, 224–240.

Nicholson, N., Cole, S. G., & Rocklin, T. (1985). Conformity in the Asch situation: A comparison between contemporary British and U.S. university students. *British Journal of Social Psychology, 24*, 59–63.

Nisan, M., & Kohlberg, L. (1982). Universality and variation in moral judgment: A longitudinal and cross-sectional study in Turkey. *Child Development, 53*, 865–876.

Nisbett, R. E., Caputo, C., Legant, P., & Maracek, J. (1973). Behavior as seen by the actor and as seen by the observer. *Journal of Personality and Social Psychology, 27,* 154–164.

Nisbett, R. E., & Ross, L. (1980). *Human inference: Strategies and shortcomings of social judgment.* Englewood Cliffs, NJ: Prentice-Hall.

Noller, P. (1980). Misunderstandings in marital communication: A study of couples' nonverbal communication. *Journal of Personality and Social Psychology, 39,* 1135–1148.

Noller, P., & Gallois, C. (1986). Sending emotional messages in marriage: Non-verbal behaviour, sex, and communication clarity. *British Journal of Social Psychology, 25,* 287–297.

Novak, D. W., & Lerner, M. J. (1968). Rejection as a consequence of perceived similarity. *Journal of Personality and Social Psychology, 9,* 147–152.

Nucci, L. P., & Nucci, M. S. (1982). Children's responses to moral and social conventional transgressions in free-play settings. *Child Development, 53,* 1337–1342.

Oakes, P. J., & Turner, J. C. (1980). Social categorization and intergroup behaviour: Does minimal intergroup discrimination make social identity more positive? *European Journal of Social Psychology, 10,* 295–301.

O'Heron, C. A., & Orlofsky, J. L. (1990). Stereotypic and nonstereotypic sex role trait and behavior orientations, gender identity, and psychological adjustment. *Journal of Personality and Social Psychology, 58,* 134–143.

Orbell, J. M., van de Kragt, A. J. C., & Dawes, R. M. (1988). Explaining discussions-induced cooperation. *Journal of Personality and Social Psychology, 54,* 811–819.

Osborn, A. F. (1957). *Applied imagination.* New York: Scribners.

Osgood, C. E., & Tannenbaum, P. H. (1955). The principle of congruity in the prediction of attitude change. *Psychological Review, 62,* 42–55.

Oskamp, S. (1971). Effects of programmed strategies on cooperation in the prisoner's dilemma and other mixed-motive games. *Journal of Conflict Resolution, 15,* 225–259.

Oskamp, S., & Perlman, D. (1965). Factors affecting cooperation in the Prisoner's Dilemma game. *Journal of Conflict Resolution, 9,* 359–374.

Osterhouse, R. A., & Brock, T. C. (1970). Distraction increases yielding to propaganda by inhibiting counterarguing. *Journal of Personality and Social Psychology, 15,* 344–358.

Ostrom, T. M., Carpenter, S. L., Sedikides, C., & Li, F. (1993). Differential processing of in-group and out-group information. *Journal of Personality and Social Psychology, 64,* 21–34.

Pagel, M. D., & Davidson, A. R. (1984). A comparison of three social-psychological models of attitude and behav-

ioral plan: Prediction of contraceptive behavior. *Journal of Personality and Social Psychology, 47,* 517–533.

Pallak, M. S., & Pittman, T. S. (1972). General motivational effects of dissonance arousal. *Journal of Personality and Social Psychology, 21,* 349–358.

Paquin, G. (1992). Coping and disputing with neighbors. *Journal of Applied Social Psychology, 22,* 1852–1870.

Park, B., & Judd, C. M. (1990). Measures and models of perceived group variability. *Journal of Personality and Social Psychology, 59,* 173–191.

Park, B., Ryan, C. S., & Judd, C. M. (1992). Role of meaningful subgroups in explaining differences in perceived variability for in-groups and out-groups. *Journal of Personality and Social Psychology, 63,* 553–567.

Parker, G. B., Barrett, E. A., & Hickie, I. B. (1992). From nurture to network: Examining links between perceptions of parenting received in childhood and social bonds in adulthood. *American Journal of Psychiatry, 149,* 877–885.

Parrott, W. G., & Sabini, J. (1989). On the "emotional" qualities of certain types of cognition: A reply to arguments for the independence of cognition and affect. *Cognitive Therapy and Research, 13,* 49–65.

Parrott, W. G., Sabini, J., & Silver, M. (1988). The roles of self-esteem and social interaction in embarrassment. *Personality and Social Psychology Bulletin, 14,* 191–202.

Parsons, T. (1955). Family structure and the socialization of the child. In T. Parsons & R. F. Bales (Eds.), *Family, socialization and interaction process.* Glencoe, IL: The Free Press.

Parsons, T. (1955). The American family: Its relations to personality and to the social structure. In T. Parsons & R. F. Bales (Eds.), *Family: Socialization and interaction process.* Glencoe, IL: The Free Press.

Pastore, N. (1952). The role of arbitrariness in the frustration-aggression hypothesis. *Journal of Abnormal and Social Psychology, 47,* 728–731.

Paulhus, D. (1982). Individual differences, self-presentation and cognitive dissonance: Their concurrent operation in forced compliance. *Journal of Personality and Social Psychology, 43,* 838–852.

Paulhus, D. L., Martin, C. L., & Murphy, G. K. (1992). Some effects of arousal on sex stereotyping. *Personality and Social Psychology Bulletin, 18,* 325–330.

Paulus, P. B., & Dzindolet, M. T. (1993). Social influence processes in group brainstorming. *Journal of Personality and Social Psychology, 64,* 575–586.

Paulus, P. B., Dzindolet, M. T., Poletes, G., & Camacho, L. M. (1993). Perception of performance in group brainstorming: The illusion of group productivity. *Personality and Social Psychology Bulletin, 19,* 78–89.

Pennington, D. C. (1987). Confirmatory hypothesis testing in face-to-face interaction: An empirical refutation. *British Journal of Social Psychology, 26,* 225–235.

Pennington, N., & Hastie, R. (1990). Practical implications of psychological research on juror and jury decision making. *Personality and Social Psychology Bulletin, 16,* 90–105.

Pepitone, A., & Triandis, H. (1987). On the universality of social psychological theories. *Journal of Cross Cultural Psychology, 18,* 471–498.

Peplau, L. A., Rubin, Z., & Hill, T. C. (1977). Sexual intimacy in dating relationships. *Journal of Social Issues, 33,* 86–109.

Peters, L. H., Hartke, D. D., & Polhmann, J. T. (1985). Fiedler's contingency theory of leadership: An application of the meta-analysis procedures of Schmidt and Hunter. *Psychological Bulletin, 97,* 274–285.

Peterson, B. E., Doty, R. M., & Winter, D. G. (1993). Authoritarianism and attitudes toward contemporary social issues. *Personality and Social Psychology Bulletin, 19,* 174–184.

Petty, R. E., & Brock, T. C. (1981). Thought disruption and persuasion: Assessing the validity of attitude change experiments. In R. E. Petty, T. M. Ostrom, & T. C. Brock (Eds.), *Cognitive responses in persuasion* (pp. 57–79). Hillsdale, NJ: Lawrence Erlbaum.

Petty, R. E., & Cacioppo, J. T. (1984). The effects of involvement on responses to argument quality: Central and peripheral routes to persuasion. *Journal of Personality and Social Psychology, 46,* 69–81.

Petty, R. E., & Cacioppo, J. T. (1986). The elaboration likelihood model of persuasion. In L. Berkowitz (Ed.), *Advances in experimental social psychology* (Vol. 19, pp. 123–205). New York: Academic Press.

Petty, R. E., & Cacioppo, J. T. (1990). Involvement and persuasion: Tradition versus integration. *Psychological Bulletin, 107,* 367–374.

Petty, R. E., Cacioppo, J. T., & Goldman, R. (1981). Personal involvement as a determinant of argument-based persuasion. *Journal of Personality and Social Psychology, 41,* 847–855.

Petty, R. E., Harkins, S. G., & Williams, K. D. (1980). The effects of group diffusion of cognitive effort on attitudes: An information-processing view. *Journal of Personality and Social Psychology, 38,* 81–92.

Petty, R. E., Harkins, S., Williams, K. D., & Latané, B. (1977). The effect of group size on cognitive effort and evaluation. *Personality and Social Psychology Bulletin, 3,* 579–582.

Petty, R. E., Schumann, D. W., Richman, S. A., & Strathman, A. J. (1993). Positive mood and persuasion: Different roles for affect under high- and low-elaboration conditions. *Journal of Personality and Social Psychology, 64,* 5–20.

Pfeifer, J. E., & Ogloff, J. R. P. (1991). Ambiguity and guilt determinations: A modern racism perspective. *Journal of Applied Social Psychology, 21,* 1713–1725.

Phillips, D. P. (1986). Natural experiments on the effects of mass media violence on fatal aggression: Strengths and weaknesses of a new approach. In L. Berkowitz (Ed.), *Advances in experimental social psychology* (Vol. 19, pp. 207–249). New York: Academic Press.

Piaget, J., & Inhelder, B. (1956). *The child's conception of space.* London: Routledge & Kegan Paul.

Piliavin, J. A., & Charny, H. W. (1988). What *is* the factorial structure of the private and public self-consciousness scales? *Personality and Social Psychology Bulletin, 14,* 587–595.

Pleck, J. H., Sonenstein, F. L., & Ku, L. C. (1991). Adolescent males' condom use: Relationships between perceived cost-benefits and consistency. *Journal of Marriage and the Family, 53,* 733–745.

Polivy, J., Herman, C. P., Hackett, R., & Kuleshnyk, I. (1986). The effects of self-attention and public attention on eating in restrained and unrestrained subjects. *Journal of Personality and Social Psychology, 50,* 1253–1260.

Porter, N., Geis, F. L., Cooper, E., & Newman, E. (1985). Androgyny and leadership in mixed-sex groups. *Journal of Personality and Social Psychology, 49,* 808–823.

Potter, S. H. (1988). The cultural construction of emotion in rural Chinese social life. *Ethos, 16,* 181–208.

Prager, I. G., & Cutler, B. L. (1990). Attributing traits to oneself and others: The role of acquaintance level. *Personality and Social Psychology Bulletin, 16,* 309–319.

Pratkanis, A. R., Greenwald, A. G., Leippe, M. R., & Baumgardner, M. H. (1988). In search of reliable persuasion effects: III. The sleeper effect is dead, long live the sleeper effect. *Journal of Personality and Social Psychology, 54,* 203–218.

Prentice, D. A., & Miller, D. T. (1993). Pluralistic ignorance and alcohol use on campus: Some consequences of misperceiving the social norm. *Journal of Personality and Social Psychology, 64,* 243–256.

Priest, R. F., & Sawyer, J. (1967). Proximity and peership: Bases of balance in interpersonal attraction. *American Journal of Sociology, 72,* 633–649.

Pruitt, D. G. (1971). Choice shifts in group discussion: An introductory review. *Journal of Personality and Social Psychology, 20,* 339–360.

Pruitt, D. G., Carnevale, P. J. D., Forcey, B., & Van Slyck, M. (1986). Gender effects in negotiation: Constituent surveillance and contentious behaviour. *Journal of Experimental Social Psychology, 22,* 264–275.

Pruitt, D. G., & Lewis, S. A. (1975). Development of integrative solutions in bilateral negotiation. *Journal of Personality and Social Psychology, 31,* 621–633.

Pryor, J. B., & Kriss, M. (1977). The cognitive dynamics of salience in the attribution process. *Journal of Personality and Social Psychology, 35,* 49–55.

Putnam, H. (1975). *Mind, language and reality.* New York: Cambridge University Press.

Pyszczynski, T., Greenberg, J., Solomon, S., Sideris, J., &

Stubing, M. J. (1993). Emotional expression and the reduction of motivated cognitive bias: Evidence from cognitive dissonance and distancing from victims' paradigms. *Journal of Personality and Social Psychology, 64,* 177–186.

Quattrone, G. A., & Jones, E. E. (1980). The perception of variability within in-groups and out-groups: Implications for the law of small numbers. *Journal of Personality and Social Psychology, 38,* 141–152.

Quittner, A. L., Glueckauf, R. L., & Jackson, D. N. (1990). Chronic parenting stress: Moderating versus mediating effects of social support. *Journal of Personality and Social Psychology, 59,* 1266–1278.

Rabbie, J. M., & Horowitz, M. (1969). Arousal of in-group-outgroup bias by a chance win or loss. *Journal of Personality and Social Psychology, 13,* 269–277.

Radikan, W. K. (1982). An evolutionary perspective on human facial displays. In P. Ekman (Ed.), *Emotion in the human face* (2nd ed.). Cambridge: Cambridge University Press.

Raggins, B. R., & Sundstrom, E. (1989). Gender and power in organizations: A longitudinal perspective. *Psychological Bulletin, 105,* 51–88.

Range, L. M., Neyra, C. J., & Goggin, W. C. (1988). The false consensus effect in unfavorable (suicide) and favorable (honor) events. *Journal of Applied Social Psychology, 18,* 597–605.

Rasinski, K. A., Crocker, J., & Hastie, R. (1985). Another look at sex stereotypes and social judgments: An analysis of the social perceiver's use of subjective probabilities. *Journal of Personality and Social Psychology, 49,* 317–326.

Raven, B. H., & French, J. R. P., Jr. (1958). Legitimate power, coercive power, and observability in social influence. *Sociometry, 21,* 83–97.

Read, S. J. (1987). Constructing causal scenarios: A knowledge structure approach to causal reasoning. *Journal of Personality and Social Psychology, 52,* 288–302.

Reddy, D. M., Baum, A., & Fleming, R. (1981). Mediation of social density by coalition formation. *Journal of Applied Social Psychology, 11,* 529–537.

Reifman, A. S., Larrick, R. P., & Fein, S. (1991). Temper and temperature on the diamond: The heat-aggression relationship in major league baseball. *Personality and Social Psychology Bulletin, 17,* 580–585.

Reis, H. T., Nezlek, J., & Wheeler, L. (1980). Physical attractiveness in social interaction. *Journal of Personality and Social Psychology, 38,* 604–617.

Reis, H. T., Senchak, M., & Solomon, B. (1985). Sex differences in the intimacy of social interaction: Further examination of potential explanations. *Journal of Personality and Social Psychology, 48,* 1204–1217.

Reis, H. T., Wheeler, L., Spiegel, N., Kernis, M. H.,

Nezlek, J., & Perri, M. (1982). Physical attractiveness in social interaction: II. Why does appearance affect experience? *Journal of Personality and Social Psychology, 43,* 979–996.

Reiss, I. L. (1966). The sexual renaissance in America: A summary and analysis. *Journal of Social Issues, 22,* 121–137.

Reiss, I. L., & Leik, R. K. (1989). Evaluating strategies to avoid AIDS: Number of partners vs. use of condoms. *The Journal of Sex Research, 26,* 411–433.

Renne, K. S. (1970). Correlates of dissatisfaction in marriage. *Journal of Marriage and the Family, 32,* 54–67.

Renne, K. S. (1971). Health and marital experience in an urban population. *Journal of Marriage and the Family, 33,* 338–350.

Reno, R. R., Cialdini, R. B., & Kallgren, C. A. (1993). The transsituational influence of social norms. *Journal of Personality and Social Psychology, 64,* 104–112.

Rice, R. W., Phillips, S. M., & McFarlin, D. B. (1990). Multiple discrepancies and pay satisfaction. *Journal of Applied Psychology, 75,* 386–393.

Riemann, R., & Angleitner, A. (1993). Inferring interpersonal traits from behavior: Act prototypicality versus conceptual similarity of trait concepts. *Journal of Personality and Social Psychology, 64,* 356–364.

Richardson, H. M. (1939). Studies of mental resemblance between husbands and wives and between friends. *Psychological Bulletin, 36,* 104–120.

Riley, D., & Eckenrode, J. (1986). Social ties: Subgroup differences in costs and benefits. *Journal of Personality and Social Psychology, 51,* 770–778.

Risman, B. J., Hill, C. T., Rubin, Z., & Peplau, L. A. (1981). Living together in college: Implications for courtship. *Journal of Marriage and the Family, 43,* 77–83.

Roberts, T.-A. (1991). Gender and the influence of evaluations on self-assessments in achievement settings. *Psychological Bulletin, 109,* 297–308.

Robinson, I., Ziss, K., Ganza, B., Katz, S., & Robinson, E. (1991). Twenty years of sexual revolution, 1965–1985: An update. *Journal of Marriage and the Family, 53,* 216–220.

Robinson, I. E., & Jedlicka, D. (1982). Change in sexual attitudes and behavior of college students from 1965 to 1980: A research note. *Journal of Marriage and the Family, 44,* 237–240.

Robinson-Stavley, K., & Cooper, J. (1990). Mere presence, gender, and reactions to computers: Studying human-computer interaction in the social context. *Journal of Experimental Social Psychology, 26,* 168–183.

Rofé, Y., Lewin, I. (1986). Affiliation in an unavoidable stressful situation: An examination of the utility theory. *British Journal of Social Psychology, 25,* 119–127.

Rogers, R. W., & Prentice-Dunn, S. (1981). Deindividuation and anger-mediated interracial aggression: Unmasking regressive racism. *Journal of Personality and Social Psychology, 41,* 63–73.

Rohrer, J. H., Baron, S. H., Hoffman, E. L., & Swander, D. V. (1954). The stability of autokinetic judgments. *Journal of Abnormal and Social Psychology, 49,* 595–597.

Rollins, B. C., & Cannon, K. L. (1974) Marital satisfaction over the family life cycle: A reevaluation. *Journal of Marriage and the Family, 36,* 271–282.

Roner, D., & Revelle, W. (1984). Personality traits: Fact or fiction? A critique of the Shweder and D'Andrade systematic distortion hypothesis. *Journal of Personality and Social Psychology, 47,* 1029–1042.

Rook, K. S. (1984). The negative side of social interaction: Impact on psychological well-being. *Journal of Personality and Social Psychology, 46,* 1097–1108.

Roseman, I. J., Spindel, M. S., & Lose, J. E. (1990). Appraisals of emotion-eliciting events: Testing a theory of discrete emotions. *Journal of Personality and Social Psychology, 59,* 899–915.

Rosen, S., Mickler, S. E., & Collins, J. E. II. (1987). Reactions of would-be helpers whose offer of help is spurned. *Journal of Personality and Social Psychology, 53,* 288–297.

Rosenberg, M. J. (1960). A structural theory of attitude dynamics. *Public Opinion Quarterly, 24,* 319–340.

Rosenfeld, P., Giacalone, R. A., & Tedeschi, J. T. (1984). Cognitive dissonance and impression management explanations for effort justification. *Personality and Social Psychology Bulletin, 10,* 394–401.

Rosenhan, D. L., Salovey, P., & Hargis, K. (1981). The joys of helping: Focus of attention mediates the impact of positive affect on altruism. *Journal of Personality and Social Psychology, 40,* 899–905.

Rosenhan, D. L., Salovey, P., Karylowski, J., & Hargis, K. (1981). Emotion and altruism. In J.-P. Rushton & R. M. Sorrentino (Eds.), *Altruism and helping behavior.* Hillsdale, NJ: Erlbaum.

Rosenhan, D. L., Underwood, B., & Moore, B. (1974). Affect moderates self-gratification and altruism. *Journal of Personality and Social Psychology, 30,* 546–552.

Rosenthal, R., & DePaulo, B. M. (1979). Sex differences in eavesdropping on nonverbal cues. *Journal of Personality and Social Psychology, 37,* 273–285.

Ross, L. (1977). The intuitive psychologist and his shortcomings: Distortions in the attribution process. In L. Berkowitz (Ed.), *Advances in experimental social psychology* (Vol. 10, pp. 173–220). New York: Academic Press.

Ross, L., Amabile, T. M., & Steinmetz, J. L. (1977). Social roles, social control, and biases in social-perception processes. *Journal of Personality and Social Psychology, 35,* 485–494.

Ross, L., Bierbrauer, G., & Hoffman, S. (1976). The role of attribution processes in conformity and dissent: Revisiting the Asch situation. *American Psychologist, 31,* 148–157.

Ross, L., Green, D., & House, P. (1977). The "false-consensus" effect: An egocentric bias in social perception and attribution processes. *Journal of Experimental Social Psychology, 13,* 279–301.

Ross, M., & Sicoly, F. (1979). Egocentric biases in availability and attribution. *Journal of Personality and Social Psychology, 37,* 322–336.

Rothbart, M., Evans, M., & Fulero, S. (1979). Recall for confirming events: Memory processes and the maintenance of social stereotypes. *Journal of Experimental Social Psychology, 15,* 343–355.

Rothbart, M., & Lewis, S. (1988). Inferring category attributes from exemplar attributes: Geometric shapes and social categories. *Journal of Personality and Social Psychology, 55,* 861–872.

Rotton, J., & Frey, J. (1985). Air pollution, weather, and violent crimes: Concomitant time-series analysis of archival data. *Journal of Personality and Social Psychology, 49,* 1207–1220.

Rozin, E. (1982). The structure of cuisine. In L. M. Barker, (Ed.), *The psychobiology of human food selection.* Westport, CT: AVI.

Rozin, E., & Rozin, P. (1981). Culinary themes and variations. *Natural History, 90,* 6–14.

Rozin, P. (1982). Human food selection: The interaction of biology, culture, and individual experience. In L. M. Barker, (Ed.), *The psychobiology of human food selection.* Westport, CT: AVI.

Rozin, P. (1991). Family resemblance in food and other domains: The family paradox and the role of parental congruence. *Appetite, 16,* 93–102.

Rozin, P., & Fallon, A. (1987). A perspective on disgust. *Psychological Review, 94,* 23–41.

Rozin, P., Millman, L., & Nemeroff, C. (1986). Operation of the laws of sympathetic magic in disgust and other domains. *Journal of Personality and Social Psychology, 50,* 703–712.

Rubin, Z. (1970). Measurement of romantic love. *Journal of Personality and Social Psychology, 16,* 265–273.

Ruble, D. N., Fleming, A. S., Hackel, L. S., & Stangor, C. (1988). Changes in the marital relationship during the transition to first time motherhood: Effects of violated expectations concerning division of household labor. *Journal of Personality and Social Psychology, 55,* 78–87.

Rusbult, C. E. (1983). A longitudinal test of the investment model: The development (and deterioration) of satisfaction and commitment in heterosexual involvement. *Journal of Personality and Social Psychology, 45,* 101–117.

Rusbult, C. E., Campbell, M. A., & Price, M. E. (1990). Rational selective exploitation and distress: Employee reactions to performance-based and mobility-based reward allocations. *Journal of Personality and Social Psychology, 59,* 487–500.

Rusbult, C. E., Insko, C. A., Lin, Y.-H. W., & Smith, W.

J. (1990). Social motives underlying rational selective exploitation: The impact of instrumental versus social-emotional allocator orientation on the distribution of rewards in groups. *Journal of Applied Social Psychology, 20,* 984–1025.

Rusbult, C. E., Verette, J., Whitney, G. A., Slovik, L. F., & Lipkus, I. (1991). Accommodation processes in close relationships: Theory and preliminary empirical evidence. *Journal of Personality and Social Psychology, 60,* 53–78.

Russell, D., Cutrona, C. E., Rose, J., & Yurko, K. (1984). Social and emotional loneliness: An examination of Weiss's typology of loneliness. *Journal of Personality and Social Psychology, 46,* 1313–1321.

Russell, D., Peplau, L. A., & Cutrona, C. E. (1980). The revised UCLA loneliness scale: Concurrent and discriminant validity evidence. *Journal of Personality and Social Psychology, 39,* 472–480.

Russell, J. A. (1991). Culture and the categorization of emotions. *Psychological Bulletin, 110,* 426–450.

Russell, J. A., Lewicka, M., & Niit, T. (1989). A cross-cultural study of a circumplex model of affect. *Journal of Personality and Social Psychology, 57,* 848–856.

Rutte, C. G., & Wilke, H. A. M. (1984). Social dilemmas and leadership. *European Journal of Social Psychology, 14,* 105–121.

Rutte, C. G., Wilke, H. A., & Messick, D. M. (1987). Scarcity or abundance caused by people or the environment as determinants of behavior in the resource dilemma. *Journal of Experimental Social Psychology, 23,* 208–216.

Ryan, R. M., Mims, V., & Koestner, R. (1983). Relation of reward contingency and interpersonal context to intrinsic motivation: A review and test using cognitive evaluation theory. *Journal of Personality and Social Psychology, 45,* 736–750.

Ryder, R. G. (1973). Longitudinal data relating marital satisfaction to having a child. *Journal of Marriage and the Family, 35,* 604–606.

Sabatelli, R. M., Buck, R., & Dreyer, A. (1980). Communication via facial cues in intimate dyads. *Personality and Social Psychology Bulletin, 6,* 242–247.

Sabini, J., & Silver, M. (1982). *Moralities of everyday life.* New York: Oxford University Press.

Sabini, J., & Silver, M. (1987). Internal and external causes of behavior. *International Journal of Moral and Social Studies, 2,* 11–22.

Sabini, J., & Silver, M. (1989). Loyalty as good and duty: A critique of Stocker. *International Journal of Moral and Social Studies, 4,* 131–138.

Sabini, J., & Silver, M. (1990). Unpublished manuscript, University of Pennsylvania, Philadelphia.

Sadalla, E. K., Kenrick, D. T., & Vershure, B. (1987). Dominance and heterosexual attraction. *Journal of Personality and Social Psychology, 52,* 730–738.

Sagan, K., Pondel, M., & Wittig, M. A. (1981). The effect of anticipated future interaction on reward allocation in same- and opposite-sex dyads. *Journal of Personality, 49,* 438–449.

Sagi, A., & Hoffman, M. L. (1976). Empathetic distress in the newborn. *Developmental Psychology, 12,* 175–176.

Saks, J. M. (1977). The limits of scientific jury selection: Ethical and empirical. *Jurimetrics Journal, 17,* 3–22.

Samelson, F. (1957). Conforming behavior under two conditions of conflict in the cognitive field. *Journal of Abnormal and Social Psychology, 55,* 181–187.

Samuelson, C. D. (1991). Perceived task difficulty, causal attributions, and preferences for structural change in resource dilemmas. *Personality and Social Psychology Bulletin, 17,* 181–187.

Samuelson, C. D., & Messick, D. M. (1986). Alternative structural solutions to resource dilemmas. *Organizational Behavior and Human Decision Processes, 37,* 139–155.

Samuelson, C. D., Messick, D. M., Rutte, C. G., & Wilke, H. (1984). Individual and structural solutions to resource dilemmas in two cultures. *Journal of Personality and Social Psychology, 47,* 94–104.

Sanbonmatsu, D. M., Shavitt, S., & Sherman, S. J. (1991). The role of personal relevance in the formation of distinctiveness-based illusory correlations. *Personality and Social Psychology Bulletin, 17,* 124–132.

Sanders, G. S. (1981). Driven by distraction: An integrative review of social facilitation theory and research. *Journal of Experimental Social Psychology, 17,* 227–251.

Sanna, L. J. (1992). Self-efficacy theory: Implications for social facilitation and social loafing. *Journal of Personality and Social Psychology, 62,* 774–786.

Sanna, L. J., & Shotland, R. L. (1990). Valence of anticipated evaluation and social facilitation. *Journal of Experimental Social Psychology, 26,* 82–92.

Santee, R. T., & Maslach, C. (1982). To agree or not to agree: Personal dissent amid social pressure to conform. *Journal of Personality and Social Psychology, 42,* 690–700.

Sarnoff, I., & Zimbardo, P. G. (1961). Anxiety, fear, and social affiliation. *Journal of Abnormal and Social Psychology, 62,* 356–363.

Schachter, S. (1951). Deviation, rejection, and communication. *Journal of Abnormal and Social Psychology, 46,* 190–207.

Schachter, S. (1959). *The psychology of affiliation: Experimental studies of the sources of gregariousness.* Stanford: Stanford University Press.

Schachter, S., Nuttin, J., De Monchaux, C., Maucorps, P. H., Osmer, D., Duijker, H., Rommetviet, R., & Israel, J. (1954). Cross-cultural experiments on threat and rejection. *Human Relations, 7,* 403–439.

Schachter, S., & Singer, J. E. (1962). Cognitive, social, and psychological determinants of emotional state. *Psychological Review, 69,* 379–399.

Schachter, S., & Singer, J. E. (1979). Comments on the Maslach and Marshall-Zimbardo experiments. *Journal of Personality and Social Psychology, 37,* 989–995.

Schafer, S. (1977). Sociosexual behavior in male and female homosexuals: A study in sex differences. *Archives of Sexual Behavior, 6,* 355–364.

Schaller, M., & O'Brien, M. (1992). "Intuitive analysis of covariance" and group stereotype formation. *Personality and Social Psychology Bulletin, 18,* 776–785.

Schank, R. C., & Abelson, R. P. (1977). *Scripts, plans, goals, and understanding.* Hillsdale, NJ: Erlbaum.

Schellenberg, J. A., & Bee, L. S. (1960). A re-examination of the theory of complimentary needs in mate selection. *Journal of Marriage and Family Living, 22,* 227–231.

Schelling, T. C. (1960). *The strategy of conflict.* Cambridge: Harvard University Press.

Scher, S. J., & Cooper, J. (1989). Motivational basis of dissonance: The singular role of behavioral consequences. *Journal of Personality and Social Psychology, 56,* 899–906.

Scherer, K. R. (1986). Vocal affect expression: A review and model for future research. *Psychological Bulletin, 99,* 143–165.

Schlegel, R. P., d'Avernas, J. R., Zanna, M. P., DeCourville, N. H., & Manske, S. R. (1992). Problem drinking: A problem for the theory of reasoned action? *Journal of Applied Social Psychology, 22,* 358–385.

Schlenker, B. R., & Trudeau, J. V. (1990). Impact of self-presentations on private self-beliefs: Effects of prior self-beliefs and misattribution. *Journal of Personality and Social Psychology, 58,* 22–32.

Schmidt, B. H., Gilovich, T., Goore, N., & Joseph, L. (1986). Mere presence and social facilitation: One more time. *Journal of Experimental Social Psychology, 22,* 242–248.

Schmidt, G. (1975). Male-female differences in sexual arousal and behavior during and after exposure to sexually explicit stimuli. *Archives of Sexual Behavior, 4,* 353–365.

Schul, Y., & Manzury, F. (1990). The effects of type of encoding and strength of discounting appeal on the success of ignoring an invalid testimony. *European Journal of Social Psychology, 20,* 337–349.

Schutte, N. S., Malouff, J. M., Post-Gordon, J. C., & Rodasta, A. L. (1988). Effects of playing video-games on children's aggressive and other behaviors. *Journal of Applied Social Psychology, 18,* 454–460.

Schwartz, S. H., & Howard, J. A. (1981). A normative decision making model of altruism. In J.-P. Rushton & R. M. Sorrentino (Eds.), *Altruism and helping behavior.* Hillsdale, NJ: Erlbaum.

Schwartz, S. H., & Tessler, R. C. (1972). A test of a model for reducing measured atttitude-behavior discrepancies. *Journal of Personality and Social Psychology, 24,* 225–236.

Sedikides, C. (1990). Effects of fortuitously activated constructs versus activated communication goals on person impressions. *Journal of Personality and Social Psychology, 58,* 397–408.

Sedikides, C., & Anderson, C. A. (1992). Causal explanations of defection: A knowledge structure approach. *Personality and Social Psychology Bulletin, 18,* 420–429.

Segal, M. W. (1974). Alphabet and attraction: An unobtrusive measure of the effect of propinquity in a field setting. *Journal of Personality and Social Psychology, 30,* 654–657.

Seligman, M. E. P., Abramson, L. Y., Semmel, A., & von Bayer, C. (1979). Depressive attributional style. *Journal of Personality and Social Psychology, 88,* 242–247.

Sermat, V., & Gregovich, R. P. (1966). The effect of experimental manipulation on cooperative behavior in a chicken game. *Psychonomic Science, 4,* 435–436.

Seyfarth, R. M., Cheney, D. L., & Marler, P. (1980). Vervet monkey alarm calls: Semantic communication in a free-ranging primate. *Animal Behaviour, 28,* 1070–1094.

Shaffer, D. R., Rogel, M., & Hendrick, C. (1975). Intervention in the library: The effect of increased responsibility on bystanders' willingness to prevent a theft. *Journal of Applied Social Psychology, 5,* 303–319.

Shanab, M. E., & Yahya, K. A. (1977). A behavioral study of obedience in children. *Journal of Personality and Social Psychology, 35,* 530–536.

Shapiro, E. G. (1975). Effect of expectations of future interaction on reward allocation in dyads: Equity or equality. *Journal of Personality and Social Psychology, 31,* 873–880.

Shapley, L. S., & Shubik, M. (1954). A method for evaluating the distribution of power in a committee system. *American Political Science Review, 48,* 787–792.

Shaver, K. G., & Drown, D. (1986). On causality, responsibility, and self-blame: A theoretical note. *Journal of Personality and Social Psychology, 50,* 697–702.

Shavitt, S., & Fazio, R. H. (1991). Effects of attribute salience on the consistency between attitudes and behavior predictions. *Personality and Social Psychology Bulletin, 17,* 507–516.

Shaw, M. E. (1954). Some effects of problem complexity upon problem solution efficiency in different communication nets. *Journal of Experimental Social Psychology, 48,* 211–217.

Shaw, M. E. (1964). Communication networks. In L. Berkowitz (Ed.), *Advances in experimental social psychology* (Vol. 1, pp. 111–147). New York: Academic Press.

Sheppard, B. H. (1985). Justice is no simple matter: Case for elaborating our model of procedural fairness. *Journal of Personality and Social Psychology, 49,* 953–962.

Sheppard, J. A., & Arkin, R. M. (1991). Behavioral other-enhancement: Strategically obscuring the link between performance and evaluation. *Journal of Personality and Social Psychology, 60,* 79–88.

Sherif, M. (1935). A study of some social factors in perception. *Archives of Psychology, 2*, 187.

Sherif, M., Harvey, O. J., White, B. J., Hood, W. R., & Sherif, C. (1961). *Intergroup conflict and cooperation: The Robbers' Cave experiment.* Norman, OK: Oklahoma Book Exchange.

Sherman, S. J., & Gorkin, L. (1980). Attitude bolstering when behavior is inconsistent with central attitudes. *Journal of Experimental Social Psychology, 16*, 388–403.

Sherman, S. J., Mackie, D. M., & Driscoll, D. M. (1990). Priming and the differential use of dimensions in evaluation. *Personality and Social Psychology Bulletin, 16*, 405–418.

Shills, E. E., & Janowitz, M. (1948). Cohesion and disintegration in the Wehrmacht in World War II. *Public Opinion Quarterly, 12*, 280–315.

Shotland, R. L., & Goodstein, L. (1983). Just because she doesn't want to doesn't mean it's rape: An experimentally based causal model of the perception of rape in a dating situation. *Social Psychology Quarterly, 46*, 220–232.

Shotland, R. L., & Goodstein, L. (1992). Sexual precedence reduces the perceived legitimacy of sexual refusal: An examination of attributions concerning date rape and consensual sex. *Personality and Social Psychology Bulletin, 18*, 756–764.

Shotland, R. L., & Stebbins, C. A. (1980). Bystander response to rape: Can a victim attract help? *Journal of Applied Social Psychology, 10*, 510–527.

Shure, G. H., Meeker, R., & Hansford, E. A. (1965). The effectiveness of pacifist strategies in bargaining games. *Journal of Conflict Resolution, 9*, 106–117.

Shweder, R. A. (1975). How relevant is an individual difference theory of personality? *Journal of Personality, 43*, 455–484.

Shweder, R. A. (1977). Illusory correlation and the MMPI controversy: A reply to some of the allusions and elusions in Block's and Edwards' commentaries. *Journal of Consulting and Clinical Psychology, 45*, 936–940.

Shweder, R. A. (1980). Factors and fictions in person perception: A reply to Lamielle, Foss, and Cavenne. *Journal of Personality, 48*, 74–81.

Shweder, R. A. (in press). The authority of voice. *New York University Law School Law Review.*

Shweder, R. A., & Bourne, E. J. (1982). Does the concept of the person vary cross-culturally? In R. A. Shweder & R. A. LeVine, (Eds.), *Culture Theory: Essays on mind, self, and emotion.* New York: Cambridge University Press (158–199).

Shweder, R. A., & D'Andrade, R. G. (1979). Accurate reflection or systematic distortion? A reply to Block, Weiss, and Thore. *Journal of Personality and Social Psychology, 37*, 1075–1084.

Siegel, K., Bauman, L. J., Christ, G. H., & Krown, S. (1988). Patterns of change in sexual behavior among gay men in New York City. *Archives of Sexual Behavior, 17*, 481–497.

Siegel, S., & Fouraker, L. E. (1960). *Bargaining and group decision making: experiments in bilateral monopoly.* New York: McGraw-Hill.

Siem, F. M., & Spence, J. T. (1986). Gender-related traits and helping behaviors. *Journal of Personality and Social Psychology, 51*, 615–621.

Sigelman, C. K., Berry, C. J., & Wiles, K. A. (1984). Violence in college students' dating relationships. *Journal of Applied Social Psychology, 5*, 530–548.

Silver, L. B., Dublin, C. C., & Lourie, R. S. (1969). Does violence breed violence? Contributions from a study of the child abuse syndrome. *American Journal of Psychiatry, 126*, 404–407.

Silverthorne, C. P. (1971). Informational input and the group shift phenomenon in risk taking. *Journal of Personality and Social Psychology, 20*, 456–461.

Simmel, G. (1908/1950). *The sociology of Georg Simmel.* Glencoe, IL: The Free Press.

Simmel, G. (1911/1971). *On individuality and social forms.* In D. N. Levine (Ed.), Chicago, IL: University of Chicago Press.

Simner, M. L. (1971). Newborn's response to the cry of another infant. *Developmental Psychology, 5*, 136–150.

Simpson, J. A. (1987). The dissolution of romantic relationships: Factors involved in relationship stability and emotional distress. *Journal of Personality and Social Psychology, 53*, 683–692.

Simpson, J. A. (1990). Influence of attachment styles on romantic relationships. *Journal of Personality and Social Psychology, 59*, 971–980.

Simpson, J. A., Campbell, B., & Berscheid, E. (1986). The association between romantic love and marriage: Kephart (1967) twice revisited. *Personality and Social Psychology Bulletin, 12*, 363–372.

Simpson, J. A., Rholes, W. S., & Nelligan, J. S. (1992). Support seeking and support giving within couples in an anxiety-provoking situation: The role of attachment styles. *Journal of Personality and Social Psychology, 62*, 434–446.

Singer, B. (1985). A comparison of evolutionary and environmental theories of erotic response: Part II. Empirical arenas. *The Journal of Sex Research, 21*, 345–374.

Skolnick, P. (1971). Reactions to personal evaluations: A failure to replicate. *Journal of Personality and Social Psychology, 18*, 62–67.

Smetana, J. G., Killen, M., & Turiel, E. (1991). Children's reasoning about interpersonal and moral conflicts. *Child Development, 62*, 629–644.

Smetana, J. G., Schlagman, N., & Adams, P. W. (1993). Preschool children's judgments about hypothetical and actual transgressions. *Child Development, 64*, 202–214.

Smith, C. A., & Ellsworth, P. C. (1985). Patterns of cognitive appraisal in emotion. *Journal of Personality and Social Psychology, 48,* 813–838.

Smith, C. A., & Ellsworth, P. C. (1987). Patterns of appraisal and emotion related to taking an exam. (1987). *Journal of Personality and Social Psychology, 52,* 475–488.

Smith, E. R. (1991). Illusory correlation in a simulated exemplar-based memory. *Journal of Experimental Social Psychology, 27,* 107–123.

Smith, E. R., Stewart, T. L., & Buttram, R. T. (1992). Inferring a trait from a behavior has long-term, highly specific effects. *Journal of Personality and Social Psychology, 62,* 753–759.

Smith, K. D., Keating, J. P., & Stotland, E. (1989). Altruism reconsidered: The effect of denying feedback on a victim's status to empathetic witnesses. *Journal of Personality and Social Psychology, 57,* 641–650.

Smith, T. W., Snyder, C. R., & Handelsman, M. M. (1982). On the self-serving function of an academic wooden leg: Test anxiety as a self-handicapping strategy. *Journal of Personality and Social Psychology, 42,* 314–321.

Smith, T. W., Snyder, C. R., & Perkins, S. C. (1983). The self-serving function of hypochondriacal complaints: Physical symptoms as self-handicapping strategies. *Journal of Personality and Social Psychology, 44,* 787–797.

Snarey, J. R. (1985). Cross-cultural universality of social-moral development: A critical review of Kohlbergian research. *Psychological Bulletin, 97,* 202–232.

Snarey, J. R., Reimer, J., & Kohlberg, L. (1985). Development of social-moral reasoning among Kibbutz adolescents: A longitudinal cross-cultural study. *Developmental Psychology, 21,* 3–17.

Snodgrass, S. E. (1992). Further effects of role versus gender on interpersonal sensitivity. *Journal of Personality and Social Psychology, 62,* 154–158.

Snyder, C. R., Smith, T. W., Augelli, R. W., & Ingram, R. E. (1985). On the self-serving function of social anxiety: Shyness as a self-handicapping strategy. *Journal of Personality and Social Psychology, 48,* 970–980.

Snyder, M. (1974). Self-monitoring of expressive behavior. *Journal of Personality and Social Psychology, 30,* 526–537.

Snyder, M. (1979). Self-monitoring processes. In L. Berkowitz (Ed.), *Advances in experimental social psychology* (Vol. 12, pp. 85–128). New York: Academic Press.

Snyder, M., Berscheid, E., & Glick, P. (1985). Focusing on the exterior and the interior: Two investigations of the initiation of personal relationships. *Journal of Personality and Social Psychology, 48,* 1427–1439.

Snyder, M., Gangestad, S., & Simpson, J. A. (1983). Choosing friends as activity partners: The role of self-monitoring. *Journal of Personality and Social Psychology, 45,* 1061–1072.

Snyder, M., & Jones, E. E. (1974). Attitude attribution when behavior is constrained. *Journal of Experimental Social Psychology, 10,* 585–600.

Snyder, M., & Kendzierski, D. (1982a). Acting on one's attitudes: Procedures for linking attitude and behavior. *Journal of Experimental Social Psychology, 18,* 165–183.

Snyder, M., & Kandzierski, D. (1982b). Choosing social situations: Investigating the origins of correspondence between attitude and behavior. *Journal of Personality, 50,* 280–295.

Snyder, M., & Monson, T. C. (1975). Persons, situations, and the control of social behavior. *Journal of Personality and Social Psychology, 32,* 637–644.

Snyder, M., & Simpson, J. (1984). Self-monitoring and dating relationships. *Journal of Personality and Social Psychology, 47,* 1281–1291.

Snyder, M., Simpson, J., & Gangestad, S. (1986). Personality and sexual relationships. *Journal of Personality and Social Psychology, 51,* 181–190.

Snyder, M., & Swann, W. B., Jr. (1978). Hypothesis-testing processes in interaction. *Journal of Personality and Social Psychology, 36,* 1202–1212.

Snyder, M., & Tanke, E. D. (1976). Behavior and attitude: Some people are more consistent than others. *Journal of Personality, 44,* 510–517.

Snyder, M., Tanke, E. D., & Berscheid, E. (1977). Social perception and interpersonal behavior: On the self-fulfilling nature of social stereotypes. *Journal of Personality and Social Psychology, 35,* 656–666.

Snyder, M., & Uranowitz, S. W. (1978). Reconstructing the past: Some cognitive consequences of person perception. *Journal of Personality and Social Psychology, 36,* 941–950.

Solano, C. H., Batten, P. G., & Parish, E. A. (1982). Loneliness and patterns of self-disclosure. *Journal of Personality and Social Psychology, 43,* 524–531.

Solomon, M. R., & Schopler, J. (1982). Self-consciousness and clothing. *Personality and Social Psychology Bulletin, 8,* 508–514.

Solzhenitsyn, A. (1973). *The Gulag Archipelago.* New York: Harper & Row.

Song, M.-J., Smetana, J. G., & Kim, S. Y. (1987). Korean children's conceptions of moral and conventional transgressions. *Developmental Psychology, 23,* 577–582.

Sorenson, R. (1972). *Adolescent sexuality in contemporary America.* New York: World.

Spanier, G. B. (1983). Married and unmarried cohabitation in the United States: 1980. *Journal of Marriage and the Family, 45,* 277–288.

Spanier, G. B., & Lewis, R. A. (1980). Marital quality: A review of the seventies. *Journal of Marriage and the Family, 42,* 825–839.

Spears, R., van der Pligt, J., & Elser, J. R. (1985). Illusory correlation in the perception of group attitudes. *Journal of Personality and Social Psychology, 48*, 863–875.

Spears, R., van der Pligt, J., & Elser, J. R. (1986). Generalizing the illusory correlation effect. *Journal of Personality and Social Psychology, 51*, 1127–1134.

Spence, J. T., & Helmreich, R. L. (1978). *Masculinity and femininity: The psychological dimensions, correlates and dimensions.* Austin: University of Texas Press.

Spence, J. T., Helmreich, R. L., & Stapp, J. (1974). The personal attributes questionnaire: A measure of sex role stereotypes and masculinity-femininity. *JSAS Catalog of Selected Documents in Psychology, 4*, 43.

Sprecher, S. (1986). The relation between inequity and emotions in close relationships. *Social Psychology Quarterly, 49*, 309–321.

Sprecher, S., McKinney, K., & Orbuch, T. L. (1991). The effect of current sexual behavior on friendship, dating, and marriage desirability. *The Journal of Sex Research, 28*, 387–408.

Sprecher, S., McKinney, K., & Orbuch, T. L. (1987). Has the double standard disappeared?: An experimental test. *Social Psychology Quarterly, 50*, 24–31.

Srull, T. K. (1983). Organizational and retrieval processes in person memory: An examination of processing objectives, presentation format, and the possible role of self-generated retrieval clues. *Journal of Personality and Social Psychology, 44*, 1157–1170.

Srull, T. K., & Wyer, R. S., Jr. (1979). The role of category accessibility in the interpretation of information about persons: Some determinants and implications. *Journal of Personality and Social Psychology, 37*, 1660–1672.

Srull, T. K., & Wyer, R. S., Jr. (1989). Person memory and judgment. *Psychological Review, 96*. 58–83.

Stake, J. E. (1983). Factors in reward distribution: Allocator motive, gender, and Protestant ethic. *Journal of Personality and Social Psychology, 44*, 410–418.

Stangor, C., & Duan, C. (1991). Effects of multiple task demands upon memory for information about social groups. *Journal of Experimental Social Psychology, 27*, 357–378.

Stangor, C., & Ruble, D. N. (1989). Strength of expectancies and memory for social information: What we remember depends on how much we know. *Journal of Experimental Social Psychology, 25*, 18–35.

Star, S. A., Williams, R. M., Jr., & Stouffer, S. A. (1958). Negro infantry platoons in white companies. In E. E. Maccoby, T. M. Newcomb, & E. L. Hartley (Eds.), *Readings in social psychology* (3rd ed.). New York: Holt, Reinhart, and Winston.

Stasser, G., & Stewart, D. (1992). Discovery of hidden profiles by decision-making groups: Solving a problem versus making a judgment. *Journal of Personality and Social Psychology, 63*, 426–434.

Stasser, G., & Titus, W. (1985). Pooling of unshared information in group decision making: Biased information sampling during discussion. *Journal of Personality and Social Psychology, 48*, 1467–1478.

Stasser, G., & Titus, W. (1987). Effects of information load and percentage of shared information on the dissemination of unshared information during group discussion. *Journal of Personality and Social Psychology, 53*, 81–93.

Staw, B. M. (1974). Attitudinal and behavioral consequences of changing a major organizational reward: A natural field experiment. *Journal of Personality and Social Psychology, 29*, 742–751.

Steblay, N. M. (1987). Helping behavior in rural and urban environments: A meta-analysis. *Psychological Bulletin, 102*, 346–356.

Steele, C. M., & Liu, T. J. (1981). Making the dissonant act unreflective of self: Dissonance avoidance and the expectancy of a value-affirming response. *Personality and Social Psychology Bulletin, 7*, 393–397.

Steele, C. M., & Liu, T. J. (1983). Dissonance processes as self-affirmation. *Journal of Personality and Social Psychology, 45*, 5–19.

Steele, C. M., Southwick, L. L., & Critchlow, B. (1981). Dissonance and alcohol: Drinking your troubles away. *Journal of Personality and Social Psychology, 41*, 831–846.

Steiner, I. D. (1966). Models for inferring relationships between group size and potential group productivity. *Behavioral Science, 11*, 273–283.

Stephan, W. G., & Rosenfield, D. (1978). Effects of desegregation on racial attitudes. *Journal of Personality and Social Psychology, 36*, 795–804.

Stepper, S., & Strack, F. (1993). Proprioceptive determinants of emotional and nonemotional feelings. *Journal of Personality and Social Psychology, 64*, 211–220.

Sternberg, R. J. (1986). A triangular theory of love. *Psychological Review, 93*, 119–135.

Stinson, L., & Ickes, W. (1992). Empathetic accuracy in the interactions of male friends versus male strangers. *Journal of Personality and Social Psychology, 62*, 787–797.

Stipek, D., Weiner, B., & Li, K. (1989). Testing some attribution-emotion relations in the People's Republic of China. *Journal of Personality and Social Psychology, 56*, 109–116.

Stoddard, T., & Turiel, E. (1985). Children's concepts of cross-gender activities. *Child Development, 56*, 1241–1252.

Stogdill, R. (1948). Personal factors associated with leadership: A review of the literature. *Journal of Psychology, 25*, 35–71.

Stokes, J., & Levin, I. (1986). Gender differences in predicting loneliness from social network characteristics. *Journal of Personality and Social Psychology, 51*, 1069–1074.

Stone, I. F. (1988). *The trial of Socrates.* Boston: Little, Brown.

Stone, L. (1977). *The family, sex, and marriage in England, 1500–1800* (Abridged edition). New York: Harper & Row.

Stoner, J. A. F. (1961). *A comparison of individual and group decisions involving risk.* Unpublished master's thesis, M.I.T., Cambridge, MA.

Storms, M. D. (1973). Videotape and the attribution process: Reversing actors' and observers' points of view. *Journal of Personality and Social Psychology, 27,* 165–175.

Storms, M. D. (1981). A theory of erotic orientation development. *Psychological Review, 88,* 340–353.

Stouffer, S. A., Suchman, E. A., DeVinney, L. C., Star, S. A., & Williams, R. M. (1949). *The American soldier: Adjustment during Army life* (Vol. 1). Princeton, NJ: Princeton University Press.

Strack, F., Martin, L. L., & Stepper, S. (1988). Inhibiting and facilitating conditions of the human smile: A nonobtrusive test of the facial feedback hypothesis. *Journal of Personality and Social Psychology, 54,* 768–777.

Stroebe, W., Diehl, M., & Abakoumkin, G. (1992). The illusion of group effectivity. *Personality and Social Psychology Bulletin, 18,* 643–650.

Strube, M. J., & Barbour, L. S. (1983). The decision to leave an abusive relationship: Economic dependence and psychological commitment. *Journal of Marriage and the Family, 45,* 785–793.

Strube, M. J., & Barbour, L. S. (1984). Factors related to the decision to leave an abusive relationship. *Journal of Marriage and the Family, 46,* 837–844.

Strube, M. J., & Garcia, J. E. (1981). A meta-analytic investigation of Fiedler's contingency model of leadership effectiveness. *Psychological Bulletin, 90,* 307–321.

Sutton, S., & Hallett, R. (1989). Understanding seatbelt intentions and behavior: A decision making approach. *Journal of Applied Social Psychology, 19,* 1310–1325.

Swann, W. B., Jr., Pelham, B. W., & Krull, D. S. (1989). Agreeable fancy or disagreeable truth? Reconciling self-enhancement with self-verification. *Journal of Personality and Social Psychology, 57,* 782–791.

Szymanski, K., & Harkins, S. G. (1987). Social loafing and self-evaluation with a social standard. *Journal of Personality and Social Psychology, 53,* 891–897.

Tajfel, H. (1982). Social psychology of intergroup relations. *Annual Review of Psychology, 33,* 1–39.

Tajfel, H., Billig, M. G., Bundy, R. P., & Flament, C. (1971). Social categorization and intergroup behavior. *European Journal of Social Psychology, 1,* 149–178.

Tajfel, H., & Turner, J. (1979). An integrative theory of inter-group conflict. In W. G. Austin and S. Worchel (Eds.), *The social psychology of intergroup relations.* Monterey, CA: Brooks/Cole.

Tanford, S., & Penrod, S. (1984). Social influence models: A formal interpretation of research on minority and majority influence processes. *Psychological Bulletin, 95,* 189–225.

Tanford, S., & Penrod, S. (1986). Jury deliberations: Discussion content and influence processes in jury decision making. *Journal of Applied Social Psychology, 16,* 322–347.

Taylor, D. M., & Jaggi, V. (1974). Ethnocentrism and causal attribution in a South Indian context. *Journal of Cross Cultural Psychology, 5,* 162–171.

Taylor, S. E., & Fiske, S. T. (1975). Point of view and perceptions of causality. *Journal of Personality and Social Psychology, 32,* 439–445.

Taylor, S. E., & Koivumaki, J. H. (1976). The perception of self and others: Acquaintanceship, affect, and actor-observer differences. *Journal of Personality and Social Psychology, 33,* 403–408.

Taylor, S. E., & Mettee, D. (1971). When similarity breeds contempt. *Journal of Personality and Social Psychology, 20,* 75–81.

Tedeschi, J. T., Schlenker, B. R., & Bonoma, T. V. (1981). Cognitive dissonance: Private rationalization or public spectacle? *American Psychologist, 26,* 685–695.

Teger, A., & Pruitt, D. G. (1967). Components of group risk taking. *Journal of Experimental Social Psychology, 3,* 189–205.

Tesser, A. (1978). Self-generated attitude change. In L. Berkowitz (Ed.), *Advances in experimental social psychology* (Vol. 11, pp. 289–338). New York: Academic Press.

Tesser, A. (1990). Smith and Ellsworth's appraisal model of emotion: A replication, extension, and test. *Personality and Social Psychology Bulletin, 16,* 210–223.

Tesser, A., & Conlee, M. C. (1975). Some effects of time and thought on attitude polarization. *Journal of Personality and Social Psychology, 31,* 262–270.

Tesser, A., & Leone, C. (1977). Cognitive schemas and thought as determinants of attitude change. *Journal of Experimental Social Psychology, 13,* 340–356.

Tesser, A., & Shaffer, D. R. (1990). Attitudes and attitude change. *Annual Review of Psychology, 41,* 479–523.

Tesser, A., & Smith, J. (1980). Some effects of task relevance and friendship on helping: You don't always help the one you like. *Journal of Experimental Social Psychology, 16,* 582–590.

Tetlock, P. E. (1979). Identifying victims of groupthink from public statements of decision makers. *Journal of Personality and Social Psychology, 37,* 1314–1324.

Tetlock, P. E., Peterson, R. S., McGuire, C., Chang, S.-J., & Feld, P. (1992). Assessing political group dynamics: A test of the groupthink model. *Journal of Personality and Social Psychology, 63,* 403–425.

Tharp, R. G. (1963). Psychological patterning in marriage. *Psychological Bulletin, 60,* 97–117.

Thibaut, J., & Kelley, H. (1959). *The social psychology of groups.* New York: Wiley.

Thibodeau, R., & Aronson, E. (1992). Taking a closer look: Reasserting the role of the self-concept in dissonance theory. *Personality and Social Psychology Bulletin, 18,* 591–602.

Thoma, S. J. (1986). Estimating gender differences in the comprehension and preference of moral issues. *Developmental Review, 6,* 165–180.

Thomas, M. H., Horton, R. W., Lippincott, E. C., & Drabman, R. S. (1977). Desensitization to portrayals of real-life aggression as a function of exposure to television violence. *Journal of Personality and Social Psychology, 35,* 450–458.

Thompson, E., & Colella, U. (1992). Cohabitation and marital stability: Quality or commitment? *Journal of Marriage and the Family, 54,* 259–267.

Thompson, L. (1990). An examination of naive and experienced negotiators. *Journal of Personality and Social Psychology, 59,* 82–90.

Thompson, W. C., Cowan, C. L., & Rosenhan, D. L. (1980). Focus of attention mediates the impact of negative affect on altruism. *Journal of Personality and Social Psychology, 38,* 291–300.

Tice, D. M. (1991). Esteem protection or enhancement? Self-handicapping motives and attributions differ by trait self-esteem. *Journal of Personality and Social Psychology, 60,* 711–725.

Tice, D. M., & Baumeister, R. F. (1985). Masculinity inhibits helping in emergencies: Personality does predict the bystander effect. *Journal of Personality and Social Psychology, 49,* 420–428.

Tinbergen, N. (1953). Fighting and threat in animals. *New Biology, 14,* 9–24.

Tisak, M. S., & Turiel, E. (1988). Variations in seriousness of transgressions and children's moral and conventional concepts. *Developmental Psychology, 24,* 352–357.

Tomkins, S. S. (1981). The role of facial response in the experience of emotion: A reply to Tourangeau and Ellsworth. *Journal of Personality and Social Psychology, 40,* 355–357.

Touhey, J. C. (1975). Interpersonal congruency, attitude similarity, and interpersonal attraction. *Journal of Research in Personality, 9,* 66–73.

Tourangeau, R., & Ellsworth, P. C. (1979). The role of facial response in the experience of emotion. *Journal of Personality and Social Psychology, 37,* 1519–1531.

Townsend, J. M., & Levy, G. D. (1990). Effects of potential partners' physical attractiveness and socioeconomic status on sexuality and partner selection. *Archives of Sexual Behavior, 19,* 149–164.

Trent, K., & South, S. J. (1989). Structural determinants of the divorce rate: A cross-societal analysis. *Journal of Marriage and the Family, 51,* 391–404.

Triandis, H. C., Bontempo, R., Villareal, M. J., Asai, M., & Lucca, N. (1988). Individualism and collectivism: Cross-cultural perspectives on self-ingroup relationships. *Journal of Personality and Social Psychology, 54,* 323–338.

Trivers, R. L. (1971). The evolution of reciprocal altruism. *Quarterly Review of Biology, 46,* 35–57.

Trope, Y., & Mackie, D. M. (1987). Sensitivity to alternatives in social hypothesis-testing. *Journal of Experimental Social Psychology, 23,* 445–459.

Tucker, J. A., Vuchinich, R. E., & Sobell, M. B. (1981). Alcohol consumption as a self-handicapping strategy. *Journal of Abnormal Psychology, 90,* 220–230.

Tuddenham, R. D., & McBride, P. D. (1959). The yielding experiment from the subject's point of view. *Journal of Personality, 27,* 259–271.

Turiel, E. (1977). Distinct conceptual and developmental domains: Social convention and morality. In C. B. Keasey, (Ed.), *Nebraska symposium on motivation* (Vol. 25, pp. 77–116). Lincoln: University of Nebraska Press.

Turiel, E., Edwards, C. P., & Kohlberg, L. (1978). Moral development in Turkish children, adolescents, and young adults. *Journal of Cross Cultural Psychology, 9,* 75–86.

Tyler, T. R. (1989). The psychology of procedural justice: A test of the group-value model. *Journal of Personality and Social Psychology, 57,* 830–838.

Tyler, T. R., & Griffin, E. (1991). The influence of decision makers' goals on their concerns about procedural justice. *Journal of Applied Social Psychology, 21,* 1629–1658.

Tyler, T. R., & Schuller, R. A. (1991). Aging and attitude change. *Journal of Personality and Social Psychology, 61,* 689–697.

Uchino, B. N., Kiecolt-Glaser, J. K., & Cacioppo, J. T. (1992). Age-related changes in cardiovascular response as a function of a chronic stressor and social support. *Journal of Personality and Social Psychology, 63,* 839–846.

United States Commission on obscenity and pornography. (nd). *Technical Report* (Vol. VI). Washington, DC: United States Government Printing Office.

Vaillant, C. O., & Vaillant, G. E. (1993). Is the U-curve of marital satisfaction an illusion? A forty-year study of marriage. *Journal of Marriage and the Family, 55,* 230–239.

Vallacher, R. R., & Solodky, M. (1979). Objective self-awareness, standards of evaluation and moral behavior. *Journal of Experimental Social Psychology, 15,* 254–262.

Van Hoof, J. A. R. A. M. (1972). A comparative approach to the phylogeny of laughter and smiling. In R. Hinde (Ed.), *Non-verbal communication.* Cambridge, MA: Cambridge University Press.

Van Ypern, N. W., & Buunk, B. P. (1990). A longitudinal study of equity and satisfaction in intimate relationships. *European Journal of Social Psychology, 20,* 287–309.

Vera, H., Berardo, D. H., & Berardo, F. M. (1985). Age

heterogamy in marriage. *Journal of Marriage and the Family, 47,* 553–566.

Vinacke, W. E., & Arkoff, A. (1957). An experimental study of coalitions in the triad. *American Sociological Review, 22,* 406–414.

Vinokur, A., & Burnstein, E. (1978). Depolarization of attitudes in groups. *Journal of Personality and Social Psychology, 36,* 872–885.

Von Neumann, J., & Morgenstern, O. (1944). *Theory of games and economic behavior.* Princeton: Princeton University Press.

Walker, L. J. (1984). Sex differences in the development of moral reasoning: A critical review. *Child Development, 55,* 677–691.

Walker, L., LaTour, S., Lind, E. A., & Thibaut, J. (1974). Reactions of participants and observers to modes of adjudication. *Journal of Applied Social Psychology, 4,* 295–310.

Wall, J. A., Jr. (1976). Effect of sex and opposing representative's bargaining orientation on intergroup bargaining. *Journal of Personality and Social Psychology, 33,* 55–61.

Wallach, M. A., & Wing, C. W., Jr. (1968). Is risk a value? *Journal of Personality and Social Psychology, 9,* 101–106.

Walster, E., Aronson, V., Abrams, D., & Rottman, L. (1966). Importance of physical attractiveness in dating behavior. *Journal of Personality and Social Psychology, 4,* 508–516.

Walster, E., Berscheid, E., & Walster, G. W. (1973). New directions in equity research. *Journal of Personality and Social Psychology, 25,* 151–176.

Walster, E., Walster, G. W., & Berscheid, E. (1978). *Equity: Theory and research.* Boston: Allyn & Bacon.

Walster, E., Walster, G. W., & Traupmann, J. (1978). Equity and premarital sex. *Journal of Personality and Social Psychology, 36,* 82–92.

Wasman, M., & Flynn, J. P. (1962). Directed attack elicited from the hypothalmus. *Archives of Neurology, 6,* 220–227.

Wason, P. C., & Johnson-Laird, P. N. (1972). *Psychology of reasoning.* Cambridge, MA: Harvard University Press.

Weber, M. (1921/1946). The sociology of charismatic authority. In H. H. Gerth & C. W. Mills (Eds.), *From Max Weber: Essays in sociology.* New York: Oxford University Press.

Weber, R., & Crocker, J. (1983). Cognitive processes in the revision of stereotypic beliefs. *Journal of Personality and Social Psychology, 45,* 961–977.

Weiss, D. S., & Mendelsohn, G. A. (1986). An empirical demonstration of the implausibility of the semantic similarity explanation of how trait ratings are made and what they mean. *Journal of Personality and Social Psychology, 50,* 595–601.

Weiss, R. F., Boyer, J. L., Lombardo, J. P., & Stitch, M. H. (1973). Altruistic drive and altruistic reinforcement. *Journal of Personality and Social Psychology, 25,* 390–400.

Weisskopf-Joelson, E., & Elisio, T. S. (1961). An experimental study of the effectiveness of brainstorming. *Journal of Applied Psychology, 45,* 45–49.

Weisz, J. R., Rothbaum, F. M., & Blackburn, T. C. (1984). Standing out and standing in: The psychology of control in America and Japan. *American Psychologist, 39,* 955–969.

Weitz, S. (1972). Attitude, voice, and behavior: A repressed affect model of interracial interaction. *Journal of Personality and Social Psychology, 24,* 14–21.

Werner, C. M., Brown, B. B., & Damron, G. (1981). Territorial marking in a game arcade. *Journal of Personality and Social Psychology, 41,* 1094–1104.

Weston, D. R., & Turiel, E. (1980). Act-rule relations: Children's concepts of social rules. *Developmental Psychology, 16,* 417–424.

Wetherell, M., Stiven, H., & Potter, J. (1987). Unequal egalitarianism: A preliminary study of discourses concerning gender and employment opportunities. *British Journal of Social Psychology, 26,* 59–71.

Whitam, F. L., Diamond, M., & Martin, J. (1993). Homosexual orientation in twins: A report on sixty-one pairs and three triplet sets. *Archives of Sexual Behavior, 22,* 187–206.

White, G. L., Fishbein, S., & Rutstein, J. (1981). Passionate love and the misattribution of arousal. *Journal of Personality and Social Psychology, 41,* 56–62.

White, L. K. (1983). Determinants of spousal interaction: Marital structure or marital happiness? *Journal of Marriage and the Family, 45,* 511–520.

Whitley, B. E., Jr. (1983). Sex role orientation and self-esteem: A critical meta-analytic review. *Journal of Personality and Social Psychology, 44,* 765–778.

Wicker, A. W. (1969). Attitudes versus actions: The relationship of verbal and overt behavioral responses to attitude objects. *Journal of Social Issues, 25,* 41–78.

Wicklund, R. A. (1975a). Objective self-awareness. In L. Berkowitz (Ed.), *Advances in experimental social psychology* (Vol. 8, pp. 233–275). New York: Academic Press.

Wicklund, R. A. (1975b). Discrepancy reduction or attempted distraction? A reply to Liebling, Seiler, and Shaver. *Journal of Experimental Social Psychology, 11,* 78–81.

Widom, C. S. (1989). Does violence beget violence? A critical examination of the literature. *Psychological Bulletin, 106,* 3–28.

Widom, C. S. (1991). A tail on an untold tale: Response to "Biological and genetic contributors to violence—Widom's untold tale". *Psychological Bulletin, 109,* 130–132.

Wierzbicka, A. (1986). Human emotions: Universal or culture-specific? *American Anthropologist, 88,* 584–594.

Wilder, D. A. (1984). Predictions of belief homogeneity and similarity following social categorization. *British Journal of Social Psychology, 23*, 323–333.

Williams, K., Harkins, S., & Latané, B. (1981). Identifiability as a deterrent to social loafing: Two cheering experiments. *Journal of Personality and Social Psychology, 40*, 303–311.

Williams, J. G., & Solano, C. H. (1983). The social reality of feeling lonely: Friendship and reciprocation. *Journal of Personality and Social Psychology, 9*, 237–242.

Williams, K. D., & Karau, S. J. (1991). Social loafing and social compensation: The effects of expectations of coworker performance. *Journal of Personality and Social Psychology, 61*, 570–581.

Willis, R. H., & Joseph, M. L. (1959). Bargaining behavior. I. "Prominence" as a predictor of the outcome of games of agreement. *Journal of Conflict Resolution, 3*, 102–113.

Wilson, D. W., & Connerstein, E. (1977). Guilty or not guilty? A look at the simulated jury paradigm. *Journal of Applied Social Psychology, 7*, 175–190.

Wilson, T. D., Dunn, D. S., Bybee, J. A., Hyman, D. B., & Rotondo, J. A. (1984). Effects of analyzing reasons on attitude-behavior consistency. *Journal of Personality and Social Psychology, 47*, 5–16.

Wilson, T. D., Dunn, D. S., Kraft, D., & Lisle, D. J. (1989). Introspection, attitude change, and attitude-behavior consistency: The disruptive effect of explaining why we feel the way we do. In L. Berkowitz (Ed.), *Advances in experimental social psychology* (Vol. 22, pp. 287–343). New York: Academic Press.

Wilson, T. D., Kraft, D., & Dunn, D. S. (1989). The disruptive effects of explaining attitudes: The moderating effect of knowledge about the attitude object. *Journal of Applied Social Psychology, 25*, 379–400.

Wilson, T. D., Lisle, D. J., Schooler, J. W., Hodges, S. D., Klaaren, K. J., & LaFleur, S. J. (1993). Introspecting about reasons can reduce post-choice satisfaction. *Personality and Social Psychology Bulletin, 19*, 331–339.

Wilson, T. D., & Schooler, J. W. (1991). Thinking too much: Introspection can reduce the quality of preferences and decisions. *Journal of Personality and Social Psychology, 60*, 181–192.

Winch, R. F. (1955). The theory of complementary needs in mate selection: A test of one kind of complementariness. *American Sociological Review, 20*, 52–56.

Winch, R. F., Ktanes, T., & Ktanes, V. (1955). Empirical elaboration of the theory of complementary needs in mate selection. *Journal of Abnormal and Social Psychology, 51*, 508–513.

Winter, L., & Uleman, J. S. (1984). When are social judgments made? Evidence for the spontaneousness of trait inferences. *Journal of Personality and Social Psychology, 47*, 237–252.

Winter, L., Uleman, J. S., & Cunniff, C. (1985). How automatic are social judgments? *Journal of Personality and Social Psychology, 49*, 904–917.

Wishner, J. (1960). Reanalysis of "impressions of personality." *Psychological Review, 67*, 96–112.

Wispe, L. (1986). The distinction between sympathy and empathy: To call forth a concept, a word is needed. *Journal of Personality and Social Psychology, 50*, 314–321.

Witte, E. H. (1990). Social influence: A discussion and integration of recent models into a general group situation theory. *European Journal of Social Psychology, 20*, 3–27.

Wittenberg, M. T., & Reis, H. T. (1986). Loneliness, social skills, and social perception. *Personality and Social Psychology Bulletin, 12*, 121–130.

Wittenbraker, J., Gibbs, B. L., & Kahle, L. R. (1983). Seat belt attitudes, habits, and behaviors: An adaptive amendment to the Fishbein model. *Journal of Applied Social Psychology, 13*, 406–421.

Wolchik, S. A., Braver, S. L., & Jensen, K. (1985). Volunteer bias in erotica research: Effects of intrusiveness of measure and sexual background. *Archives of Sexual Behavior, 14*, 93–107.

Wolchik, S. A., Sprecher, S. L., & Lisi, I. S. (1983). Volunteer bias in research employing vaginal measures of sexual arousal. *Archives of Sexual Behavior, 12*, 399–408.

Wolf, S., & Latané, B. (1983). Majority and minority influence on restaurant preferences. *Journal of Personality and Social Psychology, 45*, 282–292.

Wolfe, T. (1975). *The painted word.* New York: Bantam.

Wolff, R. P. (1974). *The anatomy of reason: A commentary on Kant's groundwork of the metaphysics or morals.* New York: Harper.

Worthy, M., Gary, A. L., & Kahn, G. M. (1969). Self-disclosure as an exchange process. *Journal of Personality and Social Psychology, 13*, 59–63.

Wood, W., Wong, F., Chachere, J. (1991). Effects of media violence on viewers' aggression in unconstrained social interaction. *Psychological Bulletin. 109*, 371–383.

Wright, E. F., Luus, C. A. E., & Christie, S. D. (1990). Does group discussion facilitate the use of consensus information in making causal attribution? *Journal of Personality and Social Psychology, 59*, 251–269.

Wright, E. F., & Wells, G. L. (1988). Is the attitude-attribution paradigm suitable for investigating the dispositional bias? *Personality and Social Psychology Bulletin, 14*, 183–190.

Wright, P. H. (1969). A model and a technique for studies of friendship. *Journal of Experimental Social Psychology, 5*, 295–309.

Wrightsman, L. S., Jr. (1960). Effects of waiting with others on changes in level of felt anxiety. *Journal of Abnormal and Social Psychology, 61*, 216–222.

Wrightsman, L. S., Jr. (1966). Personality and attitudinal correlates of trusting and trustworthy behaviors in a two-person game. *Journal of Personality and Social Psychology, 4*, 328–332.

Wyer, R. S., Jr., & Budesheim, T. L. (1987). Person memory and judgments: The impact of information one is told to disregard. *Journal of Personality and Social Psychology, 53*, 14–29.

Yamagishi, T. (1986). The provision of a sanctioning system as a public good. *Journal of Personality and Social Psychology, 51*, 110–116.

Yardley, H. O. (1957). *The education of a poker player*. New York: Simon and Schuster.

Yates, S. (1992). Lay attributions about distress after a natural disaster. *Personality and Social Psychology Bulletin, 18*, 217–222.

Yogev, S. (1981). Do professional women have egalitarian marital relationships? *Journal of Marriage and the Family, 43*, 865–871.

Yogev, S., & Brett, J. (1985). Perceptions of the division of housework and child care and marital satisfaction. *Journal of Marriage and the Family, 47*, 609–618.

Yukl, G. (1974a). The effects of the opponent's initial offer, concession magnitude, and concession frequency on bargaining behavior. *Journal of Personality and Social Psychology, 30*, 323–335.

Yukl, G. A. (1974b). The effects of situational variables and opponent concessions on a bargainer's perception, aspiration, and concessions. *Journal of Personality and Social Psychology, 29*, 227–236.

Yukl, G. A., Malone, M. P., Hayslip, B., & Pamin, T. (1978). The effects of time pressure and issue settlement order on integrative bargaining. *Sociometry, 39*, 277–281.

Zaccaro, S. J. (1984). Social loafing: The role of task attractiveness. *Personality and Social Psychology Bulletin, 10*, 99–106.

Zaccaro, S. J., Foti, R. J., & Kenny, D. A. (1991). Self-monitoring and trait-based variance in leadership: An investigation of leadership flexibility across multiple group situations. *Journal of Applied Psychology, 76*, 308–315.

Zahn-Waxler, C., Radke-Yarrow, M., & King, R. A. (1979). Child rearing and children's prosocial inclinations toward victims of distress. *Child Development, 50*, 319–330.

Zajonc, R. B. (1965). Social facilitation. *Science, 149*, 269–274.

Zajonc, R. B. (1968). Attitudinal effects of mere exposure. *Journal of Personality and Social Psychology Monograph Supplement, 9* (2, Pt. 2), 1–27.

Zajonc, R. B. (1980). Feeling and thinking: Preferences need no inferences. *American Psychologist, 35*, 151–175.

Zajonc, R. B., Adelmann, P. K., Murphy, S. T., & Nie-

denthal, P. N. (1987). Convergences in physical appearances of spouses. *Motivation and Emotion, 11*, 335–346.

Zajonc, R. B., Heingartner, A., & Herman, E. M. (1969). Social enhancement and impairment of performance in the cockroach. *Journal of Personality and Social Psychology, 13*, 83–92.

Zajonc, R. B., & Sales, S. M. (1966). Social facilitation of dominant and subordinate responses. *Journal of Experimental Social Psychology, 2*, 160–168.

Zajonc, R. B., Shaver, P., Tavris, C., & Van Kreveld, D. (1972). Exposure, satiation, and stimulus discriminability. *Journal of Personality and Social Psychology, 21*, 270–280.

Zammichieli, M. E., Gilroy, F. D., & Sherman, M F. (1988). Relation between sex-role orientation and marital satisfaction. *Personality and Social Psychology Bulletin, 14*, 747–754.

Zillmann, D. (1971). Excitation transfer in communication-mediated aggressive behavior. *Journal of Experimental Social Psychology, 7*, 419–434.

Zillmann, D., Bryant, J., & Carveth, R. A. (1981). The effect of erotica featuring sadomasochism and bestiality on motivated intermale aggression. *Personality and Social Psychology Bulletin, 7*, 153–159.

Zillmann, D., & Cantor, J. R. (1976). Effect of timing of information about mitigating circumstances on emotional responses to provocation and retaliatory behavior. *Journal of Experimental Social Psychology, 12*, 38–55.

Zillmann, D., Johnson, R. C., & Day, K. D. (1974). Attribution of apparent arousal and proficiency of recovery from sympathetic activation affecting excitation transfer to aggressive behavior. *Journal of Experimental Social Psychology, 10*, 503–515.

Zimbardo, P. G. (1969). The human choice: Individuation, reason, and order versus deindividuation, impulse, and chaos. In W. J. Arnold & D. Levine (Eds.), *Nebraska Symposium on Motivation* (Vol. 17, pp. 237–307). Lincoln, NE: University of Nebraska Press.

Zimbardo, P. (1971). *The Stanford prison experiment*, script of the slide show.

Zimbardo, P. G., & Ebbesen, E. B. (1970). Experimental modification of the relationship between effort, attitude, and behavior. *Journal of Personality and Social Psychology, 16*, 207–213.

Zimbardo, P., & Formica, R. (1963). Emotional comparisons and self-esteem as determinants of affiliation. *Journal of Personality, 31*, 141–162.

Zimbardo, P. G., Snyder, M., Thomas, J., Gold, A., & Gurwitz, S. (1970). Modifying the impact of persuasive communications with external distraction. *Journal of Personality and Social Psychology, 16*, 669–680.

Zuckerman, M. (1978). Actions and occurrences in Kelley's cube. *Journal of Personality and Social Psychology, 36*, 647–656.

Zuckerman, M., Amidon, M. D., Bishop, S. E., & Pomerantz, S. D. (1982). Face and tone of voice in the communication of deception. *Journal of Personality and Social Psychology, 43,* 347–357.

Zuckerman, M., DePaulo, B. M., & Rosenthal, R. (1981). Verbal and nonverbal communication of deception. In L. Berkowitz (Ed.), *Advances in experimental social psychology,* (Vol. 14, pp. 1–59). New York: Academic Press.

Zuckerman, M., & Feldman, L. S. (1984). Actions and occurrences in attribution theory. *Journal of Personality and Social Psychology, 46,* 541–550.

Zukier, H., & Pepitone, A. (1984). Social roles and strategies in prediction: Some determinants of the use of base-rate information. *Journal of Personality and Social Psychology, 47,* 349–360.

Acknowledgments and Copyright

Press. Copyright 1978 by PWS-Kent Publishing Co. **13.4** From Zillman, D. (1971). Excitation transfer in communication-mediated aggressive behavior. *Journal of Experimental social Psychology, 7,* 419–434. Reproduced by permission of Academic Press. **14.1, 14.2, 14.4** Reprinted from *Social pressures in informal groups* by Leon Festinger, Stanley Schachter, and Kurt Back with the permission of Stanford University Press. © 1950 by Leon Festinger, Stanley Schachter, and Kurt Back. **14.5** From Zajonc, R.B. (1968). Attitudinal effects of mere exposure. *Journal of Personality and Social Psychology Monograph Supplement, 9* (2, Pt. 2), 1–27. Copyright 1968 by the American Psychological Association. Reprinted by permission. **14.8** Tesser, A., Campbell, J., & Smith, M. (1984). Friendship choice and performance: Self-evaluation maintenance in children. *Journal of Personality and Social Psychology, 46,* 561–574. Copyright 1984 by the American Psychological Association. Reprinted by permission. **15.5** From Clark, M.S. (1984). Record keeping in two types of relationships. *Journal of Personality and Social Psychology, 47,* 549–557. Copyright 1984 by the American Psychological Association. Reprinted by permission. **16.4** From Nel, E., Helmreich, R., & Aronson, E. (1969). Opinion change in the advocate as a function of the persuasibility of his audience: A clarification of the meaning of dissonance. *Journal of Personality and Social Psychology, 12,* 117–124. Copyright 1969 by the American Psychological Association. Reprinted by permission. **16.11** From Tesser, A., & Leone, C. (1972). Cognitive schemas and thought as determinants of attitude change. *Journal of Experimental Social Psychology, 13,* 340–356. Reproduced by permission of Academic Press. **16.12** From Hovland, C.I., & Weiss, W. (1951). The influence of source credibility on communication effectiveness. *Public Opinion Quarterly, 15,* 635–650. Reproduced by permission of Elsevier North Holland, Inc. **16.15** From Petty, R.E., Hardkins, S.G., & Williams, K.D. (1980). The effects of group diffusion of cognitive effort on attitudes: An information-processing view. *Journal of Personality and Social Psychology, 38,* 81–92. Copyright 1980 by the American Psychological Association. Reproduced by permission.

TABLES

2.1 From Pruitt, D.G. (1971). Choice shifts in group discussion: An introductory review. *Journal of Personality and Social Psychology, 20,* 339–360. Originally published in Kogan, N., and Wallach, M.A., "Risktaking as a function of the situation, the person, and the group," in G. Mandler, P. Mussen, N. Kogan, and M.A. Wallach (Eds.), *New directions in psychology III.* New York: Holt, Rinehart, & Winston, 1967. Adapted by permission of Holt, Rinehart, & Winston. **3.1** Adapted from Steiner, I.D. (1966). Models for inferring relationships between group size and potential group productivity. *Behavioral Science, 11,* 273–283. Adapted by permission of the University of California Press. **3.3** Based on Laughlin, P.R. (1988). Collective induction: Group performance, social combination processes, and mutual majority and minority influence. *Journal of Personality and Social Psychology, 54,* 254–267. Copyright 1988 by the American Psychological Association. Adapted by permission. **4.1, 4.2, 4.3** Adorno, T.W., Frenkel-Brunswick, E., Levinson, D.J., & Sanford, R.N. (1950). *The authoritarian personality.* New York: Harper & Row. Reproduced by permission of HarperCollins Publishers. **6.1** Jones, E.E., & Pittman, T.S. (1982). Toward a general theory of strategic self-presentation. In J. Suls (Ed.), *Psychological perspectives on the self* (vol. 1). Hillsdale, NJ: Lawrence Erlbaum Associates. Reproduced by permission of Lawrence Erlbaum Associates, Inc. **7.4** Ekman, P. (1973). Cross-cultural studies of facial expression. In P. Ekman (Ed.), *Darwin and facial expression.* New York: Academic Press. Reproduced by permission of Academic Press and the author. **13.1** From Kanin, E.J. (1985). Date rapists: Differential sexual socialization and relative deprivation. *Archives of Sexual Behavior, 14,* 219–231. Reproduced by permission of Plenum Publishing Corporation. **14.1** Kulik, J.A., & Mahler, H.I.M. (1989). Stress and affiliation in a hospital setting: Preoperative roommate preferences. *Personality and Social Psychology Bulletin, 15,* 183–193. Reproduced by permission of Sage Publications, Inc. **15.1** Russell, D., Peplau, L.A., & Cutrona, C.E. (1980). The revised UCLA loneliness scale: Concurrent and discriminant validity evidence. *Journal of Personality and Social Psychology, 39,* 472–480. Copyright 1980 by the American Psychological Association. Reprinted by permission. **15.4** Burgess, E.W. & Wallin, P. (1953). *Engagement and marriage.* Philadelphia: Lippincott. Reproduced by permission of HarperCollins Publishers. **15.5** Levinger, G. (1965). Marital cohesiveness and dissolution: An integrative review. *Journal of Marriage and the Family, 27,* 19–28. Reprinted by permission of the National Council on Family Relations, Minneapolis, MN.

NAME INDEX

Berscheid, Ellen, 219, 321n, 460, 468, 469, 490, 496, 508n
Bersoff, D. M., 278, 279
Betancourt, H., 303, 304, 422
Bettencourt, B. A., 109
Betz, B., 360
Beyer, S., 402
Bierbrauer, G., 28
Biernat, M. R., 136
Billig, M. G., 110
Billy, J.O.G., 398
Birchler, G. R., 514
Bishop, G. D., 39
Blackburn, T. C., 262
Blair, I., 422
Blair, S. L., 513
Blalock, S. J., 586
Blank, A., 599
Blank, S., 515
Blasovich, J., 37
Blaylock, B., 505
Bless, H., 573
Bloom, B. L., 518
Blumenthal, R., 100
Blumstein, P., 514
Bodenhausen, G. V., 516
Bohner, G., 573
Bond, Charles F., Jr., 65
Bond, M. H., 264, 265, 334
Bonoma, T. V., 555
Booth, A., 519
Borden, R. J., 457
Borgatta, E. F., 70
Borgida, E., 134
Borkenau, P., 149
Bornstein, R. F., 452
Bossard, J., 450
Bouchard, T. J., 10
Bourne, E. J., 263
Bowen, G. L., 510
Bowlby, John, 485–486
Bowman, 588
Boyer, J. L., 299
Brabeck, M., 278
Bradbury, T. N., 517
Braly, K. W., 124
Bramel, D., 23
Brandt, J. R., 301
Brauer, M., 593
Braver, S. L., 296
Breaugh, J. A., 354
Brekke, N., 134
Brenner, A., 345
Brenner, M., 85
Brewer, Marilynn B., 109, 368, 369
Briggs, S. R., 221–22
Britt, T. W., 196, 214
Britton, S. D., 354
Brock, Timothy C., 554, 568
Brockner, J., 334

Brody, C. L., 26
Bromley, S., 122
Brothen, T., 460
Broussard, D. B., 378
Brown, B. R., 197
Brown, R., 107, 174, 423
Brown, Roger, 35–36, 37–38, 39
Brown, Y., 32
Browne, E. C., 371
Brownson, F. H., 415
Bruun, S. E., 73, 75
Bryan, J. H., 306
Bryant, J., 428
Buchanan, D. D., 494
Buck, M. L., 172
Buck, Ross W., 172, 248–49, 472, 516
Budd, R. J., 584, 587
Budesheim, T. L., 189
Buehler, J. A., 450
Bugelski, R., 114
Buhrich, N., 400
Bumpass, L. L., 502
Bundy, McGeorge, 82
Bundy, R. P., 110
Burgess, Ernest, 503–504, 505n
Burks, N., 514
Burman, B., 506
Burnkrant, R. E., 574
Burnstein, Eugene, 37–38, 39
Burton, S., 586
Bush, George, 264, 595
Bush, L. K., 251
Buss, Alan H., 213, 214, 221, 419
Buss, David M., 386, 390, 391, 392, 393, 506
Butcher, J. N., 407
Buttram, R. T., 185
Buunk, B., 496
Bybee, J. A., 596
Byrne, B. M., 407
Byrne, Donn, 96, 428, 450, 455–56, 505
Bytheway, W. R., 506

Cachere, J. G., 437
Cacioppo, John T., 251, 478, 529, 568–569, 571–72, 584
Calder, B. J., 439
Caldwell, M. A., 481
Camacho, L. M., 12
Camino, L., 437
Campbell, B., 508n
Campbell, Donald, 128
Campbell, J., 457
Campbell, M. A., 330
Cannon, K. L., 510
Cannon, Walter, 227, 235–36, 243, 253
Cantor, J. R., 420n
Cantor, N., 182

Capon, M., 220
Caputo, C., 157, 177
Carillo, M. J., 351
Carli, L. L., 23
Carlsmith, J. Merrill, 309, 536–40, 543, 546–47
Carlson, Michael, 310, 424
Carment, D. W., 334
Carnelley, K. B., 488
Carnevale, Peter J. D., 351, 354
Carpenter, Sandra L., 127
Carroll, L., 385
Carter, Jimmy, 84
Carter, L. F., 70
Cartwright, D., 35
Carver, Charles S., 211, 214
Carveth, R. A., 428
Caspi, A., 505
Castro, Fidel, 81, 159–61, 164
Catalan, J., 347
Cate, R. M., 497
Chaiken, A. L., 337, 481
Chaiken, Shelly, 559, 566, 569–72, 584
Chamberlain, Neville, 84
Chang, S.-J., 84
Chanowitz, B., 599
Chapanis, A., 535
Chapanis, N. P., 535
Chapman, Jean, 125
Chapman, Loren, 125
Charny, H. W., 214
Chase, T., 540
Chassin, L., 168
Chau, D. W., 149
Check, J.V.P., 429, 431
Cheek, J. M., 221–22
Chelune, G. J., 479
Chemerinski, A., 316
Chen, H. C., 571
Chen, J.-M., 593
Cheney, Dorothy, 249–50
Cherlin, A., 502
Chertkoff, J. M., 345, 373
Cheung, T.-S., 264
Chiles, C., 30
Chin, I., 102
Christ, G. H., 394n
Christy, P., 467
Chrvala, C., 23
Chwalisz, K., 229
Cialdini, Robert B., 207–08, 300–301, 308, 309–10, 312, 337, 346–47, 457, 492, 553, 584
Clark, L. F., 130
Clark, Margaret, 498–99
Clark, R. D., III, 30, 33, 394
Cline, V. B., 436
Clinton, Bill, 528
Clore, G. L., 456

Eiser, J. R., 126
Ekman, Paul, 236, 237–38, 241–42, 243, 245, 248, 250, 251–52, 270
Elisio, T. S., 9
Elkin, R. A., 547, 549, 572n
Ellen, P. S., 587
Elliot, G. C., 330
Ellis, A. L., 88
Ellis, L., 400
Ellsworth, Phoebe C., 236, 243–44, 271
Embree, M. C., 421
Emerson, R. M., 80
Emmett, 588
Engle-Friedman, M., 396
Enzle, M. E., 551
Erickson, B. E., 332
Ernst, Don, 278
Esser, J. K., 346, 351
Evans, G. W., 478
Evans, M., 130

Fallon, A., 266
Fanzoi, S. L., 479
Farber, J., 122
Fazio, Russell H., 528, 548, 553, 591–92, 594–596
Feather, Norm T., 554–55
Feeney, J. A., 488
Fein, S., 163, 427
Feingold, Alan, 391–92, 466, 467, 468
Feld, P., 84
Feldman, L. S., 173
Fenigstein, Alan, 213, 214, 220, 436
Ferguson, T. J., 419
Ferraro, Geraldine, 595
Feshbach, S., 431, 565
Festinger, Leon, 35, 79, 439, 449, 532–33, 537–39, 540, 546–47, 566–67
Fiedler, Fred, 70
Fiedler, K., 126, 178n
Figley, C. R., 510
Fincham, F. D., 174, 517
Firestone, I. J., 472
Fischer, G. W., 127
Fishbaugh, L., 23
Fishbein, Martin, 577, 579–81, 583–84, 586, 587–89, 601
Fishbein, S., 493
Fisher, G. J., 429
Fisher, J. D., 315
Fisher, William, 586
Fiske, Alan, 499–500
Fiske, Susan T., 134, 186
Fitzgerald, V., 497
Flament, C., 110
Fleishman, J. A., 369
Fleming, A. S., 512
Fleming, J. H., 163
Fleming, R., 371

Floyd, J., 462
Flynn, John P., 413
Folger, R., 329
Folkes, V. S., 599
Follette, W. C., 515, 517
Fonda, Henry, 94
Forcey, B., 354
Ford, Clellan, 389–90, 463
Ford, C. M., 437
Formica, R., 472
Foti, R. J., 71
Fouraker, Lawrence, 344–45, 348
Fox, D., 85
Fox, J., 367
Franklin, Benjamin, 317
Franklin, M. N., 371
Franzoi, S. L., 214, 510
Fraser, S. C., 442
Fraser, Scott, 551–552
Fredricks, A. J., 585
Freedman, Jonathan L., 97, 437, 550, 551–552, 554
Freedman, S., 457
French, R. L., 70
Frenkel-Brunswick, Else, 115–18
Freud, Sigmund, 112–13, 115, 119, 412, 414, 418, 420, 477, 494, 544–45, 565, 587n
Frey, Dieter, 555
Frey, J., 428
Fridlund, Alan J., 247–48
Friedland, N., 332
Friedman, D. E., 429, 432
Friedman, H. S., 249
Friedrich-Cofer, L., 437
Friend, R., 23
Friesen, Wallace V., 236, 238, 248, 250, 251–52, 270
Frieze, I. H., 404
Frijda, Nico, 236n, 271
Froming, W. J., 214
Fromkin, H. L., 468
Fuhrman, R. W., 187
Fulero, S., 130
Fultz, J., 300, 301
Furnham, A., 220
Futoran, G. C., 136

Gabrenya, William K., Jr., 74, 221
Gaelick, L., 516
Gaertner, S. L., 121
Gaes, G. G., 547
Gagnon, John H., 378, 394
Gallagher, D., 229
Gallo, P. S., Jr., 363n
Gallois, C., 516
Gallupe, R. B., 11
Gamson, William A., 371
Gangestad, S., 219, 221
Ganza, B., 385

Garcia, J. E., 70
Garland, H., 197
Gary, A. L., 479
Gebhard, P. H., 393
Geen, R. G., 423, 436
Geer, J. H., 299, 378
Geertz, Clifford, 263
Geis, F. L., 409
Gelles, R. J., 521
Genovese, Kitty, 39–43
George, J. M., 308
Gerard, H. B., 25, 472, 535
Gerbner, G., 436
Gergen, K. J., 152, 256
Gerrard, M., 385, 586
Giacalone, R. A., 556
Gibbs, B. L., 584
Gifford, R. K., 126
Gilbert, A. N., 247
Gilbert, Daniel, 137
Gilbert, D. T., 205
Gilbert, G. M., 124
Gillen, B., 162
Gillig, P. M., 564
Gilligan, Carol, 277–78, 280, 286
Gilovich, T., 68, 166
Gilroy, F. D., 510
Ginsburg, G. P., 37
Glasgow, R. E., 586
Glass, David, 121–22
Gleicher, F., 566
Gleitman, Henry, 131n, 212, 234
Gleitman, Lila Ruth, 131n
Glenn, N. D., 510, 519
Glick, Paul, 136, 219, 518, 520
Glick, R. C., 522
Glucksberg, S., 506
Glueckauf, R. L., 478
Godfrey, D. K., 204
Goethals, G. R., 543
Goffman, Erving, 193–202, 215, 216, 222, 285, 419, 540
Gold, A., 568
Goldberg, L. R., 157
Goldman, R., 571
Goldman, W., 468
Good, D. C., 404
Goodstein, L., 429, 431–32
Goore, N., 68
Gordon, S. E., 187
Gore, Al, 175, 176
Gorkin, L., 544
Gorsuch, R. L., 587
Gottesman, I. I., 435
Gottman, John M., 515, 516
Gouldner, Alvin, 345, 480
Grady, W. R., 398
Graeven, D. B., 480
Graves, J., 72
Gray-Little, B., 514

John, king of England, 258–59
Johnson, B. T., 572n
Johnson, Lyndon B., 81
Johnson, M. P., 513
Johnson, R. C., 426
Johnson, T. E., 420n
Johnson, Virginia E., 393
Johnston, L., 133
Johnston, Robert, 246–47
Jones, C., 338
Jones, C. R., 184
Jones, Ned, 127, 150–52, 154–58,
    159–61, 162–63, 164, 165–66,
    175, 190, 202–06, 221, 223, 461,
    541
Jorgenson, D. O., 367
Joseph, J. M., 419
Joseph, L., 68
Joseph, M. L., 363n
Josephs, R. A., 407
Jourard, Sydney M., 479
Judd, C. M., 127, 138, 528, 593
Jurney, J., 368

Kahle, L. R., 584
Kahn, G. M., 479
Kahneman, Daniel D., 164, 165,
    328–29, 352–353
Kale, A. R., 452
Kalick, S. M., 467
Kallgren, C. A., 312
Kalven, Harry, Jr., 90–94
Kandinsky, Vasily, 109, 111
Kandzierski, D., 218
Kane, T. R., 419
Kaniasty, K., 478
Kanin, E. J., 429
Kanki, B., 32
Kant, Immanuel, 280n
Kaplan, K. J., 472
Karabenick, S. A., 316
Karasawa, K., 304
Karau, S. J., 128, 404
Kardes, F. R., 528, 595
Karlins, M., 124
Karylowski, J., 310
Katz, I., 506
Katz, Irwin, 121–22, 124
Katz, J., 579
Katz, L. B., 187
Katz, Solomon, 268, 269, 385
Kay, A., 369, 370
Kaye, D., 567
Keating, J. P., 301n
Keiffer, M., 348
Kelem, T. T., 442
Kelley, Harold, 78, 152–55, 160, 162,
    168–69, 170–71, 173, 179–80,
    181, 190, 371–72, 560
Kelly, E. Lowell, 521–22

Kelly, George Alexander, 184
Kelman, Herbert, 22, 560, 561
Kendler, K., 478
Kendzierski, D., 600
Kennedy, John F., 81–83, 103
Kenny, David A., 70–71
Kenrick, Douglas T., 308, 309, 310,
    337, 392, 396, 492, 493
Kephart, William, 508n
Kernis, M. H., 468
Kerr, N. L., 73, 75, 95
Kessler, R., 478
Kettlewell, H., 292
Kidder, L. H., 324
Kiecolt-Glaser, J. K., 478
Kilham, W., 49
Killen, M., 278
Kim, H. S., 251, 282
Kimball, M. M., 401
Kimbell, S., 162
King, G. W., 579
King, K., 380
King, Martin Luther, Jr., 99, 113, 123
King, R. A., 306
King, Rodney, 100
Kinsey, Alfred, 378, 380, 382, 393,
    395–96, 398
Kirschner, P., 567
Kitayama, Shinobu, 259, 263
Kjos, G. L., 451
Klaaren, K. J., 597
Kleck, R. E., 466
Klee, Paul, 109, 111
Klein, S. B., 187, 190
Klein, W. M., 168
Klempner, E., 86
Klepinger, D. H., 398
Klimoski, R. J., 354
Klonsky, B. G., 404
Knapp, J. R., 316
Knibbs, C. S., 172
Knight, Hazel, 85–86
Koestner, R., 407, 550, 551
Kohlberg, Lawrence, 275–78, 280,
    283–84, 285, 286
Koivumaki, J. H., 158
Kolditz, T. A., 206
Koller, S. H., 283
Komarovsky, M., 481
Komorita, Sam S., 345–46, 361, 368,
    372–373
Koneçni, V. J., 309, 451
Konovsky, M. A., 334
Koppetsch, C., 178n
Koralewski, M. K., 429
Koslowski, L. T., 207
Koss, M. P., 428, 429
Koutsourais, H., 360
Kowalski, R. M., 197
Kraft, D., 597

Kramer, R., 276, 277
Kramer, R. M., 362, 368, 369
Krauss, R., 506
Kraut, Robert, 246–47
Kravitz, D. A., 71
Krebs, D., 467
Krebs, J. R., 250n
Kremer, J. F., 420
Krishnan, L., 334
Krismer, K., 550
Krosnick, J. A., 170, 528
Krown, S., 394n
Krueger, J., 134
Kruglanski, Arie W., 80
Krugman, H. E., 452
Krull, D. S., 202
Kryter, K., 497
Ktanes, T., 506
Ktanes, V., 506
Ku, L. C., 586
Kuczynski, L., 306
Kudoh, T., 271
Kuipers, P., 236n
Kuleshnyk, I., 212
Kulik, J. A., 423, 473
Kumagai, A. K., 264
Kumagai, H. A., 264
Kumar, P. A., 183
Kunda, Z., 136, 168
Kurdek, L. A., 505, 510, 522
Kurtz, S., 332
Kurylo, M., 586
Kutner, B., 102

LaFleur, S. J., 597
Lage, E., 32
Lalonde, Richard N., 111
Lamm, H., 10
Landy, D., 468
Lane, D. W., 323
Lang, M., 512
Lange, Carl, 227, 235, 253, 254
Langer, Ellen, 598–99
LaPiere, Robert, 138, 576–77, 579,
    584, 598, 602
L'Armand, K., 430
Larrick, R. P., 427
Latané, Bibb, 40–45, 60, 61, 72–73,
    76, 311, 314
LaTour, S., 332
Laughlin, Patrick R., 39, 87–89
Laurie, R. S., 435
Lawler, E. J., 346
Lax, D. A., 355
Layton, B. D., 458
Leary, M. R., 196, 197, 205
Le Bon, Gustav, 439
Lee, G. R., 506
LeFan, J., 462
Legant, P., 157, 177

Mathewson, G. C., 535
Matsumoto, D., 271
Maucorps, P. H., 80
Mauro, R., 271
Mauss, Marcel, 263
Mayseless, O., 32, 316
Mead, George Herbert, 192, 194, 210, 582–583, 587
Meek, D., 95
Meeker, B. F., 330
Meeker, R. J., 359
Mehlman, R. C., 174
Melburg, V., 547
Melby, J. N., 588
Mendelsohn, G. A., 149
Mesquita, B., 271
Messenger, John, 376
Messick, D. M., 368, 369
Mettee, D., 459
Meyer, T. P., 436
Michaels, J. W., 325, 497
Michela, J. L., 170
Mickler, S. E., 317
Milgram, Stanley, 12, 45, 47–55, 58, 61, 96, 162, 195, 197, 210, 315, 589
Millar, M. G., 597
Miller, Arthur, 162, 163
Miller, D., 544
Miller, Dale T., 41–42, 163, 167, 168, 172, 337
Miller, Joan G., 278–80, 286
Miller, M. L., 219
Miller, N., 424, 466
Miller, Neal E., 113, 114, 310, 418
Miller, Norman, 109
Miller, R. S., 196
Miller-Herringer, T., 249
Millman, L., 208
Mills, J., 472
Mills, Judson, 498–99, 533–35, 537, 540, 543
Mills, T. M., 80
Milne, A. B., 304
Mims, V., 550, 551
Minas, J. S., 359
Mintz, D. M., 472
Mischel, W., 182, 185
Mishal, M., 163
Mitchell, Herman, 96
Modigliani, André, 194–95, 196
Molander, P., 362
Mondale, Walter, 595
Money, J., 400, 415
Monson, T. C., 158, 177, 217
Moore, B., 308
Moore, D. J., 571
Moore, S., 435
Moran, Gary, 96–97
Moreland, R. L., 452

Morgan, B. S., 451
Morgan, M., 588
Morgenstern, Oskar, 356
Moriarty, T., 313
Morokoff, P. J., 395
Morrison, D. M., 586
Moscovici, Serge, 31–32, 39, 61
Mosher, D. C., 395
Mowrer, O. H., 418
Moyer, K. E., 414, 416
Muehlenhard, C. L., 429, 432
Mueller, C. W., 426n
Mullen, B., 168
Muller, M. M., 161
Mullis, J.-P., 566
Mummendey, A., 112
Muren, S. K., 428
Murphy, G. K., 137
Murphy, M. M., 249
Murphy, S. T., 505n
Murstein, B. I., 467, 506
Musante, L., 332
Myers, D. G., 39
Myrdal, Gunnar, 119, 122

Nadler, A., 315, 316
Naffrechoux, M., 32
Naficy, A., 543
Napoleon I, emperor of France, 77
Neale, M. A., 350, 352, 400
Neale, M. C., 478
Nel, E., 542
Nelson, C., 136
Nelson, D., 456
Nelson, T. E., 133
Nemeroff, C., 208
Nemeth, Charlan, 30, 32, 95
Netemeyer, R. G., 586
Neuberg, S. L., 134
Newcomb, Theodore, 439, 454–55
Newman, E., 409
Newman, L. S., 185
Newton, Isaac, 281
Nezlek, J., 468
Nicholson, N., 23
Nicklaus, Jack, 203, 325
Niedenthal, P. N., 505n
Niit, T., 271
Nirenberg, T. D., 396
Nisan, M., 277
Nisbett, Richard E., 155–58, 165–66, 167, 168, 175, 177, 178
Nixon, M., 70
Nixon, Richard M., 81, 84
Noller, P., 488, 516
Norris, F. H., 478
North, D., 584
Notarius, C., 515
Novak, D. W., 459
Nucci, Larry P., 280, 282

Nucci, M. S., 282
Nuttin, J., 80
Nygren, T. E., 309

Oakes, P. J., 111
O'Brien, M., 142n
Oedipus, 284
Ogloff, J.R.P., 136
O'Heron, C. A., 407
Olson, J. E., 404
O'Neil, H. K., 586
O'Quin, K., 300
Orbell, J. M., 366
Orbuch, T. L., 385
Orlofsky, J. L., 407
Ortberg, J., 587
Orthner, D. K., 510
Osborn, Alexander, 4–6, 12
Osgood, C. E., 532
Oskamp, S., 359, 360
Osmer, D., 80
Ostendorf, F., 149
Osterhouse, R. A., 568
Ostrum, T., 127
O'Sullivan, M., 250

Padgett, V. R., 73
Pagel, M. D., 587
Pallak, M. S., 547
Palmer, Arnold, 203
Palmer, R., 207
Pamin, T., 350
Panzarella, R., 49
Papciak, A. S., 367
Paquin, G., 422, 451
Parish, E. A., 483
Park, B., 127, 138
Parke, R. D., 437, 472
Parker, G. B., 488
Parks, C. D., 368
Parrott, W. G., 195–96, 598
Parsons, Talcott, 402–404, 410, 509
Pastore, Nicholas, 419, 420, 421, 423
Paulhus, D., 137, 218, 556
Paulus, P. B., 11, 12
Peckham, V., 72
Peekna, H. M., 301n
Pelham, B. W., 202
Pennington, D. C., 170
Pennington, Nancy, 97
Penrod, S., 95
Pepitone, Albert, 256, 430, 439
Peplau, L. A., 479, 481, 482, 483, 485, 495, 502
Peri, N., 316
Perie, M., 168
Perkins, S. C., 206
Perlman, D., 359
Perot, A., 428
Perri, M., 468

Stubing, M. J., 545
Suchman, E. A., 326
Suggs, Robert, 389
Sultan, F. E., 479
Sundstrom, Eric, 135n
Supanic, M., 519
Sutton, S., 584
Swander, D. V., 28
Swann, W. B., Jr., 169, 202, 597
Swedlund, M., 32
Sweet, J. A., 502
Symons, Donald, 386, 394
Syna, H., 346
Szymanski, K., 73

Tafarodi, R. W., 407
Tajfel, Henri, 109–110
Tanaka, J. S., 429
Tanfer, K., 398
Tanford, S., 95
Tanke, E. D., 158, 218, 469
Tannenbaum, P. H., 532
Tassinary, L. G., 251, 529
Taves, P. A., 547
Tavris, C., 452
Taylor, B., 172
Taylor, D. M., 140
Taylor, Shelley E., 158, 459
Tedeschi, James T., 419, 547, 555, 556
Teger, Allan L., 37
Tellegen, A., 407
Templeton, J. L., 196
ter Schure, E., 236n
Tesser, Abraham, 236, 317, 457, 528, 557–59, 597
Tessler, R. C., 587
Tetlock, Philip, 83–84
Tharp, R. G., 506, 510
Thayer, J. F., 219
Thibaut, John, 78, 331, 332
Thibodeau, R., 544
Thoma, S. J., 278
Thomas, C. M., 429, 431
Thomas, J., 568
Thomas, M. H., 435
Thompson, E., 502
Thompson, L. L., 350, 351
Thompson, V. D., 458
Thompson, W. C., 310
Thorne, A., 457
Tice, D. M., 205n, 314
Timko, C., 601
Tinbergen, Niko, 414
Tisak, M. S., 282
Titus, L. J., 65
Titus, William, 87
Todd, R. M., 301n
Tomkins, S. S., 243
Touhey, J. C., 458
Tourangeau, Roger, 243–44

Townsend, J. M., 391
Traupmann, J., 496
Trent, K., 519
Triandis, Harry, 256, 261
Trivers, Robert, 295–296, 318
Trolier, T. K., 129
Trommsdorff, G., 10
Trope, Y., 170
Trudeau, J. V., 553
Truman, Harry S, 81, 84
Tucker, A. W., 357
Tucker, J. A., 271
Tuddenham, R. D., 27
Turiel, Eliot, 277, 278, 280–83, 284–85, 286
Turner, J., 110–11
Tversky, Amos, 164, 165, 328–329, 352–353
Tyler, T. R., 333, 334

Uchino, B. N., 478
Uleman, J. S., 184, 185
Underwood, B., 308
Uranowitz, S. W., 130

Vaillant, George E., 512
Valleroy, L. Z., 268
van de Kragt, A.J.C., 366
Vanderplas, M., 300
van der Pligt, J., 126
VanderStoep, S. W., 88
Van Kleeck, M. H., 174
Van Kreveld, D., 452
Van Slyck, M., 354
Van Ypern, N. W., 496
Varey, C. A., 329
Veach, T. L., 37
Vera, H., 520
Vershure, B., 392
Vinacke, W. E., 371
Vincent, J. E., 310, 347
Vincent, J. P., 514
Vinokur, Amir, 37–38, 39
Von Bayer, C., 167
Von Neumann, John, 356

Wachtler, J., 30
Wack, D. L., 66
Wade, C., 29
Wade, G., 107
Wagenhals, W. L., 396
Walbek, N. H., 306
Walker, J. L., 351
Walker, L., 332
Walker, L. J., 278
Walker, M. R., 457
Wall, J. A., Jr., 354
Wallace, George C., 99
Wallach, M. A., 36
Wallbott, H., 271

Wallin, Paul, 503–504, 505n
Walster, Elaine Hatfield, 321n, 465, 468, 485, 490, 496
Walster, G. W., 321n, 496
Walters, G., 124
Walters, P. S., 360
Wan, K.-C., 265
Wang, Y.-E., 76
Wasman, M., 413
Weber, R., 133
Webster, D. M., 80
Weigold, M. P., 168
Weiner, Bernard, 271, 303
Weiss, D. S., 149
Weiss, R. F., 299
Weiss, R. L., 514
Weiss, W., 562, 563
Weisskopf-Joelson, E., 9
Weisz, J. R., 262
Weitz, Shirley, 119–21
Wells, G. L., 177
West, R. L., 170
West, S. G., 114
Westheimer, Ruth, 382
Weston, D. R., 282
Wetherell, M., 410
Wharton, J. D., 439
Wheeler, D., 347
Wheeler, L., 468
Whitam, F. L., 400
Whitcher-Alagna, S., 315
White, B. J., 104
White, G. L., 493
White, J. B., 601
White, S. W., 518
Whiteley, S., 385
Whitley, B. E., Jr., 407
Whitney, G. A., 517
Wiback, K., 468
Wicker, Allan, 577, 584
Wicklund, Robert, 210–11, 212, 214, 223
Widom, C. S., 435
Wierzbicka, Anna, 272
Wilder, David, 131
Wiles, K. A., 429
Wilke, H., 368, 369
Willerman, B., 462
Williams, C. J., 596
Williams, C. L., 479
Williams, J. G., 483
Williams, K., 73, 75, 76
Williams, K. D., 573
Williams, R. M., Jr., 108, 326
Willis, R. H., 363n
Wills, T. A., 478
Wilson, D. W., 90
Wilson, Margo, 386, 432
Wilson, T. D., 596, 597
Winch, Robert, 506

SUBJECT INDEX

abilities, in equity theory, 322, 324–25
abstinence, and gender differences, 397
abstract rules, application of, 311
accent, and self-presentation, 200
accessibility:
  of attitudes, 592–96
  and memory, 592
  through mere exposure, 594–96
  and priming, 594, 596
  and speed of response, 593
accommodation, in marriage, 517
actions, 173
  and emotions, 226
  intentional, 150, 154–55
  reasoned, 579–90
  responsibility for, 257
actor-observer differences:
  in attributions, 155–59, 175, 177
  experimental results on, 157
  salience in, 158–59
Adams equity theory, 321–22, 324–25
adaptation:
  and cuisine, 268–69
  and natural selection, 293
adaptive significance, 269
additive combination rules, 74
ad hoc groups, 8, 63, 89
adjustment:
  and gender, 407–9
  and self-esteem, 407
adults, attachment styles of, 486–87
adventure, romantic love as, 488–89
adversarial system, 331–34
aesthetic judgments, and pollution, 285
affect, and culture, 266
affection, and altruism, 306
affective reciprocity, 516
affiliation:
  in interpersonal attraction, 469–74
  in real-life situations, 472–73
age, and divorce, 519
aggreeableness, and autonomy, 461
aggression, 3, 411–43
  and anger, 417–18, 421–25
  animal, 411–16
  annoyance, 416
  Aristotelian account of, 417–18, 420, 421
  and aversive states, 427–28
  in children, 433–39

conceptions of, 411–12
crowd, 442
cues associated with, 423–25
danger-induced, 416
date rape as, 428–32
and deindividuation, 439–42
emotional, 411
and environment, 417
and erotica, 428
Freudian theory on, 412, 414–15, 418, 420
and frustration, 113–15, 418–25, 428
human, 417–28
impulsive, 411, 417, 439
institutional, 442
instrumental, 411–12
inter-male, 413–14, 415
irritable, 416
and jealousy, 432–33
justified, 436
and learning, 433–39
maternal, 415–16
mitigation of, 419
motives for, 417–18
predatory, 412–13
and punishment, 435
research on, 417–28
and retaliation, 419n, 420
self-defensive, 416
sex-related, 414–15, 428–33
and television, 435–39
and transfer of arousal, 425–28
and transgressions, 417–18
and weapons effect, 423
against women, 430–31
Yale group theory of, 413, 418–21
"Ah ha!" problems, 88–89
AIDS, and sexual behavior, 383
Air Corps, U.S., deprivation research in, 326
alcohol:
  and pluralistic ignorance, 41–42
  and self-handicapping, 205, 206
algorithm, defined, 569
alternatives, comparison level for, 78
altruism, 3, 289–319
  and affection, 306
  in animals, 294
  and bystander intervention, 310–11

causal attributions of, 303
and cheating, 295–96
in children, 305–7, 310
concept of, 290–94
and confession, 309–10
and decision theory, 356n
defined, 290, 293n
and discipline, 306
and distress, 298–97
and doing right thing, 310–13
and egocentrism, 305–6
and embarrassment, 309–10
and empathy, 304–7
and evolution, 291–97
existence of, 290–91
and feedback, 301n
and focusing responsibility, 313
and guilt, 309–10
and help, 289–91, 297, 300, 314–17
and inclusive fitness, 294–95
justice vs., 320
and material benefit, 290
and modeling behavior, 306
and moods, 300–301, 307–10
and perspective, 306
reciprocal, 295–97
and reducing ambiguity, 313
and rewards, 302
socialization of, 306–7, 310
and subtle cynicism, 297–99
value on, 306
and victims, 312
and vulgar cynicism, 290
and weather, 307, 309
ambiguity:
  and bystander intervention, 39–40
  and conformity, 25–28, 31–32, 59
  and disagreement, 28
  and emergencies, 20, 39–40
  reducing, 313
  Zimbardo on, 59
ambivalence:
  explicit values in, 119
  and prejudice, 119–22
  research in, 122–23
  and response amplification, 121–22
ambivalent attachment, 486
American Dilemma, The (Myrdal), 119
American Soldier, The, 107–8

androgynous subjects, 408

anger:

    and aggression, 417–18, 421–25

    and aversive states, 421–22, 428

    and blind association, 422

    cues associated with, 423–25

    degree of, 422–23

    and frustration, 418n, 422–23

    and irrationality, 417

    modulation of, 422–25

    response readiness in, 236n

    and transgression, 421

animal learning theory:

    and attitudes, 529

    and frustration-aggression theory, 113

animals:

    aggression in, 411–16

    altruism in, 294

    and care of young, 485–86

    signaling systems of, 249–50

annoyance aggression, 416

anonymity:

    and deindividuation, 442

    vs. identifiability, 366–67

anti-Semitism:

    and authoritarian personality theory, 115–19

    and deindividuation, 439

    of Nazis, 118–19, 439

Anti-Semitism (A-S) Scale, 116

anxiety:

    and being with others, 473–74

    in interpersonal attraction, 469–74

    social, 214

anxious attachments, 486

Apodaca, Cooper, and Madden v. *Oregon*, 93

apologies, 420

appeasement gestures, 416

arbitrary power, 435

arbitration, 355

arguments, quality of, 571–72

Aristotelian account of aggression, 417–18, 420, 421

Armenians, stereotypes of, 138

Army, U.S.:

    deprivation research in, 326–27, 560

    integration of, 107–8

arousal:

    and aggression, 414–15

    dissipation of, 427

    Dutton and Aron study on, 490–94

    and emotions, 225–36, 243, 270, 426

    and facial expressions, 243–45

    and films, 425–26

    in groups, 64

    and performance, 64, 66

    and rape, 428–29

    and romantic love, 490–94

    in Schachter and Singer experiment, 229–36, 243

    sexual, 494

    and social facilitation, 65–66

    transfer of, 235, 425–28

    to visual cues, 395–96

art:

    and creativity, 262

    and self, 260

Asch conformity experiment, 20, 22–25, 27–28

    and egocentric bias, 175

    focus of attention in, 210

    on influence of minorities, 30–31

    Milgram experiment and, 45, 50, 54

    rates of conformity in, 23

    results of, 23

    Sherif experiment vs., 26–28

Asch's research on attitudes, 530–32

Asch's studies of impression formation, 148–50, 179, 186–87

"as if" emotions, 229, 230

associated ideas, and priming, 594

associationism, and attitudes, 529

asymmetrical negotiations, 348

Athenian code, 275

attachment:

    and adults, 486–87

    and children, 486

    and natural selection, 485–86

    and romantic love, 485–88

attention:

    inner and outer focus of, 209–14

    selective, 554–55

attitude change:

    and conformity, 32

    influence of minorities in, 32

    majorities and, 32–33

    and persuasion, 559–74

    routes to, 568–72

    and sleeper effect, 562–64

attitudes, 525–603

    accessibility of, 592

    Asch's research on, 530–32

    and associationism, 529

    and attitude change, 527–75; *see also* attitude change

    and attraction, 454–56

    base-rate, 160, 163–65

    and behavior, 2–3, 163, 545–49, 576–603

    and cognitive dissonance, 532–59

    cognitively driven, 596

    defined, 527–28

    directly and indirectly formed, 591

    toward divorce, 519

    and drives, 581

    and emotions, 585–86

    as evaluations, 528

    and experience, 592, 597

    generality in, 577–79

    and inferences, 163, 545–49, 591

    and intentions, 580–84

    irrationality of, 530

    Lorge experiment on, 530–32

    and memory, 591–92

    and mindlessness, 598–99

    model of reasoned action in, 579–90

    old-fashioned, 429

    origins of, 581

    polarization of, 557–59

    of prejudice, 101–2

    psychological functions of, 528

    rationality of, 579–80

    reconstruction of, 577–79

    reflecting on, 596–98

    and schemata, 557–59

    and self-monitoring, 217–18

    sex-role, 510–11

    and significant others, 582–83

    similarity of, 454–56

    and social groups, 528

    social influence on, 588–90

    and subjective norms, 582–84

    uniformity of, 79–80

    and values, 581–82

Attitudes Toward Women Scale, 409

attraction, *see* interpersonal attraction

attractiveness, 3

    and being thought attractive, 469

    and culture, 463–65

    and dating, 465–66

    and evolution, 464

    of groups, 77–78

    and interpersonal attraction, 463–69

    and matching hypothesis, 466–67

    and premarital relationships, 494

    and same-gender relationships, 467

    and satisfaction, 13n

    and social skills, 468

    stereotypes of, 468

    and task evaluation, 468

attributions:

    actor-observer difference in, 155–59, 175, 177

    and behavior, 150, 170

    and candidate causes, 169–70

    causal schemata of, 154

    causes of, 173–74, 177–79

    and confirmation bias, 168–69

    and consensus, 165–66

    and considerations, 177–79

    defined, 150

    descriptive models of, 155

    and egocentrism, 165–66, 168, 175

    and emotions, 303–4

    errors and biases in, 155–59

    experimental results on, 156

    and Grice's maxims, 176–77

internal, 152
and language, 178n
management of, 192
and marital discord, 516–17
normative models of, 155
and pragmatics, 175–77
of responsibility, 140, 173–74
and salience, 158–59
situational, 156
and social knowledge structures, 171–73
and social perception, 168
and testing hypotheses, 169–70
theories of, 150–79
authoritarianism:
Berkeley group study of, 115–19
of jurors, 96
and personality scales, 116–18
syndrome of, 116–18
Authoritarian Personality, The (Berkeley group), 115, 118–19
authorities:
and interpreting moral order, 54
obedience to, 50
unanimity among, 50–51
authority, in relationships, 499
autokinetic effect, 26, 59
autonomic nervous system, and emotions, 227–29
autonomy, and agreeableness, 461
aversive states:
and aggression, 427–28
and anger, 421–22, 428
avoidant attachment, 486

baby boomers, socialization of, 384
back translation, 272
balance theory, 453, 454
and cognitive consistency, 532
bargaining:
and competition, 342
concessions in, 344–47, 362
conditions necessary for, 351
counteroffers in, 343–44
door-in-the-face effect in, 346–47
duopoly in, 342–48
equity in, 342, 362–63
face-to-face, 351
framing effects in, 351–53
ignorance vs. information in, 348
initial offers in, 343
integrative, 349–51
LOAs (Levels of Aspiration) in, 344–45
oligopoly, 351–53
opening strategies in, 351
and opponent's profits, 347–48
and problem-solving, 349–51
reciprocity in, 345–48

resistance points in, 343
in strategic interaction, 341–56
see also negotiations
bargaining theory, 373
barrier strengths, 520
base-rate attitude, 160, 163–65
base rates:
and Bayes's Theorem, 164
and fundamental attributional error, 163–65
ignoring of, 164, 174
in moral judgments, 174
use of, 165
basking in reflected glory, 207–8
Bayes's Theorem, 164
Bay of Pigs invasion, 81–83
behavior:
actor-observer differences in, 155–59
and attitudes, 2–3, 163, 545–49, 576–603
and attribution, 150, 170
causal schemata of, 154
conformity, 22
discounting of, 163
and dispositions, 149, 151, 157
and drives, 426
and emotions, 585–86
encoding of, 184–87
gender differences in, 401
and intentions, 580, 586
of leaders, 63
and mindlessness, 598–99
modeling, 306, 433, 434, 436
and model of reasoned action, 579–90
and moral choices, 280–81
and objective self-awareness, 211–12
perceived control of, 586–87
and personality, 149–50
prediction of, 579, 590–99
prey-stalking, 412–13
rationality of, 579–80
and reactions, 154
responsibility for, 173–74, 516
self as inner cause of, 209
sexual, *see* sexual behavior
and sexual scripts, 378
shaping our own, 397
social influence on, 20–21, 588–90
and social knowledge structures, 171–72
standards of, 211–12
traits and, 149–50, 184
and the will, 173
behavior exchange:
and communication, 515–16
and marriage, 514–16
physiological and affective reciprocity in, 516
behaviorism, 418n

beliefs:
in a just world, 334–38
supernatural, 281
Bem (Daryl) self-perception theory, 545–49
Bem (Sandra) Sex Role Inventory (BSRI), 137, 405–6, 407–8
beneficence, 280
Berkeley group, 115–17
bias:
in attributions, 155–59
cognitive, 166–67, 266
confirmation, 168–70
egocentric, 165–66, 168, 175
and group judgment, 85–87
of ingroups, 110–11
intergroup, *see* intergroup conflict; prejudice
and jury selection, 95–98
motivational, 167
self-serving, 166–68
in Zimbardo prison experiment, 59
binding arbitration, 355
birds, altruism in, 294
birthrate, and marriage squeeze, 383
blacks:
ambivalence toward, 119–21
divorce among, 519
lynching of, 113
in military, 108
prejudice against, 99-0, 112, 113
stereotypes of, 128, 138
blasting, in self-presentation, 207–8
blind and deaf children, nonverbal expressions of, 240
blind association, and anger, 422
bodily states, and emotions, 226
body, and self, 257
body-mind connection, 257
bogus pipeline, 556
bogus stranger technique, 455–56
bounded entities, 263
brainstorming:
and creativity, 4–6, 9–10
as experimental method, 4–13
ideas developed in, 8–12
and interference, 11, 12
and productivity, 10–11, 12
brutality, 55–60
in concentration camps, 58
and degradation, 57–58
and moral drift, 58–59
slippery slope in, 57–58
Zimbardo prison experiment on, 56–60
Burgess and Wallin on homogamy, 503–6
business organizations, gender stereotypes in, 135–36
buying and selling, *see* bargaining

in task performance, 63, 76–79
and uniformity of attitudes, 79–80
collective self-esteem, 111
collectivism:
    defined, 259
    individualism vs., 258–65, 368–69
    and Kohlberg, 283–84
    social ramifications of, 259–62
    in Western culture, 262–63
colleges and universities, admissions
    policies of, 320
combination rules, and social loafing,
    74–75
common law juries, 92
communal relationships, 498–501
communication:
    deceptive, 251, 252
    and facial expression, 246–49
    and group cohesiveness, 79–80
    and information leaks, 250
    and language, 249
    and marriage, 515–16
    in nonzero sum conflicts, 365–66
    and n-person prisoner's dilemma,
    365–66
    and pseudointeractions, 247, 248
    and self-presentation, 200–201
    senders and receivers in, 250, 252
    and signaling systems, 249–50
companionate love, 485
companionship, in marriage, 508,
    511
comparison level for alternatives, 78
compensation, in task performance, 75
compensatory tasks, 74
competence:
    and attraction, 461–62
    and self-promotion, 203
competition:
    and bargaining, 342
    and justice, 334
    and natural selection, 293
    in performance, 206–7
    response, 453n
    in zero-sum and nonzero-sum
    conflicts, 356–60
complementarity of needs, 506
compliance:
    and conformity, 21, 22
    defined, 21
    forced, 537–38
    in persuasion, 561
computer prisoner's dilemma
    tournament, 360–62
computer software, and group
    interaction, 11
concealment, and deception, 251, 252
concentration camps, 58, 284
conception, interval of opportunity for,
    387–88

concessions, in bargaining, 344–47,
    362
concrete triggers of emotion, 273
condoms, use of, 394n
confession, and altruism, 309–10
confirmation bias:
    and attribution theory, 168–69
    and candidate causes, 169–70
    for introversion and extraversion,
    169–70
conformity, 21–33
    and ambiguity, 25–28, 31–32, 59
    Asch experiment on, 20, 22–25, 27–
    28
    and attitude change, 32
    compliance and, 21, 22
    and confusion, 24–25
    defined, 21
    and embarrassment, 25
    and emperor's new clothes, 19–20
    in experiments, 22–33
    and group cohesiveness, 79
    and internalization, 21–22, 28
    and lone dissenter, 29–30
    minority influence in, 30–33
    and norms, 26, 28, 59–60
    and objectivity, 24–25, 26
    and perceptions, 21–24, 28, 31–32
    and preferences, 28–29
    and pressures, 25–27
    rates of, 23
    reasons for, 23–25
    reduction of, 28–33
    and self-awareness, 214
    and self-monitoring, 216–18
    with single supporter, 30
    and trust, 24
    types of, 23
    to unanimous majorities, 28, 50–51
confusion:
    and ambiguity, see ambiguity
    and conformity, 24–25
    and pluralistic ignorance, 41
conjunctive tasks, 74
conquest, in romantic love, 489
conscience, internalization of, 536–37
consensus information, 154
    and egocentrism, 165–66
    in moral judgments, 175
consequentialism, and moral rules, 280
consistency, in leadership, 70–71
consistency information, 154
conspecifics, mere presence of, 65–66
constant sum conflicts, 356
constituencies, representatives of, 353–
    55
Constitution, 259
constructivism, social, 274–75
construct validity, 216, 220
consummate love, 485

contamination, of self, 284–85
contingency view of leadership,
    69–70
contingent cooperation, 360
contingent goals, 582
contraceptives, 383
    and embarrassment, 197
control groups, 6–10
controlled experiments, 5
conventional stage of moral
    development, 276–77
conventions, 281
convergence of results, in
    experimentation, 8
cooperation:
    in classroom, 108–9
    contingent, 360
    and exploitation, 359–60
    and identifiability, 366–67
    in prisoner's dilemma, 358–59
    and public goods problem, 368–69
    in Tit for Tat, 360
    and trust, 366
coordination losses, and social loafing,
    71–72
corporations, gender stereotyping in,
    135–36
correlation, illusory, 125, 129–30
correlational method, 13–15
    and causality, 14–15
correlation coefficients, 13–14
correspondent inference theory, 150–
    52, 154–55, 162
    and fundamental attributional error,
    159–60
counteroffers, in bargaining, 343–44
covariation, defined, 153
covariation theory, 152–55
    and fundamental attributional error,
    160
    and reactions, 154
covetousness, and television, 438–39
creativity:
    and art, 262
    and brainstorming, 4–6, 9–10
credibility:
    in persuasion, 561–62, 571
    and sleeper effect, 562–64
crime:
    murder, 432–33
    rape, 337–38, 428–32
    and televised violence, 438–39
    and weather, 427–28
criminal justice system, 320–21
cross-cultural perspective, see culture
cross-sex-typed subjects, 408
crowd aggression, 442
Cuba:
    Bay of Pigs invasion in, 81–83
    Missile Crisis in, 81

dual representation theory, 188–90
duopoly bargaining, 342–48
    door-in-the-face effect in, 346–47
    initial offers in, 343
    LOAs (Level of Aspiration) in, 344–45
    and opponent's profits, 347–48
    reciprocity in, 345–48
    resistance points in, 343
Dutton and Aron study on romantic love, 490–94
duty, vs. caring, 278–80

eating disorders, contagion of, 84–85
Eckman study on emotional expressions, 237–42
education, and divorce, 520
egocentrism:
    and bad moods, 310
    and bias, 165–66, 168, 175
    of children, 275–76, 305
    and consensus, 165–66
    man-the-lawyer view of, 174–75
    overcoming of, 305–6
    perpetual, 305
    test for, 304–5
ego involvement, 167–68
Eichmann in Jerusalem (Arendt), 46
Eichmann trial, and obedience, 45–46, 54
elaboration likelihood model, 568
electrical activity, and facial expressions, 248
embarrassment:
    and altruism, 309–10
    avoidance of, 197
    and conformity, 25
    consequences of, 196–97
    and contraceptive use, 197
    and excuses, 195–96
    and facework, 196–97
    and interaction, 195–96
    and loss of esteem, 194–96
    and moral choices, 51
    and self-awareness, 210
    and self-presentation, 194–96
emergencies:
    and altruism, 310–11
    and ambiguity, 20, 39–40
    bystander intervention in, 310–11
    diffusion of responsibility in, 42–43
    needing help in, 315–17
    pluralistic ignorance in, 40–42
    and victims, 312
    yelling "Fire!" in, 313*n*
emotions, 2–3, 224–55, 269–74
    acting out of, 201
    and actions, 226
    and aggression, 411
    and arousal, 225–36, 243, 270, 426

"as if," 229, 230
    and attitudes, 585–86
    attributional determinants of, 303–4
    and behavior, 585–86
    and bodily states, 226
    cognition-arousal theory of, 227–36, 270, 271
    collectivist, 262–63
    complexity of, 235–36
    conceptions of, 270
    concrete triggers of, 273
    and culture, 270–73
    and deception, 249–50
    definitions of, 229
    display rules for, 241–42
    and evolution, 245–53
    and facial expression, 236–53
    fear and persuasion, 564–66
    and food, 269–74
    intensity of, 243, 244–45
    as internal and private, 227
    James-Lange theory of, 224–27, 235
    lexicalization of, 273
    and loneliness, 483
    and nervous system, 227–29, 235–36
    and perception, 225–26
    and rationality, 585–86
    response readiness in, 236*n*
    Schachter and Singer experiment in, 229–36, 243, 270
    and self-presentation, 197, 273–74
    spontaneous expressions of, 173
    and stimuli, 266, 270–71
    and tone of voice, 252
emotion transfer, 235
empathy:
    defined, 299
    development of, 304–7
    and egocentrism, 305–6
    and helping behavior, 300–301, 303
    justice vs., 320
    and moods, 307–8
    and perspective, 304
    and reducing distress, 299–303
    and socializing altruistic behavior, 306, 310
emperor's new clothes, 19–20
employment decisions, 140
    gender stereotypes in, 135–36
enduring groups, 63
enduring relationships, *see* relationships
England, sixteenth-century, love and marriage in, 507–8
entities, bounded, 263
entitlement:
    and deprivation, 328
    and equity theory, 327–28
environment:
    and adaptation, 293

and aggression, 417
    and behavior, 157
    vs. genes, 400
    influences of, 400
envy:
    and attractiveness, 467
    and friendship, 456–57
    and jealousy, 456
    and self-esteem maintenance, 456–57
    and similarity, 456
epiphenomena, 422
equal excess theory, 373
equality:
    equity vs., 321–24, 334
    in relationships, 499
equity:
    in bargaining, 342, 362–63
    defined, 321
    equality vs., 321–24, 334
    in premarital relationships, 495–97
equity theory:
    and abilities, 322, 324–25
    of Adams, 321–22, 324–25
    and cognitive processes, 322–23
    and culture, 330–31
    and entitlement, 327–28
    experimental evidence in, 322
    and justice, 321–31
    and motivation, 322–23
    and need, 329–30
    problems for, 322–25
    and relative deprivation theory, 326–29
    standard of reference in, 322, 326–29
erotica:
    and aggression, 428
    responses to, 395–96
    and transfer of arousal, 425
erotophobia-erotophilia scales, 586
ESS (evolutionarily stable strategy), 296
estrogen, and mate selection, 390
ethnocentrism:
    authoritarian personality in, 115
    and frustration-aggression theory, 114–15
    and ingroup, 115
    and minimal groups, 109–12
    in Robbers Cave experiment, 104–7
Ethnocentrism (E) Scale, 116–17
"Eureka!" problems, 88–89
evaluation apprehension, 66–68
evaluations:
    attitudes as, 528
    and competence, 461–62
    descriptions vs., 175
    and disregarded information, 189
    and extra credit effect, 461*n*
    inferred, 457–58

evaluations (*continued*)
   and ingratiation, 461
   and interpersonal attraction, 458, 459–62
   patterning of, 459
   in person perception, 179–81
   and priming, 186
   and sets, 189
   and similarity, 457–58
evolution:
   and altruism, 291–97
   and ardent males; choosy females, 397
   and attractiveness, 464
   cultural, 269
   differential success in, 292
   and facial expressions, 236–37, 241, 245–53
   and inclusive fitness, 294–95
   and mate selection, 390–93
   and morality, 397
   and self-knowledge, 386
   and sexual behavior, 385, 386–400
   see also natural selection
evolutionarily stable strategy (ESS), 296
Evolution of Human Sexual Behavior, The (Symons), 386
exchanges:
   behavior, 514–16
   remedial, 419
exchange theory:
   and communal relationships, 498–501
   and premarital relationships, 495–97
excuses, 420, 540
   and embarrassment, 195–96
exemplars, typicality of, 131–33
exemplification:
   and hypocrisy, 204–5
   in self-presentation, 204–5
expectations:
   in bargaining, 348
   of gender, 401
   and interactions, 198–99
   and relative deprivation theory, 327–28
experience, and attitudes, 592, 597
experimental methods:
   analytical use of, 8–10
   brainstorming, 4–13
   and causal relations, 4–11
   circular theories in, 540
   confederates in, 24, 27
   construct validity in, 216
   control groups in, 6–10
   controlled, 5
   convergence of results in, 8
   dependent variables in, 5–6
   experimental groups in, 6–10

factor analysis in, 214
games and simulations, 340–41
generalization in, 7–8
hypotheses in, 6, 169–70
independent variables in, 5–6
issues addressed by, 8
meta-analysis of, 65
phenomena in, 8
placebos in, 230
and popular opinions, 12–13
randomizing in, 6–7, 13, 15
reliability in, 216
for research on juries, 90–92, 94
roles of, 11, 12–13
round robin, 70–71
simulations in, 340–41
sleeper effect in, 562–64
subjects in, 5, 6–8, 13
tautological theories in, 540
validity in, 216, 393, 424–25
exploitation, and pacifism, 359–60
exposure, *see* mere exposure
expressions, universality of, 240
expressive needs, 509
extra credit effect, 461*n*
extramarital sex, 393–94
extraversion, confirmation bias for, 169–70
eyebrow flashes, 239–40

facework, and embarrassment, 196–97
Facial Affect Coding System, 250
facial expressions:
   and arousal, 243–45
   and communication, 246–49
   control of, 249, 251
   Darwin's theory of, 236–37, 241, 245–46
   and deception, 249–50
   direct readout of, 246–49
   display rules for, 241–42, 248
   and electrical activity, 248
   and emotions, 236–43
   and evolution, 236–37, 241, 245–53
   and fundamental attributional error, 163
   and intensity, 244–45
   necessity and sufficiency of, 243
   and pseudointeractions, 247, 248
   universality of, 237–42
facial feedback hypothesis, 237, 243, 245
factor analysis, defined, 214
facts:
   cultural vs. "natural," 266
   diagnostic, 164
   overall impressions and, 187–90
   recall of, 187–90

fairness:
   and obedience, 53
   see also equity; equity theory
faking:
   in self-presentation, 200–202
   see also deception
false consensus effect, 166
families:
   changing conceptions of, 508–9
   gender roles in, 403
   nuclear, 509
   socialization by, 200, 403
   as teams, 198–99
fear, *see* emotions
feedback:
   and altruism, 301*n*
   and emotions, 228–29
   facial, 237, 243
   from nervous system, 227–29
   self-enhancing, 201–2
   self-verifying, 202
feelings, *see* emotions
females, *see* gender; gender differences; women
femininity:
   and adjustment, 407–9
   measurement of, 405–6
fight or flight system, 227
films:
   and arousal, 425–26
   and attitude change, 562, 566
   as culture model, 379
   and rape myths, 430–31
   sleeper effect, 562–64
   and violence, 423–26, 428
final offer arbitration, 355
Fishbein and Ajzen model of reasoned action, 579–90
flirtation, 3
food:
   constraints on diet and, 265
   and culture, 265–69
   and eating disorders, 84–85
   and emotions, 269–74
   and neophobia, 267
   and origins of cuisine, 268–69
   poisonous, 266–67
   and status, 267–68
   taboos in, 267
foot-in-the-door technique, 551–53
forbearance, in marriage, 517
forced compliance:
   and dissonance, 537–38
   learning theory on, 539
framing effects, 351–53
free market, bargaining in, 351–53
free-rider problem, 369
Freudian theory:
   on aggression, 412, 414–15, 418, 420

and ambivalence, 119
and authoritarian personality theory, 115
displacement in, 113
and frustration-aggression theory, 113
on morality, 587n
and Northern prejudice, 119
on rationalization, 544–45
on sexual arousal, 494
and socialization, 113
Freud-Yale view of aggression, 418
friends, defined, 477–79
friendship, 477–84
    development of, 478–84
    and envy, 456–57
    expressing concern in, 482–84
    gender differences in, 481
    and loneliness, 482–84
    and propinquity, 448–50
    real vs. fake, 200–201
    and reciprocity, 479–80
    and self-disclosure, 479–82
    and self-monitoring, 219
    virtues of, 478
frustration:
    defined, 113n, 418
    and degree of anger, 422–23
    justified and unjustified, 419–21
frustration-aggression theory, 113–15, 418–25, 428
frustration anger, 418n
functional distance, 449
fundamental attributional error, 159–63
    and base rates, 163–65
    defined, 160
    investigation of, 161–62, 175
    limits of, 162–63

gambling, as adventure, 489
games, experimental, 340–41
game theory, 356–57
gay men, sexual behavior of, 394
gender, 376–410
    and adjustment, 407–9
    and BSRI, 137, 405–6, 407–8
    changing concepts of, 404–5
    division of labor by, 403
    and nonverbal cues, 252
    and PAQ, 405–6, 407–8
    roles associated with, 135–36, 402–9, 510–11
    and socialization, 403–6
    stereotypes of, 135–36, 141, 401–9
gender differences, 389–409
    and abstinence, 397
    and aggression, 414–16
    in arousal, 64
    and attractiveness, 466

in behavior, 401
in careers, 404–5, 511
cross-cultural evidence of, 389–93
on date rape, 430
discrimination based on, 404–5
and double standard, 380–81
and evolution, 397, 398–400
in friendship, 481
and gender roles, 402–9
and helping behavior, 314, 316
in intimacy, 481–82
Kinsey study on, 393–97
in knowledge of children, 388
and loneliness, 483–84
in masturbation, 396–97
in mate selection, 390–93
in math ability, 401
in mathematical ability, 401
and moral choices, 397–98
and moral development, 277–78
in negotiating, 354
normative conceptions of, 406
in parental investment, 387–88
in personality, 403, 406
in premarital and extramarital sex, 393–94
psychological, 400–402
in reproductive equipment, 386, 387
and rewards, 322, 323–24, 330
in salaries, 404–5
in self-disclosure, 480–82
in sexual arousal, 394, 395–96
in sexual behavior, 380–81, 389–98
in sexual desire, 394
in social roles, 135–36, 401, 403
in verbal ability, 401–2
in virginity, 390
generalization:
    of experiment results, 7–8
    and stereotypes, 127
generosity:
    of children, 307, 310
    and modeling behavior, 306
    and moods, 307–10
    reinforcement of, 310
    and rewards, 308
    and self-gratification, 307
    and social norms, 311
    and weather, 307, 309
genes:
    and differential success, 292
    vs. environment, 400
    and homosexuality, 398–400
    and identical twins, 399–400
    and inclusive fitness, 294–95
    and natural selection, 294
    recessive, 398
    and reciprocal altruism, 295–97
    selfish, 293–94
    and sexual behavior, 397–400

and survival, 292–93
and traits, 221
Genovese, Kitty, murder of, 39–43
Germany, gay men and lesbians in, 394
Gestalt psychology, 149
gestures:
    of appeasement, 416
    universality of, 239–40
goals:
    contingent, 582
    superordinate, 104
Goffman's self-presentation theory, 193–202
    criticisms of, 200
    on embarrassment, 194–97
    on faking, 200–202
    on interaction, 195–96
    on self-esteem, 194–95
    and self-monitoring, 215, 216
    teams in, 198–99
goose bumps, 249
greeting, eyebrow flashes in, 239–40
Grice's maxims, 176–77, 178n
group dynamics, 17–143
    in prejudice and intergroup conflict, 99–103
    social influence in, 19–61
    and task performance, 62–98
groups:
    acceptance by, 79
    ad hoc, 8, 63, 89
    alternative, 78
    arousal in, 64
    attractiveness of, 77–78
    and bias, 85–87
    brainstorming by, 4–13
    and cautious shift, 38
    cohesiveness of, see cohesiveness, group
    computer interaction of, 11
    conformity in, 21–33
    and coordination losses, 71
    costs of, 78
    defined, 62–63
    deindividuation of, 439–42
    dynamics of, see group dynamics
    enduring, 63
    experimental, 6–10
    idea production in, 8–10
    individuals vs., 9–11, 12, 33–35, 63–64, 85–89
    and ingroups, 87, 104, 110–11
    and interference, 10–11
    and intergroup conflict, 110–12
    judgment of, 85–87
    leadership of, 68–71
    loyalty in, 78–79
    minimal, 109–12
    motivation in, 11, 71–72
    negative prestige of, 78

self-esteem of, 108
social influence of, 20, 30–33
see also specific groups
misattribution studies, 548
mitigating information, 419
mixed motives, 365
mobility, differential, 330
mob violence, 439
mock juries, 90, 94
modeling behavior:
and altruism, 306
in learning aggression, 433, 434, 436
model of reasoned action, 579–90
monkeys, signaling systems of, 249–50
monogamy, 389
monozygotic twins, 399
moods:
and altruism, 300–301, 307–10
bad, 309–10
and generosity, 307–10
good, 307–9
moral authority, and individualism, 262, 263
moral choices:
base rates in, 174
and behavior, 280–81
and conformity, 21
and consensus information, 175
and contamination, 284–85
and distance from victims, 51–52
and embarrassment, 51
and food taboos, 267
gender differences and, 397–98
influence of minorities on, 30
and Milgram experiment, 45, 47–55, 60
and obedience, 46–47, 49–51, 54, 60
and responsibility, 257
slippery slopes in, 49
social influence and, 21, 52, 54, 59–60
in Zimbardo prison experiment, 58–59
see also moral development; morality
moral development:
and beneficence, 280
and culture, 275–76, 277
and gender differences, 277–78
Kohlberg theory of, 275–78
stages in, 276–77
Turiel theory of, 280–82
moral drift, and brutality, 58–59
morality:
abstract principles of, 276
and contamination, 284–85
and cultural relativism, 274–75
and evolution, 397
and perspective, 280

and pollution, 284–85
and reasoned action, 587
rules of, 278–83
and self, 274–85
and social constructivism, 274–75
universality of, 274, 275, 277, 283–85
see also moral choices; moral development
moral rhetorics, 284
moral rules:
and children, 281–82
content of, 280–81
vs. conventions, 281
and culture, 278–80
and harm, 281
and immoral acts, 282–83
moral worth, and psychological inconsistency, 541
Moscovici minority influence experiment, 31–32
motivation:
for aggression, 417–18
and equity theory, 322–23
in groups, 11, 71–72
intrinsic, 549–51
losses of, 71, 72
mixed, 365
and nonzero sum conflicts, 369–70
and prejudice, 112–15
for rape, 428–29
and self-consciousness, 212–13
social, 287–43
and social dilemmas, 369–70
and task performance, 212
in tragedy of the commons, 365
Yerkes-Dodson Law on, 212
motivational bias, 167
movies, *see* films
multiple causes of behavior, 154
murder, 432–33
of Kitty Genovese, 39–43
myths:
rape, 430–31
troubadour, 508

naive realism, 166
National Survey of Families and Households (NSFH), 501–2, 513
"natural" facts, vs. cultural facts, 266
naturalistic fallacy, 397
natural kind theory, 140–42
natural selection, 291–93
and adaptation, 293
and attachment, 485–86
and competition, 293
and genes, 294
and reproduction, 291–92, 400–401
and survival of the fittest, 292–93

variability in, 291
see also evolution
Nazis:
anti-Semitism of, 118–19, 439
army in World War II, 76–77
concentration camps of, 58, 284
and Holocaust, 45–46
ideology of, 77
neo-Nazi party and, 103
needs:
complementarity of, 506
and equity theory, 329–30
expressive, 509
instrumental, 509
and rewards, 330
need satisfaction dependence, 498
negative state relief, 300–301
negotiations:
arbitrators in, 355
gender differences in, 354
mediators in, 355
and relationships, 354–55
among representatives, 353–56
and social pressures, 354
symmetrical vs. asymmetrical, 348
and third-party interventions, 355–56
see also bargaining
neophobic tastes, 267
neotenous features, 463–64
nervous system, and emotions, 227–29
NFSH (National Survey of Families and Households), 501–2, 513
Nice and Forgiving, vs. Tit for Tat, 362
Nimitz Highway collapse, and rescue workers, 289–91, 297, 301
nonverbal cues, 240
and gender, 242, 252
nonzero sum conflicts, 356–73
and bargaining theory, 373
and coalition formation, 370–73
communication in, 365–66
cooperation in, 362
and decision theory, 356–57
defined, 356–57
double-defect outcomes of, 365n
and equal excess theory, 373
free-rider problem in, 369
and identifiability, 366–67
and minimum power theory, 372–73
and minimum resource theory, 371–72
and motivation, 369–70
and public goods problem, 368–69
rewards in, 357–58, 363n
structural solutions to, 367–68
tertius gaudens in, 371
and weighted probability theory, 373
normative conceptions, of gender differences, 406

normative models, defined, 155
normative pressure, 25, 26
norms:
  and altruism, 310–11
  and bargaining, 346
  and conformity, 26, 28, 59–60
  and gender roles, 405–6
  internalization of, 536
  paying attention to, 311–12
  vs. personal opinions, 42
  and pluralistic ignorance, 42
  of reciprocity, 480, 482
  sexual, 379
  subjective, 580, 582–84
  violation of, 311
  of virginity, 390
North, prejudice in, 119–21
n-person prisoner's dilemma, 365–66, 368
nuclear families, 509
nuclear war, as "chicken," 365n
nurturance, 506

obedience, 45–55
  and distance from victims, 51–52
  and Eichmann, 45–46, 54
  and embarrassment, 51
  and fairness, 53
  justifications for, 52
  and legitimacy, 52–53
  in Milgram experiment, 45, 47–55, 60
  and moral choices, 46–47, 50–51
  reduction of, 50–52
  and responsibility, 54
objective self-awareness, 210–14
  research on, 213
  and standards, 211–12
objectivity:
  and conformity, 24–25, 26
  and influence, 26
  in Milgram experiment, 49, 50
occupations, stereotypes about, 129, 131, 132
occurrences, classes of, 173
offspring, see children
oligopoly bargaining, 351–53
opening strategies, 351
opinions:
  vs. experimental method, 12–13
  vs. norms, 42
opponent's profits, information about, 347–48
optical illusions, 26
outgroups:
  homogeneity account of stereotypes, 125
  in minimal group research, 110
  in realistic conflict theory, 104

overretaliation effect, 426, 427
overt behavior, 226

pacifism, and exploitation, 359–60
Pakistan-Indian war, 84
PAQ (Personal Attributes Questionnaire), 405–6, 407–8
parental investment, gender differences in, 387–88
parents:
  and relationships, 487
  and socializing altruistic behavior, 306–7
  see also children
passion, 2–3, 490
Pearl Harbor disaster, 81, 83
peers, rebelling, 50–51
penicillin, and venereal disease, 383
perceptions:
  and attitude accessibility, 595
  and conformity, 21–24, 28, 31–32
  of date rape, 431–32
  and emotions, 225–26
  and reactions, 225–26
  and responsibility, 516
  and romantic love, 225
  subjective norms as, 580
performance:
  and arousal, 64, 66
  of competitor, 206–7
  of groups, 71–73, 85
  and justice, 334
  and self-presentation, 197–200
  sets and props in, 197–98
  teams in, 198–99
  see also task performance
peripheral routes to attitude change, 568–72
peripheral traits, 148
permissiveness, and sexual behavior, 385
person:
  as body, 257
  use of term, 256n
  see also self
personal ads, for mate selection, 392
Personal Attributes Questionnaire (PAQ), 405–6, 407–8
personality:
  authoritarian, 115–19
  and behavior, 149–50
  gender differences in, 403, 406
  and helping in emergencies, 314
  implicit theory of, 149
  and leadership, 69
  and prejudice, 115–19
  scales, 116
  and socialization, 403
person perception, 147–91
  and attributional critics, 170–79

  and attributional errors and biases, 155–70
  and attribution theories, 150–55
  cognitive processes in, 179–90
  and dual representation theory, 188–90
  and encoding behavior, 184–87
  and impression formation, 147–50
  organization and representation of impressions in, 186–90
  preconceptions and evaluations in, 179–81
  processes in, 179
  schemata in, 181–82, 183–84
  sensitivity to incongruent material in, 182–83
  structures of, 179
  traits in, 148–49
perspective:
  and altruism, 306
  and empathy, 304
  and morality, 280
persuasion, 559–74
  and argument quality, 571–72
  and cognition, 566–74
  compliance in, 561
  components of, 560–66
  credibility in, 561–62, 571
  and distraction, 566–68
  and fear, 564–66
  in group discussions, 37
  identification in, 561
  and information processing, 571–74
  internalization in, 561
  and issue involvement, 571, 572
persuasive argument theory, 37–38
phenomena, in experimentation, 8
physical appearance:
  in interaction, 199–200
  and socialization, 200
physical attractiveness, see attractiveness
physiological arousal, see arousal
physiological reciprocity, 516
pivotal power, 371
placebos:
  defined, 230
  in misattribution studies, 548
pluralistic ignorance:
  and alcohol, 41–42
  and bystander intervention, 40–42
  and confusion, 41
  and norms, 42
  in Zimbardo prison experiment, 59–60
point of view, and empathy, 304
polarization:
  of attitudes, 557–59
  of groups, 39

reality:
  assumptions of, 27
  shared, 20
reasoned actions:
  and cognitive dissonance, 589–90
  and emotions, 585–86
  individual limitations on, 584
  model of, 579–90
  and morality, 587
  and perceived behavioral control, 586–87
  and previous behavior, 584–85
  and social influence, 588–90
recall memory tasks, 181
reciprocal altruism, 295–97
reciprocity:
  and accommodation, 517
  affective, 516
  in bargaining, 345–48
  and expressions of concern, 482–84
  norm of, 480, 482
  physiological, 516
  and self-disclosure, 479–80
  in Tit for Tat, 361
recognition memory tasks, 181
reference groups, 326
rejection, of offer to help, 317
relationships, 2–3, 477–24
  authority in, 499
  and beneficence, 280
  communal, 498–501
  divorce, 518–23
  enduring, 447–24
  equality in, 499
  equity in, 495–97
  exchange, 499
  friendship, 477–84
  homogamy, 503–6
  interpersonal attraction in, 447–76
  investment in, 497–98
  marriage, 506–18
  and negotiations, 354–55
  parent-child, 487
  and physiological arousal, 490–94
  premarital romantic, 494–503
  rewards in, 495
  romantic, see romantic love
  same-gender, 467
  and self-monitoring, 219–20, 222
  significant, 494
relative deprivation theory, 326–29
relativism, cultural, 274–75, 283
relevance maxim, 176
reliability, of scales, 216
religion, and divorce, 520
remarriage, 502, 522–23
remedial exchanges, 419
Renaissance, 260
representativeness heuristic, 164n

representatives, negotiations among, 353–56
reproduction, and natural selection, 291–92, 400–401
reproductive equipment, 386, 387
research:
  correlational method, 13–15
  see also experimental methods
resistance points, 343
resources:
  distribution of, 370
  and dominance, 392
  and submission, 392
responses:
  amplification of, 121–22
  competition between, 453n
  readiness of, 236n
  speed of, 593
responsibility:
  for actions, 257
  of attribution, 140, 173–74
  diffusion of, 42–43
  focusing of, 313
  for injustice, 336–38
  and obedience, 54
  and perceptions, 516
retaliation, and aggression, 419n, 420
rewards:
  and altruism, 302
  and attitudes, 529
  and coalitions, 370–73
  and equity theory, 322–25
  and gender differences, 322, 323–24, 330
  and generosity, 308
  and interpersonal attraction, 461–62
  and intrinsic motivation, 550–51
  and need, 330
  in nonzero sum conflicts, 357–58, 363n
  in relationships, 495
Rhetoric, The (Aristotle), 417
rhetorics, moral, 284
riots, 427, 439
risky shift, 33–39
  and cautious shift, 38
  coining of term, 34–35
  demise of, 38–39
  explanations for, 35–38
  and group polarization, 39
  and minimum acceptable odds, 34
  and persuasive arguments, 37–38
  questionnaires on, 34
  as social comparison, 35–37
Robbers Cave experiment, 104–7
romantic love, 2–4, 484–94
  as adventure, 488–89
  arousal in, 490–94
  and attachment, 485–88

described, 484–85
elements of, 2–3
endurance of, 489–90
enhancement of, 490
features of, 485
historical view of, 507–9
and James-Lange theory, 225–26
loyalty vs. passion in, 490
and marriage, 506–18
mate selection in, 503–6
and perceptions, 225
premarital, see premarital romantic relationships
in relationships, 13
Romeo and Juliet in, 508
self-monitoring in, 219
in sixteenth-century England, 507–8
in troubadour myths, 508
as universal, 508
round robin studies, 70–71
rural areas, helping in, 314–15

salience:
  and attribution, 158–59
  and behavior standards, 212
San Francisco earthquake of 1989, 289–90
satisfaction:
  and attractiveness, 13n
  in marriage, 509–18
scales:
  personality, 116
  reliability of, 216
  validity of, 216
Schachter and Singer experiment in emotions, 229–36, 243, 270
  popularity of, 235–36
  procedure of, 230–32
  replications of, 234–35
  results of, 232–34
  and transfer of arousal, 235, 243
Schachter on anxiety and affiliation, 469–74
schemata:
  activation of, 181–82, 184
  and attitudes, 557–59
  causal, 154
  and cognitive consistency, 557–59
  and interpreting behavior, 184
  and memory, 181–83
  priming of, 183–84
  and sensitivity to incongruent material, 182–83
scripts, 181
  defined, 171
  social, 171–72
secure attachments, 486
selective attention, 554–55

self, 145–86
and art, 260
and body, 257
as bounded entity, 263
and conscious experiences, 257
contamination of, 284–85
in cultural perspective, 256–86
and emotions, 224–55, 269–74
and food, 265–69
implicit conception of, 257
as inner cause of behavior, 209–10
Mead theory of, 194, 210, 582–83, 587
as metaphor, 209–10
metaphysical notions of, 263
and morality, 274–85
and person perception, 147–91
and pollution, 284–85
presentation of, *see* self-presentation
uniqueness of, 260–61
use of term, 256*n*
Western conception of, 257–62
self-affirmation, and self-worth, 544
self-awareness:
and behavior standards, 212–13
and conformity, 214
and embarrassment, 210
inner and outer focus in, 209–14
and motivation, 212–13
objective, 210–14
as personality trait, 213–14
private and public, 214, 601
self-concept, 257
self-consciousness, *see* self-awareness
Self-Consciousness Scale, 213–14
self-deception, 208–9
self-defensive aggression, 416
self-definition, and attitudes, 528
self-disclosure:
defined, 479
and expressing concern, 482–84
and friendships, 479–82
gender differences in, 480–82
and loneliness, 483
and marriage, 509–10
and reciprocity, 479–80
self-enhancing feedback, 201–2
self-esteem:
and adjustment, 407
collective, 111
and dissonance, 543–44
and embarrassment, 194–96
and envy, 456–57
and gender roles, 407
ingroup bias and, 110–11
of minorities, 108
of people needing help, 315–17
self-evaluation, 36
self-gratification, and generosity, 307

self-handicapping, 205–6
selfish genes, and altruism, 293–94
selfishness, and demand theory, 356*n*
self-knowledge, 189–90
and evolution, 386
self-monitoring, 215–22, 599
and attitudes, 217–18
and conformity, 216–18
defined, 215*n*
and relationships, 219–20, 222
and social skills, 219
Self-Monitoring Scale, 216, 219–22
self-perception theory, 545–49
Daryl Bem on, 545–49
vs. dissonance theory, 547–49, 553
self-presentation, 192–223
appearance and manner in, 199–200
basking and blasting in, 207–8
and bogus pipeline, 556
and communication, 200–201
conformity in, 216–18
and dissonance, 555–56
and embarrassment, 194–96
and emotions, 197, 273–74
exemplification in, 204–5
faking in, 200–202
focus of attention in, 209–14
Goffman's approach to, 193–202
and identity, 193–94
ingratiation in, 202–4
intimidation in, 204–5
and performance, 197–200
self-deception in, 208–9
self-handicapping in, 205–6
self-monitoring in, 215–22
self-promotion in, 203
sets and props in, 197–98
sincerity in, 209
and social skills, 220–21
strategies of, 202–9
supplication in, 205–6
teams in, 198–99
use of term, 192
self-promotion:
and competence, 203
and ingratiation, 202–4
self-serving biases, 166–68
self-verifying feedback, 202
self-worth, and dissonance, 543–44
semantics, 141
sensitivity to incongruent material, 182–83
serviceable associated habits, principle of, 237, 246
sets:
in evaluations, 189
in experiments, 188
in performances, 197–98

settings, legitimacy of, 52–53
sex, *see* gender; sexual behavior
Sex, Evolution and Behavior (Daly and Wilson), 386
sex-related aggression, 414–15, 428–33
sex-typed subjects, 408
sexual arousal, 494
gender differences in, 394, 395–96
sexual behavior, 376–410
aggression in, 414–15, 428–33
and condom use, 394*n*
and contraceptives, 383
counterrevolution in, 384–85
and culture, 376–85
and disease, 383
double standard in, 380–81
and evolution, 385, 386–88
of gay men and lesbians, 394
gender differences in, 380–81, 389–98
genetic influences on, 397–400
on Inis Beag, 376–77
and marriage squeeze, 383
and parental investment, 387–88
passion in, 2–3, 490
and permissiveness, 385
of praying mantises, 292–93
premarital and extramarital, 393–94
and rape, 428–29
revolution in, 379, 382–83
and virginity, 390
sexual desire:
effects of deprivation on, 396–97
gender differences in, 394
sexual orientation, environmental influences on, 400
sexual scripts, 378
sexual standards, history of, 379–84
shame, response readiness in, 236*n*
shared distinctiveness account of stereotypes, 125–26
shared fate, and victim derogation, 337
Sherif and Robbers Cave experiment, 104–7
Sherif conformity experiment, 25–28
Asch experiment vs., 26–28
and performance of groups vs. individuals, 85
Zimbardo prison experiment and, 59, 60
signaling systems, 249–50
significant others, and attitudes, 582–83
similarity:
of attitudes, 454–56
and attraction, 453–59
and bogus stranger technique, 455–56

Westgate housing complex, 447–51, 453
where there's smoke there's fire, 43
will, and behavior, 173
Williams v. *Florida*, 92–93
Witherspoon v. *Illinois*, 96
women:
    aggression against, 430–31
    attitudes toward, 429
    and intuitiveness, 252
    and marriage squeeze, 383
    stereotypes of, 134, 141
    and victim derogation, 337–38
    see also gender; gender differences
working consensus, and identity, 194

working models, and attachment, 486–87
World Series, 212–13
World War II:
    deprivation research in, 326, 560
    German army in, 76–77
    and individualism-collectivism, 262
    Pearl Harbor disaster in, 81, 83

Yale group theory of aggression, 413, 418–21
Yale research on persuasion, 560–66
yelling "Fire!," 313*n*
Yerkes-Dodson Law, 212
young, *see* children

Zajonc on mere exposure, 451–53
Zajonc study of social facilitation, 63–71
zero-sum conflicts, 356–60
    see also bargaining
Zillman on transfer of arousal, 425–28
Zimbardo prison experiment, 55–60
    explanations of brutality in, 57–58
    moral drift in, 58–59
    pluralistic ignorance in, 59–60
    results of, 57
    systematic bias in, 59